I0876125

SEMITIC
and
ASSYRIOLOGICAL STUDIES

SEMITIC
and
ASSYRIOLOGICAL
STUDIES

Presented to
Pelio Fronzaroli
by Pupils and Colleagues

2003
Harrassowitz Verlag · Wiesbaden

The publication of this volume has been promoted by Paolo Marrassini, in co-operation with Alessandra Avanzini, Lidia Bettini, Marco Bonechi, Amalia Catagnoti, Giovanni Conti, Maria Vittoria Tonietti and Ida Zatelli. The general supervision has been done by Giovanni Conti with the help of Maria Vittoria Tonietti. The preparation and the realization of the editing are due to Amalia Catagnoti and Cecilia Picchi.

Bibliografische Information Der Deutschen Bibliothek:
Die Deutsche Bibliothek verzeichnet diese Publikation in der Deutschen Nationalbibliografie; detaillierte bibliografische Daten sind im Internet über http://dnb.ddb.de abrufbar.

Bibliographic information published by Die Deutsche Bibliothek:
Die Deutsche Bibliothek lists this publication in the Deutsche Nationalbibliografie; detailed bibliographic data is available in the Internet at http://dnb.ddb.de.e-mail: cip@dbf.ddb.de

© Otto Harrassowitz KG, Wiesbaden 2003
This work, including all of its parts, is protected by copyright.
Any use beyond the limits of copyright law without the permission of the publisher is forbidden and subject to penalty. This applies particularly to reproductions, translations, microfilms and storage and processing in electronic systems.
Printed on permanent/durable paper.
Printing and binding: Hubert & Co., Göttingen
Printed in Germany

www.harrassowitz.de/verlag

ISBN 3-477-04749-6

TABLE OF CONTENTS

FOREWORD

It is almost customary, in this kind of introductory note, to do some exercise in personal memories, usually with a good deal of sentimentalism. In our case, we shall limit ourselves to remember that, at the beginning of the sixties, one could meet every day a young assistant in Indo-European linguistics, and also, since a short time before, professor with an annual appointment of Hebrew and Semitic languages, seated at the end of a narrow and a little dark corridor in what was then called the "Istituto (or "Gabinetto") di Glottologia"; the approach was not entirely easy, because the floor shook a little when tramping on it, and a wooden staircase from the library creaked in an embarrassing way. But the kindness of that man encouraged every student to climb up to there and to ask him questions, also about the material contained in the two or three shelves of books in Semitics to his left; and after all, that place was one of the most important centers for the study of Indo-European and general linguistics in Italy. I do believe that in this short anecdote almost the entire essence of the personality of Pelio Fronzaroli is contained. The beginning of his career as a Indo-europeanist and a general linguist has assured him a place in Semitic studies unrivalled in Italy, and with few parallels in the world, from the point of view of the linguistic method; this was also due to the pre-eminent place held by Florence in the Humanities during the fifties and the sixties, with linguists like Giacomo Devoto, Gianfranco Contini, Bruno Migliorini, and others, and with institutions like the Circolo Linguistico Fiorentino, where fruitful discussions also with archaeologists, philologists, literary critics, were weekly held. This has also brought him to go beyond historical and comparative linguistics, and to be interested in synchronic and structural lexicography, and also in mathematical linguistics.

As for the few shelves of books, it must be remembered that during the XIX century Florence, with her "Istituto di Studi Superiori", was the main center of Oriental studies in Italy, with chairs of Hebrew, Arabic, Akkadian, Egyptian, Syriac, Chinese, and others; she was also the seat of the "Società Asiatica Italiana", with its own "Giornale". Starting from the beginning of the XX century, and with the progressive substitution of the Istituto di Studi Superiori by a University of the ordinary type, Oriental studies were also progressively, and almost entirely, destroyed, so that after the Second World War they had to be almost entirely rebuilt. In theory, this would have been relatively easy for a young men who in the meantime had perfected himself in Semitic studies in Paris; but in fact that meant to obtain funds for the library from a classical studies-oriented, and fairly poor, Faculty, to start producing pupils to cover the various fields by distracting them from the more traditional streams of research, and to earn the esteem of very authoritative, and sometimes a little arrogant, colleagues. To be sure, all this, for a novice, was not very easy, but it is exactly what has been done, and the creation of a school of pupils specialized in Arabic, Assyriology, Ethiopic, Hebrew, South Arabian, and of course Semitic and Hamito-Semitic linguistics, is maybe one of the most outstanding achievements of that novice. But this could have been almost impossible without the other element we were talking about before, that is the complete, continuous and, if it is permitted to say so, lovable capability to put himself at the disposal of every person for every question and also of every personal problem, and to infuse in the pupils a sense of confidence that only well-balanced, and so really strong, tempers can do.

Pelio Fronzaroli has been full professor of Semitic philology in the University of Florence since 1966, and also professor with an annual appointment of Biblical philology from 1968 to 1978. As for his scientific production his bibliography, which follows these lines, speaks by itself, as the contents of this volume also try to do: there are mainly articles on Semitic linguistics and on Assyriology (including Hittitology, one of the first interests of Fronzaroli), but also on Aegean philology, Arabic, Aramaic, Hebrew and Biblical Studies, North-West Semitic, Phoenician, South Arabian, Ugaritic, on Near Eastern history, and Near Eastern archaeology, this latter tied with his fairly recent interest in Eblaite philology and civilization. Here it can only be stressed, as a further testimony of his intellectual adventure, the capability of beginning a new field, that of Eblaite and Assyriological studies, in which he reached the same highs standards as in the previous period. This is not only another proof of his personal eclecticism, but above all a demonstration of how a scholar must remain open to new stimula, and not to hesitate to try new directions, if research demands it. It is also because of this further lesson that this volume is dedicated to him.

Paolo Marrassini
University of Florence
January 2003

BIBLIOGRAPHY

by Amalia Catagnoti

1953

"Ugarit-Ras Shamra", *Rivista Biblica* 1, pp. 316-330.

1955

La fonetica ugaritica, Edizioni di storia e letteratura. Sussidi eruditi, 7, Roma, pp. 102.

Leggenda di Aqhat. Testo ugaritico, Edizioni Fussi. Il melagrano, 136-137, Firenze, pp. 96.

1956

"Nota sulla formazione della lingua franca", *Atti dell'Accademia Toscana di Scienze e Lettere "La Colombaria"*, 20, pp. 211-252.

"Rapporti lessicali dell'ittita con le lingue semitiche", *Archivio Glottologico Italiano* 41, pp. 32-45.

Review of: K. Balkan, *Kassitenstudien. 1. Die Sprache der Kassiten*, New Haven, 1954, in *La Parola del Passato* 47, pp. 145-148.

Review of: G. Bedarida, *Ebrei di Livorno*, Firenze, 1956, and C. Del Monte, *Sonetti postumi giudaico-romaneschi*, Roma, 1955, in *Lingua Nostra*, XVII/4, p. 129.

Review of: C. H. Gordon, *Ugaritic Manual*, Roma, 1955, in *La Parola del Passato*, 47, pp. 467-470.

1957

Il linguaggio del bambino, Edizioni Giuseppe Malipiero. Il fanciullo nel mondo moderno, Bologna, pp. 206.

1958

"Contributo alla definizione dialettale dell'ittita", *Atti dell'Accademia Toscana di Scienze e Lettere "La Colombaria"* 22, pp. 117-179.

Review of: R. Raggiunti, *La conoscenza e il problema della lingua. Ragioni filosofiche della linguistica*, Firenze, 1956, in *I Problemi della Pedagogia* 4, pp. 956-963.

1959

"L'antefatto indeuropeo nella formazione della civiltà ittita", *La Parola del Passato* 67, pp. 260-280.

"I rapporti fra la Grecia e l'Oriente in alcuni studi recenti", *Atene e Roma* NS IV/2, pp. 65-79.

"*Su-ga-gu-um* 'sceicco'", *La Parola del Passato* 66, pp. 189-193.

Review of: F. Pasqualino, *Educazione e linguaggio*, Roma, 1957, in *I Problemi della Pedagogia* 5, pp. 728-734.

Review of: G. Tavani, *Appunti sul giudeo-portoghese di Livorno*, *Annali dell'Istituto Universitario Orientale* I/2, 1959, pp. 61-99, in *Lingua Nostra* XX/4, p. 128.

1960

"L'ordinamento gentilizio semitico e i testi di Mari", *Archivio Glottologico Italiano* 45, pp. 37-60, 127-149.

"Le origini dei Semiti come problema storico", *Accademia Nazionale dei Lincei. Rendiconti della Classe di scienze morali, storiche e filologiche*, series VIII, vol. XV/3-4, pp. 123-144.

Review of: A. Severyns, *Grèce et Proche-Orient avant Homère*, Bruxelles, 1960, in *Atene e Roma* NS V, pp. 184-185.

Review of: *Gli editti di Aśoka*, trad. e introd. di G. Pugliese Carratelli, Firenze, 1960, in *Atene e Roma* NS V, p. 185.

1961

"Metodi statistici nella classificazione delle lingue semitiche", *Groupe Linguistique d'Études Chamito-Sémitiques (Comptes rendus)* 9, pp. 47-49.

"Note di stratigrafia toponomastica toscana (foglio 106 della Carta d'Italia)", *L'Universo* 41, pp. 231-240, con 1 carta.

"Prospettive di metodo statistico nella classificazione delle lingue semitiche", *Accademia Nazionale dei Lincei. Rendiconti della Classe di scienze morali, storiche e filologiche*, series VIII, vol. XVI/7-12, pp. 348-380.

Review of: L. Gil Fernández, *Nombres de insectos en griego antiguo*, Madrid, 1959, in *Atene e Roma*, NS VI, pp. 247-248.

Review of: S. Moscati, *Chi furono i Semiti?*, Roma, 1957, in *I Problemi della Pedagogia* 7, p. 597.

Review of: S. Moscati, *Le antiche civiltà semitiche*, Bari, 1958, in *I Problemi della Pedagogia* 7, pp. 597-598.

Review of: T. Slama-Cazacu, *Relaţiile dintre gîndire şi limbaj în ontogeneză*, [Bucureşti], 1957, in *I Problemi della Pedagogia* 7, pp. 590-592.

1962

Review of: M. Pittau, *Il linguaggio. I fondamenti filosofici*, Brescia, 1957, in *I Problemi della Pedagogia* 8, pp. 592-594.

1963

"Note di stratigrafia toponomastica toscana (foglio 106 della Carta d'Italia)", *VII Congresso Internazionale di Scienze Onomastiche*, II, Istituto di Glottologia dell'Università degli Studi, Firenze, pp. 1-13 [reprint cf. 1961].

"Sull'elemento vocalico del lessema in semitico", *Rivista degli Studi Orientali* 38, pp. 119-129.

Review of: G. G. Buti, *La casa degli Indeuropei*, Firenze, 1962, *Atene e Roma* VIII, pp. 122-124.

Review of: G. Devoto, *Origini indeuropee*, Firenze, 1962, in *Rivista degli Studi Orientali* 38, pp. 272-275.

Review of: P. Graziosi, *Levanzo. Pitture e incisioni*, Firenze, 1962, in *Atene e Roma* VIII, pp. 121-122.

Review of: J. Kuriłowicz, *L'Apophonie en sémitique*, Wrocław-Warszawa-Kraków, 1961, in *Archivio Glottologico Italiano* 48, pp. 60-66.

Review of: J. Kuriłowicz, *L'Apophonie en sémitique*, Wrocław-Warszawa-Kraków, 1961, in *Rivista degli Studi Orientali* 38, pp. 73-76.

Review of: A. Parrot, *Diluvio e Torre di Babele*, Firenze, 1962, in *Atene e Roma* VIII, pp. 120-121.

Review of: *VII Congresso Internazionale di Scienze Onomastiche*, I, Firenze 1962, in *Rivista degli Studi Orientali* 38, pp. 76-77.

1964

"Studi sul lessico comune semitico. I. Oggetto e metodo della ricerca", *Accademia Nazionale dei Lincei. Rendiconti della Classe di scienze morali, storiche e filologiche*, series VIII, vol. XIX/5-6, pp. 155-172.

"Studi sul lessico comune semitico. II. Anatomia e fisiologia", *Accademia Nazionale dei Lincei. Rendiconti della Classe di scienze morali, storiche e filologiche*, series VIII, vol. XIX/7-12, pp. 243-280.

Review of: G. Herdan, *The Calculus of Linguistic Observations*, The Hague, 1962, in *Rivista degli Studi Orientali* 39, pp. 156-158.

1965

"Studi sul lessico comune semitico. III. I fenomeni naturali", *Accademia Nazionale dei Lincei. Rendiconti della Classe di scienze morali, storiche e filologiche*, series VIII, vol. XX/3-4, pp. 135-150.

"Studi sul lessico comune semitico. IV. La religione", *Accademia Nazionale dei Lincei. Rendiconti della Classe di scienze morali, storiche e filologiche*, series VIII, vol. XX/5-6, pp. 246-269.

[remarks on] G. Garbini, *Configurazione dell'unità linguistica semitica*, in *Le protolingue. Atti del IV Convegno Internazionale di Linguisti*, Paideia Editrice, Milano, pp. 137-138.

1966

"Hammurabi", in *I Protagonisti della Storia Universale*, I, Compagnia Edizioni Internazionali, Milano, pp. 169-196.

"Le figurine in terracotta. I. Presentazione", in *Missione archeologica Italiana in Siria. Rapporto preliminare della campagna 1965 (Tell Mardikh)*, Istituto di Studi del Vicino Oriente, Università, Roma, pp. 143-151.

"Il settore E. II. I reperti", in *Missione archeologica Italiana in Siria. Rapporto preliminare della campagna 1965 (Tell Mardikh)*, Istituto di Studi del Vicino Oriente, Università, Roma, pp. 89-102.

"Su alcuni problemi di tipologia morfologica in semitico", *Accademia Nazionale dei Lincei. Rendiconti della Classe di scienze morali, storiche e filologiche*, serie VIII, vol. XXI/7-12, pp. 210-223.

1967

“Il mare e i corsi d’acqua nel lessico comune semitico”, *Bollettino dell’Atlante Linguistico Mediterraneo* 8-9, 1966-1967, pp. 205-213.

“Il settore E”, in *Missione archeologica Italiana in Siria. Rapporto preliminare della campagna 1966 (Tell Mardikh)*, Istituto di Studi del Vicino Oriente, Università, Roma, pp. 79-110.

“Metodi statistici nella linguistica diacronica”, *Il Verri* 24, pp. 100-115.

1968

“Studi sul lessico comune semitico. V. La natura selvatica”, *Accademia Nazionale dei Lincei. Rendiconti della Classe di scienze morali, storiche e filologiche*, serie VIII, vol. XXIII/7-12, pp. 267-303.

1969

“Studi sul lessico comune semitico. VI. La natura domestica”, *Accademia Nazionale dei Lincei. Rendiconti della Classe di scienze morali, storiche e filologiche*, se rie VIII, vol. XXIV/7-12, pp. 285-320.

“Sulla struttura dei colori in ebraico biblico”, in *Studi Linguistici in onore di V. Pisani*, Paideia Editrice, Brescia, pp. 377-389.

Review of: G. B. Sarfatti, *Munn^{e}kē ham-mātēmātīqā bas-siprūt ham-maddāʿīt hā-ʿibrīt šel y^{e}mē hab-bēnayim*, Jerusalem, 1968, in *Rivista degli Studi Orientali* 44, pp. 171-174.

1970

“Ricostruzione interna del verbo semitico in alcuni studi recenti”, in *Mille. I dibattiti del Circolo Linguistico Fiorentino 1945-1970*, Leo S. Olschki Editore, Firenze, pp. 71-85.

Review of: I. J. Gelb, *Sequential Reconstruction of Proto-Akkadian*, *Oriens Antiquus* 9, pp. 187-191.

[remarks on] *Le lamine di Pyrgi. Tavola rotonda internazionale ... (Roma, 19 aprile 1968)*, Accademia Nazionale dei Lincei, Roma, pp. 17, 23, 29, 43-44, 46.

1971

"I cavalli del Proto-Zaccaria", *Accademia Nazionale dei Lincei. Rendiconti della Classe di scienze morali, storiche e filologiche*, serie VIII, vol. XXVI/7-12, pp. 593-601.

"L'iscrizione cuneiforme", in M. Cristofani - P. Fronzaroli, *Un'iscrizione cuneiforme su un vaso bronzeo da una tomba di Faleri*, *Studi Etruschi* 39, pp. 326-331.

"La semitistica", in *Gli studi sul Vicino Oriente in Italia dal 1921 al 1970*, I, *L'Oriente preislamico*, Istituto per l'Oriente, Roma, pp. 11-31.

"Studi sul lessico comune semitico. VII. L'alimentazione", *Accademia Nazionale dei Lincei. Rendiconti della Classe di scienze morali, storiche e filologiche*, serie VIII, vol. XXVI/7-12, pp. 603-642.

Review of: *Ugaritica VI*, Parigi, 1969, in *Journal of Semitic Studies* 16, pp. 214-221.

1972

"Problemi della lessicografia comparativa semitica", *Oriens Antiquus* 11, pp. 241-262.

1973

"Problems of a Semitic etymological dictionary", in P. Fronzaroli (ed.), *Studies on Semitic Lexicography* (= Quaderni di Semitistica, 2), Istituto di linguistica e lingue orientali. Università di Firenze, Firenze, pp. 1-24.

"Statistical methods in the study of Ancient Near Eastern languages", *Orientalia* 42, pp. 97-113.

Ugaritic Phonetics (trans. A. S. Kaye), Fullerton: California State University [English translation of *La Fonetica ugaritica*, 1955].

1974

"Classe et genre en chamito-sémitique", *Mélanges de l'Université Saint-Joseph* 48, 1973-1974,.pp. 3-20.

"Réflexions sur la paléontologie linguistique", in *Actes du premier congrès international de linguistique sémitiques et chamito-sémitique (Paris 16-19 juillet 1969)*, Mouton, The Hague-Paris, pp. 173-180.

Review of: F. Corriente, *Problemática de la pluralidad en semítico. El plural fracto*, Madrid, 1971, in *Journal of Semitic Studies* 19, pp. 275-284.

1975

"La lingua dei testi ippiatrici di Ugarit", *Archivio Glottologico Italiano* 60, pp. 34-46.

"On the common Semitic lexicon and its ecological and cultural background", in J. and Th. Bynon (eds.), *Hamito-Semitica*, Mouton, The Hague - Paris, pp. 43-52.

"Problemi di classificazione delle lingue su base quantitativa", in *Le tecniche di classificazione e loro applicazione linguistica* (= *Contributi del centro linceo interdisciplinare di scienze matematiche e loro applicazioni*), Accademia Nazionale dei Lincei, Roma, pp. 123-141.

1976

"L'espressione letteraria", in S. Moscati (ed.), *L'alba della civiltà*, vol. III, UTET, Torino, pp. 93-212.

"La trasmissione della cultura", in S. Moscati (ed.), *L'alba della civiltà*, vol. III, UTET, Torino, pp. 1-92.

1977

"L'Asia Minore e la Mesopotamia come luogo di convergenza e d'irradiazione di lingue e culture", in *Paleontologia linguistica. Atti del VI Congresso Internazionale di Linguisti*, Paideia Editrice, Brescia, pp. 105-122 e 127-128.

"L'interferenza linguistica nella Siria settentrionale del terzo millennio", in R. Ajello (ed.), *Interferenza linguistica. Atti del Convegno della Società Italiana di Glottologia, Perugia, 24 e 25 aprile 1977*, Giardini Editori, Pisa, pp. 27-43.

"Paleontologia semitica: il patrimonio lessicale semitico comune alla luce dell'affinità linguistica camito-semitica", in *Paleontologia linguistica. Atti del VI Congresso Internazionale di Linguisti*, Paidei Editrice, Brescia, pp. 155-158 e 170-172.

"West Semitic toponimy in Northern Syria in the third millennium B.C.", *Journal of Semitic Studies* 22, pp. 145-166.

1978

"Indirizzo conclusivo", in P. Fronzaroli (ed.), *Atti del Secondo Congresso Internazionale di Linguistica Camito-Semitica, Firenze 16-19 aprile 1974* (= Quaderni di Semitistica, 5), Istituto di linguistica e lingue orientali. Università di Firenze, Firenze, pp. 399-404.

1979

"Problemi di fonetica eblaita", *1*, *Studi Eblaiti* 1, pp. 65-89.

Statistical methods in synchronic and diachronic classification, *Cahiers de lexicologie* 34, pp. 19-35.

"The concord in gender in Eblaite theophoric personal names", *Ugarit-Forschungen* 11, pp. 275-281.

"Un atto reale di donazione dagli Archivi di Ebla (TM.75.G.1766)", *Studi Eblaiti* 1, 1979, pp. 3-16.

1980

"Gli equivalenti di eme-bal nelle liste lessicali eblaite", *Studi Eblaiti* 2, pp. 91-95.

"Il verdetto per A'mur-Damu e sua madre (TM.75.G.1430)", *Studi Eblaiti* 3, pp. 65-78.

"Note sul contatto linguistico a Ebla", *Vicino Oriente* 3, pp. 33-46.

"Un verdetto reale dagli Archivi di Ebla (TM.75.G.1452)", *Studi Eblaiti* 3, pp. 33-52.

1981

"La congiunzione eblaita *ap*", *Studi Eblaiti* 4, pp. 167-176.

1982

"La contribution de la langue d'Ebla à la connaissance du sémitique archaïque", in H.-J. Nissen - J. Renger (eds.), *Mesopotamien und seine Nachbarn*, XXV *RAI*, Berlin 3. bis 7. Juli 1978, Dietrich Reiner Verlag, Berlin, pp. 131-145.

"Per una valutazione della morfologia eblaita", *Studi Eblaiti* 5, pp. 93-120.

1984

"Disposizioni reali per Ti̱taw-Li'm (TM.75.G.2396, TM.75.G.1986+)", *Studi Eblaiti* 7, pp. 1-22.

"The Eblaic lexicon: problems and appraisal", in P. Fronzaroli (ed.), *Studies on the Language of Ebla* (= Quaderni di Semitistica, 13), Istituto di linguistica e lingue orientali. Università di Firenze, Firenze, pp. 117-157.

"La langue d'Ebla", *Archeologia. Les dossiers* 83/mai, pp. 42-47.

"Materiali per il lessico eblaita 1", *Studi Eblaiti* 7, pp. 145-190.

1985

"L'avverbio eblaita *ba*", *Studi Epigrafici e Linguistici* 2, pp. 25-35.

"Le lingue della Siria antica: dall'eblaita all'aramaico", in *Da Ebla a Damasco. 10.000 anni di archeologia in Siria*, Electa, Milano, pp. 56-61.

Проблемы эблаитской фонетики, в Древняя Эбла. Раскопки в Сирии, Составление и введение П. Маттиэ, Общая редакция и заключительная статья И. М. Дьяконова, Москва, Прогресс, стр. 141-162.
[Russian translation of "Problemi di fonetica eblaita, 1", 1979.]

К трактовке эблаитской морфологии, в Древняя Эбла. Раскопки в Сирии, Составление и введение П. Маттиэ, Общая редакция и заключительная статья И. М. Дьяконова, Москва, Прогресс, стр. 163-190.
[Russian translation of "Per una valutazione della morfologia eblaita", 1982.]

1986

"Semitic place names of Syria in the Ebla texts", *Orientalia Suecana* 33-35 (1984-86), pp. 139-148.

1987

"La formation des noms personnels féminins à Ebla", in J.-M. Durand (ed.), *La femme dans le Proche-Orient antique*, XXXIII *RAI*, Editions Recherche sur les Civilisations, Paris, pp. 63-73.

"Le pronom déterminatif-relatif à Ebla", *MARI* 5, pp. 267-274.

1988

"Il culto dei re defunti in *ARET* 3.178", in P. Fronzaroli (ed.), *Miscellanea Eblaitica* 1 (= Quaderni di Semitistica, 15), Dipartimento di Linguistica. Università di Firenze, Firenze, pp. 1-33.

"Tre scongiuri eblaiti (*ARET* 5, 1-3)", *Vicino Oriente* 7, pp. 11-23.

"Typologies onomastiques à Ebla", A. Archi (ed.), *Eblaite Personal Names and Semitic Name-Giving* (= *ARES* I), Missione Archeologica Italiana in Siria, Roma, pp. 1-24.

"Un'antica lingua semitica", in P. Matthiae (ed.), *Ebla. La scoperta di una città dimenticata*, *Dossier Storia* 23, Firenze, pp. 47-50.

1989

“A proposito del culto dei re defunti a Ebla”, *NABU* 1989/2.

“Il culto degli Angubbu a Ebla”, in P. Fronzaroli (ed.), *Miscellanea Eblaitica* 2 (= Quaderni di Semitistica, 16), Dipartimento di Linguistica. Università di Firenze, Firenze, pp. 1-26.

من القاموس الايبلائي (من : أضواء جديدة على تاريخ وآثار بلاد الشام، تأليف مجموعة من كبار علماء التاريخ والآثار ، تعريب قاسم طوير)، دمشق ، ص ٥٢-٥٦.

1990

“Forms of the Dual in the Texts of Ebla”, *Maarav* 5-6, pp. 111-125.

“La langue d’Ebla”, *Les Annales Archéologiques Arabes Syriennes* 40, pp. 56-63.

1991

“Lingua e testo negli Archivi di Ebla”, *La Parola del Passato* 46, pp. 220-236.

“Niveaux de langue dans les graphies éblaïtes”, in A. S. Kaye (ed.), *Semitic Studies in honor of Wolf Leslau*, I, Otto Harrassowitz, Wiesbaden, pp. 462-476.

“Noms de fonction dans les textes rituels d’Ebla”, *NABU* 1991/49.

“Une nouvelle valeur de BAD à Ebla”, *NABU* 1991/50.

1992

“The Ritual Texts of Ebla”, in P. Fronzaroli (ed.), *Literature and literary language at Ebla* (= Quaderni di Semitistica 18), Dipartimento di Linguistica. Università di Firenze, Firenze, pp. 163-185.

“Le signe 73 de la “*Sign List*” d’Ébla”, *NABU* 1992/59.

1993

“Componential Analysis”, *Zeitschrift für Althebraistik* 6, pp. 79-91.

Testi rituali della regalità (Archivio L.2769) (= *Archivi Reali di Ebla. Testi* - XI), con la collaborazione di A. Catagnoti, Missione Archeologica Italiana in Siria, Roma, pp. XVI + 183, 19 tavv.

1994

"Eblaic and the Semitic Languages", in G. Del Lungo Camiciotti - F. Granucci, - M. P. Marchese - R. Stefanelli (eds.), *Studi in onore di Carlo Alberto Mastrelli* (= *Quaderni del Dipartimento di Linguistica, Studi* 1), Firenze, pp. 89-94.

"Osservazioni sul lessico delle bevande dei testi di Ebla", in L. Milano (ed.), *Drinking in ancient societies. History and culture of drinks in the Ancient Near East* (= *History of the Ancient Near East / Studies* - VI), Sargon, Padova, pp. 121-127.

1995

"Fonti di lessico nei testi di Ebla", *Studi Epigrafici e Linguistici* 12, pp. 51-64.

"Impieghi della scrittura a Ebla", in *Studi linguistici per i 50 anni del Circolo Linguistico Fiorentino*, Leo S. Olschki Editore, Firenze, pp. 81-94.

"La lingua e la cultura letteraria di Ebla nel Periodo Protosiriano", in P. Matthiae - F. Pinnock - G. Scandone Matthiae (eds.), *Ebla. Alle origini della civiltà urbana*, Electa, Milano, pp. 156-163.

"La lingua di Ebla e le lingue semitiche", in P. Matthiae - F. Pinnock - G. Scandone Matthiae (eds.), *Ebla. Alle origini della civiltà urbana*, Electa, Milano, pp. 218-225.

"Textes de chancellerie et textes littéraires à Ebla", in F. Ismail (ed.), *Proceedings of the International Symposium on Syria and the Ancient Near East 3000 - 300 B.C.*, Aleppo, pp. 19-27.

1996

"À propos de quelques mots éblaïtes de l'orfèvrerie", in Ö. Tunca - D. Deheselle (eds.), *Tablettes et images aux pays de Sumer et d'Akkad. Mélanges offerts à M. le Professeur H. Limet*, Université de Liège, Liège, pp. 51-68.

"Notes sur la syntaxe éblaïte", *Amurru* 1, pp. 125-134.

1997

"Les combats de Hadda dans les textes d'Ebla", *MARI* 8, pp. 283-290.

"Divinazione a Ebla (TM.76.G.86)", in P. Fronzaroli (ed.), *Miscellanea eblaitica*, 4 (= Quaderni di Semitistica 19), Dipartimento di Linguistica. Università di Firenze, Firenze, pp. 1-22.

“Religione e profezia nella "Mezzaluna Fertile"”, in C. Colafemmina (ed.), *Dagli dei a dio. Parole sacre e parole profetiche sulle sponde del Mediterraneo*, Messaggi, Cassano Murge, pp. 37-48.

“Il serpente dalle sette teste a Ebla”, in E. Acquaro (ed.), *Alle soglie della classicità. Il Mediterraneo tra tradizione e innovazione. Studi in onore di S. Moscati*, Istituti Editoriali e Poligrafici Internazionali, Pisa-Roma, pp. 1135-1144.

1998

“Ebl. *wammum* "watercourse: stream"”, *NABU* 1998/89.

“*Kam$_4$-mu* in Ebla Letters”, *Subartu* IV/2, pp. 103-114.

“A Pharmaceutical Text at Ebla (TM.75.G.1623)”, *Zeitschrift für Assyriologie* 88, pp. 225-239.

1999

“Ebl. **qdm* (= igi-tùm) "to dam up (waters)"”, *NABU* 1999/47.

2001

Review of: R. Hetzron (ed.), *The Semitic Languages*, London, 1997, in *Bulletin Critique des Annales Islamologiques* 17, LoGisma editore, pp. 13-16.

2002

“Per un'interpretazione dell'ebl. *du-tum*”, in *Anatolia Antica. Studi in memoria di Fiorella Imparati* (= *Eothen*, 11), Firenze, pp. 285-287.

Testi di cancelleria: i rapporti con le città (Archivio L.2769) (= *Archivi Reali di Ebla. Testi,* XIII), con la collaborazione di A. Catagnoti, Missione Archeologica Italiana in Siria, Roma, pp. XVIII + 319, tavv. LXIV.

2003

“L'Incantation des deux haches (TM.75.G.2303)”, in J. Lentin - A. Lonnet (eds.), *Mélanges David Cohen*, Maisonneuve & Larose, Paris, pp. 223-233.

IN PRESS

“For an Interpretation of Ebl. *ne-si-in*”, *Festschrift Werner Vycichl*, pp. 3.

“The hail incantations (*ARET* 5, 4)”, *Festschrift Burkhart Kienast*, pp. 16.

"Structures linguistiques et histoire de langues au IIIe millénaire av. J. C.", in *Proceedings of 10th Meeting of Hamito-Semitic (Afroasiatic) Linguistics (Florence, 18-20 April 2001)*, pp. 10.

A MINOAN INSCRIPTION SPECIFYING CONTEMPORARY DIGNITARIES

KJELL AARTUN

University of Oslo

The inscription in question, written in the Minoan script of class A was found on a pithos in the palace of Phaistos, Crete, Magazine 33. A photograph and partial copy of it was published by L. Godart and J.-P. Olivier, in: *Recueil des inscriptions en linéaire A*, Volume IV, 1982, p. 94 = Ph(aistos), Zb 5. The whole inscription being in the Semitic idiom of the Minoans consists of 20 completely written words, one abbreviation and an illustration of a concrete object corresponding to the meaning of the abbreviated word. The content is a list of persons of rank and a statement of their cereal food. It dates from a time before the fifteenth century B.C.

Text

pi$_2$-ho-ma pa$_3$-wa-qe no-pa-ḫa a-ra-wa-qu ra-pa-pi pi-qe-si pi-qe pa$_3$-e-yo ḫa-pi-re wu-ke-zi ma-mu-re qe-ya-mi a-tu-ya qe-mi-nu da-si qe-to-wu ḫa-te-pa$_3$ ma-qi-wi o-me-no pu$_2$-nu-nu ḫu + an illustration of a special kind of bread.

Translation

" Unique persons; elegant scholars, and orators; brilliant orators, who express their words with pathos or show delicacy of feeling in their speech; chiefs or princes; (person) who does good to or takes care of a dying person of rank; (person) who is held with high regard; (person) who possesses knowledge of matters of information; (person) who is brief and concise in his speech; (person) who is acquainted with social customs or possesses legal knowledge; servants (officials or courtiers); (person) who is skilled in waiting on (somebody) knowing well how to serve kings or men of regard; a good speaker or orator or preacher; (person) who is (morally and ritually) clean; (person) in whom one trusts or confides or to whom is confided power or authority or control etc.; a sage; bre(ad) + an illustration of a special kind of bread."

Comment

pi$_2$-ho-ma < **bayhŭ̄mā*[1] (*qaytŭ̄l*-form[2] of the noun from *BHM*) (collective) "unique persons" (Arabic *bahīm*- "unique, incomparable").[3] As affirmed by the context this

1 For the phonetic changes *-*ay* > *ī*(-*ē*); *-*aw* > *ū*(/-*ō*) and **u* > *o* see Aartun II, 1997, p. 719. For the grammatical morphem -*ā* see Brockelmann I, 1961, pp. 410f.; Aartun, *op. cit.*, pp. 743f.

Minoan word (*pi$_2$-ho-ma*), appearing at the beginning of the inscription, refers to certain remarkable Minoan individuals from different territories of ancient Crete. In various regions of the Island, hitherto, the ruins of four Minoan palaces are discovered;[4]

pa$_3$-wa-qe < **pawāqā* (broken plural[5] of the participle *pāqā/ī*[6] [*PW/YQ*]) "elegant scholars, and orators" (Arabic *fawaqat-*, broken plural of *fā'iq-*, with the same meaning).[7] From a comparative point of view this Minoan broken plural (containing an *ā*-ending) parallels Arabic plural forms, as (sg. *ṯanīyat-*, pl.) *ṯanāyā*; (sg. *nadmān-*, pl.) *nadāmā*, etc.[8] The real meaning of the Minoan expression (*pa$_3$-wa-qe*) is as indicated above a rather comprehensive one. For further comment see below;

no-pa-ḫa < **nubāḫā*[9] (broken plural of a noun from *NBḪ*) "brilliant orators expressing their words with pathos/showing delicacy of feeling in their speech" (Arabic sg. *nābiḫat-*, pl. *nawābiḫ-* the same).[10] As to the morphological pattern of this Minoan plural form (*no-pa-ḫa*) compare f. ex. Arabic sg. *nadmān-*, pl. *nudāmā*; etc. (cf. Arabic dictionaries).

In the history of civilization the two above mentioned exemplifications of skilled Minoan individuals (*pa$_3$-wa-qe*, *no-pa-ḫa*) have close parallels in other contemporary societies. This provides evidence of the existence of an educational system which was based on traditional values.[11] From the available material it appears that education, in the ancient Orient as well as later in Europe in antiquity, was based largely on the study of rhetoric with the aim of producing effective public

---

2 Brockelmann I, 1961, p. 344; Aartun II, 1997, pp. 724f.

3 Kazimirski I, 1960, p. 174; Lane, 1863, p. 269; Wahrmund I, 1970, p. 268.

4 Aartun I, 1992, pp. 14ff.

5 Brockelmann I, 1961, pp. 429f.; Wright I, 1964, pp. 191f.; Beeston, 1984, pp. 26f.

6 For the *ā/ī*- ending of Minoan nouns (substantives, adjectives, participles), as frequently in the southern Semitic idioms especially in the various local languages of Ethiopia (Dillmann, 1899, *passim*; Prätorius, 1871/1972; 1879; 1886, *passim*), cf. Aartun II, 1997, pp. 743f.

7 Kazimirski II, 1960, p. 648; Lane, 1977, pp. 2462f., Wahrmund II, 1970, p. 441.

8 See Arabic dictionaries.

9 For the orthography see Aartun II, 1997, p. 718.

10 Kazimirski II, 1960, p. 1182; Lane, 1877, p. 2756.

11 Cf. Aartun I, 1992, pp. 14ff. ("[Kultur]geschichtliche Zeugnisse").

speakers.[12] Like similar speakers of the time (diviners, prophets, poets) the orators/rhetoricians as persons of rank occupied influential positions. They used a conventional rhetorical style, whereby usually four aspects were taken into consideration: diction, construction, rhythm and figurative quality;[13]

a-ra-wa-qu < **ʾarwāqu* (broken plural of a noun from *RWQ*) "chiefs/princes (literally: who exceed in excellence, or who are above/superior to, or surpass/excell [their families])" (Arabic sg. *rawq-*, pl. *ʾarwāq-* the same).[14] The latter designation (*a-ra-wa-qu*) may refer to leading members of nobility in general as well as to princes by descent. Because of their unique social and political positions the chiefs/princes belonged par excellence to the supreme class of the society. Cf. above (*pi*$_2$*-ho-ma*);

ra-pa-pi < **rapāpī* (participle/noun from *RPP*, attesting the morphological pattern *qatāl-ī* usually appearing in Ethiopian languages)[15] (Arabic *raffa-hū* "he did good to him/conferred benefit, or benefits, upon him/took care of him").[16] The Minoan expression (*ra-pa-pi*) is syntactically combined with the following two words: *pi-qe-si* < **piqāsī* (*qitāl*-form[17] of a noun from *PQS*) "person being at the point of death" (Arabic *faqasa* "be at the point of death, die");[18] *pi-qe* < **pīqī* < **piw/yqī* (*qitl*-form[19] of a noun from *PW/YQ*) "(person) being above/surpassing (his companions)"[20] (Arabic *fāqa-hum* "he was, or became, above them/surpassed them (namely his companions)" ; cf. also *fāqa bi-nafsi-hī* "he gave up his spirit i.e. he died").[21]

---

12 Junge, 1984, pp. 250ff.; Hamer, 1950, pp. 656ff.; Lamer, 1933, pp. 84ff.; Speake (editor), 1994, pp. 224f.

13 Cf. among others Hamer, 1950, pp. 658ff. Cf. also Nicholson, 1956, pp. 72ff.; Gibb, 1963, pp. 34f.; Aartun, 1994, pp. 106f.

14 Kazimirski I, 1960, pp. 954f.; Lane, 1863, pp. 1190f.

15 Brockelmann I, 1961, pp. 342, 350f.; Dillmann, 1899, *passim*; Leslau, 1987, *passim*; etc.

16 Kazimirski I, 1960, p. 892; Lane, 1863, p. 1116; Wahrmund I, 1970, p. 776.

17 Brockelmann I, 1961, pp. 350f. For further Minoan nouns of the same structure see Aartun II, 1997, pp. 726f.

18 Kazimirski II, 1960, p. 620; Wahrmund II, 1970, p. 425.

19 Brockelmann I, 1961, pp. 340f. Many Minoan examples of the same morphological type are attested in the Linear A-texts, (Aartun II, 1997, p. 720).

20 This expression may also mean "giving up (his spirit), dying". In any case, according to the context the sense of "being above/surpassing (others)" appears here to be predominant.

21 Kazimirski II, 1960, pp. 648, 655; Lane, 1877, pp. 2460f.; Wahrmund II, 1970, pp. 440f., 444f.

Also in other ancient cultures, in Sumer, Babylonia, Egypt etc., the personal servants or attendants of the noble superiors were equally looked upon and treated as men of honour. For the Minoan registration of individuals of similar professions cf. below;

pa₃-e-yo < **bāʾiyu* (participle/noun[22] from *Bʾ Y*) "who is held in high reputation" (Arabic *baʾā* "be held in high reputation").[23] Everywhere in the nations of the past men of reputation were held in high esteem. Cf. the current studies of previous civilizations in the Near East;

ḫa-pi-re < **ḫābirī* (participle/noun from *ḪBR*) "who possesses knowledge of matters of information (news, tidings, accounts, narratives, or stories)" (Arabic *ḫābir-*, *ḫabir-*, *ḫabīr-* the same).[24] In ancient times individuals of that character were likewise highly respected. Being well informed of the state of things they functioned as "historians" of their present age. In addition they possessed thorough knowledge of the past, including ethnical origin, cultural development and historical events;[25]

wu-ke-zi < **wugayzī* (*qutayl*-form[26] of the noun from *WGZ*) "who is brief and concise in his speech" (Arabic *wağaza* or *wağuza fī manṭiqi-hī* or *fī kalāmi-hī* "he was brief/concise, in his speech/language"; *mīğāz-* "[a man] who uses few words in speech and in reply").[27] As a person of high regard this Minoan individual (*wu-ke-zi*) in the first place corresponds to wellknown prophetic figures and such like of the past. In this connection prophets of the Old Testament, Arabic diviners, and above all the prophet Muḥammad deserve special attention. They employed in their sayings traditional patterns of speech often characterized by economy of words and conciseness of style. Cf. from the Biblical utterances of the Great and Small Prophets (*passim*) and from the Qurʾān especially Surah 1; 90-114; etc.;[28]

---

22 Aartun II, 1997, pp. 722f.

23 Kazimirski I, 1960, p. 81; Wahrmund I, 1970, p. 170.

24 Lane, 1863, p. 696; Kazimirski I, 1960, pp. 532f.; Wahrmund I, 1970, pp. 565, 571, 573.

25 Compare available written sources from closely related ancient cultures, above all from Babylonia, Ugarit and Israel. For further studies see von Soden, 1985; Nielsen, 1954/55; Gray, 1957; Aartun, 1978, with references.

26 Brockelmann I, 1961, pp. 352f.; Aartun II, 1997, pp., 728f.

27 Lane, 1877, pp. 2925f.; Kazimirski II, 1960, pp. 1491f.; Wahrmund II, 1970, pp. 959, 1160.

28 Cf. also the character of the sayings of the Norse visionaries and skalds and the style, motives and contents of their utterings, which no doubt are based on oriental/Semitic traditions. Evidences of oriental/Semitic art, handwork, architecture etc., and the many Semitic inscriptions in Runes and

ma-mu-re < **maʾmūrī* (passive participle/noun[29] from *ʾMR*) *qe-ya-mi* < **qiyāmi* (noun in the genitive case from *QW/YM*) (nomen rectum) "who is acquainted with social customs/possesses legal knowledge" (Gĕʿĕz *māʾĕmĕr* "learned, erudite, skilled, versed in, expert, experienced in, acquainted with, an acquaintance, wise man, prudent, intelligent, diviner, augur, wizard"; *māʾĕmarī* "who possesses knowledge"; Arabic *maʾmūr-* "authorized person, official";[30] Syriac *qĕyāmā* "standing, upright bearing; constitution, stability; statute, covenant"; *qayyāmā* "in being, existing, still alive; continuing, lasting; (legal) standing, valid"; Arabic *qiyām-* "execution, worship, cult"; *qayyām-* "immutable, unalterable"; Gĕʿĕz *qĕwwūm, qĕwwĕm* "[thing] that is in use").[31]

Linguistically as well as contextually this Minoan designation (*ma-mu-re qe-ya-mi*) in all probability refers to a skilled person who like equals in other ancient societies possesses knowledge of and supervises the standing prescriptions, of the cult and the moral orders. As an expert he is then according to ritual and social tradition at all times able to issue religious directives, mediate oracles and act as the interpreter of the law;[32]

a-tu-ya < **ʾaʿṭuyā* (*ʾaqtul*-form [broken plural][33] of a noun from *ʿṬW/Y*) "servants (officials/courtiers)" (Arabic *ʿaṭṭā, ʿāṭā* "to serve, do service for, minister to").[34] As to this type of individuals cf. Ugaritic *ʿbdm* "servants/members of a certain working group or guild"; *ʿbd mlk* "courtiers, officials of king";[35] Hebrew **ʿăḇāḏīm*: Gen. 40:20; 41:10 etc. "servants of the king, courtiers (in Egypt)"; 1 Sam.

Minoan scripts are further remnants of a previous oriental/Semitic cultural influence in this region. See Aartun, 1994, *passim*.

29 Brockelmann I, 1961, pp. 381f.; Aartun II, 1997, p. 734.

30 Leslau, 1987, p. 25; Kazimirski I, 1960, p. 55; Lane 1863, p. 95f.; Wahrmund I, 1970, p. 675.

31 Payne Smith, 1976, p. 504; Kazimirski II, 1960, p. 841; Wahrmund II, 1970, p. 542; Leslau, 1987, p. 455.

32 In comparison cf., from the Old Testament, the priest's tasks: Num. 18:5, :7 (to perform cultic service); Ez. 22:26; 44:23 (to teach); Judges 18:5f.; 1 Sam. 22:13, :15 (to mediate oracles); Hos. 4:4ff.; Zeph. 3:4; Hag. 2:11 (to interprete the law); Ez. 44:24 (to act as a judge) etc.

33 Brockelmann I, 1961, p. 433; Aartun II, 1997, p. 750. For the phonetical change see Aartun II, 1997, pp. 74, 100 etc.

34 Kazimirski II, 1960, p. 290; Lane, 1877, p. 2084; Wahrmund II, 1970, p. 272.

35 Gordon, 1965, p. 452; Aistleitner, 1963, p. 224.

8:14f.; 16-15f.; etc. the same (in Palestine); 2 Kings 22:12 *ʿæbæḏ ham-mælæḵ* "the servant of the king"; etc.

To the same main category belongs the following individual. The particular designation represents a complex expression consisting of three words: *qe-mi-nu* < **qamīnu* (noun from *QMN*, followed by a genitive; see below) "who is skilled (in)" (Arabic *qamīn-*, *qamin-*, *qaman-*, *maqman-*, *maqmanat-* the same);[36] *da-si* < **daṣṣi*/ **daḍḍi* (nomen rectum, from *DṢṢ/DḌḌ*) "waiting on (somebody)" (Arabic *daṣṣa*/ *daḍḍa* "wait on/upon or attend on [somebody]");[37] *qe-to-wu* < **qaytūwu* (*qaytūl*-form[38] from *QTW*) "who knows well how to serve kings/men of quality" (Arabic *qatā* "to know well how to serve kings/men of quality"; *maqtan-*, *maqtawayn-*, *maqtawīn-*, *maqtawīy-* "servant, slave"; Old South Arabic *mqtw(n)* "royal officer or official [civil and military]").[39] The manifold of skilled servants is a characteristic of ancient oriental cultures. For evidence cf. f. ex. Sumerian, Babylonian, Egyptian and Biblical sources;

ḫa-te-pa₃ < **ḫāṭibā*/**ḫaṭībā* (participle/noun[40] from *ḪṬB*) "a good (public) speaker, or orator, or preacher" (Arabic *ḫāṭib-*, *ḫaṭīb-* the same; *ʿilmu-l-ḫaṭābati* "rhetoric").[41] This exemplified individual of rank (*ḫa-te-pa₃*) is another type of highly-trained persons usually occurring in days of yore. Cf. already above the two designations *pa₃-wa-qe* and *no-pa-ḫa*. The art of persuasive or impressive speaking was – as generally accepted and often pointed out by scholars – an important human skill, practised in the earliest known cultures of the Near East f. ex. in Egypt from the 3rd / 2nd millennium on. It was taught, namely by "instruction", "imitation" and "exercise". Like the intention of the wall paintings the solid foundation of oratory in antiquity was the creative power of the word pictures;[42]

---

36 Kazimirski II, 1960, p. 817; Wahrmund II, 1970, pp. 528, 878.

37 Kazimirski I, 1960, p. 698; Wahrmund I, 1970, p. 663.

38 Brockelmann I, 1961, p. 344; Aartun II, 1997, pp. 724f.

39 Kazimirski II, 1960, p. 675; Wahrmund II, 1970, pp. 458, 870; Biella, 1982, p. 470; Beeston/Ghul/ Müller/Ryckmans, 1982, p. 109.

40 Brockelmann I, 1961, pp. 342f., 354f.; Aartun II, 1997, pp.737f., 739f.

41 Kazimirski I, 1960, p. 592; Lane, 1863, pp. 762f.; Wahrmund I, 1970, pp. 567, 604, 606.

42 See Junge, 1984, pp. 250ff.; Lamer, 1933, pp. 84ff.; Hoffmann, 1965, pp. 2611ff.

ma-qi-wi < **manqīwī* (*maqtīl*-form[43] of the noun from *NQW/Y*) "who is (morally and ritually) clean" (Arabic *nuqawāʾ*-, *ʾanqiyāʾ*-, *ʾanqā* "clean, pure (man)"; Hebrew and Mišnaic-Hebrew *nāqī* "clean, clear (from impurities, sin etc.)"; Ugaritic *nqy* "clean, free"; Aramaic *nĕqē*, *naqyā* "clean").[44] By this designation (*ma-qi-wi*) is more precisely meant a man of distinction who is virtuous as regards general conduct concerned with keeping carrying out law, duty, custom, ritual etc. Provable parallels of this category appear in most contemporary or later oriental cultures;[45]

o-me-no < **ʾumaynu* (*qutayl*-form[46] of the noun from *ʾMN*) "(person) in whom one trusts/confides or to whom is confided power/authority/control etc." (Arabic *ʾāmin*- "confident, reliable"; *ʾamanat*-, *ʾumanat*-, *ʾaminat*-, *ʾāminat*- "faithful, loyal, true(man), reliable; confidant, official, supervisor"; Hebrew *ʾōmēn* < **ʾāminu* "educator < who is faithful/reliable" (Isa 49:23); *næʾĕmān* "reliable, faithful (servant)" (I Sam. 22:14 etc.); Gĕʿĕz *ʾĕmūn* "faithful, true, loyal, trustworthy, reliable, sure, real").[47] Reliableness, loyalty and the like were by all people of the ancient world appreciated as good qualities. This is evident from the preserved traditions descending from distinct oriental peoples of the past especially from the wisdom literature of the nations, viz. the Egyptian teaching of Amenemope,[48] the original Mesopotamian-Assyrian book of Aḥiqar, the proverbs of the Old Testament, the Jewish book of Jesus Sirach etc. As a consequence of this, at the royal courts children (from the higher class of the people), from childhood till maturity were under constant supervision by reliable officials as their educators. By instruction and practice they were brought up following fundamental principles of wisdom;[49]

---

43 Brockelmann I, 1961, p. 381; Aartun II, 1997, p. 733. For total regressive assimilation of *n* in contact position see Aartun II, 1997, pp. 76, 100 etc. Cf. also above.

44 Kazimirzki II, 1960, pp. 1335f.; Wahrmund I, 1970, p. 141; II, p. 1060; Gesenius-Buhl, 1962, pp. 520, 918; Koehler-Baumgartner, 1953, pp. 632, 1101; Dalman, 1967, p. 277.

45 Cf. "priests", "pious ones" etc. in written sources from Mesopotamia, Israel (Palestine), Egypt. See *Wörterbuch der Mythologie* I, 1965, *passim*; *Die Religionen der Menschheit*, 10,2, 1970, *passim*; *Lexikon der Ägyptologie*, V, 1984, pp. 212ff.; Old and New Testament; post-biblical Jewish traditions; etc.

46 Brockelmann I, 1961, pp. 352f.; Aartum II, 1997, pp. 728f.

47 Kazimirski I, 1960, pp. 56f.; Lane, 1863, pp. 101f.; Wahmund I, 1970, pp. 129f.; Gesenius-Buhl, 1962, p. 48; Koehler-Baumgartner, 1953, p. 61; Leslau, 1987, p. 24.

48 See Grumach-Shirun, 1980, pp. 971f.

49 Cf. Egyptian king's letter to Ichernofret (see Brunner, 1977, p. 22); cf. also Hebrew *læqaḥ* "instruction, teaching" (Deut. 32:2; Prov. 10:21(!); *mōrǣ* "teacher" (Isa 30:20; Prov. 5:13 (!) etc.

pu₂-nu-nu < **bunūnu* (*qutūl*-form[50] of the noun from *BNN*) "a sage" (Arabic *banī n-* "wise, prudent, sagacious").[51] In all nations of the ancient Near East persons of or indicating profound wisdom, and having the wisdom of experience, were highly respected as the educational ideals of the individual people, especially of the officials of the royal court. Just as those who possess experience of life and in every way are well-informed individuals, - also as people able to write, - they were looked upon as the personalities of the society who were educated and enlightened consistent with their station in life. For that reason they could fill high offices and appear as teachers of the youth.[52] Cf. the preceding designation (*o-me-no*);

ḫu(-pV-zV) < **ḫu(bzu/ā)* (*qutl*-form[53] of the noun from *ḪBZ*) "bre(ad) + an illustration of a bread prepared in a special shape"' (Arabic *ḫubz-* "bread"; *ḫubzat-* "loaf of bread"; *ḫabīz-* "bread"; Gĕʿĕz *ḫabz-*, *ḫĕbz-* "bread"; *ḫĕbĕst* < **ḫubuztu* "loaf of bread"; Mehri *ḫabz* "bread" (the root meaning *ḪBZ* is "to knead or beat [the dough]").[54] In contrast to other common forms of bread in the ancient Near East: those in the form of flat disks or long, thick loaves,[55] the present specimen is in the shape of a long, loaf which is curved in a special way. The form of the bread being a sacral product[56] in every case originally had a symbolic meaning determined by the cult i.e. the traditional fertility cult.[57] Considering the oriental religious way of thinking the physical performance of the fertility act – regularly or principally – was regarded as a mutual act of dining.[58] Therefore – as actual cult symbols – the

---

50 Brockelmann I, 1961, p. 359; Aartun II, 1997, p. 727.

51 Kazimirski I, 1960, p. 166; Lane, 1863, p. 258; Wahrmund I, 1970, p. 261.

52 For further studies see Lambert, 1960; Morenz, 1977 ("Weisheitslehre"); Blank, 1962; Smith, 1986; *Praktisches Bibel Lexikon*, 1985; etc.

53 Brockelmann I, 1961, p. 341; Aartun II, 1997, pp. 720f.

54 Kazimirski I, 1960, p. 533; Lane, 1863, p. 697; Wahrmund I, 1970, pp. 571, 573; Leslau, 1987, p. 257.

55 Cf. Ross, 1962, pp. 461f.; Abramsky, 1971, pp. 1333f.; Währen, 1967, *passim*; and others.

56 *Meyers enzyklopädisches Lexikon*, Volume 4, 1972, p. 784; *Brockhaus Enzyklopädie*, Volume 4, 1987, pp. 24f., with references.

57 For evidence of the established Minoan fertility cult see Aartun II, 1997, pp. 567-717.

58 Cf. the Ugaritic fertility texts RIH 78/20:6-8 (Aartun I, 1991, pp. 15, 28); 52 (CTA, 23; KTU 1.23):6 (Aartun I, 1974, p. 2); 1001 obv. 8 (KTU 1.82:38) (*qḥny* "drink both!" ; from *QḤḤ*; see Aartun II, 1997, pp. 638, 643); from the Old Testament: Hab. 2:15-16; Prov. 5:15; Cant. 5:1; 8:2 etc.; and verbally Hebrew and Mišnaic-Hebrew *ʾāḵal* "to eat, consume; to sleep with" (Gesenius-Buhl, 1962, p. 35; Koehler-Baumgartner, 1953, pp. 43f.; Jastrow I, 1972, p. 63; Dalman, 1967, p. 17); Aramaic

characteristic forms of the bread always illustrated in a concrete manner (the polarity of) the main cult media in action: The flat disk i.e. the moon at full[59] as well as the long, thick loaf,[60] both naturally typifying objects, referred to the male "partner", whereas the present curved bread, exactly corresponding in shape to the physical form of the vagina,[61] symbolized the female counterpart. Following the Minoan ritual demand in force at the time, it is evident that bread in the latter form was ordered as legal food[62] for the leading men or élite of the Minoan society.[63]

Bibliography

Aartun, K. 1974 *Die Partikeln des Ugaritischen* I, Neukirchen-Vluyn.

Aartun, K. 1978 *Textüberlieferung und vermeintliche Belege der Konjunktion* pV *im Alten Testament*, *UF* 10, p. 1-13, Neukirchen-Vluyn.

Aartun, K. 1991 *Studien zur ugaritischen Lexikographie* I, Wiesbaden.

Aartun, K. 1992 *Die minoische Schrift. Sprache und Texte.* Band I, *Der Diskos von Phaistos. Die beschriftete Bronzeaxt. Die Inschrift der Tarragona-Tafel*, Wiesbaden.

Aartun, K. 1994 *Runer i kulturhistorisk sammenheng. En fruktbarhetskultisk tradisjon*, Oslo.

Aartun, K. 1997 *Die minoische Schrift. Sprache und Texte,* Band II, *Linear A-Inschriften*, Wiesbaden.

---

nahămā "bread (!); marital intercourse" (Jastrow II, 1972, p. 882; Dalman, 1967, p. 264); Arabic *ḍafaza* "to feed; cohabit"; *ḍafz-* "morsel of food(!); sexual intercourse"; *qafaša* "to eat with avidity; to sleep frequently with" (Kazimirski II, 1960, pp. 31; 789; Wahrmund II, 1970, pp. 97, 513); Accadian *asakkam akālum* (von Soden I, 1965, p. 73; CAD "A" I, pp. 245f.); Egyptian "to eat and drink" = "to cohabit" (Manniche, 1987, p. 50); and so the Minoan sacred text Kn Zb 20 (Aartun II, 1997, pp. 641f.).

59 Cf. the Minoan illustration of the phases of the moon on vessel nr. 16305 in vitrine 8 in Museum Iraklion (Aartun I, 1992, pp. 240f.). Cf. also the moon as the "bridegroom" in the Ugaritic sexual ritual 77 (CTA 24; KTU 1.24); etc.

60 Cf. the many epithets of the membrum virile in the Minoan sacred texts (Aartun I, 1992, pp. 229ff.; II, 1997, pp. 42f., 567ff.).

61 GORILA IV, 1982, p. 94; Aartun II, 1997, p. 891. Compare the anatomical structure of the vagina.

62 Cf. *Encyclopaedia Britannica* sub voce: Dietary laws and food customs; Schlichting, 1984, pp. 1126f.; and corresponding religious laws and customs in the Old Testament; Währen, 1967, *passim*; etc.

63 "Die Erotik ist der Schlüssel zum Verständnis der alten Welt und ihrer Kultur" (Vorberg, 1968, p. 5); cf. also Scott, 1966, *passim*; Helck, 1971, *passim*; Manniche, 1988, *passim*; Siems (editor), 1988, *passim*; etc.

Abramsky, S. 1971 *Bread,* in *Encyclopaedia Judaica*, Volume 4, pp. 1333f., Jerusalem.

Aistleitner, J. 1963 *Wörterbuch der ugaritischen Sprache*, Berlin.

The Assyrian Dictionary of the University of Chicago, 1963-, Chicago.

Beeston, A. F. L., Ghul M. A., Müller W. W., Ryckmans J. 1982 *Sabaic Dictionary*, Louvain-la-Neuve.

Beeston, A F. L. 1984 *Sabaic Grammar*, Louvain.

Biella, J. C. 1982 *Dictionary of Old South Arabic*, Harvard.

Blank, S. H. 1962 *Wisdom*, in *The Interpreter's Dictionary of the Bible*, pp. 852-861, New York.

Brockelmann, C. 1961² *Grundriss der vergleichenden Grammatik der semitischen Sprachen* I-II, Darmstadt.

Brockhaus Enzyklopädie, Vierter Band, 1987, *Brot*, pp. 24f., Mannheim.

Brunner, H. 1977 *Erziehung*, in *Lexikon der Ägyptologie*, Band II, pp. 22-27, Wiesbaden.

Dalman, G. 1967 *Aramäisch-neuhebräisches Handwörterbuch zu Targum, Talmud und Midrasch*, Göttingen.

Dillmann, A. 1899 *Grammatik der äthiopischen Sprache*, München.

Gesenius W., Buhl F. 1962 *Hebräisches und aramäisches Handwörterbuch*, Berlin.

Gibb, H. 1963 *Arabic literature*, Oxford.

Godart L., Olivier J.-P. 1982 *Recueil des inscriptions en linéaire A (GORILA)*, Volume IV, Paris.

Gordon, C. H. 1965 *Ugaritic Textbook*, Roma.

Gray, J. 1957 *The Legacy of Canaan*, Leiden.

Grieshammer, R. 1984 *Kultische Reinheit*, in *Lexikon der Ägyptologie*, Band V, pp. 212-213, Wiesbaden.

Grumach-Shirun, I. 1980 *Lehre des Amenemope*, in *Lexikon der Ägyptologie*, Band III, pp. 971-974, Wiesbaden.

Hamer, E. 1950 *Rhetoric*, in *Chamber's Encyclopaedia* 11, pp. 656-660, London.

Helck, W. 1971 *Betrachtungen zur grossen Göttin und den ihr verbundenen Gottheiten*, München.

Hoffmann, H. 1965 *Rhetorik*, in *Lexikon der alten Welt*, Band III, pp. 2611-2626, München.

Jastrow, M. 1972 *A Dictionary of the Targumim, the Talmud Babli and Yerushalmi, and the Midrashic Literature*, Volume I-II, Jerusalem.

Junge, F. 1984 *Rethorik*, in *Lexikon der Ägyptologie*, Band V, pp. 250-253, Wiesbaden.

Kazimirski, A. de B. 1960 *Dictionnaire arabe-français* I-II, Paris.

Koehler, L. - Baumgartner, W. 1953 *Lexicon in Veteris Testamenti Libros*, Leiden.

Lambert, W. G. 1960 *Babylonian Wisdom Literature*, Oxford.

Lamer, H. 1933 *Beredsamkait*, in *Wörterbuch der Antike*, pp. 84-87, Leipzig.

Lane, E. W. 1863-1877 *Arabic-English Lexicon*, Cambridge.

Leslau, W. 1987 *Comparative Dictionary of Gĕʿĕz*, Wiesbaden.

Manniche, L. 1987 *Liebe und Sexualität im alten Ägypten*, London.

Meyers enzyklopädisches Lexikon, Volume IV, 1972, *Brot*, pp. 781-784, Mannheim.

Morenz, S. 1977, *Ägyptische Religion*, Stuttgart.

Nicholson, R. A. 1956 *A Literary History of the Arabs*, Cambridge.

Nielsen, E. 1954/55 *Oral Tradition. A Modern Problem in Old Testament Introduction*, London.

Payne Smith, J. 1976 *A Compendious Syriac Dictionary*, Oxford.

Praktisches Bibel Lexikon, 1985, Freiburg

Prätorius, F. 1871/1972 *Grammatik der Tigriñasprache in Abessinien, hauptsächlich in der Gegend von Aksum und Adoa*, Halle/Leipzig.

Prätorius, F. 1879 *Die amharische Sprache*, Halle.

Prätorius, F. 1886 *Äthiopische Grammatik*, Leipzig.

Die Religionen der Menschheit, Band 10, 2, 1970, Stuttgart.

Ross, J. F. 1962 *Bread*, in *The Interpreter's Dictionary of the Bible*, pp. 461-464, New York.

Schlichting, R. 1984 *Speisege- und -verbote,* in *Lexikon der Ägyptologie*, Band V, pp. 1126-1128, Wiesbaden.

Scott, G. R. 1966 *Phallic Worship. A History of Sex and Sex Rites in Relation to the Religions of All Races from Antiquity to the Present Day*, London.

Siems, A. K. (editor) 1988 *Sexualität und Erotik in der Antike*, Darmstadt.

Smith, M. J. 1986 *Demotische Weisheit,* in *Lexikon der Ägyptologie*, Band VI, pp. 1192-1204, Wiesbaden.

von Soden, W. 1965 *Akkadisches Handwörterbuch*, Band I, Wiesbaden.

von Soden, W. 1985 *Einführung in die Altorientalistik*, Darmstadt.

Speake, G. 1994 *Education*, in *A Dictionary of Ancient History*, pp. 224-226, Oxford.

Vorberg, G. 1968 *Ars erotica veterum. Das Geschlechtsleben im Altertum*, Hanau.

Währen, M. 1967 *Brot und Gebäck im Leben und Glauben des alten Orients*, Bern.
Wahrmund, A. 1970 *Handwörterbuch der arabischen und deutschen Sprache* I-II, Graz.
Wörterbuch der Mythologie, Band II, 1965, Stuttgart.
Wright, W. 1964 *A G rammar of the Arabic Language* I-II, Cambridge.

I SOSTANTIVI FENICI *ʾAB* E *ʾAḤ*[*]

MARIA GIULIA AMADASI GUZZO

Università di Roma "La Sapienza"

Come nelle altre lingue semitiche, i vocaboli *ʾab* "padre" e *ʾaḥ* "fratello" presentavano originariamente in fenicio, nella declinazione singolare, una vocale lunga finale, che si è conservata in alcune situazioni. Inoltre, come in ebraico, il plurale di *ʾab* si forma mediante l'aggiunta del suffisso *-ōt*. Il presente studio, oltre a mettere in evidenza gli esempi che possono indicare la quantità e la qualità della vocale davanti ai suffissi possessivi, elenca le attestazioni del plurale di *ʾab*, che avevano finora ricevuto scarsa attenzione.

Terminazione davanti a suffissi

La prova che, anche in fenicio, *ʾab-* e *ʾaḥ-* terminavano davanti ai suffissi possessivi in vocale lunga deriva dalle grafie del sostantivo con il suffisso pronominale di 3ª persona singolare e plurale:[1] si tratta, nel primo caso, della variante grafica -Y, che si produce, di regola, dopo la terminazione del nome in vocale *-i* (sostantivo singolare al genitivo) o in vocale lunga (sostantivo plurale).[2] Infatti, la grafia ʾBY è usata sia quando il sostantivo è nominativo e accusativo ("suo padre", soggetto o complemento oggetto), sia quando è genitivo ("di/per suo padre"). La stessa constatazione vale per *ʾaḥ*, che presenta, sia al nominativo, sia al genitivo, l'ortografia ʾḤY ("di/per suo fratello"). Invece, nel nome triconsonantico "regolare", l'aggiunta del suffisso produce le seguenti grafie: singolare, nom./acc. ʾDN "il suo signore"

---

* Sono usate le seguenti abbreviazioni: AI = iscrizione latino-punica in R. Bartoccini, *Africa Italiana* 1 (1927) 233; DISI = J. Hoftijzer - K. Jongeling, *Dictionary of the North-West Semitic Inscriptions* (*Handbuch der Orientalistik* 21), Leiden 1995; EH = A. Berthier - R. Charlier, *Le sanctuaire punique d'El-Hofra à Constantine*, Paris 1952-55; IPT = G. Levi Della Vida - M. G. Amadasi Guzzo, *Iscrizioni puniche della Tripolitania (1927-1967)* (*Quaderni di archeologia della Libia* 22), Roma 1986; IRT = J. M. Reynolds - J. B. Ward Perkins, *The Inscriptions of Roman Tripolitania*, Rome / London 1952; PPG³ = J. Friedrich - W. Röllig - M. G. Amadasi Guzzo, *Phönizisch-punische Grammatik*³, Rom 1999; S 24 = iscrizione latino-punica in J. Reynolds, "Inscriptions of Roman Tripolitania: A Supplement", *Papers of the British School at Rome* 23 (1955), p. 141.

1 V. PPG³, § 241, 1-2.

2 V. PPG³, § 112; esempi: § 240, 1-2.

(*ʾadōnō*; grafia zero del suffisso); gen. ʾDNY "del/per il suo signore" (*ʾadōniyū*); plurale ʾDNY (*ʾadōnēyū* o *ʾadōnīyū*).

Con il suffisso di 3ª persona plurale *ʾab* presenta sempre la grafia ʾBNM "di/per loro padre", rispetto a nom./acc. ʾDNM "il loro signore" (*ʾadōnōm*); gen. ʾDNNM "del/per il loro signore" (*ʾadōninōm*); pl. ʾDNNM (*ʾadonēnōm* o *ʾadōnīnōm*).[3] Gli esempi sono citati in PPG³ (§ 240, 1) e non sono perciò ripetuti qui in maniera completa. Invece *ʾaḥ* non presenta esempi provvisti del suffisso di 3ª persona plurale.

La situazione dei sostantivi con il suffisso di 1ª persona singolare **-ya* è diversa e concorda con quanto è attestato per i nomi di tre consonanti. Nella fase più antica del fenicio (e nel dialetto di Biblo anche in epoca persiana), infatti, il sostantivo di tre consonanti "forti" presenta il suffisso vocalico non scritto (*-ī*) se il nome è nominativo/accusativo,[4] scritto Y (*-iy*(*a*)), se il sostantivo è al genitivo /dativo o plurale (*-ēy*(*a*) o *-īy*(*a*)).[5] Già intorno al 700 a.C. (iscrizione di Karatepe KAI 26), il suffisso possessivo di 1ª persona singolare si scrive -Y, qualsiasi sia la terminazione del nome al quale è unito.[6] Sembrerebbe quindi che la *yod* finale assuma ben presto, nella tradizione scribale più generalizzata,[7] la funzione della vocale *-ī*.

I nomi *ʾab* e *ʾaḥ* si adeguano alla stessa regola, come mostra l'iscrizione di Kulamuwa (KAI 24; ca. 825 a.C.): qui infatti è attestata la grafia ʾB "mio padre" (nom.) e ʾḤ "mio fratello" che implicano una terminazione in vocale *-ī* (forse *ʾabī*; *ʾaḥī*), e ʾBY "di mio padre" (gen.), che implica una terminazione in vocale + consonante (forse *ʾabīya* o *ʾabīy* se cade, come presunto, la vocale breve finale). Il nome *ʾaḥ* al genitivo con il suffisso di 1ª persona singolare non è testimoniato. Gli esempi di questo stadio sono: KAI 24, 3-4, WKN ʾB ḤYʾ WBL PʿL "e vi fu mio padre ḤYʾ

---

3 Sui suffissi di 3ª persona in fenicio v. da ultimo, con l'indicazione dei precedenti studi (soprattutto di Ch. R. Krahmalkov), J. Huehnergard, "The Development of the Third Person Suffix in Phoenician", *Maarav* 7 (1991), pp. 183-194.

4 In aramaico antico l'ortografia è ʾBY anche quando il nome è al nominativo: cf. l'iscrizione di Tel Dan A 2, 3; v. A. Biran - J. Naveh, "The Tel Dan Inscription: A New Fragment", *IEJ* 45 (1995), p. 12.

5 Tale regola è riscontrabile nell'iscrizione di Kulamuwa KAI 24 e nell'iscrizione di Biblo KAI 10.

6 Esempi in PPG³, § 234.

7 Si tratta del così detto Tiro-Sidonio di G. Garbini, "I dialetti del fenicio", in *Il Semitico nord-occidentale. Studi di storia linguistica*, Roma 1988, pp. 51-68 (stt. 56-58; aggiornamento e ampliamento dell'articolo di uguale titolo in *AION* 37 [1977], pp. 283-294) e di Ch. R. Krahmalkov, "Languages: Phoenician", in *The Anchor Bible Dictionary*, 4, New York / London etc. 1992, p. 222 e del "Fenicio classico" o "standard" di W. R. Garr, *Dialect Geography of Syria Palestine, 1000-586 B. C. E.*, Philadelphia 1985, in particolare p. 13.

e non si mostrò attivo"; WKN ʾḤ / (4) ŠʾL WBL PʿL "e vi fu mio fratello ŠʾL e non si mostrò attivo". Invece, con il sostantivo al genitivo, KAI 24, 5-6, KN BT ʾBY BMTKT MLKM ʾD/RM "la casa di mio padre era in mezzo a re potenti"; a l. 9, YŠBT ʿL KSʾ ʾBY "mi sedetti sul trono di mio padre". In seguito, non si possiedono attestazioni del sostantivo al nom./acc. con il suffisso di 1ª persona singolare, ma soltanto forme in funzione di genitivo, con grafia ʾBY. Come per gli altri nomi, è da supporre che quest'ultima grafia si sia generalizzata nell'uso per tutti i casi.

Qualità della vocale lunga finale

Alcune grafie puniche tarde, le trascrizioni in alfabeto latino di *ʾab* e *ʾaḥ* con suffissi personali possessivi e quelle in greco e latino di nomi di persona, dei quali *ʾab* e *ʾaḥ* costituiscono il primo elemento, permettono di ricostruire la qualità della vocale finale prevalsa in fenicio. Secondo Ch. R. Krahmalkov si tratta di *ū* dell'originario nominativo, estesa a tutti i casi; tale affermazione si basa su un'attestazione nel *Poenulus* di Plauto e su due iscrizioni latino-puniche.[8] In ciò il fenicio concorderebbe con l'aramaico, discostandosi invece dall'ebraico biblico, che presenta per tutti i casi la vocale *ī*. La situazione che rivelano i pochi esempi a disposizione non è in realtà unitaria come supposto.

Nei nomi propri[9]

I nomi propri composti con *ʾab* mostrano sempre una vocale finale *i*, che, tuttavia, solo in un caso può essere analizzata come quella dello stato costrutto. Gli esempi, nel caso di *ʾab*, sono scarsi: si tratta del cuneiforme (neo-assiro) ᴵ*A-bi-ba-aʾ-li*, e del greco Αβιβαλος (e varianti, v. nota 9); il latino è più ambiguo, con *Abius* e qualche altro esempio più incerto.[10] Nella fase tarda del punico è attestata la grafia ʿBY a

---

8 Ch. R. Krahmalkov, *JSS* 15 (1970), p. 184, nota 3; *id.*, *RSO* 44 (1969), p. 186; *JSS* 17 (1972), p. 74, n. 2; *id.*, in *The Anchor Bible Dictionary*, 4, p. 222. L'ipotesi è accolta da S. C. Layton, *Archaic Features of Canaanite Personal Names in the Hebrew Bible* (*Harvard Semitic Monographs* 47) Atlanta, Georgia, 1990, pp. 49, 101, 116 (a p. 60 il nome Ḥūrām, così vocalizzato in 1 Cron. 14: 1Q; 2 Cron. 2: 2, 10, 11, 12; 4: 11, 16; 8: 2, 18; 9: 10Q, 21, è considerato come riflesso dell'originaria forma fenicia: si tratterebbe di un nominativo "il fratello è alto"). La regola enunciata per l'aramaico non si estende con sicurezza al periodo più antico (in senso stretto) di questa lingua.

9 V. PPG³, §§ 240, 241, sub 1-2.

10 La vocale *i* rappresenterebbe, secondo K. Jongeling, la terminazione dell'ipocoristico, alla quale si aggiunge la terminazione latina *-us*; v. *Names in Neo-Punic Inscriptions*, Groningen 1984, p. 49; *id.*, *North African Names from Latin Sources*, Leiden 1994, pp. 3-4.

Mididi,[11] che presenta la stessa pronuncia del latino *Abius* e la stessa ambiguità nell'analisi di -Y.

I nomi composti con *ʾab* consistono verosimilmente in tutte le attestazioni in una frase nominale, così non si può determinare con sicurezza se la vocale finale *i* delle trascrizioni rappresenti il suffisso di 1ª persona singolare, una vocale di legamento, oppure una sopravvivenza della declinazione;[12] oltre alla sua funzione, la sua quantità non è quindi precisabile. Gli esempi in fenicio non indicano mai graficamente tale vocale finale; nel caso si tratti del pronome suffisso di 1ª singolare, questo tipo di scrittura concorda con la regola su citata della grafia Ø del suffisso pronominale di prima persona, quando *ʾab* è soggetto.[13]

Un solo esempio è discutibile. Si tratta della legenda LʾBYBʿL attestata su un sigillo (dal mercato antiquario), attribuito all'VIII secolo a.C., che appare di tipo fenicio per l'iconografia della sua raffigurazione (per la forma delle lettere potrebbe essere attribuito anche ad altre lingue che impiegano regolarmente le *matres lectionis*);[14] la classificazione dell'iscrizione è discussa proprio per la grafia "piena" del sostantivo. Ma, se davvero il sigillo è fenicio, la -Y potrebbe interpretarsi, se non come un'indicazione del suffisso di 1ª persona singolare, eventualmente come l'indicazione grafica del pronome possessivo di 3ª persona: "suo padre è Baʿl", certo non altrimenti attestato. Sembra possibile citare a confronto nomi composti con ʾB con un pronome suffisso diverso da quello di 1ª singolare, cioè ʾBNBʿL di CIS I 476, 5 o

---

11 RÉS 169, 2, nella nuova edizione di M. Sznycer, "Les inscriptions néopuniques de Mididi", *Semitica* 36 (1986), p. 10, n° 3.

12 Nonostante quanto argomentato da S. C. Layton, *Archaic Features of Canaanite Personal Names in the Hebrew Bible*, pp. 145-150 che tende a interpretare in questi casi la *ī* come l'indicazione del pronome suffisso. M. Noth, *Die israelitischen Personennamen im Rahmen der gemeinsemitischen Namengebung*, Stuttgart 1928, pp. 33-35 presume che si tratti a volte di un resto della declinazione: tra gli altri esempi, ne sarebbe una prova il nome del re di Tiro scritto ḤWRM "il fratello è alto", con la terminazione *ū* del nominativo (v. qui nota 8).

13 Si ha perciò sempre la scrittura ʾBBʿL o ʾBMLK, sia in fenicio sia in punico. Per le attestazioni e l'interpretazione v. F. L. Benz, *Personal Names in the Phoenician and Punic Inscriptions* (*Studia Pohl* 8), Roma 1972, pp. 54, 218, 257 (Benz considera che il nome abbia il suffisso pronominale di 1ª persona singolare).

14 V. N. Avigad - B. Sass, *A Corpus of West Semitic Stamp Seals*, Jerusalem 1997, p. 426, n° 1122 (con bibliografia precedente e proposte di classificazione); nel *Corpus* il sigillo non è definito: a causa della grafia piena si propone che possa essere ammonita, aramaico, o perfino ebraico (parere di J. Naveh).

ʾBNŠMŠ di RÉS 1357, 1, dove si può supporre la presenza del suffisso di 1ª persona plurale,[15] che si potrebbe riferire all'insieme della famiglia.

Nomi propri composti con *ʾaḥ* sono più frequenti. In trascrizioni assire sono attestati i nomi ¹*Ḫi-ru-um-mu* e ¹*A-ḫi-mil-ki*; il greco presenta Ειρωμος.[16] Malgrado la distanza di alcuni secoli, compare sempre la stessa vocale *-i-* (attestata anche da un esempio di scrittura piena, HYR[M], su una stele da Constantine, in Algeria, del II-I secolo a.C.).[17] Tale vocale può rappresentare sia il suffisso di 1ª persona singolare, sia la famosa "vocale di legamento". Più significative sono le trascrizioni del nome ḤMLKT "fratello della Regina", dove il sostantivo è sicuramente allo stato costrutto seguito da un nome retto. Le trascrizioni greche e latine corrispondenti sono Ιμυλκων, *Himilco*, e *Imilco*.[18] La vocale dello stato costrutto è qui in origine quella del genitivo, considerata poi, in ebraico, come la così detta *yod compaginis*.

In conclusione, nei nomi propri composti, *ʾab-* e *ʾaḥ-* presentano una vocale finale di qualità *i*; ma solo *ʾaḥ* ha un esempio sicuro di tale vocale (probabilmente in origine lunga) allo stato costrutto davanti al complemento di specificazione. Negli altri esempi si può trattare del pronome suffisso. Secondo le regole ortografiche del fenicio, tale vocale non è indicata dalla scrittura (l'ortografia consueta è ḤMLKT). Solo in epoca tardopunica (dopo il III secolo a.C.) si possono avere indicazioni grafiche della vocale, che non appaiono comunque in rapporto con la lunghezza.

Davanti a suffissi

Nella fase tarda del punico, alcune attestazioni dei vocaboli con il suffisso possessivo di 3ª singolare maschile e di 3ª plurale sono presenti sia in scrittura neopunica sia in scrittura latina e mostrano una situazione differenziata per quanto riguarda la vocale dello stato costrutto.

In funzione di soggetto, *ʾab* è attestato nella forma ʿBYʾ "suo padre" in Np 63, 2 (= JA 1917/1, 163-164); in funzione di genitivo (complemento di specificazione) la stessa grafia ʾBYʾ ricorre in IPT 79. In questi due casi -Yʾ è la scrittura "piena" del

15 V. Benz, *Personal Names*, p. 258.

16 V. PPG³ § 240, 2. Per le altre attestazioni v. Benz, *Personal Names in the Phoenician and Punic Inscriptions*, pp. 263-264.

17 *Ibid.*, p. 108 (EH n°176, 3).

18 Esempi in PPG³ § 240, 2 (con varianti nella resa di *k* fenicio; in tre casi, v. K. Jongeling, *Names in Neo-Punic Inscriptions*, p. 167, si tratta di bilingui, dove la corrispondenza con ḤMLKT – e non ḤMLK ! – è sicura).

suffisso in punico-tardo,[19] mentre la vocale lunga dello stato costrutto non è indicata in maniera specifica (si può quindi ricostruire tanto *ʾabūyū*, quanto *ʾabīyū*).

Invece, l'iscrizione neopunica da Masculula n° 3, pubblicata da J.-B. Chabot,[20] attesta in funzione di soggetto il vocabolo *ʾab* con il suffisso di 3ª persona singolare, nella grafia ʿBWYʿ (linea 4); il contesto è: ṬYNʾ Lʾ ʿBWYʿ "eresse (questa stele funeraria: ʾBN "pietra") per lui (il defunto è un uomo) suo padre". L'espressione va ricostruita *abūyū*, con il suffisso che si unisce a *ū* dell'originario nominativo, ma si deve notare l'uso inconsueto di ʿ per indicare, nel suffisso, la vocale finale *ū* (o *ō*).[21]

L'iscrizione latino-punica IRT´ 828, 1-2 presenta d'altra parte l'espressione *lobym* "per suo padre", che dovrebbe derivare, accettando lo sviluppo proposto da J. Huehnergard, da **la-ʾabī-hū* > *la-ʾabī-yū* > **lābīw* > *lobīm*,[22] sviluppo che permetterebbe di ricostruire una vocale *ī* come terminazione dello stato costrutto, in accordo con la funzione di genitivo del nome. Una certa ambiguità deriva dalla scrittura della vocale **ī* per mezzo di *y*, lettera che è adoperata per suoni vocalici variati, in qualche caso anche per *ū*.[23]

Risulta da questi due esempi, se l'ultima ricostruzione è esatta, una distinzione nella pronuncia, almeno in una fase del fenicio, tra il sostantivo al nominativo e quello al genitivo davanti al pronome suffisso di 3ª singolare (come in accadico e in arabo):[24] nominativo *ʾabūyū* "suo padre" e genitivo *ʾabīyū* "di/per suo padre": solo quest'ultima forma, nella tradizione scribale ufficiale graficamente identica alla prima (ʾBY), si sarebbe sviluppata in **lābīm* > *lobym*.

---

19 È indicata cioè mediante *alef* la vocale finale del suffisso; per ʾ che indica una qualsiasi vocale finale in punico, v. PPG³ § 105.

20 J.-B. Chabot, "Inscriptions néopuniques de Masculula", *JA* 1916/1, p. 454.

21 Chabot, *ibid.*, osserva che ʿBWYʿ è la lettura più verosimile (rispetto a ʿBYʿ). Aggiunge inoltre "Il est singulier que le ʿ final (qui est sûr) remplisse la fonction de suffixe de la 3e pers. masc., ordinairement exprimé par ʾ". Tuttavia nella stessa iscrizione a l. 2 si ha la grafia ʿWʿ "egli visse", con ʿ = *ō*, al posto del più comune ʿWʾ (mentre spesso ʿWʿ è usato per il femminile); comunque il defunto sembra sicuramente di sesso maschile.

22 V. J. Huehnergard, *Maarav* 7 (1991) 189-190.

23 V. PPG³ § 90. Va notato che il suffisso -M sostituisce in punico tardo la variante scritta -Y, sia dopo *i* del genitivo singolare, sia dopo *-ī/-ē* del plurale. Un'eventuale ricostruzione **laʾabū-hū* > **la-ʾabūw* > *lābūm*. è da escludere in base alle ortografie neopuniche (di *ʾaḥ* + suffisso *-m*) ʿYM e ḤYM, che non possono derivare, ammettendo l'ipotesi di Huehnergard, da un eventuale **ʾaḥūm*.

24 Non si possiedono esempi del sostantivo con il suffisso personale di 2ª singolare.

(Su queste basi l'accusativo doveva, in origine, terminare in *-ā-*, ma non si possiedono esempi sicuri che ne indichino la conservazione eventuale nella pronuncia.)

La situazione del sostantivo con il suffisso di 3ª persona plurale[25] è la seguente. Il nominativo ʾBNM è attestato in fenicio in KAI 40, 5 (Cipro), dove l'ortografia non dà elementi per ricostruire la vocalizzazione. In tardo-punico il genitivo ʿBNʾM è attestato in IPT 77, 2. Qui è indicata la vocale del suffisso mediante *alef*. Tale *mater lectionis* indica in origine in punico qualsiasi vocale (lunga?) (v. nota 19), ma è adoperata, in una fase successiva, spesso per *ō* (e per *ē*):[26] il suffisso si può ricostruire anche su questa base come *-nōm* (come risulta dalla trascrizione ABUNOM, v. sotto),[27] mentre ancora una volta la vocale dello stato costrutto non è indicata.

Il genitivo LʾBʿNHM è attestato in KAI 142, 4 (NP 133, da Henchir Brigitta, Tunisia). La vocale dello stato costrutto è contrassegnata da ʿ: questa faringale è usata spesso per *a* e più raramente per altre vocali. Nella stessa iscrizione KAI 142 rappresenta *a* in nomi latini trascritti, come *Gadaeus*, scritto Gʿ[D]ʿY (l. 1) e *Secunda*, scritto ŠHQNDʿ (l. 1-2; ma *Secundus*, *ibid.* è scritto ŠQNDʿ!) e in vocaboli fenici come ŠʿNʾT (l. 3) "anni" e ʿWʿ (l. 3) "essa visse". Tuttavia la stessa vocale *a* è anche indicata da ʾ, per es. in ʾQYLʾ (l. 1) forse *Aquila*. La grafia tradizionale usata in ʾB-, inoltre, rende, nella pronuncia di questo termine, ʾ, caduta precocemente, equivalente di nuovo ad *a*. H, nella presente iscrizione, è usata per *e* nel nome ŠHQNDʿ, ma per *ō* in ʿWH (l. 2) "egli visse" (*awō*). Il sistema appare dunque qui molto ambiguo[28] e si può supporre che ogni parola/espressione possa essere considerata come un'unità a sé stante: in LʾBʿNHM, l'uso dei tre diversi segni deve mostrare l'intento di indicare tre vocali diverse: *a* nella prima sillaba; *ō* nell'ultima; una vocale incerta nella seconda (*i* è indicata da Y nel nome *Aquila*, ma come si è visto gli usi non sono del tutto coerenti all'interno dell'iscrizione).

La vocalizzazione in *ū* è invece senza dubbio presente, in una forma con il nome originariamente al genitivo, nell'iscrizione latino-punica S24 (OA 2, 75, 2)[29] che ha l'espressione *labunom* "per il loro padre"; tale forma ha fornito la base a Ch. R. Krahmalkov (v. nota 8) per la ricostruzione di una vocale *ū* dello stato costrutto

---

25 Non si hanno testimonianze del nome con suffissi di 1ª e 2ª persona plurale.

26 V. PPG³ § 107, 4. In questo caso specifico ʿ è usata per *a* (ʾ era ormai caduta nella pronuncia).

27 V. Ch. R. Krahmalkov, *JSS* 15 (1970), pp. 181-188.

28 Il sistema è meno ambiguo se si presume uno sviluppo costante di *ō* > *ē*.

29 Per il significato v. G. Levi Della Vida, "Parerga neopunica", *OA* 4 (1965), p. 60; Ch. R. Krahmalkov, *JSS* 15 (1970), p. 184 e nota 3.

davanti a suffissi per tutti i casi.; ciò concorda con la grafia ʿBWYʿ (nominativo), ma non con *lobym*.

Gli esempi di *ʾaḥ* "fratello" con suffisso personale sono i seguenti:

Con il suffisso di 3ª persona singolare maschile, come nel caso di *ʾab*, la grafia punica tarda del genitivo ʾḤYʾ "di suo fratello" in IPT 10, 2 indica solo la vocalizzazione *-yū* del suffisso (**ʾaḥīyū* o **ʾaḥūyū*). Ma il nominativo ʿY̊M della NP 62, 3[30] indica (se la lettura è corretta) una pronuncia *aīm* < *ʾaḥīw* < *ʾaḥī-yū* < **ʾaḥī-hū*, analogamente a quanto ricostruito sulla base di *lobym*. Si tratterebbe perciò di una formazione basata sulla desinenza del genitivo. Il nome al genitivo scritto ḤYM è del resto attestato in JA 1916/2, 494: 10, 6, da Guelma. Si dovrebbe ricostruire una pronuncia (*ḥ*)*īm*; eventualmente *aim*, come in NP 62, ammettendo la caduta nella pronuncia della consonante Ḥ, conservatasi come grafia storica e forse usata come vocale.

Diversamente, il latino-punico fornirebbe due attestazioni di terminazione *-ū*, al nominativo e al genitivo, ambedue in IRT 826, se si segue l'interpretazione di Ch. R. Krahmalkov. Lo studioso identifica nel testo il nominativo *auia* ("suo [= di lei] fratello" e il genitivo *l<a>uia* ("per suo [= di lei] fratello").[31] Il testo dell'iscrizione è tuttavia dubbio e si trascrive come segue:

Š̊I̊D̊Ě̊N̊ F̊E/LALVIA OCLE/S FELAVIA / OCES ESRIM / XX

G. Levi Della Vida[32] aveva interpretato *Felaluia* come errore per *Felauia* (per *Flauia*) e *Oces* come errore per *Ocles*: si sarebbe trattato nei due casi della menzione dei nomi della defunta, Flavia Ocles, scritti due volte per correggere un errore (ma la seconda ne avrebbe contenuto un altro). L'interpretazione di Krahmalkov, che intende "Siden fece per suo fratello Ocles (*Siden fela l<a>uia Ocles*). Visse suo fratello Oc<l>es venti (anni) (*fel auia Oc<l>es esrim 20*) è attraente; ma lo studioso è costretto, sia a correggere il testo in FELA L<A>VIA a l. 1-2, sia a dividere a l. 3 FEL AVIA e a dare al verbo "fare" (FEL = **paʿal*) il significato di "vivere". La forma *auia* perciò non può essere accettata senza riserva, né preceduta da L-, né come soggetto. Se accettata, dimostrerebbe la presenza di una vocale *u* per tutti i casi,

30 V. J.-B. Chabot, *JA* 1917/1, p. 163 n° 30.

31 V. Ch. R. Krahmalkov, *JSS* 17 (1972), p. 74. V. anche PPG³, § 240, 2: gli esempi in scrittura neopunica non indicano mai una vocale *u*, mentre con il suffisso -M si ha sempre la vocalizzazione in *i*.

32 G. Levi Della Vida, "Sulle iscrizioni 'latino-libiche' della Tripolitania", *OA* 2 (1963), p. 84.

in alternanza con *i*, comprovata questa dal vocabolo provvisto del suffisso nella variante -M.

La vocale *u* appare, inaspettatamente, dopo il suffisso di 1ª persona singolare, nel monologo in punico di Annone, nel *Poenulus* di Plauto, unita al nome in funzione di genitivo: il v. 932 (versione recente)[33] contiene infatti l'espressione *byn ui* "il figlio di mio fratello". La forma concorda con quanto ricostruito da Krahmalkov e contrasta con quanto si desumerebbe dall'ortografia antica attestata in Kulamuwa: qui, come si è visto sopra, il gen. **ʾaḥī-* + **-ya* dovrebbe scriversi ʾḤY e pronunciarsi **ʾaḥīya*; la vocalizzazione del *Poenulus* appare perciò il riusultato di un diverso sviluppo, eventualmente secondario.

Nonostante l'esiguità delle attestazioni elencate, si può concludere che *ʾab* e *ʾaḥ* in nomi propri o davanti a suffisso mantenevano una vocale lunga; nei nomi propri tale vocale è *ī* quando *ʾaḥ* (e *ʾab*) sono allo stato costrutto seguiti da un complemento di specificazione. Nel caso dei nomi propri costituiti da una frase nominale le trascrizioni attestano una vocale *i*, che si può interpretare o come una "vocale di legamento" (derivante dal genitivo), o come il pronome suffisso di 1ª persona singolare.

Con i suffissi possessivi, nella fase antica della lingua, *ʾab* e *ʾaḥ* sembrano annettere il suffisso di 1ª persona singolare direttamente alla seconda consonante radicale quando sono al nominativo/accusativo. Nella fase tarda, il vocabolo *ʾaḥ* nel Poenulus, in funzione di genitivo, presenta invece davanti allo stesso suffisso la vocale *u*.

Davanti al suffisso di 3ª singolare e plurale si osserva un'oscillazione nella vocale che è in alcuni casi *ū*, in altri *ī*. Sulla base degli esempi tardopunici "vocalizzati", si presume che in origine la vocale fosse *-ū-* per il nominativo, *-ī-* per il genitivo (non si può dire nulla per l'accusativo). Nell'ultima fase della lingua, le terminazioni non corrispondono più con regolarità alla funzione del nome: si può trovare infatti *-ī-* con il nominativo e *-ū-* con il genitivo. Tale confusione trova un parallelo nell'uso non più "regolare" delle varianti grafiche dei suffissi di 3ª persona singolare e plurale, che erano in origine determinate proprio dalla qualità e quantità della vocale cui il suffisso era unito (v. qui pp. 13-14).[34] Così, per ritornare a *ʾab* e *ʾaḥ*, mentre *lobym* "per suo padre" e ḤYM "di suo fratello" rifletterebbero la

33 Per la data delle due versioni v. A. S. Gratwick, "Hanno's Punic Speech", *Hermes* 99 (1971), pp. 35-37.

34 V. alcuni esempi di confusione in PPG³ § 234.

variante "regolare" con il nome con la terminazione *-ī-* (genitivo), la grafia ʿYM, "suo fratello" (nominativo), corrispondendo anch'essa al genitivo del nome, mostra la caduta delle regole ortografiche tradizionali, che, nella loro generale uniformità, non permettono di verificare gli sviluppi della lingua. In epoca tarda (romana?), avrebbero forse preso il sopravvento le forme con terminazione *u* (seconda redazione del "monologo di Annone", iscrizioni latino-puniche); le varianti con suffisso *-m* devono invece avere mantenuto, anche in punico tardo (e nelle latino-puniche) la tradizionale vocalizzazione in *i*.

Va notato infine che uno sviluppo unitario del punico tardo in tutta la vasta regione del suo uso, specie in mancanza di una salda tradizione comune, non è forse da presumere; si possono essere verificate perciò, a seconda della regione di provenienza delle iscrizioni, differenze nella canonizzazione formale dei due sostantivi con il suffisso: in particolare le convenzioni ortografiche attestate dalla versione più recente del monologo punico del Poenulus e dalle iscrizioni latino-puniche tripolitane (e la varietà di punico alla loro base) sembrano rappresentare una tradizione relativamente unitaria, ma non forse l'unica.

Plurale di ʾab

Il plurale di *ʾab*, *ʾabōt*, è attestato da due esempi in scrittura fenicia e due in scrittura latina. In scrittura fenicia ʾBT è presente in un'iscrizione neopunica di Leptis Magna della fine del I secolo d.C. (KAI 126; il significato di ʾBTM in IPT 37 è discutibile) e, molto prima, intorno al 700 a.C., a Karatepe (KAI 26). Tale esempio viene esaminato per ultimo, perché la spiegazione del vocabolo è ancora incerta.

L'iscrizione neopunica KAI 126 (Trip. 27) del 92 d.C., la cui versione latina è in IRT 318 e 347, commemora la concessione dell'uso del laticlavo a un personaggio locale particolarmente benemerito, Tiberio Claudio Sestio della tribù Quirina. Il testo latino riferisce che i senatori e il popolo gli concessero tale privilegio *ob merita maiorum eius et ipsius*; il punico, nella lettura corretta in IPT 27 (l. 8), presenta, in corrispondenza, la frase LPY MʾSʾ ʾBTM WMʾSM BTM "grazie alle azioni dei suoi padri e alle sue 'proprie' azioni". Il sostantivo ʾBT, con il suffisso tardopunico di 3ª persona singolare maschile, designa qui in maniera specifica gli "antenati" (i "maggiori"). L'identico significato assume il plurale di *ʾab* anche in ebraico.

Il plurale di *ʾab* designa invece i "genitori" in un'iscrizione latino-punica da Zliten (*OA* 2, 83, 2), nella quale è presente l'espressione *lybythem lisnim*: al plurale di *ʾab* è aggiunto il numerale "due" per indicare senza possibilità di dubbio che si tratta del padre e della madre e non di “antenati”. Riguardo alla pronuncia, la consonante *y* del latino indica, dopo *l-*, una vocale breve; nel secondo caso dovrebbe indicare *ū* < *ō*, secondo lo sviluppo della desinenza **-ōt* attestato normalmente in punico tardo.[35]

Se è giusta l’integrazione *lobu<t>hem* e l’interpretazione “per i suoi genitori” nell’iscrizione latino-punica da Gasr el-Azaiz, pubblicata in Libya Antiqua 13-14, 109,[36] il vocabolo sarebbe stato usato in punico con lo stesso significato di “genitori” anche senza la specificazione del numerale.

La forma ʾBT, ancora non unanimemente analizzata, ricorre nell’iscrizione di Karatepe (KAI 26).[37] Nella versione A (porta Nord-Est o inferiore), col I, ll. 9-12. Azatiwada, il costruttore della roccaforte, ricorda:

... WY/ṬNʾ ʾNK // (10) BT ʾDNY BNʿM WPʿL ʾNK LŠRŠ ʾD/NY NʿM // (11) WYŠB ʾNK ʿL KSʾ ʾBY WŠT / ʾNK ŠLM ʾT // (12) KL MLK WʾP BʾBT PʿLN KL MLK B/ṢDQY W // (13) BḤKMTY WBNʿM LBY ...

“E io ho eretto / la casa del mio signore nel bene; e ho fatto del bene alla discendenza del mio signore / e l’ho fatta sedere sul trono di suo padre e ho stabilito / la pace con ogni re; inoltre, in (qualità di) ‘padri’ mi pose ogni re per la mia giustizia e / per la mia saggezza e per la mia bontà di cuore”.

L’espressione WʾP BʾBT PʿLN KL MLK (v. C I 21) causa tuttora difficoltà, per l’uso con il verbo PʿL della preposizione B- e per l’analisi e il significato di ʾBT. Nelle espressioni simili presenti sia a Karatepe stessa, sia a Zincirli nell’iscrizione di Kulamuwa, per esprimere il concetto del “re” come padre e madre del suo popolo vengono usate espressioni un po’ diverse. A Karatepe in A I, 3 si trova: PʿLN BʿL LDNNYM LʾB WLʾM: “Baʿl mi fece (fare) per gli Adanesi da padre e da madre; in Kulamuwa, KAI 24, 10-11: ... WʾNK LMY KT ʾB // WLMY KT ʾM WLMY KT ʾḤ ... “E io per l’uno fui un padre e per l’altro fui una madre e per il terzo fui un fratello”. Infine KAI 10, 2, usa l’espressione: PʿLTN ... MMLKT ʿL GBL “(la signora di Biblo) mi fece re su Biblo”.

35 Ad esempio il plurale di ŠT “anno”, ŠNT, è spesso trascritto *sanuth*; v. KAI 180 c, e.

36 O. Brogan, “Some ancient sites in Eastern Tripolitania”, *Libya Antiqua* 13-14 (1976-77), pp. 93-129 (foto alle tavv. XLII-XLIII).

37 V. F. Bron, *Recherches sur les inscriptions phéniciennes de Karatepe*, Genève / Paris 1979; K. L. Younger, Jr., *JSS* 43 (1998), pp. 11-47; W. Röllig, in *Corpus of the Hieroglyphic Luwian Inscriptions*, vol. II: H. Çambel, *Karatepe Aslantaş, The Inscriptions*, Berlin / New York 1999, pp. 50 e 59.

Le basi per la presente discussione possono essere considerate, andando a ritroso nel tempo, in primo luogo l'*editio princeps* dovuta a W. Röllig, quindi lo studio di F. Bron. L'analisi recente di K. L. Younger non si sofferma su questo problema in maniera più specifica rispetto ai due studi ricordati (v. nota 37).

W. Röllig (p. 51) traduce il passo " ... And indeed every king treated me as a father because of my righteousness, / and because of my wisdom, and because of my goodness of heart". Nel commento (p. 59) osserva che la spiegazione dell'espressione è incerta e rinvia per la discussione a DISI p. 8. Qui il termine è registrato sotto *ʾbt* e lo si considera un sostantivo di derivazione incerta, intendendolo come "a father's (legal) power, status of a father?". Secondo il sistema usato nel redigere il dizionario, viene riportata la bibliografia esistente, annotando le diverse proposte interpretative avanzate.

Una chiara esposizione della storia degli studi è nel lavoro di F. Bron (pp. 59-62). Lo stato della questione è il seguente, riportando solo le opinioni che non sono in contrasto con il testo luvio. Quest'ultimo è tradotto "e ogni re mi fece padre per sé".[38] Ciò rende indubbia la connessione del vocabolo con *ʾab* "padre", ma si tratterebbe secondo un gruppo di studiosi di un sostantivo astratto con il significato di "paternità", eventualmente da collegare all'accadico *abbūtu*.[39] Questa soluzione sembra quella sottintesa dal commento di W. Röllig ed è accolta con riserva in DISI e da K. L. Younger. La seconda possibilità è di analizzare ʾBT come il plurale di "padre". Questa soluzione è stata proposta per la prima volta da A. Dupont Sommer, che interpreta B- come un *beth essentiae* e spiega ʾBT come un *pluralis maiestatis*, secondo un uso noto in ebraico[40]. La spiegazione è accolta da M. Dahood, da H. L. Ginsberg[41] e dallo stesso Bron (pp. 61-62) e, più di recente, da J. C. L. Gibson.[42]

---

38 "And every king made me father to himself"; v. J. D. Hawkins - A. Morpurgo Davies, *AnSt* 28 (1978), p. 115.

39 *AHw*, 6, s. v. *abbūtu(m)* e *CAD* A (1964), p. 50, s. v. *abbūtu*. V. già F. Bron, *Recherches*, p. 61 nota 6; da ultimo, K. L. Younger, *JSS* 43 (1998), p. 16 nota 30.

40 V. F. Bron, *Recherches*, p. 61 e note 10, 11. Il riferimento a A. Dupont-Sommer è *Oriens* 2 (1949), p. 124 (v. nota 10, p. 61); per il plurale di maestà è citato, P. Joüon, *Grammaire de l'Hébreu biblique*, Roma 1923, § 136 f e i passi biblici Giud. 2: 35, Sal. 54: 6, 118: 7.

41 M. Dahood, *Biblica* (1963), p. 70; H. L. Ginsberg, "Ugaritico-Phoenicia", *JANES* 5 (1973), p. 138.

42 J. C. L. Gibson, *Textbook of Syrian Semitic Inscriptions, III. Phoenician Inscriptions* ..., Oxford 1982, p. 58, con la traduzione (p. 49), la stessa adottata nell'editio princeps, "and indeed every king treated me as a father because of my righteousness, and because of my wisdom, and because of my goodness of heart". La stessa spiegazione è citata, attribuendola al solo Ginsberg, da K. L. Younger,

E. Lipiński,[43] pur analizzando 'BT come plurale di *ʾab*, non accetta l'analisi di B- come *beth essentiae*, né quella di un plurale di maestà e propone di tradurre il passo come segue: "And every king put me among the fathers because of my righteousness and my wisdom and the kindness of my heart". In appoggio a questa interpretazione cita Gen. 45: 8 e Is. 22: 21 (confronti citati anche da J. C. L. Gibson, ai quali aggiunge Sal. 109: 14, e riproposti da K. L. Younger). Basandosi sui passi citati, attribuisce a "padri" il significato specifico di "visir", "consiglieri".[44] Ma i confronti dell'ebraico non sono stringenti: il sostantivo "padre" vi appare al singolare, il verbo usato è *hyh* e la preposizione che regge il complemento è *l-* (con questo tipo di espressioni sono invece da riavvicinare il passo di Karatepe A I, 3 e quello di Kulamuwa KAI 24, 10-11). L'attribuzione del termine "padre" ad alti funzionari, come espressione di rispetto, è indubbia; non è però dimostrato che questa sfumatura di significato sia da accogliere nel passo di Karatepe.

Mi sembra invece, anche per il confronto con il corrispondente luvio, che il significato da attribuire al termine sia proprio quello di "padri"; l'uso della preposizione *b-* indica, come è stato visto da Lipiński, l'appartenenza a una categoria, quella degli "anziani" o "predecessori" (come in KAI 126): il passo significherebbe "e tutti i re mi posero nel rango di 'padri'", cioè provvisto delle qualità caratterizzanti di "giustizia", "saggezza", "bontà" elencate in seguito. Il plurale è quindi giustificato perché designa un rango, non una persona specifica. La mancata corrispondenza nel numero tra Luvio e Fenicio si deve spiegare con l'uso in ciascuna lingua di un'espressione canonica, corrispondente per significato ma, ancora una volta, formulata un po' diversamente.

La rassegna presentata ha cercato di precisare lo schema dei vocaboli *ʾab* e *ʾaḥ*, la cui terminazione in vocale lunga davanti ai suffissi possessivi (eccetto quello di 1ª singolare) sembra aver mantenuto in Fenicio per lungo tempo la distinzione dei casi. La differenziazione della qualità delle vocali sembra persistere nel punico tardo, perdendosi tuttavia il legame con la funzione originaria del nome e prevalendo verosimilmente, almeno in alcune regioni, la vocale *ū* in tutte le funzioni. Si sono infine

---

JSS 43 (1998), p. 16 nota 30. I due autori sembrano ignorare le attestazioni del pl. 'B in punico e latino-punico, che pure sono citate in J. Friedrich - W. Röllig, *Phönizisch-punische Grammatik*², Roma 1970, § 240, 1.

43 E. Lipiński, "From Karatepe to Pyrgi: Middle Phoenician Miscellanea", *RSF* 2 (1974), p. 48.

44 V. ora J. T. Willis, "'ab as an Official Term", *Scandinavian Journal of the Old Testament* 10 (1996), pp. 130-136.

elencate le attestazioni del plurale *ʾabōt* discutendone il significato nei diversi contesti. Spero che Pelio Fronzaroli, il cui lavoro sagace permette di ricostruire una lingua che fino ad alcuni decenni fa era del tutto ignota, voglia accettare, come segno di amicizia, questo tenue contributo alla conoscenza più precisa di una lingua relativamente ben conosciuta.

IN MARGINE

ALFONSO ARCHI

Università di Roma "La Sapienza"

My regret for not having taken greater advantage of the teachings of Pelio Fronzaroli in my distant years as a student at the University of Florence (when my interests laid in different fields) is partly mitigated by the privilege of being at his side in interpreting the documents from Ebla. As a token of appreciation for his working method I here offer some marginal notes on subjects he studied.

1. 2 ká

ARET XI 2 (85) has: ^{d}Utu 2 ká é-duru$_5$ ^{d}*Ku-ra* igi-tùm *i-ba-na* "(When) the Sun advances towards the door of the chapel of Kura" (the parallel section *ARET* XI 1 [81] does not preserve the line with ká). P. Fronzaroli, *ARET* XI, p. 46, *ad* (81), comments: "Il numerale 2 davanti al sumerogramma ká 'porta' si trova anche in uno scongiuro eblaita (*ARET* V 1 v. I 1) ... si dovrà forse pensare che il numero sia riferito qui ai battenti della porta (cf. la grafia fonetica *dal-da-an*, /dalt-ayn/, *ARET* V 1 r. II 7)".

Two parallel passages mention another element of the door in the dual form:

(1) TM.75.G.2428 obv. VI 9-12: 2 NI gín DILMUN babbar:kù 2 *mu-ḫur-da wa-ra-ti-iš* 2 ká
(2) TM.75.G.2622 obv. VI 12-15: 1/2 babbar:kù 2 *mu-ḫur-tum wa-ra-ti-iš* 2 ká *A-da-ti-ig*^{ki}

The quantity of silver is minimal, roughly 5 e 4 grams respectively. This was destined to decorate the two *mu-ḫur-tum* /muḫḫurt-um/, in the dual: *mu-ḫur-da*, /muḫḫurt-ān/, that is to say the anterior part of the double leafs /dalt-ān/ of the door. See Akk. *muḫḫurtu* (from *maḫāru* D), *AHw* II, p. 669 "gegenüberliegende Seite"; *CAD M* II, p. 176: "facing, opposite direction". Thus: "x silver (for) the two fronts of the part of the entrance of the two leafs of the door". *wa-ra-ti-iš* is a terminative form, from /wârat-/, to derive from **wʾr*, see Akk. *wârum* "to go, advance".

2. Jewels and Colors

2.1. The administrative documents mention few names of colors, generally in Sumerian. Wool, siki, is "white" babbar, "black" gi$_6$, "black and white" gi$_6$ babbar", "reddish-brown" ú-ḫáb.[1] "Kilts", íb-TÚG, are white, reddish-brown, and often "mottled", gùn.[2] Other types of garments are mostly reddish-brown.[3]

ú-ḫáb is sometimes followed by sa. *ARET* VII 24 obv. V 1-4 has: 4 íb+II-TÚG ú-ḫáb 5 íb+III-TÚG ú-ḫáb sa 20 lá-3 íb+III-TÚG babbar 40 lá-1 íb+III-TÚG sa_6 gùn, that is "reddish-brown", "in reddish-brown *bands*", "white" and "first quality mottled" kilts.[4]

M. Stol has identified ú-ḫáb, the product from which this color was obtained, with "gall-nut", while "madder (*Rubia tinctorum*)" should be GIŠ-ḫáb = Akk. *ḫūratum* (a term not used at Ebla).[5] *MEE* II 29 rev. IV 2-3: 15 1/2 "KIN" siki níg-sa_{10} 6 *li-im* 2 *mi-at* ú-ḫáb "15,5 measures of wool: price of 6,200 gall-nuts", favours this identification. If we were dealing with madder root, these would not be counted

---

1 See *ARET* IV, p. 320, *sub* siki. For ú-ḫáb, a colouring agent and a colour, see B. Landsberger, *JCS* 21 (1967), pp. 169-17. In the LL 278, ú-ḫáb = *a-ša-ḫa-bù* is referred to the quality of a man, Akk. *isḫappu* "rude man", see M. Civil, *BaE*, p. 88.

2 For íb-II/III-TÚG babbar, ú-ḫáb, see *ARET* IV, p. 302; *MEE* II, p. 11 *ad* r. II 6, 7. For íb-babbar see also *ARET* I 5 (98); 20 (1) and (3) and *passim*. DAR / GÙN, in general connected with íb-II/III-TÚG, should mean gùn "mottled".

For dam gùn "women (employed) as dyers", see H. Waetzoldt, in: L. Cagni (ed.), *Ebla 1975-1985*, Napoli (1987), pp. 371-372. For passages concerning these women, see *ARET* IX, p. 381 *sub* dar, where also "young dyers" dumu-nita gùn, are quoted; see, further, *ARET* IV, p. 289: dar 1. Groups of dyers are also quoted in *MEE* VII 14 rev. I 4-5: (12+12+12 garments) gùn-gùn uru-bar "(12) dyers of the suburbs"; TM.76.G.534(+) obv. VI 6-7: 15 dumu-nita "ur_4"-"ur_4" gùn-gùn "15 young pluckers (and) dyers". A plucker was overseer of a group of dyers, in TM.75.G.2245 obv. IX 20-22: *Maš-ʾà-lu* ur_4 ugula gùn.

3 *ARET* IV, p. 328, lists *sub* ú-ḫáb: aktum-TÚG, gíd-TÚG, túg-NI.NI, $zara_6$-TÚG, and at p. 296, *sub* gi_6, only aktum-TÚG. See also *ARET* I 3 (48): 1 $zara_6$-TÚG babbar 1 $zara_6$-TÚG ú-ḫáb 12 aktum-TÚG babbar 13 aktum-TÚG ú-ḫáb; 12 (4): 1 gu-dùl-TÚG gi_6.

4 For ú-ḫáb beside ú-ḫáb sa, see also *ARET* VII 133 obv. II 5-6. The passages quoted in *ARET* I, p. 307; III, p. 392; IV, p. 318; VII, p. 237 have all the sign SA. In *ARET* VIII 528 obv. IV 8-9 have instead: 10 íb-III-TÚG ú-ḫáb 3 íb-III-TÚG ú-ḫáb ú; for ú-ḫáb ú see also *MEE* VII 2 obv. 5. Because the writing with SA is more frequent, the use of Ú can be explained as a mistake of the scribe.

For ú-ḫáb sa, see also *ARET* I 10 rev. XII 8 and 15 left edge 2. sa is explained in *ARET* IV, p. 318, as "combed (wool)", see *CAD* M, pp. 351-352, par. 3, according to the Akkadian gloss *mašādu* "to comb (wool)", a meaning which cannot be correct, because sa defines ú-ḫáb and not siki.

ú can be an abbreviation for ú-ḫab, see. TM.75.G.1913 (*MEE* X 29) rev. XIV 21 and XVI 27: ... íb-III-TÚG ú *Ma-ri*[ki].

5 M. Stol, *RlA* 6 (1980-1983), pp. 533-534. See also B. Landsberger, *JCS* 21 (1967), pp. 169-171, who is, however, in favour of the identity of ú-ḫáb with GIŠ-ḫáb, and M. van der Mieroop, *Crafts in the Early Isin Period*, Leuven 1987, pp. 31-2, who seems to agree with Landsberger. For ú-ḫáb(-)babbar, see B. R. Foster, *Umma in the Sargonic Period*, Hamden, Connecticut 1982, p. 137 (*USP* 63, l. 4).

individually but, if anything, in "bundles", sa.[6] Generally, this product was evaluated and bought in exchange for wool or silver. TM.75.G.2362 obv. XIV 10-11: 10 gín babbar:kù níg-sa$_{10}$ ú-ḫáb "10 shekels of silver: price of gull-nuts". TM.75.G.1317 obv. VII 6 registers "gull-nuts of first quality", ú-ḫáb sag. *ARET* III 609 rev. VI: 20 "KIN" siki níg-sa$_{10}$ ú-ḫáb *wa* GIŠ-ma-ir.[7] This second substance is sometimes listed together with GIŠ-a-eren, "madder",[8] *ARET* III 890 rev. II: 6 "KIN" siki níg-sa$_{10}$ GIŠ-ma-ir *wa* GIŠ-a-eren. GIŠ-ma-ir has to be another kind of plant used as a dye. It qualifies gada-TÚG, a linen garment, TM.75.G.1985+ rev. II 11: 1 gada-TÚG GIŠ-ma-ir; TM.75.G.2289 rev. I 6-7: 2 *kir-na-nu* GIŠ-ma-ir 15 *kir-na-nu* maḫ 10 *kir-na-nu* tur (*kir-na-nu* is also a type of gada-TÚG).[9]

a-gú/gi(-lu) "antimony past" and im gi$_6$ 'black earth" were also evaluated (níg-sa$_{10}$) in wool, as it was the use for goods of limited value. *ARET* II 15 X 9-10: 40 "KIN" siki níg-sa$_{10}$ *a-gú* 30 "KIN" siki níg-sa$_{10}$ GIŠ-ma-ir; IV 19 (53)-(54): 9 "KIN" siki níg-sa$_{10}$ *a-gi* 5 "KIN" siki [nig-s]a$_{10}$ GIŠ-ma-ir; TM.75.G.2163 rev. II 6-9: 10 "KIN" siki níg-sa$_{10}$ a-*gi wa* im gi$_6$; TM.75.G.2503 rev. VII 3-7: 13 "KIN" siki níg-sa$_{10}$ *a-gú wa* im gi$_6$; TM.75.G.2632 rev. X 9-13: 23 KIN siki níg-sa$_{10}$ ú-ḫáb *a-gú* im gi$_6$. This last passage, which lists *a-gú* and im gi$_6$ together with ú-ḫáb, shows that all these goods, together with GIŠ-ma-ir, were substances used in obtaining dyes or as a mordant.[10] Both *a-gú(-lu)* and im gi$_6$ were measured in *ba-rí-zú*, a measure of volume equivalent to 10 sìla (a little under ten litres). *ARET* III 847 rev. II: 10 "KIN" siki ní-sa$_{10}$ 3 *ba-rí-zú* im gi$_6$; TM.75.G.10253 rev. X 1-2: [x "KIN" siki] 6 *ba-rí-zú a-gú*.

---

6 It is not necessary to say that ú-ḫáb sa, in the passages quoted in note 6, needs another meaning.

7 See further *ARET* II 15 (21): 30 "KIN" siki níg-sa$_{10}$ GIŠ-ma-ir "5 measures K. of wool: price of G." (perhaps for the "collar of the yoke", *ḫu-lu*); IV 19 (54): 5 "KIN" siki [níg-s]a$_{10}$ GIŠ-ma-ir.

8 GIŠ-a-eren has to be identified with Sumerian a-i/ì-rí-na "root (of madder)", see Stol, *RlA* 6 (1980-1983), p. 535 § 24. According to *PSD* A, I, p. 96a, a-i/ì-rí-na is a juice which was used to treat also skins.

9 *ARET* III, p. 362: gada-TÚG *kir-na-nu* máḫ / tur; *ARET* IV, p. 306: gada-TÚG *kir-na-nu*. For túg ú-ḫáb and gíd-TÚG GIŠ-ma-ir, see *ARET* XI, p. 150 *ad* GIŠ-ma-ir.

10 im gi$_6$ is not listed in the im section of *Ḫḫ* XI 314-326, *MSL* VII, pp. 140-141. For im babbar$_x$(UD.UD) "white earth", see Landsberger, *JCS* 21 (1967), p. 140 nt. 9; H. Waetzoldt, *UNT*, pp. 173-174: "dürfte es sich um die sogenannte Walk(er)erde handeln, die sowohl Fett und Schmutz entfernt, als auch dem Stoff einen gewissen Glanz verleiht"; *CAD* G, pp. 54-55: *gaṣṣu* "gypsum, whitewash"; R. J. Forbes, *Studies in Ancient Technology*, IV, Leiden 1956, p. 84. Not only the fuller, but also the leatherworker used "white earth", see G. Th. Ferwerda, *A Contribution to the Early Isin Craft Archive*, Leiden 1985, pp. 25-26; Stol, *RlA* 6 (1980-1983), p. 531, § 10.b: "Die ... Enthaarung durch *Kalk* ist nur in den älteren Texten nachweisbar".

a-gú, genitive *a-gi*, is found in the same contexts of *a-gi-lu*, as has already been noted in *ARET* III, p. 337. *a-gú*, *ARET* IV 16 (89): 1 "KIN" siki níg-sa_{10} *a-gú*. *a-gi*, 856 rev. II: 15 "KIN" siki níg-sa_{10} *a-gi*. *a-gi-lu*, *ARET* III 463 rev. II: 10 "KIN" siki níg-sa_{10} *a-gi-lu* é en. *a-gú-lum*, TM.75.G.2154 obv. I 1-II 2: 41 ma-na šú+ša gín DILMUN *a-gú-lum* UNKEN-ak 1 la-ḫa "41; 20 minas of ... in order to make 1 jar".[11]

2.2. Jewels were coloured by the stones set in the gold. A brooch with two acorns in "rock crystal and greyish-green translucent stone" in a gold setting shows the great skill of the Ebla goldsmiths of the Amorite period in reproducing motifs inspired by nature.[12] Without doubt those of Ebla in the 24th century were no less skillful, to judge from the small stone sculptures. Unfortunately, traces of the jewels of this period remain only in the administrative documents. These reveal that, already in this period, the glodsmiths preferred the simple and compact forms of acorns.

(1) TM.75.G.2071 obv. VI 4-5: 16 *al_6-la-nu nap-ḫu* 9 *al_6-la-nu* si_4; rev. II 3-5: 3 *al_6-la-nu* gìn-gìn 6 *al_6-la-nu nap-ḫu* 4 *al_6-la-nu* si_4 "16 acorns of glass; 9 acorns of *agate*; ... 3 acorns of lapis lazuli, 6 acorns of glass, 4 acorns of *agate*"[13]

2.2.1. Of the three materials mentioned in (1), gìn is "lapis lazuli". KUR (gìn) is in fact the writing used for za-gìn in the Semitic version of "Word List B",[14] while *ARET* I 10 obv. VIII 3 has KUR.KUR: 5 ma-na gìn-gìn.[15]

---

11 This form, /ʾaguḫl-um/ (Akk. *guḫlu*, Semitic *kuḥl*, see *AHw* I, p. 296b), precises the reading of the gloss in LL no. 941: šembi-MI/ME = *A*, *B ʾa_5*(NI)*-gu-um*, *C*: *a-gu-u*[*m*]; TM.75.G.1301: *ù-gu-um*, interpreted by M. Civil, *Ebla 1975-1985*, as "antimony paste". That these forms have to be connected with *a-gú/gi* (cfr. Akk. *eg/gû*, *AHw* I, p. 191a) of the administrative documents, has been seen by G. Conti, *apud ARET* XI, p. 73 *ad* 5. Notice that the LL use the sign GU, which stays usually for /qu/; while GÚ stays for /ku/, /gu/ and sometimes for /qu/. W. Heimpel, *ZA* 77 (1987), p. 58, does not agree the meaning "antimony". Cfr. D. T. Potts - S. Parpola, *WZKM* 86 (1996), pp. 291-305.

Antimony was usually evaluated (níg-sa_{10}) in wool, siki; sometimes, however, also in silver, TM.75.G.2362 rev. XV 11-13: 1 ½ gín DILMUN babbar: kù níg-sa_{10} *a-gú*; TM.75.G.2464 rev. III 17-18: 4 gín DILMUN babbar: kù níg-sa_{10} *a-gú*.

12 See P. Matthiae *et alii*, *Ebla. Alle origini della civiltà urbana*, Milano 1995, p. 472 no 398 and the colour plate at p. 480.

13 For *al_6-la-nu* "acorn", see *ARET* IV, p. 285; H. Waetzoldt, *apud MEE* X, p. 90 *ad* rev. V 15: "(Perle in Form einer) Eichel"; Akk. *allānu(m)*, see. *AHw* I, p. 37: "'Eiche(?); Eichenzäpfchen' (Heb. *allōn*)". In TM.75.G.2622 obv. XVI 29: 2 *ri-iš-da al_6-la-nu* "two *fruits* of the oak"; /rēšt-ān/ is the dual form of *rēštum* "point".

14 Civil, in: *Ebla 1975-1985*, p. 145.

15 For KUR.KUR as the stone for 4 *bu*-DI "earrings", see *ARET* III 218 obv. V.

The gold which is occasionally linked with *al*$_6$-*la-nu* is, perhaps, that required for the setting of the jewel, see the pair of acorns in *ARET* IV 19 obv. VII 15-VIII 3, and the parallel section in *MEE* X 20 obv. rev. V 13-15.[16] The acorns were usually made of si$_4$ and *nap-ḫu*.

(2) TM.75.G.1284 obv. III 1-2: 6 *al*$_6$-*la-nu* si$_4$ 12 *al*$_6$-*la-nu nap-ḫu*
(3) TM.75.G.2078 obv. II 2-4: 8 *al*$_6$-*la-nu* kù-gi 3 *al*$_6$-*la-nu nap-ḫu* 2 *al*$_6$-*la-nu* si$_4$

The document of passage (2) presents a third kind of material:

(4) TM.75.G.1284 obv. VII 1-3: 2 *al*$_6$-*la-nu nap-ḫu wa* 1 *al*$_6$-*la-nu wa-ra-ga-tum* "2 acorns of glass and 1 acorn of greenish (stone)"; see Akk. *(w)arāqum* "greenish, yellow". TM.75.G.1679 obv. IV 1 has: 60 lá-2 *wa-ru*$_{12}$-*ga-na-tum* (followed by beads in lapis lazuli, za-gìn); the enlargement in *-ānum* individualises the single pieces of stone, therefore: "58 grains of greenish (stone)".

This term occurs also in TM.75.G.2073 rev. V 1: 13 gu *wa-ru*$_{12}$-*ga-tum* "13 strings of greenish (stone)". Other passages have gu qualified by si$_4$ (see below, 2.2.3.).

2.2.2. si$_4$, also in its reduplicate form si$_4$-si$_4$, is sometimes connected with cornelian, gug(GUL.ZA), or cornelian and lapis lazuli, GUL-gìn:za.[17] *ARET* I 30 rev. IX 5-X 1: 1 níg-lá-gaba 1 níg-lá-sag gug$_x$(ZA$_x$.GUL) gìn:za kù-gi si$_4$-si$_4$ babbar:kù 15 gín DILMUN "gug"(GUL)-gìn:za kù-gi si$_4$ babbar:kù "1 breastplate (and) 1 diadem of cornelian, lapis lazuli, gold, *agate* (and) silver: 15 shekels (is the weight) of the cornelian, lapis lazuli, gold, *agate* (and) silver".

The Sumerogramm si$_4$ (= Akk. *pelûm* "red",[18] *sāmum* "red") could be agate, which has a banded structure and is brown with white, sometimes with a little blue. Writings as ZA$_x$(-)si$_4$ and ZA$_x$(-)si$_4$-si$_4$, in *ARET* VII 13 obv. II 1, 16 obv. I 6, seem to connect cornelian (in this case: gug$_x$ = ZA$_x$.GUL) with agate, both form of chalcedony.[19] In Mesopotamia, agate is perhaps duḫ(/du$_8$)-ši-a, Akk. *dušû*,[20] a term which

16 See also the other passage of this document quoted below, 2.4.

17 For this writing, see *MEE* II, p. 115 ad v. I 5; cfr. babbar-kù-gi for babbar:kù-kù-gi)

18 According to Landsberger, *JCS* 21 (1967), pp. 141, 145: "hell rot".

19 For the use of agate, which has been found also together with cornelian, see P. R. S. Moorey, *Ancient Mesopotamian Materials and Industries. The Archaeological Evidence*, Oxford 1994, pp. 99-100.
It is unlikely that si$_4$ means "coral", as it has been suggested in *ARET* I, p. 302. Coral could have reached Ebla mostly through Mari. The documents show, however, that Ebla imported from Mari lapis lazuli, za-gìn, but not si$_4$, see Archi, *Iraq* 61 (1999), pp. 151-152. On cornelian, see W. Heimpel, *ZA* 77 (1987), p. 51.

does not appear in Ebla. Several Ebla documents list in sequence za-gìn "lapis lazuli" and si_4; the Akkadian documentation shows that also za-gìn and duḫ-ši-a / *dušû* were used in combination.[21] According to some scholars, duḫ-ši-a / *dušû* is, instead, rock crystal.[22] The beads found in Palace G are mainly of glass, a smaller number being in cornelian and rock crystal, only a few in lapis lazuli and one alone in agate.[23] This argues strongly in favour of the identification of si_4 with rock crystal. The names of the stones worked for jewels are za-gìn, gug, si_4 and *nap-ḫu* (see 2.2.3.). Rock crystal is more suitable than agate for making cups, even small ones such as that for a statue in *MEE* II 50 obv. XI 1: 1 bur-KAK an-dùl na_4-si_4-si_4 "1 cup in ...-stone (for) a statue".[24] The identification of si_4 with rock crystal is, however, excluded by the fact that si_4 indicates the colour of a cloth object, perhaps "variegated" as the agate (see 2.2.4). Akk. *dušû* is also a color given to dyed and tanned leather.[25]

Passages such as *ARET* VII 146 obv. I 1: 150 si_4; VII 147 obv. I 1-3: 60 si_4 maḫ 106 si_4 tur 12 si_4 tur-II, record grains of *agate*, which can be "large (and) small". Some of these grains were in the shape of bulbs, *ḫa-za-nu*.[26] TM.75.G.1730+ (*MEE* VII 34) rev. XX 16-22: 5 babbar:kù 15 *ḫa-za-nu* 2 KUR.KUR 2 si_4. TM.75.G.2462 rev. XXII 18-21 offers a parallel passage: 5 gín kù-gi 15 *ḫa-za-nu* 2 *ḫa-za-nu* KUR.KUR 2 *ḫa-za-nu* si_4, according to which we have to translate: "5 shekels of silver / gold (for) 15 (grains in form of) a bulb; 2 (grains in form of) a bulb of lapis lazuli; 2 (grains in form of) a bulb of *agate*". Grains of *agate* (si_4) were used to decorate bracelets. TM.75.G.2077 obv. I 3-II 1: 52 kù-gi 1 *gú-li-lum*-II 4 si_4 ša-pi kù-gi 1 *gú-li-lum*-II 3 si_4 "52 (shekels) of gold (for) 1 double bracelet (with) 4 (grains) of *agate*; 40 (shekels) of gold (for) 1 double bracelet (with) 3 (grains) of *agate*". In other cases, the number of grains or beads is not given; TM.75.G.10202 rev. XVII

20 See P. Steinkeller, *ZA* 72 (1982), pp. 249-252.

21 *CAD* D, pp. 200-202.

22 See, recently, the study by C. Michel, in: *Florilegium marianum* (*Mémoires de N.A.B.U.* 1), Paris 1992, concerning the Mari documentation.

23 See the table in: F. Pinnock, *Le perle del Palazzo Reale G*, Roma 1993, p. 61.

24 For na_4-si_4-si_4, see also TM.75.G.2520 obv. VII 10.

25 For wool dyed in the *dušû* color, see G. Bardet, in *ARM* 23, p. 7.

26 H. Waetzoldt, *apud MEE* X, p. 87 *ad* obv. III 22; cfr. P. Fronzaroli, in: *Tablettes et images aux pays de Sumer et d'Akkad*, Ö. Tunca, D. Deheselle (eds.), Liège 1996, p. 67, who quotes the LL: raš:ga-SAR, sum-SAR = *ḫa-za-nu/núm*.

21-22: ša-pi 6 gín kù-gi-IV 1 dib KUR si$_4$ "46 shekels of gold (for) 1 plate (with) lapis lazuli (and) *agate*". This stone decorated also the "handles", *ra-ʾà-tum*, of the king's chariots;[27] TM.75.G.1918 (*MEE* X 29) obv. IV 22: 1 GIŠ-gígir *ra-ʾà-tum* si$_4$; TM.75.G.1542 obv. I 3-5: 2 GIŠ-ašud-*sù* kù-gi *ra-ʾà-tum* si$_4$ "2 wheels of gold (and) the handles of *agate*".

2.2.3. Another material used for jewels in the shape of acorns is *nap-ḫu*, (see the passages in 2.2.1.). This was acquired in exchange for silver, TM.75.G.1464 rev. I 3-4: 10 gín DILMUN babbar:kù níg-sa$_{10}$ 1 ma-na 7 gín DILMUN *nap-ḫu* "10 shekels of silver: price of 1 mina 7 shekels of glass" (1 gr silver = 6,7 gr *napḫu*).

Small vessels and plates could also be made of *nap-ḫu*:

(1) *ARET* VIII 528 XV 13: 5 GIŠ-šú 4 an-zam$_x$ *nap-ḫu*
(2) TM.75.G.10202 obv. XIX 34-36: šú+ša gín DILMUN kù-gi 1 dib *nap-ḫu*

nap-ḫu frequently follows the term gu.

(3) *ARET* VIII 528 rev. XIV 20-XV 2: 1 gada-TÚG túg-mu 2 *kir-na-nu* 2 gu *nap-ḫu*
(4) *ARET* III 484 I: 2 gada-TÚG *kir-na-nu* tur 3 gu *nap-ḫu* šè-li
(5) TM.75.G.1556 rev. VIII 2-5: 3 gada-TÚG 1 gu si$_4$ 1 gu *nap-ḫu* 1 gu šè-li
(6) TM.75.G.2341 rev. VI 9: 3 gu si$_4$ 3 gu gi$_6$ 1 gu *nap-ḫu*

In the preceding passages, as in that which follows, the meaning of "string (of grains)" must be given for gu.

(7) TM.75.G.2536 obv. II 3-5: 3 gu si$_4$-si$_4$ gul-gìn-za kù-gi

It has been suggested that gu could be an abbreviation of gu-dùl-TÚG as *ʾà-da-um*-TÚG is often added to gu-dùl-TÚG (*ARET* I rev. XIV 1: ... 74 gu-dùl-TÚG *ʾà-da-um*-TÚG-I gada-TÚG).[28] This could hold true for passages such as *ARET* I 29 (1): 4 *gu-zi*-TÚG 6 gu ḫul 3 *mi-at* íb-KAK-sa$_6$; (2): 2 *gu-zi*-TÚG 1 gu *ʾà-da-um*-TÚG. In other lists of garments, gu seems, instead, to mean "string of cloth", as in *ARET* I 26 obv. I 1-II 2: 6 *mi-at* 20 túg-NI.NI 8 *mi-at* gu-dùl-TÚG 4 *mi-at* gu sa$_6$ 2 *mi-at* 20 zara$_6$-TÚG.

27 See H. Waetzoldt, *OA* 29 (1990), p. 15; other passages are quoted by G. Conti, *MisEb* 4, p. 62.

28 *ARET* I, p. 284 and III, p. 354

The LL, no. 229, have ka-diri = *na-ba-ḫu(-um)*, from **npḫ*, Akk. *napāḫum* "to blow, to light a fire".[29] The adjectival form *nab-ḫu* /napḫu/ "kindled, blazing (fire)", should here mean a material obtained from the kiln, therefore, glass.[30]

2.2.4. An object qualified by the term si_4 is *gàr-su*. This normally appears at the end of the lists of garments, after the "kilts", íb, and before or after the several kinds of bands, níg-lá-sag/gaba/DU. See, for example, *ARET* I 30 (47): 1 aktum-TÚG ... 1 íb-III-sa_6-gùn 1 *gàr-su* gi_6; III 60 obv. VII: 1 *ʾà-da-um*-TÚG 1 aktum-TÚG 1 íb-III-sa_6-gùn-TÚG 1 gada TÚG 1 *gàr-su* 1 níg-lá-DU (similarly in III 312 II; VII 24 rev. I 1). We are, therefore, dealing with a cloth object. According to TM.75.G.2190 obv. III 1, this was made of wool and flax: 3 *gàr-su* siki gada. This may have been a piece of clohing, *ARET* VII 133 obv. IV 2-3: (íb-, níg-lá-) 20 aktum-TÚG ti-TÚG 4 *gàr-su* túg-mu "... 4 g. (for) dresses". The value of a *gàr-su* varied between 12 and 3 shekels of silver. *ARET* VII 80 (6): 12 shekels 1 *gar-su* babbar; *ARET* III 274 III: 12 shekels 2 *gar-su* gi_6; TM.75.G.1730+ (*MEE* VII 34) rev. XX 11-13: 80 shekels for 33 *gar-su* (1: 2,4 shekels). The *gàr-su* could be "white", babbar, "black", gi_6, and "variegated in brown", si_4-si_4; see also TM.75.G.2359 rev. IV 17: 8 *gàr-su* gi_6 si_4-si_4. Giving the colour of the si_4 stone required a particular technique. TM.75.G.2233 obv. VI 6-10 lists the people responsible for this task separetely from the other dyers: 12 dumu-nita gùn *wa* 2 dumu-nita lú si_4-si_4 "12 young dyers and 2 young (dyers) for the si_4 colour".

An element in identifying this object is to be found in *ARET* III 787 I:] 80 *gàr-*⸢*su*⸣ GIŠ-ti, which must mean: "80 quivers (bags for arrows)". If, therefore, *gàr-su* is "bag", a comparison with the Hittite *kursa-* "bag; hunting bag" becomes likely.[31]

---

29 P. Fronzaroli, in P. Fronzaroli (ed.), *Studies on the Language of Ebla*, Firenze 1984, p. 147. Cfr. G. Conti, *MisEb* 3, pp. 102-103. The manuscripts *A* and *B* have a nominal form: *ma-ba-ḫu-um* /mappaḫum/.

30 For imitiations of precious stones in glass, called "stone x of the kiln (*kūri*)", see A. L. Oppenheim, in A. L. Oppenheim, R. H. Brill, D. Barag, and A. von Saldern, *Glass and Glassmaking in Ancient Mesopotamia*, New York 1970, p. 15; for the technology of glassmaking, *ibid.*, pp. 69-80, and Moorey, *Ancient Mesopotamian Materials*, pp. 202-215. For finds of early glass, see the survey by Moorey, *op. cit.*, pp. 189-192.

31 For Hittite *kursa-*, see S. Alp, *Beiträge zur Erforschung des Hethitischen Tempels*, Ankara 1983, pp. 93-100; H. G. Güterbock, in: *Essays in Ancient Civilization Presented to H. J. Kantor*, A. Leonard Jr., B. B Williams (eds.), Chicago 1989, pp. 113-119; now in: *Perspectives on Hittite Civilization: Selected Writings of H.G. Güterbock*, H. A. Hoffner Jr, I. L. Diamond (eds.), Chicago 1997, pp. 137-145.

2.3. iškālum "bunch of grapes"

The Lexical Lists, no. 660, offer the equivalence: še-geštin = *iš*$_{11}$*-ga-um* (*A*; *B*) *áš-ga-lum* (*D*), /ʾiṯkālu-um/, /ʾaṯkālu-um/ "bunch of grapes".[32]

The administrative documents register a few cases where both the phonetic reading and the Sumerogramm apply to a kind of jewel.[33]

(1) TM.75.G.2536 obv. I 3: 7 *iš-ga-lu* geštin kù-gi "7 bunches of grapes in gold"
(2) TM.75.G.1860 (*MEE* X 20) obv. 20: šú+ša geštin:še "20 (shekels of gold for) bunche(s) of grapes"
(3) TM.75.G.2071 obv. V 4-5: 15 *al*$_6$*-la-nu* 6 geštin:še "(gold for ...) 15 acorns (and) 6 bunches of grapes"
(4) TM.75.G.1284 obv. V 4-7: 5 kù-gi 11 še-geštin *wa al*$_6$*-la-nu* "5 (shekels = 39.15 gr) of gold (for) 11 bunches of grapes (and) acorns".

In another document *al*$_6$*-la-nu* "acorns" is connected, instead, with GIŠ-geštin, a term which in agricultural documents means "grapevine".[34]
(5) TM.75.G.1579 obv. II 6: 10 *al*$_6$*-la-nu* 10 GIŠ-geštin <kù-gi>; III 5-6: 6 *al*$_6$*-la-nu* 11 GIŠ-geštin <kù-gi>

Plates, dib, of gold (a kind of object given to important officials) were also sometimes engraved with grapevines or a vine shoot, GIŠ-geštin.[35]

2.4. tarimtum "pine cone"

The Lexical Lists have at no. 691: še-ù-suḫ$_5$ = *da-rí-ma-tum* /tarimāt-um/ (the plur. form, manuscripts *A* and *B*); *da-rí-tum* /taritt-um/ (*D*); cfr. Akk. *terinnu*; *terinnātu*

For a lexical equivalence between Eblaite and a not-Semitic language, see *a-sar-a-núm*, Hurrian *šari-yanni*, from which Akk. *sariam, siriam* "cuirass", according to G. Conti, M. Bonechi, *NABU* 1992/10; H. Waetzoldt, *OA* 29 (1990 [printed in 1992]), pp. 26-27; G. Conti, *MisEb* 4, pp. 62-63.

H. Waetzoldt, *OA* 29 (1990), p. 7, suggests to connect this term with Akk. *qe/iršu*, a strip, see *CAD* Q, p. 270; *AHw* II, p. 918. The value given to the *gar-su* is not in favour of this explanation.

32 See J. Krecher, *BaE*, p. 160; M. Krebernik, *ZA* 73 (1983), p. 26; E. Zurro, *AuOr* 1 (1983), p. 266; M. Civil, *Or* 56 (1987), p. 236; G. Conti, *MisEb* 3, p. 177, and *ibid*., p. 16, for the use of *áš* instead of *iš* and *iš*$_{11}$ in the source *D*. Beginning with the period of the minister Ibrium, the administrative documents write regularly IŠ$_{11}$ for *iṯ*; TM.75.G.2536 (text no. 5, here below) has, however, *iš*.

33 *Iš*$_{11}$*-ga-um*, a PN used in Ebla as well as in Mari, could have the same meaning. See TM.75.G.2428 rev. II 23-24: *Iš*$_{11}$*-ga-um* lú *Ìr-am*$_6$*-da-ar*; TM.75.G.1904 obv. XVI 18-19: *Iš*$_{11}$*-ga-um Ma-rí*^{ki}.

34 A. Archi, in: D. Charpin - F. Joannès (eds.), *Merchands, diplomates et empereurs. Mélanges P. Garelli*, Paris1991, 211-214.

35 See *ARET* II, p. 121, *sub* DUB-geštin, DIB+GIŠ.GEŠTIN$^!$.

"pine cone".[36] Passage no. (1) registers a pine cone in gold beside a vine shoot; no. (2) mentions a cedar tree decorated with cones of silver:

(1) TM.75.G.2382 obv. II 4-III 2: tar 3 kù-gi ù-ma na_4 1 *gú-li-lum* GIŠ-geštin *da-rí-*[*t*]*um* ᵈ*Ra-sa-ap ʾÀ-da-ni*ᵏⁱ "33 (shekels) of gold: x stone[37] (for) 1 bracelet (with) vine shoots (and) pine cones (for) DN"
(2) TM.75.G.1492 obv. IV 2-V 1: 18 babbar:kù níg-sa_{10} GIŠ-eren 2 ma-na šú+ša babbar:kù UNKEN-ak GIŠ-*da-rí-tum* "18 (shekels) of silver: the value of a cedar tree; 2 minas 20 (shekels) of silver to make (its) cones".

3. A cultic calendar

ARET XI 1-2, published by Pelio Fronzaroli, are two parallel versions of a text which sets out in great detail the ceremonies relating to the marriage of the Ebla royal couple, which lasted for many days. This is one of the principal rituals in cuneiform writing of a Semitic language in terms of its antiquity, the completness of its descriptions and also the fact that these relate to two precise historical events: respectively, the marriage of Irkab-damu and that of Išar-damu (the penultimate and last kings of Ebla). Such complex rituals prescribing each action are only found in more recent periods in Hittite Anatolia (starting from the 16th century) and Emar (13th century).

TM.75.G.12297, here below (and Plate I), is a fragment of an originally medium-seized tablet (perhaps 10 - 12 columns per side). The missing part must have been shattered into tiny pieces, difficult to identify today. There are no parallel texts.

This fragment sets out the ceremonies due to some gods in certain localities of the Ebla Kingdom which were home to well-known sactuaries. It appears, therefore, to conserve a cultic calendar covering a number of months (in II' 5 the 11th month is mentioned) and concerning not the city of Ebla but its territory.

I'	x+1	[x u]d	[the xth d]ay
		[x-]*da*-[x(-x)]	...
II	x+1	[ᵈ*Ì-d*]*a*-["*ba*]*l*"(KUL)	[Id]a[ba]l

36 See M. Civil, *Ebla 1975-1985*, p. 148: "pine cone-shaped ornament"; cfr. G. Conti, *Mis.Eb* 3, pp. 180-181.

37 For ù-ma na_4 see also TM.75.G.10189: 1 ma-na kù-gi 1 dib GIŠ-geštin ù-ma na_4 "1 mina of gold (for) 1 plate (with) a wine shoot of x stone.

LL 1130: ù-ma = *ir-ne-ne-tum* /ʾernent-um/, cfr. Akk. *erni/ettum*, Sem. **rnn*, see M. Krebernik, *ZA* 73 (1983), p. 39, is another lexeme.

		[*ʾÀ-*]*ma-du*^{ki}	of [Ha]matu.
	3	*ap*	Further,
		10 ud nídba	the tenth day: offering.
	5	30 ud iti MAxGÁNA*tenû*-sag	The thirtieth day of month XI
		in	until
	7	[	
III	x+1	⌜*in*⌝	until
		7 ud gibil	the seventh new day
	3	šeš-II-ib	the "brothers of ...".
		ʾÀ-da-ni^{ki}	(are in) Adani
	5	*in* [u]d	in order to exercise
		še[š-II-ib-]*sù*	their brotherhood office.
	7	2 [ud]	The second [day]
		[	[
IV	x+1	4 ud	The fourth day
		in	until
	3	28 ud *wa-ti-a-ti*	the twentyeighth day ...
		ḫu-mu	...
	5	^{d}*Ga-mi-iš*	of Kamiš.
		ap	Further,
	7	2 ud	the second day
		[	[
			[the xth day]
V	x+1	*i*[*n*]	in
		N[*e-a-*]⌜*ù*⌝$^{?[ki]}$[38]	Neau.
	3	8 u[d]	The eigth day
		in	until
	5	16 ⌜ud⌝ *ga*-[x-]*a*-[ ]	the sixteenth day ...
		[	

The restoration [^{d}*Ì-d*]*a*-["*ba*]*l*" [*ʾÀ-*]*ma-du*^{ki} in II 1'-2 is probable. According to the twenty monthly documents recording offerings of sheep to the gods worshiped at

38 The traces do not allow to restore: NE-*na-aš*^{ki}.

Ebla during the period immediately preceding the destruction of the city,[39] Idabal / Adabal (NI = *ì* and *ʾa*$_5$) received offerings at Ebla, mostly as Idabal of Luban. This was, therefore, considered to be the major sanctuary of this god. Idabal of Larugatu/Arugatu came then as second hypostasis. Idabal of Hamatu appears, instead, rarely in these lists. He receives an offering from the king only three times (twice in connection with the major god of the city of Ebla: "in the day of the offering for Kura", *in* ud nídba ^{d}*Ku-ra*),[40] and another time from Iraʾq-damu, the heir of the throne.[41] Idabal, instead, received many offerings in his sanctuary in Hamatu, a town to be identified with modern Hama.

For the expression: 7 ud gibil, in III 2, see *ARET* VII 24 rev. II 2-4: mu-DU *I-bí-zi-kir* 12 ud gibil iti *i-si* "(goods:) delivery of (the minister) Ibbi-Zikir (on) the 12th new day of month I" (the document is dated, rev. V 1, iti *i-si* "month I"). In the ritual *ARET* XI 1, 2, udu gibil occurs several times, and P. Fronzaroli suggests that this formula indicates the day of the month, starting from the new moon.[42]

wa-ti-a-ti and *ḫu-mu* seem to be attested only here.

ʾÀ-da-ni^{ki} (III 4) must be the ^{uru}*A-ta-an-ni*^{ki} of the Alalaḫ tablets; this is therefore to be located in the opposite direction to Hamatu, towards the Amuq. The major gods of this town were Rašap and his consort Adamma.[43] The šeš-II-ib (III 3, 6), a confraternity of people who took part in several cultic actions on behalf of the palace, are frequently connected with Adani.[44]

The traces in V 2 do not permit us to restore NE-*na-aš*^{ki}. *Ne-a-ù*^{ki} is probably the Nija of the 2nd millennium, perhaps to be identified with Qalʿat al-Mudīq, close to Apamea. His god was Idabal.[45]

---

39 Four of these tablets have been published by G. Pettinato, *OrAn* 18 (1979), pp. 85-215.

40 TM.75.G.1173+ obv. XI 27-28; TM.75.G.2598 obv. II 10-16; TM.75.G.10168 obv. I 18-II 3.

41 TM.75.G.1945 obv. II 26-III 5.

42 *ARET* XI, p. 29 *ad* (19); the list of the passages where ud gibil occurs is at p. 173.

43 See *ARES* II, pp. 124-128.

44 *ARET* IV 4 (45); III 41+ obv. IV 16-VI 1; TM.75.G.1464 obv. VII 1- 11; TM.75.G.1705 rev. IX 7-X 1; TM.75.G.1870 obv. XIII 10-14; TM.75.G.1872 obv. IX 11-X 1; TM.75.G.1875 rev. II 9-13; TM.75.G.2365 obv. III 21-IV 8; TM.75.G.10143+ obv. V 9-VI 5. See A. Archi, *Eblaitica* 4 (2002) (in print).

45 *ARES* II, p. 397.

4. NE-gar

4.1. The NE-gar was a metal object, usually not precious, the weight of which varied greatly: 56 minas of copper (26,32 kg) in text (1); 7 minas of copper (3,29 kg) in (2); 2;45 minas of gold and 21 minas of copper (11,36 kg total) in (3). It was a valuable object: according to (1) it was "delivered", mu-DU, by the king of Ebla himself. In (2) and (4) it was delivered as a gift by the king od DUlu; in (3) by the king of Dugurasu.

(1) TM.75.G.2073 rev. V 5: 56 ma-na a-gar$_5$-gar$_5$ 1 NE-gar (mu-DU en Ebla)
(2) TM.75.G.2070 obv. XI 11-12: 7 ma-na urudu 1 NE-gar (mu-DU en DU-*lu*^{ki})
(3) *ARET* VIII 528 rev. VI 8-10: 2 ma-na ša-pi 5 kù-gi 21 ma-na urudu 1 NE-gar (mu-DU *Du-gú-ra-su*^{ki} *in A-ru*$_{12}$*-ga-du*^{ki})
(4) TM.75.G.1900 obv. V 2-6: 1 NE-gar 2 KA-ma 5 gu si$_4$ 5 gu gi$_6$ ... en DU-*lu*^{ki} mu-DU

The Akkadian lists have izi-gar = *dipāru* "torch", while NE-gar occurs in the Eblaite Lists without Semitic equivalence. The quantities of metal of the Eblaite references, make us instead think of a brazier rather than a torch. The rite which took its name from NE-gar at Ebla, was celebrated in the tenth month of the year, that is in winter. It is therefore likely that this is the Brazier festival (NE: *kinūnu*), celebrated when, in the course of the year, it became necessary to fight the cold.[46] At Ebla, however, this festival was also connected to the survival of the dynasty (see 4.3).

4.2. Only four of the monthly documents listed here below and mentioning the NE-gar rite, preserve the name of the month: nos. (5), (10)-(11), (16). They are all dated to the tenth month of the "Semitic calendar", iti *i-ba*$_4$*-sa*. In some other kinds of documents, the rite could even give its name to the month. iti NE-gar appears in fact in some texts instead of iti *ḫur-mu*, the name of the tenth month according the "local calendar".[47]

(5) *ARET* VIII 542 (iti *i-ba*$_4$*-sa*: X) IV 7-13: 3 íb-III-TÚG-gùn 1 NE-gar dingir en 1 NE-gar en 1 NE-gar *ma-lik-tum* "(3 garments for) one NE-gar rite of the king's god, one NE-gar-rite of the king, one NE-gar rite of the queen".
(6) TM.75.G.1246 (iti [x]) obv. III 1-7: [(x)] 3 íb-III-TÚG-gùn NE-gar dingir en NE-gar en NE-gar *ma-lik-tum* (translation as in [5]).

46 I follow D. Charpin, *RA* 76 (1982), pp. 1-6, in considering *i-si* the first month. For the Sumerian month NE.NE-gar, see M.E. Cohen, *The Cultic Calendars of the Ancient Near East*, Bethesda, Maryland, 1993, pp. 31-32; W. Sallaberger, *Der kultische Kalendar der Ur III-Zeit*, 1, Berlin - New York 1993, pp. 125-127.

47 For the identity of iti izi-gar with iti *ḫur-mu*, see G. Pettinato, *AfO* 25 (1974-1977), p. 30.

(7) TM.75.G.2439 (iti [x]) obv. IV 4-16: (3 garments) lú NE-gar dingir en *wa* lú en *wa* lú *ma-lik-tum* (translation as in [5]).
(8) TM.75.G.10185 (iti [x]) obv. IV 1-12: (garments) PN_1-PN_8 *in* ud NE-gar dingir en "... in occasion of the NE-gar rite of the king's god".
(9) TM.75.G.2471 (iti [x]) rev. V 2-4: (garments) Šubur *in* NE-gar en "(garments for) PN in occasion of the NE-gar rite of the king".
(10) *ARET* VIII 525 (iti *i-ba₄-sa*) VII 7-9: 1 íb+III-TÚG-gùn NE-gar en "... (garments for) the NE-gar rite of the king".
(11) *ARET* VIII 525 (iti *i-ba₄-sa*) V 23-28: (garments) [*A-š*]*u-ur-ma-lik in* 1? NE-gar *ma-lik-tum* [šu-ba₄]-ti "(garments) PN has received for the NE-gar rite of the queen".
(12) TM.75.G.1936 (iti [x]) obv. II 12-III 7: (garment) *En-na-il* lú *A-ma-za*<-*ù*> níg-AN.AN.AN.AN [e]n è *ma-ba-ga-dam* é ^{d}*Ku-ra in* ud NE-gar "(garment) (for) PN_1 of PN_2 (who brought) the news (that) the king went out (for) the inspection of the temple of the god Kura on the occasion of the NE-gar rite".
(13) TM.75.G.10013 (iti [x]) obv. II' 11-III 4: (garments) *I-bí-zi-kir* lú *Iš-má-da-mu* níg-AN.AN.AN.AN *ma-lik-tum* en è *in ma-ba-ga-tum* NE-gar ^{d}*Ku-ra* "(garments) (for) PN_1 of PN_2 (who brought) the news (to) the queen (that) the king went out for the inspection for the NE-gar rite of the god Kura".

4.3. In the monthly accounts of offerings of sheep for the gods, the NE-gar rite is recorded in TM.75.G.2403, which concerns the ninth month ([iti] *ir*-[*m*]*e*), rev. IV 17-20: 1 udu NE-gar ^{d}*Ra-sa-ap ʾÀ-da-ni-du*^{ki}. This recording anticipates the following month to which TM.75.G.2397 (iti *ḫu-ru*$_{12}$*-lu*, a variant for *ḫur-mu*, the tenth month) is dedicated.

According to this last document, three sheep are sacrificed to Kura, the god of Ebla, "on the day of the NE-gar," while the sacrifices for the other gods fall on their usual days. We then have thirty-one sacrifices, each of a sheep, for the NE-gar of as an equal number of recipients (obv. IV 21-VIII 31). The first sacrifice is, again, for Kura: 1 udu NE-gar ^{d}*Ku-ra*. There then follow those for the NE-gar of four people: the king, the prince heir to the throne, Irʾaq-damu, the queen, and Zaʾaše, daughter of the minister Ibbi-Zikir and possibly betrothed to Irʾaq-damu. Among the other gods we have "the god of Enar-damu", an ancestor of the king, while later the NE-gar for "the god of the king", dingir en appears (obv. XI 9-12).

This sequence, and the fact that passages (5)-(11) of 4.2 connect the NE-gar with "the god of the king", the king himself and his queen, show that, by means of this rite, the dynasty's links with Kura, god of the city, were renewed together with the protection of the king by the tutelary god, dingir en, as well as by the ancestors (the deified Enar-damu / the god of Enar-damu).

4.4. The rite required "an invocation (to obtain) the favour (of the gods)", gù-di / du$_{11}$-ga *i-sa-rí*:[48]

(14) TM.75.G.1794 (iti [x]) rev. V 7-12: (garments) *I-da-ni-ki-mu* gù-di-II *i-sa-rí in* ud NE-gar en

(15) TM.75.G.1885 (iti [x]) obv. X 8-13: (1+1 garments) *I-da-ni-ki-mu* du$_{11}$-ga *i-sa-rí in* ud NE-gar en

4.5. Gifts of silver and gold were sent to the king of Mari, to the elders and to certain of his officials on the occasion of the NE-gar, nos. (16)-(18). While these gifts were brought (šu-mu-"tag$_4$") to Mari by people of Ebla, representatives of Mari were in Ebla and these also received gifts connected with the NE-gar, to which a GIŠ-dug-DU is related, nos. (17)-(22).

The term GIŠ-dug-DU appears in the introductory formula of TM.75.G.1444, a document with which the king confirms the dispositions of the minister Ibrium in favour three of his sons, who receive certain estates; obv. I 1-9: PN$_1$ *wa* PN$_2$ *wa* PN$_3$ GIŠ-dug-DU en *si-in* é-*sù* "PN$_1$-PN$_3$ (three of the Ibrium'sons) came to king for their estates".[49] In (19)-(21) the níg-ba is the consequence of the GIŠ-dug-DU; see further *ARET* III 2 IV: (garments for) PN GN (and) his *ma-za-lum* níg-ba GIŠ-dug-DU-*sù* "... gift (for) having come". I 14 (15): *in* ud GIŠ-dug-DU en *si-in* ḫúl na-rú-*sù* "when he came (to) the king for the festival of his stele".[50]

(16) *MEE* II 35 obv. II 11-IV 2: 10 ma-na babbar:kù 1 ma-na kù-gi níg-ba lugal 5 ma-na ša-pi 5 gín DILMUN babbar:kù níg-ba ábba-ábba *En-na-ì* di-kud *Íl-zi-da-mu* šu-mu-"tag$_4$" *in* ud NE-gar "10 minas of silver, 1 mina of gold: gift (for) the king (of Mari). 5;45 minas of silver: gift for the elders (of Mari): PN$_1$ the judge (and) PN$_2$ have brought on the occasion of the NE-gar rite".

(17) *ARET* VII 17 (1)-(2): (gifts for the king of Mari, his elders) *in* ud NE-gar PN$_1$-PN$_3$ šu-mu-"tag$_4$" "PN$_1$-PN$_3$ have brought on the occasion of the NE-gar rite". (gifts for Gulla, the brother of Enna-Dagan, king of Mari, and his agents) *in* ud NE-gar GIŠ-dug-DU " when they came (for) the NE-gar rite".

---

48 On this invocation, see M. Bonechi, *MisEb* 2, pp. 131-147.

49 *SEb* 4 (1981), p. 36. The Lexical Lists do not give an equivalence to GIŠ-dug-DU, but the following entry, no. 449, has GIŠ-dug-gíd-DU = *ga-ra-tum/du-um*, a term which G. Pettinato, *MEE* II, p. 50, derives from the same root of Akk. *karātum*, Heb. *krt* "to break off, to cut off", and translates with "assegnazione". He suggests further that: "val la pena ricordare che in ebraico *krt* è il termine tecnico per 'alleanza', sicché mi chiedo se tale significato così specifico non debba intendersi anche nei nostri casi, almeno alcune volte". There is no passages, however, which support this idea.

50 This meaning for GIŠ-dug-DU has been proposed by K. Hecker, in: *Ebla 1975-1985*, L. Cagni (ed.), Napoli 1987, p. 230.

(18) TM.75.G.10274 rev. I 5-II 12: [x ma-na] 5 gín [DILMUN] babbar:kù 1 ma-na kù-gi níg-ba [lugal] 3 [ma-na] ša-pi gín DILMUN babbar:kù níg-ba ábba-ábba *Íl-zi-da-mu Ìr-kab-ar* [PN_3] š[u-mu-]"t[ag_4"] *in* ud NE-gar 1 ma-na babbar:kù *Ìr*-NI-*il* GIŠ-dug-DU NE-gar "[x] silver, 1 mina of gold: gift (for) [the king (of Mari)]. 3;40 minas of silver (for) the elders, PN_1-PN_3 have brought on the occasion of the NE-gar rite. 1 mina of silver (to) PN' (for) having come (for) the NE-gar rite".

(19) TM.75.G.1904 obv. VII 15-20: 30 (gín) babbar:kù níg-ba *Bù-sum Ma-rí*ki GIŠ-dug-du NE-gar "30 shekels of silver: gift (to) PN of Mari, (for) having come (for) the NE-gar rite".

(20) TM.75.G.2359 rev. V 13-18: 1 ma-na babbar:kù níg-ba *Ib-gi-tum Ma-rí*ki GIŠ-dug-DU NE-gar "1 mina of silver: gift (to) PN of Mari (for) having come (for) the NE-gar rite".

(21) TM.75.G.10148 rev. IV 1-6:] níg-ba *Bù-za*-LUM *Am₆-mu-tum Ma-rí*ki GIŠ-dug-DU NE-gar "] gift for PN_1 PN_2 of Mari (for) having come (for) the NE-gar rite".

(22) *ARET* VII 16 (7): 1 ma-na babbar:kù *I-da-il* GIŠ-dug-DU NE-gar "1 mina of silver (to) PN (for) having come (for) the NE-gar rite".

(23) TM.75.G.1567 (iti *i-ba₄-sa*: X) obv. VIII 5-8: (gifts for Iram-damu) *in* ud GIŠ-dug-DU en NE-gar "when he came to the king (for) the NE-gar rite".

5. ne-sag

Sumerian ne-sag is a syllabic spelling of nesag (nisag) "first / early fruit".[51] The Eblaite Lexical Lists, no. 243, have: ne-sag = *ba-ga-lu(-um)*, whose Semitic equivalence must refer to the same root of that in no. 270: dumu-sag = *bù-ga-ru₁₂/lu*, *bù-gú-lu* "first-born".[52]

The economic documents do not give any indication to clarify this rite, which must have related to the offering of first fruits of the season. It was also the occasion for gifts to be made to the gods and did not occur in any determined month. Two documents, TM.75.G.2250 and TM.75.G.2353, which mention the ne-sag of the queen and of the king respectively, are dated to the second month of the year, iti *ig-za*. TM.75.G.2233 (ne-sag of the king's mother) and *ARET* I 11, 12 (ne-sag of several officials) concern instead the eleventh month, MAxGÁNA*tenû*-sag. The ne-sag celebration is attested for the king, the queen, members of the royal family and other people.

(1) *ARET* III 95 IV:] d*Ku-ra* en in-na-sum *in* ne-[sag-]*sù* "[(objects)] (for) Kura, (which) the king has given for his n". (*ARET* III 466 r. VII is similar).

---

51 Å.W. Sjöberg, *ZA* 63 (1973), p. 30. See also M. Civil, apud I. J. Gelb - P. Steinkeller - R. M. Whiting, *Earliest Land Tenure Systems in the Near East: Ancient Kudurrus* (OIP 104; Chicago 1991), p. 140.

52 See M. Krebernik, *ZA* 73 (1983), p. 13.

(2) TM.75.G.2245 obv. IV 10-V 8 (month: [x]): níg-ba *ma-lik-tum* ^{d}*Ra-sa-ap wa A-dam-ma-sù* lú šeš-II-ib *in* ne-sag en *wa ma-lik-tum* in-na-sum "[(garments:)] gift of the queen (for) Rašap and his (consort) Adamma, which the 'brothers of ...' have given for the n. of the king and the queen".

(3) TM.75.G.2233 rev. I 17-23: níg-ba ^{d}*Ra-sa-ap gú-nu* ama-gal in-na-sum *in* ud sag:ne-*sù* "(object) gift for Rašap *g*., (which) the queen has given on the occasion of her n.".

(4) *ARET* III 200 V:] dumu-mí en ^{d}*Ku-ra* ì-na-sum *in* sag:ne-*sù* "] the daughter of the king has given (to) Kura for her n.".

(5) TM.75.G.1834 rev. II 11-III 1: 2 íb-gùn-TÚG *Íl-zi* lú *Iš*$_{11}$*-gú-nu wa Šu-ma-lik* lú *Iš*$_{11}$*-da-mu* šeš-II-ib kéš-da *in* ud ne-sag *Ib-rí-um* "two kilts (for) PN_1 of PN_2 and PN_3 of PN_4, the 'brothers of ...' bound (to the palace) on the occasion of the n. of (minister) Ibrium".

What remains uncertain, however, is why various ne-sag rites were celebrated in the city of A(bsu):[53] *ARET* I 11 (14) and (45); TM.75.G.1322 obv. IX 4-6: PN_1 (*wa* PN_2) ne-sag *A*. TM.75.G.1363 obv. V 6-9: (garments) PN *A*. ne-sag. *ARET* I 12 (12): PN_1 (and) maškim-*sù A*. III 222 v. I; III 331 V; TM.75.G. 1318 obv. VII 8-10: (garments) ne-sag *A*. / *A*. ne-sag. See further TM.75.G.1322 obv. IX 1-2: " sag:ne *Ši-sal*^{ki}.

The gods who received gifts on the occasion of the ne-sag were: Kura and his consort Barama; Rašap of Adani and his consort Adamma; Rašap *gunum*; Idabal and his consort Baᶜaltum; Išḫara.

Plate I TM.75.G.12297

53 On *Áb-su/šu/zu/zú*^{ki}, see *ARES* II, pp. 145-147.

LA MISSIONE ITALIANA NEL DHOFAR (SULTANATO DELL'OMAN): PROSPETTIVE PER UNA RICERCA LINGUISTICA*

ALESSANDRA AVANZINI

Università di Pisa

Negli anni cinquanta una missione archeologica americana voluta da Wendell Phillips e guidata da F. P. Albright[1] iniziò lo scavo del sito di Khor Rori, ubicato nella pianura costiera del Dhofar (Sultanato dell'Oman) ad est della moderna città di Salalah, il capoluogo della regione. Gli scavi condotti dagli americani dimostrarono che Khor Rori, di cui conosciamo il nome antico, Sumhuram,[2] era un avamposto del regno dello Hadramawt fondato nel Dhofar per controllare e ricevere la produzione dell'incenso, che veniva raccolto nella regione desertica del Nejd ubicata oltre le montagne.

Nonostante che non vi siano prove certe in positivo è fortemente probabile che Khor Rori sia la Moscha Limèn citata dal *Periplo del mar Eritreo*.[3]

Dal 1996 al 1998, con brevi campagne di un mese ogni anno, la Missione Italiana nel Dhofar (MID) ha lavorato nella regione di Khor Rori. Nel 1999-2000 è prevista una più lunga presenza della missione nel Sultanato dell'Oman anche in vista dell'inizio del restauro della porta urbica e di uno scavo sistematico della città.[4]

---

* Molti i motivi di gratitudine verso il proprio maestro, ma qui ne vorrei ricordare uno strettamente personale, di cui non l'ho mai ringraziato. Molto del mio percorso lavorativo – e quindi buona parte della mia vita – è stato possibile grazie alla tranquilla sicurezza con cui Pelio Fronzaroli mi dette fiducia nel continuare studi appena intrapresi e che sembravano travolti dalla mia drammatica situazione di quegli anni lontani.

1 I risultati della missione degli anni 1952-1953 sono apparsi solo nel 1982: F. P. Albright, *The American Archaeogical Expedition in Dhofar (Oman), 1952-1953*, Washington 1982.

2 Sul nome della città cf. alcune osservazioni della scrivente: A. Avanzini, "La Missione Italiana nel Dhofar", *EVO* 19 (1996), pp. 183-184.

3 N. Groom, "The *Periplus*, Pliny and Arabia", *AAE* 6, 1995, pp. 180-195. Le prove addotte da N. Groom contro questa identificazione, oltre a non essere molto convincenti di per sé, risultano fragili essenzialmente per la mancanza di un altro porto nella zona che possa più credibilmente di Khor Rori essere identificato con Moscha.

4 Un primo, in gran parte inatteso, risultato della campagna ottobre-dicembre 1999 è stato ottenuto con la precisazione della pianta del complesso della porta. Il disegno riportato da Albright è in parte

La porta è stata costruita in vari periodi; le costruzioni, che sono state successivamente addossate alla porta urbica originaria, garantivano una maggiore capacità di difesa della città, ma davano anche una maggiore spettacolarità all'ingresso alla città. Anche dalle iscrizioni incise lungo il corridoio di accesso alla città – e non solo dal loro contenuto, ma anche dalla loro posizione nel complesso architettonico – risulta chiaramente che la porta è stata costruita in almeno due momenti.[5]

I sondaggi condotti tra il 1997 e il 1998 hanno permesso di alzare la data di fondazione di Sumhuram all'ultimo quarto del I secolo a.C.,[6] mentre l'inizio del processo di disgregazione, che portò all'abbandono del porto dell'incenso, è stato collocato intorno alla metà del IV secolo d.C. Non è possibile non rimarcare la coincidenza cronologica fra il declino di Sumhuram indicato dai dati archeologici e l'inizio del periodo di crisi dello Hadramawt, che culmina con l'annessione del regno da parte degli Himyariti alla fine del III secolo d.C.

Ma il lavoro archeologico fin qui svolto si è concentrato anche sulla zona intorno alla città.

Al termine degli scavi condotti da Albright, la città appariva come una "cattedrale" in un deserto insediativo quasi assoluto.[7] L'obiettivo storico-archeologico principale delle ricerche condotte dalla Missione Italiana in Dhofar è stato pertanto quello di collocare la città nel suo contesto territoriale, allo scopo di comprendere i modelli d'interazione culturale ed economica che collegavano fra loro gli insediamenti e le diverse entità socio-politiche esistenti in questa regione, entità socio-politiche che sono molteplici e fortemente differenziate per cultura materiale, organizzazione sociale e strategie di sussistenza.

---

errato, in particolare per quanto riguarda le dimensioni e la posizione del muro di sbarramento a nord della porta.

5 È questo un esempio di come per la comprensione dell'epigrafe non sia solo importante il testo, ma anche e forse più di tutto il suo contesto. Importanti alcune osservazioni di M. Macdonald su questo argomento nel suo interessantissimo lavoro: M. C. A. Macdonald, "Some reflextions on epigraphy and etnicity in the Roman Near East", in *Mediterranean Archaeology* 11 (1998), pp. 177-190.

6 Uno degli argomenti di Groom contro l'identificazione di Khor Rori con Moscha: la fondazione della città sarebbe successiva alla redazione del testo greco, viene così a cadere.

7 Dal 1992 al 1995 in Dhofar ha portato avanti un lavoro archeologico la missione americana diretta da J. Zarins; cf. J. Zarins, "Persia and Dhofar: Aspects of Iron Age International Politics and Trade", in G. Y. Young, M. W. Chavals and R. E. Averbeck (eds.), *Crossing Boundaries and Linking Horizons*, Bethesda 1997, pp. 615-689.

Sinteticamente il lavoro svolto dalla nostra missione ha mostrato come l'insediamento indigeno della seconda metà del I millennio a.C. e dei primi secoli d.C. in Dhofar, quindi immediatamente anteriore e contemporaneo alla fondazione di Sumhuram, si caratterizzi per un panorama estremamente composito e articolato, con tipologie insediative differenziate:

1. nella fascia litoranea esistono insediamenti occupati forse su base periodica che riflettono una strategia di sussistenza basata sulla pesca e raccolta di molluschi da parte di gruppi probabilmente mobili;
2. la piana costiera e la fascia pedemontana sono invece occupate da villaggi agricoli permanenti, controllati da fortezze. È il caso della fortezza di Ain Humrain, costruita su un'altura ai piedi delle colline presso una serie di sorgenti. La fortezza era difesa da una doppia cinta di mura con torri e controllava vari villaggi con canali d'irrigazione.[8] La strategia di sussistenza in questi siti si basa essenzialmente sull'agricoltura irrigua e sull'allevamento di caprovini e, probabilmente, di bovini;
3. nell'altopiano del Jebel Qara e nel Nejd sono invece presenti ripari in grotta connessi a gruppi pastorali, associati in alcuni casi a villaggi permanenti;
4. infine, nella regione desertica, in un'oasi ai margini delle sabbie sorge la fortezza di Shisr che controllava la via carovaniera principale.

In questo sistema insediativo caratterizzato dalla presenza di siti indigeni si colloca la fondazione di Sumhuram ad opera di coloni dello Hadramawt. La fondazione di Sumhuram va evidentemente inserita in un quadro più vasto, di tipo sovraregionale, legato allo sviluppo del commercio marittimo romano nel Mar Rosso e nell'Oceano Indiano. Il carattere intrusivo di tale operazione è riflesso in maniera molto felice dal repertorio ceramico scavato a Sumhuram, dominato da due grosse componenti non indigene: ceramica hadramautica e materiali anforacei importati dal Mediterraneo romano.

Lo studio della storia di Sumhuram si inserisce in alcune problematiche generali relative alla storia sudarabica.

La costruzione di Sumhuram da parte dei re hadramautici apre il problema del rapporto tra i regni sudarabici e la regione costiera o, più in generale, tra il potere politico e il territorio.

---

8 Zarins, *cit.*, pp. 658-660 e fig. 12.

Come è ben noto, i moduli statuali del Periodo del Ferro in Arabia meridionale si sviluppano nelle valli che scendono verso il deserto, per cui Beeston coniò il termine di cultura "sayhadica" – la cultura del deserto.

La definizione di Beeston è certo ancora, dopo molti anni, in gran parte condivisibile, anche se il concentrarsi dall'VIII secolo a.C. fino alla fine del I secolo a.C. della cultura sudarabica antica nella regione predesertica non comporta il vuoto abitativo sull'altopiano e lungo la costa. In questo senso sono importanti i risultati della missione americana sull'altopiano yemenita.[9]

La zona costiera svolge un ruolo di grande importanza nel passaggio tra protostoria e storia, come è stato messo in luce dalle ricerche archeologiche di questi ultimi anni.[10] Fino al periodo di Karibil Watar (inizio VII secolo a.C.), per rafforzare il potere sabeo, il re conduce spedizioni militari contro le regioni lungo l'Oceano Indiano.[11]

Anche se è vero che dal VII secolo tutto il potere politico-economico si è concentrato lungo la carovaniera e la nostra documentazione scritta e archeologica proviene dalla regione "sayhadica", il traffico per mare a media e lunga distanza deve essere stato delegato a comunità, che vivevano lungo la costa, dedite alla pesca e alla pastorizia, ma capaci di sviluppare una tecnologia nautica.

I seminomadi, che, come in tutta la storia vicino-orientale, interagiscono con i sedentari, nell'Arabia meridionale dovrebbero essere suddivisi in due gruppi:

1. i nomadi, dediti alla pastorizia, all'allevamento dei cammelli, che premono sulle frontiere del deserto. Alcuni di loro – come è testimoniato dalle fonti scritte – si sono sedentarizzati come, certamente, gruppi di agricoltori avranno subito fenomeni di "beduinizzazione".
2. i seminomadi della costa del mar Rosso e dell'Oceano Indiano dediti alla pesca e alla pastorizia, ma anche alla navigazione.

---

9 T. J. Wilkinson, C. Edens, "Survey and Excavation in the Central Highlands of Yemen: Results of the Dhamar Survey Project, 1996 and 1998", *AAE* 10 (1999), pp. 1-33.

10 Cf. Burkhard Vogt, "Frühe Kulturen an der Küste des Roten Meeres und des Golfs von Aden", in *Jemen*, Milano 1998, pp. 123-128. Per inciso, in questi ultimi anni le scoperte archeologiche nella regione di Sabir e lungo la Tihama hanno ridato forza alla vecchia ipotesi di Conti Rossini di una evidente koinè culturale tra lo Yemen costiero e l'Etiopia alla fine del II millennio.

11 Nella grande iscrizione RES 3945 sono ricordate otto spedizioni militari del re sabeo, di cui la prima è verso l'estremo sud dello Yemen, la terza verso la zona di Aden e l'ottava nella Tihama. Anche la guerra contro il re di Awsan, il più pericoloso ostacolo all'affermarsi del potere sabeo, ha come campo di battaglia la zona costiera della Datina: "e lo distrusse e bruciò e saccheggiò le sue terre e lo sconfisse finché non arrivò al mare e bruciò tutte le sue città che erano sul mare" (RES 3945 5).

Nel momento dello sviluppo del traffico marino romano, diventa importante per i regni sudarabici, non delegare più il commercio per mare alle popolazioni locali, ma parteciparvi in prima persona con tutte le manifestazioni proprie del potere sudarabico: fondando città e cingendole di mura, costruendo templi, scrivendo iscrizioni monumentali. La fondazione di Sumhuram sembra rientrare nel quadro storico generale ipotizzato. I coloni dello Hadramawt si inseriscono in un sistema locale – non in un territorio vuoto, ma insediato da un complesso mosaico di comunità umane, con organizzazioni socio-politiche e strategie di sussistenza economica estremamente diversificate – che aveva già creato una rete commerciale sovraregionale su lunga distanza e la controllava.

La relazione tra la città e i locali deve essere specificata, contestualizzata, non vista solo come la storia della "colonizzazione" del regno dello Hadramawt in una regione di livello tecnologico, organizzativo e culturale molto basso e che, in ogni caso, non interagisce con la città.[12]

Comprendere in maniera più precisa i modelli d'interazione economica, politica e culturale che collegavano le varie entità della regione, arrivare a una ricostruzione di tutta la storia "locale", rappresenta il compito principale della ricerca storico-archeologica della nostra missione nei prossimi anni.

La Missione Italiana in Dhofar porta avanti anche un progetto di ricerca linguistica.[13]

La situazione linguistica del Dhofar è importante per affrontare alcuni problemi generali di linguistica storica, connessi con il popolamento dell'Arabia meridionale da parte di popolazioni parlanti lingue semitiche. E non si tratta di individuare esclusivamente linee migratorie di popolazioni, ma di seguire "filoni" linguistici, non solo cioè movimenti di gruppi etnici da una zona ad un'altra, ma anche contatti tra

---

12 Non è facile uscire dalla dualistica concezione, molto persistente e pervasiva, che rappresenta la situazione coloniale come un confronto tra due entità essenzialmente distinte, ciascuna delle quali è omogenea al suo interno e chiusa verso l'esterno. Cf. sul concetto postcoloniale di "hybridity", P. van Dommelen, "Colonial Constructs: Colonialism and Archaeology in the Mediterranean", *World Archaeology* 28 (1997), pp. 305-323.

13 La ricostruzione della storia linguistica della parte orientale dello Yemen e del Dhofar è agevolata dalla migliore conoscenza, grazie alla pubblicazione delle iscrizioni della Missione Sovietica e agli studi di Frantsuzoff, dello hadramautico. È questa la lingua ASA meno sabeizzata e che presenta tratti linguistici e lessicali più strettamente connessi con il MSA.

popolazioni insediate in regioni distanti; contatto linguistico agevolato nel vicino oriente dalla presenza di gruppi di seminomadi.

Questa è, a mio parere, la forza euristica del modello "amorreo" di Garbini. Ma bisogna innanzitutto chiarire i termini del problema. Lo stesso Garbini ha perso a mio parere di vista quella che era la grande forza della sua intuizione, continuandola a vedere come un esempio di classificazione linguistica su base geografica contrapposta alla da lui tanto odiata classificazione genealogica.

Il modello prende tutta la sua importanza nel momento in cui viene relativizzato il ruolo di un popolo preciso. Se con "amorrei" intendiamo i seminomadi/nomadi – peculiarità storico-sociale della regione vicino orientale rispetto, per esempio, all'Europa – individuiamo il motore della diffusione linguistica e della creazione delle lingue semitiche.[14] Importanti inoltre alcune precisazioni di carattere generale di Fronzaroli che non vede negli "amorrei" i creatori di innovazioni linguistiche – troppo costoso supporre che gruppi di pastori, per eccellenza conservativi sul piano culturale e linguistico, fossero non solo i creatori di innovazioni linguistiche ma che fossero stati addirittura in grado di imporle alle culture urbane – ma il tramite tra gruppi di sedentari. "Sembra improbabile che popolazioni di cultura pastorale e organizzazione tribale, prive di istituzioni culturali e politiche unitarie capaci di imporre modelli linguistici, siano responsabili delle innovazioni che caratterizzano la variante amorrea. Il tipo amorreo potrebbe piuttosto aver avuto origine nelle città più meridionali dell'area siro-palestinese, città che esistevano anche se la loro lingua non è finora documentata".[15] Fascia urbana di grande importanza anche per capire i rapporti tra il semitico meridionale e quello settentrionale.

---

14 Se così intendiamo gli "amorrei" risultano, quindi, fuori luogo alcune osservazioni di Zaborski sull'inconsistenza delle nostre conoscenze linguistiche degli "amorrei" di Mesopotamia e sull'assurdità di parlare di "amorrei" nel I millennio a.C. – A. Zaborski, "Semitic Dialect Continuum", in K. Dévényi, T. Iványi (eds.), *Proceedings of the Colloquium on Arabic Grammar*, p. 366 "Another hypothesis concerning the genetic classification of Arabic has been presented in several versions by Garbini who classifies Arabic within North West Semitic and for whom the language of Amorrite names is a kind of pre-written Arabic ("una specie di arabo ante-litteram"). Unfortunately, this hypothesis by the great Italian semitist is based on rather scanty evidence (e.g. on our very limited knowledge of the Amorritic of which Garbini himself scarcely gives any concrete examples) and in general it raises more questions than it answers. Especially daring and far reaching is his hypothesis about an "amorrization" not only of North Arabic but also of South Arabian and even Ethiopic! Since most of its crucial elements cannot be verified I am unable to discuss it in this paper".

15 P. Fronzaroli, "La lingua di Ebla e le lingue semitiche", in P. Matthiae (ed.), *Ebla. Alle origini della civiltà urbana*, Milano 1995, p. 223.

L'ipotesi linguistica da cui ero partita consisteva nell'individuare un "filone" linguistico, che, partendo dalla Mesopotamia, attraverso le regioni del Golfo e il Dhofar, arrivasse in Yemen e poi fino in Etiopia. Un popolamento in periodo arcaico della zona meridionale della penisola araba, ipotizzato sul piano linguistico, è confermato da scoperte archeologiche recenti.

Di questa prima fase arcaica sarebbero testimonianza, in Arabia meridionale, le lingue sudarabiche moderne (MSA) e alcune lingue sudarabiche antiche (ASA) – o, almeno, alcuni loro tratti linguistici conservativi. La forte sabeizzazione dei dialetti epigrafici sudarabici sarebbe, inoltre, stata causa dei loro tratti linguisticamente più recenti e quindi del loro aspetto fortemente stratificato.

La mia ipotesi era in accordo con quanto sostenuto da Lonnet "Quant au sudarabique ancien, sous lequel on regroupe les langues des inscriptions antiques, il est assurément exclu, à la lumière de la comparaison lexicale et grammaticale, d'y voir l'ancêtre du sudarabique moderne; la dénomination est d'autant plus trompeuse qu'il est probable que les langues dites "anciennes" aient pénétré, venues du Nord, dans une Arabie du Sud où les langues dites "modernes" étaient déjà en place".[16]

Ultimamente, tuttavia, formulerei in modo diverso l'ipotesi generale da cui ero partita e sarei meno d'accordo con A. Lonnet.

Per quanto riguarda l'ASA, come già altrove sostenuto, a mio parere le lingue sudarabiche antiche si sono formate nell'Arabia meridionale e non sono "arrivate" dall'esterno. Le scoperte archeologiche nell'area di Marib datano insediamenti a pieno sfruttamento agricolo in un periodo molto più antico di quello fin qui noto – se non addirittura un'organizzazione del lavoro e una capacità tecnica così sviluppata da presupporre l'esistenza della grande diga nel III millennio.[17]

La forte stratificazione linguistica del sudarabico non è esclusivamente legata ad "arrivi" di nuove popolazioni, ma a una lunga protostoria di contatti all'interno dell'area yemenita. Naturalmente anche i contatti verso l'esterno sono stati di grande importanza, ma devono essere presupposti essenzialmente nella direzione sud → nord e non esclusivamente nord → sud.

Possiamo ipotizzare fenomeni di "beduinizzazione" di agricoltori dall'area yemenita – i tanto citati "Sabei del nord", che sarebbero, per l'appunto, Sabei "che

16 A. Lonnet, "Le verbe sudarabique moderne: hypothèses sur des tendances", *MAS-GELLAS* 5 (1994), p. 216.

17 U. Brunner, "Die Erfoschung der antiken Oase von Ma'rib mit Hilfe geomorphologisher Untersuchungesmethoden", *Archäologische Berichte aus dem Yemen*, 2 (1983).

sono andati a nord" e non beduini del nord dell'Arabia, che non sono ancora andati a sud, e quindi non sono ancora diventati Sabei – che avrebbero iniziato un lungo processo di contatti verso il nord, verso proprio quelle città dell'area palestinese meridionale in cui sarebbero nate le innovazioni "amorree".[18]

Altrove mi sono soffermata su quello che è a mio parere uno degli aspetti più interessanti della situazione linguistica dell'ASA: la copresenza di tratti linguistici comuni a tutte le lingue sudarabiche (le tre sibilanti sorde non enfatiche, la determinazione del sostantivo, ecc.) e di tratti diversi.[19] Restava aperto il problema – niente affatto secondario sul piano storico e linguistico – di capire se la situazione linguistica dell'Arabia meridionale preislamica era dovuta a una forte omogeneizzazione di realtà linguistiche diverse o a una base in gran parte unitaria, che si erano venuta differenziando nel tempo.

In un primo momento la prima ipotesi mi era sembrata preferibile: lingue diverse tra loro sarebbero state "sabeizzate" e rese omogenee grazie al maggior prestigio culturale sabeo (la scrittura, non a caso, sarebbe, per esempio, invenzione sabea); quest'ipotesi andava nella sostanza d'accordo – anche se veniva rifiutato il modello migratorio per periodi immediatamente precedenti le attestazioni storiche – con quanto sostenuto, per esempio, da Lonnet e da Garbini: vari filoni di lingue semitiche, distinti cronologicamente e tipologicamente sarebbero arrivati dal III millennio fino a buona parte del II nell'Arabia meridionale.

Oggi trovo preferibile, per motivi storici e linguistici, lavorare all'interno della seconda ipotesi. Gli stati sudarabici nascono grazie a un processo di differenziazione politica, religiosa, linguistica, basti pensare con quanta coerenza i sudarabici hanno per tutta la loro storia rifiutato un'identità "sudarabica".[20] Anche sul piano linguisti-

---

18 Anche il complesso problema dell'origine della scrittura ASA, come anche gli abecedari di Beth Shemesh e Ugarit, in scrittura ugaritica, ma con l'ordine alfabetico semitico meridionale, acquistano significato in questo quadro di contatti Arabia meridionale-Palestina, Siria.

19 Cf. A. Avanzini, "Brevi osservazioni sul lessico delle lingue epigrafiche dell'Arabia meridionale preislamica", *SEL* 12 (1995), pp. 27-36.

20 A. Avanzini, "La «lista degli eponimi» e l'inizio della documentazione storica nell'Arabia meridionale preislamica", in *Presentazione e scrittura della storia: storiografia, epigrafi, monumenti, Biblotheca di Atheneum* 42 (1999), p. 121: "Non vi è mai traccia in tutta la storia sudarabica, dall'inizio del I millennio a.C. almeno fino all'unificazione politica dello Yemen nel IV sec. d.C., di una consapevolezza di un'identità «sudarabica». Anche qui, di nuovo, gli stretti contatti tra stati sudarabici hanno creato uniformità culturale, ma anche forte competitività politica, e l'identità di un sudarabico è stata sempre su base politico-statuale e non culturale. Gli stati formano la propria identità su meccanismi di «differenziazione»".

co, per esempio, possiamo notare che il lessico antico sabeo è più simile a quello qatabanico, hadramautico e mineo di quanto non lo sia quello medio sabeo, che i testi hadramautici e qatabanici più "sabeizzati" sono i testi del periodo più arcaico, che l'onomastica antica è la stessa in tutta l'area sudarabica.

E proprio l'onomastica mi suggerisce un'ultima osservazione che è poi una precisazione di metodo su come impostare il processo ricostruttivo. Come dicevo, il lavoro linguistico era partito dall'ipotesi che le lingue MSA e alcuni dialetti ASA tra cui lo hadramautico rappresentassero una "fase" più arcaica del semitico dell'Arabia meridionale, mentre il sabeo era una lingua "amorreizzata" e innovativa. Uno dei tratti linguistici, come già da molti linguisti osservato, che portava a sostenere la recenziorità del sabeo era il morfema in *h* rispetto a quello in sibilante nel pronome suffisso di III persona e nel causativo.

Fronzaroli, che colloca il fenomeno in una prospettiva camito-semitica, è pienamente convincente quando attribuisce i morfemi in *s*- al semitico arcaico. Non sono quindi d'accordo con quanto sostenuto da Edzard: "the *S*-bearing forms in no way chronologically precede the *h*-bearing forms".[21] Quello che mi sembra, tuttavia, interessante osservare è che fin da una documentazione molto antica i due morfemi hanno coesistito nell'area centrale semitica; ne abbiamo prova nell'ugaritico, se non nello stesso amorreo,[22] fino ad alcune lingue MSA che usano il morfema in *h* per il pronome di III persona maschile ed in *s* per il femminile.[23] Anche nelle lingue ASA la situazione è meno lineare di quanto non sembri a una prima impressione. È vero che nel sabeo non vi è traccia dei morfemi in *s* e anche la presenza di morfemi in *h* nelle altre lingue ASA è un fenomeno più legato all'affermarsi di modelli testuali, all'imporsi della scuola scrittoria sabea, che non a fenomeni di lingua,[24] tuttavia

21 L. Edzard, *Polygenesis, Convergence, and Entropy: an Alternative Model of Linguistic Evolution Applied to Semitic Linguistics*, Wiesbaden 1998, p. 117. Il notissimo parallelo indeuropeo, citato (p. 119) a questo proposito da Edzard: "Greek *hex* «six» and *hepta* «seven» chronologically precede Latin *sex* «six» and *septem* «seven»", testimonia il contrario di quanto da lui sostenuto. Detto questo, alcune idee sostenute a proposito dei morfemi di causativo e di pronome di III persona da Edzard (cf. anche le interessanti pagine su questo stesso tema di Retsö – J. Retsö, *Diathesis in the Semitic languages*, Leiden 1989, 49-138), sono del tutto condivisibili.

22 Cf. E. E. Knudsen, "Amorite grammar. A comparative statement", in A. S. Kaye (ed.), *Semitic Studies in Honour of Wolf Leslau*, Wiesbaden 1991, pp. 876-877.

23 Difficile non pensare a un parallelismo tipologico con lo hadramautico, l'unica lingua ASA in cui il pronome suffisso di III persona è diverso per il maschile e per il femminile.

24 A. Avanzini, "*H*-forms in Qatabanian inscriptions", *Yemen* 1 (1992), pp. 13-17.

l'onomastica arcaica ASA, anche nelle documentazioni non sabee, presenta esclusivamente i morfemi in *h*.[25] La documentazione onomastica, di per sé conservativa, è testimonianza innegabile di una situazione linguistica sudarabica unitaria con morfema in *h*; anche quando le lingue non-sabee useranno regolarmente il morfema in *s*, per il pronome di III persona e per il causativo, non sentiranno la necessità di reinterpretare i nomi propri.

Ultima rapida osservazione sul rapporto ASA-MSA: la dislocazione geografica diversa tra ASA e MSA ha comportato un'evoluzione diversa con innovazioni diverse e conservazioni diverse. Le lingue MSA non sono conservative solo perché attestate in un'area geograficamente laterale, ma in primo luogo perché non hanno subito la forte sabeizzazione e successiva arabizzazione a cui sono state invece sottoposte le lingue dello Yemen occidentale. La "storia" diversa delle regioni in cui sono attestate le lingue MSA è più importante, a mio parere, delle rigide norme delle aree laterali.

Per il lavoro comparativo, intendo quindi partire dall'ipotesi che le lingue MSA e ASA possono essere fatte derivare da una matrice comune, o in qualche modo accomunante (per sfuggire all'accusa di andare in cerca di una "lingua madre" sudarabica). Matrice non unitaria – in cui sono presenti, per esempio, i due morfemi in *s* e in *h* – e da cui le lingue si sono formate con meccanismi di divergenza e di convergenza. I comparativisti sembrano aver bisogno di un'adesione metodologica di base, di una scelta di campo, che forse non è necessaria nello studio dell'evoluzione delle lingue semitiche – e forse neppure di quelle indoeuropee Se noi accettiamo che l'unità del modello ricostruito è più un postulato di certa ricostruzione, ma che le lingue naturali non sono unitarie, i due meccanismi di convergenza e divergenza possono almeno in parte immaginarsi coesistenti nella formazione delle lingue storiche.[26]

Nota: il manoscritto è stato consegnato agli inizi del 2000; i lavori apparsi dopo questa data non sono stati inclusi in bibliografia.

---

25 Cito qui, tra i tanti esempi possibili, alcuni antroponimi: *S^{1}mhyf'*, *Hbbr'l*, *Hqm'l*, *Hwfwd*, *Yhqm*, ecc., attestati nei testi arcaici provenienti dalla regione del Jawf, contemporanei a quelli antico-sabei.

26 Cf. C. Renfrew, "Time depth, Convergence theory, and Innovation in Proto-Indo-European", *JIES* 27 (1999), pp. 257-293.

A RITUAL FROM ARCHIVE L.2712 OF EBLA

MARIA GIOVANNA BIGA

Università di Roma "La Sapienza"

"Oh dark, dark night. Oh night so black of hue."
W. Shakespeare, *A Midsummer Night's Dream*,
Act 5 - Scene I

1. Preliminary analysis of the text

Tablet TM.75.G.756+771+815 was found in archive L.2712[1] where administrative texts relating to rations of food destined for palace officials and others regarding deliveries of diverse goods, in particular objects in precious woods, were conserved. Among the archive documents, text TM.75.G.756+771+815 stands out since its content is not administrative but can be considered a true ritual of the kind which Pelio Fronzaroli himself has defined as "prescriptive and descriptive" ritual. I am therefore particularly happy to dedicate to Pelio Fronzaroli, who has published the most important Eblaite rituals, the preliminary study on this ritual, certain that he, with his well-known skill in interpreting these interesting but difficult texts, will be more capable than I of improving on and completing my work.

The tablet, following a campaign of work on joints in texts and fragments from archive L.2712 undertaken some years ago by A. Archi and myself, is recomposed following the joining of three pieces; but unluckily some lines are missing and this prevents us from understanding the type of the ritual. It is not very likely that the missing fragments may be found as the archive was found all in one block and other fragments of tablets are missing, probably having crumbled to very small pieces, without leaving a trace.

The writing is good but there are some erasures and some lines are clearly written later, when the clay was already dry.

Whilst it was first thought that this text was an administrative document listing offerings in food to various gods, of the kind documented in the same archive by the text *ARET* IX 17 and 107, I later (after the joints) realised that the text was very un-

---

1 The tablet is measuring 81x87x23 cm. and will be in the volume by A. Archi and myself *ARET* X with number 57. I am indebted to A. Archi who discussed this text with me, giving some suggestions.

usual and could be read as a ritual prescription for offerings to the gods to be performed at various times according to well-established rythms and methods.[2]

The occasion on which the ritual was to be performed cannot, unfortunately, be defined with precision due to the break in the text, but without doubt involved the king. On the other hand, almost all the rituals published to date have the king as protagonist, probably as the principal religious as well as political figure. A further exceptional feature of this text is the presence of gods not attested elsewhere in the Ebla texts, be these administrative documents, rituals, lexical or literary texts.

The text, which can easily be divided into sections which denote the various phases of the ritual, starts with offerings of food, "pure breads", and various vessels containing oil, beer, wine and purifying water offered to (the statue of) a god who, to my knowledge, appears in no other Eblaite text and which I would interpret as being the (unnamed) deity of the night. There then follows the offering of a black ceremonial garment to clothe the statue of the bride of the god of the night. Offerings of food are also placed before her statue.

The ritual then speaks of offerings of oil, beer, wine and water and the sacrifice of female animals to the god of the night, who is also offered an identical piece of ceremonial black clothing. In a fragmentary form we then have further offerings of beer and wine to the god of the night.

The ritual continues with identical offerings of food, "pure breads", oil, beer, wine and purifying water (excluding, however, animals) to another god who is only attested to in this text, ^{d}NE-*ra,* in which I would, very tentatively, propose to see a Eblaite writing of the name of the god of fire. The same offerings are again made to another deity who appears only here, the goddess Abasa, wife of the god NEra. The text prescribes also a second offering to the god NEra before sunset or, more possi-

2 Examining the different types of ritual texts at Ebla, quoting this text which I discussed with him during some pleasant afternoons at Mardikh, P. Fronzaroli, *Impieghi della scrittura a Ebla, Studi linguistici per i 50 anni del Circolo Linguistico Fiorentino e i secondi mille dibattiti 1970-1995*, Firenze 1995, pp. 81-94, wrote at p. 87 and n. 22: "Di origine direttamente amministrativa è invece un altro tipo di testo rituale estremamente sobrio, che indica soltanto le offerte e l'occasione dell'atto di culto. Dal punto di vista formale esso deriva, per sottrazione dei dati non pertinenti, dalla giustapposizione dei singoli paragrafi che registrano assegnazioni cultuali (quali si trovano di frequente nei testi di consegne di tessili e di metalli). Il carattere specificatamente rituale di questa redazione è assicurato dal fatto che vi compaiono insieme offerte di cibo, di tessili e di oggetti, ordinatamente disposte e motivate secondo i momenti della giornata e secondo le divinità".

bly, before dawn. There is then an annotation relating to food rations given to a retinue of 40 people.

The text concludes by recalling that these are the offerings prescribed for the god of the night on the occasion of the ... of the king. Although I have not succedeed in reconstructing the occasion on which the ritual was to be performed, it would appear probably that this ritual for the god of the night could be a nocturnal event. It is to stress the exclusive use of black garments. But it is not matter of a funeral ritual.

The gods mentioned recall in a quite surprising way the gods of the first lines of the first tablet of the Maqlû ritual:[3] the god (or gods) of the night, the bride of the god of the night, indicated by the same term "*gal-la-tum*" which appear in the Maqlû ritual. In a type of ritual performed during the night the mention of the god of the fire and his wife would be possible.

2. The text

(1)

obv.	I.	1.	1 ⸢GIŠ-banšur⸣$^{?}$ [a]
			[.....]
		3.	[.....]
			[x] ⸢x⸣
		5.	[x GIŠ]-asar
			gaba
		7.	^{d}Gi$_{6}$-an ([A]N.MI.AN)

1 offering table ... ... an offering tray (is placed) before (the statue of) the god of the night.

---

3 Cf. K. L. Tallquist, *Die assyrische Beschwörungsserie Maqlû* (= *ASSF* 20/6), Leipzig 1895; G. Meier, *Die assyrische Beschwörungssammlung Maqlû* (= *AfO*, Beih. 2), Berlin 1937 and G. Meier, *AfO* 21 (1966), pp. 70-81. In the first two lines of the first tablet: ÉN *al-si-ku-nu-ši* DINGIR.MEŠ *mu-ši-ti / it-ti-ku-nu al-si mu-ši-tum kal-la-tum kut-tùm-tum*. For a ritual performed during the night cf. also G. Dossin, "Prière aux dieux de la nuit", *RA* 32 (1935), pp. 179-189; M. Stol, "Two Old Babylonian Literary Texts", in F. Rochberg-Halton (ed.), *Language, Literature and History: Philological and Historical Studies Presented to Erica Reiner*, New Haven 1987, pp. 383-387; W. Horowitz - N. Wasserman, "Another Old Babylonian Prayer to the Gods of the Night", *JCS* 48 (1996), pp. 57-60.

(2)

[1] GIŠ-asar *gi-l*[*a*]$^{?}$-TU[M$^{?}$ (x)]
II. 1. 1 GIŠ-⸢asar⸣ ninda-sikil
1 bur-kak ì-giš 1 an-zam$_{x}$ ŠE+TIN 1 zi-bar geštin
1 *maš-a-ḫa-tum*
3. ^{d}Gi$_{6}$-an ([A]N.MI.AN)

1 offering tray with ..., 1 offering tray with “pure breads”, 1 container-bur-kak of oil, 1 container an-zam$_{x}$ of beer, 1 container zibar of wine, 1 vase with spout for water for the god of the night.

(3)

10 lá-3 [GIŠ]-[uš]til$^{?}$
5. [.....]
[*ga-du-ma-tum*]$^{?}$
7. [gu-dùl]-⸢TÚG⸣-⸢gi$_{6}$⸣^{b}
III. 1. mu$_{4}$^{mu}
gal-la-tum
3. ^{d}Gi$_{6}$-an (AN.MI.AN)

7... ... ... for a black cloth with which to dress the (statue of the) wife of the god of the night.

(4)

10 lá-3 GIŠ-asar
5. gaba
gal-la-tum
7. ^{d}Gi$_{6}$-an (AN.MI.AN)

7 offering trays before (the statue of) the wife of the god of the night.

(5)

10 lá-3 bur-kak ì-giš
9. [10] ⸢lá⸣-[3] [an-zam$_{x}$ ŠE+TIN]
⸢10⸣ l[á-3] zi-bar gešt[in]
IV. 1. 10 lá-3 *maš-a-ḫa-tum*
1 GIŠ-kin$_{x}$ ⸢siki⸣

3. DU.DU
7 amar-sal
5. 10 lá-2 sila$_4$-sa[l]
[.....]
7. [.....]
V. 1. ZA$_x$? [-*s*]*ù*?
[AN?.MI?.]⸢AN⸣

7 containers bur-kak of oil, 7 containers an-zam$_x$ of beer, 7 containers zi-bar of wine, 7 vases for water with spout, 1 measure kin$_x$ of wool, 7 calves and 8 young sheep for the god of the night.

(6)

3. [x (x)]-*ḫa-tum*-1
[.....]
5. [.....]

(7)

rev. I. 1. ⸢10⸣ l[á-x] [g]a?-⸢*x*⸣
ga-du-ma-tum
3. gu-dùl-gi$_6$-TÚG
gaba
5. ^{d}Gi$_6$-an (AN.MI.AN)

7 ? ... for the ... of the black garment placed in front of (the statue of) the god of the night.

(8)

2 dug ŠE+TIN 1 gur$_4$(NÍGIN) geštin
7. ⸢x⸣ [...]
⸢nídba⸣
II. 1. ^{d}Gi$_6$-an (AN.MI.AN)
wa
3. ⸢x⸣ [.....]
[.....]
5. [.....]

[.....][c]
7. dub[d]
ki-gar
9. (remaining part of the col. anep.)

2 containers of beer, 1 container of wine... offering for the god of the night and ... tablet ...

(9)

III. 1. 1 GIŠ-asar ninda-sikil
1 bur-kak ì-giš 1 an-zam$_{x}$ ŠE+TIN 1 zi-bar geštin
1 *maš-a-ḫa-tum*
3. ^{d}NE-*ra*

1 offering tray with "pure breads", 1 container bur-kak of oil, 1 container anzam$_{x}$ of beer, 1 container zibar of wine, 1 vase for water with spout for the god NEra.

(10)

1 ⸢GIŠ⸣-⸢asar⸣ ninda-sikil
5. 1 bur-kak ì-giš 1 an-zam$_{x}$ ŠE+TIN 1 zi-bar geštin
1 *maš-a-ḫa-tum*
IV. 1. ^{d}*A-ba-sa*
dam
3. ^{d}NE-*ra*

1 offering tray with "pure breads", 1 container bur-kak of oil, 1 container anzam$_{x}$ of beer, 1 container zibar of wine, 1 vase for water with spout to the deity Abasa, woman of the god NEra.

(11)

gaba
5. si$_{4}$
^{d}NE-*ra* 2
7. nídba

Before the dawn (or the sunset of the following day) you must make a second offering to the god NEra.

(12)

2 é-duru^{ki} [e]
9. ninda
šu ba$_4$-ti
V. 1. [.....]
[.....]⸢nu⸣
3. [nídb]a $^?$
$^{[d]}$Gi$_6$-an([AN].MI.AN)
5. [*i*]*n*
[*x*]-*za* $^?$-*bù*
7. en

40 people receive bread (food)...; (these are) sacrificial offerings for the god of the night on the occasion of ... of the king.

[a] The sign following 1 is inscribed over an erasure.
[b] The integration is suggested by P.Fronzaroli.
[c] Followed by an erased sign.
[d] Cases 7-8 scratched.
[e] Cases 8-10 scratched.

3. *Commentary*

(1) GIŠ-asar: this term seems used in the Ebla texts to indicate a container of open shape probably smaller than the offering table, generally written as GIŠ-banšur. Normally it is of wood, but could be also of gold. It is a typical container for offerings of food to the gods; it is often used (as in our text) as a container for "pure breads" for the deities. Cf. *ARET* XI, p. 43 (80), p.148, p. 387; in *ARET* IX 17 containers GIŠ-asar with "pure breads" are offered to some deities, 1 GIŠ-asar to every god. Cf. also *ARET* IX, p. 387 s.v.

gaba: this preposition is used almost exclusively in ritual texts. In our ritual it is documented in both senses already noted by P. Fronzaroli, *ARET* XI, p. 147: 1) in front of (locative value); 2) before (temporal value).

^{d}Gi$_6$-an(AN.MI.AN): in lexical Eblaite lists gi$_6$-an is, without doubt, "the night".[4] This translation is confirmed by the text of the ritual *ARET* XI 1 (rev. XI 20: *mu-si-im*) and its parallel text *ARET* XI 2 (rev. X 12: gi$_6$-an).[5]

4 For the different glosses in Eblaites LL cf. P. Fronzaroli, *QuSem* 13 (1984), p. 147; G. Castellino, in

Considering the presence in this sole text of the determinative dingir before the night I would like to propose the possibility of considering AN.MI.AN as ^{d}Gi$_{6}$-an, the god of the night, and to define this text as a ritual to be performed to the god (or the gods) of the night.[6]

This proposed identification derives also from the quotation, after the god of the night, of his bride (*gallatum*) who receives a black dress and the same offerings as her husband. These are surprising similarities with the first tablet of Maqlû ritual where the gods of the night and the night, the veiled bride, are invoked.

Of course we may contemplate the possibility of regarding AN.MI.AN as a temporal determination; in fact, after gaba with a temporal use, we can have a temporal clause and the text could be interpretated as a nocturnal ritual, with different offerings to be performed during the night. In this case however, we would not have the receiver of the offerings. It is more probable that the offerings are destined for a deity and placed in front of the statue.

The structure of the text is clear: x offerings are to be placed in front of (the statue of) DN.

While in an administrative text (as for example *ARET* IX 107) we have only the list of offerings of food to different deities, here, in a ritual text with the prescription of different ritual acts, we have the prescription of the exact place to put the tray with food, i.e. in front of (the statue of) the god.

Finally, a temporal clause would not be repeated too many times.[7]

In the section AN of Eblaites LL there is not AN.MI.AN.[8]

(2) In this section food offerings to the god Gi$_{6}$-an are listed.

Apart from GIŠ-ASAR *gi-la*$^{?}$*-tum*$^{?}$ which appears only once, the other quantities of food and drink for the deities are standard in value and in order: pure breads, oil, beer, wine and sacred water. These are clearly standard rations of food, regular of-

---

L. Cagni (ed.), *Il Bilinguismo ad Ebla*, Napoli 1984, p. 367 and G. Conti, *QuSem* 15 (1988), p. 55 n. 109; *idem*, *QuSem* 17 (1990), pp. 195-196.

5 Cf. *ARET* XI p. 49 (gi$_{6}$-an = *mu-si-im*) with quotation of lexical lists and previous bibliography.

6 The writing AN.MI.AN could also be read dingir gi$_{6}$-an as in the case of dingir an-gub, cf. P. Fronzaroli, *QuSem* 16 (1989), p. 9.

7 The sumerogram gi$_{6}$-an is used as a temporal clause in the ritual of Angubbu, a part of which is performed during the night, cf. P. Fronzaroli, *Il culto degli Angubbu a Ebla*, *QuSem* 16 (1989), p. 4 and 25.

8 For this section cf. G. Conti, *QuSem* 17 (1990), pp. 189-196.

ferings established for deities. From other Eblaite texts we know the offerings of animals and food to the gods; here we have the list of standard offerings well known from the Mesopotamian texts; the products offered to the deities are typical of the Syrian region with wine and no dates.

gi-la$^?$*-tum*$^?$: It is attested, as I know, in this sole text. It is very probably an alimentary product because on the tray GIŠ-ASAR cereals are usually placed to be offered to deities.

For ninda-sikil cf. *ARET* IX, pp. 400-401 s.v.

The vessel bur-kak is well attested in many Eblaite texts; it could be made from gold or silver, is very precious and is used in cultic purposes and destined to contain the oil for deities and for sacred ceremonies like marriages, where the vessel-bur-kak contains the oil used to anoint the head of the bride.[9]

an-zam$_x$ ŠE+TIN: this vessel is attested many times but only here does it contain this type of beer.[10]

The beer ŠE+TIN, according to rations texts of *ARET* IX,[11] is measured by the standard of capacity for cereals and with vessels dar-áb and dug. Here there is an attestation of the use of this vessel an-zam$_x$ also for beer.

zi-bar: this is another vessel for liquid used here for wine. It is not documented in the texts of rations of the same archive L.2712, but it is frequently attested in the annual metal accounts as a vessel made of gold or silver and light.[12] It is possibly a small vessel for a regular offering, a small cup or vase. Both the vessels an-zam$_x$ and zi-bar are documented as part of the precious trousseau for the princess Dinibdulum who goes to Luban as dam-dingir in the temple of the god NIdabal of that town, cf. text TM.75.G.1860 obv. III 16-V 9 (*MEE* X, 20, pp. 59-60).

maš-a-ḫa-tum: as previously remarked by P. Fronzaroli, *ARET* XI, p. 160 is an etymological writing of *maš-ḫa-tum,* documented in the texts of king and queen's ritual. The translation of P. Fronzaroli, *ARET* XI p. 48 "*vaso con beccuccio*" (vase

---

9 Cf. *ARET* IX p. 380 s.v. bur-DÙ, where the translation "coppa" is given; it is more probably a small vessel with a closed shape. Cf. also G. Pettinato, *Thesaurus Inscriptionum Eblaicarum* B, Roma 1998, pp. 67-69, s.v. bur-KAK.

10 Cf. *ARET* IX p. 379 s.v.; cf. also G. Pettinato, *Thesaurus Inscriptionum Eblaicarum* A/2, Roma 1996, pp. 150-157.

11 Cf. *ARET* IX p. 405 s.v.; cf. also *ARET* XI pp. 139-140.

12 Cf. *ARET* VII s.v., F. D'Agostino, *MEE* VII, p. 74 at r. VIII 6 translates "oggetto z.". *Apud* P. Mander, *MEE* X, p. 87 at obv. IV 6 is quoted Waetzold's suggestion: (kleiner) Becher.

with spout) would fit in this ritual where a vase to sprinkle water could be used.[13] As it is clear from this and other sections the vessels and the quantities are standard, well codified as we would expect from a ritual prescription.

(3) GIŠ-uštil: the sign is partially broken but it is probably to read GIŠ-uštil, written here with two oblique wedges more than the usual form documented at Ebla, cf. *ARET* II 21 I 3 and p. 165; *MEE* III, pp. 359-360, numbers 302-303.

gu-dùl-TÚG gi_6 mu_4^{mu}: the lexeme mu_4^{mu} indicates here a verb "to put on a piece of clothing"; with the textile gu-dùl-TÚG it refers to a ritual dressing, of a priestess, of a statue of a deity.[14]

In the examples quoted by J. Pasquali, *La "vestizione" della statua della dea ᵈTU ad Ebla, NABU* 1996/128, the subject is the dressing of the statue of the goddess Nintu; here we have the dressing of a statue of the bride of the god of the night. As noted by Pasquali, the textile gu-dùl has a ceremonial use; it is given to female deities and to the queen. I would stress here the similarities between the dressing of the statue of the goddess Nintu with the dressing of the statue of our text. The same verb and the same textile are used. But in our ritual the color of the textile is always black, (gi_6) cf. (3) e (6), while for Nintu, (as noted also by Pasquali), the color of the textile could change and depends on whether Nintu is well-disposed (white) or angry (black). This could be further proof that this ritual has a nocturnal character. As is evident also in the Ebla texts, the chromatic symbolism has a ritual value and the color black is the color associated with mourning (and perhaps the funerary cult?) or something negative. Here there is no alternation between black and white to indicate the different and opposite moods of the deity, as in the case of the mother-goddess Nintu. The color destined for the bride and the god of the night is black.[15]

---

13 For this vessel for sprinkling cf. also P. Fronzaroli, *A Pharmaceutical Text at Ebla (TM.75.G.1623), ZA* 88 (1998), p. 234 and n. 56.

14 Cf. G .M. Urcioli, *The Term túg-mu in the AdministrativeTexts of Ebla, UF* 25 (1993), pp. 407-422; A. Archi, *The High Priestess, dam-dingir, at Ebla,* in *Und Mose schrieb dieses Lied auf* (Festschrift O. Loretz), Münster 1998, p. 43, n. 3, p. 47 with the quotation of the expression (referring to the high priestess Tinib-dulum) "on the day she took the habit".

15 Note that the color of the textile destined to the god Nidabal is always white, cf. J. Pasquali, *Il "gonnellino" del dio Hadda nei testi di Ebla, NABU* 1997/73.
Note also for example an Akkadian text from Susa (cf. G. Cunningham, *'Deliver me from Evil'. Mesopotamian Incantations 2500-1500 a.C.*, Roma 1997, pp. 59-60) describing a ritual directed against the evil eye. The negative effect of the evil eye has to be transferred to one black sheep; perhaps the color black suggests that the sheep is a neutral carrier but is black, because it is destined to

gal-la-tum: in the Eblaite LL we have: é-gi-a / *gal-la-tum*; é-gi-a / *gal-la-du*; é-gi-a / *gal-tum*; cf.: *kallātum, AHw* p. 426 and *CAD* K pp. 79-82,with two meanings: daughter-in-law and bride (in Akkadian and other Semitic languages). In the administrative texts the Sumerian term é-gi-a is used and seems to refer to daughter-in-law. We know by name some daughters-in-law, for example Damurdaseli, daughter-in-law of the last king Išar-Damu (*ARET* VIII 529 obv. VIII 24-IX 2). The princess Maud, married at the Ebla court, is always recorded, after her marriage, as princess and daughter-in-law of Durdulum; in one text (TM.75.G.1522) the scribe refers to her with the term *gal-tum*.[16] *Kallatum* can be used also as an epithet for goddesses.[17]

In our text the term could indicate the bride of the god of the night. It is clear from (4) that to the statue of this goddess are presented also food offerings like those to the statue of the god of the night. It is natural to think of the first tablet of the Maqlû ritual where we find the gods of the night and the night *kal-la-tum kut-tùm-tum* (and cf. in (7) *ga-du-ma-tum*).

(4) The quantities of food and textiles in this and in following sections are constantly seven and this can indicate that the ritual is to be performed over seven days.

The type of offering placed in the trays is not specified, but it is more than likely that the 7 trays placed in front of (the statue of) the bride of the god of the night were filled with"pure breads".

It is to be noted that the animals offered are female animals, heiffers and sheep.[18] We expect 7 sheep and not eight.

(6) An integration [*ma-sa*]-*ḫa-tum* could be possible, but not very probably.[19] An alimentary product *ma-ša-ḫa-tum* is given among other food as regular offerings to the god Enki in *ARET* IX 17 obv. II 4 and obv. IV 4, cf. *ARET* IX s.v.

---

be charged with the negative attribute. Probably there is a connection between the color of the sheep and the negative attribute to be charged on it. In the Hymn Šulgi B (cf. G. R. Castellino, *Two Šulgi Hymns (BC)*, Rome 1972) l. 142 the oracular (and expected good) omen is extracted from a white lamb ($sila_4$-babbar).

16 Cf. M. G. Biga, *Prosopographie et datation relative des textes d'Ébla*, *Amurru* I (1996), pp. 64-65.

17 *AHW* p. 426, 2); *CAD* K pp. 81-82 c. For the deity Ajja usually defined as *kallatu* of the Sun God cf. J.-M. Durand, *La religión en Siria durante la época de los reinos amorreos según la documentación de Mari,* Barcelona 1995, p. 201.

18 For amar-sal cf. also G. Pettinato, *Thesaurus Inscriptionum Eblaicarum* A/2, p. 122.

19 Cf. *ARET* XI 1 rev. XI 9: *ma-sa-ḫa-tum* as a graphic variant of the parallel *maš-ḫa-tum, ARET* XI 2 rev. X 2.

(7) *ga-du-ma-tum*: as I know this word is another *apax* of our text; it could derive from the same root as *gú-du-mu* (cf. acc. *kuttumu* fem. *kuttumtu, CAD* K, p. 611 b: covered, veiled) translated by P. Fronzaroli, *ARET* XI, p. 151 as "veil".[20]

(8) The vessel dug is documented for beer and wine, cf. *ARET* IX pp. 351-352 and p. 383. There are no attestations of a vessel NÍGIN for wine. Perhaps it is an abbreviation of the name of vessel gurgur, used in Presargonic Lagaš, cf. M. A. Powell, "Masse und Gewichte", *RlA* VII, Berlin 1987-1990, p. 506.

ki-gar: is attested many times in texts of archive L.2712; cf. for example *ARET* X 74 obv. II 5-III 7: 15 é-duru$_5$^{ki} 3 ninda-gal 3 ninda-sig$_{15}$ 3 ninda-še // ki-gar kas$_4$ *Du-lu*^{ki} 45 é-duru$_5$^{ki} 2 ninda-gal 2 ninda-sig$_{15}$ 2 ninda-še ki-gar Sa-za$_x$^{ki}. Further occurrences in other texts are often followed by a place name.

(9) The same standard offerings are made to a deity NE-*ra* attested, to my knowledge, only in this text.

In the administrative texts a category of women dam NE-ra is documented. They are at the service of the palace and of the temple of Kura cf.: TM.75.G.1743 rev. IV 13-15: 26 kin$_x$ siki bar$_6$ 13 dam NE-ra; rev. VI 17-19: 24 kin$_x$ siki gi$_6$ 12 NE-ra é-^{d}Ku-ra.

In the very similar text TM.75.G.2443 among other categories of female workers receiving rations of black and white wool at rev. VII 11-14: 30 kin$_x$ siki bar$_6$ 15 dam NE-ra é ^{d}Ku-ra; rev. VIII 24-25: 20 lá-2 kin$_x$ gi$_6$ 10 lá-1 dam NE-ra.

TM.75.G.2431 in a long list of women of the court receiving wool at rev. VII 2'-6': 22 kin$_x$ siki bar$_6$ 11 NE-ra 24 kin$_x$ siki gi$_6$ 12 NE-ra é ^{d}Ku-ra (then in the list we have the wet-nurses, singers, etc.).

Cf. also *ARET* IX s.v. p. 398 with previous bibliography.

In the LL we have: NE-ra / *sá-lum, sa-ru*$_{12}$*-um*; *ra* could be a phonetic indicator.

A deity NE-*ra* is attested only here; this deity is not quoted in the section AN of bilingual vocabularies of Ebla.

---

20 The veil is used for a bride and not for a male deity as in our text. The veil is documented for the queen of Ebla in ritual *ARET* XI 1 rev. IX 15; the parallel text *ARET* XI 2 has PAD-TÚG (cf. p. 114). For these reasons we can integrate *ga-du-ma-tum* before gu-dùl-TÚG gi$_6$ in (3). It is to note the same expression used to define the priestess of Emar in the Emar ritual; cf. D. E. Fleming, "The Installation of Baal's High Priestess at Emar", *HSS* 42, Atlanta 1992, ll. 61-62: *ki-i* É.GI$_4$.A *ú-kat-ta-mu ... ki-i-ma ka-al-la-ti e-pí-qa-ši*, where the priestess is defined as a veiled bride. And finally the night is the veiled bride (*kal-la-tum kut-tùm-tum*) in the second line of the first tablet of Maqlû. For these reasons we can propose the integration [*ga-du-ma-tum*]before gu-dùl-TÚG gi$_6$ in (3).

A reading izi for NE is accepted, for example in the month name, iti izi-gar, and in the name of the ritual izi-gar.[21] The deity AN.NE in the lexical list AN has a possible reading ^{d}izi.[22]

In *ARET* IX 17 rev. II 8 the same god receives the offering of a tray with "pure breads" (1 GIŠ-asar ninda sikil ^{d}Gibil$_4$).

^{d}NE-*ra* could be a graphic variant of ^{d}NE-*la* quoted in an Eblaite list of offerings to deities, cf. F. Pomponio-P. Xella, *Les Dieux d'Ebla,* (*AOAT* 245), Münster 1997, p. 254, where the authors consider the possibility of a reading gibil$_x$-la and to consider this deity as another form of the god of the fire. According to Pomponio-Xella, ^{d}gibil$_4$, Isadu and, probably, NEla could be different forms/manifestations of the deity of fire, cf. p. 185 (Gibil), p. 201 (Isadu).

The same authors consider Isadu as a feminine deity of the fire.

In our text ^{d}NEra is probably a male deity and his paredra is the feminine deity ^{d}Abasa, defined as dam, the usual term for woman.

The women NE-*ra* would appear to be women in charge of the fire of the palace of the king and of the temple of Kura.

Deity Abasa is another *apax* of this text.

(11) gaba si$_4$: it is a temporal clause; it could be translated "before the red" and interpreted as "before the dawn". The same temporal clause, but written gaba *sa-ma-ti*, is in the ritual of Angubbu (rev. II 11-III 1), cf. P. Fronzaroli, *QuSem.* 16 (1989), p. 4 and 16, translated "before the sunset".[23]

In our text it is also possible that the second offering to the god NEra could be performed before the sunset of the following day.

---

21 Cf. M. E. Cohen, *The Cultic Calendars of the Ancient Near East*, Bethesda 1993, pp. 31-32; M. G. Biga, *Rituali reali eblaiti e loro riflessi nei testi amministrativi, ISIMU* I (1998), p. 221.

22 Cf. i.e. W. G. Lambert, *The Section* AN, in (L. Cagni ed.), *Il Bilinguismo a Ebla,* Napoli 1984, pp. 393-401; at pp. 396-397 commentary to line 783 AN-izi=*ì-sa-tù* he writes: "izi=*ì-sa-tù* would be unworthy of comment, but AN-izi is unexpected from a Sumerian background. There is of course the Sumerian fire-god Gibil. However, in an Ebla record of offerings, *OA* 18, 134 viii 4, one is recorded to ^{d}*ì-sa-tù*, so perhaps one should read ^{d}izi and assume western influence in the presence of the divine determinative".

23 In Eblaite LL é-si-an is glossed *sa-ma-ti sa-rí-im* considered by M. Civil, *Bilingualism in Logographically written Languages: Sumerian in Ebla*, in L. Cagni (ed.), *Il Bilinguismo a Ebla,* Napoli 1984, p. 89 and translated "twilight".

(12) Probably 40 people[24] have partecipated to the rite, receiving food rations.

At the end of the text it is specified that these are offerings (nídba) for the god of the night, in the occasion of a ritual, I suppose, performed by the king. I cannot find a satisfactory integration for [x]-*za-bù,* so I cannot definc thc type of the ritual.

4. Conclusions

Without doubt the text is a ritual prescribing a series of offerings to different deities on a precise occasion, involving the king.

The perfect timing and order of the offerings to the statues of the various gods, offerings which are always the same, the same foods in the same vessels, all point to and confirm the prescriptive ritual nature of this text.

The black garments offered both to the God of the Night and to his bride make us think more of a rite for the night's deities possibly performed during the night.

All the deities quoted in this text are attested only here; they are not quoted in other administrative, lexical or literary texts of Ebla. There are no personal names as this is a prescriptive ritual which indicates only the type and sequence of the offering to be performed.

The text cannot be dated.

It is also to be noted the number of *apax* of this text not only regarding the names of gods but also objects and textiles.[25]

---

24 Cf. *ARET* IX s.v. é-duru$_5$.

25 The only two persons involved in this ritual are a bride (or a daughter-in-law) and the king. I would consider the bride as the bride of the god of the night. It is possible, but less probably, to consider this text as a ritual prescription for a bride in a particular occasion involving the king.
Or has this text also to be read in a different way and understood within the linguistic setting of the Semiticization of Sumerian as demonstrated in a wonderful way by M. Civil, G. Rubio, *An Ebla Incantation against Insonnia and the Semiticization of Sumerian: Notes on* ARET *5 8b and 9, Orientalia* 68 (1999), pp. 254-266?

TM.75.G.756+771+815 obv.

TM.75.G.756+771+815 rev.

ON THE PRESERVATION OF ANCIENT FORMS AND SOUND SHIFTS IN FREQUENT WORDS RESISTING ANALOGY IN HEBREW AND ARABIC

JOSHUA BLAU

Jerusalem

1. As well known,[1] frequent words resist analogy better than rarer vocables, being more deeply imprinted on the memory of the speaker and well remembered even under the pressure of levelling analogy. It is, therefore, that careful analysis of exceptional forms of frequent words may sometimes yield deeper understanding of sound shifts which have been cancelled by analogy and can only be reconstructed from vestiges preserved by exceptional vocables, which, because of their frequency, have not been affected by analogy. Only when applying this method does it often come to light that the product of what was alleged to be the genuine sound shift is due to analogical levelling, whereas the vestiges of the authentic sound change have been kept by a few words of high frequency.

In the following, we shall adduce some examples of this phenomenon in Hebrew and Arabic. Since analogy has affected the morphology of (classical) Arabic to a great extent and its pervasive influence is clearly felt in the homogeneous morphological structure of classical Arabic,[2] whereas Hebrew has preserved much more diversity, we shall have to rely mainly on Hebrew.

2. The alleged Biblical Hebrew sound shift *iwC*[3] > *īC*[4] is, in the main, well attested in the imperfect *qal* of those verbs I *y* that do not elide their first radical, e.g. יִיקַר 'it

---

1 See e.g. H. Bauer & P. Leander, *Historische Grammatik der hebräischen Sprache* ..., Halle, 1922, 54q; W. Havers, *Handbuch der erklärenden Syntax,* Heidelberg, 1931, p. 78, *in fine*; L. Bloomfield, *Language,* New York, 1933, pp. 409-410.

2 See G. Bergsträsser, *Einführung in die semitischen Sprachen*, München, 1928, p. 135.

3 C denotes any following consonant.

4 So e.g. A. Müller, *Hebräische Schulgrammatik*, Halle, 1878, p. 93, §§ 260-261; G. Bergsträsser, *Hebräische Grammatik*, i-ii, Leipzig, 1918-1929, i, p. 97, § 17d, who even regards it proto-Semitic (though Arabic too demonstrates that it is due to analogy; see § 2.1); J. Kuryłowicz, *L'Apophonie en Sémitique*, Wrocław, 1961, p. 22, § 27; *idem*, *Studies in Semitic Grammar and Metric*, London, 1973, p. 38, § 14c; R. Meyer, *Hebräische Grammatik*, i-iv, Berlin, 1966-1972, i, p. 99. It is, of course,

will be precious'. It stands, however, to reason that these forms arose by analogy and it is the very frequent verb יוּכַל 'he will be able' that reflects the authentic shift of *iwC*, viz. > *ū*. It is (almost)[5] only in this verb of extraordinary frequency that this shift has been preserved, giving rise to a formation of imperfect *qal* totally deviating from ordinary *qal* imperfect forms. Whereas other verbs have been adapted to the common formation of verbs (יִיקַר corresponding, e.g., to ordinary יִרְכַּב), the frequency of יוּכַל resisted the impact of analogy, since it was deeply enough imprinted on the memory of the speaker.[6]

2.1. In Classical Arabic, as a rule, *uyC* > *ūC* is considered to be the genuine sound shift,[7] since the authentic sound shift *uyC* > *īC* was only preserved when it was backed by frequency or when its action did not contravene analogy.[8] Therefore, it is reflected by *bīḍ* 'white (plural)', which was not changed to **būḍ* although the plural of colours (and bodily defects) *fuʿl* demanded it, because of its commonness. *bīd* 'deserts', on the other hand, has kept the original formation, although not very common, because it has severed it ties with colours and was, therefore, not felt as reflecting the plural *fuʿl*.[9]

3. In Biblical Hebrew, not only *-ayu* (*-ayi*)/*-ay* in final position shift to *-ɛ̄/ē* (**yitgallayu*[10] > יִתְגַּלֶּה, 'he will reveal himself'. **hitgallay* > הִתְגַּלֵּה 'reveal your-

methodologically ill-founded to postulate two parallel soundshifts, *iwC* > *īC* and *iwC* > *ūC*, as does C. Brockelmann, *Grundriss der vergleichenden Grammatik der semitischen Sprachen*, i-ii, Berlin, 1908-1913, i, p. 601, § 268fβ. For details see *Israel Oriental Studies* 1 (1971), p. 3, n. 12.

5 It is also reflected by תּוּקַד 'she will burn' (see *Israel Oriental Studies* 1 [1971], p. 3); since this verb was much less frequent than יוּכַל, it was as a rule superseded by תִּיקַד (once also תֵּקַד).

6 Similarly, Biblical Hebrew *uyC* > *ūC* (as יוּצַר 'it is formed' < **yuyṣar*) is due to analogy; the authentic sound shift is *uyC* > *īC*, as preserved in the frequent verb וַיִּישֶׂם 'and it was put'. It is rather surprising that the less common verb יִיסָךְ 'it is anointed' resisted analogy as well. For details see *Israel Oriental Studies* 1 (1971), p. 2.

7 For details see *Israel Oriental Studies* 1 (1971), p. 1 and n. 5.

8 For details see *Israel Oriental Studies* 1 (1971), pp. 1-2.

9 Similarly, Classical Arabic *iwC* > *īC* (as **ʾiwjād* > *ʾījād* 'producing') is due to analogy; the authentic sound shift is *iwC* > *ūC*, as preserved in words like *mūsā* 'razor', **tūrāṯ* > *turāṯ* 'inheritance', which were not, to be sure, very common, yet were not exposed to strong analogy. For details see *Israel Oriental Studies* 1 (1971), pp. 24-25; *Bar-Ilan Departmental Researches*, i, *Arabic and Islamic Studies*, Ramat-Gun, 1973, pp. XLII-XLV.

10 I am not paying attention to sound shifts with which we do not concern ourselves (it is therefore that we posited e.g.**yitgallayu* rather than **yatgallayu*). Pay attention that the original thematic vowel of

self!'; *śadayu/i > שָׂדֶה 'field'; *śaday > שְׂדֵה 'field' [construct])[11] but also -iyu (iyi)/-iy; e.g. *šamāniyu/i > שְׁמוֹנֶה 'eight', *piyu/i > פֶּה 'mouth'; *ḥōziyu/i > חוֹזֶה 'seer'; ḥōziy > חוֹזֵה 'seer' (construct); similarly not only -ayu- (-ayi-) in medial position shifts to -ẹ̄ (*śadayuhū > שָׂדֵהוּ 'his field')[12] but also -iyu-(-iyi-), e.g. *ʿōśiyuhū > עוֹשֵׂהוּ 'his Creator'. Again, the very frequent פֶּה 'mouth', construct פִּי preceding pronominal suffixes פִּיךָ , פִּיו / פִּהוּ , פִּינוּ may serve as touchstone for differentiating genuine sound shift from analogical formation. The absolute פֶּה proves that not only final -ayu (-ayi) > - ɛ̄ reflects genuine sound shift but also final -iyu (-iyi) > ɛ̄. It was this parallel shift to ɛ̄ that analogically transferred words in which i preceded y to the class in which y followed a; because *śadayu and *ḥōziyu exhibit the same ending ɛ̄, viz. שָׂדֶה and חוֹזֶה, the construct and the pronominal state of חוֹזֶה was restructured according to שָׂדֶה, viz. חוֹזֵה according to שְׂדֵה, rather than *ḥōzī; חוֹזֵהוּ according to שָׂדֵהוּ, rather than *חוֹז(י)הוּ. The existence of the very frequent פִּי (construct), פִּיהוּ reflects the remainders of the authentic sound shift -iy and medial -iyu- (-iyi-) to ī, which, however, as a rule, was restructured according to the analogy of -ay and (medial) -ayu- (-ayi-) (which changed to -ẹ̄-).

4. I am inclined to interpret also the exceptional behaviour[13] of the *qal* imperative and imperfect of Biblical Hebrew הלך as if it were derived from the root ילך,[14] as (partially) reflecting a sound shift that has disappeared from less frequent verbs. In the imperative *hlik,[15] which was (phonemically at least) monosyllabic,[16] the *h* was

---

הִתְפַּעֵל is *a*! The quotation of a verbal/nominal form does not necessarily imply that it occurs as such in the Bible; it may also be reconstructed by analogy to parallel forms.

11 When this sound shift occured, the construct had already lost the final case vowels.

12 Most forms preceding pronominal suffixes were, however, built as if derived from -שָׂד, arising through the re-interpretation of שָׂדַי as *śad* + *ī*, rather than *śadē* + *ī*.

13 See e.g. P. Joüon- T. Muraoka, *A Grammar of Biblical Hebrew*, Roma, 1991, pp. 194-195, W.R. Garr, *Dialect Geography of Syria-Palestine, 1000-586 B.C.E.*, Philadelphia, 1985, pp. 144-146, § 24a, b.

14 The behaviour of *hifʿil* as if derived from ילך is due to both analogy and dissimilation (*hahlīk > הוֹלִיךְ). On the other hand, Ugaritic *šhlk*, devoid of any cause for dissimilation was nor affected by analogy.

15 See *Maarav*, 2 (1980), pp. 145-146; J. Blau, A *Grammar of Biblical Hebrew*², Wiesbaden, 1993, p. 25, § 7. 2. 2.

16 It stands to reason that it was originally bisyllabic, as preserved in Accadian and Ugaritic, and hinted by Biblical Hebrew forms like זָכְרָה on the one hand, זִכְרוּ on the other. In Ugaritc, too, the *h* was elided, although the imperative *qal* is there, as mentioned, bisyillabic. Could it reflect an exceptional

elided, giving rise to *lik* > לֵךְ, from which, because of its similarity to שֵׁב., יֵלֵךְ, הוֹלִיךְ were rederived. In less frequent verbs, however, the *h*, elided in this position in *qal* imperative, was restored, as הֲרֹג 'kill',[17] which, in addition, was not attracted by verbs as שֵׁב because of the different thematic vowel.

4.1. Similarly, I tend to the opinion that the exceptional *qal* imperatives of Classical Arabic خُذْ, كُلْ, مُرْ, of أَخَذَ, أَكَلَ, أَمَرَ 'to take, to eat, to order' reflect the sound shift of the elision of the initial glottal stop followed by a consonant, which was, by analogical levelling, restored in less frequent verbs.[18]

4.2. Similarly, the very frequent Biblical Hebrew verb נָתַן 'to give' is the only Hebrew *III n* verb that assimilates the *n* to an immediately following consonant, as נָתַתִּי 'I gave'. In less frequent verbs the *n* has been analogically restored, as שָׁכַנְתִּי 'I dwelt'.

5. In verbs *I laryngeals/pharyngeals* some subphonemic changes occur, as reflected e.g. by יַעֲשֶׂה as against יִגְלֶה. Yet the verb יִהְיֶה 'to be',[19] of very high frequency, was not affected by this subphonemic change and preserved ordinary יִהְיֶה. In this case too the very frequent word imprinted itself on the memory, and has become so firmly established that it resisted subphonemic changes, just as in the preceding examples withstood the influence of analogy.

---

sound shift **hilik* > *lik* caused by the extraordinary frequency of the imperative, becoming, as a matter of fact, an interjection? I have no explanation for the distribution of Ugaritic ***hlm*** 'to strike', *prima facie*, *qal* imperative, imperfect *ylm*. Should we assume that the imperative was indeed **lm*, but it is not attested, ***hlm*** being an absolute infinitive used as command? Should we again assume that this (not attested!) **lm* lost *h* because it was used as an interjection? Admittedly, all these assumptions are rather far-fetched.

17 The development was circular: **hrog* > **rog* > (by attraction to the root √*hrg* through the analogy of ordinary verbs) *hrog* = הֲרֹג.

18 Similarly, it may be that the elision of the medial and final glottal stop in the imperative *qal* of سَأَلَ, رَأَى'to ask, to see' (which was by analogy extended to other forms), viz. سَلْ, رَ, also reflects an original sound shift, which disappeared from less frequent verbs due to analogy. On the other hand, the *qal* imperfect of Biblical Hebrew אָחַז, אָכַל, אָמַר 'to take, to eat, to say', viz. יֹאחַז, יֹאכַל, יֹאמַר is itself due to analogycal levelling, see J. Blau, *A Grammar of Biblical Hebrew²*, Wiesbaden, 1993, p. 22, n. 1.

19 And in its wake חָיָה 'to live', imperfect יִחְיֶה.

6. In Classical Arabic, final *n* exhibits the tendency of weakening.[20] Most traces of this feature have disappeared through the influence of paradigmatic analogy. *kāna* 'to be', however, has preserved (alongside with لَمْ يَكُنْ 'he was not', restored by paradigmatic analogy) also لَمْ يَكُ.

7. We shall finish with two cases in which in Classical Arabic and one in which in Hebrew frequent forms withstood morphological levelling.

7.1. Classical comparative/superlative forms are built according to the pattern *ʾafʿalu*; only the very frequent *xayr* 'better/best' and *šarr* 'worse/ worst'[21] have resisted morphological levelling.

7.2. In some Neo-Arabic dialects ordinary, not especially frequent, dual forms append pronominal suffixes without dropping the *n* of the dual ending, through the analogical influence of the forms which preserved the *n*; yet the frequent "exduals"[22] drop the *n*, since, because of their frequency, the resisted morphological analogy.

7.3. The verb הָיָה[23] resisted change in Mishnaic Hebrew. It preserved the original forms of the third person feminine singular of the perfect, viz. הָיְתָה in the context, הָיָת in the pause, whereas in less frequent verbs the context forms were influenced by the pausal ones.[24] The frequent verb הָיָה, however, resisted morphological levelling.

8. We have observed that the, *prima facie*, exceptional formation of very frequent words often does not exhibit late changes, but it rather reflects ancient sound shifts which seem exceptional only because they have disappeared from ordinary words through analogical levelling (§§ 2, 3, 4, 4.1, 4.2, 6). It is, therefore, methodologically sound to take the possibility into account that exceptional words of high frequency have preserved remainders of ancient sound shifts. Frequent words sometimes resist also morphological analogies (§ 7), as well as subphonemic changes (§ 5).

---

20 For details see H. Fleisch, *Traité de philologie arabe*, I, Beyrouth, 1961, pp. 138-139.

21 In many languages these words behave exceptionally. In Neo-Arabic analogy affected these words as well, giving rise to forms like *ʾaxyar* and *ʾašarr*.

22 H. Blanc, in his masterly paper "Dual and Pseudo-Dual in the Arabic Dialects", *Language* 46 (1970), pp. 42-57, dubs them 'pseudo-dual'; see p. 49, § 4.

23 And in its wake חָיָה.

24 For details see J. Blau, *Studies in Hebrew Linguistics*, Jerusalem, 1996, pp. 250-255.

LEOPARDS, CAULDRONS, AND A BEAUTIFUL STONE. NOTES ON SOME EARLY SYRIAN TEXTS FROM TELL BEYDAR AND EBLA

MARCO BONECHI

ICEVO - CNR - Roma

In recent years, thanks to the support of Pelio Fronzaroli, I have studied the lexicon of the 3rd millennium cuneiform texts found in Syria. It is a pleasure and a privilege to dedicate to my *Maestro* some results of such research dealing with the texts from Tell Beydar and Ebla.

In a well-made book appeared in 1996 (F. Ismahil - W. Sallaberger - Ph. Talon - K. Van Lerberghe, with contributions by M. Lebeau, D. Marien, A. Suleiman, C. Vandecasteele, P. Wambacq, *Administrative Documents from Tell Beydar (Seasons 1993-1995)*, *Subartu* II, Turnhout) a team of scholars has published 147 administrative documents found in the site of the Khabur Triangle. The book, in which some important specific studies are offered together with an exemplar publication of the evidence, shows the actual maturity of the studies on Early Syrian written materials. The following remarks, referring to the numeration of the text given by the editors, try to improve some particular points, while one peculiar text, *Subartu* II 4, will be fully discussed below:

1 obv. I:1, ká AN.GAR.KAS$_4$: among the ká listed in *Subartu* II, pp. 180f., there are some ká + DN. Also considering other clues dealing with the commercial importance of the Beydar area, I wonder if AN.GAR.KAS$_4$ may be read dingir ^{níg}kas$_4$, with reference to the unnamed "god of the caravan" (cf. also [138] obv. III:4); obv. I:3, *ìr-am*$_6$-en: after the copy, the PN may be read *ìr-am*$_6$--uru, and cf. *ìr-am*$_6$--en in obv. II:1

2 obv. I:2, *a-ḫu-tu*: it is a GN, *a-ḫu-tu* $^{<ki>}$, cf. the index, p. 191; obv. II:3, *sa* $^{?}$-[TAR]-*gu-ni*: the PN, p. 189, is compared with the PN *ša*-TAR-*gu-ni* of the text [23]; the copy, however, shows MI-[x]-*gu-ni*, or, less probably, ⸢LAK-397$^{!}$⸣-[x]-*gu-ni*; obv. II:4, *a*-⸢x⸣-*lum*: after the copy, the sign after A may be found in LAK-539ff., but it does not seem ZÉ; = LAK-547? Perhaps another broken sign follows before LUM

5 obv. I:1-2, [ki$^{?}$] še / ḪAR-ḪAR: since at Beydar dabin, "barley flour", is written ZÌ.ŠE, I wonder if our texts deals with rations of barley flour for persons grouped according to their "*district*", ká, thus [da]bin([ZÌ].ŠE) / ḪAR-ḪAR (as for ḪAR-ḪAR see the index, p. 179, "mill(ing)"); rev. IV:6, *túl-la-nu*: the first sign is LAK-770 = LAGAB×BAD = GÍGIR; therefore, I would like to read the PN, *more eblaita*, as *ḫáb-la-nu*. In such view,

note the Ebla PN normally written *ḫab-ra--ar* (*passim*), but also *ḫab-la--ar* (*ARET* III 86, 635, 866; *ARET* VIII 540) and *ḫa-ba-ra--ar* (*ARET* IV 17; *MEE* 2 33): its first element has been dubiously derived from WSem. **ḥbr*, "to be united" in PAGAN 1998:119. Therefore, I wonder if the Beydar PN may be Ḥabrānum, a form with ending /-ān-/; this would imply that the Ebla habit of writing /r/ with signs of the series LA was known and used also at Beydar

7 rev. IV:2 (= "vii 2"), É-s[ag?]: is it possible to read é-⸢gal⸣?; rev. III:5 (= "viii 5"), PA-ÍL (PN): a name of function ugula íl seems more likely to me

11 obv. I:1', x x: after the copy, I read [anše] LA-GU: in the same area, but some centuries later, cf. anše LA-GU, OBab Mari and Chagar Bazar (A. Finet in *ARM* XV, Paris 1954, p. 15; TALON 1997:142), "animaux de transport, surtout pour des personnes" (DURAND 1997:338)

17 obv. III:7, [...]-*um-ki*: more likely [...]-*um*^{ki}

19 obv. I:1, níg GÁ×MUNUS-GI: it is likely the reference is to bread, food for the workhouse of female personnel, and I wonder if in obv. III:2 ninda [é] en is a possible reading (and cf. below)

20 fragm. A obv. III:2, en-*li* (PN): at Ebla EN.LI is the current writing for the name of profession ensi (= EN.ME.LI), see for instance *ED Lú E* l. 76, MEE 15 26 rev. VI:18

23 rev. III:6, UN-gal^{ki}: kalam-gal^{ki}

26 rev. I:3, ÁŠ EN BÙ: likely a PN *áš-ru*$_{12}$*-bù*; rev. II:2, *ba-ba* apin: more likely *ba-ba* engar

29 obv. II:10, *šu-na-*⸢*na*⸣-NI munus: after the copy, read *šu-na-*⸢*na*⸣ munus

35 This interesting text will be studied in a future paper by P. Fronzaroli and myself. Note for the moment the possibility that in obv. I:2 ZAG BAR may be read zà-me. Moreover, in obv. IV:8 *a*-X(-)DU-DU is to be read ^{a}addir$_{x}$(GISAL) laḫ$_5$, while in obv. IV:10 *iš-má* (-)DU-DU is to be read *iš* má lah$_5$: context of transport by boat in riverine or lacustrine areas, confirmed by the common noun of place name má:NE^{ki} in obv. V:2. Furthermore, in obv. IV:7 read sum-*ma*, and in rev. I:10 read DU-DA-*ma*, while a reading in-du$_8$ in obv. I:11 is uncertain (*in* gaba or *in* du$_8$?): the text certainly ends with the term *li-im*, but the reference is to "one thousand" or to the social entity called *li'mum*?

42 obv. II:2, ḪI.NE.RU (PN? see the indexes): very probably a PN *ḫi-rúm*; obv. IV:9, *iš*$_{11}$-⸢x⸣: after the copy, to be read *iš*$_{11}$-[*g*]*i*

46 It is likely in the reverse the colomns were written from left to right; it may belong to the group of text 15 etc.

52 rev. I:2, ká ⸢x?⸣ [DU]-ba-[GÍN]: after the copy, read ká ⸢DU⸣-ba-⸢GÍN⸣

55 obv. III:1, nir-dingir ⸢DU?⸣: after the copy, DU is certain

57 rev. II:2, [x] GUL: I wonder if we have the name of profession [bur]-gul

58 rev. I:7, ⌜mu⌝-[...]: perhaps muḫaldim [... ...]; rev. II:5: with the index, it is a PN *mu-da*

59 rev. I:6, AN-AN lú-AL-⌜x⌝: after the copy, x is LAGAB×BAD

63 obv. III:3, géme [x] en: to be read géme [é] en (cf. also above)?; rev. II:1-2 ("v 1-2"), [...] / ⌜x⌝-lá: perhaps [šu-nígin] / [ba]-lá

64 obv. II:5, IGI^{ki}: igi^{ki}, a place called "Spring"

69 obv. II:5-6, *wa* ki / *ù*: the use of both the writings *wa* and *ù* of the conjunction "and" is remarkable, but I wonder if, after the previous PN, we have a GN PI^{ki} (geštug^{ki}?)

70 Originally the tablet had 4+4 or perhaps 5+5 columns. The extant part deals with SU of ovins ([SU x] in the broken part of the obverse, SU udu-kur and SU LAK-20; SU is read kuš by the editor, but also su, referring to pieces of meat, could be considered

74 rev. I:2, *ib-lu$_5$-il*: I prefer a reading *ib-lul--il* (**pll*)

75 After the copy, obv. I and II run as it follows: I:1 ITI.SAR ^{d}BAD igi; I:2 *íl-e-i-šar*; I:3 *in* kaskal 0;2.2; I:4 *su-a-bir$_5$*; II:1 *in* 7 ud 0;2.2 etc.

79 obv. II:5 LAK-692(GÁ×NE.É): as noted in the index, it occurs at the beginning of the *Tribute List*, and a reading ḫalub$_x$ on the ground of GÁ×ḪA.LU.ÚB = ḫalubba in *MVN* 13 15, may be considered. In such case, the reference is to the plant *ḫaluppu*, a kind of oak. Cf. the unexplained writing É.NE, var. NE.É, of the Ebla administrative records, always object of delivery (šu-mu-taka$_4$), which, therefore, may refer to a plant or to a part of a plant

85 The short texts (parallel to [114]) has been commented on *Subartu* II, p. 106. It seems to me it says that, during the month called ^{d}BAD igi (read ^{d}*be-lim* in *Subartu* II, but I think the reference is to the "Divine-Lord-Of-The-Spring"), the man (*šu*) in charge of the pasture land (ú-šim) property of the king (en) of Nagar left Tell Beydar (ba-DU), that he spent three days there (3 ud al-tuš), and that the amount of food for the donkeys of 12 teams was 2 gur 0;2.2 (anše 12 sur$_x$ še kú 2 gur 0;2.2). As for ú-šim = *marʿatum* at Ebla see *VE* 285, explained in Conti 1990:113

92 obv. I:4, máš$^?$-LUM: the copy shows a sign vaguely similar to MÁŠ, but it is not MÁŠ, and 2 or perhaps 3 erased signs, perhaps ugula$^!$ ḪI-LUM

104 obv. II':2', [x]-*gi*: after the copy read [*i*]*š$_{11}$-gi*

106 obv. II:2, AN:AN-*a-ra-tum* (PN): since AN.AN = NAB, I read *nab-a-ra-tum*, a *ma-12a3-(a)t-um* form from a second weak verb (perhaps Akk. *bâru*, "to stay firm, in good health")

114 See the remarks to text 85 above

119 obv. III:6, ⌜x x x⌝: the copy shows a rather clear MÁ after ⌜DU$^?$-x⌝; = má:laḫ$_4$$^{!?}$

122 obv. II:1, *ur-bar* ^{ki}: perhaps *daš-bar* ^{ki}

124 obv. II:2, *da-ab-rí*: perhaps *da-ab--*uru

125 rev. II:4, DI-AN: the PN may be read silim-dingir

128 Editor's interpretation of rev. II:2 as *ša* ⸢mu⸣ 23+[x] is important, since the reference may be to a long reign of the unnamed Nagar king

143 After the copy rev. II:5ff. run as it follows: [...(x+] 2 sìla / [...]-*a-bar* / ⸢x-x(-x)⸣ 4 [sìla]

145 obv. II':2, KÉŠ-*ni*: *kéš*-NI, = *kèš*--NI or perhaps *keš-bu*$_{16}$ (cf. *kéš-bù* ^{ki} in *ARET* I 7); rev. I:4, nir-AN-DU: likely nir--an-gub; rev. II:1, URI-*zi-da*: or URI-zi-da?; rev. II:8, *íl*-PA-*ba*$_4$: reading uncertain; cf. the FPN of the Mari queen wife of *ib-lul-il*?

The Tell Beydar text *Subartu* II 4 suggests the following remarks (the documentation of the relevant passages may be found at the end of the paper).

The lexical lists of the 3rd millennium as well as tablet XIV of *Ḫḫ* have sections dealing with dangerous wild animals, i.e. carnivors (see BONECHI n.d.b, with previous literature).

Lines 61-141 of *Ḫḫ* XIV show the following basic equivalences dealing with (big) carnivors (*Canoidea* and *Feloidea*):

bear	az	=	*asu, dabû*
caracal	sa-a-ri and var.	=	*zirqatu*
cat	sa-a	=	*šurānu*
(a leopard)	ur-gug$_4$-ku$_5$-da	=	*dumāmu*
dog	ur	=	*kalbu*
fox	ka$_5$-a	=	*šellebu*
cheetah	ur-gug$_4$	=	*mandinu*
hyena	kir$_4$	=	*būṣu*
jackal	ur-idim-ma	=	*zību*
leopard	nemur(PIRIG.TUR)	=	*nimru*
lion	ug	=	*ūmu*
	ur-maḫ	=	*nēšu*
	pirig	=	*lû*
lynx of the marshes	sa-a-ri-ri	=	*azaru*
wildcat	sa-a-ri	=	*murašû*
wolf	ur-bar-ra	=	*barbaru*

At the middle of the 3rd millennium the corresponding section of the *List of Animals* (sources: A = *MEE* 3 20+; B = *MEE* 3 22+; D = *MEE* 3 18+; I = *IAS* 28; see BONECHI n.d.a) was much shorter:

(63)	D	ug(ZU.PIRIG)	lion
(64)	D	ZU!(SU).PIRIG-tur	*small-lion*
(65)	D	ur-bar	wolf

(66)	B	az	bear
	D	az	
(67)	B	kìri-ma	hyena
	D	kìri	
(68)	D	ur	dog

The next entries deal with names of other wild animals, but there is no evidence they are carnivors:

(69)	D	[...]	
(70)	A	pirig-bar-kak	
	B	pirig-bar	
	D	[...]-˹x˺-LUM	
	I	˹x-x˺	
(71)	D	[...]-šáḫ	wild-boar
	I	šáḫ	
(72)	D	šáḫ:gi	wild-boar of the canebrake
	I	šáḫ:^{giš}gi	

The fact that in the ll. 70-72 of the *List of Animals* no carnivors occur is important, since it can imply that also in the three following lines no direct references to carnivors are to be found. Moreover, note that all of them start with SU followed by the name of an animal:

(73)	D	[SU].PIRIG
	I	ZU.PIRIG
(74)	D	SU.KÌRI
	I	˹SU˺<.KÌRI$^{?}$>
(75)	D	SU$^{!}$(ZU).ANŠE
	I	SU$^{!}$(ZU).[AN]ŠE

Then a different section devoted to bats and rodents begins: l. 76 in fact has SU^{mušen} (note the common element SU).

At Ebla there is another list of animals, the *Bilingual List of Animals* (see recently SJÖBERG 1996; also BONECHI n.d.a and BONECHI n.d.b), *MEE* 4 96+112+ (source A) and *MEE* 4 116 (source B). Its first 12 lines deal with big mammals, and 7-10 specifically with carnivors:

(7)	A	az$^{!}$ (ZA.PÉŠ)	*a-zú-um*	bear, *ʾasum*
	B	a-zu-um		
(8)	A	kìri-ma	*b*[*ù*$^{?}$-*zu*$^{?}$]	hyena, *būṣum*
	B	---		
(9)	A	nemur(PIRIG.TUR)	*na-me-ru*$_{12}$*-um*	leopard, *namērum*
	B	na-me-lum		
(10)	A	mun-ti-núm	*mu-da-<ne->núm*	cheetah, *mundanenum*
	B	mu-da-ne-núm		

A name of animal, a feline, commonly read ug, is therefore attested in the line 63 of the *List of Animals*. In *MEE* 3 18+ it is written ZU.PIRIG (at Ebla the writing PIRIG×SU is lacking). Consensus exists it is the name for "lion". Line 64 has the name of a smaller feline, ug-tur.

However, apparently the term ug is repeated in line 73, where the Ebla source has [SU].PIRIG, while that from Abū Ṣalābīḫ has ZU.PIRIG. An analogous, even if more compact, sequence is attested in the *Word List MEE* 3 53 = *MEE* 15 80:

List of Animals (Ebla)	Word List
(63) ZU.PIRIG	obv. IV:13 ZU.PIRIG
(64) ZU$^{!}$(SU).PIRIG-tur	obv. IV:14 ZU.PIRIG-tur
(73) [SU].PIRIG	obv. IV:15 SU.PIRIG

Rather than an unusual repetition, I suggest this situation indicate a distinction between two meanings reflected by two slightly different writings. On one side, the name of the lion currently read ug, but more likely to be read *sug, normally written sú-úg (STEINKELLER 1987:2, n. 2). On the other side, another meaning: SU pirig, very likely to be read kuš pirig, "skin of leopard" (see already D'AGOSTINO 1996:178, "pelle di leone"; as for the leopard and the cheetah in the cuneiform sources see HEIMPEL 1980-1983:599-601). Unfortunately, in the Ebla bilingual lists SU.PIRIG is left untranslated by the source B (*VE* 1018), while a similar name of animal with -tur is lacking.

Besides these occurrences of ug, at Ebla there are several cases (frequently in the administrative records dealing with multi-monthly account of precious metals) in which a writing SU.PIRIG or ZU.PIRIG (sometimes written SU.PÉŠ, cf. ARCHI 1999:155 and n. 41) can not be ug, "lion". Among them, the administrative Ebla text *MEE* 2 23, recently discussed in ARCHI 1999:154, is interesting, since it mentions one Puzurra-malku. Certainly we find here the man that elsewhere is qualified as ^{lú}su$_4$, "craftman of the carnelian": *ARET* VII 146: 1 *mi<-at>* 50 su$_4$ / puzur$_4$-*ra-ma-lik* / ^{lú}su$_4$ šu-ba$_4$-ti. It is likely we can interpret this name of profession in a broader sense, i.e. "craftman of the gems", actually a (palatine) artist also able to work with precious metals (PASQUALI - BONECHI n.d.; "goldsmith" in ARCHI 1999:154, n. 35):

[1] *MEE* 2 23

obv.			
(1)			
I	1	2 *mi-at* 3 ma-na ŠA.PI(=40) kù-sig$_{17}$ e$_{11}$	95.316 gr. of gold, expense:
	2	1 tuš 1 la-ḫa	(for) 1 base of 1 la-ḫa-jar;
	3	3 *mi-at* 12 ma-na	146.406 gr. of gold, expense:
II	1	50 kù-sig$_{17}$ e$_{11}$	
	2	*ga*-NE-LUM	(for its) *g.*
	3	1 *mi-at* 90 ma-na šušana$_x$(=20) kù-sig$_{17}$ e$_{11}$	89.076 gr. of gold, expense:
	4	1 zag	(for its) 1 shoulder;
rev.			
I	1	1 *mi-at* 31 ma-na TAR(=30) kù-sig$_{17}$ e$_{11}$	61.542 gr. of gold, expense:
	2	1 nundum$^!$(KA)^{nu}	(for its) 1 lip / rim.
	3	AN.ŠÈ.GÚ	Sum (of the expenses):
II	1	8 *mi* 40 lá-2 ma-na šušana$_x$(=20) kù-sig$_{17}$	392.340 gr. of gold,
	2	1 la-ḫa	for 1 la-ḫa-jar.
	3	*ap*	And also:
	4	5 ma-na 14 kù-sig$_{17}$	2.449,2 gr. of gold
	5	*gú-za-u$_9$*-SÙ	(for) its *g.*:
	6	nu-mu-ti	not received;
(2)			
III	1	1 ma-na TAR(= 30) ZU.PIRIG gi$_4$	702 gr. of ZU.PIRIG, to be given back,
	2	50 kù-sig$_{17}$ gi$_4$	390 gr. of gold, to be given back
	3	*si-in*	to
	4	puzur$_4$-*ra-ma-lik*	Puzurra-malku,
	5	nu-mu-ti	not received.

This document may be divided in two main parts, but it seems in both the focus is on one precious "storage jar", la-ḫa, and on its parts. In the former (obv. I:1 - rev. II:6), the expenditure of an astonishing amount of gold (almost 400 kg.) is recorded; the terms are:

la-ḫa a large container (ARCHI 1999:152ff., "storage jar"), to be compared with Mesopotamian la-ḫa-an; *passim* in the Ebla administrative records, used for foodstuff as oil or drink; as for the correspondences 1 la-ḫa = 30 sìla, 1 la-ḫa = 1,5 dug see MILANO 1990:351-352

tuš read PÚ in *MEE* 2 (a "basin", quoting Akk. *bū(r)tu*); as for the correct reading KU = tuš see ARCHI 1999:154, where it is translated as "base" of the storage jar

ga-NE-LUM it is not a PN (as for *MEE* 2). ARCHI 1999:154 and n. 32, reads *ga-bí-lum*, and explains it as "leg of a piece of furniture", comparing with Akk. *kablu*. The term can not be compared with *a*-NE-LUM of *ARET* VII 68: it could be the stand of the storage jar (a form of **wbl*), but not for the reasons in PETTINATO - D'AGOSTINO 1995:5 (since *VE* 1212 must be explained in a different way, as shown in FRONZAROLI 1995, p. 61, n. 75). Note *VE* 865, íb-lá-KAK = *ga-bí-lu-um* (source A), *ga-bí-lum* (sources C, D): the Semitic translation has been interpreted as *qabilum*, "(a kind of belt)" in CONTI 1990:205. The term íb-lá-KAK does not refer to a belt for the human body (íb^{túg} and íb-lá), but I am unable to harmonize a belt with a large container

zag "side": it frequent as a part of the wagon (CONTI 1997:36-37); in our text it may refer to the side of the la-ḫa-jar ("shoulder" in ARCHI 1999: 154, "side" *ibid.*, p. 155, said of an an-dùl-image)

nundum$^!$(KA)^{nu} read *zú-nu*, "...", in *MEE* 2, but see ARCHI 1999:154. The explanation of KA-NU is found in FRONZAROLI 1988:15: it is the Eblaic equivalent of nundum(KA×NUN), "lip", "rim". It occurs, untranslated, in *VE* 196, but an entry in the sources A and B, quoted by Fronzaroli, is nundum$^!$(KA)^{nu}-maḫ = *li-sa-ne-lu-um*/-*lum*, *lišān ʾilum*, "lofty tongue" (this Sumerogram is untranslated in the *EV* c and i). Alternatively, eme$^!$(KA)^{nu}-maḫ, with NU = *nu* as indicator that KA = eme = *lišānum* (cf. kalam-*tim* for *mātum*), could be considered. KA-NU is known in the incantation *ARET* V 1 [5] and in the lexical list *MEE* 3 70, obv. II:5, while nundum$^!$-maḫ occurs in the first incantation in *ARET* V 18: obv. III:1, 2. In an unpublished multi-monthly account of precious metals (75.2508 obv. XXIV:28-33, quoted in PETTINATO - D'AGOSTINO 1995:126 and in ARCHI 1999:154) there is another relevant occurrence of KA-NU, attested together with zag and la-ḫa: 15 gín DILMUN kù:babbar / ^{giš}*lu-lum* / zag / an-dùl-an-dùl / lú nundum$^!$ / 1 la-ḫa sagi, showing that the rim of the container was decorated. As for ^{giš}*lu-lum* cf. *VE* 430, ^{giš}TE, likely ^{giš}temen = *lu-lum* (source B), *lu-ru*$_{12}$*-um* (source A): the reference may be to the pegs used for fixing an object to a base. An attestation of gold for the decoration of the "rim" of a bur-KAK pot in ARCHI 1999:154, n. 34

gú-za-u$_9$ unexplained; also attested in *ARET* II 36 r. I:3 (said of an an-dùl-image)

In the second part of *MEE* 2 23, 0,700 kg of the material ZU.PIRIG and 0,416 kg of gold are mentioned in connection with Puzurra-malku. Therefore ZU.PIRIG is the designation of a precious material that, together with some gold, must to be given back (gi$_4$) to our artist (the ^{lú}su$_4$). About our term in this text cf. PETTINATO 1980:172 ("un minerale o metallo"), and ARCHI 1999:154 and 155 with n. 41 (with a different analysis of *MEE* 2 23 and of the other evidence): "kind of clasp for fixing the lid".

In [2-3], instead, the weight of silver or gold and of SU/ZU.PIRIG is scanty. In the former the reference is to another kind of craftsman, a "smith", while in the latter (where "knives", gír, are referred to) prince Yirḫaq-damu is mentioned, certainly as donor. In other passages too [4-7] the weight of silver and of ZU.PIRIG is scanty; the mentioned precious objects are "plates" (dib), "bracelets" (*gú-li-lum*), and "reins" (^{níg}anše-aka).

But in other passages mentioning the term under inquiry in relation with various precious items, it may be noted that (with the exception of [14]) SU/ZU.PIRIG is never counted or weighed, and that often it is preceded by the recording of a little bit of silver.

In one fragmentary text, [8], (see BONECHI 1990), belonging to the ancient phase of the Archives, some silver is recorded for the SU.PIRIG (read su-gìr, collated on the photography) of an unprecise number of bracelets (*gú-li-lum*, *kulīlum*). In other and more recent administrative passages, [9-13], we find the record of several "bracelets", often made in a-gar$_5$-gar$_5$-copper, of which the precious "ornamentation" (NU$_{11}$-za, corresponding to Ebl. *zi-du*, *sittum*, from **wsm*, FRONZAROLI 1996:61ff.) or the "lamination" (*ni-zi-mu*, *niṣmum*, likely from **nḍm*, FRONZAROLI 1996:63) sometimes are mentioned. Then our term occurs, followed by the suffix pronoun -SÙ, that appears to be used in reference to the previously mentioned objects, and not to the metals or to the techniques. Sometimes ([9-11]) the specification igi$^!$(ME)-sig / é / en follows: it is to be interpreted as a reference to the *nāṣib bayti malkim*, the "keeper of the king's house" (FRONZAROLI 1997:4, 13 as for igi-sig = *na-zi-bù*(*-um*) in *VE* 722, sources A and B). The amount of silver preceding SU/ZU.PIRIG is rather scanty. In further passages, [14-19], ZU/SU.PIRIG occurs in contexts dealing with the object - sometimes "small" (tur) - whose name is written ḪI×MAŠ. I suggest it is to be read útul, "cauldron, stock-pot", and not $šur_x$ or sùr (see below). In [14-15] SU.PIRIG may be interpreted as a reference to the material (note that it is weighed, and without the suffix -SÙ). The two small cauldrons in [14] are not so heavy: more than 2 kilos of copper for the former, more than 1,5 kilos of SU.PIRIG material for the latter (a different interpretation in ARCHI 199:157). In [20] 15 shekels of ZU.PIRIG make reference to another heavy container, the la-ḫa sagi. In [21] once again, as in the case of the bracelets mentioned above, the amount of precious metal is very scanty. The texts, dealing with la-ḫa-containers, is interesting, and I suggest a reading 1 sag-e_{11} 1 ^{giš}sal 1 an-dùl rather than 1 sag 1 ^{giš}sal-e_{11} 1 an-dùl found in D'AGOSTINO 1996:178 (1 sag 1 GIŠ-SAL.X in ARCHI 1999:155), in order to translate «2 minas and 36 D.-shekels of silver, to be exchanged with 39 D.-shekels of gold, for the lamination of 1 support and of 1 ^{giš}sal of 1 artistic image; (and) 16 D.-shekels of silver to be exchanged with 4 D.-shekels of gold, for their (of the images) ZU.PIRIG». I make reference to *VE* 249, sag-e_{11} = *dar-da-bí-gu-um* (sources A, C), *ra-ba-ga-tum* (source D), *tartapiqum* and *rapāqtum*, "support" (see CONTI 1990:108, with previous literature). The long passage [22], in the context of weapons, mentions a little silver used, in the technique *ni-zi-mu* ("lamination"), to decorate 1 á-mušen, and the ZU.PIRIG of 1 á-mušen-2. The object á-mušen is a kind of military headgear (BONECHI n.d.b, with previous literature also dealing with the bird of prey $ti_8^{mušen}$).

To sum up: (a) our term SU.PIRIG and var. is never counted, and thus there are no compelling reasons to consider it as an object; (b) the passages in which its weight is clearly given suggest SU.PIRIG is a material of some price ([1-8, 14]), used for the manufactoring of knives (gír), plates (dib), bracelets (*kulīlum*), reins (^{nig}anše-aka) and cauldrons (útul): (c) other passages ([9-13, 15-22]), in which our term is almost always followed by a pronominal suffix -SÙ referring to the previously mentioned objects, suggest that SU.PIRIG is a technique, referred to the decoration of bracelets (*kulīlum*), cauldrons (útul), la-ḫa-containers (la-ḫa sagi) and military headgears (á-mušen-2).

SU.PIRIG and var. has been read zu-pirig, "zu-pirig-objects", in MANDER 1990:81. WAETZOLDT *apud* MANDER 1990:91 suggested «ein Tier? zur Dekoration von *gú-li-lum*, an-dùl, díb, $šur_x$-tur/$šur_x$-uruda-maḫ, $á^{mušen}$, la-ḫa-sagi; Lesung wohl péš» (the reading ZU-PIRIG is adopted in WAETZOLDT 1990:34). More recently, with the reading zu-pirig, it is a part of the bracelets *kulīlum* for MANDER 1995:57-

58, which, however, rightly translates a part of [10] as: «17 silver shekels (for) their <i.e. of the bracelets> 'spotted lion' [or: for their spotting; i.e. inserted spots of silver or inserted stones bought by means of that silver?]». D'AGOSTINO 1996:177-178 considers our term in some of the mentioned administrative texts as a designation of a metal rather than that of an object, noting that the same writing in the lexical lists is not to be used in order to explain that in the administrative records (but he rightly reads it as kuš pirig). As already reported, SU.PIRIG and var. is a kind of clasp for fixing the lid in ARCHI 1999.

STEINKELLER 1987:94 has discussed the name of stone pirig-gùn (quoting other names of stone in which names of animals occur), concluding that it means «"spotted/speckled 'lion'", i.e. stone which looks like the hide of a spotted "lion"». He also quoted the gloss *la-bu-⌜ú*$^{?}$⌝ of pirig-gùn in the l. 295 of the Ugarit version of *Ḫḫ* XVI, probably *labbu*, "lion", and the inscription in the Sargonic seal BM 122125, which mentions the material of the seal itself (kišib pirig-gùn). It is to be compared with the name of stone attested in the l. 54 of *Archaic HAR-ra A*: pirig-gùn za in *MEE* 3 45+46 and *IAS* 33+; *bù-ru*$_{12}$*-gú-nu* (loanword) in the Semitic version *MEE* 3 61, see CIVIL 1987:143, 151. The Sargonic seal is composed of a black and white stone (hornblende-diorite), and Steinkeller remarks that pirig-gùn refers to characteristics as «the black and white color and the speckled or mottled appearance». The Old Babylonian inscription on the bowl A 7462, made of hornblende-diorite, dedicated by Rîm-Sîn I of Larsa to Inanna of Zabala makes reference to the bowl itself in the following way: bur ^{na_4}pirig-gùn za$^{?}$ (FRAYNE 1990:304). The name of stone pirig-gùn is interpreted as "spotty lion" also in POSTGATE 1997:209.

I suggest that all the Ebla writings under inquiry must be reduced to a basic form SU PIRIG, and that, with a reading kuš pirig, it basically means "skin of the leopard". It is in fact the same term attested in the two lexical lists above mentioned, and in several passages of the administrative records it refers to a semiprecious stone, even if na$_4$ or za do not occur. As for its use in making containers cf. l. 72 of *Archaic HAR-ra A*: bur pirig-gùn in *IAS* 33+ and 37, bur *gú-nu-gú-nu* in *MEE* 3 61, and ^{na_4}bur pirig-gùn in the Ur III texts *TCL* 2 5529:13 (see CIVIL 1987:144, 154; to his discussion on Ug. *knkn* add now *DLU* I, p. 220). Both the kuš pirig and the pirig-gùn may be kinds of diorite.

In the other passages of the Ebla administrative records mentioned kuš pirig may mean "leopard skin effect" or "leopard skin technique". This second meaning may make reference to the typical feature of the skin of the leopard, i.e. to be spotted. A good clue may be found in [22], where kuš pirig has the same syntactical rank of *niṣmum*, name of a technique ("lamination"), and, with Mander, it may be suggested the kuš pirig technique produces circular incisions. Typically the incision were filled with silver when they were made on the surface of objects in bronze or copper. Cf., in the Mesopotamian lexical lists, the terms $^{\text{pi-rig}}$pirig, $^{\text{u-ug}}$úg and $^{\text{u-ug}}$ug, equivalents of *nūrum* in the meaning "bright spot", and also the passage of the hepatoscopic Old Babylonian text *YOS* 10 42 ii 40, *šumma rēš libbi nūri itaddu*, «if the *rēš libbi* is dotted with bright spots» (*CAD* N/2, pp. 347 and 351).

No extant metal objects from Tell Mardikh documenting such a technique are known to me. However, such dotting appears in a masterpiece of the Ebla figurative art, the small leopard TM.77.G.260 in white limestone with dotted mantle, see lastly DOLCE 1995:324. Other representations of leopards or cheetahs (sometimes with drill holes which may have been inlaid) in the Near East in the mid-3rd millennium exist, see WILLIAMS-FORTE 1980-1983:601-604, showing its popularity in the art of Southern Anatolia and Syria.

Some passages ([14-19]) from the Ebla texts in which útul(ḪI×MAŠ) occurs have been already quoted. In other passages ([23-27]) this object (sometimes "big", maḫ) is mentioned, but kùš pirig is lacking. As for its meaning, it has been thought it is a weapon (PETTINATO 1980:10) or a container, a "jar" (WAETZOLDT 1990:34, with literature; PETTINATO 1996:300) or a "*pithos*" (ARCHI 1999:157, reading sùr). In the available texts its weight is rather variable. An útul relatively light is attested in [14], but in other passages its weight is astonishing huge, since it may weigh even more than 200 kilos (WAETZOLDT 1990:34, and ARCHI 1999:157).

In *VE* 1381' the sources B and A_2 do not translate ḪI×MAŠ. This sign also occurs in *EV* 0225 (*MEE* 4 80, source h, obv. II:5): zal-a-ḪI×MAŠ; cf., meaningfully, *VE* 607, zal-a = *na-za-u*$_9$ (source D; *na-za-u*[*m*] in *VE* 1330, source A_2), *nazālum*, "to pour out", and *VE* 608, zal-a-engur = *wa-rí-šu* (source D), *wa-ru*$_{12}$*-sum* (source x), *warīṯum*, *waruṯum*, from **wrṯ*, "to gush" (CONTI 1990:167-168). However, there is sufficent evidence to interpret the writing ḪI×MAŠ in all the aforementioned passages of administrative texts from the Ebla Archive L.2769 as the name of a container, to be read útul, Akk. *diqaru*. Very likely it also occurs in the royal rituals (from the same Archive) published in FRONZAROLI 1993. In these documents, with a reading šur$_x$ or sur$_x$ of ḪI×MAŠ, útul has been interpreted as a kind of bun, and translated as "focaccia" (FRONZAROLI 1993:48, 169; PETTINATO

1992:144-145; doubted in Waetzoldt 1990:34, n. 196). In fact, comparing it with ninda-sur of the Mesopotamian sources, Milano 1990:292, 404, had interpreted ḪI×MAŠ of *ARET* IX 98 (an «elenco di ingredienti ... per preparare focacce» from the Archive L.2712) as sur$_x$, "(a kind of bread or cake)", presumed to be attested also in documents from the Archive L.2769, in which, however, the term refers to a cauldron. The gastronomic nature of *ARET* IX 98 is certain: it records three foodstuff based on "semolina" (*za-la-tum*), "meal of emmer" (zíd zíz), "breads of beer" (ninda bappir), "malt" (munu$_4$), "yeast" (*ʾà-mi-zu*), "honey" (làl), and "olive oil" (ì-giš). The reading šur$_x$ of ḪI×MAŠ is based on the l. 66 of the *Ebla Sign List* (ḪI×MAŠ = *su-ru*$_{12}$*-um*, lastly Archi 1987:103). This value, variant of sùr(ḪI×AŠ), «depression, ditch», Akk. *sūru, ḫarru*, at Ebla is also attested for instance in the GN *ga-šur*$_x$(ḪI×MAŠ)^{ki}, whose reading is certain, given the variants *ga-su-lu*^{ki} and *ga-su-ru*$_{12}$^{ki} (see Archi *et alii* 1993:233-236; Bonechi 1993:153). At Ebla small signs as AŠ, DIŠ, MAŠ, TIL and PAP may be confused when they are written inside larger signs in order to modify them (cf. the cases of U$_9$, BÀD, but note that in *MEE* 3 53 = *MEE* 15 80 both ḪI×MAŠ and ḪI×DIŠ occur, obv. VI:21 and VII:9). However, among the meanings of ḪI×MAŠ there is tu$_7$, "(a soup)", Akk. *ummaru*. Attestations in texts from Mesopotamia are found in Steinkeller 1992:15-19, in reference to documents from Archaic Ur and Fara (where the form ḪI×DIŠ occurs), and (written ḪI×TIL, by-form of ḪI×MAŠ) from Pre-Sargonic Lagaš, Classical Sargonic and Ur III texts. It is unclear to me if this is the value to be found in *ARET* IX 98: the ingredients of the Eblaic ḪI×MAŠ likely refer to a sweet food in a rather solid form, but ancient gastronomy in Syria and in Lower Mesopotamia were certainly rather different, and perhaps tu$_7$ is a better reading than šur$_x$ for a foodstuff. Also note ll. 41ff. of the lexical list *MEE* 3 48+49 the foodstuff awuzu(LAK-384) (syllabic source a-wu-zu), «an early form of post-Ur III útu (written U.GA), which designates a type of cereal concoction, Akk. *tiktu* and also *šipku* ... The meaning "food preparation", perhaps "soup", with various added substances and flavourings, fits perfectly well in the context of the present word list. In lines 42ff. products added are: oil, butter, milk, cream (?), barley, emmer wheat, and two plants» (Civil 1982:15). More recently M. Civil *apud* Steinkeller 1992:16 noted about tu$_7$: «I would not be surprised if there is a connection with utu$_2$, old awuzu (<a+utu); see *OA* 21, 15, where I did not mention this possibility, though it had crossed my mind». The food LAK-384 is also attested in the l. 15 of the *Tribute List*.

In the texts published by Fronzaroli in *ARET* XI a complex ritual called *šabaʿtum* (*sa-ba-tum*, from **šaʿb-*, "seven"), a kind of holy week, occurs. There are reasons to think the central role in the ritual (distinction is made between the "first, principal", maḫ, "middle", **qbl*, and "final", **ʾaḫir*, *šabaʿtum*) was played by the sacrifice of two lambs. Night time (*nubattum*), in connection with their sacrifice (likely implying divination, I think) 4 objects were used. Besides the small cauldrons, there are tables or trays and two kinds of pots (one for beer, the other perhaps to be interpreted as *mašḫaltum*, from **slḫ*, with metathesis). The presence of the cauldrons may mean a real meal:

[28] *ARET* XI 1 [85] // 2 [90];1 [88] // 2 [93]; 1 [91] // 2 [96]

(a)

«in the 7th day of the first *šabaʿtum*» (7 ud *sa-ba-tum* maḫ)

«in the 3rd day of the middle *šabaʿtum*» (3 ud *sa-ba-tum ga-ab-li-tum* / [*ga*]-*bí*-[*li-a-tum*])

«in the *x* day of the final *šabaʿtum*» ([x] ud *sa-ba-tum a-ḫé-tum* / *a-ḫir-tum*)

(b)

«2 lambs, 7 small cauldrons, 7 pure tables/trays, 7 strainers (?), 7 jugs (of beer)» (2 sila$_4$ 7 útul tur 7 banšur sikil-sikil 7 *ma-sa-ḫa-tum* 7 *gu-/gú-mu-wa-núm* [XI 1]; 2 sila$_4$ 7 útul tur 7 ^{giš}asal [sikil] 7 *gú-mi-a-nu* ŠE+TIN 7 *maš-ḫa-tum* [XI 2])

(c)

«for the waking of the gods KUra and Barma» (*nu-ba-du* ^{d}KU-*ra ù* ^{d}*ba-ra-ma* [XI 1]; UB-u$_8$-sal ^{d}KU-*ra wa* ^{d}*ba-ra-ma* [XI 2])

These conjectures seem to be corroborated by a late pre-Sargonic text from Tell Beydar, fully quoted below, in which I suggest útul occurs. *Subartu* II 4 (related with *Subartu* II 21, 70 and 117, where more or less the same persons are mentioned in connection with hides or, more likely, meat of caprovins) deals with domestic ovins (udu) and goats (ud$_5$ and LAK-20).

The first part of the text, in fact its obverse, deals with hides of sheep if - with the editor - in obv. I:1 we read kuš udu, *mašku* (cf. *Subartu* II, pp. 112 and 128f.), or with meat of sheep if - as it seems more likely to me - we have to read su udu, *šēru*. The second part of the text (its reverse) deals with meat of goats (su ud$_5$ in rev. I$^{?}$:1 and su LAK-20 in rev. IV$^{!}$:1). The situation is depicted by the term for the "sacrifical offerings" (nídba) and for the cooking in the "stock-pot" (útul = ḪI×DIŠ; "a destination of sheep" for W. Sallaberger in *Subartu* II, p. 184; note that reading and meaning of ḪI×DIŠ in *Subartu* II 52 II:2, ká GA-ḪI×DIŠ(-)NE, are uncertain, W. Sallaberger in *Subartu* II, pp. 50, n. 10, and 180). Furthermore, the meat is "salted" (mun) or "dried" (lá). Rituals (among them, probably, divination) are involved. Even if the occurrence of ^{nig}s[a$_{10}$$^{?}$] in (1a), thereafter not repeated, is very problematic, this interpretation of the text shows its consistency. It records incomes - for the local Palace - of meat of caprovins for sacrifices and banquets of several persons, very likely in connection with the arrival of the king of Nagar at Tell Beydar (such presence is documented in other Beydar texts) and with related festivals that may have attracted many important hosts from the neighbourhood. In fact, I interpret máš lá-ŠÈ as indicative of a particular preparation of meat of a kid, on the ground of the comparison with su-lá, said of meat of various domestic mammals in the *List with Foodstuff MEE* 3 48-49 (// to Uruk *ATU* 3 "Grain", *Fara* II 15, 16 and 17, *IAS* 5 and 6, *MDP* 18, 21 and *MDP* 27 196). At Ebla some partial syllabic duplicates are attested: *MEE* 3 63 duplicates ll. 1-49, *MEE* 3 54 ll. 1-10, *ARET* V 23 ll. 50-57 (see BONECHI n.d.a, with quotation of the relevant works by M. Civil and D. O. Edzard). In l. 66 su-lá-máš occurs; other kinds of meat of máš ll. 74-76 and 78 (CIVIL 1984).

I am unable to suggest a clear philological explanation of máš lá-ŠÈ, but I interpret it as "for the drying of (meat of) kid"). Such an interpretation may find a confirmation if dam lá-ŠÈ of *Subartu* II 71 II:5 ("(a female profession)" for W. Sallaberger in *Subartu* II, p. 177) may indicate women charged with that kind of preparation of the meat. Also note the mention, in the first part of *Subartu* II 4, of ovins that are qualified through mun («"salt" ... as destination of sheep» for W. Sallaberger, *Subartu* II, pp. 177, 182), likely "salted". As for the construct ŠÈ ud_5, it is «a destination of she-goats» for W. Sallaberger, *Subartu* II, p. 184, noting that «še ud_5 as well niga:ud_5 ... seem difficult», but easy alternatives do not seems at hand.

Therefore, *Subartu* II 4 may be interpreted in the following way:

(1)		
obv. I		
1	su udu	Meat of sheep:
(1a)		
2	URI-APIN 32 su	(Income of) URI-APIN: 32 (pieces of) meat (of sheep),
3	*ša* útul(ḪI×DIŠ) [n]	n (sheep) to (be cooked in) the cauldron,
4	^{níg}s[$a_{10}$$^{?}$ n*]	[n (sheep) (for?)] purch[ases (?)] / purch[ased (?) ...],
5	mun 3	3 (sheep) to be salted.
(1b)		
6	*íl-⸢e-i⸣-šar* 20	(Income of) Yilʿey-yišar: 20 (pieces of meat of sheep),
7	nídba 1	1 (sheep as) sacrifical offering,
8	*ša* útul 1	1 (sheep) to (be cooked in) the cauldron,
(1c)		
obv. II		
1	*a-ḫu-*⸢dùg⸣ su 30 ⸢lá-2⸣	(Income of) Aḫu-ṭābu: 28 (pieces of) meat (of sheep),
2	*ša* útul 1	1 (sheep) to (be cooked in) the cauldron.

(1d)		
3	⸢x⸣-[x] ⸢su⸣ 21[+n]	[(Income of) PN]: 21+ (pieces of) meat (of sheep),
	[...]	...
(1e)		
1'	[... su] 21[+n]	[(Income of) PN]: 21+ (pieces of) meat (of sheep),
2'	nídba 2	2 (sheep as) sacrifical offering,
3'	*ša* útul 3	3 (sheep) to (be cooked in) the cauldron.
obv. III		
1	mun 1	1 (sheep) to be salted.
(1f)		
2	*ʾà-ša-*[*lu*]*m* [su n+]1	(Income of) *ʾÀ-ša-*[*lu*]*m*: 1+ (pieces of) meat (of sheep),
3	⸢nídba⸣ [n+]1	1+ (sheep as) sacrifical offering,
(1g)		
4	[... su n]	[(Income of) PN]: [n (pieces of) meat (of sheep),]
5	[nídb]a [n]	n (sheep as) sacrifical offering,
6	[*ša*] ⸢útul⸣ 2	2 (sheep) to (be cooked in) the cauldron,
7	[mu]n 1	1 (sheep) to be salted.
(1h)		
8	[... su] 11	[(Income of) PN]: 11 [(pieces of) meat (of sheep),]
9	[*ša*] útul 2	2 (sheep) to (be cooked in) the cauldron,
10	1 mun	1 (sheep) to be salted.
(1i)		
obv. IV		
1	*ìr-*[*i*]*b-sá-*[*l*]*im* [su] 13$^{?}$	(Income of) Yirḫib-šālimu: 13$^{?}$ (pieces of) meat (of sheep)
2	[...]	...
3	[...]	...
(1j)		
4	⸢x-x-x⸣ [su] 10	[(Income of) PN]: 10 [(pieces of) meat (of sheep),]
5	⸢nídba⸣ 1	1 (sheep as) sacrifical offering,
(1k)		
6	*šu-na-n*[*a*] [s]u 24	(Income of) *Šu-na-n*[*a*]: 24 (pieces of) meat (of sheep),
7	⸢*ša*⸣ ⸢útul⸣ 2	2 (sheep) to (be cooked in) the cauldron,
8	⸢1⸣ ⸢mun⸣	1 (sheep) to be salted.
(1l)		
9	*ma-na-gàr* su	(Income of) *Ma-na-gàr*: 5+ (pieces of) meat (of sheep),
obv. V		
1	[n+]5	
2	[*š*]*a* útul 1	1 (sheep) to (be cooked in) the cauldron,
3	[1] mun	[1] (sheep) to be salted.
	(blank)	
(2)		
rev. I		
1	su ud_5	Meat of she-goat:
($2a_1$)		
2	*da-da* su 25	(Income of) Dada: 25 (pieces of) meat (of she-goat),

3	ud$_5$:niga 10	10 she-goats to be fattened,
4	nídba 16	16 (she-goats as) sacrifical offering,
5	máš lá-ŠÈ 43	43 kids, (whose meat is) to be dried.
(2a$_2$)		
6	*lu-sá-lim* su 43	(Income of) *Lu-sá-lim*: 43 (pieces of) meat (of she-goat),
rev. II		
1	nídba 43	43 (she-goats as) sacrifical offering,
2	ud$_5$:⸢niga⸣ 10 lá-1	9 she-goats to be fattened (and)
3	máš lá-ŠÈ 40 lá-2	38 kids, (whose meat is) to be dried.
(2a$_3$)		
4	⸢*ḫa*⸣-*bù*-⸢*zu*⸣ su 51	(Income of) ⸢*Ḫa*⸣-*bù*-⸢*zu*: 51 (pieces of) meat (of she-goat),
5	nídba 33	33 (she-goats as) sacrifical offering,
6	ud$_5$:niga 7	7 she-goats to be fattened (and),
7	máš lá-ŠÈ 77*	77 kids, (whose meat is) to be dried.
(2a$_4$)		
8	*sal$_4$-mu* su	(Income of) Šalmu: 14 (pieces of) meat (of she-goat),
rev. III		
1	14	
2	nídba 12[+n]	12+ (she-goats as) sacrifical offering,
3	ud$_5$:⸢niga⸣ 5	5 she-goats to be fattened (and)
4	[m]áš lá-ŠÈ 30	30 kids, (whose meat is) to be dried.
(2a$_5$)		
5	lú-*ša-ma-gan* su [n+]4	(Income of) Lú-*ša-ma-gan*: 4+ (pieces of) meat (of she-goat),
6	nídba 33	33 (she-goats as) sacrifical offering,
7	ud$_5$:niga 3	3 she-goats to be fattened (and)
8	máš lá-ŠÈ 23	23 kids, (whose meat is) to be dried.
(3)		
rev. IV		
1	su LAK-20	Meat of he-goat:
(3a)		
2	*'à-kun*	(Income of) *'À-kun*: 107 (pieces of) meat (of he-goat).
3	1 *mi-at*	
4	7 su	
(3b)		
5	*nu-zú*	(Income of) *Nu-zú*: 95 (pieces of) meat (of he-goat).
6	95* <su>	
7	nídba 73*	73 (he-goats as) sacrifical offering.
(3c)		
8	su URI-ŠE:ŠE.KIN	Meat (income of) URI-ŠE:ŠE.KIN: 100 (pieces of meat of he-goat),
9	1 *mi-at* <su>	
rev.V		
1	⸢nídba⸣ 5	5 (he-goats as) sacrifical offering,

2	ud$_5$:niga 5	5 she-goats to be fattened (and)
3	máš lá-ŠÈ 7	7 kids, (whose meat is) to be dried.
(3d)		
4	su *wa*-NE-*sum*	Meat (income of) *Wa*-NE-*sum*: 106 (pieces of) meat
5	1 *mi-at*	(of he-goat),
6	6 su	
7	˹nídba˺ [n+]3	3+ (goats as) sacrifical offering,
8	˹ud$_5$˺:niga 5	5 she-goats to be fattened (and)
9	máš lá-ŠÈ 35	35 kids, (whose meat is) to be dried.

Quoted passages

[1] see above

[2] 2 kù:babbar SU.PIRIG / simug (75.1460 rev. III:5-6 quoted in D'AGOSTINO 1996:177)

[3] 1-1/2 kù:babbar / šu-bala-aka / 1/2 kù- sig$_{17}$ / 1/2 ZU.PIRIG / 2 gír / 4 gín DILMUN kù:babbar / *zi-du*-SÙ // 2 NI kù:babbar / *ru*$_{12}$-*du-ga-tum*-SÙ / *il-'à-ag-da-mu* (75.2428 rev. I:33 - II:3, quoted *ibid.*)

[4] TAR(=30) kù:babbar ZU.PIRIG UNKEN-aka 23 dib a-gar$_5$-gar$_5$ kù-sig$_{17}$ (75.2464 obv. V:1-4, quoted in ARCHI 1999:155, n. 41)

[5] 4 gín DILMUN kù:babbar ZU.PIRIG 2 dib *lu-a-tum* ^{ki} (75.10077 rev.XII:23-26, quoted *ibid.*)

[6] 10-1/2 kù:babbar ZU.PIRIG UNKEN-aka *gú-li-lum wa* ^{níg}anše-aka (75.10077 obv. III:4-9, quoted *ibid.*)

[7] ˹50˺ gín DILMUN kù:babbar ZU.PIRIG (75.1923 obv.VI:15-16, quoted *ibid.*)

[8] 6 gín DILMUN kù:babbar / SU.PIRIG / *gú*-[*li-l*]*um* [(x)] / [...] (*ARET* III 440 rev. III:6-8)

[9] 5 ma-na šušana$_x$(=20)-5 gín DILMUN kù:babbar / šu-bala-[aka] / 1 m[a-n]a 5 gín DILMUN kù-sig$_{17}$ / NU$_{11}$-za 10 *gú-li-lum* a-gar$_5$-gar$_5$ TAR(=30)-2 / 5 *gú-li-lum* a-gar$_5$-gar$_5$ šušana$_x$(=20)-2 / 10 *gú-li-lum* ˹a-gar$_5$-gar$_5$˺ [10]-˹5$^?$˺-1 / 10 *gú-li-lum* a-gar$_5$-gar$_5$ 10-1 10-1 / 2 gín DILMUN kù:babbar / ZU.PIRIG-[S]Ù / igi$^!$(ME)-sig / é / en (*MEE* 7 47 rev. IX:3-14)

[10] 10 1-3 ma-na kù:babbar / šu-bala-aka / 1 ma-na ˹TAR(=30)-4˺ gín DILMUN kù-sig$_{17}$ / NU$_{11}$-za 20 *gú-li-lum* TAR(=30)-2 / 30 *gú-li-lum* 15-1 / 1-1/2 ma-na kù:babbar / NU$_{11}$-za 10 *gú-li-lum* TAR(=30)-2 / 40 *gú-li-lum* 10:1 / 17 gín DILMUN kù:babbar / ZU.PIRIG-SÙ // igi$^!$(ME)-sig / é / en (75.2429 obv. XXI:9 - XXII:3, quoted in D'AGOSTINO 1996:177)

[11] 6 ma-na 15 gín DILMUN kù:babbar / šu-bala-aka / 1 ma-na 15 gín DILMUN kù-sig$_{17}$ / (...) / (...) / (...) / (NU$_{11}$$^?$-za$^?$ / *ni*$^?$-*zi*$^?$-*mu*$^?$) / *gú-li-lum* a-gar$_5$-gar$_5$ / ZU.PIRIG-SÙ / igi$^!$(ME)-sig / é / en (*MEE* 7 34 obv. XV:11-22)

[12] 20 gín DILMUN kù:babbar / šu-bala-aka / 10 gín DILMUN kù-sig$_{17}$ / NU$_{11}$-za 1 *gú-li-lum* 50 gín DILMUN a-gar$_5$-gar$_5$ / *an-na-aḫ* / lú-kar / *kak-mi-um*^{ki} / 1 gín DILMUN kù:babbar / ZU.PIRIG-SÙ (75.1464 rev. II:4-12, quoted in D'AGOSTINO 1996:177)

[13] 56 gín DILMUN kù:babbar / šu-bala-aka / 14 gín DILMUN kù-sig$_{17}$ / *ni-zi-mu* / 20 1-3 *gú-li-lum* a-gar$_5$-gar$_5$ / 10 gín DILMUN kù:babbar / ZU.PIRIG-SÙ (75.2508 rev. XVI:12-18, quoted in PETTINATO - D'AGOSTINO 1995:34)

[14] 10 ma-na nagga / 2 ma-na kù-sig$_{17}$ // 1 útul tur GÁ×LÁ 5 ma-na uruda / 1 útul tur GÁ×LÁ 3 ma-na TAR(=30) SU.PIRIG // é-nam-aka / é / *ni-za-ba*$_4$ (*ARET* VII 142; as for

é-nam-aka see *VE* 325, = *na-ba-um* [sources A and B], *na-ba-u*$_9$ [source D], *napālum*, «to make a supplementary payement», CONTI 1990:119)

[15] AN.ŠÈ.GÚ 4 ma-na šušana$_x$(=20) kù:babbar SU.PIRIG / UNKEN-aka 2 útul uruda // 1 *li-im* 4 *mi-at* 60 lá-1 ma-na TAR(=30) (75.1539 rev. IV:11 - III:1, quoted in D'AGOSTINO 1996:177; the quotation seems incomplete; cf. [26])

[16] 1 ma-na TAR(=30)-5 nagga / ŠUB *si-in* / 1 *mi-at* 90 ma-na a-gar$_5$-gar$_5$ / 1 útul gibil / 2 ma-na kù:babbar / ZU.PIRIG-SÙ / 4 ma-na TAR(=30) kù:babbar / [šu-b]a[la-a]ka [...] (*ARET* VIII 534 = *MEE* 5 14 rev. XII:14'-21')

[17] 4 ma-na TAR(=30) nagga / ŠUB *si-in* / 5 *mi-at* 10 lá -3 ma-na a-gar$_5$-gar$_5$ / 2 útul tur / 2 ma-na ŠA.PI(=40)-5 kù:babbar / SU.PIRIG$^!$(PÉŠ)-SÙ / *ap* / 1/2 nagga / (...) // 6 NI a-gar$_5$ / ŠUB *si-in* / 1 ma-na a-gar$_5$-gar$_5$ / (...)-SÙ (75.2428 rev. XI:32 - XIII:4, quoted in D'AGOSTINO 1996:177 and in ARCHI 1999:157)

[18] 10 lá-1 ma-na nagga šub *si-in* 9 *mi-at* ⸢55⸣ ma-na a-gar$_5$-gar$_5$ 3 ma-na 18 kù:babbar ZU.PIRIG-SÙ 2 útul maḫ (75.2622 rev.XXV:5-10, quoted in ARCHI 1999:157)

[19] 11 ma-na nagga šub *si-in* 6 *mi-at* ma-na a-gar$_5$-gar$_5$ mu-daḫ UNKEN-aka 2 útul gibil 5 ma-na [kù:babbar] ZU.PIRIG-SÙ (75.2502 obv.VIII:16-IX:6, quoted *ibid.*)

[20] [1 m]a-na [x] gín DILMUN [na]gga / [šub *si*]-*in* / ⸢10⸣ lá -1 ma-na a-gar$_5$-gar$_5$ / UNKEN-aka-UNKEN-aka / 1 la-ḫa sagi / ZU.PIRIG$^!$(PÉŠ)-SÙ 10-5 (75.2508 rev. XXIII:9-14, quoted in PETTINATO - D'AGOSTINO 1995:35, and in ARCHI 1999:156)

[21] 2 ma-na kù:babbar šu-bala-aka ŠA.PI(=40)-5 gín DILMUN kù-sig$_{17}$ *ni-zi-mu* 1 gír 3 *'a*$_5$-*bù-gu* lú an-šè 1 la-ḫa / 2 ma-na TAR(=30)-6 gín DILMUN kù:babbar / šu-bala-aka / TAR(=30)-9 gín DILMUN kù-sig$_{17}$ / *ni-zi-mu* / 1 sag-e$_{11}$ 1 ^{giš}sal 1 an-dùl / 16 gín DILMUN kù:babbar / šu-bala-aka / 4 gín DILMUN kù-sig$_{17}$ / ZU.PIRIG$^!$(PÉŠ)-SÙ / TAR(=30)-1 gín DILMUN nagga šub *si-in* 3 ma-na 9 a-gar$_5$-gar$_5$ 4 ^{giš}zú 4 *mu-a-tum* 6 ^{giš}kak lú UNKEN-aka 1 la-ḫa (75.2429 rev. XIV:3-XV:7, quoted in ARCHI 1999:155)

[22] 1 ma-na 50 gín DILMUN kù:babbar / šu-bala-aka / šušana$_x$(=20)-2 gín DILMUN kù-sig$_{17}$ / *ni-zi-mu* / 10 dib ma-na / 2 dib 50 / 2 dib ŠA.PI(=40) / 2 dib TAR(=30) / 3 dib šušana$_x$(=20)-5 / 3 dib šušana$_x$(=20) / 4 gín DILMUN kù:babbar / *ni-zi-mu* / 1 (...) / 1 íb-lá 1 gír kun / 10 gín DILMUN kù:babbar / šu-bala-aka / 2 gín DILMUN kù-sig$_{17}$ / MAŠ.MAŠ-SÙ / 3 gín DILMUN kù:babbar / *ni-zi-mu* / 2 íb-lá 2 gír kun / šušana$_x$(=20) gín DILMUN kù:babbar / [šu-b]ala-aka / ⸢4⸣ gín DILMUN kù- kù-sig$_{17}$ / [*ni-z*]*i-mu* / [N]U$_{11}$-za-[S]Ù / [n]-2 gín DILMUN kù:babbar / *ni-zi-mu* / 2 íb-lá 2 gír kun / 2 gín DILMUN kù:babbar / *ni-zi-mu* / 1 á-mušen / *wa* / ZU.PIRIG / 1 á-mušen-2 / 1 ma-na šušana$_x$(=20) kù:babbar / šu-bala-aka / 16 kù-sig$_{17}$ / *ni-zi-mu* / 16 gír šum kù-sig$_{17}$ / 2 gír mar-tu TI kù-sig$_{17}$ / *'à*-LUM / 2 gír mar-tu TI kù-sig$_{17}$ / 1 gír mar-tu (...) / 50 gín DILMUN kù:babbar / šu-bala-aka / 10 gín DILMUN kù-sig$_{17}$ / *ni-zi-mu* / NU$_{11}$-za / 1 *gú-li-lum* kù:babbar šušana$_x$(=20):2 / 1 *gú-li-lum* kù-sig$_{17}$ TAR(=30):2 / *wa* / 6 *gú-zi-na-tum* / 2 *gú-li-lum* kù:babbar-sig$_{17}$ ŠA.PI(=40):2 / *wa* / 1 *gú-li-lum* a-gar$_5$-gar$_5$ kù-sig$_{17}$ ŠA.PI(=40):2 / *ni-zi-mi* / ZA$_x$(LAK-384) / GURUŠ-GURUŠ (*MEE* 10 20 rev. XVI:25 - XVIII:15)

[23] ŠA.PI(=40)-2 a-gar$_5$-gar$_5$ / *zi-ba-du* / 1 útul / *al*$_6$ / MUNU$_4$-*ma*-NI (*ARET* VII 35 [1])

[24] 10 útul 3 la-ḫa ninda-síki (75.1383 obv. II:5, see ARCHI 1986:194-195)

[25] 5 *mi-at* 60 ma-na ⸢uruda⸣ / 1 útul maḫ uruda / 5 mi-at 30 ma-na ⸢uruda⸣ / 1 útul uruda 2 (*MEE* 2 1 obv. I:3-6)

[26] 5 *mi-at* 20 lá-1 ma-na šušana$_x$(ŠÚ+ŠA)(=20) a-gar$_5$-gar$_5$ e$_{11}$ 1 útul uruda (75.1539 obv. I:1-3, quoted in ARCHI 1999:157; cf. [15])

[27] 5 ma-na ŠA.PI(=40) zabar 2 ma-na TAR(=30) uruda 1 útul tur (75.2464 rev.XIII:2-4, quoted in ARCHI 1999:157)
[28] see above

Literature

ARCHI 1986 — A. Archi, *Berechnungen von Zuwendungen an Personengruppen in Ebla*, *AoF* 13, pp. 191-205.

ARCHI 1987 — A. Archi, *The "Sign-list" from Ebla,* in C. H. Gordon - G. A. Rendsburg - N. H. Winter (eds), *Eblaitica: Essays on the Ebla Archives and Eblaite Language*, Vol. I, Winona Lake, pp. 91-113.

ARCHI 1999 — A. Archi, *The Steward and His Jar*, *Iraq* 61 (1999), pp. 147-158.

ARCHI *et alii* 1993 — A. Archi - P. Piacentini - F. Pomponio, *I nomi di luogo dei testi di Ebla*, *ARES* II, Roma.

BONECHI 1990 — M. Bonechi, *ARET 3 145+163+358+440?*, *NABU* 1990/27.

BONECHI 1993 — M. Bonechi, *I nomi geografici dei testi di Ebla*, *RGTC* 12/1, Wiesbaden.

BONECHI n.d.a — M. Bonechi, *ED III Lexical Lists*, forthcoming.

BONECHI n.d.b — M. Bonechi, *Names of Animals at Ebla*, forthcoming.

CIVIL 1982 — M. Civil, *Studies in Early Dynastic Lexicography, I*, *OA* 21, pp. 1-26.

CIVIL 1984 — M. Civil, *Studies on Early Dynastic Lexicography II. 3. Word List D 50-57 (ARET 5 No. 23)*, *ZA* 74, pp. 161-163.

CIVIL 1987 — M. Civil, *The Early History of HAR-ra: The Ebla Link*, in L. Cagni (ed.), *Ebla 1975-1985*, Napoli, pp. 131-158.

CONTI 1990 — G. Conti, *Il sillabario della quarta fonte della lista lessicale bilingue eblaita*, in P. Fronzaroli (ed.), *Miscellanea Eblaitica* 3, *QuSem* 17, Firenze.

CONTI 1997 — G. Conti, *Carri ed equipaggi nei testi di Ebla*, in P. Fronzaroli (ed.), *Miscellanea Eblaitica* 4, *QuSem* 19, Firenze, pp. 23-71.

D'AGOSTINO 1996 — F. D'Agostino, *Testi amministrativi di Ebla. Archivio L.2769*, *MEE* 7, Roma.

DOLCE 1995 — R. Dolce, in P. Matthiae - F. Pinnock - G. Scandone Matthiae (eds), *Ebla. Alle origini della cultura urbana*, Milano.

DURAND 1997 — J.-M. Durand, *Les documents épistolaires du palais de Mari.* Tome I, *LAPO* 16, Paris.

FRAYNE 1990 D. R. Frayne, *Old Babylonian Period (2003-1595 BC)*, RIM Early Periods 4, Toronto.

FRONZAROLI 1988 P. Fronzaroli, *Il culto dei re defunti in* ARET *3.178*, in P. Fronzaroli (ed.), *Miscellanea Eblaitica* 1, *QuSem* 15, Firenze, pp. 1-33.

FRONZAROLI 1993 P. Fronzaroli (in collaborazione con A. Catagnoti), *Testi rituali della regalità (Archivio L.2769)*, *ARET* XI, Roma.

FRONZAROLI 1995 P. Fronzaroli, *Fonti di lessico nei testi di Ebla*, *SEL* 12, pp. 51-64.

FRONZAROLI 1996 P. Fronzaroli, *À propos de quelques mots éblaites d'orfèvrerie*, in: Ö. Tunca - D. Deheselle (eds), *Tablettes et images aux pays de Sumer et Akkad*, Mélanges offerts à Monsieur H. Limet, Liège, pp. 51-68.

FRONZAROLI 1997 P. Fronzaroli, *Divinazione a Ebla (TM.76.G.86)*, *Miscellanea Eblaitica* 4, *QuSem* 19, Firenze, pp. 1-22.

HEIMPEL 1980-1983 W. Heimpel, *Leopard (und Gepard).* A. *Philologish*, *RlA* 6, pp. 599-601.

MANDER 1990 P. Mander, *Administrative Texts of the Archive L.2769*, *MEE* 10, Roma.

MANDER 1995 P. Mander, *The* gú-li-lum *(Bracelets) in the Economic Texts from Ebla*, *Oriens Antiqui Miscellanea* II, pp. 41-87.

MILANO 1990 L. Milano, *Testi amministratrivi: Assegnazioni di prodotti alimentari (Archivio L.2712 - Parte I)*, *ARET* IX, Roma.

PAGAN 1998 J. M. Pagan, *A Morphological and Lexical Study of Personal Names in the Ebla Texts*, *ARES* III, Roma.

PASQUALI - BONECHI n.d. J. Pasquali - M. Bonechi, *The Early Syrian Fairs*, forthcoming.

PETTINATO 1980 G. Pettinato, *Testi amministrativi della biblioteca L. 2769*, *MEE* 2, Napoli.

PETTINATO 1992 G. Pettinato, *Il rituale per la successione al trono ad Ebla*, *SS NS* 9, Roma.

PETTINATO 1996 G. Pettinato, *Testi amministrativi di Ebla. Archivio L.2752*, *MEE* 5, Roma.

PETTINATO - D'AGOSTINO 1995 G. Pettinato - F. D'Agostino, *Thesaurus Inscriptionum Eblaicarum* A/1, Roma.

POSTGATE 1997 N. Postgate, *Mesopotamian Petrology: Stages in the Classification of the Material World*, *CAJ* 7/2, pp. 205-224.

SJÖBERG 1996 A. W. Sjöberg, *The Ebla List of Animal* MEE *4, no. 116*, *WO* 27, pp. 9-24.

STEINKELLER 1987 P. Steinkeller, *The Stone pirig-gùn*, *ZA* 77, pp. 92-95.

STEINKELLER 1992 P. Steinkeller, with Hand Copies by J. N. Postgate, *Third-Millennium Legal and Administrative Texts in the Iraq Museum, Baghdad*, *Mesopotamian Civilizations* 4, Winona Lake.

TALON 1997 Ph. Talon, with hand copies by H. Hammade, *Old Babylonian Texts from Chagar Bazar*, *Akkadica Supplementum* X, Brussels.

WAETZOLDT 1990 H. Waetzoldt, *Zur Bewaffnung des Heeres von Ebla*, *OA* 29, pp. 1-38.

WILLIAMS-FORTE 1980-1983 E. Williams-Forte, *Leopard*. B., *Archäologisch*, *RlA* 6, pp. 601-604.

Note: H. Waetzoldt, *Wirtschafts und Verwaltungstexte aus Ebla. Archiv L.2769*, *MEE* 12, Roma 2001, that appeared after this manuscript had been delivered, has not been included. I thank Tom L. McClellan for his help.

IL CIMENTO DELL'ESTRO E DELLA RAGIONE: LA DIMENSIONE SCRIBALE DELLA COSIDDETTA "TEODICEA BABILONESE"

GIORGIO BUCCELLATI

University of California, Los Angeles

Todo sucede por primera vez, pero de un modo eterno.
El que lee mis palabras está inventándolas.
Jorge Luis Borges

Sembra indubbio che il poema babilonese intitolato tradizionalmente "Teodicea" non possa a nessun titolo essere così chiamato. Non è una *teo*dicea in quanto il testo si occupa ben poco della realtà divina in genere; e non è una teo*dicea* perchè non affronta affatto il problema specifico di dover giustificare una divinità che si presume possa altrimenti venir incolpata di essere la causa del dolore umano. Anche la forma dialogica può quasi sembrare un modo di mettere a confronto due modi di sentire più che un dibattito fra due persone reali. È questa l'interpretazione che vi vuol vedere un "dialogo interiore" (sviluppata in particolare da Sara Denning-Bolle – si veda la nota bibliografica in calce all'articolo per gli opportuni riferimenti), che è sembrata a lungo anche me la più plausibile. Ma qui vorrei offrire un'alternativa che combina in un certo modo i due aspetti: un dialogo che mette in luce da un lato dei modi di sentire (il dialogo interiore), ma al contempo un dialogo fra due interlocutori concreti che si presentano, è questa la proposta, come degli scribi profondamente coinvolti nell'aspetto più intellettuale della loro arte.

Il titolo dell'articolo si riferisce a questi aspetti, e li allarga in una prospettiva che scende nel tempo fino al nostro settecento. Si tratta ovviamente solo di un collimare di interessi al livello tipologico, di un ripetersi di preoccupazioni intellettuali che trovò una delle sue espressioni più felici, e certo meglio note, nell'opera musicale di Vivaldi, quell'Opera VIII intitolata *Il cimento dell'armonia e dell'inventione* in cui si inseriscono i concerti delle Quattro Stagioni. L'altro ciclo dell'Opera III, intitolata *L'estro armonico*, esprime in maniera analoga il tendere di Vivaldi verso lo stesso ideale: il congiungersi in un'unità superiore dell'estro o invenzione da una parte e dell'armonia o tradizione dall'altra. I confronti, per l'appunto solo tipologici, attraverso distanze di migliaia di anni intendono sottolineare, come suggerito all'inizio, come ci siano delle istanze profonde che sorgono spontaneamente quando si fanno strada intenti espressivi di analoga portata. La forma dialogica contrappone come protagonisti in prima persona dei diversi modi di sentire; e, così facendo, propone una formula che accentua la dinamica delle alternative. Il "cimento" è, per l'appunto, un contrasto che porta in sè stesso la soluzione, non necessariamente nel senso che debba esserci una riposta arbitrale, ma nel senso che l'articolazione delle alternative offre la definizione della tensionalità che emerge come importante a titolo proprio. Che se poi si ottiene una composizione delle differenze, se il cimento si risolve nella vittoria di una parte sull'altra, il merito di entrambe le parti, anche di quella perdente, risulta in fondo potenziata dall'interesse accordato al cimento stesso. Quasi come il viaggiare può divenire altrettanto significativo che il raggiungere una meta, così il cimentarsi può apparire altrettanto meritorio e interessante come l'ottenere una posizione di preminenza.

Spero che il caro amico a cui è dedicato questo volume possa trovar qualche merito in questo tentativo non solo di saggiare più a fondo uno dei raggiungimenti più alti della poesia mesopotamica, ma anche di individuare la personalità di questi remoti colleghi e le affinità che ancora ci legano ad essi. Pelio Fronzaroli è un modello indiscusso di quell'ideale che tende a congiungere l'acribia filologica con l'innovazione inventiva, il metodo rigoroso con una sensibilità per i valori, insomma, l'armonia con "l'inventione", e tutto ciò con una finezza, arguzia e signorilità che sono la delizia di quanti hanno avuto il piacere di conoscerlo e ancor più di averlo come amico.

Sembra chiaro che lo sviluppo tematico proposto dal nostro poemetto possa comprendersi nel modo migliore se lo si pensi ambientato in un mondo scribale, dove il lettore è propriamente tale: un lettore invece che un uditore. In tale prospettiva, si capiscono meglio quegli aspetti che rendono in fondo il testo assai difficile, perché intenzionalmente esoterico: autore e lettore sono, per l'appunto, coinvolti in una comune atmosfera di rarefatto virtuosismo, dove l'alternanza delle strofe propone un raffinato gioco intellettuale, da cui i non-scribi sono esclusi.

Si prenda prima di tutto l'acrostico. È basato sui segni cuneiformi, più che sui valori fonologici (si vedano le strofe 3, 5, 8, 13, 24,26, 27). Ma ancor più "scribale" è il fatto che una comprensione della frase che ne risulta è assolutamente inconcepibile in chiave orale: nessun uditore potrebbe mai capire il senso della frase *Anāku Saggil-kīnam-ubbib mašmaššu kāribu ša ili u šarri* sentendo "leggere" prima la sillaba *a* ripetuta undici volte all'inizio di un verso composto di quattro piedi, poi la sillaba *na* ripetuta altre undici volte nelle stesse condizioni, e così via sino alla fine. È incontestabile che si tratti di una prova di bravura scribale, apprezzabile solo fra colleghi di una stretta elite.

Da ciò si può anche desumere che il poemetto non si basa su versioni antecedenti di cui questo sarebbe un rimaneggiamento. Può solo essere stato scritto di getto, in maniera integra. "Scritto": non dunque recepito da alcuna tradizione orale, e poi trascritto, e poi edito, e ri-edito. È un tutto unico e inscindibile, di un autore singolo, uno scriba pienamente conscio di proporre questo suo trionfo di mezzi espressivi, che sono bloccati per sempre in un meccanismo formale irreversibile. È questa una struttura dotata di quella inevitabilità che si combacia con un senso di sorpresa continuamente rinnovato di cui parla così eloquentemente la poetica di Paul Valéry. (Ed è ciò a cui mi fa pensare il distico di Borges citato all'inizio: "Tutto succede una prima volta, ma in modo eterno. / Colui che legge le mie parole le sta inventando", da *La Dicha* nella raccolta intitolata *La Cifra*.)

Nulla di popolare, dunque, ma, invece, un fenomeno di "letteratura" nel senso più intellettuale della parola. In questa prospettiva, il poema ci apre uno spiraglio sul mondo degli scribi come intellettuali, che come tali non erano pagati, ma che come tali avevano imparato a vivere. Non dimentico, ovviamente, che Saggil-kīnam-ubbib (l'individuo menzionato nell'acrostico) si qualifica come *mašmaššu* "tecnico dei riti d'incanto", e che questi deve essere, non sembra esserci dubbio, l'autore del poemetto che è al tempo stesso l'io lirico che si identifica con l'estro. Ma altrove è anche citato come *ummānu*, "maestro, capo-scuola, professore".

Visto dunque come "cimento", il poema mette in luce un aspetto proprio della dinamica insita nella vita intellettuale, l'alternativa fra la tradizione che codifica e si attiene a schemi recepiti (la "armonia" di Vivaldi) e l'apertura a esperienze nuove che oltrepassano i limiti (l' "estro" o "inventione"). Il pathos dell'io sofferente, dell'io lirico nel nostro poemetto non è da cercarsi in sofferenze straordinarie, né tanto meno in dubbi teologici sulla posizione della divinità a riguardo della sofferenza. La sua passione sta nel cercare di dare libero campo all'esperienza, di capire se stessi al di là degli schemi, anche se non necessariamente, alla fin fine, contro di essi. Il "cimento" non è un duello a morte, ma il godimento intellettuale di vedere espressi, nella loro alternanza che conduce alla fine a una reciproca comprensione, due modi di sentire inestricabilmente affiancati e ugualmente radicati nella nostra psiche. E l'alternanza, vista così, non è fra un sofferente e un amico, ma, appunto, fra l'estro (con il quale più esplicitamente si identifica l'autore) e la ragione:

dell'uno e dell'altra sono campioni due figure di scriba, che ce ne propongono, per così dire, la voce.

Si tocca con mano, a leggere attentamente il testo, il compiacimento dell'autore nella propria arte. Abbondano i termini ricercati, usati come epiteto per descrivere i due scribi, come "maestro di riflessione" (*bēl pakki*, 5), e altri che si trovano soprattutto all'inizio delle strofe in cui i due scribi si rivolgono l'uno all'altro. Queste apostrofi reciproche e a volte finemente ironiche riflettono una situazione che potremmo definire da ... consiglio di facoltà! Ciò che ricorre spesso, la vera sofferenza, si direbbe, è la difficoltà di riuscire a farsi capire:

"Tu rendi la tua reputazione simile a quella di un imbecille,
non fai che ridurre a grossolanità il tuo stile brillante."
Na'da ṭenka tumaššil lā lē'iš,
namrūtim zīmīka ukkuliš tušēmā. (14-15)

"Una sorgente, amico mio, di acqua inesauribile – tale è il tuo spirito,
immenso come il riflusso del mare che mai si ferma!
Ma comunque tu sia, lascia che ti ponga una domanda, e tu cerca di capirmi bene;
cerca di capirmi anche solo per un istante, ascolta ciò che ho da dire."
Kuppu, ibrī, libbaka ša lā iqattū nagabšu,
kumurrē gipiš tamtim ša lā išū miṭīta!
Kuāšu luṣṣiṣka, limad amātī,
qūlam-ma ana surri šemē qabāya. (23-26)

"È perché controllo la mia bocca che sono solido come una roccia,
mentre tu lasci scadere ogni riflessione ordinata in un facile chiacchierio.
Nel tuo cuore, tu tendi verso una confusione che non è metodica,
ciò che è chiaramente rosso tu lo fai apparire verdastro."
Sanqa pīya, šadūm iš[*dīya*],
sadra pakkaka dubbubīš t[*usēmī*].
Sapḫa lā ṭēmi tētemid libbaka,
samīš urqaka nussuqa tumaššī. (34-37)

"Per parte mia, mi sono inchinato a te, al mio amico, ho assorbito la tua saggezza,
ben volentieri ho lodato il tuo raffinato modo di parlare:
ma come posso trovare il modo di esprimerti il mio punto di vista?"
Aktamsakkum, rū'u''a, ātaḫaz mēreška
[*aktarrub, muštasḫi*]*pu, zikir atmīka:*
[*akka'ī p*]*akkī gana luqbīka*? (45-47)

E così via. Di fatto, lo scriba che dà voce alla ragione tende a iniziare ogni suo intervento con una tale apostrofe, che gli conferisce a volte un tono un po' sentenzioso, quasi antipatico. Al contrario, lo scriba che rappresenta l'estro e dà voce all'esperienza comincia ben presto a parlare subito in prima persona (dalla strofa 13 in avanti), come a sottolineare il bisogno di esprimersi per il bisogno di esprimersi, anche al di fuori del rapporto dialogico. (Non bisogna naturalmente dimenticare che la parte centrale del poema manca quasi totalmente, sicché è ben possibile che questa osservazione non sia applicabile al poema nella sua versione completa.) Nell'ultima strofa assegnata alla voce della ragione (26) manca una tale apostrofe, e questa è proprio la strofa in cui avviene il ravvicinamento dei due punti di vista, la sublimazione, per così dire, del cimento, mentre per converso la strofa seguente, l'ultima del poema e l'ultima in cui parla lo scriba che dà voce all'estro, troviamo un'apostrofe che non è più ironica, ma è come il riconoscimento sincero di un'amicizia nuovamente conquistata:

"Amico mio, tu condividi ciò che io sento: continua a mostrarmi che ti curi di me!
Rēmēnāt, ibrī, nissātim šite'-ma ... (287)

In questa ottica scribale, vorrei proporre di vedere in una lacuna la menzione del tempio Esagila che compare, nella forma Saggil, nel nome dell'io lirico citato nell'acrostico (vi sono per questa proposta delle basi paleografiche e filologiche che non posso discutere qui). Rivolgendosi dunque a Saggil-kīnam-ubbib, lo scriba che impersona la ragione direbbe (secondo la mia integrazione delle lacune):

"Possa il potente Esagila offrire aiuto,
possa Saggil aprire le sue porte e dispensare misericordia.
Sapṣū [*Esagila*] *tāḫanāta liškun*
[*Saggil līb*]*ēš, nakrūta līgīs.* (43-44)

È come un gioco di parole sul nome dell'interlocutore, un gioco erudito in cui viene offerto lo stesso tipo di glossa che si trova altrimenti usato negli antichi commentari cuneiformi a questo testo. Sarebbe, per così dire, fare assurgere lo strumento filologico di un apparato critico al livello di poesia.

È poi ben noto che vengono introdotte nel bel mezzo del testo poetico parole ed espressioni non solo dotte e di un tono arcano, ma anche e propriamente scribale. Il più sintomatico è il termine *šummē*:

"Tu disprezzi il buonsenso, abusi del metodo logico."
riddī [*te*]*mēš, šummē taṭpil.* (214)

Si tratta del plurale di *šumma* "se, si dia caso che", cioè quella parola chiave della letteratura scientifica mesopotamica con cui iniziano tutti i trattati di carattere tecnico. La traduzione "metodo logico" sembra dunque ben calzante. Ed è come se la voce della ragione accusasse un filosofo scolastico di usar male dei sillogismi. (In un seminario che tenni a UCLA su questo testo, Vyacheslav Ivanov suggerì molto appropriatamente che il termine *šummē* è usato qui in un senso propriamente metalinguistico). È anche interessante notare che nella stessa strofa l'ideale che viene contrapposto a tale mancanza di logica è quello di un individuo che è caratterizzato come "saggio per fama", *palkū nibissu* (217), dove il termine "saggio" viene glossato nel commentario proprio come "scriba", *tupšarru*.

Ci sono poi degli echi consistenti, anche se sfumati, ai grandi temi letterari. Si noti per esempio come queste parole dell'io lirico richiamino quelle di Ea a Utnapishtim in Gilgamesh:

"Lascia che rigetti la mia stessa casa ...
che possa mai più desiderare beni e proprietà ...
Bīta luddī [...]
bišā ayyaḫšiḫ [...] (133-134)

O ancora il richiamo a Enkidu là dove viene vagheggiata una vita nella steppa che si avvicini a quella degli animali – e l'ironia è che mentre Enkidu lasciò la steppa e "divenne un uomo", il nostro eroe è l'anti-Enkidu che vuole percorrere la strada opposta:

"Molti sono gli animali della steppa che [...]
ma chi fra di loro accumula dei beni?
Lascia dunque che mi cerchi un figlio e una figlia nella steppa:
qualunque cosa mi procuri non dovrò lasciarlo [in eredità]!
Ma'adū aṣū ṣēri, ša [...]
mannu ina birīšunū irtašī [*bušā*]?
Māra u marta lūba''ī [*ina ṣēri*]:
mala uttū ayyēziba [...]! (162-165)

Analogamente, la strofa 17 contiene dei riferimenti espliciti alla letteratura apocalittica, e la strofa 26 dei riferimenti all'*Enūma Elīš:* la citazione delle tre divinità responsabili della creazione dell'uomo (276-278), e una citazione addirittura letterale (286, cf. *En.El.* i 138).

Questa citazione si trova nella strofa 26, che marca il ravvicinamento della voce della ragione al punto di vista della voce dell'esperienza, e sembra quasi che il riferirsi alle "scritture" sia un modo intenzionale di avvalorare la conclusione raggiunta. Vi è anche un altro elemento che è più sfumato ma che mi sembra significativo. In questo testo che è così accurato nella segnalazione grafica degli aspetti metrici, manca ogni indicazione di quale sia il verso asimmetrico nelle varie strofe. Non vi sono però, per la massima parte, dubbi in merito, perché lo sviluppo logico e sintattico di ogni strofa provvede a offrire quella segnalazione che manca nell'apparato grafico. Nella strofa 26, però, ci troviamo di fronte a un certo disequilibrio, anzi, sembrerebbe quasi di dover accusare la mancanza di un verso asimmetrico vero e proprio che possa essere definito con i criteri usati altrove. La scelta comune nelle edizioni moderne cade sul verso 278, ma logicamente e sintatticamente questo appartiene ai due che precedono: i tre versi descrivono le tre divinità (Enlil, Ea e Mami/Aruru) che più direttamente sono coinvolte nella creazione dell'uomo nell'*Enūma Elīš*, come si è appena visto. E ciò che segue a questa sequenza di tre versi sono due versi che marcano il cambiamento più profondo rispetto alle posizioni prese finora dalla voce della ragione:

Il re degli dei, Narru (Enlil), creatore delle moltitudini
lo splendido Zulummaru (Ea), che ne scelse l'argilla,
la regina che diede loro forma, la signora Mami, –
  l'umanità ha da loro in dono un parlare ambiguo,
  sì, gli dei diedero in eredità falsità e insincerità.
    Šar qadmī Narru, bānī apātim,
    šarḫu Zulummaru, kāriṣ ṭiṭṭīšinā,
    šarratum patiqtašinā, šuētu Mami,
      šarkū ana amēluti itgura dabāba
      sarrāti u lā kīnāti išrukū santakka. (276-280)

L'asimmetria è dunque spostata, per l'unica volta nel poema, da un singolo verso asimmetrico a una triade a cui segue una coppia di versi nella quale si trova quella *punch line* che è per solito riservata invece al singolo verso asimmetrico. Questa è anche l'unica strofa che consiste di una singola e unica frase, e una delle poche, l'abbiamo già notato, in cui lo scriba che dà voce alla ragione non apostrofa l'altro con un epiteto più o meno benigno. È dunque una strofa importante: ciò che interessa a noi qui è solo di notare come questa complessità di modi espressivi ben si adatti allo spirito di immaginazione di questo scriba poeta che ha così bene fatto combaciare forma e contenuto, armonia e "inventione".

Ben lungi dall'essere un esercizio scribale pedante e puramente erudito, il poemetto dimostra quindi un afflato poetico di altissima qualità, ma di tale natura che non si disvela facilmente a una lettura puramente filologica. Per poterlo apprezzare nella sua piena vitalità occorre avvicinarvisi con una sensibilità particolare, e sviluppare una chiave di lettura più consona a ciò che il testo ci propone. È quanto ho cercato di fare, in maniera introduttiva, in questo breve saggio – offerto da collega a collega, e da amico ad amico, un po' proprio nello spirito di questi antichissimi colleghi di cui sentiamo ancora oggi così viva la voce.

Nota bibliografica

L'edizione principale del testo rimane quella di W. G. Lambert, *Babylonian Wisdom Literature*, Oxford 1960, pp. 65-90, 302-310, Pl. 19-26. Per titoli successivi a quella data vedi in particolare: W. G. Lambert, "A Catalogue of Text and Authors", in *JCS* 16, 1962, p. 66 (per la citazione dell'autore del nostro poemetto come *ummānu*); J. Bottéro, "La 'Theodicée'", in *Annuaire* 1966-1667, pp. 100-116; R. Labat, "La condition humaine," in *Les religions du Proche-Orient asiatique*, Paris 1970, pp. 320-349; G. Buccellati, "La teodicea: condanna dell'abulia politica", in *Oriens Antiquus* 11 (1972), pp. 161-178; P. Fronzaroli, "L'espressione letteraria. La retorica degli antichi", in S. Moscati (ed.), *L'alba della civiltà. Società, economia e pensiero nel Vicino Oriente Antico*, Torino 1976, Vol. 3, sp. p. 139; W. von Soden, "'Weisheitstexte' in akkadischer Sprache. Die babylonische Theodizee", in O. Kaiser (ed.), *Texte aus der Umwelt des Alten Testaments. Vol.3: Weisheitstexte, Mythen und Epen*, Gütersloh 1990, pp.143-157; G. J. Reinink e H. L. J. Vanstiphout, *Dispute Poems and Dialogue in the Semitic and Related Literatures*. Orientalia Lovanensia Analecta 42, Leuven 1991, specialmente pp. 1-6, 8-9, (Bottéro sulla definizione del genere), pp. 32-39 (Vanstiphout sulla dimensione scribale dei dialoghi), pp. 51-52 (Volgelzang sulla "Teodicea"), pp. 67-74 (van der Toorn con un giudizio negativo sul valore letterario della "Teodicea" e sugli scribi come intellettuali); S. Denning-Bolle, *Wisdom in Akkadian Literature. Expression, Instruction, Dialogue,* Leiden 1992, pp. 136-158; B. J. Foster, "The Babylonian Theodicy", in *Before the Muses. An Anthology of Akkadian Literature,* Bethesda (MD) 1993, pp. 806-814. – Le traduzioni proposte nell'articolo possono sembrare troppo libere, ma sono ragionate e basate su argomenti che non posso proporre qui, e su cui spero di poter tornare in una edizione multi-registro di questo poemetto. Si basano inoltre su integrazioni a volte assai diverse da quelle proposte nelle edizioni correnti, e che pure dovranno essere giustificate in altra sede. – Il volume di P. Everett, *Vivaldi. Le quattro Stagioni e gli altri concerti dell'Opera Ottava*, Venezia 1999 (edizione originaria in inglese del 1996 presso la Cambridge University Press) mette bene in luce le intenzioni intellettuali e persino la consapevolezza commerciale di Vivaldi nel compilare delle antologie programmatiche dei suoi concerti, vedi specialmente a pp. 33-37 e 104-108 per un interessante confronto con temi analoghi in Milton.

TWO SARGONIC TABLETS MENTIONING MESAG, ÉNSI OF UMMA

AMALIA CATAGNOTI

University of Florence

In a research framework directed by Pelio Fronzaroli, years ago I had the possibility to copy some Sargonic tablets housed in the British Museum. Now it is a pleasure for me to offer a short study of two of them[1] to my teacher as sign of gratitude for his constant support.

In both texts PN Mesag occurs, and, since in both he may be identified with Mesag énsi of Umma, both are relevant for the study of the so-called Umma C Archive (FOSTER 1982a:79-148), likely to be dated to Šarkališarri. As regards the debated relation between this archive and the so-called Mesag or "Sagub" Archive see BRIDGES 1981, FOSTER 1982b and FOSTER 1993:29f. and 175f. (with further literature), STEINKELLER 1992:8-10, STEINKELLER 1999:554 n. 5, VISICATO 2000: 102-124, and VAN DRIEL 2000:16f.

1. BM 140676 (1987-5-16.5)

This difficult letter, written in Sumerian, has been published in KIENAST-VOLK 1995:63-65 (photograph Taf. 6), and then republished in SALLABERGER 1996:401. In line 1 the editors read the PN as Me-nu-ḫé-[a] ("Lesung des Eigennamens nach Th. Jacobsen"), or Me-nu:sag$_7$-[di], compared with Me-ság-(nu-di). However, it is simply written ME-PA-GAN, therefore to be read Me-ság. Accordingly, BM 140676 is the second known letter written by Mesag (the other one is USP 63, while there are two letters written to Mesag, i.e. MCS 4 p. 13 no. 3 and MCS 9 251, see FOSTER 1982a:135-137):

---

[1] Published with the kind permission of the Trustees of the British Museum. I wish to thank Peter Steinkeller for his precious suggestions about the interpretation of BM 140676, and Gianni Marchesi and Marco Bonechi for their helpful suggestions.

Obv.	1	Me-ság		8	lú ma-an-⌜sum⌝
	2	na-bé-a	Rev.	9	zi-mu ba-tur
	3	*Puzur*$_4$-^{d}PA		10	ul$_4$-la-bi
	4	šeš-g̃u$_{10}$		11	si-lim-ma-na du$_{11}$-ga
	5	ù-na-dug$_4$		12	šu ḫa-ma-ab-ús-e
	6	*Gu-ti-um*^{ki}		13	2 GÁ×GI su$_{11}$-lum
	7	a-gin$_7$ ì-da-gub			

"[2]Thus says [1]Mesag: [5]say to [3]Puzur-Šullat, [4]my brother.

[7]How can one resist [6]the Gutians? [8]He (i.e. Puzur-Šullat) gave me some men (to protect me), [9]but it only reduced my food supplies. [10]Quickly, [11]whatever his well-being allows, [12]may he (i.e. Puzur-Šullat) dispatch to me! [13](For example) two baskets of dates".

ll. 6-7: gu-ti-um^{ki} a-gin$_7$ ì-da-gin, "the Gutians have come like waters!", in *PSD* A 1/I, p. 2, 1.2; "Wie kann er den Gutäern beistehen!" in KIENAST-VOLK 1995:63-64; "Der Gutäer - wie kann der ein Beistand sein?" in SALLABERGER 1996:401. Another mention of the Gutians in the correspondence of Mesag énsi of Umma occurs in MCS 4 p. 13 no. 3, letter of Iddin-Erra to Mesag, to be dated to the seventh month of, probably, Šarkališarri 6 or 7: see ll. 17-30 "See here, my people perished of hunger, while my lord knows (even) Gutians receive grain rations! Let him deal justly. Help me, My Lord!" (translation in FOSTER 1982a:135f.). As regards the Gutians and their struggles with Šarkališarri see finally WESTENHOLZ 1999:94, with literature.

ll. 8-9: l. 8 is read lú Ma-an-⌜sum⌝ in KIENAST-VOLK 1995:63-64, "der 'Mann' des Mansum hat mein(en) Leben(sunterhalt) gemindert", but lú ma-an-sum SALLABERGER 1996:401: "Einen Mann hat er (Puzur-Šullat) mir zwar gegeben, (aber) mein Lebensunterhalt wurde (dadurch nur) gemindert".

ll. 10-13: l. 11 is read si ši-ma-na-du$_{11}$-ga in KIENAST-VOLK 1995:63, "Allerschnellstens soll er (Puzuršullat) das, was er him (dem Manne des Mansum) zugesagt (?) hatte, mir schicken!", but si-lim-ma-na du$_{11}$-ga in SALLABERGER 1996:401, "Ehebaldigst soll er (Puzur-Šullat) das, was über sein Wohlergehen gesagt (werden kann), mir herschicken - (bitte:) 2 Körbe Datteln".

Once suggested that Mesag énsi of Umma is the sender of our letter, the problem of the receiver's identity becomes more interesting. It has been studied in KIENAST-

VOLK 1995:65, with reference to the previous discussions in STEINKELLER 1984:83f., in GELB-KIENAST 1990:384, and in FRAYNE 1993:297f.

In our letter Puzur-Šullat is qualified by Mesag as "brother", but it is unclear if the two men were actually brothers, or if more likely "brother" is the term used by énsi Mesag to indicate that he recognizes his same rank to Puzur-Šullat (SALLABERGER 1996:402 notes that "der Brief ... im Thema, der Strategie und der Argumentation mühelos neben altbabylonische Briefe stellen, in denen der Absender um Geschenke bittet. Die persönliche missliche Lage dient dabei als wichtiges Argument, dass man dieses Geschenkes unbedingt bedürfe").

During the Sargonic period there is one famous Puzur-Šullat, i.e. the temple administrator of a city called Dūrum (sanga Bàd^{ki}). His name occurs in the bronze inscribed bowl MBQ 26/35-62 found at Tell Mumbāqa, on the middle Syrian Euphrates, and in the British Museum cylinder seal BM 89147. Furthermore, the PN Puzur-Šullat also occurs in one tablet from Tell as-Suleimeh, in the Hamrim region (RASHEED 1981 no. 6, IV 3).

However, with the data in our possession it seems impossible to say whether Puzur-Šullat of our letter is the same Puzur-Šullat sanga of Dūrum (whose whole career, however, is actually unknown) or it is another and equally important Puzur-Šullat of the Umma area. In fact, we don't know where our letter comes from, neither if it was kept in Puzur-Šullat's archive or if it was the copy kept in Mesag's one. Furthermore, as regards Puzur-Šullat's Dūrum, it remains unclear where it must be localized: also considering the data added to the debate in OWEN 1995, at least Sumer, the Hamrin region and Syria must be taken into account. Moreover, we don't know where Puzur-Šullat resided when Mesag wrote his letter.

2. BM 140668 (1987-3-7.1)

This administrative text from Umma belongs to the group C.5 ("records of personnel") discussed in FOSTER 1982a:124-126, and in particular to C.5b, "maintenance of personnel" (other texts belonging to this group are USP 44-48 and AAS 202). USP 44, 45 and 47 present the same vertical line that cuts in two the written columns also found in the document published hereafter.

The end of our text (rev. II 16-25) includes the total, a subscription, and the date (rev. II 25, now lost).

The total (rev. II 16-17) records 31 guruš, "workers", together with 14 šeš, lit. "brothers", perhaps "monitors" (FOSTER 1982a:125; in the body of our text, as well as also in the other texts of the group C.5b, šeš may be referred to by means of the term pap), and then 3 guruš kaskal together with 4 šeš kaskal (as regards kaskal as "journey; service" see FOSTER 1982a:125, and 166, n. 83, with the following remark about the structure PN$_1$ dumu PN$_2$ kaskal PN$_3$: "the context suggests that PN$_1$ is substituting for PN$_3$ for the period of service covered by the roster"). Then this part of the text continues (rev. II 18-20) with the mention of the ugula, "foreman", and of the nu-bànda, "captain" (the engar, "cultivator", had been recorded above, rev. II 15), followed by im-si-sá-a, "on the regular roster".

The document ends with (rev. II 21-23) the usual mention of the inspection made by the énsi Mesag in the "Scepter-House" of Umma, and with (rev. II 24) the rather mysterious further annotation [*qáb*]-*la* 3 ("in the middle, 3", FOSTER 1982a:125: "perhaps this expression refers to a muster formation").

obv. I
1' [... l]ú$^{?}$/[lu]gal$^{?}$-[...]
2' [...]-ta
3' [...]⸢x⸣-da-NI(-)me
4' [...]-⸢x⸣-^{d}utu
5' [...]-kur-ra
6' [...]-⸢x⸣-ga-NI(-)me
7' [...]-na
8' [...]⸢ḫa⸣-šu-EREN
9' [... k]isal$^{?}$-lá
10' [...]-⸢x⸣-gi
11' [...]-$^{⸢d⸣}$inanna
12' [...]-⸢x⸣-za
13' [...]-zu(-)ME
14' [...-g]a$^{?}$-NI
15' [... Ur$^{?}$]-^{giš}gígir
16' [...]-si$_{4}$
17' [...]-KAL
18' [...]-DU
[...]

obv. II
1' 1 [(-x)]-⸢x⸣-⸢UR⸣-[...]
2' dumu Puzur$_{4}$-[...]
3' kaskal Ur-^{d}Išta[ran]
4' pap Lú-dingir-⸢ra⸣
5' dumu Sag-dingir išib
6' ^{I}Lugal-gaba
7' 1 Lugal-šu-nir-⸢e⸣
8' dumu Da-da iš[ib$^{?}$]
9' ^{I}Ka$_{5}^{[a(?)]}$
10' ^{I}ÌR-[...]
11' 1 ⸢Ur⸣-l[i]
12' dum[u] ⸢*I*⸣-*lu*$_{5}$-[dingir$^{?}$]
13' ^{I}Ur-[...]
14' 1 Ur-[...]
15' dumu Ì[R$^{?}$-...]
16' ^{I}Ur-[...]
[...]

rev. I
1 pap *Bur-ḫaš* [...]
2 pap Ur-^{d}nin-[...]
3 dumu Ur-^{d}[...]
4 {x}
5 {x}

6 ^{I}Lugal-pa-⸢è⸣
7 [d]umu Da-d[a]
8 [U]r$^{?}$-^{d}Išta[ran]
9 ⸢1⸣ Sipad-uru-[(na)]
10 dumu Lugal-r[a$^{?}$(-x)]
11 ^{I}Ur-⸢x⸣[...]
12 dumu Ka$_{5}^{[a(?)]}$
13 ^{I}Lugal-an-na-[túm]
14 dumu Bar-ra-a[n]
15 ^{I}Lugal-si
16 1 Zag-mu
17 dumu *Ì-lí*-x-x-x
18 ^{I}Inim-kù
19 1 Ur-[x]
20 dumu Si-GAG
21 [...]
22 1 [...]
[...]

rev. II

1 [...]-⸢mu⸣$^{?}$
2 [...]-TA$^{?}$
3 [Lugal$^{?}$]-^{giš}gígir-e
4 [...-]⸢da⸣

5 [U]r-^{d}⸢Ištaran⸣
6 [du]mu ^{d}PA-⸢x⸣-me
7 [ ] Ur-kèš^{ki}
8 [dum]u Lugal-ra
9 [ ] Ur-^{d}ki-ná
10 [...] Me-ság
11 [...] Ne-sag išib
12 [... Lug]al-níg-sa$_{6}$-ga
13 [... L]UL-gu-A[K] DU
14 (blank)
15 [...]-⸢x⸣-KID engar
16 šu-nígin 30-⸢1⸣ guruš 14 šeš
17 šu-nígin 3 guruš-kaskal
4 šeš-⸢kaskal⸣
18 ugula Du-du
19 nu-bànda Níg-UL
20 im-si-sá-a
21 Me-ság énsi-ke$_{4}$
22 [é]-gidri Umma^{ki}-ka
23 [gurum-bi] ì-aka
24 *[qáb]-la* 3
25 [x mu x iti]

Literature

BRIDGES 1981 — S. J. Bridges, *The Mesag Archive: A Study of Sargonic Society and Economy*, Yale PhD. diss.

FOSTER 1982a — B. R. Foster, *Umma in the Sargonic Period*, Hamden.

FOSTER 1982b — B. R. Foster , *Administration and Use of Institutional Land in Sargonic Sumer*, *Mesopotamia* 9, Copenhagen.

FOSTER 1993 — B. R. Foster, "Management and Administration in the Sargonic Period", in M. Liverani (ed.), *Akkad. The First World Empire. Structure, Ideology, Traditions*, *HANES* V, Padova, pp. 25-39.

FRAYNE 1993 D. R. Frayne, *Sargonic and Gutian Periods (2334-2113 BC)*, *RIM Early Periods* 2, Toronto.

GELB-KIENAST 1990 I. J. Gelb - B. Kienast, *Die altakkadischen Königsinschriften des dritten Jahrtausends v.Chr.*, *FAOS* 7, Stuttgart.

KIENAST-VOLK 1995 B. Kienast - K. Volk, *Die sumerischen und akkadischen Briefe*, *FAOS* 19, Stuttgart.

OWEN 1995 D. I. Owen, "Amorites and the Location of bàd^{ki}", in K. Van Lerberghe - A. Schoors (eds), *Immigration and Emigration within the Ancient Near East*, Fs. E. Lipinski, *OLA* 65, Leuven, pp. 213-219.

SALLABERGER 1996 W. Sallaberger, "Zur frühen mesopotamischen Briefliteratur", *OLZ* 91, pp. 389-407.

RASHEED 1981 F. Rasheed, *The Ancient Inscriptions in Himrin Area*, Baghdad.

STEINKELLER 1984 P. Steinkeller, *Old Akkadian Miscellanea*, *RA* 78, pp. 83-88.

STEINKELLER 1992 P. Steinkeller, *Third-Millennium Legal and Administrative Texts in the Iraq Museum*, Baghdad, *Mesopotamia Civilizations* 4, Winona Lake (with hand copies by J. N. Postgate).

STEINKELLER 1999 P. Steinkeller, "Land-Tenure Conditions in Southern Babylonia under the Sargonic Dynasty", in B. Böck - E. Cancik-Kirschbaum - Th. Richter (eds), *Minuscula Mesopotamica. Festschrift für Johannes Renger*, *AOAT* 267, pp. 553-571.

VAN DRIEL 2000 G. van Driel, "Institutional and Non-Institutional Economy in Ancient Mesopotamia", in A. C. V. M. Bongenaar (ed.), *Interdepency of Institutions and Private Entrepreneurs (MOS Studies 2)*, *PIHANS* 87, Leiden, pp. 5-23.

VISICATO 2000 G. Visicato, *The Power and the Writing. The Early Scribes of Mesopotamia*, Bethesda.

WESTENHOLZ 1999 A. Westenholz, "The Old Akkadian Period: History and Culture", in P. Attinger - M. Wäfler (eds), *Mesopotamien. Akkade-Zeit und Ur III Zeit*, *OBO* 160/3, pp. 17-117.

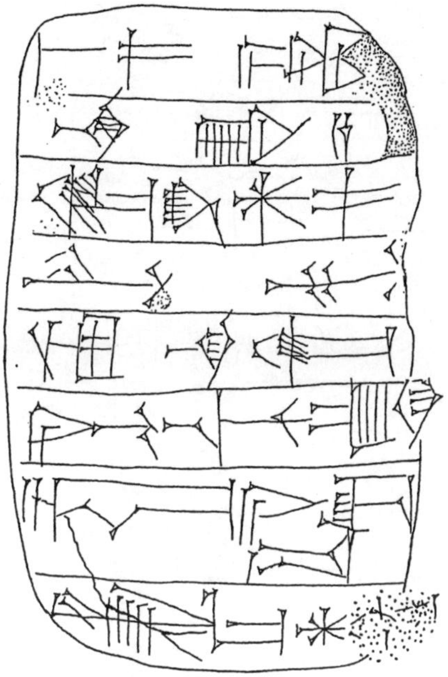

BM 140676 obv.

BM 140676 rev.

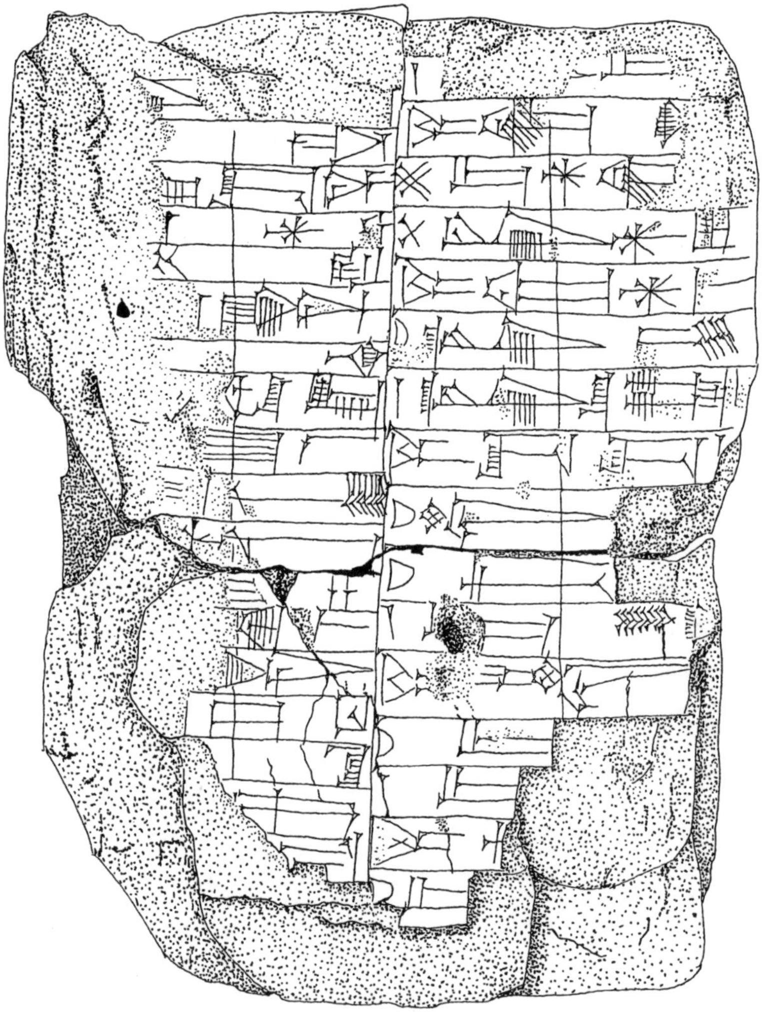

BM 140668 obv.

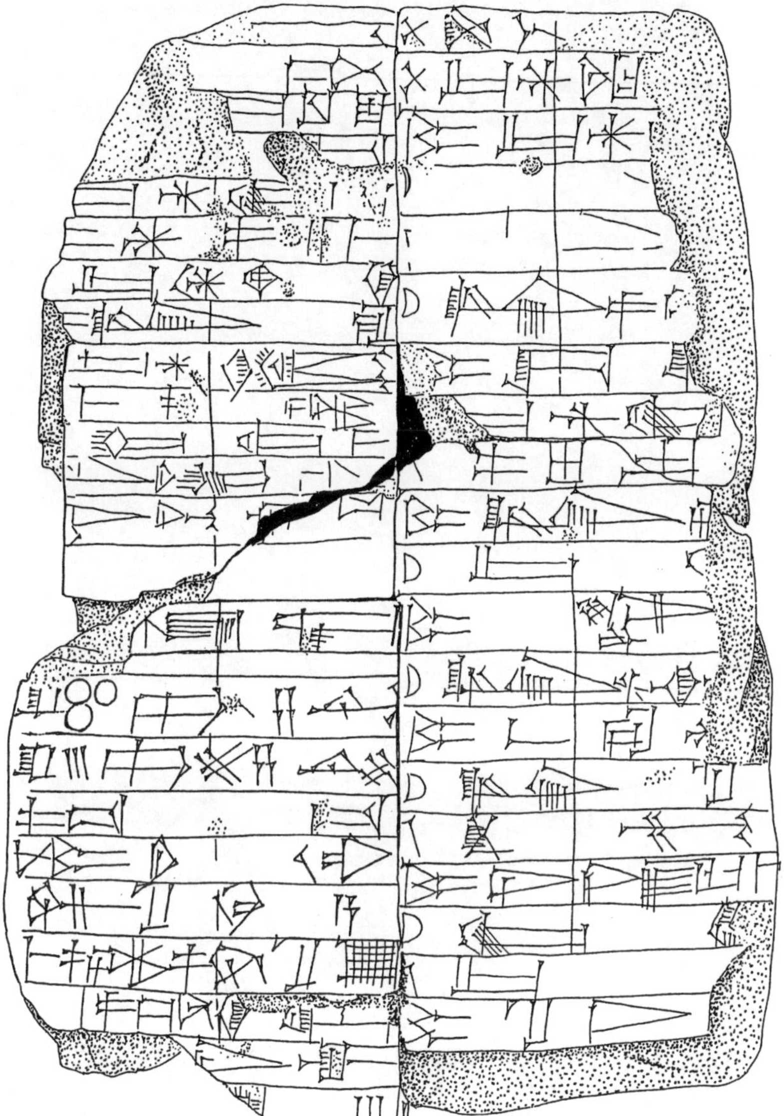

BM 140668 rev.

BM 140668 obv.

BM 140668 rev.

IL *PENNSYLVANIA SUMERIAN DICTIONARY* E IL SUMERICO DI EBLA

GIOVANNI CONTI

Università di Firenze

Fin dalla pubblicazione del suo primo volume (B) nel 1984 il *PSD* ha mostrato attenzione per le notizie derivanti dai testi di Ebla, riportando i duplicati dei testi lessicali già noti da Fara, editi in *MEE* 3, citando anche, senza commenti e senza bibliografia, la lista lessicale bilingue, edita in *MEE* 4, tra le fonti bilingui sumero-accadiche.

Con l'avanzare della pubblicazione, del *PSD* come dei testi di Ebla, l'interesse del *PSD* si è allargato, e vi sono talora anche segnalate attestazioni di un sumerogramma nei testi economici, seppur con molta parsimonia.

Così nel *PSD* A/1, p. 207, sono citate alcune attestazioni di **a:zu$_5$** (e varianti) e **a:zu$_5$-mí** nei testi economici di Ebla; l'elenco però non è completo, e non dà piena ragione della diffusione di questo nome di professione.[1] Sulle implicazioni della variante AZU.E rimane prudente (p. 208). Ma non è questo l'unico caso ad Ebla di alternanza A/E in determinativi fonetici,[2] e una lettura **e$_4$** per A in questo come in casi analoghi è da supporre con tutta evidenza. Su una possibile lettura ^{e_4}**ezu$_x$**(AZU) (o **e$_4$-zu$_5$**) si veda P. Attinger, in sede di recensione, *ZA* 85 (1995), p. 141. Le particolarità paleografiche di AZU nei testi di Ebla (NINDA*gunû*×/+ME, e la possibilità di un cuneo non canonico iniziale) non vengono segnalate; d'altra parte sono state chiarite solo recentemente da P. Fronzaroli, *ZA* 88 (1998), pp. 225-226, che anche segnala nel testo 75.G.1623 r. I 5 l'uso di **azu** per "trattamento medico" (acc. *asûtu*).

In *PSD* A/2 p.133 è citato solo un caso di AB×ÁŠ-AB×ÁŠ (*MEE* 2, 6 [= *ARET* VII 17] r. II 1) tra tanti (cf. *TIE* A/1, pp. 154-171).[3]

---

1 Per le attestazioni cf. *TIE* A/1, pp. 44-45.

2 Cf. VE 124a-c **níg**-ÈSIR.A-**sá** / **níg**-E.ÈSIR-**sá**.

3 Ma **ab-ba** (*-zú-ti-um*^{ki}) (*MEE* 2, 37 r. VI 11-12) qui inserito dal *PSD* a p. 131, § 8, è piuttosto un NP, v. *ARET* III 197, V 3-5: tessili / **dumu-nita ab-ba** / *zú-ti-um*^{ki}. Cf. M. Krebernik, *Die Personennamen der*

Col procedere della pubblicazione è allargato l'utilizzo delle glosse del VE per collocare meglio un sumerogramma, con bibliografia e proposte originali, che si avvantaggiano di un più sicuro contesto di riferimento. Così in *PSD* A/2, p. 39, il VE 549 **á-ak** = *ga-a-zu* è interpretato "to cut hair (from the body)" per via di un confronto con l'acc. *kâṣu* suggerito da attestazioni OB anche in testi bilingui.

Quando però non vi è una coincidenza lessicale evidente, come in questo caso, l'interpretazione di una glossa non è sempre valutata sufficiente dal *PSD* per considerare un sumerogramma attestato ad Ebla antecedente di un sumerogramma di attestazione successiva.

Così in *PSD* A/2, p. 109, l'interpretazione delle glosse di VE 542 (**á**-TAR = *iš-gi-da-nu* [fonte D]), e di VE 566a (**á**-TAR= [*iš*]-*gim*-[*t*]*um* [fonte D], *iš*$_{11}$-*gi-du-nu-um*/-*núm* [fonti A e B]) come /ʾiṯkitt-ān-um/ "quello che ha un difetto alla spalla" (variante lo "Spalla") (sem. **ṯkm*),[4] possibile sinonimo dell'acc. *akû*, non basta al *PSD* per identificare in **á**-TAR un antecedente di **lú-á-ku**$_5$ = *akû* "storpio", citato poche colonne prima. In alternativa il *PSD* suggerisce per le glosse eblaite un confronto con l'acc. *ašqudānu* "un serpente" (cioè un animale senza arti).

La questione può essere esaminata con un dettaglio non permesso in una voce di vocabolario:

1) *akû*: sono attestate due voci, omofone, ma distinte nell'uso, e nei sumerogrammi corrispondenti (*CAD* e *AHw*):

- *akû* A "povero, debole" (= **ḫu-ur**), attestato dal MB, in testi letterari e iscrizioni reali; ha una possibile etimologia semitica (**hkw/y*) (*DRS*, p. 407, con bibliografia);

- *akû* B "storpio, deforme" (OB/SB), attestato in testi lessicali; non ha una etimogia semitica evidente; è prestito dal sumerico in accadico per l'*AHw*; una formazione artificiale in sumerico suggerita dall'accadico per il *CAD*.

2) *ašqudānum* (Ur III, OB) è attestato solo come NP; viene derivato da *ašqudum*/*asqudum* "un roditore (criceto?)", così detto perché porta (sem. **ṯqd*) il cibo

---

Ebla-Texte, Berlin 1988, p. 137. V. anche gli esempi da inediti citati al proposito da A. Archi, *AfO* 44-45 (1997-1998), p. 275 (**ab-ba a:zu**$_5$; **ab-ba muḫaldim**).

4 P. Fronzaroli, *Niveaux de langue dans les graphies éblaites*, *Studies Leslau*, 1, pp. 466-467.

(nelle guance)[5] (sum. **péš-túm-túm**); è anche il nome di un serpente (sum. **muš-túm-túm**).

3) **á**-TAR: per le citazioni nella lista lessicale eblaita è d'obbligo tener presenti le fonti che lo attestano. Il sumerogramma è riportato dalla monolingue alla voce 566a (cf. *MEE* 15, p. 15); dalla bilingue con glossa *iš*$_{11}$*-gi-du-nu-um*/*-núm* è ripreso nelle fonti A e B alla stessa voce, (fonte C in rottura), e con glossa [*iš*]*-gim-*[*t*]*um* nella fonte D, che ripete qui il sumerogramma che aveva anticipato, con glossa *iš-gi-da-nu*, alla voce 542 (unica tra le fonti). Quindi [*iš*]*-gim-*[*t*]*um* (VE 566a) è una variazione da parte della fonte D, che aveva glossato precedentemente *iš-gi-da-nu,* in maniera analoga dalle fonti A e B in questo posto del VE; *iš* per *iš*$_{11}$ /ʾiṯ/ è una particolarità della fonte D.[6]

Concludendo, il VE ha qui inteso **á**-TAR come "quello senza braccia", e lo ha spiegato "quello simile ad un serpente *ašqudum*", per via di un modello onomastico più tardo (che però è in genere riferito al "criceto")?

Oppure è l'antecedente di un sumerogramma, **á-ku**$_5$, da riferire ad una tradizione attestata solo successivamente in testi lessicali OB, ma da cui potrebbe esser derivato, come suggerisce von Soden, l'acc. *akû* "storpio"?

O invece è da ricercare una diversa soluzione?

Da tener presente l'analisi di M. Civil sui nomi di animali nel VE (*BaE*, pp. 90-93), che ha dimostrato come in 19 casi su 44 (= il 43%) il sumerico vi è attestato in forme altrimenti note solo da liste lessicali più tarde; di questi 19 casi ben 11 hanno una traduzione autonoma. Per questo motivo una traduzione semanticamente compatibile dovrebbe essere indizio, forte quanto una concordanza lessicale, che un sumerogramma presente ad Ebla sia antecedente di un sumerogramma noto solo in testi più tardi.

---

5 *CAD* A/2, p. 340. P. Fronzaroli, *Tre scongiuri eblaiti (*ARET *5, 1-3)*, *VO* 7 (1988) pp. 18-19.

6 Questo uso del sillabario è in contrasto con l'analisi della glossa come *isqu* e *dânu* "to decree a lot", ripresa in *TIE* A/1, p. 47. Per l'unica attestazione di **á**-TAR in un testo economico lì citata v. la lettura corretta in A. Archi, in sede di rensione, *AfO* 44-45 (1997-1998), p. 274 (1 **an-dùl kù-sig**$_{17}$ **á-ku**$_5$ ND... / 2 **an-dùl kù-sig**$_{17}$ **lú á-**⌜**ku**$_5$⌝ ND *wa* ND... [TM.76.G.221]), che propone una traduzione "piedistallo". In mancanza del contesto completo, o di paralleli, l'interpretazione del passo rimane comunque non agevole.

Incrementando questa linea di tendenza, con il progredire della comprensione dell'eblaita, che tanto deve al lavoro di Pelio Fronzaroli, cui questo volume è dedicato, il terzo volume della lettera A del *PSD* perfeziona l'utilizzo del sumerico e dei sumerogrammi ad Ebla, curando, con bibliografia, l'analisi delle voci del VE, ed accrescendo le citazioni di sumerogrammi in testi economici.

Il rapido sviluppo in tempi recenti della pubblicazione dei testi di Ebla, e della loro analisi, non ha permesso sempre la completezza delle citazioni e della bibliografia. Questo vuole essere il nostro contributo al volume. Analizziamolo in dettaglio.

ad-$GI_4 \times GI_4$ (pp. 5 e 18)

Le attestazioni di **ad-gi$_4$-gi$_4$** (sic) e **ad-gi$_4$** nel VE (1035 e 1036), non glossate, sono citate unite nell'ambito delle attestazioni di **ad** A "sound", "voice" (p. 5) e di **ad-gi$_4$** (**-gi$_4$**) "advice" (p. 18).

Innanzi tutto **ad-gi$_4$** è attestato ora anche in un testo di cancelleria, *ARET* XIII 15, con significato "consigliere",[7] in accordo con la collocazione suggerita dal *PSD*. Non è però del tutto ovvio che **ad-gi$_4$-gi$_4$** ad Ebla sia variante di **ad-gi$_4$**, come non è sicuro il suo inserimento nello stesso ambito lessicografico; anche se contigue si tratta di due voci distinte da tutte le fonti del VE: **ad-gi$_4$-gi$_4$** (VE 1035), **ad-gi$_4$** (VE 1036). Le fonti bilingui (A e B), anteponendo **ad-gi$_4$**, invertono l'ordine della monoligue; l'ordine di solito osservato è che, in voci semanticamente connesse, i lemmi con secondo elemento raddoppiato seguono i lemmi con secondo elemento non raddoppiato.[8] Non è forse una regola rigida,[9] ma è comunque una forte linea di tendenza. È quindi legit-

---

7 Cf. P. Fronzaroli, *Testi di cancelleria: i rapporti con le città*, Roma 2002 (= *ARET* XIII).

8 Così VE 61-62 (**níg-du$_{10}$ / níg-du$_{10}$-du$_{10}$**), 63-64 (**níg-lu / níg-lu-lu**), 70-71 (**níg-sig / níg-sig-sig**), 73-74 (**níg-kar / níg-kar-kar**), 76-77 (**níg-sal / níg-sal-sal**), 553-554 (**á-du$_7$ / á-du$_7$-du$_7$**), 800-801 (AN.EN / AN.EN.EN), 938-939 (**dug-gur$_4$ / dug-gur$_4$-gur$_4$**), 1048 (**zi-du$_8$ / zi-du$_8$:du$_8$**), 1131-1132 (**ù-sá / ù-sá-sá**).
L'ordine inverso si ritrova in lemmi senza un rapporto, con valori e significati diversi, come in VE 38-39 (**níg**-LAGAB+LAGAB / **níg**-LAGAB, da intendere **níg-nigin / ninda-gur$_4$**), o in VE 89-90 (**níg**-NE.NE / **níg**-NE, dove il primo lemma è tradotto come "braciere" (*ga-nu-na-tum*), il secondo è attestato nei testi economici come designazione di una sostanza (*ARET* VII, p. 230, *MEE* 10, p. 168).

9 V. 574-5 (**šà-dab / šà-dab-dab**, ma la monolingue è in rottura).

timo prendere in considerazione la possibilità che i sumerogrammi facciano riferimento a realtà diverse. Ci potremmo anche domandare, in via di ipotesi, se la bilingue non abbia voluto correggere la monolingue, o non la abbia reinterpretata e riorganizzata.

Nella monolingue i due GI_4, per economia di spazio, sono sovrapposti, almeno nella fonte A disponibile in foto;[10] diversamente nella bilingue, nella fonte B (foto) come verosimilmente nella fonte A,[11] il secondo segno è in realtà $GI_4 \times GI_4$. È ormai stabilito che $GI_4 \times GI_4$ nei testi presargonici e sargonici è variante di LAK 173, e, per lo più con determinativo fonetico **e**, designa una coppia di sandali, e gli è stato attribuito il valore **esir**$_x$.[12] Appare anche connesso, nella lista lessicale bilingue eblaita, col significato "legare attorno".[13] Le due voci vanno quindi tenute separate, e **ad**-$GI_4 \times GI_4$ trova una collocazione preferibile nell'ambito di **ad** C, vocabolo attestato in sumerico in composti che fanno riferimento a parti del giogo: **ad-gú**, **ad-tab**, **ad-lá**. A conferma **ad-tab** e **ad-lá** sono anche citati nelle due voci successive del VE.

Il filo conduttore del contesto lessicografico è qui nella definizione di tipi particolari o parti del giogo o delle briglie, vocaboli in genere derivati da un significato "legare". Ciò trova conferma in una ulteriore attestazione di $GI_4 \times GI_4$, poco sopra, dove il VE (1032) traduce **gú**-$GI_4 \times GI_4$ con *gú-bí-lum/-lu-um*, una sorta di "legaccio" (del collo), se da accostare all'acc. *kapālum* "avvolgere" e a quell'insieme di radici

10 V. S. A. Picchioni, *MEE* 15, tav. II.

11 Cf. *MEE* 4 p. 8 (**gi**$_4$**:gi**$_4$ nella nota, ma **gi**$_4$×**gi**$_4$ nella trascrizione del testo a p. 7), con rimando alla nota a p. 5 ad r. IV 9 per la descrizione del segno ($GI_4 \times GI_4$).

12 P. Steinkeller, *On the Reading and Meaning of* $GI_4 \times GI_4$ *and LAK-173*, *AfO* 28 (1981-1982), pp. 140-141; dello stesso *Third-Millennium Legal and Administrative Texts in the Iraq Museum, Baghdad*, Winona Lake 1992 (= *MC* 4), p. 75.
Oltre gli esempi raccolti da P. Stenkeller, dopo, v. $^{e}GI_4 \times GI_4$, *šēnum* "Sandale", in B. Kienast - K. Volk, *Die sumerischen und akkadischen Briefe*, Stuttgart 1995 (= *FAOS* 19), s. v.; I. J. Gelb - P. Steinkeller - R. M. Whiting, *Earliest Land Tenure Systems in the Near East: Ancient Kudurrus*, Chicago 1991 (= *OIP* 104), p. 296; a Ebla VE 1323' ^{e}**esir**$_x$ = *sa-na* (duale) (M. Civil, *Bilingualism in Logographically Written Languages: Sumerian in Ebla*, *BaE*, p. 78).

13 M. Civil, *Studies on Early Dynastic Lexicography III*, *Or* 56 (1987), p. 237.

semanticamente vicine, anche se differenziale espressivamente, quali l'occ. **kbl* "catena, incatenare",[14] e l'ar. *qabala* "legare le scarpe".[15]

La voce seguente **gú-giš-gál** (VE 1033) non è tradotta; ma se l'inserimento in questo contesto della lista lessicale eblaita non è del tutto immotivato, dovrebbe essere un antecedente di quel **gú giš-gál** attestato in Urnanše 20, e in Gudea, Cil. A, Cil. B e St. D, indicandone il significato in quei passi; uno per tutti: Cil. A XV 8: **má-gan me-luḫ-ḫa kur-bi-ta gú giš mu-na-ab-gál** "Magan e Meluḫḫa, (discendendo) dalle loro montagne, si sono sottomesse a lui (= hanno messo il giogo sul (loro) collo per lui)".

ad-KID (pp. 20-23)

Il vocabolo, come segnala il *PSD*, è di larga attestazione nei testi presargonici e sargonici. Anche ad Ebla, oltre che nei duplicati dei testi lessicali sumerici, editi in *MEE* 3 (citati a p. 22), è attestato almeno una volta in un testo economico, TM.75.G.1743 v. VIII 19 (citato in M. G. Biga, *WGE*, p. 163), nel contesto di assegnazioni di lana a vari personaggi femminili:

(17-19): 11 KIN-siki gi_6-bar_6 / 11 dumu-mí / ^{ad}$adgub_x$(KID).

Quanto alla lettura del nesso, è da osservare che il corrispondente accadico, *atkuppu*, non è comunque semitico; da A. Salonen, *Die Fussbekleidung der alten Mesopotamier*, Helsinki 1969, p. 117, un vocabolo /adkub/ viene riferito al sostrato calcolitico.

La lettura **ad-kub**$_4$, abbastanza comune in letteratura, derivata dall'ipotesi che l'acc. *atkuppu* sia prestito dal sumerico, non è però considerata provata dal *PSD* in mancanza di esempi di uso autonomo di **kub**$_4$. L'ipotesi di una lettura ^{ad}**adgub**$_x$(KID), suggerita da P. Steinkeller, *FAOS* 17 (1989) p. 171, supera questa obiezione, supponendo per lo stesso segno due letture, una per il lavorante, un'altra per il frutto del suo lavoro, **adgub**$_x$ "chi intreccia stuoie di canne", e **kin** (> acc. *kîtu*) "la stuoia di canne".

14 Per le attestazioni *HALOT*, pp. 458-459; prestiti dall'aramaico nelle diverse ligue semitiche, v. la bibliografia in W. Leslau, *CDG*, p. 274.

15 Che H. Grimme, *ZDMG* 55 (1914), p. 261, avvicina al ge. *q^{w}alapa* "legare, incatenare", v. *CDG*, p. 429.

Così come ŠIM×NÍG è da intendere contestualmente **lùnga** "birraio", o **bappir** "pane di birra"; analogamente ŠIM = **lunga** o **báppir**.[16]

ad-gar B (p. 17)

Attestato solo nel VE (174). L'interpretazione della glossa *sa-da-um* (sem. **š'l* "domandare", acc. *šitūlu*) non è giudicata sufficiente per considerare questa attestazione nel VE antecedente del più tardo **ad-gar** (= **ad-gar** A) = *māliku*, **ad-mar** (ES) = *šitultu*, da cui è tenuto separato.

ad-lá (p. 23)

Solo nel VE (1038). L'identificazione del sumerogramma, di attestazione presargonica, come designazione di un tipo di bardatura, è confermata per l'attestazione eblaita dal contesto lessicografico, v. sopra **ad**-GI_4×GI_4. In tal caso la glossa *ù-nu-ù-núm* potrebbe esser considerata variante (schema 1212) di *ù-nu-nu*, glossa di **giš-éš-nu-éš**, /ʿunūnu(m)/, ar. *ʿinān*, *ʿunun* (pl.) "briglie".

ad-tab (**ad** C 3 [**ad-tab**], p. 7)

ad-tab, come segnala il *PSD*, è largamente presente nei testi presargonici e sargonici.[17]

Tra le attestazioni di **ad-tab** è da inserire l'attestazione del sumerogramma nel VE (1037: **ad**-2), identificata da H. Waetzoldt;[18] è glossata *lu-bù-ga* dall'EV r. Il sumerogramma non è attestato negli altri testi di Ebla pubblicati, che hanno invece frequentemente **níg-anše-aka** o una grande varietà di grafie fonetiche, *lu-bù-gu*, *lu-bù-gù*, *lu-bù-ga*, *lu-ba-ga*, *ru*$_{12}$*-bù-ga* (duale), sem. **rbq* "attaccare (animali)" (v. *MisEb* 4, p. 45).

---

16 Per la lettura /lunga/ v. M. Civil, *A Hymn to Beer Goddess and a Drinking Song*, *Studies Oppemheim*, p. 88.

17 V. inoltre I. J. Gelb - P. Steinkeller - R. M. Whiting, *OIP* 104, p. 296. Anche nel testo in questione, *OIP* 104, Appendix to no. 32 (= D. A. Foxvog, *Funerary Furnishings*, *Mesopotamia*, 8 [1980], pp. 67-65) III 5 il collare decorato (**za-gìn**) è verosimilmente un collare del giogo.

18 *Die eblaitische Entsprechung und die Bedeutung von* **nì-anše-aka**, *NABU* 1990/96.

giš-ád (**ád** A 2, p. 26)

giš-ád è attestato nel VE 436, con la traduzione *a-da-tum* che ne conferma la lettura e il significato, acc. *eddittu*. È anche attestato più volte nei testi economici. Il contesto completo del solo testo economico citato è:

MEE 2, 3 = *ARET* IV 4 v. VIII 18-21: 20 KIN-siki / níg-sa_{10} / giš-ád / NP.

giš-ád è attestato un'altra volta sempre nel contesto "quantità definita di KIN di lana / **níg-sa_{10}** / di una quantità non definita di **giš-ád**": *ARET* I 13 v. X 15-16; questa procedura contabile è di regola usata per sostanze coloranti, profumi e resine. Una interpretazione in tal senso è confermata da diversi testi di *ARET* IX, per esempio:

ARET IX 80 r. I 1-2: 10 *gú-bù* ì-giš giš-ši[m] / 10 *gú*-[*bù*] ì-[giš] giš-ád;

v. anche 80 r. III 1-2; 84 v. V 1-6; 94 r. IV 1-3; 103 r. I 1-II 1). E ancor meglio da TM.75.G.577 v. V 1-4 (citato in *MARI* 5, p. 530, n.46):

50 sìla ì-giš du_{10} / giš-šim / *wa* / giš-ád.[19]

addir (p. 32)

Da aggiungere la variante BI.GIŠ.A, in TM.75.G.2420 (Trattato di Abarsal) v. V 16, nel contesto **addir**(BI.GIŠ.A)**-má-gal** "traghetto", come già riconosciuto da E. Sollberger, *SEb* 3 (1980), p. 142; inoltre D. O. Edzard, *QuSem* 18, pp. 202 (che non traduce) e 217 n. n. (copia del segno). L'interpretazione è confermata da P. Fronzaroli, *ARET* XIII, pp. 66-67, e 240 s. v. **addir**(GISAL:A)**-má-gal**. Cf. ^{giš}**má-addir** = *nēberu*.

àga (**aga** B, p. 40)

Il sumerogramma **àga** come designazione di un'ascia è attestato largamente nei testi economici di Ebla; sono ricordati i tipi: 1) normale, 2) **gal**, 3) **gal-maḫ** (*MEE* 12, 35 v. VII 36), 4) **gal-tur** (*MEE* 10, 20 r. XIII 29), 5) **tur**, 6) **urudu** (*ARET* III 335 r. IV 1), 7) **tur-urudu** (*ARET* VII v. II 4); l'identificazione con un attrezzo è confermata

19 Cf. L. Milano, *Food Rations at Ebla*, *MARI* 5 (1987), p. 530.

dal trovarsi in serie complete di attrezzi da falegname, v. *ARET* III 356 r. I 1: x+2 **àga-gal** 4 **àga** 4 **dub-nagar** 4 **šum**; v. anche *ARET* I 13 r. IX 17-X 1; *ARET* III 95 r. I 5' [**àga-tur**]; *ARET* III 526 r. VI 2'; *MEE* 2, 50 v. I 8; *MEE* 10, 29 r. IV 27; TM.75.1233 r. I 4-7.

àga (p. 48)

Da inserire un rimando per **àga** come grafia presargonica di **a-ga** "retro, (stanza) posteriore" (notazione peraltro omessa anche in *PSD* A/1, p. 68), identificata da M. Civil - G. Rubio[20] negli incantesimi *ARET* V 8b // *ARET* V 9, nel contesto VII 5-6: KUR **igi**-*sù* / KUR **àga**-*uš* // II 2-3: KUR **igi**-*sù* / KUR **àga**-*sù*.

àga-kár(ŠÈ) A (p. 49)

àga-ŠÈ è considerato dal *PSD* variante di **àga-kár**,[21] il che ne conferma il significato "sconfiggere, battere" che in genere gli viene attribuito.[22] Nei testi di Ebla è attestato in contesti del tipo:

ARET VII 115 v. II 1-6: *in* / mu / *ma-rí*^{ki} / àga-ŠÈ / *áš-ti* / *'à-ti-ni*^{ki} "nell'anno in cui NL fu battuto presso NL".

MEE 12, 25 r. III 3-5: argento / níg-AN.AN.AN / lugal DU^{ki} / àga-ŠÈ "argento per (il latore del)la notizia[23] che il governatore di NL era stato sconfitto". Analogamente, nello stesso testo, r. X 1-8.

TM.75.G.2367 r. I 9-II 4, e *passim*, in contesti del tipo: NL / (*ù* NL) NP / en / *ma-rí*^{ki} / àga-ŠÈ "NP, re di Mari, ha sconfitto NL (e NL)".[24]

---

20 *An Ebla Incantation against Insomnia and the Semiticization of Sumerian: Notes on ARET 5 8b and 9*, *Or* 68 (1999), pp. 256-257.

21 Per la possibilità v. già B. Kienast, *Der Feldzugsbericht des Ennadagān in literarhistorischer Sicht*, *OA* 19 (1980) pp. 257-258.

22 F. D'Agostino, *Proposta di interpretazione del testo ARET 2, 29*, *OA* 29 (1990), p. 55, con bibliografia.

23 Per questo significato di **níg**-AN.AN.AN(.AN) v. in questo volume W. Sallaberger, *Nachrichten an den Palast von Ebla. Eine Deutung von* níg-MUL-(AN), § 3.

24 Edizione di G. Pettinato, *Bollettino militare della campagna di Ebla contro la città di Mari*, *OA* 19 (1980), pp. 238-242; per l'interpretazione v. B. Kienast, *OA* 19 (1980), pp. 247-261; dello stesso *Zum Feldzugsbericht des Ennadagān*, *OA* 23 (1984), pp. 19-32; D. O. Edzard, *Neue Erwägungen zum Brief*

àga-kár(ŠÈ) B (p. 50)

Successivamante è citato, distinto dal precedente, un secondo **àga-kár**(ŠÈ), con significato "raid". È attestato unicamente ad Ebla; il solo testo riportato è *MEE* 2, 37 r. IV 9-12: (tessuti) / **àga**-ŠÈ / 1 ÉREN-BAR.AN / NP, con la traduzione "per la razzia de 1 mercenario"; ma per **sur**$_x$-BAR.AN (**éren-bar-an**) il significato "pariglia di equidi B." ormai è accertato,[25] e la traduzione riportata dal *PSD* sarà da intendere "per la razzia di una pariglia di equidi B.".

E non è una attestazione isolata; **àga**-ŠÈ si trova spesso riferito ad animali, e gli è stato attribuito il significato "macellare",[26] che non lo differenzierebbe di molto da TIL, cui talora si oppone; per esempio:

TM.75.G.1630 r. II 3-5: *li* 3 *mi* 60 udu nídba / 8 *mi* udu ug$_7$ / 7 *li* udu àga-ŠÈ "4360 ovini offerti (in sacrificio), 800 ovini morti, 7000 ovini ..." (e *passim* nel testo).

Per questi 7000 ovini il significato "razziati", già ipotizzato dubitativamente da G. Pettinato, in alternativa a "macellati",[27] è una possibilità contestuale migliore, che trova conferma nei testi di cancelleria, elaborati da P. Fronzaroli, che precisa "rapinare, portar via (illegalmente)".[28] Per **àga**-ŠÈ riferito a **udu-udu**, v. tra altri esempi *ARET* VIII 534 r. V 1'-2', r. VIII 5'-6'; e poi:[29]

MEE 2, 41 r. V 12-VI 4: (tessuti ad altro) / NP / níg-AN.AN.AN / àga-ŠÈ / udu-udu / NP "(tessuti e altro) per NP, latore della notizia della razzia delle pecore di NP";

TM.75.1317 r. XI 3-12 (citato da A. Archi, *SEb* 1 [1979], pp. 110-111): (tessuti) / NP / *ì-mar*^{ki} / níg-AN.AN:AN.AN / *mar-tu*^{ki} / TIL / *wa* / udu / *-sù* / àga-ŠÈ "tessuti per NP di Imar, latore della notizia che i Mardu erano stati uccisi e i loro ovini razziati".

---

des Enna-Dagan von Mari, *SEb* 4 (1981), pp. 90-95; A. Archi, *I rapporti tra Ebla e Mari*, *SEb* 4 (1981), pp. 129-131.

25 Tra gli altri recentemente, H. Waetzoldt, *MEE* 12, p. 100; sugli equidi ad Ebla v. A. Archi, *Note on the equids at Ebla*, *Subartu* 4/2 (1998), pp. 11-12; per l'equide BAR.AN (**kúnga**) in ambito siriano cf. W. Sallaberger, *Subartu* 2 (1996), p. 175.

26 Cf. F. D'Agostino, *OA* 29 (1990), p. 46, con bibliografia.

27 *Il calendario semitico del 3. millennio*, *OA* 16 (1977), p. 262.

28 *ARET* XIII, pp. 110 e 241.

29 Per altre attestazioni da inediti P. Fronzaroli, *SEb* 3 (1980) p. 43. Recentemente H. Waetzoldt, *MEE* 12, pp. 190-191 ("attaccare").

Non è del tutto sicuro che vi sia motivo di tenere queste attestazioni separate dalle precedenti.[30]

àga-ús (p. 51)

àga-ús: il vocabolo è attestato anche in *ARET* IV e IX, *MEE* 2, 7 e 12 (33 r. III 4 e 8: *n* **gu$_4$-gu$_4$ àga-ús**); da espungere l'attestazione (p. 51, 1.2) *MEE* 1, 718 (= TM.75.G.1279); il testo è ora pubblicato (con foto) in *ARET* VII 115, ed è citato sopra, con la lettura corretta **àga**-ŠÈ. Per altre attestazioni v. *TIE* A/2, pp. 3-4.

È attestato anche in *ARET* V 6 III 2 // OIP 99, 326 II 8 (= *redû*).[31]

agrig (p. 62)

Il testo 75$^{!}$.G.2342, citato a p. 62, 1.4 (testi economici), non è un testo economico, ma la nota lettera di Ḫamazi, in semitico, con sumerogrammi, già pubblicata da G. Pettinato, *RBI* 27 (1977), pp. 238-240, ora in *ARET* XIII 3. Sul documento v. anche P. Fronzaroli, in *Ebla. Alle origini della civiltà urbana*, Roma 1995, p. 357.

agrig è attestato anche in TM.75.G.1444 v. VII 12 (D. O. Edzard, *SEb* 4 [1981], p. 45).

en-nun-ak (s. v. **ak** 8.50 [pp. 81-82] e Lex. 44 [p. 122])

A p. 122 sono riportate le attestazioni di **en-nun-ak** nei testi lessicali, ma a pp. 81-82 si può ora segnalare che **en-nun-ak** "sorvegliare, sorvegliante" è attestato anche come sumerogramma nel rituale di *ARET* XI 2 v. IV 11 (10-13): *wa* / **en-nun-ak** / **u$_4$ è** / ^{d}**utu** "E sorvegliamo il momento del sorgere del sole", e in testi economici, come *ARET* III 272 r. III 2' e 468 r. IV 16, e con la variante **en-nu-aka** in *ARET* IV 15 r. VII 6.

---

30 Nell'opinione di P. Fronzaroli, *ARET* XIII, p. 41, la serie **àga**-ŠÈ / TUM×SAL / **nam-ra-ak** (*MEE* 3, 44, r. IV 3-5) è di ostacolo a questa ipotesi, se da interpretare "vincere - conquistare - prendere come preda".

31 Krebernik, *Mesopotamian Myths at Ebla:* ARET *5, 6 and* ARET *5, 7*, in *QuSem* 18 (1992), pp. 73 e 112.

Inoltre da citare l'attestazione di **en-nun-ak** in OIP 99, 326, per la quale *ARET* V 6 ha il parallelo semitico: **en-nun-ak kalam** // *i-na-sar* TIM.TIM "egli protegge (/yinaṣṣar/) il paese".[32]

é-nam-aka (s. v. **ak** 8.138 [p. 95])

Le attestazioni eblaite di **é-nam-aka** nel VE sono collocate in calce alle attestazioni posteriori di **nam-ak**, di significato incerto, per le quali si propone dubitativamente un significato *šīmta nabû* "proclamare il destino". Difficilmente le attestazioni eblaite possono star qui. D'altra parte anche il passo citato di Gudea, Cil. A XXII 1 potrebbe avere una diversa interpretazione, con lettura **šim-aka** : **muš-maḫ ḫur-sag-gá šim aka-àm** "sono i grandi serpenti della montagna, che annusano".[33]

Nei testi di Ebla **é-nam-aka**, tradotto *na-ba-um*, è attestato nel VE 325; nella fonte D ha le varianti **é-nam-ki** e *na-ba-u₉*. La glossa eblaita è stata collocata da chi scrive[34] nel contesto delle attestazioni di *napālu* "pagare il saldo", che *CAD* (s. v. *napālu* II) e *AHw* (s. v. *napālu* B) differenziano dal più diffuso *napālu* (I/A) "far cadere, mandare in rovina". Quest'ultimo è di attestazione comune; nelle lingue occidentali ha il significato corrente "cadere a terra".[35] L'altro (*napālu* B) è stato confrontato dal von Soden con l'ar. *nafala* "dividere il bottino"; questo significato, con differente adattamento,si ritrova in tigré *nafla* "produrre interessi", *ʾanfala* "avere un utile". È possibile che derivi dal precedente; si ricollega comunque con tutta evidenza con le attestazioni di *napālum* in paleoaccadico e nell'accadico di Mari con significato "strappar via (pietre)",[36] che *CAD* e *AHw* inseriscono tra le attestazioni di *napālu* I/A. Da tener presenti, per una possibile motivazione dell'evoluzione semantica, anche le attestazioni

---

32 Cf. M. Krebernik, *QuSem* 18 (1992), pp. 73 e 112.

33 Cf. W. Heimpel, *Tierbilder in den sumerischen Literatur*, Roma 1968, pp. 482-483. La lettura è suggerita dalla possibilità, in altri casi, di una grafia sillabica **si-im**, per la quale cf. W. W.Hallo, *Lugalbanda Excavated*, *JAOS* 103 (1983), p. 173, l. 297: **ka-ba mu-un-sim** (var. **si-im**) "egli inspira a bocca aperta". Per un contesto analogo a quello in questione v. sotto (p. 103) **muš-ul₄-kur-ra-ke₄ si-im ḫé-em-ši-ak-dè** (Lugalbanda I, 355; 365).

34 *MisEb* 3, p. 119.

35 *ARET* XIII, p. 13.

36 Per l'acc. di Mari v. J.-M. Durand, *ARM* XXVI/1, p. 278 a).

ebraiche di *npl (hi) "attaccare, piombare addosso", "fare un'incursione" (*HALOT*, p. 710, § 8), accanto a "cadere" (qal).

Dal significato "casa depredata, saccheggiata" F. D'Agostino ipotizza un significato "debito?".[37]

Nei testi di cancelleria il sumerogramma è attestato una volta in un passo che ne illustra il significato in accordo con quanto osservato sopra:

ARET XIII 13 (= TM.G.75.2290; il passo in questione era già citato parzialmente in *ARES* I pp. 216-217) r. II 1-10 : *wa* / dam-dam / a-a / *wa* / diri / é en / *in* / *Iš-la*[ki] / é-nam-aka / *wa* / á-dab$_6$ / *am-ma-ak* "e le donne delle acque e l'abbondanza della casa del re in NL li prese come preda, dopo essersene impadronito là".[38]

Nei testi economici **é-nam-aka** è poi attestato in:

ARET VII 142 r. III 1: metallo e oggetti di metallo / é-nam-aka / é / NP.

MEE 7, 38 più volte, nel contesto di apporti mu-DU, nella formula: beni diversi / é-nam-aka / é / NP/NF.

Osserviamo che formalmente in tutti i casi l'oggetto di **é-nam-aka** è la casa (**é**).

Nel testo *MEE* 7, 38, non ostante che alcune rotture impediscano un controllo esatto dei conti, pare che i beni **mu**-DU e i beni **é-nam-aka** siano uniti nella somma finale; si tratterà di apporti volontari e di apporti non volontari; **é-nam-aka** allora "beni portati via (dalla casa)".

NE-**ra** (s. v. **ak** 8.140 [p. 95])

NE-**ra** citato nel VE 853, con glosse *sá-lum*, *sa-ru*$_{12}$*-um*, è riportato in calce alle attestazioni di **ne-ra(-aš) ak**, in opposizione dell'ipotesi di M. Civil,[39] che **ne-ra(-aš) ak** sia variante di **nam-ra(-aš) ak** "fare prigioniero".

Alcune precisazioni sono necessarie: innanzi tutto nella documentazione di Ebla NE-**ra** è attestato, oltre che nel VE, nei testi economici, come denominazione di una categoria di donne,[40] e come sumerogramma nel rituale di *ARET* XI, 2, v. V 15. Il te-

---

37 F. D'Agostino, *MEE* 7, p. 209. P. Mander, *Ebla 1975-*, pp. 401-2 propone "assegnare per decreto".

38 Così P. Fronzaroli, *ARET* XIII, pp. 13 e 137 s. v.

39 *On Mesopotamian Jails and Their Lady Warden*, in *Studies Hallo*, p. 76 n. 11.

40 H. Waetzoldt, *Frauen* (dam) *in Ebla*, *Ebla 1975-*, p. 371; L. Milano, *ARET* IX, p. 398.

sto *ARET* XI, 1, in un contesto leggermente diverso, ha, in semitico *i-da-ga-a*. Quest'ultima forma è stata interpretata dall'editore come derivata dalla radice **nqy*, /ittaqqay/ (*ARET* XI, p. 43) "offre", mentre NE-**ra**, con lettura **bí-ra**, è stato tradotto, dubitativamente "pone" (*ARET* XI, pp. 64 e 78).

Questa interpretazione suggerisce di tener separata l'attestazione in *ARET* XI dalle altre. Difficilmente il primo elemento del sumerogramma che definisce una categoria di persone può essere identificato con un prefisso verbale di coniugazione; ve ne sono esempi nei testi di Ebla, ma relativi a sumerogrammi di forme verbali.

Da verificare la possibilità di una interpretazione del sumerogramma, nell'ambito del suggerimento di M. Civil che **ne-ra(-aš) ak** sia variante di **nam-ra(-aš) ak** "fare prigioniero". In Mesopotamia NE-**ra**, attestato raramente nei testi economici, è per lo più riferito a donne di condizione servile (**géme ne-ra-ak/géme ne-ra-aš-ak**).[41] Ad Ebla **dam** NE-**ra** sono attestate in elenchi di lavoranti diverse; nel testo TM.75.G.2443 segue l'elenco delle SÙ.PA.SIKIL **ama-gi**, forse definizione di "schiave in pegno liberate/reintegrate nello status originario" (v. sotto a proposito di **ama-gi$_4$**). Allora ad Ebla **dam ne-ra** "donne prigioniere", impegnate in lavori pesanti, sarebbe una possibilità non contraddetta dai contesti; **dam ne-ra** possono opporsi a **dam**, come nell'esempio che segue:

TM.75.2443 v. VII 11-16: 30 KIN-siki bar$_6$ / 15 dam NE-ra / é / ^{d}*ku-ra* / 8 KIN-siki / 8 dam-é-^{d}*ku-ra*.

La lista lessicale bilingue eblaita, nella sua parte finale, attesta anche **nam-ra-ak** glossato *ša-la-tum* (VE 1093), acc. *šalālu* "imprigionare, catturare" (sem. **ṯll*), *šallatu* "bottino, prigioniero di guerra".[42] La stessa etimologia è impedita per *sá-lum*, *sa-ru$_{12}$-um* dall'uso del sillabario.[43] Il sumerogramma però non è attestato nei testi economici e di cancelleria editi.

---

41 Cf. le attestazioni citate da M. Civil, *St. Hallo*, p. 76 n. 11.

42 Cf. P. Fronzaroli, *SLE*, p. 150 (con bibliografia).

43 *ru$_{12}$* obbliga l'identificazione di di una seconda (o terza) /r/; *sa/sá* indica la consonante iniziale come un originario /š/, non /ṯ/.

aktum-túg (pp. 134-136)

Il *PSD* omette di segnalare che questo capo d'abbigliamento, il più diffuso nei testi di Ebla, per lo più assegnato assieme all'*ʾà-da-um*-**túg**, può esser descritto per colore o qualità: **aktum-túg**-I, **aktum-túg**-II, **aktum-túg**-I-**gùn**, **aktum-túg**-I-**sa$_6$**, **aktum-túg-bar$_6$**, **aktum-túg-sa$_6$**, **aktum-túg-ú-ḫáb**.

A p. 136 la grafia A.SU (VE 597) è citata unitamente a **aktum-túg** che la precede nel VE. Le due voci vanno però tenute distinte. Una grafia erronea A.SU per **aktum-túg** è attestata, nei testi editi, solo una volta (*ARET* IV 23 v. II 4). Nel volume precedente, lo stesso *PSD*, A/I p. 165, si domandava se per il sumerogramma A.SU nel VE non fosse possibile una lettura **a-kuš** "waterskin". La stessa grafia A.SU si trova in altre designazioni di contenitori:

- VE 632 A.SU.EDIN.TUR, grafia per **kuš**-A.EDIN-**tur** = *ḫi-ba-tum* "un piccolo contenitore per liquidi" (acc. *ḫābû*);[44]

- VE 630 A.SU-**gal** = NE-*a-tum*; per la glossa la lettura *li$_9$-a-tù*, e il confronto con l'acc. *liʾatu* "saliva", proposto da G. R. Castellino e ricordato dal *PSD*, A/I p. 166, è escluso dall'attestazione della medesima grafia nel testo seguente, dove designa con evidenza un oggetto:

ARET III 81 r. II 1'-5': argento / NE-*a-tum* / 3 BAR.AN / NP / šu ba$_4$-ti.

Un confronto possibile è con l'acc. *nādum*, *nayyādum* "otre", attestato dal paleoaccadico, ebr. *nōd*, con indebolimento di *a* pretonica[45] (/nə(y)yādum/, /nə(ʾ)ʾādum/).[46]

giš-al$_6$ C (p. 143)

(Correggi **al** in **al$_6$** qui, come in tutte le altre citazioni da Ebla).

---

44 Oltre a *PSD* cf. M. Civil, *The Early History of HAR-ra: The Ebla Link*, *Ebla 1975-*, p. 149, n. 23; per il sumerogramma v. anche J. Krecher, *Sumerische und nichtsumerische Schicht in der Schriftkultur von Ebla*, *BaE*, p. 166, n. 191.

45 Per l'indebolimento di *a* pretonica v. P. Fronzaroli, *Studies Leslau, 1*, pp. 463-465.

46 I. J. Gelb, *MAD* 3, p. 189, interpreta la grafia ^{kuš}*na-a-du-um* di media ʾ.

Nelle rare attestazioni da Ebla non può indicare un albero, come suggerisce il *PSD*. Difatti **giš-al**$_6$ è attestato anche, come sumerogramma, negli incantesimi *ARET* V 1 e 2, dove definisce l'arma di Hadda. Il parallelo **giš-uš** in *ARET* V 16 (var. di GIŠ-**bar-uš**) conferma che si tratta di un tipo di bastone puntuto, che la glossa semitica nel VE 440, *ma-ša-bù*, precisa "bastone da lancio" /maḫḏap-u(m)/, ar. *ḥḏf* "gettare lanciare", come ha dimostrato P. Fronzaroli.[47]

al$_6$**-tar**-ŠÈ

Il sumerogramma è ripetuto due volte, la prima a p. 155, con lettura **al-tar-ḫun** (da correggere in **al**$_6$**-tar-ḫun**) nell'ambito delle attestazioni di **al-tar** "(lavoro) assegnato" (**al-tar** A); la seconda a p. 156, con lettura **al-tar**-ŠÈ (**al**$_6$**-tar**-ŠÈ), isolata "di significato sconosciuto" (**al-tar** D). Ma la glossa *ar-ša-um*, per cui è citato in bibliografia P. Fronzaroli, *SLE* 139, sembra proprio collocare le attestazioni eblaite nell'ambito di **al-tar** A, se da derivare dall'ar. *rḏl* "essere basso, umile", nell'indicazione di una "forza lavoro modesta", tema del collettivo.

alam (p. 160)

Dovrebbe esser almeno ricordata la possibilità di una grafia **alam**$_x$(KÍD.ALAM) per **alam** "statua", derivata dal Sillabario di Ebla che glossa il segno *la-ʾà-núm* (A. Archi, *The "Sign-list" from Ebla*, *Eblaitica* 1 [1987] p. 95). È più che una ipotesi, dopo la pubblicazione del testo TM.76.G.86 (r. II 6 e 9), dove il sumerogramma deve designare una statua del culto (KÍD.ALAM-*ga* "la tua statua", **igi-sig** KÍD.ALAM "il custode della statua"), cf. P. Fronzaroli, *Divinazione a Ebla*, *MisEb* 4, p. 9; per altri indizi, che confermano l'identificazione, v. pp. 2-3 e p. 13.

Nei testi presargonici KÍD-**alam** è in genere un nome di professione, "lo scultore",[48] e l'uso eblaita è un uso anomalo; non è però senza esempi nei testi di Ebla la

47 Da ultimo *Les combats de Hadda dans les textes d'Ébla*, *MARI* 8 (1997), p. 285, con discussione della bibliografia.

48 Cf., tra gli altri, J. Bauer, *AWL*, p. 344, *ad* III 2; G. J. Selz, *Altsumerische Verwaltungstexte aus Lagaš. Teil 1. Die altsumerischen wirtschaftsurkunden der Eremitage zu Leningrad*, Stuttgart 1989 (= FAOS 15, 1), p. 329.

confusione, in grafia, tra nomi di professione,'e l'oggetto relativo della professione, cf. VE 1331, **nu-kiri$_6$** = *ga-rí-um*, acc. *kirû* "giardino", e **giš-nu-kiri$_6$** usato frequentemente per **giš-kiri$_6$**, in contesti del tipo *in* **giš-nu-kiri$_6$** "nel giardino".

Al difuori di Ebla si segnala forse almeno un esempio nell'iscrizione anonima, forse da Adab, della Walters Art Gallery (= *FAOS* 5/2, Anonym 3, p. 342) l. 5; KÍD.ALAM-**ni** ha un senso se interpretato "la sua statua" per il tramite del Sillabario eblaita.[49]

alim (p. 171)

alim è attestato almeno una volta in un testo economico tra animali diversi, dopo bovini, ed altri, tra cui 14 **az**: TM.74.G.2283 (= *Eblaitica* 1 [1987] p. 122) v. I 3, per un'occasione particolare (**mu**-DU / **níg-mu-sá** / *kéš-du-ut* / **dumu-mí en**).

ama-gal (p. 211)

ama-gal in effetti è riferito per lo più alla madre del re (**ama-gal en**), o ad altri personaggi della corte; v. anche

> TM.2429 (= *MEE* 12, 36) r. XX 4-12: argento / níg-du$_8$ / 1 dam / adab^{ki} / ama-gal / dumu-nita / nar / *áš-da* / *ma-rí*^{ki}.

se da intendere "... pagamento (per) una donna di Adab, madre di un giovane cantante da Mari".[50] Da considerare anche la possibilità di un significato "... riscatto[51] di una donna di Adab per la (/della$^?$) 'grande madre <del re$^?$>', quando i giovani cantanti (vennero) da Mari".

---

49 Così H. Steible - H. Behrens, *Die altsumerischen Bau- und Weihinschriften*. Teil II, Wiesbaden 1982 (= *FAOS* 5/II), p. 342; J. S. Cooper, *Studies in Mesopotamian Lapidary Inscriptions. IV*, *OA* 23 (1984), p. 160. È comunque da ricordare, con F. Pomponio, in sede di recensione a *FAOS* 5, in *AION* 45 (1985), pp. 345-346, che il Sillabario dà la lettura del segno, non il suo equivalente eblaita. La sua affinità con l'acc. *lānum* deriva dall'origine comune (prestito sumerico in accadico), se non è occasionale. Per KÍD.ALAM v. anche I. J. Gelb - P. Steinkeller - R. M. Whiting, *OIP* 104, p. 69, ad *OIP* 104, 19a r. IV 8 .

50 Così A. Archi, *Preposition at Ebla*, *Eblaitica* 4 (2002), p. 15; oppure "1 Frau (aus) Adab (und$^?$) die 'grosse Mutter' des Sohnes des Sängers (ausgelöst) von Mari", con H. Waetzoldt, *MEE* 12, p. 424. Sulla possibilità che **dumu-nita nar** possa designare anche un "discepolo" v. M.V. Tonietti, *La figura del* **nar** *nei testi di Ebla*, *MisEb* 1 (1988), pp. 108-109, che però, per l'esempio di cui tratta, preferisce la soluzione "figlio".

Le poche citazioni note di Adab nei testi di Ebla suppongono Mari come tramite per lo scambio di beni e notizie.[52]

ama-gi$_4$ (p. 210)

Il *PSD* A/III p. 210 colloca le attestazioni di questo sumerogramma nel VE tra le attestazioni di **ama-ar-gi$_4$** "liberare, libertà", e considera la glossa *ma-sa-lu-um* di significato non chiaro, pur rimandando a Krebernik, *ZA* 73 (1983), pp. 37-38.[53] Evidentemente agli autori del *PSD* non sono sembrati adeguati al sumerico né /mayšar-um/ "giustizia" (sem. **yšr*), né /mawšar-um/, acc. *wuššurum* "lasciar andare", *wuššurtum* "liberazione" (**wšr*), quest'ultimo in particolare appropriato al sumerogramma.[54] Lo conferma il fatto che *wšr* 0/2 è attestato in una forma verbale in *ARET* XI 1 v. II 1-8:

> ùz / *gú-li-lum* bar$_6$:kù / gú / ùz / *si-in* / kur^{ki} / *a-li*-NI^{ki} / *nu-wa-sa-ra-si* "una capra, un bracciale d'argento (al) collo della capra, verso la steppa di Alini la lasciamo andare".

Alla grafia sillabica, nel testo 2, corrisponde il sumerogramma GÁ×GÉME-**gi$_4$** "rinchiudere". Lo scriba ha evidentemente confuso: probabilmente ha mal interpreato la forma semitica (cf. *ARET* XI, p. 77); ma anche uno scambio tra segni simili (GÁ×GÉME / GÁ×AN) di uso non frequente potrebbe essere all'origine del fraintendimento.

Per finire, non citate dal *PSD*, sono da ricordare due attestazione di **ama-gi$_4$** / **ama-gi** in due citazioni di testi economici:

Nella prima definisce **dam** nel contesto di **dam-maḫ**, **dam giš-tag**, **dam** *a-si-ra-tum*, **dam** NE-**ra**, **dam-dar**, **dam-aktum-túg**, ecc.:

> TM.75.G.1743 v. IV 1-4 (M. G. Biga, *WGE*, p. 163): 34 KIN-siki bar$_6$ / 17 dam / PA.SIKIL.SÙ / ama-gi$_4$.

Nella seconda una serie di nomi femminili è definita X.PA.SIKIL / **ama-gi**, in un contesto di personale femminile:

---

51 Questo significato del sumerogramma, già suggerito da D. O. Edzard, *ARET* II, p. 135, è ora confermato dai testi di cancelleria, v. P. Fronzaroli, *ARET* XIII, p. 288.

52 Cf. A. Archi, *More on Ebla and Kish*, *Eblaitica* 1 (1987), p. 133 n. 43; *ARES* 1 (1993), p. 147.

53 Analogamente P. Fronzaroli, *Materiali per il lessico eblaita 1*, *SEb* 7 (1984), p. 173.

54 Cf. anche *TIE* A/2, p. 120.

TM.75.G.2443 v. VI 12-VII 9 (M. G. Biga, *WGE*, pp. 166-167): 14 KIN-siki bar_6 / NP_{1-7} / 30 KIN-<siki> / 30 dam-*sù* / 2 KIN-siki / 1 dam-maḫ / 11 KIN-siki / 11 dam-muḫaldim / 24 KIN-<siki> / NP_{1-12} / X.PA.SIKIL / $ama\text{-}gi_4$.

Seguono assegnazioni per **dam** NE-**ra** del tempio di Kura e per **dam** del tempio di Kura.

Nel testo TM.75.G.2443 il segno X è in realtà un SÙ gunuficato nella parte anteriore, all'interno del rombo,[55] come in LAK 233 il segno in esponente, diverso dal SÙ attestato correntemente ad Ebla (come in LAK 233 i segni degli esempi, v. *ARET* II, p. 162), anche nei testi di *MEE* 3 pubblicati con fotografia,[56] e come a Mari presargonica.[57] Comunque sia X.PA.SIKIL / PA.SIKIL.SÙ non può che essere identificato con SÙ.PA.SIKIL che la lista lessicale bilingue eblaita traduce *sa-ba-tum*. Per il tramite del sumerogramma che J. Bauer (*Altor. Not.* 19 [1982], pp. 6 s.) ha letto **sug_x**, designazione dello stelo maturo della spiga dei cereali, *sa-ba-tum* può essere interpretato come /šabal-t-um/ "spiga",[58] nel contesto allora "le donne della spiga" è una possibilità. Nei testi economici però SÙ.PA.SIKIL / PA.SIKIL.SÙ designa un tipo di personale femminile, definito **$ama\text{-}gi_4$** "liberato, reintegrato nello status originario";[59] in alternativa allora *sa-ba-tum* potrebbe anche essere confrontato in via di ipotesi con *sa-bar-tum*, che in *ARET* II 17, r. II 2 designa una categoria di lavoratrici, e che D. O. Edzard confronta con l'acc. *šapartum*, e traduce "Pfandsklavin". Potremmo quindi intendere le grafie SÙ.PA.SIKIL / PA.SIKIL.SÙ **$ama\text{-}gi_4$** / **ama-gi** "schiave in pegno reintegrate nello status originario". Nei testi editi SÙ.PA.SIKIL è attestato ancora solo una volta, sempre nel testo TM.75.G.2443 per definire una serie di NPF / SÙ.PA.SIKIL / **é-en**; queste evidentemente non ancora "liberate".

55 Cortesia di M. G. Biga.

56 Non si applica quindi ad Ebla la differenziazione stabilita da R. D. Biggs, *Semitic Names in the Fara Period*, *Or* 36 (1967) p. 63 n. 2 per i testi di Abu Ṣalabikh, dove il primo è usato per i testi sumerici, il secondo (la forma corrente ad Ebla), per i testi e i nomi semitici.

57 D. Charpin, *Tablettes présargoniques de Mari*, *MARI* 5 (1987), p. 127 e *passim*.

58 P. Fronzaroli, *Il culto dei re defunti in* ARET 3.178, *MisEb* 1 (1988), p. 20.

59 Per questo significato giuridico, contestualmente adeguato alle attestazioni eblaite, v. D. Charpin, *Les décrets royaux à l'époque paléo-Babylonienne, à propos d'un ouvrage récent*, *AfO* 34 (1987), pp. 38-39.

Da queste attestazioni è probabilmente da tener separato SÙ.AN.PA.SIKIL che designa un oggetto di bronzo.[60]

Un'altra attestazione di **ama-gi$_4$** si ha nel testo seguente, inedito, segnalatomi da M. G. Biga:

77.G.730 r. II 10-III 3: (oro) / šub / an-dùl DU / ^{d}*ra-sa-ap* / GIŠ-gu-gíd-kak-šub / ama-gi$_4$ / ^{d}*ra-sa-ap*.

L'esempio isolato non permette una traduzione sicura; ma **ama-gi$_4$** dovrebbe qui indicare la motivazione di un dono per il dio: "... una punta di freccia di fusione (in occasione) della 'liberazione' per ND", o "... una punta di freccia di fusione (da parte) delle (donne) 'liberate' per ND".

Il significato "liberare" è comunque sicuro in un testo di cancelleria, *ARET* XIII 14 r. III 19, riferito ad un personaggio che, avendo pagato il riscatto "(li) lasciò liberi" (*wa* / **ama-gi$_4$**-*sù*).

ama-ug$_5$-ga (p. 217)

ama-ug$_5$-ga oltre che nel VE 1058, = *gi-ba-um*, è attestato anche una volta in un testo economico, in un contesto di tipi diversi di pani:

ARET IX 35 v. I 1-II 2: 2 *mi-at* zíz bar / ninda-si-ga / 60 zíz bar ninda-síki / 30 zíz bar ama-ug$_5$-ga / 20 zíz bar ninda-sikil / ... / še-ba en 1 mu.

60 Un accessorio dello **za$_x$** v. H. Waetzoldt, *OA* 29 (1990) p. 35; *MEE* 10, 29 v. I 1; *ARET* VIII 534 v. VIII 21. Da riportare ad un significato "spiga" (come oggetto di decorazione)?

CONSIDERAZIONI SUL MEDICO EBLAITA E I SUOI STRUMENTI DI LAVORO

FRANCO D'AGOSTINO

Università di Roma

È con grande piacere che dedico questo breve saggio sul mondo della medicina ad Ebla al Prof. P. Fronzaroli, che recentemente si è occupato, con una intuizione filologica ed un'interpretazione veramente magistrale, proprio di un testo farmacologico eblaita, il primo testo con tale carattere, è da sottolineare assieme all'Autore, dell'intera storia vicino-orientale.[1] Si tratta qui di una valutazione preliminare delle informazioni su questo aspetto della cultura eblaita e le deduzioni in esso contenute vogliono essere uno spunto e uno stimolo per uno studio d'insieme sulla medicina nelle culture siriana e mesopotamica, di cui proprio l'analisi di quel testo da parte del Giubilato ci fa intuire la complessità nei rapporti e la vicinanza sia nella struttura che nei fondamenti teorici.

Nella speranza che le mie notazioni possano trovare l'interesse ed apprezzamento del Festeggiato, nelle pagine che seguono si avrà una presentazione dei personaggi qualificati come "medici" e un tentativo di enucleare il loro *status* sociale e professionale, riprendendo in esame infine tutta una serie di oggetti che si trovano nella documentazione amministrativa di Ebla e che sono stati interpretati come strumenti che il medico utilizzava nella sua pratica professionale, con ogni probabilità anche con fini chirurgici.[2]

---

1 Si tratta del testo TM.75.G.1623, che il Giubilato ha edito in *ZA* 88 [1998], pp. 225-239: "A Pharmaceutical Text at Ebla (TM.75.G.1623)" - cfr. *ibid.*, p. 235 sg.; il documento rappresenta un antecedente assai diretto delle molto più tarde serie (para)-farmaceutiche Uruanna e *šammu šikinšu*, dimostrando la profondità cronologica e la dilatazione geografica delle conoscenze mediche che saranno poi parte della tradizione assiro-babilonese (si veda uno schizzo della tradizione scritta su questo argomento in R. Biggs, "Medizin", *RlA* 7 [1990], pp. 623-629 e dello stesso Autore "Medicine, Surgery and Public Health in Ancient Mesopotamia", in J. M. Sasson *ed.*, *Civilizations of the Ancient Near East*, New York, 1995, vol. III, pp. 1911-1924 - d'ora in poi "Medicine"). Ringrazio H. Waetzoldt, che ha avuto la gentilezza di leggere il contributo discutendone con me alcuni punti.

2 Si veda A. Archi, "Lists of Tools", *Fs. W. von Soden*, *AOAT* 240, 1995, p. 7 sgg.

§ 1. I medici di Ebla: la documentazione

A più riprese nella documentazione eblaita si ritrovano personaggi qualificati con il termine "medico", a/e-/:zu$_5$,[3] e di essi i testi offrono una serie di informazioni che ci permettono, pur nella ripetitività delle attestazioni e nella loro laconicità, di tentare di enucleare la fisionomia socio-professionale di questo sofisticato artigiano[4] e il posto che l'arte medica deteneva nella struttura sociale della Ebla della metà del III millennio a.C.

Nella documentazione i personaggi a me noti definiti come "medici" sono i seguenti (citati in ordine alfabetico):[5]

§ 1.1 EN-*gi-iš-ar*

a. ARET 4, 11, v. IV, 1-3: 1 gu-súr-túg 1 aktum-túg 1 íbx3-túg-ša$_6$-dar / EN-*gi-iš-ar* / a:zu$_5$
"(stoffe 1, 1, 1) per ENgi-išar, il medico"
b. ARET 4, 20, r. III, 8-13: 2 aktum-túg 2 íbx3-túg-ša$_6$-dar / EN-*gi-iš-ar* / *ḫa-zi-ir* / a:zu$_5$
"(stoffe 2, 2) per ENgi-išar (e) Ḫazir, i medici"
c. MEE 12, 37 (= *MEE* 1, 1947 = TM.75.G.2508), r. XIX, 4-17: 8 1/2 gín-dilmun nagga / RU *ší-in* / 52 1/2 gín-dilmun a-gar$_5$-gar$_5$ / 1 *ma-š*[*a*]-*wa* / 2 *gú-za-mi-lu* / 3 šum / 3 dub-nagar-sal / 3 *ma-da-gu* / 6 LAK 60-[*al$_6^?$*][6] / 4 LAK 60-tur / EN-*gi-iš-ar*/ a:zu$_5$ / *wa* / maškim-*sù*

---

3 Sulla grafia del termine nei testi eblaiti si veda *TIE* A/1, p. 45 *s.v.* (*ibid.* per le attestazioni, riprese e commentate più oltre) e P. Fronzaroli, *ZA* 88, cit., p. 225 sg. e note relative; da ultimo si veda dello scrivente "Il medico come figura comica presso gli assiro-babilonesi", *RANL*, in stampa, alla nota 9.

4 In *MEE* 7, 48, v. III, 6 e comm. a p. 282 *ad* v. III, 2-9, ho preferito tradurre il termine "a-/:zu$_5$" con "guaritore" (nel caso specifico "guaritrice", per cui v. oltre *ad* § 1.9), parendomi la parola "medico" troppo connotata tecnicamente; proprio la pubblicazione del testo farmacologico, cit. alla nota 1, da parte di P. Fronzaroli però, permette oggi di interpretare il lemma avvertendone tutta la profondità professionale e, per così dire, la solidità dottrinale. In questo saggio, in altre parole, si usa il termine "medico" con maggiore cognizione di causa (si vedano comunque la osservazioni su questa figura professionale di R. Biggs, "Medicine", p. 1918 sgg., e E. Reiner, *Astral Magic in Babylonia*, *Transactions of the American Philosophical Society*, vol. 84/4, 1995, p. 44 sgg.). A questo proposito è però da menzionare ancora VE, l.sin. 216, dove si ha inim-a:zu$_5$ tradotto con *ʾà-za-zu, ʾà-zi-um*, messo in relazione generalmente (G. Conti, *QdS* 17, p. 98 e ancora A. Catagnoti-M. Bonechi, *SEL* 15 [1998], p. 36 sg.) con la radice **ḥzy*, "(pre)vedere, vaticinare": nel suo lavoro, cioè a dire, il "medico" utilizzava pratiche certo non *scientifiche* nella nostra ottica, se il suo "referto" era ottenuto con uso dell'attività magica cui sembra indicare la radice semitica (ma qualche dubbio ancora rimane a mio avviso sull'etimologia della glossa del VE) - v. anche la nota 32 più sotto e le considerazioni in fine di articolo.

5 Le attestazioni, come già sottolineato, sono desunte da *TIE* A/1, p. 45 sg., sino ad oggi l'unico lavoro lessicografico generale e completo sul materiale eblaita.

6 A. Archi, *AOAT* 240, cit., p. 10, nel citare il passo non integra il termine; per la lettura "*al$_6$*", e l'interpretazione semitica, rispetto a "máḫ", peraltro possibile, si veda *TIE* A/2, p. 95 *s.v. al$_6$* I.

"8,5 s.-d. di stagno da fondere con 52,5 s.d. di rame (per fare) 1 pinza$^?$, 2 coltellini$^?$, 3 seghe, 3 ciselli (a punta) fine, 3 pestelli, 6 ... [grandi$^?$] (e) 4 ... piccoli per ENgi-išar, il medico, e i(l) suo(i) assistenti(e)" [7]

Si veda anche, per b, *ad* § 1.3.

§ 1.2 EN-*ma-lik*

a. MEE 2, 37, r. VII, 2-5: 1 túg-NI.NI 1 íbx3:túg:dar / EN-*ma-lik* / a:zu$_5$ / *i-da-ad*-MU
"(stoffe 1, 1) per EN-malik, il medico di Idad-MU".

§ 1.3 ḫa-zi-ir

a. ARET 3, 17, II, 0-6': [stoffe 2; (2; 2)] / [EN-*gi-iš-ar*] / *wa* / *ḫa-zi-⌜ir⌝* / e:zu$_5$ / pa:šeš / *eb-rí-um*
"[stoffe 2, (2, 2) per ENgi-išar] e Ḫazir, i medici, funzionari-P. di Ebrium"

Si veda inoltre *ad* § 1.1, b.

§ 1.4 ìr-ì-ba

a. MEE 5, 5, r. VI, 19-23: 1 gu-súr-túg 1 sal-túg 1 íbx3-túg-dar / *ìr-ì-ba* / NI-*da-tum*^{ki} / a:zu$_5$ / en
"(stoffe 1,1,1) per Ir'iba di Nidatum, il medico del sovrano".

§ 1.5 ìr-kab-ar

a. MEE 2, 7, r. VIII, 20 - IX, 9: 1 *'à-da-um*-túg-2 // 1 aktum-túg 1 íbx3-túg-ša$_6$-dar / *ìr-kab-ar* / a:zu$_5$ / *a*-NI-*a-ù-du* / dam / en / *in* / *a-ru*$_{12}$-*kà-du*^{ki} / šu ba$_4$-ti
"(stoffe 1, 1, 1) Irkab-Ar, il medico di ANIaudu, la sposa del sovrano, ha ricevuto ad Arukadu"
b. MEE 5, 1, v. IV, 6-9: 1 *'à-da-um*-túg-2 1 aktum-túg 1 íbx3-túg-ša$_6$-dar / *ìr-kab-ar* / a:zu$_5$ / *kéš-du-ut*
"(stoffe 1,1,1) per Irkab-Ar, il medico di Kešdut"
c. MEE 5, 5, v. I, 2-4: 1 gu-súr-túg 1 aktum-túg 1 íbx3-túg-dar / *ìr-kab-ar* / a:zu$_5$
"(stoffe 1,1,1) per Irkab-Ar, il medico".

§ 1.6 i-šar

a. TM.75.G.10074, r. XVII, 31-41 (= A. Archi, *AOAT* 240, p. 10): 2 1/2 (gín) nagga / RU *ší-in* / 17 1/2 (gín) a-gar$_5$-gar$_5$ / 1 *ma-ša-wa* 3 (gín) / 1 zàḫ 2 1/2 (gín) / 2 UŠxKÍD 2 1/2 (gín) / <1> *da-bù-um* 3 (gín) / 2 *ma-ša-wa* 2 (gín) / 1 šu-i 2 (gín) / *i-šar* / a:zu$_5$
"2,5 (sicli) di stagno da fondere con 17,5 (sicli) di rame (per fare) 1 pinza (del peso) di 3 (sicli), 1 ago (del peso) di 2,5 (sicli), 2 ... (del peso) di 2,5 (sicli), <1>[8] (piccola) ascia (del peso) di 3 (sicli), 2 pinze (del peso) di 2 (sicli), 1 rasoio (del peso) di 2 (sicli) per Išar, il medico".

---

7 Si veda A. Archi, *AOAT* 240, cit., p. 10 (su questa, e l'attestazione similare di § 1.6, verterà l'analisi nel paragrafo finale, § 3, di questo saggio, cui rimandiamo per la giustificazione delle traduzioni offerte). Per la lettura del del nome, contro EN-*zi-iš-ar* di *AOAT* 240, cfr. ancora H. Waetzoldt, *MEE* 12, 37, comm. *ad* § 50, XIX 14.

8 In Archi, *AOAT* 240, cit. non si ha l'indicazione della quantità (è errore di stampa?), che qui integriamo sulla base del materiale da fusione.

§ 1.7 lu-la-NI

a. ARET 3, 5, v. IV, 6'-8': 1 gu-mug-túg *rí-ga-zi*[9] / *lu-la*-NI / a:zu_5
"1 stoffa gm. con fili di scarto per LulaNI, il medico".

§ 1.8 sine nomine

a. ARET 3, 817, II, 1'-3': [...] íbx3-túg-$ša_6$-dar 2 KIN_x-síg / e:zu_5 / *i-ib-ma-lik*[10]
"[stoffe 1,1,1] (e) 2 balle di lana per il medico di I'ib-Malik"
b. MEE 5, 12, r. III, 3-7: 1 gu-mug-túg 1 sal-túg 1 íbx3-túg-dar / a:zu_5 / du-du / *ši-in* / *'à-ra-ba-*ru_{12}^{ki}
"(stoffe 1, 1, 1) per il medico che si reca ad 'Arabaru"
c. MEE 6, 11 (= *ARET* 4, 13), v. IX, 11: 10 guruš a:zu_5
"(lana) per 10 lavoratori del medico"[11]
d. MEE 10, 30, r. X, 2-7: 3 gu-mug-túg / 1 *NA.S*[I_{11}] / *wa* / 2 dam / a:zu_5 / *eb-*al_6^{ki}
"3 stoffe-gm. per 1 persona e 3 donne del medico di Eb'al".

§ 1.9 ṭù-bí-da-mu, donna medico

a. ARET 1, 1, v. V, 1-7: 2 aktum-túg ti-túg 10 (gín) kù:babbar 2 BU.DI / *ṭù-bí-da-mu* / a-zu_5-mí / *il-'à-ak-da-mu* / *a-*da_5^{ki} / 2 *'à-da-um*-túg-1 2 aktum-túg 2 íbx3-túg-$ša_6$-dar / 2 dumu-nita-*sù*
"2 stoffe-ak., 10 (sicli) d'argento (sotto forma di) 2 spille per Ṭūbī-Damu, la donna-medico di Il'ak-Damu, (proveniente da$^?$) Ada, (e stoffe 2, 2, 2) per due suoi figli"[12]
b. ARET 1, 1, v. X, 10-14: 1 sal-túg 1 íbx3-túg-dar / dumu-nita / *ṭù-bí-da-mu* / a-zu_5-mí / *a-*da_5^{ki}
"(stoffa 1, 1) per il figlio di Ṭūbī-Damu, la donna-medico di Ada"

---

9 Si tratta di una qualifica della stoffa gu-mug-túg, che, oltre a questa, che è la più comune (cfr. *ARET* 4, 12, v. X, 12 *et passim* - si rimanda per la lista completa delle attestazioni al prossimo volume del *TIE* P-R *sub voce*), compare in un testo nella forma *rí-gi-za* (*ARET* 4, 10, v. VIII, 1; v. XIII, 10), e una volta con il segno "zú" finale, *ARET* 3, 137, v. V, 1 - ma mai con il segno "zu" alla fine, come negli indici del volume citato, p. 382, a giudicare almeno da quello che viene poi traslitterato nel corpo del volume stesso. Trattandosi per (gu)-mug di una stoffa di qualità scadente fatta con scarti della lavorazione della lana (cfr. H. Waetzoldt, *UNT*, p. 56 sg. *ad* F e *CAD* M/2, p. 187 sg. *s.v. mukku*), ritengo che il termine qualificante sia da rapportare alla rad. *rks*, "legare, riunire intrecciando", ed è qualifica che va considerata sottintesa se mancante (si tratta quindi di una "stoffa con fili di lana di scarto riuniti, legati insieme e di differente provenienza"); si veda anche J. Pasquali, *QdS* 19, 1997, pp. 261 sgg. ad 21, con ipotesi etimologica identica (ma interpretazione differente).

10 Mi chiedo se non sia significativa la presenza di un *lu-la-il* nello stesso frammento, per cui v. *ad* § 1.7.

11 Si veda anche la nota 15 più sotto.

12 Nonostante la quantità delle stoffe, mi sembra che Il'ak-Damu non sia qui da interpretare come uno dei due riceventi, non essendomi noto un personaggio omonimo legato alla città di Ada.

c. *MEE* 7, 48, v. III, 2-9: 1 aktum-túg / *ṭù-bí-da-mu* / dumu-nita / dam / a:zu$_5$-mí / *a-da$_5$*^{ki} / *ma-lik-tum* / ì-na-sum
"1 stoffa-Ak. (ciascuno) a Ṭūbī-Damu, (v. III, 6-8) la donna-medico di Ada, (v. III, 4: e suo) figlio la regina ha dato".

§ 2. Sullo status *sociale del medico eblaita*

Mi sembra che l'informazione da cui si possa prendere le mosse per identificare la figura socio-professionale del medico ad Ebla sia quella citata in § 1.8, c. La sezione del testo in cui compare l'attestazione citata abbraccia infatti da v. VII, 1 a X, 8, dove si ritrova la somma parziale (an-šè-gú), e riguarda attribuzioni di lana e stoffe per una serie di dipendenti del Palazzo (qualificati *ìr-a*-LUM e guruš ma citati senza un ordine apparente); essa comprende tanto dipendenti di singoli, elencati per nome ed eventuale qualifica,[13] quanto dipendenti di villaggi dell'area eblaita[14] e professionisti,[15] tra i quali appunto compare un "medico". Quindi, se l'interpretazione amministrativa del documento è corretta, nello *staff* del Palazzo reale era presente anche uno o più medici, come è d'altronde il caso a Mari e in Mesopotamia.[16] È da sottolineare che la mancanza nella attestazione del nome personale del medico in questione potrebbe far pensare che si tratti qui di un personaggio dedito a pazienti non abbienti e importanti della corte (benché ciò sia solo un *argumentum e silentio* che può essere smentito dai fatti e dalla constatazione delle ben 10 persone a lui addette); in ogni caso, la sua funzione non aveva una connotazione amministrativa pe-

---

13 Si veda in v. VII, 6-VIII, 13: *i-ti-^{d}aš-tár*, *i-rí-ik-ma-lik*, *bar-za-ma-li*, *ré-ti*, *a-sí-piš*, *ḫáb-ra-ar* (su questo nome v. *MEE* 7, p. 12 *ad* r. VIII, 1), *wa-da-za-ir*, *i-bí-šum*, *gi-a-ša-ru$_{12}$*; v. VIII, 22-IX, 6: *ti-ra-il*, *iš-má*-NI, *kam$_4$-mi*, qualificato ugula, su cui v. anche oltre; v. IX, 20: UR.NE, qualificato sipa; v. X, 2-5: *ma-ma*, *iš-a-ma-lik*, *ab-ra-ḫu*, qualificati ba-za.

14 Si veda in v. VIII, 14-19: *'à-šu*^{ki} (nella regione di Ebla, *RGTC* 12, p. 26 *s.v.* Aḏu), *áb-šu*^{ki} (forse ^{uru}*ap-su-na-a*, *apsny* di Alalakh/Ugarit secondo M. Astour, *WGE*, p. 145 e nota 41, quindi Tell 'Afis, 12 km a nord di Ebla; cfr. anche *RGTC* 12, p. 12 sg. *s.v.* Abḏu per altre proposte di localizzazione), *da-rí-ib*^{ki} (*Atareb*, 30 km a nord di Ebla, A. Archi, *WGE* p. 134 e nota 7; *RGTC* 12, p. 97 *s.v.* Darib).

15 Si veda, oltre al sipa e ai ba-za citati anche per nome e al "medico" riportato nel corpo del testo, al v. IX, 5-19: dumu-nita-dumu-nita-tur, "giovani apprendisti" di *kam$_4$-mi*, citato più su; ABxÁŠ e lú-kar; dumu-nita dumu-nita ir$_{11}$-ir$_{11}$; nar-nar.

16 Si veda R. Biggs, *RlA* 7, cit., p. 624. La traduzione di *MEE* 6, 11, v. IX, 11 è a mio avviso, come già proposto più su *ad* § 1.8, c, "(lana per) 10 lavoratori del medico" - v. anche dubitativamente *ARET* 4, p. 128, dove però è indubbio che la linea non deve essere unita a quella che precede.

culiare, essendo immesso all'interno di assegnazioni a gruppi professionali della più svariata natura.[17]

Va da sé che il sovrano possedeva, come d'altronde la regina e le donne dell'*entourage* reale, un medico personale e di fiducia, del quale i testi menzionano chiaramente il nome. Tale è il caso di Ir'iba, qualificato dal toponimo Nidatum, che è detto "medico (personale) del sovrano" (cfr. § 1.4), ed Irkab-Ar (cfr. § 1.5),[18] il quale è medico personale di ANIaʾudu, detta esplicitamente "donna del sovrano", e di Kešdut, la quale è senza dubbio la sposa del sovrano di Kiš e personaggio di spicco della corte di Ebla.[19] Il fatto che lo stesso personaggio Irkab-Ar sia citato una volta (cfr. § 1.5, c) con la sua qualifica ma senza la presenza di nomi di personaggi della corte può portare, a mio avviso, a due conclusioni differenti; da un lato, infatti, potrebbe trattarsi qui di un momento precedente alla sua nomina a medico delle donne - ma forse non solo, per cui v. oltre - della corte, e dall'altro l'attestazione potrebbe farci invece ritenere che non si tratti di medici personali, legati quindi ad una singola persona, ma di un gruppo di medici che operavano congiuntamente sulle stesse persone. In questo secondo caso la presenza del nome dopo la funzione potrebbe indicare la motivazione della transazione, cioè a dire: "tot a NP_1, il medico, (per avere curato) NP_2".

Assai interessante, riguardo a quest'ultimo personaggio e alla seconda delle due ipotesi prospettate, risulta il passo *ARET* 1, 44, r. IV, 5-20, dove si legge: ku_5 kù:babbar / nì-kaskal / *i*-NI-*Lum* / *ìr-kab-ar* / lú ⌜gig⌝ / 4 maškim-*su* / $sa\text{-}za_x^{ki}$ / du-du

17 Ad ogni buon conto questo, è ovvio, non deve farci immaginare che anche semplici lavoratori o artigiani della corte ricevessero una cura in caso di malattia; a questo proposito è bene sottolineare che a causa della tipologia documentaria di Ebla non siamo a conoscenza del rapporto che legava un medico ad un paziente "qualunque" e quale procedura si seguisse in questo caso.

18 Molti differenti personaggi portano ad Ebla questo nome - oltre al più famoso lugal (cfr. da ultimo G. Pettinato, *La città sepolta*, Milano 1999, p. 202) si ha ancora *ex.g.* un ugula (*ARET* 2, 25, v. I, 1), un ugula-ká (*MEE* 7, 50, v. VIII, 6-7), un *ma-za-lum* definito poi maškim in *ARET* 4, 6, v. IX, 2 sgg.; un pa:šeš di Ebriʾum (cfr. *VO* 10 [1996], p. 65; su questo aspetto si veda anche oltre nel testo) ecc. - ed è quindi difficile comprendere quando nella documentazione senza qualifica si deve ritrovare il "medico" delle nostre attestazioni.

19 Su questo personaggio, spesso citato nella letteratura eblaitologica, si veda *MEE* 7, p. 111 *ad* r. IX, 4-14, con bibliografia precedente. Anche nel passo citato in § 1.8, a, il medico in questione deve aver certo frequentato la corte, se Iʾib-Malik, e non c'è motivo per averne dubbi, è proprio il fratello della importante ed influente ama-gal-en Dušigu (si veda anche la nota 10 più sopra per la menzione di un *lu-la*-NI nello stesso frammento).

/ *ší-in* / *i-bí-sí-piš* / *ší-in* / *na-gàr*^{ki} / *ḫa-zu-lu* / maškim / *du-bù-ḫu*-^{d}*ʾà-da* / šu ba_4-⌜ti⌝, che tradurrei:

"30 (sicli) d'argento per il viaggio di INILum ed Irkab-Ar in occasione della malattia e di 4 loro funzionari-M. del Palazzo che si recano da Ibbi-Sipiš a Nagar, Ḫazulu, funzionario-M. di Dubuḫu-ʾAda ha ricevuto".[20]

L'Editore ha letto il segno in r. IV, 9, dubitativamente come "mi", ma dalla foto (Tav. LIII) sembra che si abbiano dei segni finali che indichino appunto "gig" (c'è bisogno di una collazione chiarificatrice). Questo termine è attestato comunque anche nei Bilingui, in una forma lessicalizzata sotto il gruppo "nì"; si veda infatti VE, l.sin. 100/ 0253: nì-gig, *ni-ki-tù*, *qá-dì-šum*, *ʾà-mu*, per cui si possono richiamare *nikittu*, "stato acuto d'una malattia, crisi",[21] *qadīšum* (ptc. passivo) nel senso primigenio di "ciò che si tiene separato",[22] ed eventualmente la radice **ḥmm*, "essere caldo", intendendo qui la "febbre" di un malato, sintomo spesso legato ad uno stato di crisi o attacco;[23] si tratta di tre traduzioni che "amplificano", come è spesso il caso nei testi lessicali bilingui di Ebla, il significato di un lemma e lo spiegano più che "tradurlo".[24] Nonostante INILum non sia noto nella documentazione eblaita, stante la mia conoscenza, come "medico", mi pare che sia probabile che il passo citato si riferisca ad un viaggio di lavoro di Irkab-Ar a Nagar col fine di curare Ibbi-Sipiš, certo non più giovane se la transazione è gestita da un funzionario di suo figlio Dubuḫu-ʾAda.

---

20 Il viaggio di un medico, che non viene citato per nome, si ha anche in *MEE* 5, 12, r. III, 3-7 (cfr. § 1.8, b), che si reca ad ʾArabaru per uno scopo che non viene specificato ma che con ogni probabilità è legato alla sua professionalità (sul toponimo v. *RGTC* 12, p. 47 *s.v.* Arabar); da notare, come spunto di riflessione, che nella sezione precedente del testo viene menzionata Kešdut.

21 Si veda *CAD* N/2, p. 223 *s.v. ad* 3.

22 Si veda *ex.g. HELOT* p. 872 sg. - e a quest'ultimo proposito si veda dello scrivente "Il medico come figura comica presso gli assiro-babilonesi", *RANL*, in stampa.

23 Si veda *CAD* E, p. 150 *s.v. emmu ad* b, per usi in testi medici e terapeutici (come descrizione di sintomo di malattia); ad Ebla il termine è attestato ancora in VE, l.sin. 637: a-ḫád, *ma-wu ʾà-mu-tum*, per cui v. *TIE* A/1, p. 43 *s.v.* a-UD e *MEE* 7, p. 110 *ad* r. VII, 5. È noto che anche il termine "tu-ra" è stato interpretato nella documentazione di Ebla come "malattia", per cui v. G. Pettinato, *WGE*, p. 308 sgg., ma non esiste a tutt'oggi certezza filologica dell'esattezza di questa interpretazione, considerato che altre ipotesi sono ugualmente percorribili per interpretare i *realia* che la parola nasconde (si cfr. *ex.g.* F. Pomponio, *UF* 24 [1989], p. 297 sgg.).

24 Si veda in generale *StSem* 9, p. 26 sg. Noto a margine che non mi sono noti altri esempi del termine "gig" (né nì-gig) utilizzato con questo significato ad Ebla, laddove il lemma nella documentazione amministrativa significa sempre "frumento".

L'unico "medico" del sovrano che la documentazione ci fa conoscere, come già detto, è comunque Ir'iba, qualificato ulteriormente dal toponimo Nidatum,[25] ma l'antroponimo è troppo comune perché si possa tentare di desumere informazioni dalla documentazione in assenza di qualifica professionale.[26]

Medico di un personaggio la cui valenza sociale ed amministrativa non è troppo nota è poi EN-*ma-lik* (cfr. § 1.2), essendo Idâd-MU un personaggio poco citato nei testi di Ebla.[27] Mi è nota infatti di lui una sola altra attestazione, *MEE* 10, 4, r. VI, 6-13: 4 gín-dilmun kù-sig$_{17}$ / *ni-zi-mu* / 1 díb / *i-da-ad*-MU / lú nidbá ì-giš / 18 gín-dilmun guškin / ⸢1⸣ giš-PI-lá/ dam-*sù*, "4 s.-d. d'oro per la lavorazione a sbalzo di 1 lamina per Idad-MU, l'addetto all'offerta dell'olio, (e) 1 pendaglio per sua moglie" (della donna o moglie si parla ancora nello stesso testo, r. III, 9-12: [ ] guškin / 1 šu-dub / dam / *i-da-ad-mu*): dal passo si evince che si tratta di un personaggio coin-

25 Si veda *RGTC* 12, p. 262 *s.v.* Nidadu(m): importante centro nelle vicinanze di Ebla; di un medico, di cui non viene citato il nome e che viene qualificato dal toponimo *Eb'al*, ricevono stoffe 1 suo dipendente e 2 sue donne (cfr. § 1.8, d). Colgo l'occasione per sottolineare che il toponimo che qualifica un antroponimo non sempre indica la provenienza del personaggio in questione, ma potrebbe anche rivelarsi il luogo in cui il personaggio ha svolto l'attività che fa oggetto della transazione rendicontata (aggiungo, per chiarire ciò che intendo, che *ex.g.* anche i ne-di e i nar seguiti da un nome di luogo possono avere operato professionalmente *in* quel luogo, e non essere *di* quel luogo).

26 A mo' d'esempio, si possono citare le seguenti specifiche legate a questo antroponimo (che non intendono coprire tutta la gamma nota dalla documentazione, ma soltanto sottolinearne la complessità prosopografica) - l'assenza in queste attestazioni del toponimo non necessariamente indica un differente personaggio, non essendo chiaro, a me almeno, cosa indichi la specifica geografica nei vari casi (la provenienza familiare è solo una tra altre ipotesi, per cui v. anche la nota 36 più sotto): ugula erén-bar-an en (*ex.g. ARET* 1, 4, v. IX, 19 sgg.); ugula-erén-bar-an *i-bí-sí-piš* (*MEE* 5, 2, r. IV, 17 sgg.; *MEE* 6, 12 [= TM.75.G.1436], r. III, 10 sgg.); ugula sa-za$_x^{ki}$ (*MEE* 2, 12, r. IX, 9 sgg.); maškim *i-bí-sí-piš* (*MEE* 12, 37, r. XVIII, 28 sgg.); ur$_4$ di Damur-Dašeli, figlia di Reti, é-gi-a del sovrano (*MEE* 5, 9, r. VIII, 24 sgg.); lú ká (*MEE* 5, 4, v. VI, 8 sgg. *et passim* senza lú nella documentazione); lú-kar (*MEE* 10, 3, v. II, 4 sgg.) ecc. Inoltre un personaggio con tale nome è uno dei lugal dello stato eblaita (*ex.g. MEE* 7, p. 149 *ad* testo 30) e viene detto maškim di varie altre persone di rango elevato. A solo titolo di informazione si può ancora citare il passo seguente, *MEE* 12, 36, r. XXX, 2-9: 5 gín-dilmun kù:babbar / nì-kaskal / *ìr-ì-ba* / ugula-erén-bar-an / en / du-du / *ši-in* / *na-gàr*^{ki}, laddove la motivazione del viaggio di Ir'iba, che nel passo manca, può esser messa in relazione al passo relativo ad Irkab-Ar citato più su: in assenza di conoscenza sulla professionalità di un "medico", non si può escludere *a priori* che la qualifica di ugula-erén-bar-an (en) sia detenuta contestualmente dalla stessa persona (è solo ipotesi in vista di una prosopografia generale della documentazione eblaita, necessità oramai primaria per dirimere le questioni cronologiche che tanto hanno attirato l'interesse di una parte degli eblaitologi negli ultimi anni).

27 Sulla variante col segno "a" iniziale dell'antroponimo *i-da-ad*-MU si veda *MEE* 7, p. 89 *ad* r. I, 5-II, 1.

volto con il culto (in ogni caso l'offerta dell'olio) che riceve oggetti d'oro di buon valore.

Assai interessante però può risultare il passo *MEE* 7, 50, v. V, 4-11, dove si ha: 2 *ʾà-da-um*-túg-2 2 aktum-túg 2 íbx3-túg-ša$_6$-dar / ⌜EN⌝-*ma-lik* / *i-ti-ki-da-mu* / pa$_4$:šeš / ^{d}NI.DA.KUL / *in* / *a-ru$_{12}$-kà-du*^{ki} / šu ba$_4$-ti, "(stoffe 2,2,2) EN-Malik (ed) Ittiki-Damu, funzionari-p. del dio N., in Arukatu hanno ricevuto". Benché il segno iniziale dell'antroponimo che qui interessa sia in parte in lacuna, e nonostante la presenza nella documentazione di una coppia di pa$_4$:šeš del dio Nidakul "kešda-*ma-lik* ≈ *i-ti-kà/ki-da-mu*",[28] mi chiedo se non si abbia qui un ulteriore prova della vicinanza della funzione in uno stesso personaggio del pa$_4$:šeš con quella di "medico", già sottolineata più su per Irkab-Ar.[29] Un altro personaggio definito come a:zu$_5$, infatti, è noto per essere un pa$_4$:šeš di Ebri'um, cioè Ḫazir (cfr. § 1.3, a), e già d'altronde la presenza delle due qualifiche (con l'aggiunta di quella di maškim di Ibbi-Sipiš) era stata notata per questo addetto alla corte.[30]

La realtà professionale del pa$_4$:šeš non è definitivamente chiarita nella documentazione eblaita, acquisendo questa figura funzioni non sempre univoche o facilmente identificabili.[31] Ora, mi sembra però che proprio il testo farmaceutico pubblicato dal Giubilato, unito all'informazione del legame che sembra sussistere tra medico e pa$_4$:šeš, possa fornirci una chiave di lettura del problema in parola: si tratterebbe, a mio avviso, di personaggi addetti alla cura "fisica" della persona cui vengono attribuiti, avendo varie funzioni in dettaglio (forse anche di carattere assai quotidiano ed eventualmente magico-divinatorio),[32] tra cui, come è l'esempio lampante di

---

28 Sulla coppia si veda A. Archi, *VO* 10 [1996], p. 41. In realtà, all'epoca dell'edizione come ancora oggi mi pare che il segno inciso sulla tavoletta non sia kešda, per cui v. *MEE* 7/2, Tavole, Tav. XLVIII.

29 Si veda la nota 18 più su.

30 La documentazione prosopografica si ha in A. Archi, *VO* 10, cit., p. 68 *ad* 10.

31 Si veda A. Archi, *VO* 10, cit., p. 37 sg. con bibliografia delle proposte interpretative precedenti.

32 L'aspetto della divinazione ad Ebla è giunto recentemente alla ribalta scientifica eblaitologica grazie ad un lungo ed assai interessante articolo di A. Catagnoti e M. Bonechi, "Magic and Divination at IIIrd Millennium Ebla, I. Textual Typology and Preliminary Lexical Approach", *SEL* 15 [1998], p. 17 sgg., dove una serie di transazioni economiche e la terminologia in esse coinvolta viene convincentemente considerata di origine divinatoria o comunque magica; mi sembra però di poter dire che il tema ha molto coinvolto gli Autori, che forse hanno troppo voluto cercare (e vedere) nella documentazione di Ebla: tale è il caso *ex.g.* delle motivazioni storiche che avrebbero portato Ebrium ad acquisire l'indubbio potere che ebbe, cfr. *ibid.*, p. 37 sg., dove si legge la curiosa affermazione riguardo all'etimologia del nome (**bry*): "... divination seems to us more adequate then a *simple administra-*

Ḫazir, quella di guarire con pratiche mediche. L'etimologia della funzione sarebbe quindi da derivare, come comunemente si fa e nonostante alcune perplessità di carattere grafico (la costanza, in prima istanza, della grafia rovesciata), dal verbo *pašāšu*, nel senso più generale di "essere al servizio diretto di una persona", desunto dall'originario "ungere, strofinare (il corpo) con olio",[33] aspetto dell'attività che in taluni casi è etimologicamente giustificato.[34]

Mi sembra poi assai interessante, da un punto di vista di "storia della scienza", che la funzione di "addetto alla persona", come vorrei tradurre, interpretando, il termine, e la professione di medico siano tenute distinte, indicando una chiara coscienza nella cultura siriana del III millennio a.C. delle peculiarità procedurali del medico stesso.[35]

L'unico esempio a me noto di donna-medico nella documentazione eblaita è quello di Ṭūbī-Damu (cfr. § 1.9), e i tre passi della documentazione in cui questo personaggio femminile viene citato la legano alla città di Ada(b), che sembra essere una cittadina nella Siria occidentale, comunque non distante dalla regione eblaita.[36] L'attestazione più complessa è, sintatticamente e contenutisticamente, quella di *MEE* 7, 48, v. III, 2-9 (§ 1.9, c), di cui riporto la traduzione che ne ho offerto nel volume citato (v. anche più su *ad* § 1.9, c): "1 stoffa-Ak. (ciascuno) a Ṭūbī-Damu, la donna-medico di Ada, (e suo) figlio la regina ha dato".

---

tive activity inspection ...", (corsivo mio); è comunque senza dubbio da apprezzare lo sforzo interpretativo di cercare, dietro le parole e le etimologie, la storia che esse ci indicano o ci fanno intravvedere (è la ricostruzione storica il fine di ogni ricerca).

33 Si veda *AHw*, p. 843 sg. Senza scomodare i santi, ancora nel *Nuovo Testamento*, come è noto, lo strofinare di olio il corpo è visto come segno di rispetto e sottomissione (v. Matteo, 26, 6 sgg. e paralleli; si prescinde ovviamente dalle valenze teologiche dei passi cui si allude).

34 Il fatto che l'attività del pa_4:šeš sia anche riservata alla divinità potrebbe indicare forse il tipo di rapporto che legava questa funzione alla persona cui era rivolta, benché mi sembri che la documentazione attuale non permetta un'approfondimento in alcuna direzione. Altra possibilità interpretativa è quella che vede tra le due funzioni-professioni un rapporto cronologico, laddove il pa_4:šeš, che è assai più spesso citato rispetto all'a:zu_5, è di probabile livello inferiore.

35 Si veda a questo riguardo anche la nota 4 più su e oltre nell'articolo.

36 Si veda *RGTC* 12, p. 16 s.v. Adab II (il nome femminile di *ARET* 4, 7, v. IX, 13, *da-bí-da-mu*, è forse una variante di quello di cui si tratta qui). Di nuovo, però, non è necessario che si tratti qui del luogo di provenienza della donna, anzi, a giudicare dal passo *ARET* 1, 1 (§ 1.9, a), è possibile che sia il luogo in cui ella abbia precipuamente svolto la sua attività professionale.

Già nel commento[37] avevo sottolineato l'unicità di questa formulazione, che era così tradotta sulla base delle informazioni sul personaggio che si deducono da altra documentazione (cfr. § 1.9, a e b), proponendo in alternativa che il "dumu-nita" di cui si tratta nel passo possa essere il figlio della regina stessa (eventualmente l'Irʾak-Damu di *ARET* 1, 1); ancora adesso la mancanza di ulteriore documentazione rende difficile, mi sembra, qualsiasi altra ipotesi interpretativa.

Concludendo questa sezione, si può senz'altro affermare che l'arte medica aveva un posto preciso e importante nella realtà quotidiana della corte eblaita, con professionisti specializzati che erano dediti con ogni probabilità alla cura di personaggi di spicco dell'*entourage* cortese e che venivano mandati in viaggio per offrire i loro servigi dove fosse necessario. Nulla sappiamo della preparazione teorica del medico eblaita, anche se il testo farmaceutico più volte citato è un indizio per farci intuire in quale direzione bisogna cercare (conoscenza delle erbe e delle loro proprietà);[38] forse era necessaria anche una eventuale conoscenza dell'arte divinatoria.[39] Il nome di una sola donna-medico è noto da Ebla, né, nonostante la difficoltà della documentazione a lei relativa, si hanno specifiche sulla sua attività che la possano individuare professionalmente rispetto ai suoi colleghi maschi.[40]

Va sottolineato, da ultimo, che la tipologia documentaria di Ebla impedisce di venire a conoscenza della quotidianità della professione del medico, così come ignoriamo, ed è anche più grave culturalmente, il suo ruolo fuori del mondo del Palazzo.

37 Si veda *MEE* 7, p. 282 *ad l.*

38 Questa è d'altronde la via maestra dell'arte medica anche in Mesopotamia, per cui v. R. Biggs, "Medicine", p. 1911 e per il mondo sumerico la bibliogr. in P. Fronzaroli, *ZA* 88, cit., p. 235 e nota 57 sgg.; per la Siria di Mari si veda J.-M. Durand, "Maladies et médicins", *Archives épistolaires de Mari* 1 (*ARMT* 26), 1988. L'aspetto della conoscenza delle pietre, che in Mesopotamia è altrettanto importante, sembra meno presente nella cultura del medico eblaita.

39 Si ha qui in mente l'espressione "inim-a:zu$_5$" che si ritrova nel VE, di cui si è già discusso alla nota 4 cui si rimanda. Nell'inno a Gula d'altronde si ritrova, nelle lodi che la dea fa a se stessa, questa stessa commistione di conoscenza botanica e recitazione di scongiuri (W. G. Lambert, "The Gula Hymn of Bulluṭṣa-rabi", *Orientalia* 36 [1967], soprattutto ll. 80-83, p. 120; anche R. Biggs, "Medicine", p. 1918), e a questo proposito bisogna mettere in evidenza come ad Ebla non si abbia cognizione, stante l'attuale documentazione, del rapporto che legava il medico a figure più interessate alla sfera magica (problema che in Mesopotamia coinvolge le due figure dell'*asû* e dell'*āšipu*, per cui v. K.E. Ritter, "Magic-Expert and Physician: Notes on Two Complementary Professions in Babylonian Medicine", *Studies in Honor of B. Landsberger*, *AS* 16, 1965, p. 175 sgg. e R. Biggs, "Medicine", p. 1918-1921).

40 Non è questo il caso, *ex.g.*, del mondo hittita, per cui v. G. Beckman, *RlA* 7 [1990], p. 631, Medizin B.

§ 3. Alcune considerazioni sugli strumenti di lavoro del medico eblaita

In un recente, breve articolo A. Archi ha evidenziato nella documentazione di Ebla una serie di oggetti come strumenti di lavoro del medico, sottolineando al contempo la vicinanza della terminologia di questi con quella utilizzata nei testi per esprimere gli attrezzi dei carpentieri (nagar): si tratta dei termini semitici *ma-da-gu*, *ma-ša-wa*, *gú-za-mi-lu* e *da-bù-um*, e di quelli sumerici šum, dub-nagar-sal, LAK 60 (= UŠxKÍD)-*al*$_6$/tur, zàḫ e šu-i.[41] Mi sembra che il presunto utilizzo chirurgico almeno di alcuni di questi oggetti, stante l'attuale situazione documentaria, sia più che giustificato.[42] Di altri, il testo pubblicato dal Giubilato e di cui si è fatta menzione all'inizio del saggio può essere utilizzato per comprendere in che modo, o a qual fine, essi venissero utilizzati;[43] tale è il caso essenzialmente del termine *ma-da-gu*, tradotto "pestello (per triturare erbe)", che viene convincentemente fatto derivare dalla radice *dqq*, "ridurre in polvere",[44] che trova una precisa conferma nelle azioni che il testo prescrive nella preparazione degli unguenti e delle pozioni.[45]

Nel termine *ma-ša-wa, ad sensum*, A. Archi ha voluto vedere delle "tenaglie", basandosi sulla terminazione apparentemente duale, pur non proponendo alcuna soluzione etimologica;[46] mi chiedo, come mera ipotesi di lavoro, se non si possa far derivare il termine dalla radice **šwī*, "essere incandescente", cosicché il termine indicherebbe un attrezzo, forse con due parti contrapposte, che viene usato dopo essere

41 Si veda il rimando bibliografico alla nota 2 (p. 10 per quello che qui interessa) e più su i §§ 1.1, c e 1.6, a.

42 La durezza della lega di questi strumenti è la ragione principale dell'ipotesi protratta, oltre il destinatario cui vengono riferiti (cfr. già A. Archi, *AOAT* 240, cit., p. 10 e nota 8), ma v. anche oltre. A questo proposito è bene mettere in evidenza con più forza di quanto non paia nell'articolo citato l'importanza storico-culturale di questa conclusione, se rarissimi ed assai controversi sono i richiami ad operazioni che la documentazione mesopotamica ci offre, per cui cfr. in generale R. Biggs, "Medicine", p. 1921 sg.

43 È considerazione che si ritrova anche ovviamente nell'articolo di P. Fronzaroli citato, per cui v. *ibid.*, p. 235 e nota 57.

44 Si veda già A. Archi, *AOAT* 240, cit., e P. Fronzaroli, *ZA* 88, cit., p. 235 e nota 57 (con rimando a G. Conti, *Quaderni del Dipartimento di Linguistica* 4, Università di Firenze [1993], p. 103) - ma nel lemma accadico *madakku* si ha una resa graficamente impropria della enfatica; la radice sembra attestata anche altrove ad Ebla (cfr. M. Bonechi, *NABU* 1992, p. 12).

45 Si pensa soprattutto all'espressione "tag /šub" (r. III, 6-7), che indica con ogni probabilità una doppia azione: "dopo aver triturato devi apporre (sulla carne fresca)" (mi sembra ipotesi più probabile di quella dell'Autore: "apply by smearing", che comunque è altrettanto possibile).

46 A. Archi, *AOAT* 240, cit., p. 10.

stato scaldato sul fuoco (ciò andrebbe ancora nella direzione di un uso chirurgico).[47] Altrettanto complesso, dal punto di vista dell'interpretazione, è il termine *gú-za-mi-lu*; esso compare ancora, e soltanto per quanto è a mia conoscenza, in *MEE* 11, 12 (= TM.75.G.410), v. III, 3, dove ne vengono rendicontati ben 500,[48] ma in contesto che non sembra avere nulla a che fare con l'arte medica e che quindi non aiuta a definirne il campo semantico.[49] L'ultimo oggetto espresso da un termine semitico, infine, *da-bù-um*, del peso di 3 gín (24,3 g), per il quale nessuna proposta interpretativa è stata offerta, può essere avvicinato al termine accadico *ṭapû* e varr., attestato solamente in ambito lessicale (Aa A = *nâqu*) come sinonimo di tùn; potrebbe trattarsi quindi di (un piccolo coltello in forma di) ascia.[50] Tra i termini di origine sumerica, šu-i indica senza dubbio un "rasoio", qui da intendere probabilmente come una lama molto affilata,[51] mentre šum è la "sega"[52] (si tratta di *realia*, se l'interpretazione è giusta, di uso anche in questo caso chirurgico), *LAK* 60 (= UŠxKÍD), nelle due ver-

---

47 Si veda *AHw*, p. 1206 *s.v.* *šawûm* II e *CAD* Š/1, p. 350 *s.v.* *šamû* (e *CAD* M/2, p. 282 *s.v.* *muštabbabbu*, "flasher", nome di un demone, dalla radice **šbb* che ha relazione etimologica con **šwī*); secondo l'attestazione citata in § 1.6 il peso di questo oggetto varia da 2 gín (15,6 g) a 3 (23,4; 1 gín = 7,8 g), quindi, si può aggiungere, è strumento per eseguire operazioni di precisione (v. anche oltre).

48 Si tratta nel testo di un complesso elenco di legname e affini (v. in generale E. Arcari, *BaE*, p. 320 sgg.) con la clausola finale, v. IV, 1-9: *i-bí-sí-piš* / mu-túm / *in* / *er-me* / DIŠ mu / *be* / DU.DU-a / *ar-mi*^{ki} / mu-túm é-en, su cui v. A. Archi, *Mél. Kupper*, p. 197, n. 4 (ma l'ipotesi DU.DU-a = Tuttul non è cogente).

49 A. Archi, *AOAT* 240, cit., p. 10, richiama il termine *ù*-NAM-*mi-lu* per la medesima terminazione, pur non proponendo alcuna ipotesi etimologica, mentre H. Waetzoldt considera possibile che il segno 'gú' vada staccato dal resto, per cui cfr. *MEE* 12, 37, comm. *ad* § 50, XIX 8 (anch'egli rinuncia ad ogni proposta interpretativa). Se quest'ultima ipotesi di dividere l'espressione è corretta, allora si può tentativamente mettere in relazione questo termine con l'acc. *zamirītu*, un oggetto non meglio specificato (ma probabilmente una piccola spada o un coltello), di cui nei testi di Ur III è attestato un 'eme', "lama" (cfr. *CAD* Z, p. 39 *s.v.*); in questo caso la derivazione del lemma acc. dalla città di Zamiri, proposta in *CAD*, cit. (e dubitativamente in *AHw*, p. 1508 *s.v.*) non è cogente (v. però H. Hirsch, *ZA* 24 [1967], p. 329). Niente a che fare con questo lemma, mi sembra poi di poter dire, ha il *karzillu* babilonese, "physician's lancet or scalpel" (*CAD* K, p. 240 *s.v.*), nonostante una certa assonanza dei termini.

50 Si veda *MSL* 14, p. 492, l. 129: ($^{tu-un}$tùn) *ta-*[*pu-ú*], ricostruito sul comm. AO3555, *ibid.*, p. 495, l. 11: ($^{tu-un}$tùn) *ta-pu-ú* : *ṭa-pu-ú* (l'incertezza nella resa della consonante iniziale indica una probabile origine straniera del termine); si veda ancora *AHw*, p. 1380 *s.v.* *ṭapû*. Meno probabile, perché non ne vedrei l'utilizzo medico, il raffronto con l'acc. *dappu*, di origine sumerica, con significato "(metal) plate, board" (*CAD* D, p. 106 *s.v.*).

51 Si veda già A. Archi, *AOAT* 240, cit., p. 10: *naglabtu* (il peso di 2 gín, 15,6 g, indica che si tratta di un oggetto per incisioni di precisione).

52 Così il termine si trova già tradotto in *ARET* 7, p. 235 *s.v.*

sioni "[grande$^{?}$]" e "piccolo", un oggetto non meglio identificabile[53] e dub-nagar-sal un "cisello a punta fine".[54] Anche l'oggetto espresso dal segno zàḫ, infine, sembra riportarci ad un ambito chirurgico: nel VB, l.sin. 611 esso è infatti tradotto con *da*[*m-r*]*í-gu*, che è stato rapportato alla radice **mrq*, "bucare, forare", quindi si tratterebbe, se l'interpretazione è esatta, di un "ago" o simili.[55]

Come si può notare, la terminologia eblaita, che segue quella utilizzata per gli attrezzi dei carpentieri e di altri artigiani, non sviluppa una nomenclatura tecnica dell'arte medica, e ciò porta alla conclusione che una differenziazione tra l'operare su un materiale o sul corpo umano forse non fosse chiaramente avvertita. Va notato però a questo proposito, ed è considerazione da approfondire in altra sede, che in Mesopotamia non sono noti oggetti chirurgici per operazioni complesse,[56] laddove Ebla sembra fornire al contrario una grande varietà di strumenti differenti; nonostante la difficoltà di interpretarne l'esatto significato (e ancor meno proporne un preciso scopo chirurgico), la loro durezza e piccolezza, che li distingue nettamente dai loro omonimi per fini artigianali, è indice di consumata perizia nella loro costruzione ed utilizzo.

53 A. Archi, *AOAT* 240, cit., p. 9 traduce "blade", ma è traduzione ipotetica; si vedano le considerazioni sull'oggetto in *MEE* 7, p. 270, comm. *ad* r. XIV, 18.

54 Su questo significato del lemma dub-nagar si veda *TIE* D, *s.v.* (con bibliografia precedente; v. anche H. Waetzoldt, *NABU* 1995, 104, che lo interpreta come un termine generale per oggetti appuntiti o con punta affilata), mentre "fine" traduce sal, *raqqu*; lo stesso lemma va letto in *MEE* 7, 47, r. XIV, 16 (correggi la lettura lì proposta).

55 Si veda G. Conti, *QdS* 17, 1990, p. 169; in realtà, il sumerico non si addice alla glossa eblaita, e ciò getta un'ombra sull'interpretazione avanzata (ma meglio, interpretativamente, non sono in grado di fare).

56 Si veda in generale R. Biggs, "Medicine", p. 1921.

ḤORŌN, DER HERR ÜBER DIE SCHLANGEN. DAS VERHÄLTNIS VON MYTHOS UND BESCHWÖRUNG IN KTU 1.100

MANFRIED DIETRICH - OSWALD LORETZ

Universität Münster

Bei den Ausgrabungen im Bereich südlich der Akropolis fand sich während der 24. Kampagne 1961 im Haus des "hurritischen Priesters" die fast unversehrt erhaltene Tafel RS 24.244 (KTU 1.100),[1] die seit ihrer Publikation durch Ch. Virolleaud 1968[2] wiederholt als eine Beschwörung[3] gegen giftige Schlangen und Schlangenbiß[4] bezeichnet worden ist.[5]

Die Interpretation des einzigartigen Textes hängt im wesentlichen von strukturalen, kolometrischen und philologischen Vorentscheidungen sowie der Bestimmung des Verhältnisses zwischen göttlicher und menschlicher Sphäre ab, die man bei einem Studium des ersten Teils desselben (Z. 1-60) trifft. Denn es kann keinem Zweifel unterliegen, daß nach KTU 1.100 Schlangengift, das durch einen Biß seitens einer giftigen Schlange übertragen wird, nur dann beseitigt werden kann, wenn auf göttlicher Ebene der hierfür zuständige Gott gefunden und sein Handeln zum Vorbild für menschliches genommen wird. Also setzt der Text voraus, daß zwischen der Tätigkeit eines menschlichen und des göttlichen Vernichters von Schlangengift das Verhältnis von Abbild und Urbild besteht. Die Brücke zwischen beiden bildet der

---

1 W. H. van Soldt 1991, S. 642; P. Bordreuil – D. Pardee 1989, S. 299.

2 Ch. Virolleaud 1968, S. 564-572, tituliert den Text: *Šapaš, la déesse du Soleil, et les serpents.*

3 Wiederholt in den neuesten Publikationen: W. G. E. Watson 1999, S. 166; K. Spronk 1999, S. 270; N. Wyatt 1999, S. 575; J. C. L. Gibson 1999, S. 202 ("charm"); vgl. N. Wyatt 1998, S. 378: "A Spell against Snakebite". – D. Pardee 1997, S. 295, nennt den Text *Ugaritic liturgy against venomous reptiles.*

4 Zur strittigen Frage, ob es sich bei KTU 1.100 um eine Beschwörung gegen giftige Schlangen oder gegen einen giftigen Schlangenbiß handelt, siehe unten Abschnitt 2.3.2.2. zu *nṯk nḥš* ‖ *šmrr nḥš ʿqšr.*

5 Vgl. zu diesem Textgenre noch KTU 1.82; 1.107; RS 1992.2014; siehe zu letzterem Text D. Pardee 1997, S. 327-328.

Mythos, der in eine Beschwörung eingebaut[6] oder mit einer solchen verbunden wird.[7]

Der besondere Reiz des mythischen Geschehens in KTU 1.100 liegt darin, daß erst nach einem langwierigen Verfahren feststeht, was jedermann ohnehin schon weiß: Nur Ḥorōn ist für die Beschwörung gegen Schlangen und deren Gift zuständig (Z. 61-76). Der erste Teil von KTU 1.100 (Z. 1-60) stellt uns folglich erstens vor das Problem, wie das Verhältnis zwischen menschlichem und göttlichem Beschwörer zu bestimmen ist, und konfrontiert uns angesichts der zwölfmal an verschiedene Gottheiten wiederholten Bitte zweitens mit der Frage, warum ein langes Vorspiel nötig ist, bis man bei der richtigen Adresse ankommt. Während die erste Frage die Ordnung und Zuständigkeitsbereiche in der göttlichen Welt berührt, führt uns die zweite in die ugaritische Kultgeographie ein.

Die nachfolgenden Ausführungen sollen sich eher mit der Ordnung in der göttlichen Welt als mit der Kultgeographie – diese soll in einem anderen Zusammenhang zur Sprache kommen – befassen und darlegen, daß KTU 1.100 keine Beschwörung gegen Schlangen oder Schlangenbiß abbildhaft auf menschlicher,[8] sondern urbildhaft auf mythischer Ebene ist. Wir haben es mit einer Beschwörung zu tun, in der der göttliche Schlangenbeschwörer Ḥorōn Handlungsträger ist. Somit ist KTU 1.100 als ein mythischer Begleittext zu einer Beschwörung einzustufen. Unser Augenmerk legen wir dabei vornehmlich auf den ersten Hauptteil des Textes, Z. 1-60, weil dieser auf Ḥorōn und dessen Tätigkeiten (Z. 61-76) zuführt.

In diesem umfangreichen ersten Abschnitt spielt das Inzipit (Z. 1-7) erwartungsgemäß eine besonders wichtige Rolle. Da dessen Aussagen vielfach oberflächlich und darum fehldeutend behandelt worden sind, werden wir uns seinen epigraphischen, kolometrischen, philologischen und strukturalen Gegebenheiten besonders widmen und uns bemühen, dort, wo dies nötig erscheint, von früheren, voreiligen Ergebnissen zu entlasten (Punkt 2).

Bevor wir uns den Problemen der Analyse von KTU 1.100:1-60 zuwenden, greifen wir einleitend drei Sonderfragen auf (Punkt 1): Epigraphie, die kolometrische Gliederung von KTU 1.100 und das Phantom einer Pferdegöttin.

---

6 A. Falkenstein 1931, 74-76, zeigt, daß in einigen sumerischen Beschwörungen z.B. die ursprüngliche Marduk-Ea-Formel durch die Einfügung einer mythologischen Erzählung erweitert wird.

7 M. Dietrich – O. Loretz 1980, S. 166.

8 Siehe M. Tsevat 1979.

Zum Schluß werden wir zusammenfassende Bemerkungen zum Thema *Mythos und Realität in KTU 1.100:1-60* unterbreiten (Punkt 3).

1. Einleitende Sonderfragen

1.1. Epigraphie: Schreibfehler, Auslassungen

Die bestens erhaltene und leicht lesbar geschriebene Tafel RS 24.244 weist im Bereich des ersten Hauptteils Z. 1-60 eine Reihe von Schreibfehlern und Auslassungen auf.[9]

Während als Schreibfehler nur *ʿt* für *ʿm* (Z. 20) und zwei falsch gesetzte Trenner (*ʿ*{.}[[x]]*ṯtrt*, Z. 20; *ʿq*{.}*šr*, Z. 39) zu vermerken sind,[10] sind dem Schreiber etliche Auslassungen unterlaufen. Kleinere Auslassungen wie die eines einzelnen Wortes (*nḥš*, Z. 6) oder einzelner Buchstaben (*y*<*ʿ*>*db*, Z. 12; *u*<*m*>*h*, Z.14; *b*<*l*>, Z. 30) stehen einer größeren gegenüber, die sich auf die Anrufung einer Göttin bezieht und am linken Rand nachgetragen worden ist (Z. 77-79).[11]

Angesichts dieser Schreibfehler und Auslassungen überrascht es nicht, daß der Schreiber(schüler) einmal auch eine ungewöhnliche Pleneschreibung verwendet hat: *mnty*, Z. 9.

1.2. Die kolometrische Gliederung von KTU 1.100[12]

Der Schreiber hat KTU 1.100:1-60 zwar mittels Trennstrichen in elf Abschnitte gegliedert, innerhalb dieser aber den Text fortlaufend geschrieben und auf eine Anordnung nach poetischen Einheiten verzichtet. Daß dieser erste Teil trotzdem hochpoetisch ist, wurde generell angenommen.[13]

---

9 M. Dietrich – O. Loretz 1980, S. 163-164.

10 Zu einem korrigierten Trenner in Z. 47 siehe KTU^{2} S. 115 Anm. 3.

11 An dieser Stelle ist eine Bemerkung zu dem Abschnitt über die Anrufung des Ḥorōn (Z. 57-60) nötig: Entgegen I. Kottsieper 1984, S. 99, der annimmt, daß Ḥorōn das Bittformular frühzeitig abbreche, haben wir es hier mit einer vom Aufbau des Textes her bedingten Verkürzung des Formulars zu tun, weil Ḥorōn als zuständige Gottheit natürlich anders reagiert als die vor ihm angerufenen Gottheiten und gegen die Schlange aktiv wird. Der Abschnitt Z. 61-76 beschreibt die Vernichtung des Schlangengiftes und die damit zutage tretende Beherrschung der Schlangen durch Ḥorōn.

12 M. Dietrich – O. Loretz 1980, S. 164-165.

13 M. Dijkstra 1999, 152, charakterisiert KTU 1.100:1 als eine Kette von Epitheta, die er als Beleg für poetische Prosa ("poetic prose with repetition and even occasional parallelism within a prose context") ansieht. Es dürfte jedoch kaum zulässig sein, Z. 1 isoliert von Z. 2-60 zu interpretieren.

Größere Meinungsverschiedenheiten treten bei der Gliederung des Inzipits erst nach dem Tetrakolon *Einführung der Sprecherin* (Z. 1-2a, siehe unten Punkt 2.3.1) für die Unterabschnitte *Bitte der um "Mutter", eine Botschaft an die Sonne zu übermitteln* (Z. 2a-3, siehe unten Punkt 2.3.2.1) und *Botschaft der um "Mutter" mit anschließendem Ersuchen um Legitimation für die Beschwörung* (Z. 4-6a, siehe unten Punkt 2.3.2.2) auf, wo aus sachlichen Gründen mitunter viel zu lange Kola in Kauf genommen werden.[14]

1.3. Das Phantom einer Pferdegöttin in KTU 1.100:1-7

Ch. Virolleaud beginnt die Erstveröffentlichung von RS 24.244 mit der Bemerkung, daß er es hier nicht nur mit einer beachtenswert großen, perfekt erhaltenen Tafel zu tun habe, sondern auch mit einer, die durch ein neues Thema ausgezeichnet werde. Darauf dürfte ihn vor allem sein Verständnis von Z. 1-3 gebracht haben, da er in *Pḥlt* eine mythische Gestalt, eine göttliche "cavale" erkannte.[15] So zog die "göttliche Stute" ("la Cavale",[16] "Mare"[17]) als Mutter des "göttlichen Hengstes" in die Ugaritologie ein, wo nach Ausweis der neueren Übersetzungen[18] beide trotz berechtigter Kritik weiterhin wie wild herumgaloppieren und sich wachsender Beliebtheit erfreuen. Sie sind ohne Untermauerung ihrer Existenz sogar zu Mitgliedern eines Pantheons avanciert, obwohl sie jeglicher Unterstützung durch Parallelbezeugungen entbehren.[19]

Dagegen wird diskutiert, ob KTU 1.100:61-76 poetische Strukturen aufweise; W. G. E. Watson 1999, S. 177 – dazu siehe M. Dietrich – O. Loretz 2000, S. 346-377.

14 So bildet M. C. Astour 1968, S. 13, für Z. 2-3 mit *ʿm il mbk nhrm b ʿdt thmtm* ein überlanges Kolon von 29 Konsonanten, und E. Lipiński 1974, S. 170, springt beispielsweise in Z. 4-5a von 9 auf 18 Konsonanten.

15 Ch. Virolleaud 1968, S. 564, 566. – Zur weiteren Diskussion siehe unten, Punkt 2.3.1., anläßlich des Wortpaares *pḥl* ‖ *pḥlt* in Z. 1.

16 P. Xella 1981, S. 226, "La madre dello stallone, la Giumenta"; P. Bordreuil 1985, S. 545, "La mère de l'étalon, la Cavale"; D. Pardee 1988, S. 202, "La mère de l'étalon, la cavale"; A. Caquot 1989, S. 82, "La mère de l'étalon, la Cavale".

17 M. C. Astour 1968, S. 15, "The mother of the Stallion, the Mare"; D. Pardee 1997, S. 295, "the mare"; S. B. Parker 1997, S. 219, "The Mare and Horon"; N. Wyatt 1998, S. 378, "The Myth of Shapsh and the Mare".

18 Selbst in die repräsentative Textsammlung COS I hat D. Pardee 1997, S. 295-298, diese Deutung eingebracht.

19 A. Caquot 1989, S. 79, sucht diese Schwierigkeit dadurch zu beheben, daß er für die Verbindung von Pferd und Sonne einen hethitischen Ursprung in Erwägung zieht.

Interpreten, die KTU 1.100 als eine Schlangenbeschwörung mit einem Mythos über eine Stute und die Sonne oder Ḥorōn verstehen, finden zwar breite Zustimmung,[20] haben aber mit dem Problem zu kämpfen, die Funktion der angeblich in Z. 1 angeführten "Mutter" der Pferde, der Stute, im Abschnitt Z. 1-7 und in den parallelen folgenden zwölf Wiederholungen zu erklären.

S. B. Parker, der besonders herausstellt, daß noch keine befriedigende Gesamterklärung des Textes KTU 1.100 vorliege, geht überraschenderweise von der Feststellung aus, daß nur eines sicher sei: Die Mutter der Pferde bitte ihre eigene Mutter, die Sonne, eine Botschaft zu einer Reihe von Gottheiten zu bringen.[21]

Über Verlauf und Inhalt der Aktion finden sich mehrere Interpretationsvarianten:

- N. Wyatt weitet den Gedanken von der Pferdemutter, deren göttlicher Status für ihn nicht ganz sicher ist,[22] dahingehend aus, daß das Fohlen einer Stute von einer Schlange gebissen worden sei. Die Stute wende sich aus diesem Grund an elf Götter(-Paare) und zuletzt an Ḥorōn.[23]

- Nach D. Pardee erreichen die ersten elf Götter(-Paare) mit ihren Beschwörungen nur ein partielles Ergebnis. Erst Ḥorōn gelinge es, alles Gift zu vernichten. Mit ihm wolle die Pferdemutter eine Ehe eingehen.[24]

- S. B. Parker deutet die Rede der Stute an die Sonne als eine Bitte um eine Beschwörung, die es einem Exorzisten ermögliche, das Gift zu beseitigen. In den ersten elf Versuchen werde keine endgültige Beseitigung des Giftes erreicht. Der Exorzist binde nur und füttere die Schlange.[25]

---

20 D. R. West 1995, S. 106, "The Greek mare goddess Demeter and the Ugaritic mare goddess *pḥlt*"; D. Pardee 1988, S. 204-205; *id.* 1997, S. 295, umschreibt Z. 1-60 folgendermaßen: "*The Mare Seeks an Ally Capable of Vanquishing Venomous Serpents*"; S. B. Parker 1997, 219, "The Mare and Horon"; N. Wyatt 1998, 378, "*KTU 1.100: The Myth of Shapash and the Mare: A Spell against Snakebite*".

21 S. B. Parker 1997, S. 219, stellt fest: "What is clear is that the mother of horses asks her mother, Shapash, the sun goddess, to take a message to a series of deities."

22 N. Wyatt 1998, S. 378 Anm. 1., er zu Mare folgendes: "A mare-goddess?".

23 N. Wyatt 1998, S. 378, formuliert das Problem folgendermaßen: "This text ... is in the form of a myth of a mare whose foal has been bitten."

24 D. Pardee 1997, S. 295-296.

25 S. B. Parker 1997, S. 219.

- J. C. de Moor versteht die Botschaft, die Šapaš im Namen der Pferdemutter den einzelnen Gottheiten überbringen soll, als längeren Wortlaut einer Beschwörung, die Z. 4b-7 umfaßt.[26]
- Nach D. R. West besteht die Bitte der Pferdemutter um Beseitigung des Giftes durch einen Beschwörer sogar aus Z. 4-7.[27]

Falls man von der Annahme ausgehen will, daß in KTU 1.100 eine "Pferdeheroin" als Hauptakteurin auftritt,[28] steht man vor dem Problem, daß es für diese Art von Beschwörung in der altorientalischen Literatur keine Parallele gibt. M.C. Astour und D.R. West finden hier einen Ausweg, indem sie einen Vergleich mit der griechischen Pferdegöttin Demeter anstellen.[29]

2. Das Inzipit (Z. 1-7) und seine Bedeutung für die Interpretation von KTU 1.100:1-60

2.1. Bisherige Vorschläge zur Gliederung des Inzipits Z. 1-7

Während über die kolometrische und syntaktische Gliederung von Z. 1-2a keine Differenzen bestehen, gehen die Meinungen für den Abschnitt Z. 2b-7 auseinander – es sind u.a. folgende Gliederungen unterbreitet worden:

D. Pardee[30]

4-5a	5b-6a	6b-7
Rede der *um*	Botschaft der *um*	Beschwörungsversuch der einzeln Gottheit

A. Caquot[31]

4-6		7
Rede der *um*		Verweigerung einer Antwort

---

26 J. C. de Moor, ARTU 1987, S. 146-147, übersetzt zwar *pḥl* und *pḥlt* mit "He-ass" bzw. "She-ass" (vgl. auch M. C. A. Korpel 1990, S. 240; M. Dijkstra 1999, S. 152), verweist aber zugleich auf die griechische Göttin Demeter als Parallele.

27 R. D. West 1995, S. 109.

28 D. Pardee 1997, S. 295, formuliert z.B., daß im ersten Hauptabschnitt von zwölf Untergliedern folgendes geschehe: "In these subsections the equine heroine, seeking a vanquisher of venomous serpents, sends a message to twelve deities."

29 M.C. Astour 1967, S. 265; R. D. West 1995, S. 108-113; siehe ferner J. C. de Moor, ARTU 1987, S. 146 Anm. 1.

30 D. Pardee 1997, S. 295-296.

31 A. Caquot 1989, S. 79-84.

J. C. de Moor[32]

3-4a	4b-7
Rede der *um*	Wortlaut der Beschwörung der *um*

N. Wyatt[33]

2b-7	4-7
Rede der *um*	Botschaft der *um*

S. B. Parker[34]

2b-6a	6b-7
Rede und Botschaft der *um*	Bericht über die Tätigkeit der Gottheit

Wie dieser Forschungsüberblick zeigt, rühren die bisherigen, zum Teil stark divergierenden Diskussionen über die Deutung des Inzipits Z. 1-7 und infolgedessen auch die über die Gesamtinterpretation des Abschnitts KTU 1.100:1-60 letztlich von unterschiedlichen Auffassungen über die kolometrische Gliederung und die syntaktische wie parallele Position einzelner Wörter her. Darum untersuchen wir im folgenden abschnittweise dezidiert die Kolometrie und die Wortpaare, um einen wohlbegründeten Zugang zum Text zu finden.[35]

Übersichtshalber bieten wir, unter Vorwegnahme unserer Ergebnisse, zunächst die von uns erarbeitete Interpretation des Inzipits (Punkt 2.2) und begründen sie anschließend (Punkt 2.3).

2.2. Kolometrie und inhaltlicher Aufbau des Inzipits

Den aufgeführten Gliederungsvorschlägen stellen wir für das Inzipit folgende gegenüber und gehen davon aus, dabei den Rahmen für den ersten Hauptteil des Textes, Z. 1-60, inhaltlich abstecken zu können.

I *Einführung der Sprecherin (um pḥl etc.) und deren Aufforderung an ihre Mutter, die Sonne.*

[1]*um pḥl pḥlt*	9	Die Mutter von männlichem Zuchttier (und) weiblichem Zuchttier,
bt ʿn bt abn	9	die Tochter der Quelle (und) Tochter des Steins,
bt šmm w thm	9	die Tochter des Himmels und der Meerestiefe
[2]*qrit l špš umh*	11	ruft zur Sonne, ihrer Mutter (folgendes):

32 J. C. de Moor 1987, S. 146-147.

33 N. Wyatt 1998, S. 379-380.

34 S. B. Parker 1997, S. 218-219.

35 M. Dietrich – O. Loretz 1980, S. 164-165.

II *Rede an die Sonne und Nennung der Bitte, die die Sonne an die einzelnen Gottheiten überbringen soll.*[36]

– 1 *Der Auftrag:*[37] *Bitte an die Sonne, gewissen Göttern und Göttinnen eine Botschaft zu übermitteln.*

špš um ql bl	9	"Sonne, (meine) Mutter, trage die Nachricht
ʿm [3]*il mbk nhrm*	11	zu El an die Quelle der beiden Ströme,
b ʿdt thmtm	9	an den Treffpunkt der beiden Meere:
– – – – – –		– – – – – –

– 2 *Inhalt der Botschaft: Bitte um eine effektive Beschwörung von Schlangenbiß und Schlangengift, Ersuchen um Legitimation der Beschwörung des von der Schlange gebissenen Kranken.*

[4]*mnt nṯk nḥš*	9	'Meine Rezitation der Beschwörung betrifft den Biß der Schlange,
šmrr nḥš [5]*ʿqšr*	11	die Vergiftung durch die gehäutete Schlange!
– – – – – –		– – – – – –
lnh mlḫš abd	10	Von ihm der Beschwörer vernichte,
lnh ydy [6]*ḥmt*		von ihm entferne er das Gift!'"

III *Ablehnendes Verhalten der um Hilfe ersuchten Gottheit.*

hlm yṯq nḥš	9	Aber siehe da, er stärkte die Schlange,
yšlḥm <nḥš> ʿqšr	<12>	fütterte die gehäutete Schlange.
– – – – – –		– – – – – –
[7]*yʿdb ksa w yṯb*	11	Er bereitete einen Stuhl und setzte sich.

2.3. Einzelbemerkungen zu Kolometrie, Philologie und Syntax des Inzipits

2.3.1. ***Z. 1-2a****: Einführung der Sprecherin*

Über die Gliederung des Abschnitts Z. 1-2a, der die Einleitung zu KTU 1.100 ist, in vier Kola besteht Konsens:

[1]*um pḥl pḥlt*	9	Die Mutter von männlichem Zuchttier (und) weiblichem Zuchttier,
bt ʿn bt abn	9	die Tochter der Quelle (und) Tochter des Steins,
bt šmm w thm	9	die Tochter des Himmels und der Meerestiefe
[2]*qrit l špš umh*	11	ruft zur Sonne, ihrer Mutter (folgendes):

36 I. Kottsieper 1984, S. 99, spricht von einem Bittformular.

37 D. W. Young 1979, S. 840, nennt Z. 2-3 "The Commission".

Die kolometrische Anordnung der ersten drei Kola führt zu vier Wortpaaren, von denen eines vertikal und drei horizontal angeordnet sind:

vertikal: *um* ‖ *bt* ‖ *bt*
horizontal: *pḥl* ‖ *pḥlt*, *ʿn* ‖ *abn*, *šmm w thm*

um ‖ *bt* ‖ *bt* "Mutter ‖ Tochter ‖ Tochter" — gleichgültig, ob die Wörter *um* "Mutter" und *bt* "Tochter" hier metaphorisch oder real zu verstehen sind:

In Symmetrie zu den drei horizontalen Parallelismen ist hier von einem dreifachen, allerdings vertikal angeordneten Parallelismus auszugehen, der eine Totalität umschreibt. Diese ist auf die drei Bereiche *pḥl pḥlt*, *ʿn abn* und *šmm w thwm* zu beziehen und ohne Namensnennung der göttlichen Gestalt als deren Funktionsbestimmung aufzufassen: Es handelt sich um eine weibliche Figur aus dem Kreis der Sonne, die in besonderer Weise mit den aufgezählten drei Bereichen der Natur verbunden ist, also als Personifikation der jeweiligen Bereiche gelten darf.

Aus Z. 1-7 wurde aufgrund der Position des Wortes *um* "Mutter" gemeinhin gefolgert, daß *um* metaphorisch gebraucht sei und eine besondere Theogonie voraussetze: Entgegen der üblichen Vorstellung, daß El Schöpfer und Vater aller Geschöpfe sei, werde hier die Sonnengöttin Šapaš an die Spitze der Götter gestellt — sie sei die Mutter von Himmel und Erde, sie habe Quelle und Stein geboren, sie sei die Mutter der ersten Geschöpfe ("He-ass", "She-ass"). Möglicherweise stamme diese Theogonie, so die weiteren Überlegungen, aus einer hethitisch-hurritischen Quelle. Bemerkenswert sei jedoch, daß damit die Aussage des Inzipits (Z. 1-7) gewissermaßen in Widerspruch zum folgenden Teil des Textes stehe, in dem El die Reihe der Götter anführe.[38]

Die Vertreter eines realen Verständnisses von *um* "Mutter", die "La mère de l'étalon, la cavale"[39] übersetzen und die die *um* mit der Pferdemutter identifizieren, entheben sich zwar der Mühe, für die namenlose Gestalt eine Identifikation vorzunehmen, haben aber in der Folge das Problem, für *bt* "Tochter" eine plausible Erklärung zu finden. So wird beispielsweise vermutet, daß die postulierte "Mutter des Hengstes"

---

38 J. C. de Moor 1987, S. 146 Anm. 3; M. C. A. Korpel 1990, S. 240, schließt sich der Anschauung an, daß in KTU 1.100:1-7 *Šapaš* die Mutter der Schöpfung sei: "The Ugaritic sun-goddess Schapshu is called the mother of Heaven and Flood who gave birth to Spring and Stone, the parents of the She-ass, the first animated creature. The She-ass called Shapshu her mother ... In this text Shapshu has been placed at the top of the list of gods as the first mother."

39 D. Pardee 1988, S. 204; *id.* 1997, 295.

nach Maßgabe von *bt ʿn bt abn* in der Steppe wohne, und daß *bt šmm w thm* auf ihre himmlische Abkunft als Tochter der Sonne anspiele.[40]

um "Mutter" — metaphorisch gebrauchter Ehrenname:

um wird hier auf eine Göttin oder eine weibliche Figur aus dem göttlichen Bereich der Sonne angewendet.[41]

bt "Tochter" – metaphorisch auch als Anrede einer Höhergestellten.[42]

pḥl ‖ *pḥlt* "männliches Zuchttier" ‖ "weibliches Zuchttier":

Daraus, daß *p/bḥl* an allen ug. Belegstellen (KTU 1.4 IV 5.9.15; 1.19 II 4.9.11; 4.377:24[43]) für den jungen Eselhengst gebraucht wird, muß man für KTU 1.100:1 nicht schließen, daß *pḥl* auch hier "junger Eselhengst" bedeutet.[44] Die Beiordnung des Wortpaares *pḥl* ‖ *pḥlt* zu den Parallelismen *ʿn* ‖ *abn* und *šmm w thm* zeigt vielmehr an, daß dem *pḥl* nur eine allgemeinere Bedeutung wie "männliches Zuchttier"[45] zugrundeliegt.[46]

Aus den Belegen für *pḥl* wurde schon früher zu Recht geschlossen, daß *pḥl* in KTU 1.100:1 aufgrund der Verbindung mit "Mutter" ganz allgemein ein fruchtbares, zeugungs- bzw. tragfähiges männliches oder weibliches Tier meine und daß die Übersetzungen "Hengst" für *pḥl* und "Stute" für *pḥlt*, die sich letztlich auf das ar. *faḥl*[47]

---

40 D. Pardee 1988, S. 204-205, sucht für die Rechtfertigung seiner Erklärung schließlich bei der Originalität des Autors von KTU 1.100 seine Zuflucht.

41 Vgl. hierzu akk. *ummu* für Göttinnen (*AHw*, S. 1417: *ummu* I "Mutter" 8 von Göttinnen) sowie den metaphorischen Gebrauch des Wortes in akkadischen und hebräischen Quellen (*AHw*, S. 1416: *ummu* I "Mutter" 5 bildl.; *HAL*, S. 59: *ʾm* Mutter – 2. metaph.; Ehrenname für eine Frau: Ri 5,7).

42 Fürs Hebr. siehe Ges.[18] 185: bt_1 – 7. Anrede des Lehrers od. Höhergestellten.

43 M. Dietrich – O. Loretz 1985, S. 103, leiten aus dem Nebeneinander von *bḥ[lm]* und *ḥmrm* in KTU 4.377:24.25.30 ab, daß es sich bei *pḥl* in diesem Text um einen Pferdehengst handle und folglich ug. *pḥl* eine Bezeichnung für den Zuchthengst von Pferd und Esel sei. Diese Schlußfolgerung ist nicht zwingend. Wir belassen es auch in KTU 4.377:24 bei *pḥl* "männliches Zuchttier; Hengst (v. Esel)".

44 Vgl. dagegen oben die in Anm. 26 erwähnten Autoren.

45 Vgl. *AHw*, S. 875: *puḫālu*, Am. *puḫīlu* (ar. *faḥl* Hengst) "Zuchtwidder, -stier, -hengst"; M. Dietrich – O. Loretz 1985, S. 101-103.

46 Vgl. auch den Parallelismus *ʿr* ‖ *pḥl* in KTU 1.4 V 14-15; 1.19 II 8-9.10-11 (zu *ʿr* siehe *AHw*, S. 328: *ḫârum, ajarum* "Eselhengst" aB, Māri; *HAL*, S. 778: *ʿr* "Hengst [v. Esel]"); in KTU 4.377 geht *bḥ*[lm] (Z. 24) einem *ḥ*[mrm] "Esel" (Z. 25) voran; zu *bḥl* siehe G. Del Olmo Lete 1979, S. 194 (: "stallion"); M. Dietrich – O. Loretz 1985, S. 101-103; DLU 106: *bḥl*.

47 F. Renfroe 1985, S. 410-411.

stützt, die Gefahr einer irreführenden semantischen Einengung der Wörter auf das Pferd in sich berge.[48]

An dieser Stelle ist ein Rekurs auf das Thema *Das Phantom einer Pferdegöttin in KTU 1.100:1-7* (siehe oben Punkt 1.3) nötig: Da es im Alten Orient eine Reihe von Hinweisen gibt, die eine Verbindung zwischen Pferd und Sonne nahelegen,[49] schloß M.C. Astour schon bald nach dem Bekanntwerden von KTU 1.100, daß hier ein Zeugnis für diese Tradition vorliege. Er folgte im Verständnis von KTU 100:1, wie oben schon angedeutet, Ch. Virolleaud und interpretierte das Wort *pḥlt* wie dieser als "mare" und dachte dabei an einen Namen der Tochter der Sonne.[50] Ch. Virolleaud faßte seinerseits sowohl *pḥl* als auch *pḥlt* aber auch als Namen zweier unterschiedlicher göttlicher Wesen auf, so daß er Z. 1a folgendermaßen übersetzte: "La mère de *Pḥl* (à savoir) *Pḥlt*".[51] Dagegen stellte M. Tsevat überzeugend fest, daß *pḥl pḥlt* eine asyndetische Beiordnung zweier Substantive sei und wohl einen Merismus meine: "Mutter aller Pferde".[52] Diese Deutung einer Beziehung zwischen *pḥl* und *pḥlt* findet jedoch nur begrenzt Zustimmung.[53]

Aus der poetischen Position des Wortpaares *um* ‖ *bt* ergibt sich jedoch zwingend, daß nur der mit *um – bt* bezeichneten namenlosen Gestalt ein göttlicher oder quasigöttlicher Status eigen sein kann. Demgegenüber kommt den Parallelpaaren *pḥl* ‖ *pḥlt* "männliches Zuchttier" ‖ "weibliches Zuchttier" und *ʿn* ‖ *abn* "Quelle" ‖ "Stein" aus dem Blickpunkt der Kosmologie allenfalls eine untergeordnete göttliche Stellung zu.

ʿn abn "Quelle (und) Stein":

Das Wortpaar *ʿn abn*, das den Parallelismus *ʿn* ‖ *abn* voraussetzt, ist in Symmetrie zu den vorangehenden und nachfolgenden Parallelismen auch merismisch zu deuten. Denn es beschreibt den Gegensatz zwischen Wasser und wasserlosem Gestein und

---

48 M. Dietrich – O. Loretz 1985, S. 103; vgl. dagegen D. Pardee 1979, S. 405.

49 Siehe z.B. M. J. Mulder 1972, S. 89-90 mit Anm. 71; A. Caquot 1989, S. 79, und E. Lipiński 1999, S. 765, zu 2 Kön 23,11-12.

50 M. C. Astour 1967, S. 265.

51 Ch. Virolleaud 1968, S. 566; A. Caquot 1989, S. 82, "La mère de l'étalon, la Cavale"; N. Wyatt 1998, S. 378, "The Mother of the stallion, Mare".

52 M. Tsevat 1979, S. 760-761.

53 Siehe z.B. J. C. de Moor, ARTU 1987, S. 146; D. R. West 1995, S. 109; D. Pardee 1997, S. 295; S. B. Parker 1997, S. 219, 223, entscheidet sich zwar für "The mother of stallion and mare", erwägt aber auch "the stallion's mother, the mare".

könnte vielleicht jenen vertikalen Parallelismen gleichgestellt werden, die beispielsweise Tal und Berg zusammensehen.[54]

šmm w thm "Himmel und Meer(estiefe)":

Dieser Ausdruck[55] sieht merismisch die höchsten Höhen und die tiefsten Tiefen zusammen und ist *ġrm w thmt* "Berge und Meer" (KTU 1.148:6.43; RS 1992.2004:29) an die Seite zu stellen.

qrit "sie ist rufend" (G Part.f.Sg.: *qāriʾt-*[56]) – in den Wiederholungsabschnitten (Z. 8 et par.), in denen die *um* "Mutter" die Sonne um die Übermittelung ihrer Worte an weitere Gottheiten bittet, steht das narrative *tqru* "sie rief" (G PK 3.f.Sg.: *tiqraʾu*) für die konkrete Durchführung.

2.3.2. ***Z. 2b-6a****: Rede der um "Mutter" an Špš, die Sonne*

Die *Rede der um "Mutter" an Špš, die Sonne*, die El zum Ziel hat, wird im gesamten Text zehnmal wiederholt (Z. 8-9, 14-15, 19-20, 25-26, 30-31, 35-36, 40-41, 45-46, 51-52, 57-58)[57] und richtet sich jeweils an eine andere Gottheit mit Nennung des Ortes ihrer Verehrung. Dabei beschreibt der Text in beeindruckender Weise den kultgeographischen Horizont Ugarits – im folgenden analysieren wir jedoch nicht alle Abschnitte mit ihren unterschiedlichen Gottheiten und Kultorten, sondern lediglich den ersten Abschnitt aus dem Inzipit mit El als intendiertem Ansprechpartner.

Die Rede läßt sich in zwei Abschnitte gliedern: Der erste (Z. 2b-3) enthält die Bitte, eine Botschaft an die Sonne zu übermitteln, und der zweite (Z. 4-6a) bietet den Wortlaut der Botschaft mit anschließendem Ersuchen um Legitimation für die Beschwörung.

2.3.2.1. ***Z. 2b-3****: Bitte der um "Mutter", eine Botschaft an die Sonne zu übermitteln*

špš um ql bl	9	"Sonne, (meine) Mutter, trage die Nachricht

---

54 J. Krašovec 1977, S. 94-96, *hr* ‖ *ʾpq, bqʿh, gyʾ, ʿmq, śdh*; O. Loretz 1998, 229, zu ug. *ġr - arṣ* ‖ *gbʿ - šdm*.

55 B. Alster 1999, 868-869; he. *šmym + thwm* und *šmym* ‖ *thwm* siehe J. Krašovec 1977, S. 154, Nr. 257p-t; M. Dahood, RSP I 1972, S. 358-359, Nr. 560, *šmm + thm*.

56 Vgl. dagegen E. Lipiński 1974, S. 171: *qrit* Stativ (*qariʾta*) zur Beschreibung eines dauernden Zustandes; I. Kottsieper 1984, S. 99, deutet die Form als berichtendes *tqṭl*.

57 Impliziert ist diese Rede auch für den Nachtrag auf dem linken Rand der Tafel (KTU 1.100:77-79): Der Schreiber hat stichwortartig die aus Versehen ausgelassene Ansprechpartnerin *ʿṯtrt* von Māri ins Gespräch gebracht, siehe M. Dietrich – O. Loretz – J. Sanmartín 1975, S. 124.

ʿm ʾil mbk nhrm	11	zu El an die Quelle der beiden Ströme,
b ʿdt thmtm	9	an den Treffpunkt der beiden Meere:
------		------

Sachlich ist bemerkenswert, daß die in Z. 1 als *um* "Mutter" eingeführte Sprecherin *Špš*, die Sonne, als "(ihre) Mutter" anspricht und sie als Übermittlerin ihres Anliegens wünscht.

Da innerhalb des Trikolons sowohl *ʿm il* "zu El" als auch *b* "in" Doppelfunktionen wahrnehmen, ergeben sich die beiden Wortpaare *mbk* ‖ *ʿdt* und *nhrm* ‖ *thmtm*. Beide Parallelismen dienen dazu, den Wohnsitz des Hochgotts El zu umschreiben.[58]

Dem Bild von den beiden Strömen und Meeren als Sitz des Schöpfergottes liegen altmesopotamische[59] und antike Anschauungen zugrunde, daß der Erdboden, die bewohnte Welt von diesen Wassermassen umgeben ist.[60]

2.3.2.2. ***Z. 4-6a****: Botschaft der um "Mutter" mit anschließendem Ersuchen um Legitimation für die Beschwörung*

In Z. 4-6a folgt die Botschaft, die die Sonne im Auftrag der *um* "Mutter" an El – der Wortlaut der Botschaft wird zehnmal wiederholt und hat jeweils eine andere Gottheit im Blick (Z. 9-11, 15-17, 20-22, 26-28, 31-33, 36-38, 41-43, 46-48, 52-54, 58-60[61]) – übermitteln soll. Das Ersuchen hat zum Ziel, die Legitimation für die Beschwörung am Kranken zu gewinnen. Denn der Beschwörungspriester braucht nach altorientalischer Anschauung eine göttliche Legitimation, die ihn befähigt, eine Beschwörung erfolgreich durchzuführen. Dabei muß ihm die für die Beschwörung zuständige Gottheit die Beschwörungsformel in den Mund und die beschwörungsgemäßen Mittel in die Hand legen. So berufen sich beispielsweise die Beschwörungspriester in den sumerischen Beschwörungen auf die Götter der "weißen Magie", in deren Auftrag sie die Beschwörungshandlung an Kranken vornehmen. Dadurch, daß hier die Götter des Ea-Kreises mit ihrer Macht hinter dem Beschwö-

58 Siehe M. Dietrich – O. Loretz 1997, S. 136-139; zur den Quellwassern (*mê nagbi*) in der akk. Kosmologie siehe W. Horowitz 1998, S. 314-315.

59 Zum Wohnort Enki/Eas im Wasser siehe H. D. Galter 1981, S. 52-84; M. Dietrich – O. Loretz 1997.1998, S. 136-139; W. Horowitz 1998, S. 315. – Zum Thema der Rezeption des mesopotamischen Schöpfergottes Enki/Ea im Westen mit den ältesten Zeugnissen aus Ebla siehe F. Pomponio – P. Xella 1997, S. 164-169.

60 W. Horowitz 1998, S. 40-42, 325-326 zur babylonischen bzw. griechischen Weltkarte. – Es versteht sich, daß dann, wenn eine andere Gottheit als Ansprechpartner auftritt, der Kultort wechselt.

61 Zum Nachtrag Z. 79 siehe Anm. 57.

rungspriester stehen, wird dessen Kraft in dem Maße erhöht, wie sie für die Beschwörung erforderlich ist. Da er nun auf höheren, göttlichen Befehl die Beschwörung am Kranken vollzieht, ist er vor Dämonen geschützt, die sich durch seine Beschwörungshandlung angegriffen fühlen könnten.[62]

Botschaft und Ersuchen um Legitimation haben folgenden Wortlaut:

[4]*mnt nṯk nḥš*	9	'Meine Rezitation der Beschwörung betrifft den Biß der Schlange,
šmrr nḥš [5]*ʿqšr*	11	die Vergiftung durch die gehäutete Schlange!
------		------
lnh mlḫš abd	10	Von ihm der Beschwörer vernichte,
lnh ydy [6]*ḥmt*	9	von ihm entferne er das Gift!'"

Bevor wir auf Einzelheiten dieses Redeabschnitts zu sprechen kommen, unterbreiten wir ein Florilegium bisheriger Übersetzungen und Deutungen:

– A. Caquot 1989, S. 83-84:

> (4) "(Voici) ma conjuration:
> Un serpent a mordu
> un serpent (5) venant de muer *a craché* son poison.
> De son fait l'incatateur *a péri*,
> (car) sur lui il a lancé (6) le venin.

Der Interpret[63] gelangt zu dieser Übersetzung, weil er wie J. C. de Moor (siehe unten) davon ausgeht, daß *mnt* "meine Beschwörung" wegen der Pleneschreibung *mnty* in Z. 9 nur einen Nominalsatz meinen kann. Gleichzeitig betont er, daß Übersetzungen, die eine Determination des *mnt* durch das nachfolgende *nṯk* "Biß" voraussetzen,[64] abzulehnen sind.

– S. B. Parker (1997, 220) bindet Z. 4-5 syntaktisch an die Rede an die Sonne in Z. 2-3 an und faßt Z. 5-6 als letzten Teil dieser Rede auf:

> "Shapsh, mother, carry my cry
> To El at the source of the Rivers,
> At the confluence of the Deeps,
>
> For a spell for a viper's bite,
> For a sloughing viper's venom.

62 A. Falkenstein 1931, S. 20-27.

63 1989, S. 83-84: Anm. 253.

64 C. H Bowman – R. B. Coote 1980, S. 136, "By the recitation for the bite of the snake"; P. Xella 1981, S. 227, "Incantesimo per il morso del serpente"; D. Pardee 1997, S. 295, "My incantation for serpent bite"; S. B. Parker 1997, S. 220, "For a spell for a viper's bite"; N. Wyatt 1998, S. 379, "A spell against the bite of a snake".

Let the exorzist banish the bane,
Expel from it the poison."

– D. Pardee (1997, 295) deutet Z. 4-6a als Botschaft der *um* "Mutter" (Z. 1) durch die Sonne an die einzelnen Götter. Innerhalb derselben interpretiert er Z. 5b-6a als die Beschwörung seitens der *um* "Mutter":

My incantation for serpent bite,
for the scaly serpent's poison:
From it, O charmer, destroy,
from it cast out the venom.

– J. C. de Moor (1987, 147) schließlich erkennt in Z. 4-6a einen Teil der Beschwörung, die er bis Z. 7 ausdehnt:

"Shapshu, my mother, carry my voice,
. . .
My incantation is:

'A poisonous serpent has bitten,
a serpent which has sloughed its skin!
Is there someone to charm for its destructive venom?
is there someone to expel its poison?
Look! Let him bind the serpent,
let him feed the serpent which has sloughed its skin,
let him place a chair and sit down!'"

Entgegen diesen Interpretationen, die sehr unterschiedliche Positionen hinsichtlich der Kolometrie einnehmen, dürfte daran festzuhalten sein, daß die Botschaft, die die Sonne im Auftrag der *um* "Mutter" an die einzelnen Götter zu überbringen hat, weder eine Beschwörungsformel enthält, noch mit einer solchen identisch ist.[65] Die Botschaft bringt vielmehr den Wunsch zum Ausdruck, daß die jeweils angesprochene Gottheit der Beschwörung der Bittstellerin Kraft verleihe, das Schlangengift unschädlich zu machen, damit ein Schlangenbeschwörer mit ihr sein Ziel erreiche, das Gift des Schlangenbisses zu tilgen.

Um Klarheit zu gewinnen, halten wir zunächst fest: Die beiden Bikola weisen folgende, für die Definition des Wunsches der *um* "Mutter" (Z. 1) an El und die anderen Gottheiten wichtigen Wortpaare auf: *ṯk nḥš* ‖ *šmrr nḥš ʿqšr; nṯk* ‖ *šmrr, nḥš* ‖ *nḥš, lnh* ‖ *lnh* und *abd* ‖ *ydy*.

65 I. Kottsieper 1984, S. 104, scheint *ql* und *mnt* (Z. 2b-4) innerhalb einer syntaktischen Einheit gleichzusetzen.

Diesen Wortpaaren lassen sich bei einer sorgfältigen Analyse u.a. folgende Aussagen entnehmen:

mnt "Rezitation einer Beschwörung, Beschwörung".[66]

Wie die Pleneschreibung in Z. 9 (*mnty*: |minût-ı|) zeigt, ist bei *mnt* ein Suff.1.Sg. zu implizieren und auf die Auftraggeberin *um* "Mutter" (Z. 1) zu beziehen.

ntk nḥš ‖ *šmrr nḥš ʿqšr* "Biß der Schlange" ‖ "Vergiftung der gehäuteten Schlange":[67]

Die Formulierung dieses Begriffspaars dürfte zu erkennen geben, daß es sich bei KTU 1.100 nicht um eine prophylaktische Beschwörung gegen bissige und giftige Schlangen handelt,[68] sondern um die Beschwörung gegen das in einem konkreten Fall durch einen Schlangenbiß in einen Menschen oder ein Tier eingedrungene Gift.[69]

nṯk ‖ *šmrr* "Biß"[70] ‖ "Vergiftung".[71]

---

66 *mnt(y)* ist wohl dem Akk. entlehnt, vgl. *AHw*, S. 657: *minûtu* I 3 Rezitation einer Beschwörung; *CAD* M/2, S. 98-99: *minûtu* 3. recitation (of an incantation). – I. Kottsieper 1984, S. 100-101, weist zu Recht darauf hin, daß an einigen der in den Lexika zitierten Stellen weniger "Rezitation einer Beschwörung" als "Beschwörung" in Frage kommt.

Das *bhtm*/*bt mnt* "Haus der Beschwörung" in Z. 70-71 ist mit *bt ḥrš* "Haus des Zauberers" von KTU 1.12 II 61 vergleichbar.

67 Zu anderen Kolagliederungen vgl. beispielsweise J. Tropper 1990, S. 89, der *šmrr* "sehr giftig" mit dem vorangehenden *nḥš* verbindet und dabei ein wenig symmetrisches Bikolon in Kauf nimmt: *nṯk nḥš šmrr* ‖ *nḥš ʿqšr* (10 ‖ 7). – Oder: A. Caquot 1989, S. 83, der nach T. H. Gaster einen asymmetrischen Parallelismus bildet: *nšk nḥš* ‖ *šmrr nḥš ʿqšr* (6 ‖ 11) "Un serpent a mordu ‖ un serpent venant de muer *a craché* [= *šmrr* Š G SK) son poison." – Oder: E. Lipiński 1974, S. 169, 171-172, postuliert folgendes Bikolon: *šmrr* [= *šu-um-r*[*i-ir*], EA 185:74] *nḥš* [5]*ʿqšr lnh mlḫš* ‖ *abd lnh ydy* [6]*ḥmt* (18 ‖ 12) "'Chasse le serpent, l'ophidien qui siffle contre lui, ‖ fais périr celui qui, sur lui, crache du venin!'"; auch gegen diese Lösung sprechen die asymmetrischen Überlängen.

68 Vgl. dagegen Ch. Virolleaud 1968, 569, der betont, daß die Beschwörung nicht den Zweck habe, einen Schlangenbiß zu heilen, sondern einen solchen zu verhindern; siehe ferner D. Pardee 1988, 223, "La cavale, mère de l'étalon, demande à sa mère, le Soleil, de transmettre un message à *ʾIlu* ... Dans le message est rapportée la conjuration de la cavale contre les serpents: celle-ci consiste en une invitation adressée à un charmeur en vue d'extirper le venin du serpent."; id. 1997, 295, "Ugaritic liturgy against venomous reptiles".

69 C. H. Bowman – R. B. Coote 1980, S. 135; S. B. Parker 1997, S. 219; N. Wyatt 1998, S. 378, "A Spell against Snakebite".

70 Die Interpreten, die in *mnt(y)* einen selbständigen Nominalsatz erkennen, betrachten *nṯk* als finite Verbform (SK 3.Sg.): J. C. de Moor 1987, S. 147; A. Caquot 1989, S. 85.

71 Zur Diskussion dieses Nomen actionis vom Š-Stamm siehe D. Pardee 1978, S. 257; I. Kottsieper 1984, S. 106: *mrr* Š Inf. cstr. "das Vergiften"; vgl. dagegen J. C. de Moor 1987, S. 147; J. C. de Moor – K. Spronk 1987, S. 171, die *šmrr* als Adj. auffassen: "poisonous"; ähnlich J. Tropper 1990, S. 89: Š-Verbaladjektiv des Typs *šuqtul* mit elativischer Bedeutung: "überaus giftig".

lnh ‖ *lnh* “von ihm” ‖ “von ihm”:

Das Bezugsobjekt von *lnh* “von ihm” ist, wie der Fortgang der Rede in Z. 6b-7 zu erkennen gibt, der (oder die) vom Schlangenbiß Betroffene, in dem/der sich das Gift nun befindet.[72]

mlḫš “Flüsterer, Beschwörer”.[73]

ʾbd ‖ *ydy* D “vernichten” ‖ G “vertreiben”.

2.3.2.3. ***Z. 6b-7****: Das ablehnende Verhalten der um Hilfe ersuchten Gottheit*

hlm ytq nḥš	9	Aber siehe da, er stärkte die Schlange,
yšlḥm <*nḥš*> *ʿqšr*	<12>	fütterte die gehäutete Schlange.
------		------
[7]*yʿdb ksa w ytb*	11	Er bereitete einen Stuhl und setzte sich.

In diesem letzten Abschnitt des Inzipits, der drei Kola umfaßt und aus einem Bikolon und einem abschließenden Monokolon zusammengesetzt ist,[74] finden sich nur die beiden Wortpaare: *ytq* ‖ *lḥm* Š und *nḥš* ‖ *nḥš*.

Bei einer Interpretation dieses Abschnitts ist im Blick zu halten, daß hier der Bericht über das Verhalten der um Legitimation ersuchten Gottheit steht. Alle Gottheiten, die vor Ḥorōn (Z. 57-60) angesprochen worden sind, gehen ebensowenig gegen das Schlangengift vor wie an dieser Stelle El und behandeln die Schlange eher freundlich: Sie pflegen sie und vermehren damit sogar ihr gefährliches Gift.[75]

---

72 Vgl. dagegen E. Verreet – J. Tropper 1988, S. 342, “Von ihr (der Schlange), oh Beschwörer, vernichte, von ihr treibe aus das Gift!”. – Anders auch Ch. Virolleaud 1968, S. 569, der *ʿqšr* mit *lnh* verbindet und hierzu vermerkt: “*ʿqšr lnh*, c’est-à-dire d’un serpent doué d’*ʿqšr*, littéralement à qui appartient le *ʿqšr*.”; E. Lipiński 1974, S. 169, *ʿqšr lnh mlḫš* ... *lnh ydy ḥmt* “l’ophidien que siffle contre lui ... celui que, sur lui, crache du venin”; C. H. Bowman – R. B. Coote 1980, S. 136, *šmrr nḥš* ... *lnh mlḫš abd* “For the pain of the snake ... For it let the charm destroy”.

73 Vgl. hebr. *HAL*, S. 501: *lḥš* pi. Ptz. Beschwörer (zu den vergleichbaren Stellen des Alten Testaments Jer 8,17; Ps 58,5 und Qoh 10,11 siehe u.a. M. C. Astour 1968, S. 17; S. D. Sperling 1993, S. 226 Anm. 16.); Akk. *mulaḫḫišu* “Flüsterer”: *AHw*, S. 670; *CAD* M/2, S. 188: *mulaḫḫišu* whisperer (as a name of a god).

74 P. Xella 1981, S. 227; A. Caquot 1989, S. 84-85; S. B. Parker 1997, S. 220; vgl. dagegen Autoren, die ein asymmetrisches Trikolon ansetzen: D. Pardee 1997, S. 295; N. Wyatt 1998, S. 380.

75 Vgl. dagegen zB. D. Pardee 1997, S. 295 mit Anm. 8, der den Text auf die einzeln angerufenen Gottheiten bezieht, von denen jede nur fähig sei, eine limitierte Anzahl von Schlangen zu beschwören. Dagegen erfülle Ḥorōn schließlich alle in ihn gesetzten Erwartungen und zerstöre das ganze Gift; ähnlich S. B. Parker 1997, S. 219-220.

Die Tatsache, daß die Gottheiten sich zum Schluß auf einen Stuhl setzen und die fressende Schlange beobachten, gibt unmißverständlich zu verstehen, daß sie sich voll mit deren Aktion identifizieren[76] und eine Legitimierung des Beschwörungspriesters ablehnen.[77]

wṯq ‖ *lḥm* Š "stärken" ‖ "füttern":

A. Caquot (1989, 84 Anm. 261) versucht, die finiten Verbformen, die auch bei einem femininen Subjekt (Z. 20; siehe Z. 77-79) masculin bleiben, dadurch zu erklären, daß er in *nḥš* das Subjekt sieht und die Verbformen passivisch deutet. Dieses Problem ergibt sich für A. Caquot von der Annahme her, daß in Z. 6b die Gottheit um ein Eingreifen gebeten werde. Stattdessen läßt sich die fehlende Kongruenz in Z. 23 damit erklären, daß das Schema von Z. 6b-7 als formelhaft angesehen wurde und deswegen darauf verzichtet werden konnte, den Text im Einzelfall umzuformulieren.

Der Bedeutungsansatz von *wṯq* "stärken"[78] war lange umstritten,[79] liegt aber aufgrund des parallelen *lḥm* Š "zu essen geben, füttern"[80] auf der Hand.

76 M. C. Astour 1968, S. 19, zieht dafür zwei Erklärungsmöglichkeiten in Betracht: erstens, Füttern der Schlange, um ihr das Gift durch eine andere Ernährung zu entziehen; zweitens, Füttern der Schlange, um zu demonstrieren, daß sie letztlich zahm ist – das Füttern von Schlangen mit kleinen Tieren werde selbst in modernen Vivarien als Spektakel durchgeführt.

77 M. Tsevat 1979, S. 759, 763, bezieht Z. 6b-7 lediglich auf El, der nicht daran denke, sich von der Schlange zu trennen. Die Szene schließe damit, daß er sich einen Stuhl heranhole und sich setze – ein Bild der Zufriedenheit; D. W. Young 1979, S. 840, "The Response"; C. H. Bowman – R. B. Coote 1980, S. 138; A. Caquot 1989, S. 85, "(Mais le dieu) dispose un trône et s'assied."

78 *yṯq* "er stärkte", G PK 3.m.Sg.; vgl. ar. *waṯiqa* vertrauen, fest sein, II fest, solid machen, stärken (Wehr 1374a); C. H. Bowman – R. B. Coote 1980, S. 136.

79 Ch. Virolleaud 1968, S. 569, hatte ar. *wṯq* "ligoter" zur Diskussion gestellt, an das sich M. C. Astour 1968, S. 18, anschloss, gleichzeitig aber betont, daß hier "binden" im Sinn von akk. *kaṣāru* vorliege, folglich ein Binden durch Beschwörung. Die weniger wahrscheinliche Ableitung von *šqy* "trinken, zu trinken geben" erwog Ch. Virolleaud 1968, S. 569, auch: "Mais peut-être le scribe a-t-il écrit *yṯq* pour *yšq* "il donne à boire").
Vgl. dagegen M. J. Mulder 1972, S. 90 Anm. 75, *ṯwq* "einengen", he. *šwq*, akk. *sâqu* D "'einengen'(?)"; M. Tsevat 1979, S. 759, 762-763, ar. *waṯiqa* "vertrauen" u.ä., "Doch dieser steht mit der Schlange gut"; D. W. Young 1979, S. 843, 845, *ṯqq* "to forage", he. *šqq* (Prov 28,15; Jl 2,9; Jes 33,4); M. Dietrich – O. Loretz 1980, S. 160, *ṯqy* D "erhöhen".

80 *yšlḥm* "er fütterte" Š PK 3.m.Sg. – Vgl. dagegen E. Lipiński 1974, 169, 172, *yšlḥm* "il combat"; C. H. Bowman – R. B. Coote 1980, S. 136, *yšlḥ+m* "He ... Sends off (<the snake>)".

3. Mythos und Realität in KTU 1.100:1-60 – Sitz im Leben von KTU 1.100 als mythischem Begleittext zur Beschwörung

Die Bitte an die einzelnen Götter hat den Zweck, dem Beschwörer (*mlḫš*, Z. 5b) Kraft und Legitimation zu verleihen, die Rezitation einer Beschwörung gegen das tödliche Gift eines Schlangenbisses erfolgreich einzusetzen. Denn der Beschwörer kann die Beschwörung der *um* "Mutter" erst dann wirksam umsetzen, wenn die Gottheit zustimmt, die für Schlangen- und Schlangengiftbeschwörungen zuständig ist.[81] Ihre Tätigkeit wird als Nachahmung eines mythischen Urbildes gedeutet, wie der zweite Teil, KTU 1.100:61-76, verdeutlicht.

Während die Besuche bei den ersten elf Gottheiten in ihren Heiligtümern (Z. 3-55.77-78) offensichtlich ergebnislos verlaufen, bringt der zwölfte bei Ḥorōn den gewünschten Erfolg: Seine Macht über Schlangen und Schlangengift verhilft der nach der Macht der Beschwörung rufenden *um* "Mutter" (Z. 1) dazu, in der Welt der Menschen eine Beschwörung gegen Schlangengift durchführen zu lassen.

Hinsichtlich des Sitzes im Leben von KTU 1.100 läßt sich daraus ableiten, daß er als Mythos während der Durchführung einer Beschwörung vorgetragen wurde und der Beschwörung ihre mythologische Rechtfertigung lieferte. Dies ist letztendlich der wichtigste Grund dafür, KTU 1.100 nicht als eine Beschwörung einzustufen.

Das ablehnende Verhalten der angerufenen Gottheiten im Rahmen von KTU 1.100:1-56 und das eingreifende des Ḥorōn in Z. 61-76 führen zum Schluß, daß Ḥorōn als der alleinige Herr über die Schlangen[82] und deren Gift angesehen war. Nur er ist befugt und imstande, Vergiftungen durch Schlangenbiß zuzulassen oder deren Beseitigung zu bewirken.[83] Im Rahmen der magischen Medizin ist eine Beseitigung nur mittels Rezitation einer Beschwörung durch einen göttlich legitimierten Beschwörungspriester möglich.

---

81 Vgl. z.B. das Verhältnis zwischen Asarluḫi und Enki in der Beschwörung VS 10, 193, und die diesbezüglichen Ausführungen von N. Veldhuis 1993, S. 161-168.

82 Siehe O. Keel 1992, S. 224-226, zu Herr und Herrin der Schlangen in Vorderasien, allerdings ohne Bezugnahme auf Ḥorōn.

83 O. Keel 1992, S. 229, deutet Schlangenappliken aus Ton auf Gefäßdeckeln oder an Gefäßausgüssen, -rändern und -schultern nach dem Prinzip *similia similibus curantur*. Sie hätten die Funktion gehabt, den Inhalt der Gefäße vor Verlust und Vergiftung zu schützen, gleichzeitig aber auch ihn mit der Vitalität der Schlange anzureichern.

Literatur[84]

Aartun, K., 1974 "Die Partikeln des Ugaritischen", *AOAT* 21/1.

Alster, B., 1999 "Tiamat", in *Dictionary of Deities and Demons in the Bible*, S. 867-869.

Astour, M., ²1967 *Hellenosemitica*, Leiden.

Astour, M., 1968 "Two Ugaritic Serpent Charms", *JNES* 27, S. 13-28.

Bordreuil, P., 1983 "'Venin de printemps, venin foudroyant': A propos de RS 24.244 l. 5", *UF* 15, S. 299-300.

Bordreuil, P., 1985 "Ashtart de Mari et les dieu d'Ugarit", *M.A.R.I.* 4, S. 545-548.

Bordreuil, P. – D. Pardee, 1989 *La trouvaille épigraphique de l'Ougarit. 1. Concordance*, *RSOu* 5.

Bowman, C. H. – R. B. Coote, 1980 "A Narrative Incantation for Snake Bite", *UF* 12, S. 135-139.

Caquot, A., 1989 "KTU 1.100", *TO* II, S. 79-94.

Dahood, M., 1972 "Ugaritic-Hebrew Parallel Pairs", *RSP* I, S. 71-382.

Dahood, M., 1989 *Ugaritic-Hebrew Philology*, Second Reprint (With Minor Corrections), *BibOr* 17.

Del Olmo Lete, G., 1979 "Quantity Precision in Ugaritic Administrative Texts (*ṣmd*, *ḥrṣ*, *aḥd*)", *UF* 11, S. 179-186.

Dietrich, M. – O. Loretz, 1975 "Untersuchungen zur Schrift- und Lautlehre des Ugaritischen (III): "Formen und ugaritisch-hurritische Lautwert(e) des keilalphabetischen Zeichens 'ẓ'", *UF* 7, S. 103-108.

Dietrich, M. – O. Loretz, 1980 "Die Bannung von Schlangengift (KTU 1.100 und KTU 1.107:7b-13a.19b-20)", *UF* 12, S. 153-170.

Dietrich, M. – O. Loretz, 1985 "Die akkadischen Tierbezeichnungen *immeru*, *puḫādu* und *puḫālu* im Ugaritischen und Hebräischen", *UF* 17, S. 99-103.

Dietrich, M. – O. Loretz, 1993 "Ein "hurritisches" Zusatzzeichen des Keilalphabets?", *UF* 25, S. 137-142.

Dietrich, M. – O. Loretz, 1996 *Analytic Ugaritic Bibliography 1972-1988*, *AOAT* 20/6.

Dietrich, M. – O. Loretz, 1997-1998 "Wohnorte Els nach Ugarit- und Bibeltexten. Eine Studie zu ug. *ġr ll* ‖ *hr mʿd* und *he. hr mwʿd* ‖ *yrkty ṣpwn* (KTU 1.2 I 20; Jes 14,13)", *UF* 29, S. 123-149.

84 Siehe ferner M. Dietrich – O. Loretz 1980, S. 153 Anm. 1; *id.* 1996, S. 480-483; D. Pardee 1988, S. 194.

Dietrich, M. – O. Loretz – J. Sanmartín, 1973 "Die ugaritischen Verben *MRR* I, *MRR* II, und MRR III", *UF* 5, S. 119-122.

Dietrich, M. – O. Loretz – J. Sanmartín, 1975 "Bemerkungen zur Schlangenbeschwörung RS 24.244 = Ug. 5, S. 564ff. Nr. 7", *UF* 7, S. 121-125.

Dijkstra, M., 1999 "Ugaritic Prose", in W. G. E. Watson – N. Wyatt, *Handbook of Ugaritic Studies*, *HdO* 39, S. 140-164.

Falkenstein, A., 1931 *Die Haupttypen der sumerischen Beschwörung literarisch untersucht*, *LSS* NF 1.

Galter, H. D., 1981 *Der Gott Ea/Enki in der akkadischen Überlieferung. Eine Bestandsaufnahme des vorhandenen Materials*, Dissertationen der Karl-Franzens-Universität Graz 58.

Gibson, J. C. L., 1999 "The Ugaritic Literary Texts", in W. G. E. Wastson – N. Wyatt, *Handbook of Ugaritic Studies*, *HdO* 39, S. 193-202.

Hendel, R. S., 1999 "Serpent *nḥš*", *Dictionary of Deities and Demons in the Bible*, S. 744-747.

Horowitz, W., 1998 *Mesopotamian Cosmic Geography*, *MC* 8.

Keel, O., 1992 *Das Recht der Bilder gesehen zu werden. Drei Fallstudien zur Methode der Interpretation altorientalischer Bilder*, *OBO* 122.

Korpel, M. C. A., 1990 *A Rift in the Clouds. Ugaritic and Hebrew Descriptions of the Divine*, *UBL* 8.

Kottsieper, I., 1984 "KTU 1.100 – Versuch einer Deutung", *UF* 16, S. 97-11.

Krašovec, J., 1977 *Der Merismus im Biblisch-Hebräischen und Nordwestsemitischen*, *BibOr* 33.

Kutler, L., 1984 "A 'Strong' Case for Hebrew *mar*", *UF* 16, S. 111-118.

Lipiński, E., 1974 "La légende sacrée de la conjuration des morsures de serpents", *UF* 6, S. 169-174.

Lipiński, E., 1999 "Shemesh *šmš*", in *DDD*, S. 764-768.

Loretz, O., 1998 "Akkadisch-ugaritisch *ḫalbu*/*ḥlb* – hebräisch *ḥlb* (Ps 81,17)", in M. Dietrich – O. Loretz, ed., *dubsar anta-men. Studien zur Altorientalistik. Festschrift für Willem H. Ph. Römer*, *AOAT* 253, S. 223-244.

Moor, J. C. de, 1987 "Myth and Ritual VI (KTU 1.100)", *ARTU*, S. 146-156.

Moor, J. C. de – K. Spronk, 1987 *A Cuneiform Anthology of Religious Texts from Ugarit. Autographed Texts and Glossary*, Leiden.

Mulder, M. J., 1972 "Hat man in Ugarit die Sonnenwende begangen?", *UF* 4, S. 79-96.

Pardee, D., 1978 "The Semitic Root *mrr* and the etymology of Ugaritic *mr*(*r*) // *brk*", *UF* 10, S. 249-288.

Pardee, D., 1979 "*m*^e*rôrăt-p*^e*tanîm*, 'Venom', in Job 20,14", *ZAW* 91, S. 401-416.

Pardee, D., 1988 "Ḥôrānu et les serpents", *RSO* 4, S. 193-226.

Pardee, D., 1997 "Ugaritic liturgy against venomous reptiles (1.94)", in *COS* I, S. 295-298.

Parker, S. B., 1997 "The Mare and Ḥorōn. 25. CAT 1.100", in *UNP*, S. 219-223.

Pomponio, F. – P. Xella, 1997 Les dieux d'Ebla. Étude analytique des divinités éblaïtes à l'époque des archives royales du IIIe millénaire, AOAT 245.

Renfroe, F., 1985 "Arabic Evidence for Ugaritic *pḥl* 'Stallion'", *UF* 17, S. 410-411.

Renfroe, F., 1992 Arabic-Ugaritic Lexical Studies, ALASP 5.

Sasson, J. M., 1972 "Flora, Fauna and Minerals", *RSP* I, S. 383-452.

Sperling, S. D., 1993 "Ḥbr and Friends", in M. E. Cohen – D. C. Snell – D. B. Weisberg (eds.), *The Tablet and the Scroll. Near Eastern Studies in Honor of William W. Hallo*, Bethesda, S. 225-229.

Spronk, K., 1999 "The Incantations", in W. G. E. Watson – N. Wyatt, *Handbook of Ugaritic Studies*, *HdO* 39, S. 270-286.

Tropper, J., 1990 *Der ugaritische Kausativstamm und die Kausativbildungen des Semitischen*, *ALASP* 2.

Tropper, J. – E. Verreet, 1988 "Ugaritisch *ndy*, *ydy*, *hdy*, *ndd* und *d*(*w*)*d*", *UF* 20, S. 339-355.

Tsevat, M., 1979 "Der Schlangentext von Ugarit. UT 607 – KTU 1.100 – Ug V, 564ff. – RS 24.244", *UF* 11, S. 759-778.

Xella, P., 1981 "KTU 1.100", *TRU* I, S. 224-240.

van Soldt, W. H., 1991 *Studies in the Akkadian of Ugarit. Dating and Grammar*, *AOAT* 40.

Veldhuis, N., 1993 "An UR III Incantation against the Bite of a Snake, a Scorpion, or a Dog (VS 10, 193)", *ZA* 83, S. 161-169.

Verreet, E., 1988 *Modi ugaritici*, *OLA* 27.

Virolleaud, Ch., 1968 "Nouveaux textes mythologiques et liturgiques de Ras Shamra (XXIVe Campagne, 1961), 7. – RS 24.244", *Ugar.* 5, S. 564-572.

Ward, W. A., 1980 "Egypto-Semitic *MR*, 'Be Bitter, Strong'", *UF* 12, S. 357-360.

Watson, W .G. E., 1999 "Ugaritic Poetry", in W. G. E. Watson – N. Wyatt, *Handbook of Ugaritic Studies*, *HdO* 39, S. 165-192.

West, D. R., 1995 *Some Cults of Greek Goddesses and Female Daemons of Oriental Origin*, *AOAT* 233.

Wyatt, N., 1999 "The Religion of Ugarit: An Overwiew", in W. G. E. Watson – N. Wyatt, *Handbook of Ugaritic Studies*, *HdO* 39, S. 529-585.

Wyatt, N., 1998 "KTU 1.100 – The Myth of Shapsh and the Mare: A Spell against Snakebite", *RTU*, S. 378-387.

Young, D. W., 1979 "The Ugaritic myth of the god Ḥōrōn and the mare", *UF* 11, S. 839-848.

ENLIL, VATER DER GÖTTER*

DIETZ OTTO EDZARD

Universität München

1.1. Piotr Steinkeller hat 1988 bei einem AOS Meeting in Chicago auf den merkwürdigen Umstand ingewiesen, dass der Enlil gelesene Göttername bis in die Ur III-Zeit hinein ^{d}EN-É geschrieben wird, während die Frau Enlils, Ninlil, sich vom ältesten uns bekannten Beleg an (WF 1 vi 26) ^{d}Nin-KID schreibt.[1]

Erst während der Ur III-Zeit beginnen sich die Schreibungen in ein einheitliches ^{d}En-líl (KID) und ^{d}Nin-líl zu vereinigen.[2]

Steinkeller schloss aus diesem epigraphischen Befund, dass eine Deutung des Namens ^{d}En-líl als "Lord Wind" oder "Air God" nicht möglich sei. Aber auch die Bedeutung von líl spräche dagegen: "ghost, haunting spirit" (*zaqīqu, lilû*), nicht "wind".[3] Zu líl, vgl. unten 4.

Steinkeller meinte, dass die älteste uns überlieferte syllabische Schreibung, $^{(d)}$*I-li-lu* in Ebla,[4] möglicherweise auf ein **il-ilī* "god of (all) the gods" zurückgehe.

Enlil sei eine aus dem nördlichen Babylonien nach Nippur importierte Gottheit. "Enlil was a typical universal god, lacking any clear individual traits and without any specific domain, and therefore being very much Dagan (with whom he was identified at Mari probably already in ED times), El, and Ashshur". Steinkeller hält die ältere Schreibung ^{d}EN.É für ein Logogramm, "whose literal sense is 'master of the household, paterfamilias'".

1.2. Unmittelbare Reaktion auf Steinkellers Vortrag von 1988 war ein Aufsatz von Th. Jacobsen in der Fs. Å. Sjöberg (1989) 267-276, "The líl of ^{d}En-líl" (s. dort S.

---

* Für eine Durchsicht des Entwurfs, Kritik und viele sehr nützliche Hinweise habe ich W. Sallaberger zu danken.

1 S. jetzt P. Steinkeller, in: (ed.) K. Watanabe, *Priests and Officials in the Ancient Near East* (1999) 103-137, "On Rulers, Priests and Sacred Marriage", dort S. 114 Anm. 36.

2 M. Krebernik, *Beschwörungen aus Fara und Ebla* (1984) 279, hat jedoch erkannt, dass in der UD.GAL.NUN-Orthographie das zweite Element sowohl von Enlil als auch von Ninlil durch NUN wiedergegeben wird, so dass die Unterscheidung aufgehoben ist.

3 Zu *CAD* Z 60 s. unten 4.2.

4 In D. O. Edzard, *ARET* 5 no. 1 v 2-4, vi 1-3, 10-12: *I-li-lu*, A.MU, DINGIR.DINGIR.DINGIR; no. 3 i 6-ii 2, ii 8-iii 2: *I-li-lu*, ...

267 Anm. 1 Ende). Am Anfang seines Artikels (S. 267-269) hat Jacobsen den epigraphischen Befund zusammengefasst und in einer Tabelle veranschaulicht. Jacobsen versucht, das von Steinkeller gezeigte Dilemma dadurch zu beheben, dass er dem Zeichen É (REC 423) auch den Wert líl, zuschreibt, während er für KID (REC 425) die Lesung lil_x bietet. Jacobsen hält an einer Deutung von líl als "Wind" fest.

1.3. 1992 hat sich F. Wiggermann für eine Übersetzung "Lord Ether" ausgesprochen in seinem Beitrag "Mythological Foundations of Nature", in: (ed.) D. J. W. Meijer, *Natural Phenomena. Their Meaning, Depiction and Description*, 279-306. Besonderes Gewicht legt Wiggermann beim Begründen seiner Übersetzung auf den von Enlil vollzogenen Trennungsakt von Himmel und Erde, wie er andeutungsweise überliefert ist:[5] s. S. 282 und S. 299 Anm. 77.

1.4. P. Attinger, *Eléments de linguistique sumérienne* (1993) 709, meint bei der Behandlung von šu líl-lá du_{11}, wörtlich "faire la main de 'lil'", dass *CAD* Z 60 die Bedeutung "Wind" von *zaqīqu* zu Unrecht nur als sekundär anerkannt habe.[6] "Cette disctinction me semble trop tranchée, car les 'deux acceptions' sont connotativement voisines: un lieu voué au 'lil' est un lieu abandonné, ouvert à tous les vents et hanté de fantômes".[7]

1.5. Piotr Michalowski hat in seinem Eröffnungsreferat auf der Prager Rencontre assyriologique internationale 43 (1996) die Etymologie des Namens Enlil erneut zur Debatte gestellt: "The Unbearable Lightness of Enlil", in: (ed.) J. Prosecký, *Intellectual Life of the Ancient Near East* (1988) 237-247. Hinter dem geistreich anspielenden Titel verbirgt sich die These, der Name Enlil/Ellil sei semitischer Herkunft und stelle ursprünglich die Reduplikation von *ʾil* "Gott" dar, also **ʾilʾil*. "The writing Enlil represents a Sumerianization, through dissimilation, resulting in something that looks Sumerian - with the initial element en - but which was in reality a loan from another language" (S. 242). Wie Steinkeller weist Michalowski damit Versuche zurück, das Namenselement líl sumerisch zu deuten und in Enlil einen "Lord Wind", "Seigneur Air", "Herrn Luft" zu sehen.[8]

---

5 Prolog des Preisliedes auf die "Hacke" (^{giš}al); s. C. Wilcke, *RlA* 4 (1972-1975) 36.

6 S. unten 4.2.

7 Attinger zitiert S. 710 Jacobsen (*Fs. Sjöberg* S. 272 mit Anm. 26), der líl, und líl-lá als Partizipien eines Verbums "to blow" erwägt.

8 Auch Edzard, *Wörterbuch der Mythologie* 1 (1962) 59 schlug für Enlil "Herr Windeshauch" vor. - Michalowski betont in Lamentation over the Destruction of Sumer and Ur (1989) 98 (Komm. zu Z. 345): "líl = *zaqīqu* means 'phantom, ghost, haunted place', never 'wind'".

Wie Steinkeller beruft sich Michalowski bei seinem Deutungsvorschlag auf die in Ebla bezeugte Schreibung $^{(d)}$*I-li-lu* (s. oben Anm. 3). Der Autor zitiert S. 242 Anm. 9 den ihm vorgetragenen Einwand, dass in eblaitischer Orthographie ein anlautendes I- nur [yi-] darstellen könne, nicht aber [ʾi-], so dass die Rückführung auf *ʾilʾil schwer denkbar sei. Er reagiert mit dem Argument, dass sein Etymologie-Vorschlag weit in die prähistorische Zeit zurückreiche, "and that the Ebla spelling represents a secondary stage, in which the Semitic phonological structure of the name had long been adapted to the Sumerian language".

2. Theoretische Erwägungen zu ^{d}*En-É*

2.1. En-É ist am ältesten belegt in der Ǧamdat-Naṣr-zeitlichen Verbindung En-É-tìl, falls diese, wie erstmals A. Falkenstein 1936 vorschlug,[9] als PN zu deuten ist, der die Elemente "Enlil" und "Leben" enthält.[10] Wenn wir einen GN ^{d}En-É unbefangen deuten, werden wir entweder eine Genitivverbindung "Herr des Hauses" oder eine appositionelle Verbindung "Herr, (der) das Haus (ist)" vermuten, wobei offen bleiben würde, ob É das Heiligtum des Gottes meint oder nicht. Spätestens in Ean. 1 xvi 14-15 šuš-gal-^{d}En-É-lá(-k) "Fangnetz des Enlil" stellen wir fest, dass der betr. GN eine appositionelle Verbindung darstellt und dass das zweite Namenselement auf -l endet. Es gibt keinen Hinweis darauf, dass das Wort für das "Haus", das wir als *hay rekonstruieren können,[11] ursprünglich auf -l geendet habe. Es wäre daher, wenn wir den GN sumerisch etymologisieren wollen, ein anderes nominales Element, das auf -l endete, anzunehmen - einschliesslich des später KID = líl geschriebenen Elements.

2.2. Sowohl Steinkeller (s. oben 1.1) als auch Michalowski (oben 1.5) stellen eine semitische Etymologie eines logographisch, ^{d}EN.É geschriebenen Gottes zur Debatte. Während Steinkeller die Problematik des Anlauts *I-* in $^{(d)}$*I-li-lu* nicht disku-

9 Archaische Texte aus Uruk S. 38.

10 Belegübersicht bei R. K. Englund - J.-P. Grégoire, *The Proto-cuneiforms Texts from Jemdet Nasr* (1991) 98 s.v. E_{2a}; 99-102 s.v. EN_a; 152 s.v. Ti_a Weniger wahrscheinlich ist, dass die Verbindung $En_a.E_{2a}$ die Stadt Nippur meinte.

11 So wegen des Reflexes von é-gal als haykal im Hebräischen (> *hēḵal*), Arabischen (*haykal*), Türkischen (*heykel*).

tiert, ist Michalowski sich der Sache bewusst. Jedoch verweist er den semitischen Ursprung des Namens in eine unbestimmte und unbestimmbare Vergangenheit zurück.

2.3. Unbefangener Angang der Ebla-Schreibung $^{(d)}$*I-li-lu*: Steinkeller und Michalowski unterscheiden sich von der sonst meist üblichen Reaktion von Assyriologen, wenn sie mit Ebla-Orthographie konfrontiert werden. Man ist sonst eher bereit, Ebla-Orthographie anzuerkennen als Quelle für die Kenntnis der Aussprache des Sumerischen in der Zeit vor Sargon, d.h. mehrere Jahrhunderte vor den Ausspracheglossen der altbab. Serie Proto-Ea (MLS 14).

Hier nur drei Beispiele: sila$_4$ "Lamm" hat in Ebla den Zeichennamen *sa-la-um* (A. Archi, *Eblaitica* 1 [1987], 93 ff.); d.h. eine Form, [sala] steht der jüngeren [sila] gegenüber.[12]

šinig "Tamariske" lautet *ša-na-gúm* (ebd. 97:9); d.h. [šanag] steht jüngerem [šinig] gegenüber.[13]

Für ter/tir "Wald" bietet Ebla *ti-i-ru*$_{12}$*-um* (ebd. 96:75). Hier ist mit *ti-i-r* eine zweisilbige Form [tiyir] bezeichnet gegenüber jüngerem einsilbigen [te/ir].[14]

Solche Beispiele lassen sich vermehren.[15] Angesichts einer 'Gleichung' $^{(d)}$*I-li-l*(*u*) = ^{d}En-É fühlt man sich herausgefordert, die beiden Formen zu harmonisieren, d.h. ^{d}En-É möglichst nahe an [Yil(l)il(u)] heranzuführen. Falls É für [lil] steht, wäre *li-l*(*u*) ganz und gar unproblematisch. Auch die Assimilation des auslautenden -n von [en] an ein folgendes [l] lässt sich unschwer erklären.[16] So reduziert sich die

12 si-la = GÁ×PA MSL 14, 114 no. 4: 19 (Proto-Ea, secondary branch).

13 [ši]-ni-ig = ŠIN[IG] Proto-Ea 820 (MSL 14, 61).

14 te-er = TIR Proto-Ea 457 (MSL 14, 50). - Bei einer Schreibung CV-VC ist in Texten des III. Jahrtausends oft unsicher, ob CVC oder CV'VC zu lesen sei. Vgl. das Beispiel des Heiligtums ti-ra-áš im präsargonischen Lagaš. Hier ist eher dreisilbig tira'aš zu lesen als zweisilbig tiraš, da die Schreibung schoh bei Ur-Nanše vorkommt (Urn. 25 v 8): ti-áš:ra. Bei zweisilbigem *tiraš würden wir nach dem orthographischen Brauch der präsargonischen Zeit eher *ti-ra(-š) erwarten unter Vernachlässigung der Notierung des silbenschliessenden Konsonanten. Vgl. auch Edzard, Gudea (= RIME 3/1) S. 75 Anm. zu Cyl. A x 15.

15 Vgl. jetzt Y. Gong, *Die Namen der Keilschriftzeichen* (= AOAT 268, 2000) 78-83, "Zeichennamen aus Ebla".

16 J. Bauer, OBO 160/1 (1998) 435 nennt als Beispiele für die Assimilation des auslautenden -n von NIN an folgenden Konsonenten ^{d}Níĝ-ĝír-su (RTC 5 i 2, v 2) für [Ninĝirsu] und ^{d}Nim$_5$(NÍG)-mú (RTC 8 ii 6) für [Ninmu].

Aufgabe, eine Formannäherung vorzunehmen, auf den Anlaut von EN. Wir müssten bei einer interpretatio sumerica folgerichtig ein mit [y] anlautendes EN ansetzen, also *[yen] oder - mit neutralem V(okal) - *[yVn]. Das führt zur Frage nach der Aussprachetradition von EN.

3. Die Aussprachetradition von EN

3.1. Proto-Ea 416 (MSL 14, 48) verfährt tautologisch: en = EN. Der Zeichenname lautet *e-nu*, seltener EN-*nu*,[17] und ebenso lautet das ins Akkadische entlehnte *ēnu*(*m*). Häufige Schreibungen sind *e-nu*(*-um*), *e-ni*, *i-ni*, EN-*um* (*CAD* E 177-179) gegenüber sehr seltenem, EN-*nu* und EN-*na* (ebd.). Der Befund spricht für einen langen Vokal in EN.[18]

3.2. Sum. en ist durch in vertreten in Šulgi (TIM 9, 35:18(!)) in he-a = *lu e-nu-um* "sei es ein ēn". Hierher gehören auch syllabische Schreibungen wie Il-li-il; s. A. Falkenstein, *ZA* 55 (1962) 60.

3.3. Die Götterwaffe an-kár(a) in Gudea Cyl. A vi 21 wird en-kár(a) geschrieben in Cyl. B vii 13.[19]

3.4. In Ebla steht bei Verbalformen (theophorer Personennamen) EN in Anfangsstellung oft dort, wo man eine 3. Person masc. mit Präfix *y*- erwartet. Das hat M. Krebernik 1985 festgestellt.[20] J. M. Pagan führt 1998[21] 52 entsprechende Fälle auf (S. 23, 305-308).

3.5. EN wäre wohl nicht so häufig als akk. Syllabogramm für [yi(n)] verwendet worden, wenn es nicht ein sumerisches Vorbild mit y-Anlaut gegeben hätte, also *[yVn]. Auf der anderen Seite konnten wir Gründe dafür anführen (s. oben 3.1),

---

17 Gong (wie Anm. 15) S. 115.

18 Der Hinweis, dass die Vokalquantität sumerischer Lehnwörter im Akkadischen wie auch die Vokalquantität in Zeichennamen Rückschlüsse auf Kurz- oder Langvokal im sumerischen Ausgangswort erlauben, wurde dem Verfasser vor vielen Jahren von Th. Jacobsen nahegebracht. Man ist dem bisher nie systematisch nachgegangen. - D. Fleming, *The Installation of Baal's High Priestess at Emar* (= *HSS* 42, 1992) 81 mit Anm. 43 fragt, ob EN-tu in Emar *ittu* zu lesen sei. W. G. Lambert, *BiOr*. 52 (1995) 88 zieht *ettu* vor. Eine Vokalverkürzung nach Kontraktion wäre als sekundär zu betrachten.

19 Vgl. auch á-an-kár(a) in Inanna und Ebeh 2: P. Attinger, *ZA* 88 (1998) 168.

20 Vgl. AfO 32 (1985) 57 Anm. 22: "Nach Ausweis zahlreicher in PN erscheinenden Verbalformen (3. m.) stehen *íl*, *ìr*, *en*/*e*$_x$ überwiegend für [yil], [yir], [yi(n)]".

21 ARES 3, A Morphological and Lexical Study of Personal Names in the Ebla Texts.

dass EN einen langen Vokal hatte.[22] Unsere Rekonstruktion lässt sich folglich erweitern zu *[yV̄n], wobei V̄ = "ē" oder "ī".[23]

3.6. Wenn wir unter solchen Voraussetzungen ^{d}En-É (= Enlil) und in Ebla $^{(d)}$*I-li-l*(*u*) vergleichen, so können wir in *I-li-l*(*u*) den Reflex eines Namens *Yēn/Yīn-lil sehen, ohne dass wir ad hoc geschaffene Lautgesetze anwenden oder gar überstrapazieren müssten.

3.7. A n h a n g. Eine phonetische Diskussion von sum. EN wäre unvollständig, wenn die Emesal-Form [umun] ausser Betracht bliebe. Sowohl für en als auch für lugal steht in Emesal-Götternamen *ù-mu-un* oder eine verkürzte Form mu-uC (C = assimilierter Konsonant wie in ^{d}Mu-ul-líl). Vgl. M. K. Schretter, *Emesalstudien* (1990) 263 f. In jüngerer (nach altbab.) Überlieferung ist syllabisches ù-mu-un durch das Logogramm U = umun ersetzt.

Sind en und umun lautlich verwandt? Die Diskussion ist bei Schretter lakonisch zusammengefasst zu "Die Grundform ist im H(aupt)D(ialekt) *emen > *ewen > en, im ES umun". Der u-Vokalismus in der Emesal-Form liesse sich erklaren als Labialisierung der Vokalqualität unter dem Einfluss eines labialen Nasals (m) oder eines stimmhaften bilabialen Reibelauts (w).

Ebenso gut können wir aber auch an ein heteronymisches Paar (y)ēn : umun denken, so wie wir ja ganz zweifelsfreie Heteronymie haben bei nin : gašan "Herrin". Zwar erscheint (in unserer Latein-Transliteration!) die lautliche Nähe bei (y)Vn / (y)ēn und VmVn / umun grösser zu sein als bei nin und gašan, die man selbst bei kühnster Strapazierung hypothetischer Lautentwicklungen nicht auf einen gemeinsamen Nenner bringen könnte. Aber wir wollen die Frage auf sich beruhen lassen, da sie sich nicht eindeutig beantworten lässt.

---

22 W. Sommerfeld, *Die Texte der Akkade-Zeit. 1. Das Dijala-Gebiet: Tutub* (1999) 20 Anm. 29 stellt für das babylonische Altakkadisch die folgende Verteilungsregel von (Ì, IL), IN, (IR) und (I, ÍL), EN, (ÌR) auf: Die erste Reihe wird verwendet, wenn eine geschlossene Silbe CVC mit den beiden Zeichen CV+VC geschrieben wird (z.B. *i-dì-in*) oder wenn Stimmabsatz am Wortanfang ausgedrückt werden soll.

Die zweite Reihe steht in allen anderen Fällen, u.a. am Wortanfang beim Verbalpräfix *yi*(*n*)-. Anlautendes *yin-* verwendet EN, nie IN.

EN und IN sind nach Sommerfeld nicht im Sinne eines Kontrastes zweier Vokalqualitäten zu verstehen.

23 Wenn es schon im Akkadischen oft schwierig ist, die Qualität eines Vokals auf [e] oder [i], festzulegen, so wächst die Unsicherheit im Sumerischen noch um das Mehrfache an.

4. líl

4.1. Wir kommen zurück auf das Dilemma, das sich uns darbietet in der Schreibung [d]En-É mit seit Eanatum von Lagaš nachweisbarem Auslaut auf -l. Wir können auf eine - sehr knappe - Diskussion von líl nicht verzichten; denn ausser líl steht uns kein anderes sumerisches Lemma zur Verfügung, das einem É-l entprechen würde.

Hätte das Sumerische einmal ein Wort É-l besessen, das im Verlauf der Sprachentwicklung noch im III. Jahrtausend untergegangen wäre; das dann aber lautlicher Nähe wegen mit líl gleichtgesetzt worden sei? Dergleichen ist leicht vermutet und als Hypothese ausgesprochen; es führt uns aber wegen Unbeweisbarkeit nicht weiter.

4.2. Im ausführlichen Diskussionsabschinitt am Ende des Artikels *zaqīqu* (*CAD* Z 60) ist man bestrebt, eine Bedeutung "wind, storm" für *zaqīqu* auszuschliessen, da *šāru*, "Wind" als akkadische Entsprechung von líl sowie als "Synonym" von *ziqīqu* (Lautvariante von *zaqīqu*) nur in lexikalischen Texten, nicht aber auch in Bilinguen vorkäme. B. Landsberger hatte in DLZ 1928, 2098 für *zaqīqu* die Bedeutungen "Hauch, Schemen, Geist" vorgeschlagen (zitiert bei Falkenstein, *ZA* 45 [1939] 24). W. von Soden hat dagegen in *AHw* III 1530, seinem Lemma *zīqīqu* (*zāqīqu*) die Bedeutungen "Wind, Hauch; Geist; Traumgott" zuerkannt, also an erster Stelle "Wind".

4.3. Th. Jacobsen (s. oben 1.2) hat S. 270 seine Übersetzung "Lord Wind" für Enlil bekräftig. Dabei fügt er aber präzisierend hinzu, dass líl in der Bedeutung "Wind" der älteren Sprache angehöre. Diese Bedeutung habe sich nur in bestimmten festen Verbindungen erhalten. Es sei also nicht mehr als ein frei verwendbares lexikalisches Lemma anzusehen. Jacobsen nahm an, "that the god was seen as a personification of the wind and the numinous power in it much as the name of the god An presents him as the deified sky ..." (S. 270).

4.4. Unbestreitbar ist die Bedeutung "windig, phantomhaft, Niemand" im Vermerk der Sumerischen Königliste über den "alten Mann" (ab-ba) des Gilgameš. Er sei ein líl-lá gewesen, ein Niemand.[24]

4.5. Sonstige Verbindungen mit líl oder auch das Wort allein lassen sich teils mit dem "Wind" als solchem verbinden, teils auch mit der "Windigkeit", dem

---

24 Vgl. W. Heimpel, *ZA* 82 (1992) 10. Jacobsen hatte in seiner Edition von 1939 (AS 11) S. 89 Anm. 128 schon auf die bei Aelian, *De natura animalium* xii 21 überlieferte Geschichte von der Geburt des Gilgamos hingewiesen, der "by an obscure person" gezeugt worden wäre (ék tinos andròs aphanoûs).

"Heimgesuchtsein", dem "Phantomhaften" bis hin zum "Nichts" oder, mit -a verbunden, "Niemand". Oft steht die Übersetzung im Ermessen des Interpreten, und eine Entscheidung in der einen oder anderen Richtung lässt sich bei unbefangenem Angang der Belege nicht erzwingen.

Der folgende sehr knappe Überblick ist reduziert auf das uns am nötigsten Erscheinende, und er soll in keiner Weise einer Untersuchung des Wortes líl gleichkommen.[25]

4.5.1. líl in Genitivverbindungen

4.5.1.1. é-líl-lá. "haunted place" Innin-šagurra 16: Å. Sjöberg, *ZA* 65 (1975) 178 (Var. -lá-e, lá-lá, líl S. 202); = *bīt zaqīqi* (s. S. 212). Alternativübersetzung "Haus, das dem Wind ausgesetzt ist".

É/GÁ-líl-lá = GÁ×LÍL.LÁ = É *za-qí-qu*, [É ...], É *ṣe-ri*, É ⌜x⌝-[x(-x)], É *er-ṣe-tú*, É [...], É ⌜*qa*⌝-[*ab-rum*(?)], [É ...] Aa 1V/4, 193-200 (MSL 14, 387).[26]

In Aa IV/4, 193-200 ist neben É *zaqīqu* der einzige voll erhaltene Eintrag É *erṣetu*. Man könnte vermuten (aber für definitive Schlüsse ist zu wenig erhalten), dass líl lexikalisch negativ belastet war.

Nicht hierher gehört é-líl-lá als Variante von e-líl-lá, wozu unten 4.5.1.7.

4.5.1.2. eden-líl-lá, Th. Jacobsen, *JNES* 12 (1953) 168 Anm. 28, "desert of the wind". Alternativübersetzung "haunted desert", "windige, von Geistern heimgesuchte Steppe".

4.5.1.3. lú-líl-lá ist nach OB lú B vi 26 f. (MSL 12, 186) = *a-wi-il za-qí-qi-i*[*m*], *Su-tu-u*[*m*]; es folgen weiter Sutäer und Amurriter. Der Kontext legt eine Übersetzung "der aus der windigen (Zone)" oder "der aus der Leere" nahe, was eine passende Beschreibung des Nomaden wäre. Hier ist wohl nicht Gespenstisches impliziert.

Auch lú-líl-lá ḫur-sag̃-g̃á tuš-a "der aus der Leere, der im ansteigenden Land wohnt" ist der Nomade; s. Išme-Dagān von Isin A 271-272.[27]

---

25 Ich bin St. Tinney sehr zu Dank verpflichtet für die Möglichkeit, seine über das Internet zu erreichende Datenbank zu benutzen. - Vor Jacobsen (s. oben 1.2) hat sich am ausfürlichsten J. Krecher, *SKL*, (1966) 178-180, mit líl, auseinandergesetzt, für das er "Schemen" empfahl.

26 Da É und GÁ neubab. zusammengefallen sind, lässt sich É/GÁ - zumindest in CT 12,22 a iii 6' - nicht auf eine der beiden Lesungen festlegen.

27 Bezogen auf die MAR.TU-Nomaden; s. W. H. Ph. Römer, *SKIZ* (1965) 53.

Lú-líl-lá als Variante von lú-lil-lá = *lillu* "Tölpel" bleibt, da nicht zugehörig, aus unserer Diskussion ausgeschlossen; s. *CAD* und *AHw.* s.v. *lillu.*

4.5.1.4. sug-líl-lá (oder: ambar-líl-lá) ist mir unklar; s. K. Volk, Balag (= FAOS 18, 1989) 141:48 und 172 f. (Kommentar).

4.5.1.5. šu-líl-lá ba-ab-du$_{11}$ P. Michalowski, LSUr (1989) Z. 143, 149 und *Kommentar* S. 73 (zu Z. 29): "was haunted" (vom Heigtum gesagt); Attinger (s. oben 1.4) S. 710: "fut voué à l'abandon". Alternativübersetzung: "war der Hand des Windes ausgesetzt".

4.5.1.6. TÚG.LÍL.LÁ = *taḫapšu,* etwa "Pferdedecke" (hurritisches Lehnwort). Man könnte, falls der Deutungsansatz zutrifft, an die ad hoc-Schaffung eines Sumerogramms für ein Stück Stoff denken, das das Pferd vor Zugluft, Kälte schützen sollte.[28]

4.5.1.7. ub-líl-lá "Ecke von lil" = *ibratu* (Etymologie unbekannt): "open-air shrine (a niche in a corner on the street or in a court)", "Kultnische an Aussenwänden".

Die Babylon-Beschreibung Tintir V 86 (A. George, *Bab. Topographical Texts* [1992] 68) summiert 180 UB.LÍL.LÁ der Ištar (vorher 300 *parakku* der Igigi und 600 *parakku* der Anūna-Götter). Vgl. die Diskussion dort S. 369, wo auch Ištars Epithet ^{d}NIN$^{be\text{-}let}$ *ib-ra*[*t-ti*] "Herrin der *i.*" genannt ist. Die Zahl ist sehr hoch; das Verhätnis zwischen *parakku* (900) und *ibratu* (180) ist - zufälligerweise? - 5:1.

Zu E. I. Gordon, SP 1.142, s. *CAD* I s.v. *ibratu* und George 1992, 369.

Falls das líl von ub-líl-lá überhaupt mit dem hier besprochenen líl zusammenhängt, ist vielleicht an eine Grundbedeutung "windige, zugige Ecke" zu denken. Es dürfte hier kaum etwas Geisterhaft-gespenstisches im Spiel sein.

[4.5.1.8.] Nicht zu unserer Thematik gehören - wohl meist lautmalende - Ausdrücke für Ausrufe, Zurufe, Lieder o.ä, wie e-líl-lá, ù-líl-lá, a-la-la und andere, die u.a. M. Civil und P. Attinger zusammengestellt haben.[29]

4.5.2. líl ausserhalb von Genitivverbindungen

Hier ist der Diskussion durch Krecher (s. Anm. 25) trotz erheblicher Vermehrung der Belege wenig entscheidend Neues hinzuzufügen, so dass wir uns sehr kurz fassen.

4.5.2.1. Im Folgenden nur je ein Beispiel für die Verbindung von líl mit den Verben dù, g̃ar, ku$_4$(-r), sàg, sù.

---

28 Falls diese Deutung zutrifft, wäre noch mit lebendigem Verständnis des Sumerischen zu rechnen.

29 Civil, *Fs. S. N. Kramer* (= *AOAT* 25, 1976) 90; Attinger (wie oben 1.4) 556-562 s.v. i-lu du$_{11}$.

amaš líl-àm al-dù "der Schafpferch ist (als lil hingesetzt =) zum Wind / zur Leere geworden" Dumuzi's Dream 40 (B. Alster, Mes. 1 [1972] 56 und Kommentar S. 97).

ki-ùr ... èš líl-lá ba-ab-g̃ar "Kiur ... das Heiligtum wurde (zu lil gesetzt =) den Winden / den Schemen ausgeliefert" *LSUr* 347.

é-zi lí[l-lá àm-m]a-ni-in-k[u$_4$] "das rechte Haus ist (zu lil zurückgekehrt =) zu einem Schemen geworden" SKL 57 iii 51 und Kommentar S. 179 f.

líl-e a-gim íb-sàg "wie ist (die Hürde) (an lil geschlagen =) leer geworden?" Nippur Lament 2, 6, 11; s.a. Z. 104; St. Tinney, *Kommentar* S. 129 f.

ešemen-ba líl ba-e-su "auf dem Spielplatz (der Stadt) (hat sich lil ausgebreitet =) ist alles leer geworden" Cohen. Eršemma 111 no. 1.1:34; s. dort S. 114 no. 22.2:50.

4.5.2.2. Weitere Beispiele. en-iri-bar-ra ... líl-e ḫa-ba-ab-laḫ$_5$-e-eš "die (nicht durch eine Mauer geschützten) en der Aussenstadt ... hat der Wind fortgeweht" *LSUr* 345.[30]

In SBH 50a r. 18 f. steht líl-lá in Parallele zu ùlu^{lu} "Südwind"; s. SKL 179. Diese Stelle legt Zeugnis davon ab, dass líl (auch) als eine Art von Wind aufgefasst worden ist.

Als letztes Beispiel der Refrain aus der Ur-Klage Z. 1 ff.: (tùr-ra-na mùš mi-ni-in-ga) amaš-a-na líl-e "(in seiner Hürde hat (Enlil) zu walten aufghört), in seinem Schafpferch <hat> lil <...>". Tinney in Nippur Lament S. 127 übersetzt "He (Enlil) ceased working in the cattle-pen, in his sheepfold, the phantoms ..." und ist sich dabei der syntaktischen Problematik bewusst.[31]

4.5.3. Ich habe in den vorangehenden Beispielen bewusst auf den Versuch verzichtet, líl einheitlich zu übersetzen. An Stellen, an denen "Wind" plausibel erscheint, habe ich - eingedenk der Diskussion Attingers (s. 1.4) - diese Übersetzung eingesetzt oder als Alternative geboten. Wir kehren nach diesem Exkurs über líl zum Gottesnamen Enlil zurück.

---

30 Michalowski: "were carried off by phantoms". Es besteht aber kein Zwang, líl als Plural aufzufassen, da sich das auf die verbale Basis [lah] folgende [eš] auf die Pluralität der en bezieht.

31 In der Erstedition, *AS* 12 (1940), hatte Kramer übersetzt "He has abandoned his stable, his sheepfold (has been delivered) to the wind". In seinem *Kommentar* S. 72 f., wo er auf ba-nin-in-g̃ar in Z 32 als Auffänger der elliptischen Zeile hinwies, rechtfertigte Kramer seine Übersetzung mit der Annahme, der Lokativ amaš-a-na stünde als Variante für amaš-a-ni. A. Falkenstein, SAHG (1953) 192 ff., "... sein (ihr) Pferch ist leer", lässt nicht erkennen, wie er die Zeilen syntaktisch auffasste. Th. Jacobsen, *The Harps* (1987) 448 ff., "... and his sheepfold, to the winds" scheint den Lokativ in amaš-a-na nicht zur Kenntnis zu nehmen.

5. Wir wissen nach wie vor nicht genau, was der anfangs ^{d}En-É geschriebene Name bedeutet. Er kann nicht der "Herr Wind" gewesen sein, wie sehr wir uns auch auf die lexikalische 'Gleichung' líl: *šāru* (Idu II 236; Ea IV 8) stützen wollten (wobei nicht übersehen werden soll, dass *šāru* in der Reihe der Entsprechungen von líl sogar an erster Stelle steht). Denn ein *šāru* in der Gestalt von líl war auf keinen Fall jene Naturgewalt, die sich segensreich oder verderblich auswirken konnte und die durch den Wettergott Iškur (Adad) verkörpert war.

Man könnte mit Wiggermann (s. oben 1.3) argumentieren, Enlil sei Herr über dasjenige gewesen, was u n t e r An, dem Himmel, und ü b e r der Erde war. Aber hat es schon im III. Jahrtausend v. Chr. die (griechische) Idee von *aithēr* gegeben, dem (lufterfüllten) leuchtend klaren Himmel im Gesatz zu *ouranós*, dem Himmel(sdach)? Nur unter solcher Voraussetzung könnte Wiggermanns "Lord Ether" angenommen werden.

Wir haben oben gesehen (4.5), dass líl an den Stellen, wo man auch eine Übersetzung "Wind" vermuten kann, grundsätzlich negativ belastet ist. líl kann daher auf keinen Fall eine gewöhnliche Entsprechung von *šāru* und ein Synonym von im, tum_9 "Wind" sein. Zwar konnte auch *šāru* negative Konnotationen haben;[32] aber die Grundbedeutung ist positiv oder neutral.

Dort wo wir eine Übersetzung "(böser) Wind" nicht vertreten können, bleiben uns die Bedeutungen "Schemen'", "Phantom", "Leere", "Nichts". Über etwaige ältere Bedeutungen von líl zu spekulieren, ist müssig.

Hat es im sumerischen Pantheon einen "Herrn Schemen" gegeben? Hat ein Gott, und zwar ein in der Götterhierarchie sehr hoch angesiedelter Gott, einen Bereich verkörpert, der un-fassbar, schwer zu be-greifen war? Wäre es denkbar, dass man den Namen eines so gestalteten Gottes ausweichend, 'tabuisierend' schrieb: ^{d}En-É?[33] Betont werden muss, dass die Zeichen KID (líl) und É einander sehr ähnlich sind. Ob etwa auch líl und é in der ersten Hälfte des III. Jahrtausends v. Chr. einander lautlich näher waren, als unsere Latein-Transliteration preisgeben kann, lässt sich nicht herausfinden.[34]

---

32 "flatus" (*CAD* Š/2 *šāru* A 3 b), "emptiness, nothingness, vanity, (said of words) lies, falsehoods" (ebd. 5).

33 Mir ist freilich sonst kein Fall 'tabuisierender' Schreibungen bekannt.

34 Zu é < *hay s. oben Anm. 10. KID = líl ist in Proto-Ea 245 (MSL 14, 41) li-il glossiert; für Schreibungen le-el, le-e-la s. A. Sjöberg, *ZA* 83 (1993) 7 f. le-e-l(a) spricht vielleicht für Langvokal; dass womöglich sogar eine Form mit Diphthong, *[layl], zugrunde liegt, bleibt aber reine Hypothese.

6. Wie dem auch sei, die interpretatio sumerica des Namens Enlil erscheint mir als die einzig zu rechtfertigende. Wir haben gesehen (besonders oben 3.6), dass sich die Ebla-Schreibung ([d])*I-li-l*(*u*) problemlos mit einer sumerischen Form *Yēn-lil verbinden lässt. Die These von Steinkeller und P. Michalowski, Illil/Ellil/Enlil sei ein aus dem semitischen Bereich stammender uralter Eindringling im sumerischen Pantheon, müsste mit kräftigeren Argumenten untermauert werden.

Enlil hat, so wie ihn die sumerische und akkadische Literatur schildert, oft etwas Ausweichendes, negativ 'Windiges' an sich gehabt. Er herrscht in Willkür, bricht sein Wort, lässt seinen Sohn für sich in den Kampf ziehen, und am Anfang von Atra-ḫasīs ist er gar als Feigling porträtiert. Wir empfinden Enlil - ganz im Gegensatz zu seinem Bruder Enki - als einen zutiefst unsympathischen Gott. Wenn die altmesopotamische Götterwelt ihre liebe Not mit ihm gehabt hat, sollte es uns da besser ergehen?

SEMITICO, INDEUROPEO E SOSTRATO INDOMEDITERRANEO

GIOVANNI GARBINI

Università di Roma “La Sapienza”

Nel 1956 Pelio Fronzaroli dedicò uno dei suoi primi lavori ai “Rapporti lessicali dell’ittita con le lingue semitiche” (Fronzaroli 1956); la finezza della sua indagine linguistica lo portò a scoprire quanti diversi tipi di contatto linguistico possono venire a crearsi tra due idiomi sostanzialmente diversi che le vicende storiche hanno per un certo tempo messo in rapporto tra loro. Dopo tanti anni forse non gli dispiacerà ricordare certi suoi giovanili interessi attraverso queste pagine che un suo antico condiscepolo affettuosamente gli dedica.

Lo studio dei più antichi rapporti tra le lingue semitiche e quelle indeuropee, realizzatisi in età preistorica, ha trovato in Italia assai meno adepti che all’estero, ma in compenso possiamo affermare che si è avuta da noi quella consapevolezza critica che ha evitato ai nostri studiosi di cadere negli eccessi che hanno reso giustamente sospetto questo tipo di ricerche. Dopo il grande nome di Graziadio Isaia Ascoli, i cui classici saggi del 1864 introdussero in Italia le indagini sull’“ario-semitico”, bisognerà arrivare agli anni Venti di questo secolo per incontrare quelli di Piero Meriggi, che più tardi ripudierà il suo studio giovanile (Meriggi 1961, p. 32), e di Carlo Tagliavini; nel 1949 Luigi Heilmann pubblicò la sua informatissima monografia (Heilmann 1949) che faceva il punto della situazione dopo un secolo e mezzo di studi. Era un bilancio particolarmente esauriente per il fatto di aver potuto prendere in considerazione l’ultimo libro di Albert Cuny (Cuny 1946), lo studioso che per vari decenni si era dedicato a tali ricerche.

A conclusione della sua indagine, Heilmann dichiarava che i rapporti tra indeuropeo e camito-semitico “sono innegabili e numerosi: accordi nel fonetismo, contatti nella struttura e nell’uso di alcuni morfemi, convergenze lessicali cospicue” (p. 79), ma che tuttavia questi non sono tali da giustificare la tesi di una discendenza dei due gruppi linguistici da un antenato comune, come voleva la teoria “nostratica” di Cuny; essi testimoniano invece “di contatti e di livellamenti interrotti in età molto remote e costituiscono la prova di una ‘affinità’ che si potrebbe anche brevemente esprimere con l’appellativo di ‘nostratica’, qualora da questo si escluda ogni significazione genealogica di tipo schleicheriano” (p. 81; cfr. anche Heilmann 1983).

Contemporaneamente al libro di Heilmann appariva un articolo di Vittore Pisani (Pisani 1949), nato anch'esso come reazione all'ultimo lavoro di Cuny, che discuteva la tesi dello studioso francese e nel quale Pisani applicando la sua teoria delle leghe linguistiche affermava che gli elementi comuni al semitico e all'indeuropeo erano il risultato della confluenza in gruppi linguistici diversi di "dialetti formanti un tempo una certa unità, portando così seco nelle famiglie di nuova formazione elementi uguali" (Pisani 1949, p. 336). Con queste parole il problema dell'affinità tra semitico e indeuropeo veniva impostato su basi del tutto nuove, perché si indicava un tipo di soluzione che teneva conto dei due elementi chiaramente rilevati da Heilmann, e cioè l'innegabile esistenza di tratti linguistici comuni ai due gruppi e l'impossibilità di stabilire una parentela di tipo genealogico.

Lo sviluppo degli studi nella seconda metà del secolo non è stato quello che si poteva prevedere dopo le prese di posizione di Heilmann e di Pisani. In Italia le idee di quest'ultimo sono state accettate da qualche semitista (Garbini 1981; Durand 1994, p. 174) e sviluppate da alcuni allievi dello stesso Pisani (ricorderò Maria Luisa Mayer, Francesco Aspesi e Vermondo Brugnatelli) ai quali si deve anche l'iniziativa di periodiche "Giornate di studi camito-semitici e indeuropei". Nel quadro generale che stiamo delineando possono considerarsi emblematiche le vicende di queste "giornate"; iniziate in sordina a Venezia nel 1978, dopo aver raggiunto il magico numero di sette nel 1993 con un volume che recava il significativo titolo *Sem Cam Iafet* (Milano 1994) esse hanno dovuto cedere alle nuove mode culturali: l'ottava "giornata" svoltasi a Napoli nel 1996 non solo segnò la sostituzione di "camito-semitico" con "afroasiatico" ma eliminò ogni riferimento all'indeuropeo. Fuori d'Italia la posizione di Pisani circa i rapporti tra semitico e indeuropeo ha trovato un sostanziale parallelo in quella, definitasi autonomamente, dello statunitense Saul Levin (Levin 1971 con Pisani 1971, pp. 324-326; Levin 1995); nella sua opera più recente questi rifiuta la parentela genealogica nostratica ed esprime fondati dubbi su quella genealogica camito-semitica; egli lavora invece sull'ipotesi che "there were important prehistoric periods of perceptible contact, not so far back in the past, and probably recurrent rather than continuous" (p. 4), giungendo alla conclusione che "the IE-Semitic combinations ... testify, if not to a common prehistoric language, at least to prehistoric language-communities in truly intimate contact" (p. 12). La debolezza dell'opera di Levin risiede nel metodo impressionistico più che critico dei suoi accostamenti linguistici.

Mentre estremamente rari sono stati i contributi validi allo studio dei rapporti tra semitico e indeuropeo (mi limito a citare Petráček 1981 e 1982), fuori del nostro paese è da rilevare il nuovo vigore della teoria nostratica di Cuny e del suo predecessore più illustre, Hermann Møller. Linus Brunner (Brunner 1969 con Neu 1971) e Allen R. Bomhard nella sua prima fase (Bomhard 1984 con Helimski 1987) si muovevano ancora in questo senso, ma in Russia le cose sono andate diversamente. Sulla scia delle idee di Nikolaj Marr, ammiratore e seguace di Alfredo Trombetti, si è sviluppata fin dagli anni Sessanta una vivace scuola di "nostratisti" (Vladislav M. Illič-Svityč, Aron Dolgopolsky poi trasferitosi in Israele, A. Lamprecht, M. Čejka) che allargano il concetto di nostratico a comprendere numerosi altri gruppi linguistici, come il caucasico meridionale, l'uralico, il dravidico, l'altaico ed altri ancora. Questa impostazione delle ricerche, che ricalca vie già battute nei primi decenni del secolo, ha trovato seguaci anche fuori della Russia (cfr. Koskinen 1980; Bomhard-Kerns 1994) per una serie di ragioni che vale la pena di ricordare.

In primo luogo va rilevato che negli ultimi decenni si è imposta prepotentemente negli studi camito-semitici, specialmente ad opera di studiosi statunitensi e russi, la vecchia *Stammbaumtheorie* nella sua versione più tipicamente schleicheriana, con le sue "protolingue" largamente distribuite nelle varie ramificazioni di un albero sempre più gigantesco. Il criterio della parentela genetica, già in crisi verso la fine del secolo scorso, è ritornato in auge quasi all'improvviso, senza alcuna discussione scientifica, ed è diventato per i più un dogma accettato acriticamente trasformandosi di fatto in un postulato utilizzato per le più spericolate operazioni di classificazione linguistica.

L'inopinata nuova fortuna della teoria dell'albero genealogico non costituisce l'unico esempio della profonda involuzione subita dai nostri studi. Un successo analogo hanno incontrato i tentativi di identificare popolazioni di lingua indeuropea con determinate "culture" individuate dagli archeologi preistorici. Sull'esempio delle ricerche avviate da Vere Gordon Childe nella prima metà di questo secolo e poi riprese da Marija Gimbutas (ricerche che sedussero perfino un grande linguista come Giacomo Devoto [Devoto 1962]), verso la fine degli anni Ottanta alcuni archeologi anglosassoni riesumarono il problema dei primi indeuropei in Europa e della loro eventuale provenienza; secondo Colin Renfrew, lo studioso rapidamente diventato il più noto di quel gruppo, furono genti indeuropee quelle che introdussero in Europa l'agricoltura da esse inventata in Anatolia intorno al 6.000 a.C. (Renfrew 1987 con Campanile 1989). Nonostante le apparenze, gli studi sulle parentele linguistiche e quelli degli archeologi sulle origini indeuropee sono intimamente collegati, dato che questi ultimi ricercano il loro fondamento teorico negli schemi "nostratistici" dei primi, che a loro volta assumono i dati archeologici a conferma della grande antichità delle loro "protolingue": non è certo un caso che Bomhard abbia scritto la seconda versione del suo libro in collaborazione con John C. Kerns, che condivide le idee di Renfrew (Bomhard-Kerns 1994), e che questi porti a conferma delle proprie vedute gli studi dei già ricordati linguisti russi e di Joseph Greenberg (Renfrew 1995).

Il nome di Greenberg ci introduce nel vestibolo del terzo edificio che concorre a formare il complesso in cui risiede attualmente l'ultima moda della ricerca interdisciplinare sulle più antiche genti dell'Asia Anteriore e dell'Europa centro-orientale. Sono state le idee di Greenberg, con le sue macrofamiglie linguistiche, a guidare le ricerche genetiche di Luigi Luca Cavalli-Sforza che per vari decenni ha insegnato nella Stanford University, la stessa in cui insegnava Greenberg (cfr. Cavalli-Sforza 1996, pp. 202-207), e che ha impostato la scelta dei geni in modo da fornire risultati che concordassero con le vedute di Albert J. Ammerman, un archeologo americano stretto collaboratore di Cavalli-Sforza fin dall'inizio degli anni Settanta (Ammerman-Cavalli-Sforza 1986, pp. 135-39). È difficile negare che le indagini del genetista italiano sono state condotte con degli obiettivi prefissati e sono quindi poco attendibili nei loro risultati; a conferma di ciò basterà ricordare che Bryan Sykes, genetista dell'università di Oxford, lavorando nello stesso settore è pervenuto a conclusioni completamente diverse che smentiscono totalmente la teoria di Cavalli-Sforza e quella di Renfrew sul neolitico europeo (Powledge-Rose 1996). Non siamo certamente in grado di esprimere un giudizio di merito: possiamo soltanto prendere atto che gli studi svolti con grande apparato di metodi matematici possiedono un grado di incertezza non inferiore a quello degli studi storici e linguistici quando hanno per oggetto le fasi preistoriche dell'umanità.

Il quadro offerto attualmente dalla ricerca sui rapporti tra lingue semitiche e lingue indeuropee appare in definitiva dominato dall'ipotesi della parentela genealogica, finalizzata alla dimostrazione della monogenesi del linguaggio; questa ha trovato un sostegno nella teoria genetica sull'origine unica dell'*homo sapiens sapiens*. D'altra parte si assiste a tentativi di retrodatare di svariati millenni le origini indeuropee. In tal modo è stato trovato un accordo tra chi si ispira più o meno consapevolmente al modello biblico per l'origine dell'umanità e della diversità linguistica e chi rivendica un primato almeno cronologico degli indeuropei da contrapporre alle realizzazioni culturali dei semiti nel Vicino Oriente a partire dal III millennio a.C. Si tratta di un quadro poco esaltante di diffuso dilettantismo scientifico e che ci riporta a più di un secolo addietro. Non vale la pena di spendere parole per sottolineare la totale inconsistenza di ipotesi come quelle che proiettano indietro di millenni una realtà linguistica, qual'è l'indeuropea, chiaramente percepibile solo nel II millennio a.C., o che legano un fatto linguistico a un determinato tratto di cultura materiale o che pretendono di individuare il momento in cui un certo gene diffuso nel Vicino Oriente è giunto nell'Europa meridionale, quando sappiamo con certezza che da almeno quattromila anni esiste nell'area mediterranea un flusso etnico ininterrotto da est verso ovest. Un'indagine seria sulle affinità tra semitico e indeuropeo deve ripartire dal punto a cui essa era giunta nel 1949 con le posizioni di Heilmann e Pisani.

L'impossibilità di provare l'esistenza di una parentela genealogica tra le lingue semitiche e quelle indeuropee rende indispensabile l'individuazione di un punto di contatto geografico e cronologico tra almeno alcuni gruppi di parlanti le rispettive lingue, in un momento ovviamente anteriore all'età storica. Dal punto di vista geografico la realtà semitica impone dei grossi limiti: l'area originariamente semitica a prescindere dalle note espansioni di età storica, è compresa tra il Mediterraneo e la valle del Tigri, estendendosi dalla zona stepposa siro-anatolica a nord fino all'estremo confine meridionale della penisola araba a sud; questa è la situazione già fissata nel III millennio a.C. Le lingue definite camitiche, dall'antico egiziano al ciadico, si trovano tutte in Africa; per chi, come lo scrivente, le considera come il risultato di più o meno superficiali processi di semitizzazione di lingue africane, svoltisi nel corso dei millenni, esse non costituiscono un problema per l'argomento che stiamo trattando. Chi invece sostiene la parentela genetica del camito-semitico (anzi dell'afroasiatico) e di conseguenza l'origine africana del semitico deve lavorare di fantasia per giustificare come mai un berlinese dica *siebzig*, una parola molto vicina a *sabaʾin* usata per dire la stessa cosa da un abitante di Nguru.

L'area coperta dalle lingue indeuropee è molto ampia attualmente, ma se risaliamo nel tempo le cose cambiano radicalmente. Nelle grandi pianure europee a nord delle Alpi gli archeologi hanno voluto trovare indeuropei fin dal VII millennio a.C., ma la realtà linguistica è assai diversa. La spinta verso ovest delle lingue balto-slave ha costretto quelle germaniche, a loro preesistenti, ad espandersi verso occidente, a spese delle lingue celtiche, ora quasi completamente estinte e relegate nell'estremo ovest dell'Europa; l'arrivo dei Celti, provenienti dall'est, non è però anteriore al VI secolo a.C. e non esiste alcuna prova sicura che vi fossero nell'Europa continentale precedenti popolazioni di lingua indeuropea. Nella penisola italiana varie lingue indeuropee sono attestate nel I millennio a.C. Passando all'Asia, indeuropei sono documentati nel Turkestan orientale solo nel VII secolo d.C.; in India la documentazione scritta non è anteriore al III secolo a.C., anche se una serie di argomenti linguistici e culturali rendono probabile una presenza indeuropea verso l'inizio del I millennio a.C. Genti iraniche gravitavano dall'altopiano iranico verso la Mesopotamia nel VII secolo a.C. e a questa data risalgono le più antiche iscrizioni frigie. La grande espansione indeuropea si è dunque realizzata essenzialmente nel I millennio a.C. Nel II millennio a.C. l'area sicuramente indeuropea era molto più ristretta e si estendeva dalla Grecia, con il cosiddetto miceneo, a buona parte della penisola anatolica, mentre una sporadica presenza indo-iranica è documentata nel XVII secolo a.C. nell'alta Siria e nell'alta Mesopotamia. Dati linguistici precisi in Anatolia e toponomastici nell'area egea rivelano con chiarezza il carattere intrusivo dell'indeuropeo in queste aree, vale a dire che le lingue indeuropee usate in tali regioni nel II millennio a.C. si erano sovrapposte alle lingue locali in una data non molto anteriore a quella della loro più antica documentazione. Questa constatazione fa risalire all'inizio del II millennio o al massimo agli ultimi secoli del III millennio a.C. il momento della prima comparsa di genti indeuropee. I numerosi tentativi compiuti per collegare queste vicende linguistiche con la documentazione archeologica sono tutti rimasti al livello di ipotesi indimostrate (Jasink 1983), come ipotetica è l'asserita provenienza balcanica delle suddette genti. La grande mobilità mostrata dai popoli indeuropei nel corso della storia rende assai verosimile la supposizione che la loro penetrazione nella penisola anatolica, nel bacino dell'Egeo e nella penisola italiana sia avvenuta in fasi successive e con diverse zone di provenienza da parte di gruppi relativamente omogenei ma ben differenziati dialettalmente.

Nel quadro estremamente fluido delle lingue, delle popolazioni e dei movimenti che costituivano la realtà indeuropea nei secoli a cavallo del 2000 a.C. esiste un punto fermo: almeno una parte di queste genti di lingua indeuropea era stata abbastanza lungamente in contatto con genti di lingua semitica. E poiché nessuna lingua semitica è mai stata parlata a nord del Caucaso e ad est dei monti Zagros l'area in cui per un certo tempo semitico e indeuropeo vissero l'uno accanto all'altro non può essere altro che la Transcaucasia (Armenia, Kurdistan) e la regione dell'alto Tigri e dell'alto Eufrate, dove la presenza semitica testimoniata dagli attuali dialetti neoaramaici orientali era documentata tremila anni orsono dallo stato aramaico di Bit Zamani.

Soffermiamoci un momento su questo confine settentrionale dell'area linguistica semitica. Lo stato residuale della presenza aramaica in zona sia semitica (Iraq settentrionale) sia non semitica (Iran nordoccidentale, Turchia sudorientale) lascia facilmente intendere che l'estensionc dell'aramaico doveva essere in antico molto maggiore e più compatta; all'inizio del I millennio a.C. la città arameofona di Samal, a nord-est di Adana, costituiva probabilmente l'estremità occidentale di un sostanziale *continuum* linguistico. Ciò non significa che nella regione non esistessero altre lingue (è documentato il neo-ittito nella parte occidentale e l'urarteo in quella orientale), ma soltanto che i parlanti aramaico dovevano essere molto numerosi e in stretti rapporti con gli allofoni: basterà ricordare che il fondatore dello stato urarteo, in Armenia, verso la metà del IX secolo a.C., era un arameo, Arame di Agushi; solo col suo successore Sarduri compare l'onomastica e la documentazione epigrafica urartea. Se volessimo definire una linea di tendenza nella storia linguistica della Transcaucasia e dell'Anatolia orientale, risulterebbe abbastanza evidente una regressione delle lingue semitiche nei confronti di quelle indeuropee (iranico, armeno, neo-ittito, greco), che hanno subito un arresto in età moderna grazie all'arrivo del turco. Appare pertanto ragionevole l'ipotesi che nel II e nel III millennio a.C. le lingue semitiche, e più precisamente i dialetti amorrei, erano diffuse in queste regioni più di quanto emerge dalla documentazione storica.

Individuato il punto di contatto geografico tra semitico e indeuropeo, è relativamente facile definire quello cronologico. Se i primi movimenti di genti di lingua sicuramente indeuropea sembrano collocarsi al più presto nei secoli finali del III millennio a.C., saranno questi il *terminus ante quem*; semiti e indeuropei si trovarono dunque vicini per buona parte del III millennio a.C. e presumibilmente anche nel IV millennio, almeno nella seconda metà di esso. Questo periodo storico è particolarmente significativo, perché corrisponde alla cosiddetta "rivoluzione urbana" e alla prima urbanizzazione, un evento di durata abbastanza lunga che ebbe profonde ripercussioni anche sulle popolazioni non direttamente interessate alla formazione delle città. Sul piano linguistico le tribù amorree, con la loro economia a base pastorale che comportava continui spostamenti e la pratica della transumanza, reagirono alla formazione della cultura urbana con un atteggiamento di contrapposizione realizzatosi in una serie di innovazioni che portarono alla formazione di un tipo linguistico che possiamo definire "medio-semitico", distinto da quello antico rappresentato dall'eblaita e dall'accadico e da quello recente dell'ultimo millennio. Ho già avuto modo di rilevare (Garbini 1981) come alcune affinità dell'indeuropeo con il semitico si notino più con l'amorreo che con le lingue di tipo arcaico, il che conferma l'ambito cronologico ora definito e nello stesso tempo accomuna amorrei e indeuropei sul piano del comportamento socio-linguistico. Dal punto di vista storico è importante osservare la contemporaneità della grande espansione demografica e linguistica amorrea nell'area della Mezzaluna Fertile e di quella indeuropea verso occidente; due grandiosi movimenti etnici che si conclusero, nei primi secoli del II millennio a.C., con un pressoché totale dominio politico amorreo e indeuropeo e che diedero l'avvio a un processo di trasformazione linguistica che in pochi secoli fece scomparire tutte le lingue non semitiche e non indeuropee dalla valle del Tigri alla Grecia.

In conclusione, il quadro entro cui studiare i rapporti tra semitico e indeuropeo (senza escludere eventualmente qualche altro gruppo di lingue, come quelle caucasiche meridionali) è, in linea generale, quello di una lega linguistica costituitasi con molta verosimiglianza nel IV millennio a.C., e durata per quasi tutto il III, nella Transcaucasia e nell'Anatolia orientale; una lega caratterizzata da molti elementi lessicali comuni e da alcune innovazioni linguistiche in parte parallele. Appare ovvio, naturalmente, che la definizione di semitiche e di indeuropee che diamo alle lingue parlate da queste popolazioni non indica altro che il definirsi storico di un certo tipo linguistico attestato poco più tardi. Prima di questo, cioè prima del IV millennio a.C., esistevano tipi linguistici parzialmente diversi, che potremmo chiamare rispettivamente pre-semitico e pre-indeuropeo, che con ogni probabilità erano collegati tra loro e con altri gruppi linguistici in maniera diversa da quella che si determinò nel IV millennio: ma tutto ciò si sottrae completamente alla nostra indagine. È questa la ragione che rende assurdo parlare di indeuropeo nel V o nel VII millennio a.C. o di camito-semitico nell'VIII o nel X millennio a.C. Le lingue e le parentele linguistiche si trasformano continuamente, specialmente laddove, come nella preistoria, non esistono fattori che favoriscano la coesione linguistica, come solidi organismi politici o lingue di prestigio.

Prima di chiudere il discorso sui rapporti tra semitico e indeuropeo è necessario affrontare ancora un problema di storia linguistica ad esso collegato, quello del cosiddetto sostrato indomediterraneo. L'arrivo relativamente recente delle lingue indeuropee in Europa offre una piena giustificazione alle ricerche tendenti a individuare la situazione linguistica di questa nella fase anteriore alla diffusione dell'indeuropeo. Che i risultati raggiunti siano pienamente soddisfacenti è un altro discorso, nonostante l'impegno di studiosi come Giovanni Alessio, Carlo Battisti e Vittorio Bertoldi, per ricordare solo gli italiani che hanno lavorato maggiormente sul "sostrato mediterraneo", su cui si sarebbero poi impiantate le lingue indeuropee. Un articolo di Vittore Pisani apparso verso la fine degli anni Trenta (Pisani 1938) ampliò poi la prospettiva storica del sostrato dal Mediterraneo fino all'India, avendo lo studioso riscontrato significative consonanze linguistiche e culturali che univano la Grecia all'India interessando tuttavia anche le più antiche culture del Vicino Oriente; a questo sostrato indomediterraneo si sarebbero a un certo momento sovrapposte le lingue semitiche e quelle indeuropee. Gli studi in questo settore non sono stati molto numerosi (oltre a diversi articoli di Pisani stesso menzionerò Belardi 1954 e 1955) e hanno trovato in Domenico Silvestri un attento indagatore (Silvestri 1974 e 1982, pp. 96-157); dopo le messe a punto di quest'ultimo si possono citare Silvestri 1985, Chiera 1983 e 1986, Durand 1993, Garbini 1993.

A proposito del sostrato indomediterraneo bisogna tuttavia fare una precisazione preliminare che modifica sostanzialmente l'impostazione originaria di Pisani: se per l'Europa e l'India è legittimo parlare di sostrati anarî, quali che siano, questo non è possibile per l'Asia Anteriore, perché a parte il sumerico in Mesopotamia non esiste un sostrato linguistico sottostante al semitico. Accanto a questo vi sono lingue non semitiche come il khurrito, ma non esiste alcun indizio che faccia supporre un sostrato non semitico nell'area in cui troviamo le lingue semitiche nel III millennio a.C. Come ho detto poco fa, prima del semitico, cioè prima del IV-III millennio a.C., possiamo individuare solo un semitico che doveva essere alquanto diverso da quello che conosciamo, che possedeva lo stesso lessico ma una struttura radicale e una morfologia certamente diverse, anche se ignoriamo quanto. In altri termini, tra il Mediterraneo e l'Eufrate il semitico costituiva un segmento dello strato linguistico "indomediterraneo", un segmento che a oriente si univa al sumerico come questo proseguiva poi con l'antico elamita e così via, nell'ambito di una grande comunità culturale che si estendeva fino all'Indo e all'Asia Centrale. Ma dopo quanto si è detto nelle pagine precedenti, risulta evidente un altro fatto: anche la fase più antica dell'indeuropeo e quella immediatamente precedente facevano parte dello stesso strato linguistico, e così pure il khattico ed eventualmente il khurrito (se entrò nell'area prima del III millennio), nonché le lingue non indeuropee dell'Anatolia. Quando troviamo in greco, completamente isolato, un verbo come *agapàō* che trova un'ampia serie di corrispondenze fonetiche e semantiche nelle lingue semitiche, sarebbe suggestivo ipotizzare un sostrato "mediterraneo" in Grecia che comprendeva anche elementi semitici; è però molto più verosimile supporre che *agapàō* sia stato portato in Grecia da quegli indeuropei che vi hanno introdotto il greco e che avevano appreso il termine semitico nell'Anatolia orientale; viceversa, ai semiti era rimasta solo una radice, nelle varianti *ʾlm* e *wlm*, fra le tante a base *al-* che usavano gli indeuropei per indicare la "alimentazione" (cfr. Garbini 1988).

L'ipotesi, ora suggerita, secondo cui la parte non indifferente del lessico greco che presenta evidenti affinità con quello semitico avrebbe fatto parte fin dall'inizio del patrimonio lessicale greco offre una spiegazione più soddisfacente di quella comunemente accettata, che parla di *emprunts* o *loan words* più o meno numerosi (mi limito a ricordare l'importante studio Szemerényi 1974); è infatti difficile immaginare in quale cornice storica si possa collocare l'imponente flusso di termini semitici in una lingua greca già fissata intorno all'Egeo.

È un dato innegabile che molti termini comuni al semitico e all'indeuropeo affondano le loro radici nella cultura neolitica e che questa si diffuse dal Vicino Oriente a tutta l'Europa, rendendo possibile che molte parole viaggiassero insieme con essa; sul piano metodologico l'ipotesi più economica resta tuttavia sempre quella che tali termini, definitisi nella lega linguistica di età neolitica che univa semiti e indeuropei, siano stati portati in Europa e fino in India dagli indeuropei che giunsero, in età protostorica, in queste regioni. È presumibile che anteriormente alle migrazioni indeuropee qualche parola di origine mesopotamica o siriana si sia propagata nell'ambito delle culture neolitiche vicino-orientali; è tuttavia probabile che la parte più consistente del lessico "indomediterraneo" sia stata diffusa dagli indeuropei. È stato il diverso destino dell'evoluzione storica del semitico e dell'indeuropeo che ha fatto attribuire a un inesistente sostrato indomediterraneo quelle parole che appartenevano al lessico comune dei semiti e degli indeuropei.

Bibliografia

Ammerman-Cavalli-Sforza 1986: A. J. Ammerman - L. L. Cavalli-Sforza, *La transizione neolitica e la genetica di popolazioni in Europa*, Torino 1986 (titolo originale: *The Neolithic Transition and the Genetics of Populations in Europe*, Princeton 1984).

Belardi 1954: W. Belardi, *Una nuova serie lessicale indomediterranea*, in *Rendiconti dell'Accademia Nazionale dei Lincei*, ser. VIII, 9 (1954), pp. 610-644.

Belardi 1955: W. Belardi, *Un'innovazione nel sostrato*, in *Rendiconti dell'Accademia Nazionale dei Lincei*, ser. VIII, 10 (1955), pp. 308-331.

Bomhard 1984: A. R. Bomhard, *Towards Proto-Nostratic. A New Approach to the Comparison of Proto-Indo-European and Proto-Afroasiatic*, Amsterdam 1984.

Bomhard-Kerns 1994: A. R. Bomhard - J. C. Kerns, *The Nostratic Macrofamily. A Study in Distant Linguistic Relationship*, Berlin - New York 1994.

Brunner 1969: L. Brunner, *Die gemeinsamen Wurzeln des semitischen und indogermanischen Wortschatzes*, Bern - München 1969.

Campanile 1989: E. Campanile, recensione di Renfrew 1987, in *Kratylos*, 34 (1989), pp. 53-56.

Cavalli-Sforza 1996: L. L. Cavalli-Sforza, *Geni, popoli e lingue*, Milano 1996.

Chiera 1983: G. Chiera, ʾṯkl-ʾškr *"grappolo": una base mediterranea nel lessico semitico*, in *Rivista degli Studi Orientali*, 57 (1983) [1985], pp. 43-51.

Chiera 1986: G. Chiera, *Rapporti tra la base mediterranea* (a)skal *e il semitico* aškil, in *Annali dell'Istituto Universitario Orientale di Napoli*, 46 (1986), pp. 291-293.

Cuny 1946: A. Cuny, *Invitation à l'étude comparative des langues indo-européennes et des langues chamito-sémitiques*, Bordeaux 1946.

Devoto 1962: G. Devoto, *Origini indeuropee*, Firenze 1962.

Durand 1993: O. Durand, *A propos du "substrat méditerranéen" et des langues chamito-sémitiques*, in *Rivista degli Studi Orientali*, 67 (1993) [1994], pp. 27-38.

Durand 1994: G. Garbini - O. Durand, *Introduzione alle lingue semitiche*, Brescia 1994.

Fronzaroli 1956: P. Fronzaroli, *Rapporti lessicali dell'ittita con le lingue semitiche*, in *Archivio Glottologico Italiano*, 41 (1956), pp. 33-45.

Garbini 1981: G. Garbini, *Camito-semitico e indeuropeo*, in *Atti del Sodalizio Glottologico Milanese*, 21 (1979-80) [1981], pp. 4-18 (ristampato in *Le lingue semitiche*[2], Napoli 1984, pp. 253-268).

Garbini 1988: G. Garbini, *Convergenze indeuropeo-semitiche tra preistoria e protostoria*, in *AIΩN. Annali del Dipartimento di Studi del Mondo Classico*. Sez. Ling., 10 (1988), pp. 67-80.

Garbini 1993: G. Garbini, Argaman *"porpora"*, in *Semitica. Serta philologica Constantino Tsereteli dicata*, Torino 1993, pp. 77-80 (ristampato in *Note di lessicografia ebraica*, Brescia 1998, pp. 22-28).

Heilmann 1949: L. Heilmann, *Camito-semitico e indoeuropeo. Teorie e orientamenti*, Bologna 1949.

Heilmann 1983: L. Heilmann, *Linguaggio, lingue, culture. Saggi linguistici e indologici*, Bologna 1983, pp. 149-155 (lo studio, intitolato *Strutturalismo e rico-*

struzione di protolingue. A proposito del nesso "ario-semitico", era apparso la prima volta nel 1965).

Helimski 1987: E. Helimski, *A "New Approach" to Nostratic Comparison*, in *Journal of the American Oriental Society*, 107 (1987), pp. 97-100 (recensione di Bomhard 1984).

Jasink 1983: A. M. Jasink, *Movimenti di popoli nell'area egeo-antolica. III-II millennio a.C.*, Firenze 1983.

Koskinen 1980: K. E. Koskinen, *Nilal. Über die Urverwandschaft des Hamito-semitischen, Indogermanischen, Uralischen und Altaischen*, Tampere 1980.

Levin 1971: S. Levin, *The Indo-European and Semitic Language*, Albany N.Y. 1971.

Levin 1995: S. Levin, *Semitic and Indo-European: the Principal Etymologies with Observations on Afro-Asiatic*, Amsterdam-Philadelphia 1995.

Meriggi 1961: P. Meriggi, *Affinità strutturali fra indeuropeo e altre famiglie linguistiche*, in *Indeuropeo e protostoria. Atti del III Convegno Internazionale di linguisti. Milano 1958*, Milano 1961, pp. 31-38.

Neu 1971: E. Neu, recensione di Brunner 1969, in *Indogermanische Forschungen*, 76 (1971), pp. 218-228.

Petráček 1981: K. Petráček, *K teorii laryngál*, in *Slovo a Slovesnost*, 42 (1981), pp. 262-268.

Petráček 1982: K. Petráček, *La racine en indoeuropéen et en chamitosémitique et leurs perspectives comparatives*, in *Annali dell'Istituto Universitario di Napoli*, 42 (1982), pp. 381-402.

Pisani 1938: V. Pisani, *L'unità culturale indo-mediterranea anteriore all'avvento di Semiti e Indeuropei*, in *Scritti in onore di Alfredo Trombetti*, Milano 1938, pp. 199-213 (ristampato con un'appendice in *Lingue e culture*, Brescia 1969, pp. 53-70; qui Pisani dà al suo articolo la data del 1936, probabilmente quella prevista inizialmente per il volume, uscito con molto ritardo).

Pisani 1949: V. Pisani, *Indeuropeo e camito-semitico*, in *Annali dell'Istituto Universitario Orientale di Napoli*, 3 (1949), pp. 333-339 (ristampato in *Saggi di linguistica storica*, Torino 1959, pp. 71-78).

Pisani 1971: V. Pisani, *Parentela fra le grandi famiglie linguistiche*, in *Paideia*, 26 (1971), pp. 317-326 (ristampato in *Mantissa*, Brescia 1978, pp. 55-68).

Powledge-Rose 1996: T. M. Powledge - M. Rose, *The Great DNA Hunt*, in *Archaeology*, 49, 5 (1996), pp. 36-44.

Renfrew 1987: G. Renfrew, *Archaeology and Language. The Puzzle of Indo-European Origins*, London 1987.

Renfrew 1995: G. Renfrew, *Towards a New Synthesis?*, in *Cambridge Archaeological Journal*, 5 (1995), pp. 258-261.

Silvestri 1974: D. Silvestri, *La nozione di indomediterraneo in linguistica storica*, Napoli 1974.

Silvestri 1982: D. Silvestri, *La teoria del sostrato. Metodi e miraggi*, vol. III, Napoli 1982.

Silvestri 1985: D. Silvestri, *Etimologie 'mediterranee' rivisitate,* in *Tra linguistica storica e linguistica generale. Scritti in onore di Tristano Bolelli*, Pisa 1985, pp. 281-301.

Szemerényi 1974: O. Szemerényi, *The Origins of the Greek Lexicon*: *Ex Oriente lux*, in *Journal of Hellenic Studies*, 94 (1974), pp. 144-157.

DIE VEREHRUNG DES GOTTES EL UNTER DEN ISRAELITEN

WOLFRAM HERRMANN

Stuttgart

Seit durch die Entdeckungen von Ras Schamra die Fragen um die westsemitische Gottheit El die Semitisten und Bibelwissenschaftler immer wieder beschäftigten, ist bis heute keine einhellige Klärung aller anstehenden Probleme erzielt. Das gilt in besonderem Maße für den Bereich der Wissenschaft vom Alten Testament. Als in ihm angesiedelt, will der Autor vorstehenden Beitrages seine Sicht der Dinge in die Waagschale werfen, um dadurch vielleicht dem Gespräch einen neuen Impuls zu verleihen.

Immerhin hat sich schon weitestgehend die Erkenntnis durchgesetzt, daß man unter den religiösen Gegebenheiten, wie sie uns aus Ugarit bekannt geworden sind, auch die El betreffenden nicht unmittelbar auf die Verhältnisse unter den Israeliten übertragen kann. Dagegen sprechen schon einmal der räumliche und zeitliche Abstand und sodann die Tatsache, daß die kanaanäischen und aramäischen Inschriften, die dem biblisch Bezeugten zumeist näher liegen, in mancher Hinsicht anders geartete Auffassungen wahrnehmen lassen, als sie die ugaritischen Texte dokumentieren. Freilich bedeutet das keine absolute Isolierung Israels gegenüber diesen, wie nicht wenige literarische Ähnlichkeiten bis hin zu einzelnen formalen Übereinstimmungen bestätigen. Derartige Realien leiten sich indessen von einem gemeinsamen kulturellen Hintergrund her und nicht aus unmittelbarer Abhängigkeit aus einer Richtung.

Auf Grund solcher Überlegungen muß man nun allerdings nicht so weit gehen, völlig auszuschließen, die Gottheit El in der alttestamentlichen Literatur als eine eigenkonturierte Gestalt vorzufinden, mithin das Nomen אל nicht allein als Appellativum zu erklären, weil schon der Inschriftenbestand die Benennung im Sinne eines nomen proprium ausweist.[1] Sie ist sicher zutreffend in dem Gottesnamen Rakab-El

1 Daß El auch als Eigenname im Alten Testament vorkommt, wurde teilweise bereits betont; siehe letzthin R. Rendtorff, "*ʾEl* als israelitische Gottesbezeichnung", *ZAW* 106 (1994), S. 4-21 [7].

enthalten,[2] eindeutig nachgewiesen durch die Nebenordnung zu anderen namentlich genannten Gottheiten.[3]

Dazu fügen sich einige Belege im alttestamentlichen Schrifttum, und man wird kaum fehlgehen, an den hergehörigen Stellen hinter dem Namen El eine klar erkennbare, gegenüber Jahwe eigenständige, Gottheit zu gewahren, wie sie gleichfalls in den oben genannten phönikischen und aramäischen Inschriften hervortritt.[4]

In erster Linie figurieren in der Beziehung die alte Überlieferung verkörpernden Formulierungen אל אלהי ישראל[5] und האל אלהי אביך.[6] Der Kontext spricht zwar vom Erzvater Jakob, und traditionell sieht man im Gott Jakobs allein Jahwe. Dem steht allerdings der eindeutige Wortlaut entgegen,[7] und es kann kein Zweifel an der Erkenntnis aufkommen, Israel sei tatsächlich mit dem Gotte El vertraut gewesen, unabhängig davon, wann und in welchem Ausmaße die Verehrung Jahwes Raum griff.[8] Wir sind nämlich zur Begründung dessen nicht nur auf die beiden Stellen der Genesis angewiesen. El rangiert Jes 14,13 in der Genitivverbindung 'die Sterne Els'.[9] Wenn es dort heißt, der Tyrann beabsichtigte, über den Sternen Els zu thronen,

2 KAI 24,16; 25,4.5f; 214,2.3.11.18; 215,22; 216,5; 217,7f. - Die Annahme äußerte bereits W. W. Graf Baudissin in *Kyrios als Gottesname im Judentum und seine Stelle in der Religionsgeschichte* Teil 3 (1929), S. 11; siehe die Erläuterungen Rölligs zu KAI 24,16.

3 KAI 214,2.11.18; 215,22; 222 A 11; vielleicht auch in Deir Alla II,6; endlich bezeugt durch Philo von Byblos: Eusebius, Praeparatio Evangelica I,10,16.20.29.44.

4 Vgl. zur Sache O. Eißfeldt, "El and Yahweh", *JSS* 1 (1956) 25-37 = El und Jahwe, Kl. Schr. III (1966) 386-397; E. Jacob, "El", *BHH* 1 (1962), S. 386-389; M. J. Mulder, *Kanaänitische Goden in het Oude Testament*, 1965, pp. 13-24.

5 Gen 33,20.

6 Gen 46,3.

7 Jos 8,30 ist El bewußt durch Jahwe ersetzt, um klar zu machen, er und kein anderer sei der Gott Israels. Die Wiedergabe der Bezeichnung in der griechischen Septuagintaübersetzung von Gen 33,20 läßt vielleicht auf eine andere Textüberlieferung schließen, in welcher der Name El ausgemerzt war. Der Artikel vor dem Namen El in Gen 46,3 muß nicht irritieren, denn dort ist grammatisch El als Leitwort konstruiert, das eine Apposition näher erläutert; vgl. C. Brockelmann, *Hebräische Syntax*, 1956, § 66 a. Der sprachlichen Formulierung von Gen 46,3 gleich sind Gen 31,13; Jes 42,5; vgl. Ps 85,9.

8 Vgl. die Erklärung von Gen 33,20 durch C. Westermann, Genesis, BK, 2. Teilbd. (1981, ^{2}1989). Freilich heißt es bei ihm zu generalisierend, der Kult des Gottes Israels sei an die Stelle des El-Kultes getreten, und es verlautet nichts darüber, wann das geschehen sein soll. Vorher sagt W., El, der Schöpfergott, sei zum Gott der Israeliten geworden, und zwar als El, nämlich Gott schlechthin. Beides ist exakter zu bestimmen: El huldigten von Hause aus Leute, die zu den Israeliten zählten, und während der geschichtlichen Zeit ist in Israel die El-Verehrung nicht durchweg abgekommen.

9 Man bedenke dazu die kritische Note a bei H. Wildberger, "Jesaja", *BK*, 2. Teilbd. (1978, ^{2}1989).

folglich dem Höchsten ebenbürtig zu sein,[10] dann will das besagen, er wollte an der Herrschaft über das All partizipieren, die nur dem Götterherrn El zukommt. Dahinter stehen kanaanäische Reminiszenzen, die - obwohl nur in den Texten von Ras Schamra modifiziert faßbar - eine solche mythologische Bildwelt ermöglichten, wie nicht zuletzt die Aufnahme im Alten Testament beweist.

Ferner mag Ez 28,2aα wenigstens auf den Gott El hinweisen.[11] Da im Fortgang des Wortlauts appellativisch von 'Gott' die Rede ist, sollte man, wenngleich die Erinnerung an die persönliche Gottheit mitschwingen und den Hintergrund für das an der Stelle Ausgesprochene abgeben dürfte,[12] das Gleiche auch zu Anfang voraussetzen,[13] zumal im Buch Ezechiel außer hier V. 2 und 9 das Nomen אֵל sonst nicht vorkommt. Dennoch erinnert der Bericht an das Wissen um die Gottheit El. Der in dem Gerichtswort wegen seines Hochmuts getadelte König von Tyrus hielt sich für einen Gott und meinte, er habe einen Wohnsitz mitten im Meer eingenommen: מושב אלהים ישבתי בלב ימים.[14] Der Satz enthält unverkennbar mythologisches Kolorit, denn die ugaritischen Mythen erwähnen den Wohnsitz Els als *mṯb ʾil*[15] und umschreiben ihn durch *mbk nhrm / ʾapq thmtm* - Quellort der beiden Ströme, Quellbecken der beiden Tiefen.[16] Die Rede vom Wohnsitz des tyrischen Königs mitten im Meer darf man infolgedessen nicht nur von der geographischen Gegebenheit her deuten wollen.

Zu alledem mag man erwägen, ob nicht das Vorkommen von אל in zwei althebräischen Inschriften die Gottheit El nennt. In einer dem 9. Jh. entstammenden Inschrift von Kuntillet 'Ağrud[17] steht es zweimal in Parallele zu Baal. Das Verständnis

10 V. 14.

11 Befürwortet von Eißfeldt, aaO., 28f = 389.

12 Ähnlich F. M. Cross, אֵל ThWAT I (1973), S. 259-279 [271]; vgl. A. Cooper - M. H. Pope, *RSP* III (1981) IV 2j.

13 Siehe zur Stelle W. Zimmerli, "Ezechiel", *BK*, 2. Teilbd. (^{2}1979), S. 667.

14 Vgl. Ps 29,10a (Jahwe wohnt über dem Himmelsozean). Siehe auch O. Loretz, "Der Wohnort Els nach ugaritischen Texten und Ez 28,1-2.6-10", *UF* 21 (1989), S. 259-267.

15 KTU 1.3,IV,48 (erg.); V,39; 1.4,I,12; IV,52.

16 KTU 1.2,III,4 (erg.); 1.3,V,6f (erg.); 1.4,IV,21f; 1.6,I,33f; 1.17,VI,47f (erg.) [lies *mbk* statt *mbr*]; vgl. 1.100,3 [hat *ʿdt* anstelle von *ʾapq*]. - Zu den El als Wohnsitz zugeschriebenen Orten vgl. jetzt M.Dietrich - O. Loretz, "Wohnorte Els nach Ugarit- und Bibeltexten. Eine Studie zu ug. *ǵr ll* || *hr mʿd* und he. *hr mwʿd* || *yrkty ṣpwn* (KTU 1.2 I 20; Jes 14,13)", *UF* 29 (1997), S. 123-149 [siehe hier speziell, S. 136-138].

17 KAgr (9): 7,1.3.

als Eigenname liegt von daher sehr nahe. Und die Deutung der in das Ende des 8. Jh. zu datierenden Schale von Ḫirbet el - Kōm als Libationsgefäß[18] läßt das allein auf die Unterseite eingeritzte אל ebenso als Gottesname verstehen.[19]

Man kann auf Grund all der bisher gemachten Beobachtungen nicht leugnen, daß in der Erlebniswelt Israels und dem ihm vertrauten mythologischen Gut gerade auch der Gott El seinen Platz einnahm.

Endlich darf man das theophore Element *el* in Personennamen[20] für die Bezeugung einer eindeutig umrissenen Gestalt in Anspruch nehmen. Bleibt auch die Etymologie des Namens ישראל umstritten, ist das theophore Element in ihm doch der kanaanäische Gott El.[21]

Beachtung verdient außerdem, daß im Unterschied zu der Vorstellung in Ugarit die Inschriften El nirgends über die anderen Götter herausgehoben zeigen, er demnach nicht wie dort als deren Oberhaupt fungiert. Man wird von daher die Verhältnisse in Israel kaum different verstehen können.[22] Die himmlische Heerschar von 1 Kö 22,19[23] setzt sich nicht aus den anderen neben Jahwe verehrten Gottheiten zusammen, kann mithin keineswegs als Götterversammlung gelten. Es werden ja auch keine diesbezüglichen Namen genannt. Das durch הָרוּחַ gekennzeichnete Einzelwesen dieser Gruppierung[24] macht hinlänglich deutlich, daß an keine sonst angeru-

---

18 Kom (8): 8.

19 Siehe zu beiden Inschriften J. Renz, *Die althebräischen Inschriften*, Teil 1 (1995), S. 57-59. 199f. 215.

20 Bezüglich Ugarits siehe O. Eißfeldt, *El im ugaritischen Pantheon*, 1951, S. 46-52; F. Gröndahl, *Die Personennamen der Texte aus Ugarit*, 1967, S. 94-97; in Hinsicht auf den übrigen geographischen Raum einschließlich des Alten Testaments M. Noth, *Die israelitischen Personennamen im Rahmen der gemeinsemitischen Namengebung*, 1928, S. 82-99; neuerdings J. H. Tigay, *You shall have no other Gods*, 1986; betreffs des Bestandes nur aus den kanaanäischen und aramäischen Inschriften KAI III,[2]1969, S. 45-56; vgl. dazu die Erwägungen von P. Bordreuil, "Les Noms propres Transjordaniens de l'Ostracon de Nimroud", *RHPhR* 59 (1979), S. 313-317; U. Hübner, *Die Ammoniter*, 1992, S. 256; P. M. M. Daviau - P. E. Dion, "El, the God of the Ammonites ? The Atef-crowned Head from Tell Jawa / Jordan", *ZDPV* 110 (1994) S. 158-167.

21 Die Erinnerung an die El-Gottheit ist ferner enthalten in Nu 23,8.19.22f; 24,4.8.16.23; 2 Sam 23,5. Man vergleiche zu El als Eigenname im Alten Testament auch die Übersicht in RSP III (1981) IV,2.

22 Vgl. R. Rendtorff, "El, Baʿal und Jahwe. Erwägungen zum Verhältnis von kanaanäischer und israelitischer Religion", *ZAW* 78 (1966), S. 277-291 = Gesammelte Studien, 1975, S. 172-187; ders., *ʾEl* als Gottesbezeichnung, 5.7.

23 Parallel dazu steht 2 C 18,18.

24 1 Kö 22,21; 2 C 18,20.

fenen Götter gedacht ist. Vielmehr handelt es sich um eine Schar von Dienern oder Boten, wie sie sonst religionsgeschichtlich nachgewiesen sind und aus dem Gang der Erzählung hier unmißverständlich hervorgeht.[25]

Dem widerstreitet auch nicht das einmalige Vorkommen von עדת אל in Ps 82,1. Obwohl eine genaue sprachliche Parallele in KTU 1.15,II,7.11 existiert, können daraus keine schwerlich verifizierbaren Schlüsse gezogen werden. Die in ihm enthaltenen Konturen erweisen Ps 82 als relativ spätes Gebilde, und der Gebrauch des Gottesnamens אל geht auf die in babylonischer Zeit erfolgte Anwendung kanaanäischen Traditionsgutes im Rahmen des Jahweglaubens zurück. Entgegen der Auffassung, bei den Elohimwesen von V. 1b handele es sich um menschliche Richter, wird doch diejenige im Rechte sein, welche tatsächliche göttliche Wesen annimmt. Freilich sollte man sich davon distanzieren, eine depotenzierte Göttergruppe zu behaupten, die Jahwe untergeordnet erscheine.[26] Vielmehr ist hier Jahwe den anderen gleichwertigen Göttern konfrontiert. Die Juden trauten ihm allein alles Heilvolle zu. Sie hegten die Überzeugung, er sei machtvoller als die anderen,[27] die nicht in der Lage sind, das Recht aufzurichten. Das muß Jahwe tun. Man begegnet in dem Bezug einer speziellen Art der sogenannten Götzenpolemik, die kein anderes Ziel hat, als die göttliche Überlegenheit Jahwes in jedem Belang hervorzuheben.[28]

Weiterhin kursiert bis in die Gegenwart hinein die Annahme, Jahwe sei unter den Israeliten im Lauf der Geschichte mit dem Gotte El geglichen worden und habe dessen Position eingenommen.[29] Die Auffassung ziehen jedoch gewichtige Gründe in Zweifel.[30] Denn in der frühesten Zeit erlebte man Jahwe als Helfer im Kampfgeschehen. Diese Eigenschaft erkannten die Israeliten ihm in der Folgezeit bleibend zu, und das unterschied ihn offenkundig von der uns in den Inschriften und auch in Ras Schamra bezeugten El-Gestalt. Dazu zählen dann auch Deskriptionen der Art, wie Jahwe den Israeliten wirksam erschien, und die kaum anderweitig kanaanäische

---

25 Vgl. Ps 103,21; 148,2.

26 Man stützt diese These gern mit Belegen wie Gen 6,2.4; Dt 32,8.43a LXX; 1 Kö 22,19; Jes 6,1-3; Ps 29,1; 89,6-8; Hi 1,6; 2,1; 38,7.

27 Vgl. etwa Ps 95,3; 96,4.

28 Zur Ausdeutung von Ps 82 siehe P. Kleinert, "El", Abhandlungen zur semitischen Religionskunde und Sprachwissenschaft, Festschrift W. W. Graf Baudissin, 1918 (*BZAW* 33), S. 261-284 [280-282].

29 Siehe z. B. W. H. Schmidt, "אֵל *'ēl* Gott", *THAT* I (1971), S. 142-149 [148].

30 Vgl. M. J. Mulder, "Jahwe en El, identiteit of assimilatie?", *Rondom het Woord* 13 (1971), S. 402-418.

Herkunft nahelegen. Das gilt für 'lebendig, zuverlässig, groß, stark' und 'furchtbar'.[31]

Auf der anderen Seite gibt es einige Prädizierungen, die am kanaanäischen El hafteten und auch Jahwe beigelegt auftreten. Dazu zählt die Charakterisierung Jahwes als אל רחום וחנון ארך אפים ורב חסד[32] die eine Beziehung zu dem Epitheton Els von Ugarit als *lṭpn ʾil dpʾid*[33] hat. Und man muß voraussetzen, diesen Wesenszug Els kannte man offenbar ebenso in den südlichen Landstrichen des kanaanäischen Siedlungsgebiets. Andere Prädikate sind König[34] und Vater.[35] Endlich heißt es mehrfach, Jahwe sei ein 'eifernder Gott'.[36] So wird El niemals charakterisiert. Die Literatur von Ras Schamra redet hingegen vom eifernden, ungestümen Verhalten der Göttin Anat.[37]

Es wird also sein Bewenden damit haben müssen, daß Israel Jahwe nicht mit El gleichsetzte, ihm aber Eigenschaften dieses Gottes beilegte, insofern sich der Glaube mehr und mehr auf Jahwe hin konzentrierte. Man muß demnach davon ausgehen, beide Gottheiten haben während der geschichtlichen Zeit nebeneinander ihre Verehrung genossen.[38]

Eine letzte Frage betrifft die nach der Auffassung Els als Schöpfer. Man bezieht sich dabei in erster Linie auf die in der phönikischen Inschrift von Karatepe und ein weiteres Mal in einer neupunischen Inschrift von Leptis Magna vorkommende Be-

---

31 Dt 7,9.21; 10,17; Jos 3,10; Jes 9,5; 10,21; Jer 32,18; Ho 2,1; Ps 42,3; 84,3; 86,15; 95,3; Ne 9,32.

32 Ex 34,6; Dt 4,31; Jn 4,2; Ps 86,15; Ne 9,17.31 (teilweise in abweichender sprachlicher Gestalt).

33 (teilweise ergänzt:) 1.1,III,21f; IV,13.18; 1.4,IV,58; 1.5,VI,11f; 1.6,I,49f; III,4.10.14; 1.15,II,13f; 1.16,IV,9; V,10.23; 1.18,I,15; 1.24,44f [liest *lẓpn*]; fraglich 1.6,VI,39 - von El *lṭpn* allein: 1.1,II,18; III,6; 1.6,IV,11; 1.16,I,11.21.23; II,44.49; IV,2; *pʾid* allein: 1.4,II,10; III,31.

34 Die Inschriften wenden diesen Titel freilich nicht auf El an. Das ist nur in den Texten von Ugarit der Fall. Es wird aber wohl richtig sein, hier von einem kanaanäischen Erbe zu sprechen: KTU 1.2,III,5; 1.3,V,8 [erg.]; 1.4,I,5; IV,24.38.48; 1.6,I,36; 1.14,I,41; 1.17,VI,49; 1.117,3f [erg.]; - 1 Sam 12,12; Jes 6,5; 33,17.22; 41,21; 43,15; 44,6; Ze 3,15; Sa 14,9.16f; Ma 1,14; Ps 10,16; 24,8-10; 29,10; 44,5; 47,3.7f; 48,3; 74,12; 84,4; 95,3; 98,6; 145,1; 149,2.

35 Die Dinge liegen hier geradeso wie bei der Titelei König: KTU 1.1,III,26; 1.2,I,16.33.36; III,16.17.19.21; 1.3,V,10.35; 1.4,IV,47; 1.6,IV,10; VI,27; 1.13,21; 1.14,I,37.41.43; II,6.24; III,32.47; IV,6; 1.17,I,23; 1.92,15; 1.114,14; 1.117,3; - Jes 63,16; 64,7; Jer 3,4.19; 31,9; Ma 1,6; 2,10.

36 Ex 20,5; 34,14; Dt 4,24; 5,9; 6,15; Jos 24,19; Na 1,2.

37 KTU 1.3,II,5-35; V,22-25; 1.17,VI,41-45; 1.18,I,9-12; - mit dem in KTU 1.3,II,5-35 geschilderten Gemetzel Anats mag man immerhin Jes 63,1-6 vergleichen.

38 So auch Eißfeldt, *El und Jahwe*, 389; Mulder, Kan. Goden, 95.

stimmung אל קן ארץ.[39] Die gleiche Formulierung vermutet man schon lange in dem Götternamen ᵈEl-ku-ni-ir-ša eines in Boğazköj entdeckten Mythus.[40] Danach sah die kanaanäische Bevölkerung in El den Schöpfer der Erde.[41] Nun redet Gen 14,19.22 von אל עליון קנה שמים וארץ, in dessen Namen Melchisedek, der König von Salem, Abram segnet. Aus dieser Bezeugung schloß man vielfach, die Israeliten hätten in alter Zeit Jahwe mit dem Schöpfergott El von Jerusalem in eins gesetzt. Die Redefigur verrät freilich durch die Zueinanderordnung der nomina propria divina *ʾēl* und *ʿäljôn* sowie die Erweiterung durch den Himmel, womit El zum Schöpfer des Alls gemacht wird, eine relativ späte Entstehung.[42] Wo man im übrigen verstreut Bemerkungen über das Schöpferwirken Jahwes findet, handelt es sich um spätere Interpolationen oder generell erst relativ spät entstandene Stücke.[43]

Hat einerseits Lipiński erklärt, dem Verb *qny* eigne nicht die Bedeutung ‘schaffen’, sondern ‘besitzen’,[44] angesichts dessen man erwägen mag, ob zwischen ‘erwerben, besitzen’ und ‘schaffen, erschaffen’ ein grundlegender Kontrast besteht, so ist auf der anderen Seite die Idee in Ugarit[45] von der im übrigen kanaanäischen Raum unterschieden. In der ugaritischen Mythologie sind keine Anhaltspunkte gegeben, die erkennen ließen, El habe die Erde bzw. die Menschen geschaffen,[46] wie schon von anderen gesehen.[47]

---

39 KAI 26 A III,18 (Karatepe, 8. Jh. v. Chr.); 129,1 (Tripolitana 13, 2. Jh. n. Chr.).

40 H. Otten, “Ein kanaanäischer Mythus aus Boğazköy”, *MIOF* 1 (1953) 125-150.

41 Zu den Zeugnissen können vielleicht zwei weitere gerechnet werden, die in ihrem Verständnis allerdings nicht absolut gesichert sind: palmyrenisch *ʾlq(w)nrʿ*, spätes 1. Jt. v. Chr.; hebr. *ʾl*]*qn ʾrṣ*, frühes 7. Jh. v. Chr. (vgl. N. Avigad, “Excavations in the Jewish Quarter of the Old City of Jerusalem”, 1971, *IEJ* 22 (1972), S. 193-200 [195]).

42 Vgl. A. Caquot, “Schöpfungsmythen der Kanaanäer”, *Quellen des Alten Orients, I: Die Schöpfungsmythen*, hg. von M. Eliade, 1964 (1980), S. 173-182 [177f].

43 Das betrifft vornehmlich Gen 2,8f. 19; 24,3a; Ex 20,11a; Jos 2,11b; 1 Sam 2,8b; 2 Kö 19,15b; Jes 37,16b; Am 4,13; 5,8; 9,5f; Ps 19 A; 24,1f; 89,12; 93,1b; Prov 16,4.

44 E. Lipiński, “קָנָה *qānāh*”, *ThWAT* VII (1993), S. 63-71 [64.67-69].

45 Aufgelistet von Cross, אֵל, 262.

46 Dafür sind die appositionellen Ausdrücke *ṯr* und *ʾab ʾadm* nicht eindeutig genug, ebensowenig die Wortfolge *bny bnwt*; vgl. M. Dietrich - O. Loretz - J. Sanmartín, “Bemerkungen zur Schlangenbeschwörung RS 24.244 = UG. 5, S. 564ff. Nr. 7”, *UF* 7 (1975), S. 121-125; S. Segert, *A basic Grammar of the Ugaritic Language*, 1984.

47 Rendtorff, *El, Baʿal und Jahwe*, 287 [= Ges. St. 182]; M. H. Pope, “The Status of El at Ugarit”, *UF* 19 (1987) 219-230; J.-L. Cunchillos, “Peut-on parler de Mythes de Création à Ugarit?”, F. Blanquart (Éd.), *La Création dans l'Orient Ancien* (Congrès de l'ACFEB, Lille 1985), 1987, S. 79-96 [95f].

Wieweit in Israel bezüglich Erde und Menschen dem Gotte El Eigentumsrecht oder die erschaffende Funktion zugesprochen war, wird deutlich, wenn man sich vergegenwärtigt, daß die frühesten Zeugnisse über die Erschaffung des Menschen durch Jahwe aus dem 7. Jh. v. Chr. stammen.[48] Und als Schöpfer der Welt - an der in Mesopotamien nachgewiesenen Mythologie orientiert[49] - ist er nicht früher als im babylonischen Zeitalter bezeugt,[50] teilweise im Bilde des Kampfes gegen lebensfeindliche Mächte.[51]

Auf Grund dieser Gegebenheiten leuchtet die Annahme ein, in Israel sei bis gegen Ende der geschichtlichen Ära das Schöpfungshandeln dem Gotte El zugeschrieben worden[52]. Selbst bei denen, die Jahwe vornehmlich anhingen, löste er El in allen Belangen nicht entscheidend vor dem Übergang der prophetischen in die babylonische Epoche ab. Welches Gewicht die Gottheit El in der mythischen Vorstellungswelt der Israeliten und Judäer hatte, läßt sich hinzukommend an der Tatsache ermessen, daß in der nachgeschichtlichen Zeit der Name El vermehrt Jahwe beigelegt erscheint.[53] Es ist das offensichtlich ein bewußt archaisierender Vorgang. Man mag darin den Willen erkennen, die Suprematie Jahwes gebührend hervorzuheben, sein

---

48 Gen 2,7.22; Ex 4,11; Dt 4,32; 32,6.15; Jes 29,16; 43,1.15; 44,2; 45,11f; 51,13aα; 54,5; Ho 8,14; Prov 14,31; 17,5; 22,2; 29,13; vgl. 20,12; Ps 139,13 - Zu der Erwägung, die sog. jahwistische Schöpfungserzählung sei nicht früher als gegen Ende der geschichtlichen Zeit entstanden, kann als älterer Kronzeuge B. Stade genannt werden: Der Mythus vom Paradies Gn 2.3 und die Zeit seiner Einwanderung in Israel, *ZAW* 23 (1903) 172-179. Vgl. ferner H. H. Schmid, Der sogenannte Jahwist. Beobachtungen und Fragen zur Pentateuchforschung, 1976, und die in seinen Bahnen laufenden Äußerungen.

49 Vgl. O. Kaiser, *Die mythische Bedeutung des Meeres in Ägypten, Ugarit und Israel*, [2]1962, 76.144f; S. E. Loewenstamm, "The Ugaritic Myth of the Sea and its Biblical Counterparts", *ErIs* 9 (1969), S. 96-101 [Hebrew Section].

50 Gen 1,1-2,4a; 1 Sam 2,8b; Jes 40,22b.26.28a; 42,5; 44,24b; 45,7.12.18; 48,13a; 51,13aα.16bα; Jer 10,11f; Am 4,13; 5,8; 9,5f; Ps 19,2; 24,1f; 74,15-17; 89,12f; 93,1b - Immerhin leitet man die Belege vielfach aus älterer Zeit her oder erkennt in ihnen andererseits ältere Überlieferung. Hier ist zugestandenermaßen noch manches umstritten. - Von dem so dokumentierten Glauben leben dann Stellen wie Gen 24,3a; Ex 20,11a; Jos 2,11b; 2 Kö 19,15b = Jes 37,16b.

51 Jes 44,27; 50,2bα; 51,9f.15aβ = Jer 31,35bα; Na 1,4a; Ps 74,13f; 89,10f.

52 Vgl. die Reflexionen von W. H. Schmidt, *Königtum Gottes in Ugarit und Israel*, [2]1966 (*BZAW* 80) 63; H. Vorländer, "Der Monotheismus Israels als Antwort auf die Krise des Exils", B. Lang (Hg.), *Der einzige Gott. Die Geburt des biblischen Monotheismus*, 1981, 84-113 (108). Die Überzeugung, das Schöpferwirken sei erst relativ spät auf Jahwe übertragen worden, teilen beispielsweise B. Stade, *Geschichte des Volkes Israel*, 2. Bd. (1888) 30; J. P. Hyatt, "Was Yahweh originally a Creator Deity?", *JBL* 86 (1967) 369-377; H. Wildberger, "Jesaja", *BK*, 3. Teilbd. (1982), S.1427.

53 Z. B. schon Jes 40,18; 42,5; 43,10.12; 45,14f.21f; 46,9; vgl. Cross, aaO., 277f.

Handeln mythologisch als seit den ältesten Zeiten übermächtig und alles umgreifend zu beschreiben, gleichzeitig aber auch die mit El ursprünglich verbundenen Eigenschaften lebendig zu erhalten und die ererbte Gläubigkeit auf Jahwe zu übertragen.

REMARKS ON THE SEMANTICS AND TRANSLATION OF *KIMʿAṬ* IN BIBLICAL HEBREW*

JACOB HOFTIJZER

Leiden

The nominal lexeme *mʿṭ* refers semantically to undefined smallness. A further specification of the type of smallness concerned is not provided by the use of the lexeme itself, but by contextual means.[1] Therefore, there is no reason to consider this lexeme as such as being polysemic. Not the lexeme in question, but its various translational equivalents display semantic diversity.[2]

In this article the author will discuss only a special group of *mʿṭ* instances, namely those occurring in the prepositional phrase *kimʿaṭ*. First, those instances where *kimʿaṭ* functions as a modifier in a verbal or nominal clause will be discussed.

In Ps. 2:12 *kimʿaṭ* is a modifier in a verbal clause (*ky-ybʿr kmʿṭ ʾpw*). A modal translation of this instance of *kimʿaṭ* seems less than suitable.[3] An interpretation that the wrath of the Lord could/can (very) easily flare up, does not fit the context, which speaks of the certainty of the divine punishment of the king's enemies (cf. v. 5).[4] This makes a non-modal, temporal interpretation the most probable one (cf. already

---

* The author thanks Mrs. Dr.J.W.Dyk for correcting the English of this article.

1 For the various types of smallness concerned in the different context types (smallness of what?), cf. the dictionaries and H.J.Zobel (1984). Also from a quantitative standpoint, the smallness in question is unspecified. The semantic difference between *mʿṭ* and its antonyms is only a difference in degree, not allowing for a specific semantic definition of the quantitative side of *mʿṭ*, cf. Wehrle (1991), 579.

2 Against Zobel (1984), pp. 1031, 1032, who speaks of "die verschiedenen Bedeutungsnuancen" of *mʿṭ*.

3 Against, e.g., Hupfeld (1855), pp. 15, 34: "leicht könnte entbrennen sein Zorn"; Delitzsch (1894), pp. 69, 76: "denn entflammen möchte schier sein Zorn"; Gunkel (1926), pp. 5, 12: "denn leicht kann entbrennen sein Zorn"; Podechard (1949), pp. 13, 18: "car en un instant peut s'enflammer son courroux"; Buttenwieser (1969), p. 792: "for his wrath may soon be kindled"; van Uchelen (1971), pp. 15, 21: "want zeer licht ontbrandt zijn toorn"; Dahood (1965), p. 6: "for his ire flares up quickly"; Craigie (1983), pp. 63, 68: "for his anger flares up quickly". Also against Wehrle (1991), p. 583; Jenni (1994), p. 161. Cf. also Kraus (1978a), p. 154: "Das in v. 5 angekündigte Hervorbrechen des göttlichen Zornes kann sehr schnell, «unversehens» ... geschehen".

4 Cf. Duhm (1922), p. 12; Zenger (1987), p. 505; cf. also Baethgen (1904), p. 7.

the LXX).[5] The temporal interpretation in question implies that God's wrath will certainly start "burning" within a short time, if the rulers do not obey the Lord (cf. also vv. 10f.). This does not imply, that it will start "burning" under all circumstances in a near future.[6] Divine wrath is presented in the context as being avoidable: *pn-yʾnp wtʾbdw drk* (v. 12). The idea that God's wrath is conceived of as starting to "burn" "within a short time", finds its parallels in a number of Biblical texts in which divine punishment or the flaring up of the divine wrath is presented as being imminent.[7]

In Ps. 81:15 *kimʿaṭ* occurs also as a modifier in a verbal clause (*kmʿṭ ʾwybyhm ʾknyʿ*). Within the context this clause must be translated in a modal way, as is clear from v. 14 (*lw ʿmy šmʿ ly yśrʾl bdrky yhlkw*). Both clauses express an imaginary condition (cf. also v. 12). The verbal clause from v. 15, quoted above, describes what would happen if the people would fulfill this condition and obey the Lord. However, this fact does not justify a semantic interpretation of the relevant *kimʿaṭ* as such as being modal.[8] Here a temporal interpretation (the subduing of the enemies taking place within a short period of time), would also fit well into the context.[9] In the translations of this verse the word "soon" is often used to represent *kimʿaṭ*. For this context this translation is acceptable (not, as we have seen, for Ps. 2:12), but one

5 Cf., e.g., van der Ploeg (1971), p. 40: "want zijn toorn ontvlamt in een ogenblik"; Auffret (1977), p. 9: "for it flames up in a moment"; Rogerson-Mc Kay (1977a), p. 19: "for his anger flares up in a moment"; von Mutius (1981), p. 44: "denn sein Zorn entbrennt im Nu".

6 Against, e.g., Duhm (1922), p. 11: "denn bald wird entbrennen sein Zorn"; Brownlee (1971), p. 336: "for his wrath will soon be kindled". Cf. also Baethgen (1904), p. 7: "Der Sänger erwartet das baldige Ausbrechen des Gerichtstages"; Zenger (1987), p. 505: "ist ... temporal im Sinne von "bald" zu deuten"; Seybold (1996), p. 33: "erwartet die Reaktion Gottes im Balde".

7 Cf. Numb. 16:21 (*krgʿ*); 17:10 (*krgʿ*); Jer. 4:20 (*ptʾm // rgʿ*); 15: 8 (*ptʾm*); Pss. 64:8 (*ptʾwm*); 73:19 (*krgʿ*); Job 9:23 (*ptʾm*); 34:20 (*rgʿ*); Lam. 4:6 (*kmw-rgʿ*). Cf. also below.

8 Against Jenni (1994), p. 161. A modal interpretation as proposed by the translation "easily" is also not probable. Against, e.g., Hupfeld (1860), pp. 395, 405; Hitzig (1865), p. 187; Seybold (1996), p. 321. Also against Delitzsch (1894), p. 540: "schier würde ich ..." and Wehrle (1991), p. 583: "es bräuchte nur wenig", "es wäre ein Geringes".

9 Cf. Briggs-Briggs (1925), p. 210: "in a little while their enemies I would subdue"; van der Ploeg (1974), p. 47: "dan zou ik hun vijanden in een oogwenk doen bukken"; Auffret (1993), p. 287: "en un instant j'abattrais ses ennemis".

must not forget, that the reference to the short period of time for the subjugation is expressed by *kimʿaṭ*, but not, at least not explicitly, by "soon".[10]

In Job 32:22 Elihu considers the imaginary circumstance that he would be able to flatter (for his attitude in this matter, cf. also Job 33:3). If that were the case, the Lord would punish him (*kmʿṭ yśʾny ʿśny*). Here also *kimʿaṭ* is a modifier in a verbal clause. The fact that this last-mentioned clause expresses the consequences of a fictitious situation, does not justify a semantic interpretation of the relevant *kimʿaṭ* as such as being modal. As in Ps. 2:12 and 81:15, a temporal interpretation (the speaker being taken away within a short period of time), fits the context very well.[11] A modal translation of this *kimʿaṭ* with "easily" seems less probable. It is more probable, that the text states that if Elihu were to act in a way unacceptable to God, the Lord would punish him, than that the text would assert, that in such a case there was a fair chance He would punish him.[12] With regard to a translation with "soon", which one often finds in commentaries, the same remarks already made in the discussion of Ps. 81:15 are valid.[13]

In Ps. 94:17 *kimʿaṭ* is again a modifier in a verbal clause (*lwly YHWH ʿzrth ly kmʿṭ šknh dwmh npšy*). Many scholars interpret this text as meaning, that if the Lord had not helped the Psalmist, he would have almost died.[14] J.Ridderbos has justly refuted this interpretation by observing that the implication that the Psalmist would have survived the attacks of his enemies, albeit in a bad condition, would weaken

10 For this translation, cf., e.g., Baethgen (1904), p. 256; Duhm (1922), p. 316; Gunkel (1926), p. 356; Kissane (1954), pp. 53, 55; Weiser (1955), p. 376; Buttenwieser (1969), p. 55; Rogerson-McKay (1977b), p. 160; Booij (1994), p. 7; Goulder (1996), p. 153. Comparable problems arise with the translation "straightway", cf. Dahood (1968), p. 263; Tate (1990), p. 318.

11 Cf., e.g., Kroeze (1961), p. 366: "zo maar zou zijn Schepper hem wegnemen"; Terrien (1963), p. 219: "mon Créateur m'enlèverait en un instant"; Dhorme (1967), p. 485: "my Maker would carry me off in a flash!"; van Selms (1983), p. 114: "dan zou het oordeel van zijn Schepper hem doen omkomen, en dat in een ogenblik tijds".

12 Against, e.g., Dillmann (1891), p. 282; Fohrer (1963), p. 449; Wehrle (1990), p. 91; Wehrle (1991), p. 584; Jenni (1994), p. 161. For the reason mentioned here the translation of *kimʿaṭ* with "vielleicht" (cf. Ehrlich [1913], p. 310) is still less probable.

13 For this translation, cf. Duhm (1897), p. 156; Budde (1913), p. 204; Driver-Gray (1921), p. 283; Kissane (1946), p. 217; Hölscher (1952), p. 78; Tur-Sinai (1957), p. 463; Pope (1973), p. 241; Habel (1985), p. 442. The same problems arise with the translation "speedily" proposed, e.g., by Gordis (1978), p. 360.

14 Cf., e.g., Delitzsch (1894), p. 605; Briggs-Briggs (1925), p. 291; Schmidt (1934), p. 176; Kraus (1978b), p. 821; Stolz (1983), p. 43; Wehrle (1991), pp. 587f.; Jenni (1994), p. 161.

the Psalmist's expression of gratitude. It is more likely that the Psalmist is relating that he could survive only due to the Lord,[15] the more so, since the enemies are described as killing vulnerable people (v. 6) and as being intent on killing the righteous (v. 21). The same objection can be made against an interpretation/translation of *kimʿaṭ* with "easily".[16] The interpretation of the *kimʿaṭ* in question with "within a short period of time" does fit the context very well.[17] In this interpretation the death of the Psalmist is presented as being certain, if the Lord had not helped him.[18]

In Psalm 73:2 *kimʿaṭ* occurs in a clause in which the predicate is a participle Qal passive (*wʾny kmʿṭ nṭwy rgly*).[19] It is possible to take the form *nṭwy* as a form in the absolute state, in which case *rgly* functions as a modifier to it. Such a construction occurs elsewhere as well, cf., e.g., the *qaruʿa kuttonto* in 2 Sam. 15:32 and the *lavuš baddim* in Ez. 9:2.[20] However, it is also possible to take the *nṭwy* in question as a form in the construct state, cf., e.g., the *qeruʿe vegadim* in 2 Sam. 13:31, the *levuš*

---

15 Cf. Ridderbos (1958), p. 433.

16 For this interpretation, cf., e.g., Hupfeld (1862), p. 35; Hitzig (1865), p. 251; van der Ploeg (1974), p. 134; Booij (1994), pp. 139, 143.

17 Cf. also texts which mention disasters overtaking people within a short period of time, like Is. 47:9 (*rgʿ bywm ʾḥd*); Jer. 6:26 (*ptʾm*); 51:8 (*ptʾm*); Hab. 2:7 (*ptʿ*); Pss. 6:11 (*rgʿ*); 64:5 (*ptʾm*); 73:19 (*krgʿ*); Prov. 6:15 (*ptʾm, ptʿ*); 24:22 (*ptʾm*); 29:1 (*ptʿ*); Lam. 4:6 (*kmw-rgʿ*). Cf. also below.

18 For interpretations which present the death of the Psalmist as certain, if the Lord had not helped him, cf., e.g., Duhm (1922), p. 352; Gunkel (1926), pp. 413, 415: "wenn ihn nicht Gott geholfen hätte, so wäre er schon längst in der Unterwelt"; Weiser (1955), p. 425; Dahood (1968), p. 346: "I would have directly dwelt in the Fortress"; Conti (1997), p. 4: "già abiterebbe nel luogo di silenzio la mia anima". A translation with "soon" is contextually acceptable. For this translation, cf., e.g., Kissane (1954), p. 118; Rogerson-McKay (1977b), p. 212; Tate (1990), p. 482; Howard (1997), p. 45. However, cf. the remarks made above about the use of the translation "soon". An interpretation that the Psalmist "would be dead soon", instead of "would have been dead soon", is also possible. For this interpretation, cf., e.g., Baethgen (1904), p. 292; Wutz (1925), p. 251; Ridderbos (1958), pp. 428, 433; Buttenwieser (1969), p. 637; Seybold (1996), p. 371. For a suffix conjugation form referring to the future, cf. below the discussion of Ps. 119:87.

The author considers the relevant *kimʿaṭ* as belonging only to the following clause and not to the preceding one as well. In this connection, cf. the remarks of Ben- Zvi (1991), p. 100 n. 16 on the use of the *shalshelet gadol*.

19 This interpretation means, that I prefer the reading of the *Ketiv*. For this decision, cf., e.g., Hupfeld (1860), p. 285; Hitzig (1865), p. 123; Baethgen (1904), p. 227; Buttenwieser (1969), p. 531; Irsigler (1984), pp. 11f.; Goulder (1996), p. 56. Cf. also Caquot (1971), pp. 34f.

20 Cf., e.g., Gesenius-Kautzsch-Cowley (1910), § 116k; Waltke-O'Connor (1990), § 37.3b; Joüon-Muraoka (1991), § 121o; Gibson (1994), § 111a.

habbaddim in Ez. 9:11 and the *neṭuyot garon* in Is. 3:16.[21] In the last-mentioned case one can consider the phrase *nṭwy rgly* as a substantivated clause, in which *rgly* functions as a modifier. Normally the *kimʿaṭ* in this clause is interpreted/translated as "nearly", "almost".[22] This means that the feet of the Psalmist did not really slip.[23] However, in the opinion of the author, this interpretation is far from certain. In the context (especially vv. 21f.) the Psalmist speaks depreciatingly about himself. He calls himself a *bʿr* and *bhmwt* in his relation to God. The nominal form *bʿr* is used as a parallel to *ksyl* (Pss. 49:11; 92:7; cf. also the Qal Participle *bʿrym* parallel to *ksylym* in Ps. 94:8) and the nominal form *bhmh* is used in Job 18:3 referring to human beings in a very depreciating manner. Therefore, one seriously has to consider the possibility that in Ps. 73:2 *kmʿṭ* has to be interpreted with "within a short period", "within a moment". If this is true, the Psalmist starts with the remark that his feet slipped (v. 2) because of his attitude towards life (v. 3).[24]

One finds a comparable case in Prov. 5:14 where *kimʿaṭ* is modifier in a nominal clause (*kmʿṭ hyyty bkl-rʿ btwk qhl wʿdh*).[25] Most scholars translate *kimʿaṭ* here with "well-nigh", "nearly", "almost",[26] meaning that the worst did not happen.[27] How-

21 Cf., e.g., Gesenius-Kautzsch-Cowley (1910), § 116k; Waltke-O'Connor (1990), § 37.3c; Joüon-Muraoka (1991), § 121o; Gibson (1994), § 111b.

22 Cf., e.g., Hupfeld (1860), pp. 281, 285; Delitzsch (1894), pp. 486, 488; Duhm (1922), p. 278; Gunkel (1926), pp. 311, 313; Kissane (1954), p. 3; Dahood (1968), p. 186; Buttenwieser (1969), p. 524; Ross (1978), p. 161; Stolz (1983), pp. 46f.; Tate (1990), p. 318; Wehrle (1991), p. 587; Jenni (1994), p. 161; Hauge (1995), pp. 269f.; Brueggemann-Miller (1996), p. 50; Seybold (1996), p. 279.

23 Cf., e.g., Kraus (1978b), p. 668: "es ist nicht geschehen! Jahwe hat ihn nicht fallen lassen". For comparable remarks, cf. Hitzig (1865), p. 123; Ridderbos (1958), p. 323.

24 One may compare Ps. 38 where the Psalmist speaks about *ḥṭʾty* (v. 4), *ʾwlty* (v. 6) and *ʿwny* and *ḥṭʾty* (v. 19). He also speaks about the tottering of his feet in v. 17.
The parallel *kʾyn* in Ps. 73:2 will be discussed below.

25 For the use of the term "nominal clause" in this connection, cf., e.g., Waltke-O'Connor (1990), § 4.5c; Joüon-Muraoka (1991), § 154m; Gibson (1994), § 50.

26 Cf., e.g., Wildeboer (1897), p. 15; Toy (1914), pp. 108, 110; Oesterley (1929), p. 36; van der Ploeg (1952), p. 29; Gemser (1963), p. 34; McKane (1970), p. 218; van der Weiden (1970), p. 56; Ringgren in Ringgren-Zimmerli (1980), p. 28; Plöger (1984), p. 52; Wehrle (1991), p. 588; Jenni (1994), p. 161; Whybray (1994), p. 88.

27 Cf., e.g., Frankenberg (1898), p. 43: "Der Ehebrecher ist froh, dass er wenigstens dem schlimmsten Unheil der öffentlichen Aburteilung in der Gerichtsversammlung entzogen ist"; Meinhold (1991), p. 114: "Der Weise lässt den Schüler allerdings knapp entkommen". Cf. also Tuinstra (1996), p. 142. For the interpretation of "being in all evil", cf., e.g., Boström (1935), p. 141; McKane (1970), p. 317; Plöger (1984), p. 57.

ever, as Lang has remarked already, this interpretation is somewhat improbable from a contextual standpoint.[28] In v. 12 a young man (cf. v. 1) is being introduced, who regrets that he has been ensnared in the nets of the "strange woman". His words end at the end of v. 14. They imply that the young man in question really had undesirable contacts with this woman, contacts which of necessity led to his downfall (vv. 9-11; cf. also v. 23). Therefore, another interpretation, implying that he actually underwent the consequences of his sin, is preferable. In the author's opinion, an interpretation of the relevant *kimʿaṭ* with "within a short period of time", "within a moment" would fit well in the context.[29]

In Ps. 119:87 *kimʿaṭ* functions as a modifier in a verbal clause (*kmʿṭ klwny bʾrṣ*). Normally this *kimʿaṭ* is translated/interpreted as "well-nigh", "nearly", "almost".[30] However, this translation of *kimʿaṭ* is less probable for Ps. 73:2 and Prov. 5:14 (see above). For that reason, we have to ask ourselves whether it is inevitable for Ps. 119:87. In the author's opinion this is not the case. An interpretation with "within a short time" is certainly possible. From the context it is clear that the Psalmist fears that he will not live a long time (*kmh ymy-ʿbdk*; v. 84, especially in relation to the preceding clauses). He requests to be kept alive (*kḥsdk ḥyny*; v. 88). One can say with Soll, that he has the idea that "his time is running out".[31] Cf. in this connection also v. 126 (*ʿt lʿśwt lYHWH*). Against this background an interpretation of Ps. 119:87a as "within a short time they will eradicate me ..." has to be considered seriously.[32]

The preceding instances describe a change for the worse. However, *kimʿaṭ* is also attested in some texts involving a change for the better.

---

28 Cf. Lang (1990), p. 195 (n. 34).

29 Lang (1990), p. 195 translates with "sofort".

30 Cf., e.g., Hupfeld (1862), p. 231; Hitzig (1865), p. 356; Delitzsch (1894), pp. 714, 725; Baethgen (1904), p. 365; Duhm (1922), p. 421; Kittel (1922), p. 378; Gunkel (1926), p. 526; Schmidt (1934), p. 216; Kissane (1954), p. 231; Deissler (1955), p. 186; Weiser (1955), p. 506; Buttenwieser (1969), p. 866; Dahood (1970), p. 166; van der Ploeg (1974), p. 324; Kraus (1978b), p. 990; Allen (1983), p. 130; Wehrle (1991), p. 588; Jenni (1994), p. 161; Seybold (1996), p. 465.

31 Cf. Soll (1991), p. 101 (cf. also p. 153). Soll (1991), p. 165 translates *kimʿaṭ* in Ps. 119:87 with "almost".

32 In this interpretation the suffix conjugation form *klwny* has been interpreted as referring to the future and not to a fictitious past, as is normally done. For the possibility of such an interpretation, cf. Driver (1892), §§ 13, 14; Gesenius-Kautzsch-Cowley (1910), § 106m, n; Waltke-O'Connor (1990), § 30.5.1e; Joüon-Muraoka (1991), § 112g. Among the instances quoted one finds not only examples from prose, but also from poetic texts, cf. also Michel (1960), pp. 90ff.

In 2 Chr. 12:7 *kimʿaṭ* is a modifier in a verbal clause (*wntty lhm kmʿṭ lplyṭh*). A number of scholars take *kimʿaṭ* as the direct object of *ntty*,[33] in which case *lplyṭh* is treated as an apposition (with so-called *l* objecti) or as an attribute to *kimʿaṭ*. There is an interesting parallel text (relating to a comparable situation: relief for the people, although they remain subjects to a foreign power)[34] in Ezra 9:13 (*wntth lnw plyṭh* ...). This makes it probable, that *lplyṭh* in 2 Chr. 12:7 functions as (a paratactic element of) the object. In Ezra 9:13 one finds (after *plyṭh*) a *k*-phrase as clause modifier (*kzʾt*). Consequently, one has to ask oneself whether the interpretation of *kimʿaṭ* in 2 Chr. 12:7 as object is inevitable. Some scholars interpret the relevant *kimʿaṭ* in a temporal way: "within a short time".[35] In the opinion of the author, one has to consider this interpretation seriously. As we have seen, *kimʿaṭ* indicating "within a short period of time" is used in cases describing divine punishment, the flaring up of divine wrath or disasters overtaking people. One may ask oneself whether, if it is used in contexts describing changes for worse, it cannot also be used in contexts describing changes for better. Moreover, there are some instances where the text indicates that a change for better takes place within a short period of time, cf. Is. 29:5 (concerning the downfall of enemies; *whyh lptʿ ptʾm*); 2 Chr. 29:36 (the reinstitution of the Temple service; *bptʾm hyh hdbr*).[36] Against this background the temporal interpretation must be considered seriously.

In Ezra 9:8 *kimʿaṭ-regaʿ* functions as modifier in a nominal clause (*wʿth kmʿṭ-rgʿ hyth tḥnh mʾt YHWH ʾlhynw* ...). The use of *rgʿ* here gives us the certainty that we have to do with a modifier with a temporal function; therefore, this phrase is normally interpreted in a temporal way. Some authors translate it with "for a short mo-

33 Cf., e.g., Galling (1954), p. 104: "Ich ... will ihnen ein wenig "Errettung" widerfahren lassen"; van den Born (1960), p. 159: "Ik zal ... hun een weinig uitkomst geven"; Myers (1965b), p. 72: "I will grant them some measure of deliverance"; Mason (1990), p. 35: "I will grant them some respite", cf. also p. 36; Japhet (1993), p. 673: "I will grant them some deliverance". Cf. also Kelly (1996), p. 60: "Rehoboam and the leaders of Judah ... are granted a partial deliverance".

34 They remain subject to the Persian kings (Ezra 9:9) and to Sisak (2 Chr. 12:8) respectively.

35 Cf., e.g., Nowack (1902a), p. 128: "und werde ihnen in kurzem Rettung schaffen"; Curtis-Madsen (1910), p. 371; Rudolph (1955), p. 234: "im Balde", with reserve; Michaeli (1967), p. 171: "dans peu de temps, je les ferai échapper"; Jenni (1994), p. 160: "in kurzer Frist". Cf. also Wehrle (1991), p. 585. Williamson (1982), p. 248 seriously considers the possibility of the translation "in a short while".

36 Cf. also Mal. 3:1: the coming of an Angel of the Lord preparing the coming of the Lord; *wbptʾm ybwʾ* ...

ment",[37] which could suggest, that "the times of grace will not last long".[38] For that reason, one has to consider an alternative temporal interpretation. Because changes for the good or for the better can be described as taken place "within a short period of time" (see above), one must seriously consider the possibility that such an interpretation is applicable here.[39] In view of the discussion of the other texts, this interpretation has, in the author's opinion, to be given the preference.

In Is. 26:20 *kimʿaṭ-regaʿ* functions as modifier in a verbal clause (*ḥby kmʿṭ-rgʿ*). As in Ezra 9:8 the use of *rgʿ* provides certainty that we have to do with a modifier with a temporal function. Therefore this phrase is normally interpreted in a temporal way: "for a short period of time".[40] This interpretation is contextually possible,[41] but it is also conceivable from a contextual standpoint, that the people are asked to hide themselves within a short period of time (a translation with "soon", "quickly" is possible, with the reservations mentioned above). In view of the remarks made about the other texts and especially in view of the fact that a translation of the *kimʿaṭ-regaʿ* in Ezra 9:8 with "for a short period of time" seems less probable (see above), a translation with "soon", "quickly" should be considered seriously.[42]

---

37 Cf., e.g., Bertholet (1902), p. 40; Batten (1913), p. 323; Rudolph (1949), p. 88; De Fraine (1961), p. 65; Myers (1965a), p. 74; Williamson (1985), p. 125; Jenni (1994), p. 160. Michaeli (1967), p. 301 and Jobsen (1997), pp. 83, 87 have interpreted/translated with "since a short time". We have to do, probably, with a contextual interpretational adaption, which, however, is not allowed by the Hebrew. Nor is the interpretation of Ehrlich (1914), p. 177 "vor kurzer Zeit" allowed by the Hebrew.

38 Cf. Blenkinsopp (1988), p. 181. Cf. van Oorschot (1994), p. 77: "Die Zuwendung Jahwes erscheint ... als zeitlich oder in anderer Weise eng begrenzt". The interpretation of Williamson (1985), p. 135: "he intends only to contrast the eighty years since the decree of Cyrus with the long centuries of oppression ..." is less convincing. For a comparable interpretation, cf. also, e.g., Grosheide (1963), p. 258; Clines (1984), p. 123.

39 Cf., e.g., Delekat (1964), p. 64: "ganz plötzlich", "ganz unerwartet"; Galling (1964), p. 62 (n. 1): "in einer plötzlichen Wende"; Blenkinsopp (1988), p. 180: "suddenly"; cf. also p. 183. In der Smitten (1973), p. 28 n. 83 has argued that this interpretation is less probable, because of the *mʿṭ* in *mḥyh mʿṭ* in the same verse: "Seine Übersetzung wird dem zweimaligen *mʿṭ* in Vers 8 zu wenig gerecht". However, the delivery from the worst evils (v. 7) is described as a sign of undeserved mercy (cf. v. 13). This delivery, however small it may be relatively speaking, is considered something special, which ought not to be endangered (cf. vv. 10, 14). This means, that it was understood as a real, unexpected change for the good.

40 Cf., e.g., Procksch (1930), pp. 331f.; Kissane (1960), p. 284; Duhm (1968), p. 188; Schoors (1972), p. 158; Millar (1976), p. 54; Wildberger (1978), p. 890 (cf. also p. 902); Kaiser (1983), p. 168; Jenni (1994), p. 160.

41 Cf. also Is. 10:25.

42 Cf. also Delekat (1964), p. 64.

An instance of *kimʿaṭ* also occurs in the third tale about a Patriarch presenting his wife as his sister. In this case *kimʿaṭ* functions as modifier in a verbal clause (Gen. 26:10; *kmʿṭ škb ʾḥd hʿm ʾt-ʾštk*). In the first and second tale the king of the country takes the Patriarch's wife into his house (Gen. 12:15; 20:2). In the third tale this does not happen. In the first and second tale the truth comes to light because the Lord punishes the king in question (Gen. 12:17) or threatens to punish him (Gen. 20:3). In the third tale the truth comes out purely by chance (Gen. 26:8), without the Lord interfering. In all three tales the king reacts angrily, in the first and second tale, because of the intervention of the Lord (Gen. 12:18f.; 20:9f.), in the third tale, because of the risks he and his people incur (Gen. 26:10). The clause we study here is part of the king's reproach in the third tale. Some scholars have translated the relevant *kimʿaṭ* with "almost".[43] This interpretation is not convincing from a contextual point of view. It implies that an incident had already happened, through which the wife in question was really endangered. This is not appropriate in a tale in which the king discovers the real situation by chance. Quite a number of scholars translate the *kimʿaṭ* in question with "easily", implying that the honour of the wife could have been endangered easily.[44] However, the king reacts by uttering an official decree for this special case, "in form similar to apodictic law" (v. 11).[45] This heavy decree is to safeguard the wife, while the Patriarch and his wife remain in the same city (they leave only later for a different reason, Gen. 26:16f.). In other words the aim of the decree is to safeguard her in the future. Therefore, it appears that in the first place the king is thinking of what may happen, not what could have happened. For that reason, the author suggests that one consider another interpretation of the relevant clause in Gen. 26:10, namely, that it refers to a future threat to the honour of the Patriarch's wife, not to a threat in the past. In that case the suffix conjugation form *škb* has to be interpreted as referring to the future, which is grammatically possible.[46] The king sees that a situation, in which Isaac's wife is presented as his sister, must

43 Cf., e.g., B. Jacob (1934), pp. 549f.; Speiser (1964), p. 201; Gispen (1983), p. 26; Wehrle (1991), pp. 585ff.; Jenni (1994), p. 161; Soggin (1997), p. 348. The translation of Wenham (1994), p. 182: "Almost any of the people could have lain ...", is less convincing, because it relates *kimʿaṭ* especially to *ʾḥd hʿm*, which is syntactically improbable.

44 Cf., e.g., Gunkel (1910), p. 301; Heinisch (1930), p. 287; Gemser (1953), § 247; De Fraine (1963), p. 199; von Rad (1972), p. 215; Westermann (1981), p. 513; Fischer (1994), p. 185.

45 Cf. Van Seters (1975), p. 181. Cf. also, e.g., B.Jacob (1934), p. 550; Keel-Küchler (1971), p. 125.

46 Cf. the grammatical references given in n. 32.

certainly lead to disaster. To stave off this disaster, he utters a decree, that anyone who harms Isaac and Rebekkah, will be severely punished. This decree is formulated in such a way, that the fact that they are husband and wife, is underscored (*ʾyš hzh* ... *ʾštw*; v. 11). In discussing other texts, we have already seen that a change for the worse can be described as happening unexpectedly, within a short period of time. For these reasons the author proposes to translate the relevant clause from Gen. 26:10 as follows: "before you are aware of it, one of the people will ...".[47]

In Ez. 16:47 *kimʿaṭ qaṭ* is an extra-clausal constituent functioning as modifier to the verbal predicate in the following clause (*kmʿṭ qṭ wtšḥty mhn bkl-drkyk*). Some scholars translate it with "almost".[48] This interpretation is less probable from a contextual standpoint. In v. 46 two sisters of the "you" in the text (Jerusalem, cf. v. 3) are mentioned, the big sister being Samaria, the little one being Sodom. In v. 47 the prophet says that Jerusalem did not act in the same way as her sisters. In v. 48 the text says that Sodom did not do what Jerusalem did. These contextual facts speak against an interpretation of the *kimʿaṭ* in question with "almost".[49] For that reason a temporal interpretation, "within a short period of time" is preferable. A translation with "soon" is contextually acceptable, with the reservations mentioned above.[50]

In 2 Sam. 19:37 *kimʿaṭ* functions as modifier in a verbal clause (*kmʿṭ yʿbr ʿbdk ʾt-hyrdn ʾt-hmlk*). After the revolt of Absalom, King David, who had fled to the Israelite community east of the Jordan, returns to Jerusalem. On his journey back he is ac-

47 Some authors consider the reaction of the king in v. 11 somewhat exaggerated, cf., e.g., Skinner (1930), p. 365; Aharoni (1978-1979), p. 222; Coats (1983), p. 190; Boecker (1992), p. 34; Fischer (1994), p. 185. Weimar (1977), p. 87 and Levin (1993), p. 206 suggest, that vv. 10 and 11 could not be of the same author. The interpretation of Gen. 26:10 in this article makes the relation between vv. 10 and 11 more clear: they belong together. On this point, cf. also Blum (1984), p. 302 n. 6.

48 Cf., e.g., Bertholet (1897), p. 88; Ehrlich (1912b), p. 59; Fohrer (1955), p. 91; Eichrodt (1959), p. 118.

49 Cf. Zimmerli (1969), p. 340.

50 Cf., e.g., Aalders (1955), p. 274; Wevers (1969), p. 130; Zimmerli (1969), p. 333; Greenberg (1983), pp. 272, 289; Brownlee (1986), p. 242; Maarsingh (1988), p. 46; Allen (1994), pp. 225, 231; Jenni (1994), p. 160. For a temporal interpretation, cf. also Wehrle (1991), p. 583. In the opinion of the author, the interpretation of *qṭ* given by Eitan (1923), pp. 137f. with "little" is still the most probable (cf. also Brownlee [1986], p. 243). An emendation of the text on this point seems less probable (cf. also Wehrle [1991], p. 583 n. 37). Against, e.g., Bertholet (1897), p. 87; Ehrlich (1912b), p. 59; Fohrer (1955), p. 91; Wevers (1969), p. 130; Zimmerli (1969), p. 340. Cf. also the interpretation given by Greenberg (1983), p. 272 for *qṭ* as serving "to intensify the adverb" *kmʿṭ* (cf. Allen [1994], p. 231).

companied by Barzillai (v. 32).[51] During this journey the king invites Barzillai to go with him to Jerusalem to dwell at his court (v. 34). Barzillai asks to be allowed to return home, pleading his age (vv. 35-36). Later, he proposes that his son Kimham will accompany David to Jerusalem (v. 38), a proposal accepted by the king (v. 39). After crossing the Jordan, David takes his leave of Barzillai (v. 40).[52] The clause we discuss here is part of Barzillai's plea. It is clear that a temporal interpretation of the relevant *kimʿaṭ*, as proposed for the texts discussed above, is not possible here. Most scholars interpret it in a locative way "for a short distance".[53] From a contextual standpoint, this seems to be the most probable interpretation. Barzillai, being asked to go with the king to Jerusalem (*ʾth ʿbr ʾty wklklty ʾtk ʿmdy byrwšlm*), makes a polite counterproposal (*kmʿṭ yʿbr ʿbdk*). If we take this counterproposal as a contrast to the proposal to go all the way to Jerusalem, a locative interpretation of this *kimʿaṭ* seems quite acceptable, albeit one cannot be absolutely certain.[54]

A number of texts where *kimʿaṭ* does not function as modifier in a verbal or nominal clause will be discussed as well.

In Prov. 10:20 *kimʿaṭ* functions as predicate in a nominal clause (*lb ršʿym kmʿṭ*). There can be no reasonable doubt about its contextual meaning: the clause asserts that the "heart" of the wicked is of little value.[55]

---

51 The most probable interpretation of the *hyrdn* in v. 32 is "in the direction of the Jordan" (cf., e.g., Dhorme [1910], pp. 407f.; Driver [1913], p. 337; Fokkelman [1981], p. 305; Langlamet [1983], p. 153; Stoebe [1994], p. 427). The interpretation of this *hyrdn* as "over the Jordan" is less probable, because the king still has to cross this river (v. 40; against, e.g., Hertzberg [1956], p. 295 [n. 2]). The proposal to delete this *hyrdn* as a later gloss, is less convincing, against, e.g., Wellhausen (1871), p. 205; Budde (1902), pp. 292f.; Smith (1912), p. 366.

52 Cf., e.g., Fokkelman (1981), p. 310. Against, e.g., Dhorme (1910), p. 408; Hertzberg (1956), p. 298; Langlamet (1983), pp. 153f.; Stoebe (1994), pp. 427, 428.

53 Cf., e.g., Klostermann (1887), p. 224: "ein wenig"; Nowack (1902b), p. 230; Budde (1902), p. 293: "ein wenig"; Dhorme (1910), p. 408: "un peu"; Smith (1912), p. 366; Hertzberg (1956), p. 295; Goslinga (1962), p. 348; Langlamet (1983), pp. 154f.; Wehrle (1991), pp. 581f.; Jenni (1994), p. 161; Stoebe (1994), p. 427f.

54 Other interpretational proposals are: a) "barely" (van den Born [1956], p. 202, a less probable interpretation); b) "only" (Ehrlich [1910], p. 326; cf. also Stoebe [1994], p. 428); c) "for a short time" (Keil [1875], p. 349). On the subject, cf. also Driver (1913), pp. 337f. Langlamet (1983), p. 154 considers an interpretation of *kmʿṭ* as *kī meʿaṭ* possible. In the author's opinion such a reading is unnecessary.

55 Cf., e.g., Toy (1914), p. 211; Oesterley (1929), p. 79; Gemser (1963), p. 50; van der Weiden (1970), p. 94; Ringgren in Ringgren-Zimmerli (1980), p. 45; Plöger (1984), pp. 121, 128; Snijders (1984), pp. 72, 77; Westermann (1990), p. 93; Meinhold (1991), pp. 177f; Krüger (1995), p. 427. Also Jenni

In Ps. 105:12 *kimʿaṭ* is one of a string of three paratactic predicates in a substantivated nominal clause (*bhywtm mty mspr kmʿṭ wgrym bh*). Here again there can be no reasonable doubt as to its contextual meaning: "few".[56] It is not impossible, that here, besides the quantitative feature, a qualitative feature plays a role as well.[57]

According to the Massoretic accentuation, the *kimʿaṭ* in Is. 1:9 belongs to the preceding clause, an *atnaḥ* being placed under it. This accentuation indicates (probably) that it is taken as a paratactic element in a nominal phrase (*śryd kmʿṭ*).[58] The idea of a small remnant which alone remains is also found elsewhere (cf., e.g., Is. 16:14). A number of scholars follow the Massoretic interpretation.[59] It remains, however, also possible, that this *kimʿaṭ* belongs to the following clause, in which it would be a modifier in a nominal clause (*kmʿṭ ksdm hyynw*). If one prefers this interpretation, as a number of scholars do, one has to interpret the *kimʿaṭ* in question as "within a short period of time" as in other texts discussed above, referring to a change for the worse.[60]

(1994), p. 160, who translates it with "etwas Geringes", considers it to have a qualitative function. Cf. also Wehrle (1991), p. 584: "Die *mʿaṭ* inhärente quantitative Bedeutung erhält durch die semantische Opposition qualitativ bewertenden Charakter". Compare the use of *kimʿaṭ* here with the use of *mʿṭ* in Gen. 30:15; Numb. 16:9, 13; Josh. 22:17; Is. 7:13; Ez. 34:18.

56 Cf., e.g., Hupfeld (1862), pp. 111, 118; Hitzig (1865), p. 292: "ihrer wenig"; Baethgen (1904), p. 316: "so wenige"; Gunkel (1926), p. 457: "gar wenige"; Buttenwieser (1969), p. 803: "very few"; Kraus (1978b), p. 888: "nur wenige"; Allen (1983), p. 36: "a tiny group"; Ceresko (1983), p. 22: "a mere handful"; Wehrle (1991), p. 584; Jenni (1994), p. 160: "nur wenige"; Seybold (1996), p. 412: "zu wenig". Dahood (1970), p. 55 interprets *kmʿṭ* here as *kī meʿaṭ*, and translates, *ibid.* p. 49: "a mere handful". This interpretation is, in the author's opinion, unnecessary.

57 Cf., e.g., Delitzsch (1894), p. 647: "gar winzig"; Bentzen (1939), p. 536: "som en ubetydelighede, en quantité négligable"; Anderson (1972), p. 729: "of little account". The interpretation of Booij (1994), p. 228: "only during a short time" ("nog maar kort") seems less probable, because it implies that *kimʿaṭ* is here a modifier, which it is not (also against Duhm [1922], p. 378).

58 That *kimʿaṭ* is a paratactic element here is made probable by the fact that it can have the same function as *meʿaṭ* without preceding preposition. Compare the use of *kimʿaṭ* in Ps. 105:12 with the use of *meʿaṭ* in Numb 13:18 (*hmʿṭ hwʾ ʾm-rb*); Eccl. 9:14 (*wʾnšym bh mʿṭ*); Neh. 2:12 (*wʾnšym mʿṭ ʿmy*); 7:4 (*whʿm mʿṭ btwkh*). See also the remarks made below in the discussion about Cant. 3:4.

59 Cf., e.g., Kissane (1960), pp. 5, 10; Duhm (1968), p. 27; Wildberger (1972), p. 18; E.Jacob (1987), p. 38; Wehrle (1991), p. 582; Jenni (1994), p. 160; Oesch (1994), p. 441. It is possible, that the Massoretic accentuation in 1 Chr. 16:19, which differs from that of the parallel text Ps. 105:12, takes *kmʿṭ* as paratactic element belonging to a nominal phrase *mty mspr kmʿṭ*, cf. van Uchelen (1981), p. 157.

60 Cf., e.g., Marti (1900), p. 8; Ehrlich (1912a), p. 4; Barth (1977), p. 190; Kaiser (1981), p. 33; van Uchelen (1981), p. 158. The translation of van Uchelen (1981), p. 158: "surely", is not in contradiction with the context, but does, in the opinion of the author, not indicate the temporal aspect which *kimʿaṭ* has in such a context. A translation with "almost" is contextually improbable. A destruction

Another instance of *kimʿaṭ* is attested in Cant. 3:4. Most scholars interpret it as a phrase with temporal function ("scarcely", "hardly").[61] A temporal interpretation seems most probable in view of the fact that the girl has searched for her beloved for a long time during the night.[62] The grammatical description of the context is not simple. In the author's opinion, the most probable solution is to take *kmʿṭ šʿbrty mhn* as subject and *ʿd šmṣʾty ʾt šʾhbh npšy* as predicate, both phrases together forming a nominal clause, indicating that it was only a short time after the girl saw the watchmen that she found her beloved.[63]

Summing up the results of this study, one comes to the following conclusions. The number of attested *kimʿaṭ* instances is relatively low, making the drawing of general conclusions difficult. The impression one gets is that the grammatical function of *kimʿaṭ* influences its semantic scope. If it is a clause modifier and occurs in clauses describing a fundamental change for the better or for the worse, it most probably had a special temporal function ("within a short period of time"). (In these instances the translation "soon" is possible, if the period of time concerned starts at a fixed moment.) In the only case where such a change is not involved (the text speaks about moving on), it has a different (locative) function: 2 Sam. 19:37. If *kimʿaṭ* does not have the function of clause modifier, it has semantic values which are also attested for *meʿaṭ* (cf. nn. 55, 58, 63). It is difficult to decide to what degree *kimʿaṭ* and

---

like that of Sodom and Gomorrha is a complete one. If the destruction is almost like that one, it means that a small remnant is left. If one translates the clause in question in this way, there would be no contrast with the preceding clause, as is suggested by the context (cf. Gray [1928], p. 6). Against, e.g., Marti (1900), p. 8; Barth (1977), p. 190 n.1; Kaiser (1981), p. 33.

61 Cf., e.g., Hitzig (1855), p. 44; Budde (1898), p. 14; Rudolph (1962), p. 137; Goulder (1986), p. 27; Murphy (1990), pp. 111, 144, 146; Mulder (1991), p. 35; Wehrle (1991), p. 584; Jenni (1994), p. 160.

62 Van den Oudenrijn (1962), p. 24 has interpreted the *kimʿaṭ* in question in a locative manner: "iets verder op". Although such an interpretation remains possible, the author prefers a temporal one for contextual reasons.

63 The remark of Blau (1959), p. 131, that the relevant *kimʿaṭ šè* "scheint ... in nichts von *kimʿaṭ* verschieden zu sein", is, in the opinion of the author, less convincing. Inasfar as *kimʿaṭ* functions as clause modifier with temporal function, it means probably "within a short time" (see above). This interpretation would not fit in a clause *kmʿṭ ʿbrty*. I differ from Blau in that I take the relevant *š*-clause as apposition to *kimʿaṭ*. I agree with Blau that an emendation of the clause is unnecessary, cf. Blau (1959), p. 131 n. 2; *idem* (1977), p. 30 n. 30. Blau (1959), pp. 131f.; *idem* (1977), p. 30 and Wehrle (1991), p. 584 take *kmʿṭ šʿbrty mhn* as nominal clause (cf. also Snaith [1993], pp. 48f.).
One must compare the use of *kimʿaṭ* indicating "a short period of time" with the use of *meʿaṭ* in, e.g., Gen. 47:9; Lev. 25:52; Prov. 6:10; 24:33; Job 10:20; Ruth 2:7 (cf. also the plural *meʿaṭim* in Ps. 109:8).

meʿaṭ are interchangeable in such contexts, for it may dependent on the special type of context and not only on the meanings as such. It seems less probable that *kimʿaṭ* in itself has any type of modality as a semantic feature. If clauses are to be interpreted as being modal, this feature is not added or strengthened by the use of *kimʿaṭ*.[64] It is impossible to give a precise semantic definition of *kimʿaṭ*, in its relation to *meʿaṭ* and to words like *mzʿr* (which can be temporally used: Is. 10:25; 29:17 (*mʿṭ mzʿr*)), *zʿyr* (which can be temporally used: Job 36:2), *rgʿ*, *ptʾm*, *ptʿ* and *kʾyn* (Ps. 73:2, parallel with *kimʿaṭ*).[65]

The author is very grateful to be able to show his great appreciation for an eminent scholar in this way.

References

Aalders G. Ch. (1955), *Ezechiël verklaard*, I, *hfdst. 1-24*, Kampen.

Aharoni R. (1978-1979), " ʿAl Sheloshet Sipurim domim beSefer Bereshit", *Beth Miqra* 24, pp. 213-223.

Allen L. C. (1983), *Psalms 101-150*, Dallas, Texas.

Allen L. C. (1994), *Ezekiel 1-19*, Dallas, Texas.

Anderson A. A. (1972), *The Book of Psalms*, Vol. II, *Introduction and Psalms 73-150*, London.

Auffret P. (1977), *The literary Structure of Psalm 2* (= *JSOT* Supplement Series 2), Sheffield.

Auffret P. (1993), ""Écoute, mon peuple!", Étude structurelle du Psaume 81", *SJOT* 7, pp. 285-302.

Baethgen F. (1904), *Die Psalmen übersetzt und erklärt*, Göttingen.

Barth H. (1977), *Die Jesaja-Worte in der Josiazeit, Israel und Assur als Thema einer produktiven Neuinterpretation der Jesajaüberlieferung*, Neukirchen-Vluyn.

Batten L. W. (1913), *A critical and exegetical Commentary on the Books of Ezra and Nehemiah*, Edinburgh.

64 Against Wehrle (1991), pp. 588f. The "beinahe-Relation" proposed by Wehrle (1991), pp. 585ff. is not very probable, because the interpretation of *kimʿaṭ* as "almost" is less probable for a number of texts, see above.

65 It seems probable that *kʾyn*, although interchangeable with *kimʿaṭ*, has a more strictly definable semantic field, cf. Tsmudi (1992), p. 162.
It seems probable that *kimʿaṭ* also occurred in context types for which it is not attested in the Hebrew Bible. In such cases it can have had other semantic values than those discussed above. Cf., e.g., the *kimʿaṭ* in Sir. 51:16 (variant text, cf. Beentjes [1997], p. 125): *hṭyty kmʿṭ ʾwzny whrbh mṣʾty lqḥ*.

Beentjes P. C. (1997), *The Book of Ben Sira in Hebrew, a Text Edition of all extant Hebrew Manuscripts and a Synopsis of all parallel Hebrew Ben Sira Texts* (= SVT 68), Leiden-New York-Köln.

Bentzen A. (1939), *Fortolkning til de gammeltestamentlige Salmer*, København.

Ben-Zvi E. (1991), "Isaiah 1,4-9, Isaiah and the events of 701 BCE in Judah, a Question of Premise and Evidence", *SJOT* 1, pp. 95-111.

Bertholet A. (1897), *Das Buch Hesekiel erklärt*, Tübingen.

Bertholet A. (1902), *Die Bücher Esra und Nehemia erklärt*, Tübingen.

Blau J. (1959), "Adverbia als psychologische Subjekte/Praedikate im Bibelhebræisch", *VT* 9, pp. 130-137.

Blau J. (1977), *An adverbial Construction in Hebrew and Arabic, Sentence Adverbials in frontal Position, separated from the Rest of the Sentence* (= *The Israel Academy of Sciences and Humanities*, Proceedings, Volume VI no 1), Jerusalem.

Blenkinsopp J. (1988), *Ezra-Nehemiah, a Commentary*, Philadelphia.

Blum E. (1984), *Die Komposition der Vätergeschichte* (= *Wissenschaftliche Monographien zum Alten und Neuen Testament*, Band 57), Neukirchen-Vluyn.

Boecker H. J. (1992), *1.Mose 25,12-37,1, Isaak und Jakob*, Zürich.

Booij Th. (1994), *Psalmen*, deel III, (*81-110*), Nijkerk.

van den Born A. (1956), *Samuel uit de Grondtekst vertaald en uitgelegd*, Roermond-Maaseik.

van den Born A. (1960), *Kronieken uit de Grondtekst vertaald en uitgelegd*, Roermond-Maaseik.

Boström G. (1935), *Proverbiastudien, die Weisheit und das fremde Weib* (= *Lunds Universitets Årsskrift*, N.F. Avd. 1. Band 30 Nr. 3), Lund.

Briggs C. A. - Briggs E. G. (1925), *A critical and exegetical Commentary on the Book of Psalms*, Vol. II, Edinburgh.

Brownlee W. H. (1971), "Psalm 1-2 as a coronation Liturgy", *Biblica* 52, pp. 321-336.

Brownlee W. H. (1986), *Ezekiel 1-19*, Waco, Texas.

Brueggemann W. - Miller P. D. (1996), "Psalm 73 as a Canonical Marker", *JSOT* 72, pp. 45-56.

Budde K. (1898), in K. Budde - A. Bertholet - G. Wildeboer, *Die fünf Megillot (das Hohelied, das Buch Ruth, die Klagelieder, der Prediger, das Buch Esther) erklärt*, Freiburg i.B.-Leipzig-Tübingen.

Budde K. (1902), *Die Bücher Samuel erklärt*, Tübingen-Leipzig.

Budde K. (1913), *Das Buch Hiob übersetzt und erklärt* (2nd edition), Göttingen.

Buttenwieser M. (1969), *The Psalms chronologically treated with a new Translation*, New York.

Caquot A. (1971), "Le Psaume LXXIII", *Semitica* 21, pp. 29-55.

Ceresko A. R. (1983), "A poetic Analysis of Ps. 105, with Attention on its Use of Irony", *Biblica* 64, pp. 20-46.

Clines D. J. A. (1984), *Ezra, Nehemiah, Esther*, Grand Rapids.

Coats G. W. (1983), *Genesis with an Introduction to narrative Literature*, Grand Rapids, Michigan.

Conti M. (1997), "Dio difensore della causa degli oppressi secondo il Salmo 94", *Antonianum* 72, pp. 3-37.

Craigie P. C. (1983), *Psalms 1-50*, Waco, Texas.

Curtis E. L. - Madsen A. A. (1910), *A critical and exegetical Commentary on the Books of Chronicles*, Edinburgh.

Dahood M. (1965), *Psalms I, 1-50, Introduction, Translation, and Notes*, Garden City, New York.

Dahood M. (1968), *Psalms II, 51-100. Introduction, Translation, and Notes*, Garden City, New York.

Dahood M. (1970), *Psalms III, 101-150, Introduction, Translation, and Notes with an Appendix the Grammar of the Psalter*, Garden City, New York.

Deissler A. (1955), *Ps 119 (118) und seine Theologie. Ein Beitrag zur Erforschung der anthologischen Stilgattung im Alten Testament* (= *Münchener Theologische Studien im Auftrag der Theologischen Fakultät München*, I Historische Abteilung, 11. Band), München.

Delitzsch F. (1894), *Biblischer Kommentar über die Psalmen* (5th edition), Leipzig.

Delekat L. (1964), "Zum hebräischen Wörterbuch", *VT* 14, pp. 7-66.

Dhorme P. (1910), *Les Livres de Samuel*, Paris.

Dhorme E. (1967), *A Commentary on the Book of Job* (trsl. H. Knight, with a prefatory note by H. H. Rowley), London, etc.

Dillmann A. (1891), *Hiob* (4th edition), Leipzig.

Driver S. R. (1892), *A Treatise on the Use of the Tenses in Hebrew and some other syntactical Questions* (3rd edition), Oxford.

Driver S. R. (1913), *Notes on the Hebrew Text and the Topography of Samuel with an Introduction on Hebrew Palaeography and the ancient Versions and Facsimiles of Inscriptions and Maps* (2nd edition), Oxford.

Driver S. R. - Gray G. B. (1921), *A critical and exegetical Commentary on the Book of Job*, Edinburgh.

Duhm B. (1897), *Das Buch Hiob erklärt*, Freiburg i.B.-Leipzig-Tübingen.

Duhm B. (1922), *Die Psalmen erklärt* (2nd edition), Tübingen.

Duhm B. (1968), *Das Buch Jesaja übersetzt und erklärt* (5th edition), Göttingen.

Ehrlich A. B. (1910), *Randglossen zur hebräischen Bibel, Textkritisches, Sprachliches und Sachliches*, dritter Band, *Josua, Richter, I u. II Samuelis*, Leipzig.

Ehrlich A. B. (1912a), *Randglossen zur hebräischen Bibel, Textkritisches, Sprachliches und Sachliches*, vierter Band, *Jesaia, Jeremia*, Leipzig.

Ehrlich A. B. (1912b), *Randglossen zur hebräischen Bibel, Textkritisches, Sprachliches und Sachliches*, fünfter Band, *Ezechiel und die kleinen Propheten*, Leipzig.

Ehrlich A. B. (1913), *Randglossen zur hebräischen Bibel, Textkritisches, Sprachliches und Sachliches*, sechster Band, *Psalmen, Sprüche und Hiob*, Leipzig.

Ehrlich A. B. (1914), *Randglossen zur hebräischen Bibel, Textkritisches, Sprachliches und Sachliches*, siebenter Band, *Hohes Lied, Ruth, Klagelieder, Koheleth, Esther, Daniel, Esra, Nehemia, Könige, Chronik, Nachträge und Gesamtregister*, Leipzig.

Eichrodt W. (1959), *Der Prophet Hesekiel Kapitel 1-18 übersetzt und erklärt*, Göttingen.

Eitan I. (1923), "The Bearing of Ethiopic on Biblical Exegesis and Lexicography", *JPOS* 3, pp. 136-143.

Fischer I. (1994), *Die Erzeltern Israels, feministisch-theologische Studien zu Genesis 12-36* (= *BZAW* 222), Berlin-New York.

Fohrer G. (1955), *Ezechiel mit einem Beitrag von* Kurt Galling, Tübingen.

Fohrer G. (1963), *Das Buch Hiob*, Gütersloh..

Fokkelman J. P. (1981), *Narrative Art and Poetry in the Books of Samuel, a full Interpretation based on stylistic and structural Analysis*, Vol. I, *King David (II Sam. 9-20 & 1 Kings 1-2)*, Assen.

De Fraine J. (1961), *Esdras en Nehemias uit de Grondtekst vertaald en uitgelegd*, Roermond-Maaseik.

De Fraine J. (1963), *Genesis uit de Grondtekst vertaald en uitgelegd*, Roermond-Maaseik.

Frankenberg W. (1898), *Die Sprüche übersetzt und erklärt*, Göttingen.

Galling K. (1964), *Studien zur Geschichte Israels im persischen Zeitalter*, Tübingen.

Gemser B. (1953), *Hebreeuse Spraakkuns, Vormleer, Sinsleer en Oefeninge*, Pretoria.

Gemser B. (1963), *Sprüche Salomos* (2nd edition), Tübingen.

Gesenius-Kautzsch-Cowley (1910), *Gesenius' Hebrew Grammar as edited and enlarged by the late E. Kautzsch* ..., second English edition *revised ... by A. E. Cowley*, Oxford.

Gibson J. C. L. (1994), *Davidson's introductory Hebrew Grammar - Syntax* (4th edition), Edinburgh.

Gispen W. H. (1983), *Genesis vertaald en verklaard*, III, *Genesis 25:12-36:43*, Kampen.

Gordis R. (1978), *The Book of Job, Commentary, new Translation and special Studies*, New York City.

Goslinga C. J. (1962), *Het tweede Boek Samuel verklaard*, Kampen.

Goulder M. D. (1986), *The Song of fourteen Songs* (= JSOT Supplement Series 36), Sheffield.

Goulder M. D. (1996), *The Psalms of Asaph and the Pentateuch, Studies in the Psalter III* (= JSOT Supplement Series 233), Sheffield.

Gray G. B. (1928), *A critical and exegetical Commentary on the Book of Isaiah, I-XXXIX* by G. B. Gray, *XL-LXIV* by A. S. Peake, Vol. I, *Introduction and Commentary on I-XXVII*, Edinburgh.

Greenberg M. (1983), *Ezekiel 1-20, a new Translation with Introduction and Commentary*, Garden City, New York.

Grosheide H. H. (1963), *Ezra-Nehemia verklaard*, I, *Ezra*, Kampen.

Gunkel H. (1910), *Genesis übersetzt und erklärt* (3rd edition), Göttingen.

Gunkel H. (1926), *Die Psalmen übersetzt und erklärt* (4th edition), Göttingen.

Habel N. C. (1985), *The Book of Job, a Commentary*, London.

Hauge M. R. (1995), *Between Sheol and Temple, Motif, Structure and Function in the I-Psalms* (= JSOT Supplement Series 178), Sheffield.

Heinisch P. (1930), *Das Buch Genesis übersetzt und erklärt*, Bonn.

Henry M.-L. (1966), *Glaubenskrise und Glaubensbewährung in den Dichtungen der Jesajaapokalypse* (= *Beiträge zur Wissenschaft vom Alten und Neuen Testament*, Fünfte Folge, Heft 6), Stuttgart-Berlin-Köln-Mainz.

Hertzberg H. W. (1956), *Die Samuelbücher übersetzt und erklärt*, Göttingen.

Hitzig F. (1855), *Das Hohe Lied erklärt, die Klagelieder erklärt*, Leipzig.

Hitzig F. (1865), *Die Psalmen übersetzt und ausgelegt*, zweiter Band, Leipzig-Heidelberg.

Hitzig F. (1874), *Das Buch Hiob übersetzt und ausgelegt*, Leipzig-Heidelberg.

Hölscher G. (1952), *Das Buch Hiob* (2nd edition), Tübingen.

Howard D. M. Jr. (1997), *The Structure of Psalms 93-100*, Winona Lake, Indiana.

Hupfeld H. (1855), *Die Psalmen übersetzt und ausgelegt*, Erster Band, Gotha.

Hupfeld H. (1860), *Die Psalmen übersetzt und ausgelegt*, Dritter Band, Gotha.

Hupfeld H. (1862), *Die Psalmen übersetzt und ausgelegt*, Vierter Band, Gotha.

In der Smitten W. Th. (1973), *Esra, Quellen, Überlieferung und Geschichte*, Assen.

Irsigler H. (1984), *Psalm 73, Monolog eines Weisen, Text, Programm, Struktur* (= *Arbeiten zu Text und Sprache im Alten Testament* 20), St.Ottilien.

Jacob B. (1934), *Das erste Buch der Tora Genesis übersetzt und erklärt*, Berlin.

Jacob E. (1987), *Ésaïe 1-12*, Genève.

Japhet S. (1993), *I & II Chronicles, a Commentary*, London.

Jenni E. J. (1994), *Die hebräischen Präpositionen*, Band 2, *Die Präposition Kaph*, Stuttgart-Berlin-Köln.

Jobsen A. (1997), *Ezra en Nehemia, een praktische Bijbelverklaring*, Kampen.

Joüon P. - Muraoka T. (1991), P. Joüon, *A Grammar of Biblical Hebrew translated and revised by* T. Muraoka (Vol. I-II), Roma.

Kaiser O. (1981), *Das Buch des Propheten Jesaja, Kpitel 1-12* (5th edition), Göttingen.

Kaiser O. (1983), *Der Prophet Jesaja, Kapitel 13-39 übersetzt und erklärt*, Göttingen.

Keel O. - Küchler M. (1971), *Synoptische Texte aus der Genesis*, Zweiter Teil, *Der Kommentar mit einer Einführung in die literarischen Schichten der Genesis*, Fribourg.

Keil C. F. (1875), *Die Bücher Samuelis* (2nd edition), Leipzig.

Kelly B. E. (1996), *Retribution and Eschatology in Chronicles* (= JSOT Supplement Series 211), Sheffield.

Kissane E. J. (1946), *The Book of Job, translated from a critically revised Hebrew Text with Commentary*, New York.

Kissane E. J. (1954), *The Book of Psalms, translated from a critically revised Hebrew Text with Commentary*, Vol. II, *Psalms 73-150*, Dublin.

Kissane E. J. (1960), *The Book of Isaiah translated from a critically revised Hebrew Text with Commentary*, Dublin.

Kittel R. (1922), *Die Psalmen übersetzt und erklärt* (3rd-4th edition), Leipzig-Erlangen.

Klostermann A. (1887), *Die Bücher Samuelis und der Könige*, 1887.

Kraus H. J. (1978a), *Psalmen*, 1. Teilband, *Psalmen 1-59* (5th edition), Neukirchen-Vluyn.

Kraus H. J. (1978b), *Psalmen*, 2. Teilband, *Psalmen 60-150* (5th edition), Neukirchen-Vluyn.

Kroeze J. H. (1961), *Het Boek Job verklaard*, Kampen.

Krüger Th. (1995), "Komposition und Diskussion in Proverbia 10", *ZThK* 92, pp. 413-433.

Lang B. (1990), "Schule und Unterricht im alten Israel", *La Sagesse de l'Ancien Testament*, nouvelle édition mise à jour (ed. M. Gilbert), pp. 186-201.

Langlamet F. (1983), "David et Barzillaï, 2 Samuel 19:32-41a: le Récit primitif et sa "Forme"", *Isac Leo Seeligmann Volume, Essays on the Bible and the Ancient World* (edd. A. Rofé - Y. Zakovitch), Vol. III, Non-Hebrew Section, Jerusalem, pp. 149-169.

Levin Chr. (1993), *Der Jahwist*, Göttingen.

Maarsingh B. (1988), *Ezechiël*, Deel II, Nijkerk.

Marti K. (1900), *Das Buch Jesaja erklärt*, Tübingen.

Mason R. (1990), *Preaching the Tradition, Homily and Hermeneutics after the Exile*, Cambridge-New York-Port Chester-Melbourne-Sydney.

McKane W. (1970), *Proverbs, a new Approach*, London.

Meinhold A. (1991), *Die Sprüche*, Teil 1: *Sprüche Kapitel 1-15*, Zürich.

Michaeli F. (1967), *Les Livres des Chroniques, d'Esdras et de Néhémie*, Neuchatel.

Michel D. (1960), *Tempora und Satzstellung in den Psalmen* (diss. Bonn).

Millar W. R. (1976), *Isaiah 24-27 and the Origin of Apocalyptic* (= *Harvard Semitic Monograph Series* 11), Missoula, Montana.

Mulder M. J. (1991), *Hooglied, een praktische Bijbelverklaring*, Kampen.

Murphy R. E. (1990), *The Song of Songs, a Commentary on the Book of Canticles or the Song of Songs*, Minneapolis.

von Mutius H. G. (1981), "Die Bezeugung einer aussertiberiensischen Punktationsform in Ps 2.12 durch mitteralterliche jüdische Gelehrte", *BN* 15, pp. 44-45.

Myers J. M. (1965a), *Ezra-Nehemiah, Introduction, Translation and Notes*, Garden City, New York.

Myers J. M. (1965b), *II Chronicles, Translation and Notes*, Garden City, New York.

Nowack W. (1902a), *Die Bücher der Chronik übersetzt und erklärt*, Göttingen.

Nowack W. (1902b), *Die Bücher Samuelis übersetzt und erklärt*, Göttingen.

Oesch J. M. (1994), "Jes. 1,8f. und das Problem der "Wir-Reden" im Jesajabuch", *ZKTh* 116, pp. 440-446.

Oesterley W. O. E. (1929), *The Book of Proverbs with Introduction and Notes*, London.

van Oorschot J. (1994), "Nachkultische Psalmen und spätbiblische Rollendichtung", *ZAW* 106, pp. 69-86.

van den Oudenrijn M. A. (1962), *Het Hooglied uit de Grondtekst vertaald en uitgelegd*, Roermond-Maaseik.

van der Ploeg J. (1952), *Spreuken uit de Grondtekst vertaald en uitgelegd*, Roermond-Maaseik.

van der Ploeg J. P. M. (1971), *Psalmen uit de Grondtekst vertaald en uitgelegd* (deel 1), Roermond.

van der Ploeg J. P. M. (1974), *Psalmen*, deel II, *Psalmen 76 t/m 150 uit de grondtekst vertaald en uitgelegd*, Roermond.

Plöger O. (1984), *Sprüche Salomos (Proverbia)*, Neukirchen-Vluyn.

Podechard E. (1949), *Le Psautier, Traduction littérale et Explication historique* (= *Bibliothèque de la Faculté Catholique de Théologie de Lyon*, Vol. 3), Paris.

Pope M. H. (1973), *Job, Introduction, Translation, and Notes*, Garden City, New York.

Procksch O. (1930), *Jesaia I übersetzt und erklärt*, Leipzig.

von Rad G. (1972), *Das erste Buch Mose Genesis übersetzt und erklärt* (9th edition), Göttingen.

Ridderbos J. (1958), *De Psalmen vertaald en verklaard,* II *Ps 42-106*, Kampen.

Ringgren H. - Zimmerli W. (1980), *Sprüche/Prediger übersetzt und erklärt* (3rd edition), Gòttingen.

Rogerson J. W. - McKay J. W. (1977a), *Psalms 1-50*, Cambridge-London-New York-Melbourne.

Rogerson J. W. - McKay J. W. (1977b), *Psalms 51-100*, Cambridge-London-New York-Melbourne.

Ross J. F. (1978), "Psalm 73", *Israelite Wisdom, theological and literary Essays in Honor of Samuel Terrien* (edd. J. G. Gummie and others), New York, pp. 161-175.

Rudolph W. (1949), *Esra und Nehemia samt 3.Esra*, Tübingen.

Rudolph W. (1955), *Chronikbücher*, Tübingen.

Rudolph W. (1962), *Das Buch Ruth, das Hohe Lied, die Klagelieder*, Gütersloh.

Schmidt H. (1934), *Die Psalmen*, Tübingen.

Schoors A. (1972), *Jesaja* [Vol. I], Roermond.

van Selms A. (1983), *Job II*, Nijkerk.

Seybold K. (1996), *Die Psalmen*, Tübingen.

Skinner J. (1930), *A critical and exegetical Commentary on Genesis* (2nd edition), Edinburgh.

Smith H. P. (1912), *A critical and exegetical Commentary on the Books of Samuel*, Edinburgh.

Snaith J. G. (1993), *The Song of Songs*, Grand Rapids.

Snijders L. A. (1984), *Spreuken, een praktische Bijbelvertaling*, Kampen.

Soggin J. A. (1997), *Das Buch Genesis, Kommentar* (trsl. Th. Frauenlob), Darmstadt.

Soll W. (1991), *Psalm 119: Matrix, Form and Setting* (= *The Catholic Biblical Quarterly Monograph Series* 23), Washington.

Speiser E. A. (1964), *Genesis, Introduction, Translation, and Notes*, Garden City, New York.

Stoebe H. J. (1994), *Das zweite Buch Samuelis*, Gütersloh.

Stolz F. (1983), *Psalmen im nachkultischen Raum* (= *Theologische Studien* 129), Zürich.

Tate M. E. (1990), *Psalms 51-100*, Dallas, Texas.

Toy C. H. (1914), *A critical and exegetical Commentary on the Book of Proverbs*, Edinburgh.

Tsmudi J. (1992), “"Iyov haqaton" (Tehilim 73) le’Oro shel "Iyov" hagadol”, *Beit Miqra* 37, pp. 157-169.

Tuinstra E. W. (1996), *Spreuken I*, Baarn.

Tur-Sinai N. H. (1957) (H.Torczyner), *The Book of Job, a new Commentary*, Jerusalem.

van Uchelen N. A. (1971), *Psalmen*, Deel I (*1-40*), Nijkerk.

van Uchelen N. A. (1981), “Isaiah 1:9 - Text and Context”, *OTS* 21, Leiden, pp. 155-163.

Van Seters J. (1975), *Abraham in History and Tradition*, New Haven-London.

Waltke B. K. - O’Connor M. (1990), *An Introduction to Biblical Hebrew Syntax*, Winona Lake, Indiana.

Wehrle J. (1990), "Zur syntaktisch-semantischen Funktion der PV *k˙=mʿaṭ* in Ijob 32,22", *BN* 55, pp. 77-95.

Wehrle J. (1991), "Die PV *k˙=mʿaṭ* als Indikator für den Satzmodus in Sprechakten", *Text, Methode und Grammatik, Wolfgang Richter zum 65. Geburtstag* (edd. W. Gross, H. Irsigler, Th. Seidl), St. Ottilien, pp. 577-594.

van der Weiden W. A. (1970), *Le Livre des Proverbes, Notes philologiques* (= *Biblica et Orientalia* 23), Rome.

Weimar P. (1977), *Untersuchungen zur Redaktionsgeschichte des Pentateuch* (= BZAW 146), Berlin-New York.

Weiser A. (1955), *Die Psalmen übersetzt und erklärt* (4th edition), Göttingen.

Wellhausen J. (1871), *Der Text der Bücher Samuelis untersucht*, Göttingen.

Wenham G. J. (1994), *Genesis 16-50*, Dallas, Texas.

Westermann C. (1981), *Genesis*, 2. Teilband, *Genesis 12-36*, Neukirchen-Vluyn.

Westermann C. (1990), *Wurzeln der Weisheit, die ältesten Sprüche Israels und anderer Völker*, Göttingen.

Wevers J. W. (1969), *Ezekiel*, London, etc.

Whybray R. N. (1994), *Proverbs*, Grand Rapids.

Wildberger H. (1972), *Jesaja*, 1. Teilband, *Jesaja 1-12*, Neukirchen-Vluyn.

Wildberger H. (1978), *Jesaja*, 2. Teilband, *Jesaja 13-27*, Neukirchen-Vluyn.

Wildeboer G. (1897), *Die Sprüche erklärt*, Leipzig-Tübingen.

Williamson H. G. M. (1982), *1 and 2 Chronicles*, Grand Rapids.

Williamson H. G. M. (1985), *Ezra, Nehemiah*, Waco, Texas.

Wutz F. (1925), *Die Psalmen textkritisch untersucht*, München.

Zenger E. (1987), ""Wozu tosen die Völker ...?", Beobachtungen zur Entstehung und Theologie des 2.Psalmes", *Freude an der Weisung des Herrn, Beiträge zur Theologie der Psalmen, Festgabe zum 70. Geburtstag von Heinrich Gross* (= Stuttgarter Biblische Beiträge 13), Stuttgart, pp. 495-509.

Zimmerli W. (1969), *Ezechiel*, 1. Teilband, *Ezechiel 1-24*, Neukirchen-Vluyn.

Zobel H. J. (1984), "*mʿṭ*", *ThWAT* 4, Stuttgart-Berlin-Köln-Mainz, coll. 1030-1036.

SIGNIFICATO POLITICO DELL'INVESTITURA SACERDOTALE NEL REGNO DI ḪATTI E IN ALCUNI PAESI VICINO-ORIENTALI AD ESSO SOGGETTI[1]

FIORELLA IMPARATI

Università di Firenze

È ben noto dalla documentazione ittita che la consacrazione di qualcuno al sacerdozio della principale divinità del pantheon di Ḫatti equivaleva alla sua nomina come re di questo paese.[2]

Conosciamo inoltre casi in cui un sovrano ittita, concedendo ad un suo figlio l'investitura del sacerdozio di una o più importanti divinità di un paese straniero inglobato nel regno di Ḫatti o ad esso subordinato, gli conferiva in tal modo il governo di questo paese.

1. Si ricorda il famoso esempio di Telipinu, figlio di Šuppiluliuma I, che era stato prima nominato sacerdote del dio della Tempesta, di Ḫepat e di Šarruma in Kizzuwatna, ed al quale poi il padre aveva conferito il governo dello stato siriano di Aleppo.[3] Del resto, come ha evidenziato R. Beal,[4] anche il decreto di insediamento di Telipinu come sacerdote in Kizzuwatna da parte di Šuppiluliuma I, della regina Ḫenti, del principe ereditario Arnuwanda e di Zida, Capo delle guardie del corpo, ha l'aspetto di un trattato di subordinazione.

---

1 A Pelio Fronzaroli, con simpatia e stima, ricordando i primi comuni studi orientalistici nella Facoltà di Lettere di Firenze.

Per le abbreviazioni bibliografiche nel presente articolo si sono seguite quelle utilizzate in *The Hittite Dictionary of the Oriental Institute of the University of Chicago* (= *CHD*), Chicago 1980 ss.

2 V. in ultimo G. Beckman, *Civilizations of the Ancient Near East* (= *C.A.N.E.*) I, New York 1995, p. 530.

3 V. A. Goetze, *Kizz.*, New Haven 1940, pp. 12-17; H. Klengel, *Gesch. Syr.* 1, Berlin 1965, pp. 196 s.; e inoltre *Syria*, Berlin 1992, pp. 114, 128 s.; "Die historische Rolle der Stadt Aleppo im vorantiken Syrien", in *Die Orientalische Stadt: Kontinuität, Wandel, Bruch* (I. *Internationales Colloquium der D.O.G. 9-10 Mai 1996*), Saarbrücker 1997, pp. 370 s.; *Geschichte des Hethitischen Reiches* (= *GHR*), Leiden - Boston - Köln 1999, pp. 165 s.; R. Beal, *Or NS* 55 (1986), pp. 435 s.; *THeth* 20, Heidelberg 1992, pp. 321 s. ; T. Bryce, *Hethitica* 11 (1992), pp. 5-18.

4 *Or NS* 55, p. 435 con n. 51.

Della nomina di Telipinu come re di Aleppo si ha finora notizia soltanto da due testi più tardi, dell'epoca di Ḫattušili III,[5] mentre le altre fonti in cuneiforme e in geroglifico cronologicamente più vicine menzionano questo Telipinu soltanto come "sacerdote" o "gran sacerdote", come se il conferimento di questa carica avesse costituito l'elemento basilare della sua nomina al governo di Aleppo: sappiamo infatti che questa località già fin da epoca antica, antecedentemente alla dominazione ittita, era un importante centro di culto del dio della Tempesta, ma anche delle due divinità ad esso legate, Ḫebat e Šarruma.[6]

Di particolare interesse è un passo in un documento di Muršili II, in cui questo sovrano conferisce ad un "sacerdote" – del quale non si specifica il nome, ma in cui è stato a ragione riconosciuto il Telipinu in questione, fratello appunto di questo re – il ruolo di giudice rispetto a controversie sorte fra altri stati siriani subordinati a Ḫatti:[7] emerge da ciò l'importanza di questo "sacerdote" anche in àmbito politico-amministrativo a livello internazionale.

Accettando l'ipotesi di identificare questo "sacerdote" con Telipinu, il fatto che egli fosse menzionato soltanto con questo titolo anche sotto Muršili II mi sembra far presumere che il padre Šuppiluliuma I gli avesse conferito il governo di Aleppo, ma non il titolo di re di questo paese. Ciò poteva essere stato fatto nel preciso intento di tenere sotto un maggiore controllo Aleppo, rafforzando invece il potere di Karkemiš, sul cui trono Šuppiluliuma aveva posto un altro suo figlio, Piyaššili/Šarri-Kušuḫ.[8] Appare significativo, in tale contesto, il famoso passo dell'editto in cui Muršili II stabilisce la posizione cerimoniale alla corte ittita del fratello Piyaššili e dei suoi discen-

5 KUB XIX 9 (CTH 83.I.A) I 18; KBo VI 28 + KUB XXVI 48 (CTH 88) Ro 21.

6 V. per ultimi V. Haas, *Gesch. Rel.*, Leiden - Boston - Köln 1994, pp. 553-555; H. Klengel, *Die historische Rolle der Stadt Aleppo im vorantiken Syrien*, pp. 359-374, *infra*.

7 KBo III 3 + III 27'-29': v. H. Klengel, *Or* NS 32 (1963), pp. 38, 44, 51; T. Bryce, *Hethitica* 11, pp. 16 s. In III 29'-33' dello stesso testo si specifica che, in caso di dispute di grande importanza, spettava al sovrano ittita il compito di dirimerle; del resto, ciò avveniva anche nell'amministrazione della giustizia all'interno del regno ittita: v. in ultimo F. Imparati, in H. Klengel, *GHR*, pp. 330 s.

8 Sul problema se Aleppo in quel periodo avesse avuto rispetto a Karkemiš una posizione di parità o di subordinazione, v. in ultimo T. Bryce, *Hethitica* 11, pp. 17 s., e H. Klengel, *Die historische Rolle der Stadt Aleppo im vorantiken Syrien*, p. 371 con n. 50.

denti che saliranno in futuro sul trono di Karkemiš, e cioè che il re di questo paese sarà secondo per importanza soltanto al principe ereditario ittita (^{lú}*tuḫ(u)kanti*).[9]

Una ulteriore conferma del carattere politico che rivestiva una tale investitura sacerdotale in Aleppo verrebbe dall'ipotesi già formulata da A. Archi ed ora ripresa e sviluppata da Th. van den Hout, e cioè quella di identificare lo Ḫalpaziti che sembra aver svolto una funzione sacerdotale con l'omonimo re di Aleppo,[10] noto dalla lettera IBoT I 34 Ro 8,[11] dell'epoca di Tutḫaliya IV.

Secondo Th. van den Hout,[12] il fatto che Tutḫaliya avesse insediato Ḫalpaziti – che non era stato trattato bene da Ḫattušili – sul trono della "politically unimportant and subordinate city of Ḫalpa, could then be considered an effective measure of compensation and remuneration by Tutḫaliya".

A mio avviso, si trattava di qualcosa di più di una semplice volontà di offrire un compenso a Ḫalpaziti: era piuttosto un'abile mossa politica di Tutḫaliya per cercare di recuperare quella fazione che era stata ostile a suo padre ed ora anche a lui. Questa iniziativa non doveva apparire troppo rischiosa – poiché Ḫalpaziti era ormai

---

9 KBo I 28 Ro 6-19; sull'integrazione delle rr.17-19 v. F. Imparati - F. Pecchioli Daddi, *EOTHEN* 4, Firenze 1991, p. 34, n. 23; per gli studi su questo documento v. G. Beckman, *DiplTexts*, Atlanta 1996, p. 177, nr. 29.

10 V. A. Archi, *AoF* 6 (1979), p. 8, il quale aveva proposto di riconoscere nello Ḫalpaziti presente in KUB XXII 35 III 9' il re di Aleppo per "il richiamo agli dèi di Aleppo nella l.13'"; Th. van den Hout, *AoF* 25 (= *Fs Klengel*) (1998), pp. 68-74; *The Purity of Kingship*, Leiden - Boston - Köln 1998, pp. 55-59; a p. 57 di tale volume questo studioso rileva che "the fact that this title (= priest) is now attested for two kings of Ḫalpa could point to a certain tradition of priest-rulers there", pur riconoscendo che "Talmišarruma is never mentioned as <<Priest>> in our sources". S. Alaura, nella sua recensione a questo libro (in stampa in *OLZ*), non concorda, per vari motivi che sarebbe troppo lungo esporre qui, con questa ipotesi di identificazione. Le sue obiezioni si basano, fra l'altro, anche sul fatto che lo Ḫalpaziti coinvolto in alcune controversie all'epoca di Muwattali II – e quindi già adulto in questo periodo – non poteva essere, a causa dell'età, il re di Ḫalpa presente nella lettera su menzionata, che Th. van den Hout (*Fs Klengel*, p. 69; *The Purity of Kingship*, p. 56) ritiene si debba datare ad una fase tarda del regno di Tutḫaliya IV (cioè, intorno al 20° anno di regno di questo sovrano). Abbiamo tuttavia vari esempi di persone – ovviamente di ceto sociale elevato e che potevano quindi godere di un miglior tenore di vita rispetto alla gente comune – vissute molto a lungo, come lo stesso Ḫattušili III, Bentešina di Amurru, Mašduri, re del paese del fiume Šeḫa, il faraone Ramses II ecc. Bisogna inoltre aggiungere che sulla datazione di IBoT I 34 i pareri degli studiosi non sono concordi, anche se oggi appare verosimile una collocazione di questo documento all'epoca di Tuthaliya IV: v. in ultimo H. Klengel, *GHR*, p. 282.

11 V. H. Klengel, *Or NS* 32 (1963), pp. 280-291; A. Hagenbuchner, *THeth*. 16, Heidelberg 1989, pp. 313-315; v. inoltre bibliografia in H. Klengel, *Syria*, p. 130, n. 234, e *GHR*, p. 282.

12 *The Purity of Kingship*, p. 59.

molto vecchio a quell'epoca (v. n.10) e non sarebbe rimasto troppo a lungo sul trono di Ḫalpa – ed avrebbe inoltre mostrato la buona volontà del sovrano ittita di venire incontro ai suoi avversari.

Come ho già avuto modo di rilevare altrove, Tutḫaliya in alcune occasioni aveva preso le distanze dalla politica paterna, stigmatizzando certi atteggiamenti di personaggi che avevano favorito l'ascesa al trono del padre[13] o cercando di recuperare personaggi messi da parte da quest'ultimo, allo scopo di sedare vecchi contrasti politici e di tutelare così la stabilità del suo potere e di quello dei suoi eredi legittimi, soprattutto in una situazione politica che si presentava spesso instabile, anche per le possibili rivendicazioni al trono ittita da parte di Kurunta.

A proposito dell'utilità di insediare, in taluni casi, una persona di età molto avanzata sul trono di un paese subordinato a Ḫatti, si ricorda quanto si è osservato altrove per un eventuale collocamento di Ulmi-Teššup sul trono di Tarḫuntašša.[14]

2. Per quanto riguarda Kizzuwatna, già prima di Telipinu abbiamo l'esempio di Kantuzzili, principe del Medio Regno ittita, ritenuto da alcuni studiosi come figlio di Tutḫaliya I/II e Nikkalmati[15] e da altri come figlio di Arnuwanda I.[16] Come è noto,

13 Senza però rinnegare, ovviamente, l'azione politica di questo, in virtù della quale Tutḫaliya aveva conseguito il potere regio: si ricorda, a titolo esemplificatorio, la deplorazione di questo sovrano verso il comportamento di Mašduri espressa – sia pure strumentalmente allo scopo di salvaguardare i diritti dei suoi discendenti alla successione al trono – nel trattato con Šaušgamuwa di Amurru, o la presumibile diffidenza sempre di Tutḫaliya nei riguardi di Bentešina di Amurru: v. F. Imparati, *Seminari dell'Istituto per gli Studi Micenei ed Egeo-Anatolici* (1991), Roma 1992, pp. 64-67 e 69; v. inoltre p. 77 s., dove si rileva che l'azione politica di Tutḫaliya, una volta salito al trono, "si trovò drammaticamente costretta a fluttuare tra una severa presa di distanza dal comportamento scorretto del padre e dei sostenitori di questo ... e al contempo un inevitabile riconoscimento della legittimità dell'operato paterno per non indebolire se stesso nel potere ...".

14 V. F. Imparati - F. Pecchioli Daddi, *EOTHEN* 4, p. 67, dove si osserva: "L'insediamento sul trono di Tarḫuntašša di Ulmi-Teššup – più fedele e forse anche meno pericoloso (di Kurunta), perché presumibilmente non facente parte della famiglia di Muwattalli e inoltre già in età avanzata – poteva servire a Tutḫaliya per ridimensionare una regalità rivelatasi troppo incomoda".

15 V. F. Imparati, *Fs Laroche* (1979), p. 173; *Fs Meriggi* I (1979), p. 299; *Archivum Anatolicum* 3 (1997) (= *Gs Bilgic*), p. 302, n. 19; S. Košak, *AnSt* 30 (1980), pp. 37-38; V. Haas, *ChS* I/1, Roma 1984, p. 9; *AoF* 12 (1985), p. 274; S. de Martino, *EOTHEN* 4, p. 17. Negli articoli qui sopra citati ho proposto l'identificazione della regina che officia in *KUB* XLV 47 con Nikkalmati, basandomi non soltanto sul fatto che il nome di questa regina è composto con il nome della dea Ningal, che fino a quel tempo non pare aver tenuto alcun ruolo nel culto ittita (v. J. Klinger, *ZA* 85 (1995), p. 96, n. 84), ma anche perché essa è la prima a portare un nome così composto e inoltre perché la figlia di lei, Ašmunikkal, reca – certo non casualmente – un nome contenente quello della stessa dea. La documentazione pervenutaci non mi sembra in contrasto con tale ipotesi.

egli era stato insediato come "sacerdote" in Kizzuwatna: tale nomina aveva verosimilmente un valore politico.

A tal proposito, è interessante ricordare una lettera rinvenuta a Maşat (HKM 74),[17] scritta da un "sacerdote", di cui non si indica né il nome né la provenienza, a Kaššu, personaggio presente in molte lettere di Maşat col titolo di "sovrintendente degli araldi delle truppe".[18] La lettera in esame è una replica al rifiuto di Kaššu di restituire *volontariamente* (ZI-*it*) al "sacerdote" alcune persone, evidentemente sudditi di quest'ultimo passati al servizio di Kaššu in Zikašta;[19] Kaššu aveva addotto come motivazione del suo rifiuto il fatto che questa località (situata nel distretto di Tapik(k)a, odierna Maşat) costituiva il posto di frontiera più avanzato ed aveva suggerito al "sacerdote" di far presente la situazione al Palazzo. Il "sacerdote", dopo aver affermato che avrebbe notificato *ripetutamente* il fatto al Palazzo, dice che egli pure non restituirà i sudditi di Kaššu che si recheranno in Kizzuwatna, poiché anche questo luogo costituisce il posto di frontiera più avanzato. Mi sembra interessante notare che il "sacerdote" in Ro 11 usa il verbo *tarkummai-/tarkummiya-* "far presente, notificare" all'iterativo – diversamente da Kaššu in Ro 9 – quasi per voler evidenziare l'importanza del fatto e la sua intenzione che esso non venga accantonato.

Dal contesto della lettera risulta che questo "sacerdote" doveva tenere un posto di rilievo in Kizzuwatna, dato che si occupa della importante questione della restituzione dei fuggiaschi. Egli viene per lo più identificato dagli studiosi con il Kantuzzili sopra ricordato.[20]

È noto che il problema di coloro che fuggivano per rifugiarsi in altri paesi era molto sentito dai vari stati vicino-orientali antichi sia nel loro interno, cioè nel passaggio da una provincia all'altra, sia nei loro rapporti internazionali.

Il fatto che tale problema affliggesse fortemente il paese di Kizzuwatna emerge dal trattato stipulato da un sovrano ittita del Medio Regno con Paddatiššu di Kizzu-

16 V. R. Beal, *Or NS* 55, p. 445; *THeth* 20, pp. 320-321 con n. 1225; J. Klinger, *ZA* 85, pp. 93-99 *infra*. Secondo J. Freu, *Hethitica* 13 (1996), p. 23, Kantuzzili sarebbe stato figlio di Ḫuzziya II.

17 V. S. Alp, *HBM*, Ankara 1991, pp. 262 s.; R. Beal, *THeth* 20, pp. 321 e 404; F. Imparati, *Gs Bilgic*, p. 202 n. 19.

18 V. in ultimo R. Beal, *THeth* 20, pp. 396-407.

19 Su questa località v. S. Alp, *HBM*, pp. 46 s.; G. F. del Monte, *RGTC* 6/2, Wiesbaden 1992, p. 195.

20 V. R. Beal, *THeth* 20, p. 321 e J. Klinger, *ZA* 85, pp. 93 ss.; F. Imparati, *Gs Bilgic*, p. 202 n. 19. S. Alp, *HBM*, p. 342, pensa ad un personaggio vissuto precedentemente a Telipinu; G. F. del Monte, *loc. cit.*, ritiene che si tratti di Telipinu, il "sacerdote" di Kizzuwatna di cui si è parlato sopra.

watna,[21] laddove, oltre ai paragrafi relativi alla loro restituzione, analoghi a quelli presenti in altri trattati, si contemplano anche casi legati a movimenti di popolazioni transumanti attraverso i confini di questo paese.[22]

Nel caso della lettera di Maşat in esame appaiono significative sia l'affermazione di Kaššu in Ro 7-9, e cioè che egli non avrebbe restituito *volontariamente* al "sacerdote" i sudditi di questo, sia la convergente opinione dei due interlocutori – sia pure espressa con toni e, evidentemente, finalità diversi – sull'opportunità che il "sacerdote" notificasse il caso in questione al Palazzo. È infatti noto da vari documenti ittiti che, se qualcuno catturava un fuggiasco, doveva per la maggior parte dei casi consegnarlo al re.[23] Conosciamo due lettere provenienti sempre da Maşat – HKM 9 e 24 – scritte appunto dal re, in cui egli informa il loro destinatario di aver ricevuto i fuggiaschi che quest'ultimo gli aveva mandato; è interessante rilevare che la prima di queste lettere è diretta proprio a Kaššu.

Sappiamo inoltre, come si è detto sopra, che quando una controversia fra sudditi di Ḫatti, sia all'interno del regno sia a livello internazionale, si presentava importante dal punto di vista politico, economico, amministrativo, militare, si doveva ricorrere al giudizio del sovrano ittita.[24] Per il caso discusso nella nostra lettera non è certo se in essa si facesse riferimento al Palazzo situato nella capitale: è anche possibile che vi si alludesse al famoso Palazzo posto in Šapinuwa, dove il re si recava spesso e dove poteva trovarsi in quel determinato periodo.[25] In ogni caso, per i motivi sopra esposti, anche per la questione discussa in questa lettera era necessario richiedere il giudizio dell'organo più competente a dirimerla.

Quindi Kaššu nella lettera in esame, a sostegno del suo rifiuto, si faceva forte del fatto che non spettava a lui prendere una decisione in proposito; può darsi, inoltre, che egli si sentisse sicuro dell'appoggio del re, almeno in quel periodo della sua carriera. Esiste tuttavia anche la possibilità che Kaššu volesse far credere al "sacerdote", allo scopo di impressionarlo, di godere del favore regio più di quanto ciò corrispondesse alla realtà. Infatti, come si è avuto modo di esporre altrove, anche in altre lettere di Maşat – HKM 68 e 54 – Kaššu parla della possibilità di un suo

21 V. in ultimo H. Klengel, *GHR*, p. 98, con bibliografia.

22 V. i §§ 5-9, rr. 17'-40' di questo trattato presso G. Beckman, *DiplTexts*, pp. 12 s., v. anche p. 171; v. inoltre T. Bryce, *Tel Aviv* 13-14 (1986-1987), pp. 95 s.

23 V. alcuni esempi in proposito in *CHD* P, p. 362, *infra*.

24 V. sopra n. 7.

25 V. F. Imparati, *Gs Bilgic*, pp. 201-206, e in particolare p. 202, n. 19.

ricorso all'intervento del Palazzo o del re, forse per voler intimidire la parte con cui egli era in contrasto: ci sono, tuttavia, pervenute alcune lettere dalle quali si può dedurre che egli non aveva goduto ininterrottamente della fiducia e del favore del re.[26]

Dalla lettura della lettera in esame sorge anche il problema relativamente alla posizione del "sacerdote" e, quindi, di Kizzuwatna rispetto a Ḫatti in quell'epoca. Tale posizione appare, chiaramente, di subordinazione: in quanto Kizzuwatna era uno stato assoggettato al regno ittita o in quanto faceva parte di questo come provincia? Secondo S. Alp[27] il "sacerdote" di Kizzuwatna nella nostra lettera sembra aver avuto una certa autonomia nei riguardi di Ḫattuša perché in Vo 15 ss. egli minaccia di rappresaglia Kaššu, dignitario del Gran Re ittita. A me pare, invece, che l'accettazione del "sacerdote" di presentare la faccenda al Palazzo e di richiedere *ripetutamente* il giudizio del sovrano ittita riveli piuttosto una forte dipendenza di Kizzuwatna da Ḫatti.

A mio avviso, in questa lettera si tratta piuttosto di un contrasto fra dignitari dipendenti da Ḫatti – sia pur di rango e con competenze diverse – che di una controversia fra un alto dignitario di una sede provinciale ittita e il capo di uno stato subordinato a Ḫatti. Ciò si accorda con l'opinione di R. Beal[28] che Kizzuwatna fosse stata incorporata in Ḫatti durante i regni congiunti di Tutḫaliya I/II e di Arnuwanda I.[29] È quindi possibile che la nomina di Kantuzzili come "sacerdote" in Kizzuwatna fosse posteriore al trattato di Tutḫaliya I/II con Šunaššura,[30] verosimilmente l'ultimo re di Kizzuwatna.

In caso contrario, se si ritenesse Kizzuwatna, nel periodo della lettera in esame, come uno stato soggetto a Ḫatti, si dovrebbe allora addurre come sostegno della risposta negativa di Kaššu alla richiesta del "sacerdote" il fatto che nei trattati stipulati da sovrani ittiti con paesi a loro soggetti la restituzione dei fuggiaschi veniva effettuata soltanto dal paese assoggettato, mentre il re ittita li restituiva soltanto eccezio-

---

26 V. S. de Martino - F. Imparati, *Atti II CIH* (*StMed* 9), Pavia 1995, pp. 112-114.

27 *HBM*, p. 342.

28 *Or NS* 55, pp. 436-445.

29 Sulla possibilità che Kizzuwatna confinasse con Tapik(k)a v. S. Alp, *HBM*, p. 342; di opinione diversa è invece R. Beal, *THeth* 20, p. 404 n. 1522. È anche possibile che fra queste due località esistessero zone non appartenenti a strutture locali organizzate, ma abitate da genti semi-nomadi che avevano per questo la possibilità di spostarsi più facilmente da una provincia all'altra (cfr. sopra, a proposito del trattato con Paddattiššu); comunque, questo non è il caso trattato nella lettera HKM 74, dove si allude specificamente a fuggiaschi sudditi di Kaššu o del "sacerdote".

30 V. in ultimo H. Klengel, *GHR*, p. 106 [A 7], con bibliografia.

nalmente.[31] Anche in questo caso, tuttavia, sarebbe sempre valida la decisione di ambedue le parti di presentare la questione al Palazzo.

Riepilogando, mi sembra plausibile presumere che – mentre la nomina di Kantuzzili come "sacerdote" in Kizzuwatna avesse lo scopo di inglobare definitivamente questo paese nel regno di Ḫatti – con l'insediamento di Telipinu come "sacerdote" in Aleppo si intendesse creare al momento una situazione transitoria, in previsione di fare successivamente di questo paese un regno subordinato a Ḫatti, retto appunto da membri della famiglia reale ittita.[32]

3. Tornando di nuovo a Kantuzzili, mi sembra interessante soffermarci brevemente su un problema che sorge dalla lettura di una lettera[33] dell'epoca del Medio Regno ittita, proveniente da Kuşaklı, antica Šariš(š)a.[34] Questa lettera è inviata da un *ḪAZAN(N)U*, non sappiamo di quale località,[35] ad un "capo degli impiegati di Palazzo" (GAL DUMU^{meš} É.GAL)[36] per informarlo su una consultazione oracolare fatta allo scopo di conoscere lo stato di salute di una persona definita come DUMU MUNUS SANGA.[37] Questa espressione sumerica può essere interpretata o come "figlia del sacerdote" o come "figlio della sacerdotessa" o come un'unica espressione per indicare una particolare designazione sacerdotale con implicazioni forse relative all'età o al rango:[38] G. Wilhelm,[39] l'editore della lettera, preferisce la secon-

31 In alcuni trattati stipulati con sovrani di paesi dell'Anatolia occidentale il sovrano ittita stabilisce che i fuggiaschi da questi paesi nel suo territorio, nel caso in cui esercitino una attività nel settore produttivo, sia in ambito agricolo che artigianale, non verranno trattenuti a Ḫatti: v. i trattati di Muršili II con Targašnalli di Hapalla (KBo V 4 Ro 39'-40') e con Kupanta-Kurunta di Mira-Kuwaliya (KUB VI 44 IV 41'-45').

32 Infatti, come si è detto sopra, di una eventuale nomina di Telipinu come re di Aleppo non si ha finora notizia in testi a lui contemporanei, mentre è la documentazione coeva che ci informa che Muršili II nominò il figlio di Telipinu, Talmi-Šarruma, re di Aleppo: cfr., fra gli altri, H. Klengel, *Syria*, pp. 128 s.; G.F. del Monte, *L'Annalistica ittita*, Brescia 1993, pp. 96 s., n. 79. Di diversa opinione è T. Bryce, *Hethitica* 11, pp. 17 s., il quale ritiene che anche a Telipinu fosse stato conferito il titolo di "re".

33 KuT 49: v. G. Wilhelm, *MDOG* 130 (1998), pp. 177-180.

34 V. *RGTC* 6, 1978, pp. 351 s., 6/2, p. 141.

35 Sulla possibile presenza di questo dignitario anche in sedi ittite diverse da Ḫattuša, v. bibliografia presso F. Imparati, in *GHR* p. 341 n. 77.

36 V. F. Pecchioli Daddi, *Mestieri*, Roma 1982, pp. 529-535.

37 Ro 4, 14, 22, 23.

38 Piuttosto che per indicare la minore capacità o esperienza professionale del sacerdote, che sembra espressa mediante l'espressione ^{lú}SANGA.TUR: v. F. Pecchioli Daddi, *Mestieri*, p. 426, ed anche pp. 365 s.

39 *MDOG* 130, p. 178 n. 10.

da possibilità; a me pare invece che possano esservi dei motivi per giustificare la prima ipotesi interpretativa.

Purtroppo non si indica nel testo né il nome di questo/a eventuale sacerdote/ssa né la località a cui esso/a è legato/a.[40] Doveva verosimilmente trattarsi di una persona molto importante, per la preoccupazione che traspare dalla lettera e che coinvolge dignitari di rilievo, e inoltre ben nota, dato che se ne parla senza darne alcuna specificazione.

Poiché, come si è visto, nella lettera di Maşat sopra esaminata, sempre del Medio Regno ittita, laddove si parla di un "sacerdote" senza alcuna specificazione è possibile che si facesse riferimento a Kantuzzili – mentre in un'altra lettera ancora di Maşat, HKM 57,[41] dove si tratta il caso di un servo di un LÚ DUMU SANGA/ ^{lú}DUMU.SANGA/ ^{lú}DUMU SANGA,[42] si trova alla r.11 l'indicazione del luogo dove questo esercitava il sacerdozio, cioè in Urišta[43] – appare lecito chiedersi se anche nella lettera di Kuşaklı su ricordata non si parlasse della figlia di un "sacerdote" non ulteriormente definito e non si alludesse in tal modo a Kantuzzili.[44]

---

40 Non conosciamo neppure il luogo di provenienza della lettera, cioè se si trattasse di una lettera in arrivo a Šariš(š)a o la copia di archivio di una lettera in partenza da Šariš(š)a. Nella prima ipotesi, è possibile che il "capo degli impiegati di Palazzo" avesse chiesto l'esecuzione delle operazioni mantiche nella capitale e il *ḪAZAN(N)U* di Ḫattuša avesse fornito le informazioni relative; inoltre, dato che il "capo degli impiegati di Palazzo" era un dignitario che stava di solito molto vicino al re (v. F. Imparati, *SMEA* 18, 1977, pp. 54 s. con n. 133), non è da escludere che in quel tempo anche il sovrano si trovasse a Šariš(š)a. Nella seconda ipotesi il "capo degli impiegati di Palazzo" sarebbe stato nella capitale e si sarebbe rivolto per le consultazioni al *ḪAZAN(N)U* di Šariš(š)a, ciò che dimostrerebbe l'importanza di questo centro per l'esecuzione di operazioni mantiche.

41 S.Alp, *HBM*, pp. 226 s., e p. 336.

42 V. S. de Martino - F. Imparati, *Atti II CIH*, pp. 109-111 con n. 46, dove si è proposta una spiegazione della presenza e del valore che poteva avere LÚ in questa espressione, ma non si è affrontato il problema del significato di DUMU in essa.

43 Su questa località v. in ultimo S. Alp, *HBM*, p. 46, con bibliografia, e G. F. del Monte, *RGCT* 6/2, p. 180.

44 Di una "figlia", senza alcuna specificazione, si parla in un'altra lettera (KuT 50 Ro 7) proveniente, come quella in esame, dall'edificio C di Kuşaklı e ad essa contemporanea in base al *ductus*: v. G. Wilhelm, *MDOG* 130, pp. 175 s. e pp. 180-186. Anche in questa seconda lettera si parla di consultazioni oracolari relative a questa figlia; purtroppo, però, non abbiamo altri elementi per individuare chi fosse questa persona, la quale dal contesto della lettera appare essere stata di alto rango, verosimilmente appartenente alla famiglia reale: v. G. Wilhelm, *art. cit.*, p. 181. Di essa infatti si occupa addirittura la regina, la quale non sente alcuna necessità di fornire su di lei ulteriori indicazioni. È difficile anche stabilire la possibilità di un legame tra questa "figlia" e un'ipotetica "figlia del sacerdote" presente nella lettera KuT 49: si rileva però che, se in quest'ultimo caso si fosse trattato di una figlia

A tal proposito vorrei ricordare quanto ho avuto modo di rilevare altrove,[45] a proposito della menzione in alcuni testi – sempre di epoca medio-ittita – di Kantuzzili insieme ad alcuni personaggi, quali Manninni, Pariyawatra, Tulpi-Teššup, e della menzione in due testi contemporanei di un ^{lú}SANGA, non altrimenti denominato, ancora insieme con questi personaggi:[46] mi sembra importante notare che in questi ultimi due casi, dove è presente questo "sacerdote", non compare Kantuzzili.

Purtroppo, però, non sono in grado di presentare elementi concreti a sostegno di una possibile presenza di Kantuzzili "sacerdote" nella lettera in esame di Kuşaklı.

4. Sempre nell'ottica di considerare certe investiture sacerdotali col valore di nomine a carattere politico, sono ben noti i casi di Ḫattušili III e di Tutḫaliya IV, ai quali, prima della loro ascesa al trono di Ḫatti, fu conferito – rispettivamente al primo dal fratello Muwattalli II e al secondo dal padre Ḫattušili III – il sacerdozio del dio della Tempesta di Nerik e della regalità di Ḫakpiš/Ḫakmiš,[47] probabilmente allo scopo di costituire in questa zona un "vice-reame" di Ḫatti.[48]

---

di Kantuzzili, avrebbe anche questa fatto parte della famiglia reale. Da notare la presenza in questa lettera degli "impiegati di Palazzo".

A proposito della menzione in alcuni testi di questi "sacerdoti-capi" di qualche paese soggetto a Ḫatti con il solo titolo sacerdotale, senza altre specificazioni, si ricorda come confronto anche un passo del documento di Muršili II su menzionato (v. n. 7), dove si parla appunto di un "sacerdote" senza altra indicazione e nel quale è stato riconosciuto quel Telipinu, figlio di Šuppiluliuma I, posto dal padre al governo di Aleppo.

45 V. *Fs Laroche*, p. 173.

46 V. F. Imparati, *Fs Laroche,* pp. 169-172.

47 See V. Haas, *KN*, Roma 1970, pp. 13 s., 15, 24, 175 ss.; questa regalità fu conferita certamente a Ḫattušili e con molta probabilità a Tutḫaliya; v. anche F. Imparati, *Fs Houwink ten Cate*, p. 155, e Th. van den Hout, *The Purity of Kingship*, p. 86.

48 V. in ultimo F. Imparati, in *GHR*, pp. 372-373 ; cfr. anche R. Beal, *THeth* 20, pp. 324 s. Mi sembra interessante ricordare il ben noto passo del §3, I 13-18, dell' "autobiografia" di Ḫattušili III (v. H. Otten, *StBoT* 24, Wiesbaden 1981, pp. 4-5), laddove si dice che questo, ancora fanciullo e di salute molto cagionevole, era stato posto dal padre al servizio della dea Ištar come suo "sacerdote", su richiesta della dea stessa, richiesta fatta pervenire a Muršili proprio tramite il fratello di Ḫattušili, Muwattalli, il futuro re di Ḫatti. Dato l'intento fortemente strumentale che caratterizza tutto questo testo, non appare ben chiaro il reale significato di questo passo. Si possono, a mio avviso, formulare tre ipotesi: 1) Ḫattušili voleva soltanto enfatizzare anche qui, come fa in tutto il testo, l'interessamento di Ištar nei suoi riguardi fin dalla sua fanciullezza e la continua volontà della dea di conferirgli il potere su Ḫatti; 2) Muršili, probabilmente anche sotto l'influenza dello stesso Muwattalli – il quale è presentato nel testo, forse non casualmente, come latore del messaggio della dea al padre – intendeva allontanare dalla scena politica Ḫattušili, conferendogli appunto un sacerdozio prestigioso, probabilmente allo scopo di vanificare ogni sua eventuale aspirazione futura al trono di Ḫatti; 3) forse Muršili

Appare verosimile che Ḫattušili III avesse conferito al figlio Tutḫaliya il sacerdozio del dio della Tempesta di Nerik e con ciò, presumibilmente, anche la vice-regalità in Ḫakpiš in un periodo precedente alla deposizione del fratello più anziano di quest'ultimo dalla carica di *tuḫ(u)kanti*.

Quando poi era avvenuta questa deposizione, o per lo meno questa era già nei programmi di Ḫattušili, egli aveva affidato al figlio Tutḫaliya il sacerdozio di Ištar, che, a mio avviso, ne preludeva l'investitura ad erede al trono di Ḫatti.[49]

5. In questo contesto mi sembra interessante ricordare il caso di Ḫešni, DUMU. LUGAL – verosimilmente figlio di Ḫattušili III e fratello di Tutḫaliya IV – organizzatore della famosa "congiura".[50]

Th. van den Hout[51] propone di identificare questo Ḫešni col personaggio omonimo che è menzionato in alcuni testi ittiti col titolo di "sacerdote", o che, pur non essendo accompagnato da questo titolo, sembra però aver esercitato una funzione sacerdotale.

Tale proposta di identificazione si basa sulla lettera KBo XVIII 48,[52] diretta da un sovrano ittita, verosimilmente Ḫattušili III, a Ḫešni "DUMU-[*YA*]", che lì risulta aver svolto la mansione di "Orakelpriester" o "auf jeden Fall die Funktion eines solchen Beamten ausüben konnte". Si deve rilevare che dal contesto di questa lettera Ḫešni sembra aver rivestito anche un ruolo politico di rilievo, poiché viene consultato e informato proprio dal re riguardo a situazioni di politica internazionale.

Improduttivo per la sua estrema frammentarietà è il frustulo KBo XVIII 134, lettera inviata presumibilmente sempre da Ḫattušili III a Ḫešni, dove sembra si contemplino anche situazioni a carattere internazionale per la menzione alla r. 2 del paese di Babilonia (INIM KUR *Karan*[*duniaš*]); appare inoltre significativa, in rap-

---

pensava alla possibilità di una successiva utilizzazione di questo sacerdozio, in previsione cioè di conferire un giorno a Ḫattušili un "regno di appannaggio" o qualcosa di simile.

49 V. F. Imparati, *Fs Houwink ten Cate*, pp. 143-157; cfr. anche H. Tadmor, in H. Tadmor - M. Weinfeld (edd.), *History, Historiography and Interpretation*, Leiden 1983, pp. 54 ss.

50 Su questo personaggio v. in ultimo Th. van den Hout, *StBoT* 38, Wiesbaden 1995, pp. 206-211, con bibliografia precedente.

51 *StBoT* 38, pp. 207 s.

52 V. A. Hagenbuchner, *THeth* 16, pp. 7-12, dove a p. 10 si deve cancellare l'attestazione di Ḫešni fra i testimoni presenti nel testo relativo all'eredità dei beni di Šaḫurunuwa; cfr. anche H. Klengel, *GS* I, pp. 62 s., 82, 94 n. 57.

porto a quanto osservato per la lettera precedente, la presenza alla r. 3 del termine oracolare *TE*^{meš}.[53]

Gli altri casi in cui Ḫešni è menzionato esplicitamente col titolo di "sacerdote" non sembrano particolarmente rilevanti per l'identificazione proposta da Th. van den Hout.[54]

Questa ipotesi di identificare il "principe" Ḫešni con il "sacerdote" dello stesso nome viene ad assumere per noi un particolare interesse se accettiamo la proposta di N. Tani[55] di riconoscere nello Ḫešni organizzatore della famosa "congiura" proprio quel fratello maggiore di Tutḫaliya IV, che dalla Tavola Bronzea risulta essere stato nominato *tuḫ(u)kanti* prima di lui dal padre Ḫattušili III e poi deposto da questo in favore appunto di Tutḫaliya.[56]

In tal caso, sarebbe allora plausibile ipotizzare che l'investitura di Ḫešni come "sacerdote" avesse avuto, almeno in un primo tempo, anche una valenza politica, cioè la sua nomina come erede al trono di Ḫatti.

Purtroppo, data la natura dei documenti in cui è ricordata la funzione sacerdotale di questo personaggio, non abbiamo notizia sul contesto politico e sul periodo entro il quale egli fu nominato "sacerdote", né se fosse legato al culto di qualche particolare divinità. L'importanza della sua posizione, risultante soprattutto dalla lettera KBo XVIII 48 sopra menzionata, induce a datare questo documento ad un periodo anteriore alla nomina di Tutḫaliya quale erede al trono; così pure la carica sacerdotale rivestita da Ḫešni, presumibile anche da questo documento, porta a collocare la sua investitura a "sacerdote" antecedentemente al conferimento a Tutḫaliya della carica di successore al trono di Ḫatti.

6. Nell'ottica di intendere in taluni casi la consacrazione sacerdotale di qualcuno come un conferimento a questo del governo di qualche paese, mi sembra interessante riprendere in esame un passo del § 3 del "Testamento di Ḫattušili I",[57] la cui

53 V. A. Hagenbuchner, *THeth* 16, pp. 12 s.

54 *StBoT* 38, p. 208.

55 Ipotesi formulata nella sua tesi di laurea su "I processi ittiti per malversazione", discussa a Firenze il 6 luglio 1998; tale ipotesi è stata rielaborata da N. Tani in un articolo sull'argomento, tuttora in fase di ultimazione.

56 Sulle diverse ipotesi proposte per l'identificazione di questo fratello di Tutḫaliya v. in ultimo F. Imparati, *Fs Houwink ten Cate*, pp. 151-153.

57. V. F. Sommer - A. Falkenstein, *HAB*, München 1938, pp. 4-5 ; per la traduzione della versione ittita, v. T. R. Bryce, *MHT*, Brisbane 1983, pp. 100-101.; per la versione accadica v. M. Marazzi, *AkkBoaZ*, Roma 1986, pp. 7-12, entrambi con bibliografia.

versione ittita è integrata secondo la versione accadica. Com'è noto, Ḫattušili – dopo aver ricordato nei paragrafi precedenti che egli aveva nominato il nipote Labarna suo figlio e suo successore al trono di Ḫatti e che lo aveva poi deposto da questa carica a causa del suo cattivo comportamento – ribadisce alla reazione drammatica ed esasperata della madre del giovane a questa decisione: "(KUB I 16 + H II 16-19)[58] ... (Ma io), il re, feci a lui q[ualcosa] di male? [*Non lo feci sacerdote*] e lo po[rtai avanti sempre] in modo buono?[59] [Ma egli non] tenne in considerazione [il volere] del re! C[ome allora può egli in considerazione della bontà del suo proprio cuore][60] a[vere] affetto per Ḫattuša?".[61]

Mi sembra possibile ritenere che Ḫattušili in questo passo, ricordando con una certa enfasi quanto si era impegnato a favore del nipote, addirittura *facendolo sacerdote* (A I 16/H II [16]), si riferisse in tal modo ad un periodo anteriore al momento attuale, alludendo cioè con tale espressione alla precedente investitura di questo nipote come erede al trono di Ḫatti. Che il re facesse qui riferimento al periodo precedente la deposizione del nipote da questa carica mi sembra confermato dal §6 (A I 30-36/H II 30-36), dove si parla invece di ciò che Ḫattušili aveva assegnato a Labarna, dopo averlo deposto dalla successione al trono, e di come questi da allora in avanti aveva il dovere di comportarsi.

È da notare che nel passo del § 3 sopra esaminato il re non specifica in quale paese e di quale divinità egli avesse conferito il sacerdozio al nipote, contrariamente a quanto abbiamo visto a proposito di Kantuzzili, Telipinu, ed anche di Ḫattušili III e Tutḫaliya IV rispetto alla regalità di Ḫakpiš/Ḫakmiš. Ciò poteva esser dovuto al fatto che ormai la deposizione di Labarna era già avvenuta e quindi una specificazione più ampia e precisa della sua precedente consacrazione sacerdotale non si riteneva più necessaria. Inoltre, essendo l'investitura sacerdotale di Labarna un evento non lontano dalla redazione del "testamento" e quindi ben noto ai contemporanei, appariva inutile fornire ulteriori indicazioni.

---

58 Integrato secondo KUB I 16 + A I 16-19.

59 Su quest'ultima espressione v. J. Puhvel, *HED* 1, Berlin - New York - Amsterdam 1984, p. 200: "I have constantly singled him out for good treatment"; su tutta la frase v. *CHD* P, p. 119: "[Did I not make him a priest] and pr[omote] him [always] in a good way?".

60 Letter. "di quel cuore".

61 V. J. Puhvel, *HED* 4, Berlin - New York 1997, p. 156.

LA CLASSIFICAZIONE DELL'UGARITICO: PROBLEMA PRIMA STORICO E POI LINGUISTICO

FELICE ISRAEL

Università di Trieste

0. Premessa

Chi scrive ha avuto modo di conoscere personalmente il professor Fronzaroli circa ventotto anni fa in occasione del colloquio la Lessicografia semitica, quando giovane studente venne a Firenze per accompagnare il p. G. Rinaldi. Di questo colloquio egli ricorda l'epica discussione tra M. Dahood, poi suo professore al Pontificio Istituto Biblico, e J. De Moor. Chi scrive oggi crede che, proprio al problema posto dalla classificazione dell'ugaritico sia possibile proporre una soluzione non solo grazie all'attuale progresso degli studi ma anche tenendo conto contemporaneamente della più antica storia dei popoli semitici della regione siro-palestinese.

La classificazione dell'ugaritico è uno di quei problemi che si è presentato in tutte e tre le fasi della storia degli studi ugaritici: la fase della descrizione, la fase della definizione e la fase della sistemazione.[1] Resta significativo che in ognuno di questi periodi degli studi sia in opere generali sulle lingue semitiche o in descrizioni specifiche dell'ugaritico si sia fatto concordemente riferimento alla situazione di stallo della ricerca[2] nel proporre una classificazione sicura della lingua di Ugarit. A

---

1 La prima fase che si può denominare di "descrizione" inizia, dopo la decifrazione della scrittura ugaritica e finisce quasi dopo l'inizio della seconda guerra mondiale con la pubblicazione di *Ugaritic Grammar* di C. H. Gordon. La seconda fase, quella della definizione, si estende si può dire fino al 1973 anno di pubblicazione di *KTU* – oggi *CAT* – La terza ed ultima fase, quella della sistemazione dalla la pubblicazione di *KTU* è ancora in corso. Nel mare di stampa sono apparsi J. Tropper, *Ugaritische Grammatik*, Münster 2000 (*AOAT* 273) e M. P. Streck, *Das Amurritische Onomastikon der altbabylonischen Zeit. I Die Amurriter, Die Onomastische Forschung, Orthographie und Phonologie Nominalmorphologie*, Münster 2000 (*AOAT* 271/1), nonché l'articolo di D. Arnaud, "Prolegomènes à la redaction d'une histoire d'Ougarit II: les borderaux de rois divinisés", *SMEA* 41 (1999), pp. 153-173. Ad essi nelle note ci si riferirà rispettivamente come Tropper, Streck e Arnaud bis.

2 G. Rinaldi, *Le lingue semitiche. Introduzione generale storica e bibliografica*, Torino 1954 (*La Sacra Bibbia, Volumi Sussidiari*), p. 43; S. Moscati (a cura di), *An Introduction to the Comparative grammar of the Semitic Languages, Phonology and Morphology*, Wiesbaden 1964 (*Porta linguarum orientalium* VI), p. 9 § 3.9; C. H. Gordon, *UT*, p.144 § 14.1; W. Leslau, *Semitic Languages Enc Brit*

nostro avviso il problema può essere risolto rinunciando come ha ben sottolineato nell'ultima fase degli studi J. Blau[3] al metodo genealogico per sostituirlo con la teoria delle onde: va ricordato che tale prospettiva era già stata segnalata da J. Friedrich[4] nella fase di descrizione. Chi scrive crede che il problema globale della classificazione dell'ugaritico con le sue aporie metodologiche emerse nel corso degli studi potrà chiarirsi solo mediante un'attenta rivisitazione degli studi più antichi e non solo di quelli più recenti:[5] tale procedimento renderà comprensibili i presupposti intellettuali che hanno influenzato i diversi studiosi, ma sfortunatamente in questa sede, non c'è spazio per procedere ad una rassegna completa degli studi precedenti.[6]

Il recente emergere del problema amorreo dopo anni di silenzio[7] sulla questione amorrea – cfr. § 1.2 – ci ha invece indotto ha riproporci il problema delle relazioni ugaritico-amorree sollevate la prima volta nella fase di descrizione da parte di A. Goetze.[8] Dopo il noto articolo dello studioso di Yale e l'analisi comparativa dei dati onomastici condotta da J. Aistleitner[9] la classificazione dell'ugaritico come amorreo

---

20, p. 208; Ch. Rabin, *Semitic Languages. An Introduction, The Biblical Encyclopaedia Library* V, Jerusalem 1991, pp. 36-37; St. Segert, *A Basic Grammar of the Ugaritic Language with Selected Texts and Glossary*, Berkeley, Los Angeles-London 1984, p. 14 § 12.3; J. Tropper, "Ugaritic Grammar", in W. G. E. Watson - N. Wyatt, *Handbook of Ugaritic Studies*, Leiden 1999 (*HdO* 93) pp. 91-121, p. 91 § 3.1.1 in particolare.

3 J. Blau, "Hebrew and North West Semitic: Reflections on the Classification of the Semitic Languages", *HAR* 2 (1979), pp. 21-44, pp. 36-37 § 6.2.

4 J. Friedrich, "Kananäisch und Westsemitisch", *Scientia* 84 (1949), pp. 220-223, in particolare p. 222.

5 Tra i lavori più recenti cfr. D. Cohen, in J. Perrot, *Les langues dans le monde ancien et moderne. Trosième partie Les langues chamito-sémitiques. Textes reunis par David Cohen*, Paris 1988, pp. 58-60; B. Isaksson, "The Position of Ugaritic among the Semitic Languages", *Or. Suec.* 38-39 (1989-1990), pp. 54-69; A. S. Kaye, "Does Ugaritic go with Arabic in Semitic Genealogical Sub-Classification?", *Folia Orientalia* 28 (1991), pp. 115-128.

6 Chi scrive si propone di presentare in altra sede una tavola sinottica delle diverse classificazioni proposte per l'ugaritico, perché crede tali dati possano comunque essere di giovamento per quanti incomincino a dedicarsi agli studi ugaritici: spesso percorrendo la letteratura scientifica si ha la sensazione che non vi sia una piena consapevolezza dei problemi e delle soluzioni precedentemente prospettate né tantomeno dei presupposti metodologici e ideologici che hanno determinato tali ipotesi.

7 Cfr. dapprima S. Moscati, "La questione degli Amorrei", *RANL* 1958, pp. 356-365 e M. Liverani, "The Amorites", in D. J. Wiseman, *People of Old Testament Times*, Oxford 1973, pp. 100-133.

8 A. Goetze, "Is Ugaritic a Canaanite Dialect?", *Language* 17 (1941), pp. 127-138, in particolare pp. 133-138.

9 J. Aistleitner, "Studien zur Sprachverwandtschaft des Ugaritischen II", *Acta Orientalia Hungarica* 8 (1957), pp. 51-98, cfr. in particolare pp. 88-92 per le isoglosse amorreo-ugaritiche nell'onomastica.

è stata dapprima proposta da G. Garbini[10] e recentemente riproposta prima da S. Parpola[11] e poi da D. Pardee.[12] Lo studioso finlandese, nel quadro di uno studio specifico dedicato alle evoluzioni dell'accadico e dei suoi rapporti con l'eblaita, ha proposto una nuova classificazione genealogica delle lingue semitiche disegnando un albero genealogico in cui cananaico e ugaritico sono due entità distinte e l'ugaritico in particolare è visto come il discendente diretto dell'amorreo. Purtroppo in questo contributo S. Parpola non si intrattiene specificatamente sul tema delle relazioni linguistiche intercorrenti tra ugaritico e amorreo e conseguentemente le concezioni di questo studioso possono essere dedotte dal lettore soltanto mediante un'interpretazione dell'albero genealogico disegnato dallo studioso finlandese.[13] D. Pardee invece nel corso di una sintetica presentazione dell'ugaritico ha avuto modo di definire questa lingua "a remnant of a Western "Amorite" Dialect" conservante tratti cananaici arcaici. Contemporaneamente e nella stessa sede A. Faber[14] ha definito l'ugaritico "a Northwest Semitic sibling of Canaanite". Sullo stesso piano, ma ben quindici anni prima, debbono essere messe le parole di W. Von Soden[15] che ha definito correttamente e lapidariamente l'ugaritico come una "lingua siriana con superstrati cananei". Precedentemente lo stesso studioso[16] nel definire il *Nordsemitisch* aveva scritto che "Die von vielen vertretene Meinung, das Ugaritische sei eine

---

10 G. Garbini, *op. cit*, 1972[1], p. 64, 1984[2], p. 144. Un'analoga posizione seppure meno dettagliata nella motivazione si riscontra pure nel successivo manuale di G. Garbini e O. Durand, *Introduzione alle lingue semitiche*, Brescia 1994 (*Studi sul Vicino Oriente Antico* 2), pp. 134-135.

11 S. Parpola, "Proto-Assyrian", in H. Waetzoldt - H. Hauptmann, *Wirtschaft und Gesellschaft von Ebla. Akten der internationalen Tagung Heidelberg 4.-7. November 1986*, (*Heidelberger Studien Zum Alten Orient* 2), pp. 293-297.

12 D. Pardee, "Ugaritic", in R. Hetzron, *The Semitic Languages*, London 1997, pp. 131-144, in particolare p. 131.

13 *Art. cit.*, alla precedente nota 11 cfr. in particolare a p. 298 per l'albero genealogico.

14 A. Faber, "Genetic Subgrouping of the Semitic Languages", in R. Hetzron, *The Semitic Languages*, London 1997, pp. 3-15 in particolare p. 10-11.

15 W. Von Soden, *Introduzione all'orientalistica antica*, Brescia 1989 (*Studi sul Vicino Oriente antico*), p. 38.

16 W. Von Soden, *Das Nordsemitische in Babylonien und in Syrien*, in L. Cagni, *La lingua di Ebla, Atti del convegno internazionale (Napoli, 21-23 aprile 1980)*, Napoli 1981, pp. 355-361, in particolare p. 358 ripreso in W. Von Soden, *Aus Sprache, Geschichte und Religion Babyloniens, Gesammelte Aufsätze hereausgegeben von L. Cagni und H. P. L. Mülller*, Napoli 1989 (*Istituto Universitario Orientale Dipartimento di Studi Orientali Series Minor* XXXII), pp. 269-275, in particolare p. 272.

kananäische Sprache, habe ich nie teilen können. Dem Gesamkeiten stehen in Sprachbau und Wortschatz zu vielen Verschiedenheiten gegenüber".

Oggi i legami amorreo-ugaritici debbono, a nostro avviso, essere valutati con maggior attenzione per due motivi: il primo di questi è la concezione del ruolo dell'amorreo e del tipo linguistico amorreo proposti da G. Garbini[17] nella sua opera di sintesi storico-linguistica *Le lingue semitiche*. Il secondo motivo è costituito dall'emergere tramite i testi di Mari della cultura amorrea in genere e non solo quanto a organizzazione tribale[18] ma anche come un rinnovato interessamento alla lingua e ai problemi generali posti in genere da questa più antica cultura semitica siriana.

Alternativamente alla classificazione dell'amorreo come lingua amorrea l'attribuzione più frequentemente proposta per l'ugaritico è stata quella al Cananaico a partire dalla fase di descrizione fino ai giorni nostri.[19] Purtroppo però il concetto di

---

17 G. Garbini, *Le lingue Semitiche. Studi di storia linguistica*, Napoli 1984² cfr. in particolare pp. 115-118 e p. 119.

18 Dopo i pionieristici studi di J. R. Kupper, *Les nomades en Mesopotamie aux temps des rois de Mari*, Paris 1957 (*Bibliothèque de la Faculté de Philosophie et Lettres de l'Université de Liège* 142), D. O. Edzard, *Die Zweite Zwinschenzeit Babyloniens*, Wiesbaden 1957 cfr. più recentemente M. Anbar (Bernstein), *Les tribus amurrites de Mari*, Freiburg-Göttingen 1991 (*OBO* 108) e soprattutto D. Charpin - J. M. Durand, ""Fils de Sim'al": les origines tribales des rois de Mari", *RA* 80 (1986), pp. 141-183. Cfr. da ultimo Streck pp. 39-65.

19 La prima definizione come "fenicio" è dovuta a E. Dhorme in *JPOS* 11 (1931), p. 5, *RB* 39 (1930), p. 575 ed è stata poi sviluppato da Ch. Virolleaud in *Syria* 12 (1931), p. 20 e anche da un punto di vista culturale sempre da parte dello stesso Ch. Virolleaud, *La légende de Keret roi des Sidoniens publiée d'après une tablette de Ras - Shamra*, Paris 1936, introduzione alle pp. 1-33. Tale teoria è stata poi diffusa da R. Dussaud, *Les découvertes de Ras Shamra (Ugarit) et l'Ancien Testament*, Paris 1937, pp. 55-63. La definizione dell'ugaritico come "proto-ebraico" è dovuta a Th. H. Gaster in *JRAS* 1932, p. 857 mentre la sua definizione come "an early Hebrew dialect" è dovuta a J. A. Montgomery - Z. S. Harris, *The Ras Shamra Mythological Texts*, Philadelphia 1935 (*Memoirs of the American Philosophical Society* IV 1935), notamente a p. 8. La prima definizione dell'ugaritico come lingua cananea è dovuta a W. F. Albright il quale in *BASOR* 46 (1932), p. 208 ha definito l'ugaritico "an early Canaanite dialect" per poi precisare la sua definizione come "Northern Canaanite" in *JPOS* 12 (1932), pp. 207-208, e *JPOS* 14 (1934), pp. 104-115; la stessa definizione è proposta sempre da parte di W. F. Albright, *The Northwest Semitic Tongues before 1000 b.C.*, *Atti del XIX Congresso Internazionale degli orientalisti, Roma 23-29 Settembre 1935*, Roma 1938, pp. 445-450, p. 448 in particolare e W. F. Albright, "Recent Progress in North Canaanite Research", *BASOR* 70(1938), pp. 18-24, p. 21 in particolare. In questi due ultimi studi appena citati lo studioso americano divide in il semitico nordoccidentale a) in North Canaanite - l'ugaritico - b) in South Canaanite - Palestina e Fenicia - c) East Canaanite affiancati da un Proto-Hebrew e da un Proto-Aramaic. La definizione dell'ugaritico come "coastal Canaanite" è stata proposta da Z. S. Harris, *Development of the Canaanite Dialects.*

Cananaico resta ambiguo sia da un punto di vista linguistico che geografico e su tale problematica ci si dovrà soffermare al seguente § 1.1.

Al successivo § 2. saranno segnalati i riflessi culturali amorrei deducibili dai testi ugaritici ed in particolare al § 2.1. ci si intratterrà sul problema posto dall'antenato mitico *ditanu* ed il contributo offerto da questo elemento come conferma dell'ipotesi amorrea. In particolare al § 2.1.1. ci si soffermerà su *ditanu* a Ugarit, poi al § 2.1.2. su *ditanu* nella documentazione amorrea e siriana ed infine al § 2.1.3. su *ditanu* quale elemento storicamente fondante l'unità dei popoli amorrei. Al successivo § 2.2. si segnaleranno gli altri elementi siro-amorrei presenti nella mitologa ugaritica. Al § 2.3. ci si soffermerà sul sigillo di *yaqarum*, sigillo dinastico di epoca amorrea. Al § 3.1. si segnaleranno i tratti linguistici amorrei presenti nell'ugaritico e al successivo Al § 3.2. invece si segnaleranno i tratti linguistici cananaici presenti nell'ugaritico. Infine al § 4. proprio sulla base dei dati precedentemente raccolti sarà possibile trarre delle conclusioni in cui sia dato linguistico che quello storico-culturale trovino reciproca giustificazione.

1.1. Canaan concetto linguistico e geografico

Dal punto di vista linguistico il concetto di cananaico non corrisponde simmetricamente all'impiego geografico del toponimo Canaan.[20] Tale toponimo dal punto di vista della geografia storica è una prima volta un concetto egiziano – la provincia di Canaan con capoluogo Gaza[21] –, poi un concetto biblico[22] – la terra assegnata dal Signore agli Israeliti Num. 34: 1-12 e quello meno idealizzato di Ez. 47: 15-20 – ed in-

An Investigation in Linguistic History, New Haven 1939 (*American Oriental Series* 16), pp. 10-11, p. 98. La definizione dell'ugaritico come lingua canaea è stata anche proposta da St. Segert, *op. cit.*, alla precedente nota 2, p. 14 § 12.1-12.3. Recentemente la definizione dell'ugaritico come "Northern Canaanite" è stata proposta da J. Tropper cfr. *infra* alla seguente nota 134. Significativo resta l'atteggiamento in merito di C. H. Gordon il quale in UG 1940 p. 90 § 13.5 definì l'ugaritico un "hymnical-epic dialect of Canaan", per fare autocritica in *UH* a p. 116 § 14.8 e ritenere l'ugaritico una lingua a indipendente ibidem p. 116 § 14.9, posizione poi mantenuta in *UM* p. 123 § 14.9.

20 Prescindendo dalle nuove acquisizioni linguistiche – il cananeo di EA – e dalle nuove acquisizioni di testi vicino orientali lo studio di S. Moscati, *I Predecessori di Israele. Studi sulle più antiche genti semitiche in Siria e Palestina*, Roma 1956 (*Studi Orientali pubblicati a cura della Scuola Orientale* IV) rimane sempre opera magistrale.

21 W. Helck, *Die Beziehungen Ägyptens zu Vorderasien im 3. und 2. Jahrtausend v. Chr.*, Wiesbaden 1971^2, pp. 249-250.

22 Cfr. Y. Aharoni, *The Land of the Bible. A Historical Geography*, Philadelphia 1979^2, p. 67-77 e "Kanaan im Alten Testament", in O. Keel - M. Küchler, *Orte und Landschaften der Bible*, vol. I, Göttingen 1984, pp. 244-252.

fine ultimo un concetto fenicio.[23] Sulle attestazioni extrabibliche del termine il lavoro di N. P. Lemche[24] presenta un'esauriente *status quaestionis* e le nuove attestazioni del toponimo nel secondo millennio nei testi di Emar[25] o di Alalaḫ[26] non sono risolutive nel fissare i confini del paese di Canaan che appaiono precisati solamente nel testo biblico il quale a sua volta pone ben noti problemi di datazione. L'esame dei dati ci mostra che in epoca amarniana[27] grazie alla lettera di EA 148 = LA 122:46 il paese di Canaan si estendeva fino a Sidone e Haṣor. Il dato ugaritico – prescindendo da EA 151: 44 = LA 125[28] invece esclude l'appartenenza politica del regno di Ugarit al mondo cananeo perché la menzione tra diversi NNPP di stranieri del NP *yʿl* seguita dall'aggettivo etnico *knʿny* alla linea 7 della lista nominale RS11.840 = CAT 4.96 nonché la denominazione degli Ugaritiani come *maru ugarit* contrapposta ai *maru Kinaḫḫi* nel testo RS 20.182 = Ugaritica V nº 36[29] ll.5'-9' fanno automaticamente escludere l'appartenenza di Ugarit al mondo cananeo come da tempo rilevato da A. F. Rainey.[30] Il dato fenicio infine resta tardivo ed è costituito da una serie di monete da Beirut[31] dell'epoca di Antioco IV Epifane recanti la legenda *ʾš bknʿn* oppure *ʾm bknʿn*. Solo in epoca ellenistica il paese di Canaan viene esplicitamente identificato con la Fenicia come provano le traduzioni dei LXX a Gios 5:12 χώρα τῶν Φοινίκων e Es 16:35 Φοινικίσση per *ʾrṣ knʿn* oppure a Deut 3:9 οἱ Φοίνικες per Ṣidonîm e Φοίνικες per Ṣdwn in Is. 23:2. In epoca romana i passi dei Vangeli sinottici di Mt. 15:22 e Mc 7:26, rispettivamente ambientati a Tiro e

23 G. Bunnens, *Dictionnaire de la civilisation phénicienne et punique*, Brepols Turnhout 1992, p. 87.

24 N. P. Lemche, *The Canaanites in their Land. The Tradition of the Canaanites*, Sheffield 1991 (*JSOT Supplement* 110). Per un'integrazione dei dati vicino orientali antichi su Canaan cfr. la recensione a quest'opera di N. Na'aman, "The Canaanites and their Land. A Rejoinder", *UF* 26 (1994) pp. 397-418.

25 D. E. Fleming, ""The Storm God of Canaan" at Emar", *UF* 26 (1994), pp. 127-130.

26 R. S. Hess, "Occurrences of "Canaan" in Late Bronze Age Archives of the West Semitic World", *IOS* 18 (1998), pp. 365-371.

27 Per un'analisi delle medesime sempre valido S. Moscati, *op. cit.*, alla precedente nota 20, pp.46-50.

28 LA = M. Liverani, *Le lettere di el-Amarna*, vol I-II, Brescia 1998-1999 (*Testi del Vicino Oriente Antico, Letterature Meospotamiche* 3, 1-2).

29 Editio princeps in *Ugaritica* V, pp. 111-114.

30 A. F. Rainey, "A Canaanite at Ugarit", *IEJ* 13 (1963), pp. 43-45; A. F. Rainey, "Ugarit and Canaanites again", *IEJ* 14 (1964), p. 101.

31 Cfr. Beyrouth, in *Dictionnaire de la civilisation phénicienne et punique*, Brepols Turnhout 1992, pp. 71-72. Riproduzione fotografica a cura di P. Bordreeuil - N. Tabet in *Syria* 22 (1985), p. 180 e p. 181 fig. 7; e *Syria* 63 (1986) p. 421 e p. 423 fig. 6, p. 424 fig. 8.

Sidone e a Tiro, indicano la donna di quei luoghi nel testo con le parole γυνὴ Χαναναία e Συροφοινικίσση τῷ γένει. Questi testi tardi continuano ad attestare l'identificazione tra Fenicia e Canaan ancora presente qualche secolo dopo nell'area coloniale punica, come si desume oltre che da un passo ben noto di Agostino[32] anche dall'iscrizione di El Hofra 102[33] dove alla linea 4 dove *ʿbdʾšmn bn mʾdr* si definisce *ʾš knʿn*, ossia proveniente dalla Madrepatria. Si deve in conclusione presumere che la consapevolezza da parte dei Fenici di appartenere al mondo cananeo sia un'eredità dell'epoca del Bronzo come provano le lettere di EA 131: = LA 166: 61, 148 = LA 122: 86 che situano rispettivamente Biblo, Tiro e Sidone nel paese di Canaan. L'applicazione di quella definizione di Cananeo proposta da C. Brockelmann[34] sulla base delle isoglosse intercorrenti tra Fenicio Ebraico e Moabita mostra come confini geografici e dato linguistico non coincidevano perché i testi biblici concorrono unanimemente a dare come limite orientale al paese di Canaan il corso del Giordano.[35] L'acquisizione della lingua degli Ammoniti unitamente a quella dei Moabiti e degli Edomiti, avvenuta tramite recenti ritrovamenti epigrafici non fa che confermare la non coincidenza tra Canaan geografico e Canaan linguistico, lasciando vedere invece un'anfizona linguisticamente cananaica ai limiti dell'area geografica cananaica.

Il progresso degli studi di filologia semitica nordoccidentale consente oggi allo studioso di ritenere meno difficile la definizione del termine cananaico nel secondo millennio[36] essendo possibile contrapporre contrastivamente nel secondo millennio amorreo, ugaritico e cananaico.[37] La concezione del Cananaico proposta da C. Brockelmann oggi può essere ampliata e verificata geograficamente sito per sito

32 Unde interrogati rustici nostri quid sint, punice espondentes Chanani, corrupta scilicet, sicut in talibus solet, una littera, quid aliud respondent quam, Chananaei? PL XXXV col. 2096. Per il passo cfr. F. Vattioni, "Sant'Agostino e la civiltà punica", *August* 8 (1968), pp. 434-467, p. 444 in particolare e S. Moscati, "Unde interrogati rustici nostri" in S. Moscati, *Scritti fenici minori*, Roma 1988, p. 615-620.

33 Edizione a cura di A. Berthier - R. Cherlier, *Le sanctuaire punique d'El-Hofra à Constantine*, Paris 1952-1955, vol. I pp. 83-84, vol II pl. XI A.

34 C. Brockelmann, *Grundriss der vergleichenden Grammatik der semitischen Sprachen* I, Berlin 1908, p. 8 § 10.

35 N. Na'aman, *art. cit.*, alla precedente nota 24, p. 410.

36 J. C. Grennfield, "Amurrite, Ugaritic and Canaanite", in *Proceedings of the International Confrence on Semitic Studies held in Jerusalem 19-23 July 1965*, Jerusalem 1969, pp. 92-101.

37 F. Israel, "La conquête de Canaan: observation d'un philologue", *Antiquités Sémitiques* 4, Paris 1999, pp. 63-77.

perché i contributi di W. L. Moran e di A. F. Rainey[38] hanno fatto emergere pienamente i tratti cananei – ciò significa strettamente affini ed anticipatori dell'ebraico e del fenicio – presenti nella documentazione amarniana. Le isoglosse che indubitabilmente uniscono la documentazione di El Amarna con l'ugaritico e l'ebraico da tempo segnalate da H. L. Ginsberg[39] sono a loro volta un'ulteriore conferma della non coincidenza tra Canaan geografico e Canaan linguistico. Oggi il termine cananaico risulta meno ambiguo dal punto di vista linguistico proprio grazie al progresso degli studi che hanno consentito di definire tale ramo del Semitico nel suo divenire storico a partire dal secondo millennio e nella sua frammentazione nel primo millennio. Purtroppo nella classificazione dell'ugaritico come lingua cananaica un notevole peso è stato esercitato da fatti culturali affrettatamente detti cananei: significative restano le diverse definizioni proposte per l'ugaritico da C. H. Gordon.[40] Tale ambiguità è stata recentemente segnalata da D. Pardee[41] che sinteticamente ha descritto tali fattori come una "confusion of categories, namely between linguistic and literary criteria". Tale confusione è avvenuta malgrado l'avvertimento, lanciato quasi quarantanni fa e purtroppo inascoltato, di J. Cantineau[42] che faceva notare

38 Abbiamo desunto i dati da A. F. Rainey, "Canaanite in the Amarna Tablets. A Linguistic Analysis of the Mixed Dialect used by the Scribes from Canaan", Leiden 1996 (*HdO* XXV: 1-IV), vol. I, "Orthography, Phonology, Morphosyntactic Analysis of the Pronouns, Nouns, Numerals"; vol. II, "Morphosyntactic Analysis of the Verbal System"; vol. III, "Morphosyntactic Analysis of the Particles and Adverbs"; vol. IV, References and Index of textes cited. Per i principi che hanno permesso di individuare il sistema verbale cananeo cfr. in particolare vol. II, p. 11-16.

39 Dapprima H. L. Ginsberg, *The Classification of the North-West Semitic Languages, Atken des XXIV Internationalen Orientalisten-Kongresses, München 28 August bis 4. September 1957*, München 1959, pp. 256-257 e poi H. L. Ginsberg, "The Northwest Semitic Languages", in B. Mazar, *World History of the Jewish People*, II, Givataim 1970, pp. 102-124 (edizione originale 1960), in particolare pp. 104-105.

40 Ad esempio UG apparsa nel 1940 p. 90 § 13.5 l'ugaritico è definito "hymnical-epic dialect of Canaan", ma poi in UH del 1947 C. H. Gordon riconosce che molti studiosi – se stesso compreso – facendo così un'autocritica implicita a p. 114-115 § 14.4 "have approached Ugaritic from an Old Testament view for it as had so much to do with the preponderance of the Canaanite school of thought to which I have adhered" dicendo poi a p. 116 § 14.8 "I feel less inclined to subsume Ugaritic and Hebrew in the category of Canaanite than I wrote Ugaritic Grammar in 1940" [cfr. il capitolo XII, pp. 78-87 e pp. 88-89 §§ 13. 2-4] e concludendo a p. 116 § 14.9 "meanwhile , we would do best to treat Ugaritic as a separate Semitic language rather than a dialect of another language, or of some subgroup, in the Semitic family".

41 D. Pardee, *art. cit.*, alla precedente nota 12, p. 131.

42 J. Cantineau, "La langue de Ras Shamra. (Deuxième article)", *Syria* 21 (1940), pp. 38-61, in particolare p. 38.

come a fini classificatori "une question de langue" non poteva "être tranchée que par des arguments linguistiques". Chi scrive crede che oramai siano emersi sufficienti elementi atti a dimostrare come quegli elementi formali di lingua poetica presenti sia nei testi ugaritici che nel testo biblico[43] non siano prova di affinità a fini classificatori – quindi di cananeicità dell'ugaritico – ma piuttosto spia dell'esistenza di una lingua poetica semitico siro-palestinese[44] da paragonare – con tutte le prudenti riserve del caso – all'analogo fenomeno presente in ambito indoeuropeo.[45] Questo approccio permette, secondo noi, una volta per tutte inquadrare i parallelismi ebraico ugaritici nella loro giusta prospettiva fenomenologica pur non levando nessun merito ai primi e pionieristici[46] lavori di U. Cassuto o di M. Held che ebbero modo di individuarli. Inoltre oggi l'emergere degli stessi fenomeni sia nelle iscrizioni fenicie[47]

43 Cfr. il magistrale G. B. Gray, *The Forms of Hebrew Petry Considered with Special Refrence to the Criticism and Interpretation of the Old Testament*, New York 1962 (*The Library of Biblical Studies*), Prolegomenon by D. N. Freedman VII-LIII. Utile il prolegomeno in particolare pp. XLI-XLVI e pp. LI-LIII, per la valorizzazione della documentazione ugaritica per la comprensione della poesia biblica. Un'ottima presentazione dei problemi in W. G. E. Watson, *Classical Hebrew Poetry. A Guide toits Techniques*, Sheffield 1984 *JSOT* Supplement 26 e dello stesso *Traditional Techniques in Classical Hebrew Verse*, Sheffield 1994, *JSOT Supplement* 170.

44 Chi scrive ha introdotto en passant questo concetto in F. Israel, "Reflexions methodologiques sur le classement linguistique de DAPT", in J. Hoftijzer - G. Van der Kooij, *The Balaam Text from Deir 'Alla Re-evaluated. Proceedings of the International Symposium Held at Leiden 21-24 August 1989*, Leiden 1991, pp. 305-317, in particolare p. 316.

45 G. Costa, *Le origini della lingua poetica indeuropea. Voce, coscienza e transizione neolitica*, Firenze 1998 (*Accademia Toscana di Scienze e Lettere "La Colombaria", Studi* 164. Si consulti in particolare pp. 11-133 per per la storia della ricerca e la bibliografia finale, valutata criticamente, dopo la pubblicazione della fondamentale monografia di R. Schmitt, *Dichtung und Dichtersprache in indogermanischer Zeit*, Wiesbaden 1967.

46 Per la storia di questi studi cfr. W. Watters, "Formula Criticism and the Poetry of the Old Testament", Berlin 1976 (*BZAW* 138), pp. 20-27 in particolare. Il culmine di questi studi è dato dalle liste di M. Dahood in RSP I-III per cui cfr. M. Dahood, "Ugaritic-Hebrew Parallel Pairs", *RSP* I, pp. 71-382, *RSP*, II pp. 1-33, *RSP*, III 1-178, Idem, "Ugaritic-Hebrew Parallel Pairs", Supplement in *RSP* II, pp. 34-39, e *RSP* III, pp. 178-206.

47 Per il problema generale delle coppie di parole cfr. il ricco materiale raccolto da Y. Avishur, *Stylistic Studies of Word-Pairs in Biblical and Ancient Semitic Literature*, Neukirchen Vluyn 1984 (*AOAT* 210). Questa monografia è stata preceduta dagli studi dello stesso Y. Avishur, "Word Pairs Common to Phoenician and Biblical Hebrew", *UF* 7 (1975), pp. 13-47, e "Studies of Stylistic Features Common to the Phoenician Inscriptions and the Bible", *UF* 8 (1976), pp. 1-22. Per quanto concerne la documentazione fenicia purtroppo meno noto ma non di inferiore valore è il volume di F. Stéphan, *Les inscriptions phéniciennes et leur style*, Beyrouth 1985 (*Publications de l'Université Libanaise, Section des études archéologiques* III).

che nella documentazione aramaica più o meno recente[48] unitamente alla presenza di veri e propri specimina di lingua poetica sia nell'iscrizione di Deir ʿallā[49] che nel papiro Amherst 63[50] crediamo siano la miglior prova dell'esistenza di questa "lingua

48 Per uno sguardo d'insieme sulla letteratura aramaica antica sopravissutaci: A. Lemaire, "Traditions littéraires araméeennes dans la litterature hébraïque du 1er milénaire avant notre ère", *JA* 274 (1986), p. 479, A. Lemaire, "Aramaic Litterature and Hebrew Litterature. Contacts and Influences in the First Millennium BCE". *Proceedings of the Ninth World Congress of Jewish Studies, Jerusalem, August 4-12 1985*, Jerusalem 1988, pp. 9-24. Etude de tecnique poetique et parallelisme de mots. St. Segert, "Preliminary Notes on the Structure of the Aramaic Poems in the Papyrus Amherst 63", *UF* 18 (1986) pp.272-276, 289-297; St. Segert, "Parallelistic Structeres on the Aramaic Henoch Fragments", in Z. J. Kapera, *Intertestamental Essays in Honor of J. T. Milik*, Krakow 1992, pp. 187-203; G. E. Watson, "The Ahiqar Sayings. Some Marginal Comments", *AO* 2 (1984), pp. 253-261, lista delle coppie di parola pp.260-261. Cfr. anche J. C. Greenfield, "Early Aramaic Poetry", *JANES* 11 (1979) pp. 45-51 e dello stesso J. C. Greenfield, "On Mandaic Poetique Techniques", in M. Macuch - Chr. Kessler Müller - B. G. Fragner, *Studia semitica necnon iranica Rudolpho Macuch septuagenario ab amicis et discipulis dedicata*, Wiesbaden 1989, pp. 101-108, sempre sulla poesia mandea cfr. St. Segert, "Parallelism in the Qolasta", *ibidem* pp. 263-301.

49 Per l'ampia problematica connessa a questa documentazione cfr. gli atti del congresso tenutosi a Leida vent'anni dopo la pubblicazione del testo J. Hoftijzer - G. Van der Kooij, *The Balaam Text from Deir ʿAlla Re-evaluated. Proceedings of the International Symposium Held at Leiden 21-24 August 1989*, Leiden 1991.

50 R. A. Bowman, "An Aramaic Religious Text in Demotic Script", *JNES* 3 (1944), pp. 219-231; traduzione completa a cura di R. C. Steiner , "The Aramaic Text in Demotic Scripts", in W. W. Hallo (editor), *The Context of the Scripture*, I *Canonical Compositions from the Biblical World*, Leiden 1997, pp. 319-27, "Lessico" in *DISI*, pp. 1255-1266. Pubblicazione di singoli passi C. F. Nims - R. C. Steiner - A. Paganized, "Version of Psalm 20:2-6 from the Aramaic Text in Demotic Script", *JAOS* 103 (1983), pp. 261-274; C. F. Nims - R. C. Steiner, "You cant'offer Your sacrifice and Eat it too . A Polemical Poem from the Aramaic Text in Demotic Script", *JNES* 43 (1984), pp. 89-114; C. F. Nims - R. C. Steiner, "Ashurbanipal and Shamash-shum-ukin. A Tale of two Brothers from the Aramaic Text in Demotic Script, Part I", *RB* 92 (1985), pp. 60-81; R. Steiner, "The Aramaic Text in Demotic Script: The Liturgy of a New Year's Festival Imported from Bethel to Syene by Exiles from Rasha", *JAOS* 111 (1991), pp. 362-363; R. C. Steiner, "Papyrus Amherst 63: A New Source for the Language, Literature, Religion, and History of Arameans", in J. M. Geller - J. C. Greenfield - M. Weitzman, *Studia aramaica Supp. JSS* 4) Oxford 1995, pp. 199-207. S. P. Vleeming - J. W. Wesselius, "An Aramaic Hymn from the Fourth Century B.C., *BO* 39 (1982), pp. 501-509; S. P. Vleeming - J. W. Wesselius, "Bethel the Saviour, Papyrus Amherst 63 col. 7:1-18", *JEOL* 28 (1983-1984) pp. 110-142; S. P. Vleeming - J. W. Wesselius, *Studies in Papyrus Amherst 63*, vol. I, Amsterdam 1985; studi M. Weinfeld, "The Pagan Version of Psalm 20:2-6. Vicissitudes of a Psalmodic Creation in Israel and its Neighbours", *EI* 18 (1985), pp. 130-140 (ebraico moderno); St. Segert, "Preliminary Notes on the Structure of the Aramaic Poems in the Papyrus Amherst 63", *UF* 18 (1986), pp. 272-276, 289-297; Kh. Th. Zauzich, "Der Gott des aramäisch-demotischen Papyrus Amherst 63", *GM* 85 (1985), pp. 89-90; E. Bresciani, "Le sixième satrapie: L'Egypte perse et ses sémites", in *Le livre de traverse, de l'exegese biblique à l'anthropologie*, Paris 1992, pp. 87-99; I. Kottsieper, "Die literarischen Aufnahme assyrischen Begebenheiten in frühen aramäischen Texten",

poetica semitica dell'area siro-palestinese" sulla quale contiamo di soffermarci in studi futuri.

1.2. Il riemergere della questione amorrea

La questione amorrea, che tanto peso ha avuto tra la fine degli anni Cinquanta e l'inizio degli anni Sessanta, oggi[51] sembra riemergere per l'apparire di tutta una serie di studi che affrontano la questione non solo dal punto di vista linguistico ma anche storico. Dal punto di vista linguistico dopo gli studi di Th. Bauer,[52] I. J. Gelb,[53] G. Buccellati,[54] di H. B. Huffmon[55] nuovi strumenti di lavoro quali il repertorio onoma-

---

in D. Charpin - F. Joannès, *La circulation des biens, des personnes et des idées dans le Proche Orient Ancien*, Paris 1992 (*Editions Récherches sur les Civilisations*) *Actes de la XXXVIII^è Rencontre Assyriologique Internationale (Paris , 8-10 jullet 1991)*, pp. 283-289; F. H. Polak, *The Daniel Tales in their Aramaic Literary Milieu*, A. S. Van der Woude, *The Book of Daniel in the Light of New Findings*, Leuven 1993 (*Bibliotheca Ephemeridum Theologicarum Lovaniensium* 106), p. 249-265 in particolare pp. 249-253; I. Kottsieper, "El-ferner oder naher Gott? Zur Bedeutung einer semitischen Gottheit in verschiedenen sozialen Kontexten", in I Jts v. Chr., in R. Alberz - S. Otto, *Religion und Gesellschaft. Studien zu ihren Wechselbeziehung in den Kulturen des Antiken Vorderem Orient*, vol. I, Münster 1997 (*AOAT* 248), pp. 25-74, Anhang I "Zur Interpretation von ḥrn in Pap. Amherst 63", in particolare pp. 51-55, Anhang II "Zur Interpretation von Pap. Amherst 63", 13, pp. 13-27 in particolare pp. 56-63, Anhang III "Papyrus Amherst 63", 18 1-4a in particolare pp. 63-67; I. "Kottsieper, Anmerkungen zu Pap. Amherst 63", Teil II-V, *UF* 29 (1997), pp. 385-434. Per il salmo K. A. D. Smelik, "Een Aramees Parallel voor Psalm 20", *Nederlands Theologisch Tjdschrift* 37 (1983), pp.89-103; K. A. D. Smelik, "The Origin of Psalm 20", *JSOT* 20 (1985), pp. 75-81; M. Weinfeld, "The Pagan Version of Psalms 20:2-6.Vicissitudines of a Psalmodic Creation in Israel and its Neighbors", *EI* 18 (1985), pp. 130-140; I. Kottsieper, "Anmerkungen zu Pap. Amherst 63: I 12,11-19 Eine aramäische Version von Ps 20", *ZAW* 100 (1988), pp. 217-244; Z. Zevit, "The Common Origin of the Aramaic Prayer to Horus and of Psalms 20", *JAOS* 110 (1990), pp.213-228; M. Delcor, "Remarques sur la datation du Ps. 20 Comparée à celle du psaume araméen apparenté dans le papyrus Amherst 63", in M. Dietrich - O. Loretz, *Mesopotamica-Ugaritico-Biblica, Festschrift für K. Bergerhof zur Vollendung seiner 70 Lebensjahres am 7. Mai 1992*, Neukirchen 1993 (*AOAT* 232), pp. 25-43.

51 Cfr. le sintesi più recenti di G. M. Schwartz, "Pastoral Nomadism in Ancient Asia", in J. Sasson, *Civilizations of the Ancient Near East*, New York 1995, vol. I, pp. 249-258 e R. M. Whiting, "Amorite Tribes and Nations of Second Millennium Western Asia", in J. Sasson, *Civilizations of the Ancient Near East*, New York 1995, vol. II, pp. 1231-1242.

52 Th. Bauer, "Die Ostkananaer. Eine philologisch-historische Untersuchung über die Wanderschicht der sogennanten "Amoriter" in Babylonien", Leipzig 1926, p. 64. Cfr. ora Streck p. 131 § 1.107.

53 I. J. Gelb, "La lingua degli Amoriti", *RANL* 1958, pp. 143-64. Cfr. ora Streck p. 131 § 1.108.

54 G. Buccellati, *The Amorites of the Ur III Period*, Napoli 1966 (*Pubblicazioni del Seminario di Semitistica Ricerche* I). Cfr. ora Streck p. 132 § 1.110.

stico di I. J. Gelb[56] con la relativa rielaborazione grammaticale ad opera di E. E. Knudsen,[57] lo studio sulla fonologia amorrea di G. Buccellati[58] e la breve descrizione linguistica dell'amorreo di C. H. Gordon[59] costituiscono dei punti di partenza ottimi per riconsiderare dal punto di vista descrittivo – seppure nei limiti di una lingua residuale – l'insieme della documentazione linguistica amorrea. Dal punto di vista storico gli studi di G. Buccellati,[60] le sintesi di D. O. Edzard[61] sia sul termine geografico e sul teonimo MAR-TU, la riedizione della geografia di Sargon a cura di W. Horowitz,[62] i nuovi testi apparsi sul dio Martu[63] lo studio storico sul regno di Amurru dovuto a I. Singer,[64] obbligano, dopo tanto tempo di silenzio, a rivedere la questione amorrea nel suo complesso sia dal punto di vista storico che linguistico, tanto più che la pubblicazione di nuovi testi da Mari è stata rivelatrice non solo di dati onomastico-linguistici ma anche della cultura amorrea:[65] in particolare è emerso

55 J. B. Huffmon, *Amorite Personal Names in the Mari Texts. A Structural and Lexical Study*, Baltimore 1965. Cfr. ora Streck p. 132 § 1.109.

56 I. J. Gelb, *Computer Aided Analysis of Amorite*, Chicago 1980 (*Assyriological Studies* 21). Cfr. ora Streck p. 132 § 1.111.

57 E. E. Knudsen, "Amorite Grammar. A Comparative Statement", in A. S. Kaye, *Semitic Studies in Honour of Wolf Leslau on the Occasion of his Eighthy-fifth Birthday, November 14th 1991*, Wiesbaden 1991, pp. 866-885. Cfr. ora Streck p. 133 § 1.113.

58 G. Buccellati, "Akkadian and Amorite Phonology", in A. S. Kaye - P. T. Daniels, *Phonologies of Asia and Africa (Including the Caucasus)*, Winona Lake Indiana 1987, vol. 1, pp. 3-38.

59 C. H. Gordon, "Amorite and Eblaite", in R. Hetzron, *The Semitic Languages*, London 1997, pp. 100-113, in particolare pp. 102-104. Cfr. ora Streck pp. 133-134 § 1.114a.

60 G. Buccellati, "Ebla and the Amorites", in *Eblaitica* 3 (1992), pp. 83-104 e G. Buccellati, "Gli Amorrei e l'"addomesticamentro" della steppa", in O. Rouault - M. G. Masetti Rouault, *L'Eufrate e il tempo. La civiltà del medio Eufrate e dell Gezira siriana*, Milano 1993, pp. 67-69; G. Buccellati, "Amorites in The Oxford Encyclopedia of Archaeology" in *The Near East* vol 1, pp. 107-111.

61 D. O. Edzard, "Martu A Gott", *RLA* VII, pp. 433-438, B. Martu (Mardu), "Bevölkerungsgruppe", *RLA* VII, pp. 438-440.

62 W. Horowitz, *Mesopotamian Cosmic Geography*, Winona Lake Indiana 1998.

63 O. R. Gurney, "N° 1 Hymn to Amurru", in *OECT* XI (1989), pp.15-19, W. W. Hallo, "Two Letter-Prayers to Amurru", in M. Lubetski - Cl. Gottlieb - Sh. Keller, "Boundaries of the Near Eastern World. A Tribute to C. H. Gordon", *JSOT Suppl.* 273, Sheffield 199, pp. 397-410 con bibliografia aggiornata. Per la rielaborazione di testi precedenti cfr. J. Klein, *The Marriage of Martu: The Urbanization of ' Barbaric Nomads' Michmanim* 9 (1996), pp. 87-96. Cfr. ora Streck pp. 70-72 § 7.1.13.

64 I. Singer, "Appendix III, A Coincise History of Amurru", in Sh. Izreʾel, *Amurru Akkadian: A Linguistic Study*, Atlanta 1991, vol. II, pp. 135-195. (*Harvard Semitic Studies* 40-41).

il fatto che l'amorreo era percepito in ambito mariota come una una lingua[66] ed una volta studiata la lista *malku* = *šarru*[67] potrà apparire il lessico amorreo, oggi noto soprattutto attraverso l'onomastica. Tutti questi fatti non possono lasciare sordo chi si interessa alla storia linguistica dell'area siro-palestinese perché proprio il posto dato all'amorreo nello sviluppo delle lingue semitiche da G. Garbini[68] che all'inizio degli anni Sessanta assieme a Ch. Rabin,[69] individuava l'area centrale ed innovativa del semitico, costituisce la premessa all'individuazione dell'area semitico centrale da parte di R. Hetzron,[70] definita precedentemente e correttamente soprattutto da un punto di vista geografico "amorrea" da G. Garbini. L'emergere della cultura amorrea ha permesso – indipendentemente – sia allo scrivente che a I. Singer[71] di trovare un punto di contatto non solo tra cultura amorrea e ugaritica ma anche come si vedrà al seguente § 2.1.3. tra cultura aramaica e amorrea. Questo punto di contatto, chi scrive, crede sia un punto fermo di non indifferente importanza nel supportare l'"ipotesi amorrea" di G. Garbini per la quale come aveva rilevato D. Cohen[72] mancavano proprio gli elementi storici atti a suffragarla.

---

65 J. M. Durand, "Unité et diversité au Proche Orient Ancien à l'époque amorrite", in D. Charpin - F. Joannès, *La circulation des biens, des personnes et des idées dans le Proche Orient Ancien, Actes de la XXXVIIIe Rencontre Assyriologique Internationale (Paris, 8-10 Jullet 1991)*, pp. 97-128.

66 J. M. Durand, *art. cit.*, alla precedente nota 65 in particolare pp. 123-126 testo n° 7930 citato a p. 124 nota 196, testo A. 109 citato a p. 125 nota 205. Cfr. ora Streck pp. 76-80 § 8.1.

67 Per questa lista lessicale cfr. le notizie in A. Cavigneaux, "Lexicalische Listen", in *RLA* VI pp. 609-840, p. 639. Cfr. i doucmenti nel frattempo pubblicati da E. Von Weiher, *Spätbabylonische Texte aus Uruk III (Ausgrabungen dee Deutschen Forschungsgemeinschaft in Uruk Warka 12)*, Berlin 1988, pp. 244-249 nr. 119 tavola II, pp. 250-254 nr. 120 tav. III.

68 G. Garbini, "Configurazione dell'unità linguistica semitica", in *Atti del IV Convegno internazionale dei linguisti*, Milano 1963, Milano 1965, pp. 35-47, ripreso con modifiche in G. Garbini, *Le lingue Semitiche. Studi di storia linguistica*, Napoli 1972, pp. 23-37, nella seconda edizione pp. 23-42.

69 Ch. Rabin, "The Origin of the Subdivision of Semitic", in D. W. Thomas - W. D. McHardy, *Hebrew and Semitic Studies Presented to G. R. Driver in Celebration of his Seventieth Birthday, 20 August 1962*, Oxford 1963, pp. 104-115.

70 R. Hetzron, "Semitic Languages", in B. Comrie, *The World's Major Languages*, London-Sydney 1987, pp. 654-663 e p. 656 in The World Major Languages e precedentemente R. Hetzron, "La division des langues sémitiques", in A. Caquot - D. Cohen, *Actes du premier congrès international de linguistique sémitique et chamito-sémitique, Paris 16-19 juillet 1969*, The Hague 1973, pp. 180-194, cfr. in particolare p. 185 per la rappresentazione grafica e p. 192.

71 I. Singer, "A Political History of Ugarit", in W. G. E. Watson - N. Wyatt, *Handbook of Ugaritic Studies*, Leiden 1999 (*HdO* 39), pp. 603-733, in particolare pp. 613-614.

72 D. Cohen, *op. cit.*, alla precedente nota 5: p. 58.

2. Riflessi amorrei nella cultura ugaritica

2.1. Ditanu e l'ipotesi amorrea

2.1.1. Ditanu nella documentazione ugaritica

A Ugarit l'elemento ditanu *-dtn* e *ddn* - è messo in relazione con la casa regnante[73] non solo nel poema di Keret CAT 1. 15: III, 4 e 15 b dove l'espressione *pḫr qbṣ dtn* è impiegata per designare l'insieme dei re di Ugarit ma anche nel rituale funerario dell'ultimo re di Ugarit Hammurapi RS 34.126[74] = CAT 1.161 alle linee 3 e 10 dove la medesima espressione *qbṣ d*[*dn*].si riferisce senza alcun dubbio ai precedenti re di Ugarit. Il dossier ugaritico su Ditanu si completa con il testo paramitologico RS 24.272 = CAT 1.126,[75] linee 1-2, che menziona una visita del dio El presso Ditanu per ricevere delle istruzioni rituali. Ditanu appare come un elemento divino oggetto di culto nel testo frammentario RIH 78/11:2 = CAT 1.170[76] dove riceve un un montone in olocausto. Nell'onomastica ugaritica è attestato infine il NP *bn ddn* in CAT 4.69 VI:29, 4.633:6, 4.760:5: con questo elemento, salvo future scoperte, si chiude il dossier ugaritico su Ditanu.

2.1.2. Ditanu nella documentazione amorrea e siriana

La tavoletta BM 80328 tratta dall'oscurità in cui si trovava da parte di J. J. Finkelstein[77] ci offrirà diverse sorprese come vedremo al seguente § 2.1.3); qui ci basti ricordare che essa alla linea 6 presenta il nome tribale *ditanu* Per tale elemento,

---

73 Cfr. da ultimo I. Singer, *art. cit.*, alla precedente nota 71.

74 P. Xella, "I testi rituali di Ugarit", I, *Testi*, Roma 1981 (*Studi semitici* 54), pp. 279-287, A. Caquot - J. M. de Tarragon, "Textes ougaritiques", II, *Texte religieux et rituels, Introduction, Traduction, Commentaire, Littératures du Proche Orient Ancien*, Paris 1989 a cura di A. Caquot pp. 103-110. Da ultimo P. Bordreuil, "Une bibliothèque au sud de la ville", Paris 1991 *RSO* VII, pp. 151-163 e *TUAT* II, p. 328, pp. 331-333 e J. Tropper, "Morphologische Besonderheiten des Spätugaritischen", *UF* 25 (1993), pp. 389-393.

75 D. Pardee, "Les textes paramythologiques de la 24ᵉ campagne (1961)", *RSO* IV Paris 1988, p. 179-192, P. Xella *TRU*, pp. 173-177, J. M. de Tarragon, in *LAPO* II, pp. 119-123, *TUAT* II, pp. 329-331.

76 = *LAPO* II p. 236, *TRU* 357-58

77 J. J. Finkelstein, "The Genealogy of the Hammurapy Dynasty", *JCS* 20 (1966), pp. 95-118 e per i rapporti con le tribù mariote cfr. D. Charpin - J. M. Durand, *art. cit.*, alla precedente nota 18 in particolare p. 159-163. Per i legami con il mondo aramaico cfr. *infra* alle seguenti note 83 e 84.

precedentemente, studiato da E. Lipiński[78] qui ci limiterà a ricordare – senza pretesa all'esaustività – alcuni elementi tra i più significativi che lo legano al mondo amorreo. Nella lessicografia mesopotamica esso appare come sinonimo di Amurrum,[79] nell'iscrizione B di Gudea[80] si ricorda come dei blocchi di alabastro siano stati portati da *tidanum* "la catena montagnosa degli Amorrei". Questa antichissima connessione tra Amorrei e Ditanu[81] è stata proprio recentemente confermata dal testo eblaita MEE 5,[82] 11 perché tale testo VI r ll. 25-26 menziona dapprima il sovrano di *martu*^{ki} e poi VII r ll. 4-5 menziona il sovrano di *da-da-nu*^{ki}, ossia Ditanu.

2.1.3. Ditanu elemento storicamente fondante l'unità dei popoli amorrei

Il procedere mediante il processo logico dell'associazione ha indotto lo scrivente a combinare i dati offerti dalla mitica genealogia di Hammurabi presenti nella tavoletta BM 80328 con altri testi apparsi successivamente ove i medesimi elementi appaiono. La tavoletta del British Museum presenta gli antenati mitici di Hammurapi alcuni dei quali e più precisamente i Hanei della l. 5 e i Numḫu della l. 8 riappaiono anche nel testo di Mari A 12803[83] alla colonna I l. 20 e i Numḫu ibidem l. 21. Come si vede da un punto di vista verticale le tribù amorre di Hana e di Numḫu insediate a Mari reclamavano per se stesse quello stesso antenato mitico Ditanu comune agli Ugaritiani: questo stesso elemento Ditanu antenato mitico di Hammurapi da un

78 Per Ditanu fondamentale il materiale raccolto da E. Lipiński, "Ditanu", in Y. Avishur - J. Blau, *Studies in the Bible and Ancient Near East Presented to S. E. Loewenstamm, on his Seventieth Birthday*, Jerusalem 1978, pp. 95-110.

79 *MSL* III, p. 209 ti-id-nu = a-mur-ru-u.

80 *RIME* 3/1, p. 34 VI: 13-20. Cfr. ora Streck pp. 31-36 § 4.3, p. 337 § 1.201.

81 Per Ditanu cfr. G. Buccellati, *op. cit.*, alla nota 54, pp. 243-244 e D. O. Edzard, *op. cit.*, alla precedente nota 18, p. 31, 33.

82 Testo citato da G. Pettinato, "Il regno MAR-TU nella documentazione di Ebla", in K. Van Leberghe - A. Schoors, *Imigration and Emigration whithin the Ancient Near East, Festschrift E. Lipinski*, Leuven 1995 (*OLA* 65), pp. 229-243 a p. 234; con bibliografia precedente sul problema. Cfr. ora Streck p. 31 § 1.14.

83 Editio princeps par A. Birot, "Fragment de rituel de Mari relatif au kispum", in B. Alster, *Death in Mesopotamia, Papers read at the XXVIe Rencontre assyriologique internationale*, Kopenhagen 1980 (*Mesopotamia Copenhagen Studies in Assyriology* 8), pp. 139-150, texte succesivement publié par J. M. Durand, "Les rituels de Mari", in D. Charpin - J. M. Durand, *Florilegium Marianum III, Recueil d'études à la mémoire de Marie-Thérèse Barrelet, Memoires de Nabu* 4, Paris 1997, pp. 19-78, in particolare pp. 63-70. Cfr. aussi la traduction par M. Dietrich et O. Loretz en TUAT II, pp. 325-326, et J. M. Durand, *Mitología y Religión del Oriente Antiguo*, II/1, *Semitas Occidentales (Ebla, Mari)*, Barcelona 1995, pp. 286-287.

punto di vista orizzontale sarà poi quell'elemento che collegherà orizzontalmente ad Amorrei ed Ugaritiani gli Aramei grazie alla pubblicazione di un gruppo di nuovi testi – gli annali di Suḫu e Rapiqu – pubblicati da A. Cavigneaux e B. Khalil Ismail.[84] Da questi testi emerge come nel primo millennio il governatore di Suḫu Ninurta-kudurri-uṣur pretende di discendere da un Hammurapi.[85] L'effetto esercitato da queste genealogie mitiche non può essere che quello di rafforzare storicamente quella percezione già presente negli studi di un origine comune non solo di Amorrei ed Aramei ma anche degli Ugaritiani. Tale percezione già intravista precedentemente[86] combinata al dato genealogico e al fatto che una parte di queste due popolazioni fossero stanziate in un medesimo territorio non può non fare riflettere anche da un punto di vista linguistico sul problema delle relazioni amorreo-aramaiche. Da un punto di vista territoriale l'insediamento dei Hanei resta rivelatore di questa con-

---

84 A. Cavigneaux - B. Khalil Ismail, "Die Statthalter von Suhu und Mari im 8 Jh. v. chr. anhand neuer Textes aus den irakischen Grabungen im Staugebiet des Qadissiya-Damms", *BM* 21 (1990), pp. 321-456. Per questi testi P. E. Dion, "Les Araméens à l'âge du fer: histoire politique et structures sociales", Paris 1997 (*Etudes bibliques NS* 34), pp. 61-63 e successivamente P. E. Dion, "Les araméens du Moyen-Euphrate au VIIIe siècle à la lumière des inscriptions des maîtres de Suhu et Mari", *SVT* 61 (1995), pp. 53-73. Per la storia di Suhu cfr. N. Haklar, "Die Stellung Suḫis in der Geschichte: Ein Zwischenbilanz", *OA* 22 (1983), pp. 25-36. Per una successiva menzione di Hana nei testi Emar cfr. St. Bassetti, "Anat in a Text from Emar", in D. I. Owen - G. Wilhelm, *Studies in the Civilization and Culture of Nuzi and the Hurrian* 8, R. F. S. Starr, *Memorial Volume Bethesda*, Maryland 1996, pp. 245-46. Per i testi di Emar cfr. *MSK EMAR* VI/1, p. 58 n° 26.

85 11-14, 2:I 1-4, 4:1-4, 5:1-4, 16 :1-3, 17:9-14, 18:I 1-5. Si tenga presente che tale NP era comune in ambito siro-amorreo come prova la sua popolarità nell'onomastica regale: tale è il caso di Hammurapi di Yamkhad cfr. H. Klengel, *Syria 3000 - unto 300 B.C.E. A Handbook of Political History*, Berlin 1992 pp. 58-59 e a Ugarit dove oltre all'ultimo re menzionato in RS RS 34.126 = *CAT* 1.161 alla l. 31 – cfr. precedente nota 73 – anche nella lista regale RS 24.257 = *CAT* 1.113: 20 – cfr. alla seguente nota 111 – ricostruita da K. A. Kitchen – cfr. *art. cit.*, alla seguente nota 111 è stato possibile ricostruire verso il 1800-1740 l'esistenza di un sovrano dal medesimo NP. Per l'etimologia del NP cfr. A. F. Naccache, "ʿAmmurafi et ses cousins", in M. Yon - M. Sznycer - P. Bordreuil, *Le pays d'Ougarit autour de 1200 av. J.-C. Histoire etarchéologie. Actes du Colloque International, Paris 28 juin - 1er Jullet 1995*, (*RSO* XI), pp. 263-268. Sulla lista reale di Ugarit vedasi la prima pubblicazione dei testi RS 94.2518, RS 88.2012, RS 94.2528 e RS 94.2501 in Arnaud bis da cui emerge una tradizione diversa denominata B dallo studioso francese.

86 J. R. Kupper, *op cit.*, alla nota 18, pp. 111-141 e St. A. Kaufman, *The Akkadian Influences on Aramaic*, Chicago 1974 (*Assyriological Studies* 19), pp. 23-24. Cfr. anche R. Zadok, Elements of Aramean Pre-History, M. Cogan - I. Ephʿal, Ah, Assyria ... Studies in Assyrian History and Ancient Near Eastern Historiography Presented to H. Tadmor, Jerusalem 1991, (Scripta Hierosolymitana XXXIII) pp. 104-117, in particolare § 4, p. 107. Per le isoglosse ugaritico-aramaiche cfr. St. Segert, "Ugaritisch und Aramäisch", in St. Segert, *Studia Semitica Philologica necnon philosophica Ioanni Bakoš dicata*, Bratislava 1965, pp. 215-226.

tinuità: all'epoca della documentazione mariota il territorio in questione risulta di occupazione amorrea,[87] i testi di Emar[88] ne documenteranno una presenza aramaica e tale presenza aramaica sarà successivamente confermata dagli annali di Tiglat Pileser I.[89] Questa continuità amorreo – aramaica – hanea troverà degli echi nell'interpretazione proposta da A. R. Millard[90] per la titolatura del re Zakkur[91] (=KAI 202) e nella venerazione rivolta da questo re al dio Mer,[92] divinità tipicamente amorrea.[93] La medesima coincidenza di stanziamento oltre che per la zona tra Hana Rapiqu e Suḫu si riscontra anche per il Gebel Bishri dove dapprima gli Amorrei sono vinti da Šar-kali-Šarri[94] e successivamente Gudea, nell'iscrizione B[95] si vanta di avere apportato da questo luogo delle pietre da costruzione dal Gebel Bishri definito "catena montagnosa degli Amorrei". Anche per il territorio del Gebel Bishri si può constatare la medesima continuità di insediamento prima amorreo e poi aramaico grazie agli annali di Tiglat-Pileser I.[96]

---

87 Per l'epoca di Mari cfr. lo studio di M. Anbar (Bernstein), "La région au Sud du district de Mari", *IOS* 5b (1975), pp. 1-17.

88 D. Arnaud, Emar VI, 3 n. 263 ll. 17-20.Cfr. successivamente R. Zadok, *art. cit.*, alla precedente nota 86, p. 116 § 14.

89 *RIMA* 2, pp. 37-38, 29-35 = ARI § 83 e *RIMA* 2, p. 43, 34-36 = ARI § 97 ; Cfr. anche J. A. Brinkman, *A Political History of Post-Kassite Babylonia*, Rome 1968 (*Analecta Orientalia* 43), pp. 183-184, nota 127. Cfr. ora Streck p. 32 § 1.16.

90 A. R. Millard, *The Homeland of Zakkur*, *Sem.* 39 (1990), pp. 57-52, in particolare p. 50-51; a questo proposito cfr. P. E. Dion, *op. cit.*, alla precedente nota 83, pp. 147-149.

91 KAI 202 A: 2 'š 'nh.

92 KAI 202 A: 1.

93 Sul dio Wer prescindendo dalle speculazioni etimologiche di A. T. Clay, *The Empire of the Amorites*, New Haven 1919 YOS VI) pp. 68-70 vedasi oggi più correttamente M. Bonechi, "Lexique et idéologie royale proto-syrienne", *MARI* 8 (1997), pp. 477-535 in particolare pp. 494-497, p. 481 e § 2.1.2. 5.2, pp. 494- 497.

94 RIME 2, p. 184 Cfr. Buccellati, *op. cit.*, alla precedente nota 53, pp. 236-237, D. O. Edzard *op. cit.*, alla precedente nota 18, p. 31, 33, 35-36. Cfr. più recentemente per un'indagine archeologica del sito O. J. Zarins, "Jebel Bishri and the Amorite Homeland: The PPNB phase", in M. C. Haex - H. H. Curvers P. M. M. G. Akkermans, *To the Euphrates and Beyond. Archaeological Studies in Honour of M. N. Van Loon*, Rotterdam 1989 pp. 29-51.

95 RIME 3/1, p. 34-33-12. Per il Gebel Bishri in epoca medio-babilonese cfr. R. Zadok, *art. cit.*, alla precedente nota 86, pp. 108-110 § 8.

96 RIMA 2 p. 23, V 44-63 = ARI § 34 Cfr. lo studio di G. M. Schwartz, "The Origins of the Arameans in Syria and Northern Mesopotamia. Research Problems and Potential Strategies", in M. C. Haex - H. H. Curvers P. M. M. G. Akkermans, *To the Euphrates and Beyond. Archaeological Studies in*

2.2. Altri elementi siro-amorrei nella mitologa ugaritica

Oltre all'elemento Ditanu – sul quale cfr. precedente §§ 2.1.1 - 2.1.3 – altri elementi ci obbligano ad inserire la mitologia ugaritica nel contesto amorreo: essi sono dei dati precisi di geografia mitologica – qui volutamente non sono state prese in considerazione ipotetiche interpretazioni globali dei miti – e cioè la constatazione che il contesto geografico in cui si svolgono i miti ugaritici, – diversa considerazione richiedono i testi economici[97] – fa vedere abbastanza chiaramente come il paese di Canaan[98] non era il naturale teatro della mitologia ugaritica.

Il testimone più evidente di questa estraneità è in primo luogo il fatto che la battaglia tra Yam e Baal si svolge sul Gebel Akra[99] subito identificato con la montagna dello Sapon. Tale montagna è sacra a Baᶜal come provano le diverse menzioni della divinità bᶜl ṣpn nei testi cultuali[100] come pure su di essa, sempre nei testi cultuali,[101] era venerata la dea Anat, che forse aveva la sua origine su di essa.[102] La lotta tra

---

Honour of M. N. Van Loon, Rotterdam 1989, pp. 275-291. Cfr. R. Zadok, *art. cit.*, alla precedente nota 86 pp. 108-110 § 8.

97 P. Xella, "Ugarit et les Phéniciens. identité culturelle et rapports historiques", in M. Dietrich - O. Loretz, *Ugarit. Ein Ostmediterranees Kulturzentrum im Alten Orient. Ergebnisse und Perspektiven der Forschung, I, Ugarit und seine altorientalische Umwelt*, Münster 1995 (*ALASP* 7), pp. 239-266, particolarmente per i rapporti con il mondo fenicio la lista della documentazione a pp. 257-260; D. Arnaud, "Les ports de la "Phénicie" à la fin de l'âge du bronze réecent (XIV-XIII siècles) d'après les textes cunéiformes de Syrie", *SMEA* 30 (1988), pp. 179-194, particolarmente utile la lista della documentazione alle pp. 192-194 dove sono citati dei testi ancora inediti.

98 Cfr. sopra § 1.1. Per una delimitazione dl paese di Canaan dal punto di vista della geografia storica cfr. da ultimo N. P. Lemche, *op. cit.*, alla precedente nota 24 pp. 25-52 e precedentemente M. Weippert, "Kanaan", *RLA* V, pp. 352-355 nonché R. De Vaux, "Le pays de Canaan", *JAOS* 88 (1968), pp. 23-30 in particolare p. 27.

99 Per una primissima identificazione cfr. O. Eissfeldt, *Baal Zaphon, Zeus Kasios und der Durchzeug der Israeliten durchs Meer*, Halle 1932 (*Beiträge zur Geschichte des Altertums* 1. p. 5, 1. P. Bordreuil, "Arrou Gourou et sapanou: Circonscriptions Administratives et géographie mythique du Royaume d'Ougarit", *Syria* 61 (1984), pp. 1-10; P. Bordreuil, *Recherches Ougaritiques*, I Où Baal a-t-il remporté la victoire contre Yam?, *Semitica* 40 (1991), pp. 17-27. Per la stele RS 4.427 cfr. il recente studio di M. Yon, in M. Yon (a cura di), *Arts et industries de la pierre*, *RSO* VI, Paris 1991, pp. 294-299, n° 5, p. 326 fig. 5, p. 331, fig. 11a, p. 330 fig. D per il dettaglio della base.

100 bᶜl ṣpn nei testi cultuali *CAT* 1.39:10, 1.41:33, 1.46:12,14, 1.87:36, 1.109:5,9, 29, 32, 1.112:22, 1.118:4, 1.130:22, 1.148:2, 26, 27, 1.173:5.

101 ᶜnt ṣpn nei testi cultuali 1.46:17, 1.109:13,17, 1.130:13.

102 Per questa ipotesi cfr. P. Bordreuil, "La deesse ᶜAnat et les sources du Sapon", in B. Geyer, *Techniques et pratiques hydro-agricoles traditionelles en domaine irrigué. Approche pluridisciplinaire des modes de culture avant la motorisation en Syrie, Actes du Colloque de Damas 27 Juin 1er juillet 1987*, tome 2, Paris 1990 (*BAH* 136), pp. 257-268.

Baʿal e Yam, che è uno degli elementi centrali della mitologia ugaritica, trova degli antecedenti a Mari[103] nel testo A 1968 studiato recentemente da J. M. Durand[104] e subito paragonato ai testi CAT 1.2 IV 4-30, CAT 1.6 V: 1-6 da P. Bordreuil e D. Pardee[105] e CAT 1.3:III 37- IV 4.

Un'altra testimonianza di questa estraneità geografica del paese di Canaan è offerta dal testo RS 24.244 = CAT 1.100[106] che invoca divinità siriane e più precisamente Dagan di Tuttul – linea 15 – ṯṯ wkmṯ di ḫryth[107] – linea 36 – e Astarte di Mari[108] linea 78.

Volendo prendere in considerazione un'ulteriore elemento e ben noto tra le affinità bibliche e ugaritiche non si può non fare un accenno alla mitica figura del Leviatano, presente nella Bibbia ebraica[109] dove si presenta con gli stessi epiteti di "serpente guizzante e tortuoso" in Is. 27:1 e di mostro a più teste in Ps 74:14 come nei passi CAT 1.5: I,1-3//CAT 1.5: I, 27-30 e CAT 1.3: III, 41-42, ma anche questa

---

103 P. Bordreuil - D. Pardee, "Le combat de Baʿlu avec Yammu d'après les textes ougaritiques", *MARI* 7 (1993), pp. 63-70; J. M. Durand, "Le mythologème du Combat entre le dieu de l'orage et la Mer en Mésopotamie", *MARI* 7 (1993), pp. 41-61.

104 J. M. Durand, "Le mythologème du Combat entre le dieu de l'orage et la Mer en Mésopotamie", *MARI* 7 (993), pp. 41-61, specificatamente pp. 43-46 per la pubbicazione ed il commentario del testo A 1968. A questo proposito cfr. anche P. Bordreuil - D. Pardee, *art. cit.*, alla seguente nota 105, p. 69.

105 P. Bordreuil - D. Pardee, "Le combat de Baʿlu avec Yammu d'après les textes ougaritiques", *MARI* 7 (1993), pp. 63-70, per *CAT* 1.2 IV 4-30 cfr. pp. 63-64, per *CAT* 1.6 V: 1-6 cfr. p.65, per *CAT* 1.3:III 37-IV 4 cfr. pp. 65-66.

106 P. Xella, *I testi rituali di Ugarit*, I, *Testi*, Roma 1981 (*Studi semitici* 54), pp. 224-240; A. Caquot - J. M. de Tarrragon, *Textes ougaritiques*, II, *Texte religieux et rituels, Introduction, Traduction, Commentaire, Littératures du Proche Orient Ancien*, Paris 1989 a cura di A. Caquot, pp. 79-94. D. Pardee, *op. cit.*, alla precedente nota 74, pp. 192-226. *TUAT* II, pp. 329, 345-350; P. Bordreuil, "Des serpents et des dieux. Magie et divinités syrienne dans le mythe ougaritique de Horon et les serpents", in *Simposium International. Histoire de Deir ez-zûr et ses antiquités, Deir Ez Zor 2-6 octobre 1983*, AAAS 34 (1986) pp. 183-188.

107 D. Pardee, *op. cit.*, alla precedente nota 74, p. 212 nota 64. Su questa divinità cfr. da ultimo H. P. Müller, *DDD*, pp. 186-189, p. 187 in particolare. Per Kamiš a Ebla cfr. F. Pomponio - P. Xella, *Les dieux d'Ebla. Etude analytique des divinités eblaïtes à l'époque des archives royales du III millénaire*, Münster 1997 (*AOAT* 245), pp. 175-181, U. Worschech, "Der Gott Kamosch. versuch einer Charakteriesierung", *UF* 24 (1992), pp. 393-401; F. Israel, "ṯṯ wkmṯ les avatars de l'enigmatique dieu ṯṯ", *Sem* 41-42 (1991-1992), pp. 59-62.

108 P. Bordreuil, "Ashtart de Mari et les dieux d'Ougarit", *MARI* 4 (1985), pp. 545-547.

109 Is 27:1, Ps 74:14, Ps 104:26, Job 3:8, Job 40:25.

figura ha antecedenti siriani in diversi testi eblaiti dove appare un mostro a sette teste come emerge da due recenti studi dovuti proprio a P. Fronzaroli.[110]

2.3. Il sigillo dinastico amorreo di yaqarum

Nella lista regale d'Ugarit RS 24.257 = CAT 1.113[111] fatta oggetto di un dettagliato ed acuto studio da parte di K. A. Kitchen[112] appare il nome del primo re di Ugarit *yqr* – linea 26. Questo nome corrisponde a quello *yaqarum* menzionato nel sigillo dinastico ugaritico, che porta la seguente legenda *ya-qa-rum mar ni-iq-ma-du šar ^{al}u-ga-ri-it*. Questo sigillo dinastico, di chiara ispirazione paleoebabilonese,[113] quanto a iconografia, ma d'epoca culturalmente amorrea, è stato fatto oggetto innanzitutto di un dettagliato studio da parte di J. Nougayrol[114] per quanto concerne il suo uso nei testi amministrativi ugaritici; recentemente esso è stato riesaminato da D. Arnaud[115] dal punto di vista epigrafico e secondo lo studioso francese esso deve essere ritenuto più recente di quanto proposto da J. Nougayrol.[116] Tuttavia il motivo iconografico d'epoca culturalmente amorrea costituisce un secondo elemento che concorre a connettere la casa regnante ugaritica al mondo amorreo. Il fatto che esso sia stato perso e poi riprodotto ci sembra essere il miglior testimonio di questa consapevolezza da parte dei sovrani ugaritici.

3. Tratti linguistici amorrei e cananei nell'ugaritico

3.1. Tratti linguistici amorrei nell'ugaritico

Oggi grazie alla recente rielaborazione dei dati linguistici amorrei di E. E. Knudsen[117] sulla base dei materiali raccolti da I. J. Gelb[118] si deve tenere presente

---

110 P. Fronzaroli, "Les combats de Hadda dans les textes d'Ebla", *MARI* 8 (1997), pp. 283-290, in particolare pp. 285-286 per l'interpretazione dei diversi passi. Cfr. successivamente dello stesso P. Fronzaroli, "Il serpente dalle sette teste a Ebla", in A. Acquaro, *Alle soglie della classicità Il Mediterraneo tra tradizione e innovazione, Studi in onore di S. Moscati*, Roma 1996, pp. 1135-1144.

111 Cfr. il commentario di D. Pardee, *op. cit.*, alla nota 75, pp. 165-178.

112 K. A. Kitchen, "The King List of Ugarit", *UF* 9 (1977) pp. 131-142. Cfr. ora Arnaud bis p. 163.

113 E. Auerbach, *Heirloom. Seals and Political Depicting in Late Bronze Age Syria*.

114 *Ugaritica* III, pp. 67-77 cui aggiungasi *PRU* III, pp. XXIV-XXV e XL-XLIII.

115 D. Arnaud, "Prolegomenes à la rédaction d'une historie d'Ugarit I: Ougarit avant Suppilluliuma 1er" *SMEA* 39 (1997), pp. 151-161, pp. 158-161 in particolare.

116 Cfr. indipendentemente da noi anche I. Singer, *art. cit.*, alla precedente nota 71, pp. 611-612.

117 Cfr. E. E. Knudsen, *art. cit.*, alla precedente nota 57.

118 I. J. Gelb, *op. cit.*, alla precedente nota 56.

che alcuni tratti morfologici scelti da A. Goetze[119] che allora erano di incerta attestazione, oggi invece appaiono non solo di sicura attestazione nell'amorreo ma sono di natura contrastiva con il cananaico. Qui ci si soffermerà sui seguenti tratti morfologici:

1) Pron. pers. ind. di 1° p. s. comune = nr. 11 della lista di A. Goetze. La forma anāku dell'ugaritico[120] e dell'amorreo[121] si oppone alla forma amarniana *anōkî*[122] – poco attestata ma sicuramente presente perché strutturalmente legata alla forma dell'affisso verbale di 1° p. s. del perfetto[123] che sarà esaminata al seguente punto 2.

2) Affisso verbale -tî 1° p. s. del perfetto = nr. 8 della lista di A. Goetze. Seguendo la ricostruzione proposta da J. Blau[124] è lecito ricostruire nell'ugaritico la forma *-tu*[125] che si oppone alla forma *-tî* comune in tutta la documentazione amarniana.[126]

3) Affisso verbale ed il suffisso pronominale di 1. p. pl. = nr. 13 della lista di A. Goetze.[127] L'ugaritico presenta una chiara attestazione vocalizzata di tale tratto

---

119 Cfr. *art. cit.*, alla precedente nota 8 in particolare lista alla p.128-130.

120 D. Sivan, *A Grammar of Ugaritic Language*, Leiden 1997 (*Handbuch der Orientalistik* 28), pp. 49-59 con confronto con *Ugaritica* V 130 III 12' a-na-ku cfr. J. Huehnergard, *Ugaritic Vocabulary on Syllabic Transcription*, Atlanta 1987 (*HSS* 32), p. 108.

121 E. E. Knudsen, *art. cit.*, alla precedente nota 57: in particolare p. 876. Voir aussi I. J. Gelb, *op. cit.*, alla precedente nota 55, p. 560, n° 471, a-na-ku-DINGIR-LAMMA, n° 472 a-na-ku-la-ma.

122 Cfr. Rainey I p. 47-56, specialmente p. 47 per la lettera di Gerusalemme EA 287= LA 38: ll. 66, 79.

123 Condividiamo la ricostruzione di J. Blau, "Zu Lautlehre und Vokalismus des Ugaritischen", *UF* 11 (1979), pp. 55-62, in particolare p. 61 § 9.

124 J. Blau, "Zu Lautlehre und Vokalismus des Ugaritischen", *UF* 11 (1979), pp. 55-62, in particolare p. 61 § 9.

125 Cfr. ora Tropper p. 465 § 73.331.4.

126 Per le attestazioni cfr. Rainey 2, pp. 284-287, per una valutazione geografica cfr. F. M. Th. Böhl, *Die Sprache der Amarna Briefe mit besonderer Beücksictigung der Kanaanismen Leipzig*, 1909 (*Leipziger Semitistischen Studien* V, 2, pp. 46-48 § 27 n-r. Per la distribuzione geografica delle forme ibride cfr. *ibidem*, pp. 58-59 § 29 b-c). Distribuendo i dati raccolti da A. F. Rainey per le forme non ibride questo tratto morfologico appare nella Fenicia a Byblos e Tiro, sulla costa a Gezer, nella Palestina settentrionale, centrale e meridionale, nella valle dell'Oronte a Qadesh e a Kumidi. Per quest'ultima località si aggiungono altre forme nel documento pubblicato da cfr. D. Arnaud, "Une lettre de Kamid el Loz", *Sem* 40 (1991), pp. 7-16;: *uš-ši-ir-ti* ll. 7, 11, *ḫa-al-ti* l. 12, che si accompagnano ad altri perfetti cananaici *šap-ra-ta* l.5, *ḫa-al-ta* l.8 e alla glossa *nu-ḫu-uš-ti* linea 24. Per l'utilizzazione linguistica dei testi di Kamid el Loz cfr. in Rainey 4 p. 187. Al dossier di Byblos va aggiunta la lettera pubblicata da J. Huehnergard, "A Byblos Letter. probably from Kamid el Loz", *ZA* 86 (1996), pp. 97-113 dove alle linee 18, 22 compare la forma ibrida *iš-ši-ir-ti*.

127 Cfr. A. Goetze, *art. cit.*, alla precedente nota 8, p. 121 nota 51.

morfologico nel NP dAddu-la-na.[128] Tale NP mostra il suffisso *-na* che converge con l'amorreo[129] e nel primo millennio con l'aramaico[130] ma diverge dal cananeo di El Amarna che impiega sia come affisso verbale[131] che come pronome suffisso[132] *-nu* attestato nell'area cananaica con sicurezza solo nell'ebraico[133] sia in funzione di affisso verbale che di pronome e suffisso.

3.2. Tratti linguistici cananaici dell'ugaritico

Tra gli elementi addotti da J. Tropper[134] come significativi per sostenere l'appartenenza dell'ugaritico al Cananaico alcuni ci sembrano certi mentre altri richiederebbero una discussione più approfondita perché passibili di diversa interpretazione.

---

128 RS 8.213:3 editio princeps F. Thureau Dangin, "Trois Contrats de Ras Shamra", *Syria* 18 (1937), pp. 245-55, pp. 251-253. Da un punto di vista semantico cfr. per questo NP il parallelo *ya-a-ḫu-u-la-ki-im* cfr. M. D. Coogan, *West Semitic Personal Names in the Murašu Documents*, Missoula Montana 1976 (*Harvard Semitic Monographs* 1), p. 27, p. 109.

129 Per le attestazioni cfr. G. Buccellati, *op. cit.*, alla precedente nota 54, p. 192 § 3.1.1.1.8.

130 K. Tsereteli, "Grammatica generale dell'aramaico", *Henoch* 17 (1995), pp. 3-102, in particolare p. 46 per il pron. suffisso p. 50 per il suffisso del perfetto.

131 Attestazioni in Rainey 1, pp. 85-88 in Byblos, a Gezer, nella Palestina meridionale a Gerusalemme, nella Palestina centrale a Megiddo e nella Palestina settentrionale, e nella valle dell'Oronte.

132 Per le attestazioni Rainey 1, pp. 66-68 che segnala che il tratto morfologico è distribuito geograficamente in tutti i dossier.

133 La sola trascrizione fenicia certa appare a Costantina KAI 175:2 ρυβαθων che non lascia vedere quale sia la vocale finale. Altri tentativi di individuare il nostro suffisso sono stati fatti ma si sono rivelati superati: ad es la sua attestazione è stata proposta in Poenulus 939 *ynnynu* da Friedrich e da St. Segert, St. Segert, *A Grammar of Phoenician and Punic*, München 1976, p. 60, § 51.224, pp. 99-100 per Poenulus 936 *tnu* "con noi". Tali interpretazioni devono essere abbandonate grazie alle diverse interpretazioni di M. Sznycer, *Les passages puniques en transcription latine dans le "Poenulus" de Plaute*, Paris 1967 (*Etudes et Commentaires* LXV) per i versi suddetti, cfr. in particolare p. 89 per *tnu* e pp. 106-107 per *ynnynnu*. Per quanto concerne il suffisso verbale J. Friedrich - W. Röllig, *Phönizisch-Punische Grammatik*, Rom 1970², § 112 pp. 47-50 -nu fanno uso dell'ebraico e per il suffisso pronominale ricorrono a EA 264 = LA 74:18 - Palestina meridionale - *ru-šu-nu* e per il suffisso verbale ricorrono a p 57 § 128 a EA 174 = LA 224: 8 *e-ba-ša-nu* - dalla Beqaʿ -.

134 J. Tropper, "Is Ugaritic a Canaanite Language", in G. I. Brooke - A. H. W. Curtis - J. F. Healey, *Ugarit and the Bible. Proceedings of the International Symposium on Ugarit and the Bible, Manchester, September 1992*, (*UBL* 11), pp. 343-353. lo studioso tedesco in particolare alle pp. 346-347 non accetta i punti fermi stabiliti da J. Huehnergard perché egli ricostruisce *quttil* e *šuqtil* per i temi verbali D e Š nel cananeo di El Amarna, il fatto che anōkî sia attestato a Samal e in Palmireno - ma in reltà si tratta di un unicum Tadmorea 18 per il quale cfr. J. T. Milik, *Recherches d'épigraphie proche-orientale I Dédicacs faites par des dieux (Pqalmyre, Hatra, Tyr) et des thiases sémitiques à l'époque romaine*, Paris 1972 (*BH* 92). pp. 289-292, e se attestato indice di ā > ō. per il pronome di I p. pl. non tiene conto del dato onomastico ugaritico da noi citato.

Tra gli elementi che allo stato attuale della nostra ricerca possono essere considerati sicuramente cananaici vanno posti:

1) l'operatività della legge Barth Ginsberg[135] che si riscontra anche nel cananeo di El Amarna[136] ma non nell'amorreo[137] e che nel primo millennio sarà operativa prima nell'ebraico ma solo posteriormente nell'aramaico,[138]

2) il pronome interrogativo *miya,*[139]

3) la flessione del plurale maschile e del duale,[140]

4) la terminazione locativa *ah,*[141]

5) il comportamento del verbo *hlk,*[142]

6) il sistema modale,[143]

---

135 J. Barth, "Zur vergleichenden semitischen Grammatik", *ZDMG* 48 (1894), pp. 1-21, in particolare pp. 4-6. A. F. Rainey, A. F. Rainey, "The Barth-Ginsberg Law in the Amarna Tablets", *EI* 14 (1978), pp. 9*-13*; J. Barth, "Zur vergleichenden semitischen Grammatik", *ZDMG* 48 (1984), pp. 1-21, in particolare pp. 4-6.

136 J. Tropper, *art. cit.*, alla precedente nota 134, p. 348. Per El Amarna cfr. per la funzionalità della legge a El Amarna cfr. Rainey vol. 2, p. 10, pp. 61-75 e precedentemente A. F. Rainey, "The Barth-Ginsberg Law in the Amarna Tablets", *EI* 14 (1978), pp. 9*-13*. Si fanno seguire le attestazioni tenendo conto della distribuzione geografica: *yi-ša-al-šu* EA 60 = LA 235:21 da Lakish, *yi-il$_5$-ma-ad* EA 64= LA 33:8, Palestina meridionale, *yi-iḫ-na-nu-ni* EA 137 = LA 192:81 Medio Giordano, *ir-ka-ab-mi* EA 245= LA 93:11da Megiddo, *yi-il-ma-du* EA 251 = LA 87:9 dalla Palestina centrale, *yi-il-ma-ad* EA 264 = LA 74:23 dalla Palestina centrale, *iḫ-la-aq* EA 270=LA 47:29 da Gezer, te-e"-la-aq EA 274=LA 84:14 dal Medio Giordano. A questi esempi si aggiunga dal dossier di Gerusalemme il NP *e-en-ḫa-mu* EA 286 - LA 40:28 e la variante grafica *ye-e'-en-ḫa-mu* Nella lettera di Kumidi pubblicata da D. Arnaud, cfr. *infra* nota 61- alla l. 20 si può forse aggiungere la forma *]i-ka-lu* come pure nella letera da Byblos pubblicata da J. Huehnergard cfr. nota 61 le forme *yi-i-de* l.19 e *yi-il-qa* l. 32. Per la sua funzionalità in ugaritico riconosciuta come operativa in ugaritico già da H. L. Ginsberg, *Tarbi* 4 (1932-1933), pp. 382-383 difficilmente accessibile. Più facilmente accessibile anche se oggi gli esempi in grafia alfabetica *ilak, išal* confermano l'operatività della legge, l'articolo di H. L. Ginsberg, "Two Religious Borrowings in Ugaritic Literature I: A Hurrian Myth in Semitic Dress", *Or.* 8 (1939), pp. 317-327, in particolare pp. 318-322.

137 C. H. Gordon, "Amorite and Eblaite" in R. Hetzron, *The Semitic Languages*, London 1997, pp. 100-113, p.103 e precedentemente S. Moscati, *op. cit.*, alla nota 20, p. 91 § 10.

138 Kl. Beyer, *Die Aramäischen Texte vom Toten Meer*, Göttingen 1984, pp. 108-112.

139 J. Tropper, *art. cit.*, alla precedente nota 134, p. 349. Cfr. ora Tropper pp. 238-239 § 44.11.

140 J. Tropper, *art. cit.*, alla precedente nota 134, p. 349. Cfr. ora Tropper pp. 289 ss. § 53.2 per il duale, p. 293 ss. § 53.3 per il plurale.

141 J. Tropper, *art. cit.*, alla precedente nota 134, p. 349. Cfr. ora Tropper pp. 320 s. § 34.3.

142 J. Tropper, *art. cit.*, alla precedente nota 134, p. 349. Cfr. ora Tropper pp. 624-625 § 75.3.

143 J. Tropper, *art. cit.*, alla precedente nota 134, p. 350.

7) l'impiego dell'infinito assoluto come tempo narrativo.[144]

Altri fatti addotti dal collega tedesco invece ci sembrano attualmente destinati ad un ulteriore approfondimento:

1) la presenza delle laterali śin e ḍad in ugaritico e in cananeo,[145]

2) l'evoluzione di dittonghi,[146]

3) gli imperfetti dei verbi *primae aleph yubd*, *yuhb*, *yuḫd*, *yukl*, *yusp*,[147]

4) il prefisso verbale della 3a p. pl. + suffisso *n*.[148]

4. Conclusioni

Riprendendo qui quanto esposto in un nostro precedente studio[149] dobbiamo subito precisare che a fini classificatori l'innovazione euristica introdotta da J. Huehnergard[150] si è rivelata per noi quanto mai utile perché grazie ad alcuni punti fermi da lui stabiliti si sono potuti stabilire dei punti fermi contrastivamente divergenti tra Amorreo e Cananaico – per il concetto di Cananaico cfr. § 1.2) – . Ora si è anche visto che tra Ugaritico e Cananeo di El Amarna vi sono dei punti di convergenza alcuni dei quali si prolungano fino al fenicio ed all'ebraico. Questi punti richiamati da molto tempo all'attenzione degli studiosi da parte di H. L. Ginsberg[151] e più recentemente da parte di J. Tropper[152] apparentemente obbligherebbero ad iscrivere l'Ugaritico nel Cananaico ma ciò non è possibile per due motivi: la presenza di tratti amorrei nell'Ugaritico e la mancata appartenenza geografica di Ugarit all'area cananaica – cfr. sopra § 1.1) –. La compresenza di due tipi linguistici era stata in parte

144 J. Tropper, *art. cit.*, alla precedente nota 134, p. 350. Cfr. ora Tropper pp. 491-492 § 75.531 e per la vocalizzazione pp. 479-485 § 73.51.

145 J. Tropper, *art. cit.*, alla precedente nota 134, pp. 347-348.

146 J. Tropper, *art. cit.*, alla precedente nota 134, p. 348. Cfr. ora Tropper pp. 187-193 § 33.31.

147 J. Tropper, *art. cit.*, alla precedente nota 134, pp. 348-349. Cfr. ora Tropper pp. 610-616 § 75.21.

148 J. Tropper, *art. cit.*, alla precedente nota 134, p. 349. Cfr. ora Tropper pp. 44 s. § 73.233.43.

149 F. Israel, *art. cit.*, alla precedente nota 37.

150 J. Huehnergard, "Remarks on the Classification of the Northwest Semitic Languages", in J. Hoftijzer - G. Van der Kooij, *The Balaam Text from Deir ʿAlla Re-evaluated. Proceedings of the International Symposium Held at Leiden 21-24 August 1989*, Leiden 1991, pp. 282-293, nonché per gli stessi elementi protocananaici in *ABD* IV p. 160 e albero genealogico p. 157.

151 H. L. Ginsberg, *art. cit.*, alla precedente nota 39.

152 J. Tropper, *art. cit.*, alla precedente nota 134.

intuita nel corso degli studi sia da parte di C. Brockelmann,[153] di H. Goeseke[154] e di J. F. Brent[155] che avevano constato tale situazione. Di particolare rilievo restano le conclusioni di J. F. Brent che dopo aver riassunto le diverse posizioni espresse sul problema della classificazione dell'ugaritico, concludeva che l'ugaritico non andava escluso della storia comune del semitico nordoccidentale e che le differenze tra Cananeo e Ugaritico andavano spiegate alla luce della conservazione e del relativo isolamento dai centri di innovazione linguistica. I pareri di questi studiosi appena citati vengono a coincidere con il parere di W. Von Soden[156] e di D. Pardee[157] ricordati all'inizio di questo studio. In conclusione la compresenza, enucleabile dalla documentazione ugaritica, di elementi amorrei – elencati al precedente § 3.1) – e di elementi cananei – elencati al precedente § 3.2) – è da intendersi in termini di sostrato – i primi – e di astratto – i secondi – . In questa prospettiva storica si dovranno abbandonare a fini classificatori i criteri della logica binaria dell'inclusione e dell'esclusione che sono tipici della classificazione genealogica: in tal modo la classificazione dell'ugaritico non diventerà altro che la descrizione storica della formazione dello stato ugaritico. In questa prospettiva fatto storico e dato linguistico troveranno una mutua giustificazione. La definizione già citata di W. Von Soden dell'ugaritico come "lingua siriana con superstrati cananei" rimane pertanto quella che più sinteticamente rende conto della formazione della lingua di Ugarit. Gli elementi amorrei, i.e. siriani nella terminologia di W. Von Soden, infatti trovano la ragione della loro presenza non solo alla luce di quanto esposto al § 2) ma anche dal fatto che non bisogna dimenticare come i secoli ancora oscuri di Ugarit siano stati dei secoli amorrei come provano gli indizi attualmente disponibili forniti dal dossier relativo al viaggio effettuato da Zimri Lim nel periodo che va dall'ultimo mese del suo ottavo anno di regno ai primi quattro mesi del nono, recentemente studiato da P.

---

153 C. Brockelmann, "Kananäisch und Ugaritisch", *HdO* III, 1 *Semitistik*, Leiden 1953, pp. 40-58, in particolare pp. 45-46 per la descrizione dei fatti essenziali ossia fonetica, flessione nominale, preposizione l, sistema verbale a due tempi a prefisso, sistema modale, a p. 46 il lessico. Brockelmann sottolinea sempre a p. 46 gli elementi cananei nella mitologia.

154 H. Goeseke, "Die Sprache der semitischen Texte aus Ugarit und ihre Stellung innerhalb des Semitischen", *Wissenschaftliche Zeitschrift der Martin Luther-Universität*, Halle-Wittenberg VII/3 1959, pp. 623-652.

155 J. F. Brent, "The Problem of the Placement of Ugaritic among the Semitic Languages", *Westminster Theological Journal* 41 (1978), pp. 83-107, in particolare pp. 104-107.

156 W. Von Soden, *art. cit.*, alle precedenti note 15 e 16.

157 Cfr. *art. cit.*, alla precedente nota 12.

Vilard.[158] Altri elementi di quest'epoca per il momento restano ancora da scoprire e sarà compito delle generazioni future occuparsene. Alla luce dei dati storici che allora emergeranno la posizione linguistica dell'ugaritico potrà essere ulteriormente chiarita confermando, noi lo crediamo fermamente, l'ipotesi qui proposta. Allora sarà possibile proporre per l'ugaritico anche una periodizzazione – cosa oggi quasi impossibile[159] – se non limitatamente ad alcuni testi che rendono etimologicamente le consonanti interdentali segnalati anche da P. Fronzaroli[160] più di quaranta anni fa.

158 Cfr. *Ugaritica* I, pp. 16-18, testo tradotto da G. Dossin, in *Syria* 18 (1937), p. 74 nota 1 e poi dossier completato da P. Vilard, "Un roi de Mari à Ugarit", *UF* 18 (1986), pp. 387-412.

159 St. Segert, *op. cit.*, alla precedente nota 2, p. 15 § 13.1 e D. Pardee, *art. cit.*, alla precedente nota 12, p. 131.

160 Ci si riferisce ai testi RS 2.002 = *CAT* 1.23, RS 5.300 = *CAT* 1.71 non sfuggiti nella loro peculiarità all'attenzione C. Brockelmann, *Kananäische Miszellen, Festschrift O. Eissfeldt zum 60 Geburtstage 1. September 1947*, Halle 1947, pp. 61-67, in particolare cfr. "Dialektmischung" in *Ugarit*, pp. 61-63, e P. Fronzaroli, "La fonetica ugaritica", Roma 1955 (*Sussidi eruditi* 7), pp. 22-24 § 13 per il testo RS 2.012 = *CAT* 1.12 e pp. 34-35 § 19 per il testo RS 5.194 = *CAT* 1.24.

IL RUOLO DI TARḪUNTAŠŠA
DA MUWATALLI II A ŠUPPILULIUMA II

ANNA MARGHERITA JASINK

Università di Firenze

Le interpretazioni tradizionali sullo spostamento della capitale ittita da Ḫattuša a Tarḫuntašša da parte di Muwatalli sono state ridiscusse di recente.[1] Tale spostamento è stato considerato il punto cruciale di un disegno a carattere soprattutto religioso che avrebbe forse avuto anche la conseguenza di suddividere il regno fra i due figli, Urḫi-Tešup e Kurunta. Non si tratterebbe pertanto di un'esigenza dettata soltanto da una insicurezza dei confini settentrionali e dall'opportunità di una maggior vicinanza alle operazioni militari in Siria ma di un progetto di ben più ampia portata. Se una tale ipotesi è esatta ne consegue che il nuovo regno di Tarḫuntašša negli intenti di Muwatalli doveva avere un'estensione molto ampia, col controllo strategico sia del Paese Basso che delle vie di transito meridionali. I due rilievi di Muwatalli rinvenuti a Sirkeli e la costruzione della fortezza di Meydancikkalesi potrebbero rappresentare una testimonianza dell'importanza assunta dal sud dell'Anatolia in questo periodo: i primi,[2] nell'area orientale della pianura cilicia, in posizione cen-

1 V. Houwink ten Cate 1994, p. 233, il quale ritiene che la spartizione voluta da Muwatalli sia da applicare fra lui stesso e Ḫattušili, che avrebbe mantenuto il controllo del nord come re di Ḫakpis; in tal modo quella parte della corte ostile a Muwatalli avrebbe potuto optare per Ḫattušili, senza altri tentativi di rovesciamento dell'autorità di Muwatalli. Il Singer, 1996, pp. 191 sgg., 1998, pp. 539 sgg., propone invece di riconoscere nella decisione di Muwatalli di creare una nuova capitale l'atto conclusivo di una operazione a carattere religioso, intesa a riconquistare il favore del dio della tempesta. In tale operazione i centri religiosi dell'area centro-meridionale e sud-orientale dell'Anatolia avrebbero avuto un nuovo impulso in un culto di stato che vedeva in posizione preminente il dio della tempesta *piḫaššašši*, assunto a divinità personale di Muwatalli, al quale venne appunto dedicata la nuova capitale Tarḫuntašša. La motivazione addotta dal Singer, pur molto diversa da quella di Houwink ten Cate, non contrasta con una suddivisione del regno che comunque privilegiava l'area centro-meridionale: Urḫi-Tešup, l'erede al trono, avrebbe dovuto prendere il posto del padre a Tarḫuntašša, mentre si può presumere che il secondogenito avrebbe sostituito lo zio, alle cure del quale era stato affidato forse proprio con questa finalità, nell'area centro-settentrionale dell'Anatolia. Non possiamo sapere con certezza se l'intento di Muwatalli fosse quello di una reale suddivisione del regno o se Kurunta avrebbe in qualche modo dovuto esser soggetto al fratello maggiore.

2 Sul secondo rilievo, pubblicato di recente da Ehringhaus 1995, p. 118 e Neve 1996, pp. 19 sgg., v. Börker-Klähn 1996, pp. 39 sgg., con conclusioni negative sulla proposta che Sirkeli rappresentasse il

trale lungo il corso del Ceyhan sia rispetto alle vie provenienti dal nord (dalla zona di Kozan e da quella delle Porte Cilicie) che in direzione est verso la Siria, volti a sottolineare per i passanti la presenza dell'autorità del sovrano su una zona particolarmente strategica; la seconda,[3] come baluardo militare a difesa della valle del Calycadnos e forse del porto di Ura. La localizzazione della città di Tarḫuntašša rimane in ogni caso un problema aperto. Delle varie aree di ubicazione proposte[4] ritengo la più plausibile l'area a nord delle pendici del Tauro, in quanto appare come la meglio rispondente alle esigenze di Muwatalli. È una zona ricca di centri abitati, noti da numerosi testi ittiti di diverso contenuto,[5] non localizzabili con certezza ma che costituiscono nel loro insieme una fascia che da est, nella zona di Ereğli, raggiunge e oltrepassa ad ovest Konya fino a Beyşehir. Si tratta nel suo complesso dell'area meridionale della conca centrale formata dall'altopiano anatolico, che in età ittita era definita come Paese Basso. Come rileva Alp,[6] Ḫattušili nella sua "Apologia" (I 75 sgg.) ribadisce lo spostamento di Muwatalli nel Paese Basso dietro ordine della sua divinità; nella preghiera di Muwatalli, antecedente allo spostamento della capitale, hanno un grosso rilievo sotto il profilo del culto una serie di città localizzabili in questa stessa zona.[7] Sembrano tutti indizi di un interesse precipuo del sovrano per questa area. Quindi aver creato una nuova capitale proprio in tale zona

---

^{NA_4}*ḫekur* di Muwatalli. Sull'abitato localizzato in cima alla collina e una sua possibile identificazione col centro ittita di Arušna v. Forlanini 1979, p. 169.

3 Fortificazioni ittite del periodo tardo-imperiale sono ben visibili a Meydancikkalesi. Meno leggibile la stele che nella parte superiore "montre encore les traces sévèrement érodées du cartouche royal de Muwatalli" (Laroche 1981, p. 359).

4 Per un elenco delle proposte v. Alp 1995, pp. 2 sg., Hawkins 1995, pp. 56 sg. Ritengo due di esse quelle più compatibili con quanto si sostiene nel presente lavoro: l'ubicazione presso Karaman (Gordon 1967, p. 81), nelle cui vicinanze è stato rinvenuto un ampio sito dell'età del Bronzo (French in Hawkins, *cit.*, n. 201) e l'ubicazione sulla collina di Kizildağ (Alp, *cit.*, pp. 6 sgg.) sorretta da convincenti argomentazioni sia di ordine archeologico che filologico (v. anche Hawkins, *cit.*, p. 63 e n. 259). Sulla difficoltà di riconoscervi invece il forte di Meydancikkalesi v. Forlanini 1988, pp. 198 sg. Anche una generica collocazione in "the interior of Cilicia Aspera, to the south-west of the Lamus River" (Houwink ten Cate 1992, p. 252), collegata ad una ubicazione dei confini orientali di Tarḫuntašša lungo il fiume Lamas, non mi trova concorde. Ancor più improbabile mi appare quindi una collocazione presso Sirkeli, troppo spostata ad est rispetto ai confini dello stato di Tarḫuntašša (v. n. 2 su un'eventuale identificazione di Sirkeli con Arušna).

5 V. in particolare Forlanini 1986, TAV. XVI.6; *Id.* 1988, pp. 135 sgg.

6 Alp 1995, pp. 5 sg.

7 Singer 1996, pp. 191 sgg.

risulta ben comprensibile. L'esistenza di un precedente santuario al dio della tempesta nel sito dove sorse la "grande" Tarḫuntašša è per ora solo oggetto di ipotesi.[8]

Con la presa del potere da parte di Ḫattuşili III si ha la restaurazione del regno di Ḫatti nella sua totalità. È ovviamente abbandonata l'idea della creazione di uno stato di ampie dimensioni come ipotizzato probabilmente da Muwatalli, ma la città di Tarḫuntašša rimane il centro di un nuovo stato, con confini molto più ristretti e in ruolo subordinato a Ḫatti, che viene affidato al figlio di Muwatalli Kurunta. Oltre a servire come una sorta di risarcimento per colui che in realtà avrebbe potuto legittimamente rivendicare il trono di Ḫatti, mi sembra che lo stato di Tarḫuntašša risponda anche a un'esigenza politica ben precisa: il suo ruolo si configura come quello di uno stato cuscinetto, saldamente (almeno nell'intento del sovrano di Ḫatti!) dipendente dal regno ittita, nei confronti della turbolenta area sud-occidentale, cioè i territori dei paesi di Arzawa e di Lukka.[9] Tale ruolo può a mio parere essere documentato da due tipi di fonti: quelle di ordine geografico, rappresentate in modo specifico dai confini fra Ḫatti e Tarḫuntašša e quelle più propriamente "politiche", che concernono gli interventi di Ḫatti nell'area sud-occidentale. Ha sempre destato meraviglia il fatto che nell'elenco dei confini fra Ḫatti e Tarḫuntašša dopo la menzione di una lunga serie di nomi geografici che delimitano una direttrice ovest-est che divideva in linea "orizzontale" il territorio di Ḫatti (a nord) da quello di Tarḫuntašša (a sud), manchi un riferimento ai confini che separavano Tarḫuntašša da Ḫatti lungo l'area orientale, mentre l'elenco si sposta bruscamente lungo la direttrice occidentale.[10] È possibile che per i contraenti non vi fosse alcun bisogno di una precisazione dettagliata dei confini fra la zona di Šaliya e la costa meridionale, forse privi di particolari insediamenti e che non presentavano particolari problemi. Ḫatti aveva saldamente in mano il controllo delle Porte Cilicie e l'area della Cilicia piana, inseriti nel territorio di Kizzuwatna, parte integrante dell'impero. Lungo la costa cilicia ri-

8 Forlanini 1988, p. 148 e n. 91; Singer 1996, pp. 185 sgg., il quale propone un'origine in area hurrita del dio della tempesta *piḫaššašši* (come ipostasi di Tešup). Su tale appellativo e sul nuovo valore di FULGOR dato al segno geroglifico *200 v. Hawkins 1992, pp. 71 sg.

9 V. Singer 1984, p. 214.

10 Lo stacco avviene, nel trattato con Ulmi-Tešup, con l'espressione *araḫzenaz* "dall'esterno" (Kbo IV 10 Ro 29), cui sembra corrispondere nella Tavoletta bronzea *arunaz(-) pedaz* "dalla parte del mare" (I 56). È da notare tuttavia che questa seconda espressione è preceduta da altre due formule introduttive, "dalla parte di Ušaula"(I 50) e "dalla parte di Ḫawaliya"(I 53), seguite ciascuna da una serie di nomi di località che "appartengono al paese del fiume Ḫulaya". La descrizione dei confini occidentali sembra cominciare quindi con la zona nord-occidentale e proseguire da lì verso e lungo la costa.

tengo fosse in mano ittita anche il porto di Ura alle foci del Calycadnos, non come appartenente direttamente a Ḫatti ma legato da particolari vincoli di dipendenza.[11] Se Ura fosse rientrata sotto la giurisdizione di Tarḫuntašša sicuramente ne avremmo traccia nel trattato. Lo sbocco diretto al mare era comunque assicurato a Tarḫuntašša in un'area più occidentale, che comprendeva a ovest la foce del fiume Kastaraya (da identificare col classico Kestros e con l'odierno Akşu Çayi) e che si può supporre si estendesse ad oriente lungo la costa fino ai margini del territorio di Ura.[12] Da qui è probabile che i confini di Tarḫuntašša si allontanassero dal mare lungo le zone impervie dell'area montuosa della Cilicia Tracheia.[13] Non ve ne sarebbe menzione specifica nel trattato per la mancanza di una precisa delimitazione costituita da cittadelle di confine.[14] In questo quadro mi sembra possibile che Meydancikkalesi non

11 Riguardo a Ura già nel periodo medio-ittita v. il trattato stipulato fra Arnuwanda I e questa città (KUB XXVI 29+) e il precedente (?) accordo fra Arnuwanda e Ḫuḫazalma con cui viene ristabilita la sovranità di Ḫatti su Ura e Mutamutašši (KBo XVI 47): v. De Martino 1996, pp. 73 sgg. e Forlanini 1988, pp. 161 sg. limitatamente al secondo testo. Per una menzione di Ura oltre che nelle fonti ittite in quelle ugaritiche v. Lemaire 1993, pp. 227 sgg. (con precedente bibliografia). Si ricorda che gli Ittiti si servivano anche del porto di Lašti[, menzionato accanto a Ura in Bo 2810 II 14' (v. Del Monte 1978, p. 245). Ma sfortunatamente non abbiamo altre notizie di questa città, di cui anche il nome è incerto, e non è quindi possibile collocarla se non genericamente sulle coste dell'Anatolia.

12 "Etwa im Bereich Silifke-Anamur-Alanya" (Otten 1988, pp. 36 sg. e n. 35; *Id.*1989, p. 18). La località di Šaranduwa (KBo IV 10 Ro 30' / TavBr. I 57.60) sembra costituire in entrambi i testi la città sul mare più ad oriente (v. Beal 1992, p. 70; Giorgieri 1998, p. 180). La presenza di mercanti di Tarḫuntašša a Ugarit (RS 17.42 e 17.158: PRU IV pp. 169 sgg.), nel periodo in cui é "vicere" il re di Karkemiš Ini-Tešup, e quindi gran re di Ḫatti Ḫattušili o Tutḫaliya, non è necessariamente collegata ad un loro uso del porto di Ura, perché potrebbero imbarcarsi anche in una delle città costiere del loro paese.

13 In favore di una netta separazione geografica fra i confini orientali di Tarḫuntašša e quelli occidentali di Kizzuwatna v. Jasink 2000a (in stampa). Per una diversa ipotesi sull'estensione dei confini di Tarḫuntašša lungo la costa fino al Lamas Çay e su una loro presunta coincidenza con i confini che in precedenza avevano diviso Hatti da Kizzuwatna v. Houwink ten Cate 1992, pp. 251 sgg., seguito da Hawkins 1995, pp. 50 sgg.; v. anche Liverani 1995, p. 49, il quale propone inoltre di riconoscere nel toponimo Qode dei testi egizi Tarḫuntašša piuttosto che Kizzuwatna (*ibid.*). Tuttavia la menzione di Kizzuwatna nel passo della Tavoletta bronzea che concerne le esenzioni da oneri e dalla fornitura di aiuto al sovrano ittita da parte di paesi appartenenti al dio della tempesta *piḫaššašši* e ad altre divinità (III 47-50) mi sembra rientrare in una sequenza di località non necessariamente confinanti con Tarḫuntašša ma appartenenti a quella zona più ampia che aveva interessato in modo particolare Muwatalli sotto l'aspetto religioso (v. ad esempio la zona di Sirkeli, facente indubbiamente parte di Kizzuwatna).

14 Sarebbe stato di grande interesse poter controllare il rilievo sulla collina di Bezciler presso Ermenek, fotografato e discusso dal Bittel, 1939, p. 126, che purtroppo è andato distrutto. Una sua datazione al periodo ittita, più tarda di quella proposta dal Bittel a Muršili II, avrebbe potuto confermare

rappresentasse una fortificazione di Tarḫuntašša intesa come confine con il territorio di Ḫatti ma piuttosto una roccaforte ittita con un ruolo di deterrente nei confronti di Tarḫuntašša nel caso di sue eventuali ambizioni su Ura. Si può supporre che la parte superiore della valle del Calycadnos o almeno le sue sponde occidentali rientrassero nel territorio di Tarḫuntašša e che per un certo tratto il fiume segnasse il confine naturale fra i due stati: il traffico per Ḫatti era convogliato, superato il Tauro, ad est verso Šaliya, mentre il nord (Karaman, Karadağ) apparteneva a Tarḫuntašša. La sola menzione di Šaliya come zona di confine appartenente a Ḫatti, che delimitava l'estensione di Tarḫuntašša a nord-est,[15] risultava sufficientemente chiara per definire come fosse saldamente in mano a Ḫatti[16] una striscia di territorio che si estendeva ad ovest di Ereğli,[17] attraverso la quale Ḫatti poteva mantenere un collegamento diretto con il porto di Ura.[18] La differenza fra i dati succinti forniti dai confini orientali

---

l'esistenza di una via di transito che dal Calycadnos si dirigeva verso occidente, costituendo la "via di Tarḫuntašša" distinta dalla "via di Ḫatti". Ma v. Kohlmeyer 1983, pp. 102 sgg., che propone una datazione molto più tarda per questo monumento, ovviamente solo sulla base della fotografia del Bittel (*ibid.*, Abb.15), risalente addirittura al periodo romano. Recenti campagne di scavo intraprese dal 1994 a Kilise Tepe (v. per ultimi Hansen→Postgate 1999, pp. 111 sgg.) hanno riportato alla luce anche un abitato dell' età del Bronzo Tardo, che presenta tipiche caratteristiche ittite (per l' implicazione della presenza di frammenti micenei v. Jasink 2000b, n. 16, in stampa). È comunque difficile stabilire, allo stato attuale delle conoscenze, se si trattava di una città di Ḫatti o dello stato vassallo di Tarḫuntašša. Secondo la ricostruzione qui proposta propenderemmo per una stazione ittita. I quattro sigilli in geroglifico anatolico ivi ritrovati non sono sufficienti a risolvere la questione. È comunque interessante che uno di essi appartenga ad un certo Tarḫunta-piya che porta il titolo di "auriga".

15 Šaliya viene descritta come il punto di confine più orientale della direttrice ovest-est che divideva in linea "orizzontale" il territorio di Ḫatti (a nord) e quello di Tarḫuntašša (a sud). Per prime vengono elencate le singole località di confine che fanno parte o di Ḫatti o del paese del fiume Ḫulaya (da intendere in un'accezione molto più ampia rispetto al suo significato originario che includeva la sola vallata del fiume, identificato con il Çarşamba Suyu; viene ora a coincidere o con la stessa Tarḫuntašša, secondo Gurney 1993, pp. 13 sgg., seguito da vari studiosi fra cui la scrivente, o almeno con i suoi confini settentrionali e occidentali, secondo Houwink ten Cate 1992, p. 253 e Hawkins 1995, p. 50 e n. 167). Il testo prosegue con i confini nord-orientali, che terminano con Šaliya: "Šaliya è il confine, ma Šaliya appartiene al paese di Ḫatti" (KBo IV 10 Ro 29; TavBr. I 49-50).

16 V. Forlanini 1988, p. 149.

17 Si ritiene improbabile che tale zona si estendesse fino a Karaman, situata a sud del Karadağ, che siamo propensi a ritenere il "fulcro" di Tarḫuntašša (v. n. 4).

18 Quasi concordemente è accettata l'ubicazione di Ura nei pressi della foce del Calycadnos. Il rilievo rupestre ritrovato presso Keben nella valle del Calycadnos a 23 Km. da Silifke potrebbe rappresentare una prima tappa del percorso che partiva appunto dalla foce del Calycadnos, ma v. Kohlmeyer 1983, p. 102 e Taf.40, che mette in dubbio una datazione così antica. È stata proposta anche una ubicazione di Ura più ad occidente, nei pressi dell'odierna Aydincik, dove sorgeva in età classica il

di Tarḫuntašša a mio parere motivati da una situazione di sicuro controllo e di stabilità da parte di Ḫatti, e il dettagliato elenco dei confini che concerne invece l'area occidentale di Tarḫuntašša risponde, a mio parere, ad una situazione politica di questa seconda zona completamente diversa, molto più fluida e soggetta se non a capovolgimenti almeno a tentativi di ribellione nei confronti di Ḫatti. Tale situazione è ben documentabile dalle fonti "politiche" sia di Ḫattušili III che di Tutḫaliya IV;[19] in tale contesto il ruolo affidato a Kurunta avrebbe potuto costituire una carta vincente per i sovrani di Ḫatti.[20] Non solo la presenza di Kurunta sembra attestata in alcuni testi concernenti le "campagne occidentali"[21] ma anche alcune delle città di confine

---

porto di Kelenderis (Beal 1992, pp. 69 sgg.). Una tale localizzazione meglio si accorderebbe con la fondazione di una fortezza ittita a Meydancikkalesi, che proteggeva la via di comunicazione verso l'interno (cfr. la situazione per l'età ottomana, in cui Aine Bazar (Gülnar), vicino a Meydancikkalesi, costituiva la residenza estiva del governatore del distretto e dei mercanti di Gilindere (Kelenderis)). Contro tale ipotesi v. Lemaire 1993, pp. 231 sgg.

19 Si accetta la datazione a Ḫattušili III per la "lettera di Tawagalawa" e a Tutḫaliya IV per la "lettera di Milawata" (Singer 1983, pp. 205 sgg; Poetto 1993, p. 77). Si ricorda che nei primi anni del suo regno Ḫattušili dovette opporsi ad una ribellione delle terre di Lukka che raggiunse anche il Paese Basso, almeno fino a Kuwalapaša (classica Kolbasa in Pisidia, a nord del lago Kestel). I frammenti KUB XXI 6 e 6a (attribuiti ad una composizione annalistica di Ḫattušili) più volte discussi sono stati nuovamente commentati da Otten 1988, p. 38, Houwink ten Kate 1992, pp. 256 sgg., Hawkins 1995, p. 52 n. 181 e pp. 56 sg. e nn. 198.199, in base ai dati offerti dalla Tavoletta bronzea; Otten e Hawkins propongono la collocazione di vari siti, ritenuti in precedenza in una zona più a nord-est, lungo la costa della Panfilia (v. in particolare Šalluša = Selinus e Naḫita = Nagidos). Di diversa opinione Houwink ten Cate, *cit.*, pp. 258 sg. Di particolare interesse le recenti considerazioni di Forlanini 1998, pp. 218 sgg., sulla condizione di vita tribale delle genti di Lukka e sulla possibilità di interpretare i vari toponimi come nomi tribali piuttosto che di città.

20 V. Singer 1983, p. 214 "the kingdom of Tarḫuntašša... may have served as a buffer-state and as a basis for military operations in the southwest, considerably shortening the supply lines for the Ḫittite armies"; Forlanini 1988, p. 166: "Vediamo intervenire lo stesso re di Tarḫuntašša, con la funzione di preparare le grandi offensive imperiali".

21 V. "Lettera di Tawagalawa" I 73-74, in cui Kurunta (^{md}KAL-*aš*) viene designato come "re potente"(*šarkuš* LUGAL), in confronto ai due "grandi re"(LUGAL.GAL) di Ḫatti e di Aḫḫiyawa (si segue l'interpretazione del testo di Singer 1983, p. 212; sull'identificazione di ^{md}KAL-*aš* con Kurunta v. già Houwink ten Cate 1974, pp. 150 sg.); "Lettera di Milawata" Vo 39', in cui secondo la nuova lettura di van den Hout (1984, p. 91; 1994, p. 91) Kurunta sarebbe coinvolto nel recupero di documenti importanti per il sovrano ittita, riguardanti Walmu di Wiluša (per una lettura diversa v. Hoffner 1982, p. 131; Singer 1983, p. 215); framm.KUB VI 47 (CTH 214.3) 1'', in cui "Kurunta, re del paese x" (]LAMMA LUGAL KUR $^{u[ru}$) sembrerebbe menzionato in un testo concernente le aree occidentali (sono nominati infatti anche un Alantalli (prob. l'omonimo re di Mira) e Maššan(a)uzzi/ Matanazzi (prob. la sorella di Ḫattušili sposa di Mašduri re del paese del fiume Seḫa) (si segue l'interpretazione del testo di Imparati 1992, pp. 308 sg. e *Id.*1992a, pp. 67 sg.).

sia dalla parte ittita che da quella di Tarḫuntašša sono ben note perchè ripetutamente attraversate da sovrani di Ḫatti a partire dal medio regno nelle loro spedizioni verso sud-ovest. Si tratta pertanto di una zona "calda" che da sempre ha dato preoccupazioni a Ḫatti. La creazione di uno stato cuscinetto, pronto ad affrontare in prima istanza eventuali ribellioni, può costituire una mossa tattica di Ḫattušili, mascherata da un riconoscimento per Kurunta.

Con Tutḫaliya IV la situazione in occidente si fa nuovamente pesante,[22] pertanto l'aiuto di Kurunta può risultare essenziale. Degna di particolare interesse mi appare la lettera che Tutḫaliya invia alla regina, scritta poco dopo la morte del padre, in cui si parla di una ribellione in Lalanda e di una possibile generale insurrezione nel Paese Basso.[23] È probabile che la rivolta sia fomentata dalle genti dell'occidente piuttosto che dal re di Tarḫuntašša. Mi sembra pertanto difficile una identificazione di Lalanda con Karaman,[24] a sud del Karadağ, in quanto tutta la zona sembrerebbe far parte dello stato di Tarḫuntašša.[25] Una localizzazione più settentrionale a nord del Karadağ, in quella parte del Paese Basso che invece era nelle mani di Ḫatti, cioè nella fascia che da Konya raggiunge Ereğli, appare più probabile. Le vittorie di Tutḫaliya descritte nel monumento di Yalburt sembrano aver scongiurato il pericolo. La lunga iscrizione in geroglifico che celebra le imprese del sovrano, inserita in un complesso cultuale come il bacino per la raccolta delle acque, che presenta anche un carattere di pubblica utilità, fa parte, come è stato detto più volte,[26] di un nuovo modo di concepire la regalità, che deve essere ben "visibile" da parte dei sudditi sia interni che esterni. La sua edificazione nei pressi di Yalburt ne fa un monumento di propaganda politica rivolto proprio a quelle popolazioni occidentali che sono state vinte. Yalburt, insieme al monumento di Eflatunpinar e al pilastro di Fasillar sono considerate le opere edilizie più occidentali di Tutḫaliya IV. Tuttavia è necessario

---

22 La già citata lettera di Milawata, da attribuire con certezza a questo sovrano, ben esemplifica la complessità dei rapporti degli stati "vassalli" dell'occidente sia con Ḫatti che fra di loro (Singer 1983, pp. 214 sgg.).

23 KUB XIX 23; v. Singer 1983, p. 214.

24 Del Monte 1978, pp. 240 sgg. (voci Lalanta, Lanta); *Id.*1992, pp. 92 sgg. (voci Lalanta, Lanta, Laranta).

25 Si è già indicata come molto probabile un'ubicazione della città stessa di Tarḫuntašša nell'area del Karadağ e di Karaman (v. n. 4).

26 V. ultimamente Giorgieri-Mora 1996, p. 72.

considerare come ad eccezione della prima[27] non si siano conservate delle iscrizioni che ne indichino inequivocabilmente l'autore. È a tal punto da tener presente la recente scoperta del rilievo rupestre di Kurunta presso Hatip, che sembra "rompere" la supremazia dichiarata ostentatamente da Tutḫaliya in occidente.[28] Tuttavia è possibile che Hatip, a sud di Konya, rientrasse nei confini nord-occidentali del territorio di Tarḫuntašša fronteggiando Ikuna/Ikuwaniya (identificata appunto con l'odierna Konya), che sembra rientrasse invece nell'area di controllo ittita.[29] Si deve anche tener presente come questo monumento, a differenza degli altri prima considerati, sia su un piano completamente diverso: rappresenta infatti un tipico monumento rupestre, che sfrutta l'ambiente roccioso naturale, quali sono venuti alla luce in altre zone del paese ad opera di principi locali[30] e non un'opera monumentale paragonabile ai "bacini lustrali". Il problema è piuttosto rappresentato dalla titolatura, con l'inserimento del titolo "gran re" e la rivendicazione di Kurunta di una diretta discendenza da "Muwatalli gran re eroe". Non è da escludere che la creazione di questo monumento sia da collegarsi alla generale debolezza di Tutḫaliya che non riesce ad imporsi completamente a questo suo "vassallo" il quale, almeno all'interno dei propri confini, si fregia di un titolo parallelo a quello del cugino; ma la presenza delle impronte di sigillo di "Kurunta gran re" ritrovate a Ḫattusa[31] farebbe piuttosto pensare al tentativo di un colpo di mano, forse fallito. Sulla vicenda di Kurunta varie ipotesi di datazione sono state fatte, senza che sia possibile al momento raggiungere

---

27 A cui si può forse aggiungere anche il blocco isolato di Köylütolu (Meriggi 1975, pp. 265 sg.; Masson 1980, pp. 106 sgg.), che probabilmente faceva parte di una più lunga iscrizione inserita in un bacino lustrale. La sua appartenenza a Tutḫaliya IV è basata sulle somiglianze con le altre iscrizioni di questo sovrano. Tuttavia sul blocco sono leggibili solo le due titolature di *labarna* e "grande re" ed è stato ipotizzato (Woudhuizen 1994-1995, pp. 158 sgg.) che l'autore dell'iscrizione sia invece Šaušgakurunti (*šaušga*-CERVUS-*ti*), alto funzionario palatino e membro della famiglia reale, già noto da alcuni sigilli, indicato nel testo cone difensore della città di Titarma.

28 Scoperta e descrizione del monumento in Dinçol 1998 e 1998a. Proprio in conseguenza a questa scoperta è stata proposta un'attribuzione a Kurunta anche dei monumenti di Eflatunpinar, Fasillar e Köylütolu (Bahar et al. 1996, citati in Dinçol 1998, p. 33). Già Singer 1996, p. 65, n. 7, nota brevemente come i monumenti di Eflatunpinar e Fasillar sembrerebbero rientrare nel territorio di Tarḫuntašša, se i suoi confini occidentali arrivavano al fiume Akşu Çayi.

29 Cfr. TavBr. II 48, in cui KUR [uru]*Ikkuwaniya* viene ricordato come una delle zone, distinte da Tarḫuntašša, dedicate al dio della tempesta *piḫaššašši*. Sulla sua possibile occupazione da parte del sovrano di Tarḫuntašša all'epoca di Šuppiluliuma v. oltre.

30 Cfr. ad occidente i rilievi di Karabel e Sipylos, ad oriente quelli di Tasçi, Imamkulu, Hanyeri, Hemite: v. Kohlmeyer 1983; Jasink (in corso di pubblicazione).

31 Neve 1987, pp. 401 sgg.; *Id.* 1991, pp. 330 Abb. 35,332 sgg.

una soluzione certa. Sono propensa a seguire quella che individua nel tentativo di Kurunta un momento di particolare debolezza nel corso del regno di Tutḫaliya, successivo alla stipulazione del trattato redatto sulla Tavoletta bronzea. Non è probabile una collocazione dell'evento alla morte di Ḫattušili,[32] in quanto dalla Tavoletta bronzea[33] traspare una sorta di alleanza di Tutḫaliya con il cugino, quando ancora Ḫattušili è in vita e Kurunta è già insediato sul trono di Tarḫuntašša, probabilmente volta a favorire la propria candidatura al trono di Ḫatti. Non ritengo d'altronde possibile un tentativo di colpo di mano alla morte di Tutḫaliya, che può essere proposto solo accettando l'identificazione di Kurunta con Ulmi-Tešup,[34] oppure ipotizzando una sequenza Kurunta - Ulmi-Tešup - Kurunta. Comunque è da tener presente come il monumento di Kurunta non sia stato eraso e questo potrebbe denotare l'impossibilità della sovranità di Ḫatti ad intervenire.[35] È possibile considerare d'altro canto gli altari di Emirgazi[36] come una voluta dimostrazione da parte di Tu-

32 Beckman 1989-90, p. 293.

33 V. in particolare l'intervento di Tutḫaliya presso il padre perchè conceda a Kurunta del personale legato a determinate località (Ro I 68-90) e l'enfatizzazione del legame personale fra i due cugini (Ro II 31-32). V. inoltre il riferimento alla fedeltà di Kurunta a Tutḫaliya al momento della morte del padre (Ro II 53-57). Sui rapporti fra i due cugini v. Klengel 1991, pp. 228 sgg.

34 Proposta già da Güterbock 1961, p. 86 n. 3, riproposta anche dopo la scoperta della Tavoletta bronzea da vari studiosi fra cui Klengel 1991, pp. 231 sg.; Sürenhagen 1992, pp. 355 sgg.; Gurney 1993, pp. 19 sgg. e accettata da Hawkins 1995, p. 62. Di parere contrario Otten 1988, pp. 6 sg., 32 e, fra gli altri, van den Hout 1989, pp. 100sgg.; *Id.*1994, pp. 11 sgg.; Imparati - Pecchioli-Daddi 1991, pp. 61 sgg., che si oppongono con considerazioni a mio parere ben valide anche ad una sequenza Kurunta (Ḫattušili III) - Ulmi-Tešup (Ḫattušili III) - Kurunta (Tutḫaliya IV); Houwink ten Cate 1992, p. 243; Giorgieri 1998, p. 180.

35 La reazione di Tutḫaliya avrebbe portato all'annullamento del trattato con Kurunta quale risulta dalla Tavoletta bronzea: una conferma di ciò si avrebbe dal luogo stesso di ritrovamento della tavoletta (Neve 1987, p. 408; *Id.*1993, p. 19; v. anche Beckman 1989-90, p. 293, n. 20. Per altre ipotesi sul luogo di ritrovamento della tavoletta v. Imparati 1992a, p. 60). È stato anche ipotizzato (Neve, *ibid.*) che il livello di distruzione che precede la caduta finale di Ḫattuša sia da ascrivere all'attacco di Kurunta contro la capitale; a mio parere è tuttavia difficile che un evento di tale portata non sia stato ricordato in qualche documento ittita posteriore.

36 La loro collocazione nei pressi di Gölörem a nord del massiccio del Karakadağ (a esso o al più alto Kasandağ può riferirsi nel testo l'espressione (DEUS)MONS.MENSA, v.Hawkins 1995, p. 93; cfr. anche Marazzi 1990, pp. 201 sg. sulla lettura MENSA/THRONUS e sul problema della identificazione della montagna con l'ittita Šarpa, proposta da Forlanini 1987, pp. 73 sgg.) appare una conferma a una possibile linea di confine fra Ḫatti e Tarḫuntašša che procede in direzione ovest-est da Konya direttamente verso Karapinar (nei cui pressi è da ubicare la città ittita di Uda, v. Forlanini 1990, p. 119), mentre il massiccio del Karadağ a sud della linea di confine rientra completamente nel territorio di Tarḫuntašša; il confine piega poi verso sud-est lasciandosi sulla sinistra il Karacadağ in territorio

tḫaliya del proprio potere sul Paese Basso, che nella sua parte meridionale appartiene a Tarḫuntašša.

Sotto Šuppiluliuma la situazione si va ancor più deteriorando. Il problema di Tarḫuntašša esplode: mentre nei periodi precedenti Tarḫuntašša era uno stato vassallo, il cui legame con Ḫatti era ripetutamente ribadito da accordi scritti, dalla iscrizione del Südburg si ricava come Tarḫuntašša sia messa sullo stesso piano delle terre ribelli di Lukka. Ormai è vanificato totalmente l'intento di Ḫatti di avere in questo stato un baluardo nei confronti dei turbolenti paesi occidentali. Anche Tarḫuntašša è divenuta terra ostile. In questa chiave di lettura è a mio parere possibile reinterpretare il vocabolo CAPUT.VIR non come un titolo di Šuppiluliuma ma piuttosto come un personaggio che a lui si oppone e guida alla rivolta Tarḫuntašša.[37] Partendo dalle terre di Lukka la ribellione si estende lungo tutta la fascia del Paese Basso. Il programma di riconquista di Šuppiluliuma sembra seguire un ordine geografico, da occidente verso oriente. I paesi attaccati da Šuppiluliuma si possono distinguere in tre aree principali: i §§ 1-7 concernono le terre di Lukka, i §§ 8-11 il monte IUDEX (?).QUINQUE, i §§ 12-17 il paese di Tarḫuntašša. Su tutti e tre si estendeva il controllo di CAPUT.VIR, anche se ottenuto in modo diverso. Per il § 5 proporrei la traduzione "CAPUT.VIR ha portato via a Ḫatti tutte le terre alle frontiere di Ḫatti, (cioè) al Sole queste (terre)".[38] A mio parere con questa espressione si vuol intendere che il principe di Tarḫuntašša ha esteso i suoi possessi verso ovest – inglobando l'area costituita genericamente dalle terre di Lukka di pertinenza dei confini occidentali di Ḫatti – a scapito appunto del regno di Ḫatti.[39] Anche il monte

ittita, e infine verso sud-ovest - rimanendo anche la zona di Eregli (con la città di Šaliya) in mano ittita - perdendosi nella catena del Tauro, con la zona di Karaman e l'alta valle del Calycadnos nel territorio di Tarḫuntašša.

37 Per un'analisi dettagliata di tale proposta e per l'ipotesi di una identificazione fra CAPUT.VIR e Ḫartapu v. Jasink 2000 (in stampa).

38 Südburg 3, § 5. CAPUT.VIR *ḪATTI* REGIO *430 *FINES-zi/a ḪATTI* *416-*wa/i-ní zi/a ARḪA* CAPERE. Hawkins 1995, p. 23 traduce "'Prince-man' (to?) Ḫatti all the land(s) - (to?) the frontiers of Ḫatti the *Sun* (?) took away this (?)". Per una traduzione leggermente diversa v. Giorgieri 1998, p. 183 "zu Ḫatti (ich), der Prinz (?), die Sonne (?), das nahm weg, and zwar die Grenze/Gebiete aller (jener?) Länder".

39 Da notare come l'ultimo dei cinque territori conquistati da Šuppiluliuma sia il paese di Ikuna, che sicuramente sotto il sovrani precedenti era stato sotto il controllo ittita ma vicinissimo ai confini di Tarḫuntašša (v. p. 000 e n. 29). Probabilmente l'area di Konya fu la prima ad essere annessa a Tarḫuntašša nel momento del suo distacco da Ḫatti ed è l'ultima ad essere riconquistata: Šuppiluliuma parte infatti nella sua riconquista dalle zone più esterne a Tarḫuntašša, con una mano-

IUDEX.QUINQUE è oggetto di contesa fra i due sovrani. Mi sembra possibile ipotizzare una ubicazione alternativa a quella proposta da Hawkins a nord-ovest di Tarḫuntašša in posizione intermedia fra questa e le terre di Lukka. Proporrei, ovviamente a livello di ipotesi[40] dal momento che il nome di questa montagna è noto solo dall'iscrizione del Südburg,[41] una ubicazione a nord-est di Tarḫuntašša in un quadro che vede un'espansione di questo stato anche in tale direzione. Prima di attaccare direttamente Tarḫuntašša forse Šuppiluliuma, procedendo con un attacco a tenaglia, si impadronisce anche dei suoi confini nord-orientali, come ha fatto in precedenza con quelli nord-occidentali. L'attacco finale viene sferrato nel cuore di Tarḫuntašša con la sottomissione del suo re e la presa della sua capitale.

Se questa ricostruzione è esatta, il primo problema da risolvere consiste nell'identità di CAPUT.VIR. Questo titolo non è mai stato usato in precedenza da alcun sovrano ittita e mi sembra poco probabile che proprio Šuppiluliuma, il quale in una situazione di difficoltà si riallaccia sotto ogni aspetto alla tradizione, si appropri di un titolo estraneo a tale tradizione.[42] Due unici esempi sono noti in iscrizioni in geroglifico del secondo millennio che potrebbero raffrontarsi con questo titolo. Il primo appartiene all'iscrizione rupestre di Tasçi,[43] in cui "sembra" ricorrere la sequenza VIR.CAPUT,[44] da intendere "forse" come una delle titolature di un certo Lupaki. Se si accetta tale interpretazione e non quella che vi riconosce il nome proprio Ziti/a, il titolo sarebbe prerogativa di un funzionario al servizio di Ḫattusili, preposto insieme ad altri alle operazioni in quella zona, e un'identificazione di questo titolo con il cuneiforme LÚ.SAG può essere considerata probabile.[45] Il secondo

---

vra che potremmo definire di accerchiamento (v. oltre sulla ubicazione del monte IUDEX. QUINQUE).

40 V. oltre una possibile identificazione con la zona di Burunkaya.

41 Sia la sua traduzione di "Mount *Five-Labarnas*" (intendendo i due segni che compongono il nome logograficamente) che quella di monte *Tapapanuwa* (cercando nei due segni un valore logografico) restano a livello speculativo (v. Hawkins 1995, pp. 39 sg.).

42 L'unico possibile equivalente in cuneiforme è rappresentato da LÚ.SAG (con i segni in sequenza opposta) che indicava l' "eunuco" o più genericamente il "principe" (v. Pecchioli Daddi 1977, pp. 178 sgg.), comunque un funzionario reale molto vicino alla persona del re.

43 Per un'analisi dettagliata dell'iscrizione v. Jasink (in corso di pubblicazione).

44 "Sembra", in quanto il secondo segno è una via di mezzo fra il *10 CAPUT, di cui rappresenterebbe una forma semplificata e il *19, cioè il "profilo", che viene trascritto con *á* (che è attestato nella stessa iscrizione in unione a VAS, dando luogo al titolo trascritto come HEROS).

45 Molto più difficile al contrario una identificazione con il CAPUT.VIR dell'iscrizione del Südburg inteso come titolo o di Šuppiluliuma o del re di Tarḫuntašša.

esempio appartiene all'iscrizione Kizildağ 4, in cui si legge la sequenza MAGNUS. REX VIR *416-*wani,* tripla titolatura per Ḫartapu. Il segno VIR da solo non è attestato altrove, mentre appare ripetutamente in espressioni composte, soprattutto come elemento onomastico nella formazione di nomi di persona[46] ma anche, più raramente, nelle titolature.[47] Nessuno di questi casi può adattarsi al titolo VIR usato da Ḫartapu. Potrebbe invece essere proposta una connessione col titolo "nuovo" che appare nell'iscrizione del Südburg, estraneo alle titolature portate sia dai sovrani di Ḫatti che dai loro funzionari. VIR rappresenterebbe cioè una abbreviazione di CAPUT.VIR,[48] e dal momento che Kurunta di Tarḫuntašša non si fregia di tale titolo né nei suoi sigilli né nell'iscrizione di Hatip, si potrebbe ipotizzare che il CAPUT. VIR menzionato da Šuppiluliuma, al quale ovviamente non viene riconosciuto nessun titolo[49] se non quello di "uomo a capo (di uomini)", distinto da qualsiasi titolatura dei sovrani di Ḫatti, fosse proprio Ḫartapu. Una retrodatazione di questo personaggio alla fase finale della potenza ittita, già proposta dal Singer,[50] ben si inquadrerebbe in una storia di Tarḫuntašša il cui crollo sarebbe avvenuto parallelamente a quello del regno di Ḫatti; anzi, alla sua indipendenza avrebbe posto fine già Šuppiluliuma, con la sua "campagna di un anno"[51] descritta nell'iscrizione del Südburg. I monumenti di Kizildağ, Karadağ e Burunkaya[52] rappresenterebbero il momento di massima espansione di Tarḫuntašša a scapito del regno di Ḫatti, ridimensionato dalle imprese di Šuppiluliuma. Questa sua conquista dell'area meridionale a mio parere rappresenta un consolidamento del potere di Šuppiluliuma sul ter-

---

46 Corrisponde all'elemento LÚ/*ziti* degli antroponimi ittito-luvi.

47 Per MAGNUS.VIR, corrispondente al cuneiforme LÚ.GAL, v. Böhmer-Güterbock 1987, n° 191 e n° 192; per PITHOS.VIR.DOMINUS v. Nowicki 1991, p. 253 e Hawkins 1993, p. 717.

48 Sulla possibile corrispondenza del titolo VIR con CAPUT.VIR v. Hawkins 1992, p. 267, senza ulteriori considerazioni.

49 Cioè quelli di MAGNUS.REX e *416-*wani*, che sono invece i titoli reali dei sovrani di Hatti.

50 1996, pp. 69 sg.

51 Un riferimento alla "campagna di un anno" condotta in Siria da Šuppiluliuma I non è forse casuale! Sul formulario dell'iscrizione che inizia con un "quando"(REL+*ra/i*) e termina con "in quell'anno"(*pa-ti-'* ANNUS) e sul suo probabile significato in senso letterale v. Hawkins 1995, pp. 45.53 e n. 188.

52 Proprio quest'ultima zona costituirebbe insieme alle frontiere di Lukka un ampliamento recente di Tarḫuntašša. In tale ottica una identificazione di Burunkaya o, meglio, della zona montuosa adiacente, con (MONS)IUDEX(?).QUINQUE non mi pare da escludere.

ritorio anatolico meridionale e precede la spedizione e relativa vittoria su Alašiya,[53] descritta nella seconda parte di KBo XII 38, che con ogni probabilità rappresenta la copia in cuneiforme della mal conservata iscrizione in geroglifico di Nişantaş.[54] Questa seconda spedizione può essere inquadrata nei tentativi compiuti da parte di Ḫatti, in unione con l'area dell'alta Siria (Ugarit),[55] per fermare l'avanzata dei "popoli del mare"[56] e può essere considerata l'ultima testimonianza[57] a noi pervenuta

---

53 V. già Hoffner 1992, p. 48.

54 V. per ultimo Hawkins 1995, p. 59 e nn. 225.226. Quanto al problema della differenza stilistica fra le iscrizioni di Nişantaş e del gruppo Karadağ-Kizildağ-Burunkaya, che si rifanno alle precedenti iscrizioni di Tutḫaliya, e l'iscrizione del Südburg, intesa o come volutamente arcaicizzante (Hawkins 1995,p. 21) o come innovativa (Giorgieri 1998, pp. 175 sg.), è possibile che tale differenza sia dovuta alla diversa funzione dei monumenti cui appartengono, indipendentemente dalla loro sequenza cronologica.

55 La presenza sia delle truppe di Ugarit in Ḫatti che della flotta di Ugarit davanti alle terre di Lukka (RS 20.238,22-23; v. Lehmann 1970, pp. 53 sgg.; Klengel 1992, p. 150) è da connettere a questi tentativi di arginare i "popoli del mare" piuttosto che alla spedizione condotta da Šuppiluliuma nelle terre di Lukka descritta nell'iscrizione del Südburg, come propone Hawkins 1995, p. 61, diretta in realtà, a mio parere, contro il re di Tarḫuntašša.

56 Lehmann 1970, pp. 63 sg.

57 Di diversa opinione Singer 1996, pp. 67sgg., il quale ritiene che l'iscrizione del Südburg non sia il risultato di una guerra fra due sovrani anatolici, il gran re ittita e il re di Tarḫuntašša, ma piuttosto una vittoriosa reazione di Šuppiluliuma contro le invasioni dei "popoli del mare", preceduta da una vittoria su Alašiya, occupata per prima da quelle stesse genti. A mio parere tale interpretazione, che non ci sentiamo di escludere con certezza in quanto i dati in nostro possesso si prestano a diverse soluzioni, presenta alcuni punti deboli. Due vittorie consecutive di così ampia portata quali una conquista dei mari e una conquista dell'Anatolia meridionale da parte di Šuppiluliuma e dei suoi alleati mi sembra avrebbero portato ad un arresto almeno momentaneo delle forze eversive rappresentate dai "popoli del mare": ma questo non avvenne, anzi dai testi di Ugarit traspare un progressivo accrescersi di una situazione deterioratasi anche ad opera di fattori endemici quali la carestia. Le richieste del re di Ḫatti di navi, truppe, viveri dalla Siria sembrano riflettere una mancanza di controllo ben diversa da quanto è stato oggetto di vanto nelle iscrizioni in geroglifico. Sarei pertanto propensa a separare questi eventi, legati invece a episodi indipendenti dalla nascente presenza dei "popoli del mare". L'episodio descritto nel Südburg rappresenta una riconquista dell'Anatolia a un "vassallo" che è diventato troppo potente (Ḫartapu), che ha cercato di estendere i propri territori, mirando come il predecessore Kurunta ad un colpo di mano sulla stessa Ḫatti. La conquista di Alašiya viene descritta come un'impresa analoga a quella del padre, a glorificazione del controllo di Ḫatti su Cipro, scalo fondamentale nella rotta fra l'Anatolia e la Siria e parte di un percorso comerciale che include Ura e Ugarit. Probabili avversari non sono gli abitanti di Cipro ma i pirati che spadroneggiavano lungo tutte le coste del Mediterraneo orientale e che rappresentano le avvisaglie dei "popoli del mare". Mi sembra che la spedizione contro Tarḫuntašša sia completamente distinta da quella contro Cipro, essendo la prima condotta contro un "vassallo" ribelle, mentre la seconda ha lo scopo di dimostrare la potenza ittita anche sul mare, all'"esterno", nel tentativo di frenare un nemico minaccioso e non ben definibi-

prima del crollo di Ḫatti e delle distruzioni che colpirono tutta la fascia costiera dell'Anatolia e della Siria. In questa fase finale Tarḫuntašša non esiste più come entità politica a se stante[58] e probabilmente la sua "capitale" segue la sorte di Ḫattuša.

Bibliografia

Alp, S., 1995 "Zur Lage der Stadt Tarḫuntašša", in *Atti del II Congresso internazionale di Hittitologia* (Pavia 1993), *Studia Mediterranea* 9, Pavia.

Beal, R. H., 1992 "The location of Cilician Ura", *AnSt* 42, pp. 65 sgg.

Beckman, G. M, 1989-90 Rec. a Otten 1988, *WO* 20-21, pp. 289 sgg.

Bittel, K., 1939 "Archäologische Funde aus der Türkey 1934-1938", *AA*, pp. 94 sgg.

Boehmer, R. M. - Güterbock, H. G, 1987 *Glyptic aus dem Stadtgebiet von Boghazköy. Grabungskampagnen* 1931-1939, 1952-1978, Berlin.

Börker-Klähn, J, 1996 "Grenzfälle: Šunaššura und Sirkeli oder die Geschichte Kizzuwatnas", *UF* 28, pp. 37 sgg.

Del Monte, G. - Tischler J, 1978 *Die Orts- und Gewässernamen der hethitischen Texte,* RGTC 6, Wiesbaden.

De Martino, S., 1996 *L'Anatolia occidentale nel medio regno ittita*, in *Eothen* 5, Firenze.

Dinçol, A. M., 1998 "Die Entdeckung des Felsmonuments in Hatip und ihre Auswirkungen über die historischen und geographischen Fragen des Hethiterreichs", *TÜBA-AR* 1, pp. 27 sgg.

Dinçol, A. M., 1998a "The Rock Monument of the great king *KURUNTA* and its Hieroglyphic Inscription", in *Acts of the 3rd International Congress of Hittitology* (Çorum, September 16-22,1996), Ankara, pp. 159 sgg.

Forlanini, M., 1979 "Appunti di geografia etea", in *Studia Mediterranea Piero Meriggi dicata*, Pavia, pp. 165 sgg.

Forlanini, M., 1986 *Anatolia: L'impero hittita*, *Atlante storico del Vicino Oriente antico* (= *ASVOA* 4.3), Roma.

Forlanini, M., 1987 "Le mont Šarpa", *Hethitica* 7, pp. 73 sgg.

le. La possibilità, da me proposta, di riconoscere in CAPUT.VIR un personaggio ben preciso, come unico avversario di Šuppiluliuma, non è compatibile con una sua identificazione con uno dei capi di forze nemiche composite quali i "popoli del mare".

58 È stata rinvenuta a Ugarit una lettera inviata dal re di Tarḫuntašša a Ammurapi di Ugarit, con richiesta di scambi di prodotti fra i due paesi (RS 34.139, Malbran-Labat 1991, pp. 41 sg). Si può tuttavia suporre che pur appartenendo all'età di Ammurapi/Šuppiluliuma preceda l'iscrizione del Südburg e risalga quindi al periodo di massima espansione di Tarḫuntašša.

Forlanini, M., 1988 "La regione del Tauro nei testi hittiti", *VO* 7, pp. 129 sgg.

Forlanini, M., 1990 "Uda, un cas probable d'homonymie", *Hethitica* 10, pp. 109 sgg.

Forlanini, M., 1998 "The geography of Hittite Anatolia in the light of the recent epigraphical discoveries", in *Acts of the 3rd International Congress of Hittitology* (Çorum, September 16-22,1996), Ankara, pp. 217 sgg.

Giorgieri, M., 1998 Rec. a Hawkins 1995, *OLZ* 93, pp. 174 sgg.

Giorgieri, M - Mora, C., 1996 Aspetti della regalità ittita nel XIII secolo a.C., Como.

Gordon, E. I., 1967 "The meaning of the ideogramm dKASKAL.KUR = 'Underground water-course' and its significance for Bronze Age historical geography", *JCS* 21, pp. 70 sgg.

Güterbock, H., 1961 "The north-central area of Hittite Anatolia", *JNES* 20, pp. 85 sgg.

Gurney, O. R., 1993 "The Treaty with Ulmi-Tešub", *AnSt* 43, pp. 13 sgg.

Hansen, C. K. - Postgate, J. N., 1999 "The Bronze to Iron Age transition at Kilise Tepe", *AnSt* 49, pp. 111 sgg.

Hawkins, J. D., 1992 "What does the Hittite Storm-God Hold?", in *Natural Phenomena,* Amsterdam, pp. 71 sgg.

Hawkins, J. D., 1993 "A bowl epigraph of the official Taprammi", in *Aspects of Art and Iconography: Anatolia and its Neighbors. Studies in Honor of Nimet Özgüç*, Ankara, pp. 715 sgg.

Hawkins, J. D., 1995 *The Hieroglyphic Inscription of the Sacred Pool Complex at Hattuša SÜDBURG*, Studien zu den Bogazköy-Texten, Beiheft 3, Wiesbaden.

Hoffner, H. A., 1982 "The Milawata Letter Augmented and Reinterpreted", *AfO* Beiheft 19, pp. 130 sgg.

Hawkins, J. D., 1992 "The last Days of Khattusha", in *The Crisis Years: the 12th Century B.C.*, Dubuque, pp. 46 sgg.

van den Hout, T. P. J., 1984 "Kurunta und die Datierung einiger hethitischen Texte", *RA* 78, pp. 89 sgg.

van den Hout, T. P. J., 1989 "A Chronology of the Tarḫuntašša-Treaties", *JCS* 41, pp. 100 sgg.

van den Hout, T. P. J., 1994 *Der Ulmitešub-Vertrag. Eine prosopographische Untersuchung,* Studien zu den Bogazköy-Texten 38, Wiesbaden

Houwink ten Cate, P. H. J., 1974 "Anatolian evidence for relations with the West in the late Bronze Age", in *Bronze Age Migrations in the Aegean. Archaeological and linguistic problems in Greek prehistory*, London, pp. 141 sgg.

Houwink ten Cate, P. H. J., 1992 "The Bronze Tablet of Tudhaliyas IV and its Geographical and Historical Relations", *ZA* 82, pp. 233 sgg.

Houwink ten Cate, P. H. J., 1994 "Urhi-Tessub revisited", *BiOr* 51, pp. 233 sgg.

Imparati, F., 1992 "A propos des témoins du traité avec Kurunta de Tarḫuntašša", in *Hittite and other Anatolian and Near Eastern Studies in Honour of Sedat Alp*, Ankara 1992, pp. 305 sgg.

Imparati, F., 1992a "Significato politico della successione dei testimoni nel trattato di Tuthaliya IV con Kurunta", in *ISMEA Seminari* 1991, pp. 59 sgg.

Imparati, F. - Pecchioli Daddi, F., 1991 "Le relazioni politiche fra Hatti e Tarḫuntašša all'epoca di Hattusili III e Tuthaliya IV", in *Quattro studi ittiti, Eothen* 4, Firenze pp. 23 sgg.

Jasink, A. M., 2000 "Šuppiluliuma and Ḫartapu: two "great Kings" in conflict?" (in stampa).

Jasink, A. M., 2000a "Kizzwatna and Tarḫuntašša. Their historical evolution and interactions with Ḫatti" (in stampa).

Jasink, A. M., 2000b "Presenze micenee e greche nella Cilicia preclassica" in Studi in onore di M. Cataudella (in stampa).

Klengel, H., 1991 "Tuthalija IV. von Hatti: Prolegomena zu einer Biographie", *AoF* 18, pp. 224 sgg.

Klengel, H., 1992 *Syria, 3000 to 300 B.C.*, Berlin.

Kohlmeyer, K., 1983 *Felsbilder der hethitischen Grossreichszeit*, Acta Praehistorica et Archaeologica 15.

Laroche, E., 1981 "Le fouilles de Meydandjik Près de Gulnar (Turquie)", Académie des Inscriptions & Belles-Lettres, Comptes Rendus 1981, Paris, pp. 356 sgg.

Lehmann, G. A., 1970 "Der Untergang des Hethitischen Grossreiches und die neuen Texte aus Ugarit", *UF* 2, pp. 39 sgg.

Lemaire, A., 1993 "Ougarit, Oura et la Cilicie vers la fin du XIIIe s. av. J.-C.", *UF* 25, pp. 227 sgg.

Liverani, M., 1995 "Le royaume d'Ougarit", in *Le pays d'Ougarit autour de 1200 av. J.-C., Ras Shamra-Ougarit XI*, Actes du Colloque International Paris, 28 juin-1er Juillet 1993, Paris, pp. 47 sgg.

Malbran-Labat, F., 1991 "Lettre n° 14", in *Une Bibliothèque au sud de la ville. Les textes de la 34e campagne (1973).* Ras Shamra-Ougarit VII, Paris, pp. 41 sg.

Masson, E., 1980 "Les inscriptions Louvites Hiéroglyphiques de Köylütolu et Beyköy", *Kadmos* 19, pp. 106 sgg.

Marazzi, M., 1990 *Il geroglifico anatolico: Problemi di analisi e prospettive di ricerca*, Roma.

Meriggi, P., 1975 *Manuale di eteo-geroglifico*, Parte II: Testi - 2a e 3a Serie, Roma.

Neve, P., 1987 "Die Ausgrabungen in Boğazköy-Ḫattuša 1986", *AA*, pp. 381 sgg.

Neve, P., 1991 "Die Ausgrabungen in Boğazköy-Ḫattuša 1990", *AA*, pp. 299 sgg.

Neve, P., 1993 *Ḫattuša - Stadt der Götter und Tempel. Neue Ausgrabungen in der Hauptstadt der Hethiter*, Mainz am Rhein.

Nowicki, H., 1981 "Bemerkungen zur hier.-luw. Inschrift von Karahöyük-Elbistan", *KZ* 95, pp. 251 sgg.

Otten, H., 1988 *Die Bronzetafel aus Boğazköy*, Studien zu den Boğazköy-Texten, Beiheft 1, Wiesbaden.

Otten, H., 1989 *Die 1986 gefundene Bronzetafel. Zwei Vorträge*, Innsbrucker Beiträge zur Sprachwissenschaft - Vorträge und Kleinere Schriften 42, Innsbruck.

Pecchioli Daddi, F., 1977 "Il ^{LÚ}*KARTAPPU* nel regno ittita", *SCO* 27, pp. 169 sgg.

Poetto, M., 1993 *L'iscrizione luvio-geroglifica di Yalburt*, Studia Mediterranea 8, Pavia.

Singer, I., 1983 "Western Anatolia in the Thirteenth Century B.C. according to the Hittite Sources, *AnSt* 33, pp. 205 sgg.

Singer, I., 1996 "Great Kings of Tarḫuntašša", *SMEA* 38, pp. 63 sgg.

Singer, I., 1998 "From Ḫattuša to Tarḫuntašša: some thoughts on Muwatalli's reign", in *Acts of the 3rd International Congress of Hittitology* (Çorum, September 16-22,1996), Ankara, pp. 535 sgg.

Sürenhagen, D., 1992 "Untersuhungen zur Bronzetafel und weiteren Verträgen mit der Sekundogenitur in Tarḫuntašša", *OLZ* 87, pp. 341 sgg.

Woudhuizen, F. C., 1994-1995 "Luwian Hieroglyphic monumental rock and stone inscriptions from the Hittite empire period", *Talanta* 26-27, pp. 153 sgg.

NON-TRIVIAL SEMANTIC SHIFTS IN SEMITIC. S. MAISEL'S "ISOSEMANTIC SERIES" APPLIED TO ANATOMIC LEXICON

LEONID KOGAN - ALEXANDER MILITAREV

Russian State University for the Humanities

While working on the first volume of the Semitic Etymological Dictionary (SED) the authors faced, alongside with a wide range of phonological and morphological problems, specific difficulties in the semantic comparison of presumed cognates. Apart from trivial cases of identical or evidently related meanings ("tooth" vs. "molar", "hand" vs. "arm" vs. "elbow", "sleep" vs. "dream", etc.), there are many cases of phonetically compatible words having quite different, sometimes remote, meanings. To decide whether to treat such cases as homonyms or cognates we have consistently applied a procedure of "isosemantic series" to the most difficult and controversial instances. The method of isosemantic series was worked out by Moscow Semitist Solomon Maisel (1900-1952) in his study on root variation in Semitic (Maisel 1983). The procedure consists in confirming etymological identity of two lexemes by adducing another pair (or other pairs) of lexemes, manifesting the same meaning shift, or one lexeme synchronically combining both meanings in question. The more is the number of pairs adduced, the more reliable is a given isosemantic series. The pairs may be taken from the same language or related languages; they may also be taken from other linguistic families, in which case semantic shifts in question can be regarded as semantic *frequentalia* or *universalia.*

In fact, weighing a semantic plausibility of this or that comparison by scanning one's memory in search of similar meaning shifts is a common mental operation for an etymologist; sporadically, similar meaning shifts figure as indirect arguments elsewhere in etymological studies. The merits of Maisel's method, however, are (1) in his efforts to create a theoretical basis for the very phenomenon of repeated semantic shifts in a given language or linguistic family or even in unrelated languages, (2) in making the adduction of similar meaning shifts a regular and necessary procedure in cases of non self-evident semantic comparison, and (3) in presenting around 60 isosemantic series from Semitic and non-Semitic languages.

In the present paper, two series adduced by Maisel, with *addenda* and *corrigenda* by the authors, are analyzed, together with four newly compiled series, namely:

1. "Mouse" ~ "muscle";
2. "Womb, uterus" ~ "mercy";
3. "Eye" ~ "(water) spring, well";
4. "Daughter/girl/baby (of the eye)" ~ "pupil/apple of the eye";
5. "Leg/knee/loins" ~ "part of a people, tribe";
6. "Bone" ~ "to be sturdy, strong; to be big, corpulent; to be fearsome".

1. "Mouse" ~ "muscle"

1.1. Arab. *ʿaḍal-* 'rat des champs' (BK 2: 281) ~ *ʿaḍalat-*, *ʿaḍīlat-* 'muscle; morceau de chair ferme et compacte' (*ibid.*). The example is quoted from Maisel 1983: 196.

Neither of the words in question has a sound etymology so far. The Arab. *ʿaḍal-* has some, not quite convincing, parallels in Ethiopian Semitic languages. One of those is the Tgr. word combination *ʿaṭal ṭäbe* 'sorte de belette' (LH: 489; *apud* d'Abbadie). Semantically, "a weasel" can be well compared to "a rat". However, if we suppose that it is the element *ʿaṭal* that conveys the required meaning within this construction, it is necessary to remark that Arab. *ḍ* (< PSem. **ṣ́*) normally corresponds to Tgr. *ṣ* or *č̣*, but not to *ṭ*, which derives from Sem. **ṭ* only. As for the second element of the construction, *ṭäbe,* its meaning is impossible to establish on the basis of this, or any other, Ethiopian dictionary.

For Arab. *ʿaḍa/īlat-* 'muscle' cf. MSA: Mehri *ʿaẑalét,* Hars. *ʾaẑéylḗt* 'upper arm, biceps' (*SSL*: 209), which may be Arabic loanwords.

1.2. Syr. *ʿuḳbartā* 'mus; musculus' (Brock.: 542).

Although the possiblity of a calque translation from Greek (cf. 1.5.) cannot be ruled out, the term quoted is connected semantically and phonetically with another case of this semantic shift in Semitic languages where Greek influence is impossible, namely:

1.3. Mehri *ʾārḳayb ḏə-fām* 'Achilles' tendon' (JM: 28), Hars. *ʾarḳáyb ḏe-fām id.* (JH: 10).

The literal meaning of both phrases is "mouse of the leg" (the Jib. cognate *ʿarḳéb* means nothing but 'mouse', cf. JJ: 15). We are inclined to think, however, that in this particular case we are dealing with a case of a secondary contamination rather than that of a direct semantic shift "mouse" > "muscle, tendon". Such a conclusion follows from the fact that cognate forms meaning "Achilles' tendon" are well attested in other Semitic languages: Post-bibl. Heb. *ʿarḳūb* 'hough, ham, the inner part of the knee, the inner angle of the joint which unites the thigh and the leg of an animal' (Ja.: 1223), Syr. *ʿarḳūbā* 'genu(?), calx, tendo Achillis' (Brock.: 551), Arab. *ʿurḳūb-* 'tendon d'Achille; jarret; le tibia (chez certains oiseaux); coude' (BK 2: 232).

On the other hand, there is a certain similarity between the MSA term for "mouse" and the PSem. name for that animal, **ʿakbar-*: Heb. *ʿakbār* (KB: 823, with parallels from other Semitic). There are substantial phonetic differences in MSA, though: the emphatic *ḳ* and the metathesis. There is, however, Syr. *ʿuḳbartā* 'mouse' a curious intermediate case of sorts in that it differs from Sem. **ʿakbar-* only by the nature of its velar, and from MSA **ʿaḳbār* only by the metathesis. One can imagine that the two terms, anatomical and zoological, affected one another in MSA: "mouse" underwent phonetic changes due to the influence of "Achilles' tendon" (for similar phonetic irregularities see Syr. *ʿuḳbartā* in Brock.: 542 and *ʾagbərā* 'mus' *ibid.*: 3), while "Achilles' tendon" had ceased to be felt as an independent word and merged with "mouse" completely so that an attribute *ḏə-fām* "that of the leg" was necessary to preserve the anatomic meaning of the term. Needless to say, these complex changes presuppose a close association of the notions "mouse" and "muscle" as early as proto-MSA.

Lastly, there is another curious fact bearing on the word **ʿarḳūb-* 'Achilles' tendon' itself: it shows such an astounding similarity to the two well-known Semitic anatomical terms **ʿarḳ-* 'tendon, vein' and **ʿaḳib-* 'heel' - that one cannot exclude an exotic possibility of a phonetic and semantical "merger" of the two words. Indeed, stretching from muscles of the shin to the heel bone, *tendo Achillis* is nothing but the "heel tendon"! Cf. SED: 22-23; also, with somewhat different conclusions, Steiner 1982.

1.4. Kemant *yešwā* 'souris' (Conti Ross.: 271) ~ *inšuwā* 'biceps' (*ibid.*: 169; note that in SIFKY: 142 *inšuwā* is quoted as Qwara).

Both words are most likely to be variants of the same stem derived from Central Cush. **Hinçuwā* 'mouse': Bilin *inšuwā,* Xamir *yeč̣uwā,* Xamta *ač̣uwā,* Aungi *ençā,* Damot *inc̣ī* (see SIFKY: 142), which descends from the PCush. **ʿi/ançaw-,* a form reconstructed on the basis of both Central Cush. **Hinçuwā* and East Cush. **ʿançaw-* ~ **ʿawwaç-*: Afar *andawā* 'Maus' (RAfar: 812), Saho *ʿandawa* 'rata' (SIFKY: 142, *apud* Welmers), Oromo *wawwaçoo* 'mongoose' (Gragg: 402). Note that instead of the latter Dolgopolsky quotes Oromo *antuta* 'mouse, rat' (SIFKY: 142), which is not acceptable, as Oromo *t* does not correspond to *ç. Cush. *ʕi/ançaw-*, in its turn, derives from the Afrasian **ʕay(n)ç-* 'mouse, rat':

Omot. **(H)i/unç-* 'mouse, rat': Ometo (Chara) *uçā* (Cer. Om.: 163), Mocha *īč̣č̣e,* Kafa *ič̣č̣ō* (LMč: 15), Shinasha *iinça,* Gimirra *uç* (Lamberti: 269);

Sem. **Hayyaṣ-* 'weasel' (and **Hanṣaw/y-* 'mouse'?): Akk. *ayyaṣu* 'Wiesel' OB on (AHw: 25), Gez. *ʾanṣawā* 'mouse, weasel' (LGz: 32; also *ḥanṣawā* 'mouse' *ibid.*: 238), Tgr. *ḥanṣawā* 'mouse' (*ibid.*: 238) and *ʕ/ʔanṣay* (*ibid.*: 32), Tna. *ʾanč̣əwa* 'mouse' (*ibid.*: 32). According to Leslau, all Eth. forms are Cushitisms which looks plausible. In this case, Akk. is the only reliable parallel to this root in Sem.

1.5. Numerous examples of this semantic shift in Indo-European languages are quoted in WH 2: 132 (sub *mūs*). The most widely known of those - Greek *mũs* 'mouse; muscle' and Latin *musculus* 'young mouse; muscle' - are also adduced in Maisel 1983: 196 together with Russian *мышь* 'mouse' ~ *мышца* 'muscle' (both Latin and Russian examples are sometimes treated as calque translations from Greek).

Of interest are somewhat similar Indo-European semantic shifts, such as Sanskrit *muškaḥ* 'Hode' (Mayrhofer: 657-658; with a remark: "ursprünglisch 'Mäuschen'") and Middle High German *muselîn* 'Membrum' ("from 'Mäuschen'" *ibid.*).

As obvious from the examples quoted above, the "mouse" > "muscle" semantic shift is fairly widespread and not confined to Semitic languages alone. The first ready explanation occurring to a student is that the shift is based on a visual metaphor: a muscle resembles a mouse moving under the skin. Although it is not quite clear what was the precise nature of the ancients' concept behind the shift, it would have been very strange indeed if the meaning had developed in the opposite direction.

2. "Womb, uterus" ~ "mercy"

2.1. PSem. **raḥim-* 'womb, uterus' ~ **rḥm* 'to be merciful'.

PSem. **raḥim-* 'womb, uterus': Akk. *rēmu, rīmu* 'Mutterleib' OB on (AHw: 970), Ebl. *ri-ʾe$_x$*(EN)*-mu, ri-mu-um /reḥmum/* 'uterus' (Krebernik: 14), Heb. *räḥäm, raḥam* 'womb' (KB: 1217), Jud. *raḥămā, raḥmā* 'orifice of the matrix, womb' (Ja.: 1467), Syr. *raḥmā* 'uterus' (Brock.: 724), Arab. *raḥim-, riḥm-* 'utérus' (BK: 1 838), Tgr. *rəḥm* 'womb; descent' (LH: 146), Tna. *rəḥm-u* 'bocconi, a ventre a terra' (Bassano: 141; with the meaning shift "womb" > "belly, abdomen"), Mehri *raḥm* 'womb' (JM: 321), *mərḥām* id. (*ibid.*: 322), Jib. *raḥm* 'womb' (JJ: 210), East Jib. *mərḥám* 'womb' (JM: 322). Cf. SED: 204-205.

PSem. **rḥm* 'to be merciful': Akk. *rêmu* 'sich erbarmen, Mitleid haben' (AHw: 970), Ugar. *rḥm* 'mitleidsvoll, liebevoll sein' (Aist:. 291), Heb. *rḥm* (ḳal, piʿ) 'to love, to meet someone with love, to take pity on someone' (KB: 1217) and *raḥămīm* 'a feeling of love, loving sensation, mercy' (*ibid.* 1218; with an unaccountable vocalism instead of the expected **rəḥāmīm),* Aram. bibl. *rəḥūm* 'merciful' (KB_g: 1123), *raḥămīn* 'compassion' (*ibid.*: 1124), Jud. *rəḥēm* (Ja.: 1469), Syr. *rəḥēm* 'miseratus est; amavit' (Brock.: 723-724), Mand. *rhm* 'to love, to have pity' (DM: 426), Arab. *rḥm* 'être compatissant, avoir pitié de qn' (BK 1: 838), Sab. *rḥm* 'to be merciful' (SD: 116; treated as an Aram. loanword in Beeston 42), Mehri *rəḥām* 'to be kind to so.' (JM: 321), Hars. *reḥām* 'to pity' (JH: 103), Jib. *raḥám* 'to be kind' (JJ: 210). Cf. also the Common Semitic derivatives **raḥmān-* and **raḥmāniyy-* 'merciful': Akk. *rēmēnû* (AHw: 970), Heb. *raḥămānī* (KB: 1219), Aram. Anc. Off. Palm. *rḥmn* (HJ: 1071), Syr. *raḥmānā* (Brock.: 724), Mand. *rahmana* (DM: 419). Both Arab. *raḥmān-,* and Sab. (monotheistic period) *Rḥmn-n* are customarily considered Aramaic borrowings (Wagner: 106, Beeston: 42).

In Eth. a metathetic variant of this consonantal root, viz. **mḥr*, dates back to the Common Ethiopian stage: Gez. *mḥr* (LGz: 336), Tgr. *mäḥarä* (LH: 111), Tna. *mäḥarä* (Bassano: 78), Amh. *marä* (K: 171) etc. Curiously enough, in most Eth., words derived from this root have no anatomical connotations (except for the above-quoted examples from Tgr. and Tna. which were not, as a rule, taken into account in the comparative studies). The situation is much the same with Mandaic *rhm* (< **rḥm*, meaning 'to love, etc.' with no anatomic term derived from this root attested).

2.2. PSem. **ḥann(-at)-* 'womb, uterus' ~ *ḥnn* 'to be merciful'.

Sem. **ḥann-* 'womb, uterus': Aram. Off. *ḥn* 'vagina' (HJ: 387), Syr. *ḥannā* 'sinus; penis; cunnus, vagina' (Brock.: 242), *ḥannūtā* 'uterus' (*ibid.*), Arab. *ḥann-at-* 'femme, épouse' (BK 1: 499; with a frequent semantic shift), Tgr. *ḥənot* 'foetus' (LH: 85), *ḥannä* 'to be with child' (*ibid.*: 84; the term *ḥante* 'lap, the lower parts' given *ibid.*: 83 probably also belongs here). In Aram. see possibly also Jud. *ḥēnā* 'lap, bosom' (*Ja.*: 481), Mand. *hana* 'lap, loins, embrace, privy parts' (DM: 124) which may derive alternatively from **ḥayn-* < **ḥaʾn-* < **ḥaʿn-* < **ḥaṣ́n-* 'lap, womb' for which see e.g. LGz: 226 (sub *ḥəḍn* 'bosom, lap'). Cf. SED: 111-112.

Sem. **ḥnn* 'to be merciful': Akk. *enēnu* 'to pray, ask for mercy' (CAD E: 162, AHw: 217, attested in OB, NA; note that *enēnu* 'to grant a privilege, to do favour', attested from OAkk on, is treated in CAD E: 164 as a homonymous verb), Ugar. *ḥnn* 'sich erbarmen, Gunst verschaffen' (Aist.: 105), Heb. *ḥnn* 'to favour so.' (KB: 334),

Arab. *ḥnn* 'être ému, être dans une vive émotion de tristesse, de joie mêlée d'agitation; avoir une grande tendresse pour qn; avoir compassion de qn' (BK: 1 499).

To be objective, we have to point out the weak spot of this series: the nominal stem with the hypothetical original meaning "womb, uterus" is not as widespread in Semitic languages as its presumed derivative, the verbal stem "to be merciful".

Both semantic series (2.1. and 2.2) are from Maisel 1983: 221-222.

2.3. Hittite *genzu* 'Schoss; Geschlechtsteile; Liebe, Zuneigung, Freundlichkeit' (Tischler: 555; suggested by A. S. Kasyan).

In this case, we cannot exclude the possiblity of the Akkadian influence on the presumed meaning shift (from either the above-mentioned *rêmu* 'sich erbarmen, Mitleid haben' or its derivatives).

3. "Eye" ~ "water spring, well"

3.1. PSem. **ʿayn-* 'eye' ~ '(water) spring, well'.

Akk. *īnu, ēnu* 'eye; bubble, spring' (from OAkk, OA on; CAD I: 153, AHw: 383), Ugar. *ʿn* (Aist.: 235-236), Pho. *ʿn, ʿyn* (T: 252), Heb. *ʿayin* (KB: 817), Jud. *ʿayin*, det. *ʿēnā, ʿaynā* (Ja.: 1071), Syr. *ʿaynā* (Brock.: 522), Mand. *aina*, constr. *ʿin* (DM: 15, 348), Arab. *ʿayn-* (BK 2: 425), Gez. *ʿayn* (LGz: 79), Mehri *ʾāyn* (JM: 38), Jib. *ʿíhn* 'eye; spring' (JJ: 20). Cf. SED: 28-29.

Cf. also derived forms with **mV-* prefixation meaning "spring": Heb. *maʿyān* (KB: 612), Syr. *məʿīnā* (Brock.: 523), Arab. *maʿīn-* (BK: 2 427), Sab. *mʿynt* (SD: 23).

Semitic **ʿayn-* 'eye' has cognates in other Afras. languages: Egyp. *ʿ(y)n*, a grapheme depicting the eye (EG 1: 189); East Cush.: Afar, Saho *intī́* 'Auge' (RAfar: 814; <**ʿin-t-*); Omot.: Gimirra *an* 'eye' (SIFKY: 150, *apud* Bulatovich); Berb. **ənHi* ~ **i-Hanəy* (intensive imperfective) 'to see' (Prasse: 84; both with metathesis); Chad. **ʿiyan-* 'to see' (Stolbova 1987: 78).

A similar root **HVnw-* 'spring, water source' is likely reconstructed on the common Afras. level: **HVnw-* (**H-* = **ʿ-* ?): Omot.: Kafa *īnō* 'sorgente salina', *unnō* 'sorgente' (Cer. Caff.: 400), Anfilla *ino* '(water) spring' (SIFKY: 150); Berb. **Hanw* 'spring': Siwa *anu* (Laoust: 284), Ghadames *anu* (Lanfry: 229), Ahaggar *ânu* (Foucauld: 1283), Qab. *anu* (Dallet: 537) etc. The common origin of Afras. **HVnw-* 'spring' and Afras. **ʿayn-* 'eye' is very probable, though not entirely certain.

3.2. Afras. **ʿi/all-* (**ʿil-* according to OS: 247) 'eye' ~ **ʿa/ila* '(water) source, spring, reservoir' (cf. Militarev: 23)

Afras. *ʿi/all- 'eye':

Berb. *(w)all: Ghadames *a-we/all,* pl. *wa/ell-en* (Lanfry: 389), Ahaggar, Izayan *all-ən,* Semlal *wall-ən* (all pl.), Shawiya *ṯ-ala* (Aikh. Mil.: 258); Cush. *ʿil(l)- (SIFKY: 144): Centr. Cush.: Bilin *ʿil* (RBil: 63), East Cush.: Somali *íl* (Abraham: 127), Oromo (Borana) *ila,* Kambatta *illé* etc.; Centr. Chad. *ʾil-: Buduma *ye/il,* Gulfei *el,* Lamang *ili* (OS: 247).

Afras. *ʿa/ila '(water) source, spring, reservoir':

Sem.: Gez. *ʿelā* 'fountain', Tgr., Tna. *ʿela* 'cistern', Har. *ela* 'stagnant water' (LGz: 60); Berb.-Canar. *Halaw 'spring': Ahaggar *ta-hăla* (pl. *ti-hāliw-īn*), East Tawllemmet *t-āla,* Seghrushen *t-äla,* Qab. *ṯ-ala,* Canar. (Gomera, Hierro) *aala* 'water'; Centr. Cush.: Bilin *ʿelā, ʿäla* 'Brunnen' (RBil: 63), East Cush.: Somali *íl* 'a spring of water' (Abraham: 126; also *ʿèel* 'well' *ibid.*: 73), Afar *elā* 'Brunnen, Cisterne' (RAfar: 807), Oromo *ela*, Kambatta *elo* (LHar: 24).

That Afras. *ʿi/all- 'eye' and *ʿa/ila 'spring' are cognate stems, and not partial homonyms is far from being obvious (cf. certain differences between the two terms - primarily as regards vocalic patterns - in those languages where both are present). However, in view of the wide spread of the semantic series "eye" ~ "spring" throughout Afrasian as well as outside it may be regarded as a plausible, though indirect, argument in favor of the former supposition.

3.3. Berb. *t-iṭṭ 'eye; spring (of water)'.

Siwa *ṭ-eṭṭ* (Laoust: 297), Ahaggar *t-iṭ* (Foucauld: 253), Qbl. *t-iṭ* (Dallet: 832). Further cognates see in Aikh. Mil.: 258.

The meaning "eye" is primary, which follows from Afras.: East Cush. *ʾinṭ/d-: Somali pl. *ínḍó* (Abraham: 127), Rendille *indo,* Gidole *iinda,* Arbore *iynḍa* 'eye' (SIFKY: 150); Chad. *ʾi/u(n)d/ṭ- 'eye': West: Hausa *ido,* Bolewa *ʾido,* Bele *ido,* Gera *iiḍi*; Centr.: Tera *idi,* Dghvede *nde*; East: Dangla *udā,* Migama *ʾiḍe,* Jegu *ʾude,* Sokoro *id-* (OS: 25, 29; Stolbova 1996: 108-109; with other interpretations in both sources). The Afras. protoform can be reconstructed as *ʾinṭ/d- 'eye'.

3.4. Beḍawye *gŭad* 'Auge, Gesicht; Quelle' (RBeḍ: 90; cf. SIFKY: 297).

The same (or similar) semantic shift is attested in Indo-European languages and in Basque:

3.5. Middle and New Pers. *čašm*, Baluchi *čam* 'Auge' ~ Middle Pers. *čašmak*, New Pers. *čašme*, Baluchi *čamay* 'Quelle' (Horn: 98).

3.6. Spanish *ojo de agua* = 'punto de afloramiento de un manantial' (attested since 1280, Corominas: 422).

3.7. Basque *urbegi* 'spring' (< *ur* 'water' + *begi* 'eye'; DVE: 366). Example suggested by M. Daniel.

4. "Daughter/girl/baby (of the eye)" ~ "pupil/apple of the eye"

4.1. Heb. *bat ʿayin* (KB: 166), Arab. *bintu-l-ʿayni* (BK: 1 169), Gez. *bənta ʿayn* 'pupil of the eye, eyeball' (LGz: 99).

The Gez. form is remarkable because it is the only relic in Ethiopian languages of the Common Semitic stem **bin-/*bin-t-* 'son/daughter' supplanted in these languages by other terms, in particular by derivatives of the root **wld* 'to give birth (to)': Gez. *wald* 'son', *walatt* (< **walad-t*) 'daughter' (LGz: 613, with other Ethiopian forms).

Word-combinations of the same type, and with the same meaning are widely represented in other Eth. (all examples below are quoted from LGz: 613):

4.2. Tgr. *wälätt ʿayn* 'pupil of the eye, eyeball' (*wälätt* 'girl, daughter' and *ʿayn* 'eye').

4.3. Tna. *gʷal ʿayni* 'pupil of the eye, eyeball' (*gʷal* 'girl' and *ʿayni* 'eye').

4.4. Amh. *yayn mammito* 'pupil of the eye, eyeball' (*ayn* 'eye', the nota genitivi *yä-* and *mammit* 'girl').

4.5. Of special interest are Amh. *yäayn b(ə)rät* (K: 884), Muher *yen brät* and Zwai *yīn bərät* 'pupil of the eye' (LGur: 156), in which the element *b(ə)rät* most probably derives from **bar-(a)t-* 'daughter', a fem. form of Common Semitic **bar-* 'son' (not to be identified with Sem. **bin-/*bin-t- id.* discussed in 4.1): Jud. *bərat-* 'daughter', *bar-* 'son' (Ja.: 188, 198), Sab. *brw* 'son' (SD: 32), Mehri *bərt* 'daughter', *bər* 'son' (JM: 54). On the basis of the above-quoted Eth. examples, it is possible to reconstruct Common South Eth. word-combination **(ya-)ayn b(ə)rat* 'pupil of the eye' (= "daughter of the eye").

The identification of the element *bərät* with Amh. *bərät* 'iron' (so K: 884 and - as one of the possible interpretations – LGz: 99 and LGur: 156), which is based on a would-be visual comparison of pupil of the eye to a light-reflecting polished metal surface, is much less convincing than the "daughter-of-the-eye" interpretation, not because the association with iron is utterly impossible, but because such a semantic shift does not seem to be attested elsewhere.

4.6. Soddo, Wolane *in gäräd* (and other forms) 'pupil of the eye' (LGur: 290; *in* 'eye' and *gäräd* 'daughter, girl').

4.7. Jib. *nónú* 'pupil of the eye; little baby' (JJ: 198), Mehri *náwnəw* (JM: 307), Hars. *ʾenūnū* (JH: 172, English-Ḥarsūsi Wordlist only) 'pupil of the eye'.

The meaning "child" was apparently lost in Mehri and Harsusi but survived in Jibbali. Semitic and Afrasian parallels indicate that this meaning is primary to "pupil of the eye". Jib. *nónú* 'child' can be compared to Heb. *nīn* 'descendants' (KB: 697) while comparison of this term to Soq. *nínhin* 'frère aîné, maître' (LS: 268) is less plausible for semantic considerations. See further East Cush. Konso *ina* 'child' (SIFKY: 175), South Cush.: Burunge *nana* 'sibling, cousin' (Ehret: 292) and possibly Iraqw, Gorowa *nâʾāai* 'child, cub (of an animal)' (SIFKY: 175); Omot.: Shinasha *naʾa,* Anfillo *nao,* Shekko *naʾo,* Yemsa *naa,* Gimirra (She) *nia* etc. 'Kind; Sohn' (Lamberti: 365). Cf. SIFKI: 175, Militarev: 23-24.

4.8. Centr. Sem. **ba/u(ʾ)ba/u(ʾ)-(at)-* 'pupil of the eye': Heb. **bābā* 'eye-ball' (KB: 106; in the phrase *bābat hā-ʿayin* 'b. of the eye'), Jud. *bābītā, babtā* 'pupil of the eye' (Ja.: 136; in combination with *ʿēnā* 'eye'), Syr. *bābətā* 'pupilla (oculi); oculus' (Brock.: 62), Arab. *buʾbuʾ-* 'prunelle, pupille (de l'oeil)' (BK: 1 78; attested without, and in combination with, *ʿayn-* 'eye').

Although the meaning "pupil of the eye" can be safely reconstructed on the Central Semitic level, the important fact is that, in part of the languages, the word occurs in combination with "eye"; this points to the possibility of an ultimately non-anatomical origin of the element **ba/u(ʾ)ba/u(ʾ)-*. The PSem. term from which the element in question is likely to descend is **bab(b)-*, a descriptive word which survived only in Akk. *bābu* 'child, baby' (CAD B: 27, AHw: 95) and Arab. *babb-, babbat-* 'jeune garçon gros et gras' (BK: 1 81); note, though, phonetical differences between the two Arabic forms compared, *buʾbuʾ-,* with *-ʾ* absent from corresponding Hebrew and Aramaic forms, and *babb(-at)-*.

4.9. Egyp. (Pyr.) *ḥwn.t ỉmy.t ỉr.t* 'Pupille' (EG III: 53), lit. "the girl that is in the eye": *ḥwn.t* 'Mädchen, Jungfrau' (*ibid.*); *ỉmy.t,* an adjective (nisbah) meaning "that one (f.) which is in, she who is in", derived from the preposition *ỉm* 'in' (*ibid.* I: 72); *ỉr.t* 'Auge' (*ibid.*: 106).

A similar semantic shift is attested in Indo-European:

4.10. Lat. *pūpula, pūpilla* (WH: 2 390; < *pūpa* 'Mädchen; Püppchen'). Borrowed into English (*pupil of the eye*), German (*Pupille*) and other languages.

4.11. Greek *kórē* 'Jungfrau, Mädchen', übertr. 'Pupille, Puppe' (Frisk: 920).

4.12. Spanish *niña* (*niñilla*) *del ojo*, lit. "girl of the eye" (since 1438, Corominas: 414).

5. "Leg/knee/loins" ~ "part of people, tribe" (discussed in M. Cohen 1928)

5.1. Sem. **paḫiḏ-* 'thigh, haunch; tribe, people'.

Sem. **paḫiḏ-* 'thigh, haunch': Heb. *paḥad* 'thigh, haunch' (KB: 757; hapax in Job where *-d* instead of **-z* probably implies the Aramaic origin of the word; for an alternative tradition to render it as "testicle" see Pope: 272), Jud. *paḥdīn* (pl.) 'testiculi' (Ja.: 1151), Syr. *puḥdā* 'femur, clunis' (Brock.: 562), Arab. *faḫiḏ-/faḫḏ-/fiḫḏ-* 'cuisse' (BK 2: 552), Sab. *fḫḏ* 'hip' (SD: 43), Hars. *efḫāḏ* 'thigh' (JH: 37), Mehri *əfḫāḏ* (JM: 110), Jib. *faḫḏ* 'flesh and bone of upper leg from knee to hip' (JJ: 67); as for Soq. *fáḫid* 'cuisse' (LS: 335), it is, in all likelihood, an Arabic loan – otherwise, it would be difficult to account for *ḫ* instead of the expected *ḥ*. Cf. SED: 186-187.

Sem. **paḫiḏ-* 'tribe, people': Aram.: DAlla *pḥz,* Palm. *pḥd/pḥz* 'clan, tribe' (HJ: 905), Arab. *faḫiḏ-/faḫḏ-/fiḫḏ-* 'la plus petite subdivision d'une tribu' (BK 2: 552), Qat. *fḫḏ* 'clan, family, sub-tribe' (Ricks: 129), Mehri *fəḫə́ḏət* 'tribe' (JM: 110), Jib. *fḫə́ḏət* id. (JJ: 67), Soq. *fâḥid* 'peuple' (LS: 335).

5.2. It is by a similar semantic shift from "knee" [Sem. **birk-/*bark-*: Akk. *bi/urku* (OB on; CAD B: 255, AHw: 129, 140), Ugar. *brk* (Aist: 58), Heb. *bäräk* (KB: 160), Jud. *birkā* (Ja.: 195), Syr. *burkā* (Brock.: 96), Arab. *bārikat-* (BK 1: 116), Gez. *bərk* (LGz: 105), Tgr. *bərək* (LH: 278), Selti Wolane *bərk* (LGur: 153), Mehri *bark* (JM: 52), Jib. *bɛrk* (JJ: 28), Soq. *bərk* (LS: 96); cf. SED: 36-37] that we may explain the Arab. *burkat-* 'famille ou troupe d'hommes qui demandent le prix du sang' (BK 1: 117), an expression meaning, most probably, a group of people related by blood. Cf. also Tgr. *bərək* 'community', *təbaräkä* 'to have fellowship' (LH: 278).

5.3. Syr. *šāḳā* 'femur, crus; gens, stirps' (Brock.: 765).
The primary meaning is "thigh", from Sem. **šāḳ-* 'thigh, leg': Akk. *sīḳu* 'lap, thigh' MA on (AHw: 1049, CAD S: 305; with *s-* instead of the expected *š-*), Ugar. *šḳ* 'thigh' (Gordon: 488), Heb. *šōḳ* 'Schenkel, Wadenbein' (KB_g: 1344), Bibl. *šāḳōihī* (du. suff.) 'Schenkel' (*ibid.*: 1795), Jud. *šāḳā, šaḳḳā, šōḳā* 'joint, leg, foreleg' (Ja.: 1620, Sokoloff: 564), Arb. *sāḳ-* 'jambe, tibia' (BK 1: 1167), Tgr. *səḳuḳa* 'forearm, lower part of the leg' (LH: 182). Cf. SED: 212-213.

5.4. Russ. *колено* 'knee; a part of people, tribe' (Vasmer 2: 289, with discussion).

5.5. On the possibility of relating Lat. *genū* 'knee' to *genō*, *gigno* 'to give birth, to generate' (whence derivatives like *genus*, *gēns* 'kin, tribe, people') see EM: 273; doubts as to this relation are expressed in WH 1: 593.

6. "Bone" ~ "to be sturdy, strong", "to be big, corpulent", "to be fearsome"

6.1. Sem. **ʿaṯm-(at-)* 'bone' ~ **ʿṯm* 'to be big, large, numerous', 'to be sturdy, strong, powerful', 'to be fearsome'.

Sem. **ʿaṯm-(at-)* 'bone': Akk. *eṣemtu* (from OB on; CAD E: 341, AHw: 251), Ebl. *a-za-mu-um /ʿaẓmum/* (Krebernik: 16), Ugar. *ʿẓm* (Aist.: 240), Pho. *ʿṣm* (T: 255), Heb. *ʿäṣäm* (KB: 869), Jud. *ʿăṭam* (det. *ʿiṭmā*) (Ja.: 1063), Arab. *ʿaḏm-* (BK 2: 293), Gez. *ʿaṣm, ʿaḍm* (LGz: 58), Tgr. *ʿaṣəm, ʿačəm* (LH: 491). Cf. SED: 25-26.

Sem. **ʿṯm* 'to be big, large, numerous', 'to be sturdy, strong, powerful', 'to be fearsome': Ugar. *ʿẓm* 'gross, viel' (Aist.: 240), Heb. *ʿṣm* 'to be mighty, numerous' (KB: 727), Arab. *ʿḏm* 'être grand, grave, important, terrible, effrayant', *ʿi ḏm-* 'grandeur, au physique; grand taille' (BK 1: 293), Tgr. *ʿəṣṣum* 'strong' (LH: 490-491).

6.2. Sem. **garm-* 'bone' ~ **grm* 'to be sturdy, strong', 'to be big, corpulent', 'to be fearsome, to intimidate'

Sem. **garm-* 'bone': Heb. *gäräm* (KB: 203), Aram. Off. *grmyk* (pl. suff.; HJ: 235), Jud. *garmā* (Ja.: 270), Syr. *garmā* (Brock.: 32), Mand. *girma* 'bone; knuckle' (DM: 92), Arab. *ǯarām-, ǯurām-* 'noyau de dattes' (BK 1: 282; also *ǯurum-, ǯurūm-, ʾaǯrām-* 'corps, tout ce qui a quelque volume' *ibid.*), Sab. *grm* 'body (of animal)' (SD: 50). Cf. SED: 87-88.

Sem. **grm* 'to be sturdy, strong', 'to be big, corpulent', 'to be fearsome, to intimidate (s.o.)': Jud. *gərēm* 'to be substantial, strong' (Ja. 269), Syr. *garmānāyā* 'fortis, firmus' (Brock.: 133), Arab. *ǯrm* IV 'être grand, gros, d'un grand volume' (BK 1: 282), Gez. *garama* 'to be frightful, awesome, to become formidable, admirable' (LGz: 203). Modern Eth. verbs meaning "frighten" and "astound, astonish" derived from this root see *ibid.*

6.3. Hittite *ḫaštai* 'Knochen, Gebein(e); Widerstandskraft' (Tischler: 202; suggested by A. S. Kasyan).

The example is commented by Tischler in the following way: "Nach semitischem Vorbild? vgl. hbr. *ʿṣm*". It can be observed that Akkadian, the only Semitic language which was in contact with Hittite for a long period, knew no such semantic development (at least for *eṣemtu* 'bone') whereas direct contact between Hittite and other Semitic languages (Hebrew among them) is difficult to prove.

Semantic shifts quoted under this heading are not fully obvious. It is quite possible that we are dealing with homonymous stems here; the more so as the hypothetically secondary meanings show a wide divergence. Thus, while a relation between the concepts "sturdy, strong" and "big, corpulent" is quite natural, the development towards "fearsome, horrible" is not self-evident.

Abbreviations of languages, dialects and linguistic periods

Afras. = Afrasian (Afroasiatic, Semito-Hamitic)
Akk. = Akkadian
Amh. = Amharic
Anc. = Ancient Aramaic
Arab. = Arabic
Aram. = Aramaic
Berb. = Berber
Bibl. = Biblical Aramaic
Canar. = Canarian
Chad. = Chadic
Cush. = Cushitic
DAlla = Aramaic of the inscription from Deir Alla
Ebl. = Eblaite
Egyp. = Egyptian
Eth. = Ethiopian
Gez. = Geʿez
Har. = Harari
Hars. = Ḥarsūsi
Heb. = Hebrew
Jib. = Jibbāli
Jud. = Judaic Aramaic
Lat. = Latin
MA = Middle Assyrian
Mand. = Mandaic
MSA = Modern South Arabian
NA = Neo-Assyrian
OA = Old Assyrian
OAkk = Old Akkadian
OB = Old Babylonian
Off. = Official Aramaic
Omot. = Omotic
Palm. = Palmyrene
Pers. = Persian
Pho. = Phoenician
Post-bibl. = Post-biblical Hebrew
Pyr. = Egyptian texts of the Pyramids
Qab. = Qabyle
Qat. = Qatabanian
Sab. = Sabaic
Sem. = Semitic
Syr. = Syriac
Soq. = Soqotri
Tgr. = Tigre
Tna. = Tigrinya
Ugar. = Ugaritic

References

Aikh. Mil. = A. Yu. Aikhenvald - A. Yu. Militarev, in *Liviysko-guanchskiye yazyki. - Afraziyskiye yazyki* (Yazyki Azii i Afriki IV, kn. 2. Moskva 1991) /A. Yu. Aikhenvald, A. Yu. Militarev, *Libico-Guanche Languages*, in *Languages of Asia and Africa* IV 2, Moscow, 1991, in Russian./

Abraham = R. C. Abraham, *Somali-English Dictionary*, London, 1962.

AHw = W. von Soden, *Akkadisches Handwörterbuch*, Wiesbaden, 1965-1981.

Aist. = J. Aistleitner, *Wörterbuch der ugaritischen Sprache*, Leipzig, 1963.

Bassano = F. da Bassano, *Vocabolario tigray-italiano e repertorio italiano-tigray*, Roma, 1918.

Beeston = A. F. L. Beeston, *Foreign Loanwords in Sabaic*, in *Arabia Felix. Festschrift Walter W. Müller*, Wiesbaden, 1994, pp. 39-45.

BK = A. de Biberstein-Kazimirski, *Dictionnaire arabe-français*, Paris, 1860.

Brock. = C. Brockelmann, *Lexicon Syriacum*, Halle, 1966.

CAD = *The Assyrian Dictionary of the Oriental Institute*, the University of Chicago, 1956-.

Cer. Caff. = E. Cerulli, *Studi etiopici*. IV. *La lingua caffina*, Roma, 1951.

Cer. Om. = E. Cerulli, *Studi etiopici*. III. *Il linguaggio dei giangerò ed alcune lingue sidama dell'omo*, Roma, 1938.

Conti Ross. = C. Conti Rossini, *La langue des Kemant en Abyssinie*, Wien, 1912.

Corominas = J. Corominas, *Breve diccionario etimológico de la lengua castellana*, Madrid, 1996.

Dallet = J.-M. Dallet, *Dictionnaire kabyle-français*, Paris, 1982.

DM = E. S. Drower - R. Macuch, *A Mandaic Dictionary*, Oxford, 1963.

DVE = J. M. Azkue, *Diccionario Vasco-Español*, Madrid, 1983.

EG = A. Erman - H. Grapow, *Wörterbuch der aegyptischen Sprache*, Berlin, 1955.

Ehret = Ch. Ehret, *The historical reconstruction of Southern Cushitic phonology and vocabulary*, Berlin, 1980.

EM = A. Ernou - A. Meillet, *Dictionnaire étymologique de la langue latine. Histoire des mots*, Paris, 1967.

Foucauld = Ch. de Foucauld, *Dictionnaire touareg-français*, Paris, 1951.

Frisk = H. Frisk, *Griechisches etymologisches Wörterbuch*, Heidelberg, 1954.

GAG = W. von Soden, *Grundriss der Akkadischen Grammatik*, Roma, 1995.

Gragg = G. Gragg, *Oromo Dictionary*, East Lansing, 1982.

HJ = J. Hoftijzer - K. Jongeling, *Dictionary of the North-West Semitic Inscriptions*, Leiden - New York - Köln, 1995.

Horn = P. Horn, *Grundriss der neupersischen Etymologie*, Strassburg, 1893.

Ja. = M. Jastrow, *A Dictionary of the Targumim, the Talmud Babli and Yerushalmi, and the Midrashic Literature*, New York, 1926.

JH = T. M. Johnstone, *Ḥarsūsi Lexicon*, Oxford, 1977.

JJ = T. M. Johnstone, *Jibbāli Lexicon*, Oxford, 1981.

JM = T. M. Johnstone, *Mehri Lexicon*, London, 1987.

K = T. L. Kane, *Amharic-English Dictionary*, Wiesbaden, 1990.

KB = L. Koehler - W. Baumgartner, *The Hebrew and Aramaic Lexicon of the Old Testament. Revised by W. Baumgartner and J. J. Stamm*, Leiden-New York-Köln, 1995.

KB_g = L. Koehler - W. Baumgartner, *Hebräisches und Aramäisches Lexikon zum Alten Testament* (*neu bearbeitet von W. Baumgartner und J. J. Stamm*), Leiden, 1967-1990.

Krebernik = M. Krebernik, *Zu Syllabar und Orthographie der lexikalischen Texte aus Ebla. Teil 2* (*Glossar*), *ZA*, Band 73, 1 Halbband, 1983, pp.1-47.

Lamberti = M. Lamberti, *Die Shinassha-Sprache. Materialen zum Boro*, Heidelberg, 1993.

Lanfry = J. Lanfry, *Ghadamès*, II. *Glossaire* (*parler des Ayt Waziten*), Alger, 1973.

Laoust = E. Laoust, *Siwa*, T. 1, Paris, 1931.

LGur = W. Leslau, *Etymological Dictionary of Gurage*, Wiesbaden, 1979.

LGz = W. Leslau, *Comparative Dictionary of Geʿez* (*Classical Ethiopic*), Wiesbaden, 1987.

LH = E. Littman - M. Höfner, *Wörterbuch der Tigre-Sprache*, Wiesbaden, 1956.

LHar = W. Leslau, *Etymological Dictionary of Harari*, Berkeley-Los Angeles, 1963.

LMč = W. Leslau, *A Dictionary of Moča* (*Southwestern Ethiopian*), Berkeley-Los Angeles, 1959.

LS = W. Leslau, *Lexique Soqotri*, Paris, 1938.

Maisel 1983 = S. S. Maisel, *Puti razvitiya kornevogo fonda semitskikh yazykov*, Moskva, 1983. /*Ways of Root Derivation in Semitic*, Moscow, 1983, in Russian/

Mayrhofer = M. Mayrhofer, *Kurzgefasstes etymologisches Wörterbuch des Altindischen*, Heidelberg, 1956.

M. Cohen 1928 = M. Cohen, *Genou, famille, force dans le domaine chamitosémitique*, in *Mémorial Henri Basset*, Paris, 1928, pp. 203-210.

Militarev = A. Militarev, *Home for Afrasian: African or Asian? Areal Linguistic Arguments*, in *Cushitic and Omotic Languages. Proceedings of the Third International Symposium, Berlin, March 17-19, 1994*, Köln, 1996.

OS = V. Orel - O. Stolbova, *Hamito-Semitic Etymological Dictionary*, Leiden-New York-Köln, 1995.

Pope = M.Pope, *Job. Introduction, Translation and Notes*, New York, 1965.

Prasse - K. G.Prasse, *A propos de l'origine de H touareg* (*tahaggart*), Köbenhavn, 1969.

RAfar = L. Reinisch, *Die Afar-Sprache. Sitzungsberichte der philosophisch-historischen Klasse der Kaiserlichen Akademie der Wissenschaften zu Wien*, 1886, Bd. 111 (cpt. 5-112), Bd. 113 (cpt. 795-916), 1887, Bd. 114 (cpt. 89-127).

RBeḍ = L. Reinisch, *Wörterbuch der Beḍauye-Sprache*, Wien, 1895.

RBil = L. Reinisch, *Wörterbuch der Bilin-Sprache*, Wien, 1897.

Ricks = S. D. Ricks, *Lexicon of Inscriptional Qatabanian*, Roma, 1989.

SD = A. F. L. Beeston et al., *Sabaic Dictionary*, Louvain-la-Neuve, 1982.

SED = A. Militarev - L. Kogan, *Semitic Etymological Dictionary*, Vol. I Anatomy of Man and Animals, Münster, 2000.

SIFKY = A. B. Dolgopol'skiy, *Sravnitel'no-istoricheskaya fonetika kushitskikh yazykov*. Moskva, 1973, /A. B. Dolgopolsky, *Comparative-Historical Phonetics of Cushitic*. Moscow, 1973, in Russian./

Sokoloff = M. Sokoloff, *A Dictionary of Jewish Palestinian Aramaic*, Jerusalem, 1990.

SSL = M.-C. Simeone-Senelle, A. Lonnet, *Les noms des parties du corps dans les langues sudarabiques modernes. Deuxieme partie: les membres.* - MAS-GELLAS. Materiaux arabes et sudarabiques. 1988-1989. Nouvelle série 2.

Steiner 1982 = R. C. Steiner, Review of T. M. Johnstone's JH, in: *Afroasiatic Linguistics* 8/4, pp. 9-20.

Stolbova 1987 = O. V. Stolbova, *Sravnitel'no-istoricheskaya fonetika i slovar' zapadnochadskikh yazykov*, in *Afrikanskoye istoricheskoye yazykoznaniye i problemy rekonstruktsii*, Moskva, 1987, /*Comparative-Historical Phonetics and Lexicon of West Chadic*, in *Historical Linguistics and African Languages: Problems of Reconstruction*, Moscow, 1987, in Russian./

Stolbova 1996 = O. V. Stolbova, *Studies in Chadic comparative phonology*, Moscow, 1996.

T = R. S. Tomback, *A Comparative Semitic Lexicon of the Phoenician and Punic Languages*, Missoula, 1978.

Tischler = J. Tischler, *Hethitisches Etymologisches Glossar*, Innsbruck, 1977.

Vasmer = M. Vasmer, *Etimologicheskiy slovar' russkogo yazyka*, Moskva, 1967 /*Etymological Dictionary of Russian*, Moscow, 1967, in Russian./

Wagner = M. Wagner, *Die lexikalischen und grammatikalischen Aramaismen im alttestamentlichen Hebräisch*, Berlin, 1966.

WH = A. Walde, *Lateinisches Etymologisches Wörterbuch (3, neubearbeitete auflage von J.B.Hofmann)*, Heidelberg, 1938.

LEXIKALISCHES AUS TUTTUL

MANFRED KREBERNIK

Friedrich-Schiller-Universität Jena

Professor Fronzaroli hat sich als Semitist und Philologe große Verdienste um das Verständnis der Ebla-Texte erworben. Die Archive des Palastes G in Ebla erwähnen neben vielen anderen Orten auch Tuttul, das Kultzentrum Dagans. Von dort möchte ich ihm zwei lexikalische Miszellen als Geburtstagsgrüße nach Ebla senden. Die Ausgrabungen in Tell Bīᶜa - Tuttul haben in den vergangenen Jahren etwa 380 keilschriftliche Funde erbracht - bisher allerdings noch keine "Ebla-zeitlichen". Als deren Vorbote könnte sich jedoch einst eine aus dem Kunsthandel stammende Bronzeaxt erweisen, deren Inschrift einen Herrscher (EN) von Tuttul namens Jil'e-Li'm (*il-e-li-im*) nennt.[1] Die überwiegende Mehrheit der bisherigen Textfunde aus Tuttul datiert in die Regierungszeit Jasmaḫ-Adads. Im Laufe der Grabungskampagne von 1994 wurde jedoch ein Hort von 49 Tafeln entdeckt, die sich von jenen durch ein älteres Schriftsystem abheben.[2] Drei weitere Tafeln derselben Art wurden 1997 gefunden.[3] Die Texte dieser älteren - in sich wohl zweischichtigen - Gruppe tragen keine Jahres- oder Līmu-Daten. Paläographisch und orthographisch teilen sie viele Gemeinsamkeiten mit den "Šakkanakku-zeitlichen" Texten aus Mari. Im folgenden möchte ich zwei lexikalische Besonderheiten herausgreifen. Die Tafeln, aus denen die Belege stammen, sind im Anhang vollständig wiedergegeben. Sie gehören zu einer Gruppe von 25 Tafeln, die in Listenform den "Ausgang" (*ṣītum*)[4] bzw. "Eingang" (*nērbum*)[5] von Schafen und Ziegen verbuchen. Die Texte als ganze können an dieser Stelle allerdings nicht ausführlich kommentiert werden (dazu sei auf die bevorstehende Gesamtpublikation der Tuttul-Texte in WVDOG 100 verwiesen).

---

1 Publikation: Morrison 1984.

2 Bi.29/50:151,1-49.

3 Bi.27/49:103-105.

4 Vgl. die logographische Rubrik È.A in Šakkanakku-Texten aus Mari (*ARM* 19, *passim*).

5 < **nērebum*. Die Elision ist auffällig, doch wird die Deutung durch paralleles *ṣītum* bestätigt.

1. Die Präposition *iš*

Eine Präposition *iš*, die standard-akk. *ana* entspricht, war zunächst aus präsargonischen und Šakkanakku-zeitlichen Mari-Texten bekannt. In Ebla wollte man das Lemma in zwei – importierten – literarischen Texten erkennen,[6] doch ist keiner der beiden Belege sicher. Eindeutige Belege boten dann wieder die Texte aus Tell Beydar.[7] Tuttul gesellt sich nun als dritter zu den Orten, in denen *iš* bezeugt ist: eine Liste, welche den "Ausgang" von Schafen verzeichnet, enthält den Eintrag

1 UDU *iš* ^{I}*ʾà-a* (Text 1: 7)

wobei *iš* ^{I}*ʾà-a* offenbar den Empfänger (des Opfertieres) ausdrückt: "für Ea".[8] Einen weiteren Beleg enthält möglicherweise Text 4: 1 (s.u. mit Anm. 48). In zwei anderen Texten der Gruppe findet sich hingegen *a-na*.[9]

O. Gensler hat unlängst vorgeschlagen, IŠ als Akkadogramm für *ana* zu interpretieren.[10] Ausgangspunkt seines Aufsatzes ist die auffällige lautliche und funktionelle Übereinstimmung der akk. Kasusendung *-iš* mit der Präposition *iš*. Ein etymologischer Zusammenhang scheint auf der Hand zu liegen. Genslers Hauptanliegen ist es, die sprachtypologische Unwahrscheinlichkeit eines genetischen Zusammenhangs aufzuzeigen, der voraussetzt, daß eine Präposition *iš* im Akkadischen zur Kasusendung geworden sei. Er möchte das Problem dadurch lösen, daß er der Präposition *iš* die Existenz abspricht.

Wie Gensler einräumt, ist es aber bei einem Lemma, das durch ein einzelnes Zeichen ausgedrückt wird, schwierig, logographische oder phonographische Lesung zu beweisen, da die Chance variierender Schreibungen gering ist.[11] Drei mögliche Fälle sind zu diskutieren:

6 *ARET* 5, 6 ix 2; 7 ii 5. Vgl. Lambert 1992; Krebernik 1992.

7 *Subartu* 2, 180 (Index): 7 Belege.

8 Auch sonst kommen Schreibungen von Götternamen mit Personenkeil vor, vgl. Annunītum mit Personenkeil in Text 2: 3c oder Bi.29/50:151,7: 1: 2 UDU.UDU É ^{I}*na-ʾà-rí-im* "2 Schafe: Haus des Flußgottes". In Bi.29/50:151,42: 7f. stehen Naharum und Ea ohne Personenkeil, in Text 2: 2b wird Dagan mit Personenkeil und Gottesdeterminativ geschrieben.

9 Text 7: 19: (Schaf) *a-na* ^{d}UTU. Bi29/50:151,2: 2-4: 36 UDU *a-na mu-tu*$^{!?}$*-mi-il pa-<aq>-da-a* "36 Schafe wurden dem PN übergeben".

10 Gensler 1997.

11 Gensler 1997, S. 145.

1) IŠ und AN erscheinen als Varianten in Z. 71 der frühdynastischen Vogelliste.[12] AŠ.IŠ^{mušen} // ÁŠ.AN^{mušen}; hier ist es jedoch der Textzeuge aus Fāra, welcher IŠ schreibt, während der Textzeuge aus Ebla AN hat. Die Lesung des Namens und die Interpretation der Schreibvarianten sind noch ungewiß.

2) Eine andere mögliche Schreibvariante, die für syllabisches *iš* sprechen würde, ist ein mit dem Zeichen ŠÈ geschriebenes Wort in den Ebla-Texten. Es wurde zunächst generell als Präposition gedeutet, für die man eine Lesung *éš* als Schreibvariante von *iš* in Erwägung ziehen konnte. ŠÈ ist jedoch in Ebla syllabisch nur mit dem Lautwert *šè* gebräuchlich. Das Wort *šè* ist, wie P. Fronzaroli gezeigt hat, Genitiv Singular des maskulinen Determinativ- bzw. Relativpronomens: /d̲ī/ oder /t̲ī/.[13] Wahrscheinlich lassen sich alle Belege für die mutmaßliche Präposition ŠÈ in diesem Sinne deuten.[14]

3) Als dritte potentielle Variante von *iš* sei $iš_{11}$ erwähnt, das in ARET 7, 75 ii 3 als Präposition interpretiert wird. Hierzu ist zunächst zu bemerken, daß die beiden Zeichen IŠ und $IŠ_{11}$ in Ebla, in Tell Beydar (und wohl auch in den präsargonischen Texten aus Mari)[15] sowie im aAK Syllabar auseinandergehalten werden und verschiedene Auslautkonsonanten bezeichen, nämlich /š/, /ś/ (bzw. das Produkt aus deren Zusammenfall) versus /d̲/, /t̲/. Ferner ist die Interpretation der betreffenden Stelle unsicher: 3 Minen Silber; PN; LÚ $IŠ_{11}$ ZÌ. Vielleicht ist $IŠ_{11}$ hier ein Fehler für $IŠ_{11}$.KI (s. Anm. 21).

Die syllabische Lesung von IŠ läßt sich also bislang durch Schreibvarianten ebensowenig beweisen wie die logographische Interpretation. Gensler versucht zunächst, mögliche Einwände gegen seine These zu entkräften, um sie dann durch Plausibilitätsargumente zu untermauern. Mir scheinen allerdings gewichtige Gründe gegen die Deutung von IŠ als Akkadogramm zu sprechen. Zunächst ist es schriftgeschichtlich wenig wahrscheinlich, daß zu dem vorausgesetzten frühen Zeitpunkt ein Endungsmorphem (das keiner Wortsilbe entsprach!) isoliert und zu einem Logogramm für eine Präposition abstrahiert worden sein sollte – und zwar innerhalb derselben Sprache. Für einen solchen Vorgang gibt es keine Parallele. Ferner wird die Beobachtung, daß gerade Präpositionen zu den frühesten syllabisch geschriebenen Elementen gehören, durch Genslers Hinweis auf IGI.ME = *qidmay* "vor" nicht ent-

---

12 So die Umschrift in *MEE* 3, S. 112; vgl. M. Civils Kommentar, o.c. S. 276, sowie Owen 1981, S. 38.

13 Fronzaroli 1987, S. 268f., setzt die Formen mit /d̲/ an, doch spricht die enge Verwandtschaft des Eblaitischen mit Akkadischen (dort *šū* < **t̲ū* etc.) vielleicht eher für /t̲/; vgl. auch hebr. *šä*-.

14 Zwei Belege, in denen der Genitiv des Pronomens nicht ohne weiteres erklärlich ist, bespricht Fronzaroli 1987, S. 269. Möglicherweise wird die Genitivform verselbständigt und adverbiell bzw. konjunktionell gebraucht, wie dies später vor allem durch aram. *d(ī)* bezeugt ist. Auch die gewöhnliche Form des entsprechenden hebr. Pronomens, masor. *zä*, geht auf **d̲ī* zurück.

15 Die von Charpin 1987 und 1990 publizierten Texte enthalten nur IŠ. $IŠ_{11}$ ist aber aus dem inschriftlich belegten Königsnamen $iš_{11}^{!}$(LAM)-gi_4-*ma-rí* zu erschließen.

kräftet. Charakteristisch für die ältesten syllabisch geschriebenen Präpositionen ist nämlich nicht nur ihre Wortart, sondern auch ihre Form: es handelt sich um ein- und zweisilbige Partikeln, die sich nicht ohne weiteres auf ein logographisch darstellbares Nomen oder Verbum beziehen lassen – genau dies ist aber bei *qidmay* leicht möglich, da es zu der gemeinsemitischen Wurzel q-d-m "vorn sein" gehört. Zu dieser existierten mit größter Wahrscheinlichkeit mehrere – verbale und nominale – Ableitungen, darunter wohl auch ein Nomen der Bedeutung "Vorderseite", das logographisch durch IGI dargestellt werden konnte.[16] Vielleicht ist es nicht zu kühn, von der Präposition ausgehend auf eine PiRS-Form zu schließen, also **qidmum*.[17] Auf dieses (oder ein ähnlichlautendes) Lemma bezog man sich bei der logographischen Darstellung der Präposition durch IGI, wobei die Aussprache durch das phonetische Komplement *me* verdeutlicht wurde.[18] Die räumliche und zeitliche Verteilung der Verwendung von IŠ läßt sich auf der Sprachebene leichter erklären als auf der Schriftebene. Mari, Tell Beydar und Tuttul wären demnach Repräsentanten eines Dialektgebietes, das nach bisherigem Kenntnisstand etwa der heutigen Ǧazīra entsprach. Die Belege erstrecken sich über eine Spanne von drei- bis vierhundert Jahren. Während die frühesten Quellen (präsargonische Texte aus Mari und Beydar) ausschließlich *iš* verwenden, kommen in den späteren, Šakkanakku-zeitlichen *iš* und *a-na* nebeneinander vor. Akzeptiert man Genslers These, so stellt sich die Frage, warum das Logogramm IŠ für *ana* – bereits vor der Babylonisierung des Šakkanakku-zeitlichen Schriftsystems! – aufgegeben worden sein sollte, während die Präposition selbst weiterexistierte. Interpretiert man die Schreibung jedoch syllabisch, so reflektiert ihr Verschwinden einen gewöhnlichen sprachgeschichtlichen Vorgang: eine Präposition (*iš*) stirbt aus und wird durch eine andere (*ana*) ersetzt, die offenbar im größeren Teil des akk. Sprachgebietes gebräuchlich war.

Ungeklärt bleiben freilich die Etymologie der Präposition *iš* sowie ihr Verhältnis zur Endung des Terminativs. Gegen die Annahme, daß eine einzelne Präposition im Akkadischen zur Kasusendung geworden sei ("preposition hopping"), führt Gensler überzeugende Argumente ins Feld, und so wird man wenigstens vorläufig damit le-

16 Vgl. im späteren Akkadischen IGI = *pānum*.

17 Im Unterschied zu akk. *qudmum*.

18 Ich nehme an, daß die Schreibung als IGI^{me} zu verstehen ist und auf einem Dialekt fußt, in dem /ay/ zu /ē/ monophthongisiert war.

ben müssen, daß zwei – fast![19] – gleichlautende und gleichbedeutende Morpheme etymologisch nicht direkt miteinander verknüpft werden können. Außerakkadische Entsprechungen der Präposition *iš* lassen sich nicht mit Sicherheit nachweisen. Die ḥaḍramitische Präposition *h*-, scheidet, wie Gensler zurecht feststellt, aus. Sie ist offenbar auf lautlichem Wege aus *l*- entstanden, welches ihr in den anderen altsüdarabischen Sprachen entspricht: parallel zur Präposition *l*- hat sich im Ḥaḍramitischen auch das Prekativpräfix *l*- zu *h*- entwickelt.[20] Als potentielle Verwandte nicht ganz von der Hand zu weisen sind aber Gəʿəz *ʾəs(sə)ma* "wegen" und *ʾəska* "bis".[21] Ein alternativer etymologischer Ansatz könnte in der Hypothese bestehen, daß die Präposition *iš* selbst aus einem alten (und vielleicht verschliffenen) Nomen lokaler Bedeutung im *iš*-Kasus hervorgegangen sei (rein formal vergleichbar wäre akk. *ʾay-iš* > *ēš* "wohin").

19 Im Unterschied zur Kasusendung muß die Präposition mit einem Konsonanten, der keilschriftlich nicht explizit ausgedrückt ist, anlauten. Auch läßt die Keilschrift keine Schlüsse auf die möglicherweise differierende Vokalqualität (etwa /e/ versus /i/?) und -quantität zu.

20 Den Hinweis verdanke ich N. Nebes (Jena).

21 Von Soden 1987, 362, zählt *ʾəs(sə)ma* zu den Wörtern, die seiner Ansicht nach eine außer Gebrauch gekommene, akkadisch *ina* entsprechende Präposition enthalten, doch sind die Beispiele mit angeblicher n-Assimilation – außer *ʾəs(sə)ma* noch *ʾəmma* "wenn" und *ʾəm(mə)na* "von, aus" – problematisch, da diese im Gəʿəz nicht üblich ist. Führt man *ʾəs(sə)ma* dagegen auf **iš ši/um(i)* zurück, so wäre die Analogie zu akkadisch *ana šumi* > *aššum* vollkommen. Voraussetzung ist allerdings, daß die Aussprache *ʾəssəma* (gegenüber modernem *ʾəsma*) richtig rekonstruiert ist, wozu von Soden auf einen von A. Schall entdeckten, mittelalterlichen Beleg in lateinischer Umschrift hinweist. *ʾəska* kombiniert nach von Soden "das dem akkadischen Terminativ-Adverbial auf *-iš* entsprechende Dativ-Element *əs* mit dem 'deiktischen Element' *-ka*". Diese Analyse ist allerdings sehr hypothetisch, da es dazu keine Parallele gibt. Von Soden vergleicht *ʾəska* mit *iš*$_{11}$*-ki* in Ebla, das nach der communis opinio syllabische Schreibung einer Präposition mit der ungefähren Bedeutung "für" ist. Auf die Ähnlichkeit beider hatte bereits F.A. Pennacchietti hingewiesen, jedoch getrennte Etymologien vorgeschlagen (apud G. Pettinato, *MEE* 2, S. 101; Pennacchietti 1981, S. 299). Die Verbindung von *ʾəska* mit *iš*$_{11}$*-ki* würde derjenigen mit *iš* widersprechen, da *iš* und *iš*$_{11}$ verschiedene Auslaute repräsentieren. Lesung und Bedeutung von IŠ$_{11}$.KI bedürfen allerdings noch weiterer Klärung. Auffällig ist, daß es nur in sehr eingeschränkten Kontexten gebraucht wird (vor Personen und Orten, meist in Zusammenhang mit Kauf), und daß KI ein Zeichen ist, das nicht zum aktiven Bestand des eblaitischen Syllabars gehört. In *ARET* 1, 42 Rs. ii 1 findet sich die reduplizierte Form IŠ$_{11}$.KI.IŠ$_{11}$.KI vor einer Leerzeile. In den lexikalischen Texten rangiert IŠ$_{11}$.KI einerseits als eigenes Lemma (*MEE* 4, VE 1114; ohne Gleichung), andererseits findet es sich innerhalb einer Erklärung: É.RA = *ba-du* IŠ$_{11}$.KI (*MEE* 4, VE 336b); letzteres kann kaum anders denn als *ba-du* = /baytu/ "Haus" mit abhängigem Genitiv IŠ$_{11}$.KI verstanden werden. Diesen Belegen zufolge ist IŠ$_{11}$.KI keine Präposition – zumindest keine primäre –, sondern ein Nomen, dessen Schreibung eher logographisch als syllabisch zu interpretieren ist.

2. UDU *Zamrum.*

2.1. In zwei 1985 von Ph. Talon veröffentlichten Wirtschaftstexten aus Mari tauchten bis dahin unbekannte Termini auf, die offenbar Schafe bezeichnen oder qualifizieren.[22] Der Vokalisation nach lassen sich auf der Schriftebene drei, anscheinend zur selben Wurzel gehörige Nominalformen unterscheiden, die alle ein (singularisches oder pluralisches) Femininmorphem enthalten: *Za-mu-ra-tum*, *Za-ma-ra-tum/tim*, *Zu-mu-ra-tum*. Die Zeichen ZA/ZU lassen hinsichtlich des Anlauts verschiedene Lesungen zu: *za/zu*, *ṣa/ṣú* und – neben *sa/su* weniger gebräuchlich – *sà/sú*. Die Belege stellen sich, nach Formen gegliedert, folgendermaßen dar:

1 U$_8$ *Za-mu-ra-tum* (*ARM* 24, 45: 4)

76 UDU *ḫa-la'-at' Za-ma-ra-tim* (*ARM* 24, 51: 2)
74 SILA$_4$.GA <*ša?*> *Za-ma-ra-tim* (*ARM* 24, 51: 3)
1 *me-at* 76 UDU.NÍTA$^{\text{ḫi.a}}$ *ša Za-ma-ra-tim* (*ARM* 24, 51: 7)
1 *me-at* 91 *Za-ma-ra-tum'* (*ARM* 24, 51: 8)
2 ME 58 UDU.NÍTA *ša Za-ma-ra-tim* (*ARM* 24, 51: 11)
2 ME 70 *Za-ma-ra-tum*$^{\text{ḫi.a}}$ (*ARM* 24, 51: 16)
79 *ḫa-la-at Za-ma-ra-tim* (*ARM* 24, 51: 20)
1 *šu-ši* 8 SILA$_4$.GA; *ša Za-ma-ra-tim* (*ARM* 24, 51: 21-22)

98 UDU *ḫa-la-at Zu-mu-ra-tim* (*ARM* 24, 51: 1)
94 SILA$_4$.GA *ša Zu-mu-ra-tim* (*ARM* 24, 51: 4)
2 ME 7 *Zu-mu-ra-tum* (*ARM* 24, 51: 5)
1 *me-at* 4 UDU.NÍTA$^{\text{ḫi.a}}$ *ša Zu-mu-ra-tum* (*ARM* 24, 51: 6)
1 ME 30 UDU.NÍTA *ša Zu-mu-ra-tim* (*ARM* 24, 51: 12)
2 ME 72 *Zu-mu-ra-tum* (*ARM* 24, 51: 17)
72 *ḫa-la-at Zu-mu-ra-tim* (*ARM* 24, 51: 18)
72 SILA$_4$.GA *ša Zu-mu-ra-tim* (*ARM* 24, 51: 19)

Die Formen werden entweder selbständig gebraucht, oder sie treten im Genitiv zu Bezeichnungen von Schafen. Die Belege für selbständigen Gebrauch sind:

1 U$_8$ *Za-mu-ra-tum* (*ARM* 24, 45: 4)

1 *me-at* 91 *Za-ma-ra-tum'*[23] (*ARM* 24, 51: 8)

---

22 Den Hinweis auf diese Lemmata sowie auf *ra-ba-ba-tam* (s.u. 2.2) verdanke ich M. P. Streck (München), der in seiner noch unveröffentlichten Habilitationsschrift zum amurritischen Onomastikon der altbab. Zeit auch die amurritischen Lehnwörter zusammenstellt. *ARM* 24, 51 (und wohl auch 45) gehört nach Durand 1987, S. 171, zu den "documents datant des tous premiers moments de la 'babylonisation' de Mari".

23 Zur Umschrift: Beschädigte Zeichen sind durch unmittelbar folgendes einfaches Anführungszeichen (') gekennzeichnet. Diese Notation hat gegenüber halben eckigen Klammern sowohl visuelle (leich-

2 ME 70 *Za-ma-ra-tum*$^{\text{ḫi.a}}$ (*ARM* 24, 51: 16)

2 ME 7 *Zu-mu-ra-tum* (*ARM* 24, 51: 5)
2 ME 72 *Zu-mu-ra-tum* (*ARM* 24, 51: 17)

Die Belege für genitivischen Gebrauch sind:

76 UDU *ḫa-la'-at' Za-ma-ra-tim* (*ARM* 24, 51: 2)
79 *ḫa-la-at Za-ma-ra-tim* (*ARM* 24, 51: 20)

98 UDU *ḫa-la-at Zu-mu-ra-tim* (*ARM* 24, 51: 1)
72 *ḫa-la-at Zu-mu-ra-tim* (*ARM* 24, 51: 18)

74 SILA$_4$.GA <*ša?*> *Za-ma-ra-tim* (*ARM* 24, 51: 3)
1 *šu-ši* 8 SILA$_4$.GA; *ša Za-ma-ra-tim* (*ARM* 24, 51: 21-22)

94 SILA$_4$.GA *ša Zu-mu-ra-tim* (*ARM* 24, 51: 4)
72 SILA$_4$.GA *ša Zu-mu-ra-tim* (*ARM* 24, 51: 19)

1 *me-at* 76 UDU.NÍTA$^{\text{ḫi.a}}$ *ša Za-ma-ra-tim* (*ARM* 24, 51: 7)
2 ME 58 UDU.NÍTA *ša Za-ma-ra-tim* (*ARM* 24, 51: 11)

1 *me-at* 4 UDU.NÍTA$^{\text{ḫi.a}}$ *ša Zu-mu-ra-tum* (*ARM* 24, 51: 6)
1 ME 30 UDU.NÍTA *ša Zu-mu-ra-tim* (*ARM* 24, 51: 12)

Als nomina regentia der Genitivverbindungen kommen vor: *ḫa-la-at*, SILA$_4$.GA "Milchlamm" und UDU.NÍTA "Hammel". *ḫa-la-at* gehört wohl zu ʿ-w-l "ernähren" und wurde als "milchgebend(es Schaf)" gedeutet;[24] morphologisch handelt es sich um ein nach nordwestsem. Weise gebildetes Partizip des G-Stammes: /ʿāl-at/.

Wie sind nun die unterschiedlichen Bildungen der Wurzel Z-m-r in den Mari-Texten morphologisch zu beurteilen?

Za-mu-ra-tum ist nach Kontext (*ARM* 24, 45: 4: 1 U$_8$ *Za-mu-ra-tum*) ein femininer Singular. Wahrscheinlich handelt es sich um ein zu U$_8$ gehöriges Adjektiv; weniger wahrscheinlich, aber nicht ganz auszuschließen, ist die Möglichkeit, daß U$_8$ als

tere Lesbarkeit) als auch EDV-technische Vorteile. Man könnte ferner differenzieren zwischen ' zur Kennzeichnung noch eindeutig lesbarer Zeichen und " zur Kennzeichnung konjizierter Lesungen. Mit x werden beschädigte, unkenntliche Zeichen wiedergegeben, X steht für erkennbare, aber nicht identifizierte Zeichen.

24 Durand 1987, S. 171, stellt die Verbindung mit ÙZ *a-lá-tum* in *ARM* 19, 462: 4 her. Zadok 1992 setzt als Wurzel ġ-w-l an aufgrund von arab. *ġālat*, doch scheint "säugen" nicht die Grundbedeutung des arab. Verbums zu sein: "she suckled her child while she was compressed/pregnant" (nach E. W. Lane, Arabic-English Lexicon, London 1877). Heimpel 1999 weist darauf hin, daß die Anzahl der Lämmer in *ARM* 24, 51 in etwa mit der Anzahl der *ḫa-la-at* übereinstimmt, was darauf schließen lasse, daß *ḫa-la-at* "ewes with milk" seien. Dazu passe das in *ARM* 19, 462: 2 zu *a-lá-tum* parallele *ya-bi-sa-tum* /yabisātum/ in der Bedeutung "trockene", d.h. nicht-milchgebende, (sc. Ziegen).

Determinativ fungiert, wonach *Za-mu-ra-tum* substantiviertes Adjektiv oder Substantiv wäre.

Za-ma-ra-tum und *Zu-mu-ra-tum* sind durch selbständigen Gebrauch nach den Zahlen 191 (*ARM* 24, 51: 8), 270 (*ARM* 24, 51: 16) bzw. 207 (*ARM* 24, 51: 5), 272 (*ARM* 24, 51: 17) als feminine Plurale (im Nominativ) ausgewiesen. Auch bei den Genitiven *Za-ma-ra-tim* bzw. *Zu-mu-ra-tim* wird es sich um Plurale handeln, da auch die übergeordneten Nomina im Plural stehen und die Zuordnung einer größeren Anzahl von *ḫa-la-at*, $SILA_4$.GA oder UDU.NÍTA zu jeweils einem Exemplar von *Za/Zu-ma-ra-tim* unwahrscheinlich ist.

Was die Nominalformen betrifft, so stehen, wie schon Talon feststellte,[25] *Za-ma-ra-tum/tim* und *Zu-mu-ra-tum/tim* zueinander in Opposition. Diese Tatsache sowie die a/u-Alternanz lassen an ein Nebeneinander von G-stämmiger und D-stämmiger Nominalform denken, also etwa PaRaS-āt versus PuRRuS-āt. Ein dem morphologischen entsprechender semantischer Gegensatz wäre dann "einfach" versus "viel, in höherem Maße".[26] Fraglich ist, ob *Za-mu-ra-tum* eine dritte Nominalform darstellt (etwa PaRuSS-at) oder, was wahrscheinlicher ist, als Variante einer der beiden anderen aufzufassen ist: in letzterem Falle kommt vor allem PaRRuS als (ältere) Variante von PuRRuS[27] in Frage. Ob die zugehörige maskuline Form in dem Toponym BÀD *Za-mu-ri-im*^{ki} vorliegt,[28] ist unsicher. Ist *Za-mu-ra-tum* hingegen der Singular zu *Za-ma-ra-tum*, so müßte eine lautlich bedingte Variante von PaRS-at vorliegen, s.u. 2.3.

Schon der lexikalische Befund legt nahe, daß wir es mit – amurritischen[29] – Lehnwörtern zu tun haben. Auch lassen sich Flexion und Nominalbildung nur mit Mühe in allen Punkten akkadisch deuten. Bei *Za-ma-ra-tum* = /Zamarātum/ müßte man annehmen, daß wie in akk. *labirum* wegen des folgenden /r/ ein Kurzvokal erhalten blieb, der sonst elidiert worden wäre. *Za-mu-ra-tum* ist akkadisch nur erklärbar, wenn man eine Nominalform PaRuSS-at ansetzt, ansonsten würde man **Zamurtum* bzw. **Zammurtum* erwarten.

---

25 *ARM* 24, S. 33.

26 Zum akk. D-Stamm vgl. Kouwenberg 1997, zur Opposition von PaRvS versus PuRRuS s. o.c. 361-364.

27 Vgl. ass. PaRRuS gegenüber bab. PuRRuS. In Ebla sind beide Bildungen belegt.

28 Zadok 1993, S. 322. Das Toponym dürfte zu ḏ-m-r "schützen" gehören.

29 Inwieweit der traditionelle altorientalische Terminus großräumige sprachliche Homogenität des "Amurritischen" voraussetzt, sei dahingestellt. Er wird hier als Bezeichnung nicht-akkadischer semitischer Sprachen in der Nachbarschaft von Mari bzw. Tuttul gebraucht.

2.2. Die Texte aus Tuttul liefern nun ergänzendes Material zu den oben behandelten Termini der Mari-Texte, wobei allerdings das Formenspektrum noch bunter wird. In 6 Texten erscheint als Bezeichnung oder Qualifikation von Schafen ein Lemma *Zamrum*, das maskuline und feminine Formen bildet. Die morphologische Analyse ergibt sich aus den Kontexten. Belegt sind:

Za-am-ru-um (Sg. m. Nominativ): Text 2: 3b; Text 3: 2; 6; Text 4: 5; 6
Zu[!]*-am'-ra'-am'* (Sg. m. Akkusativ): Text 7: 4; 6
Za-am-ra-tum (Sg. f. Nominativ): Text 2: 3a
[*Zu*]*-am*[!]*-ra-ta-am* (Sg. f. Akkusativ): Text 7: 12
Za-am-ra-tá-an (Dual f. Nominativ): Text 5: 7
Zu'-am[!]*-ra-ta-in* (Dual f. Akkusativ): Text 7: 1
Za-ma-ra-tum (Pl. f. Nominativ): Text 6: 1

Etwas problematisch hinsichtlich Lesung und Orthographie sind die Belege aus Text 7. Die erste Silbe wird hier konsequent mit einer "gebrochenen Vokalschreibung" notiert, darüberhinaus auch die Endung des Obliquus Dual (falls hier nicht ein Diphthong angedeutet werden soll). Derartige Graphien begegnen innerhalb unserer Textgruppe noch in einem weiteren Text.[30]

In allen Belegen geht dem syllabisch geschriebenen Wort das Zeichen UDU voraus, das hier eher Logogramm als Determinativ ist. Dafür spricht insbesondere die Formulierung 2 UDU *Za-am-ra-tum ú Za-am-ru-um'* "2 Schafe – (nämlich) ein männliches und ein weibliches Zamrum", da hier die Zahl 2 nur zusammen mit dem Oberbegriff UDU "Schaf" sinnvoll ist.

Zamrum ist augenscheinlich ein Substantiv oder substantiviertes Adjektiv. Die Formenbildung weicht von der akkadischen ab. Falls ein Adjektiv vorläge, würde man im Akkadischen im Sg. und Dual des Femininums Formen mit Vokal zwischen 2. und 3. Radikal erwarten, also etwa **Zamartum*, **Zamartān*. Geht man von der Nominalform PaRS aus, so fügen sich allerdings der feminine Sg. und Dual *Zamratum*, *Zamratān* ins akkadische Paradigma. Besonders auffällig ist jedoch der feminine Plural *Za-ma-ra-tum*; hier sollte im Akkadischen keinesfalls ein Vokal zwischen 2. und 3. Radikal auftreten. Falls die Schreibung ernst zu nehmen ist und nicht etwa eine Kv-Kv-Schreibung für KvK (*Za-ma* für /Zam/) enthält,[31] wird hier

---

30 Bi.29/50:151,1: *na-bi-na-ta-im* (PN im Gen.; Z.1) *ba-iq-rum* (Z.6), *ša-la-ta-im* (Z.7)

31 Diese in den Ebla-Texten sehr häufige Schreibweise kommt sehr sporadisch vielleicht noch in unseren Šakkanakku-zeitlichen Tuttul-Texten vor, die möglichen Fälle beschränken sich allerdings auf Personennamen, deren Interpretation in jedem Falle mit Unsicherheiten behaftet ist. So könnte

die Nominalform des Singulars durch a-Einschub erweitert. Leider ist der maskuline Plural mit einer zu postulierenden analogen Bildeweise **Za-ma-ru* nicht belegt. Theoretisch lassen sich die Schreibungen durch zwei Typen der Pluralbildung erklären:

	Singular	Plural
1.	PaRvS-at-um > ParSatum	PaRRaS-āt-um
2.	PaRS-at-um	PaRaS-āt-um

Der erste Typus ist nur ansatzweise im Akkadischen bezeugt und hier wenig wahrscheinlich.[32] Der zweite dagegen ist bei der Pluralbildung der Nominalformen PaRS, PiRS, PuRS und zugehöriger Feminina aus den nordwestsem. Sprachen, aber auch aus dem Arabischen, gut bekannt. Im Ugaritischen finden sich beispielsweise zu *riš* /raʾšu/ "Kopf" die Plurale *rḁšm* /raʾašū-ma/ und *rḁšt* /raʾašātu/ neben *rišt* /raʾšātu/; das Hebräische[33] bildet zu **malk* "König" und **malkā* "Königin" die Plurale **malakīm* bzw. **malakōt*; im Arabischen sind Fälle wie *ḥalqatun* "Ring" mit Kollektiv *ḥalaqun* und Plural *ḥalaqātun* zu vergleichen. Trifft unsere paradigmatische Interpretation der oben zusammengestellten Belege zu, so sind sie von doppelter Bedeutung: erstens stellen sie das bislang älteste Zeugnis für den a-Einschub bei der Pluralbildung dar, zweitens dokumentieren sie diese Erscheinung zum ersten Mal für das Amurritische. Ergänzend sei auf ein weiteres mögliches Zeugnis für die Pluralbildung mit a-Einschub in den Tuttul-Texten hingewiesen, nämlich den Ortsnamen *qa-ra-a-a-tu-li-im*,[34] falls dieser als /qarayātu-liʾm/ "Dörfer des Liʾm" zu interpretieren und zu einem Singular **qaryatu(m)* zu stellen ist. Ein etwas jüngeres Beispiel könnte schließlich ein Textzeuge der "Insurrection générale contre Narām-Sîn" aus Mari enthalten: dort findet sich eine zu *rabbatum* "10 000"[35] gehörige Form

sich hinter der Schreibung *Bu-Zu-Bu-Za-an* (Text 1: 4) ein /BuZBuZān/ verbergen, hinter *mi-ri-mi-ru* (Bi.29/50:151,1: 14) ein /mirmiru/.

32 Dieser Typus wurde von E. Reiner für das Akkadische angenommen (Reiner 1966, S. 64), ihr Ansatz jüngst von Kouwenberg 1997, S. 52-57, wieder aufgegriffen. Es handelt sich jedoch nicht um ein allgemeingültiges Paradigma. Betroffen ist eine kleine Anzahl von Adjektiven, die auch gewöhnliche Plurale bilden. Umgekehrt kommt PaRRaS auch singularisch vor.

33 Rekonstruierte Formen in Anlehnung an die von W. Richter entwickelte Transkription, vgl. Richter 1983.

34 Bi.29/50:151,17: 2: 5 <UDU> *in qa-ra-a-a-tu-li-im*.

35 Die Form ist möglicherweise akkadisiert (logographisch GAL geschrieben; Angleichung an *rabûm* "groß"?). In Ebla, Alalaḫ, aber auch im Šakkanakku-zeitlichen Mari sind Formen mit /i/ in der ersten Silbe üblich (*ribba* oder *ribab*, *ribbat-*), s. Durand 1984.

ra-ba-ba-tam: *4 ra-ra-ba-tam di-*[*ku*] "40 000 wurden getötet"[36] Ein anderer Mari-Text bietet allerdings den Plural *rabbātim*[37] Die Akkustivendung /-am/ muß, insbesondere wenn ein Plural /rababāt-/ intendiert ist, fehlerhaft sein.Vielleicht liegt hier jedoch eine mit *rabbatum* konkurrierende (aus dem Plural rückgebildete?) Singularform *rababatum* zugrunde, vgl. hebr. **ra/ibabā* neben *ribbō*.

2.3. Wie verhalten sich nun die Formen aus Mari und Tuttul zueinander? Akzeptiert man die Hypothese, daß ein Teil der Formen aus Mari zum D-Stamm gehört, so beschränkt sich der direkte Vergleich auf die mutmaßlich zum G-Stamm gehörigen Bildungen. Deren Pluralform *Za-ma-ra-tum* findet sich sowohl in Mari wie auch in Tuttul. Ausgehend von dieser Gemeinsamkeit und von den in Tuttul gut bezeugten Singularformen *Zamrum*, *Zamratum* liegt es nahe, auch *Za-ma-ra-tum/tim* in Mari auf ein dort (noch) nicht belegtes **Zamr*(*at*)*um* zu beziehen und die einzige in Mari vorkommenden Singularform *Za-mu-ra-tum* entweder mit den mutmaßlich D-stämmigen Formen *Zu-mu-ra-tum/tim* zu verbinden oder aber als lautlich bedingte Variante von *Zamratum* anzusehen.[38] Somit ergibt sich das folgende hypothetische Paradigma, das, wie zu hoffen ist, weitere Belege korrigieren oder bestätigen werden (fett = in Tuttul belegte Form; unterstrichen = in Mari belegte Form):

	Singular	Dual	Plural
1. m.	***Zamr-um***	—	—
f.	***Zamr-at-um***	***Zamr-at-ān***	***Zamar-āt-um***
2. f.	*Zammur-at-um*(?), **Zummur-at-um*	—	***Zummur-āt-um***

2.4. Die genaue Bedeutung der verschiedenen Termini ist aus den Kontexten nicht zu erschließen. Aus der Existenz maskuliner und femininer Formen ergibt sich, daß der Grundbegriff nicht geschlechtsspezifisch ist. Das Nebeneinander zweier, vermutlich auf G- bzw. D-Stamm bezogener Nominalformen läßt vermuten, daß *Zamrum* eine Qualität bezeichnet, bei der einfaches und gesteigertes Maß lexikalisch unterschieden werden. Aufgrund der Mehrdeutigkeit der Syllabogramme ZA/ZU bieten sich verschiedene etymologische Anknüpfungspunkte:

---

36 Charpin 1997, S. 10f., A.1252+M.8696 Rs. 8': 4; danach zu ergänzen Rs. 6': 5 *ra-ba*'[*-ba-tam di-ku*]. Vgl. ug. *rbt* "10 000" mit Plural *rbbt*.

37 Dossin 1974, S. 181, A.1153: 16: 5 *ra-ab-ba-tim*.

38 Mit epenthetischem Vokal vor /r/, u-Färbung unter Einfluß des Labials /m/?

1) **ḍamr-* "Wolle" (Gəʾəz *ḍamr*, hebr. **ṣamr*, syr. *ʿamrā*). Diese Etymologie würde einen Wechsel der Bedeutung bzw. der Wortart voraussetzen: "Wolle" > "wolltragend(es Schaf)".

2) Hebr. **zamr* "ein Capride".[39]

3) ḏ-m-r "schützen".

4) Wenig wahrscheinlich ist eine Verbindung mit arab. *ʾasmaru* "braun, gelb", da die Farbbezeichnung offenbar erst innerarabisch entstanden ist und zudem die Wurzel (s-m-r oder š-m-r?) nicht feststeht.

Anhang: Die Texte aus Tuttul.

Text 1 (Bi.29/50:151,45)

1	2 UDU	*ni-iš-ni'-i*$^{?}$'	2 Schafe: PN(?).[40]
2	1 UDU	É ^{d}*da'-gan*	1 Schaf: Haus des Dagan.
3	1 UDU	*ra-pí-qa'-u'*	1 Schaf: die Rapiqäer(?).[41]
4	1 UDU	*Bu-Zu-Bu-Za-an*	1 Schaf: PN.
5	1 UDU	*šu-mu-na-ʾà-rí*	1 Schaf: PN.
6	1 UDU	*aḫ-lu-lá-*^{d}IM	1 Schaf: PN.
7	1 UDU	*iš* ^{1}ʾ*à-a*	1 Schaf: Für Ea.
8	*ṣí-tum*		Ausgang.

Text 2 (Bi.29/50:151,25)

1a	1 UDU *a-lu-um*[42]	1 Edelschaf:
b	*in ki-rí-i-im*	im "Garten"(?).
2a	1 UDU *sá a-bu-ni-im*	1 Schaf von PN:[43]
b	*in* É $^{I.d}$*da-gan*	im Haus des Dagan.
3a	2 UDU *Za-am-ra-tum*	2 Schafe – 1 weibliches Zamrum,
b	*ú Za-am-ru-um*	1 männliches Zamrum:
c	É '*a-nu-ni'-tim*$_{x}$(TIN)'	Haus der Annunītum.
d	*sá a-ḫu-na*	von Aḫuna.
4	*ṣí-tum*	Ausgang.

---

39 So Zadok 1992 und1993, S. 322.

40 Vgl. Text 4: 1.

41 *ra-pí-qa-u* auch in Text 5: 5. Formal handelt sich um eine Nisbe, die auch als Eigenname gebraucht sein könnte. Auffällig ist hier wie auch bei *a-am-a-Ti-u* in Text 5 (und anderen mutmaßlichen Nisben) das Fehlen der Mimation im Vergleich mit *a-am-a-Ti-u-um* (Text 3) oder *ì-ma-ra-u-um* "Emaräer" (Bi.29/50:151,10: 4); daher vielleicht pluralisch zu verstehen.

42 Beachte die syllabische Schreibung gegenüber gewöhnlichem *a-lum*.

43 *a-bu-ni-im* /ʾabu-niʿm/ ist als PN auch in Bi.29/50:151,41: 1 bezeugt.

Text 3 (Bi.29/50:151,39)

1	*a-za-tum* É *an-nu-ni-tim*$_{x}$(TIN)	Eine Ziege:[44] Haus der Annunītum.
2	1 UDU *Za-am-ru-um*	1 Zamrum-Schaf:.
3	É $^{I.d}$*da-gan-ì-lí*	Haus des PN
4	1 UDU *a-tu-rí-u'-um*	1 ...-Schaf:[45]
5	*in tu-x-NI*^{ki}'	in ...[46]
6	1 UDU *Za-am-ru-um*	1 Zamrum-Schaf:
7	*a-am-a-Ti-u-um*	der Jamḫadäer(?).[47]
8	*ṣí-tum*	Ausgang.

Text 4 (Bi.29/50:151,19)

1	*u-um a-Ga* X *ni-iš-ni*-x [?]	(Am) Tage als PN (?) ...[48]
2	[1?] UDU É *ba-al-da-ku-ra*$^{!?}$'	[1?] Schaf: Haus von PN.
3	6 UDU *in 2 u-me-in'*	6 Schafe: in ...[49]
4a	UDU *a-tu-dum* É'	<1> Widder; Haus von ...[50]
4b	*ru-X-ba-a-an*	
5	1 UDU *Za-am-ru-um* É [*ba*$^{?}$]-*al*$^{?}$'-*da-ku-ra*	1 Zamrum-Schaf: Haus des PN.
6	1 UDU *Za-am-ru-um* É.MÍ	1 Zamrum-Schaf: "Frauenhaus".
7	[n] UDU' *bi-rí-im*	1 Opferschau-Schaf.
8	[n UDU] TUR *sá bi-rí-im*	1 junges Opferschau-Schaf.
9	[n] UDU' SILA$_{4}^{?}$' TUR *i-ga-li-im*	[1] junges ...-Schaf: PN.
10	[n] UDU *ša/ta*$^{?}$'-*ra-lá-NI*	[1] Schaf: PN.
11	[1] UDU *a-lu-um ra-Ti-ú-tum*	[1] Edelschaf: PN(?).[51]
12	1 UDU *x-ti-a-um*	1 Schaf: PN.

44 Zu vergleichen ist Bi.29/50:151,5: 1: 1 UDU *a-za-tan*. Es liegt *ʿazzatum* < **ʿanzatum* "Ziege" vor, das auch in Chagar Bazar und in Nuzi belegt ist, s. *CAD* s.v. *azzatu* und *AHw*. s.v. *ḫazzatu*. "1" vor dem Dual in Bi 29/50:151,5: 1 ist vohl fehlerhaft.

45 Kaum in *a-tu-du*$^{!}$-{*u*}-*um* "Widder" zu emendieren, das in Text 4: 4 *a-tu-dum* und in Bi.29/50:151, 321: 5 *a-tu-dú-um* geschrieben wird.

46 Das zweite Zeichen ist mir unklar, evt. liegt eine ältere Graphie für Tuttul vor: *in tu-tu*$_{x}$*-li*^{ki}.

47 Vielleicht als /yamʿadīyum/ zu interpretieren. S.a. Anm. 41.

48 Der Anfang könnte auch 10 UM/MES$^{!}$/DUB$^{!}$ zu lesen sein, was aber nicht in den folgenden Kontext (Schafe) paßt. Die Lesung *u-um* /yōm/ "Tag" (status constructus) impliziert ein Tagesdatum, das an dieser Stelle freilich ebenfalls unerwartet ist, immerhin scheint aber auch Bi.29/50:151,2 mit einem Tages- oder Monatsdatum einzusetzen: UD'/ITI' MI TA/ŠA GA'/BI' SIG$_{5}$/AR$^{!}$. *a-Ga* ist vielleicht PN, vgl. *a-Ga-a* in Bi.29/50:151: 5. X könnte ZU, SU oder IŠ sein, letzteres dann vielleicht die oben behandelte Präposition. Am Ende könnte dasselbe Lemma (PN?) wie in Text 1: 1 vorliegen.

49 Die orthographisch naheliegende Interpretation "in 2 Tagen" paßt schlecht ins Formular; sollte *u-me-in* ein Toponym sein?

50 Derselbe Name (einer Gottheit?) kommt auch in Bi.29/50:151,21: 6 vor. Das zweite Zeichen ist mir unklar, es ähnelt DAG, KAL oder UN.

51 Oder: "die Soldaten" (*rādiʾūtum*)?

13	2 UDU *in' x-NI-*[*x*]	2 Schafe: in ...
14	1 UDU É *an-nu-ni-tim*$_{x}$(TIN)	1 Schaf: Haus der Annunītum.
15	1 UDU *qú-ra'-da'-an*	1 Schaf: PN.
16	*ṣí-tum*	Ausgang.

Text 5 (Bi.29/50:151,16)

1	12 UDU ITI ^{d}*da-gan*	12 Schafe: Monat(sfest) des Dagan.[52]
2a	1 UDU DAM.MUNUS	1 Schaf: Gattin des PN.
2b	*ab-dú-*^{d}*da-gan*	
3	[n] UDU *ab-da-an*	[1] Schaf: PN.
4	[n] UDU *ḫu-Tu-Tum*	[1] Schaf: PN.
5	[n] UDU' *ra-pí-qa-u'*	[1] Schaf: die Rapiqäer(?).
6	[n] UDU *a-bu-la-ú*	1 Schaf: PN.
7	2 UDU *Za-am-ra-tá-an*	2 Zamrum-Schafe:
8	*a-am-a-Ti-u*	die Jamḫadäer(?).
9	*ṣí-tum*	Ausgang.

Text 6 (Bi.29/50:151,6)

1	77 UDU *Za-ma-ra-tum*	77 weibliche Zamrum-Schafe
2	8 UDU *x-lu*	8 ...-Schafe.
3	9 UDU' x.x	9 ...-Schafe.
4	12 UDU' *KU*$^{?}$*-ra'-tum'*	12 ...-Schafe.[53]
5	ŠUNIGIN' [1] *me'-at* 6 UDU	Insgesamt: [1] hundert 6 Schafe.
6	*x-x-ra-tum*	...
7	n' UDU ÙZ	n Ziegen.
8	4 UDU ÙZ TI.x	4 ...-Ziegen.
9	6 UDU *lá-lá-ú* x	6 ...-Zicklein.
10	16 UDU *lá-lá-a-ú*	16 Zicklein.
11	ŠUNIĞIN 97 UDU ÙZ	Insgesamt: 97 Ziegen.
12	DUB *né'-re'-eb'* UDU	Tafel über den Eingang von Kleinvieh,
13	*sá a-mu-na-ga-ma*	gehörig dem PN
14	x *i-x-x-NI-lu-ma*	... PN(?).
15	ITI NI.X.SAĞ	(Im) Monat ...[54]
16	DUB$^{?}$ *sá-ṭir*$_{5}$(TIR)	wurde die Tafel geschrieben.

52 ITI ^{d}*da-gan*' ist Zweckbestimmung von 2 Rindern in Bi.29/50:151,42: 10. Das fragliche Zeichen findet sich auch in Text 6: 15 sowie in dem "Pseudo-Šakkanakku-Text" Bi.28/46:88: 5 (vorläufige Publikation: Krebernik 1990, S. 75f.; dazu J.-M. Durand1991, S. 86f.) als Element des PN *Za-mu*-X. Mit X = ITI wäre der Name *sà-mu-eraḫ* zu lesen.

53 Wohl kaum das ansonsten erst mA bezeugte (*a*)*gurratu* "Mutterschaf".

54 Der Monatsname ist vohl NI.NÌ$^{!}$.SAĞ zu lesen, vgl. NI.NÌ.SAĞ im Šakkanakku-zeitlichen Mari.

Text 7 (Bi.29/50:151,31)

1	2 UDU' *zu'-am*$^{!}$*-ra-ta-in*	2 Zamrum-Schafe
2	*pu-ul-sú-mi-il*	hat PN
3	*ú-ra-bi*	aufgezogen.
4	1 UDU *zu*$^{!}$*-am'-ra'-am'*	1 Zamrum-Schaf:
5	*ì-lí-ka-bar*$^{!}$(MAŠ)	PN.
6	1 UDU *zu*$^{!}$*-am*$^{!}$*-ra-am'*	1 Zamrum-Schaf:
7	*e-NI-su-ma-bu'-um'*	PN.
8	1 UDU *ša-ta-am*$^{!}$	1 Zamrum-Schaf:
9	*mi-ki-nu-um'*	PN.
10	1 UDU *ša-ta-am*$^{!}$	1 weibliches Schaf:
11	*i'-x-a-ḫu-x-*[?]	PN.
12	1' UDU' [*zu*]*-am*$^{!}$*-ra-ta-am*	1 Zamrum-Schaf:
13	*Ta'-am-ka'-ru-um*	der Kaufmann.[55]
14	4$^{?}$' UDU *ia-ḫa'-ad-x-*[...]	4? Schafe: PN.
15	*ner'-bu'-um'*	Eingang.
16	1 [UDU] x *x-x-ri-ta-im'*	1 ...-[Schaf],
17	1 UDU' [*x*]*-ú*$^{?}$*-ri-im*	1 ...-Schaf,
18	1 UDU *zu'-am-ra-tum*	1 (weibliches) Zamrum-Schaf:
19	*a-na* ^{d}UTU	für Šamaš.
20	*ṣí-tum*	Ausgang.

Bibliographie

D. Charpin, "Tablettes présargoniques de Mari", *MARI* 5 (1987), S. 65-127.

D. Charpin, "Nouvelles tablettes présargoniques de Mari", *MARI* 6 (1990), S. 245-252.

D. Charpin, "La version mariote de l'"insurrection générale contre Narâm-Sîn"", in D. Charpin - J.-M. Durand (ed.), *Florilegium Marianum* 3, *Recueil d'études à la mémoire de Marie-Thérèse Barrelet*, Paris 1997, S. 9-17.

G. Dossin, "Une opposition familiale", in A. Finet (ed.), *La voix de l'opposition en Mésopotamie*, Brüssel 1974, S. 179-188.

J.-M. Durand, "A propos du nombre 10 000 à Mari", *MARI* 3 (1984), S. 278f.

J.-M. Durand, "Histoire du royaume de Haute-Mésopotamie, I", *MARI* 5 (1987), S. 155-198.

J.-M. Durand, "Nouvelles de Tuttul", *NABU* 1991/114.

---

55 Als Eigenname zu verstehen?

P. Fronzaroli, "Le pronom déterminatif à Ebla", *MARI* 5 (1987), S. 267-274.

O. D. Gensler, "Mari Akkadian IŠ "to, for" and Preposition-Hopping", *Or.* NS 66 (1997), S. 129-156.

W. Heimpel, "*Hallatum, hālātum, ha-la-tum*", *NABU* 1999/44.

N. J. C Kouwenberg, *Gemination in the Akkadian Verb*, Assen 1997.

M. Krebernik, "Die Textfunde aus Tall Biʿa", *MDOG* 122 (1990), S. 67-87.

M. Krebernik, "Mesopotamian Myths at Ebla", in P. Fronzaroli (ed.), *Literature and Literary Language at Ebla*, Firenze 1992, S. 63-149.

W. G. Lambert, "The Language of *ARET* V 6 and 7", in P. Fronzaroli (ed.), *Literature and Language at Ebla*, Firenze 1992, S. 41-62.

M. M. Morrison, "A New Anchor Axehead", *OrAnt.* 23 (1984), S. 45-48; Tav. I-II.

D. I. Owen, "On Birds, Eggs and Turtles", *ZA* 71 (1981), S. 29-47.

F. A. Pennachietti, "Indicazioni preliminari sul sistema preposizionale dell'Eblaita", in L. Cagni (ed.), *La lingua di Ebla*, Napoli 1981, S. .

W. Richter, *Transliteration und Transkription*, St. Ottilien 1983.

W. von Soden, "Äthiopisch-akkadische Isoglossen", in H. Jungraithmayr – W. W. Müller (ed.), *Proceedings 4th International Hamito-Semitic Congress* (Amsterdam/Philadelphia 1987), S. 559-566.

R. Zadok, "On the Names of Two Animals", *NABU* 1992/58.

R. Zadok, "On the Amorite Material from Mesopotamia", in M. E. Cohen e.a. (ed.), *The Tablet and the Scroll. Near Eastern Studies in Honor of William W.Hallo* (Bethesda 1993), S. 315-333.

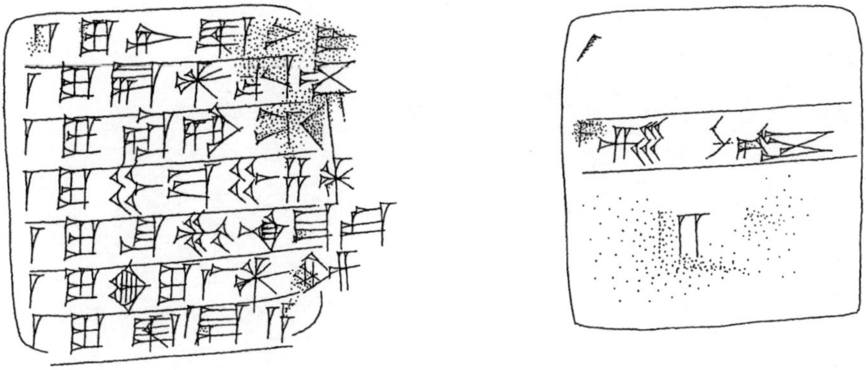

Text 1 (Bi.29/50:151,45)

Text 2 (Bi.29/50:151,25)

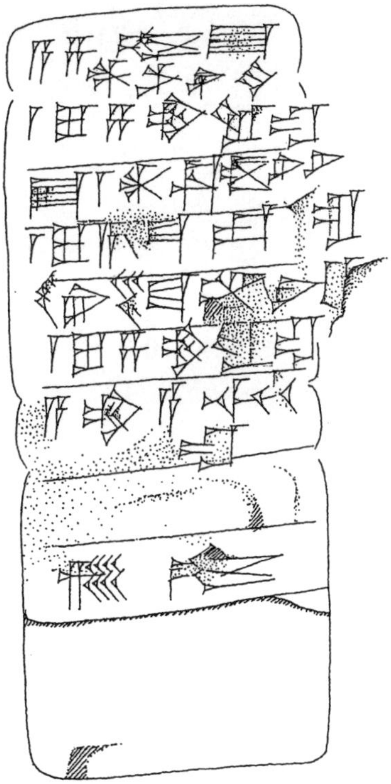

Text 3 (Bi.29/50:151,39)

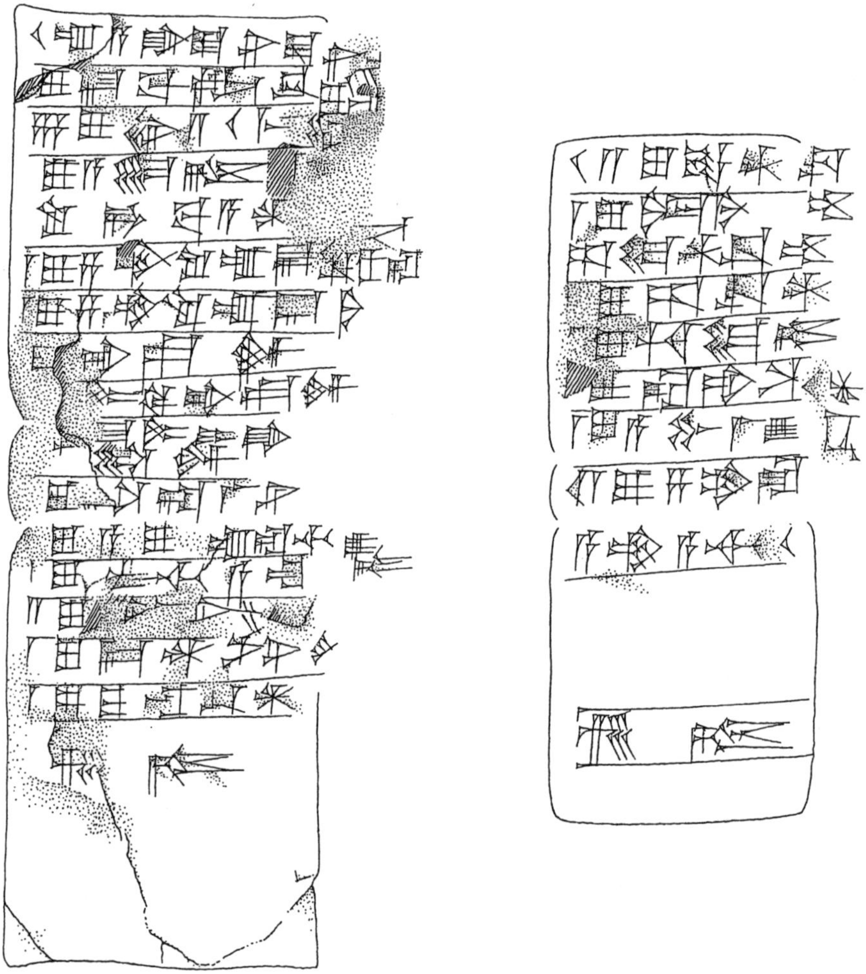

Text 4 (Bi.29/50:151,19)

Text 5 (Bi.29/50:151,16)

Text 6 (Bi.29/50:151,6)

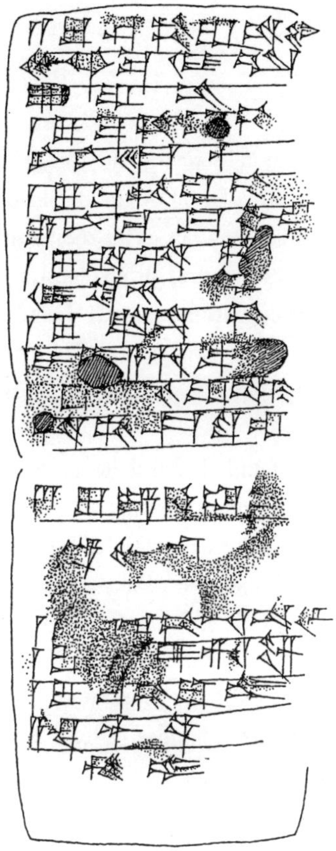

Text 7 (Bi.29/50:151,31)

LES PARTICULES DU DISCOURS DANS LES TEXTES DE LA RÉGION DU MOYEN-EUPHRATE IIE MILLÉNAIRE

HENRI LIMET

Université de Liège

Le langage sert avant tout à communiquer: on échange des idées, on raconte des événements, on donne des informations ou on en demande. Le dialogue (le mot étant pris au sens large: un récit suppose un lecteur ou un auditeur, une lettre s'adresse à un destinataire) progresse ou se charge de nuances au moyen de divers mots que, comme le remarque Cl. Hagège [1985, p. 237], les grammaires académiques signalent à peine ou rangent "sous l'étiquette condescendante de particules". Ce sont, en réalité, des mots importants et très employés, car ils constituent l'articulation d'un texte.

Quand il s'agit de langues "mortes", comme l'accadien, qui est en outre fort éloigné de nous dans l'espace et dans le temps, il n'est pas facile de dégager le rôle exact de ces "particules". Il est cependant permis de tenter cette recherche grâce aux témoignages sur l'accadien parlé, que nous trouvons dans les lettres, des passages de jugements et, c'est le cas pour la région du Moyen-Euphrate, au IIe millénaire, dans les "testaments" ou les déclarations d'adoption. C'est, en effet, dans la langue courante, celle qu'emploient normalement les gens dans la conversation, que nous avons des chances de voir se révéler l'usage de ces petits mots, bien embarrassants parfois pour le traducteur moderne.

La méthode à laquelle nous avons eu recours est celle de la *grammaire textuelle*, exposée, pour le français, par H. Weinrich, 1989. Le principe en est que le texte doit être la donnée première, parce qu'il se caractérise par une structure globale: un segment de phrase, et même souvent une phrase, "ne sont pas des unités significatives"; il convient de les mettre en rapport de sens avec la totalité du texte [Weinrich, 1989, pp. 24-25]. Pour rester dans le cadre imposé du présent volume, nous avons limité notre enquête aux textes d'Emar et environs.[1]

---

1 Dans les pages qui suivent, les renvois aux documents seront référencés selon les abréviations suivantes: E = Arnaud, 1986; TS = Arnaud, 1991; RE = Beckman, 1996.

1. Les "testaments" dont il est question ici, sont oraux et écrits, cela signifie que le "notaire" a enregistré les dispositions prises par le testateur dans les termes où elles ont été énoncées par lui.[2]

Pour la clarté de l'exposé, nous donnons ci-après un de ces "testaments" (le "testament" de Dame N. [E. 30]), en laissant en accadien et non traduites les particules étudiées ainsi que les conjonctions; toute ponctuation a été omise volontairement; quant à la distinction en cinq paragraphes, elle reproduit celle qui est marquée par des lignes de séparation sur l'original. Cette disposition est celle des documents du type dit "syro-hittite", par opposition au type "syrien".[3]

1) *Dame N.* **akanna** *a dit* **mâ anumma**
J'ai institué Q. comme mon mari **ù** B. comme mon fils j'ai fait qu'il soit son fils **ù** ma maison tous mes biens j'ai donné à Q. mon mari **ù** je l'ai institué le père de ma maison **ù** B. son fils durant les jours où Q. vivra B. son fils l'honorera **kimê** il l'honorera après que son destin l'aura emporté qu'il prenne ma maison tous mes biens.
2) **Šumma** Q. en face de B. son fils disait **mâ** toi-**mi** tu n'es pas mon fils il n'aura pas ma maison mes biens qu'il dépose son vêtement sur un tabouret qu'il aille où il veut **ù šumma** où B. en face de Q. son père disait **mâ** tu n'es pas mon père toi-**mi mâ** je ne t'honorerai plus que B. prenne la main de son épouse de ses fils qu'il dépose son vêtement sur un tabouret-**ma** il n'aura pas la maison tous mes biens qu'il aille où il veut
3) **Šumma** mes oncles ...
4) **enuma** pour la maisonnette de A. fils de H. **ù** A. au sujet de cette maisonnette **ù kimu** la maisonnette 12 sicles d'argent moi **ù** [...] j'ai donné à A. fils de H. **ù** mes frères n'ont pas donné d'argent avec moi **ù** à l'avenir ils ne réclameront pas ma maison...**Anumma** j'ai donné 20 sicles d'argent à ma fille A. **anumma** j'ai rendu 16 sicles d'argent à mon fils A. **anumma** ma fille T. m'a donné 30 sicles d'argent **ù** je lui ai rendu 10 sicles d'argent i**nanna** dans la suite à propos de leurs dots ils ne réclameront pas contre elles ...
5) **anumma** mes oncles avec mon père ont fait le partage ...

Ce document ne présente aucune ponctuation marquée par des signes quelconques. La compréhension est heureusement facilitée a) parce qu'il est divisé en cinq

---

2 Le terme "testament" est-il correctement employé pour désigner ce type de document? Oui, si l'on admet que "fixer le destin de ..." (*šimti ... išîm*) signifie que le *pater familias* prend des dispositions pour déterminer ce que deviendront sa famille et ses biens après sa mort (voir E.15 ou E.32: "après que mon destin m'aura emportée". En revanche, les textes qui débutent par "à partir de ces jours" (*ištu umi annî*) énoncent des décisions qui prennent effet immédiatement. Les clauses sont toujours révocables si certaines conditions ne sont pas remplies. Pour Arnaud, 1981, p. 7, *šimtu* est le mot qui signifie "testament"; plus récemment, le *CAD* Š/3, p. 18, s.v. *šimtu*, § 4, a entériné ce sens: "legal disposition referring to the last will".

3 Arnaud, 1991, p. 7, a établi la distinction, admise généralement, entre un groupe "syrien" de tablettes et un groupe "syro-hittite".

paragraphes, séparés par une ligne (numérotés ici de 1 à 5) et b) parce que des adverbes, des conjonctions, et même des variations dans les modes verbaux (par ex. les optatifs: qu'il dépose son vêtement, ... qu'il aille où il veut...) indiquent des changements de phrases. Sans cette aide, l'audition ou la lecture de ce texte se révéleraient très difficiles.

L'analyse montre que:

- le document est censé dit par la testatrice dont les paroles sont introduites par *akanna mâ* (*iqbi*);
- les paroles prononcées par des tiers sont signalées à la fois par *mâ* et par l'enclitique *-mi*;
- les différentes dispositions qu'elle déclare vouloir prendre ou avoir déjà prises sont précédées de *anumma*, si elles n'ont aucun rapport entre elles;
- en revanche, les mentions d'actions qui se suivent et font partie d'un ensemble, sont reliées par *ù*; l'enclitique *-ma* unit des faits concomitants, formant une structure unique;
- enfin, *inanna* ne saurait se traduire ici par "maintenant".

Ces observations préliminaires sont développées dans les pages qui suivent.

2. Akanna

Le *CAD* A/1, p. 259 a, sous *akanna* A, traduit: *thus, in the following way*; cette particule introduit le style direct. Cf. aussi W. von Soden, *GAG* § 120 c: *folgendermassen* (étymol. *ak*(*i*)*anna*). D. Arnaud traduit par "ainsi". Ces vues sont confirmées par van Soldt [1991, p. 465] et par Huehnergard [1989, p. 193] pour la grammaire d'Ugarit.

On notera que *akanna* annonce une citation[4] mais il est accompagné de *mâ*, éventuellement complété par *-mi*, qui introduit vraiment les paroles prononcées. Il s'agit d'un signifiant discontinu.[5] Parfois, *anumma* présente le premier sujet traité.

2.1. E.5, 1-2: *a-kan-na iq-bi ma-<a> a-nu-<um>-ma ...-mi* (E. 70, 2-4; 117, 2-4; 215, 2-3; TS 23, 1-5; 42, 1-6; RE 63, 1-4).

---

4 On peut se demander si c'est *akanna* qui introduit le style direct ou si c'est *mâ* qui suit *iqbi*, avec le renfort de *-mi*. Par *akanna*, le texte annoncerait seulement qu'un discours va suivre.

5 On entend par "morphème discontinu" un signifiant dont les éléments sont séparés; par ex., en français, la négation /ne ... pas / (dans "je ne te connais pas") ou, dans la graphie, la 1re pers. sing. exprimée par le pronom /je/ et le /s/ final du verbe.

2.2. Sans *-mi* mais avec *anumma*: E. 16,1: *a-kan-na iq-bi ma-a a-nu-ma* (pas de *-mi,* comme dans E. 30,1; 32, 2; 91, 2; 93, 4; 128, 3; 213, 3; TS 22, 1-2; 28, 1 et 19; 31, 2; 39, 2; 41, 3; 71, 1-2; RE 18, 1-2; 26, 1-2 et 16-17; 87, 2).

2.3. Sans *-mi*, ni *anumma* E. 18, 2: *a-kan-na iq-bi ma-a*, dans un rescrit royal, comme en E. 19, 2; voir aussi 33, 1-2 (procès); 252, 6; 257, 6 (décision royale).

2.4. Sans *anumma*, mais avec *-mi*: RE 13, 1-3: NP *a-kan-na iq-bi ma-a ... él-qa-an-ni-mi* (et plusieurs verbes également affectés de *-mi*); RE 76, 2 et 6; 88, 16'-17'.

Les formules 1 à 4 apparaissent dans les documents "syro-hittites".

2.5. Ce type d'introduction n'est pas le seul employé dans les documents étudiés: ainsi *akanna* peut être remplacé par *(a)kiamma* dans les documents de type "syrien".

E. 15, 6-7: *a-ki-ia-am-ma iq-bi um-ma šu-ma a-nu-ma* (E. 197, 5); sans *anumma*: RE 37, 4-5; 69, 5-6;

E. 34, 6-7: *ki-ia-am iq-bi a-nu-um-ma* (E. 181, 3; 183, 5; 256, 3; RE 8, 4-5; 15, 4-5; 23, 5-6; 28, 5-6).

Remarque sur des cas particuliers: en E. 201, 10, *iq-bi um-ma-a*, et à la ligne 26: *a-kan-na iq-bi um-ma* (paroles royales); TS 36, 9, *a-na* NAM.ÉRIM *a-kan-na id-din ma-a ...-mi* "le soumit au serment (pour qu'il dise) ..."; RE 85, 10-14: *a-kan-na iq-bi um-ma-a a-nu-um-ma ... e-te-pu-uš-ši-mi ... li-ip-la-ah-mi ... id-di-na-am-mi ... at-ta-din-mi.*

3. mâ

Cf. *CAD* M/1, p. 2, § 3 (attestations à partir des textes en babylonien et assyrien moyens, ainsi qu'à Ugarit); *GAG* § 121 b (p. 176). Cette particule est écrite *ma-a* ou *ma.*

3.1. Elle introduit le discours direct qui a été annoncé par *akanna*, voir en 2.

3.2. *mâ* est annoncé par *um-ma*:

E. 18,13: *um-ma* LUGAL *ma-a*; sans verbe déclaratif, *mâ* est employé seul en E. 18, 9. En revanche, l'expression est renforcée par *-mi* dans les exemples suivants:

E. 212, 8-9: *um-ma* NP-*ma ma-a ... la-a at-ta-din-mi*

E. 28, 6-7: *um-ma* NP *ma-a id-ni ... la-a ta-al-lak-mi*

Voir aussi RE 66,1.

3.3. Dans le cas de loin le plus fréquent, le verbe *qabû* "dire" est suivi de *mâ*. Le verbe de la phrase qui reproduit les paroles, est marqué par la particule *-mi*: *i-qab-bi ma-a ul* AMA-*ia at-ti-mi* ... *ma-a ul a-pal-làh-ki* (E. 32, 13-14); s'il y a deux verbes, seul le premier est affecté de *-mi*, voir aussi la lettre E. 264, 23-26: *iq-ta-bi ma-a*... *a-lak-mi* ... *ip-pa-aš-ma*).

E. 117, 10: *šum-ma* NP1 *a-na pa-ni* NP2 *i-qab-bi ma-a iš-tu* É-*ia at-lak-mi* "si NP1 dit devant NP2: sors de ma maison".

E. 205,19: i-*qab-bu-u ma-a* ... *ni-pa-tar-mi*

RE 13,18-19: *i-qab-bi ma-a ul a-pal-làh-ka-mi* (RE 10-24; dans 63, 20, l'éditeur a ajouté, peut-être à tort: <*akanna iqabbi*> qui ne figure pas sur la tablette).

Cette construction est celle de la formule souvent citée: "s'il dit: tu n'es pas mon fils" et les autres du même type:

TS 39, 16: *i-qab-bu-u ma-a ul* DUMU-*ni at-ta-mi* "s'ils disent: tu n'es pas notre fils" et, à la ligne 20: *i-qab-bi ul* DUMU-*ru-ku-nu a-na-ku-mi* "s'il dit: je ne suis pas votre fils". Cf. TS 40, 12-13 et 16; 41, 15-16; 42, 20-21; 43, 11-12 et 17-18; 72, 12-13 et 17-18.

4. Anumma

Pour le *CAD* A/2, p. 147 a, *anumma* a le sens général de *now, here*; sous la rubrique b 2', il est dit que cet adverbe introduit le message, son porteur et son contenu. C'est la définition que reprend van Soldt, 1991, p. 465, qui observe qu'à Ugarit, c'est plus une interjection qu'un adverbe. Pour Rainey, 1988, p. 211, qui distingue des "now-particles" et des "behold-particles" (autrement dit, des particules temporelles et des particules déictiques), *anumma* est passé de la première à la seconde catégorie. L'étymologie n'est pas claire; *anumma* n'a rien à voir avec *annu*, le démonstratif, comme le voulait Dhorme, *Recueil*, p. 477. Pour von Soden, *GAG* § 20 i, toutefois, *anumma* équivaut à *annumma*, mais la traduction "*nun, nunmehr*" est loin d'être satisfaisante. Peut-être faut-il songer à l'arabe *ʾan* qui introduit certaines subordonnées. Ce pourrait être une particule *inu/enu* renforcée par *-ma*; en E. 30, 17, *e-nu-ma* remplit les fonctions d'*anumma* (voir aussi E. 260, 9 et 21; 263, 17 et 32).

L'écriture est normalement *anumma*, mais on rencontre fréquemment *a-nu-ma*: E. 128, 3; 213, 3, 10, 17, 19; TS 41, 3, 5, 26, 27, 30; 71, 2, 16, 19.

4.1. Comme on l'a vu plus haut, *anum(m)a* se place immédiatement après l'ensemble de mots qui signalent que les dispositions testamentaires sont reproduites telles que le testateur les a énoncées oralement, d'où la formule: *akanna iqbi mâ anumma*. Le terme *anumma* introduit le premier sujet traité.

4.2. Quand le testateur, après avoir fixé le sort d'une personne ou de biens, passe à un autre sujet, il présente sa décision par *anum(m)a*: qui se traduirait alors correctement par "quant à ..." ou "d'une part ... d'autre part ...". Exemple: B. et I., son épouse, ont vendu leur fille à l'épouse de T. pour 30 sicles; quant à (*anumma*) B., il a restitué 15 sicles à sa fille (RE 67). Autre exemple: d'une part (*anumma*), elle a donné sa fille à NP comme épouse; d'autre part (*anumma*), NP a donné sa propre fille ... (RE 61; on pourrait traduire aussi: elle a donné ...; quant à NP, il a donné ...). Voir aussi TS 70, 8'; RE 57, 5, 8; 67, 6; E. 93, 9: *a-nu-ma* commence un nouveau paragraphe, qui, en outre, est isolé visuellement sur la tablette par deux lignes de séparation. Sans ligne de séparation: E. 185, 19'; TS 28, 9 appartiennent au type "syrien".

Anumma signale donc un changement d'orientation du discours. Il joue un rôle analogue à celui de *šanîtam*, très prisé par les scribes de Mari dans les lettres, où il se traduirait bien par "en outre", "de surcroît" (Finet, 1956, p. 119, § 47 f); cette suggestion serait aussi d'application pour *anumma*.

4.3. Souvent, si le testateur (ou, de façon plus générale, le déclarant) annonce plusieurs décisions successives, en prévoyant des situations différentes, il introduit chacune d'elles par *anumma*. La traduction française utiliserait, dans ce cas, des termes comme: "d'abord ... ensuite ... enfin ..." ou: "d'une part ... d'autre part ...".

On s'en fera clairement une idée à la lecture du § 4, lignes 24-26, du texte E. 30 cité plus haut. Cf RE 30, 8: "d'une part (*anumma*) la maison principale ...; 15: d'autre part (*anumma*) ...; 23: enfin (*anumma*), mes deux fils ...".

Elle apparaît également en E. 70: *anumma* figure successivement aux lignes 5, 9, 11. Voir aussi TS 41, 5, 26-27, 30. Sans ligne de séparation: E. 181, 3, 9, 13; RE 8, 5, 6, 19, 28, 35; 15, 5, 9; 28, 6, 8, 30, 40, 43; ces tablettes appartiennent au type "syrien".

RE 10, 10, 20, 30; 13, 12, 14, 26 (deux documents de type "syro-hittite").

4.4. *ù a-nu-ma* introduit un ajout et commence une autre partie de l'exposé; l'ensemble figure souvent après une ligne de séparation (E. 5,11; 202, 13 et 17; 213, 10 et 24; 215, 12; TS 71, 16-19). Exemple: "en outre, quant à Illina, je l'ai libéré ... " (RE 25, 20).

4.5. En E.117, 29, les deux lignes qui débutent par *anumma* apparaissent comme un ajout; celui-ci figure, en effet, à la fin du document, après l'énumération des témoins qui ont apposé leurs sceaux. Il semble bien qu'il s'agisse d'une note qui répare un oubli; en recourant à *anumma*, on peut insérer une clause qui aurait dû être mentionnée dans le corps du texte. Le sens et la fonction de la particule se dégagent très clairement dans un cas comme celui-là.

4.6. Après une hypothèse dont le verbe est mis en évidence par *-ma*, la proposition principale commence par *anumma*. Voir par ex. E. 15, 24: *šum-ma* NP. *a-ba-šu ù* AMA-*šu it-ta-na-bal-ma a-nu-um-ma* "si NP entretient bien ses père et mère, alors ...". RE 23, 11 et 13: *ù šum-ma* NP DUMU-*ya im-tù-ut ù* NUMUN.MEŠ NU.TUKU, *a-nu-um-ma* ... "si NP, mon fils, meurt et n'a pas de postérité, alors ..."; même cas *ibid.*, 20 et 24.

Remarque: *šumma* joue le même rôle et occupe la même place sur le document que *anumma,* mais en y ajoutant, bien entendu, l'idée d'éventualité.

5. Inanna

Pour le *CAD* I/J, p. 142, *inanna* signifie *now, just now*; p. 144: c'est l'équivalent de *anumma*, mais celui-ci introduit le premier sujet et *inanna* le second et toujours le dernier. Selon van Soldt, 1991, p. 465, *inanna*, dans la grammaire d'Ugarit, sert à renforcer le contraste dans le temps entre un fait et un autre qui l'a précédé. Il faut ajouter qu'à Emar, il souligne, en outre, une situation nouvelle par rapport à celle qui vient d'être exposée.[6]

5.1. L'adverbe *inanna* conserve parfois son sens premier de "maintenant". Par ex. E. 114, 4: NP a acheté une maison pour telle somme d'argent; maintenant ...; voir aussi E. 80: a) une maison a été achetée, b) maintenant (*inanna*), elle a été achetée par un autre, c) à l'avenir (*urram šēram*) ... À Ugarit, le sens temporel n'est attesté que rarement (Huehnergard 1989, p. 193).

5.2. Inanna introduit un nouvel élément dans une affaire, un récit, un raisonnement, sans que la notion temporelle soit perdue. E. 16, 2-4 est articulé sur trois niveaux: *a-nu-ma* ... *i-na-an-na* ... *ù* "Bazila me doit 41 sicles d'argent, or il a remboursé 20

6 J. Nougayrol, dans *Ugaritica* V, p. 69, note 3, à propos de la lettre n° 20, avait finement observé que *inanna* revenait souvent dans le document: "À ce trait, et à d'autres du même genre, on devine chez le rédacteur un souci d'enchaînement et d'articulation de la pensée assez particulier".

sicles... alors je lui ai donné ...". Cas analogue en E. 117, 3. Voir aussi E. 205, 3: NP1 devait 25 sicles d'argent à NP2; or (*inanna*, l. 3) NP1 est mort et maintenant ses enfants ... (*ù inanna*, l. 6). On retrouve cette expression dans RE 13, 3: j'ai adopté NP, *ù inanna la-a i-ma-gur-mi* "or/ mais, maintenant, il n'est plus d'accord". Voir aussi E. 256; RE 10, 2; 63, 5.

D'autres exemples: dans TS 34, 4: l'épouse et les enfants de S. sont retenus comme garantie d'une dette; or (*inanna*) S. a pris leur place, ils sont donc libérés. Même remarque pour TS 39: NP est mon débiteur; "or (*inanna*) moi, j'ai annulé sa dette et (*ù*) j'en ai fait mon fils et (*ù*) je lui ai donné ma fille pour épouse".

Dans le testament cité plus haut (E. 30, au § 4): *inanna* apporte une conclusion après trois *anumma*; on le traduira par "dans ce cas (ou: c'est pourquoi), il n'y a pas lieu de contester".

L'adverbe *inanna* demande des traductions différentes selon le contexte. Une traduction par la conjonction "or", en français, est souvent recommandable.

5.3. Inanna marque les étapes successives d'une procédure (une traduction par "maintenant" ne se justifierait absolument pas). Soit le procès relaté par E. 33: une dame fait d'abord l'inventaire de ses biens et produit des témoins; ensuite (= *inanna*, à la l. 12) elle convoque son fils adoptif; ensuite (*inanna*, l. 18), ... Autre cas du même genre (TS 21): le document décrit trois états successifs d'une famille; le second et le troisième sont introduits par *inanna* "ensuite ... ensuite ..." (l. 5 et 7).

5.4. Dans une lettre (E. 259 et 261), *inanna*, après l'en-tête et le rappel de la teneur du message précédemment reçu, introduit la réponse qui y est donnée. En E. 268, 16: "or (*inanna*) je ne suis pas venu (alors que tu me l'avais demandé); maintenant (*inanna*), puisque ...".

6. -mi

Il y a peu de choses à ajouter à ce que nous avons dit plus haut à propos de *akanna* et de *mâ* qui annoncent le discours direct, celui-ci étant, en outre, marqué par l'enclitique *-mi*. Voir aussi *GAG* § 123 c et 155 a. L'emploi de *-mi* se justifie lorqu'il importe de rapporter textuellement les paroles, souvent celles d'un tiers (même observation pour Mari, Finet, 1956, p. 124). Comme l'observe Weinrich, 1989, p. 565, le discours direct exige normalement "une marque de citation".

Remarque: dans RE 13, au début, dans la citation des paroles du testateur luimême, les verbes sont affectés de l'enclitique *-mi*.

6.1. Nous avons vu plus haut le préambule des "testaments": *akanna iqbi mâ...mi*, syntagme en deux parties qui figure également dans un récit (E. 18, 11). L'enclitique *-mi* est cependant souvent négligé par les rédacteurs des documents.

6.2. Le discours direct est signalé par *mâ* et l'enclitique *-mi* est, ou n'est pas utilisé.

E. 16, 14: *i-qab-bu-u ma-a ... te-er-ra-mi iš-tu* É-*ni at-lak-mi* "ils dirent: "... rends et hors de notre maison va-t-en""; voir aussi les l. 18-19.

6.3. La présence de *mâ* seul suffit, parfois même sans verbe déclaratif (voir ci-dessus).

6.4. L'enclitique *-mi* ne doit pas nécessairement être accolé à un verbe, mais il peut l'être à tout mot jugé important:

E. 30, 9 et 11: *at-ta-mi*; RE 25, 15; 63, 17 et 21: *at-ta-a-mi* (avec une "pause" en /â/; E. 33, 21: *ù* DAM-*tu at-tu-ka-mi* "et l'épouse est bien la tienne"; RE 26, 14: *at-tu-nu-mi.*

6.5. Aucune "marque de citation" autre que le verbe déclaratif, par ex. dans E. 17, 14: *iq-ta-bi a-nu-um-ma* (ce dernier mot étant l'adverbe de présentation portant sur l'énoncé qui suit). Le verbe déclaratif fait défaut au début de E. 180 et de 202. Toutefois, le verbe déclaratif peut être remplacé par une formule telle que: *a-na di-ni iz-zi-iz um-ma* NP-*ma ma-a ... at-ta-din-mi* (E. 212,8 sv) "il se présenta au procès, ainsi (parla) NP: ... 'je lui ai donné'".

Remarque: il semble qu'une ébauche de discours indirect s'amorce dans le langage, si on se réfère à des cas comme celui-ci (E. 33, 13-14): Dame Išarte fit comparaître (*ul-te-ziz*) NP (en disant) que (*ki-i*) NP avait une dette; la conjonction *kî*, en l'absence de verbe et de toute marque de citation, introduit la déclaration de la demanderesse. Voir aussi E. 212, 12: les témoins (déclarant) que (*ki-i*) ...

7. -ma

Cf. *GAG* § 123, sous 1 a. Cette particule lie deux phrases pour autant qu'il y ait entre elles un lien logique,[7] à la différence de *ù* qui unit deux mots ou deux phrases en produisant un effet d'accumulation. On sait que *-ma* est enclitique; il s'adjoint au premier verbe de la séquence et il annonce un second verbe.

---

7 Weinrich, 1989, p. 366. En fait, les deux notions vont de pair: les "joncteurs" simples unissent des signes linguistiques fonctionnellement équivalents et les deux termes appartiennent à la même classe linguistique.

7.1. Le cas le plus fréquemment rencontré est celui d'expressions figées comme: "qu'il prenne (*liṣbat-ma*) la main de sa femme et qu'il aille [= et ensuite il pourra aller] où il veut (*ašar libbi-šu lillik*)". Il s'agit d'une personne (enfant adopté par ex.) qui a commis une faute et est déshérité (E. 69, 10; 16, 8 et 16; TS 28, 22; 39, 112-13; 40, 17; 72, 18-20).

Autre formulation de même type: "qu'il dépose (*liškun-ma*) son vêtement sur un tabouret et qu'il s'en aille (*lillik*)" ou mieux: "ensuite il pourra aller ..." (E. 32, 17; 112, 17-18; 181, 12; TS 39, 23; 41, 25; TS 71, 14-15). E. 197, 13: *lirubu-ma lizûzu* "qu'ils entrent et qu'ils partagent": les héritiers doivent d'abord avoir le droit de pénétrer dans la maison pour pouvoir partager les biens entre eux; c'est une métaphore pour exprimer qu'ils "entrent" en possession des biens.

Séquence de trois verbes: *liṣbat-ma* ... *liddinuni-šu* ... *lillik* (TS 43, 13-14). Les deux premiers verbes forment groupe, le troisième reste à part (voir un autre exemple en 7.2). Voir aussi E. 5, 21-22.

On notera que les actions se suivent dans le temps; la première est légèrement antérieure à la suivante; la seconde apparaît dès lors comme une conséquence ou une suite logique. On le constate dans cet exemple: E. 257, 2 NP ... vola (*išriq-ma*) et il fut pris (*iṣṣabat*). On en trouve plusieurs exemples dans les lettres:

E. 258, 21-22: *li-qa-am-ma šu-bi-la* "prends (le turban?) et apporte-le moi" (Arnaud: "prends pour me l'apporter"); 262, 10: "(les frères de NP), ...envoie-les ici (*ab-ka-nim-ma*)... et qu'ils aillent (*lil-li-ku-ni*) ..." (= pour qu'ils puissent aller). Voir aussi 264, 27. Dans des exemples comme ceux-ci, la première action permet d'accomplir la seconde.

7.2. Cette observation vaut également dans les documents suivants:

E. 70, 10: qu'elle donne (*liddin-ma*) les deux fils en mariage et qu'elle prenne (*lilqi*) la dot. La seconde action est possible seulement si la première est réalisée. E. 16, 21: qu'il donne (*liddin-ma*) 61 sicles d'argent à... et qu'il aille (*lillik*) (voir aussi ligne 36); TS 41, 27-29: "à la maison d'un beau-père il la livrera (*liddin-ši-ma*), il prendra la "dot" (*lilqi*) et ainsi il prendra une épouse (*aššata lihuz*); TS 42, 22-23.

7.3. Le préambule des "testaments" se présente parfois comme suit:

E. 15 et 176, début: NP fit siéger (*ušēšib-ma*) ses frères et fixa (*išīm*) le destin...; RE 15 et 37. En revanche, au n° 180 *ušēšib* est suivi de *ù*, avec le même sens que -*ma*. La simple juxtaposition suffit souvent: E. 181; RE 23; 28; 57.

7.4. *-ma* met en évidence et n'a pas la fonction de liaison dans cet exemple: E. 15, 21-24, si NP entretient (*it-ta-na-bal-ma*) ses père et mère, alors (*a-nu-um-ma*)... et (à la l. 14): *tuššab-ma* "elle continuera à résider dans la maison". Cette valeur de *-ma* est particulièrement évidente quand elle est accolée au prédicat d'une phrase nominale (*GAG* § 123, sous 1 s).

E. 15, 10: *ši-it-ma* "(les père et mère de la maison) c'est bien elle" (voir aussi 185, 6; TS 50, 9; RE 28, 7; 58, 8). TS 47, 12: "NP1 et NP2, ce sont bien eux les père et mère de la maison". Voir aussi E. 213, 10: *ana* ÌR-*ut-ti ša* NP ... *iš-tu* SAG-DU-*šu-ma e-te-ru-ub* "dans la servitude de NP je suis vraiment entré de mon plein gré".

Il faut signaler un cas d'emploi assez rare, en E. 70, 7-8: 2 tabourets de bronze, 1-*en* ... 1-*en-ma* "un de 400 sicles ... et un autre de 200". Dans ce cas, *-ma* attire l'attention.

Rappelons simplement ici que *-ma* indique la personne qui envoie une lettre: *umma* NP ÌR-*ka-ma* "ainsi (parle) NP, ton serviteur".

8. u

Cf. *GAG* § 117 b (sous la rubrique conjonction), correspond à l'arabe *wa* et signifie "et, et aussi".

8.1. La conjonction *u* (généralement écrite *ù*) lie des signes linguistiques qui sont de même nature, c'est-à-dire qui ont la même fonction et, souvent, sont de la même classe grammaticale.

a) unit deux substantifs: E. 91, 3: *a-na a-bi ù* AMA-*mì*; 31, 3: *a-na a-bu-ut-ti ù* AMA-*mi* et 12: *a-na a-ba-šu-nu ù* AMA-*šu-nu*; 185, 5': *a-bu ù* AMA *ša* É-*ti-ia* "le père et la mère de la maison"; et *passim.*

b) unit deux noms propres: E. 16, 5; 17, 10-11; 31, 8; 34, 14 et *passim.*

c) E. 16, 10-11: *a-na Sîn-a-bi ù* DAM-*šu*; *ù* unit ici un nom propre et un nom commun, soit des noms qui, sans être de même catégorie, ont la même fonction.

d) normalement, dans une énumération, *ù* ne figure qu'entre l'avant-dernier et le dernier élément de la série dont, en fait, elle annonce la fin.[8] Exemples: E. 117, 19 *bušu bašitu-šu ù kaianzu-šu* "<son> bien, ses possessions et son trésor"; RE 30, 15-16 "une grande maison, des petites maisons et (*ù*) une nouvelle maison".

8 Weinrich, 1989, p. 367, pense que la jonction (par "et" en français) étant faible, on peut rattacher autant de "compléments" que l'on veut, on obtient alors une série. Cette remarque vaut pour l'accadien.

Rem. Un substitut possible de *ù* est *qadu* "avec" (cf. *CAD* A/1, s.v. *adi* B) qui comporte aussi la nuance additionnelle de "en y incluant ..., ensemble".[9]

8.2. Dans les "testaments" d'Emar, comme on le voit dans le texte cité au § 1 (= E. 30), *ù* relie des phrases qui s'ajoutent les unes aux autres, mais traitent de faits et d'actions relevant d'un thème unique. Au § 1, la testatrice règle les rapports de son mari et de son fils; puis, au § 2, *ù* réunit ce qui, d'une part, concerne l'attitude éventuelle du père et, d'autre part, celle du fils, l'un à l'égard de l'autre. Au § 4 (l. 17-22), il y a accumulation de faits au sujet d'une petite maison (*kirṣitu*); les phrases sont reliées par *ù* qui, à la ligne 20, a le sens de "mais, or" et, à la ligne 22, celui de "donc, c'est pourquoi".

8.3. La conjonction *ù* peut, en effet, avoir un sens adversatif comme nous venons de le voir.[10]

a) Prenons l'exemple de RE 76: "NP1 et (*ù*) NP2 ont donné leur sœur à NP3 pour qu'elle soit É.GI$_4$.A, mais (*ù*) NP3 ne l'a pas prise et, en outre (*ù*), il l'a donnée comme épouse à NP4 et enfin (*ù*) il a pris l'argent de la 'dot'"; dans ce texte se mêlent plusieurs valeurs de la conjonction *u*.

b) En particulier, quand *ù* est suivi de *šumma*, il a le sens adversatif.

E. 15: à une première hypothèse (l. 17) s'opposent une seconde (l. 21): "mais si..." et une troisième (l. 26): "mais si...". Même opposition dans E. 5 entre les lignes 17 sv et 23 sv.; E. 16, l. 13: *šumma* ..., 17: *ù šumma* ..., 23: *ù šumma* ..., et, à l'intérieur du § 5, opposition entre les lignes 30: *ù šumma* ... et 33: *ù šumma* ....; la traduction "mais si ..." s'impose dans ces exemples. Voir aussi RE 25, 14; 63, 19; 88, 15'.

8.4. *ù* suivi de *anumma*: E. 70, 9; 201, 49; 202, 13 et 17; 213, 10; 217, 9 et 11. Voir aussi au § 4.4.

---

9 E. 212, 2: NP *qadu* DAM-*šu* 2 DUMU.MEŠ-*šu* *ù* 3 DUMU.MÍ-*šu* "NP avec son épouse, deux fils et deux filles". La préposition *qadu* indique que les objets ou les personnes forment un tout indissociable (à la différence de *itti* "en compagnie de"). Voir aussi: E. 31, 4 "un lit avec (*qadu*) des tissus d'Accad"; RE 29,1 "une maison avec (*qadu*) ses fondations de pierre"; RE 37, 5 et 7.

10 Weinrich, 1989, p. 372, à propos de la conjonction française *mais*, explique que ce morphème signale un contraste entre les deux termes qu'il unit. Généralement, tandis que le premier "provoque une attente positive", le second "a une signification négative". Dans les textes d'Emar, *ù* relie aussi parfois deux éventualités dont la seconde est moins favorable que celle qui a été énoncée en premier lieu, ou même la contredit.

8.5. *ù* introduit une phrase sans qu'il y ait liaison. E. 185, 14'-16': "mais si (*ù šumma*) NP1 n'a pas de descendance, alors (*ù*) NP 2..."; E. 212, 3 sv: "mais quand (*ù ki-i-me-e*) NP 1 alla à son destin, alors (*ù*) NP 2 avec NP 3 se présenta devant le roi"; E. 215, 5-7: "en échange (*ki-i-mu-u*) de mes dettes ..., alors moi (*ù a-na-ku*) ...".

8.6. La conjonction *ù* est parfois omise quand les deux éléments forment un signe linguistique indissociable:

E. 16, 16: ŠU DAM-*šu* DUMU.MEŠ-*šu* "la main de sa femme (et) de ses enfants"; 69, 9: *qa-ti* DAM-*šu* DUMU.MEŠ-*šu*. On peut tenir pour possible une influence du sumérien.

9. La nature et la présentation des messages écrits expliquent l'emploi des "particules" et adverbes étudiés ici.

9.1. Ces mots étaient nécessaires dans le Proche-Orient ancien lorsque la communication orale était très développée. Les idées s'enchaînaient les unes aux autres, tantôt s'accumulant, tantôt s'opposant; dès lors, tout discours devait être structuré. Les particules servaient à marquer les étapes de l'énoncé.

9.2. Les tablettes, dans la tradition babylonienne, sont disposées, sommairement dit, selon les caractéristiques suivantes.

Les signes (ou mieux: graphes) sont gravés les uns à la suite des autres, en *scriptio continua*, comme le furent les lettres dans les inscriptions grecques plus tard[11] et dans les manuscrits latins médiévaux. Rien ne met en évidence un signe qui, comme nos lettres majuscules, indiquerait le début d'une phrase; aucun espace, point ou tiret pour séparer les mots.

Toutefois, la lecture était facilitée par la disposition des tablettes en cases dans lesquelles étaient rangés des signes formant un syntagme (par ex., un substantif à l'état construit et son complément). Une autre aide venait des déterminatifs (ou classificateurs, pour signaler les toponymes, les noms propres de personnes, les objets

---

11 Voir cependant, dans Bonfante *et al.*, 1994, p. 355-357, fig. 14 et fig. 15, les exemples d'inscriptions grecques présentant des points en haut pour séparer les mots. Dans l'alphabet ougaritique, il existait un "séparateur de mots", de même qu'en vieux-perse et en élamite, au temps des Achéménides, cf. *ibid.*, p. 79, fig. 25; p. 84, fig. 28; p. 85, la fig. 30 montre que la version babylonienne de la précédente ne présente pas le clou oblique de séparation.

en métal, en bois, etc), voire des indices phonétiques (comme AMA-*mi* pour *ummi*).[12] La récurrence des formules juridiques aidait certainement.

Dans les documents accadiens d'Ugarit et d'Emar, le système des cases a été abandonné; en revanche, une ligne sépare, dans les tablettes du type "syro-hittite", les différents sujets traités ou isole l'en-tête du document. Par conséquent, et y compris à l'intérieur de paragraphes ainsi déterminés, les phrases se suivent sans qu'aucun indice matériel (espace, point ou barre) signale la fin d'une phrase et le début d'une autre.

9.3. Les clercs pratiquaient peut-être la lecture silencieuse. Ils devaient, dans ces conditions, séparer mentalement les mots; un signe comme *ù* ou un groupe de signes comme *a-nu-um-ma*, figurant ici et là dans un texte, étaient aisément repérables pour leur œil exercé. Toutefois, selon certains spécialistes (G. Cavallo, 1997, p. 90), "l'ouïe est mieux à même que la vue de saisir la succession des mots, le sens de la phrase". Il est possible qu'au lieu de parler de "lecture silencieuse", on devrait dire "lecture individuelle (ou en privé) et murmurée".

Il fallait, dans certaines circonstances, que les clercs fassent une lecture orale, à haute voix. Comme secrétaires, ils devaient faire en sorte que le destinataire de la lettre qu'ils avaient en main, ou les parties à un "testament", entendent le message. L'acte de "lire" est rendu en accadien par *šasû* et *šemû*: l'un "crie" le texte qu'il voit (voir et crier, c'est lire) et l'autre l'écoute.[13]

9.4. Dès lors, la conclusion s'impose à nous. À défaut d'indices matériels, le texte à transmettre doit être structuré. Pour cela, divers mots (particules ou adverbes) annoncent que l'on a changé de sujet, que l'on reproduit les paroles d'un intervenant, puis la réponse éventuelle; ils signalent que ce qu'on va lire est la teneur d'une lettre ou d'une conversation antérieures, mais ils précisent que la situation a changé, etc.

---

12 Gelb, 1952, p. 113, signale les classificateurs et les "auxiliary marks".

13 À propos de *šasû*, *CAD* Š/2, p. 147 et sv., en particulier la section 10, p. 165, où est donné le sens de "lire" (*šitassû*, forme Gt, mais von Soden, *AHw*, s.v. *šasû*, rubrique 13, pense à une forme Gtn). Le verbe *šasû* seul peut déjà signifier "lire", ceci implique qu'on ne se bornait pas à parcourir des yeux la lettre, mais qu'on prononçait le texte à haute voix. À propos de *šemû*, *CAD* Š/2, p. 277, 1 d: "entendre une lettre que le secrétaire lit"; *šušmu* (généralement accompagné d'un complément: *tuppam*, *awātam*): "faire entendre une lettre, un message". Exemple tiré de *Ugaritica* V, n° 57 (tr.): *tuppa ... kimê ana pani-šu išasu-šu* [*u an*]*a pan belti*-[*ya l*]*ilšusi, belti-ya li*[*šme*]"comme on a lu à haute voix la lettre devant lui, qu'on la lise à haute voix devant ma Dame, que ma Dame l'entende".

Pour pouvoir être compris par le destinataire, le message est décodé aisément parce qu'il se présente de façon intelligible, tant à la lecture qu'à l'audition.

Tout le jeu de particules et adverbes disponibles, à quoi s'ajoutent les conjonctions (*kima, šumma* ...) facilite visuellement la lecture silencieuse et sa compréhension lors de la lecture orale. Ces "petits mots" se révèlent indispensables, autant que nos points, virgules, guillemets, parenthèses et majuscules.

Bibliographie

Arnaud D., "Humbles et superbes à Emar", dans *Mélanges orientaux en l'honneur de M. Henri Cazelles* (= *AOAT* 212), 1981, pp. 1-14.

Arnaud D., *Recherches au pays d'Aštatta.* Emar VI/3. Textes sumériens et accadiens, Paris, Ed. Recherche sur les civilisations, 1986.

Arnaud D., *Textes syriens de l'âge du Bronze récent* (= *Aula Orientalis. Supplementa*, 1), Barcelona, 1991.

Beckman G., *Texts from the vicinity of Emar in the Collection of J. Rosen* (History of the Ancient Near east/ Monographs-II), Padova, Sargon, 1996.

Bonfante Larissa, Chadwick J. *et al.*, *La naissance des écritures*, Paris, éd. du Seuil, 1994 (pour la trad. française citée ici).

Cavallo G., "La lecture dans le monde romain", dans Cavallo G. et Chartier R., *Histoire de la lecture dans le monde occidental*, Paris, éd. du Seuil, 1997, pp. 79-107.

Dhorme E., "La langue de Canaan" (article paru dans la *Revue biblique* en 1913-1914) dans *Recueil Ed.Dhorme*, Paris, 1951, pp. 405-487.

Finet A., *L'accadien des lettres de Mari*, dans Acad. Royale de Belgique, Cl. des Lettres, Mémoires, t. LI, Bruxelles, 1956.

Gelb I. J., *Writing*, Chicago, 1952.

Hagege Cl., *L'homme de paroles, Contribution linguistique aux sciences humaines*, Paris, Fayard, 1985.

Huehnergard J., "Five Tablets from the vicinity of Emar", *RA* 77, 1983, pp. 11-43.

Huehnergard J., *The Akkadian of Ugarit* (*HSS* 34), Atlanta, 1989.

Rainey A. F., "Some Presentation Particles in the Amarna Letters", *UF* 20, 1988, pp. 209-220.

van Soldt W., *Studies in the Akkadian of Ugarit, Dating and Grammar* (*AOAT*, t. 40), 1991.

Weinrich H., *Grammaire textuelle du français*, Paris, Alliance française, Didier-Hatier, 1989 [trad. franç. de la *Textgrammatik der französischen Sprache*, Stuttgart, 1982].

"BROKEN" PLURAL IN "ARAMAIC" TRIBAL NAMES

EDWARD LIPIŃSKI

Katholieke Universiteit Leuven

Tiglath-pileser III's inscriptions contain a list with the names of thirty-five tribes of southern and southeastern Babylonia qualified as "Aramaean", and other passages refer to some additional tribes, like the *Puqūdu*. The main list probably goes back to the king's first regnal year, i.e. 745 B.C.,[1] since it is practically identical with the one introduced by the formula "at the beginning of my reign, in my first *palû*", occurring on slab NA 9/76 from the Polish excavations at Nimrud.[2]

B. Moritz had proposed that the so-called "Aramaeans" of that area had come from the Arabian peninsula.[3] His opinion was heavily criticized,[4] but the material has never been properly analyzed. In particular, North-Arabian onomastics has not been taken seriously into account and the grammatical patterns of the tribal names have not been examined.[5] Yet, the mixed constitution of the South-Babylonian population was clearly expressed in Sennacherib's annals:[6] ^{lú}*Úr-bi* (or *Uru*$_8$*-bi*) ^{lú}*A-ra-mu* ^{lú}*Kal-du*, "Arabs, Aramaeans, Chaldaeans". True, ^{lú}*Úr-bi* is not identical with

---

1 H. TADMOR, *The Inscriptions of Tiglath-pileser III, King of Assyria. Critical Edition with Introduction, Translation, and Commentary*, Jerusalem 1994 (quoted further *Tigl. III*), p. 272 with n. 10.

2 *Tigl. III*, p. 37; see the transliteration by E. FRAHM, rec. in *AfO* 44-45 (1997-1998), p. 401. Beside the omission of Nos. 1 and 2 of the well-known list of Tadmor's Summary 7 and the insertion of ^{lú}*Li-'-ta-ú* between Nos. 12 and 13, the sequence of the names is identical to that appearing in *Tigl. III*, pp. 158-161, lines 5-8. Nos. 20 ff. are missing.

3 B. MORITZ, *Die Nationalität der Arumu-Stämme in Südost-Babylonien*, in *Oriental Studies published in commemoration of the Fortieth Anniversary of Paul Haupt*, Baltimore-Leipzig 1926, pp. 184-211.

4 T.W. ROSMARIN, *Aribi und Arabien in den babylonisch-assyrischen Quellen*, in *Journal of the Society of Oriental Research* 16 (1932), pp. 1-23 (see pp. 2-3); F. ROSENTHAL, *Die aramaistische Forschung*, Leiden 1939, pp. 11-12; I. EPH'AL, "Arabs" in Babylonia in the 8th Century B.C., in *JAOS* 94 (1974), pp. 108-115 (see pp. 108-109).

5 R. ZADOK, *On West Semites in Babylonia during the Chaldean and Achaemenian Periods: An Onomastic Study*, 2nd ed., Jerusalem 1978 (quoted further ZADOK, *WSB*), pp. 185-187, considers most tribal names as toponyms and does not examine their nominal patterns.

6 D. D. LUCKENBILL, *The Annals of Sennacherib* (OIP 2), Chicago 1924 (quoted further *Sennacherib*), p. 25, line 39; p. 54, line 52; p. 57, line 12; E. FRAHM, *Einleitung in die Sanherib-Inschriften* (*AfO. Beih.* 26), Wien 1997 (quoted further *Sanherib*), p. 51, line 10.

Classical and Literary Arabic *ʿUrūb* or *Aʿrub*, "Arabs", and lú*Úr-bi* has been interpreted as a military term designating a special kind of warriors,[7] but the nominal pattern *fuʿul*, often abridged to *fuʿl*, also forms "broken" plurals, and the form *ʿUrb(u)* is actually attested in the pre-Classical and later language.[8] Thus, Assyrian *Urbi* must have been borrowed from Old Arabian, and it appears only in contexts dealing with South Mesopotamia and with Judaea, because these areas actually had an Arab population. Of course, the *Urbi* may have formed special military units in the Assyrian army due to their accoutrements and particular warfare, but their name basically has an ethno-social meaning.

If this is the case, one can assume that also some "Aramaean" tribes of South Babylonia bear names that are "broken" plurals of a noun or an adjective, derived from an occupation, such as Warrior, Herdsman, Camelherd, Wanderer, Shepherd, Kneader, or the like. These characteristics occur in tribal names of modern Bedouin, with plurals like Ḥaweyṭāt, Ḥamāʾid, Ġannāmāt, ʿAzeyzāt, etc. For example, the Ḥaweyṭāt pretend that their ancestor was called Ḥaweyṭ, "guardian", but the Ḥamāʾid - a plural of Ḥamīd, "laudable", – believe for some unspecified reason that their ancestor was called Fāḍel.[9] As for the Ġannāmāt, they are simply "shepherds", and the ʿAzeyzāt have ʿAzīz as eponymous ancestor, i.e. the "powerful" or "noble" man.

One of the more prominent Aramaean tribes of South Babylonia between the mid-8th century and 626 B.C. are the *Puqūdu* or *Piqūdu*, which sometimes are simply called "Aramaeans".[10] Their name is vocalized *Pəqōd* in the Hebrew Bible,[11] while the Septuagint has the form Φακουδ in Ez. 23, 23, perhaps by identification with the town of uru*Pa-qu-ud* in Babylonia, in the province of Laḫīru.[12] The original

---

7 I. EPH'AL, *art. cit.* (n. 4), pp. 110-111, n. 16.

8 D. NEIMAN, *Urbi = "Irregulars" or "Arabs"*, in *The Jewish Quarterly Review* 60 (1969-1970), pp. 237-258; J. ŁACINA, *Słownik arabsko-polski*, Poznań 1997, p. 611b. E. FRAHM, *Sanherib*, pp. 104-105, does not seem to be aware of the fact that Urbi is borrowed from Arabic.

9 Cf. A. JAUSSEN, *Coutumes des Arabes au pays de Moab*, Paris 1908, pp. 108-116.

10 St.W. COLE, *Nippur IV. The Early Neo-Babylonian Governor's Archive from Nippur* (OIP 114), Chicago 1996 (quoted further *Nippur* IV), No. 27, 16.20.

11 Jer. 50, 21; Ez. 23, 23.

12 *SAA* VI, 287, 11. The transliteration *Pa-qu-tú* and the transcription *Pāqutu* (*ibid.*, p. 231 and 341) reflect a misinterpretation of the place name which is certainly related to the Puqūdu tribe. In fact, the town belonged to the province of *Laḫīru*, the governor of which has sealed the tablet (*SAA* VI, 287, 1-2), and the territory of the Puqūdu is certainly situated in this area, as apparent in No. 46 of the ar-

pronunciation of the name was *Puqūdu*, already attested as *Pu-qu-du, Pu-qu-u-du-ú, Pu-qu-ú-da, Pu-qu-da-a-a* in the early Neo-Babylonian archive from Nippur.[13] This form does not result from a Neo-Assyrian vowel harmonization,[14] but represents the "broken" plural of *pāqidu*, a noun used as personal name in Amorite.[15] There seems to be little doubt, in fact, that Early Aramaic made use of "broken" plurals like Arabic and other Semitic languages.[16] The pattern *fuʿūl*, as in *Puqūdu*, is used especially in Classical Arabic as the "broken" plural of verbal adjectives,[17] e.g. *quʿūdu(n)*, plural of *qāʿidu(n)*, "sitting", but also as the plural of a name like "Arab", thus *ʿUrūb*, "Arabs". This and related patterns occur in the name of several tribes attested in southern Babylonia by Assyro-Babylonian texts:

Gurūm(u)	*Rummūl(utu)*
Luḫūʾ(ātu)	*Rupūʾ(u)*
Nugūʿ(u)	*ʿUbūd(u)*
Puqūd(u)	*ʾUbūl(u)*
Rubbū	*ʾUtūʾ*

chive published in *Nippur* IV and in Sennacherib's annals, where ^{uru}*La-ḫi-ru* and ^{lú}*Pu-qu-du* are associated: *Sennacherib*, p. 43, line 48.

13 See the index in *Nippur* IV, p. 443. The Neo-Assyrian references to the Puqūdu are collected in S. PARPOLA, *Neo-Assyrian Toponyms* (AOAT 6), Kevelaer-Neukirchen-Vluyn 1970 (quoted further *Toponyms*), pp. 280-281. – The Neo-Babylonian spellings clearly exclude the interpretation of the tribal name in the same sense as the proper names of the *quttul* pattern, which were examined by H. HOLMA, *Die assyrisch-babylonischen Personennamen des Form* quttulu *mit besonderer Berücksichtigung der Wörter für Körperfehler. Eine lexikalische Untersuchung*, Helsinki 1914.

14 This was the opinion of ZADOK, *WSB*, p. 131.

15 *Pa-qì-du-um* in Th.G. PINCHES, *CT* 45, London 1964, No. 89, II, 32. – Paqīdā was an Aramaic deity, attested in Graeco-Roman times: L.-H. VINCENT, *Le dieu saint Paqeidas à Gérasa*, in *RB* 49 (1940), pp. 98-129; J.T. MILIK, *Les papyrus araméens d'Hermoupolis et les cultes syro-phéniciens en Égypte perse*, in *Biblica* 48 (1967), pp. 546-622 (see pp. 559-560).

16 E. LIPIŃSKI, *Studies in Aramaic Inscriptions and Onomastics* II (OLA 57), Leuven 1994, pp. 54-56, 63, 68, 77-78, 98; cf. E. LIPIŃSKI, *Semitic Languages: Outline of a Comparative Grammar* (OLA 80), Leuven 1997 (quoted further *Semitic*), § 31.23-34. A recent study of the "broken" plural in Semitic languages, based on an unpublished doctoral dissertation, is provided by R.R. RATCLIFFE, *Defining Morphological Isoglosses: The 'Broken' Plural and Semitic Subclassification*, in *JNES* 57 (1998), pp. 81-123.

17 A. MURTONEN, *Broken Plurals: Origin and Development of the System*, Leiden 1964, p. 2; W. FISCHER, *Grammatik des klassischen Arabisch*, Wiesbaden 1972, p. 51, § 88, Anm. 1, and p. 68, § 122.

Puqūdu should therefore be considered as a grammatical "broken" plural of *pāqidu.*[18] The later Neo-Babylonian and Late Babylonian spelling *Pi-qu-du*[19] reveals the weakening of the short vowel *u* > *ə* and already announces the Masoretic Hebrew vocalization *Pəqōd.*

Since Arabic *fāqid* means "deprived", it is unlikely that the name of the tribe would derive from this word. This meaning conforms to the connotation "to miss" of *faqada* in Arabic and of *fqd* in Epigraphic South Arabian. In Aramaic instead, the *pāqid* is the "care-taker" or "overseer", a connotation which is close to the basic meaning of *pqd* in Semitic, "to look for/at". Used in the plural, as the name of a tribe of shepherds, *puqūdu* must mean "herdsmen". This use of the root is illustrated by the clause *wə-pāqadtā nāwəkā* in Job 5, 24: "may you be informed that all is well with your tent, take care of your transhumant flock,[20] and suffer no loss". In fact, the Puqūdu were shepherds, who sometimes were selling the wool of their sheep for a price that merchants judged too high in consideration of its inferior quality.[21]

The first tribe of the main Tiglath-pileser III's list is called ^{lú}*I-tu-ʾa*, but the earlier form of its name, attested in 885 B.C., is ^{kur}*Ú-tu-ʾ*. The vocalisation of the *alif* is provided by the variant spelling ^{kur}*I-tu-ʾa-a*. The name of the tribe seems thus to go back to an original form **ʾUtūwa* which is the "broken" plural of **ʾātiw* > **ʾātī*, "(home)comer",[22] based apparently on the "absolute" or citation form **ʾātiwa.*[23] The

18 An objection might be raised against this interpretation because of the patronymic *Pu-qú-du-um* that occurs in a text from the time of king Mananāya (1799-1786 B.C.) in central Babylonia; cf. M. RUTTEN, *Un lot de tablettes de Mananâ*, in *RA* 52 (1958), pp. 208-225; 53 (1959), pp. 77-96; 54 (1960), pp. 19-40, 147-152, in particular p. 77, No. 11, 24: witness *Ì-li-ia mār Pu-qú-du-um*. This name must be read *Puquddûm*, in Assyro-Babylonian "trust", something committed to a person's care; cf. *AHw*, p. 880a. There is also a similar Assyro-Babylonian name *Paqūdu* or *Paquddu* meaning "intrusted"; cf. A.Y. AHMAD, *The Archive of Aššur-mātu-taqqin found in the New Town of Aššur and dated mainly by Post-Canonical Eponyms*, in *Al-Rāfidān* 17 (1996), pp. 207-288, especially ^{m}*Pa-qud-du* in text 9, r. 29; text 15, line 15; text 16, line 13; text 24, line 10; ^{m}*Pa-qu-du* in text 18, line 14; text 22, lines 1 and 5; text 32, line 13; text 34, r. 18; cf. *AHw*, pp. 826b-827a.

19 K. L. TALLQVIST, *Neubabylonisches Namenbuch*, Helsinki 1905, p. 298b.

20 For the meaning of the noun *nāweh*, see F. R. KRAUS, *Akkadische Wörter und Ausdrücke XI. – nawûm*, in *RA* 70 (1976), pp. 172-179.

21 *Nippur* IV, No. 46, 16b-19a.

22 The verb "to come", widely employed in Aramaic, in Arabic, in South Arabian, and in poetical Hebrew, occurs under two variant forms *ʾtw* and *ʾty*, best recognizable in Sabaic: A. F. L. BEESTON – M. A. GHUL – W. W. MÜLLER – J. RYCKMANS, *Sabaic Dictionary / Dictionnaire sabéen*, Louvain-la-Neuve - Beyrouth 1982 (quoted further *Sabaic Dictionary*), p. 9. Because of the usual monophthongization *iw* > *iy* > *ī* when *w* closes the syllable, the identification of the variant *ʾtw* is of-

later spelling of the tribal name with initial *i-* stands for **ʾItūwa* which reflects the frequent alternation *i/u*,[24] unless it should be explained by the influence of the Babylonian word *itū*, "neighbour". The singular personal name "(home)comer" occurs in Thamūdic at Taymāʾ (*ʾtw*),[25] in Aramaic (*ʾytw*),[26] and in Hebrew (*ʾty*, *ʾyty*),[27] where the forms *ʾytw* and *ʾyty* seem to witness the same phonetic phenomenon as Arabic *ʾimāla šadīda* which consists in a change *ā* > *ī* next to an apical consonant like *t*.

The second tribe in Tiglath-pileser III's main list is ^{lú}*Ru-pu-uʾ*. The tribe is attested throughout the 8th century B.C., first in Syria, near the Middle Euphrates, later in southeastern Babylonia. Its name is spelt in cuneiform ^{lú}*Ru-pu-ʾ*, ^{kur}*Ru-pu-ʾ*, or ^{lú}*Ru-pu-ú*. The second sign of the name is usually read *bu*,[28] but *Ru-bu-ʾ/ú* does not provide any etymology that would fit a tribal name, while *Rpwʾ* is possibly the very name of the Aramaean tribe used as patronymic in Numb. 13, 19[29] and a clan or a tribe *ḏ-Rfʾm* is attested in South-Arabian.[30] *Rupūʾ* is a "broken" plural like *Puqūd*, formed accordingly to the same nominal pattern and derived from the same adjectival or participial stem *qātil*, viz. *rāpiʾ*, "healer", "restorer".[31] This noun is used as

ten impossible in the other tongues. – As for the "broken" plural, it follows the same *qutūl/fuʿūl* pattern as in the tribal names *Puqūdu* and *Rupū'*.

23 For this explanation of the final *-a*, cf. LIPIŃSKI, *Semitic*, § 32.6.

24 *Ibid.*, § 21.8.

25 G. LANKESTER HARDING, *An Index and Concordance of Pre-Islamic Arabian Names and Inscriptions* (Near and Middle East Series 8), Toronto 1971 (quoted further *Arabian Names*), p. 19.

26 *TAD* II, B2.2, 16; *RÉS* 1295, 4. Cf. W. KORNFELD, *Onomastica Aramaica in Ägypten*, Wien 1979, p. 41.

27 II Sam. 15, 19. 21.22; 18, 2.5.12; 23, 29; I Chron. 11, 31.

28 S. PARPOLA, *Toponyms*, pp. 295-296; *Nippur* IV, p. 443.

29 This verse belongs to a postexilic passage and a real anthroponym *Rpw'* would have a parallel *Ra-pu-ú-um* only in Amorite: G. DOSSIN, *Deux listes nominatives du règne de Sûmu-Iamam*, in *RA* 65 (1971), pp. 37-66, 184-190 (see p. 41, col. II, 30).

30 Hadramic inscription Ingrams I from ʿAqaba Fatura, republished by A.J. DREWES, *Some Hadrami Inscriptions*, in *BiOr* 11 (1954), p. 93-94 and Pl. III, see line 7: *w-s*^{1}*ṭrn yf[d] ḏ-Rfʾm*, "and the scribe was *Yfd* of the *Rfʾm*".

31 In Ugaritic and in the "Canaanite" languages, the word may also designate an ancestor, but we do not know whether this was the case also in Aramaic. Cf. H. ROUILLARD, *Rephaim*, in *DDD*, 2nd ed., Leiden-Grand Rapids 1999, pp. 692-700 with literature.

anthroponym in various Semitic languages, also in Aramaic as shown e.g. by the name of the Ḫindaru sheikh *Ra-a-pi-ʾ*.[32]

The fourth place in Tiglath-pileser III's list is taken by the [lú]*Lu-ḫu-ú-a-tu*.[33] This tribe is called [lú]*Lu-ḫu-ú-a-a* in a Sūḫu inscription,[34] where the gentilic suffix is used instead of the plural ending. The form of the name **Luḫūʾātu* strongly suggests a North-Arabian origin of the tribe, since this is the nominal pattern of the so-called "individual" plural formed from a "broken" plural of the *fuʿūl* stem, like Classical Arabic *buyūtātu(n)*, "distinguished families", plural of *buyūtu(n)*, "families", which is the "broken" plural of *baytu(n)*.[35] The root itself is certainly *lḥy*, which is well represented in Old Arabian onomastics,[36] especially by the North-Arabian personal name *Lḥy*.[37] Considering that there is also a Ṣafaitic proper name *ʾlḥ*,[38] i.e. *ʾalḥā*, the elative "long-bearded", we assume that *lḥy* meant "bearded" in Old Arabian and was pronounced *lāḥiy* or *laḥīy*.[39] The implications of such a name are revealed by the importance attached to the beard among modern Bedouin. For instance, they say *liḥyatahū ṭayyiba*, "his beard is good", to signify that someone is "whole-hearted", while a "good-for-nothing" is called *mā lahū liḥya*, "he has no beard".[40] In consequence, the biblical *Bĕʾer Laḥay Rōʾī*[41] probably was "the Well of the Bearded Seer" and the **Luḥūʾātu* were "distinguished bearded men". The substitution of *hamza* for intervocalic *yāʾ* is normal in Classical Arabic, but the phonetic influence of the

32 *APN*, p. 186a; ZADOK, *WSB*, p. 121.

33 *Tigl. III*, p. 158, line 5; cf. p. 130, line 4; p. 194, line 5; p. 196, line 5. They are missing in the sequence of slab NA 9/76; cf. *ibid.*, p. 272, n. 10.

34 *RIMB* II, text S.0.1002.2, p. 295, line 10.

35 W. FISCHER, *op. cit.* (n. 17), pp. 60-61, § 106.

36 HARDING, *Arabian Names*, pp. 512-513; E. A. KNAUF, *Ismael*, 2nd ed., Wiesbaden 1989, pp. 47-48.

37 HARDING, *Arabian Names*, p. 512.

38 *Ibid.*, p. 65.

39 This name is attested: W. CASKEL, *Ǧamharat an-nasab, das genealogische Werk des Hišam ibn Muḥammad al-Kalbi*, Leiden 1966, vol. II, p. 375b.

40 H. LAMMENS, *Le berceau de l'Islam* I, Rome 1914, p. 311. It should be noticed that the pronunciation *laḥya* is attested besides *liḥya*, "beard"; cf. C. RABIN, *Ancient West-Arabian*, London 1951, p. 101.

41 Gen. 16, 4; 24, 62; 25, 11. An inconclusive survey of the opinions is given by A. DE PURY, *Lahai-Roi*, in *DDD*, 2nd ed., Leiden-Grand Rapids 1999, pp. 500-502.

original **Luḥūyātu* may still be perceived in the variant spelling [lú]*Li-ḫu-ú-a-ta-a-a*[42] of the tribal name with vowel *i* in the first syllable, dissimilated from *ū*.

The [lú]*Ru-ub-bu-ú* come in the sixth place.[43] This tribe is not attested in other sources. The pattern of the name indicates a "broken" plural *Rubbū*, probably "the great" or "numerous ones", either in Aramaic or in Arabic.

An interesting case is provided by the [lú]*Ru-um-mu-lu-tu,* known only from Tiglath-pileser III's list.[44] These tribesmen are literally "desert people", since the expected *Rummūlatu*[45] seems to be the "broken" plural of a derivative of *raml*, "sand", "sand desert".[46] That derivative certainly corresponds to the Ṣafaitic proper name *Rml*.[47] If this was *rammāl*, the "geomancer" who practices divination by means of figures or lines in the sand, the *rummūlatu* would have been "geomancers", but this is just a possibility. In any case, the name indicates that this was an Arab tribe of desert nomads.

The eigteenth and nineteenth positions are taken in the list by the [lú]*Ú-bu-du*[48] and the [lú]*Gu-ru-mu*.[49] Both are mentioned also in Sennacherib's inscriptions.[50] There is a lack of concrete information about the [lú]*Ú-bu-du*, but the name seems once again to be a "broken" plural **ʿubūd*, "servants" of a deity. This "broken" plural is not the same as the one of Classical Arabic but the abstract term *ʿubūda*, "worship", implies the former existence of a "broken" plural **ʿubūd*. The length of the second vowel is

42 *ABL* 468 = *SLA* 247, r. 8.

43 *Tigl. III*, p. 158, line 5; cf. p. 194, line 5; p. 196, line 5; p. 272, n. 10.

44 *Tigl. III*, p. 158, line 6; cf. p. 272, n. 10.

45 Here we can reckon with a Neo-Assyrian harmonization of the vowels, affecting a short *a* in open syllable. The gemination of *m* might be non-phonemic.

46 W. FISCHER, *op. cit.* (n. 17), p. 52, § 98b, sub *fuʿūblatun*. This tribal name was already related to Arabic *raml*, "sand", by F. HOMMEL, *Ethnologie und Ethnographie des Alten Orients* (Handbuch der Altertumswissenschaft III/1, 1), München 1926, p. 436. The word *rml* occurs also in Sabaic: *Sabaic Dictionary*, p. 117.

47 HARDING, *Arabian Names*, p. 287.

48 *Tigl. III*, p. 158, line 6; cf. p. 272, n. 10.

49 *Tigl. III*, p. 158, line 6; cf. p. 64, line 13; p. 194, line 6. Neo-Assyrian references are collected in S. PARPOLA, *Toponyms*, pp. 137-138.

50 *Sennacherib*, p. 25, line 44; p. 49, line 12; p. 54, line 55; p. 57, line 14; *Sanherib*, p. 51, line 12.

confirmed by the probable variant spelling $^{\text{lú/kur}}$*Bu-ú-du*,[51] besides the gentilic variant $^{\text{lú/kur}}$*Bu-da-a-a*[52] indicating the same tribe.

It is difficult to relate the tribal name ^{lú}*Gu-ru-mu* to the use of the root *grm* in Arabic: the verb *ǧarama* can mean "to bone the meat", "to shear sheep", "to pick a bone", "to cut fruit". The fundamental idea is that of cutting off, and it explains the Syriac use of *gəram* in the sense of "cutting short", "deciding". This general meaning was known in Early Aramaic as well, at least if the exceptional Babylonian *garāmu* in astrological context is an Aramaic loanword. According to this text, the Venus planet "cuts across in front or her", *ana pānīša igarrim*, what a commentary explains by *illak*, "she goes".[53] According to some authors, this verb is used in Arab names of the Hellenistic period, like *Šmšgrm* (Σαμσιγεραμος) and *Grmʾl* (Γαραμηλος), where Syriac *gəram* would indicate that the deity "has decided" the child's birth or destiny.[54] However, the Ethiopic verb *garama* means "to be the object of veneration, respect",[55] and this verb is certainly related to Classical Arabic *karuma*, Stem I of which means "to be precious" and Stem II, "to venerate". It is surprising that Old Arabian anthroponomy provides only a couple of names with the element *krm*,[56] while there are several hundred names with the element *grm*,[57] which is hard to explain. The obvious conclusion is that this particular root *krm* was pronounced in many ancient dialects with an initial voiced velar,[58] like in Ethiopic. The

51 *Tigl. III*, p. 42, line 7; p. 84, line 7. E. FRAHM, rec. in *AfO* 44-45 (1997-98), p. 401, questions the identity of the two names.

52 *Tigl. III*, p. 66, lines 5 and 6; p. 86, Ann. 2, lines 4 and 5.

53 *AHw*, p. 282a.

54 A. CAQUOT, *Sur l'onomastique religieuse de Palmyre*, in *Syria* 39 (1962), pp. 231-256 (see pp. 246-247). The reference to Syriac *gəram* occurs first in J. CANTINEAU, *Le Nabatéen* II, Paris 1932, pp. 78-79, and J. STARCKY, *Inventaire des inscriptions de Palmyre* X, Damas 1949, pp. 26-27.

55 This explanation has been taken into account by J. CANTINEAU, *op. cit.* (n. 54), p. 79, and it was followed by W. CASKEL, *Liḥyan und Liḥyanisch*, Köln 1954, p. 146.

56 HARDING, *Arabian Names*, p. 61, s.v. *'KRM*, and p. 499, s.v. *KRM*.

57 *Ibid.*, p. 23, s.v. *'JRM*; pp. 159-160 and 368, s.v. *ŠMSJRM*; p. 609; *Safaitic Cairns*, p. 564, 565, 586, 618; K.L. STARK, *Personal Names in Palmyrene Inscriptions*, Oxford 1971, p. 14, 53, 82, 115; A. NEGEV, *Personal Names in the Nabatean Realm* (Qedem 32), Jerusalem 1991, pp. 19-20, Nos. 242-256; p. 65, No. 1162; H. WUTHNOW, *Die semitischen Menschennamen in griechischen Inschriften und Papyri des Vorderen Orients*, Leipzig 1930, p. 39, 105, 134, 172.

58 For similar cases, see LIPIŃSKI, *Semitic*, § 10.8.

absence of the element *grm* in Aramaean onomastics[59] proves that the lú*Gu-ru-mu* are a North-Arabian tribe and that its name should most likely be interpreted as a "broken" plural *Gurūmu* of *garīmu*,[60] "noble, distinguished". The later attested form uru*Ge-ru-mu*[61] reflects the weakening of the short vowel *u* and most likely stands for **Gərūm*, but this place name has probably no direct link with the tribe.

The lú*Ú-bu-lu* appear on the twenty-seventh place in Tiglath-pileser III's list. They are known from the inscriptions of Tiglath-pileser III, of Sargon II, and of Sennacherib.[62] In Neo-Babylonian sources, the *ʾUbūlu* appear only in two letters from Nippur, in the mid-8th century,[63] and in one document from Ur.[64] Like other "Aramaean" tribal names, *ʾUbūl* is a "broken" plural corresponding to the singular *ʾābil*, the camel-driver or rather the man who takes care of the dromedaries, the camelherd. This word is not attested so far in Aramaic texts, but the man in charge of David's camels was called *ʾwbyl* (ωβιλ) according to I Chron. 27, 30. This is an Hebrew form, characterized by the change *ā* > *ō*; it goes back to an original *ʾābil* and therefore does not correspond to Arabic *ʾabbāl*, "camel-driver". David's *ʾōbīl* is explicitly identified in I Chron. 27, 30 as Ishmaelite, what the Targum has rightly translated by "Arab".[65] True, a driver seated on a dromedary is already represented on a relief from Tell Ḥalaf dating from the 9th century B.C.[66] and the camel-driver had to be designated in Aramaic by some word, but we cannot simply assume that *ʾābil* was an Early Aramaic term meaning "camel-driver". An Old Arabian word suits the biblical context better. In any case, the regular "broken" plural of *ʾābil* can be *ʾubūl*,[67] and the name of the ʾUbūlu tribe can therefore mean "camel-drivers" or

---

59 The names *Grmw* and *Grmy* occur in Syriac, but the overwhelming North-Arabian evidence indicates that they should be considered as Arabian names.

60 *Grymw* is well attested in Nabataean and *Grymy* occurs in Palmyrene. Many of the Ṣafaitic attestations of *Grm* may belong here too, but others may correspond to Γαρμος. *Krym* is mentioned by IBN DURAID, *Kitāb al-ištiqāq* ("Book of Etymology"), ed. by F. WÜSTENFELD, Göttingen 1854, p. 165, where the author (A.D. 837-934) deals with the etymology of Arab tribal names.

61 *RGTC* 8, p. 141.

62 For the attestations, see S. PARPOLA, *Toponyms*, p. 364.

63 *Nippur* IV, Nos. 32, 8 and 98, 17.

64 H.H. FIGULLA, *UET* V, London 1953, No. 140, 8. See *RGTC* 8, p. 317.

65 A. SPERBER, *The Bible in Aramaic* IVA, Leiden 1968, p. 29.

66 *ANEP*, No. 188.

67 The plural *'ubbal* is attested in the classical period.

"camelherds". This noun was probably a denominative formation based on *ibil(u)*, "camel(s)" or rather "dromedaries" in both Assyro-Babylonian and Arabic.

The [lú]*Ú-bu-lu* are followed by the [lú]*Kar-ma-a'*.[68] It is unlikely that there is any connection between this tribe and the [uru]*Kar-me-e* of some Nineveh texts from the time of the Sargonids.[69] This town is undoubtedly identical with the Nestorian bishopric of *Karmē*, located on the left bank of the Tigris, somewhere opposite to Tikrīt. It is still attested in the 5th and 6th centuries A.D. by the names of its bishops who had taken part in various councils.[70] It is also unlikely that [lú]*Kar-ma-'* derives from a tribalized place name *Karmā'*, "the vineyard" or "barren hill", if the toponym is a derivative of Assyro-Babylonian *karmu*. One should rather assume that *Karmā'* is related to Arabic *karīm*, "noble", pronounced with an initial unvoiced velar, contrary to *Gurūmu*. Now, the classical "broken" plural of this North-Arabian noun is *kuramā'*, but unstressed short vowels following upon a syllable with short vowel were normally elided in the Eastern dialects, whereas they changed the quality of the preceding vowel. This combined process of vowel harmony and elision produced *kilma* for *kalima*, "word", *ṣudqa* for *ṣaduqa*, "dowry", *fiḫḏ* for *faḫiḏ*, "thigh", *ʿuḍd* for *ʿaḍud*, "elbow",[71] and *karmā'* can thus stand for *kuramā'*, "nobles". However, it cannot simply be said that the West-Arabian forms are older and the Eastern forms produced by elision. As the example of Arabic *malik* and Phoenician *milk* proves, there was a good deal of wavering between monosyllabic and bisyllabic noun forms in Semitic. For the same reason, *karmā'*, "nobles", can actually be older than *kuramā'* in North-Arabian. If this interpretation is correct, the allegedly Aramaean tribe of *Karmā'* is in fact a North-Arabian group and its name seems to reveal the existence of aristocratic clans among pre-Islamic North-Arabians.

The *Karmā'* tribe is followed in Tiglath-pileser III's list by [lú]*Am-la-tu*,[72] which raises a similar problem. In fact, *'amlā'* is the Arabic "broken" plural of *mala'*,

---

68 *Tigl. III*, p. 160, line 7.

69 *ABL* 574, 6; *SAA* XI, 231, 6'.

70 For the bishops mentioned in A.D. 486, 497, 554, see E. SACHAU, *Zur Ausbreitung des Christentums in Asien* (APAW. PH 1919-I), Berlin 1919, pp. 26-38, in particular No. 21.

71 These examples have been collected by C. RABIN, *op. cit.* (n. 40), p. 97.

72 *Tigl. III*, p. 160, line 7; cf. p. 66, line 3. This name should be distinguished from [m]*Am-li-ta Na-pi-šá-a-a* (S. PARPOLA, *CT* 53, London 1979, No. 289, r. 7), that is probably identical with [m]*A-mi-li-'-ti* (*APN*, p. 21b; *PNA* I/1, p. 105), "My Ancestor is my strength". Other interpretations are taken into consideration by R. ZADOK, *Remarks on Ezra and Nehemiah*, in *ZAW* 94 (1982), pp. 296-298 (see pp. 296-297, n. 11).

"crowd", and a plural morpheme *-ātu(n)* can be added in Arabic to the collective "broken" plural in order to form the so-called "individual" plural,[73] e.g. *baytu(n)*, "family", *buyūtu(n)*, "families", *buyūtātu(n)*, "distinguished families". Similarly, *ʾamlāʾ* most likely meant "crowds" and *ʾamlātu* < *ʾamlāʾātu* could designate "popular assemblies" or the like. There is a serious doubt therefore whether ^lú^*Am-la-tu* is an actual tribe or rather an Arabic name for assemblies of tribesmen. The doubt increases when one sees Tiglath-pileser III's annals reporting that "600 captives of ^uru^*Am-la-te* from the ^lú^*Da-mu-ni*" tribe were deported in 738 B.C. to ʿUmq-Pattin.[74] It appears therefore that *ʾamlātu* was no tribe at all and probably not even a town in the territory of the Damūnu, but the site of the "popular assemblies" of the tribe whose members have been dragged into captivity by the Assyrians.

Tiglath-pileser III's list further mentions the ^lú^*Ru-ʾ-a* in the thirtieth position. The ^lú^*Ru-ʾ-a*[75] or ^lú^*Ru-ùʾ-a*[76] exactly corresponds to the Arabic "broken" plural *ruʿāʾ*, "shepherds", which is formed on the rarely used pattern *fuʾāl*.[77] The cuneiform spelling ^lú^*Ru-ú-a-a*[78] probably reflects a *w*-glide between *u* and *a*, while ^lú^*Ru-u-ʾ-a-a*[79], ^uru^*Ru-ʾ-ú-a*,[80] and ^lú^*Ru-ʾ-u/ú/ùʾ-a*,[81] are a kind of *lectiones conflatae*. Instead, it does not appear that KUR *Ru-u/ú-a* mentioned in Tiglath-pileser III's inscriptions[82] has some relation to the name of the tribe.

Finally, the ^lú^*Li-ʾ-ta-a-ú* tribe comes in the thirty-second place.[83] The name of this

---

73 W. FISCHER, *op. cit.* (n. 17), pp. 61-62, § 106b.

74 *Tigl. III*, p. 66, line 3.

75 *Tigl. III*, p. 160, line 7. References to the Neo-Assyrian texts are collected in S. PARPOLA, *Toponyms*, pp. 294-295.

76 A. FUCHS, *Die Inschriften Sargons II. aus Khorsabad*, Göttingen 1994 (quoted further *Sargon II*), p. 136, Ann. 258; p. 146, Ann. 281; p. 147, Ann. 286.

77 W. FISCHER, *op. cit.* (n. 17), p. 53, § 90.

78 *ABL* 287 = *SLA* 84, 6; *ABL* 1468, r. 6; NBC 6142, 13 (unpubl.: *RGTC* 8, p. 427).

79 *ABL* 1222, r. 6.

80 *ABL* 268 = *SLA* 253, 10.

81 *Tigl. III*, p. 122, line 12; p. 130, line 5; *Sargon II*, p. 195, Displ. 19; p. 227, Displ. 127; Pavem. IV 74; *Sennacherib*, p. 25, line 47; p. 43, line 49; p. 49, line 13; p. 54, line 56; p. 57, line 15; *Sanherib*, p. 51, line 13.

82 *Tigl. III*, p. 72, line 6; p. 132, line 9; p. 164, line 32.

83 *Tigl. III*, p. 160, line 7; cf. p. 122, line 12; p. 130, line 6; p. 194, line 6; p. 196, line 6.

tribe is spelt also ^{lú}*Li-ʾ-ta-u*, ^{lú}*Li-ʾ-it-ta-a-a*, ^{lú}*Li-ʾ-ta-a-a*, ^{lú}*Li-ta-a-a*,[84] and one should probably add the Babylonian settlement of ^{uru}*Li-ta-mu*[85] and the personal or ethnic name ^{m}*Li-ta-mì*.[86] Since the suffix *-āʾu/-āwu* is a typically Arabian morpheme, the base of the name should not be linked with the Aramaic element **liʾt*.[87] Besides, one of the variant spellings indicates that the *t* was geminated and this confirms the statement by Arab grammarians that there was a plural pattern *fiʿillāʾu*, which is not attested in the classical language,[88] but was obviously not invented by the grammarians themselves. Since North-Arabian *ṯ* is regularly expressed in cuneiform script by signs with *t*,[89] especially *ta* and *at*, the name of the tribe should most likely be considered as a "broken" plural **liʾṯṯāʾu/*liyiṯṯāwu* of the noun *layṯ*, "lion", which was used also as personal name.[90] This pattern is of course different from the classical plural *luyūṯ*, "lions", but the apparent replacement of *-āʾu* by *-āwu* (Babylonian *-ta-mu/-ta-mì*) reminds us of the *ʾibdāl* rules of Arab grammarians and strengthens the assumption that the name of the tribe is North-Arabian.

In a later period, Bēl-ibni's letters addressed to king Ashurbanipal mention the ^{lú}*Nu-gu-ú-ʾ*[91] or ^{lú}*Nu-gu-ḫu*.[92] The two different spellings of the name in question favour the reading ^{lú}*Nugūʿu*, which is the exact "broken" plural *nuǧūʿ* of the Arabic noun *naǧʿ*, "hamlet, small village". The first letter seems to suggest that Bēl-ibni refers to the important city of Laḫīru and to the "small villages" or settlements in its surroundings. This may be either a common noun or the proper name of a determined group of hamlets, not necessarily an actually distinct tribe.

---

84 The references are collected in S. PARPOLA, *Toponyms*, p. 226; J.A. BRINKMAN, *A Political History of Post-Kassite Babylonia: 1158-722 B.C.* (AnOr 43), Rome 1968 (quoted further *PKB*), pp. 270-271, n. 1738; W. RÖLLIG, *Li'ta'u*, in *RLA* VII, Berlin 1987-90, p. 33.

85 *RGTC* 8, p. 213.

86 Babylonian tablet BM. 40548, dated to the 9th year of Erība-Marduk (*ca.* 765 B.C.) and quoted by BRINKMAN, *PKB*, pp. 270-271, n. 1738.

87 For this element, see ZADOK, *WSB*, pp. 98-99.

88 W. FISCHER, *op. cit.* (n. 17), p. 52, § 90, Anm. 1.

89 LIPIŃSKI, *Semitic*, § 13.9.

90 Hebrew in I Sam. 25, 44; II Sam. 3, 15. Arabic in W. CASKEL, *op. cit.* (n. 39), vol. II, p. 376b, s.v. *Laiṯ*. In Ṣafaitic names, *layṯ* is monophthongized to *lṯ*: HARDING, *Arabian Names*, p. 510, also in Thamūdic *ʾblṯ*, "My father is a lion" (*ibid.*, p. 15).

91 *ABL* 280 = *SLA* 40, 19-20.

92 *ABL* 1000 = *SLA* 42, 6-7. 13-14.

The result of this analysis of tribal names raises a double question: Why are these tribes considered as "Aramaean", while they apparently are Arab? And: Can we admit that some of these tribes are actually Aramaean despite the fact that their name is a "broken" plural?

The majority of the so-called "Aramaean" tribes of southern and southeastern Babylonia are demonstrably of Arab descent, as can be shown by an etymological and morphological analysis of their names. They were all called "Aramaeans" because their way of life was similar to that of better known Aramaean semi-nomads: they did not reside in large cities of their own, were roaming with their flocks between winter and summer grazing places, and appear often as members of raiding parties. The distinction between these "Aramaeans" and the "Chaldaeans" seems therefore to have been basically cultural and social-economic. The question whether the Chaldaeans themselves were Aramaeans or not must be answered by analyzing their names, especially the names of their tribes and clans, and by attempting to determine the language that they were using among themselves. Since there are no texts preserved in the "Chaldaean" language, only non-Akkadian words and phrases in Assyro-Babylonian letters written by Chaldaeans can give a clue in this matter. However, this is not the topic of the present essay in honour of Prof. Pelio Fronzaroli.

The second question is linked directly with the problem of the "broken" plural. The existence of Aramaic "broken" plurals can hardly be denied in the inscription of Tell Faḫarīya,[93] which is the oldest written document in Aramaic from Upper Mesopotamia. Unless we are ready to assume the presence of unexplainable mistakes in this text, we must reckon with "broken" plurals in phrases like *nhr klm*, "all the rivers" (line 4), and *mt kln*, "all the lands" (line 5). In Arabic, *nuhūr* is the "broken" plural of *nahr*, but the often abridged pattern *fuʿul* > *fuʿl* may offer a more suitable explanation, since a form **nuhr* preserving the *h* avoids the problem that *nuhūr* might create, for intervocalic *h* disappears at Tell Faḫarīya in *klm* < *klhm* and in *kln* < *klhn*. Another pattern of "broken" plural may be represented by *ʾdqwr*, "jugs" (line 3), since the interpretation by Akkadian *adagurru* or *adakurru*, "libation vessel", does not explain the long vowel *ū* indicated by *w*. Instead, the pattern *ʾafʿūl* of a "broken" plural of *dqr*, "jug", corresponding to Akkadian *diqāru*, "pot", would

93 See here above, n. 16.

parallel the frequent Ethiopic "broken" plural with the vowel *u* < *ū*, as in *ʾahgur*, "cities", from *hagar*, "city", *ʾaḥqul*, "fields", from *ḥaql*, etc.

The Arabic patterns *fawāʿilu* and *fawāʿila(tun)* of "broken" plurals are used generally with nouns having a long *ā* in the first syllable.[94] They would explain the form *mwddt* in line 13 of the Tell Faḫarīya inscription, since the corresponding Arabic noun is precisely *mādda*, "fundamental constituent", "base". This perfectly fits the Aramaic phrase *mwddt krsʾh*, "the foundations of his throne". Also *swr*, "cows", in line 20 of the Tell Faḫarīya inscription must be the "broken" plural of **ṯūrā*, possibly **ṯuwar*, like Arabic *ṣuwar* is the plural of *ṣūra(tun)*, "shape", "figure". However, another pattern is used in the traditional curses of the Sefire treaties, found near Aleppo, which are posterior by one century to the Tell Faḫarīya inscription. There, the words *ssyh*, "mares", and *šwrh*, "cows", are used each with the verb in the plural (*yhynqn*, "they give suck")[95] and must thus be considered as collective nouns. It stands then to reason that they should be interpreted like Arabic *qirada(tun)*, the "broken" plural of *qird*, "ape, monkey", or *dibaba(tun)*, the Arabic "broken" plural of *dubb*, "bear". In fact, the pattern *fiʿala(tun)* is used mainly to form the "broken" plural of animal names[96] and we might have corresponding "broken" plurals **sisayā* and **ṯiwarā*, "mares" and "cows", in the Sefire inscription. These words can be used as masculine or feminine, like other animal names, and the use of different patterns, like *swr* at Tell Faḫarīya in the 9th century and *šwrh* at Sefire in the 8th century, does not constitute a difficulty when one knows that Arabic *ḥimār*, "ass, donkey", has three different "broken" plurals, namely *ḥamīr, ḥumur*, and *aḥmira*, beside the feminine *ḥamāʾir*, "she-asses". The basic question is whether Early Aramaic preserves traces of "broken" plurals or not, although their patterns do not need to be exactly the same as those of Classical Arabic. In the light of this evidence, there is no reason why the "broken" plurals *Puqūdu* and *ʾUtūʾ*, for instance, could not be genuine Aramaic forms. The name of these tribes is certainly older than their first written attestations in the 9th and 8th centuries B.C. and thus reflect the Early Aramaic morphology.

---

94 W. FISCHER, *op. cit.* (n. 17), p. 56, § 97 with Anm. 1.

95 Sefire stela I, A, 22-23.

96 W. FISCHER, *op. cit.* (n. 17), p. 52, § 89b.

THE DISGRACED COMMISSIONER. THE TURNOVER IN AMARNA OFFICIALDOM

MARIO LIVERANI

Università di Roma "La Sapienza"

A couple of Amarna letters provide information about a rather unusual event: the dismissal (by Pharaoh) of an Egyptian commissioner and the appointment of a replacement. The first letter (EA 326) has long been understood in this sense. The letter is the answer by Yidya, king of Ascalon, to a Pharaonic message. The central passage of the letter runs as follows:

"I have heard the words of the king my lord about his commissioner, that he was unable to protect the land of the king my lord. Behold (now) the king my lord has installed Rianappa (as) commissioner of the king my lord".[1]

The passage is followed by statements of obeisance. Yidya is clearly taking note of the new dispositions communicated by the royal message. The appointment of a new commissioner had to be formally communicated to the vassal kings of the area under concern.

In the second letter (EA 315), Pu-Baʿlu king of Yursa (a town close to Ascalon) takes note, in rather a similar way, of the same royal message, although previous interpretations do not seem to have caught the meaning of the message, nor the link with Yidya's letter. After routine statements of obeisance, Pu-Baʿlu goes on:

"(Concerning) Rianappa, the commissioner of the king my lord, whom the king my lord, strong like the Sun in the heaven, has designated: who is the dog that does not observe the words of the king my lord, the Sun in the heaven?"[2]

---

1 J. A. Knudtzon, *Die el-Amarna-Tafeln*, I, Leipzig 1907, p. 937 and W. L. Moran, *The Amarna Letters*, Baltimore 1992, p. 353 have partly misunderstood it, by translating a-na LÚ.MAŠKIM-*šu* "zu seinem Vorsteher", "to his commissioner" where I translate "about his commissioner" (obviously "the words of the king" is the message addressed to Yidya, not to the commissioner!). The *enūma* which follows is clearly declarative or substantive, cf. A. Rainey, *Canaanite in the Amarna Tablets*, III, Leiden 1996, pp. 77-83, and p. 200 for this passage.

2 The passage was misunderstood by Knudtzon (*cit*., p. 919), who relates "strong like the Sun" to Rianappa, and by Moran (*cit*., p. 348), who links it to "what the king ordered". Neither translation makes sense of the letter as a whole. Cf. my own traslation in *Le Lettere di el-Amarna*, I, Brescia 1999, pp. 67-68 (LA3).

The person is the same, bearing the same title (*rābiṣu*) in the same geographical area, and the situation (new appointment) is the same. What is different is the term employed: *šakānu* "to put" (in the sense of "install") in EA 326, *qebû* "to say" (in the sense of "nominate, appoint"[3]) in EA 315. The first term is the more common with such a meaning,[4] and reminds one of the title *šaknu* or *šakin māti* sometimes used as a synonym for *rābiṣu*.[5] The second term could be a semantic calque from Egyptian *s3*, which means both "to order" and "to appoint, assign". Notice that the verb *paqādu* "to entrust" also belongs to the same semantic (and institutional) field, but is only applied to local kings, not to Egyptian officials (a significant nuance in institutional terms).[6]

Rianappa (Egyptian *Rʿ-nfr*)[7] belongs to the later part of the reign of Amenophis IV,[8] so that we should not be surprised at the fact that there was little opportunity for him to carry out an active role in the Amarna archive. But he is mentioned in a third letter, EA 292 from Gezer (not far from Ascalon and Yursa). Here is the relevant passage:

"I had built a house, Manhate by name, in order to make provision in view of (the arrival of) the Egyptian troops of the king my lord. But Maya took it out of my hands, and put his commissioner inside it! Entrust Rianap(pa) my commissioner with (the task of) giving me back my citadel, and I will prepare in view of (the arrival of) the Egyptian troops of the king my lord."

This letter, too, may belong to the moment of the appointment of the new commissioner – with the difference that the senders of EA 315 and EA 326 simply take note of the pharaonic order, while the sender of EA 292 takes the opportunity to recriminate and gain some advantage. The entire letter in fact uses the well-known line

3 *CAD* Q, p. 39 (meanings 7 and 8).

4 Cf. e.g. EA 107: 22-23; 149: 47-48; 211: 21-22; etc.

5 Cf. EA 7: 77; EA 256: 9.

6 Cf. E. F. Campbell, "Two Amarna Notes", in *Essays in Memory of G. E. Wright*, Garden City NY 1976, pp. 49-51; M. Liverani, "Aziru servitore di due padroni", in *Studi orientalistici in ricordo di F. Pintore*, Pavia 1983, pp. 115-116.

7 Cf. W. F. Albright, in *JNES* 5 (1946), pp. 19-20; R. N. Hess, *Amarna Personal Names*, Winona Lake 1993, n. 139.

8 E. F. Campbell, *The Chronology of the Amarna Letters*, Baltimore 1964, pp. 128 and 135.

of reasoning "I should protect, but how can I do so unless you provide me with the necessary conditions?".[9]

If this reconstruction is correct, we have the name of the disgraced commissioner: Maya. The previous commissioner, Maya, committed the offence of appropriating Manhate from the king of Gezer; the new commissioner, Rianappa, must restore Manhate to its legitimate owner, to the advantage of the correct functioning of the Egyptian imperial administration (hosting travelling troops).[10]

Maya – one of the few officials in the Amarna archive also known from Egyptian sources[11] – is named in a complete set of letters (EA 216-218, 300, 320, 328, 337, all from southern Palestine), whose content and tone are quite normal: answers by local kinglets to pharaonic messages announcing the arrival of Maya at the head of an armed contingent. Only one of the letters (EA 300, from Gezer) hints at problems, but these are local in nature and do not affect Maya's position. It is hard to say whether all the letters refer to one and the same inspection tour by Maya, or to several tours, given the routine character of the procedure and related messages.[12]

An interesting item, however, has recently been added to the "dossier" of Maya, thanks to an ingenious proposal by N. Na'aman. I am speaking of EA 230, written by an otherwise unknown Yama, whom Na'aman suggests reading as a mistaken (metathetical) rendering of Maya.[13]

According to Na'aman's suggestion, EA 230 yields an excellent sense. First of all, the sender is not a local king but an Egyptian *rābiṣu*, who has to protect the local

9 On the various kinds of answers, inside the Egyptian administrative procedure, cf. my article "A Seasonal Pattern for the Amarna Letters", in *Studies in Honor of W. L. Moran*, Atlanta 1990, pp. 337-348; *Le lettere di el-Amarna*, I, pp. 34-37.

10 On the function of Manhate cf. F. Pintore, "La prassi della marcia armata nella Siria egiziana dell'età di el-Amarna", in *OA* 12 (1973), p. 301. Manhatu, labelled as *bītu* (l. 30) and *ālu* (l. 38) is a kind of citadel or caravanserai, a (fortified) building serving as "post station" (this is precisely the meaning of the toponym **manāḫtu*, from *nwḫ* "to rest", cf. R. Zadok, in *UF* 27 [1995], pp. 627-628). Moran's translation "village" is inappropriate.

11 Cf. Campbell, *Chronology*, pp. 75-76, 126-130; M. Valloggia, *Recherches sur les "messagers" dans les sources égyptiennes*, Genève 1976, pp. 105-106; the texts concerning him have been translated most recently by W. J. Murnane, *Texts from the Amarna Period in Egypt*, Atlanta 1995, pp. 143-147.

12 Cf. fn. 9, above.

13 N. Na'aman, "Praises to the Pharaoh in Response to His Plans for a Campaign to Canaan", in *Studies Moran*, p. 401. Notice that the same metathesis *ia-ma* for *ma-ia* happens also with the name of *I-ri-ma-ia-aš-ša* (EA 130: 11) / *I-ri-ia-ma-[aš-ša]* (EA 370: 8).

ḫazānu.[14] Secondly, we are dealing with a commissioner who had problems with Pharaoh, to the point of addressing to him a unique letter of self-justification, which remains incomprehensible in the traditional interpretation:

"To the king my lord, say: message of Yama your servant. At your feet I fall down. Behold, I am your servant in the place in which I reside. Behold, the places where I reside are your cities, all of them. I protect your servants and your regents (*ḫazānu*). If an (Egyptian) soldier comes to me, I protect him; and the cities where I reside are well protected, all of them, for you. Ask your regents, whether they are protected (or not). May you know that all your cities are safe."

The commissioner (*rābiṣu*) is in charge of protecting a set of cities ruled by local regents (*ḫazānu*). The implicit charge against which Yama tries to react is the very one of which, in EA 326, Maya was accused, to be "unable to protect the land of the king" (*la-a yi-la-ú na-ṣa-ar māti šarri*).

The crime of inefficiency is typical of a system like the Egyptian one, centred on the correct "protection" of the "king's places" (*ašru šarri*, Egypt. *t3 st pr-ʿ3*), i.e. the local nodal points in the network of communication and displacement of people and goods that is the empire. We cannot be sure that the "official charge" was in fact substantiated by specific malfunctions, mistakes or abuses (like the one concerning Gezer, EA 292). It is also possible that the disgrace of Maya had a properly Egyptian matrix, within the royal court, or even in his personal relationships with Pharaoh, and that the "official charge" was just an excuse, carefully selected to show the vassals that Pharaoh was concerned with their own interests and safety.

In any case, around the middle of Amenophis' reign, Maya fell into disgrace and was removed from the office of commissioner in the province of Canaan (or perhaps, more specifically, in the area between Ascalon and Yursa on the coast, and Gezer and Lachish in the Shephelah). The information in the Amarna archive is confirmed by the archaeological data. Work in the tomb being built for Maya in the Amarna necropolis,[15] as appropriate for a good official under the protection of his sovereign, stopped abruptly, his name and figure were deleted from the already

---

14 In the old interpretation, the two terms were oddly inverted, cf. fn. 170-171 in my *Lettere di el-Amarna*, I, pp. 110-111.

15 Tomb 14, published by N. de G. Davies, *The Rock Tombs of el Amarna*, V, London 1908, pp. 1-5 and pls. I-V; identification with the Maya of the letters by W. F. Albright, in *JNES* 5 (1946), p. 15; 6 (1947), p. 59.

decoraded walls, and covered with plaster.[16] Maya could not use the tomb, which was set aside to await another official; but the abandonment of Amarna, a few years later, left the tomb incomplete and unassigned.

16 Davies, *cit.*, p. 5; on the chronological implications cf. Campbell, *cit.*, pp. 75-76, 128-129.

MUSICIANS FROM HAZOR AT MARI

ABRAHAM MALAMAT

The Hebrew University of Jerusalem

The corpus of Manatan's letters has recently been published by G. Ozan.[1] Manatan was a Mari official active towards the end of King Zimri-Lim's reign (1774-1761 B.C. according to the Middle Chronology). The corpus consists of fifteen letters, almost all addressed to the king of Mari. The most intriguing letter for the Palestinian scene reports to Zimri-Lim the return of a caravan sent to Hazor and bringing three musicians from there to Mari (No. 143 in Manatan's corpus, sigla M. 5117).[2] This is the twentieth Mari document mentioning Hazor – a significant number. First we shall translate the letter:

To my lord
Speak
Thus (speaks) Manatan
Your servant.
The [city of Mari], the palace,
[the sanctuaries], the work houses
and my [guar]ds are well.
A caravan (*teḫitum*) has arrived from Hazor.
Ibni-Addu,
the servant of my lord,
Abdi-Erah,
a person from Hazor,
his escort,
and 3 Amorite (mar-tu) musicians (lú nar meš),
who are with him, (came) to my lord.
Yarpa-Addu,

1 The corpus of Manatan at Mari has been published by G. Ozan, *Les lettres de Manatan*, *FM* 3 (*à la mémoire de M.-Th. Barrelet, Mémoire de NABU* 4), Paris 1997, pp. 291-305; for our document see pp. 296-297. For the previously published four documents of Manatan, see Ozan, *ib.* , p. 292 n. 1.

2 On the relations between Mari and Hazor see A. Malamat, *Mari and the Early Israelite Experience* (The Schweich Lectures 1984), London-Oxford 1989, pp. 55-62 and more recently M. Bonechi, *Relations amicales syro-palestiniennes: Mari et Haṣor au XVIIIe siècle av. J.C.*, *FM* 1 (*Mémoires de NABU* 2), Paris 1992, pp. 14-21.

Kibsi-Addu,
2 men from Qatna
(20) came to Mari.

The caravan (or group of messengers) returned from Hazor, the most distant site to the south-west of the Mari political and economic horizon. The caravan was led by Ibni-Addu (or Ibni-Adad), whose name is identical with the name of the ruler of Hazor in the Mari documents.[3] According to the custom at Mari, the caravan was escorted on its way back to Mari by a special envoy from Hazor.

The Akkadian term (lú) nar (meš), "musician", was a Sumerian loan word, which denoted players of musical instruments as well as singers, i.e. persons who possessed certain skill in the realm of music.[4] Some idea of the monetary value of a musician at the time may be gathered from a new document from Mari, according to which Zimri-Lim procured for Haya-Sumu an expert female musician for half a mina of silver.[5] The musicians were designated as "Amorites" (lú mar-tu), that is, persons coming from the West (here the term does not refer to nomads). Recently, have been attested among others eleven female musicians in Zimri-Lim's harem at the Mari palace, specified as "Amorites".[6] In the light of the document dealt with here, several of them might have been brought from the city of Hazor. The emphasis on "Amorites" indicates experts in the art of singing and in the playing of musical instruments characteristic of Syria-Palestine, such as the *kinnārum, kinnōr*, "lyre". Now this West Semitic term appears also in Ebla, in Mari and in Ugarit[7] and above all, in the Bible (cf. in particular Gen. 4:21). At the end of the document two persons are mentioned as coming from Qatna (some 300 km to the north of Hazor), who must surely have joined the caravan on its way back to Mari. One of the persons, Yarpa-Addu, is mentioned explicitly as a messenger (*mar šiprim*) in the context of

3 His West Semitic name, as was common at Hazor, was Yabni-Addu. The first name element easily became Yabin, the name of the king of Hazor in the Bible; see A. Malamat, *Mari* (*op.cit.* 2), p. 58 and n. 111, and a reference there to Albright.

4 On the term for musician in Sumerian and Akkadian cf. *CAD* N, s.v. *naru*, pp. 376-379 (and references there on Mari p. 378 [3']).

5 See now J.-R. Kupper, *Lettres du temps de Zimri-Lim* (*ARM* 28), Paris 1998, no. 86, ll. 24-28 (p. 122).

6 See now N. Ziegler, *Le Harem de Zimri-Lim*, *FM* 4 (*Mémoires de NABU* 5), Paris 1999, pp. 118f., 130, 216.

7 See, *e.g.*, *CAD* K, p. 387, s.v. *kinnāru*; A. D. Kilmer, *RlA* 6 (1980-1983), p. 573 b (s.v. Leier).

another caravan reaching Mari (*ARM* 6 14:22). Thus it is likely that we have here the very same messenger.

The letter conforms in format to other letters of Manatan's corpus, as well as to letters published some forty years ago, dealing with caravans, especially from the West. A very similar document mentions caravans sent from Hazor and Qatna to Mari and Babylon (*ARM* 6 78).[8] Yet this document does not specify the items carried by the caravan (possibly they were mentioned in the damaged part of the document). The musicians were, like other artists and artisans, a mobile element, passing from one city to another.[9] Thus, unpublished documents from Mari attest to the presence of musicians in the West not only at Hazor but also at Qatna, Aleppo, Carchemish, and to the east of Mari in the city of Assur.[10]

Our document testifies that Hazor, in addition to being the center of a school of higher learning at the time, as is proven by several documents unearthed at Hazor,[11] was also most likely the seat of a music "academy" of widespread renown.

---

8 Cf. A. Malamat, *Hazor "The Head of All those Kingdoms"*, *JBL* 79 (1960), pp. 35-36. On a similar letter mentioning Yarpa-Addu from Qatna (Hazor is absent), see *ARM* 6 14: 7-24 and cf. D. Elgavish, *The Diplomatic Service in the Bible and Ancient Near Eastern Sources* (Hebrew), Jerusalem 1998, p. 143 (bottom).

9 Cf., *e.g.*, J. M. Sasson, *Instances of Mobility among Mari Artisans*, *BASOR* 190 (1968), pp. 46-54.

10 On these cities see J.-M. Durand, *Unité et diversité au Proche-Orient à l'époque amorrite*, in *La circulation des biens, des personnes et des idées dans le Proche-Orient ancien*, *RAI* XXXVIII, Paris 1992, p. 127.

11 On these documents see references in A. Malamat, *Mari* (*op.cit.* 2), p. 55 and n. 105 and in addition A. Horowitz, *A Combined Multiplication Table on a Prism Fragment from Hazor*, *IEJ* 47 (1997), pp. 190-197.

THREE OLD-BABYLONIAN CONTRACTS FROM THE KINGDOM OF LARSA[1]

PIETRO MANDER

Istituto Universitario Orientale di Napoli

While studying epigraphic material supposedly coming from Larsa, in order to single out particular archives for prosopographical purposes, the present writer came across the following three texts. It is a great pleasure for him to dedicate their edition to Prof. Fronzaroli, whose contributions have always given great momentum to philological studies on cuneiform documents.

The three present tablets have been spotted thanks to Dr. C. Walker's and Prof. Dr. M. Sigrist's invaluable cataloguing work on the texts of the British Museum of London, coded below number BM 24.000.[2] The present writer is deeply indebted to their courtesy and liberality for accessing still unpublished drafts and computer files.

The relevant texts are:

1) BM 24168
2) BM 24169
3) BM 24349

These texts preserve the year names; they have been described, in the unpublished file of CBT 3, as loans records[3] and the year name is there given in transliteration: the respective dates are.[4]

---

1 The present writer would like to thank the Trustees of the British Museum for allowing him the permission to study and publish the here presented material. He would like to thank Prof. W. G. Lambert, Prof. F. Pomponio and Dr. C B. F. Walker, who discussed some passages of these texts with him. Of course, the full responsibility rests with the present writer.

2 The closing figure in CBT 2 is 23618.

3 Dr. C. B. F. Walker - who is studying the Old-babylonian epigraphic material in the British Museum - kindly informed me that in his opinion the place of origin of these texts should be Kisurra. As a matter of fact, the present texts - as will be seen below - provide evidence corroborating this opinion. Furthermore, as already pointed out by Skaist, the use of the technical expression sum-mu-dam - occurring here in text 1 obv. 7 - is limited to the area of Nippur and Kisurra (see Skaist, A., *The Old Babylonian Loan Contract*, Ramat Gan 1994 (henceforth: *Loan*), p. 198 f.).

1. Loan of silver; Sumuel 20
2. Loan of barley; Sumuel 20
3. Silver loan without interest; Sumuel 28

Texts 1 and 2 show traces, unfortunately illegible, of seal impressions.

T.1 BM 24168

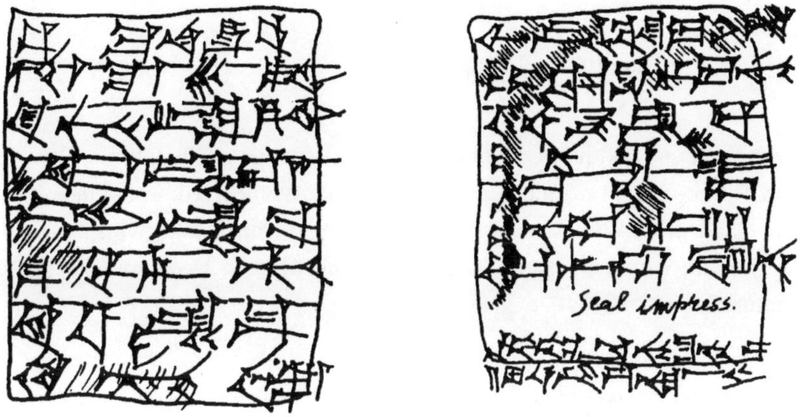

Seal 

Obv 1) 1/3 ma-na kù-babbar
2) máš 1 gín 1 še-ta
3) ki *nu-mat* É-*ra-bi*
4) ^{I}Inim-^{d}En-líl-lá / dumu Lú-^{d}EN.ZU
5) šu ba-an-ti
6) iti u$_4$-bur$_{14}$-šè
7) sum-mu-dam

4 According to Sigrist's Year Name List (to be found in internet: http://www.mpiwg-berlin.mpg.de /Yearnames/HTML/T10K1.htm) that we follow.

Rev 8) igi ^{d}EN.ZU-*ki-ma-ì-lí-*⌜*a*$^{?}$⌝ / dumu *Puzur*$_{4}$-^{d}*Da-mu*

9) igi *Na-bi-*^{d}EN.ZU / d[umu] *Be-e-lum*

10) igi *Ma-nu-um* / d[umu] *Nu-úr-*^{d}A-a

11) i[gi] ⌜Ur$^{??}$⌝-MAŠ (=$^{d?}$)Dub-šen-na

blank - seal impression

12) iti gan-gan-è mu *Su-mu-e*[*l*] / ^{id}Burun-na$^{?}$ ba-an-keš[da]

Seal (edges and blank space on the reverse only)

1) *lost*

2) dum[u? ... ?] lú-agrig

3) x x x

"1/3 silver minas, (its) interest per 1 shekel (is) 1 (bariga of) barley, from the household of Bîtum-rabi, Inim-Enlila, son of Lu-Suena has received; in the month of harvest he shall give. Witness: Sîn-kīma-ilia, son of Puzur-Damu; witness: Nabi-Sîn, son of Bêlum; witness: Manum, son of Nûr-Aja; witness: Ur-Dubšenna (?). Month Kisilimum, year: Su 20"

obv. 2)

Expressing the interest clause by a nominal sentence is a practice of the regions south of Sippar: see Skaist, *Loan*, p. 98 f. and 109 ff.

The interest rate here recorded is extensively discussed by Skaist, *Loan*, p. 109-113, who examines its correspondence to 20% stated by Kienast. This interest rate is found in the northern region of South Babylonia (see map in Skaist, *Loan*, p. 111).

obv. 3)

Tentative interpretation.

obv. 6)

On this time definition and the expression u$_{4}$-bur$_{14}$-šè, see Skaist, *Loan*, p. 149 ff.

rev. 8)

Sîn-kīma-ilija, son of Puzur-Damu is mentioned in Kienast, B., *Die altbabylonischen Briefe und Urkunden aus Kisurra*, I. Teil + II. Teil (Freiburger altorientalische Studien 2), Wiesbaden 1978 (henceforth: FAOS 2/1 aut 2), I. Teil, p. 6 ff. where he is taken as "index fossil"; his existence is to be dated to the reign of Manabalti-El.

rev. 9)
The spelling Be-e-lum for Bēlum occurs in Kisurra texts: see Kienast, FAOS 2/2, p. 191.

rev. 11)
The sign DINGIR is written in a peculiar way by the present text's scribe: cf. the shape of this sign in rev. 2 and 6: . In the sign at hand, the two heads of the wedges are closer than in the above-mentioned occurrences of the sign DINGIR, and this makes it uncertain whether the determinative for divine names is actually meant here.

T.2 BM 24169

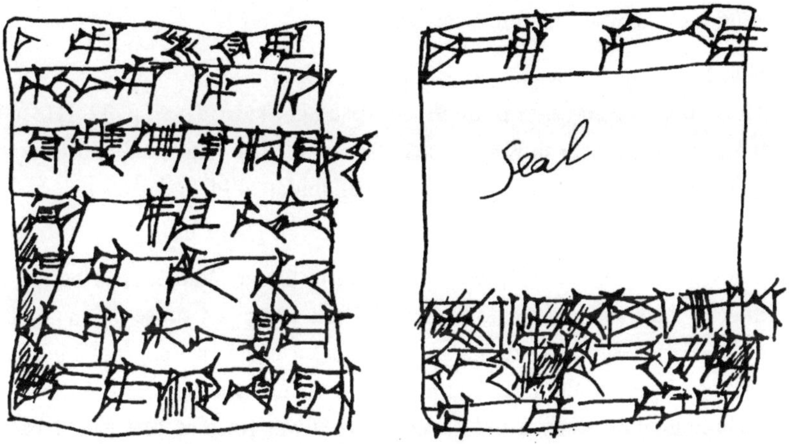

Obv	1)	10 gur še-ur$_5$-ra
	2)	máš 1 gur 1/5 4/30 <še>-ta
	3)	ki ^{d}EN.ZU$^{!}$-*e-ri-ba-am*
	4)	*Ša-ra-kum*
	5)	šu ba-an-ti

	6)	igi *Bur-*^{d}EN.ZU
	7)	dumu *Ku-bi-na-da*
Rev	8)	dumu *E-ni-hum*
	9)	mu ^{id}Burun-na
	10)	*Gu-un-gu-nu*$^{!}$*-um*
	11)	ba-an$^{!}$-kešda

Seal (edges and blank space in the reverse only)

	1)	[*Š*]⸢*a*⸣$^{??}$*-r*[*a-kum*] (?)
	2)	[...] A.NI.x[...]

"10 kūr of barley , ur$_5$-ra-type loan, (its) interest (being) per 1 kūr: 1 bariga and 4 sūt (i.e. = 33 1/3%), from Sîn-eribam, Šarakum has received. Witness: Bur-Sîn, son of Ḳūbi-nādā, son of Enihum. Year: Su 20"

obv. 1)

The expression še-ur$_5$-ra is amply discussed in Skaist, *Loan*, p. 33-41. On the occurrence of ur$_5$-ra loans in Kisurra, see ibid. p. 38. The reign of Sumu-El is included in their spreading period, as stated by Skaist, ibid. p. 49 f.

obv. 2)

Skaist (*Loan*, p. 115-18), when referring to the geographic distribution of the two interest rates, namely 33 1/3 % (1 máš 1 gur 1 bariga 4 sūt še-ta) and 20 % (1 máš 1 gur 1 bariga še-ta),[5] outlines two regions, a northern one, including texts of the Manana Dynasty and from Nippur, where the rate was 33 1/3%, and a southern one, including either Kisurra and Larsa, where it was fixed at 20% (see maps on p. 116-117).

The passage at hand provides new evidence that the distribution of one of the two interest rates, i.e. 33 1/3%, was wider than previously known, overlapping with the area where the 20% rate was applied. On the ground of the present evidence, it is possible to provide a different interpretation for two passages in FAOS 2 texts, where it was previously read: text 38 obv 2) máš 1 gur 1 (PI) ⸢še$^{!}$⸣-ta, and text 52 obv 2) máš 1 gur 1 (PI) ⸢še$^{!}$⸣-[ta]. From the traces visible in the copies, it can be read, respectively: 1 máš 1 gur 1 bariga ⸢4 sūt⸣ <še>-ta; 1 máš 1 gur 1 bariga ⸢4 sūt⸣ [<še>-ta].

---

5 Because of a misprint, in p. 115 the position of the 2 figures, in Skaist, *Loan*, must be inverted: to *Ai* II i 38 must correspond 20% and to *Ai* II i 39, 33 1/3%.

rev. 7-8)

A witness named Kūbi-nādā, son of E.NI.[...] is mentioned in FAOS 2 112 11'

rev. 8)

Notwithstanding a crack on the tablet's surface of, the first sign of the line reads clearly (more clearly than it appears on the photograph) DUMU. The present writer can recognise no trace of a PN on the lower edge of the tablet, so it must be assumed either that Bur-Sîn's father and grandfather are both mentioned, or that the scribe dropped the name of Bur-Sîn's father and by mistake added the name of the next witness.

rev. 9 ff.)

The present variation of the 20th year of the reign of Sumuel is not - at the present writer's knowledge - recorded elsewhere. It could be tentatively translated: "Year in which the Euphrates (of) Gungunum was dammed", meaning that the damming work had been made where a canal or a previous damming were built by Gungunum, unless the present form is a shortened variation of a still unknown fuller year name. A town named after Gungunum is mentioned once in the Larsa texts (Groneberg, B., *Rép Géo* 3 p. 82 *s. v.* URU^{ki} *gu-un-gu-nu*: The context does not help locating it near to that great river), but the absence of the determinative KI rather suggest interpreting the quotation as referring to the homonymous king. Neither year names of Gungunum nor his royal inscriptions mention digging or construction works by the Euphrates. It is then possible that Sumuel's dam was erected where a canal dug by Gungunum crossed the river: 3 canals are mentioned in Gungunum year names (namely: Annepadda, Imgur-Sîn and the Išartum; a fourth canal was placed at Girsu).

T.3 BM 2434

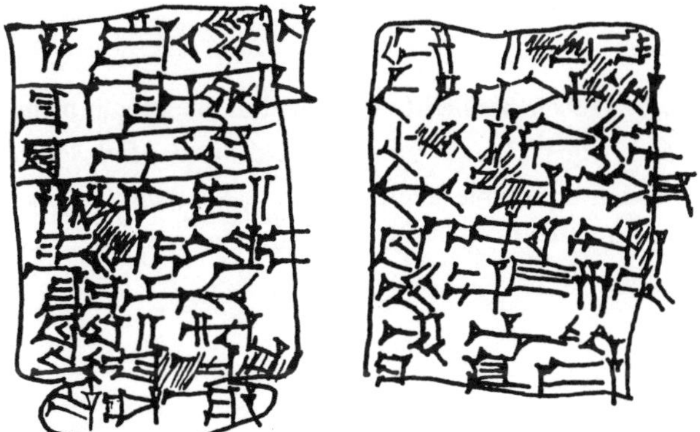

Obv	1)	4 gín 10 še kù-babbar
	2)	šu-lá-šè máš nu-tuku
	3)	ki ^{d}Nanna
	4)	*Sà-al-lí-ja*
	5)	dumu *Tu-ga-ru-um*
	6)	šu ba-an-ti
	7)	iti *Te-a-ri*
	8)	Uri$_5$-ma^{ki} (sic!)
Inf. Edge	9)	kù$^{!}$ ì-lá-e
Rev	10)	igi *Sà-a-*⸢x⸣-⸢*la*⸣
	11)	igi Nì-ga-⸢^{d}⸣[Nann]a (⸢^{d}⸣[ŠEŠ].KI)
	12)	igi ⸢*Ha*$^{?}$⸣*-a-ni-bu-um*
	13)	igi *Nu-úr-ì*$^{!}$*-lí-šu*
	14)	iti ab-è
	15)	mu-ús-sa 6-kam
	16)	en-^{d}nanna
	17)	ba-hun-gá
		Unsealed

"4 shekels and 10 grains of silver, loan of šu-la$_2$-type, without interest, from (the temple) of Nanna, Salija, son of Tugarum, has received; in that Simānum, (in) Ur, (that) silver he shall repay. Witness: Sa...la; witness Niga-Nanna; witness Hanibum; witness: Nūr-ilišu. Month Kislimum; year: Su 28"

obv. 3)
On temple loans, see Skaist, *Loan*, p. 172 ff. and reference at p. 11 fn 4. The occurrence of Nanna's temple loans is documented in Kisurra: see Kienast, FAOS 2/1, p. 42.

obv. 7)
Dr. C. B. F. Walker pointed to my attention the month name Tīrum (see RlA 5 p. 301 b; Landsberger, B., *Der kultische Kalender der Babylonier und Assyrer*, Leipzig 1915, p. 85) as a possible interpretation of the name of this month. He quoted the still unpublished BM 29673, a tablet of unknown provenience, where this month name occurs.

rev. 10)
The tablet is deeply chipped with only a horizontal wedge on the lower level surviving. This trace could match with AL, that may be inferred because of the respectively preceding and following signs A- and -LA.

Conclusion

In the texts at hand we came across textual and prosopographical data that relate these same texts to the epigraphic corpus from Kisurra. The latter set of data is of a particular relevance to outline the political changes in Larsa at the time of Sumu-El.

Kienast, when studying cross-connections and the prosopography of the person mentioned in the single archives he was able to single out,[6] noted the dating of the archives and the deeds of Sîn-kīma-ilija, whom he identified with the son of Puzur-Damu, of the Kisurra kings Itūr-Šamaš and Manabalṭi-El.[7]

The very same two persons, Sîn-kīma-ilija and his father Puzur-Damu occur in text 1, a text dated to the king of Larsa Sumu-El; furthermore, the texts at hand add two year names of Sumu-El in addition to those listed by Kienast.[8] Unfortunately the date of FAOS 2 112 (see above, ad text 2 rev. 7-8), where very likely Kūbi-nādā and his father Enihum are mentioned, is not recorded, so it is impossible to relate this occurrence to the documentation of text 2.

It is possible to assert that in the 20th reign year of Sumu-El, king of Larsa, Sîn-kīma-ilija, the son of Puzur-Damu was still living, businesslike and trustworthy enough to act as a witness in the stipulation of a loan contract.

Besides these few data, some guesses could be made: Nabi-Sîn and his father Bēlum, recorded in the witness tally of text 1 are homonymous with two merchants (dam-gàr) mentioned in FAOS 2 texts, and Sîn-eribam is creditor in text 2 and in FAOS 2 61. At present, the above considerations cannot be used to develop a chronological analysis, but could be confirmed by the edition of further texts.

6 See Kienast, FAOS 2/1 p. 7 f. (§ 6).

7 See Kienast, FAOS 2/1 p. 6 (§ 5f); p. 19.

8 See Kienast, FAOS 2/1 p. 15, where Sumu-El 6, 19 (= 20 in Sigrist's list), 23 and 26 regnal years are enumerated.

Text 1 = BM 24168

Text 2 = BM 24169

Text 3 = BM 24349

"GENETIC SUBGROUPING" IN SEMITIC

PAOLO MARRASSINI

University of Florence

In recent years there has been a remarkable flowering of works on the Semitic languages, from Lipiński[1] to Bennett[2] to Stempel[3] to Kienast.[4] One of the most important is surely *The Semitic languages*, edited by the late Robert Hetzron,[5] whose introductory chapter, by Alice Faber, contains some principles for *Genetic subgrouping of the Semitic languages*,[6] and therefore is best suited for a general discussion.

What strikes first, here as in almost every contribution coming from the USA, is the persistent appearance of some "Proto", either explicit or understood; it is as genealogy would be the only relevant phenomenon in historical linguistics, without any reference to linguistic geography (on which Moscati's criteria were essentially based),[7] or to parallel development and *drift*. To take an example for the first case, the change *ā* > *o* is not necessarily "Proto-Canaanite"[8] - quite apart from the fact that it is also extant in Lebanese Arabic (clearly as a substratum phenomenon),[9] and elsewhere[10] - but could also be only "common Canaanite", deriving from a later, geographical innovation. Historically speaking, this is the case, for example, of the connecting vowel/diphthong *ē/ay* in the plural noun before possessive suffixes. This *ē/ay* is obviously the oblique case of the dual (Sem. *-ay*), used here instead of the

---

1 E. Lipiński, *The Semitic languages*, Leuven 1997.

2 P. R. Bennett, *Comparative Semitic linguistics. A Manual*, Winona Lake 1998.

3 R. Stempel, *Abriss einer historischen Grammatik der semitischen Sprachen*, Frankfurt am Main - Berlin - New York - Paris - Wien 1999.

4 B. Kienast, *Historische semitische Sprachwissenschaft*, Wiesbaden 2001.

5 R. Hetzron, *The Semitic languages*, London 1997.

6 *Ibid.*, pp. 3-15. Cp., by the same author, *Genetic subgrouping of the Semitic languages*, University of Texas at Austin diss., 1980, DA 41/4 (1980), 1568-A.

7 Cp. e.g. *Nordarabico, sudarabico, etiopico*, RSO 34 (1959), p. 38.

8 Faber, *cit.*, p. 4.

9 H. Fleisch, *Le changement* ā > o *dans le sémitique du nord-ouest et en arabe dialectal libanais*, *CRAI* 1963, pp. 111-115.

10 E.g. in Western Syriac, or in the Semitic Ethiopian clitics, like pl. noun *-āt* > Amh *-očč*, etc.

oblique case of the plural (which could be more natural, and is in fact employed in South Semitic)[11] because of the frequency of its usage in the parts of the body,[12] and, curiously enough, it has been clearly utilized as a Northwest Semitic isogloss only by Garr;[13] but what is important here is that it is not a genetic feature, but a geographical one, born at the earliest at the end of the 2nd millennium, when Northwest Semitic was already extant as a separate entity, and Canaanites were already firmly established in their homeland since at least a millennium or two, if not from eternity.

For the second case, it must be said that parallel development is perhaps the most dangerous enemy of historical and genetic linguistics, as noted already by Antoine Meillet in 1900;[14] the excellent studies by Blau, Cohen, Gai, Kapeliuk, and Morag[15] should encourage to carry on a very promising direction, which will presumably wipe out many "Proto-Semitic" features. Here we come to the problem of the traits which F. calls "idiosyncratic", i.e. non-banal innovations, valid for grouping dialects together. This is the problem of the well-known parallelism between comparative linguistics and textual criticism:[16] in their genealogical tree the manuscripts of a given text are to be grouped according to their errors, and an error is the same as an innovation in comparative linguistics; but to avoid taking into account parallel production of them, and so false connections, these errors must be unusual and un-

11 Cp. J. Cantineau, *Accadien et sudarabique*, BSL 33 (1932), p. 184; W. Leslau, *South-East Semitic (Ethiopic and South-Arabic)*, JAOS 63 (1943), p. 8; A Goetze, *The Akkadian masculine plural in -ānū/ānī*, "Language" 22 (1946), pp. 126-127.

12 Th. Nöldeke, *Beiträge zur semitischen Sprachwissenschaft*, Strassburg 1904, p. 51.

13 W. R. Garr, *Dialect geography of Syria-Palestine 1000-586 B.C.E.*, Philadelphia 1984, p. 93.

14 *Note sur une difficulté générale de la grammaire comparée*, printed later in *Linguistique historique et linguistique générale*, Paris 1948, pp. 36-43; cp. the very opportune warning by J. Blau, *Some problems of the formation of the old Semitic languages in the light of Arabic dialects*, in: *Proceedings of the International Conference on Semitic Studies ... 1965*, Jerusalem 1969, pp. 39-40.

15 J. Blau, *On some Arabic dialectal features paralleled by Hebrew and Arabic*, JQR 74 (1985), pp. 5-12; D. Cohen, *Egyptien, araméen et éthiopien: parallélisme et symetries morphogénétiques dans l'évolution des systèmes verbaux*, in: S. Segert - A. J. Bodrogligeti (eds.), *Ethiopian studies dedicated to Wolf Leslau*, Wiesbaden 1983, pp. 81-98; A. Gai, *Structural similarities between Tannaitic Hebrew and Arabic*, Mus 101 (1988), pp. 43-49; O. Kapeliuk, *Some common traits in the evolution of Neo-Syriac and Neo-Ethiopian*, JSAI 12 (1989), pp. 294-320; Sh. Morag, *Biblical Hebrew and modern Arabic dialects: some parallel lines of development*, JSAI 12 (1989), pp. 94-117.

16 Cp. A. Ronconi, *Appunti per un parallelo fra filologia e linguistica*, "Rivista di cultura classica e medievale", 6 (1964), pp. 3-16; S. Timpanaro, *Die Entstehung der lachmannischen Methode*, 2. erw. u. überarb. Auflage, Hamburg 1971, pp. 73-92 (Kap. III: *Textkritik und Sprachwissenschaft und ihre Krisen ...*).

repeatable, that is *not-polygenetic*, i.e. "idiosyncratic" in F. terminology. If an error is non-polygenetic is a *connecting error*, i.e. an error capable of unite two or more mss. in a single family; and so is also a non-polygenetic linguistic innovation. But when a feature is to be classified as (almost) surely "non-polygenetic"? This is a difficult task in textual criticism, an even more in comparative linguistics, where it cannot be fulfilled before the general tendencies of the system itself are clearly and completely enucleated. But this in turn is not very easy. For example, the passage *a* > *e* in the neighbourhood of laryngeals could have seemed strange in Akkadian before a similar phenomenon in Modern South Arabian was known,[17] or the interdentals[18] before Eblaic confirming Old Akkadian,[19] or even, for **yaqattal*, the many late formations with a vowel between the I and the II radical (see below).

Among the innovations of West Semitic against East Semitic, F.[20] follows Hetzron and includes perfect *qatala* among them; but is it really true that this form differs "in crucial aspects" from the Akkadian stative? The question of the West Semitic perfect and the East Semitic stative must be inserted in the much more complicated framework of the suffixed "conjugations" in the Semitic languages, i.e. must include also the recent Aramaic constructions like the Neo-Aramaic suffix-conjugation (e.g. *qātl-en* < *qātil* + *ʾana*) and the construction *šemīʿ l-*, the Ethiopic gerundive, and at least the Egyptian forms of the so-called "Old perfective" (e.g. *sḏm.kwi* < *sḏm+ink*), the *sḏm.f* and the *sḏm.n.f.* It was Castellino who clearly approached the Ethiopic gerundive to the Akkadian stative,[21] but D. Cohen[22] rejected his hypothesis by grouping the Akkadian stative together with the West Semitic perfect, the suffix conjugation of Neo-Aramaic, and Egyptian "Old perfective", mainly

---

17 In the dialect of Abd el-Kuri (E. Wagner, *Der Dialekt von Abd el Kuri*, "Anthropos" 52, 1959, pp. 477-478) and elsewhere (T. M. Johnstone, *The Modern South Arabian languages*, Malibu 1976, p. 96).

18 An "Amorite" innovation according to G. Garbini, see e.g. his *Le lingue semitiche*, II ed., Napoli 1984, pp. 51-53 and 199-120.

19 P. Fronzaroli, *Problemi di fonetica eblaita*, SEb 1/5-6 (1979), pp. 66-89.

20 Faber, *cit.*, p. 8.

21 G. R. Castellino, *The Akkadian personal pronouns and verbal system in the light of Semitic and Hamitic*, Leiden 1962.

22 D. Cohen, *La phrase nominale et l'évolution du système verbal sémitique*, Paris 1984; cp. earlier *Égyptien, araméen, et éthiopien. Parallélisme et symétries morphogénétiques dans l'évolution des systèmes verbaux*, in: S. Segert - A. J. E. Bodrogligeti (eds.), *Ethiopian studies dedicated to W. Leslau*, Wiesbaden 1983, pp. 81-98.

on the basis of the fact that in all these cases one has to do with *a nominal sentence* made by a nominal predicate to which abridged forms of the independent personal pronoun are attached with the function of subject. Instead, in the case of the Ethiopic gerundive, of the Aramaic constructions of the type *šemīʿ leh*, and the Egyptian forms *sḏm.f* and *sḏm.n.f* it is only question of a *simple name* (usually an adjective) to which a possessive suffix pronoun is added; the subject is external to the syntagme. Probably this general picture is even more complicated than Cohen thinks: the paramount importance of the adjective should be stressed, as indicated by cases like the Egyptian Old Perfective, where a substantive must be "adjectivized" by the *nisba* ending *-y*, and the Ethiopic, where also adjectives with possessive suffixes exist (e.g. *tekuzeya* "I (being) sad");[23] but above all, two problems remain, that also the constructions like Aramaic *semīʿ leh* and Egyptian *sḏm.n.f* are to be classified as *nominal sentences* by virtue of the preposition, and that the Ethiopic gerundive is a non-finite form, whereas Egyptian *sḏm.f* is finite. So, leaving aside the problem of ergativity,[24] in view of what has been said, of the fact that adjectives are predominating in the Akkadian stative and in the stative themes of the West Semitic perfect,[25] and maybe also of the fact that many of these conjugated forms seem to derive from a scheme *qatil* (Akkadian stative, stative verb in West Semitic) or *qatīl* (Aramaic *šemīʿ leh*, Ethiopic gerund), we can conclude that the distance between both forms is not so big as it could appear at a first sight.

---

23 H. Satzinger, *Äthiopische Parallele zum ägyptischen* sḏm.f, MDAIK 23 (1968), pp. 163-166; Id., *Ein semitisches* sḏm.f *(Resumé)*, ZDMG Supplementa I, XVII. Deutscher Orientalistentag, Teil 1, 1968, p. 39.

24 Cp. I. M. Diakonov, *Semito-hamitic languages*, Moscow, 1965, pp. 15-18 e 86-88; F. I. Andersen, *Passive and ergative in Hebrew*, in: H. Goedicke (ed.), *Near Eastern studies in honor of W. F. Albright*, Baltmore-London, pp. 1-15; H.-P. Müller, *Die Konjugation von Nomina im Althebräischen*, ZAW 96 (1984), pp. 245-263; *Ebla und das althebräische Verbalsystem*, Bibl 65 (1984), pp. 154-162; *Ergativelemente im akkadischen und althebräischen Verbalsystem*, Bibl 66 (1985), pp. 385-417; *Das Bedeutungspotential der Afformativkonjugation*, ZAH 1 (1988), pp. 74-98 and 159-190; *Zur Theorie der historisch-vergleichenden Grammatik dargestellt am sprachgeschichtlichen Kontext des Althebräischen*, in: A. S. Kaye (ed.), *Semitic studies in honor of Wolf Leslau*, II, Wiesbaden 1991, pp. 1112-114. Contrary to Diakonov, I believe that one can speak of ergative elements in a typological sense, and not in a historico-genealogical perspective: cp. the doubts by D. O. Edzard, *Die semitohamitischen Sprachen in neuer Sicht*, RA 61 (1967), pp. 143-145 (review.-article of Diakonov) and H.-J. Sasse, *Afroasiatisch*, in: B. Heine et al. (Hrsg.), *Die Sprachen Afrikas*, Hamburg 1981, p. 145; see also M. Z. Kaddari, *Ergativity in Modern Hebrew*, in: *Proceedings of the Eleventh International Conference of Linguistics*, I, Firenze 1974, pp. 661-666.

25 That the West Semitic perfect derived from a conjugated adjective was already held by H. Bauer, *Die Tempora im Semitischen*, BA 8 (1910), pp. 1-53.

F., following Hetzron, considers the imperfect *yaqtulu* as an innovation of Central Semitic (but why not of Western Semitic in its entirety?), as compared with the older *yaqattal*, "a form that is preserved in Ethiopian Semitic, South Arabian, and Akkadian".[26] But all this is far from being established. First of all, this new form is not indentified by the fact of being "non-geminate", but by that of having a vowel between the I and the II radical; although considered very important at the beginnings, gemination is a less significant feature. The approach between Akkadian and Ethiopic was first proposed by P. Haupt in 1878,[27] and it was sometimes utilized, together with Modern South Arabian,[28] until Landsberger called the attention to it in 1926,[29] and finally a vigorous discussion between Greenberg and Leslau arose in the Fifties.[30] Apart from the sporadic attempts to find traces of *yaqattal* in North West Semitic,[31] all of them unsuccessful[32] as even more that to find it in a dialect of South Arabian,[33] it must be said that today is *yaqattal* itself which is in danger of being

---

26 Faber, *cit.*, pp. 8-9.

27 *Studies in the comparative grammar of the Semitic languages*, JRAS 1878, pp. 244-251.

28 E. g. in the famous article by V. Christian, *Akkader und Südaraber als ältere Semitenschichte*, Anthropos 14-15 (1919-20), pp. 729-739.

29 *Prinzipienfragen der semitischen, speziell der hebräischen Grammatik*, OLZ 29 (1926), pp. 867-976.

30 J. H. Greenberg, *The Afro-Asiatic (Hamito-Semitic) present*, JAOS 72 (1952), pp. 1-9; W. Leslau, *The imperfect in South-East Semitic*, JAOS 73 (1953), pp. 164-6; Greenberg, *A reply*, *ibid.* pp. 167-168.

31 Discussed in T. L. Fenton, *The absence of a verbal form* *yaqattal *from Ugaritic and North-West Semitic*, JSS 17 (1970), pp. 31-44. For El-Amarna cp. A. F. Rainey, *Morphology and the prefix-tenses of West Semitized El-'Amarna tablets*, UF 7 (1975), pp. 394-426 (esp. p. 423).

32 A. Goetze, *The tenses of Ugaritic*, JAOS 58 (1938), pp. 297-300; against him Fenton, *cit.*, pp. 35-36; O. Rössler, *Eine bisher unbekannte Tempusform im Althebräischen*, ZDMG 111 (1961), pp. 445-451; *Die Präfixkonjugation* qal *der verba Iae* nun *im Althebräischen und das Problem der sogenannten Tempora*, ZAW 74 (1962), pp. 125-141; on the contrary A. Bloch, *Zur Nachweisbarkeit einer hebräischen Entsprechung der akkadischen Verbalform* iparras, ZDMG 113 (1963), pp. 41-50.

33 According to A. Avanzini, *Linguistic data and historical reconstruction: between Semitic and Epigraphic South Arabian*, in: A. S. Kaye (ed.), *Semitic studies in honor of Wolf Leslau*, I, Wiesbaden 1991, pp. 108-109. Without knowing it, Avanzini makes use of the old device (assimilation of the first consonant n in the verb) already employed by Goetze for Ugaritic, and generally rejected (see the preceding footnote). There is plenty of examples of an assimilated *n* in ESA imperfects (e.g. *yḏrn*, *yḍ'n*, *yfṣn*, *ygwn*, *ys2n*, *yṣrn*, maybe *yḍwn*). True, all of them are forms with final *-n*, which A. excludes from her reasoning, but it is she herself who afterwards quotes *yfṣn*. This discovery in Sabaic should indicate a mean to avoid any similarity between indicative and subjunctive, resulting from the absence of *b-* in the first, and so one is compelled to invent a *yaqattal* form for every Arabic dialect in which such a distinction, and prefixed *b-*, do not exist; Sabaic,

considered secondary, as a verbal form originated independently by parallel development (cp. Meillet, above), in different area for different reasons, semantic for Ethiopic (universal tendency towards the renewing of the verbal aspect for the expression of concomitance, here through the utilization of the intensive),[34] and phonetic in Modern South Arabian (fall of the *u* in internal open syllable in **yaqtulu*, and "réssaut" of the final -*u* to a position between the I and the II radical, as in many modern Arabic dialects).[35] Of course, from the semantic point of view the real obstacle remains Akkadian, where the intensive form is perfectly alive; but from the phonetic point of view Cohen's position was somewhat anticipated by E. Wagner:[36] the insertion of a vowel between the I and the II radical is neither rare nor fortuitous, and follows phonological rules which are found in Iraqi Arabic, in many Arabic dialects of the Maghreb, and in Hebrew in the verbs of I laryngeal.[37] But what is very significant, in my opinion, is that in Qumran many fragments from Cave I[38] have been found with a vowel between the I and the II radical when pronominal suffixes are attached. Although R. Meyer[39] tried to interpret them as a Proto-Semitic *yaqattal*, most probably they are an example of a very widespread

---

usually considered (by A. herself) as the most innovating ESA dialect, would so be in this case the most conservative, and in it the narrative imperfect would derive from the subjunctive.

34 See, with different nuances, J. Kuryłowicz, *Le système verbal du sémitique*, BSL 45 (1949), pp. 47-56; *L'apophonie en sémitique*, Warszawa 1962, pp. 48-85; *On the methods of internal reconstruction*, in: *Proceedings of the Ninth International Conference of Linguists*, 1964 > *Esquisses lingustiques*, II, München 1968, pp. 93-120; M. Cohen, *Sémitique, égyptien, libyco-berbère, couchitique et méthode comparative*, BO 10 (1953), pp. 88-90; *Renouvellements des modes du verbe. Exemples observés dans l'évolution ds langues sémitiques méridionales*, Scientia 94 (1959), pp. 166-172; F. Rundgren, *Intensiv- und Aspektkorrelation ...*, Stockholm 1959. Note that, as Cohen (below) stresses, Geez *yeqattel* is phonetically not from **yaqattal*, but from the intensive **yuqattil*.

35 D. Cohen, *La forme verbale à marques personnelles préfixées en sudarabique moderne*, in: *IV Congresso Internazionale di Studi Etiopici*, II, Roma 1974, pp. 63-70; *La phrase nominale*, cit., pp. 62-78; on the contrary G. Goldenberg, *The Semitic languages of Ethiopia and their classification*, BSOAS 40 (1977), pp. 475-477, with a not very pleasant appendix in *The modern South Arabian prefix conjugation: addendum to BSOAS XL*, 3, 1977, BSOAS 43 (1979), pp. 541-546.

36 E. Wagner, *Die Möglichkeit der Entstehung einer* yeqatel-*Form im Südsemitischen*, in: *Proceedings of the Twenty-Sixth International Congress of Orientalists*, New Delhi, 4-10th January, 1964, II, New Delhi 1968, pp. 46-49.

37 Cp. already C. Brockelmann, *Grundriss der vergleichenden Grammatik der semitischen Sprachen*, Berlin 1908, pp. 212 e 555-556.

38 J. T. Milik, *Discoveries in the Judaean Desert*, I, Oxford 1955.

39 *Spuren eines westsemitischen Präsens-Futur in den Texte von Chirbet Qumran*, in: W. F. Abright et al. (hrsg.), *Von Ugarit nach Qumran. Beiträge ... O. Eissfeldt* (BZAW 77, 1958), pp. 118-128.

phenomenon of insertion of such a vowel, common in the Babylonian vocalization of Hebrew, as well as in Palestinian and Samaritan Aramaic,[40] and in Mandaic-[41] Contrary to Qimron,[42] the current explanation of such forms is today that of an anaptyctic vowel;[43] and this reminds us of the extensive usage of such vowels also in Galilean Arabic, just to form verbal imperfects like *yímisku*, *yilibsu*, *yínidru*, etc.;[44] if we add cases like those quoted by Garbini for Punic,[45] it becomes apparent that the proto-semiticity of *yaqattal* is not so clear as it would seem.

The perfect endings[46] of the I and II persons in *-t* are labelled as "Central Semitic" (i.e. Arabic). But in fact they are "West-Semitic", the situation being the same in Amorite, El-Amarna, Ugaritic, Ya'udic, Moabite, Hebrew, Phoenician, Aramaic as well. From where can it be affirmed that in West Semitic "the initial consonant for the first person singular suffix was *k*"? Moreover, the generalization of *-k* is rightly treated as a South Semitic innovation.[47] But there is the problem of the real weight of which this phenomenon can be credited. As a matter of fact, Cantineau[48] considered it "une preuve sérieuse de l'unité du domaine sudarabique à une certaine époque", but Goldenberg[49] pointed out similar phenomena in Neo-Assyrian[50] and in Samaritan Aramaic as clear products of parallel development, concluding that this isogloss is "much less neat than one would desire". Of course,

---

40 Z. Ben-Hayyim, *Studies in the traditions of the Hebrew language*, Madrid-Barcelona, Institutd "Arias Montano" 1954, pp. 87-88.

41 M. H. Goshen-Gottstein, *Studies in the language of the Dead Sea scrolls*, JJS 4 (1953), p. 107; *Philologische Miszellen zu den Qumrantexten*, RQ II/1, n. 5 (1959), pp. 43-46.

42 E. Qimron, *The Hebrew of the Dead Sea scrolls*, Atlanta 1986, pp. 52-53.

43 Sh. Morag, *Biblical Hebrew and modern Arabic dialects. Some parallel lines of development*, JSAI 12 (1989), pp. 94-117; *Qumran Hebrew. Some typological observations*, VT 38 (1988), pp. 148-164.

44 H. Palva, *Lower Galilean Arabic. An analysis of its anaptyctic and prothetic vowels with sample texts*, (Studia Orientalia XXXXII) Helsinki 1965, pp. 52-55, 59-62.

45 G. Garbini, *Note semitiche*, AION-Ling 4 (1962), pp. 89-90 (two inscriptions, one from el-Hofra/Costantina, III-II c. B.C., the other from Volubilis, II-I c. B.C).

46 Faber, *cit.*, pp. 9 and 11.

47 For ESA see J. Ryckmans - W. W. Müller - Y. M. Abdallah, *Textes du Yémen antique inscrits sur bois*, Louvain 1994, p. 87, and earlier M. Höfner, *Über sprachliche und kulturelle Beziehungen zwischen Südarabien und Äthiopien im Altertum*, in: *Atti del Convegno Internazionale di Studi Etiopici*, Roma 1960, p. 463 fn. 6 (cp. A. F. L. Beeston, *Sabaic grammar*, Manchester 1984, p. 14).

48 *Accadien et sudarabique*, BSL 33 (1932), pp. 180-181.

49 *The Semitic languages of Ethiopia and their classification*, BSOAS 40 (1977), p. 478.

50 In fact, already in Middle Babylonian (Gelb, BO 12, 1955, p. 106).

an influence by the possessive pronoun must also be taken into account, as Goldenberg himself suggests, and as it has been proposed since the XVI century by Angelo Canini.[51] Anyway, being the result of an analogic unification, it is very difficult to consider this phenomenon as a proof of the *genetic* unity of each of the two groups.

Following Huenergard, F. proposes,[52] as one of the two "major innovations" of Northwest Semitic as compared with Arabic, the double plural marking of certain nouns, i.e. an internal plural, to which an external desinence is added. But this is an extremely trivial phenomenon, clearly due to the fact that the internal plural is no more understood as such, but only as one of the many schemes of the singular. This happens with extreme frequency in the Geez,[53] but it is also well documented in Arabic,[54] and accordingly cannot be taken as a significant proof of relationship.

As an isogloss of Central Semitic F.[55] quotes the pharingealized emphatics of Arabic and Hebrew, as opposed to the glottalized ones in other Semitic languages. If it is so, "Central Semitic" (which for F. includes only Arabic) must be another mistake for "West Semitic" (see above). Moreover, Modern Aramaic has also glottalized emphatics, as shown by Dolgopolsky (quoted by F.), who has also tried to show the process of evolution from glottalized to pharingealized emphatics. But the problem is more of substance. That glottalized emphatics were also typical of Jewish Aramaic was suggested by the present writer on the basis of the fact that the loanwords with ṣ have *ṣ* in Geez if they come from Jewish Aramaic, but only *s* if they come from Arabic.[56] On the other hand, although F. very astutely considers Akkadian as belonging to the second group because of the Geer's law,[57] she goes

51 A. Canini, *Institutiones linguae Syriacae, Assyriacae atque Thalmudicae, una cum Aethipicae atque Arabicae collatione* ..., Parisiis 1554, p. 31.

52 Faber, *cit.*, pp. 10-11.

53 C. F. A. Dillmann (- J. A. Crichton), *Ethiopic grammar*, London 1907 (= Amsterdam 1974), par. 141 pp. 314-317; according to Dillmann, Geez is "in this matter unapproached by any other Semitic speech", p. 314.

54 C. Brockelmann, *Grundriss etc.*, Berlin 1908 = Hildesheim 1961, pp. 429-430.

55 Faber, *cit.*, p. 8.

56 P. Marrassini, *Semitico e camitosemitico nella linguistica etiopica*, OA 15 (1976), p. 337.

57 Cp. now also F. Corriente, *Introducción a la gramática comparada del semítico meridional*, Madrid 1996, p. 17. Very near to this solution also J. Aro, *Pronunciation of the "emphatic" consonants in Semitic languages*, SO 47 (1977), pp. 12-13, and A. S. Kaye, *Some remarks on Proto-Semitic phonology*, "Language Sciences" 8 (1986), p. 41. That Geer's law is now valid also for Eblaic has been demonstrated by G. Conti, *Il sistema grafico dell'eblaita e la legge di Geers*, Quaderni del Dipartimento di Linguistica dell'Università di Firenze 4 (1993), pp. 97-114.

maybe too far in utilizing the same criterion for classifying also Hebrew in the same way; the fact that in Hebrew the *t* of the *hitqattel* form becomes *ṭ* if in contact with a *ṣ*[58] does not necessarily demonstrate this. It is true that Cantineau's old proofs for glottalization in Hebrew did not stand,[59] although the famous sentence by Jerome ("... *sade, quam aures nostrae penitus reformidant*") seems to suggest a glottalized, rather than a pharingealized (and, so, more domestic) sound; but the fact is that the *t* is part of a morpheme, and as such it may be submitted to special phonetic laws;[60] besides, the same Akkadian assimilates a non-emphatic to a following emphatic,[61] and in particular the infix *-ta-* becomes *-ṭa-* if preceded by *q* in Middle and Neo-Assyrian,[62] and sometimes also in Late Babylonian.[63] As in Akkadian *q* just dissimilates *ṭ* in Geer's law, and taking into account the evolution sketched by Dolgopolsky, one can wonder whether also Akkadian had produced an evolution from glottalized to pharingealized emphatics as in Aramaic (and in Arabic) - i.e. if this evolution is not the normal one in many Semitic languages.

From the isoglosses of Aramaic, the postponed article has been eliminated,[64] because of Huenergard's opinion that "most of the innovations generally considered Aramaic are not observed in the oldest Aramaic inscriptional material". This proba-bly[65] derives from the quasi-absence of the article from some of the oldest Aramaic

58 For pharingealized emphatics in Modern Aramaic, with other examples of assimilation, see K. Tsereteli, *On one Suprasegmental Phoneme in Modern Semitic*, JAOS 102 (1972), pp. 343-346; R. D. Hoberman, *Emphasis Armony in a Modern Aramaic Dialect*, Lg 64 (1988), pp. 2-26.

59 G. R. Cardona, *Per la storia fonologica del «ṣādē» semitico*, AION NS 18 (1968), p. 4.

60 Cp. e.g. the evolution **š > h* in the causative and the pronominal suffixes in some Semitic languages (cp. M. M. Bravmann, *The Semitic causative prefix Š/SA*, Mus 82 (1969), p. 519 = *Studies in Semitic philology*, Leiden 1977, p. 202); see also F. Aspesi, *Sistema fonematico 'complessivo' e sistemi fonematici 'morfologici': un'interpretazione di alcuni fatti semitici*, AION 37 (NS 27) (1977), pp. 393-401.

61 W. von Soden, *Grundriss der Akkadischen Grammatik*, par. 26c p. 27; confirmed by Gelb, BO 12 (1955), p. 102.

62 von Soden, *Grundriss*, *cit.*, par. 29e p. 29 and 96f p. 124.

63 W. von Soden, *Ergänzungsheft zu GAG*, Rom (1969), p. 20**.

64 Faber, *cit.*, p. 10.

65 Unfortunately I have not seen the article by Huenergard (*Recent research in early Northwest Semitic grammar*) quoted here by F.

texts, above all the Tell Fekheriyeh inscription[66] (that from Deir ‘Alla is very difficult to interpret),[67] but cannot base itself on Ya'udic, which is not Aramaic, but only Northwest Semitic *prior* to the distinction Canaanite-Aramaic, as Moscati firmly held since the Fifties. Apart from the fact that Old Aramaic in general has of course the article -ʾ,[68] the reasoning is somewhat circular: if we admit that the post-poned article is typical of Aramaic (and it is difficult to deny it), why do we consider as Aramaic those dialects which do not possess this article? Here the real problem maybe lies in a too "genealogic" conception of the linguistic development: inside of the Northwest Semitic languages, no group was already born as "Aramaic", but one (or more) *became* it, thanks to innovations different in time and space, and possibly crossing each other in various *Wellen* (a case in point is e.g. the development **ḏ > d* in Ugaritic). Talking about the article, a prefixed definite article (*ʾ/h/ḥ(a)* and many other forms) is pointed out as a "primary innovation separating Modern South Arabian from the rest of South Semitic", but also in this case the validity of this statement depends on what this separation is meant to indicate. Quite apart from the doubts raised by Pennacchietti,[69] the Modern South Arabian article is clearly a part of the general phenomenon of the prefixed article *h/ʾan/m/l*, which was born at almost the same time in Syria-Palestine and the Peninsula at the end of the II millennium B.C./beginning of the I. From this point of view, it is an areal phe-nomenon which does not separate genetically Modern South Arabian from Epigraphic South Arabian and Ethiopic - any more than the *h(n)*- article unites genetically Thamudic, Lihyanic, Safaitic, Hasaean, and parts of early Arabic, with Hebrew and Phoenician; but in terms of genealogical affiliation, it can be confi-dently said that when the general trend of creating a definite article in Semitic had begun (at the epoch just indicated), ESA (which has *-n*) and Geez (which has none, or the suffixed pronoun *-u*) were already separated from all the rest (which has *h/ʾan/m/l*), and of course from each other. It also follows that, as far as the article is

66 Only the first word (*dmwtʾ*), as it seems. For the problem of the article see e.g. T. Muraoka, *The Tell-Fekheriye bilingual inscription and early Aramaic*, "Abr-Naharain" 22 (1983-84), pp. 94-95, who is in favour of the "Aramaicity" of this text.

67 Cp. J. A. Hackett, *The Balaam text from Deir 'Alla*, Chico 1984, pp. 113-114.

68 Cp. R. Degen, *Altaramäische Grammatik*, Wiesbaden 1969, pp. 55, 83-84; S. Segert, *Altaramäische Grammatik*, Leipzig 1974, (II ed. 1984), p. 188 (as it is well known, Segert's "Altaramäisch" also includes Imperial Aramaic). On the problem of the article in the oldest Aramaic texts see already S. Segert, *Altaramäische Studien*, AO 26 (1958), pp. 578-584.

69 *Un articolo prepositivo in neosudarabico?*, RSO 45 (1970), pp. 285-293.

concerned, neither Ethiopic nor Modern South Arabic can derive from ESA as it is presently known.[70]

For Ethiopian languages, the treatment by F. understandably draws even more heavily from Hetzron. First of all, as an Ethiopicist I think I can afford to assert that, even from a purely graphic point of view,[71] a schema of Semitic family with such a material space dedicated to Ethiopian languages is frankly exaggerated, as a kind of monstrous outgrowth: why not to subdivide, say, also Akkadian, maybe the most granitic languages in our lists, differentiating Old Akkadian, with its interdental(s) (see above), from Old Babylonian, which according to Goetze possessed special sibilants,[72] from Middle Babylonian and Neo-Assyrian, with their second persons of the stative ending in *-k* (see above), from Middle and Neo-Assyrian, which according to Garbini gave birth to the laterals with their evolution *št* > *lt*,[73] from Assyrian, with its vowel harmony, or with its evolution *š* > *s*,[74] and so on? But in spite of that, full justice is still to be done to the complexity of the problems. As I have treated some of them in a paper now in the press for the *Proceedings* of the XIV Conference of Ethiopian Studies, I shall limit myself to quote a few cases, without discussing them: the evolution of the interdentals into sibilants, as frequently in ESA, perhaps prevents us from connecting ESA with MSA, where the evolution is towards dentals; the presence in Geez of three genitival constructions (construct state in *-a*, analytical construction with *z-*, analytical construction with *l-* plus "pronom de rappel") has no parallel in the other Semitic languages (which have only two of them), except maybe Punic, and this perhaps suggests a composite nature of Geez; the Geez perfect endings *-ka* and *-na* are *-kā* and *-nā* in Tigrinya, as in Geez itself before pronominal suffixes, i.e. in an older stage, from which or from a language similar to which (and not from Geez as it stands) Tigrinya should derive; the construct and accusative marker *-a* of Geez is present in Tigrinya in personal names (usually from Geez), but frequently absent from place names which would

70 For ESA cp. the famous letter by Beeston in Ullendorff's *The Semitic languages of Ethiopia*, London 1955, n. 30 pp. 8-9.

71 Faber, *cit.*, genealogical tree on p. 6.

72 A. Goetze, *The sibilants of Old Babylonian*, RA 52 (1958), pp. 137-141.

73 Garbini, *Le lingue semitiche*, cit., p. 150.

74 Cp. also S. Parpola, *The alleged Middle/Neo-Assyrian irregular verb* *nass *and the Assyrian sound change* /s/ > /š/, "Assur" 1 (1974), pp. 1-10; E. A. Knauf, *Aššur, Šūaḥ und der stimmlose Sibilant des Assyrischen*, BN 49 (1989), pp. 13-16.

theoretically demand it at the origin,[75] and so one can wonder whether Tigrinya ever possessed this *-a*; this construct *-a* seems to be connected with names with a construct in *-a* in Old Babylonian, as already noted by von Soden, and maybe it can also be connected with the predicative *-a* of Old Akkadian, Eblaic and Amorite personal names; the external plural, so alive in North Ethiopic and in MSA, makes it difficult to derive them from ESA; the plural *-ān* of Geez, Akkadian, part of MSA, and Hamito-Semitic, represents an archaic belt on which *-īn* (Aramaic, Arabic, ESA, part of MSA) was superimposed, Ethiopic being already separated at that epoch; a possible origin of SE different from NE could be suggested by the II person feminine of the perfect *-š*, which is maybe not from the northern *-ki* (palatalization of velars is extremely rare in Ethiopic), but from the *-š* so widespread in the south of the Peninsula; the many *living*[76] archaisms of South Ethiopic, connecting it to Geez outside Tigre and Tigrinya are also to be noted (Amharic genitive *ya-* from **za* or **la*; old *-i-* in the plural noun before possessive suffixes, preserved in SE *-Vč(c)*).

So, it is clear that a search for rules governing genetic interpretation is most welcome. F. has done much in this direction, but sometimes our analysis has to rest on even sounder foundations.

75 E.g. *Māy 'angog* "Water of the iguana", *Falag dā'ro* "River of the sycomore", etc.

76 I.e. not crystallized like the accusative *-a*, etc.

ISHTAR OF EBLA AND HADAD OF ALEPPO: NOTES ON TERMINOLOGY, POLITICS AND RELIGION OF OLD SYRIAN EBLA

Paolo Matthiae

Università di Roma "La Sapienza"

After the publication in 1955 of the final report of the excavations at Tell Atshanah by Sir Leonard Woolley, the glyptic documented in the level VII of Alalakh began to be called with the new definition of Old Syrian glyptic.[1] U. Moortgat-Correns was the first scholar who noticed that a large part of the production of cylinder seals, attested in Alalakh VII mostly in seal impressions, corresponded to a style which several years before H. Frankfort classified under the definition of Second Syrian Group.[2] Notwithstanding minor differences in the chronological attribution in the conventional Middle Chronology, the glyptic material collected in Alalakh VII could with some certainty be dated between around 1725 BC and 1650/1625 BC, when is plausible that Hattusili I conquered and destroyed precisely the town of Alalakh VII.[3] On the contrary, according to the classification system proposed by H. Frankfort in his very authoritative essay of 1939, the Second Syrian Group had to be dated, in the lack of sure stratigraphic evidences descending from regular excavations, to the Mitannian period, namely after, and not before, the reigns of the great Old Hittite kings Hattusili I and Mursili I.[4] Therefore, in general terms, H.

---

1 C. L. Woolley, *Alalakh*, Oxford 1955. The new terminology has been introduced by U. Moortgat-Correns, *ZA* 51 (1955), pp. 88-101 and by W. Nagel, E. Strommenger, *JCS* 12 (1958), pp. 109-123.

2 H. Frankfort, *Cylinder Seals*, London 1939, pp. 260-273. After the founded critical observations by Moortgat-Correns, *ZA* 51 (1955), pp. 97-101, H. J. Kantor, *JNES* 15 (1956), pp. 158-160 has tried, without success, to support Frankfort's classification.

3 D. Collon, *The Seal Impressions from Tell Atchana/Alalakh*, Neukirchen-Vluyn 1975, pp. 143-144, who considers that Alalakh conquest happened early during Hattusili I's reign, but it is very probable that Alalakh VII was conquered at the time of the second expedition by Hattusili I: C. Kühne, in H.-J. Nissen, J. Renger (eds.), *Mesopotamien und seine Nachbarn*, I, 1, Berlin 1982, pp. 243-244 note 68; M. Heinz, *Tell Atchana/Alalakh. Die Schichten VII-XVII*, Neukirchen-Vluyn 1992, p. 197.

4 On the base of the strongly incomplete evidence of Alalakh VII and IV seal impressions published in the C. L. Woolley's final report, the conclusion of U. Moortgat-Correns, *loc. cit.*, that the First and Second Syrian Groups of H. Frankfort were approximately contemporary was, in general terms, not

Frankfort's geographic attribution of those classes of seals, defined of the Second Syrian Group to inner and, in part at least, coastal Syria, and to central and upper Mesopotamia, was correct, but his chronological attribution after around 1650/1600 BC, and not before that date, was not correct.

Yet, with the new definition of Old Syrian style, for a group, already numerous at the time, of cylinder seals, frequently called, until that time, with the ambiguous, and certainly wrong name of Syro-Hittite, what did they wish to mean?[5] First of all, they certainly wished to make the chronological precision clear, which was conveyed by the discoveries of Alalakh VII. However, it looks quite certain that the new terminology clearly implied two other facts. On the one hand, in fact, they wished to make clear, by means of the adopted definition, that the Old Syrian style was contemporary with the Old Babylonian style.[6] On the other hand, they clearly meant to maintain that this western style, chronologically parallel, was independent, in its iconographic contents and formal values, from that of contemporary Babylonia. These two considerations were basic ones as they discarded not only H. Frankfort's chronological evaluation, but also his interpretative structure of the glyptic of Syria in the first half of 2nd millennium BC.: in fact, he had maintained that, before the more original Second Syrian Group of the Mitannian period, the First Syrian Group could be singled out precisely for the strong influence of the Old Babylonian style.[7]

Of course, the identification of an autonomous Old Syrian style in the glyptic from Aleppo and Alalakh between around 1725 and 1625 BC, set, as a matter of fact, the problem of the independence and originality of the whole culture which had produced that style. A strong suggestion in this direction had already been given, even before 1955, by H. Frankfort himself, who had drawn attention precisely on several elements of independence and originality of the architectural tradition, which linked the palaces of Alalakh VII and IV, respectively of Middle Bronze II and of Late Bronze I, with the later so-called *khilani* of Iron II in Syria.[8] The acknow-

---

incorrect: in this respect the judgement of D. Collon, *The Seal Impressions*, p. 197 is too much negative.

5 G. Contenau, *La glyptique syro-hittite*, Paris 1922: it is on the background of this kind of very rough critical evaluations that may be appreciated the importance of the new terminology for its implication in the perspective of a historical consideration.

6 B. Buchanan, *JCS* 11 (1957), pp. 45-52; E. Porada, *JNES* 16 (1957), pp. 192-197.

7 H. Frankfort, *Cylinder Seals*, pp. 252-260.

8 *Id.*, *Iraq* 14 (1952), pp. 120-131.

ledgement, particularly in bronze-working from Ugarit to Qatna but also in stone reliefs from Karkemish, of works which, in other artistic genres, were clearly the product of that same style, allowed to extend from glyptic to the whole of the figurative culture, the definition Old Syrian.[9] The problem of the verification of the historical interpretation, which saw in the region of inner Syria, including Alalakh, Aleppo, Karkemish, and Qatna, the core of the autonomous and original Old Syrian culture, produced the beginning of the excavations at Tell Mardikh in 1964.

In 1977, a series of work seasons had already allowed to identify, in 1968, Tell Mardikh with ancient Ebla, but had also revealed, with the excavations of 1975 and 1976, one first basic sector of the Royal Palace G, and the State Archives of Mardikh IIB1, which was defined Early Bronze IVA.[10] In that same year, in a synthesis about the complex of the results at Tell Mardikh, I proposed to divide Middle Bronze (ca. 2000-1600 BC) in Middle Bronze I, until around 1800 BC, and Middle Bronze II, starting from that date, and to call the first of the two phases archaic Old Syrian period, and classic Old Syrian period the second one.[11] The choice of a date around 1800 BC for the beginning of the second phase descended from the belief that in the history of inner Syria the emergence of Yamkhad, by the end of the reign of Sumuepukh of Aleppo, and particularly at the beginning of Yarim-Lim I's reign, had been an event of special and long lasting importance, which had brought to the hegemony of Aleppo, over a large part of northern Syria, until Hattusili I's and Mursili I's Syrian conquests between 1625 and 1595 BC.[12]

According to this proposal of interpretation, Ebla had been the dominating political power in inner Syria in the early Old Syrian period, like Isin and Larsa had been in lower Mesopotamia in the early Old Babylonian period.[13] Shortly after 1800 BC, the rise of Aleppo as dominating power in upper Syria, under Yarim-Lim I, since 1780 BC, probably came a few years before the rise of Babylon under Hammurabi, between 1770 and 1760 BC in lower Mesopotamia. The classic Old Syrian period could thus be defined the age of the rise and predominance of Yamkhad in upper Syria, like the classic Old Babylonian period was the age of the

9 P. Matthiae, *Ars Syra*, Roma 1962; *Id.*, in *Studi in onore di E. Volterra*, VI, Roma 1967, pp. 623-637.

10 P. Matthiae, *Ebla, un impero ritrovato*, Torino 1977, pp. 33-44.

11 *Ibidem*, pp. 48-50.

12 P. Matthiae, *I tesori di Ebla*, Roma-Bari 1984, pp. 103-125.

13 *Ibidem*, pp. 146-150.

achievement of Babylon in lower Mesopotamia. Around 1595 BC Mursili I put an end to both hegemonies with the conquests of Aleppo and Babylon.[14]

It is evident, from these considerations, that the designation of around 1800 BC for the passage from Middle Bronze I to Middle Bronze II, and from the archaic to the classic Old Syrian period for inner western Syria, was based on events of the political history, and not on data of the development of material culture. Moreover, the kind of political event chosen certainly had a strong historical impact – suffice to think that, after Yarim-Lim I's ascent, the king of Yamkhad became a "great king", and such he remained in the conscience of his contemporaries, including the Hittites of Hattusili I, for nearly two centuries, until around 1600 BC –, but it is quite likely that for the Syrian world it was of a "processual", not "punctual" kind.[15] In other words, while in correspondence with the end of Middle Bronze II, around 1600 BC, the archaeological evidence from the North Syrian sites reveals in the majority of instances, and not occasionally, extensive, albeit not everywhere final, destructions of the urban and rural centres, in correspondence with Middle Bronze I end, it is probable that only rare traces of traumatic events, like a destruction, were preserved in the archaeological evidence.

In fact, as regards the passage from Mardikh IIIA to Mardikh IIIB, around 1800 BC, nowhere in the great urban settlement of Ebla we could find a destruction. Therefore, one might ask oneself, in terms of political history, which events were at the origin of the situation very efficaciously described from two Mari letters, where Aleppo appears as acknowledged political power up to lower Mesopotamia, and at same level as very few other political centres of those years. On the one hand, in fact, in Iturasdu's letter, they say that the king of Aleppo is "followed by twenty kings", while the kings of Babylon, Larsa, Eshnunna, and Qatna are "followed by ten or fifteen kings",[16] and, on the other hand, in Yamsum's letter to Zimri-Lim they maintain that, after the death of Shamshi-Addu I of Assyria, the "great kings" were only four, namely Hammurabi of Babylon, Rim-Sin of Larsa, Amutpi-El of Qatna, and Yarim-Lim of Yamkhad.[17] It is quite likely that the Yarim-Lim I's prestige and

---

14 See now H. Klengel, *Syria 3000 to 300 B.C.*, Berlin 1992, pp. 80-83.

15 For a recent picture of the city during Middle Bronze I-II see P. Matthiae, in E. D. Oren (ed.), *The Hyksos*, Philadephia 1997, pp. 379-414.

16 G. Dossin, *Syria* 19 (1938), pp. 119-121.

17 *ARM* XXVI n. 303, pp. 56-59.

hegemony, unlike Hammurabi's, who conquered and destroyed Eshnunna, Larsa, and Mari, asserted themselves not as a consequence of victories against other towns of northern Syria, but of a great success in the scenery of international politics, to which acts of great political skilfulness followed. The military success might have been a final victory against Shamshi-Addu, between 1781 and 1776 BC, at the very beginning of the reign of the king of Yamkhad,[18] while the placement of Zimri-Lim on the throne of Mari at Yasmakh-Addu's place, and the visit to the king of Ugarit with the new king of Mari are examples of the immediately following politics.[19]

Thus, in a completely parallel way as was ascertained in Palestine for the passage from Middle Bronze IIA, roughly corresponding to Middle Bronze I in Syria, to Middle Bronze IIB, roughly equivalent to Middle Bronze II of Syria, when, in the same years as Yamkhad, the powerful kingdom of Hazor emerged, the changes in material culture, between Middle Bronze I and Middle Bronze II at Ebla, and in north inner Syria are slow, and not sudden.[20] They can be perceived most of all in the evaluation of ceramic shapes, in the progressive quit of archaic types and in the gradual affirmation of new types in a phase of changes, which stretches from late Middle Bronze I to early Middle Bronze II, perhaps between 1850 and 1750 BC. This situation is particularly clear at Ebla, where, as seems now certain, no trace of a relevant destruction may be dated from around 1800 BC or slightly later.[21] It is quite likely that the king of Ebla recognised the predominance of Aleppo around 1770 BC, becoming one of the most powerful among the "twenty kings who followed" the great king of Yamkhad. This acknowledgement might have marked the beginning of a new cultural phase in Ebla itself, in which one may legitimately maintain that also a religious influence from Aleppo may have asserted itself.

The hypothesis that the recognition by Ebla, around 1770 BC, of the political predominance of Aleppo were at the origin of the strong presence of the figure of Hadad of Aleppo in works of Ebla related with kingship, dating from the 17th century BC is based upon three considerations. The first one is that the main deity of

18 H. Klengel, *Syria*, pp. 54-55.

19 *Ibidem*, pp. 56-58: the great political importance of Yamkhad had influence very probably till beyond the Tigris and arrived to strongly support, during some heavy difficulties, Babylon itself: H. Klengel, in *De la Babylonie à la Syrie* (Fs. J.-R. Kupper), Liège 1990, pp. 190-195.

20 A. Mazar, *Archaeology of the Land of the Bible*, New York-London 1990, pp. 191-195.

21 L. Nigro, in M. al-Maqdissi, V. Matoïan (eds.), *La céramique de l'âge du Bronze en Syrie*, Damas in print.

Ebla during the archaic Old Syrian period was by no means a god of the kind of Hadad, but rather that Ishtar Eblaitu, who was remembered with this appellative alone as a great goddess adored in the god Ashur's temple in the city of Ashur, still around 1250 BC, nearly four centuries after the final destruction of Ebla as a great urban centre.[22] The second consideration is that originally the Ishtar of Ebla was by no means related with the weather-god of Aleppo, but was the spouse of another male deity, whose personality is elusive, but who can be traced in the iconographic patrimony of the archaic Old Syrian glyptic. The third consideration is that, while at Ebla, in the archaic Old Syrian period, the deity protecting kingship is the Ishtar of Ebla, in the classic Old Syrian period this role was carried out by Hadad of Aleppo, flanked by his spouse Khebat.[23]

The role of main deity Ishtar had at Ebla in Middle Bronze I is shown by the peculiar presence in the city of two temples dedicated to the goddess, one in the Lower Town north-west, and one at the western periphery of the Citadel.[24] These two temples, which are the biggest in the town, were, as is clearly pointed out at by their different topographic location, the first one the public cult place of the great goddess for the needs of the community, and the second one the cult place of the same goddess reserved to the ruling dynasty.[25] To these two different functions corresponds the different architectural formulation of the two cult buildings, and the different placement of the two edifices in the respective sacred areas of the Lower Town and of the Citadel. In fact, the so-called Temple P2 in the Sacred Area of Ishtar in the Lower Town, though certainly being the more monumental in size, has exactly the same typology as the other temples in the Lower Town of Ebla, namely Rashap's Temple B, and Shamash's Temple N, with one cella only, with longitudinal structure and axial entrance.[26] On the contrary, Temple D of the Acropolis had a longitudinal tripartite structure, with vestibule, antecella, and cella, which, also on the base

---

22 R. Frankena, *Takultu*, Leiden 1954, p. 8, 12, 92 note 77; G. van Driel, *The Cult of Aššur*, Leiden 1969, p. 65

23 This goddess is documented already in the Ebla Archives with a non secondary role and some arguments are presented in order to show that her name originally meant "That of Aleppo": A. Archi, *Or* 63 (1994), pp. 249-251.

24 P. Matthiae, *Ebla, un impero ritrovato. Dai primi scavi alle ultime scoperte*, Torino 1989 (2nd Ed. 1995), pp. 157-160, fig. 35; *Id.*, *CRAI* 1990, pp. 410-414, fig. 13-15.

25 *Id.*, *PdP* 46 (1991), pp. 320-325, fig. 10; *Id.*, *CRAI* 1993, pp. 640-662, fig. 21.

26 About the identification of the gods titulary of the Ebla temples see P. Matthiae, *CMAO* 1 (1986), pp. 335-362.

of the evidence offered by the later Iron II temples of Tell Taʿyinat and Jerusalem, is usually considered typical of the palatial temples with function of dynastic chapels.[27]

The deity owner of Temple D of the Citadel was certainly Ishtar, as is proved by the fact that in a small chapel, called Shrine G3, built in front of the great cult building, Ishtar's Stele was placed, where, in one of the upper registers of the main face, there was the goddess' image in a winged chapel placed on a bull, between two standing bull-men, holding spears.[28] Moreover, in the carved limestone basin, found intact in a corner of the cella, the king and a high priestess take part to the rite of the sacred banquet depicted on the main face (Fig. 1), and their presence seems certainly related with a cult act of the kind of the holy weddings, obviously connected with the goddess Ishtar.[29] Lastly, the entrance to the antecella, or to the cella of Temple D, was decorated with figures of crouching lions, the animals sacred to the great goddess.[30]

On the other hand, in Temple P2 in the Lower Town north, a fragment, albeit very short, of a carved basin shows that this was the only ritual basin of Ebla thus far known, which had in the middle of the main side the front facing naked figure of the great winged goddess, while in one side there was represented, naked and front facing as well, a hierodule, certainly peculiar to Ishtar's sanctuaries.[31] Moreover, while also this temple, the only one in the Lower Town, had its entrance decorated with standing figures of the great goddess' lions,[32] in the *favissae* in the Cisterns Square, in front of the main façade of Temple P2 we found, with beads of stone and precious metals, clay figurines of naked women, bronze torques and snakes, and two miniature carnelian figures of couching lions, all elements hinting at the great goddess' fertility.[33] In one of the *favissae* also an archaic Old Syrian cylinder seal was found (Fig. 2), with a symbol, which has been defined the ancestor of the *semeion* of

---

27 A. Kuschke, in *Das Ferne und Nahe Wort* (Fs. L. Rost), Berlin 1967, pp. 124-132; Ch. J. Davey, *TyndBull* 31 (1980), pp. 107-146; A. Mazar, in A. Kempinski, R. Reich (eds.), *The Architecture of Ancient Israel*, Jerusalem 1992, pp. 161-187.

28 P. Matthiae, in *ScAn* 1 (1987), pp. 447-495.

29 *Id.*, *Ebla* (2nd Ed.), pp. 191-192, pl. 127.

30 M. Floriani Squarciapino, in *Missione archeologica italiana in Siria, 1966*, Roma 1967, p. 65, pl. XXII 1, XXIV 1, XXXVII 1.

31 P. Matthiae, *StMisc* 30 (1996 = Ds. L. Guerrini), pp. 3-12.

32 *Id.*, *CRAI* 1990, p. 424 note 118.

33 N. Marchetti, L. Nigro, *JCS* 49 (1997), pp. 1-44.

Atargatis' Temple at Hierapolis, where, in front of this sacred standard the high priestess is represented, the same personage who appears also on the carved basin from Temple D.[34]

The two Old Syrian temples of Ebla dedicated to Ishtar not only were the biggest and most monumental in town, but they also were both topographically related with kingship. In fact, the fortified Citadel Temple D was placed immediately to the west of the central region of the Royal Palace E, of which only the northern edge is known, but which certainly stretched over all the central part of the Acropolis.[35] A very similar topographic situation related, in fact, at Alalakh the so-called Yarim-Lim's Palace and Temple VII.[36] On the other hand, Ishtar's Sacred Area in the Lower Town developed at the north-western feet of the Citadel between two other important palatial buildings with a sure royal function: the Northern Palace, which had in its central sector an important throne room with a dais against one of the short walls, probably with representance functions, and the Western Palace;[37] this large palatial building was certainly related with the Royal Cemetery, which for a large part stretched below its floors, with the Temple of Rashap, the god of Netherworld, where was found another carved basin with a sacred banquet to whom participate the king and perhaps the Crown Prince (Fig. 3),[38] and with Sanctuary B2, for the cult of the royal ancestors.[39] The Northern Palace, as the very fragmentary, but quite meaningful fragments of Egyptianising ivories certainly belonging to a royal throne lead to presume,[40] was most likely a ceremonial royal building, probably connected with public rites in relation with Ishtar's adjacent Sacred Area. The Western Palace was the residence, and possibly also the administrative seat, of the Crown Prince, one of whose main ritual duties was certainly to watch over the correct accomplish-

---

34 P. Matthiae, *CRAI* 1993, pp. 659-660, fig. 25.

35 *Id.*, *Ebla* (2nd Ed.), pp. 160-162, fig. 36.

36 C. L. Woolley, *Alalakh*, pp. 90-106, fig. 35.

37 P. Matthiae, *Ebla* (2nd Ed.), p. 162-175, fig. 37-40; *Id.*, in E. D. Oren ed., *The Hyksos*, pp. 384-387, fig. 14.4-6.

38 *Id.*, *I tesori di Ebla*, pl. 58.

39 *Id.*, *PdP* 46 (1991), pp. 325-327.

40 G. Scandone Matthiae, *AAAS* 40 (1990), p. 146-160; Ead., *PdP* 46 (1991), p. 372-393; Ead., *ScAn* 5 (1991), pp. 423-459; Ead., in E. D. Oren (ed.), *The Hyksos*, pp. 420-425.

ment of the funerary rites for the deceased king, and on the strict observance of the cult for the deified royal ancestors.[41]

Thus, in different ways, apparently in a more public way in the Lower Town, both sanctuaries of the Ishtar Eblaitu had a close connection with kingship. This consideration can be proved also by the observation that only in the sacred areas of the great goddess remains of votive royal statues were found, as if only in the temples of the patron deity of kingship they used to dedicate votive images of the kings. In fact, in the sacred area of the Citadel they had probably dedicated Ibbit-Lim's famous statue, which was found re-employed south of Temple D, and also another very damaged statue, kept in Shrine G3, where had been placed Ishtar's stele.[42] Moreover, in the vestibule of Temple P2 in the Lower Town, on the contrary, we found the important remains of two couples of archaic statues of a sitting king and of a standing queen, and of a similar couple of later statues in the classic Old Syrian style.[43]

That Ishtar was the dynastic deity of the archaic Old Syrian Ebla is proved, however, not only in architecture and topography, by the typology and location of her temple in the Citadel, near the palace. The inscription on Ibbit-Lim's statue, which refers precisely to the temple on the Acropolis, and probably also to one of the two carved basins found in that sacred building, shows clearly that Ishtar was the goddess of Eblaic kingship.[44] In the figurative sphere Ishtar's stele from Shrine G3, in the sacred area in the Citadel, is the clearest evidence of the fact that the goddess was considered the patron deity of kingship at Ebla. In this monument, which had, in the main face, with the uranian and chtonic symbols of the goddess,[45] scenes of liturgical celebration in the goddess's honour, were two remarkable scenes on the lateral and back faces: the royal hero killing the lion, and two kings represented mir-

---

41 P. Matthiae, UF 11 (1979 = Fs. Schaeffer), pp. 563-569; *Id.*, *ArOr* 48 (1981), pp. 55-65; *Id.*, *Beiträge zur Gesellschaft und Kultur Vorderasiens. II. Internat. Tagung der Keilschriftforscher Sozialistischer Länder*, Berlin 1982, pp. 167-174; *Id.*, *BiArch 45* (1984), pp. 18-32.

42 *Id.*, *SEb* 3 (1980), pp. 60-61, fig. 13; *Id.*, *Ebla* (2nd Ed.), pp. 186-187, pl. 76.

43 *Id.*, in B. Hrouda *et al.* (eds.), *Von Uruk nach Tuttul. Eine Festschrift für E. Strommenger*, München-Wien 1992, pp. 111-128.

44 I. J. Gelb, *StOr* 55 (1984), pp. 3-19.

45 P. Matthiae, *ScAn* 1 (1987), 455-461, fig. 4-7.

ror-like while smiting a prisoner.[46] Moreover, it has been supposed that the mythical beings represented on the back face – the winged sphinx, the human-headed bull, and, perhaps, a griffin – were the same beings represented in the famous painting of Zimri-Lim's Investiture at Mari, whose protagonist is the warrior Ishtar.[47]

The artistic works discovered at Ebla do not allow to identify the god who in the archaic Old Syrian Ebla flanked Ishtar as great male deity at the head of the pantheon of the city. Yet some, albeit rare, archaic Old Syrian cylinder seals show a god together with the front facing naked goddess (Fig. 4), which is the licentious, and probably popular iconography of the great goddess of Ebla (Fig. 5).[48] This deity is not frequently represented, but he has constant characteristics, and he disappears later on in the classic Old Syrian glyptic: he wears a peculiar head-dress with a plume, holds a mace or a peculiar flamed weapon and sometimes treads on a snake (Fig. 6).[49] The companion goddess of this god is precisely Ishtar of Ebla, as he appears on seals where is represented also the king with the peaked cap,[50] who in one case is surely the king of Ebla (Fig. 7a-b) and in other cases is associated with the antecedent of the so-called *semeion* of Hierapolis, (Fig. 8) which certainly stood in Temple P2 in Ishtar's Sacred Area.[51]

---

46 *Id.*, in L. De Meyer, E. Haerinck (eds.), *Archaeologia Iranica et Orientalis. Miscellanea in honorem L. Vanden Berghe*, Ghent 1989, pp. 369-391.

47 A. Parrot, *Syria* 18 (1937), pp. 343-345; M.-Th. Barrelet, in *Studia Mariana*, Paris 1949, pp. 9-35; A. Parrot, *Mission archéologique de Mari, II, Peintures murales*, Paris 1958, pp. 53-66; J. Margueron, in B. Hrouda et al. (eds.), *Von Uruk nach Tuttul*, pp. 103-110.

48 P. Matthiae, in M. Lebeau, Ph. Talon (eds.), *Réflets des deux fleuves* (Fs. A. Finet), Leuven 1989, pp. 127-133.

49 T. Özgüç, N. Özguç, *Ausgrabungen in Kültepe, 1949*, Ankara 1953, pl. LXII n. 692; B. Teissier, *Sealing and Seals on Texts from Kültepe* kārum *Level 2*, Leiden 1994, p. 178, 187, n. 530, 581; E. Williams-Forte, in O. White Muscarella (ed.), *Ladders to Heaven*, Toronto 1981, p. 131, n. 129.

50 For this personage see provisionally B. Teissier, in M. J. Mellink et al. (eds.), *Aspects of Art and Iconography: Anatolia and Its Neighbors* (Fs. N. Özgüç), Ankara 1993, pp. 601-612, who considers this figure generally representing archaic Old Syrian kings, but it is very probable that the crown was specifically typical of the Ebla kings: the sovereigns of Ebla on the carved basins of Temple D and Temple B wear precisely this crown: P. Matthiae, *I tesori di Ebla*, pl. 58-59.

51 The seal impression with the royal inscription of Eb-Damu of Ebla has been recently newly published by B. Teissier, *Sealing and Seals*, p. 177, 233, n. 529. For one seal with the *semeion*, the high priestess identical to the female figure of the carved basin of Ebla Temple D and the royal figure with peaked cap see *Ibidem*, p. 179, 233, n. 536. On the Ebla *semeion* P. Matthiae, *CRAI* 1993, pp. 659-661, fig. 25.

It is certain that the mysterious god wearing the plume head-dress and holding the mace or a peculiar flamed weapon of the archaic Old Syrian glyptic was a weather-god who in the myth triumphed over the snake. Now, it is very interesting that the Early Syrian incantations of the State Archives hint precisely at the god Hadad's triumph over a mythical primeval creature presented as a snake.[52] Although the question is quite problematic, one can even ask oneself if this male divine figure of the first rank in Old Syrian Ebla were the heir of the enigmatic god Kura who in the Archives period was the head of the pantheon, and had a clear patronage of Early Syrian kingship.[53] Like the celestial and chtonic Old Syrian Ishtar Eblaitu was the result of a syncretistic process between the older Ishtar and the Early Syrian Ishkhara, who apparently was the most important goddess of the Archives period,[54] so the god with the plume head-dress, the mace or the flamed weapon and the snake might be the result of a syncretism between the Early Syrian gods Kura and Hadad.

Another hint strengthens the hypothesis that the Ishtar of the Old Syrian period were precisely the goddess of the dynasty of Ebla. In fact, the enigma of the word *mēkum*, which appears in several sources, since the Neo-Sumerian period,[55] seems to be nowadays satisfactorily solved, as a specific title of the king of Ebla: this word is clearly, as has been recently supposed, a peculiar alteration of the title *mālikum* "king".[56] In Babylonia during the 3rd dynasty of Ur, as well as in Anatolia in the "Epos der Freilassung",[57] and very probably also in the "Story of Sinuhe" in Egypt,[58] it was understood as the specific title of the lord of Ebla. But the invaluable bilingual Hittite and Hurrian "Epos der Freilassung", recently discovered at Boghazköy, when it names the king of Ebla it calls him *mēkum*, but with the appellative "the Star of Ebla".[59] Now, this appellative, which is similar to other ones of the peripheral re-

---

52 P. Fronzaroli, *M.A.R.I.* 8 (1997), pp. 284-286; *Id.*, in *Fs. Kienast*, in print.

53 F. Pomponio, P. Xella, *Les dieux d'Ebla*, Münster 1997, pp. 245-248.

54 A. Archi, in H. Otten et al. (eds.), *Hittite and Other Anatolian and Near Eastern Studies in Honour of S. Alp*, Ankara 1992, pp. 9-13; D. Prechel, *Die Göttin Isḫara*, Münster 1996.

55 D. Owen, in L. Cagni (ed.), *Ebla 1975-1985*, Napoli 1987, pp. 263-291; *Id.*, in M. Chavalas, J. L. Hayes (eds.), *New Horizons in the Study of Ancient Syria*, Malibu 1992, p. 120.

56 M. V. Tonietti, *M.A.R.I.* 8 (1997), pp. 225-242.

57 H. Otten, in H. Waetzoldt, H. Hauptmann (eds.), *Wirtschaft und Gesellschaft von Ebla*, Heidelberg 1988, pp. 291-292.

58 G. Scandone Matthiae, *M.A.R.I.* 8 (1997), pp. 249-250.

59 H. Otten, *Das hurritische Epos der Freilassung I*, Wiesbaden 1996, p. 277, 282-83.

gions of Mesopotamia, like "the Sun of the country of Nagar" for the king of that important city of upper Mesopotamia, recently identified with Tell Brak,[60] certainly hints at Ishtar as goddess of the planet/star Venus.

On the other hand, a series of data leads to believe that the royal ideology of Ebla underwent a change during the classic Old Syrian period, when the role of divine patron of the kingship of Ebla passed from Ishtar to Hadad of Aleppo. The final phase of this important religious and political change, evidently descending from the great prestige of the god of Aleppo,[61] but certainly also from the political authority of the kings of Yamkhad, is revealed by the extraordinary, certainly dynastic, seal of the personage who, in the inscription on the same cylinder, presents himself as Indilimgur's son (Fig. 9).[62] The exceptionality of this seal, kept only in some impressions on jars, found mainly in the Western Palace, identified with the Crown Prince's residence, is proved by three elements at least. First, its size, with a height of 7,5 cm, is nearly three times that of the most important contemporary Old Syrian cylinders. Second, the style of the engraving, which can be fully appreciated in the preserved impressions, is of a very high level, and can be compared with the best cylinder seals from upper Syria of Middle Bronze II.[63] Third, the compositional pattern, with the prince receiving life, under the form of an Egyptian *ankh*, from Hadad of Aleppo and from his consort Khebat, is clearly derived from the dynastic seals of Yamkhad.

The evidence offered by this exceptional document of the classic Old Syrian glyptic art is basic for two converging reasons. On the one hand, in fact, the personage represented on the cylinder wears the royal cloak of the kings of Yamkhad and certainly also of other important towns of upper Syria during the classic Old Syrian period,[64] but he is bare-headed, and does not wear the usual ovoid tiara, which usually appears with the cloak with swollen edges in the kings' figures of

---

60 D. Matthews, J. Eidem, *Iraq* 55 (1993), pp. 201-207.

61 H. Klengel, *JCS* 19 (1965), pp. 87-93.

62 P. Matthiae, *Syria* 46 (1969), pp. 1-43.

63 *Id.*, *I tesori di Ebla*, p. 124, pl. 87.

64 J. Nougayrol, P. Amiet, *RA* 56 (1962), pp. 169-174; for a seal surely depending from the dynastic cylinders of Yamkhad, with the name of a servant of one Hammurabi, who must be the successor of Yarim-Lim I or the last king of Aleppo, see. D. Collon, *First Impressions*, London 1987, p. 128, fig. 544.

Middle Bronze II inner Syria.[65] On the other hand, the name of the father of the seal owner, Indilimgur, appears in a fragmentary year name on the only one cuneiform tablet found in the same Western Palace where the majority of impressions of the seal were found on jars.[66]

These two combined data lead to believe that the owner of the cylinder seal were the Crown Prince of the years immediately before the destruction of the city by the Hittites, and quite likely the prince's father, Indilimgur, was one of the last, but most probably precisely the last king of Ebla, who saw the town fall at the end of Hattusili I's or more probably Mursili I's siege. The jars with the impressions of the seal of king Indilimgur's son were found in the destruction level of the Western Palace, because this Crown Prince was the last one to live in the palatial building of the Lower Town west.[67] But for the destruction of the city he was not able to seat on his father's throne, though he had been designated Crown Prince.

The compositional pattern of the seal of Indilimgur's son is an evident dilatation of the scheme of the dynastic seals of the kings of Yamkhad, where in front of the king only the goddess Khebat appears in the presence of a minor goddess with both hands raised, though a constant protocol element of the inscriptions of these seals is the appellative "Beloved of the god Hadad" (Fig. 10).[68] Thus, if in the figurative tradition of the royal workshops of Aleppo the king of Aleppo, certainly for ritual reasons which we cannot reconstruct any more, is shown while receiving kingship from the goddess Khebat of Aleppo, the combination of the figure and of the titles certainly reveals that the kingship of Yamkhad was under Hadad's and Khebat's protection.[69] This same ideology was completely accepted at Ebla in Indilimgur's time: also at Ebla, like at Aleppo, kingship was no more given by the Ishtar Eblaitu, but rather by the two great gods of Aleppo, who, therefore, had become patron deities also for the kings of Ebla, clearly as a consequence of the political predominance and prestige of the dynasty of Yamkhad.[70]

---

65 D. Collon, *The Seal Impressions*, pp. 186-199, pl. XXIX-XXXI.

66 J.-R. Kupper, *SEb* 9 in print.

67 P. Matthiae, *Ebla* (2nd Ed.), pp. 204-207.

68 D. Collon, *The Seal Impressions*, pp. 6-13, n. 3-11.

69 The very recent extraordinary discovery of an imposing temple on the Aleppo Citadel reveals that the famous Old Syrian sanctuary of Hadad was there, probably not far from the royal palace: W. Khayata, K. Kohlmeyer, *DaM* 10 (1998), pp. 69-95.

70 H. Klengel, *Syria*, pp. 49-64.

Other considerations confirm this observation. In the first place, Hadad's iconography in the seal of Indilimgur's son is the classical and peculiar one of the god of Aleppo and does not have any of the several iconographic variants of other weather-gods' figures in the Old Syrian glyptic, which probably were forms of Hadad adored in other cult centres of northern Syria.[71] In the second place, the same Hadad with the identical Aleppo iconography appears in another big seal in front of a high dignitary, without Khebat's figure,[72] showing that around 1650/1600 BC the cult for Hadad of Aleppo had an important role in the milieu of Ebla court, even beyond the strictly ideological and religious aspects of kingship. In the third place, in some other seals of Ebla, always known from impressions, in part at least certainly slightly older, Khebat's iconography appears, without the figure of the god of Aleppo,[73] proving the diffusion of the cult for the great gods of Aleppo among the high officials of Ebla during Middle Bronze II. Lastly, it is quite peculiar, yet meaningful, that the great front facing naked goddess, who was the traditional image of Ishtar of Ebla, does not appear in these seals of refined style and belonging to personages of the upper classes of the town, who in 17th century BC apparently also preferred the politically oriented devotion of their kings for the great gods of Aleppo, instead of the traditional local cult for the goddess of Ebla.

Another important figurative document of Ebla, which probably dates back from around 1750 BC, albeit quite incomplete, might be the proof of the beginning, in chronological terms, of this special deference of the Eblaic kings to the great god of Aleppo. This is a meaningful fragment of a basalt stele, where the god Hadad's figure appeared, with other certainly human personages.[74] Most probably he was represented according to the specific iconography of Aleppo and at bigger size than the other protagonists of the probably cultic scene. In this stele, which was certainly of royal commitment and where, by the way, there is the most ancient representation of Hadad's in inner Syria besides glyptic, the substitution of the cult for the ancient Eblaic god with the plume head-dress and the mace or the flamed weapon by Hadad of Aleppo in the role of patron deity of the Ebla kingship, seems to be documented

---

71 P. Amiet, *Akkadica* 28 (1982), pp. 26-36.

72 P. Matthiae, *I tesori di Ebla*, pl. 88.

73 *Id.*, *Ebla* (2nd Ed.), pp. 204-205, pl. 161.

74 *Id.*, in Mellink et al. (eds.), *Aspects of Art and Iconography*, pp. 389-397, pl. 69-71.

in a certainly not advanced phase of the classic Old Syrian period, probably not a long time after Yarim-Lim I's reign.[75]

Although the lack of the licentious iconography of Ishtar of Ebla, as front facing naked female figure or unveiling herself, in the Old Syrian cylinder seals found at Tell Mardikh is quite disconcerting, in the large evidence of the Old Syrian glyptic concerning the great goddess there are a few, not frequent, seals of the greatest interest, because they reveal a peculiar development of religious feeling in some centres of inner Syria in Middle Bronze II. In fact, in a few Old Syrian seals there is a peculiar iconography of the great goddess, closely related with the figure of Hadad of Aleppo.[76] The front facing naked goddess, in the typical traditional aspect already well attested in the archaic Old Syrian glyptic, appears standing on a bull, which, although present in the goddess' ancient iconography, as is proved at Ebla by the same Ishtar's Stele, in this instance is Hadad's bull: the goddess' bull, in fact, is at the same time the bull of the god of Aleppo, who is represented at the goddess' side, holding all his usual insignia and the reins of the sacred animal.[77]

It appears clearly that in these instances, during the classic Old Syrian period, some religious milieus, which cannot yet be identified, developed a meaningful conjunction between Ishtar of Ebla and Hadad of Aleppo, which might be a theological elaboration based on mythical episodes unknown to us, but which is a secondary development with respect to the original independence of the two deities. Before these syncretistic formulations among different local traditions, clearly inspired by the prevailing role of the great sanctuary of Aleppo, descending from the new political prestige of the kings of Yamkhad, the companion of Ishtar of Ebla was the weather-god with the plume head-dress, the mace or the flamed weapon and the snake, while the spouse of Hadad of Aleppo was Khebat.[78] In other words, on the one hand, the reception by the kings of Ebla of the ideology of the kingship of

75 *Ibidem*, pp. 396-397.

76 C. H. Gordon, *Iraq* 6 (1939), p. 17, n. 38, pl. V; E. Porada, *CANES*, p. 130, n. 967, pl. CXLVI, B. Teissier, *Ancient Near Eastern Cylinder Seals from the Marcopoli Collection*, Los Angeles-London 1984, pp. 242-243, n. 477.

77 P. Matthiae, in M. Lebeau, Ph. Talon (eds.), *Réflets*, p. 133.

78 It has to be observed that the cult of Hadad and Khebat of Aleppo was already well known in the Early Syrian Ebla, but the unique importance of the specific royal ideology of the divine couple of Yamkhad is something completely new in the classic Old Syrian Ebla, after the emergence of Ishtar Eblaitu in the archaic Old Syrian Ebla: F. Pomponio, P. Xella, *Les dieux d'Ebla*, pp. 52-64, 66-67.

Aleppo and, on the other one, the close, not original, relation between Ishtar and Hadad are two, presumably independent, important consequences of the political achievement of Yamkhad in upper Syria around 1800 BC.

On the base of these considerations, founded on the archaeological evidence offered by the recent researches at Ebla, there are important corroborations for the proposal of terminological subdivision of the Old Syrian period, advanced precisely on the base of the Ebla excavations. But most of all it is important that nowadays, when basic progresses have been made for the historical consideration of the archaeological and epigraphic materials of the Syrian world in Middle Bronze I-II, the results of the most recent researches contribute to a more and more mature historicisation of the Old Syrian culture: this clearly is the main trend for future years, under the impulse of the new developments of the excavations at Ebla. It is with a special pleasure that these considerations are presented, with the warmest affection and the most sincere gratitude, in a volume of contributions in the honour of Pelio Fronzaroli. He, in fact, with his acute interpretations and evaluations of the literary texts from the State Archives of Ebla, through a constant attention to the archaeological evidence from Ebla and other Syrian centres, did and is doing so much in order to fully bring to light the successive most ancient cultures of Syria.

List of the Figures

Fig. 1 – Aleppo, Archaeological Museum: carved limestone basin from Temple D, Acropolis, of Ebla. Detail of the sacred banquet with the king with the peaked cap and the high priestess, ca. 1800 BC.

Fig. 2 – Idlib, Archaeological Museum: impression of an archaic Old Syrian steatite cylinder from a *favissa* of the Sacred Area of Ishtar, Lower Town, of Ebla. The *semeion* is represented in front of the high priestess, ca. 1850-1800 BC.

Fig. 3 – Damascus, National Museum: carved basalt basin from Temple B, Lower Town, of Ebla. Detail of the sacred banquet with the king with the peaked cap and, perhaps, the Crown Prince, ca. 1850 BC.

Fig. 4 – Impression of a cylinder seal of Kültepe II with the king with the peaked cap in front of a sitting deity and the couple of the god with plume head-dress, flame weapon and snake, and the naked goddess, ca. 1850 BC (Özgüç, *Kültepe 1949*, pl. LXII 692).

Fig. 5 – Drawing by B. Teissier of the impression of the cylinder seal of Kültepe II of Fig. 4, with the king and the couple of the god with plume head-dress and the naked goddess, ca. 1850 BC (Teissier, *Sealing and Seals*, p. 581, p. 235).

Fig. 6 – Collection Borowski: impression of a steatite archaic Old Syrian cylinder, with a sitting personage and the couple of the god with the plume head-dress, the mace and the snake, and the naked goddess, ca. 1850 BC (White Muscarella, *Ladders to Heaven*, n.129, p. 131).

Fig. 7a-b – Drawings by B. Teissier of two impressions of an archaic Old Syrian cylinder seal with the figure of the king with the peaked cap and the inscription of king Eb-Damu of Ebla, ca.1850 BC (Teissier, *Sealing and Seals*, fig. 529a-b, p. 233).

Fig. 8 – Drawing by B. Teissier of an impression of an archaic Old Syrian cylinder seal with the king with the peaked cap in front of a sitting god and the high priestess in front of the antecedent of the *semeion* of Hierapolis temple, ca. 1850 BC (Teisssier, *Sealing and Seals*, fig. 536, p. 233).

Fig. 9 – Idlib, Archaeological Museum: impression on a jar shoulder of the seal of king Indilimgur's son, represented in front of Hadad and Khebat of Aleppo giving him the life, ca. 1650/1620 BC.

Fig. 10 – Antakya, Archaeological Museum: drawing by D. Collon of the impression of the dynastic seal of king Abba-El, son of Hammurabi I, of Yamkhad, from the Palace VII of Alalakh, ca. 1700-1675 BC (Collon, *The Seal Impressions*, fig. 3, p. 6).

Fig. 1

Fig. 2

Fig. 3

Fig. 4

Fig. 5

Fig. 6

Fig. 7a

Fig.7b

Fig. 8

Fig. 9

Fig. 10

THE MOUNTAINS AND THE STARS*

PIOTR MICHALOWSKI

University of Michigan, Ann Arbor

The discovery of the Ebla tablets from the third millennium opened up a new chapter in the study of the religions of ancient Syria. At first, it appeared that the religious practices of the inhabitants were unique, as were many of the deities that they worshipped. Further study revealed many practices that were specific to this time and place, but also much continuity with later Syrian traditions. The royal ancestor cult, the worship of deities such as Rasap, later Rešef, of Baʾal and Haddad under the joint guise of Hadda-baʿal (ᵈʾì-*da-bal*), the veneration of stone monuments, as well as other religious cultural elements, are documented for millennia after the fall of Ebla.[1] Still, there remain religious matters that appear to be particular to the cultural complex documented in the clay tablets from Tell Mardikh. Among these is the posited Semitic deity Kabkabum, whose name apparently means, "star".[2]

This "god" occurs exclusively in two parallel incantations written in the "Eblaite" language. These were originally published by D. O. Edzard as *ARET* V 1 and 3 and have been elucidated more recently by P. Fronzaroli.[3] The two passages that are our concern read as follows:

---

* I would like to thank Gary Beckman, Jerry Cooper, and Norman Yoffee for comments and suggestions.

1 Much of our knowledge of these matters is due to the efforts of Prof. Pelio Fronzaroli. It was he who realized that the apparently unique Eblaite deity IdaBAL, who had been the subject of much speculation (e.g. W. G. Lambert, "The Identity of the Eblaite God NIdaKUL", *OA* 23 [1984], pp. 43-44), was actually Hadda-baʿl (ʾa_5-*da-bal*; "Les combats de Hadda dans les textes d'Ébla", *M.A.R.I.* 8 [1997], pp. 288-289).

2 See, most recently, P. Mander, "El término mul", in G. del Olmo Lete, ed., *Mitología y Religión del Oriente Antiguo* II/1 (Sabadell, 1995), pp. 103-108; F. Pomponio and P. Xella, *Les dieux d'Ebla. Étude analytique des divinités éblaïtes à l'époque des archives royales du III*ᵉ *millénaire* (Münster, 1997), p. 222.

3 "Tre scongiuri ebailiti (*ARET* 5, 1-3)", *VO* 7 (1988), pp. 18-19. He also returned to these texts in his article on "Lingua e testo negli archivi di Ebla", *La Parola del Passato* 46 (1991), pp. 230-235. See also M. Krebernik, *Die Beschwörugen aus Fara und Ebla* (Hildesheim, 1984), p. 324, as well as A. Catagnoti and M. Bonechi, "Magic and Divination at IIIrd Millennium Ebla, 1. Textual Typologies and Preliminary Lexical Approach", *SEL* 15 (1998), pp. 24-25.

ARET V 1 v 5-vi 3 *wa iš*$_{11}$*-da-ga-sù* 1 SUD maškim.e.gi$_4$*-ma si-in i-li-lu* a.mu dingir. dingir.dingir

ARET V 3 ii 3-iii 2 *wa iš*$_{11}$*-da-ga-sù ga-ga-ba-bù dag-da-su* *si-in* ^{d}*i-li-lu*

"And he brought the m.-official SUD before Enlil, the father of the gods"

Moreover, *ARET* 5 1 bears a subscript UD-du$_{11}$-ga 1 SUD, "Incantation against/for SUD". This same version of the charm mentions SUD earlier in a passage:

iv 2-6: *na-zi-a-du* munus DIŠ SUD *mi-nu ti-na-ì-si-du*

which has been rendered by P. Fronzaroli as "l'(offerta di) *olio fino* della donna di Kabkab da parte degli uomini".[4]

All commentators, beginning with M. Krebernik and D. O. Edzard, have interpreted the signs *ga-ga-ba-bù* as Kabkab(um) and translated the divine name as "Star", from common Semitic *kbkb*. The Sumerogram SUD has resisted interpretation.[5] If the Semitic name indeed means "star", one would expect the Sumerian to be mul. Indeed, a ^{d}mul is listed in the large bilingual "Ebla Vocabulary", rendered in the explanatory column as *gag-gáb*.[6] P. Fronzaroli attempted to correlate SUD with the southern Mesopotamian goddess Sud (written ^{d}SU.KUR.RU, i.e. ^{d}sùd), the daughter of Nisaba. I hope that the recipient of this volume will not be too displeased if I do not find this convincing. As he points out, the verbal forms associated with SUD are masculine, not feminine. More important, he draws attention to the sequence of deities who served as guarantors of the treaty between Ebla and AbarSAL: ^{d}utu, ^{d}*ʾà-da* and ^{d}mul.[7] Even if one were to speculate that ^{d}mul and SUD were identical, the daughter of Nisaba does not really belong with the sun goddess and the storm god Hadda. There is another clue that appears to have gone unnoticed. Neither SUD, who is mentioned three times in text 1 nor Kabkabu in text 3 are preceded by the divine determinative. The scribe who wrote the former used the classi-

4 "Tre scongiuri eblaiti (*ARET* 5, 1-3)", *VO* 7 (1988), p. 17.

5 M. Krebernik, *Die Beschwörungen*, p. 324, noted the entry SUD = *ga-ba-ga-bu*$_x$(NI) in *MEE* 4, 1185b, but the significance of this equation seemed enigmatic. The sources for the line are: *ga-ba-ga-bu*$_x$(NI) (text T) and *ga-ba-*⌜*ga*⌝-N[I] (text AZ [collated] courtesy of G. Conti). This may indeed be a writing for *kbkb*. See now also M. Civil and G. Rubio, "An Ebla incantation against insomnia and the Semiticization of Sumerian: Notes on ARET 5 8b and 9", *OrNS* 68 (1999), p. 257, n. 10.

6 See, already, P. Fronzaroli, "Un verdetto reale degli Archivi di Ebla (TM.75.G.1452)", *SEb* 3 (1980), p. 40 n. 27.

7 Discussed by P. Fronzaroli, *VO* 7 (1988), p. 22.

fier in the logographic writing of the name of the Sun Goddess (^{d}UTU), but not before the syllabic spelling of the Semitic name *I-li-lu* ("Enlil"). In text 3 both divine names are preceded by the dingir sign, but Kabkabu is not. In text no. 1 SUD follows the DIŠ sign; perhaps we should be speaking not of a logogram SUD, but of DIŠ.SUD, as it is highly improbable that the first part of the compound is a "Personenkeil". All of this leads one to suspect that we are not dealing with a divine name, strictly speaking; perhaps another etymology and another explanation are in order.

So far all discussions of Kabkab(um) have been limited to the Ebla material described above. There are interesting well-known parallels from later Semitic onomastics and that may be brought into the discussion. Among personal names, certainly the best known is Ila-kabkabu, the father of the Amorite ruler Šamši-Addu. Among geographical names of the third millennium the name Kakkabān immediately comes to mind.[8] The latter, formed with the derivational morpheme */-ān/*, designated a place that was "of Kakkab" and leads us to a completely different interpretive path.

A few years ago A. Catagnoti and M. Bonechi published a fascinating communication on the ancient name, of the extinct volcano whose impressive mass dominates the horizon of part of the Habur triangle in the area close to modern Hasseke, demonstrating that it was originally designated as Kakkab or Kabkab.[9] The authors persuasively argued the continuity of the name from pre-Sargonic to modern times, and published an Old Babylonian Mari letter that includes mention of the volcano, written *ka-ab-ka-ab*. The Mari texts also preserve names such as *ka[b-k]a-bu-um*,[10] and *kab-ka-bi-im* which must be interpreted as gentilics, as well as *ka-ab-ka-ba*, *ka-ab-ka-ba-an* and *ka-ab-kab-ti-el*.[11] These names may derive from the geographical term

8 Attested in a tablet from Tell Brak, *AOAT* 3/1 69, line 11.

9 "Le volcan Kawkab, Nagar et problèmes connexes", *N.A.B.U.* 1992/50-53. For the Ebla references see also M. Bonechi, *RGTC* 12/1 (1993), pp. 141-142 sub Kakkab and Kakkaban.

10 G. Dosssin, *RA* 65 (1972), p. 52 col. x 77 (time of Sumu-iamam).

11 See J.-M. Durand, "Études sur les noms propres d'époque amorrite, I (Liste A)", *M.A.R.I.* 8 (1997), p. 602 n. 35. H. B. Huffmon, *Amorite Personal Names in the Mari Texts: A Structural and Lexical Study* (Baltimore, 1965), p. 220. Note also the name of an Old Assyrian *līmu* Šu-Eshtar, qualified as *kà-kà-ba-nu-um*, presumably implying that he was from Kakkabān, although this city is not otherwise attested in the published Kanesh tablets (K. Balkan, *Observations on the Chronology of Kārum Kaniš*

or they may be linked more directly to the word for "star" as an endearment, a usage paralleled in other languages, including modern Arabic, in which Kawkab is a popular feminine name. One must also mention here the unique form of address documented in the Mari correspondence. Female members of the royal family addressed Zimri-Lim as *kakkabī*, "my star", marking a rare form of intimacy, alternating it with the more familiar *šamšī*, "my sun", which was used in various periods to address kings.[12] These facts notwithstanding, is it possible that the Kabkabu(m) of the Ebla incantations, who also appears in later Amorite onomasticon, was not a "star", but a personification of a sacred mountain?

The occurrence of a divinity in a literary text from Tell Mardikh by no means implies a presence in the local cult. The incantations from the site are in two languages: Sumerian and "Eblaite", and while it is clear that the former were imported, opinion is divided on the origins of the latter. In southern Mesopotamian magical texts there are deities that do not have any major role in the cults of most Sumerian cities, and thus one has to be careful in using the pantheon of incantations for establishing the origins of these texts. Outside of the incantations there is no trace of any god SUD and ᵈmul is attested only in a lexical text and in one treaty. There have been suggestions that ᵈmul is to be connected with the more commonly attested níg-mul-mul, which has been the subject of much speculation, but the latter has now been definitively identified as the Eblaite logogram for "letter, missive".[13] There is a remote possibility that SUD is to be read bu and that this is a unique defective writing for <an-gub>-bu. But even if only a small number of references can be linked to the topographical feature, we have here clear traces of one more interesting link between the mental world of third millennium Syria and later times.

[Ankara, 1955], p. 95). See already *ga-ba-ga-bù*, the name of a prince of Manuwat in the Ebla archives (*ARET* 3 35 rev. vi 2).

12 See J. Sasson, "The Posting of Letters with Divine Messages", *Birot Memorial Volume*, p. 305 n. 21.

13 Thus W. Sallaberger, this volume. For earlier interpretations see P. Fronzaroli, *N.A.B.U.* 1991, 49 and previously, A. Archi, *N.A.B.U.* 1988, 44. G. Pettinato, *Il rituale per la successione al trono ad Ebla* (Rome, 1992), p. 244 reads ᵈmul and translates "appannaggio delle divinità". A full, investigation of various aspects of "mul" in Ebla texts was the subject of an unpublished 1989 doctoral dissertation from la Universidad Complutense de Madrid, under the title *La ofrenda en Ebla: el caso de mul*. I know this only through the summary by P. Mander in the essay cited above on note 1. A. Catagnoti and M. Bonechi, *SEL* 15 (1998), pp. 34-35, comment on the uncertainty of the meaning of the term.

There is evidence in third millennium texts that points to a system of sacred spaces that were not the focus of the official cult, but were clearly part of the world view of people in various parts of Western Asia. The fact that such mountains, rivers, and cities can be traced primarily through personal names indicates that sacred sites must have been part of the broader culture. Deified aspects of the two prominent mountain ranges of northern Mesopotamia and Syria - Jebel Hamrin (Ebih), the Jebel Sinjār (^{d}sággar)[14] are well attested in early historical times. Ebih is documented in personal names beginning with the Early Dynastic period and the name of a third mountain range, Dibar, identified as the Jebel ʿAbd el-ʿAzīz, is attested already in Old Akkadian, albeit without divine determinative.[15] There is, to date, no evidence of such elements in the small sample of pre-Sargonic personal names from Sumer and Babylonia. The widest attestation of mountain, river, and city names as "theophoric" elements is documented in the Amorite onomasticon.[16] The ranges of the Jebel Bishri, the Hamrin, the Amanus, the Jebel Sinjār, as well as other mountains are attested in names from the Mari documents.[17] In Old Babylonian names one finds general topographic features such as the "steppe" (*ṣērum*) or "mountains", (*šadûm*) taking the place of gods.[18] This whole phenomenon deserves a fuller treatment; we take for granted that these names all provide evidence that the ancients in certain contexts thought that certain elements of their environment were divine, but other explanations should also be considered. However one may choose to interpret this phenomenon, it is of interest that it may have a longer history than we suspected, reaching back at least as far as the middle of the third millennium.[19]

---

14 See M. Stol, *On Trees, Mountains, and Millstones in the Ancient Near East* (Leiden, 1979), p. 26. On the deified Sinjār see also J.-M. Durand, *Mélanges Birot*, pp. 80-81 n. 4. Note also kur sá-gar = MIN (= *ša-du-u*) *e-ri-tum* in Hh XXII 1 A i: 25 (*MSL* XI 23).

15 M. Stol, *idem*. See also W. G. Lambert, "The God Aššur", *Iraq* 54 (1983), p. 84.

16 Note the cult of the "divine" Balikh at Ebla and the cult of other rivers in Assyria, as described by Lambert, *ibid*. In the same article he suggests that the god Aššur was originally the god of a holy site located at the hill which later became the city of Assur.

17 J.-M. Durand, "L'emploi des toponymes dans l'onomastique d'époque amorrite (I): les noms en Mut-", *SEL* 8 (1991), pp. 84-96.

18 See M. Stol, "Old Babylonian Personal Names", *SEL* 8 (1991), pp. 202-203.

19 Human use of topography for mythological and ideological purposes has been extensively studied. For two very different, but instructive, case studies, see Jean Richter, *Géographie sacrée du monde Grec. Croyances astrales des anciens Grecs* (Paris, 1966) and Keith H. Basso, *Western Apache Language and Culture: Essays in Linguistic Anthropology* (Tucson, 1990), pp. 99-173.

Why, one must ask, would anyone name a mountain "Star"? The ancients did not know that Kawkab was once an active volcano and only airplane pilots or astronauts would recognize a star-like pattern seen from above. We may never know the answer; for now we can only speculate. As noted above, the Jebel Sinjār was named ^{d}sággar (HAR) in third and second millennium texts, going back at least as far as the time of the Ebla archives.[20] E. Laroche and S. Dalley have identified Saggar as a name of the moon god in late second millennium Syria, primarily in the Emar texts.[21] Dalley goes so far as to suggest that *šgr* at Ugarit and in the Deir ʿAlla Balaam text is to be identified as this aspect of the moon god, and proposes to take this as far back as ^{d}*sa-nu-ga-ru*$_{12}$ of Ebla. If the deity and the mountain range are one and the same - and one must note here Durand's important objections to this identification[22] - then we would have two ancient Syrian mountain names that referred to nocturnal celestial phenomena - the moon and the stars. If Dibar, the ancient name of the Jebel ʿAbd el-ʿAzīz, can be linked to the Akkadian *dipāru*, "torch", then the pattern would be complete.

In Mesopotamian mythology the torch, Sumerian gi-izi-lá, Akkadian *dipāru*, was associated with the fire god Gibil/Girra.[23] Most important, this god manifested himself at night; in the ritual series *Maqlû* he appears only during nocturnal ceremonies;[24] earlier in Ugarit he is associated with the moon.[25] In a previous article I argued that Gibil/Girra was associated with some form of nocturnal fire, and if this interpretation can be extended beyond the Sumero-Babylonian world, it could well be that some such celestial phenomenon was associated with such a deity, and with his torch, in the broader Syro-Mesopotyamian cultural complex. A deity whose name was written logographically as ^{d}gibil$_{4}$(IZI), presumably an equivalent of

20 The oldest extant reference is presumably sag-gàr^{ki}, see M. Bonechi, *RGTC* 12/1 327 sub Zaggar.

21 See E. Laroche, *Akkadica* 22 (1981), p. 11, as well as St. Dalley and B. Teissier, "Tablets from the Vicinity of Emar and Elsewhere", *Iraq* 65 (1992), pp. 90-91.

22 J.-M. Durand, "La religión en Siria durante la época de los reinos amorreos según la documentación de Mari", in G. del Olmo Lete, ed., *Mitología y religión del Oriente Antiguo* II/1 (Sabadell, 1995), pp. 183-184. See also F. Pomponio and P. Xella, *op. cit.*, pp. 319-320.

23 P. Michalowski, "The Torch and the Censer", pp. 151-163 in M. Cohen, *et al.*, eds., *The Tablet and The Scroll: Near Eastern Studies in Honor of William W. Hallo* (Bethesda, 1993).

24 See T. Abusch, "Mesopotamian Anti-Witchcraft Literature: Texts and Studies. Part 1: The Nature of *Maqlû*: Its Character, Divisions, and Calendrical Setting", *JNES* 33 (1974), pp. 258-259.

25 RS 1992.2004:14 ^{d}har ù ^{d}gìr; F. Pomponio and P. Xella, *op. cit.*, p. 320.

^{d}BIL.GI (to be read as ^{d}gibil$_{6}$ or ^{d}gibil$_{4}^{gi}$) is attested in an Eblaite document, although there is no assurance that this is the same god as the Mesopotamian Girra.[26] In order to speculate on the etymological link between *dipāru* and Dibar, one must first establish the exact nature of the first two consonants of the latter. In third millennium texts the first syllable is written ti and the second consonant is expressed with the signs ba (*ti-ba-a*[*r*])[27] and bar (in the names KAL-*ti-bar šu-ti-bar*).[28] This suggests that the word began with /d/, but the evidence for the nature of the second consonant is more ambiguous evidence: both spellings could represent /b/ as well as /p/. First millennium references all use bar; they are anachronistic and clearly retain earlier spellings, compounding our etymological woes.[29]

As a final note I would like to take a look at the name of Samsi-Addu's father, conventionally rendered as Ila-kakkabu. His name was written as DINGIR-*kab-ka-bi*[30] by the late compilers of the Assyrian King List, but second millennium sources provide the spelling *i-la-kab-ka-bu-ú* and *ì-lí-ka-ab-ka-bu*.[31] I. J. Gelb argued forty years ago that these spellings imply an analysis *il-a kakkabu-hu,* with the predicate use of /-a/ on the first element and Amorite third person pronoun /-hu/ on the second.[32] Huffmon was not convinced by this interpretation and argued that the writing of the final vowel did not necessarily imply such an analysis. The existence of such names as ʾIla-bínī, ʾIla-hadnuhu, and ʾIla-hāluhu speaks in favor of I. J. Gelb's interpretation.[33] These probably have to translated as "My son is divine", "His 'pleasure' is divine", and "His maternal uncle is divine". The semantic range of the subjects, kinship terms and a possible endearment suggest that the proper interpretation of the

26 See F. Pomponio and P. Xella, *op. cit.*, p. 185.

27 Naram-Sin E2.1.4.23 l. 11 (D. R. Frayne, *RIME* 2 127).

28 Old Akkadian references in J. J. M. Roberts, *The Earliest Semitic Pantheon* (Baltimore, 1972), p. 53. Old Assyrian: *šu-ti-bar* (Lambert, p. 84).

29 The writing *di-bar* is found in the "*Lipšur* Litanies" (E. Reiner, *JNES* 16 [1956], p. 14, preceded by *da-bar*), in Hh XXII 1 A i: 14 (*MSL* XI 23), and in *takūltu* (B. Menzel, *Assyrische Tempel* II T 14; see Lambert, p. 85).

30 Two copies of the late AKL preserve this spelling (I. J. Gelb, "Two Assyrian King Lists", *JNES* 13 [1954], pp. 210-211).

31 I. J. Gelb, *Computer-Aided Analysis of Amorite* (Chicago, 1980), p. 23.

32 "La lingua degli Amoriti", *Atti della Accademia Nazionale dei Lincei*, serie VIII, Rendiconti XIII (1958), p. 144, maintained by the same author in *Computer-Aided Analysis,* p. 7.

33 For attestations see *Computer-Aided Analysis*, p. 217.

royal name is “My ‘Star’ is divine”, which finds an amazing parallel in his son’s name: “Hadda is ‘my sun’”. One cannot disassociate the names of the two rulers of Ekallatum from the Mari usage of *kakkabī* and *šamšī* described above.

I am fully aware that I have presented readers with a series of highly speculative propositions, full of semantic and etymological ambiguities. Nevertheless, there is a probability that at some point in the remote past the mountains of Syria were named after celestial phenomena: the stars, the moon and some form of celestial fire. By historical times the mythology behind this was lost, and the meanings, as well as the etymologies, may very well have been forgotten. We can conclude, however, that in early Semitic onomastica the work *kabkabu* (*kakkabu*) had a limited range of secondary meanings, either as an endearment, derived from the notion of protection, or as a designation of the mountain Kawkab.[34]

34 In *Subartu* IV/1 (1998), p. 220 M. Bonechi announced a study, to be published in *QuSemM* 3, in which he will provide a “reason for this apparently quite strange denomination” of the volcano Kawkab.

LES AFFAIRES DE MONSIEUR GĪDA-NA'IM*

LUCIO MILANO

Università Ca' Foscari di Venezia

1. Le commerce éblaïte

Pour expliquer le développement rapide de la puissance politique d'Ébla à l'époque des archives on s'est souvent servi de l'argument du commerce: un commerce de grande envergure, qui aurait constitué le réseau de base de son expansion politique vers la fin de l'époque dynastique archaïque. Ce n'est pas mon intention de minimiser cet argument: cependant, ce qu'on sait des modalités, des frontières et du volume du commerce éblaïte est encore une question ouverte, qu'on a réussi à approcher plus facilement à partir des données archéologiques[1] que par rapport à la documentation textuelle. Une fois franchi le malentendu de voir du commerce dans la circulation intense des textiles et d'objets de luxe, qui se réfère essentiellement à la sphère de la redistribution interne du royaume, il reste encore à definir le cadre d'ensemble dans lequel s'inscrivent les pratiques commerciales sur la longue distance, où l'échange de dons et l'activité des marchands se mêlent parfois de façon inextricable.[2]

---

* Cet article est offert à Pelio Fronzaroli avec admiration et gratitude.

1 Cf. F. Pinnock, *About the Trade of Early Syrian Ebla*, dans *MARI* 4 (1985), pp. 85-92; *Ead.*, *The Lapis Lazuli Trade in the Third Millennium and the Evidence from the Royal Palace G*, dans *BM* 21 (1986), pp. 221-228; *Ead.*, *Considerazioni sul sistema commerciale di Ebla protosiriana*, dans *PdP* 46 (1991), pp. 270-284; J. Mellart, *Archaeological Evidence for Trade Routes between Syria and Mesopotamia during the Early and the Beginning of the Middle Bronze Age*, dans *SEb* 5 (1982), pp. 15-32.

2 Pour une vue d'ensemble du commerce d'Ébla sur la base des données épigraphiques voir H. Klengel *Ebla im Fernhandel des 3. Jahrtausends*, dans H. Waetzoldt - H. Hauptmann (éd.), *Wirtschaft und Gesellschaft von Ebla*, Heidelberg 1988, pp. 245-251 et A. Archi, *Trade and Administrative Practice: the Case of Ebla*, dans *AoF* 20 (1993), pp. 45-58. A. Archi a remarqué que, du point de vue documentaire, la situation d'Ébla pourrait être pareille à celle de la Mésopotamie à l'âge akkadienne, où les biens de luxe (surtout les métaux), étant proprieté personnelle du roi et des hauts fonctionnaires, n'étaient pas comptabilisés dans les archives d'état. À Ébla, on sait que des grandes quantités d'objets d'or et d'argent étaient stockés et enregistrés comme faisant partie du trésor du palais, mais la provénance de ces biens n'est pas notée de façon systematique.

Une enquête équilibrée sur les pratiques commerciales éblaïtes doit se baser évidemment sur une évaluation du vocabulaire et de la typologie des textes: quels sont les mots qui identifient les marchands? Quelle est la valeur des mots-clé du lexique administratif qui sont en rapport avec l'activité de ceux derniers? Et finalement, y a-t-il des typologies spécifiques de textes pour l'enregistrement de transactions commerciales?

Quant au dernier point, la réponse semble être non. Des "merchant's accounts", du type bien connu à Umma pendant la IIIème dynastie d'Ur, ne sont pas attesté à Ébla, même s'il y a des indices que la rédaction de véritables bilans, où les recettes et les dépenses se balancent, pouvaient resulter particulièrement utiles pour des marchands qui agissaient en tant que chargés du palais. Très intéressant à cet égard est le texte TM.75.G.1353,[3] une balance de comptes qui est épitomée dans le colophon comme un "enregistrement des sorties (et) des entrées du roi dans la 5ème(?) année" (dub-gar è mu-túm en 3[+2$^{?}$] mu), où plusieurs postes semblent se référer à l'activité de marchands.[4] Mais malheureusement ce document est unique. Par conséquent, la plupart des témoignages sur le commerce d'Ébla est à chercher dans les comptes-rendus qui s'occupent de façon générale des sorties et des entrées de biens du palais.

Comme on l'a souvent remarqué, les données sur l'activité des marchands d'Ébla concernent essentiellement la région de Mari, et, plus en particulier, les villes de Tuttul, de Imar et de Mari.[5] Un ensemble, beaucoup moins nombreux, d'occurrences se réfère à la Syrie du nord-est (de l'Euphrate au Habur, le long de la ligne marquée par les villes d'Abarsal, de Ḫarran et de Nagar). On ne devrait pas avoir de doutes à propos de la fonction du lú-kar – le terme le plus fréquemment attesté pour "marchand" dans les textes d'Ébla –, mais le statut d'autres types de marchands est au contraire problématique, comme c'est le cas pour le gá'eš,[6] le dam-gàr (très rarement attesté[7]) et le u_5 "courrier, messager", qui certainement exerçait la fonction de

3 Cf. L. Milano, *Due rendiconti di metalli da Ebla*, dans *SEb* 3 (1980), pp. 12-21.

4 Cf. en particulier l'occurrence de "prix/achats" (níg-sa_{10}) aux §§ 1, 2, 8, 13, 15, et la mention de marchands et courriers (dam-gàr, u_5) aux §§ 12, 13, 14, 15, 16.

5 Un répertoire des occurrences se trouve dans *ARES* 2, sous les différents toponymes.

6 Ce terme pourrait se référer, comme en sumérien, au commerce maritime ou fluvial. Pour ga'eš dans le texte littéraire *ARET* 5, 6 (et le parallèle d'Abu Ṣalabikh), cf. W. G. Lambert, *JCS* 41 (1989), p. 10 et M. Krebernick, *QuSem* 18 (1992), p. 115: "merchant, trader", mais aussi "goods, foreign trade(?)".

7 *ARET* 3, 147 r. II 3; *ARET* 4, 9 v. IV 6; *ARET* 7, 70 r. II 3, TM.75.G.1353 (*SEb* 3 [1980], p. 13) r. VIII 3; TM.75.G.2420 (= *QuSem* 18, pp. 195 ss.) bd 5; *MEE* 7, 34 r. IX 1'; r. XVII 15.

marchand dans certaines occasions.[8] Du moment que types différents de "marchands" sont parfois mentionnés dans les mêmes textes,[9] il est clair qu'ils impliquent des prérogatives spécifiques.[10]

Un groupe de documents qui semble être particulièrement rattaché au commerce est celui qui est caractérisé par l'enregistrement d'opérations comptables référées à "voyages, expéditions (commerciales)" (kaskal-kaskal).[11] Dans ces documents – qui d'ailleurs ne s'occupent pas exclusivement d'expéditions – il y a une co-occurrence de trois éléments typiques: a) la mention des "marchands" (lú-kar, gá'eš) et des "courriers" (u_5) comme agents des transactions; b) les expressions níg-sa_{10} "prix, achat"[12] ou šu-bal-AG "échange" pour définir la nature des transactions; c) l'énumération en séquence des expéditions (1, 2, 3, etc. kaskal-kaskal)[13] au cours desquelles une certaine opération a été accomplie. Dans un des colophons (TM.75.G.1928 v. IX 1-6) le type de transaction est défini par le terme til (dont on va parler par la suite[14]): "Total: 19 mines et 14 sicles d'argent: compte rendu des dépenses (effectuées) dans les pays, pour la 7ème année" (dub-gar til-til kalam-*tim* kalam-*tim áš-du* 7 mu). D'autres colophons mettent en évidence le personnage qui est en charge des opérations: ainsi par ex. TM.75.G.1222 (v. X 1-4): "Total: 16 mines et 6 sicles d'argent, 2 mines et 42 sicles d'or, supplément d'argent d'Enna-Il, le représentant du marchand-ga'eš" (diri babbar:kù *En-na-Il* maškim gá'eš) et TM.75.G.1738 (v. VI 1-5) "Total: 7 mines et 40 sicles d'or, 3 mines d'étain en échange: expédition de Sa-Damu" (šu-bal-AG kaskal *Sa*$_{12}$-*Da-mu*).

---

8 Dans *MEE* 2 G. Pettinato traduit má-ḫu (= u_5) par "mercante". Cf. aussi H. Waetzoldt, *BaE*, p. 418 ss. et P. Steinkeller, *OrAnt* 23 (1984), p. 34 ("mounted messanger"). Un indice intéressant pour le rapport entre le "courrier" u_5 et le milieu du commerce est fourni par les textes qui ont affaire avec des expéditions commerciales (kaskal-kaskal), du type de *ARET* 7, 11 et *ARET* 7, 16.

9 Cf. par ex. la co-occurrence de gá'eš et dam-gàr dans *MEE* 7, 34; de gá'eš et u_5 dans *ARET* 7, 11, *ARET* 7, 16, *MEE* 2, 35; de dam-gàr et u_5 dans TM.75.G.1353 (=*SEb* 3 [1980], pp. 12-15); de lú-kar et u_5 dans *ARET* 3, 193. Dans le Traité avec Abarsal (TM.75.G.2420) on a lú-kar et dam-gàr.

10 Le dam-gàr a été mis en rapport avec le commerce maritime sur la base du contexte du Traité avec Abarsal.

11 Une étude de ces textes est en cours de préparation.

12 Pour la construction de níg-sa_{10} dans les textes d'Ébla cf. G. Conti, *La legge di Geers e il sistema grafico eblaita*, dans *Quaderni del Dipartimento di Linguistica - Università di Firenze* 4 (1993), p. 98s, n. 2.

13 Parmi les textes déja publiés, qui contiennent des séquences de kaskal-kaskal, il y a par ex. *ARET* 7, 1; 16; 17 et *MEE* 10, 23.

14 Voir ci-dessous, pp. 13 ss.

Il est assez clair, à mon avis, que les textes énumérant des kaskal-kaskal offrent un témoignage important d'une activité commerciale gérée directement par le palais d'Ébla, même si parfois les "voyages" des marchands pouvaient être finalisés à la livraison de dons et de tributs.[15] À juger par cette documentation, on a l'impression d'un *commerce administré* (qui se déroule surtout en direction de Mari), dans un cadre de circulation généralisée de marchands qui sont au service d'une multiplicité de centres différents.[16] Il faut ajouter que dans beaucoup de listes de "prix" (níg-sa_{10}), qui présentent souvent des liens prosopographiques avec les listes des "voyages" (kaskal-kaskal), les quantités de métaux enregistrées représentent des véritables *dotations* des marchands pour l'achat de biens,[17] qui peuvent être non seulement des biens de luxe, mais aussi du bétail et des produits alimentaires.[18]

C'est à partir du contrôle du palais sur l'activité des marchands qu'on peut mieux comprendre les clauses relatives au commerce qui figurent dans les traités internationaux, en particulier ceux d'Ébla avec Abarsal[19] et avec Mari.[20] Dans ce dernier, il y a un passage concernant des règles à suivre dans la pratique commerciale, qui engagent Ébla d'un coté, et Mari et Kish de l'autre coté.[21] Ce n'est donc pas par hasard que dans *ARET* 7, 9 – où il s'agit d'argent et or livrés à Mari pendant plusieurs expéditions – une des expéditions (qui n'est pas reportée dans le colophon) concerne la ville de Kish: les deux villes avaient évidemment des liens très étroits en matière de

---

15 C'est le cas, par ex., de *ARET* 7, 9, où il s'agit de livraisons mensuelles d'argent et d'or pour le roi de Mari (lugal *Ma-rí*^{ki}) dans la ville de DU^{ki}.

16 Dans *ARET* 7, 14 et 15 il s'agit justement de quantités de biens reçus par (šu ba_4-ti), ou bien "au compte de" (*al_6*), marchands de Mari.

17 Quelques exemples de ces textes ont été donnés par A. Archi, *cit.*, dans *AoF* 20 (1993), pp. 45-58.

18 Cf. par ex. TM.75.G.2630 v. VI 1'-2. Il s'agit en total de 87 mines d'argent, "sortie au temps d'Ibrium" (è *in* u_4 *Ib-rí-um*). Pour le commerce de céréales voir aussi *ARET* 7, 14; pour l'achat de fourrage TM.75.G.1529.

19 TM.75.G.2420. Cf. E. Sollberger, *The So-Called Treaty Between Ebla and "Ashur"*, dans *SEb* 3 (1980), pp. 129-160 and D. O. Edzard, *Der Vertrag von Ebla mit A-BAR-QA*, dans *QuSem* 18 (1992), pp. 187-217. L'activité de commerçants et messagers est traitée en particulier aux §§ 6-10, 14-15, 18-19, 22-25, 33, 1'-3'.

20 TM.75.G.2268. De ce texte seulement quelques passages ont été publiés: cf. G. Conti, *Index of Eblaic Texts* (= *QuSem Materiali* 1), Firenze 1992, p. 93. Le document est défini dub *ù-su-rí Ma-rí*^{ki} "document de l'accord(?) avec Mari" (cf. *ARET* 2, 32 v. VI 1-3: dub *ù-su-rí Ḫa-zu-um* "document de l'accord(?) avec Ḫazum).

21 Le passage est cité par A. Archi, *Les rapports politiques et économiques entre Ebla et Mari*, dans *MARI* 4 (1985), p. 67.

circulation des marchands, non pas seulement pour le fait d'être situées sur le même itinéraire.[22]

2. *Le texte* ARET *2, 29*

Les traités mis à part, il est assez rare de trouver dans les archives royales d'Ébla des documents qui illustrent de façon articulée des missions entreprises par des marchands. Un rapport de ce type est représenté pourtant par un texte qui a été publié par D. O. Edzard dans *ARET* 2 (texte n. 29), et qui a été repris et commenté par F. D'Agostino dans un article paru quelques années plus tard.[23] Il s'agit de la description d'une série de transactions qui se déroulent autour d'un personnage, un tel Gīda-naʿim, probablement le fils d'une nourrice résidante au palais, et qui concernent d'autres personnes gérants leurs affaires en rapport direct avec lui, ou agissants dans le même milieu géographique que lui. Ce n'est pas ceci le seul exemple disponible d'un rapport sur des activités commerciales conduites par un marchand particulier: un autre document du même type, par exemple, celui de l' "accord (relatif) à Ḫazum" (dub *ù-su-rí Ḫa-zu-um*),[24] se réfère vraisemblablement à une controversie entre ce dernier et d'autres marchands.

Etant donné l'intérêt du document *ARET* 2, 29 pour la problématique du commerce – comme D'Agostino l'a correctement remarqué –, c'est à ceci que je prêterai mon attention par la suite, en proposant une traduction qui sera suivie par quelques observations d'ordre général. Dès maintenant, il me paraît nécessaire de souligner que, dans mon interprétation, tous les evénéments relatés dans le texte ont affaire à des opérations d'achats et de vente de biens de la part de marchands qui se trouvaient dans des régions au nord-ouest de Mari. Le terme til, un des mots-clé occurrant à plusieurs réprises dans le document, n'aurait pas à mon avis la valeur de "perdre (relativement à l'argent)",[25] mais la valeur de "dépenser, verser (à titre de pay-

22 Les villes de Mari et de Kish se trouvent souvent associées dans la comptabilité, comme on peut voir dans la liste d'attestations rassemblée par A. Archi, *Kiš nei testi di Ebla*, dans *SEb* 4 (1981), pp. 77-87, à intégrer par *ARES* 2, s.v. Kiš^{ki}.

23 F. D'Agostino, *Proposta d'interpretazione del testo* ARET *2, 29 (Ipotesi per uno studio della legislazione commerciale di Ebla)*, dans *OrAnt* 29 (1990), pp. 39-55. En 1996 le texte a été inclu par le même D'Agostino dans *MEE* 7 (texte n. 42).

24 *ARET* 2, 32 (cf. aussi *MEE* 7, 10). Ḫazum est qualifié comme un agent-maškim d'Ibrium dans *ARET* 4, 10 r. 6-8.

25 Cf. F. D'Agostino, *cit.*, dans *OrAnt* 29 (1990), p. 46: "perdita", "non utilizzazione (a fini commerciali)".

ment)". Plutôt qu'à un document portant sur des quantités d'argent plusieurs fois perdues et remboursées, il faudrait donc penser à une liste de dépenses effectuées par des marchands qui étaient en rapport entre eux.

§ **1.** (Recto I 1) 2 *mi-at* 60 udu (2) lú *Gi-da-na-im* (3) ì-na-sum (4) *si-in* (5) *Ma-ri*[ki] (6) *áš-da* (7) *Ḫa-ra-an*[ki] (8) šu ba$_4$-ti (II 1) -*sù*
"260 moutons que Gīda-naʿim a donné à Mari, de Ḫarran il les a reçus."[26]

§ **2.** (2) 2 *ma-na* babbar:kù (3) lú 2 KU.TU (4) til (5) *Ga-da-mu*[ki] (6) mun (7) *Ar-kir-ra-tum* (8) *wa* (9) ì-na-sum (10) babbar:kù (11) bur tar
"2 mines d'argent que 2 agents fiduciaires[27] (de Gīda-naʿim?) ont dépensé à Gadamu pour le sel[28] d'Ar-kirratum[29]: et ils ont donné l'argent (sous forme) de vases de 30 (sicles)".[30]

§ **3.** (III 1) 1 BAR.AN.SAL (2) *Ga-da-mu*[ki] (3) *Puzur$_4$-ra-Ma-lik* (4) til (5) *wa* (6) lul-gu-AG-*sù* (7) 2 ma-na babbar:kù
"1 mule-BAR.AN[31] Puzra-Malik a déboursé à Gadamu et on lui a remboursé[32] 2 mines d'argent".[33]

---

26 Les prépositions *si-in* et *áš-da* semblent indiquer ici une opposition spatiale, qui est marquée ailleurs par l'opposition *si-in* / *mi-nu*, (cf. *ARET* XI, glossario). D'autre part, on ne peut pas exclure pour *áš-da* une valeur locale "près de".

27 Pour KU.TU et sa traduction voir plus loin, pp. 11 s.

28 Je garde l'interpretation du signe donnée par Edzard ("guniertes DIM": *ARET* 2, p. 150), qui transcrit dim$_x$ et traduit "mât" (*ibid.*, p. 121). L'occurrence au § 9 de MUN lú *in* 1 GIŠ-má-gibil$_4$ permet de comprendre tout aussi bien "sel" que "mât". La valeur de 4 sicles d'argent pour un mât (§ 9) semblerait être très modeste. S'il est vrai que le sel n'est pas attesté ailleurs dans les textes d'Ébla, on le connait bien dans la région de Mari, jusqu'à Tuttul et dans l'Idâ-maraṣ (cf. J.-M. Durand, *Le sel à Mari (II): Les salines sur les bords du Habur*, dans *MARI* 6 [1990], pp. 629-634 et M. Guichard, *Le sel à Mari (III): les lieux du sel*, dans *Florilegium Marianum* 3 [1997], pp. 167-200), et il est aussi maintenant attesté dans les textes de Tell Beydar (*Subartu* 2 [1996], p. 182 s.v.): il s'agit donc de la région qui fait l'objet des affaires de Gīda-naʿim. La correction de F. D'Agostino, *OA* 29 (1990), p. 46 *ad* r. II 6 (GÍRx*gunû*) et l'hypothèse d'une désignation géographique (même en absence du déterminatif): "Gadamu (nel territorio di) Ziqaqapu (?)" n'est pas justifiée par la forme du signe: voir p. ex. la graphie de GÍR*gunû*[ki] dans *MEE* 10, 2 v. IV 3 et dans TM.75.G.1353 v. VI 4 (*SEb* 3 [1980], fig. 2f.).

29 L'interprétation de ce nom (est-ce un nom de personne?) n'est pas sans problèmes: cf. J. M. Pagan, *ARES* 3 (1998), p. 215 (s.v. harr-). À ma connaissance, il n'y a pas d'autres attestations d'Arkirratum à Ébla.

30 Voir par ex. *ARET* 7, 45 r. I 1-3: 2 ma-na tar babbar:kù / kù-gi / 5 bur-KAK tar / en "2 mines 30 (sicles) d'argent (et) or: 5 vases-KAK de 30 (sicles), (pour) le roi". Pour la tournure de phrase cf. par ex. *ARET* 2, 5 v. IV 1-4: 1 ma-na šú+ša babbar:kù til babbar:kù *in Zi-na-tum*[<ki>], "1 mine 20 sicles d'argent: dépense d'argent dans (la ville de) Z." (Pour une différente traduction voir *MEE* 10, p. 5).

31 Sur les mulets BAR.AN, hybrides de l'âne et de l'onagre (*E. asinus* x *hemionus*), qui étaient particulièrement appreciés dans la région de Nagar et exportés jusqu'à Ébla, cf. dernièrement A. Archi, *Subartu* 4,2 (1998), pp. 8-12 et K. Van Lerberghe, *Subartu* 2 (1996), pp. 112-114 (avec bibliographie

§ 4. (8) 70 udu (9) *Ir-i-tum*^{ki} (10) *wa* (11) ì-na-sum-*sù* (12) *Gi-da-na-im* (13) *si-in* (14) *Nab-ra-la-du*^{ki}
"70 moutons (appartiennent à) Ir'itum: et Gīda-naʿim les a donné à Nabraladu".

§ 5. (IV 1) 1 udu 3 gu_4 3 IGI.NITA (2) *Ù-šu-mu*^{ki} (3) *Puzur₄-ra-Ma-lik* (4) lul-gu-AG-*sù*
"1 mouton, 3 boeufs, 3 ânes-I. Puzra-Malik lui (= à Gīda-naʿim) a remboursé à Ušumu".[34]

§ 6. (5) 4 gu_4 (6) lú nin-ni$^!$(DÙ) (7) *Mi-na-lum* (8) *Du-du-lu*^{ki} (9) *wa* (10) šu ba_4-ti-*sù* (11) *áš-da* (V 1) KU.TU (2) nin-ni$^!$ (DÙ) (3) *Mi-na-lum* (4) *Du-du-lu*^{ki} (5) *wa* (6) ì-na-sum-*sù* (7) *Gi-da-na-im* (8) *si-in* (9) 2 šu (Verso I 1) *Mi-na-lum* (2) *Du-du-lu*^{ki}
"4 boeufs de la soeur de Minalum de Tuttul, de la part d'un agent fiduciaire la soeur de Minalum de Tuttul les a reçus, et Gīda-naʿim les a remis entre les mains de Minalum de Tuttul".[35]

---

précedante). Cf. aussi TM.75.G.1872 r. I 1-II 2: "100 mines d'argent pour le roi de Nagar: 12ème expédition; 6 mines, 10 sicles d'argent pour son représentant-e-gi_4 (e-gi_4-maškim-*sù*): 10ème expédition; 40 mines d'argent, prix des mulets (níg-sa_{10} BAR.AN-BAR.AN nita); 1 mine d'argent pour le fourrage des mulets du roi (še-kú BAR.AN-BAR.AN en)".
Les textes de Tell Beydar ont confirmé l'importance de l'exploitation de ces hybrides dans la région du Haut Khabur, qu'il est intéressant de retrouver ici dans le contexte de transactions commerciales dans la Syrie de nord-est.

32 Cf. F. Pomponio, *The Meaning of the Term lul-gu-aka*, dans *WdO* 13 (1982), pp. 95-96.

33 Le prix (níg-sa_{10}) d'une mule BAR.AN.SAL n'est pas attesté. Pour le BAR.AN (mâle) on trouve des équivalences en argent qui sont assez variables: le "prix" de **2 mines** est assez frequemment attesté (cf. par ex. TM.75.G.1928 r. IX 5-7; TM.75.G.1402 r. I 5-7), mais on trouve aussi **25 sicles**: *MEE* 10 29 v. I 3-14; **45 sicle**: *ARET* 1, 44 r. VI 4-5; **1 mine**: *ARET* 7, 71 r. II 5-III 1, III 4-5, IV 3-4, V 2-3, v. I 2-3, II 4-5; TM.75.G.1460 v. IV 5-6; TM.75.G.2543 r. III 5-7; **1 mine 3 sicles**: TM.75.G.1872 r. XI 4-5; **1 mine 5 sicles**: *ARET* 7, 71 r. I 1-2, II 1-2; **1 mine 30 sicles**: *ARET* 7, 75 r. I 1-2; **5 mines**: *MEE* 10, 29 v. I 7-8. Tous ces "prix" pourraient bien inclure un surplus attribué à l'agent pour sa transaction.
En principe, on pourrait admettre que la phrase du § 3 se termine avec lul-gu-AG-*sù*, comme au § 5. C'est l'hypothèse de Edzard, éditeur du texte, suivi par F. D'Agostino, *cit.*, dans *OrAnt* 29 (1990), p. 40, qui traduit: "1 onagro femmina (a) Gadamu Puzra-Malik ha perduto e ha rimborsato" (-*sù* n'est pas traduit explicitement). Il me semble cependant que mon intérpretation soit plus convenable si l'on considère que 2 mines d'argent correspondent au prix courant pour un mulet BAR.AN et que 2 mines pour 70 moutons (au § 4) ne donneraient pas un chiffre rond par tête de bétail. La valeur d'un mouton n'est pas toujours la même et elle est généralement supérieure à 2 sicles d'argent. Dans *ARET* 2, 5 on trouve en effet **7 sicles**; **4 ½ sicles**; **3 sicles**; **2 sicles**. Des valeurs inférieures à 2 sicles sont rares: voir pourtant *ARET* 2, 6 (**1 sicle** par tête de bétail) et TM.75.G.2508 r. XIII 16-22 (**1 sicle** et **1 ⅓ sicles** par tête de bétail).

34 Le texte a bien *Ù-šu-mu*^{ki}, comme dans la translitération de Edzard, et non pas *Ù-šè-mu*^{ki}, comme il a été corrigé par D'Agostino.

35 La situation illustrée par cette poste semble être liée à la clause juridique contenue dans TM.75.G.1444 r. X 9-v. II 13: cf. D.O. Edzard, *Der Text TM.75.G.1444 aus Ebla*, dans *SEb* IV (1981), pp. 41-42. Le texte a été subdivisé par Edzard de la façon suivante: (§ 16) *en-ma* / *Ib-rí-um* / *si-in* / en / (§ 17) giš-ba-tuku / du_{11}-ga / *Ti-lu-du* / *Ti-a-Da-mu* / *Kir-su-ud* / *Da-mur-Da-mu* / ⌜*Ḫa*⌝-*lu-*

§ 7. (3) šú+ša gín-DILMUN babbar:kù (4) níg-du$_8$ (5) ir$_{11}$ (6) *Ma-rí*^{ki} (7) *Sal-ba-du*^{ki} (8) níg-du$_8$-*sù*
"20 sicles d'argent, dépôt du fonctionnaire-ir$_{11}$[36] de Mari, dans la ville de Salbadu il (= Gīda-naʿim?) les a déposés".[37]

§ 8. (9) 2 KU.TU (II 1) ⸢DU⸣^{ki} (2) *wa* (3) 1 KU.TU (4) *Ma-rí*^{ki} (5) *wa* (6) *ḫa-mi-zu* (7) *in* (8) *ʾÀ-du*^{ki} (9) *wa* (10) ⸢zàḫ⸣ (11) *si-in* (12) ki-sur (3) *Ḫa-ra-an*^{ki} (III 1) *wa* (2) šu-du$_8$-*sù* (3) ME.SE$_{11}$ (4) Kur^{ki} (5) *wa* (6) ì-na-sum-*sù* (7) *Gi-da-na-im* (8) *si-in* (9) 2 šu (10) *Ma-rí*^{ki}
"2 agents fiduciaires de la ville de DU et 1 agent fiduciaire de Mari: on les surveillait(?)[38] donc dans la région de ʾAdu et ils se sont enfuits[39] vers la frontière[40] de Ḫarran; alors un fonctionnaire-ME.SE$_{11}$[41] du Pays les a pris et Gīda-naʿim les a remis entre les mains de Mari".[42]

---

ud / (§ 18) *Ḫa-sum* / 2 u$_4$ / *wa* / ⸢x⸣ / ⸢u$_4$⸣ / KU.TU KU.TU / nu šu ba$_4$-ti / (§ 19) *si-a-ma* / MÍ du$_{11}$-ga / *áš-da* / 2 / dumu-nita dumu-nita / al$_6$-tuš / (§ 20) *ap* / nu MÍ du$_{11}$-ga / é en / al$_6$-tuš / (§ 21) *si-a-ma* / KU.TU šu ba$_4$-ti / KU.TU / AMBAR-ti-gi / en / ḫi-til . Voilà la traduction que je propose: "(§ 16) Ainsi dit Ibrium au roi: (§ 17) que Tia-Damu, Kirsud, Damur-Damu, Ḫaludu (et) Ḫasum écoutent le décret de (= à l'égard de) Tiludu (§ 18): pour deux jours, pour n jours les agents fiduciaires elle ne recevra pas. (§ 19) (Si) elle veut, elle habitera chez (ses) deux fils; (§ 20) mais (si elle) ne veut pas, elle habitera dans la maison du roi. (§ 21) Si elle reçoit un agent fiduciaire, l'agent fiduciaire déboursera le ... du roi". Il s'agit de cinq femmes d'Ibrium (cf. *ARES* 1, p. 260). Pour *Ḫa-sum* (qui n'est pas considerée un nom de personne par Edzard) cf. aussi la graphie *Ḫa-šu* dans *MEE* 10, 20 r. II 3 (*Ḫa-su* est une faute dans *ARES* 1, p. 260). Les fils de Tiludu avaient été mentionnés au § 3 du même texte.

36 Sur cette catégorie sociale, qui n'a rien à voir avec des esclaves, voir L. Milano, *Lessicografia e storia sociale: gli "schiavi di Ebla"*, dans *SEL* 12 (1995), pp. 121-134; J. P. Grégoire - J. Renger, *Die Interdependenz der wirtschaftlichen und gesellschaftlich-politischen Strukturen von Ebla. Erwägengen zum System des Oikos-Wirtschaft in Ebla*, dans H. Hauptmann - H. Waetzoldt (éd.), *Wirtschaft und Gesellschaft von Ebla* (= *Heidelberger Studien zum Alten Orient*, 2), Heidelberg 1988, p. 221 ss.

37 Il n'est pas facile de dire si ce montant d'argent est en rapport avec les quatre boeufs livrés à Minalum par Gīda-naʿim au § 6. En effet, le prix d'un boeuf n'est jamais au dessus de 20-30 sicles (cf. *ARET* 7, 78 r. I 5-6), ce qui donnerait au moins 80 sicles pour 4 boeufs. Mais si le sens de níg-du$_8$, "depôt", est celui d'une anticipation sur le total du versement, il est possible qu'il ait été versé par Minalum même au fonctionnaire de Mari.

38 Pour *ḫa-mu-zu* dans les listes lexicales cf. les obsérvations de F. D'Agostino, *cit.*, dans *OrAnt* 29 (1990), p. 50, qui traduit *ḫa-mi-zu* comme un nom de fonction: "sorvegliante".

39 Cf. l'attestation de *MEE* 2, 32 v. I 10: zàḫ Kur^{ki} "un fugitif du Pays", qu'on ne peut pas pourtant mettre en relation directe avec le passage du § 8.

40 Cf. *ʾa$_5$-na* ki-sur *Ib-la*^{ki} "à la frontière d'Ébla" dans le Traité entre Ébla et Abarsal: D. O. Edzard, *QuSem* 18 (1992), p. 207, v. XIII 15-17 (voir aussi v. I 7-8: *al*$_6$ ki-sur. Pour la valeur de *al*$_6$ voir M. V. Tonietti, *MisEb* 4 [1997], p. 77). L'interprétation de "frontière, confins" est sûre dans *ARET* 7, 156 r. II 14-III 2, qui est un cadastre de biens fonciers: 5 *mi-at* gána-kešda-ki / *A-da-bí-gú*^{ki} / *in* / ki-sur / *Du:ur*^{ki}. Elle est aussi plausible dans *ARET* 1, 13 r. III 9-11 (textiles pour deux personnes qui "sont allées aux confins", lú DU.DU / ki-sur / ki-sur) et dans *ARET* 1, 13 r. IV 3-7 (textiles pour les mêmes personnes, comme "livraison additionnelle quand ils se rendaient aux 'lamentations sur la frontière'", tag$_4$ / ì-ti / *in* / *da-ma-ti* / ki-sur).

§ 9. (11) 1 ma-na babbar:kù (12) níg-sa$_{10}$ 1 GIŠ-má-⌜gibil$_4$⌝ (IV 1) 4 gín-DILMUN babbar:kù (2) mun (3) lú *in* (4) 1 GIŠ-má-⌜gibil$_4$⌝ (5) til (6) *Ma-rí*^{ki} (7) 2 KU.TU (8) DU^{ki} (9) *wa* (10) *Sa-mu-za*^{ki}
"1 mine d'argent, prix d'un bateau(?)[43] (et) 4 sicles d'argent du sel[44] qui (se trouve dans) le bateau, 2 agents fiduciaires des villes de DU et Samuza[45] ont dépensé à Mari".

§ 10. (11) 2 KU.TU (12) DU^{ki} (13) *in* (14) ki (15) *Ḫal*$^{!}$*-sum*^{ki} (16) *wa* (V 1) ḫi-mu-túm (2) 4 IGI.NITA-*sù* (3) *wa* (4) šu-du$_8$ (5) IGI.NITA-IGI.NITA-*sù* (6) *wa* (7) ì-na-sum (8) *si-in* (9) 2 ⌜til⌝-*sù* (10) *ap* (11) 2 KU.TU (12) tùn-šè (13) IGI.NITA-IGI.NITA-*sù* (14) šu-du$_8$ (15) é (16) ir$_{11}$ (17) ⌜*Ma-rí*⌝^{ki}
"2 agents fiduciaires de la ville de DU (se trouvaient) dans le territoire de Ḫalsum, et devaient faire parvenir leur 4 ânes-IGI.NITA; alors ils ont pris leurs ânes-IGI.NITA et ils (les) ont donnés pour (= à titre de) leurs deux déboursements. Mais les 2 agents fiduciaires ont été tués (et) leur ânes-IGI.NITA a pris la maison du/des fonctionnaire(s)-ir$_{11}$ à Mari".[46]

3. Gīda-naʿim et les autres protagonistes

Comme on l'a déja dit, le personnage central du texte est un certain Gīda-naʿim, qui pourrait bien être le fils de la nourrice Gišadu,[47] dont le nom est plusieurs fois attesté

---

41 Selon M. Astour, *History of Ebla*, dans *Eblaitica* 3 (1992), p. 60 et note 362 il s'agit du même mot que l'Akk. *mēsu(m)* or *mēšu* (^{giš}MES), un type de bois. Il faut plutôt penser à un nom de fonction, comme G. Pettinato a bien compris dans *MEE* 2. Cf. aussi, par ex., *MEE* 7, 35 r. IV 9-13: une parure de vêtements pour NP ME.SE$_{11}$ ZA$_x$ en.

42 Ces gens avaient evidemment commis un crime, car la libre circulation des marchands est prevue, par ex., par le Traité entre Ébla et Abarsal: "En ce qui concerne les marchands d'Ébla, Abarsal les laissera rentrer (chez eux); en ce qui concerne les marchands d'Abarsal, Ébla les laissera rentrer (chez eux)" (cf. Edzard, *cit.*, pp. 202-203, §§ 24-25).

43 Il n'y a aucun doute que le signe mal visible qui se trouve après GIŠ-má soit le même ici et dans IV 4. Faute de mieux, je propose une graphie defective de NE = gibil$_4$, la seule qui me paraît possible dans ce contexte (une restitution má-gur$_8$ est impossible). L'imbarcation GIŠ-má-gibil$_4$ est attestée dans le Traité entre Ébla et Abarsal r. VIII 7, r. IX 12.

44 Voir la note 28 ci-dessus.

45 Transliteré *sa mu* 6 par Edzard, *ARET* 2, 29. La lecture ZA.KI (sandhi) pour le dernier groupe de signes a eté proposée par D'Agostino, *OA* 29 (1990), p. 55 n. 51. Puisque le toponyme est inconnu, l'incertitude demeure.

46 Pour cette traduction voir L. Milano, *cit.*, dans *SEL* 12 (1995), p. 124.

47 Un Gīda-naʿim fils de la nourrice Gišadu (dumu-nita ga-du$_8$ *Gi-ša-du*) est attesté dans *ARET* 1, 5 v. VIII 18-21. Autres occurrences du nom: *ARET* 3, 11 v. III 5'; *ARET* 3, 134 v.$^?$ VIII 2; *ARET* 4, 10 v. III 16 (*Dab*$_6$*-bù-lu* lú G. Sa-za$_x$^{ki}) où il s'agit toujours de livraisons de textiles. Pour l'interprétation du nom cf. J. M. Pagan, *ARES* 3 (1998), p. 311 ("Naʿim is good"). Pour l'analyse morphologique des éléments *gi-da* (de GYD "être bon") et *na-im* (NʿM "être gracieux, favorable") cf. *ibid.*, pp. 115-116 et 142-143, avec bibliographie et commentaire.

dans les listes des "femmes du roi" (dam en).[48] Dans notre texte, Gīda-naʿim est essentielment en charge de bétail (§§ 1, 4, 5, 6), mais il agit aussi comme mandataire du roi d'Ébla, du moment qu'il est chargé de la restitution à Mari des "agents fiduciaires" qui s'étaient enfuis vers la frontière de Ḫarran (§ 8). Bien que Gīda-naʿim ne soit pas qualifié comme "marchand", le contexte général suggère qu'il avait cette fonction:[49] il conduit ses affaires sur place, à Mari (§ 1), à Ušumu (§ 5), à Tuttul (§ 6), et probablement à Salbadu (§ 7). La restitution des fugitifs semble, elle aussi, avoir lieu à Mari (§ 8), dans le cadre d'une opération où les prérogatives du marchand se mêlent à celle d'un fonctionnaire d'état.

D'autres personnages sont mentionnés dans le texte à coté de Gīda-naʿim. Le premier est Puzra-Malik, qui pourrait être identifié avec un haut fonctionnaire que l'on trouve attesté à la fois comme consignataire de quantités d'or, comme percepteur de taxes et comme responsable de mulets-BAR.AN. Il est actif dans la région de Nagar, c'est à dire pas loin du théâtre des opérations commerciales décrites dans notre texte.[50] Puzra-Malik est mentionné au § 3 comme quelqu'un à qui l'on a remboursé (lul-gu-AG) de l'argent en échange d'une mule, mais sa liaison d'affaires avec Gīda-naʿim est évidente d'après le § 5, où il s'agit d'un autre remboursement, cette fois-ci à sa charge, concernant des têtes de bétail.

48 Cf. *ARES* 1, pp. 252, 257-258.

49 L'hypothèse est déja suggérée par D'Agostino, *OrAnt* 29 (1990), p. 44.

50 Pour les livraisons (ì-na-sum) d'or cf. *ARET* 7, 30, *ARET* 7, 31, *ARET* 7, 63 et *MEE* 2, 23. Dans les premiers trois textes on trouve une somme finale en or qui "reste au compte de" (al_6) Puzra-Malik. Pour d'autres attestations voir encore TM.75.G.2062 v. II 10, TM.75.G.2542 r. VII 11 et TM.75.G.2543 r. IV, qui ont affaire avec la gestion de métaux et avec des opérations commerciales. Dans TM.75.G.1452 r. VI 3-v. I 5 (=*SEb* 4 [1981], p. 7), Puzra-Malik figure comme percepteur d'argent provenant de deux villages (*Ba-zu-ḫa*-WA^{ki}, *Ša-na-ru*$_{12}$*-gú*^{ki}). Il est très probable que le personnage en question soit aussi le "responsable des attelages des mulets-BAR.AN" qui porte le même nom dans *ARET* 1, 4 v. IX 24, *ARET* 4, 1 r. III 7, *ARET* 8, 522 r. IV 11, *ARET* 8, 525 v. III 20 (ugula bìr-BAR.AN en), *ARET* 1, 6 v. XII 19 (ugula bìr-BAR.AN *I-bí-Zi-kir*). En effet, le Puzra-Malik attesté dans TM.75.G.2542 r. VII 11 est en même temps quelqu'un qui: a) gère de l'argent, b) est responsable (ugula) des mulets BAR.AN, c) est actif dans la région del Nagar (DU.DU *Na-gàr*^{ki}), c'est à dire le milieu géographique de notre texte. L'identification avec un Puzra-Malik qui est engagé à son tour dans des transactions concernant les textiles présente plus d'incertitude: cf. *ARET* 1, 11 r. XII 11 (textiles *P.* šu-du$_8$ maškim *Du-bí*), *ARET* 3, 215 v. I 6' (textiles *P.* maškim *Du-bí* šu-du$_8$), *ARET* 4, 13 r. X 6 (textiles *Zi-kir-ra-ar wa Puzur*$_4$*-ra-Il* 2 maškim *Du-bí* šu-du$_8$), *ARET* 4, 8 r. III 7 (*Puzur*$_4$*-rí* ... maškim-maškim *I-bí-Zi-kir*), *ARET* 4, 23 v. VIII 7 (textiles *P. Ì-mar*^{ki} šu-mu-tag$_4$), *ARET* 7, 134 r. I 4 (laine *áš-da* NP *P.* še-SAGxḪA.AN.AN.AN).

Un autre personnage en rapport avec Gīda-naʿim est un certain Minalum de Tuttul, qui au § 6 est présenté comme le destinataire de 4 boeufs appartenants à sa soeur, qui lui sont remis par l'intermédiation de Gīda-naʿim lui même (§ 6). Le nom Minalum est attesté une autre fois seulement dans les textes d'Ébla (à moins que ce personnage ne se cache parfois sous l'hypocoristique MinaNI[51]), là où il s'agit d'une livraison de vêtements à des personnes, dont certaines proviennent de la ville de DU, qui est mentionné aussi dans notre texte (§§ 9 et 10).[52] Puisque DU se trouvait près de Tuttul,[53] c'est là le seul, très faible indice qu'on ait affaire avec le même personnage.

A propos des agents des transactions illustrées par *ARET* 2, 29, il y a finalement la question des personnages qualifiés par le mot KU.TU, qui ne sont jamais appelés par leurs noms propres. L'hypothèse que dans ce contexte il s'agit d'un groupe de personnes a été suggérée par Edzard[54] et se révèle en effet comme la plus plausible, même si le terme KU.TU est parfois utilisé comme nom propre[55] ou comme une composante de noms propres.[56] Quant au sens du terme, l'opinion de A. Westenholz, qui rapproche l'élément KU.TU à l'akkadien *kuttu / kittum*,[57] me paraît suggestive, bien que le recours à *kattû* "garant" (de *katāʾum* "prendre en garantie") soit aussi très plausible:[58] je proposerais par conséquent une traduction "(agent) fiduciare", qui

51 Pour ce *Mi-na*-NI cf. par ex. *ARET* 9, 68, *passim*.

52 Cf. *MEE* 2, 40 v. IV 3.

53 Voir la note 70 ci-dessous.

54 Cf. *ARET* 2, p. 131 s.v. KU-tu.

55 C'est très probablement le cas de *ARET* 1, 17 v. I 5; *ARET* 2, 24 r. III 1; *ARET* 4, 15 r. I 6; *ARET* 7, 9 v. II 3; v. IV 3; *MEE* 7, 46 r. III 8 (KU.TU ur_x NP)

56 L'élément KU.TU est présent en deuxième position dans les noms suivants: NI-*ba*-KU.TU (*ARET* 7, 64 r. II 2), *A*-KU.TU (*ARET* 3, 651 r. III 1'; *ARET* 8, 532 r. VII 19: *A*!-KU.TU), *Ga-ʾà*-KU.TU (*ARET* 8, 526 r. XV 17), *In*-KU.TU (*ARET* 8 542 r. VII 7); *Iš-la*-KU.TU (TM.75.G.2627 [*CRAI* 28, p. 182], v. VII 4); *Ma-na*-KU.TU (*ARET* 4, 13 v. III 19); *Zi*-KU.TU (*ARET* 8, 542 v. III 16); *Zi-li*-KU.TU (*ARET* 4, 13 r. II 10). En première position il est attesté dans le nom KU.TU-*ʾà-bù* (TM.75.G.1761 [*ARES* 1, p. 281] v. III 5.

57 Cf. A. Westenholz, *ARES* 1, p. 100 n. 4: "An element *ku-tu* [....] may contain the form *kuttu*, equivalent of Babylonian *kittum*. The Babylonian form is attested already in the Fara period: *ki-núm* [...]." L'élément KU.TU a été aussi interprété dans l'onomastique en faisant recours au mot ouest-sémitique pour "chevreau": cf. F. Pomponio, *Peculiarità della grafia dei termini semitici nei testi amministrativi eblaiti*, dans L. Cagni (ed.), *Il Bilinguismo a Ebla. Atti del Convegno Internazionale (Napoli 19-22 aprile 1982)*, Napoli 1984, pp. 311-312 et J. M. Pagan, *ARES* 3 (1998), p. 213 s.v. gudy-.

58 Cf. D'Agostino, *OrAnt* 29 (1990), pp. 45-46. Pour *katāʾum* cf. W. von Soden, *Or.* NS 26, p. 131s.

pourrait bien s'adapter à la fonction d'une catégorie de marchands agissant pour le compte de quelqu'un, et même d'une ville, comme ce serait le cas des §§ 2 et 6 et, respectivement, des §§ 8, 9 et 10.[59] Notre texte mis à part, cette traduction apparaît convenable dans d'autres passages de documents administratifs[60] et juridiques éblaïtes: en particulier dans TM.75.G.1444, où l'on trouve la réduplication du terme KU.TU en fonction du pluriel.[61]

4. L'horizon géographique (fig. 1)

Parmi les lieux qui sont mentionnés dans notre texte, il y en a qui sont bien connus, tandis que d'autres ne sont jamais attestés ailleurs. L'activité de Gīda-naʿim se développe entre Mari, Tuttul, Ḫarran et Irʾitum[62] (§§ 1, 4, 6), donc sur la route qui va du Moyen Euphrate jusqu'au Baliḫ et qui touche des villes mineures comme Salbadu[63] (entre Tuttul et Mari, § 7) et Nabraladu[64] (§ 4). Pour les villes de Gadamu[65] (§§ 2, 3) et d'Ušumu (§ 5), où se situent les traffics de Puzra-Malik et des agents-KU.TU, on peut penser à une localisation à l'est de l'Euphrate, mais il n'y a pas d'eléments pour une identification plus précise.

59 Dans *ARET* 9, 13 r. IV 10 on a le passage suivant: 2 dar-áb ŠE+TIN 6 dug / inim-di / KU.TU / en / *Ḫu-ti-mu*[ki], que je propose d'interpréter "2 mésures-d. de bière (et?) 6 jarres pour le porte-parole, agent fiduciaire du roi de Ḫutimu". Pour l'interprétation de inim-di = *dal-da-gi-lum* /taltak(k)irum/, /taštak(k)irum/ "celui qui parle" cf. G. Conti, dans *MiSeb* 3 (1990), pp. 95-96. Il faut distinguer entre KA.DI = *dal-da-gi-lum* et KA.DI II = *ba-a-lu-um, ba-la-lum* /palālum/ "invoquer" (Cf. *ARET* XI, p. 155), comme a été remarqué par M. Bonechi, *MiSEb* 2, p. 135 note 11.

60 Cf. *MEE* 7, 23 r. IV 9-17: (une parure de vêtements et du metal) *A-šum Ur-sá-um*[ki] GIŠ.DUG.DU *wa* ḫi-mu-DU 1 KU.TU *Za-bur-rúm*[ki] "pour A. d'Ursaʾum sont parvenus, et un agent fiduciaire de Zaburrum devra les remettre" (dans le contexte il s'agit de marchands). Voir aussi la note précedante.

61 Voir la note 35. Pour la réduplication du terme cf. aussi TM.75.G.2429 r. XIV 24-27 (photo dans P. Matthiae, *Ebla: un impero ritrovato*, Torino 1989^2, tav. 66): KU.TU KU.TU *Ḫu-sa-um*[ki] *wa Ša-za-bi-ig*[ki].

62 Le royaume d'Irʾitum (probablement l'Irrite/a du deuxième millénaire) était situé au nord-est de Karkamish, dans la région caracterisée par la présence des *badalum*: cf. M. Bonechi *RGTC* 12/1, p. 206, (avec bibliographie précedente) et, pour le contexte géographique, L. Milano - E. Rova, *Ceramic Provinces and Political Borders in Upper Mesopotamia in the Late Early Dynastic Period*, dans *Studi in memoria di L. Cagni*, Napoli 2000, à paraitre.

63 Pour *Sal-ba-ad*[ki] / *Sal-ba-du*[ki] cf. *ARES* 2 (1993), p. 423.

64 C'est la seule attéstation du toponyme avec cette graphie. Cf. la variante *Nab-ra-ra-du*[ki] dans TM.75.G.2429 r. XXII 10.

65 Il n'y a pas d'autres textes d'Ébla où ce toponyme soit attesté. *Ga-da-mu* est attesté pourtant comme nom de personne: *ARET* 3, 197 r. II 5, r. III 2 (dumu-nita G. ugula *La-ša*[ki]); *MEE* 2, 36 v. V 2, 6 (mu-túm G. en / *ma-lik-tum*).

Quant à Kur, dont le nom devrait correspondre ici à une région, plutôt qu'à une ville, il est possible que ce toponyme désigne une zone au nord-est de Mari et de Tuttul,[66] sur le versant sud-occidental du Tûr Abdin: d'après certains textes éblaïtes ce serait le pays d'origine d'une plante particulière (kaskal-SAR).[67] L'association (au § 8) de Kur avec Mari, Harran et ʾAdu – un royaume qui se trouvait au nord-est de Tuttul, sur le Baliḫ[68] – ferait penser à un espace géographique compris entre Mari et le Haut Ḫabur occidental. C'est donc ici que se situe l'affaire des fugitifs, qui se dirigent vers la frontière de Ḫarran pour être ensuite reconduits à Mari par Gīda-naʿim.

Les événements du § 9 ont lieu plus à l'ouest, car le royaume de Ḫalsum[69] est souvent associé à celui d'Irʾitum, et devrait être localisé au nord de ce dernier, les deux faisant partie de la zone caracterisée par la présence des *badalum*.

Pour la localisation de DU (§§ 8, 9, 10), l'hypothèse la plus probable est celle d'une contiguïté à la région de Tuttul,[70] probablement du côté ouest de l'Euphrate, en direction de Ḫalsum: c'est ici, en effet, que se trouvent les agents-KU.TU en charge d'une livraison d'ânes, qui semble être compliquée par la mort des agents mêmes. La référence à un bateau mené par un agent de DU jusqu'à Mari (§ 9) raffforce l'idée d'une localisation fluviale de cette ville.

5. Le lexique du commerce: le sens de til

Au début de cet article on a fait allusion au terme til, occurrant plusieurs fois dans *ARET* 2, 29 comme un des mots-clé qui qualifient des postes de bilan. De ce terme se sont occupés à plusieurs reprises G. Pettinato et F. Pomponio, qui ont abouti à des

---

66 Pour les références cf. M. Bonechi, *RGTC* 12/1, pp. 165-166. Cf. en particulier l'occurrence de Kur^{ki} dans le document des affaires de Ḫazum, *ARET* 2, 32 v. IV 1.

67 Cf. *ARES* 2, p. 330.

68 Dans l'introduction au traité entre Ébla et Abarsal ʾAdu est mentionné comme une cité-état soumise à Ébla. Pour l'histoire de ʾAdu et les événements politiques qui la mettent en rapport avec Mari et Ébla, cf. L. Milano, *Le dossier éblaïte sur l'affaire de ʾAdu*, dans *Eothen* 10 (1999), pp. 133-148.

69 Le toponyme est attesté avec les graphies *Ḫal-sum*^{ki}, *Ḫal-šum*^{ki}, *Ḫal-su*^{ki}: cf. *ARES* 2, pp. 267-269 (où la réference à notre texte est omise, car on propose une lecture *Ti*$_x$*-sum*^{ki}) et M. Bonechi, *RGTC* 12/1, p. 173. En particulier, pour les rapports entre Ḫalsum et Mari, cf. TM.75.2400 (*cit.* dans A. Archi, *Les rapports politiques et économiques entre Ebla et Mari*, dans *MARI* 4 (1985), p. 77: un vêtement LÚxGÁNA*tenû Ma-ri*^{ki} lú *si-in Ḫal-sum*^{ki} DU.DU *mi-nu Sá-bù*^{ki}.

70 Cf. A. Archi, *Tuttul-sur-Baliḫ à l'âge d'Ebla*, dans *Mélanges Kupper* (1990), p. 202. Voir aussi M. Bonechi, *RGTC* 12/1, p. 105.

conclusions tout à fait différentes. Selon le premier, til aurait essentiellement le sens de "mourir" (qualifiant une personne), ou "détruire" (qualifiant une ville),[71] tandis que Pomponio a suggéré le sens de "finir (un voyage), arriver".[72] Dans le contexte spécifique d'*ARET* 2, 29, F. D'Agostino a proposé à son tour la traduction "perdu". Mais justement dans ce contexte, il me paraît préférable d'attribuer à til le sens de "dépenser, utiliser (completement), délivrer", qui peut se référer soit à l'argent, soit à des biens, et qui est bien connu pour *gamāru*, particulièrement dans le lexique commercial des lettres paléo-assyriennes, et dans l'epistolaire amarnien.[73] C'est la même valeur qu'on retrouve en ougaritique pour la racine KLY et pour des locutions comme *d nkly* "qui a été dépensé / épuisé", typiques du langage administratif.[74] Tel que *gamāru* en akkadien, l'emploi de til dans les textes éblaïtes peut avoir des différentes nuances: appliqué à la catégorisation du bétail, par exemple, il sert à distinguer les moutons abattus par rapport à ceux qui sont offerts en sacrifice (udu nídba);[75] mais appliqué à la comptabilité des textiles, il indique des quantités de vêtements qui ont été "déboursés" par l'administration, en opposition aux vêtements "en entrée" (mu-túm), ou "au compte de" (al_6) quelqu'un.[76] La traduction de til par "débourser, déboursement" permet d'interpréter de façon à mon avis convaincante des documents comptables où il s'agit de livraisons d'objets (comme par exemple des poignards, des textiles, de la laine[77]) et de livraisons de personnes, affectées à des tâches déterminées.[78]

---

71 Cf. surtout G. Pettinato, *Nascita, matrimonio, malattia e morte a Ebla*, dans H. Hauptmann - H. Waetzoldt (éd.), *Wirtschaft und Gesellschaft von Ebla*, *cit.*, pp. 311-313.

72 F. Pomponio, *Epidemie e* revenants *a Ebla*, dans *UF* 21 (1989), pp. 301-305.

73 Cf. surtout *CAD* G, p. 26s, b) et c) ; p. 29s b) et c).

74 Cf. L. Milano, *KLY nel lessico amministrativo del semitico di nord-ovest*, dans *Vicino Oriente* 1 (1978), pp. 83-97.

75 Cf. L. Milano, *Distribuzione di bestiame minuto ad Ebla: criteri contabili e implicazioni economiche*, dans *QuSem* 13 (1984), pp. 205-223.

76 Cf. par ex. *ARET* 7, 24 v. II 8-III 5: 83 gu-dùl-TÚG mu-túm 73 gu-dùl-TÚG til 52 gu-dùl-TÚG al_6 ugula engar.

77 Cf. TM.75.G.1669 (*SEb* 2 [1980], pp. 11ss.) où, dans toute une série de postes, des poignards d'or et d'argent sont assignés à des personnages et "déboursés" (til) par un ou deux "préfets des équipes" (ugula é-$duru_5$^{ki}). Cf. aussi TM.75.G.1865 r. V: (poignards d'argent et or pour NP) lú *Iš-má-Da-mu* til *Ma-ri*^{ki} "ce que *I.* a déboursé à Mari"; TM.75.G.2335 r. II 1-5: (objets d'or) níg-ba *I-bí-Zi-kir* lú til *Ma-ri*^{ki} "don d'*I.*, qu'il a déboursé à Mari". Selon Archi, *loc. cit.*, p. 14 til devrait être traduit "finished (operation)", une indication qui serait trop générique pour un compte rendu. Cf. aussi *ARET* 7, 113 r. II 1-4: vêtements et argent NP šu ba_4-ti lú til NP_2, "NP a reçu: ce que NP_2 a déboursé"; *ARET*

Dans les textes qui enregistrent des expéditions commerciales (kaskal-kaskal) til est employé de façon similaire, pour indiquer des dépenses faites par les marchands: un des exemples le plus intéréssant à ce propos est TM.75.G.1928 qui enregistre des quantités d'argent remises à des personnnes, ou bien utilisées pour acheter des objets ou des animaux. Dans certains cas on parle explicitements des expéditions (kaskal) qui fournissent l'occasion des achats, et le colophon specifie qu'il s'agit d'un "compte-rendu des dépenses (effectuées) dans les pays, pour la 7ème année" (dub-gar til-til kalam-*tim* kalam-*tim áš-du* 7 mu).[79] Une expression pareille est fournie par un passage d'un autre texte administratif, où le total de 7 mines d'or est annoté comme une "sortie: le jour qu'Irkab-Damu (le roi d'Ébla) a payé ses 'prix'" (è *in* u_4 *Ìr-kab-Da-mu si-mi* til-*sù*).[80]

Cela dit, il est difficile d'établir si l'emploi de til est lié exclusivement à des transactions commerciales, ou, plus en générale, à n'importe quelle opération de comptabilité. De plus, il faut remarquer que l'interprétation suggerée ici pour til dans certains contextes n'exclue pas, dans des autres contextes, ni des traductions qui se rattachent au sens de base de *gamāru* ("accomplir, méner à terme"),[81] ni la

4, 5 r. VI 2-10: vêtements NP lú til NP_2 *wa* ì-na-sum dumu-nita NP_3 "pour NP: ce que NP_2 a déboursé et que le fils de NP_3 a donné"; *ARET* 8, 542 v. IX 1'-2': [...] lú NP til-*sù*; *MEE* 2, 28 v. I 2-II 3: argent NP šu ba_4-ti *si-in* NL lú til NP_2 "NP a reçu pour NL: ce que NP_2 a déboursé".Voir encore le passage de TM.75.G.1444 mentionné à la note 35. On peut démontrer que dans *ARET* 7, 145 til n'indique pas un "produit ou une surface agricole" (p. 236, s.v. TIL), mais le mot-clé habituel pour "déboursement", referé à des vêtements.

78 Cf. par ex. *ARET* 8, 522 v. IV 4-12: (une parure de vêtements pour NP ...) šeš *Ba-*^{d}*Eš*$_4$*-dar* šu-du_8 *wa* 1 *mi-at* 20 *na-se*$_{11}$ *Ar-mi*^{ki} *wa* 1 *mi-at* 80 *na-se*$_{11}$ *A-ba-tum*^{ki} til *in* uru^{ki}-uru^{ki} *Gú-da-da-núm*^{ki} "le frère de *B.* a pris, et 120 personnes de Armi et 180 personnes de Abatum il a delivré aux villes de Guddanum"; *MEE* 10, 43: 3 *li-im* 2 *mi-at na-se*$_{11}$ til *Ba-da-nu*^{ki} *wa Ma-sa-nu*^{ki} lú *Ib-al*$_6$^{ki} itu *ig-za* "3200 personnes delivrées à *B.* et à *M.* de (la région de) *I.* Mois *i.* ".

79 Cf. le passage suivant du traité entre Ébla et Abarsal (Edzard, *QuSem* 18 [1992], p. 198, § 11), dont l'interprétation n'est pas claire: [...] nu / *ba-li* / kalam-*tim* / al_6-til / gu_4 / áb / níg-du_8 / kalam-*tim* / til /.

80 *MEE* 10, 4 r. VIII 6-11. La traduction donnée par P. Mander et suggeré par G. Pettinato (cf. p. 35) est au contraire la suivante: "expense on the occasion (of) the end of Irakb-Damu's destiny." L'expression *in* u_4 til(.til) NL (cf. Pomponio, *cit.*, *UF* 21, pp. 301-302) est attestée aussi, par ex., dans *ARET* 2, 4 r. VI 6-8; *ARET* 3, 459 r. VI 1ss. et TM.75.G.2508 v. IX 18'-24' "à l'occasion du/des payment(s) à NL".

81 Par ex., dans l'expression níg-AN.AN.AN.AN NP til *in* / *áš-du* NL (et similaires), où l'action définie par níg-AN.AN.AN.AN serait "accomplie" dans/près d'une ville. L'expression est attestée plusieurs fois à propos de remises de vêtements: cf. *ARET* 8, *passim*, *ARET* 3, 167 r. II 2-4; 412 r. II 2'-4'; 470 r. VI 14-VII 2; *ARET* 4, 3 r. VIII 6-12; 10, r. VIII 6-8; *MEE* 2, 1 v. VII 3-5; 37 *passim*. D'autres

possibilité que le signe TIL soit occasionnelement employé dans le sens de úš "mourir".

6. La circulation des biens e l'activité de Gīda-naʿim

Il reste à faire quelques remarques à propos des activités menées par Gīda-naʿim et du type de transactions illustreés par notre texte, qui montrent emblématiquements certains des caractères de la circulation des biens à l'époque d'Ébla.

On a déja parlé d'une probable appartenance du personnage à une catégorie de marchands qui, au cours de leurs activités, pouvaient aussi intervenir dans des matières qui relevaient d'un intérêt politique, comme c'est le cas de la restitution des fugitifs à Mari. Tout cela présuppose un contrôle considérable de l'état sur la gestion des traffics, qui est d'ailleurs demontré par le fait que la comptabilité des expéditions commerciales (celle de Gīda-naʿim y comprise) était gardée dans les archives du palais. On a eu de même l'occasion de souligner que la région dans laquelle se déroule l'activité de Gīda-naʿim et des autres individus mentionnés dans *ARET* 2, 29 est la même où se situe la plupart des traffics commerciaux d'Ébla: notamment, la région entre le Baliḫ, sa confluence avec l'Euphrate et le haut Ḫabur occidental. On peut aussi ajouter que ce texte nous confirme l'existence d'un *réseau* établi par fonctionnaires et marchands, qui se déplacent eux mêmes, ou bien envoient des biens d'une place à une autre par des intermédiaires. Ce qu'il faut noter n'est pas seulement la mobilité des sujets, mais aussi la *décentralisation* des opérations comptables. A coté d'un contrôle effectif sur la provénence et la destination des biens, il y a de la part de l'administration centrale un intérêt spécifique pour le contrôle de *l'espace de l'intermédiation*, du point de vue géographique (les lieux de l'intermédiation), substantiel (types d'opérations comptables) et humain (personnages impliqués). Tout cela peut s'expliquer seulement dans la perspective d'un commerce administré où l'envergure des activités commerciales trouve sa limite naturelle dans le contrôle politique de l'état, et, par conséquent, dans la contrainte effective représentée par des frontières.

Il peut être utile, à ce propos, d'examiner plus en particulier le rôle de Gīda-naʿim par rapport aux opérations qui le regardent, qu'on peut schématiser de la façon suivante:

---

exemples sont cités par Pomponio dans *UF* 21, *cit.*, pp. 302-304, où il suggère que "in questo tipo di contesti TIL indichi uno spostamento del nì-AN.AN.AN.AN verso una città o un individuo" (p. 303).

a) Il est avant tout un intérmediaire dans la gestion du bétail (ì-na-sum / šu ba_4-ti)

§ 1. Il donne à Mari 260 moutons reçus de Ḫarran

§ 4. Il donne à Nabraladu 70 moutons appartenants à Irʾitum

§ 6. Il donne à Minalum de Tuttul 4 boeufs appartenants à la soeur de Minalum, qu'elle a reçu par des agents fiduciaires (KU.TU)

b) Il réalise des transactions pour le compte de tiers contre un remboursément (lul-gu-AG) en argent ou en d'autres biens

§ 5. Il reçoit un remboursément en bétail à Ušumu, probablement par Puzra-Malik

§ 7. Il dépose (níg-du_8) de l'argent d'un fonctionnaire (ir_{11}) mariote à Salbadu

c) Il s'occupe de faire respecter la legalité en ce qui concerne l'activité d'autres marchands, grâce à un statut qui lui est évidemment reconnu par une pluralité de partenaires commerciaux (Mari, Ébla, peut-être ʾAdu)

§ 8. Il confie à Mari des agents fiduciaires (KU.TU) rétenus dans le royaume de ʾAdu et échappés illégalement vers la frontière de Ḫarran

d) Il est en rapport avec d'autres individus qui, comme Puzra-Malik, semblent avoir un type d'activité similaire. En effet, Puzra-Malik reçoit des remboursements en argent pour des livraisons effectuées (§ 3), et donne à son tour des remboursements à Gīda-naʿim pour des livraisons qu'il a evidemment reçues (§5).

L'implication de Gīda-naʿim dans les affaires illustrées aux §§ 2, 9 et 10 n'est pas explicite, mais plausible. En effet, au § 2 on parle d'un achat de sel en échange de 2 mines d'argent effectué par des agents fiduciaires. Du moment qu'au paragraphe précedant il s'agit d'une opération gérée par Gīda-naʿim, il est bien possible que ces fiduciaires dépendent de lui.

La situation présentée aux §§ 8, 9 et 10 est différente, car il s'agit de fiduciaires attachés à des localités spécifiques, notamment les villes de Mari, de DU, de Samuza et la région de Kur. Si dans ces cas un lien directe avec Gīda-naʿim est peu probable, on peut penser cependant à une sorte de contrôle de notre personnage sur leur activité. Les evénéments du § 8, en particulier, ont de ce point de vue des affinités avec ceux du § 10, en s'agissant toujours d'opérations qui ne sont pas menées à bonne fin et qui ont leur conclusion à Mari: dans le premier cas les agents fiduciaires sont en fuite vers Ḫarran, dans le deuxième ils sont tués après avoir au moins partiellement exécuté leur mission. C'est justement Gīda-naʿim qui amène les fugitifs à Mari, et c'est probablement lui même qui s'occupe de ramener à Mari les ânes (avaient-ils une charge?) des agents tués.

7. Une conclusion et un regret

Le rapport sur les activités de Gīda-naʿim nous offre une occasion inattendue de suivre pas à pas la mission et les déplacements d'un haut fonctionnaire éblaïte dans la vallée de l'Euphrate, à une distance considérable de son pays. Dans une région où il est possible d'immaginer une intensité de traffics telle que les textes de Mari nous la montrent à une époque postérieure, Gīda-naʿim avait été chargé par son roi d'un certain nombre de transactions, comprénant la livraison de troupeaux et d'animaux de prix – de boeufs et des ânes-IGI.NITA –, le dépôt d'argent, la riscossion de remboursements et l'intermédiation dans des autres affaires. Ses rapports avec Puzra-Malik et avec des fiduciaires de plusieurs villes de la région de l'Euphrate mettent en lumière un réseau qui a les traits typiques des réseaux commerciaux. En effet, le lexique et les situations illustrées par *ARET* 2, 29 sont tout à fait caractéristiques soit des textes administratifs qui concernent le commerce (comme par exemple les textes qui mentionnent les missions, kaskal-kaskal, des marchands), soit des textes juridiques (comme par exemple les traités) qui s'occupent, dans certains passages, du même sujet.

Dans le rapport sur l'activité de Gīda-naʿim il ne s'agit pas d'une circulation de biens de luxe, métaux ou produits exotiques, qui, comme on l'a rémarqué au début, ne sont pas considérés d'habitude dans la comptabilité des marchands. Il s'agit, au contraire, de livraisons d'animaux, de quantités de sel qui voyagent sur des bateaux, de payements en argent: le tout melé à des accidents de parcours (fuite et mort des agents KU.TU), qui se sont probablement passés pendant une seule mission du marchand.

On aimerait bien lire, dans le colophon de ce texte, la rubrique: dub-gar til-til *Gi-da-na-im in* u_4 kaskal-*sù*. Malheurésement, le scribe nous a nié cette pièce d'évidence, qui aurait confirmé le cadre d'ensemble. C'est à nous, donc, d'y croire ou pas.

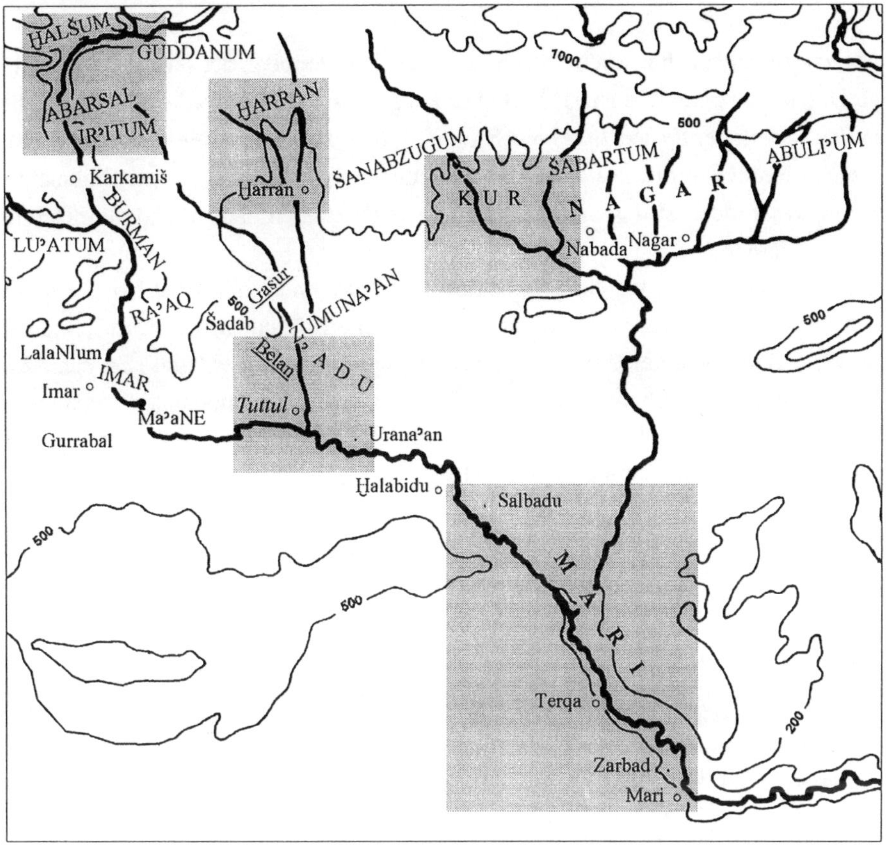

Fig. 1. La Syrie de l'est d'après les textes d'Ébla et les zones interessées par les traffics de Gīda-naʿim.

GRAMMATISCHE ATAVISMEN IN SEMITISCHEN SPRACHEN[1]

Hans-Peter Müller

Münster

Atavismen begegnen in allen Sprachen und in allen Perioden der jeweiligen Sprachgeschichte. Ihre Ursache ist das Fortleben älterer Formative entweder als Fossile, die in den jeweiligen Systemzusammenhang eingehen und darum selbst einer synchronischen Betrachtungsweise allenfalls als Redundanz auffallen, oder als Rudimente, die im synchronen System nutzlos oder gar dysfunktionell bleiben und nur diachronisch erklärbar sind.[2]

Im folgenden werden einige grammatische Atavismen in semitischen Sprachen bezeichnet, die schwer verständliche grammatische Phänomene in diesen erklärbar machen. Damit soll ein Gelehrter geehrt werden, dessen hohes Verdienst nicht zuletzt im Bereich der Semitistik liegt, von der ugaritischen Phonologie angefangen (1955) über "Studi sul lessico comune semitico" (1964-1971) bis hin zur eblaitischen Sprache, Religion und Literatur (1979 ff.).

---

1 Bibliographische Abkürzungen nach W. von Soden, *Akkadisches Handwörterbuch* (= *AHw*) III, Wiesbaden 1981, IX -XVI. Ferner werden gebraucht:

- *ARET*	*Archivi reali di Ebla. Testi*, Roma 1981 ff.
- *BZ*	*Biblische Zeitschrift*, Paderborn.
- *BZAW*	*Beihefte zur Zeitschrift für die alttestamentliche Wissenschaft*, Berlin - New York.
- *HAL*	L. Köhler u.a., *Hebräisches und aramäisches Lexikon zum Alten Testament* 1-5, Leiden ^{3}1967-1995.
- *HO*	*Handbuch der Orientalistik*, Leiden.
- *KAI*	H. Donner - W. Röllig, *Kanaanäische und aramäische Inschriften* 1-3, Wiesbaden ^{2}1967-1969.
- Krael	E. G. Kraeling, *The Brooklyn Museum Aramaic Papyri*, New Haven 1953.
- *MEE*	*Materiali epigrafici di Ebla* (Istituto universitario orientale di Napoli. Seminario di studi asiatici. Series maior), Napoli 1979 ff.
- *VT*	*Vetus Testamentum*, Leiden.
- *WZ*	*Wissenschaftliche Zeitschrift.*
- *ZAH*	*Zeitschrift für Althebraistik*, Stuttgart u.a. 1988 ff.
- *ZAW*	*Zeitschrift für die alttestamentliche Wissenschaft*, Berlin - New York.

GAG wird nach der 3., ergänzten Auflage von 1995 zitiert.

2 Zur Unterscheidung sprachlicher 'Fossile' und 'Rudimente' vgl. Vf., "Zur Theorie der historisch vergleichenden Grammatik dargestellt am sprachgeschichtlichen Kontext des Althebräischen", in: A. S. Kaye (ed.), *Semitic Studies in honor of Wolf Leslau*, Wiesbaden 1991, 1100-1118, bes. 1100.

1. Phonologie: mehrfache [*L*]- *und* [*R*]-*Laute*[3]

Scheinbare Unregelmäßigkeiten in der Schreibung von [*L*]- und [*R*]-Lauten im Eblaitischen erklären sich m. E. am leichtesten, wenn man annimmt, daß es im ältesten Semitischen mehr als einen [*L*]- und [*R*]-Laut gab; mindestens ein zweifacher [*L*]-Laut lebt auch in jüngeren semitischen Sprachen fort.

a. Der häufige Wechsel *< *r* > > < *l* > in der eblaitischen Schrift, etwa in *ma-ḫi-la* für *[*maḫira*] "er hat empfangen" TM. 75.G.1782 VIII 1 (*ARET* II, 21), läßt vermuten, daß es neben velarem [*r*] ein apikoalveolares [*r*] gab,[4] das mit einem ebenfalls apikoalveolaren [*L*]-Laut leicht verwechselt werden konnte. – Eine solche Vermutung suggeriert umgekehrt, da [*R*]- und [*L*]-Laute eng verwandte Sonorlaute (Liquide) sind, das Vorhandensein zweier [*L*]-Phoneme: neben dem apikoalveolaren [*l*] kann es einen anderen [*L*]-Laut gegeben haben, der einem Wechsel < *l* > > < Ø > unterlag; so würde sich der Fortfall von < *l* > am Silbenanfang, etwa bei < *a* > für *[*la*], < *um* > für *[*lum*], gelegentlich auch am Silbenende, etwa bei < *ḫa* > für *[*ḫal*], erklären.[5] Der zweite [*L*]-Laut könnte ein lateralalveolares [*l*], wie wir es aus dem Englischen kennen, oder ein (semi)vokalisches [*l̥*] sein, das insbesondere am Silbenanfang wegen der geringen artikulatorischen Stärke der betreffenden Laute in der Schrift fortgefallen wäre. – Rechnen wir mit [*l̥*], so legt sich zugleich der Gedanke an (semi)vokalisches, silbenbildendes [*r̥*] nahe, zumal wir beides aus einigen slawischen Sprachen und aus dem Altindischen kennen.[6] Aus dem Vorhandensein eines silbenbildenden [*r̥*] erklärt sich der Wechsel [*r̥*] > [*ā*], vielleicht in eblaitisch *ma-ʾà-um* für [*maʾāʾum*] < *[*mar̥āʾum*] "Herr (sein, besitzen)" von der Wurzel *mr̥ʾ*

---

3 Vgl. zum folgenden für die Einzelnachweise und für weitere Details Vf., "Eblaitische Konjugation in Kontexten und Personennamen", in: A. Archi (ed.), *Eblaite Personal Names and Semitic Name-Giving* (*Archivi reali di Ebla. Studi* 1), Roma 1988, 71-87, hier 72-78; ders., "Die aramäische Inschrift von Tel Dan", *ZAH* 8, 1995, 121-139, bes. 126-133. - Zu "weakness of the liquids" im Eblaitischen und allgemein im Semitischen vgl. jetzt E. Lipiński, *Semitic Languages. Outline of a Comparative Grammar* (*Orientalia Lovaniensia Analecta* 80), Leuven 1997, 133f.

4 Zum Wechsel [*R*] > [*L*] im Eblaitischen vgl. P. Fronzaroli, "L'interferenza linguistica nella Siria settentrionale del III millennio", in: R. Ajello (ed.), *Interferenza linguistica. Atti del convegno della società italiana di glottologia*, Perugia, 24 e 25 aprile 1977, Pisa 1978, 36-43.

5 Vgl. Vf., "Eblaitische Konjugation" (Anm. 3), 73[6]; G. Conti, *Il sillabario della quarta fonte della lista lessicale bilingue eblaita*, in: P. Fronzaroli (ed.), *Miscellanea Eblaitica*, 3, Firenze 1990, 34, zu < *r* > 32 f.

6 Vgl. M. Mayrhofer, *Sanskrit-Grammatik mit sprachvergleichenden Erörterungen*, Berlin - New York 1987, § 12.

(= ^{d}en VE 800)[7] oder sicherer in *wa-ʾà-um* für [*w̯aʾāʾum*] < *[*w̯ar̥āʾum*] "führen" (= šu-ra VE 506; vgl. *ta-lá*-PI [*tar̥āʾu*] oder [*tar̥āw̯u*] VE 1339) und zu [*l̥*] > [*ā*] *ʾà-a-ku*$_{17}$(TIK)*-um* für [*haʾākum*] < *[*hal̥ākum*] (= al-du VE 984, vgl. 635.1000, ferner *a-a*-GÚM = al-du 984 und *a-a-ku*$_{17}$(TIK)(*-um*) *li-sa-nu* = eme-lá 073).[8]

b. Die hier versuchsweise aufgezählten Merkmale des Altsemitischen vermögen eine Reihe von auffälligen Tatbeständen in jüngeren semitischen Sprachen zu erklären und damit rückbezüglich die bleibende Unsicherheit der eblaitischen Befunde kompensieren.

Dem eblaitischen Wechsel [*R*] > [*L*] entspricht im Hebräischen der Wechsel in *ʾarmôn* neben seltenerem, also wohl abgeleitetem *ʾalmôn*, beides "Palast", *ʾrr* neben seltenerem *ʾlh* I, bei gemeinsamen Wurzelkonsonanten *ʾr* / *ʾl*, beides "fluchen", *ʿrm* Niphʿal "sich sammeln" Ex 15,8 neben *ʿlm* III Hitpaʿʿel "sich häufen" Hi 6,16b (Vulgata: *inruit*), wenn *ʿlm* mit A. Fitzgerald als Dialektvariante zu *ʿrm* aufzufassen ist,[9] u.a. Häufiger freilich ist im Semitischen der Wechsel [*L*] > [*R*],[10] auch beim Übergang von Fremdwörtern aus einer semitischen Sprache in eine andere. In vielen, wenn nicht den meisten Fällen ist die Richtung des Wechsels nicht auszumachen.

Insbesondere aus silbenbildendem [*l̥*] im Unterschied zu einem oder mehreren anderen [*L*]-Laut(en) erklärt sich der Wechsel [*l̥*] > [*â*] in aramäischen Bildungen wie *jsq* "er stieg auf" Tel Dan 2 (vgl. *ʾässâq* Ps 139,8, aramäisches Haphʿel *hassiqu* Dan 3,22 und Hophʿal *hussaq* 6,24) von einer Wurzel *sl̥q* und *jhk* "er ging" Tel Dan 3 (vgl. *wjhk* ebd. 5, *jᵉhâk* Esr 6,5, *mᵉhâk* 7,13) von einer Wurzel *hl̥k*. Aus dem Phönizischen ist möglicherweise *tk* [*tâk*] < *[*tiʾâk*] < *[*tihâk*] "sie ging" KAI 26 A II 5

7 Vgl. F. Vattioni, "L'aramaico è attestato a Ebla?", in: L. Cagni (ed.), *Il bilinguismo a Ebla* (Istituto universitario orientale. Dipartimento di studi asiatici. Series minor XXII), Napoli 1984, 257-266, hier 263 (Lit.); anders Conti, aaO. (Anm. 5), 192. Zur Verbreitung der Wurzel *mrʾ* im Semitischen vgl. die Isoglossen in *AHw* 615 f. (akkadisch seit dem aAK!) und *HAL* 1740.

8 Die Stabilität von [*l̥*] in dem Partizip *ʾà-lik* "gehend" TM.75.G.1443 Rs. III 9 (vgl. *ʾà:lik* G. 1233 Rs. IX, ferner *il-iš-ʾà-lik MEE* 2, 1980, Register S. 344b) liegt wohl daran, daß [*l̥*] hier nicht zwischen den beiden ihm homogenen Vokalen [*a* - *a*] steht.

9 "The interchange of *L*, *N* and *R* in Biblical Hebrew", *JBL* 97, 1978, 481-488. - Zu arabischen Beispielen vgl. C. Brockelmann, *Grundriß der vergleichenden Grammatik der semitischen Sprachen* I, Berlin 1908, § 48 c (vgl. 84 b.2a); R. Růžička, *Konsonantische Dissimilation in den semitischen Sprachen*, Leipzig 1909, 17-23, u.v.a.

10 Beispiele hierfür und für das unmittelbar folgende bei Vf., "Eblaitische Konjugation" (Anm. 3), 76.

von *(j)l̥k* zu vergleichen[11] – neben *wjlk* ebd. II 19, worin < *l* > erhalten blieb; der Wechsel [*l̥*] > [*â*] wäre dann nicht auf das Aramäische beschränkt.

c. Die unter 1b aufgezählten Tatbestände in jüngeren semitischen Sprachen stellen zumindest innersemitisch Atavismen dar: ein differenzierter Bestand von [*L*]- und [*R*]-Lauten ließ sich schon in Ebla, vollends aber später nicht mehr graphemisch darstellen, vielleicht auch schon nicht mehr phonemisch unterscheiden;[12] aramäisches *j*^{e}*hâq* u.ä. macht wahrscheinlich, daß einzelne der früher unterschiedenen Laute, also [*l̥*] im Gegensatz zu [*l*], jetzt auch phonemisch fortfielen. Wenn einige der differenten [*L*]- und [*R*]-Laute im Eblaitischen auch auf phonetischen Einfluß des Sumerischen zurückgehen können,[13] so zeigen doch das Vorhandensein von (semi)vokalischem [*l̥*] und [*r̥*] u.a. im Altindischen sowie Übereinstimmungen zwischen Fällen von innerindogermanischen und solchen innersemitischen Lautwandels,[14] daß die Phonologie der ältesten semitischen Sprachen Berührungen mit der der indogermanischen Sprachen aufweist, was das Recht des Begriffs des 'Nostratischen' für das Semitisch-Hamitisch-Indogermanische bestärkt.

2. *Pronomina*

a. Das Femininmorphem [*i*]. – Das im Pronominalbereich und in davon abhängigen Konjugationsformen begegnende Femininmorphem [*i*] steht in der semitischen Morphologie isoliert da. Es findet sich im selbständigen Personalpronomen 2. fem. sing. in akkadisch *attī*, hebräischem K^{e}tîb *ʾtj* Jdc 17,2, arabisch *ʾanti* und Isoglossen sowie in der 3. fem. sing. in akkadisch *šī*, hebräisch *hîʾ*, arabisch *hija* und Isoglos-

11 So unter Voraussetzung der Worttrennung *ʾšt tk lḥd/j dl plkm* "eine Frau ging allein mit Spindeln" entsprechend dem bildluwischen Text; anders M. Heltzer, *Anuario de filologia* 8, Barcelona 1982, 171-175.

12 Vgl. zum Akkadischen *GAG* § 8e (mit Verweisen), 34a, 35a.

13 So zitiert M.-L. Thomsen (*The Sumerian Language* [*Mesopotamia* 10], Kopenhagen 1984, § 28) im Blick auf die Alternanz von [*l*] und [*r*] im Sumerischen einen Satz von A. Cavigneaux: "wenn man /*r*/ als primär ansetzt ..., muß es sich um alveolares /*r*/ handeln (bei einem velaren /*r*/ wäre die Verwechselung mit /*l*/ nicht zu erklären)". An apikoalveolares [*r*] läßt sich auch denken, wenn im Sumerischen aus Ebla din-gi-li für *dingir "Gott" steht; vgl. G. Pettinato, *OrAnt* 18, 1979, 333: 10//22.

14 Ein Wechsel [*r̥*] > [*L*] liegt etwa vor, wenn altindisches *pr̥thu* "breit" griechisch als πλατύς erscheint (vgl. Mayrhofer, aaO. [Anm. 6], § 12), was den o.g. Fällen von innersemitischem Wechsel [*R*] > [*L*] entspricht. - Daß es auch im Lateinischen lateralalveolares [*l*] gegeben haben muß, zeigen Wechsel wie *altus* > *haut, falsus* > *faux* u.ä.; vgl. M. Schubiger, *Einführung in die Phonetik*, Berlin - New York 1977, 78.

sen; im Plural entsprechen ihm im Akkadischen 2. fem. *attina* und 3. fem. *šina*. [*i*] kehrt in den akkadischen Pronominalsuffixen 2. fem. sing., 2. fem. pl. und 3. fem. pl. wieder, wobei wir auf die Aufzählung von Isoglossen verzichten können. – Derivate sind akkadisches [*ī*] beim Imperativ (= Imp.) fem. sing.[15] und in den Präformativkonjugationen (= PKK, sing. PK) 2. sing. fem. (*taprusī* u. ä.). In der akkadischen Afformativkonjugation (= AK) findet sich [*i*] in der 2. fem. sing. [-*āti*] und der 2. fem. pl. [-*ātina*], nicht dagegen in der 3. fem. pl., wo mit [-*ā*] die Dualendung eingetreten ist.

Ein Femininmorphem [*i*] findet sich auch beim altindischen Nomen, insbesondere beim Adjektiv.[16] Offenbar liegt also auch in der Gemeinsamkeit von rezessivem [*i*] für Fem. ein nostratisches Erbe vor.

b. Das Femininmorphem /-*na*/. – Als isoliert erscheint weiterhin [-*na*] im akkadischen, hebräischen und arabischen fem. pl., und zwar sowohl beim selbständigen Personalpronomen (akkadisch 2. fem. pl. *attina*, 3. fem. pl. *šina*; hebräisch *ʾattēnā* > *ʾattēn, hēnā*; arabisch *ʾantunna, hunna*) und in den entsprechenden Pronominalsuffixen, als auch im Imp. fem. pl. und in den PKK 2. und 3. fem. pl.;[17] im Arabischen ist [-*na*] in der 2./3. fem. pl. – anders als [-*na*] nach [-*ī*] in der 2. fem sing. und nach [-*ū*] in der 2./3. masc. pl. – nicht auf den Indikativ (im Gegensatz zu Subjunktiv und Apokopat) beschränkt. Offenbar also ist [-*na*] als Markierung der 2./3. fem. pl. von [-*na*] als Indikativmarkierung der 2. fem. sing. und der 2./3. masc. pl. im Reichsaramäischen und Arabischen genetisch zu unterscheiden.[18]

Im Akkadischen ist beim Imp. fem. pl. und in den PKK der 2./3. fem. pl. [-*na*] nach [-*ā*] sekundär ausgefallen.

---

15 Vgl. zum rudimentären [-*i*] für Imp. fem. sing. im Koptischen E. Edel, *Altägyptische Grammatik*, Roma 1955, § 660 und 661 Anm. 1.

16 Vgl. Mayrhofer, aaO. (Anm. 6), § 41.45.49.50.52.

17 Zu [-*i*] und [-*nà*] für 2. fem. sing. (*ti-dbil-i*) und 2./ 3. pl. (*ti-dbil-nà* / *ʾi-dbil-nà*) einer beja-kuschitischen PK vgl. A. Zaborski, *Studies in Hamito-Semitic I: The Verb in Cushitic*, Krakau 1975, 13.

18 Zum Pronominalsuffix -*ṯn* 2. fem. sing. und pl. mit -*ṯnj* für Dual und dem entsprechenden enklitischen Pronomen im Ägyptischen vgl. Edel, aaO. (Anm. 15), § 159, bes. bb, § 166, bes. cc.

3. Trennung von Nomen und Verb

Daß das Verb sich vorgeschichtlich erst relativ spät vom Nomen getrennt hat,[19] geht aus seiner vielfältigeren Verwendbarkeit, d.h. seiner geringeren Spezifizität, hervor: morphologisch gibt es vor allem in älteren semitischen Sprachen, etwa dem Akkadischen, vom Nomen (in der bezeugten Sprache freilich am häufigsten vom Adjektiv) sowohl Deklinations- als auch Konjugationsformen;[20] syntaktisch kann das Nomen – und das Partizip als nominale Ableitung vom Verb – ebenfalls im Gegensatz zum Verb als Subjekt, Prädikat, Objekt einschließlich anderer Adverbiale, und als Attribut gebraucht werden. Das älteste und elementarste sprachliche Kommunikationsmedium, nämlich dasjenige für die Appellfunktionen und den emotionsgeladenen Ausdruck, ist das Nomen als Holophrase ('Einwortsatz'); es fungiert als solches noch hinter Aufmerksamkeitserregern wie hebräisch *hinnē*, arabisch *ʾinna* "siehe" u.ä.[21] Der Infinitiv (= Inf.) als 'Nomen actionis' repräsentiert einen Übergang von Nomen und Verb und hat so an der Vielfalt der nominalen Verwendungsmöglichkeiten Anteil; die einfachsten Formen des semitischen Inf., also etwa der hebräische Inf. constructus, sind wie der oft lautgleiche Imp. masc. sing. das Formativ mit der

---

19 Daß "in der primitiveren Sprache" und in der Syntax der Sprache des Kleinkindes die Nominalbildung bzw. das nominale Syntagma aufgrund der größeren Bedeutung gegenständlicher Vorstellungen überwiegt, hat schon W. Wundt (*Völkerspychologie* II/2, Leipzig ^{3}1912, 314-320) erkannt. Vgl. für den Ablauf des frühkindlichen Spracherwerbs die differenzierteren Beobachtungen zum Nomen, zur attributiven Nominalphrase und zu zweiteiligen (dyadischen) Sätzen mit den nun eine eigene Kategorie bildenden Verben, mit prädikativen Adjektiven und schließlich auch prädikativen Substantiven R. Jakobson, *Der grammatische Aufbau der Kindersprache* (Rheinisch-Westfälische Akademie der Wissenschaften, Vorträge. G 218), Düsseldorf 1977, bes. 11 f. 15-17.21, zum prädikativen Nominalsatz vgl. den Diskussionsbeitrag von H. Gipper ebd. 18 f. - Freilich wird man heute mit einer Analogie von sprachlicher Phylogenese und Ontogenese vorsichtiger umgehen, als es Wundt tat, und in bezug auf die sprachliche Ontogenese beachten, daß die kreative Entwicklung der Kindersprache von der Nachahmung der Erwachsenensprache unterlaufen wird: die Eigengesetzlichkeit der sprachlichen Entwicklung wirkt hier bei der Nachahmung selektiv, wobei sich die in der Eigengesetzlichkeit angelegte Synchronie gegenüber der Diachronie des Außeneinflusses geltend macht; bei den phylogenetisch älteren, 'archaischen' Sprachen gibt es für die letztere dagegen keine Analogie.

20 Vgl. zum Akkadischen und Hebräischen Vf., "Die Konjugation von Nomina im Althebräischen", *ZAW* 96, 1984, 245-263, zum Eblaitischen und Hebräischen ders., "Ebla und das altsemitische Verbalsystem", *Biblica* 65, 1984, 145-167.

21 Vgl. Vf. "Die Konstruktionen mit *hinnē* "siehe" und ihr sprachgeschichtlicher Hintergrund", *ZAH* 2, 1989, 45-76. Zur übergeneralisierten Holophrase im Spracherwerb des Kleinkindes vgl. nach dem Vorangang von H. E. Lenneberg, R. Jakobson, aaO. (Anm. 19), 11.25, u.v.a. E. Oksaar, "Spracherwerb und Kindersprache in evolutiver Sicht", in: A. Peisl - A. Mohler (edd.), *Der Mensch und seine Sprache*, Frankfurt M. u.a. 1979, 145- 166, hier 159 f.

geringstmöglichen Anzahl morphematischer Bestandteile und ursprünglich kurzen Vokalen;[22] der Imp. scheint das älteste verbale Kommunikationsmedium zu sein, von dem die PKK morphologisch ausgehen.

Der morphologischen Trennung von Nomina und Verben entspricht syntaktisch diejenige von Nominal- und Verbalsätzen, wobei wir unter Nominalsätzen Sätze ohne finites Verb verstehen. Die Nominalsätze, jetzt auf bestimmte Funktionen beschränkt, eröffnen Möglichkeiten des Darstellens, ohne auf die Verwendung einer Wortklasse Verb angewiesen zu sein, und repräsentieren als solche einen sonst überwundenen Entwicklungsstatus der Sprache. Nominale Einwortsätze können adverbiell subordiniert werden: *ʿäräb* "wenn es Abend ist", *ûbōqär* "und wenn es Morgen ist" Ex 16,6 f.,[23] jeweils ohne *b*ᵉ-, aber mit folgendem Wāw apodoseos.

4. Ergativische und akkusativische Morphosyntax[24]

a. Die Konjugation von Nomina ist in den semitisch-hamitischen Sprachen, wie vor allem das Akkadische und das Ägyptische zeigen, von der beschreibenden Afformativkonjugation ausgegangen; entsprechend bleibt die akkadische Konjugation von Substantiven weithin auf die AK, den Stativ, beschränkt. Die der beschreibenden Funktion eigene Aktiv-Passiv-Neutralität hat zur Folge, daß beim Übergang der AK auf fientische Verben passivische transitive Verben im Akkadischen, Ägyptischen u.a., in Resten auch noch im Hebräischen,[25] morphologisch ebenso behandelt werden wie aktivische intransitive Verben: akkadisches *parṣāku* "über mich ist entschieden" und *balṭāku* "ich lebe" haben die gleiche morphologische Struktur, was an Ergativsprachen erinnert,[26] wie wir sie unter anderem in Afrika finden;[27] wenn die

---

22 Altertümlich sind wohl auch die zahlreichen Typen von Nomina actionis mit [*t*]-Präfix im Semitischen (vgl. zum Akkadischen *GAG* § 56k-m), wobei viele eblaitische Beispiele gleichzeitig [*ta*]-Infixe enthalten, was in keiner jüngeren semitischen Sprache wieder vorkommt; vgl. Vf., "Eblaitische Konjugation in Personennamen und Kontexten", in: L. Cagni (ed.), *Ebla 1975-1985. Dieci anni di studi linguistici e filologici* (Istituto universitario orientale. Dipartimento di studi asiatici. Series minor XXVII), Napoli 1987, 101-122, hier 117 ff.

23 Vgl. C. Brockelmann, *Hebräische Syntax*, Neukirchen 1956, § 13a.

24 Vgl. zum folgenden für die Einzelnachweise und weitere Details Vf., "Ergativelemente im akkadischen und althebräischen Verbalsystem", *Biblica* 66, 1985, 385-417; ders., "Ergative Constructions in Early Semitic Languages", *JNES* 54, 1995, 261-271.

25 Vgl. Vf., "Das Bedeutungspotential der Afformativkonjugation", *ZAH* 1, 1988, 74-98.159-190.

26 Zur Verbindung des Afroasiatischen mit Kaukasussprachen in der Gemeinsamkeit einer ursprünglichen bzw. rezenten ergativischen Syntax vgl. I. M. Diakonoff, *Semitic-Hamitic Languages*, Moskau 1965; ders., *Afrasian Languages*, Moskau 1988, bes. 59-61.

Semiten im 4. Jt. vor Chr. aus Nordafrika über Syrien-Palästina nach Mesopotamien kamen, wo sie das älteste semitische Stratum im Sumerischen und die von W. von Soden so genannten 'nordsemitischen' Elemente des Eblaitischen, Altamurritischen, Ugaritischen u.ä. hinterließen,[28] besteht auch ein historischer Zusammenhang.

Die vom Imp. ausgehenden PKK vorwiegend fientischer Verben fügten sich wohl von vornherein in eine akkusativische Morphosyntax; zusammen mit der ursprünglich ergativischen AK fientischer Verben entsteht so ein System 'gespaltener Ergativität', wie wir es aus vielen Sprachen kennen.[29] Unter syntaktischem Einfluß der mit einem direkten Objekt verbundenen ägyptischen *sḏm.f*-Bildungen bzw. der semitischen PKK auf die AK ergab sich schon früh, etwa im Ägyptischen des Alten Reichs sowie dem Frühmittelägyptischen[30] und im Altbabylonischen,[31] eine aktivisch-präteritale Funktion der AK: aus dem "Stativ" wird, zugleich durch Metonymie, das "Perfekt", das den perfektiven Aspekt mit der punktualen Aktionsart und dem präteritalen Tempus verbindet.[32] In jüngeren semitischen Sprachen wie dem Hebräischen gibt es nun für das Präteritum rudimentär und redundant zwei konkurrentielle Ausdrucksmöglichkeiten, die AK fientischer Verben und die Kurzform der PK (= PKKF, konventionell: 'Imperfectum consecutivum'), meist, aber nicht immer mit *wa-*. Die ältere ergativische Struktur wird auf abgeleitete Stämme, etwa das hebräische Niph'al mit Isoglossen,[33] abgedrängt und wirkt im System als Fossil.

---

27 Vgl. Lipiński, aaO. (Anm. 3), 24 u.ö., auch zur Ergativität im Afroasiatischen.

28 Vgl. Vf., "Zur Bildung der Verbalwurzeln im Eblaitischen", in: H. Hauptmann - H. Waetzoldt (edd.), *Wirtschaft und Gesellschaft von Ebla* (*Heidelberger Studien zum Alten Orient* 2), Heidelberg 1988, 279-289, hier 286 ff.

29 Vgl. etwa E. A. Moravcik, "On the distribution of ergative and accusative patterns", *Lingua* 45, 1978, 233-279, zum Sumerischen Thomsen, aaO. (Anm. 13), § 38-43 (Lit.).

30 Vgl. Vf., "Wie alt ist das jungsemitische Perfekt? Zum semitisch-ägyptischen Sprachvergleich", in: H. Altenmüller - D. Wildung (edd.), *Festschrift W. Helck* (*Studien zur altägyptischen Kultur* 11), Hamburg 1984, 365-379.

31 Vgl. M. B. Rowton, "The use of the permansive in Classic Babylonian", *JNES* 21, 1962, 233-303; J. Huehnergard, ""Stative", predicative form, pseudoverb", *JNES* 46, 1987, 215-232.

32 A. Loprieno (*Das Verbalsystem im Ägyptischen und im Semitischen* [*Göttinger Orientforschungen* IV 17], Wiesbaden 1986, bes. 38-50, 144-146) sucht nach einer gemeinsamen Basis für den ergativischen Gebrauch des stativischen Aspekts und den akkusativischen Gebrauch des perfektischen Tempus und findet sie im gemeinsamen Merkmal der 'Perfektivität'; der enge Zusammenhang zwischen perfektivem Aspekt und Passiv sei umgekehrt "eine der bedeutendsten indogermanisch-afroasiatischen Isoglossen" (42).

33 Vgl. Vf., *ZAW* 96 (Anm. 20), 258-260, vor allem ders., *Biblica* 66 (Anm. 24), 404-410.

b. Die ergativische Morphosyntax, der ein Wirklichkeitsverständnis vom *patiens* (Handlungs- und Wahrnehmungsobjekt) her entspricht, für die also das *patiens* die merkmallose, selbstverständliche, das *agens* (Handlungsträger) die merkmalhafte Instanz ist, die durch das Ergativmorphem markiert werden muß, ist gegenüber der akkusativischen Morphosyntax wohl weltweit die ältere Struktur; in den nostratischen Sprachen stellt sie einen Atavismus dar, der Systemwidersprüche zeitigt.[34] Aus einer ergativischen Substruktur erklären sich, was ich an anderen Stellen gezeigt habe,[35] eine Reihe sonst schwer interpretierbarer Phänomene in verschiedenen Grammatikbereichen, die sich auf die semitischen Sprachen bis in diejenigen der Gegenwart verteilen.

5. Kurzform und Langform der Präformativkonjugation (PKKF und PKLF)

Die präteritale PKKF ohne *wa-* findet sich im Hebräischen vor allem in der für sprachliche Atavismen anfälligen Personennamengebung, aber auch in der Poesie und in besonderen Konstruktionen, selbst der Prosa.[36] Semantisch verwirklicht sie den perfektiven Aspekt, die punktuale Aktionsart und das präteritale Tempus;[37] darin entspricht sie der fientisch-akkusativisch gebrauchten AK, dem 'Perfekt'. Umgekehrt ist die Reihung von AKK in der Erzählung, die die eben genannte Redundanz ausschließt, auch im Hebräischen keine auf Einfluß des Aramäischen zurückgehende späte Innovation.[38]

---

34 Morphosemantische Beispiele bei Vf., *JNES* 54 (Anm 24), 270 f.

35 Vgl. *Biblica* 66 (Anm. 24); *ZAH* 1 (Anm. 25); *ZAH* 2 (Anm. 21), 50-62; *JNES* 54 (Anm. 24), zuletzt: "Zu den semitisch-hamitischen Konjugationssystemen", *ZAH* 11, 1998, 140-152, bes. 142-145.

36 Vgl. Vf., Zur Theorie (Anm. 2), 1101 f.; zum weitgehenden promiscue-Gebrauch von PK und AK G. Bergsträßer, *Hebräische Grammatik II: Verbum*, Leipzig 1929, § 6i, zu "marginal uses" der präteritalen PK(KF) R. S. Hendel, "In the margins of the Hebrew verbal system", *ZAH* 9, 1996, 152-181, zu *ʾāz* + PK S. 160.

37 Zur Vielfalt der Funktionen semitischer Konjugationsthemen vgl. Vf., "Polysemie im semitischen und hebräischen Konjugationssystem", *Or.* 55, 1986, 365-389; zum Ineinandergreifen von Aspekt, Aktionsart und Tempus Vf., *ZAH* 11 (Anm. 35).

38 Vgl. R. Meyer, "Auffallender Erzählstil in einem angeblichen Auszug aus der "Chronik der Könige von Juda"", in: J. Herrmann (ed.), *Festschrift F. Baumgärtel*, Erlangen 1959, 114-123; Vf., *ZAH* 1 (Anm. 25), 170; W. von Soden, "Gab es im vorexilischen Hebräisch Aramaismen in der Bildung und der Verwendung von Verbformen?", *ZAH* 4, 1991, 32-45, wonach die *w*^{e}-AK (das 'Perfectum copulativum') "eine auf den Stativ zurückgehende habitative Vergangenheitsform" darstellt, die mit dem Narrativ (scil. dem 'Imperfectum consecutivum') "nicht funktionsgleich ist und auch im nachexilischen Hebräisch ... nicht an dessen Stelle tritt" (45).

Die Langform der PK (=PKLF) ist im Hebräischen im Grundstamm der Verben II und III inf. und im Hiph'il der starken Verben von der Kurzform zu unterscheiden, nämlich bei Verba II inf. durch die Länge des zweiten, bei Verba III inf. durch die Länge des dritten, in beiden Fällen vokalischen Radikals,[39] im Hiph'il starker Verben durch Länge des Stammvokals.[40]

Die aus dem Akkadischen bekannte *iparras*-Struktur für die durative Aktionsart, den imperfektiven Aspekt und das präsentisch-futurische Tempus mit Länge des zweiten Radikals ist hebräisch im Pi''el einiger Durativverben erhalten geblieben, da hier ebenfalls Längung des zweiten Radikals stattfindet: neben die PK konnte nun eine AK treten, so daß es wieder zwei 'Tempora' mit den betreffenden Konnotationen (Aspekten, Aktionsarten) gab;[41] innerhalb des Pi''el stellt die durative Funktion einen Atavismus dar. Die Kategorien 'Tempus' und 'Stamm' können sich ursprünglich aber auch fließend verhalten haben: diachronisch kann in den semitisch-hamitischen Sprachen sowohl 'Temporalisierung' einer Stämmedifferenz, als auch Übergang von 'Tempora' zu Stämmen vorliegen.[42]

---

39 Da bei Verba II inf. der zweite Radikal ursprünglich lang ist, erscheint hier eher die PKLF im Vergleich mit der PKKF als die merkmallosere Form. - Das Gleiche gilt von Verba III inf., wenn auch hier mit ursprünglicher Kürze des dritten, vokalischen Radikals gerechnet werden muß; vgl. J. Wellhausen, "Über einige Arten schwacher Verben im Hebräischen", in: *Skizzen und Vorarbeiten* 6, Berlin 1899, 250-260, bes. 257.259. Dafür spricht, daß der dritte Radikal sowohl bei Verbal-, als auch bei Nominalbildungen vor vokalischen Afformativen, dazu bei Verbalbildungen vor Pronominalsuffixen und in den sog. apokopierten Formen ausfällt, was bei Vokallänge schwerer erklärlich ist. Anders stellen sich die genetischen Verhältnisse dar, wenn die Verba III inf. ursprünglich zweiradikalig (besser: zweikonsonantig) gewesen sein sollten, womit Wellhausen, ebd. 255-260, rechnete (vgl. unsere Anm. 56); dann wäre die PKKF auch hier die merkmallosere Form.

40 Die Länge des /*ī*/ in der Stammsilbe des Hiphʿil ist für das Hebräische im Gegensatz zu allen anderen semitischen Sprachen typisch. Ob die Längung von *einem* der Konjugationsthemen des Hiphʿil ausgegangen ist und gegebenenfalls von welchem, weiß ich nicht zu sagen; so bleibt offen, ob die PKKF oder die PKLF hier die merkmalhaftere Bildung ist.

41 Dagegen sind einige Verbalnomina beim Qal verblieben, etwa *bārûk, dôbēr, ḥôkā̂, kᵉsûj* (Part. pass. constr.) u.a. - Vgl. zum Problem B. Landsberger, "Prinzipienfragen der semitischen, speziell der hebräischen Grammatik", *OLZ* 29, 1926, 967-976, hier 972[12]; Vf., "Zur Geschichte des hebräischen Verbs", *BZ* 27, 1983, 34-57, hier 43f.; *ZAH* 1 (Anm. 25), 80[28]. 166; W. von Soden, "Tempus und Modus im älteren Semitischen", in: Vf. (ed.), *Babylonien und Israel* (*Wege der Forschung* 633), Darmstadt 1991, 463-493, hier 478.

42 Vgl. H.-J. Sasse, "Afroasiatisch", in: B. Heine u.a. (edd.), *Die Sprachen Afrikas*, Hamburg 1981, 129-148, hier 141, ferner im gleichen Band S. 180 (E. Wolff zum Berberischen) und 236 (Sasse zu akkadisch *iparras*, das "von einer in den westsemitischen Sprachen unbekannten Basis -$C_1aC_2C_2aC_3$

6. *Infinitiv mit Pronominalsuffix*[43]

Neben AK und PK gibt es, offenbar fossil, ein aus dem Inf. mit Pronominalsuffix gebildetes Verbalformativ, das in der wohl aus einem Nomen actionis gebildeten ägyptischen *sḏm.f*-Form ("sein Hören" > "er hört") mit Derivaten[44] seine erfolgreichste Ausprägung gefunden hat, aber auch in einem hebräischen Adverbial wie *k^ešom^cô* "als er hörte" subordinativ fortlebt. Auch andere Nomina können in Verbindung mit Pronominalsuffixen Sätze sein: *w^eḥoljô* "und seine Krankheit" > "er wurde krank" Koh 5,16.

Im Altsüdarabischen,[45] Ugaritischen,[46] Amarna-Kanaanäischen,[47] aber auch noch in jüngeren semitischen Sprachen, etwa im Phönizischen,[48] wird der Inf. narrativ gebraucht, vor allem in der für Atavismen spezifischen 1. P. sing.; vgl. *w^ešabbē^aḥ ^ʾanî* "da pries ich" Koh 4,2, dazu in der 3. P. in *jôsîp da^cat jôsîp mak^ʾōb* "wer das Wissen vermehrt, vermehrt den Kummer" 1,18 und in *nišlô^aḥ* "wurden gesandt" Est 3,13; *naḥ^apôk* "er wandte sich" 9,1.

Altertümlich sind die infinitivischen Verbalformative insofern, als sie, allein herrschend, eine Flexion ohne die Wortklasse Verb konstituieren würden – falls man den nominalen Charakter des Inf. hervorhebt, also die *sḏm.f*-Form als 'genitivische Flexion'[49] versteht, die das Verhältnis von Handlung und *agens* nach Analogie eines Possessivverhältnisses auffaßt.

abgeleitet ... und als eine innerakkadische Uminterpretation eines ursprünglichen Intensiv-Frequentativs anzusehen" sei).

43 Vgl. zum folgenden Vf., *ZAH* 11 (Anm. 35), 141 f.

44 Vgl. W. Schenkel, *Die altägyptische Suffixkonjugation. Theorie der innerägyptischen Entstehung aus Nomina actionis* (*Ägyptologische Abhandlungen* 32), Wiesbaden 1975.

45 Narrative Infinitive folgen hier auf finite Formen und bilden dann Reihen; vgl. M. Höfner, *Altsüdarabische Grammatik*, Leipzig 1943, § 54; A. F. L. Beeston, *Sabaic Grammar* (*JSS*, *Monograph* No. 6), Manchester 1984, § 8:2.

46 D. Sivan, *A Grammar of the Ugaritic Language* (*HO* I 28), Leiden u.a. 1997, 124 f. (Lit).

47 W. L. Moran, "The use of the Canaanite infinitive absolute as a finite verb in the Amarna letters from Byblos", *JCS* 4, 1950, 169-172; A. F. Rainey, *Canaanite in the Amarna Tablets. A Lingustic Analysis of the Mixed Dialect Used by the Scribes from Canaan II*, Leiden u.a. 1996, 383-390.

48 J. Friedrich - W. Röllig - M. G. Amadasi Guzzo - W. R. Mayer, *Phönizisch-punische Grammatik*, Rom, ³1999, § 267b; St. Segert, *A Grammar of Phoenician and Punic*, München 1976, § 64.613.

49 Vgl. C. E. Sander-Hansen, *Ägyptische Grammatik*, Wiesbaden 1963, § 356-359 und ff.

7. *Indikativ und Jussiv*[50]

Sowohl Nominalsätze, als auch AK und PKKF können indikativisch wie jussivisch gebraucht werden. Aus der jussivischen AK, dem akkadistisch so genannten 'stativischen Prekativ',[51] hat sich vor allem nach *wᵉ*- das 'perfectum consecutivum' entwickelt, indem die ursprünglich tempusneutrale jussivische Funktion metonymisch den imperfektiven Aspekt und infolgedessen das präsentisch-futurische Tempus aus sich entließ. Daß die PKKF auch als 'fientischer Prekativ' gebraucht werden könnte,[52] hat zur Folge, daß beim hebräischen 'Imperfekt' Indikativ und Jussiv morphologisch oft nicht mehr unterscheidbar sind.[53] Es handelt sich um Rudimente eines Sprachstatus, der den Ausdruck des Seins von dem des Sollens noch nicht unterschied.

8. *Verba infirma*[54]

a. Beiläufig zeigte bereits der Wechsel [r̥] > [*ā*] im Falle von eblaitisch *ma-'à-um* < *[*mar̥āʾum*] und der von [*l̥*] > [*â*] im Falle von aramäisch *jᵉhâk,* daß nicht nur (semi)vokalisches [r̥] und [*l̥*], sondern auch, davon abgeleitet, vokalisches [*â*] als Radikal fungieren kann. Es gibt im Semitischen zwar nur wenige echt zweiradikali-

---

50 Vgl. zum folgenden Vf., "Assertorische und kreatorische Funktion im althebräischen und semitischen Verbalsystem", *Aula orientalis* 2, Barcelona 1984, 113-125.

51 Vgl. *GAG* § 81b; zum Ausfall der Wunschpartikel *lū* und entsprechender Jussiv-Indikatoren in anderen semitischen Sprachen, auch des hebräischen *wᵉ*-, Vf., *Aula orientalis* 2 (Anm. 50), 121. Zum jussivischen Gebrauch des ägyptischen 'Pseudopartizips' vgl. Edel, aaO. (Anm. 15), § 591-594.906bb. 910.

52 Vgl. zum Akkadischen *GAG* § 81c, zum Ausfall von *l*- Vf., *Aula orientalis* 2 (Anm. 50), 117/8.

53 Die massoretische Differenzierung zwischen ultimabetontem Jussiv (*jāqṓm,* vgl. AK *wᵉqāṭaltā́*) und paenultimabetontem Indikativ (*wajjā́qom*, vgl. AK *qaṭáltā*) ist phonetisch bedingt und sekundär; vgl. Vf., "Zur Wechselbeziehung von Wirklichkeitswahrnahme und Sprache", in: *Mythos - Kerygma - Wahrheit* (*BZAW* 200), Berlin - New York 1991, 264-309, hier 293-295.

54 Vgl. zum folgenden Vf., "Zur Bildung der Verbalwurzeln" (Anm. 28); "Die Sprache der Texte von Tell Deir ʿAllā im Kontext der nordwestsemitischen Sprachen mit einigen Erwägungen zum Zusammenhang der schwachen Verbklassen", *ZAH* 4, 1991, 1-31, hier 19 ff. (Lit.).

ge,[55] wohl aber viele zweikonsonantige Verbalwurzeln, deren dritter Radikal ein Vokal ist.[56]

Auf Vokale als ersten Radikal gehen wohl auch die Verba I: ʾ, nämlich [*a*], I: *j*, nämlich [*i*], und I: *w/j*, nämlich [*u*], zurück, was die Annahme eines Wurzelaugments als erstem Radikal erübrigt; die Vokale wurden teilweise zu den homogenen Semikonsonanten. Zweikonsonantige Wurzeln mit ursprünglich gelängtem ersten Konsonanten (*KK*) und kurzem Binnenvokal können infolge nasalierender Geminatendissimilation (besser: Auflösung der Längung) beim ersten Konsonanten einem Wechsel *KK* > *ñK* unterliegen, was den bedeutungsklassenspezifischen Typ der Verba I: *n* ergibt, soweit [*n*-] nicht wie etwa bei akkadisch *nawāru*(*m*) "leuchten" Wurzelkonsonant einer dreikonsonantigen Bildung ist.[57] Das Aramäische scheint eine ähnliche Nasalierung bei Verba I: *w/j* zu kennen, etwa in *jindaᶜ* "er kennt" Dan 2,9 und *mandaᶜ* "Kenntnis" 2,11 sowie bei einem Verb II: *l̥* > *â*, nämlich *sl̥q* > *sâq*, in *hansâqā* "hinaufbringen" Dan 6,24 und wohl auch in *mnsq* "hinaufsteigen" Krael 9,15; auch hier kann eine Nasalierung der Geminatendissimilation dienen, wenn wir einen Wechsel *jdᶜ* > *-ddᶜ* > *-ñdᶜ* > *ndᶜ* ansetzen.[58] Auch das Hebräische und das

55 Zweiradikalige (einkonsonantige) Wurzeln liegen bei den doppelt schwachen Verben vor; so besteht hebräisches *nṭh* mit Isoglossen nur aus [*ṭ*] und einem wohl ursprünglich kurzen [*u*] (vgl. zur Kürze des dritten Radikals bei Verba III inf. Anm. 39), das in den 'apokopierten' Bildungen fehlt (PKKF *jēṭ* u. ä.).

56 Gesteht man zu, daß Radikale sowohl konsonantisch als auch vokalisch sein können, ergibt sich die Unterscheidung von 'Wurzel' und 'Basis' als gegenstandslos. *Insoweit* ist der These J. Troppers ("Die infirmen Verben des Akkadischen", *ZDMG* 148, 1998, 7-34) nicht zu widersprechen, "daß die sogenannten infirmen Verben des Akkadischen einem einheitlichen dreiradikaligen Grundparadigma folgen" (31). Tropper übt Kritik an der durch W. von Soden u.a. vertretenen "Biradikalismus-These", wobei er Biradikalismus als Bikonsonantismus (miß-)versteht; eine Einzelauseinandersetzung ist hier nicht möglich. - Zu zweikonsonantigen Verbalwurzeln im Eblaitischen vgl. G. Conti, "Arcaismi in Eblaita", in: P. Fronzaroli (ed.), *Studies on the Language of Ebla* (*Quaderni di Semitistica* 13), Firenze 1984, 159-172.

57 Vgl. Růžička, aaO. (Anm. 9), zur Nasalierung anstelle einer ursprünglichen Konsonantenlängung im Akkadischen *GAG* § 32bc, zum Aramäischen mit besonderer Berücksichtigung der Verben I: *n* K. Beyer, *Die aramäiischen Texte vom Toten Meer*, Göttingen 1984, 89-95. Dagegen dachte von Soden (*n* als Wurzelaugment im Semitischen, WZ Halle 17, 1968, G Heft 2/3, 175-184; dort auch zu [*l̥*] in *sl̥q* und *hl̥k* S. 178) zu den Verba I: *n* nicht an Nasalierung; daß die Verba I: *n* zum Teil lautmalend Geräusche bezeichnen oder ein richtungsbestimmendes Semelement enthalten (vgl. *GAG* § 102b), bleibt von dieser Differenz unberührt. - Zu *nawāru*(*m*) u.a. vgl. § 102a.

58 Nur analoge Haphᶜel-Bildungen eines Verbs II gem., nämlich *ᶜll*, sind *tnᶜl* Krael 12,22, *hanᶜēl* Dan 2,25 und *hanᶜālā* 4,3 (gegenüber *häᶜālā* 5,7 ohne [*n*-]), wo nasalierende Dissimilation von [ᶜᶜ] schwer vorstellbar ist; vielleicht handelt es sich auch um graphemische Standardisierungen.

Aramäische kennen den Wechsel *-jK* > *-KK* bei Verba I: *w/j*, nämlich in hebräisch *ʾäṣṣōq* "ich werde ausschütten" von *jsq* Jes 44,3 und in *wᵉ-/waʾäṣṣorkā* von *jṣr* Jes 42,6; 49,8 (vgl. Jer 1,5) bzw. in aramäisch *jittib* "er sitzt/ wird sitzen" von *jtb* Dan 7,26 sowie *jikkul* "er kann" 3,29 und *tikkul* Qᵉrê "du kannst" 5,16, beides von *jkl*.[59]

b. Die Verba II gem. gehen auf zweikonsonantige Wurzeln mit kurzem, die Verba II inf. auf solche mit langem Binnenvokal zurück.[60] Die fälschlich sog. aramaisierenden Bildungen im Hebräischen,[61] insbesondere bei Verba II gem., beruhen auf Längung des ersten der beiden Wurzelkonsonanten, aber auch des letzten oder beider; ähnlich wird neben anderen Wurzeln akkadisches *i/uzuzzu(m)* "stehen" von *ziz* gebildet, während 'aramaisierende' Bildungen bei Verba II inf. an akkadischem *i/utūlu(m)* "liegen" von *tīl* Parallelen haben; solche Lexeme sind im Akkadischen die eigentlichen Verba II gem.[62] Die betr. Struktur ist also älter als vermutlich das Aramäische, wo es in *taddiq* "sie wird zerschlagen" von *dqq* Dan 7,26 und, mit Ersatzdehnung für das nicht längbare [*r*], in *tērōᵃᶜ* "sie wird zermalmen" von *rᶜᶜ* Dan 2,40[63] begegnet, was offenbar zu der Bezeichnung 'aramaisierende Bildungen' geführt hat.

c. Die zweikonsonantigen Wurzeln mit Vokalen als erstem (so ursprünglich bei I: *ʾ*, I: *j*, I: *w/j*), zweitem (kurz bei II gem., lang bei II inf.) oder drittem (III inf. einschließlich III: *ʾ* < III: *a/ā*)[64] Radikal, sind strukturelle Atavismen. Die semitischen Sprachen ziehen in wachsendem Maße die Dreikonsonantenstruktur vor, ohne daß

---

59 Das Akkadische kennt sogar einen Wechsel I: *w* > I: *t*: *(w)abālu(m)* > *tabālu(m)*.

60 Ein kurzer Binnenvokal scheint in der AK *qamtā, qamtî* u.ä. nachzuwirken; in den AKK *qām, mēt, bān* u.ä. liegt nur Tonlänge vor (vgl. Wellhausen, aao. [Anm. 39], 252 f.); anders in der AK *bîn* als Allomorphem zu *bān* und in der AK *bôš* mit 1. sing. *bôštî* (gegenüber *qamtā, qamtî*), dem akkadisch *bâšu(m)* entspricht, so daß beim zweiten Radikal Wechsel [*â*] > [*ô*] vorliegt; das Hiphʿil wird zum Teil nach I: *w* gebildet. Die AK von *bôʾ*, entsprechend akkad. *bâʾu(m)*, behält [*â*] auch in *bâʾtā, bâʾtî* u.ä. bei, entspricht also weder *qām* noch *bôš*, was ich nicht erklären kann. *ʾôr* und *ṭôb* sind konjugierte Nomina. Vgl. zum Problem K. Beyer, *Althebräische Grammatik*, Göttingen 1969, 62.

61 Vgl. Vf., "Aramaisierende Bildungen bei Verba mediae geminatae - ein Irrtum der Hebraistik?", *VT* 36, 1986, 423-437; von Soden, *ZAH* 4 (Anm. 38), 34; Vf., *ZAH* 4 (Anm. 54), 23-25.

62 Vgl. W. von Soden, "Die unregelmäßigen Verben im Akkadischen", *ZA* 50, 1952, 163-181; *GAG* § 107, ferner vorläufig Vf., *VT* 36 (Anm. 61), 428-430.

63 Vgl. St. Segert, *Altaramäische Grammatik*, Leipzig 1975, § 5.7.3.3.1-3.

64 Zur Kürze oder Länge des [*a*] vgl. entsprechend Anm. 39, zu Verba III: *a/ā* im Akkadischen *GAG* § 105c. - Die Bildung von einer hebräischen Wurzel *ʿzʾ* < *ʿ*zḻ* liegt vielleicht vor, wenn der Dämonenname עֲזָאזֵל aus *ᶜᵃ*zaḻʾel* abzuleiten ist; vgl. GKa § 30n, ferner *HAL* s.v.

dabei freilich eine lineare Entwicklung absehbar wäre. Schon das Eblaitische zeigt die Tendenz, bei Verba II inf. durch die Zeichen *a, i* oder *ì* Hiatus und bei Verba II inf. und III inf. durch PI ([*wa*] oder [*wu*]) Gleitlaut oder Hiatustilger anzuzeigen.[65] Auch das Altakkadische[66] und das Altassyrische[67] haben bei Verba II inf. die Dreikonsonantenstruktur bekanntlich weitgehender verwirklicht als das Altbabylonische.[68] Darstellung des zweiten Radikals von Verba II inf. durch < *j* > oder < ʾ > finden sich schon im älteren Aramäischen, die des dritten Radikals bei Verba III inf. im Phönizischen und späten Hebräischen, wozu auf Einzelnachweise verzichtet werden kann. Im Arabischen und Äthiopischen werden die Verba I: *n* 'regelmäßig' konjugiert.

9. Folgerungen

Das Vorhandensein von Atavismen verbietet eine rein synchronische Sprachbetrachtung – es sei denn, man behandelt die synchrone Systematik als eine Struktur mit großer Widerspruchstoleranz. Jede Sprachengruppe, ja auch jede Einzelsprache konserviert Strukturen des Wirklichkeitsumgangs vieler Jahrhunderte, ja Jahrtausende. Die Interferenz älterer und jüngerer humanbiologischer, auch humanethologischer Befindlichkeiten ist als Hintergrund nicht auszuschließen. Vor allem: so wie an Lexemen religiöse, philosophische und politische Vorstellungen haften, die nur durch historische Analyse wieder zum Bewußtsein kommen, enthält auch die Grammatik mit ihren Atavismen die allmählich verschwindenden Spuren von Anordnungsbedürfnissen lang zurückliegender Generationen, die alle, die sie danach benutzen, an längst nicht mehr normative Bewußtseinsformationen binden, ja ihr Denken mit naiven Vorurteilen infizieren.[69] Daran kann gegenüber unbefragten Selbstverständlichkeiten, die die Suggestivwirkung des Gegenwärtigen haben, aller-

---

65 Vgl. Vf., "Zur Bildung der Verbalwurzeln" (Anm. 28), 280-285.

66 Vgl. I. J. Gelb, *Old Akkadian Writing and Grammar* (*MAD* II), Chicago ^{2}1961, 178 f.

67 *GKT* § 94.

68 *GAG* § 100a, 104. - Das Graphem < *h* > in ugaritischem *bhṯ* statt geläufigerem *bṯ* als Isoglosse zu hebräisch *bôš,* in *nhmmt* "Schlaf" von *nūm* oder in altsüdarabisch *bhʾ* als Isoglosse zu hebräisch *bôʾ* ist Dehnungszeichen, das wie in hebräisch *ʾabrāhām* neben *ʾabrām* doppelgipflige Aussprache anzeigen will.

69 Anknüpfend an einschlägige Formulierungen F. Nietzsches nannte L. Wittgenstein das "Mißtrauen gegen die Grammatik die erste Voraussetzung des Philosophierens", wobei er unter Philosophie derzeit "die Lehre von der logischen Form wissenschaftlicher Sätze" verstand (*Aufzeichnungen über Logik* [1913], in: H. T. Costello [ed.], *Ludwig Wittgenstein, Schriften* I, Frankfurt M. 1960, 186).

dings auch eine Chance liegen, insofern gerade Widerspruchstoleranz in dissipativen grammatischen Strukturen und 'unscharfe Logik' (fuzzy logic) den Anforderungen des konkreten, alltäglichen Lebens, an denen sich Sprache primär zu bewähren hat, besonders angemessen erscheinen.

UNE FORMULE ÉPISTOLAIRE EN OUGARITIQUE ET ACCADIEN

DENNIS PARDEE

University of Chicago

La lettre RS 8.315, découverte en 1936 et publiée en 1938,[1] comportait le premier exemple de la double formule d'état de bien-être des correspondants. Depuis la mise au jour de ce document, la formule est revenue plusieurs fois dans les documents épistolaires en langue ougaritique et elle a trouvé son parallèle en accadien.

Nous avions l'intention de présenter les données suivantes dans notre réédition des documents épistolaires actuellement en préparation. La décision d'avancer cette présentation et de la dédier au professeur Fronzaroli a été prise pour deux raisons: (1) l'édition en préparation ne paraîtra sûrement pas avant le troisième millénaire, et celui-ci risque même d'être déjà assez avancé lorsqu'elle verra le jour; (2) une grammaire ougaritique parue récemment en anglais et qui fera certainement autorité n'admet pas l'interprétation d'une partie de cette formule qui nous semble être aussi solide qu'un élément de la grammaire ougaritique puisse l'être.[2] Nous verrons que cette interprétation est appuyée non seulement par l'analyse interne de l'ougaritique mais aussi par l'existence de la même formule dans des lettres en langue accadienne provenant de Ras Shamra et d'Émar.

Suivent les exemples de la formule qui sont actuellement attestés en ougaritique.[3] La formule-type se traduit littéralement: "Voici que chez moi tout va bien; là-bas chez toi, (pour ce qui concerne) quoi qu('il y ait) de bien, renvoie m'en la parole", autrement dit: "Chez moi, ça va bien; renvoie-moi de tes nouvelles". La première

1 Dhorme, *Syria* 19 (1938), pp. 142-146.

2 Sivan, *Grammar* (1997), p. 59. Il s'agit de l'interprétation de la particule *mnm*; le rattachement ou non de la clause où figure cette particule à la suivante dépendra de cette analyse, comme nous le verrons.

3 Nous citons uniquement des textes publiés; la formule se rencontre encore plusieurs fois dans les textes inédits de la "Maison d'Ourtenou": RS 92.2005 (cette tablette porte deux lettres dont chacune comporte la double formule); RS 92.2010 (double formule; forme modifiée de la demande de retour de nouvelles); RS 94.2479 (double); RS 94.5003$^+$ (double). Au sujet des découvertes effectuées dans cette maison, voir Yon, Bordreuil et Malbran-Labat, *CRAI* 1995, pp. 427-449; Malbran-Labat, *SMEA* 36 (1995), pp. 103-111; Yon, *La cité d'Ougarit* (1997), pp. 96-98.

partie de la formule rapporte donc le bien-être de l'expéditeur, la seconde demande en retour les nouvelles du destinataire. Comme on le verra en parcourant la liste suivante,[4] cette formule de base est attestée sous plusieurs formes, et l'une ou l'autre des deux parties de la formule peuvent s'exprimer indépendamment. Lorsque les deux éléments de la formule sont présents, l'expéditeur parle toujours de son bien-être avant de demander les nouvelles du destinataire, et le rang respectif des correspondants n'exerce donc aucun effet sur l'ordre de ces éléments.

(1) RS 8.315 (*CTA* 51) {(1) l . ʾumy. ʾadtny (2) rgm (3) tḥm . tlmyn (4) w . ʾaḫtmlk . ʿbdk (5) l . pʿn . ʾadtny (6) mrḥqtm (7) qlny . ʾilm (8) tǵrk (9) tšlmk (10) **hnny** . **ʿmny** (11) **kll** . **mʾid** (12) **šlm** . (13) **w** ⌜.⌝ **ʾap. ʾank** (14) **nḫt** . **ṯmny** (15) **ʿm** . **ʾadtny** (16) **mnm** . **šlm** (17) **rgm** . **ṯṯb** (18) **l** . **ʿbdk**}, "A ma mère, notre dame, (2) dis: (3) Message de *Talmiyānu* (4) et de *ʾAḫātumilki* tes serviteurs: (5) Aux pieds de notre dame (6) de loin (7) nous tombons. Que les dieux (8) te protègent, (9) qu'ils te soient salutaires! (10) Voici (que) chez nous (11) tout va très (12) bien. (13) Et quant à moi, (14) je me suis reposé. Là-bas (15) chez notre dame, (16) (pour) tout ce qui va bien, (17) renvoie un rapport (à ce sujet) (18) à tes serviteurs" (formule double, avec insertion atypique d'un court message entre les deux parties de la formule).

(2) RS 9.479A (*CTA* 52) {(1) l . mlkt (2) ʾadty (3) rgm (4) tḥm . tlmyn (5) ʿbdk (6) l . pʿn (7) ʾadty (8) šbʿd (9) w . šbʿʾid (10) mrḥqtm (11) qlt (12) **ʿm** . **ʾadty** (13) **mnm** . **šlm** (14) **rgm** . **tṯṯb** (15) **l** . **ʿbdh**}, "A la reine, (2) ma dame, (3) dis: (4) Message de *Talmiyānu* (5) ton serviteur: (6) Aux pieds de (7) ma dame (8) sept fois (9) et sept fois (10) de loin (11) je tombe. (15) Chez ma dame, (16) (pour) tout ce qui va bien, (17) qu'elle renvoie un rapport (à ce sujet) (18) à son serviteur" (formule simple, adressée à la destinataire).

(3) RS 11.872 (*CTA* 50) {(1) l . mlkt (2) ʾumy. rgm (3) tḥm . mlk (4) bnk . (5) l . pʿn . ʾumy (6) qlt . l . ʾumy (7) yšlm . ʾilm (8) tǵrk . tšlmk (9) **hlny** . **ʿmny** (10) **kll** . **šlm** (11) **ṯmny** . **ʿm** . **ʾumy** (12) **mnm** . **šlm** (13) **w** . **rgm** . **ṯṯb** . **ly**}, "A la reine, (2) ma mère, dis: (3) Message du roi, (4) ton fils: (5) Aux pieds de ma mère (6) je tombe. Puisse ma mère (7) se porter bien . Que les dieux (8) te protègent, qu'ils te soient salutaires! (9) Ici chez moi (10) tout va bien. (11) Là-bas chez ma mère, (12) (pour) tout ce qui va bien, (13) renvoie moi un rapport (à ce sujet)" (formule double).

(4) RS 15.008 (*PRU* II 15) {(1) tḥm . ⌜t⌝lm[y]⌜n⌝ (2) l ṯryl . ʾumy (3) rgm (4) yšlm . lk. ʾily (5) ʾugrt. tǵrk (6) tšlmk ... (14) **ʿmny** . **šlm** (15) **kll** (16) **w mnm** . (17) **šlm** . **ʿm** (18) **ʾumy** (19) **ʿmy** . **tṯṯb** (20) **rgm**}, "Message de *Talmiyānu*: (2) A *Ṯarriyelli*, ma mère, (3) dis: (4) Puisses-tu bien te porter. Que les dieux (5) d'Ougarit te protègent, (6) qu'ils te soient salutaires! ... (14) Chez moi tout (15) va bien. (16) (Et pour) tout ce qui (17) va bien chez (18) ma

4 Pour que les indicateurs au sujet de l'expéditeur et du destinataires soient disponibles au lecteur, nous fournissons le début du texte et mettons la formule que nous étudions ici en caractères gras. L'espace ne permet pourtant d'indiquer ni les sources secondaires, ni nos propres raisons invoquées pour adopter telle interprétation des éléments des lettres traduites ici qui ne sont pas en rapport avec la formule visée par notre étude.

mère, (19) qu'elle me renvoie (20) un rapport (à ce sujet)" (formule double, servant de conclusion atypique au corps de la lettre).

(5) RS 16.137[bis] (*PRU* II 14)[5] {(1) l . mlkt (2) ʾadty. rgm (3) tḥm . ʾillḏr (4) ʿbdk (5) l ⸢.⸣ pʿn [.] ʾa⸢d⸣ty (6) šbʿ⸢d⸣ [.] ⸢w⸣ [. š]b[ʿ(ʾi)d] (7) mrḥq⸢t⸣[m .] ql[t] (8) **[hln]⸢y⸣** [. **ʿm]⸢ny⸣** (9) **[kll . šlm]** (10) **ṯm[ny . ʿm .]** ⸢**ʾa**⸣**[dty]** (11) **mn⸢m⸣** [. **šlm]** (12) **rgm [tṯtb . l ʿbdh]**}, "A la reine, (2) ma dame, dis: (3) Message de *ʾIlaliḏarru*, (4) ton serviteur: (5) Aux pieds de ma dame (6) sept et [s]e[pt fois] (7) de loi[n je] tombe. (8) [Ic]i [che]z moi (9) [tout va bien.] (10) Là-b[as chez ma] d[ame], (11) (pour) tou[t ce qui va bien], (12) [qu'elle renvoie] un rapport (à ce sujet) [à son serviteur.]" (formule double).

(6) RS 16.379 (*PRU* II 13) {(1) ⸢l⸣ mlkt . ⸢ʾu⸣[m]⸢y⸣ (2) ⸢r⸣gm . tḥ⸢m⸣[...] (3) mlk . bn⸢k⸣[...] (4) ⸢l⸣ . pʿn . ⸢ʾu⸣m⸢y⸣ (5) qlt ⸢. l⸣y . ⸢ʾu⸣[m]y (6) yšlm . ʾil [m] (7) tǵ⸢r⸣k . tš[l]⸢m⸣k (8) **⸢h⸣lny** . **ʿmn⸢y⸣** [. **š]lm** (9) **w** . **ṯm⸢n⸣** . **⸢ʿm⸣** [. **ʾu]my** (10) **mnm** . **š⸢l⸣[m]** (11) **w** . **rgm** [. **ṯṯb** .] **⸢l⸣y**}, "A la reine, ma m[è]re, (2) dis: Message du (3) roi, ton fils: (4) Aux pieds de ma mère (5) je tombe. Puisse ma mère (6) se porter bien. Que le[s] dieu[x] (7) te protègent, qu'ils te soient sa[l]utaires! (8) Ici chez moi cela v[a b]ien. (9) Et là-bas chez ma mère, (10) (pour) tout ce qui va bi[en], (11) [renvoie] moi un rapport (à ce sujet)" (formule double).

(7) RS 17.139 (*PRU* V 9) {(1) tḥm . mlk (2) l . ṯryl . ʾumy. rgm (3) yšlm ⸢.⸣ lk . ʾilm (4) tǵrk. tšlmk (5) lḥt . šlm . k . lʾik⸢t⸣ (6) ʾumy. ʿmy . **ht** . **ʿm⸢ny⸣** (7) **kll** . **šlm** . **ṯmny** (8) **ʿm** . **ʾumy**. **mnm** . **šlm** (9) **w** . **rgm** . **ṯṯb** . **ly**}, "Message du roi: (2) A *Ṯarriyelli*, ma mère, dis: (3) Puisses-tu bien te porter. Que les dieux (4) te protègent, (5) qu'ils te soient salutaires! (6) Pour ce qui concerne (le fait qu'un message sur) tablette (7) ma mère m'a envoyé: Voici (que) chez moi (8) tout va bien. Là-bas (9) chez ma mère, (pour) tout ce qui va bien, (10) renvoie moi un rapport (à ce sujet)" (formule double, la première partie introduite atypiquement par l'allusion à une lettre précédente qu'avait reçue l'expéditeur de celle-ci de la part du destinataire de celle-ci).

(8) RS 17.434+ (*Ugaritica* VII, p. 121-134) {(1) [tḥ]m . pdǵb . mlk[t ...]⸢--⸣[...] (2) [l .] ⸢n⸣qmd . rgm. **h⸢l⸣[ny. ʿm .] šp[š]** (3) **⸢w⸣ . ʿm . mlkt . kll[. šlm]** (4) w . šlm . d . ḥw[t]k . ⸢w⸣ [. d] ⸢. bt⸣ [.] ⸢ml⸣k [...]}, "[Messa]ge de *Pudugépa*, rein[e de ...:] (2) [A] *Niqmaddu* dis: I[ci chez] le Sole[il] (3) et chez la reine tout [va bien.] (4) Et le bien-être de ton pa[y]s et [de] la maison du roi [... .]" (formule concernant le bien-être de l'expéditeur suivie probablement par une autre formule à l'égard du destinataire, peut-être celle qui comporte le verbe ŠʾL).

(9) RS 18.031 (*PRU* V 59) {(1) l . mlk . ʾugrt (2) ʾaḫy. rgm (3) tḥm . mlk . ṣr . ʾaḫk (4) yšlm . lk . ʾilm (5) tǵrk. tšlmk (6) **hnny** . **ʿmn** (7) **šlm** . **ṯmny** (8) **ʿmk** . **mnm** ⸢.⸣ **šlm** (9) **rgm** . **ṯṯ⸢b⸣**}, "Au roi d'Ougarit, (2) mon frère, dis: (3) Message du roi de Tyr, ton frère: (4) Puisses-tu bien te porter. Que les dieux (5) te protègent, qu'ils te soient salutaires! (6) Voici (que) chez moi (7) cela va bien. Là-bas (8) chez toi, (pour) tout ce qui va bien, (9) renvoie moi un rapport (à ce sujet)" (formule double).

(10) RS 18.038 (*PRU* V 60) {(1) tḥm . špš (2) l . ʿmrpʾi. rgm (3) **ʿm** . **špš** . **kll** . **mʾidm** (4) **šlm**}, "Message du Soleil: (2) A *ʿAmmurapiʾ* dis: (3) Chez le Soleil tout va très bien" (formule simple, concernant le bien-être de l'expéditeur).

---

5 Voir notre rapport de collation de cette tablette (*UF* 19 [1987], pp. 202-204), où est indiquée l'existence de deux fragments jointifs au fragment principal publié dans l'*editio princeps*.

(11) RS 18.147 (*PRU* V 61) {(1) tḥm . pgn [.] ⸢ʾabk⸣ (2) l . mlk . ʾugrt [. bny] (3) rg⸢m⸣ (4) yšlm . lk . ⸢ʾil⸣m (5) tǵrk. tšlmk (6) **hnny . ʿmn . š⸢l⸣m** (7) **ṯmny . ʿ[m .] bny** (8) **mnm . [š]lm** [.] ⸢**r**⸣**gm . ⸢ṯṯb⸣ [. ly]**}, “Message de *Pugana*, ton père :[6] (2) Au roi d’Ougarit, [mon fils,] (3) dis: (4) Puisses-tu bien te porter. Que les dieux (5) te protègent, qu’ils te soient salutaires! (6) Voici (que) chez moi cela va bien. (7) Là-bas ch[ez] mon fils, (8) (pour) tout ce qui [va b]ien, renvoie [moi] un rapport (à ce sujet)” (formule double).

(12) RS 18.287 (*PRU* V 128) {(1’) [tǵrk . tšl]⸢mk⸣ (2’) [l . pʿn . bʿ]ly . šb[ʿd] (3’) [w . šbʿ(ʾi)d .] ⸢m⸣rḥq⸢t⸣[m] (4’) [qlt . **ʿmk .**] ⸢**m**⸣**nm** (5’) **[šlm . rgm .] ṯṯb** (6’) [l . --- . **ʿb]dk**}, “[... te protègent, qu’ils] te soient salu[taires!] (2’) [Aux pieds de] mon [maît]re se[pt] (3’) [et sept fois] de loi[n] (4’) [je tombe. Chez toi,] (pour) tout (5’) [ce qui va bien,] renvoie [un rapport (à ce sujet)] (6’) [à ...,] son serviteur” (formule simple, adressée au destinataire).

(13) RS 19.102 (*PRU* V 115) {(13) l . ybn[n ...] (14) bʿly . r⸢g⸣[m] (15) tḥm . ʿbd[...] (16) ʿbdk (17) l pʿn . bʿly (18) ṯnʾid. šbʿd (19) mrḥqtm (20) qlt . **ʿm** (21) **bʿly . m⸢n⸣m** (22) **šlm** (23) ⸢**r**⸣**gm [. ṯṯ]b** (24) **[l .] ⸢ʿb⸣⸢dk⸣**}, “Aux pieds de mon maître (18) deux fois, sept fois (19) de loin (20) je tombe. Chez (21) mon maître, (au sujet de) tout (22) ce qui va bien (23) [renvo]ie un rapport (à ce sujet) (24) [à] ton serviteur” (formule simple, adressée au destinataire; il s’agit de la seconde lettre que porte cette tablette).

(14) RS 19.158B (*PRU* V 171) {(2’) [---]y . **hnn**[...] (3’) ⸢**ʿm**⸣**n . šlm** (4’) ⸢**ṯ**⸣**mn . ʿmk** (5’) ⸢**m**⸣**nm . šlm** (6’) **[r]⸢g⸣m . ṯṯb . ⸢l⸣**[...]}, “(2’) [---] voic[i (que) ...] (3’) chez moi, cela va bien. (4’) Là-bas chez toi, (5’) (au sujet de) tout ce que va bien, (6’) renvoie un [ra]pport (à ce sujet) à [...]” (formule double; texte perdu avant et après).

(15) RS 20.199 (*KTU*/*CAT* 2.68)[7] {(1) ⸢l .⸣ mlkt . ʾadty (2) ⸢r⸣gm (3) [t]ḥm . ʾurǵṯb . ʿbdk (4) l . pʿn . ʾadty (5) mrḥqtm (6) šbʿd . w . šbʿd (7) qlt . ly (8) ʾadty. ⸢yš⸣lm (9) [ʾi]⸢l⸣m . t⸢ǵ⸣rk (10) [tšl]⸢mk⸣ (11) **[hnn]⸢y⸣** (12) **[ʿmn .] ⸢k⸣ll** (13) **[mʾi]d . šlm** (14) **ṯmny . ʿm** (15) **ʾadty. mnm** (16) **šlm . rgm** (17) **ṯṯb . l . ʿbdk**}, “(1) A la reine, ma dame, (2) dis: (3) Message de *ʾUrǵiteṯṯub*, ton serviteur. (4) Aux pieds de ma dame, (5) de loin (6) sept fois et sept fois (7) je tombe. Puisse (8) ma dame puisse se porter bien. (9) Que les [di]eux te protègent, (10) [qu’ils te soient sal]utaires! (11) [Voici q]ue (12) [chez moi] tout (13) va très bien. (14) Là-bas chez (15) ma dame, (pour) tout (16) ce qui va bien, (17) renvoie à ton serviteur un rapport (à ce sujet)” (formule double).

---

6 Celle-ci est la seule attestation de *ʾab*, “père”, comme titre de l’un des correspondants dans le corpus épistolaire en langue ougaritique. Par ailleurs, c’est le mot *ʾadn* qu’emploie un fils en s’adressant à son père (RS 92.2005, *ʿAzzīʾiltu*, à son père *ʾUrtēnu* – on sait qu’il s’agit du père au sens familial parce que cette lettre est adressée aussi à sa mère et la seconde lettre que porte cette tablette est adressée à sa sœur; probablement RS 19.102, première lettre, *Talmiyānu* à *Yabnīnu*; RS [Varia 4] pose un problème plus compliqué, car le destinataire est nommé *bny ʾaḫy*, “mon fils, mon frère”, et l’expéditeur se nomme *ʾaḫk ʾadnk*, “ton frère, ton seigneur”) – voir la ré-édition de ce texte par Bordreuil, *Semitica* 32 (1982), pp. 5-9.

7 Ce texte et le suivant n’ont pas encore été l’objet d’une *editio princeps* proprement dite, et nous citons donc la transcription préliminaire dans *KTU*/*CAT*. Dans notre étude préliminaire du premier texte (*AfO* 31 [1984], pp. 213-215), nous avons pu mettre au point l’expression des formules dans cette lettre, propositions agréés pour la plupart par les auteurs de *CAT*.

(16) RS 29.095 (*KTU/CAT* 2.71)[8] {(1) tḥm . tlmyn (2) l pzy . rgm (3) ⸢y⸣šlm ⸢.⸣ lk (4) ʾilm ⸢.⸣ tšlmk (5) tǵrk [.] **hnny** (6) **ʿmn . ⸢š⸣[l]m** (7) **ṯmny . ʿmk** (8) **rgm ṯṯb . ly**}, "(1) Message de *Talmiyānu*: (2) A *Pizziya* dis: (3) Puisses-tu bien te porter. (4) Que les dieux te soient salutaires, (5) qu'ils te protègent! Voici (que) (6) chez moi cela [va] bien. (7) Là-bas chez toi, (8) <(pour) tout ce qui [va b]ien>?, renvoie moi un rapport (à ce sujet)" (formule double).

(17) RS 34.124 (RSO VII 88) {(1) [l . mlkt . ʾumy] (2) [rgm] (3) [tḥm .] ⸢m⸣[lk . bnk] (4) [l p]ʿn . ʾumy ⸢.⸣ [qlt] (5) [l]⸢y⸣ . ʾumy <. y>šlm ⸢.⸣ [ʾilm] (6) [t]ǵrk . tšl⸢m⸣[k] (7) **⸢h⸣nny . ʿmn . šl[m . kl]⸢l⸣** (8) **ṯmny . ʿmk- . mnm** (9) **šlm . rgm . ṯṯ<b> . ly**}, "[A la reine, ma mère] (2) [dis:] (3) [Message du] r[oi, ton fils:] (4) [Aux p]ieds de ma mère [je tombe.] (5) [Pui]sse ma mère se porter bien. [Que les dieux] (6) te protège[nt] et [te] soient salutaires. (7) Ici chez moi [tou]t va [bien]. (8) Là-bas chez toi, (pour) tout (9) ce qui va bien, renvo<ie> moi un rapport (à ce sujet)" (formule double).

(18) RIH 77/21A (*Syria* 56 [1979], p. 307) {(1) tḥm . ⸢š⸣[pš . mlk] (2) rb . l ⸢m⸣[...] (3) rgm (4) **hlny [. ʿm . špš . mlk]** (5) **rb . ⸢k⸣[ll . šlm** ...]}, "Message du S[oleil, le (2) grand [roi]: A [...] (3) dis: (4) Ici [chez le soleil, le] (5) grand [roi], t[out va bien ...]" (malgré l'état abîmé de la tablette, il est probable que, comme en RS 18.038, autre lettre du "Soleil", seule la première partie de la formule s'y trouvait).

Analyse

La formule n'est attestée que dix-huit fois sur une soixantaine de textes qui sont assez bien conservés pour permettre de trancher, et on peut donc qualifier de fréquente son omission complète. Cela arrive surtout lorsque l'expéditeur est de rang supérieur, mais aussi lorsqu'il s'agit d'une lettre d'inférieur à supérieur. Comme la liste le montre, on rencontre parfois seulement l'un ou l'autre des deux éléments: le rapport de l'expéditeur est parfois omis lorsque l'auteur est de rang inférieur au destinataire (RS 9.479A, RS 18.287, RS 19.102 [seconde lettre]), la demande de retour de nouvelles lorsque l'expéditeur est de rang supérieur (RS 18.038, RIH 77/21A?). En revanche, on ne rencontre jamais l'un seul de ces deux éléments sans l'autre lorsque le vœu de santé *yšlm l* ...est présent.[9] Cela ne veut pas dire que la formule accompagne toujours *yšlm l* – au contraire elle est souvent absente dans cette circonstance.

Si la formule de retour de nouvelles n'est pas exprimée dans des lettres dont l'auteur est socialement supérieur au destinataire, elle se trouve dans une lettre où la

8 Voir la note précédente; pour ce texte-ci, nous n'avons pas proposé d'édition préliminaire, mais le texte proposé dans *KTU/CAT* reflète bien les formules de la lettre.

9 En accadien, on ne trouve aucun exemple de la séquence "*lū šulmu* ... formule d'état de l'expéditeur", deux exemples de la séquence "*lū šulmu* ... formule d'état du destinataire" (RS 17.078; RS 20.013 [seconde lettre] – passage cité plus bas, note 55).

supériorité est exprimée par un terme familial (RS 18.147 de “père” à “fils”).[10] On peut aussi citer le cas mixte de RS 34.124: un “fils” (normalement terme d'infériorité) qui est aussi “roi” (normalement terme de supériorité) demande des nouvelles de sa “mère” (normalement un terme de supériorité).[11]

La séparation des correspondants dans l'espace est le plus souvent indiquée par des adverbes: *hn-/hl-*,[12] “voici/ici”,[13] introduit l'expéditeur, *ṯm-*, “là-bas”, le destinataire. *ṯm-* est omis plus souvent que *hn-/hl-*, et l'omission de *ṯm-* se rencontre le plus souvent, comme dans les textes accadiens, lorsque la première formule est entièrement omise.[14]

A ces adverbes s'ajoute presque toujours la préposition *ʿm*, “avec, auprès de, chez”, devant le nom ou le pronom qui désigne l'expéditeur et le destinataire.[15] L'expéditeur se désigne le plus souvent par le pronom suffixe: “avec moi = chez moi”.[16] Toutefois, le roi-soleil a tendance à indiquer ici son titre.[17] L'expression pré-

---

10 On trouve deux cas similaires en accadien: RS 16.111, de mère à fille (probablement un véritable rapport familial), et RS 17.078, où l'expéditeur s'adresse au destinataire comme à son “fils” (il s'agit vraisemblablement d'un rapport social exprimé par un terme familial). Dans son étude de cette formule, Kristensen, *UF* 9 (1977), p. 155, ne fait pas la distinction entre rapport familial et rapport social.

11 On ne trouve pas de cas semblable en accadien parce que la correspondance personnelle entre membres de la famille royale était normalement rédigée en ougaritique.

12 La forme de l'adverbe que l'on rencontre le plus souvent est celle où figurent les allongements par *-n-* et par *-y*, qu'il ne faut pas confondre avec le morphème du duel qui est homographe. On trouve une fois *ht*, “voici” (RS 17.139), mais dans ce cas la formule fait partie de la formule plus large *lḥt* ... *ky*.

13 Certains textes permettent d'établir une distinction sémantique entre *hn-* et *hl-*: il s'agit de l'usage du seul *hl-* pour introduire le corps de la lettre lorsqu'il ne s'agit pas de la formule de bien-être, toujours en rapport avec la situation de l'expéditeur. En plus du sens présentatif, “voici”, ce mot comporte donc la nuance locale d'“ici”.

14 La particule *ṯm-* est absente après l'omission de la première partie de la formule en RS 9.479A, RS 18.287, et RS 19.102 (seconde lettre); elle est absente après la formule introduite par *hnn* en RS 92.2010, mais dans une variante de la formule de retour de nouvelles; les particules *ṯm-* et *hn-/hl-* sont toutes deux absentes en RS 15.008; la particule *hn-* ou *hl-* n'est absente qu'une fois lorsque la formule de retour de nouvelles est omise, en RS 92.2010 (ce cas ne se rencontre pas dans les textes accadiens provenant d'ougaritains, mais on le trouve une fois dans une lettre du roi du Ḫatti, RS 20.212).

15 La préposition est omise seulement dans RS 92.2005, dans la formule *ṯm-*, probablement dans les deux lettres que portent cette tablette. En RS 92.2010 et RS 94.2479 on trouve d'autres formules, *šlm* à l'état construit (à la place de la formule *ṯm-*... *ʿm-*) et *b bt mlk* (après *hlny hnn*), respectivement.

16 Le pronom est attesté au singulier ({ʿmy}) et, en RS 8.315, au duel ({ʿmny}).

positionnelle désignant le destinataire peut être nominale (par ex., "avec ma mère = chez ma mère") ou pronominale ("avec toi = chez toi"), la seconde forme étant moins fréquente.[18]

Le noyau du rapport donné et de celui qui est demandé est toujours identique: l'expéditeur dit qu'il se porte bien et il demande que le destinataire lui renvoie des nouvelles de son bien-être.[19] Si le sujet de la seconde formule est invariable, toujours *mnm šlm*,[20] dans la première formule on rencontre davantage de variété: (1) *kll šlm* (RS 11.872, RS 16.137bis, RS 17.139, RS 94.2479); (2) *šlm kll* (RS 15.008, RS 34.124); (3) *kll mʾid(m) šlm* (RS 8.315, RS 18.038, RS 20.199); (4) seulement *šlm* (RS 16.379, RS 18.031, RS 18.147, RS 29.095, RS 92.2005); (5) *mʾid šlm* (RS 92.2010). La distribution des éléments autour de *šlm* dans le rapport de l'expéditeur nous oblige à conclure qu'il s'agit là d'une phrase verbale. Cette conclusion est appuyée par la formule accadienne correspondante, où la forme est toujours *šulmu*, à savoir le nom *šulmu* employé au permansif: la forme correspondante en ouest-sémitique est le parfait d'un verbe statif. Nous ne sommes pas en mesure de déterminer si l'emploi de cette forme verbale est partout absolu, à savoir sans sujet exprimé ("(ça) va bien"), et dans ce cas *kll* lorsqu'il est présent serait à analyser comme à l'accusatif adverbial ("ça va entièrement bien"),[21] ou si *kll* est le sujet du verbe là où il est présent ("tout va bien").[22]

---

17 En RS 18.038:3 on trouve *ʿm špš*, en RS 17.434⁺:2-3 on peut vraisemblablement restituer, comme nous l'avons indiqué plus haut, *h⸢l⸣[ny] ʿm šp[š] ⸢w⸣ ʿm mlkt*, et en RIH 77/21A:4-5 on peut restituer *hlny* [*ʿm špš* ...], comme nous l'avons aussi indiqué plus haut.

18 Elle est attestée cinq fois: RS 18.031, RS 18.287, RS 19.158B, RS 29.095, RS 34.124.

19 Ainsi l'allusion à ces nouvelles de bien-être prend la forme de *lḥt šlm*; dans la seule attestation de cette expression (RS 17.139:5), elle signifie: "(message sur) tablette (demandant des nouvelles concernant) le bien-être (du destinataire)". Il ne faut pas donner trop de poids à ces allusions au "bien-être" des correspondants: la formule ne constitue guère plus qu'une façon d'exprimer ce que nous appelons "des nouvelles". Comme nous l'avons dit une fois: "It is part of the psychology of Ugaritic epistolography to ask for good news" (*UF* 19 [1987], p. 211).

20 L'omission de *šlm* dans la formule de bien-être en RS 94.2479:8 nous paraît fautive. Le cas de l'omission de *mnm šlm* dans RS 29.095 est plus délicat mais nous semble relever aussi d'une erreur de scribe (voir notre traduction plus haut).

21 Rainey, *IOS* 3 (1973), p. 56 (à propos de RS 15.008:14-15); *idem*, *JAOS* 94 (1974), p. 191 (de même); Levine, *Presence* (1974), pp. 10-11, n. 21; cf. Dietrich et Loretz, *UF* 18 (1986), p. 114 ("ist vollständiges Wohlbefinden" [traduction de RS 15.008:14-15]); *idem*, *UF* 26 (1994), p. 68 ("ist das Wohlergehen vollkommen").

22 Ginsberg, *BASOR* 72 (1938), p. 19 "all has been very well"; Gordon, *Ugaritic Grammar* (1940), § 5.43 (p. 28) "all is quite peaceful"; *idem*, *Or* 12 (1943), pp. 73-74 "all is very well"; *idem*, *Ugaritic*

En revanche, le caractère consonantique de l'écriture ougaritique permet deux analyses des premiers éléments de la formule de retour de nouvelles, soit verbale: /mannama šalima/, "quoi (que ce soit qui) va bien", soit nominale: /mannama šalāmu/, "quoi (que ce soit) de bien".[23] Par souci d'uniformité avec la première for-

---

Handbook (1947), § 6.43 (p. 32) "all is quite peaceful"; *idem, Ugaritic Literature* (1949), p. 117 "all is very well"; *idem, Ugaritic Manual* (1955), § 20.916 (p. 278) "everything is (very) peaceful"; *idem, Ugaritic Textbook* (1965), § 19.1240 (p. 419-420) "'everything is (very) peaceful' = 'all is well'"; Virolleaud, *PRU* II (1957), p. 31 "tout va bien" (traduction de RS 15.008:14-15); Aistleitner, *WUS* (1963), § 1320 (p. 150) "Gesamtheit, Alles"; Parker, *Studies* (1967), p. 19 "everything is fine"; Ahl, *Epistolary Texts* (1973), p. 407 (*et passim*) "all is very well"; Cunchillos, *Naissance* (1982), p. 180 "tout va pour le mieux"; *idem, Alonso Schökel* (1983), p. 64 "todo va muy bien"; *idem, Díez Macho* (1986), p. 261 "tout va bien"; *idem, MB* 48 (1987), p. 29 "tout va pour le mieux"; *idem, Estudios* (1989), p. 82 "todo va muy bien"; idem, *TO* II (1989), p. 284 (*et passim*) "tout va très bien"; Pardee, *AfO* 31 (1984), p. 214 "everything is very well" et p. 228 "kalīlu [ma']da šalima" (RS 20.199:12-13); p. 220 "everything is well" et p. 229 "šalima kalīlu" (RS 15.008:14-15); pp. 224, 227 "everything is well" et p. 230 "kalīlu šalima" (RS 11.872:10 et RS 17.139:7); cf. *idem, Les textes rituels* (2000), p. 649, n. 28 à propos de RS 24.260; Widbin, *East Archives* (1985), p. 42 "Everything is well" (traduction de RS 15.008:14-15). Loewenstamm a traduit *kll šlm* et *šlm kll* par "perfect well-being", sans indiquer explicitement ni son analyse de *kll*, ni sa façon de comprendre la formule *kll mi'd(m) šlm* (*Bib* 56 [1975], p. 112).

Pour Dahood, *Or* 45 (1976), p. 339, *kll* serait un nom commun lorsque ce mot précède *šlm*, qui serait toujours un nom commun (*kll šlm* = "the perfection of peace"), un adjectif lorsqu'il le suit (*šlm kll* = "perfect peace"). Cette explication de *šlm* comme à l'état construit lorsqu'il précède *šlm* est contredite par la formule *kll mi'd(m) šlm*.

Dans les textes accadiens cités plus bas, le mot correspondant, *gabbu*, est attesté trois fois au nominatif (RS 17.247; RS 20.212; RS 20.227 – les deux premiers textes proviennent de la cour du Ḫatti), deux fois à l'accusatif (RS 17.383; RS 34.173). La forme à l'accusatif est placée deux fois devant *šulmu* (RS 17.383 [*gabba šulmu*], RS 34.173 [*gabba danniš danniš šulmu*]); on trouve une fois le nominatif dans cette situation (*gabbu šulmu*: RS 17.247). Dans les deux autres textes, on rencontre soit *gabbu bītu šulmu*, "toute la maison(née) va bien", soit *gabbu danniš šulmu*, "tout va très bien" (voir les notes à propos de RS 20.212:3' et de RS 20.227:11'). La seconde lecture correspond évidemment mieux à la formule ougaritique, où l'on trouve *kll mi'd(m) šlm*, mais non pas *kll bt(h) šlm*.

23 Le premier à comprendre la structure de cette formule, Ginsberg (*BASOR* 72 [1938], p. 19) a traduit *šlm* comme nom: "what welfare", et en cela fut suivi par Gordon (*Or* 12 [1943], pp. 73-74, et toutes ses publications ultérieures), et par plusieurs autres spécialistes (Richardson, *JBL* 66 [1947], pp. 322-323; Parker, *Studies* [1967], p. 19; Ahl, *Epistolary Texts* [1973], p. 139; Gevirtz, *Or* 42 [1973], p. 171; Kristensen, *UF* 9 [1977], p. 154, première interprétation; Römer, *Hulst* [1977], pp. 136, 139; Brooke, *UF* 11 [1979], p. 70; Cunchillos, *AF* 5 [1979], p. 74; idem, *Naissance* [1982], p. 180; idem, *MB* 48 [1987], p. 29 – un changement d'avis est signalé dans la note 27; Widbin, *East Archives* [1985], p. 42 – à propos de RS 15.008:16-17; Smith, *Milgrom* [1995], p. 797).

mule, nous avons dans le passé préféré vocaliser comme formule verbale.[24] C'est l'examen des formules correspondantes en accadien (voir plus bas) qui nous a convaincu que l'analyse comme expression nominale était préférable. En effet, 1° en accadien on trouve invariablement le nom *šulmānu*, et 2° la rareté de la double formule en accadien laisse penser qu'elles sont d'origine étrangère dans cette langue, peut-être même ougaritique - dans ce cas la forme accadienne serait vraisemblablement le reflet fidèle de l'expression ouest-sémitique. Un troisième argument dans ce sens vient de la variante de la formule rencontrée en RS 4.475:16-17, où *mnm* est suivi sans aucun doute par un nom commun (*mnm rgm d tšmᶜ*);[25] aussi parle dans ce sens la formule modifiée de RS 92.2010, où *mnm* est absent, mais *šlm* est sans doute possible un nom commun, car l'expéditeur demande au destinataire de lui renvoyer (T̠T̠B) des nouvelles de diverses personnes (*šlm* + NP, etc.). Ces trois considérations font pencher, nous semble-t-il, en faveur l'analyse de *mnm šlm* comme pronom indéfini suivi du nom commun[26] (au lieu de pronom indéfini + verbe). Cette partie de la formule constitue donc un *casus pendens* en apposition avec le complément d'objet direct de la clause verbale, *rgm*: "Là-bas avec toi (pour ce qui concerne) quoi que (ce soit) de bien, renvoie-moi une parole (à ce sujet)".[27]

---

24 Par exemple, dans *BiOr* 34 (1977), p. 3; *AfO* 31 (1984), pp. 228-230; *JNES* 49 (1990), pp. 365-366; Bordreuil et Pardee, RSO VII (1991), p. 144; Pardee et Whiting, *BSOAS* 50 (1987), pp. 5, 8, 9.

25 Voir Gordon, *Ugaritic Textbook* (1965), § 6.29 (p. 41).

26 A notre connaissance, il n'existe toujours pas d'indice provenant de Ras Shamra concernant la vocalisation du nom commun *šlm* signifiant "bien-être, paix". Nous vocalisons conventionnellement /šalām-/. Suivant l'usage majoritaire qu'attestent les textes accadiens cités plus bas, nous avons vocalisé le mot signifiant "le bien-être" comme un nominatif, bien que les trois cas soient possibles, comme le montrent les textes accadiens (nominatif = apposition avec *mannama* dans une construction *casus pendens*; génitif = *mannama* à l'état construit; accusatif = apposition dans une construction où *mnm šlm* est marqué comme complément d'objet direct du verbe dans la clause principale). Sur vingt-neuf exemples accadiens, on rencontre dix-huit cas de *šulmānu* au nominatif, trois au génitif, deux à l'accusatif, et le mot est restitué dans six des textes cités.

27 Cette analyse syntaxique des éléments *mnm šlm* est à la base des interprétations des auteurs cités plus haut, note 23, et aussi de la nôtre (note 24), où nous avons pourtant pris *šlm* pour une forme verbale.

Rien ne permet de penser que la fonction de *mnm* ait été interrogative, selon l'interprétation usuelle de Virolleaud dans ses *editiones principes* (suivi par Kaiser, *ZDPV* 86 [1970], pp. 19-20; Loewenstamm, *Lešonenu* 23 [1958-59], p. 75 [cf. *idem*, *Comparative Studies* [1980], p. 60, supplément à la note 26]; *idem*, *UF* 5 [1973], p. 210-211; *idem*, *Comparative Studies* [1980], p. 451, n. 7a [ici la fonction de *mnm* est définie comme celle d'un pronom indéfini, mais la phrase est toujours traduite comme interrogative: "'Is whatsoever welfare with', i.e. 'is all right with'"]; Aartun, *Partikeln* I [1974], pp. 5, 55-56; *idem*, *Partikeln* II [1978], pp. 57, 77, 79; Milano, *OrAn* 16 [1977], p. 23; Lipiński, *OLP* 12 [1981], pp. 93, 94, 99; Hoftijzer, *Schrijvend Verleden* [1983], pp. 95, 97; Sivan,

Le verbe de la formule de retour de nouvelles est toujours ṮB[28] au schème-Š (avec assimilation – selon le norme ougaritique – du /š/ à la première consonne de la

Grammar [1997], p. 59; cf. Kristensen, *UF* 9 [1977], p. 154, seconde interprétation). En effet, la fonction normale de *mnm* en prose est celle d'un pronom indéfini (Gordon, *Ugaritic Textbook* [1965], § 19.1504 [p. 435] – le seul cas de *mnm* interrogatif cité est en poésie [*CTA* 3 IV:48], et dans ce texte *mnm* est en parallèle avec *mn* [III:34] et elle consiste sans aucun doute en *mn* + *m* enclitique, en rapport de toute façon avec un être animé, donc /mīnama/ non pas /mannama/ [ou /mīnummê/ selon la vocalisation adoptée traditionnellement par comparaison avec l'accadien]; Loewenstamm, *Lešonenu* 23 [1958-1959], pp. 75-77 – dans cette étude, Loewenstamm analysait *mnm* dans les textes épistolaires de la même manière que dans *CTA* 3 IV:48; ce n'est que dans *Comparative Studies* [1980], p. 451, n. 7a, qu'il a senti la valeur de la formule parallèle dans les textes accadiens, mais toujours en traduisant la phrase entière comme interrogative, comme nous venons de le voir). Nous verrons plus bas (note 41) que Nougayrol de son côté a interprété la version accadienne de cette formule comme interrogative jusque dans ses dernières publications (du reste, c'est la traduction de Nougayrol que cite Loewenstamm [1980, p. 451, n. 7a] comme autorité en la matière). Pourtant, *mī nummê* n'est pas plus interrogatif en accadien qu'en ougaritique (*AHw*, p. 656; *CAD* M_2, p. 97; Huehnergard, *Akkadian* [1989], p. 138-140; Van Soldt, *Studies* [1991], pp. 407-409). D'ailleurs, la formule accadienne montre que l'analyse de *mnm* dans la formule correspondante en ougaritique comme pronom indéfini personnel (Aartun, *Partikeln* I [1974], pp. 55-56 "jedermann") est aussi inadmissible.

Virolleaud a envisagé l'interprétation du seul cas de cette formule dans les textes publiés dans *PRU* II comme un vœu ("et que tout aille (ou: tout va-t-il) bien pour ma mère" [p. 31]), alors qu'en *PRU* V il est revenu à l'interprétation comme formule interrogative (pp. 16-17). Caquot (*SDB* 9 [1979], col. 1415) et à sa suite Cunchillos (*Díez Macho* [1986], pp. 259-266; *Alonso Schökel* [1983], p. 64; *TO* II [1989], p. 259; *Manual* [1992], p. 176 – changement d'avis, voir la note 23), Althann (*Jeremiah 4-6* [1983], p. 61) et Dietrich et Loretz (*UF* 18 [1986], p. 114; *UF* 26 [1994], p. 68) ont adopté l'interprétation de la formule comme vœu. Cette interprétation n'est pourtant pas plus admissible que l'interprétation comme question. On peut citer les raisons suivantes: (1) la forme est *šlm* (non pas *yšlm*) et le parfait "précatif" ou "optatif" (*šlm* = "que ça aille bien") n'est pas attesté dans ces lettres alors que la phrase nominale "précative" (*šlm* = "qu'il y ait du bien") n'est pas courante; (2) le vœu de santé est souvent exprimé plus avant dans la lettre par *yšlm* (il s'agirait donc d'une double expression du vœu dans ces lettres); (3) la préposition dans le vœu de bien-être est *l*, dans cette formule on trouve *ʿm* presque partout (voir plus haut et la note 15); (4) la formule correspondante dans les lettres en langue accadienne ne constitue pas un vœu: le vœu est *lū šulmu* (≈ *yšlm* en ougaritique) alors que la formule correspondant à *mnm šlm* est *mīnummê šulmānu* (textes cités plus bas); (5) l'interprétation comme souhait ne sert pas mieux à la compréhension des lettres composées de formules où figure celle-ci (comme le pense Cunchillos, *Díez Macho* [1986], p. 265), car selon les deux interprétations de *mnm šlm* la fonction de la formule entière est de demander le retour de nouvelles. Sur la double formule amarnienne où la seconde partie est constituée par un vœux, voir plus bas, la note 73.

28 Plusieurs aspects de la demande de retour de nouvelles en RS 4.475 (*CTA* 53) s'écartent de la formule épistolaire proprement dite. Le passage se lit: {(14) hm . nṯkp (15) mʿnk (16) w . mnm (17) rgm . d . tšmʿ (18) ṯmt . w . št (19) b . spr . ʿmy}, que l'on peut traduire, "S'ils ont été vaincus, ta réponse et quelque parole que tu entends là-bas, informe m'en par écrit". L'un de ces écarts se voit dans la

racine: {ṯṯb}) signifiant le "renvoi" de ses nouvelles par le destinataire.[29] Ce verbe peut s'exprimer soit à l'impératif, soit plus rarement au jussif,[30] avec pour complément d'objet direct le nom commun *rgm*, "parole → message/rapport". Le complément d'objet direct précède normalement le verbe,[31] et la phrase verbale peut ou non être introduite par le *w* d'apodose.[32] Par l'uniformité de l'usage du verbe ṮṮB,

formule "ŠT + *b* + *spr*" à la place de "ṮṮB + *l*". Un autre est la présence de *rgm* après *mnm*, non pas *šlm*, comme dans la formule courante; ce qui présente pourtant l'avantage de fournir encore une preuve contre l'analyse de *mnm* dans la formule que nous étudions comme à fonction interrogative (voir plus haut). Deux autres textes comportant des formules de retour de nouvelles fournissent des traits d'union entre l'expression de RS 4.475 et la double formule que nous étudions ici. En effet, dans RS [Varia 4] on trouve aussi l'allusion à une situation précise et une demande de retour de nouvelles, mais l'expression utilisée emploie le verbe ṮṮB avec comme complément d'objet direct *rgm*: {(15) w h⸢-⸣ . ʾaḫy (16) bny . yšʾal (17) ṯryl . w rgm (18) ṯṯb . l ʾaḫk (19) l ʾadnk}, "Et voici, que mon frère, mon fils fasse la demande auprès de *Ṯarriyelli*, et ensuite renvoie un rapport à ton frère, ton seigneur" (traduction reflétant la lecture de {h⸢t⸣} à la ligne 15; si la bonne lecture est {h⸢m⸣} il s'agissait d'une phrase conditionnelle: "Si mon frère demande ..."). En RS 94.2284:24 on trouve en plein milieu de la lettre la formule {w mnm . rgm . w ṯṯb ...}, qui semble signifier "Et quoi qu'il y ait comme rapport, renvoie(-le moi) ...". Ces trois textes se situent donc à l'écart de la double formule épistolaire, mais en ce faisant ils permettent d'établir l'identité de fonction de la particle *mnm* dans les formules *mnm rgm* et *mnm šlm*. C'est sur ce point précis que nous nous séparons de Sivan (*Grammar* [1997], pp. 59, 60), pour qui la particule serait simplement indéfinie dans l'expression *mnm rgm*, interrogative dans l'expression *mnm šlm*.

29 La formule ne s'applique pas au messager mais au destinataire, et la traduction anglaise n'est donc pas "bring back" (Levine, *Numbers* [1993], p. 356), mais "send back".

30 On rencontre *rgm ṯṯb* en RS 9.479A, *ṯṯb rgm* en RS 15.008 et *w rgm ṯṯb* en RS 94.2479, toutes des lettres d'inférieur masculin à supérieur féminin. La formule n'était pourtant pas de rigueur dans cette situation, comme le montre RS 20.199, adressée par inférieur masculin à supérieur féminin. Cf. Kristensen, *UF* 9 (1977), p. 155 (qui cite aussi RS 16.137bis, où le verbe est entièrement restituée); Cunchillos, *TO* II (1989), pp. 260-261.

31 ṮṮB suivi de *rgm* se trouve en RS 15.008, RS 16.137bis (en grande partie restitué), et RS 16.379 (cf. De Moor, *Verse* [1993], p. 193, n. 9).

32 La formule avec *w* d'apodose se rencontre moins fréquemment que l'autre: quatre fois avec la particule (RS 11.872, RS 16.379, RS 17.139, RS 94.2479), contre quinze d'exemples de l'expression simple (RS 8.315, RS 9.479A, RS 15.008, RS 16.137[bis], RS 18.031, RS 18.147, RS 19.102, RS 19.148, RS 20.199, RS 29.095, RS 34.124, RS 92.2005 [les deux lettres], RS 92.2010 [*šlm* ... *ʾat ṯṯb*], RS 95.5003⁺). Méconnaissant l'usage du *w* d'apodose, Dietrich et Loretz ont cité la présence de cette conjonction comme preuve de l'analyse comme deux clauses indépendantes, dont la première exprimerait un vœu (*UF* 18 [1986], p. 114, n. 32). On doit aussi repousser l'explication du *w* comme "emphatic" (Kristensen, *UF* 9 [1977], p. 155): le *w* dit "d'apodose" est trop fréquent dans les langues nord-ouest sémitiques pour penser à autre chose dans cette formule (voir Groß, *Pendenskonstruktion* [1987]). Il va sans dire que la méconnaissance de la nature de la particle *mnm* (voir plus haut et la note 27) va de pair avec celle de la clause suivante comme indépendante; l'usage du *w* d'apodose dans deux expressions où figurent des variantes de la formule de retour de nouvelles (RS 4.475 et RS

l'ougaritique marque sa différence par rapport à l'accadien, où l'on rencontre deux verbes, "renvoyer" et "écrire",[33] et où l'on rencontre l'omission du complément d'objet direct (voir plus bas).[34] La préposition qui accompagne le verbe ṮṮB pour marquer le complément d'objet indirect est *l* ou *ʿm*, la première étant plus fréquente.[35] Le complément d'objet indirect lui-même peut consister soit en un pronom ("renvoie-moi une réponse"), soit en un nom commun ("renvoie à ton serviteur une réponse"), sans préférence marquée pour l'une ou l'autre de ces formes.[36]

La formule en langue accadienne

Les expressions accadiennes correspondant à la formule ougaritique étant assez mal connues, mais en même temps précieuses pour la bonne compréhension de la version ougaritique, il vaut la peine de les citer *in extenso*. Nous les citons ici avec traduction[37] et dans l'ordre des numéros "RS".[38]

94.2284:24, surtout le second – textes cités note 28) ne laisse aucun doute quant à la bonne interprétation du *w* dans les quatre exemples de la double formule où figure *w*.

33 Voir plus bas, citations des textes accadiens et notre analyse comparative. La formule "ŠT + *b* + *spr*" en RS 4.475 fournit l'exemple en ougaritique d'une autre façon d'exprimer la demande de retour de nouvelles, mais parce que le contexte aussi est particulier et que cette expression ne revient plus dans ces textes, on doit conclure que cette formule n'est pas stéréotypée au même point que "*rgm* + ṮṮB" (cf. plus haut, la note 28). En RS [Varia 4] on trouve la formule "*rgm* + ṮṮB", mais sans la formule "*mnm* X", et il s'agit là aussi d'une expression adaptée à une situation particulière (texte cité note 28).

34 *rgm* n'est omis en ougaritique que dans la formule allongée *šlm* ... *ṯṯb* de RS 92.2010:12-20.

35 "*rgm* + ṮṮB + *ʿm*" en RS 15.008, RS 92.2005 (première lettre) et RS 94.2479 (cf. "*šlm* + ṮṮB + *ʿm*" en RS 92.2010:13-20), "*rgm* + ṮṮB + *l*" dix fois: ici, RS 9.479A, RS 11.872, RS 16.379, RS 17.139, RS 19.102, RS 19.158B, RS 20.199, RS 29.095, RS 34.124 (cf. Rainey, *Proceedings* [1969], p. 206); la formule prépositionnelle n'est située au début de l'apodose que dans un seul de ces cas (RS 15.008). L'usage n'est pas lié à la forme de la référence à l'expéditeur, c'est-à-dire par nom commun ou par pronom, car les deux formes de l'expression s'emploient avec les deux prépositions (voir la note suivante). Dans la formule où paraît le jussif de ṮṮB, on trouve une fois *l* (RS 9.479A: *rgm tṯṯb l ʿbdh*), deux fois *ʿm* (RS 15.008: *ʿmy tṯṯb rgm*, RS 94.2479: *w rgm tṯṯb ʿm ʿbdh*).

36 Parmi les textes assez bien conservés pour y lire l'expression, on trouve quatre fois *ṯṯb* ... *ʿbdk* (RS 8.315, RS 18.287, RS 19.102, RS 20.199), une fois *tṯṯb* ... *ʿbdh* (RS 9.479A) et une fois *tṯṯb* ... *ʿbdk* (RS 94.2479); on rencontre huit fois le syntagme où le pronom est attaché à la préposition, *l* (RS 11.872, RS 16.379, RS 17.139, RS 29.095, RS 34.124) ou *ʿm* (RS 15.008, RS 92.2005, RS 92.2010 [*šlm*-X ... *ṯṯb*]).

37 Voulant faire ressortir la structure des formules, les traductions attachées à ces textes sont les nôtres, à la place des traductions moins littérales proposées par les éditeurs.

38 Comme nous l'avons fait pour les textes ougaritiques, nous indiquons entre parenthèses à la fin de la traduction la forme précise, à savoir double ou simple, que manifeste la formule dans chaque texte. Aussi, pour alléger cette présentation, nous n'indiquons pas ici tout le début de la lettre, et pour cette

(1) RS 1.[057]:5'-6': {[i]t-ti EN-ia mi-nu-um-me-e (6') [š]ul-ma-nu ṭé-ma li-te-ru-[ni]},[39] "Chez mon maître, quoi que (ce soit de) bien, qu'il me renvoie un rapport (à ce sujet)" (formule simple, adressée au destinataire; inférieur social).

(2) RS 12.005:0'-3' (*PRU* III, pp. 16-17): {[aš-ra-nu] (1') [it-ti-ka] ù it-ti DUMU-ia (2') [mi-nu-me-e] šul-ma-nu (3') [ṭé-ma šap-p]a-ra}, "Là-bas chez toi et chez mon fils, quoi que (ce soit de) bien, écris-moi[40] un rapport (à ce sujet)" ([?] + formule adressée au destinataire; rapport de supérieur à inférieur avec terme familial [destinataire = "fils"], mais on ne sait pas s'il s'agit de l'usage social du terme).[41]

(3) RS 15.033:7-15 (*PRU* III, pp. 15-16): {aš-šum šul-ma-na (8) im-ma-ti$_4$-ma la aš-pu-ra-ak-ku (9) an-na-ka-nu ú-ul aš-ba-ku (10) i-na KUR-ḫa-at-ti aš-ba-ku (11) aš-šum an-ni-i (12) šul-ma-na ú-ul aš-pu-ra-ak-ku (13) i-na-an-na it-ti ŠEŠ-ia (14) mi-nu-um-me-e šul-ma-nu (15) ṭé-ma-ti šap-pa-ra}, "Quant au fait que (des nouvelles de ma) santé je ne t'ai jamais mandée(s): je n'habite plus ici, j'habite en pays hittite; c'est pourquoi je ne t'ai point mandé (des nouvelles de ma) santé. Or, chez mon frère, quoi que (ce soit de) bien, écris-moi des rapports (à ce sujet)" (formule double, la première partie étant de forme particulière; égal).

(4) RS 16.111:7-9 (*PRU* III, p. 13-14): {it-ti LUGAL KUR-u-ga-ri-it (8) ù it-ti-ki mi-nu-me-e (9) šul-ma-nu ṭé-ma te-er-ri}, "Chez le roi d'Ougarit et chez toi-même, quoi que (ce soit de) bien, renvoie(-moi) un rapport (à ce sujet)" (formule adressée en même temps à la destinataire et au roi; supérieur familial [destinataire = "fille" mais aussi "reine"]).

(5) RS 16.116:6 (*PRU* III, p. 10): {[a-n]a ^{d}UTU-ši-i[a šul-mu]}, "Chez le soleil cela va bien" (formule simple, concernant le bien-être, chez l'expéditeur, du roi du Ḫatti; le rapport entre les correspondants eux-mêmes est inconnu).

---

raison nous indiquons la relation de l'expéditeur par rapport au destinataire. On se souviendra que "frère" est ambigu, utilisé régulièrement pour les rapports d'ordre social aussi bien que familial, et que les autres termes familiaux s'emploient aussi pour exprimer un rapport social, bien que moins fréquemment que "frère".

39 Ce texte a été publié en copie par Virolleaud, *Syria* 10 (1929), pl. LXXVI, n° 2; première transcription et traduction par de Langhe ("grâce au concours de M. G. Dossin"), *Textes* (1945) I, pp. 115-117; nouvelles transcription et traduction par Ahl, *Epistolary Texts* (1973), pp. 187-188.

40 Ahl remarque: "This verb looks like a G stem imperative formed from the present tense, perhaps by analogy to the imperative formed from the imperfect in Ugaritic. The final *a* is a ventive suffix" (*Epistolary Texts* [1973], p. 525, n. 59). On peut objecter que l'impératif n'est "formed from the imperfect" que par les grammariens de l'époque moderne, mais cela n'amoindrit en rien l'explication par analogie, qui implique, ajoutons-nous, que le YQTL ougaritique était pour les scribes de ces textes en prose l'équivalent du présent-futur en accadien, et non pas donc de l'accadien IPRUS. Cela cadre bien avec notre constat de l'absence du YQTL-parfait dans ces textes (voir la note 27).

41 Remarquons à propos du premier de ces textes publiés par Nougayrol que celui-ci a pris la formule *mīnummê* ... pour interrogative dans toutes ses publications jusqu'à *PRU* VI (1970), où il propose pour la première fois l'interprétation générale de: "Ici tout va bien: puissent (également) de bonnes nouvelles me parvenir de chez toi!" (p. 12, n. 3 [cf. plus haut, note 27]). Profitant de la longue expérience de Nougayrol, Arnaud traduit *mīnummê* comme introduisant une clause déclarative: "Qu'avec mon seigneur tout va bien: qu'on m'en envoie nouvelle!" (*AuOr* 2 [1984], p. 181, cf. p. 186, traduisant textes d'Émar).

(6) RS 17.078:6-7 (*PRU* IV, pp. 196-197): {it-ti-ka mi-nu-um-me-e (7) [šu]l-ma-ni ṭé-ma-ti šap-pa-ra}, "Chez toi, quoi que (ce soit de) bien, écris(-moi) des rapports (à ce sujet)" (formule simple, adressée au destinataire; supérieur social, rapport exprimé par terme familial [destinataire = "fils" mais aussi "préfet"]).

(7) RS 17.247:4-5 (*PRU* IV, p. 191): {a-nu-ma a-na DINGIR.UTU-ši (5) gab-bu šu-ul-mu}, "Voici (que) chez le Soleil tout va bien" (formule simple, concernant le bien-être, chez l'expéditeur, du roi du Ḫatti; supérieur social).

(8) RS 17.383:6-9 (*PRU* IV, p. 221-23): {e-nu-ma it-ti LUGAL ù it-ti-ia (7) gáb-bá šul-mu aš-ra-nu it-ti (8) LUGAL EN-ia mi-nu-me-e šul-ma-nu (9) ṭé-ma li-te-er-ru-ni}, "Voici (que) chez le roi (du Ḫatti) tout va bien; là-bas chez le roi (d'Ougarit) mon maître, quoi que (ce soit de) bien, qu'il me renvoie un rapport (à ce sujet)"[42] (formule double; la première partie rapporte le bien-être du roi du Ḫatti, la seconde demande les nouvelles du destinataire, qui est le supérieur social de l'expéditeur).

(9) RS 17.422:8-10 (*PRU* IV, p. 223-25): {it-ti EN-ia mi-nu-me-e (9) šul-ma-nu ṭé-ma (10) li-te-er-ru-ni}, "Chez mon maître, quoi que (ce soit de) bien, qu'il me renvoie un rapport (à ce sujet)" (formule simple, adressée au destinataire; inférieur social).

(10) RS 17.428:4-7 (*PRU* VI 9): {e-nu-ma [i]t-ti-ia š[ul-mu] (5) aš-ra-nu it-ti ⸢LÚ⸣-[sà-ki-ni] (6) mi-nu-me-e šul-ma-nu (7) ṭé-ma [li]-te-ru-ni}, "Voici (que) chez moi cela va bien; là-bas chez le préfet, quoi que (ce soit de) bien, qu'il me renvoie un rapport (à ce sujet)" (formule double; égal).

(11) RS 18.089:6-9 (*PRU* VI 15): {[e-nu-ma it-ti-ia šu]⸢l-mu⸣ (7) [aš-ra-nu it-ti-k]⸢a⸣ (8) [mi-nu-me-e šul-]ma-na (9) ṭ[é-ma šu-up]-ra}, "Voici (que) chez moi cela va bien; là-bas chez toi, quoi que (ce soit de) bien, écris-moi un rapport (à ce sujet)" (formule double; égal).

(12) RS 19.006:5-7 (*PRU* VI 1): {⸢i⸣[-nu-m]a ⸢EN⸣-ia ⸢il⸣-tap-ra (6) [a-na] š[u]l-ma-⸢ni⸣-ia (7) [EN-i]a a-na muḫ-ḫ[i-i]a šul-m[u]}, "Puisque mon maître a écrit au sujet de mon bien-être: mon maître, pour moi cela va bien" (formule simple, concernant le bien-être de l'expéditeur; inférieur).

(13) RS 19.050:6-8 (*PRU* VI 14): {e!-nu-ma it-ti-ia š[ul-mu] (7) aš-ra-nu i[t-t]i-k[a mi-nu-ú]-m[e]-e (8) šul-ma<-ni/nu> ṭ[é-ma] šu-u[p-r]a}, "Voici (que) chez moi cela va bien; là-bas chez toi, quoi que (ce soit de) bien, écris-moi un rapport (à ce sujet)" [43] (formule double; probablement égal [sans terme précis]).

---

42 En raison de l'ambiguïté de l'usage de *šarru* en RS 17.383, désignant et le roi d'Ougarit et celui du Ḫatti, la traduction de ce passage dans *CAD* A_2, p. 454, est fautive: *ašrānu* ne signifie pas "ici", mais "là-bas"; *šarru* dans la phrase commençant par *enūma* désigne le roi du Ḫatti, dans la phrase commençant par *ašrānu* le roi d'Ougarit (voir Rainey, *UF* 3 [1971], p. 161, n. 48; Loewenstamm, *UF* 5 [1973], p. 211, n. 10).

43 Cette formule de retour de nouvelles est précédée immédiatement par des vœux de bien-être (l. 3 {... lu-ú šul-m[u] (4) a-n[a] É[-k]a [g]áb-bi mim-m[u-ú ša(?)] (5) a-n[a] m[uḫ-ḫ]i-ka da[n-ní]š lu-ú[(?) šul-mu]}), le seul exemple de cette séquence dans ces textes (on trouve aussi un exemple de la seule formule d'état du destinataire précédée de *lū šulmu* [RS 20.013, seconde lettre – passage cité plus bas, note 55] et un cas de la double formule précédée d'une forme verbale de *šalāmu* [RS 34.164]). Normalement lorsque le vœu exprimé par *lū šulmu* s'accompagne de la formule d'état de bien-être, la formule NṢR s'insère après *lū šulmu*.

(14) RS 19.070:8-16 (*PRU* IV, p. 294): {a-nu-um-ma ^{m}DINGIR-mil-ku (9) LÚ.DUMU.KIN-ni a-na ša-a-li (10) šul-mi ša LUGAL EN-ni (11) [n]a-al-ta-pár-šu (12) [ù m]i-[n]u-[u]m-m[e-]e (13) [šul-ma-nu ṭé-ma] (14) [ša ^{m}tu-ud-ḫa-l]i-ya (15) [LUGAL EN-ni] (16) [li-te-er-ru-ni]}, "Voici (que) nous envoyons[44] Ilimilkou, notre messager, pour demander d'après le bien-être du roi, notre maître. Ainsi, quoi que (ce soit de) bien, qu'on (nous) renvoie un rapport concernant Toudḫaliya" (formule simple, concernant le bien-être, chez l'expéditeur, du roi; inférieur [terme familial, "père", employé pour le destinataire]).

(15) RS 20.013:19-20 (*Ugaritica* V_N 49): {⸢ù⸣ ak-kà-ši[45] aš-r[a]-n[u mi]-nu-me-e šul-ma-ni (20) ṭé-ma te-e[r]-r[a ...]}, "Et quant à toi, là-bas, quoi que (ce soit de) bien, renvoie (-moi)[46] un rapport (à ce sujet)" (formule simple, adressée au destinataire; égal).

(16) RS 20.019:6-7 (*Ugaritica* V_N 48): {it-ti GAŠAN-ia mi-nu-me-e šul-ma-nu (7) ṭé-ma li-te-er-ru-ni}, "Chez ma dame, quoi que (ce soit de) bien, qu'on me renvoie un rapport (à ce sujet)" (formule simple, adressée au destinataire; inférieur social).

(17) RS 20.023:6-8 (*Ugaritica* V_N 54): {e-nu-ma ID-ia šul-mu (7) aš-ra-nu ID-ka mi-nu-mé-e (8) šul-ma-na ṭé-(ma te)[47]-er-an-nu}, "Voici (que) chez moi cela va bien; là-bas chez toi, quoi que (ce soit de) bien, renvoie(-moi) un rapport (à ce sujet)" (formule double; rapport social de l'expéditeur par rapport ou desinataire inconnu, mais il s'agit soit d'égaux, soit de supérieur à inférieur).

(18) RS 20.023:24-28 (*Ugaritica* V_N 54): {e-nu-ma ID-ia š[u]l-mu (25) aš-ra-nu ID EN-ia (26) ù ID GAŠAN-ia mi-nu-me-e (27) šul-ma-ni ṭé-(ma te)-er<-ra-nu>$^{?}$[48] (28) a-na ÌR-MEŠ-ka}, "Voici (que) chez moi cela va bien; là-bas chez mon maître et chez ma dame, quoi que (ce soit de) bien, renvoie(-moi) un rapport (à ce sujet)" (formule double; inférieur social).

(19) RS 20.178 *recto*:13-17 (*Ugaritica* V_N 55): {[a-nu-ma i]t-tu šul-mu (14) [aš-ra-nu i]t-tu ⸢NIN⸣-i[a] (15) [mi-nu-um-me-e] š[ul-ma-nu] (16) [ṭé-ma te-er-ri a-na] (17) [ŠEŠ-ki]},[49] "Voici (que) chez moi! cela va bien; là-bas chez ma sœur, quoi que (ce soit de) bien, renvoie à ton frère un rapport (à ce sujet)" (formule double; égal).

(20) RS 20.178 *verso*:6'-10' (*Ugaritica* V_N 55): {a-nu-ma i[t-tu šul-mu] (7') aš-ra-nu it-t[u MÍ.AM]A-ia (8') mi-nu-um-me-e šul-ma-nu (9') ṭé-ma te-er-ri a-na (10') DUMU-ki},

---

44 Parfait épistolaire: il ne s'agit pas d'une correspondance dans le passé. Le document actuel est vraisemblablement un brouillon, la lettre à laquelle ce texte fait allusion ayant été livrée au destinataire par *ʾIlīmilku*.

45 Cette lecture est proposée par Huehnergard, *Akkadian* (1989), pp. 123, 350.

46 La fin de la forme verbale n'étant pas conservée, on ne sait pas si le complément d'objet indirect était exprimé.

47 A propos de cette graphie bizarre qui revient à la ligne 27 (voir le texte suivant), voir Huehnergard, *Akkadian* (1989), p. 181, n. 312, préférant la lecture et l'interprétation de Nougayrol ({ŠE} = {KUR}? = /mate/ = /ma te/) à d'autres qui ont été proposées ultérieurement.

48 Voir la note précédente.

49 Restitution de Nougayrol d'après la formule correspondante de la seconde lettre inscrite sur cette tablette (citée ici à la suite).

"Voici (que) chez moi! cela va bien; là-bas chez ma mère, quoi que (ce soit de) bien, renvoie à ton fils un rapport (à ce sujet)" (formule double; inférieur familial).

(21) RS 20.189D:1'-4' (*Ugaritica* V_N 73): {[e-nu-]m[a it-ti-ia šul-mu] (2') [aš]-ra-nu [it-ti-ka] (3') mi-nu-um-me-e [šul-ma-nu] (4') ṭé-ma te-er[-ra ...]},[50] "Voici (que) chez moi cela va bien; là-bas chez toi, quoi que (ce soit de) bien, renvoie(-moi) un rapport (à ce sujet)" (formule double; rapport social de l'expéditeur par rapport ou desinataire inconnu).

(22) RS 20.212:3'-4' (*Ugaritica* V_N 33): {it-ti DINGIR.UTU-ši gab-bu dan-ní[š][51] (4') šu-ul-mu}, "Chez le Soleil, tout va très bien" (formule simple, concernant le bien-être, chez l'expéditeur, du roi du Ḫatti; supérieur social).

(23) RS 20.219:7-9 (*Ugaritica* V_N 44): {it-ti LUGAL KUR-ú-ga-rit$_x$ (8) [E]N-ia mi-nu-me-e šul-m[a-nu] (9) [ṭé-]ma te-er-ra a-na Ì[R-ka], "Chez le roi d'Ougarit mon maître, quoi que (ce soit de) bien, renvoie à ton serviteur un rapport (à ce sujet)" (formule simple, adressée au destinataire; inférieur social).

(24) RS 20.227:9'-14' (*Ugaritica* V_N 57): {e-nu-ma it-t[i]-[ia] (10') ù it-ti Ì[R-MEŠ ša it-ti-ia] (11') aš-bu gab-bu ⸢É⸣[-ia[52] šul-mu] (12') it-ti ŠEŠ-ḫi-ia a[š-ra-nu[?]][53] (13') mi-nu-um-me-e [šul-ma-nu ṭé-ma] (14') te-er[-ra ...]},[54] "Voici (que) chez moi et chez les serviteurs qui résident avec moi, toute ma maisonnée va bien; chez mon frère là-bas, quoi que (ce soit de) bien, renvoie(-moi) un rapport (à ce sujet)" (formule double; égal).

(25) RS 20.227 *tranche gauche*:1-2 (*Ugaritica* V_N 57): {[šul-mu aš-ra-n]u it-ti GAŠAN-ia mi-nu-um-me-e (2) [šul-ma-nu ṭé-ma l]i-te-er-ru-ni}, "... va bien; là-bas chez ma dame, quoi que (ce soit de) bien, qu'on me renvoie un rapport (à ce sujet)" (formule double; inférieur social).

(26) RS 21.201:3'-5' (*PRU* VI 20): {e-nu-ma it-ti-ia šul-mu (4') aš-ra-nu it-ti-ka[!] mi-nu-me-e (5') šul-ma-nu ṭé-ma li-te-er-ru-ni}, "Voici (que) chez moi cela va bien; là-bas chez toi, quoi que (ce soit de) bien, qu'on me renvoie un rapport (à ce sujet)" (formule double; rapport social de l'expéditeur par rapport ou destinataire inconnu).

(27) RS 32.204 *recto*:5-9 (RSO VII 19): {⸢a-nu-um-ma⸣ it-ti LUGAL (6) [lu[?]] dan-⸢níš⸣ dan-níš šul-mu (7) ⸢aš⸣-ra-a-nu it-ti MÍ-šar-ra-ti (8) ⸢mi⸣-nu-me-e šu-ul-ma-nu (9) ⸢be⸣-el-ti ṭé-ma li-te-ru-ú-nu}, "Voici (que) chez le roi tout va très, très bien; là-bas chez la reine, quoi que (ce soit de) bien, ma dame, qu'on me renvoie un rapport (à ce sujet)" (formule double; la lettre a été dictée par un personnage socialement inférieur à la destinataire, mais le

---

50 La fin de la forme verbale n'étant pas conservée, on ne sait pas si le complément d'objet indirect était exprimé.

51 La lecture du premier signe de ce mot comme {dan} a été proposée par Rainey (*IOS* 5 [1975], p. 25); l'éditeur avait lu {É-š[u]}, "sa maison".

52 Bien que l'éditeur n'ait pas dessiné les petits clous qui permettraient ici la lecture de *danniš*, le point d'interrogation qu'il attache au mot *bītu* dans sa transcription permet de penser que la lecture de l'adverbe est à considérer. On restituerait dans ce cas {⸢dan⸣-[níš (dan-níš) šul-mu]}.

53 L'éditeur avait raison d'indiquer comme douteuse cette lecture, car *ašrānu* ne suit jamais la formule "*itti* X" (seule la formule difficile de RS 20.013:19-20 s'approche de celle-ci – voir la note 55).

54 La fin de la forme verbale n'étant pas conservée, on ne sait pas si le complément d'objet indirect était exprimé.

rapport de bien-être concerne le roi (de Karchemish), socialement supérieur à ces deux personnages).

(28) RS 32.204 *verso*:6-7 (RSO VII 19): {it-ti LUGAL EN-ia mi-nu-me-e (7) šul-ma-nu ṭé-ma li-te-er-ru-ni}, "Chez le roi mon maître, quoi que (ce soit de) bien, qu'il me renvoie-moi un rapport (à ce sujet)" (formule simple, adressée au destinataire; inférieur social).

(29) RS 34.134:7-10 (RSO VII 31): {e-nu-ma it-ti-ia šul-mu (8) aš-ra-nu it-ti ŠEŠ-ḫi-ia (9) mi-nu-me-e šul-ma-nu (10) lu-ú ti-šap-pa-ra}, "Voici (que) chez moi cela va bien; là-bas chez mon frère, quoi que (ce soit de) bien, que tu m'écrives (à ce sujet)" (formule double; égal).

(30) RS 34.134:27-30 (RSO VII 31): {e-nu-ma it-ti-ia ù it-ti DUMU-ka (28) šul-mu aš-ra-nu it-ti ŠEŠ-ia (29) mi-nu-me-e šul$^{!}$-ma-nu (30) lu-ú ti-šap-pa-ra}, "Voici (que) chez moi et chez ton fils cela va bien; là-bas chez mon frère, quoi que (ce soit de) bien, que tu m'écrives (à ce sujet)" (formule double; égal).

(31) RS 34.139:4 (RSO VII 14): {[a]-nu-um-ma it-ti-ia SILIM-mu "Voici (que) chez moi cela va bien" (formule siumple; égal).[55]

(32) RS 34.141:8-10 (RSO VII 32): {e-nu-ma it-ti-ia šul-mu aš$^{!}$-ra-nu (9) it-ti ŠEŠ DU$_{10}$-GA-ia mi-nu-me-e (10) šul-ma-nu lu-ú ta-šap-pa-ra}, "Voici (que) chez moi cela va bien; là-bas chez mon doux frère, quoi que (ce soit de) bien, que tu m'écrives (à ce sujet)" (formule double; égal).

(33) RS 34.161:6-9 (RSO VII 22): {e-nu-ma it-ti-ia šul-mu (7) aš-ra-nu it-ti ŠEŠ-ia (8) mi-nu-me-e šul-ma-nu (9) ṭé-ma li-te-ru-ni}, "Voici (que) chez moi cela va bien; là-bas chez mon frère, quoi que (ce soit de) bien, qu'il me renvoie un rapport (à ce sujet)" (formule double; égal).

(34) RS 34.164:11-20 (RSO VII 34): {e-nu-ma an-na-ka-nu (12) a-na ŠEŠ-ku-nu (13) a-na É.MEŠ-ku-nu (14) ù iš-tu li-it (15) DUMU.MEŠ-ri-ku-<nu> dan-niš (16) dan-niš šul-mu aš-ra-nu (17) iš-tu li-it (18) [ŠE]Š.MEŠ-ia mi-nu-me-e (19) [šul-ma-na] ṭe$_4$-ma te-ru (20) [at-tu]-ú-nu}, "Voici (qu')ici pour tes frères, pour tes maisons et pour tes fils cela va très, très bien; là-bas du côté de chez mes frères, quoi que (ce soit de) bien, renvoyez(-moi) vous-même un rapport (à ce sujet)" (formule double; égal).

(35) RS 34.165:3-5 (RSO VII 46): {[... a-na[56] É.ḪI.]A-ia DAM.MEŠ-i[a ...] (4) [...]-ia ANŠE.KUR.RA.MEŠ-i[a ...] (5) [da-an-ni-i]š da-an-ni-i[š šul-mu]}, "... pour mes mai-

---

55 La deuxième partie de la formule, qui serait à sa place dans une lettre entre personnages de rang égal, est dans cette lettre remplacée par un vœu de bien-être, mais ce vœu commence par la préposition *itti*, anormale dans les vœux: {(5) [i]t-ti-ka ù it-ti ÉRIN.MEŠ-ka (6) [A]NŠE.KUR.RA.MEŠ-ka i-na ŠÀ KUR-ka (7) dan-⸢níš⸣ [dan-níš] lu-ú SILIM-mu}, "Que chez toi, chez tes troupes, les chevaux dans ton pays, cela aille excellemment bien". Cette formule ressemble par l'usage de la préposition *itti* à la formule de retour de nouvelles du destinataire, mais la présence de {lu-ú SILIM-mu} et l'absence de la formule de renvoi de nouvelles assurent qu'il s'agit d'une salutation. On peut comparer l'usage de *ana* sans *muḫḫu* en RS 20.013, seconde lettre (*Ugaritica* V$_N$ 49): {(14) a-nu-um-ma a-[n]a É-ka (15) ù a-na a-bi-ka [MÍ](?).AMA-ka (16):DAM-ka ù a-na gab-ba (17):mim-mu-ú ša ŠEŠ DU$_{10}$.GA-ia (18) dan-níš dan-níš lu-ú šu[l]-mu}, "Voici: à ta maison, et à ton père, ta mère, ta femme, et à tout ce qui est à mon cher frère, grandement, grandement, salut!".

sons, mes épouses, [...], mes [X], mes chevaux, [...}, cela va très, très bien" (formule simple, concernant le bien-être de l'expéditeur; égal).

(36) RS 34.173:6-8 (RSO VII 33): {[a]-nu-ma it-ti-ia gáb-bá dan-níš (7) [šu]l-mu aš-ra-nu it-ti ŠEŠ DU_{10}-GA-ia (8) [mi-n]u-me-e šul-ma-nu lu-ú tal-ta-nap-pa-ra}, "Voici (que) chez moi cela va bien; là-bas chez mon doux frère, quoi que (ce soit de) bien, que tu m'écrives continuellement (à ce sujet)" (formule double; égal).

(37) RS [Varia 26]:19-26 (RSO VII 30): {e-nu-ma i-na URU-e-mar (20) ak-tal-da a-na muḫ-ḫi-ia (21) ÌR ù GEMÉ-ka (22) dan-níš dan-níš šul-mu (23) aš-ra-nu it-ti (24) ŠEŠ-ḫi-ia mi-nu-me-e (25) šul-ma-nu (26) lu-ú ti-šap-pa-ra}, "Voici (que) je suis arrivé à Émar. Pour moi, ton serviteur et ta servante cela va très, très bien; là-bas chez mon frère, quoi que (ce soit de) bien, que tu m'écrives (à ce sujet)" (formule double; égal).

Analyse comparative

La formule accadienne de retour de nouvelles se différencie de la formule ougaritique en ce qu'elle manifeste davantage de variété dans l'expression verbale. En effet, si en ougaritique on ne trouve que ṮṮB, en accadien on rencontre deux verbes principaux: (1) *šapāru*, "écrire", à la deuxième personne du singulier, impératif ou présent-futur; (2) *târu*, schème-D, qui correspond par son sens à ṮB, schème-Š, en ougaritique, à savoir "renvoyer", attesté à l'impératif, comme en ougaritique, et au précatif de la troisième personne, ce qui n'est pas attesté en ougaritique.

Une autre classification correspond plus directement aux usages attestés par les lettres ougaritiques, à savoir selon la distribution des deux parties de la formule: il existe (1) vingt-six exemples de l'expression particulière à l'envoi des nouvelles concernant le bien-être de l'expéditeur (le n° 3 n'est pas inclus dans ce total, étant de forme très particulière); (2) trente et un exemples de la formule requérant retour de nouvelles; (3) vingt textes comportant les deux parties de la formule;[57] (4) six textes comportant seul le rapport de l'expéditeur; (5) dix exemples de seule la demande de retour de nouvelles.

Comme en ougaritique, lorsque les deux parties de la formule sont présentes, l'expéditeur fait toujours état de son bien-être avant de demander des nouvelles du destinataire. Aussi comme en ougaritique, la présence de la seule première partie de

---

56 Nous maintenons ici la restitution de l'éditeur, mais, si l'orgine en dehors de l'Ougarit ne favorise pas la restitution de cette préposition, on pourrait aussi restituer *itti*, plus fréquent dans cette formule (voir les remarques qui suivent cette liste).

57 RS 12.005 n'est pas compté ici et dans les deux totaux suivants parce que l'état du texte ne permet pas de déterminer si ce texte comportait la première partie de la formule.

la formule se rencontre surtout lorsque l'expéditeur est le supérieur social.[58] En revanche, on trouve deux exemples de l'omission du rapport de l'expéditeur lorsque celui-ci est de rang supérieur (mais uniquement d'ordre familial: RS 16.111 et RS 17.078) et deux exemples lorsqu'il est l'égal du destinataire (RS 15.033 et RS 20.013) – cela est attesté en ougaritique uniquement si l'expéditeur est de rang inférieur.

La demande de retour de nouvelles n'est exprimée par un expéditeur de rang supérieur que si le rapport est familial (RS 12.005, RS 16.111, RS 17.078); toutes les autres attestations de cette partie de la formule sont dans des lettres d'inférieur à supérieur (onze exemples) ou entre égaux (quinze exemples).

Aussi comme en ougaritique la situation respective des correspondants est indiquée par les particules *enūma/anumma*[59] et *ašrānu*. L'adverbe *ašrānu* est souvent absent lorsque la première partie de la formule est omise, mais les scribes d'Ougarit ne laissaient pas tomber la particule introduisant la première partie.[60] Le nom ou le pronom par lequel on mentionne le correspondant est introduit normalement par la préposition signifiant "avec" (*itti* ≈ *ʿm* en ougaritique), rarement par *ana*,[61] préposi-

58 Pourtant à la différence de l'ougaritique, on rencontre ici trois exemples de l'emploi de seule la première partie de la formule par un personnage de rang inférieur ou égal au destinataire: le premier (RS 19.006), d'inférieur à supérieur, comporte une explication de la raison de cet envoi de nouvelles; le deuxième (RS 34.139), entre "frères", remplace la formule de retour de nouvelles par une bénédiction; le troisième (RS 34.165) est constitué par un roi qui se nomme "frère" de son correspondant mais qui se sent vraisemblablement supérieur à celui-ci.

59 On peut envisager que l'usage d'*enūma* et d'*anumma* correspond à l'usage de *hn-* et *hl-*, respectivement, en ougaritique; du moins d'après *CAD A_2*, pp. 147-148, *anumma* prend la nuance d'"ici" plus facilement qu'*enūma*. Loewenstamm (*UF* 5 [1973], pp. 210-211; *Comparative Studies* [1980], pp. 451-454) a nié toute distinction entre les particules, tant en ougaritique qu'en accadien, et Huehnergard n'a pas trouvé de différence entre les deux particules accadiennes (*Akkadian* [1989], pp. 196-197). D'ailleurs, si l'usage des deux particules ougaritiques n'est pas identique, elles paraissent interchangeables dans cette formule, et il est donc impossible de fonder sur les textes épistolaires un jugement quant à l'usage des particules accadiennes.

60 Là où le début de la formule est conservé, on trouve l'absence de la particule uniquement dans les lettres provenant de la cour hittite: RS 16.116 et RS 20.212.

61 Dans le rapport de l'expéditeur on trouve une fois *anumma ana* X (RS 17.247), deux fois *enūma* ... *ana muḫḫi-* ... (RS 19.006 et RS [Varia 26]), et une fois *enūma annakānu ana* X (RS 34.164) – cette dernière formule correspond de près à *hlny hnn* en RS 94.2479. Dans l'une des deux lettres de la cour hittite où la particule d'introduction est omise (voir la note précédente), la préposition est *ana* (RS 16.116), et l'éditeur de RS 34.165 a restitué *ana* dans la formule de l'expéditeur de cette lettre (voir plus haut, note 56). Dans la formule de retour de nouvelles, on trouve une fois *ana* X *ašrānu*, si l'analyse de {AG-GA-ŠI[!]} en RS 20.013:19 par Huehnergard est admise (voir plus haut, la note 45),

tion qui correspond au plus près à *l* en ougaritique (nous rappelons que *l* n'est pas attesté dans cette formule en ougaritique, *b* une seule fois), une fois par *ištu lēt*, "du côté de chez" (RS 34.164, dans la formule de retour de nouvelles).

Suivant les règles de la morphologie accadienne, le complément d'objet indirect du verbe exprimant le renvoi de nouvelles est exprimé par une formule prépositionnelle seulement s'il s'agit d'un nom; si un nom n'est pas présent, on trouve soit que le pronom datif est attaché au verbe, soit que le verbe est au ventif, soit que la notion du datif n'est pas exprimé. Si le verbe est *târu*, le complément d'objet direct *ṭēmu* (≈ *rgm* en ougaritique) est toujours exprimé, mais, s'il est *šapāru*, ce nom peut être omis.[62]

A notre connaissance, cette formule n'est attestée ni dans les lettres accadiennes d'el-Amarna,[63] ni dans celles de Mari. En revanche, on la retrouve dans les textes d'Émar.[64] Cette absence dans d'autres corpus bien connus est d'autant plus frappante

---

au lieu de *ašrānu itti* X. Dans le seul autre cas où la seconde partie de la formule ne commence pas par *ašrānu*, la préposition est *itti* (RS 20.227:12': {it-ti ŠEŠ-ḫi-ia a[š-ra-nu]}). La formule aberrante qu'a proposée Nougayrol à titre de restitution de RS 19.070 est aussi à remarquer.

62 Le nom *ṭēma* est présent en RS 12.005 (restitué, mais l'espace disponible ne laisse pas en doute la justesse de la restitution), RS 17.078; RS 19.050; RS 18.089. Il est absent en RS [Varia] 26, RS 34.134 (bis), RS 34.141, RS 34.173.

63 En revanche, on trouve assez souvent (comme Robert C. Hawley a eu l'amabilité de nous le rappeler) un rapport sur la situation de l'expéditeur suivi de vœux (par ex., dans les lettres du roi hittite à la cour égyptienne, EA 26:2-3, etc., ou du roi d'Alashia, EA 33:3-4), les vœux étant souvent de la sorte que consiste en un longue série à l'intention du roi, de sa famille, etc. (connus en ougaritique par RIH 78/3^{+} – voir Bordreuil et Caquot, *Syria* 57 [1980], pp. 356-358). L'existence de cette double formule amarnienne est vraisemblablement à l'origine de l'interprétation de la seconde partie de la formule ougaritienne comme un vœu (voir plus haut, la note 27).

Les formules de EA 149:56-57, 151:50-51, et Taanach 1:15-18, sont du type attesté en ougaritique par RS 4.475 (voir plus haut, la note 28) et RS [Varia 4] (voir plus haut, notes 6 et 28). En effet, il s'agit dans ces textes de demandes de retour de nouvelles exprimées en rapport avec des situations précises, non pas de la formule plus générale par laquelle on demande des nouvelles concernant le bien-être du correspondant. On en trouve aussi un exemple clair dans un texte accadien de Ras Shamra: RS 34.137:6-13 (RSO VII 37) {il-te-mi na-ma-ši (7) ŠEŠ-ia iš-tu KUR u-ga-ri-it (8) ú ŠÀ-ia it-ti-šu (9) U$_4$-ma ù mu-ši (10) ù at-ta mì-nu-um-[me-]e (11) [ta]l-te-me iš-tu (12) muḫ-ḫi ŠEŠ-ia (13) ṭé-ma te-er-ra-an-ni}, "J'apprends le voyage de mon frère hors du pays d'Ougarit et mon cœur est evec lui nuit et jour. Et quant à toi, tout [ce] que [tu aur]as entendu de le part de mon frère, renvoie-m'en un message". Tant par sa position dans la lettre que par son allusion précise à un sujet abordé dans la lettre elle-même, cette expression ressemble à celle de RS 4.475 et se sépare de la formule figée qui est l'objet de notre recherche ici.

64 A parcourir les lettres du temple M$_1$ (cf. Arnaud, Emar VI/3 [1986], pp. 255-267), on se croirait – en ce qui concerne les formules épistolaires – devant un corpus ougaritien. Voir aussi l'exemple, publié

lorsqu'on constate que la formule sous l'une ou l'autre de ses formes se rencontre dans environ 25% des lettres en accadien trouvées à Ras Shamra (37 exemples dans quelque 150 textes recensés) et dans environ 30% des textes ougaritiques (18 exemples dans une soixantaine de textes assez bien conservés pour déterminer si la formule était présente). L'absence de la formule dans les corpus classiques explique sa nouveauté manifeste pour les assyriologues,[65] mais elle laisse ouverte la question de savoir si elle est d'origine ouest-sémitique, mais syrienne, ou d'origine anatolienne.[66] Il paraît en tout cas difficile de parler tout simplement d'origine accadienne, car rien n'indique dans l'état actuel de nos connaissances qu'elle ait été d'origine mésopotamienne; si donc à Ougarit ou à Émar il s'agit de traductions de l'accadien, le rôle joué par l'accadien a dû être celui d'intermédiaire pour la formule dont l'origine se serait trouvée dans une autre langue.[67] Soulignons que diverses formes

---

par le même auteur (*SMEA* 30 [1992], p. 196), de la seule demande du retour de nouvelles; le destinataire est de rang supérieur à l'expéditeur. L'origine de la lettre est inconnue, mais identifiée par l'éditeur comme provenant de la région du moyen Euphrate ("ME" 127:8-9).

65 Cf. l'hésitation de Nougayrol quant à l'analyse de la formule *mīnummê* (plus haut, note 41); la difficulté qu'a présentée l'analyse de RS 17.383:6-9 pour les auteurs du *CAD* (plus haut, note 42). Cf. aussi la méconnaissance de la formule de retour de nouvelles chez Virolleaud (voir plus haut, note 27); l'absence de mention des parallèles très étroits entre les formules ougaritiques et accadiennes dans le travail de Rainey sur le scribe à Ougarit où sont cités d'autres parallèles entre des textes dans les deux langues ("Scribe" [1968], pp. 126-147); la méconnaissance de la nature de la formule de retour de nouvelles chez Cunchillos (voir plus haut, notes 23 et 27). Parker (*Studies* [1967], p. 27) et Ahl (*Epistolary Texts* [1973], pp. 139-140, cf. pp. 84-88, 120-121) furent les premiers à comparer explicitement les versions ougaritiques et accadiennes de la double formule en connaissance de leur véritable signification, Parker très brièvement, Ahl en détail (cf. Kristensen, *UF* 9 [1977], pp. 153-156; Römer, *Hulst* [1977], p. 139; Kaiser avait comparé la formule dans les deux langues mais en l'interprétant comme interrogative: *ZDPV* 86 [1970], pp. 19-20).

66 Hagenbuchner cite quatre exemples de la formule hittite par laquelle l'expéditeur rapporte son bien-être (*Korrespondenz* I [1989], pp. 73-77) et trois exemples de la formule propre au retour de nouvelles du destinataire (*ibid.*, pp. 71-73); les deux parties de la formule se rencontrent aussi dans un même document (pp. 77-79). La présence de ces formules en hittite nous oblige de penser à une origine commune à l'usage au Ḫatti, à Émar, à Ougarit (et sûrement en d'autres corpus que nous ne connaissons pas ou qui sont encore à découvrir). L'aire d'usage actuellement connue correspondant au territoire sous contrôle hittite, on peut penser que l'usage ougaritien et émariote constitue un calque sur l'usage hittite.

67 Pour pouvoir parler de traductions de l'accadien (Kaiser, *ZDPV* 86 [1970], p. 20), il faudrait expliquer pourquoi cette formule ne se trouve en accadien que dans les lettres d'Ougarit et d'Émar, et pourquoi elles font défaut dans les autres corpus, que ce soit en Mésopotamie ou dans le Levant. Pour Kristensen (*UF* 9 [1977], p. 154), il ne s'agit pas de "word for word translations", mais, tout en indiquant l'absence de parallèles dans d'autres corpus (*ibid.*), il ne nie pas l'origine accadienne de la formule. Dans la révision de son article dans *UF* 5 publiée dans *Comparative Studies* (1980),

du rapport de bien-être de l'expéditeur et diverses formes de demandes de retour de nouvelles se rencontrent dans d'autres corpus épistolaires,[68] et même en ougaritique;[69] c'est donc l'ensemble de la forme précise du rapport de bien-être jointe à la demande de retour de nouvelles qui constitue la nouveauté.

Il nous paraît nécessaire d'insister sur le caractère stéréotypé de la formule de base. On ne voudrait pas repousser l'analyse de la structure du document épistolaire ougaritique par Cunchillos, pour qui la lettre ougaritique est bipartite: "La *structure* d'une épître ougaritique est simple: à l'*introduction* fait suite *le corps du message*", et "La deuxième partie de la lettre ou *corps du message* se caractérise pour une structure dialogique ponctuée dans certains cas par les adverbes *hnny* 'ici' et *ṯmny* 'là-bas'".[70] D'après certains indices, il est clair que la double formule que nous venons de présenter appartenait au corps de la lettre: (1) en ougaritique, on ne rencontre pas un seul cas où cette formule soit insérée avant l'une des formules appartenant clairement à la *praescriptio*;[71] (2) une fois (RS 15.008) la double formule sert de clôture au lieu d'introduction au corps de la lettre (ici aussi le seul élément qui pourrait être identifié comme le corps de la lettre, à savoir la phrase *w ʾap ʾank nḫt*, s'insère entre les deux parties de la formule - voir plus bas); (3) une fois la double formule est incorporée dans une autre formule épistolaire, moins fréquemment attestée, celle qu'emploie l'expéditeur pour faire allusion à une lettre précédente (RS 17.139:5-9); (4) lorsque la demande de retour de nouvelles sert de clôture, on peut trouver des variantes appropriées aux circonstances de la lettre (plus haut, nous avons signalé le cas de RS 4.475 qui comporte des différences majeurs; en RS [Varia 4] on trouve la formule *rgm ṯṯb ʿm* sans *ṯmny* et attachée à une formule d' introduction qui n'a rien de commun avec la formule *hnny/hlny*).[72] Dans les textes en accadien, on trouve ces caractéristiques, y compris trois exemples clairs de l'insertion de la formule dans le corps de la lettre (en RS 15.033 et en RS [Varia 26] la situation

Loewenstamm reconnaît l'absence de parallèles dans les lettres de Mari et suggère que les formules attestées à Ougarit pourraient être d'origine ougaritique ou même hourrite (p. 454).

68 Cf. Virolleaud, *Syria* 19 (1938), p. 342, n. 1; Kristensen, *UF* 9 (1977), p. 154; Hagenbuchner, *Korrespondenz* I (1989), pp. 76-77.

69 Voir les demandes de retour de nouvelles dans des situations précises qui sont attestées en RS 4.475 et RS [Varia 4] (cités plus haut, note 28).

70 *TO* II (1989), pp. 243, 257.

71 Pourtant, on trouve une fois en accadien la bénédiction *lū šulmu* à la suite du rapport de nouvelles de l'expéditeur (cf. RS 34.139).

72 Cf. plus haut, les notes 6, 28 et 63.

géographique de l'expéditeur est indiquée avant cette formule, longuement dans le premier exemple [ll. 7-12, non citées plus haut], brièvement dans le second [ll. 19-20, citées plus haut]; en RS 19.006 on trouve une allusion à une lettre précédente qui ressemble au texte ougaritique RS 17.139 que nous venons de citer, mais avec seule la formule de rapport de nouvelles de l'expéditeur). Toutefois, la position qu'occupent normalement cette formule, à savoir soit entre la *praescriptio* et le message neuf et original ou après ce message, et la forme stéréotypée qu'elles affectent ne laissent pas de doute qu'il s'agit d'une formule épistolaire au sens étroit du terme.[73] Le caractère stéréotypé se remarque particulièrement dans l'usage de *šlm* dans la formule de retour de nouvelles,[74] car c'est cet élément qui tombe lorsque l'expéditeur exprime son désir d'apprendre ce qui ce passe dans une situation précise.[75] L'identification du caractère stéréotypée de la formule n'est pas sans importance, car la méconnaissance de sa fonction a eu pour fâcheux résultat qu'on a identifié le corps de la lettre en tant que message comportant de véritables nouvelles comme un post-scriptum.[76]

La fonction principale de la double formule ou de l'une ou l'autre de ses deux parties est donc soit d'introduire le corps de la lettre (même dans les cas cités où elles ne constituent pas les premiers mots du corps de la lettre, elles sont incorporées dans cette introduction), soit de clore la lettre entière. Leur signification, malgré le degré de formalisme qu'elles manifestent, est de rapporter le bien-être de l'auteur de la lettre et de demander au correspondant de renvoyer de ses nouvelles. Que leur valeur communicative n'eût pas complètement disparu est indiqué par les lettres qui consistent entièrement en formules (RS 9.479A, RS 20.199),[77] car de telles lettres permettaient à l'expéditeur de rassurer son correspondant quant à son bien-être et de demander que le destinataire n'oublie pas de le rassurer en retour.

---

73 Kaiser, *ZDPV* 86 (1970), pp. 19-20; Ahl, *Epistolary Texts* (1973), pp. 84-88, 120-121, 139-140; Kristensen, *UF* 9 (1977), pp. 153-156.

74 Cf. Pardee, *UF* 19 (1987), pp. 210-211.

75 RS 4.475, RS [Varia 4]; RS 94.2284:24 (textes cités plus haut, note 28).

76 Virolleaud (*Syria* 21 [1940], p. 253; cf. Richardson, *JBL* 66 [1947], p. 323) à propose de RS 11.872:14-18.

77 RS 8.315 est presque à compter parmi ces exemples, car la seule phrase qui ne constitue pas une formule épistolaire consiste en quatre mots: *w ʾap ʾank nḫt*.

Abbréviations

AB	Anchor Bible.
AF	*Anuario de Filología.*
AHw	W. von Soden, *Akkadisches Handwörterbuch* (Wiesbaden: Harrassowitz, 1958-1981).
ALASP	Abhandlungen zur Literatur Alt-Syrien-Palästinas (Münster: UGARIT-Verlag).
AnOr	Analecta Orientalia (Roma: Pontificium Institutum Biblicum).
AOAT	Alter Orient und Altes Testament (Kevelaer: Butzon & Bercker; Neu-kirchen-Vluyn: Neukirchener Verlag).
ATSAT	Arbeiten zu Text und Sprache im Alten Testament (St. Ottilien: EOS Verlag).
AuOr	*Aula Orientalis.*
BAH	Bibliothèque Archéologique et Historique.
BibOr	Biblica et Orientalia (Roma: Pontificium Institutum Biblicum).
BiOr	*Bibliotheca Orientalis.*
CAD	*The Assyrian Dictionary of the Oriental Institute of the University of Chicago* (Chicago: Oriental Institute, 1956-).
CRAI	*Comptes Rendus de l'Académie des Inscriptions et Belles Lettres.*
CTA	Herdner, A., *Corpus des tablettes en cunéiformes alphabétiques découvertes à Ras Shamra-Ugarit de 1929 à 1939* (MRS 10; BAH 79; Paris: Imprimerie Nationale; Geuthner, 1963).
EA	Texte accadien de Tell el-Amarna, cité d'après l'édition par J. A. Knudtzon, *Die el-Amarna-Tafeln mit Einleitung und Erläuterungen*, 2 vol. (Vorderasiatische Bibliothek 2; Leipzig: Hinrichs, 1915; réimpression Aalen: Zeller, 1964).
HSS	Harvard Semitic Studies.
IOS	*Israel Oriental Studies.*
JAOS	*Journal of the American Oriental Society.*
JBL	*Journal of Biblical Literature.*
KTU/CAT	Dietrich M., Loretz O., Sanmartín J., *Die keilalphabetischen Texte aus Ugarit einschließlich der keilalphabetischen Texte außerhalb Ugarits. Teil 1 Transkription* (AOAT 24/1; 1976); idem, *The Cuneiform Alphabetic Texts from Ugarit, Ras Ibn Hani and Other Places (KTU: second, enlarged edition)* (ALASP 8; 1995).

LAPO	Littératures Anciennes du Proche-Orient (Paris: Les Éditions du Cerf).
MB	*Le Monde de la Bible.*
MRS	Mission de Ras Shamra.
MVEOL	Mededelingen en Verhandelingen van het Vooraziatisch-egyptisch Genootschap "Ex Oriente Lux" (Leiden: Zutphen).
Or	*Orientalia n.s.*
OrAn	*Oriens Antiquus.*
PRU	*Le Palais Royal d'Ugarit.*
PRU II, V	Texte publié par Ch. Virolleaud dans *PRU* II (1957) ou *PRU* V (1965).
PRU III, IV, VI	Texte publié par J. Nougayrol dans *PRU* III (1955), *PRU* IV (1956) ou *PRU* VI (1970).
RSO VII	P. Bordreuil *et al.*, *Une bibliothèque au sud de la ville* (Ras Shamra-Ougarit VII; Paris: Éditions Recherche sur les Civilisations, 1991).
SDB	*Supplément au Dictionnaire de la Bible* (Paris: Letouzey et Ané, 1928-).
SMEA	*Studi Micenei ed Egeo-Anatolici.*
Taanach	Texte accadien de Tell Taanach cité d'après l'édition par F. Hrozný, "Keilschrifttexte aus Taᶜannek", in E. Sellin, *Tell Taᶜannek. Bericht über eine mit Unterstützing der kaiserlichen Akademie der Wissenschaft ... unternommene Ausgrabung in Palästina* (Denkschriften der kaiserlichen Akademie der Wissenschaften in Wien, Philosophisch-Historische Klaase 50 (1904), pp. 113-122; "Die neugefundenen Keilschrifttexte von Taᶜannek", in E. Sellin, *Eine Nachlese auf dem Tell Taᶜannek in Palästina* (*ibid.*, vol. 52; 1905), pp. 36-41.
TO II	A. Caquot, J.-M. de Tarragon, J.-L. Cunchillos, *Textes ougaritiques, tome II Textes religieux, rituels, correspondance* (LAPO 14; 1989).
UF	*Ugarit-Forschungen.*
Ugaritica V	MRS 16; BAH 80; Paris: Imprimerie Nationale; Geuthner, 1968.
Ugaritica V_N	Texte publié par J. Nougayrol dans *Ugaritica* V, pp. 1-446.

Ugaritica VII	MRS 18; BAH 99; Paris: Mission Archéologique de Ras Shamra; Geuthner, 1978.
WUS	J. Aistleitner, *Wörterbuch der ugaritischen Sprache* (1963).
ZDPV	*Zeitschrift des Deutschen Palästina-Vereins.*

Ouvrages cités

Aartun, K., *Die Partikeln des Ugaritischen.* 1. Teil (AOAT 21/1; 1974).

Aartun, K., *Die Partikeln des Ugaritischen.* 2. Teil (AOAT 21/2; 1978).

Ahl, S. W., *Epistolary Texts from Ugarit: Structural and Lexical Correspondences in Epistles in Akkadian and Ugaritic* (thèse, Brandeis; Ann Arbor, MI: University Microfilms, 1973).

Aistleitner, J., *Wörterbuch der ugaritischen Sprache* (éd. O. Eissfeldt; Berichte über die Verhandlungen der sächsischen Akademie der Wissenschaften zu Leipzig; Philologisch-historische Klasse, Band 106, Heft 3; Berlin: Akademie-Verlag, 1963).

Althann, R., *A Philological Analysis of Jeremiah 4-6 in the Light of Northwest Semitic* (BibOr 38; 1983).

Arnaud, D., "La Syrie du moyen-Euphrate sous le protectorat hittite: l'administration d'après trois lettres inédites", *AuOr* 2 (1984), pp. 179-88.

Arnaud, D., *Recherches au pays d'Aštata. Textes sumériens et accadiens* (Emar VI/1-3; Paris: Éditions Recherche sur les Civilisations, 1985-1986).

Arnaud, D., "Les ports de la 'Phénicie' à la fin de l'âge du Bronze récent (xiv-xiii siècles) d'après les textes cunéiformes de Syrie", *SMEA* 30 (1992), pp. 178-194.

Bordreuil, P., "Quatre documents en cunéiformes alphabétiques mal connus ou inédits (U.H. 138, RS 23.492, RS 34.356, Musée d'Alep M. 3601)", *Semitica* 32 (1982), pp. 5-14.

Bordreuil P., Caquot A., "Les textes en cunéiformes alphabétiques découverts en 1977 à Ibn Hani", *Syria* 56 (1979), pp. 295-315.

Bordreuil P., Caquot A., "Les textes en cunéiformes alphabétiques découverts en 1978 à Ibn Hani", *Syria* 57 (1980), pp. 343-373.

Bordreuil P., Mabran-Labat F., "Les archives de la maison d'Ourtenu", *CRAI* 1995, pp. 443-449.

Bordreuil P., Pardee D., "Les textes en cunéiformes alphabétiques", RSO VII (1991), pp. 139-172.

Brooke, G. J., "The Textual, Formal and Historical Significance of Ugaritic Letter RS 34.124 (= KTU 2.72)", *UF* 11 (1979), pp. 69-87.

Caquot, A., "La lettre de la reine Puduḫepa", *Ugaritica* VII (1978), pp. 121-134.

Cunchillos, J.-L., "Le texte ugaritique KTU 2.30", *AF* 5 (1979), pp. 73-76.

Cunchillos, J.-L., "Tablette en cunéiforme alphabétique d'Ugarit: lettre privée", in *Naissance de l'écriture, cunéiformes et hiéroglyphes* (catalogue d'exposition au Galeries nationales du Grand Palais, 7 mai-9 août 1982; éd. N. André-Leicknam, C. Ziegler; Paris: Éditions de la Réunion des musées nationaux, 1982), p. 180.

Cunchillos, J.-L., "Una carta paradigmática de Ugarit (KTU 2.11). La carta de Talmiyanu y Aḫatmilku", *El misterio de la palabra. Homenaje al profesor L. Alonso Schökel* (éd. V. Collado, E. Zurro; Valencia-Madrid: Ediciones Cristiandad, 1983), pp. 61-74.

Cunchillos, J.-L., "Que tout aille bien auprès de ma mère! Un qatala optatif en ugaritique?", *Salvación en la palabra. Targum - Derash - Bertith. En memoria del profesor Alejandro Díez Macho* (éd. D. Muñoz León; Madrid: Ediciones Cristiandad, 1986), pp. 259-266.

Cunchillos, J.-L., *Traduction de texte*, *MB* 48 (1987), p. 29.

Cunchillos, J.-L., *Estudios de epistolografía ugarítica* (Fuentes de la Ciencia Bíblica 3; Valencia: Institución San Jerónimo, 1989).

Cunchillos, J.-L., "Correspondance", *TO* II (1989), pp. 239-421, 446-478.

Cunchillos, J.-L., *Manual de estudios ugaríticos* (Madrid: Consejo Superior de Investigaciones Científicas, 1992).

Dahood, M., "Hebrew Lexicography: A Review of W. Baumgartner's *Lexikon*, Volume II", *Or* 45 (1976), pp. 327-365.

De Langhe, R., *Les textes de Ras Shamra-Ugarit et leurs rapports avec le milieu biblique de l'Ancien Testament* (Universitas Catholica Lovaniensis, Dissertationes ad gradum magistri in Facultate Theologica vel in Facultate Iuris Canonici consequendum conscriptae, Series II, Tomus 35; Gembloux: Duculot; Paris: Desclée de Brouwer, 1945).

De Moor, J. C., "Syntax Peculiar to Ugaritic Poetry", *Verse in Ancient Near Eastern Prose* (éd. J. C. De Moor et W. G. E. Watson; AOAT 42; 1993), pp. 191-205.

Dhorme, E., "Nouvelle lettre d'Ugarit en écriture alphabétique", *Syria* 19 (1938), pp. 142-146.

Dietrich M., Loretz O., "Orthographie und Inhalt im ugaritischen Brief KTU 2.16", *UF* 18 (1986), pp. 111-114.

Dietrich M., Loretz O., "Ugaritisch i<u>t</u>, <u>t</u>yndr und hebräisch *ʾšh*, *šy*, (KTU 1.14 IV 38; 2.13:14-15; 2.30:12-14a)", *UF* 26 (1994), pp. 63-72.

Gevirtz, S., "On Canaanite Rhetoric. The Evidence of the Amarna Letters from Tyre", *Or* 42 (1973), pp. 162-177.

Ginsberg, H. L., "Two North-Canaanite Letters from Ugarit", *BASOR* 72 (1938), pp. 18-19.

Gordon, C. H., *Ugaritic Grammar: The Present Status of the Linguistic Study of the Semitic Alphabetic Texts from Ras Shamra* (AnOr 20; 1940).

Gordon, C. H., "The Poetic Literature of Ugarit", *Or* 12 (1943), pp. 31-75.

Gordon, C. H., *Ugaritic Handbook: Revised Grammar, Paradigms, Texts in Transliteration, Comprehensive Glossary* (AnOr 25; 1947).

Gordon, C. H., *Ugaritic Literature: A Comprehensive Translation of the Poetic and Prose Texts* (Roma: Pontificium Institutum Biblicum, 1949).

Gordon, C. H., *Ugaritic Manual: Newly Revised Grammar, Texts in Transliteration, Cuneiform Selections, Paradigms, Glossary, Indices* (AnOr 35; 1955).

Gordon, C. H., *Ugaritic Textbook: Grammar, Texts in Transliteration, Cuneiform Selections, Glossary, Indices* (AnOr 38; 1965).

Groß, W., *Die Pendenskonstruktion im Biblischen Hebräisch* (ATSAT 22; 1987).

Hagenbuchner, A., *Die Korrespondenz der Hethiter, 1. Teil: Die Briefe unter ihren kulturellen, sprächlichen und thematischen Gesichtspunkten* (Texte der Hethiter 15); 2. Teil: *Die Briefe mit Transkription, Übersetzung und Kommentar* (Texte der Hethiter 16; Heidelberg: Carl Winter/Üniversitätsverlag, 1989).

Hoftijzer, J., "Ugaritische brieven uit de tijd van de ondergang van de stad", *Schrijvend Verleden. Documenten uit het oude nabije oosten vertaald en toegelicht* (éd. K. R. Veenhof; MVEOL 24; 1983), pp. 94-99.

Huehnergard, J., *The Akkadian of Ugarit* (HSS 34; Atlanta: Scholars Press, 1989).

Kaiser, O., "Zum Formular der in Ugarit gefundenen Briefe", *ZDPV* 86 (1970), pp. 10-23.

Kristensen, A. L., "Ugaritic Epistolary Formulas: A Comparative Study of the Ugaritic Epistolary Formulas in the Context of the Contemporary Akkadian Formulas in the Letters from Ugarit and Amarna", *UF* 9 (1977), pp. 143-158.

Levine, B. A., *In The Presence of the Lord. A Study of Cult and Some Cultic Terms in Ancient Israel* (Studies in Judaism in Late Antiquity 5; Leiden: Brill, 1974).

Levine, B. A., *Numbers 1-20. A New Translation with Introduction and Commentary* (AB 4A; 1993).

Lipiński, E., “Aḫat-milki, reine d'Ugarit, et la guerre du Mukiš”, *OLP* 12 (1981), pp. 79-115.

Loewenstamm, S. E., “הערות לתורת הבינוניים באוגריתית לאור הכנענית”, *Lešonenu* 23 (1958-59), pp. 72-84 (traduction anglaise dans *Comparative Studies* [1980], pp. 55-77).

Loewenstamm, S. E., “Lexicographical Notes on 1. *ṭbḫ*; 2. *hnny/hlny*”, *UF* 5 (1973), pp. 209-211 (= *Comparative Studies* [1980], pp. 449-454).

Loewenstamm, S. E., Recension, *Bib* 56 (1975), pp. 103-119 (= *Comparative Studies* [1980], pp. 473-495).

Loewenstamm, S. E., *Comparative Studies in Biblical and Ancient Oriental Literatures* (AOAT 204; 1980).

Malbran-Labat, F., “La découverte épigraphique de 1994 à Ougarit (les textes akkadiens)”, *SMEA* 36 (1995), pp. 103-111.

Milano, L., “Sul presunto giubileo a Ugarit (*PRU* V 9)”, *OrAn* 16 (1977), pp. 23-33.

Pardee, D., “A New Ugaritic Letter”, *BiOr* 34 (1977), pp. 3-20.

Pardee, D., “Ugaritic: Further Studies in Ugaritic Epistolography”, *AfO* 31 (1984), pp. 213-230.

Pardee, D., “Epigraphic and Philological Notes”, *UF* 19 (1987), pp. 199-217.

Pardee, D., *Les textes rituels* (Paris: Éditions Recherche sur les Civilisations, (2000).

Parker, S. B., *Studies in the Grammar of Ugaritic Prose Texts* (thèse, Johns Hopkins University, 1967).

Rainey, A. F., “The Scribe at Ugarit, His Position and Influence”, *Proceedings of the Israel Academy of Sciences and Humanities* 3/4 (1968), pp. 126-147.

Rainey, A. F., “Observations on Ugaritic Grammar”, *UF* 3 (1971), pp. 151-172.

Rainey, A. F., “Gleanings from Ugarit”, *IOS* 3 (1973), pp. 34-62.

Rainey, A. F., “The Ugaritic Texts in Ugaritica 5”, *JAOS* 94 (1974), pp. 184-194.

Rainey, A. F., “More Gleanings from Ugarit”, *IOS* 5 (1975), pp. 18-31.

Richardson, H. N., “A Ugaritic Letter of a King to His Mother”, *JBL* 66 (1947), pp. 321-324.

Römer, W. H. Ph., “Zur Deutung zweier Briefe aus Ugarit in alphabetischer Keilschrift”, *Übersetzung und Deutung. Studien zu dem Alten Testament und seiner Umwelt Alexander Reinhard Hulst gewidmet von Freunden und Kollegen* (Nijkerk: Callenbach, 1977), pp. 135-153.

Sivan, D., *A Grammar of the Ugaritic Language* (Handbuch der Orientalistik I, Band 28; Leiden: Brill, 1997).

Smith, M. S., "The **qatala* Form in Ugaritic Narrative Poetry", *Pomegranates and Golden Bells. Studies in Biblical, Jewish, and Near Eastern Ritual, Law, and Literature in Honor of Jacob Milgrom* (éd. David P. Wright et al.; Winona Lake: Eisenbrauns, 1995), pp. 789-803.

Van Soldt, W. H., *Studies in the Akkadian of Ugarit: Dating and Grammar* (AOAT 40; 1991).

Virolleaud, C., "Les inscriptions cunéiformes de Ras Shamra", *Syria* 10 (1929), pp. 304-310, pl. LXI-LXXX.

Virolleaud, C., "Fragments alphabétiques divers de Ra Shamra", *Syria* 19 (1938), pp. 335-344.

Virolleaud, C., "Lettres et documents administratifs provenant des archives d'Ugarit", *Syria* 21 (1940), pp. 247-276.

Virolleaud, C., *Textes en cunéiformes alphabétiques des archives est, ouest et centrales* (*PRU* II; MRS 7; Paris: Imprimerie Nationale; Klincksieck, 1957).

Virolleaud, C., *Textes en cunéiformes alphabétiques des archives sud, sud-ouest et du petit palais* (*PRU* V; MRS 11; Paris: Imprimerie Nationale; Klincksieck, 1965).

Widbin, R. B., *The East Archives in Le Palais Royal d'Ugarit: A Structural and Socio-Economic Analysis* (thèse Brandeis; Ann Arbor, MI: University Microfilms, 1985).

Yon, M., "La maison d'Ourtenou dans le quartier sud d'Ougarit (fouilles 1994)", *CRAI* 1995, pp. 427-443.

Yon, M., *La cité d'Ougarit sur le tell de Ras Shamra* (Paris: Éditions Recherche sur les Civilisations, 1997).

FROM AKKAD TO ḪATTUŠA: THE HISTORY OF GURPARANZAḪ AND THE RIVER THAT GAVE HIM ITS NAME *

Franca Pecchioli Daddi

University of Florence

The Akkad empire, for the Hittites as well as for other peoples in the Near East, represented a constant reference point on an ideological and cultural plane: at the court of Ḫattuša one could read works translated into Hittite that narrated the heroic deeds of the great Akkadian sovereigns and the city - the heart of that 'heroic kingship', recognised as a model by the Anatolian sovereigns, also became the place of the myth.[1]

Akkad is, in fact, the setting of the story,[2] with strong epic features in which the protagonists are the young Ailanuwa king, Gurparanzaḫ, and his eponymous divinity, the river Aranzaḫ. The original composition must have been rather extensive,[3] however, we know only of two episodes,[4] partially preserved, on some fragments that belong to different tablets:

A. 1. KUB XXXVI 67 (Bo 2865)
2. KBo XXII 98 (Bo 69/683): parallel to A. 1 II 15'-19'
3. KBo XXVI 104 (1622/u)

B. KUB XVII 9 (Bo 631)

---

* For the citations we refer to H. G. Güterbock - H. A. Hoffner (ed.), *The Hittite Dictionary of the Oriental Institute of the University of Chicago* (= CHD), Chicago 1997, pp. vii-xxvi (*List of Abbreviations*).

1 See the work, still fundamental, of H. G. Güterbock, *Die historische Tradition und ihre literarische Gestaltung bei Babyloniern und Hethitern bis 1200. Zweiter Teil: Hethiter*, ZA 44 NF 10 (1938), pp. 45-145.

2 CTH 362.

3 Cf. the colophon of fragment KUB XVII 9 IV 1', where we read "Second tablet [...] Gurpara[nzaḫ ...]".

4 The order of succession of the two episodes, known as "Gurparanzaḫ and the bow" (test A) and "Gurparanzaḫ and the Tigris" (test B), is very uncertain, according to E. von Schuler, in H.W. Haussig (ed.), *Wörterbuch der Mythologie*, Stuttgart 1983, p. 170; B. De Vries, *The Style of Hittite Epic and Mythology* (diss.), Ann Arbor 1967, p. 47, also holds their belonging to the same composition uncertain.

It is possible that another two fragments belong to this story: KUB XXXVI 64 (Bo 3114)[5] and - but the attribution is in this case extremely uncertain - KBo XXII 70 (Bo 69/233).[6]

These fragments, of which H. G. Güterbock[7] published a partial edition, have been touched on by various scholars[8] in their works regarding the texts of literary and mythological character coming from the Hittite archives, often with divergent interpretations depending on whether the emphasis lies more on the 'historic' or 'mythical' character of this composition.

Everyone, however, has recognised the connection of this text with the Hurrian cultural tradition from the time when most personages mentioned bear names belonging to this language: Gurparanzaḫ, taken from the Hurrian name of the river Tigris, Aranzaḫ, and from a *gurp-/gurbe* term perhaps indicating a particular type of quiver, may, according to M. Salvini,[9] be a programmatic name probably put together to mean something like the " turcasso del Tigri". The name of his wife, Tatizuli, in which we recognise the Hurrian word *tad-* "to love", is interpreted by V. Haas and H. J. Thiel[10] as " geliebt ist das Antlitz".[11] The names of Impakru's subordinate kings (?) and Gurparanzaḫ's companions, Eniadali e Ešiadali, are formed by the term *adal* " strength ", already frequent in the oldest Hurrian onomasticon, and by *ene* "god" and *eše* "land" respectively.

The name of the Akkad king,[12] Impakru, that we are unable to analyse for the present, does not appear to have come from Hurrian.[13]

---

5 CTH 354; see further ahead, text C.

6 CTH 370; see further ahead, text D.

7 *op. cit.*, pp. 84-90: transcription, translation and comment of A.1 Obv II 5'-35'; *idem*, *Kumarbi. Mythen von churritischen Kronos*, Zürich-New York 1946, p. 118: translation of B I 14-22.
See also recently, A. Ünal, TUAT III/4 (1994), pp. 852-853: translation of A. 1. II 10'-32'; B I 7-39.

8 See, in particular, B. De Vries, *op. cit.*, pp. 47-49; E. von Schuler, *op. cit.*, pp. 169-170; G. Wilhelm, *The Hurrians*, Warminster 1989, p. 62; F. Pecchioli Daddi, in F. Pecchioli Daddi - A. M. Polvani, *La mitologia ittita*, Brescia 1991, pp. 23-24; A. Archi, CANE IV (1995), p. 2373; cf. also G. Beckman, RlA VIII, 7/8 (1997), p. 572, who inserts this work in the paragraph *Hittite Tales* and attributes the fragments KBo XXII 96, 98, 104.

9 SEL 8 (1991), pp. 176-177.

10 AOAT 31 (1978), p. 35.

11 The meaning could also possibly be "the face shows love".

12 Even if Impakru is never defined as the "king of Akkad", this is implied from the context: cf. also A. Archi, *loc. cit.*

In my opinion, the overall analysis of what remains[14] of the Gurparanzaḫ tale provides further interesting and valuable elements.

I. The texts

Text A.1 (KUB XXXVI 67)

Obv. II

x + 3'	-]⸢ma?-al?-la?-x-x-x⸣[
4'	]x nu-kán ḫu-u-⸢ya-wa?-an?⸣[-zi
5'	]-pu ḫu-u-da-⸢ak⸣ ^{m}Gur-pa-[
6'	]x ú-da-aš nu-za ⸢šar?-ga?⸣[-
7'	^{m}]Im-pa-a-ak-ru-uš tar-aḫ-t[a
8'	]-ma-aš gi-im-ri ⸢i?-ya?⸣-[

9'	[gi-im-r]i?-ya-kán ḫu-u-e-da-ar (traces) [
10'	[PÌRIG.TU]R ḫar-tág-ga-an ^{m}Gur-pa-a-ra-an-za-ḫu-uš [
11'	[ḫu-u-]da-a-ak ku-en-ta gi-im-ra-an ⸢ša-ra⸣-a [
12'	[nam-m]a ^{URU}Ag-ga-ta an-da pa-a-ir [
13'	[^{URU}]Ag-ga-ta URU-ri ^{m}Im-pa-a-ak-ru-uš [
14'	[*Š*]*U-ŠI* LUGAL^{MEŠ} 70 šar-ga-u-e-eš an-da-an pa-[a-ir

---

15'	[ḫ]a-na-za-an-za-an a-wa-an ⸢kat⸣-ta a-še-ša-nu-ut [
16'	^{m}Gur-pa-a-ra-an-za-ḫu-un a-pí-el ^{LÚ}*ḪA-TA-NI-*⸢*ŠU*⸣ [
17'	e-te-ir-ša-ma-aš e-ku-ir nu-uš-ma-ša-at x-x [ ]
18'	nu ^{GIŠ}PAN$^{\text{ḪI.A}}$ ú-e-ki-ir ⸢^{KUŠ}⸣*IŠ-PA-DU* AN.ZA.GÀR x[-x-x-x-x]-x-⸢ir⸣
19'	ma-aḫ-ḫa-an ú-nu-wa-a-ir na-at *A-NA* ^{m}Gur-pa-⸢a-ra-an⸣-za-ḫu
20'	pí-ra-an kat-ta ti-⸢i⸣-e-ir ši-ya-iš-ki-iz-zi
21'	^{m}Gur-pa-a-ra-an-za-ḫa-[aš n]u-uš-ši-kán GI-aš
22'	*IŠ-TU* ^{GIŠ}PAN pa-ri-⸢ya-an⸣ MUŠEN-iš ma-a-an i-ya-at-ta-ri
23	*ŠU-ŠI* ⸢LUGAL⸣^{MEŠ} 70 ^{LÚ}GURUŠ-⸢za?⸣ ši-ši-ya-u-wa-an-zi tar-aḫ-ta

---

24'	^{m}Im-pa-a-ak-ru-uš[ ]ša-aš-ti pa-it na-aš-za ⸢kat?-ta? še⸣-eš-ta
25'	^{m}Gur-pa-a-ra-an-za-⸢ḫa-aš-ša⸣ ša-aš-ti pa-it
26'	Ì.DÙG.GA-ma-aš-⸢ši pí⸣-ra-an pa-ap-pár-še-eš-kán-z[i]x
27'	KASKAL^{MEŠ} *IŠ-T*[*U* i]š-pár-ri-ir na-at![15]-kán É[.ŠÀ

13 H. G. Güterbock, *op. cit.*, p. 89, puts forward, dubitatively, the hypothesis that Impakru might be identified with the first king of the Gutean dynasty, Imbia. Cf. however the name of the vizir of the Sea, Impaluri, in the songs of the Kumarbi cycle.

14 As for the indications of Obverse and Reverse, we follow what is reported in the reproductions in autography; but see further ahead.
For KUB XXXVI 67 Obv. I the last signs of only two lines remain: x+1 -]*wa-an-zi*, 2'-]*za?-a?-aš*; for Rev. IV some signs of three lines remain: x+1 -*z*]*i?*, 2']*x ne-pí-*[, 3']*x-x*[).

28' na-aš-kán ⸢ša-aš-ti⸣ še-ir *IŠ-TU* ^{GIŠ}KUN$_{5}$ pa-i[t
29' DAM-*ZU*-za ^{f}Ta-ti-zu-li ta-ma-i UD-a[t
30' še-eš-ḫa-aš nu *A-NA* ^{m}Gur-pa-a-ra-an-zi-ḫu k[u-(?) / t[e-(?)
31' [š]a-li-qa-aš li-e-wa-za ku-it-ma-an[
32' [tar?-aḫ?]-ti nu-wa-an-na-aš-kán ŠÀ É.ŠÀ-ni/*NI* in[-

33']x ^{f}Ta-ti-zu-li-⸢iš⸣[ ]x[
34']x É $^{\text{NA}_4}$KIŠIB pa-ra-a d[a-
35' -]šu-uš 1$^{\textit{NU-TIM}}$ AN.B[AR(?)
36' -z]a-an-za na-an-k[án
37' -a]n-za šu-u[š
38' -u]š-⸢za⸣[

Obv. III

x+1]x-x
2]
3' ^{m}Im-pa-]a-ak-ru
4' -r]u *IQ-BI*
5' -]nu-wa
6']^{LÚ}ga-i-na-an-ni
7']

8' -z]i-za an-da
9' -]e-eš
10' ^{m}Im-pa-]⸢ak⸣-ru-uš-kán
11']ti-ya-at
12']x-⸢a?-aš?-ši?⸣ x x LUGAL^{MEŠ}
13']ki-iš-ša-an *IQ-BI*
14' (-)a]n-na-za LUGAL KUR ^{URU}A-i-la-nu-wa
15']nu-wa-an-na-aš MUNUS-an LÚ-an-ni gu[l-

16' -]e-eš ^{m}E-ni-a-da-liš x[
17' ^{m}]E-ši-a-da-li pa-r[a-a
18' me]-mi-ir ^{m}E-ši-a-d[a-li
19' -r]u EN-*YA* ki-i *IQ*[-*BI*
20' -ká]n?/-a]t? iš-ta-ma-aš-ti [
21']x-⸢ir?⸣ MUNUS-za ^{m}Gur-pa-a-ra-an-⸢za⸣[-
22' ⸢a⸣-da-an-na-za a-ku-wa-an-na 70 $^{\text{⸢LÚ⸣}}$[GURUŠ
23' nu-za a-pí-⸢el⸣ i-wa-ar[
24' *Ú-UL* ⸢*IQ*⸣-[*BI*
25' nu a-pí-e[l

---

15 Instead the sign is AP.

Translation

A.1 II

4'] and they fl[ee
5' [the ba]nk [of the river (?)] immediately Gurpa[ranzaḫ
6']he brought and [of the (?)]young man [
7']Impakru wo[n
8'] then he (or: and with them) on the steppe he went for[ward

9' And on the [steppe] the wild animals[
10' [a leopa]rd, a bear Gurparanzaḫ[
11' [at on]ce killed, the steppe up there [he/they left?
12' [Th]en they entered Akkad,[
13' in Akkad, in the city, Impakru,[Gurparanzaḫ(?),]
14' 60 kings, 70 young men enter[ed.]

15' In front he seated him down,
16' Gurparanzaḫ, his son-in-law;
17' with them they ate, drank and they en[joyed(?)] themselves.
18' Then the bows they asked for, quiver and target (lit.: pillar) [they ask]ed for (?);
19' when they were ready (lit.: they had prepared), in front of Gurparanzaḫ
20' they descended / they sat down. He shoots,
21' Gurparanzaḫ and the arrow from him,
22' from the bow flies like a bird:
23' 60 kings, 70 young men he won at shooting (with the bow).

24' Impakru went to bed and lay down;
25' also Gurparanzaḫ went to bed,
26' but in front of him they sprinkle perfume,
27' they covered the route with [carpets] and [in the bed] room [they accompanied him].
28' And he in bed went onto the step[;
29' for? his wife Tatizuli another day[
30' he had established; then to Gurparanzaḫ ...[
31' she approached: "You must not [...] until [
32' [...]...; to us in the bedroom ...[..."].

33' [Thus spoke (?)] Tatizuli [
34' from the] storehouse outside[
35']... a set of ir[on (?)

Rev. III is too fragmentary to attempt a translation.

Notes

Obv. II 5': the term [*wap*]*pu-* "bank of the river, wadi" should probably be restored. It is supposed that the hunt, organised by Impakru, took place near the Tigris. Gurparanzaḫ, who found himself on the riverbank, persuaded by Impakru, distances himself from his protector in order to take part.

Obv. II 6': perhaps *šar-ga-*[*wa-aš*, a genitive form referring to Gurparanzaḫ.

Obv. II 8': possible restorations: [*nu nam-*]*ma-aš* "and then he" or [*nu-uš-*]*ma-aš* "and with them"; *i-ya-a*[*n-ni-eš* "he went" or *i-ya-a*[*t-ta-* ..., for which cf. H. G. Güterbock, *op. cit.*, p. 85, n. 5, who sees traces of two horizontals.

Obv. II 10': restoration from context. H. G. Güterbock, *op. cit.*, p. 85, n. 6, points out that the traces at the end of the gap allow for signs like AZ or UK.

Obv. II 12': [*nam-m*]*a* or, like H. G. Güterbock, *op. cit.*, p. 84, [*na-a*]*t*, with a proleptic pronoun.

Obv. II 13': "in Akkad, in the city" - similar locutions are frequent in mythological texts: see the Song of Gilgameš (1.A. KUB VIII 57 I 11; 18. KUB VIII 62 I 8, 26),[16] the poems of the Kumarbi cycle (e.g. the Song of god LAMMA/KAL,[17] I A. KUB XXXVI 2b II 26']; the Song of Silver,[18] 2 A. KUB XXXIII 115 III [14']-15', 2 B'. KUB XXXVI 18a ll. 3', 5'; the Song of Ḫedammu,[19] 2. KUB VIII 67 Rev. IV? 3', 4'; the Song of Ullikummi,[20] I B. KUB XXXIII 98 I 11-12), the Song of release[21] (e.g. I. 6. KBo XXXII 15 III 20; I. 9. KBo XXXII 19 II 24, III 49').

Obv. II 13'-14': A. Ünal's translation is different, *op. cit.*, p. 852: "In der Stadt Agade [hat sie] Impakru [empfangen(?)]. 60 Könige (und) 70 Helden gingen (?) hinein (in die Stadt)".

Obv II 15': restoration from context; for the adverbial use of *ḫanza*, cf. J. Puhvel, *HED* 3 (1991), p. 91. Here the pronoun *-an* has a proleptic function.

---

16 The episodes are cited according to E. Laroche, RHA 82 (1968), pp. 7-24.

17 For this song, see E. Laroche, *op. cit.*, pp. 31-38; H. A. Hoffner, *Hittite Myths*, Atlanta 1990[1], pp. 43-45; 1998[2], pp. 46-47.

18 Edition by H. A. Hoffner, FsOtten[2] (1988), pp. 143-166.

19 Edition by J. Siegelová, StBoT 14 (1971), pp. 35-88.

20 Edition by H. G. Güterbock, JCS 5 (1961), pp. 135-161; 6 (1952), pp. 8-42.

21 Edition by E. Neu, StBoT 32 (1996).

Obv. II 17': according to H. G. Güterbock, ZA 44 (*cit.*), p. 86, n. 1, "Zeichen eher LA als AT"; in reality the signs in autography seem to compel us to read ⌜*UM-MA*⌝. If however the second sign was not reproduced correctly, we could think of a form of *dušk-* which is well suited to the context; cf. for example the description of the reception the town arranges for Gilgameš and Enkidu on their return from their victorious expedition to the region of cedars, episode 6. KUB VIII 52 + KUB XXIII 9 l. 9' *nu-uš-ma-ša-at du-uš-ki*[*-iš*]*-kán-zi*[.

Obv. II 27': A. Ünal, *loc. cit.*, restores [Blumen(?)].

Obv. II 29' ff.: the text is not very clear here and its interpretation depends on whether the name of Gurparanzaḫ's bride, ᶠTatizuli, is really dative and not nominative without an ending, as H. G. Güterbock retains, *op. cit.*, pp. 87-88:[22] in the former case it would be Gurparanzaḫ, and not the woman, who wants to postpone the consummation of their marriage to a later date (*tamai* UD-*a*[*t*]),[23] while Tatizuli tries to overcome the bridegroom's resistance by using her feminine charm to seduce him (*salik-* is also used to indicate the sexual encounter: cf. § 195 of the Laws) and by convincing him of the secretness of their act. If instead - as is more likely - Tatizuli is the subject, it would be the woman who refuses the sexual act; in this case, considering the signs before the gap at line 30', we suggest the following translation: "[For him] his wife Tatizuli fixed another day and, to Gurparanzaḫ, sai[d: "Why did you] come near me? Absolutely not, until [...] you [win(?)]; then in our(?) bedroom spo[ntaneously] we will [unite"]. For constructions with *le* after the verb, cf. CHD 3/1 (1980), pp. 55-57.

Obv. II 32': H. G. Güterbock, *op. cit.*, p. 86, restores [*na-a*]*ḫ*(?)*-ti*. The implied restoration in A. Ünal's translation, *loc. cit.*, ("Solange [ich ... bin, sollst du dich mir] nicht [nähern.]") does not seem possible, as there is not enough space in the gap for more than two signs.

in[-probably *in*[*-nara* "willingly, spontaneously".

Obv. III 5': perhaps [LUGAL KUR ᵁᴿᵁ*Aila*]*nuwa* should be restored.

Obv III 14': if the attestation is complete, *annaza* is probably an adverb ("one time").

---

22 This interpretation also matches B. De Vries, *op. cit.*, p. 48; A. Ünal, *op. cit.*, p. 852.

23 The translation of these words given by B. De Vries, *loc. cit.*, "another matter", clearly presupposes a reading *ut-tar*.

Obv III 15' ff: l. 15' - possible translation: "]now they assigned us (a form of the verb *gulš* -) a woman in place of / instead of a man". In my view, the words reported here belong to Impakru (cf. l. 19': "Impakr]u, my lord, has said this"), who has no son as heir and searches for a son-in-law; news, passed by word-of-mouth (ll. 16'-17'), then probably gets reported to Ešiadali, who in turn informs Gurparanzaḫ.

Obv. III 23': "in the manner of him, like he (did)". For *iwar*, see. J. Puhvel, HED 1-2 (1984), pp. 499-502.

Text A.2 (KBo XXII 98)

x+1]x [
2' a-]da-an-na a-ša-a[n-zi

3' ^{m}G]ur-pa-ra-an-za-ḫu-uš [
4' LUGAL?]^{MEŠ} an-da a-še-ša-nu-ut[
5' a-]wa-an a-še-ša-nu-ut x[
6']x ^{GIŠ}PAN$^{ḪI.A}$ ú-e-ki-i[r
7' -]*U*$^{ḪI.A}$AN.ZA.GÀR$^{ḪI.A}$[
8' ^{m}Gu]r-pa-ra-an-za-ḫu [

9']x [

This fragment, which belongs to a different, perhaps longer, version (cf. ll. 2'-5'), describes the banquet in detail in which the members of the hunt take part.

Text A.3 (KBo XXVI 104)

x+1 ^{m}Im-pa-a]k-ru-u[š
2' a]n-da-an-wa-x[
3' -]nu-wa
4' -a]n-za-ḫu-uš nu-wa ^{LÚ}GURUŠ
5' -a]n-zi

6' -r]a-an-za-ḫu-i
7']x x x x x x x x x

The fragment that belongs to the right column of the tablet (a trace of the edge remains) is probably parallel to the text A.1 III: in fact, a direct discourse of (?) Impakru is related there and Gurparanzaḫ is mentioned.

For l. 3' it might be possible to restore [LUGAL KUR ^{URU}*Aila*]*nuwa*.

Text B (KUB XVII 9)

Obv. I

1]x-wa-za ÍD[
2]x EN-*YA* wa-aš-x[
3]x-an-na-za DUMU.MUNUS x-x-x[
4 -]e-ir ma-a-wa-mu-kán EN-*Y*[*A*
5 -]ni ḫar-pi-ya-ši nu u-ni-u[š?
6 -y]a- š[i

---

7 ^{URU}Ak-]ka-ta-az-za *IŠ-TU* É[
8]x-at-ti nu-wa-at-ta *ŠUM*-za x[
9 -m]a-kán *ŠUM*-an gul-aš-mi [
10] EN-*YA* ḫa-an-da-an-ta-tar me-m[i-
11 *I*-]*NA* ^{URU}A-ag-ga-dè pa-a-i-mi x[
12]^{m}Gur-pa-ra-an-za-ḫi-iš ku-it pa-a-i [
13]a-pád-da-ya e-eš-du

---

14 [nu ^{f}]^{D}A-ra-an-za-ḫa-aš Á^{MUŠEN}-aš GIM-an tar-na-aš
15 [na-]aš ^{URU}Ag-ga-dè an-da-an pa-it
16 [na]-aš-za ^{URU}Nu-u-a-du DÙ-at na-aš-za-kán *I-NA* ^{GIŠ}KUN$_5$
17 ša-ra-a e-ša-at nu-za ^{m}Gur-pa-ra-an-za-ḫu-uš
18 a-la-la-am-ni-⸢iš-ki⸣-iz-zi šar-ga-u-e-eš-ši
19 kat-ta-an ar-⸢ku?/ú?-iš⸣-kán-zi nu ^{fD}A-ra-an-za-ḫa-aš
20 *A-NA* ^{m}Gur-pa-ra-an-za-ḫu *IQ-BI* ku-wa-at-wa [
21 ú-e-eš-ki-ši nu-wa-⸢ták⸣-kán šu-up-pa-ya-za [
22 [ša-k]u-wa-za iš-ḫa-aḫ-ru pa-ra-a a-ar-aš [

---

23 [LUGAL KUR] ^{URU}A-i-la-nu-wa ⸢ku-wa⸣-at-wa ú-e-eš[-ki-ši
24 ⸢na-aš⸣[-ta-kán ^{m}Gu]r⸢-pa⸣-ra-an-za-ḫu *A-NA* ÍD[
25 nu-wa-z[a(?)]⸢zi⸣-ik nu-u-wa ki-e-da-ni pí[-di

---

26 *UM-MA* ^{ÍD}A-ra-an-za-ḫi am-mu-uk-wa-⸢za⸣[
27 ^{D}U-aš SAG.DU-aš SAG.DU-aš wa-a-tar x[
28 at-ta-aš AMA-aš uš-ki-⸢iš-kat-tal⸣[-la-aš
29 *UM-MA* ^{m}Gur-⸢pa⸣-ra-an-za-ḫu DUMU.MUNUS[
30 nu-wa-mu i-wa-ru ku-it pa-a-i nu[
31 ^{URU}A-ag-ga-ta-⸢az⸣-za du-uš-qa-⸢ra⸣[-wanza?
32 am-mu-uq-qa-za ú-nu-wa-⸢aḫ⸣-ḫa-ri nu-u[n-na-aš / nu-u[n-taraš
33 kat-ta pa-a-ši[

---

34 ^{fD}A-ra-an-za-ḫu-uš *IŠ-ME* na-aš-za ⸢*IŠ-TU*⸣[
35 Á^{MUŠEN}-aš GIM-an tar-na-aš na-aš *I-N*[*A*
36 *IT-TI* ^{D}MAḪ pa-it ^{D}Gul-šu-uš[

37 ^{ÍD}A-ra-an-za-ḫa-an a-ú-e-ir x[
38 a-ku-wa-an-na pí-⸢i-e⸣-ir e-iz-za-at[-ta
39 1-*ŠU* 2-*ŠU* 3-*ŠÚ* 4-*ŠÚ* 5-*ŠÚ* 6-*ŠÚ* 7-*ŠÚ* x[

---

40 ^{ÍD}A-⸢ra-an-za⸣[-]x [
41 ^{D}Gul[-
42 x x[

Rev. IV (Colophon)

]⸢DUB.2^{KAM}⸣[*ŠA* ^{m}]⸢Gur-pa-ra-a⸣-a[n-

Translation

1]... the river[
2 o]f? my lord the lac[k ?
3]...... the young girl ......[
4 they [said ??], if with me my lord[
5 in [friendship/matrimony???] you are united, then the aforementioned thing[/ persons [
6]you ...[

7]and from [Ak]kad from home[
8]you [...]... and you by name [
9]but the name I will inscribe [
10]the providence of my lord [I will] say[
11]to Akkad I will go [
12]this that Gurparanzaḫ gives [
13]and there he/it must be! [

---

14 [Then] the river Aranzaḫ like an eagle departed
15 [and] entered Akkad.
16 [Now] it has gone (lit.: made) to Nuadu and on the stairs
17 it sat. Gurparanzaḫ
18 is crying, the young men around him (at his feet)
19 are invoking/are prostrate. Then the river Aranzaḫ
20 said to Gurparanzaḫ: "Why
21 do you lament and from your pure
22 [ey]es tears flow?

---

23 [King of] Ailanuwa, why do you lament?"
24 And the[n Gurparanzaḫ to the river [said:
25 "And you (are) still in this pla[ce!"

---

26 So the river Aranzaḫ: "I [
27 of the Storm God of the head/person (I am) of the head/person the water [
28 of the father and of the mother (I am) the keep[er!"

29 So Gurparanzaḫ: “The young girl [
30 and the dowry that (s)he will give me, then[
31 and from Akkad [(s)he] happy[
32 I will adorn myself and with u[s (opp.: readily)
33 you will come!”[

---

34 The river Aranzaḫ listened and it from [
35 like an eagle departed and in[
36 with the Mother Goddess it went; the Fate Goddesses [
37 the river Aranzaḫ saw ...[... to eat and
38 to drink they gave [to it], it at[e and drank]
39 once, twice, three times, four times, five times, six times, seven times [

Notes

Obv. I 1-13: here remains part of a dialogue between two personages, one of whom is certainly the river Aranzaḫ, given that it goes away at the end (l. 14). The identity of the other interlocutor is instead more problematic: if it is Gurparanzaḫ, as B. De Vries retains, *op. cit.*, p. 48, who asks for help from his god and protector and addresses him by calling him “my lord”, the subsequent scene with the meeting of Gurparanzaḫ and Aranzaḫ in Akkad would be repetitive and, in part, superfluous (in particular, ll. 29-33), as the river would have already been advised by the young man of his difficult relationship with his wife. It seems therefore more reasonable to say that the interlocutor is a different person: it might be the woman who tells her husband’s god and protector what has happened and who, to solicit the intervention of the river, promises to glorify its name and exalt its divine providence. Both hypotheses imply, however, that in this text - contrary to Hittite belief - a male character is attributed to the fluvial divinity (see ll. 2, 4, 10: EN-*YA*); to avoid this possible incongruance - after all it is not totally unusual in mythological texts,[24] it could be supposed that Tatizuli tells the divinity the words she related to her husband: in this case EN-*YA* would be appellative for Gurparanzaḫ[25] and not for the river.

---

24 See, for example, the fragment belonging to the Kumarbi cycle, KUB XXXIII 118, in which the Wašitta mountain is female in character: cf., recently, F. Pecchioli Daddi, *op. cit.*, p. 117, n. 12 (with previous bibliography).

25 According to KUB I 1 I 48 (*para*) *ḫandandatar* (l. 10) is also the prerogative of the sovereign: cf. P. Cotticelli, in A. Kammenhuber (ed.), *Materialien* 11 (1989), p. 149, Nr. 33; F. Pecchioli Daddi, BiOr 48 (1991), p. 216.

Obv. I 16: ^{URU}*Nuadu* is a *hapax*, not recorded in RGTC 6: if it is not an error of the ancient scribe,[26] it could be the name of an Akkad quarter. A. Ünal, *op. cit.*, p. 853, translates: "Es geschah in der Stadt Nuadu, (dass) ...".

Obv I 19: reading uncertain due to abrasion of the tablet.

Obv I 26-28: the river Aranzaḫ alleges with these words, which do not find a parallel in other Hittite texts, its role as the young man's divinity and affirms its own divine power, that is derived from its ties to the Storm God: "(I am) the water of the person of the Storm God of the person". For the Storm God "of the person/head" (^{D}U SAG.DU/*ḫaršannaš*) as a personal divinity, cf. H. M. Kümmel, StBoT 3 (1967), p. 84; for the attestations, see B. H. L. van Gessel, *Onomasticon of the Hittite Pantheon*, Leiden-New York-Köln 1998, pp. 777, 784.

The privileged relationship of the river Aranzaḫ with the Storm God sets, as noted, a mythical precedent in the Kumarbi Song, according to which, the two divinities are both Kumarbi's offspring, born from the seed of Anu that the father of the gods swallowed. This is well testified in the rituals in the Hurrian language discovered in Ḫattuša: see the Middle Hittite ritual KBo XXIII 6 + KBo XXVII 100 + KBo XX 129 + KBo XL 123 + FGH 23 + ABoT 39 + FHG 20 + KUB XXXII 29 + 33 + KBo XXXIII 47[27] (= ChS I/1 [1984], pp. 51-65, Nr. 5[28]) II 27, 31; the fragment KBo XXVII 110 Obv.? 9', 10' (Privat Wuppertal), where Aranzaḫ is called as "river of the god Tešub"; the list of offerings for the worship of the Storm God of Šapinuwa, KBo (XVII 86 +) XV 62[29] III 14'.

The role of the river Tigris in the mythological tradition of the Hurrian matrix and its ties with the city of Akkad, testified by the Gurparanzaḫ story, is confirmed in Ḫattuša in another two documents:

- in a strange and difficult text,[30] KUB XXXVI 55 (CTH 351) III 22', that shows close analogies with the Theogony and other songs of the Kumarbi cycle - a more precise connection cannot be found at present - where the birth is narrated, or better

26 Possible amendment: [*na*]-*aš-za* URU *nu-u-a* GUB DÙ-*at* "and he was found still on his feet in the city" (?).

27 CTH 777. For the joins, see D. Groddeck, AoF 23 (1996), p. 305, Nr. 39; AoF 26 (1999), p. 308, Nr. 90; S. Košak, StBoT 39 (1995), p. 63.

28 Second tablet of the series *itkalzi*, the conjuration of the water.

29 CTH 786.2. For the join, cf. S. Košak, StBoT 42 (1998), p. 37.

30 For this text, see now A. Archi, Fs Popko, Warsaw 2002, pp. 1-10.

still, the conception of Aranzaḫ, together with that of other divinities (III 25' -]*ši-pa-an*; III 27']ᴰZA.BA₄.BA₄; III 29' -*a*]*n*);

- in KBo XXII 6[31] (CTH 310.5) I 16', where Sargon sacrifices an ox and seven sheep to the river in order to favour his expedition to Purušḫanda and spur his army.

I 29-33: it is not clear here if Gurparanzaḫ confides his desire to the river or rather, does not relate to it the conditions placed by his wife, who will leave Akkad with joy, and adorn herself and yield to her husband only when she receives the dowry that is due her.

Other fragments (?)

Text C. KUB XXXVI 64 (Bo 3114): from CTH 354
Obv.? II

x+1]x
2']
3' i]š-ta-ma-aš-š[a-an-z]i
4' a]n-na-aš-wa [ ]
5']a-pu-u-un m[e-mi-an iš-]ta-ma-aš-mi
6']x me-mi-eš-ki[-
7']x-an-du [ ]x
8']x-ta-ru [

Rev.? III

x+1]x

2' ⁽ᶠ⁾]ᴰA-ra-an-za-ḫa-an-na
3' kap?-p]u-u-wa-an-zi
4']x-a-an-ta-ri
5']

6' wa?-a]t?-ru wa-at-ku-an
7']i-ya-mi 5 *LI-IM*
8']ar-nu-mi
9']*Ú-UL* da-ri-ya[-
10']an-da ú[-
11' -]ša[

The attribution of this small fragment to the text discussed is suggested by the mention of the river Aranzaḫ, by the presence of direct discourse and the verb

---

31 Edition by H. G. Güterbock, MDOG 101 (1969), pp. 19, 21.

kappuwai-, which might be connected with the mention of "storehouse" in KUB XXXVI 67 Obv. II 34' and of "dowry" in KUB XVII 9 Obv. I 30.

According to the reproduction in autography, the fragment might belong to the same tablct of KBo XXVI 104; the hypothesis however must be checked with the original.

Text D. KBo XXII 70 (Bo 69/233): from CTH 370
Obv.

x+1]x-ri-[
2']še-ir a-pa-˹aš?-ma?˺
3' -]˹ir˺

4' -]˹za˺-kán ^{D}U-˹ta?˺-aš
5' ma-a]ḫ-ḫa-an-ma-za ^{D}UTU-uš
6' -ḫ]u-u-wa-ar-za-ma-kán
7' ma-aḫ-]ḫa-an-ma-kán GAL-iš
8']x x-x-ma-at
9']x-˹zi˺

Rev.

x+1]x-˹ti˺-x AMA-aš?[
2' -]˹e˺-ša-an-te-eš
3']uš-ki-eš-kán-zi
4' ^{GIŠ}na-a]t-ḫi-ši kat-ta-an še-eš-ta
5' u]š-ki-eš-kán-zi
6']GIŠ-ru GAM-an
7']še-eš-mi
8']-˹i˺
9']x

It is extremely uncertain to say that this fragment belongs to the composition; however, it can be taken into consideration for its references to the sexual act of Rev. 4' "he laid down in his bed" and Rev. 7' "I will lay me down".

II. The literary composition

1. Typology

As mentioned, this work originally must surely have been somewhat lengthy, and was part of the collection of texts, like other compositions of mythological character,[32] deposited in the library of the great temple 1: the two fragments of which the place of discovery is known, KBo XXII 98 and KBo XXVI 104, come, in fact, from this area (from the debris of excavations at square K/19 and square L/19 respectively).[33]

The only colophon we have does not preserve the complete title of the work; however, because of the size of the gap in KUB XVII 9 Rev. IV and especially for the analogies with other compositions in structure, style[34] and content,[35] the text dedicated to Gurparanzaḫ might also belong to the genre of "songs".[36]

Such literary genre, as we know, was prolific in Ḫattuša; this included compositions different in their content and inspiration, yet analogous in structure.[37]

The element of major differentiation is seen by the nature of the protagonists and by the setting. In fact, they are clearly distinguished: on one hand, the songs of the Kumarbi cycle that are all played out on the divine level where the great celestial and chthonian deities are the protagonists who struggle among themselves for supremacy and where the human presence is sporadic and marginal; on the other, the songs in which the protagonists are heroes - deified like Gilgameš or human beings such as Gurparanzaḫ, Kešši, Atramḫaši - who move about in the world of men and interact with the gods.

However, the structure of the various songs is developed according to a well-defined compositive model that provides a proem in which the (anonymous) author speaks in the first person and exhalts the personage as protagonist (god or hero, whoever it may be) of the exploits that will then be narrated in unrelenting rhythm and refined style.

The model for this type of composition of which mortal beings are the protagonists, and for the text on Gurparanzaḫ in particular, seems to be the Gilgameš Song,

32 For example, the myth of Illuyanka, the history of Appu, the Hurrian version of the Kešši song, the songs of the Kumarbi cycle, etc.

33 The fragment KBo XXII 70 (text D) comes from the same area: debris from K/19.

34 See further ahead.

35 G. Wilhelm, *Grundzüge der Geschichte und Kultur der Hurriter*, Darmstadt 1982, p. 87; *idem*, *The Hurrians* (*cit.*), p. 62, thinks that Gurparanzaḫ, like Kešši the protagonist of the homonymous song, represents the type of hunter that, in his opinion, had an important role in authentic Hurrian mythology.

36 Cf. for this H. G. Güterbock, *Hethitische Literatur*, in W. Röllig (ed.), *Neues Handbuch der Literaturwissenschaft. I*, Wiesbaden 1978, p. 241; F. Pecchioli Daddi, *op. cit.*, p. 23.

37 Cf. F. Pecchioli Daddi, *op. cit.*, pp. 17-25.

which the Ḫattuša scribes knew and drew up copies of in Akkadian (and in Hittite and Hurrian) already in the Middle Hittite period. In fact, also in this work, when the event passes from the world of the gods to the world of men, the protagonist is presented as a hero (Gilgameš confronts the $^{LÚ.MEŠ}$GURUŠ of Uruk and wins); and the steppe - i.e. the non-urban territory where wild animals lived and hunters roamed - constitutes the prime scenery; also the role of the female appears important here (the sacred prostitute who subdues Enkidu), as does the role of the Mother Goddess.

2. Content

On the basis of the tablets that have come down to us, the following sequence of events is reconstructed: The young Gurparanzaḫ displays his courage by killing the wild animals on the steppes during a hunt organised by the king of Akkad, Impakru, who receives him with full honours in the city and chooses him as his son-in-law. During the nuptial banquet in Akkad, Gurparanzaḫ gives yet one more proof of his skills by beating everyone in an archery competition and demonstrates his worth by being chosen by Impakru. At this point, the nuptial procession accompanies him to the bride who is waiting for him in the matrimonial bedroom, but who refuses to consummate the marriage and follow her husband until she receives the dowry that is due her. Impakru, informed about this, becomes very critical towards his son-in-law who is seen to be weaker than his wife. Gurparanzaḫ cries desperately and does not know how to resolve the situation. Help then comes from his divinity and protector, the river Aranzaḫ, that goes for advice to the Fate Goddesses and to the Mother Goddess, on whom the destinies of human beings depend.

3. Purpose

The rest of this epic, mythical story does not, in my view, involve Hurrian military exploits against the Akkad reign;[38] nor does it date back to an ancient Hurrian myth of the hunt:[39] the hunt and the archery competition effectively talked about in A. 1 Obv. II are not in fact central to the narration; they are presented rather as a typical entertainment of male reunions at a high-level, which offer Gurparanzaḫ the occasion to demonstrate those abilities that, according to the ideology of the kingship affirmed in the Late Bronze Age, render one worthy to reign.

---

38 Cf. H. G. Güterbock, ZA 44 (*cit.*); E. von Schuler, *loc. cit.*

39 Cf. G. Wilhelm, *loc. cit.*

Instead, central to the narration is the relationship between Gurparanzaḫ and his wife (the young girl is mentioned more often in the text, even in a fragmentary context[40]) and especially the consummation of their marriage, which the woman opposes if her conditions are not met.

Since the young man's god and protector turns to the Mother Goddess and Fate Goddesses that preside over birth, it is reasonable to suppose that the consummation of the stymied union between the king of Ailanuwa and the daughter of the Akkad king is the theme of the story together with the prelude of the birth of a child who is presented as heir of the Hurrian and Akkadian traditions.[41]

Thus we are dealing with an epic mythical story that is etiological in character, i.e. with a well-documented text typology in the Anatolian world up to the Ancient Reign, in some way similar to the text about Zalpa[42] and to the story of the young shepherd.[43] However, compared to these compositions linked to the origins of the dynasty and of the Hittite reign that were composed in an ancient era, the tablets of the Gurparanzaḫ story don't show any element (paleographic or linguistic) that make us think they derive from the ancient original ones.

The stylistic elements employed (see, for example, the simile of the eagle and the locution "Akkad, in the city") and the contents refer to other mythological texts of various origin (Mesopotamian, Hurrian and Anatolian; see in particular the role of Akkad, the presence of the Fate Goddesses and the Mother Goddess, the problem of the dowry and the consummation of the marriage, and the possible birth of an heir); instead the onomasticon and the setting clearly derive from Hurrian culture.

Therefore it appears to be a work, fruit of the elaboration and *contaminatio* of themes and narrative motifs of different traditions, that the Ḫattuša scribes composed in the late imperial period to give a literary form to a Hurrian etiological myth, probably related to the beginning of an ancient local dynasty, which perhaps, up to that time, had remained faithful to oral tradition only. The absence, at the present time, of Hurrian fragments attributable to this myth or in which

---

40 A. 1 Obv. II 29', 33', Rev .III 15', 21'; B Obv.I 3, 29.

41 For the role of Akkadian tradition in the Hurrian world, see G. Wilhelm, *The Hurrians* (*cit.*), *passim*; for the early Hurrian state formations that occurred in the reign of Akkad, *ibidem*, pp. 8 sgg.; cf. also M. Salvini, *Bibliotheca Mesopotamica* 26 (1998), pp. 99-115.

42 CTH 3.

43 CTH 2.

Gurparanzaḫ, is mentioned, and the name of the king of Akkad, Impakru,[44] confirmation of whom has not been found in the Hurrian world where the names of Akkad sovereigns were well known (cf. KUB XXVII 38 IV 13-28 = ChS I/5 Nr. 87), make it improbable that the text that has reached us on Gurparanzaḫ is the Hittite translation of an original composed in the Hurrian language.

Although it is not possible to define the dynasty that the myth refers to, given the vastness of the area concerned (Eastern Anatolia, Upper Mesopotamia), it appears fairly reasonable to think of a reign in northern Mesopotamia, situated in the piedmont of the upper Habur near the upper course of the Tigris, and in the center of which are located Tell Mozan/Urkiš, Tell Brak/Nagar, Tell Barri/Kaḫat, Tell Leilan/Šeḫna/Apum/Šubat-Enlil. Ailanuwa, the name of the city where Gurparanzaḫ is king, might refer to this area if we take into consideration the hypothesis that this *hapax* is really "Hittite-isation" (with reduction of intervocalic *l*[45] and addition of suffix *-(u)wa*) of the toponym Alilanum, the city that, according to the indications provided by the tablets of Tell Leilan[46] is situated in the area between the Djebel Sinjar and the Habur plains, where a sovereign by the Hurrian name of Masum-atal[47] reigned in the paleo-Babylonian era.

4. Reconstruction

Based on the abovementioned comments, I believe that reconstruction of the plot of this composition is possible, according to a sequence that perhaps shows greater coherence by inverting Obv. and Rev. of KUB XXXVI 67:

- KUB XXXVI 67 Obv. I (presently Rev. IV) - lost: [The proem, exposition of the theme, and beginning of the narration].

- KUB XXXVI 67 Obv II (presently Rev. III) - fragmentary: Impakru, the king of Akkad, does not have a male son to succeed him and searches for a son-in-law; 60 kings in his service, many of whom are Hurrian (see the names of Ešiadali and

44 Also note that Impakru's daughter, Tatizuli, oddly bears a Hurrian name.

45 The loss of the intervocalic *l* could be configured as a phenomenon of palatalization, in case of oral transmission of the myth; instead, if we suppose (but, as said, this seems less probable) that the Hittite scribes depended on a written compilation, there could be an error in reading the original syllabogram.

46 Cf. J. Eidem, RA 85 (1991), p. 122.

47 Masum-atal is mentioned in the Mari text: see J. R. Kupper, RHA XXXVI (1978), pp. 123, 126; cf. J. Eidem, AAAS 37/38 (1987-88), p. 120, n. 29.

Eniadali), show their concern. They make the news known to the king of Ailanuwa, Gurparanzaḫ, who steps forward along with seventy other young men;

- KUB XXXVI 67 Rev III (currently Obv. II): The suitors gather together at Akkad and, together with Impakru, participate in a hunt along the banks of the river Aranzaḫ, which is the eponymous divinity and protector of Gurparanzaḫ; he, aided by the river, is distinguished for his skills and Impakru chooses him as his son-in-law. At the banquet, which is held in Akkad on their return from the hunt, Gurparanzaḫ again shows his abilities by exceeding all the others (the 60 kings and 70 young men) in an archery competition. At the end of the celebrations he is accompanied with full honours to the nuptial bed, but the young woman, Tatizuli, refuses to consummate the marriage and follow her spouse until she receives the dowry that she is due from her father to allow the bride and groom to be independent and build their own dominion;

- KUB XXXVI 67 Rev. IV (currently Obv. I): lost: [Gurparanzaḫ is torn between the loyalty towards his father-in-law and the longing for his wife; at the end he decides to remain in Akkad at the side of his father-in-law. The two are separated: the woman goes in search of help to the river Aranzaḫ, her husband's protector, while Gurparanzaḫ stays in the city].

- KUB XVII 9 Obv. I: The river Aranzaḫ intervenes in helping the two young people; it first speaks with the woman, who explains her reasons, and then goes to Akkad where Gurparanzaḫ is. The river finds him in tears surrounded by the young men of his retinue. It comforts him assuring him of its willingness and capacity to help; the young man then reveals his sorrow. The river then goes to the Mother Goddess for advice and together her reach the Fate Goddesses who welcome the river according to the rules on palatine hospitality.

- KUB XVII 9 Obv. II- Rev. IV - lost: [The goddesses find a way to resolve the conflict between the two young people and the marriage is consummated. A son is born who receives a paternal and maternal inheritance and becomes the sovereign of a new powerful reign].

UN PALAZZO RITROVATO

PAOLO EMILIO PECORELLA

Università di Firenze

All'amico Pelio, in ricordo dei giovani tempi

L'identificazione della città di Kahat, nota da numerose fonti come sede del dio della tempesta oltre che di un palazzo fatto erigere da Tukulti-Ninurta II (890-884 a.C.),[1] con il sito di Tell Barri nell'alta Siria è opera di G. Dossin.[2] La questione è stata discussa più volte in connessione con gli scavi che la Missione Archeologica Italiana[3] ha in corso dal 1980; anche se negli ultimi anni si è cercato di attribuire il toponimo ad altro sito archeologico i risultati degli scavi hanno confermato la correttezza dell'identificazione.[4] Questa, come è noto, si fonda sulla lastra,[5] conservata nel Museo di Aleppo e segnalata nel 1960 dal funzionario del Dipartimento alle Antichità e ai Musei, Mahmud Heretani (che ne aveva avuto notizia durante un viaggio di ricognizione nella regione e l'aveva fatta ricoverare al vecchio posto di polizia di Tell Brak insieme a due frammenti iscritti del medesimo testo cuneiforme), dove si cita espressamente la costruzione di un palazzo nella città di Kaḫat.

1 Si veda M. Salvini, "I dati storici" in P. E. Pecorella, M. Salvini, *Tell Barri/Kaḫat 1. Relazione Preliminare sulle campagne 1980-1981 a Tell Barri/Kaḫat nel bacino del Ḫabur* (con contributi di R. Biscione, P. Ferioli, E. Fiandra, N. Parmegiani, R. Ricciardi Venco, U. Scerrato, S. Sorda e G. Ventrone Vassallo), Roma 1982, pp. 13-28.

2 G. Dossin, "Le site de Kaḫat", in *Les Annales Archéologiques de Syrie* XI-XII, 1961-1962, pp. 197-206. Si veda anche W.J. van Liere, "Notice géographique sur la ville de Kaḫat-Tell Barri", in *Les Annales Archéologiques de Syrie* XI-XII, (1961-1962), pp. 163-164.

3 Per un inquadramento generale si veda M. Salvini, "Le cadre historique de la fouille de Tell Barri (Syrie)", in *Akkadica* 35, (nov.-déc. 1983), pp. 24-41; *Idem*, "Kahat nella documentazione cuneiforme: repertorio delle fonti" in P.E. Pecorella cur., *Tell Barri/Kaḫat 2. Relazioni sulle campagne 1980-1993 a Tell Barri/Kaḫat, nel bacino del Ḫabur* (*Siria*), *con contributi di M.G. Amadasi, S. Anastasio, L. Bettini, R. Biscione, V. Francaviglia e A.M. Palmieri, N. Parmegiani, P.E. Pecorella, R. Pierobon Benoit, L. Tondo, M. Salvini*, Roma 1998, (citato in seguito come *Kaḫat 2*), pp. 29-34.

4 Si veda M. Guichard, "Au pays de la dame de Nagar", in D. Charpin, J.-M. Durand curr., *Florilegium Marianum II. Recueil d'études à la mémoire de Maurice Birot* (*Mémoires de N.A.B.U.* 3, Paris 1994), pp. 240.

5 *Kaḫat 2* fig. 3 a p. 18.

Oltre alla lastra, sin dalla prima visita con il collega Mirjo Salvini nel 1978, erano evidenti i "cippi" che costellano l'acropoli; si tratta di oltre un centinaio di blocchi in basalto e in calcare biancastro[6] che, a partire dal momento della sedentarizzazione della regione intorno agli anni '40, sono stati reimpiegati dalla popolazione dei villaggi vicini per segnalare le sepolture dei congiunti, poste intorno al piccolo mausoleo dello Sceicco Barri. L'evidente conclusione circa questo materiale lapideo era che provenisse dal palazzo di Tukulti-Ninurta II, proprio per l'uso del paramento esterno delle murature nei palazzi aramaici e neoittiti.

Nel corso degli anni a questo materiale si sono aggiunti due altri blocchi, uno reimpiegato come lastra tombale[7] e l'altro rinvenuto sulla pendice del *tell*, durante l'inverno del 1986, che presentano una decorazione di rosette a rilievo ed excise.

La ricerca della struttura palaziale è stata infruttuosa sino al 1997. La presenza di un livello medievale con la costruzione di un muro di terrazzamento aveva fatto pensare ad uno smantellamento degli strati superiori dell'acropoli e alla conseguente perdita dei dati archeologici che riguardavano i periodi dell'Età del Ferro. In realtà la situazione era molto più complessa, come si è poi visto nello scavo dell'Area G, sulle pendici meridionali del *tell*, dove sono stati recuperati materiali pertinenti ai periodi tra l'Achemenide e quello Romano imperiale.[8] Una sequenza "tarda" è stata registrata nell'Area H, in alto, sulla pendice occidentale, con un livello partico-romano e uno bizantino-sasanide, oltre che a lacerti dell'insediamento medievale islamico, fortemente danneggiato dall'inserimento delle tombe moderne. Era quindi possibile che l'acropoli celasse anche un livello neoassiro, registrato per altro anche alla sommità dell'Area G.

Nel 1996, per approfondire l'indagine sul livello del III millennio, messo in luce nei primi anni di scavo sul fianco occidentale,[9] si è aperta la trincea di saggio, Bs, per accertare la sequenza del II millennio. Come spesso accade, la limitatezza del

---

6 *Kaḫat 2* fig. 6 a p. 18.

7 *Kaḫat 2* figg. 4 e 5 a p. 18.

8 Per un quadro complessivo dei risultati si veda R. Pierobon-Benoit, "Tra l'Ellenismo e il Medioevo: dati e problemi a Tell Barri", in *Kaḫat 2,* pp. 199-256. Anche: P.E. Pecorella, R. Pierobon Benoit, "Tell Barri e la Siria nord-orientale dopo la fine dell'impero assiro", in *Studi Miscellanei* 30 (*Studi in memoria di Lucia Guerrini, Vicino Oriente, Egeo-Grecia, Roma e mondo romano - Tradizione dell'antico e collezionismo di antichità*, a cura di M. G. Picozzi e F. Carini), Roma 1996, pp. 13-21. R. Pierobon Benoit, "Eracle e il leone nemeo in una falera da Tell Barri", in *L'incidenza dell'antico, Studi in memoria di Ettore Lepore*, Napoli 1996, pp. 607-614.

9 Si veda R. Biscione, "La sequenza del III millennio a Tell Barri/Kaḫat : l'area B", in *Kaḫat 2,* pp. 35-64.

saggio non ha dato risultati certi, per gli interventi posteriori che hanno modificato la sequenza dei livelli. Si è deciso, quindi, nel 1996, di aprire l'area di scavo J, al di sotto del ciglio dell'acropoli verso occidente, su un fronte di dieci metri ed una profondità di cinque. I risultati sono stati incoraggianti, per quello che riguarda l'occupazione "tarda", specie per il periodo posteriore alla caduta dell'impero assiro alla fine del VII secolo. Dati interessanti sono stati raccolti per il periodo achemenide, anche con il ritrovamento di una tomba da cui proviene un anello d'oro con la rappresentazione di una figura femminile, del tipo noto come greco-persiano.[10] L'elemento più cospicuo, anche da punto di vista della potenza degli strati, è il livello neobabilonese che mostra una occupazione incentrata su produzioni artigianali.[11]

La scoperta della struttura palaziale è giunta nel 1997 con la individuazione degli ambienti le cui murature in crudo erano di particolare consistenza e accuratezza. Si tenga comunque presente che l'area di scavo interessa il margine occidentale della china e che al di sopra delle strutture murarie vi sono diversi metri di strati e livelli posteriori che, al momento, impediscono di penetrare verso il cuore del palazzo.[12]

In sostanza, riassumendo il lavoro di tre campagne nell'Area J,[13] si è giunti ad identificare una serie di vani che si scaglionano lungo la china, ciascuno dei quali, al momento, è preceduto da un vano lastricato con mattoni cotti. In superficie, durante l'ultima campagna, sono emersi muri che indicano un proseguimento del "fronte" lungo la china attuale del *tell*, confermando così la sostanziale continuità della mor-

---

10 P. E. Pecorella, R. Pierobon Benoit, "Tell Barri - Kaḫat. Una città dell'alta Siria", in *Studi e testi I* (*Eothen 9*), Firenze 1998, pp. 93-116 e fig. 14.

11 Per quanto riguarda più direttamente i livelli dell'Area J, occorre dire che nel 1996 alcuni strati ed i relativi materiali vennero interpretati come appartenenti al periodo neoassiro; in realtà, come si è visto quasi contemporaneamente nei settori superiori dell'area G, la testimonianza della ceramica era fuorviante in quanto, pur seguendo assai da vicino la produzione neoassira, si trattava in realtà di materiali prodotti durante il controllo neobabilonese della regione. Nel riempimento del vano 57 sono stati recuperati numerosi materiali che attestano un uso "domestico" su vasta scala: infatti sono presenti numerose spatole in osso e fusajole in argilla cruda, elementi da connettere ad attività di tessitura e filatura. La stessa situazione si è riscontrata nel livello neobabilonese dell'area G e questo è forse un indizio per far risalire la fase di riuso al momento immediatamente posteriore alla caduta dell'impero assiro.

12 A questo inconveniente si cerca di ovviare, al momento, ampliando la vicina area A, il cui scavo ha raggiunto il livello achemenide.

13 Il resoconto dei lavori si trova in P. E. Pecorella, *Tell Barri - Kahat. Relazione preliminare della campagna del 1997, Firenze 1997; Idem, Tell Barri - Kahat. Relazione preliminare della campagna del 1998*, Firenze 1999; Idem, *Tell Barri - Kahat. Relazione preliminare della campagna del 1999.* Firenze 2000.

fologia del monticolo, sino al canalone meridionale (da dove proviene la lastra con l'iscrizione di Tukulti-Ninurta II), dove si trovava evidentemente una delle vie d'accesso all'acropoli.

Al momento la struttura consta di quattro ambienti, l'uno arretrato rispetto all'altro, per seguire l'andamento della china. È da dire che i cortili lastricati, a cielo aperto, potevano essere chiusi da muri verso valle, a meno di non voler immaginare una serie di terrazze aperte verso occidente. Le murature sono in mattoni crudi di notevole spessore, assai ben costruite, tanto da far pensare alla possibilità di un piano superiore. Tra i vani 71 e 57, quelli settentrionali, il muro è raddoppiato come se si fosse proceduto ad un ampliamento in un secondo momento o forse per assicurare maggiore stabilità alla struttura. Il vano 107 pare essere un elemento di servizio, date le dimensioni, mentre dalla corte 105 ai accede ad un altro vano che si trova alle spalle dell'area. La struttura continua verso l'area A come testimoniano le tracce di altri muri di cospicuo spessore e gruppi di mattoni cotti legati con bitume che devono appartenere ad altri ambienti a cielo aperto; la fronte è al momento lunga all'incirca una cinquantina di metri.

Le vicende della struttura hanno fornito una serie di elementi interessanti: che si tratti di ambienti di rappresentanza è attestato dalla presenza, nel vano 71, di una sorta di "tappeto", costituito da quattro grandi lastre di pietra, ben connesse tra di loro, ai cui limiti corre una decorazione di rosette incise. Le lastre sono collocate se non al centro dell'ambiente, di cui non si è raggiunto ancora il limite settentrionale, in una posizione tale da potervi accedere da tutti i lati; in tal modo si esclude la possibilità che si tratti di un podio, anche perché le lastre sono allo stesso livello del pavimento. La superficie è molto consunta e le lastre sono parzialmente calcinate dall'uso di porvi sopra dei bracieri, durante la stagione invernale, come mostra il caso analogo di Nimrud (comunicazioni di D. Oates).

È evidente che gli ambienti hanno subito le ingiurie del tempo e che sono stati reimpiegati come è emerso immediatamente nella prima campagna di scavo. Infatti il vano 57 ha mostrato un rialzamento del suolo, in argilla battuta, al di sopra dell'originario pavimento in mattoni crudi, e su questo nuovo suolo sono stati trovati alcuni pesi e macine in basalto, una delle quali del tipo rettangolare a sella e le altre del tipo rettangolare con scanalatura, tipiche del periodo neoassiro e di quello neobabilonese. La soglia che porta dal cortile al vano, costituita da due belle lastre in pietra calcarea, le cui estremità si trovano al di sotto degli stipiti, venne rialzata, ponendovi un blocco più o meno quadrato con un incavo semicircolare asimmetrico, tipico delle porte monumentali. Poiché il blocco non copriva tutta la luce della porta, alcuni mattoni crudi riempivano il varco. Il blocco o ganghero è simile a quelli delle porte monumentali di Tell Halaf, specie del periodo di Kapara,[14] e ben si addice ad una costruzione del IX secolo,[15] dove furono impiegate probabilmente maestranze della regione. In base alle misure si può ritenere che la porta originaria avesse una luce di circa 2,40 metri. È plausibile che lo smantellamento di queste imponenti strutture sia dovuto al crollo, lungo la pendice, dei terrazzamenti sui quali si ergeva, sul ciglio, il palazzo. Tra l'altro, uno dei blocchi rinvenuto in superficie, è parte di un altro ganghero. Questi due blocchi recano una decorazione di rosette a bassorilievo entro un modulo quadrato con triangolini excisi, circondato da serie di rosette doppie e semplici entro listelli che si ripetono regolarmente.[16] Anche in questo caso è rispettato l'uso di procedere alla decorazione una volta che le lastre fossero *in loco*, come dimostra l'irregolarità della tessitura disegnativa. La datazione del reimpiego è attestato da un *goblet* del tipo detto "di Palazzo", neoassiro, immediatamente al di fuori della porta.

Per altro, al momento del reimpiego dei vani 57 e 71 le pareti presentavano ancora la decorazione originaria: si tratta di uno strato di argilla fine coperto da uno strato di intonaco di color bianco sul quale sono tracciate serie di rosette a sei petali, di bande e fasce parallele in colore azzurro, nero e talvolta in rosso. Secondo i dati in nostro possesso, le pareti hanno ceduto probabilmente a causa del crollo della copertura lignea, in parte recuperata in antico e in parte combusta da un incendio di modeste proporzioni, visibile nel riempimento dei vani ed anche sul bordo della corte 85.

Il rimaneggiamento della struttura è attestato anche dalla situazione della porta che mette in comunicazione i vani 57 e 107. Qui le soglie sono state reimpiegate: si

---

14 Nella *Südburgtor* e nel *Tempel-Palast;* si veda M. Frh. von Oppenheim, R. Naumann, *Tell Halaf II. Die Bauwerke*, Berlin 1950, pp. 134-136, fig. 67 e tav. 26. Il tipo esiste anche nel periodo cosiddetto antico aramaico, oltre che nello *Stadttempel* neoassiro.

15 Lo studio di P. Albenda, "Assyrian Carpets in Stone", in *JANESCU* 10, (1978), 1-34, comprende tutta la documentazione disponibile all'epoca. Stupisce, per altro che l'Autrice non prenda in considerazione il materiale di Tell Halaf, che è il più antico e che specifichi come il primo esempio di blocco pavimentale decorato risalga a Tiglat-pileser III (745-727 a.C.).

16 Il pezzo che ha maggiore somiglianza con le nostre lastre proviene dal Palazzo Bruciato di Nimrud (*ibid*. pl. 6), dove la sequenza va dal Periodo medioassiro a quello neoassiro; quindi la lastra in questione potrebbe risalire, appunto, a una fase strutturale del IX secolo a.C. anche se è stata datata al regno di Sargon II, Albenda, *ibid*., p. 5.

tratta di una lastra (118) con decorazione di rosette, molto consunta, che non copre tutta la luce del varco, di una seconda (129), più grande che in origine doveva avere una diversa collocazione come si desume dal fatto che la parte non decorata è a vista e di una terza (120), simile ai gangheri già citati. Inoltre la pavimentazione del vano 107 è irregolare e sommaria; si distingue solamente la lastra 92, probabilmente anch'essa una soglia asportata dal luogo originario.

Ben poco, quindi, è stato trovato che risalga alla fase più antica di vita del palazzo, dato lo stato di riuso delle strutture; salvo qualche pezzo frammentario come una piccola base di pietra basaltica compatta con tracce di perni in ferro, alcuni frammenti di un oggetto in osso con cerchi concentrici incisi e poco altro. La datazione, come si evince da quanto esposto, si basa al momento sulla qualità e tipologia delle soglie e sulla decorazione parietale che attestano la qualità dell'edificio, ascrivibile certamente a Tukulti-Ninurta II, in sintonia evidentemente con quanto dice l'iscrizione della soglia pubblicata dal Dossin.

La scoperta del palazzo di Tukulti-Ninurta II, oltre a confermare l'identificazione di Tell Barri con la città di Kaḫat ed a porre fine alla discussione di carattere geografico-topografico, conferma alcune l'ipotesi sulla morfologia del *tell* durante il periodo preclassico; al momento la sommità si presenta a pianta ovoidale con una sorta di bordo rilevato e due profondi canaloni che costituiscono i resti delle vie d'accesso. In origine, riteniamo che l'acropoli fosse di minori dimensioni e spostata verso occidente; l'ampliamento verso gli altri tre punti cardinali dovrebbe essere avvenuto dopo il periodo neobabilonese con la costruzione di strutture come il *Grande Muro di Difesa,* che circonda l'acropoli, e di terrazzamenti, tesi ad ampliare la superficie sommitale che si veniva restringendo. Questo ampliamento dell'occupazione sembra trovare conferma dalle vicende che gli scavi delle ultime campagne rivelano per le fasi tarde. Si è sempre considerato l'anello che circonda il *tell* su tre lati (il quarto è delimitato dal corso del fiume) come il resto del muro di fortificazione del II millennio, distrutto durante la conquista neoassira della regione. In realtà, lo scavo dell'area M, nella città bassa, ha portato alla luce un cospicuo edificio, costruito con mattoni cotti e calce, che si prolunga al disotto della eminenza a semiluna. Al di sopra si trovano un livello bizantino-sasanide e uno medievale. È ben vero che un ristretto saggio in profondità sulla eminenza più ad occidente aveva portato alla luce ceramica del Ḫabur, oltre a materiale "tardo" ma è troppo difficile poter trarre dati sicuri da così pochi elementi che possono essere anche sporadici. Anche se le mura urbane del II millennio si trovano al di sotto della semiluna, occorrerà ampliare e approfondire l'esplorazione della città bassa e saggiare la consistenza dello "stagno" o fossato che circonda il *tell*. Oltre al ritrovamento del palazzo ci attende adesso quello del tempio del dio della tempesta (con l'archivio che i testi ricordano) che è ben probabile si trovasse proprio sull'acropoli originaria dell'insediamento.

Illustrazioni

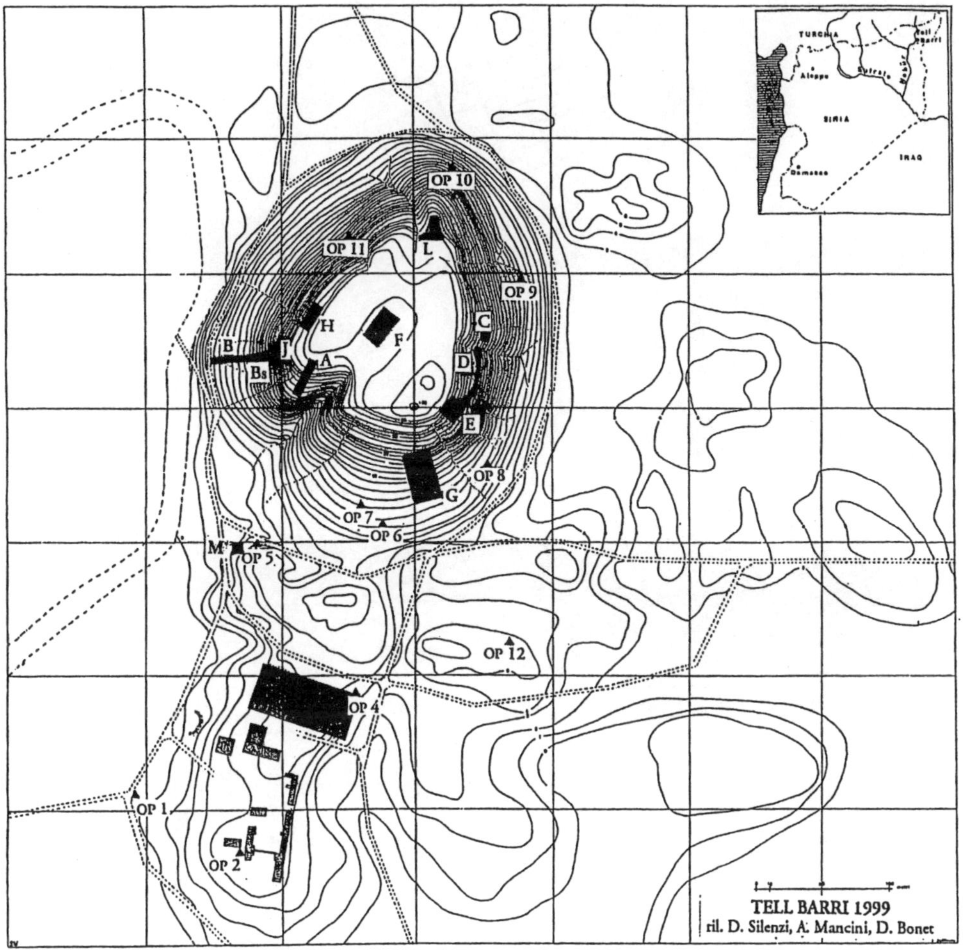

1. Pianta generale di Tell Barri.

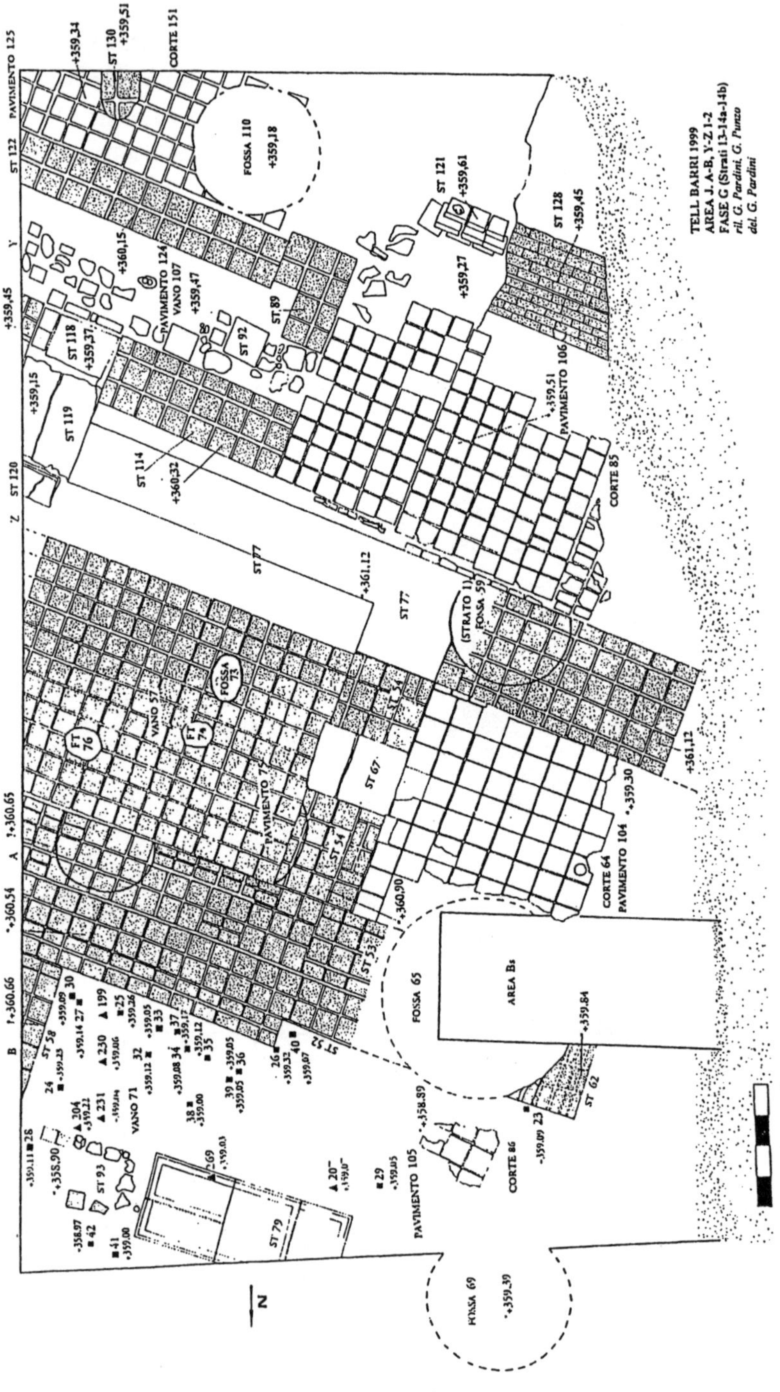

2. Pianta del palazzo, strato 14 (1999).

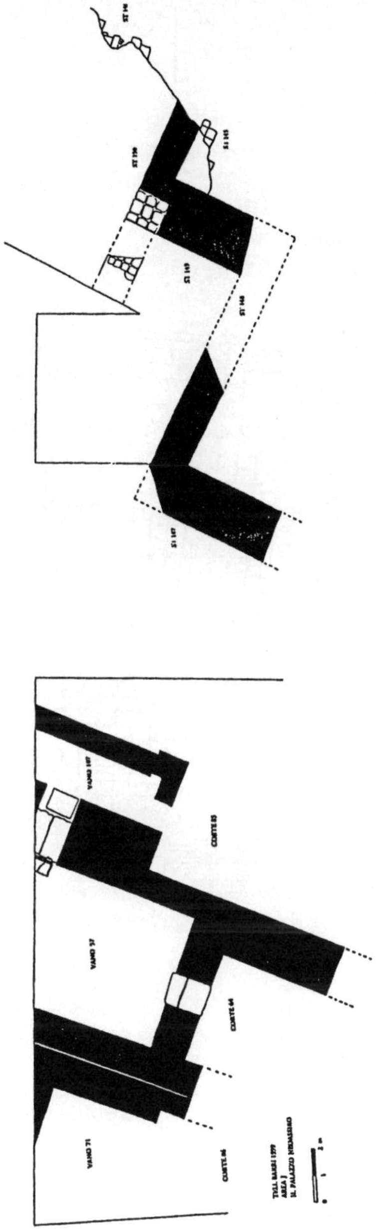

3. Schema delle strutture.

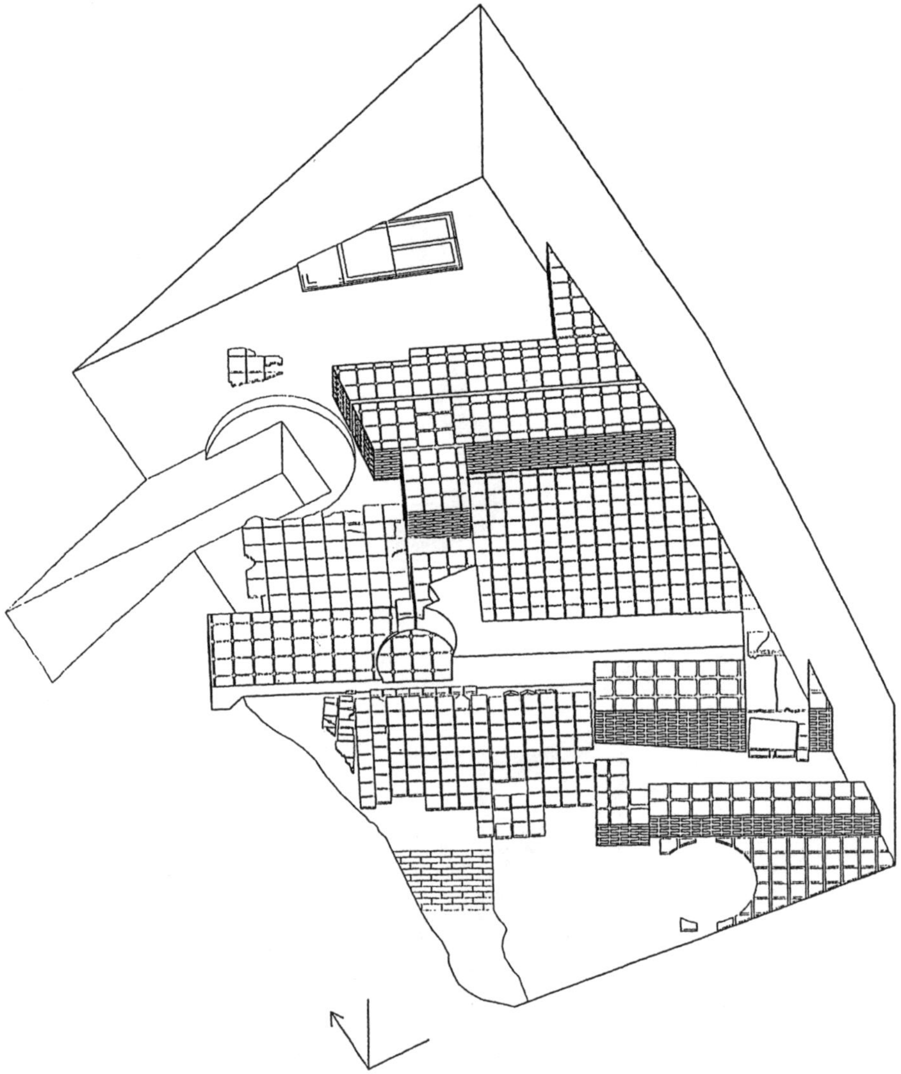

TELL BARRI 1999 - AREA J - STRATI 13 & 14
ASSONOMETRIA DEL PALAZZO NEOASSIRO
SCALA 1:70
ril. G. Pardini, S. Punzo; *del.* G. Pardini

4. Assonometria delle strutture.

5. Veduta generale delle strutture.

6. Ganghero.

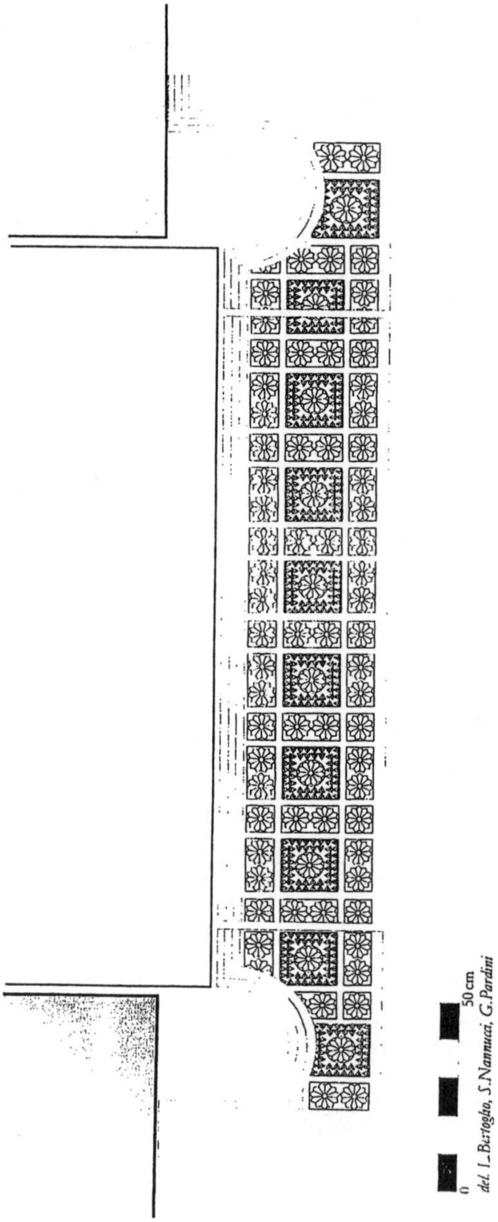

7. Ricostruzione della porta con il ganghero.

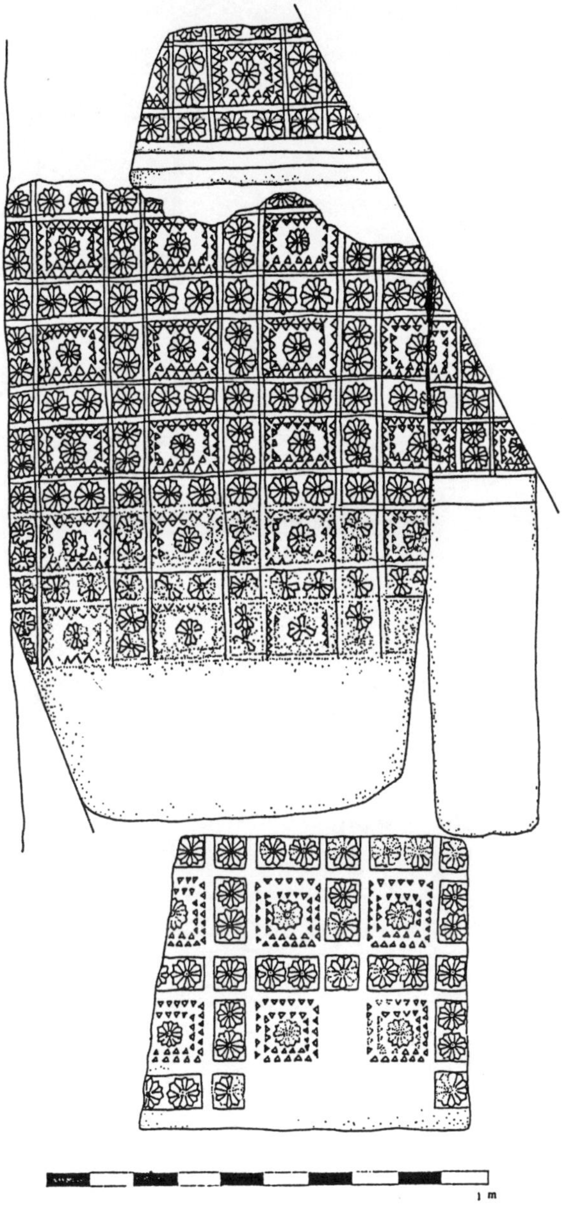

8. Le tre lastre del vano 107.

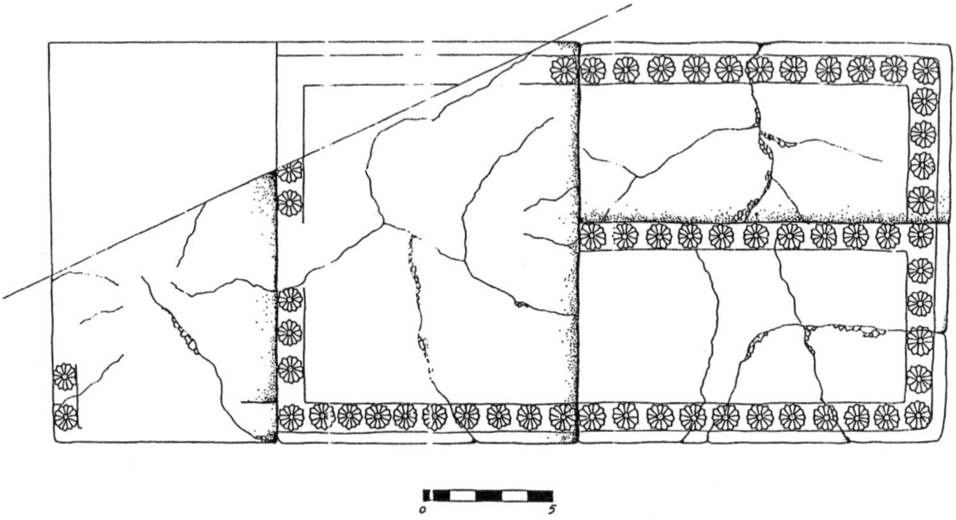

9. Il "tappeto".

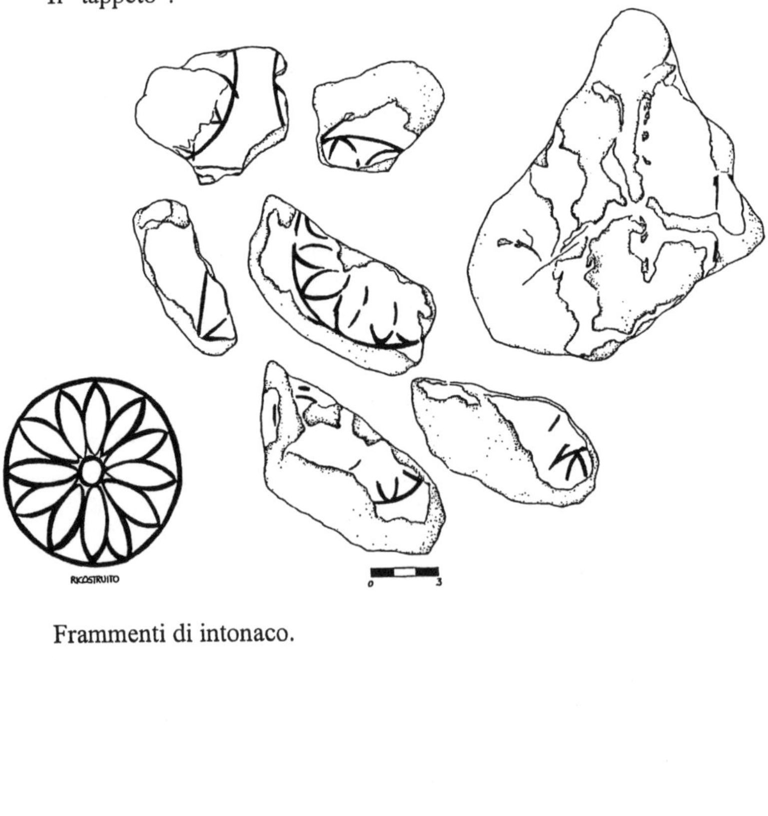

10. Frammenti di intonaco.

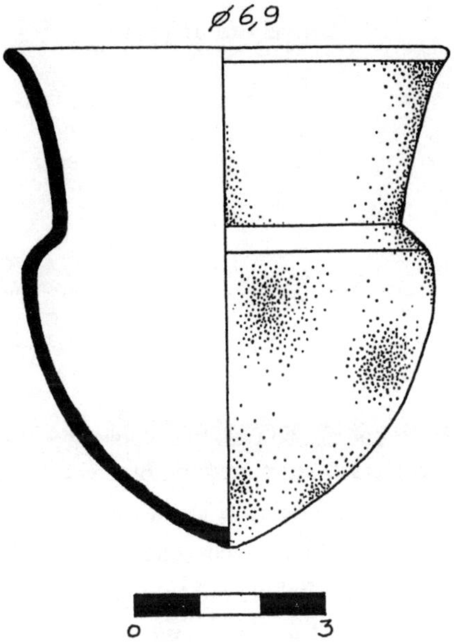

11. Il *goblet* della soglia 67, inv. 2089.

LO SPECCHIO DELL'ANIMA E IL MANTO DI LUCE NEL *TESTAMENTO DI ABRAMO*[1]

FABRIZIO A. PENNACCHIETTI

Università di Torino

"*Verrà la morte e avrà i tuoi occhi*"
Cesare Pavese

"*La morte verrà all'improvviso,
avrà le tue labbra e i tuoi occhi*"
Fabrizio De André

1. Gli occhi della Morte

1.1. Il *Testamento di Abramo*,[2] un'opera apocrifa databile al I sec. d.C., è forse il testo più antico della letteratura di area mediterranea che si sia posto il problema di come l'uomo prenderà piena coscienza di se stesso al momento del trapasso. Vi si racconta che, quando il Signore Iddio decise che i giorni di Abramo erano giunti al termine, comandò all'arcangelo Michele di annunciargli la morte affinché ordinasse le sue cose in tempo. Visto che il patriarca invocava ogni pretesto per non lasciare questo vano mondo, e poiché l'arcangelo non osava contraddirlo per il rispetto che gli portava, il Signore convocò la Morte in persona, ingiungendole di rivestirsi di tutta la sua bellezza e di tutto il suo splendore e di prendere Abramo con dolcezza e con i dovuti riguardi.[3]

Quando Abramo vide quell'essere meraviglioso sedersi al suo fianco fu investito da una soave fragranza e dal riverbero della sua luce.[4] Ciò nondimeno turbato da

---

1 Ricerca effettuata con fondi erogati dal Ministero dell'Università e della Ricerca Scientifica e Tecnologica.

2 Per la relativa bibliografia si consulti Haelewyck, *Clavis Apocryphorum*, pp. 56-61: n. 88 - *Testamentum Abrahae (De morte Abrahami)*; Nickelsburg, *Review*, Colafemmina, *Testamento* e Rosso Ubigli, *Testamento*.

3 Cfr. la recensione greca lunga, detta A, cap. 16, 1-5. Secondo la recensione greca breve, detta B, cap. 13, 1-3, il Signore incaricò Michele di adornare la Morte con grande bellezza in modo che Abramo potesse mirarla con i suoi propri occhi, cfr. Colafemmina *Testamento*, pp. 69 e 91.

4 Recensione greca A, cap. XVI, 8: καὶ ἰδοὺ ὀσμὴ εὐωδίας ἤρχετὸ πρὸς αὐτὸν, καὶ φωτὸς ἀπαύγασμα.

quella presenza che avrebbe dovuto essere rassicurante, il patriarca chiese alla Morte chi fosse e se apparisse a tutti con simile avvenenza e splendore. Al che la Morte rispose che quella bellezza non le apparteneva, ma che dipendeva unicamente dalle buone opere di Abramo e dal suo grande amore per Dio. Ai giusti compariva con grande serenità e seduzione; ai peccatori invece con putredine e ferocia.[5]

Visto che anche con lei il patriarca faceva resistenza, la Morte gli tese un tranello pregandolo di baciarle la mano. Ne avrebbe ottenuto letizia, forza e vita. Nell'istante stesso in cui Abramo sfiorò con le labbra la mano della Morte, la sua anima vi rimase incollata. La Morte allora sfilò l'anima dal corpo del patriarca e la consegnò a Michele e a una schiera di angeli.[6]

La Morte, o meglio l'angelo della morte, è dunque lo specchio che riflette la bellezza o la bruttezza interiore dell'anima del defunto. È nel momento del trapasso che l'uomo, in un impatto emotivo che coinvolge tutti i sensi, dall'olfatto all'udito, conosce pienamente la verità insperata o inconfessata della propria coscienza. Un'idea senza dubbio affascinante e unica nel suo genere. Non credo che essa trovi riscontro in altri antichi testi religiosi dell'Oriente mediterraneo. Dove è nata allora, da dove proviene?

1.2. Nel 1971 Francis Schmidt[7] ha creduto di individuare la fonte originaria di questa idea in Iran, segnalando in Böklen (1902),[8] von Gall (1926)[9] e Widengren

5 Cfr. rec. A, cap. 17, 6-8: "Le disse Abramo: 'Ti prego, dal momento che sei la Morte, dimmi, appari a tutti con simile avvenenza, splendore e bellezza?' Gli rispose la Morte: 'No, mio signore. Le tue opere giuste, la tua incommensurabile ospitalità e la grandezza del tuo amore per Dio sono divenute una corona sul mio capo. Io compaio ai giusti con avvenenza, grande serenità e seduzione; ai peccatori invece io mi presento con grande putredine e ferocia, con la massima asprezza e con lo sguardo crudo e spietato'"; rec. B, cap. 13, 12-13: "Disse Abramo alla Morte: 'Come osi mentire? Io vedo che la tua bellezza non è di questo mondo'. Rispose la Morte ad Abramo: 'Non pensare, Abramo, che questa bellezza sia mia o che io mi presenti così ad ogni uomo. No! Solo se uno è giusto come te, prendo la sua giustizia, m'incorono la testa con essa e mi reco da lui. Se uno è peccatore, vado da lui con grande putredine, mi faccio dei suoi peccati una corona per il mio capo e li sconvolgo con grande terrore perché rimangano sgomenti'". Traduzione di Colafemmina, *Testamento*, pp. 71 e 92. Nella versione etiopica (Delcor, *Testament*, p. 219, cap. VIII) si ha "Questo splendore è tuo. Secondo le opere di ciascuno io mi vesto venendo da lui".

6 Cfr. rec. A, cap. 20, 8-9. Il particolare del bacio alla mano manca alla rec. B.

7 Cfr. Schmidt, *Testament*, nota 35, vol. I, pp. 99-100.

8 Cfr. Böklen, *Verwandtschaft*, p. 47.

9 Cfr. von Gall, *Basileia tou Theou*, pp. 350-351.

(1957)[10] gli studiosi che hanno paragonato prima di lui questa originale rappresentazione della Morte con la dottrina zoroastriana sulla manifestazione della vergine *Daênâ*.[11]

Sulla *Daênâ* esiste una ricchissima letteratura.[12] Essa non è la Morte né l'angelo della morte. È piuttosto la personificazione dei pensieri, delle parole e delle azioni buone o cattive compiute dall'uomo, la custode dei meriti e dei demeriti accumulati nel tesoro celeste, il "doppio" trascendente dell'anima, in conclusione la vera coscienza dell'uomo. Sulla modalità del suo incontro con l'anima del giusto ci istruisce lo *Hāδōxt Nask*, ovvero il 12° Yašt, un poema escatologico molto antico che risale sicuramente a un archetipo avestico (*Hāδōxt Nask*, II, 7-14):

7 - Alla fine della terza notte, quando appare l'aurora, l'anima del giusto crede di essere tra piante e di respirare profumi. Sembra che un vento odoroso, più odoroso di ogni altro, dalle regioni meridionali soffi verso di essa.
8 - E l'anima del giusto sembra respirare quel vento e dire a se stessa: "Donde soffia questo vento, che è il più profumato di quelli che le mie narici abbiano mai respirato?"
9 - All'arrivo di questo vento, la propria *Daênâ* le appare sotto forma di una giovane fanciulla, bella, raggiante, dalle bianche braccia, robusta, dal viso grazioso, slanciata, dal bel seno vigoroso, di nobile sembianza, di rango elevato e glorioso, quindicenne all'aspetto, di forme più belle della più bella di tutte le creature.
10 - E l'anima del giusto le domanda: "Che donna sei tu, che sei la più bella che io abbia mai visto?"
11 - Allora la propria *Daênâ* le risponde: "O tu, giovane di buon pensiero, di buona parola, di buona azione, di buona visione, sono la tua *Daênâ*". "E chi ti ha amata, per avere questa maestà, questa bontà, questa bellezza, questo profumo, questa forza vittoriosa, questo potere sui nemici con cui mi appari?".
12 - "O giovane di buon pensiero, di buona parola, di buona azione, di buona visione, tu mi hai amata per questa maestà, questa bontà, questa bellezza, questo profumo, questa forza vittoriosa, questo potere sui nemici con cui mi vedi apparire.
13 - Quando tu, vedendo qualcuno bruciare i morti e adorare gli idoli, opprimere il prossimo e abbattere gli alberi, giacevi a cantare le *gâthâ*, sacrificavi alle buone acque e al fuoco di Ahura Mazdâ e davi accoglienza all'uomo giusto venuto da vicino o da lontano,
14 - così, amabile, tu m'hai resa più amabile; bella, tu m'hai fatta più bella; desiderabile, più desiderabile; seduta in un luogo eccelso, tu m'hai fatta sedere ancora più in alto".[13]

---

10 Cfr. Widengren, *Juifs et Iraniens*, p. 238.

11 Cfr. Pavry, *Future life*, pp. 39-45. Ultimamente anche Colafemmina (*Testamento*, p. 71, nota 75) e Rosso Ubigli (*Testamento*, p. 42, nota 149) si sono richiamati alla credenza zoroastriana sulla *Daênâ*.

12 Si veda Colpe, *Daênâ*; Widengren, *Daênâ*; Gnoli, *Daênâ*; Piras, *Hāδōxt Nask*.

13 Traduzione di Morano, *Libero arbitrio e destino*, pp. 87-88.

Ovviamente l'anima del malvagio incontrerà una *Daênâ* differente. L'Arda Wirâz Nâmag (cap. 17), un testo pahlavico, avverte che un vento freddo e puzzolente che viene dal nord preannuncia l'arrivo di una giovane orribile e repellente, dalla voce stridula e assordante, che, piena di rancore, gli rinfaccia di averla ridotta in quello stato deplorevole.[14] Mentre la *Daênâ* del giusto, lieta e riconoscente, aiuta l'anima di lui a varcare il ponte Činwad (l'islamico aṣ-Ṣirāṭ), che è teso sull'inferno, e la introduce in paradiso, la *Daênâ* del malvagio, per vendetta, fa precipitare quest'ultimo nel baratro.[15]

Secondo Bausani il motivo islamico delle urì, le fanciulle celesti promesse ai beati, è stato influenzato dall'idea della *Daênâ*.[16] Ma, mentre è solo opinabile che il pio musulmano finalizzi la sua buona condotta all'incontro con le urì, per il pio zoroastriano ogni buon pensiero, ogni buona parola e ogni buona azione hanno principalmente lo scopo di rendere più bella e più splendente la propria *Daênâ*, ovvero la propria anima celeste. Nei suoi occhi radiosi egli spera di poter rispecchiare i propri occhi il terzo mattino dopo il trapasso. Il bene viene dunque fatto *ruwān ī xwēš rāy* "per amore della propria anima".[17] Similmente i cristiani, che operano il bene per amore di Cristo, aspirano a contemplare in eterno la luce del suo santo volto.

2. Tre notti d'attesa

All'interno del *Testamento di Abramo* è stato individuato un altro tema che potrebbe riecheggiare un motivo iranico. Secondo Shaked[18] è il tema delle tre notti che il corpo di Abramo ha dovuto attendere prima che lo ungessero d'unguenti e d'aromi e lo seppellissero presso la quercia di Mamre (rec. A, cap. XX, 11). Lo *Hāδōxt Nask*, che ho citato più sopra, riporta infatti che l'anima del defunto deve attendere tre notti

---

14 Cfr. Pavry, *Future life*, pp. 41-44.

15 Una raffigurazione dell'incontro del giusto con la propria *Daênâ*, accompagnata dai due cani che proteggono il ponte Činwad, con sullo sfondo la Città della Luce, la si è potuta ammirare nel sito internet http://www.walker.reston.va.us/hmgs/gallery.htm È opera di Hannah M. G. Shapero, Falls Church, Virginia.

16 Cfr. Bausani, *Persia religiosa*, p. 143.

17 Cfr. Shaked, *For the sake of the soul*, p. 17: espressione in pahlavico.

18 Cfr. Shaked, *Iranian influence*, p. 323.

in uno stato di sospensione e di sconcerto, restando vicina alla testa del cadavere.[19] Solo alla fine della terza notte essa incontra il suo destino di salvezza o di perdizione.

3. Il "drappo divinamente intessuto" è il "manto di gloria"?

3.1. A questo punto vien fatto di chiedersi se non sia da collegare con concezioni escatologiche iraniche anche il "drappo divinamente intessuto" (ἐν σινδόνι θεουφαντῷ) in cui l'arcangelo Michele depose l'anima di Abramo prima di portarla in cielo.[20]

Il passo è interessante perché richiama un particolare della morte di Giuseppe, padre putativo di Gesù, così come viene narrato nella versione copta, in quella araba e in quella latina della *Storia di Giuseppe il Carpentiere*.[21] Quando Giuseppe morì, gli arcangeli Michele e Gabriele avvolsero la sua anima in un lenzuolo luminoso che, secondo le versioni copta e araba, sarebbe stato di seta. Merita attenzione il fatto che Gesù, rivolgendosi alla Morte, la chiama "O tu che vieni dal sud!". Anche il vento odoroso descritto nello *Hāδōxt Nask* (v. 7) soffia dalle regioni meridionali, mentre quello fetido che accoglie i peccatori proviene da nord.

Ho l'impressione che tanto il "drappo divinamente intessuto" quanto il "lenzuolo luminoso" siano più adatti ad avvolgere l'anima di un infante che ad accogliere l'anima gloriosa di un giusto al suo ingresso in paradiso. Prospetto pertanto l'ipotesi che entrambi i drappi siano il frutto di un antico fraintendimento. Alle loro spalle ci sarebbe il "manto di gloria",[22] l' "abito di luce"[23] o la "veste di splendore"[24] che ricevono in cielo i salvati e che sono entrati nei rituali battesimali cristiano e mandaico.[25]

Nello zoroastrismo e nel manicheismo troviamo una concezione non molto dissimile da questo particolare aspetto della "teologia dell'abbigliamento" - come la definisce Brock: l'anima salendo al cielo riceve un abito di luce che simboleggia

---

19 Cfr. Pavry, *Future life*, cap. II "The soul of the righteous during the first three nights after death" (pp. 9-20) e cap. III "The soul of the wicked during the first three nights after death" (pp. 21-27).

20 Cfr. rec. A, cap. XX, 10: "Nel medesimo istante sopravvenne l'arcangelo Michele con una moltitudine di angeli, ed essi deposero la sua anima in un drappo divinamente intessuto", traduzione di Colafemmina, *Testamento*, p. 76.

21 Cfr. Barnes, *Extracts*, p. 57; Delcor, *Testament*, p. 173: cap. XXIII "Venerunt itaque Michael et Gabriel ad animam patris mei Josephi, et acceptam involverunt involucro lucido".

22 In greco στολὴ δόξης, in siriaco *esṭal šubḥā, esṭlā d-šubḥā*.

23 In siriaco *esṭal nuhrā*.

24 In mandaico *ʿuṣṭlia ḏ-ziua* "vesti di splendore".

25 Cfr. Brock, *Perspectives*, pp. 98-104.

l'immagine che preesiste al corpo e che dimora nella regioni celesti.[26] Questo simbolismo traspare anche nell'*Inno della perla*, il testo poetico gnostico contenuto negli apocrifi *Atti di Tommaso*. Qui un giovane principe, mandato in Egitto a recuperare una perla preziosa, si perde dimenticando lo scopo del suo viaggio, ma poi, richiamato dai genitori mediante una lettera inviata da un'aquila, compie la sua missione e si ricongiunge con loro indossando l' "abito di luce" che aveva lasciato a casa. Quest'abito nel frattempo si era miracolosamente ingrandito adeguandosi alla crescita tanto fisica quanto spirituale del principe.[27] Un modo per dire che il giovane aveva ritrovato il "doppio" celeste della sua anima.

3.2. Vale la pena esaminare a che cosa corrisponda nelle versioni copta, araba ed etiopica del *Testamento di Abramo* l'espressione "drappo divinamente intessuto" della recensione greca A.

Dal cap. IX della versione copta apprendiamo che, presa l'anima di Abramo, l'arcangelo Michele l'avvolse in bende di lino finissimo e la portò via su di un carro di luce.[28]

Il testo arabo corrispondente non dipende direttamente né dalla stessa versione copta né dalla recensione greca A. In ogni caso esso presenta un grave errore scribale, sicché al cap. IX si legge quanto segue: "Dopodiché il capo degli angeli Michele prese l'anima di nostro padre Abramo *e la trovò fredda come neve bianca* [*wa-talaqqāhā bāridīya ka-l-talğ al-abyaḍ*][29] e la trasportò sul suo carro di luce".[30] Che da chiedersi che senso abbia questa constatazione attribuita a Michele. Che si tratti di un caso clinico di ipotermia da spavento? Certo che Abramo non ci fa una bella figura.

È chiaro che il testo originario suonava diversamente. La parte che ci interessa può infatti essere ricostruita come segue: ... *wa-talaqqāhā bi-ʾardiya bayḍāʾ ka-l-talğ* ... "e la accolse con manti bianchi come la neve". La sequenza consonantica di *bāridīya* < B'RDYH > (una variante anomala dell'aggettivo *bārida* "fredda") è la

26 Cfr. Albrile, *Zurvân*, p. 216.

27 Cfr. Albrile, *op. cit.*, p. 223; Beyer, *Das syrische Perlenlied*, pp. 248-249, versi 72-98.

28 Cfr. Delcor, *Testament*, p. 195.

29 Ms. arabo n° 132 della *Bibliothèque Nationale* di Parigi, fol. 10v, linee 6-7. È stato scritto da un cristiano egiziano in un arabo scorretto e incolto.

30 Cfr. Delcor, *op. cit.*, p. 251: "Puis, le prince des anges, Michel, prit l'âme de notre père Abraham et *il la trouva froide comme de la neige blanche* et il la transporta sur son char de lumière", traduzione di Marius Chaîne, rivista da Philippe Marçais. (Il corsivo è mio).

stessa di *bi-ʾardiya* "con manti" (la preposizione *bi-* più il plurale di *ridāʾ* "manto, mantello, soprabito"). Suppongo che, quando *bi-ʾardiya* è stato letto *bāridīya*, l'aggettivo *bayḍāʾ* "bianca" è stato spostato e accordato con *at-talǧ* (*al-abyaḍ*) "la neve (bianca)" per assicurare comunque un senso al testo. Finora la migliore traduzione di questo brano l'ha fatta W. E. Barnes nel 1892 con l'aiuto di W. Robertson Smith: "... and received it in garments like white snow...".[31] La specificazione di "bianca" riguardo alla neve è comunque superflua.

Veniamo ora alla versione etiopica del *Testamento di Abramo*. In essa sta scritto (cap. IX) che "Michele allora prese l'anima di Abramo; *egli la trovò fredda e bianca come la neve*.[32] La fece montare su un carro". È evidente che questa versione dipende direttamente dalla versione araba perché traduce pedissequamente, anzi peggiorando, il testo corrotto presente in quella.

3.3. Un indizio indiretto circa la natura spuria del "drappo divinamente intessuto" di cui parla la rec. A (nella rec. B questo dettaglio è assente) è rappresentato dalla descrizione che il *Testamento di Isacco* fa della morte del secondo patriarca. Quest'opera apocrifa, collegata con il *Testamento di Abramo*, si è conservata solo in copto, in arabo e in etiopico. Ebbene, di Isacco al cap. VII si dice che "il Signore tolse la sua anima dal suo corpo. *Essa era bianca come la neve*".[33]

A mio avviso questa inutile constatazione sul colore dell'anima di Isacco nasconde il fraintendimento di un'espressione tipo "e ricevette un manto candido come la neve", la quale doveva trovarsi sia nell'archetipo greco andato perduto del *Testamento di Isacco* sia nell'archetipo a monte della rec. A del *Testamento di Abramo*.

4. Conclusione

Ho colto l'occasione di questo volume in onore di Pelio Fronzaroli, collega che da sempre ammiro e della cui amicizia vado fiero, per segnalare nel "drappo divina-

---

31 Cfr. Barnes, *Extracts*, p. 139.

32 Così nel ms. etiopico n° 107 della collezione d'Abbadie della *Bibliothèque Nationale* di Parigi, cfr. Delcor, *op. cit.*, p. 220: "Michel prit alors l'âme d'Abraham; *il la trouva froide comme la neige blanche*". Nel ms. etiopico n° 134 del catalogo Zotenberg della *Bibliothèque Nationale* di Parigi il testo è leggermente differente, cfr. Delcor, *op. cit.*, p. 223: "Michel, prenant l'âme d'Abraham, *la trouva froide et blanche comme la neige*". (Il corsivo è mio).

33 Cfr. Delcor, *op. cit.*, versione copta, p. 205: "Le Seigneur enleva son âme de son corps. *Elle était blanche comme la neige*"; versione araba, p. 260: "Lorsqu'il eut dit cela, le Seigneur prit son âme de son corps et *elle était blanche comme la neige*"; versione etiopica, p. 232: "Après cela notre Seigneur arracha l'âme du corps de Jacob (sic), *blanche comme la neige*". (Il corsivo è mio).

mente intessuto" un ulteriore possibile riflesso di concezioni escatologiche iraniche nel *Testamento di Abramo*. Un testo, questo, unico nel suo genere nella letteratura apocrifa giudaica per l'accentuato universalismo della sua soteriologia, che non fa distinzione tra ebrei e gentili.[34] Delicata è certo la questione su quanto e come abbia inciso sul giudaismo e sul cristianesimo la cultura religiosa iranica.[35] Numerosi sono comunque i paralleli e le affinità che sono stati da tempo individuati tra testi religiosi iranici da una parte e gli apocrifi e gli pseudoepigrafi giudaici e la letteratura qumranica dall'altra.

L'influenza che lo zoroastrismo può aver esercitato sull'escatologia giudaica dovrebbe risalire non oltre l'epoca ellenistica, quando anche in Palestina sono maturate esperienze spirituali finalizzate al conseguimento della salvezza individuale. È probabile che, in questo nuovo clima di apertura intellettuale, le autorevoli comunità giudaiche della Mesopotamia e della Persia abbiano funto da tramite delle idee zoroastriane.

Bibliografia

Albrile, *Zurvân* = Albrile, E., "Zurvân tra i mandei? Un *excursus* sulle origini dello Gnosticismo", *Teresianum*, 47, 1 (1995), pp. 193-244.

Barnes, *Extracts* = Barnes, W. E., *Extracts from the Arabic version of the Testaments of Abraham, Isaac and Jacob*, in M. Rh. James (ed.), *The Testament of Abraham. The Greek text now first edited with an introduction and notes*, Cambridge 1892, pp. 131-161.

Barr, *Religious Influence* = Barr, J., "The Question of Religious Influence: The Case of Zoroastrianism, Judaism, and Christianity", *Journal of the American Academy of Religion*, 53, 2 (1985), pp. 201-235.

Bausani, *Persia religiosa* = Bausani, A., *Persia religiosa da Zaratustra a Bahâ'ul-lâh*, Milano 1959.

Beyer, *Das syrische Perlenlied* = Beyer, K., "Das syrische Perlenlied. Eine Erlösungsmythos als Märchengedicht", *Zeitschrift der Deutschen Morgenländischen Gesellschaft*, 140, 2 (1990), pp. 234-259.

34 Cfr. Sanders, *Testament*, pp. 876-879.

35 Cfr. Widengren, *Juifs et Iraniens* (1957); Winston, *Iranian component* (1966); Shaked, *Iranian influence* (1984); Barr, *Religious Influence* (1985).

Böklen, *Verwandtschaft* = Böklen, E., *Die Verwandtschaft der jüdisch-christilichen mit der parsischen Eschatologie*, Göttingen 1902.

Brock, *Perspectives* = Brock, *Syriac Perspectives on Late Antiquity*, London 1984: Variorum Reprints.

Colafemmina, *Testamento* = Colafemmina, C. (a cura di), *Il testamento di Abramo. Introduzione, traduzione e note*, Roma 1995, Città Nuova Editrice.

Colpe, *Daênâ* = Colpe, C., "Daênâ, Lichtjungfrau, Zweite Gestalt. Verbindungen und Unterschiede zwischen zarathustrischer und manichäischer Selbst-Anschauung", in R. van den Broek - M. J. Vermaseren (eds.), *Studies in Gnosticism and Hellenistic Religions presented to G. Quispel*, Leiden 1981, pp. 58-77.

Delcor, *Testament* = Delcor, M. (ed.), *Le Testament d'Abraham. Introduction, traduction du text grec et commentaire de la recension grecque longue suivi de la traduction des Testaments d'Abraham, d'Isaac et de Jacob d'après les versions orientales*, Leiden 1973, E. J. Brill.

Gnoli, *Daênâ* = Gnoli, Gh., "Über die Daênâ: Hāδōxt nask, 2, 7-19", in Ch. Elsas *et alii* (Hrsg.), *Tradition und Translation. Zum Problem der interkulturellen Übersetzbarkeit religiöser Phänomene. Festschrift für C. Colpe*, Berlin-New York 1994, pp. 292-298.

Haelewyck, *Clavis Apocryphorum* = Haelewyck, *Clavis Apocryphorum Veteris Testamenti*, Turnhout 1998: Brepols.

Morano, *Libero arbitrio e destino* = Morano, E., "Libero arbitrio e destino dell'uomo nella dottrina zoroastriana", in A. Bongioanni - E. Comba (a cura di), *Libertà o Necessità? L'idea di Destino nelle culture umane*, Torino 1998, Ananke, pp. 85-97.

Nickelsburg, *Review* = Nickelsburg, G. W. E., "Review of the literature", in G. W. E. Nickelsburg (ed.), *Studies on the Testament of Abraham*, Missoula, Montana, 1976, pp. 9-22.

Pavry, *Future life* = Pavry, J. D. C., *The Zoroastrian doctrine of a future life from death to the individual judgment*, New York 1929, Columbia University Press.

Piras, *Hāδōxt Nask* = Piras, A., "Il testo avestico dell'Hāδōxt Nask 2" (Tesi per il conseguimento del Dottorato di Ricerca in Studi Iranici - VI Ciclo - IUON), Napoli 1995.

Rosso Ubigli, *Testamento* = Rosso Ubigli, L. (a cura di), *Testamento di Abramo*, in P. Sacchi (a cura di), *Apocrifi dell'Antico Testamento*, vol. IV, Brescia 2000, Paideia, pp. 17-101.

Sanders, *Testament* = Sanders, E. P. (ed.), *Testament of Abraham. A new translation and introduction*, in J. H. Charlesworth (ed.), *The Old Testament Pseudepigrapha*, vol. 1, *Apocalyptic Literature and Testaments*, Garden City N. Y. 1983, pp. 869-902.

Schmidt, *Testament* = Schmidt, F. (ed.), *Le Testament d'Abraham: Introduction, édition de la recension courte, traduction et notes* (tesi dattilografata, 2 voll., Bibliothèque Nationale et Universitaire, Strasbourg 1971).

Schmidt, *Two recensions* = Schmidt, F., "The two recensions of the Testament of Abraham: in which direction did the transformation take place?", in G. W. E. Nickelsburg (ed.), *Studies on the Testament of Abraham*, Missoula, Montana, 1976, pp. 65-83.

Shaked, *Iranian influence* = Shaked, Sh., "Iranian influence on Judaism. First Century B.C.E. to Second Century C.E.", in W. D. Davies - L. Finkelstein (eds.), *The Cambridge History of Judaism. Vol. One. Introduction; the Persian Period*, Cambridge 1984, pp. 308-325.

Shaked, *For the sake of the soul* = Shaked, Sh., ""For the sake of the soul": A Zoroastrian idea in transmission into Islam", in Sh. Shaked, *From Zoroastrian Iran to Islam. Studies in Religious History and Intercultural Contacts*, Aldershot, Hampshire GB, 1995, chap. XI, pp. 1-32.

von Gall, *Basileia tou Theou* = von Gall, A. F., *Basileia tou Theou*, Heidelberg 1926.

Widengren, *Juifs et Iraniens* = Widengren, G., "Quelques rapports entre Juifs et Iraniens à l'époque des Parthes", *Volume du Congrès Strasbourg 1956*, Leiden 1957 (Supplements to *Vetus Testamentum*, vol. IV), pp. 197-241.

Widengren, *Daênâ* = Widengren, G., "La rencontre avec la *daênâ*, qui représente les actions de l'homme", in Gh. Gnoli (ed.), *Iranian Studies* (= *Orientalia Romana. Essays and Lectures* 5), Serie Orientale Roma LII, IsMEO, Roma 1983, pp. 41-79.

Winston, *Iranian component* = Winston, D., "The Iranian Component in the Bible, Apocrypha, and Qumran: A Review of the Evidence", *History of Religions*, 5, 2 (1966), pp. 183-216.

LE LINGUE SEMITICHE DI EBLA, MARI E TELL BEYDAR NEL PANORAMA LINGUISTICO DEL VICINO ORIENTE ANTICO DEL III MILLENNIO A.C.

GIOVANNI PETTINATO

Università di Roma "La Sapienza" - Heidelberg

Ho accolto volentieri l'invito rivoltomi a partecipare con un contributo al volume in onore del collega Pelio Fronzaroli, scegliendo un tema, certo a lui gradito, quale è quello della collocazione linguistica dei testi in cuneiforme documentati nei tre centri siriani di Ebla, Mari e Tell Beydar. P. Fronzaroli, da sempre attivo nella ricerca comparata delle lingue semitiche, si è egregiamente cimentato nell'indagine filologica e linguistica dell'idioma di Ebla, affrontando anche, e non se ne poteva fare a meno, il problema del rapporto tra la nuova lingua di Ebla e la nota lingua semitica della Mesopotamia, denominata "Accadico", con risultati chiarificatori e fondamentali sul difficile tema dei rapporti linguistici all'interno del variegato mondo semitico del terzo millennio. È un piacere, ora, poter contribuire alle sue trentennali ricerche, inserendo nel quadro dei nuovi tasselli, Mari e Tell Beydar, che ci aiuteranno meglio a comprendere il difficile panorama linguistico della Fertile Mezzaluna. Il collega vorrà scusare, lo spero di cuore, il taglio prevalentemente assiriologico del mio intervento, ed accogliere le mie osservazioni come un modesto apporto alla difficile tematica da lui padroneggiata.

*

* *

Il panorama linguistico della Fertile Mezzaluna in generale e del mondo chiamato, secondo una classificazione ottocentesca, semitico, in particolare, è molto complesso e variegato. Grazie ad approfonditi studi comparativi si è ormai raggiunta un'unità di vedute per quanto riguarda la tipologia delle lingue e dei dialetti semitici del primo millennio, suddivisi per lo più secondo le aree geografiche. Si ha così un semitico orientale, riferito alla lingua parlata in Mesopotamia, nella fattispecie assiro e babilonese; quindi un semitico meridionale che abbraccia l'arabo e i dialetti affini; infine un semitico nord-occidentale con le due grandi famiglie del cananeo e dell'aramaico.

Questa classificazione, riferita alle lingue documentate nel primo millennio, è stata estesa senza molto successo a quelle esistenti nel secondo millennio, anche perché la documentazione epigrafica non è molto abbondante. Comunque sono state individuate due grandi aree, quella del semitico orientale, sempre rappresentata dall'assiro e dal babilonese, e l'altra del semitico occidentale, caratterizzata dall'amorreo e dal cananeo.[1]

Venendo poi al terzo millennio, sembrava che la divisione linguistica del semitico orientale e occidentale, con l'accadico da una parte e l'amorreo dall'altra, non dovesse subire variazioni di sorta, sicché gli studiosi si affannavano a ricostruire il "proto-semitico", quella lingua cioè da cui nel quarto millennio avrebbero avuto origine i due tronconi linguistici identificati appunto come accadico ed amorreo. È merito del semitista italiano G. Garbini aver attirato l'attenzione su alcuni fenomeni particolari e su specifici termini, per cui anche nel terzo millennio bisognava ipotizzare l'esistenza del cananeo.[2]

Questa, a grandi linee, era la situazione degli studi attorno al 1974, prima cioè della scoperta degli Archivi Reali di Ebla databili senza ombra di dubbio al terzo millennio, e nulla faceva prevedere grandi sconvolgimenti. Sono comprensibili quindi la meraviglia e lo scetticismo degli studiosi in generale e dei semitisti in particolare, quando nel 1975, sei mesi dopo il rinvenimento delle prime 40 tavolette del terzo millennio a Tell Mardikh-Ebla, annunziammo di aver decifrato una nuova lingua semitica differente dall'accadico (semitico orientale) e dall'amorreo (semitico occidentale).[3]

È più che naturale che questi primi dieci anni di studio del materiale epigrafico rinvenuto a Ebla siano stati dedicati all'approfondimento della lingua semitica ivi documentata. Va precisato che in nessun momento è stata messa in discussione la qualifica di "semitico" della nuova lingua: il dibattito verteva soprattutto sull'attribuzione o meno della lingua di Ebla all'area orientale od occidentale; si trattava, cioè, di un dialetto dell'accadico oppure di un dialetto o lingua occidentale? Come ricordavo più su, a venti anni di distanza dalla scoperta di Ebla, è stata raggiunta

---

1 P. Fronzaroli, "West Semitic Toponymy in Northern Syria in the Third Millennium B.C.", *JSS* 22 (1977), pp. 145 sgg; G. Garbini - O. Durand, *Introduzione alle lingue semitiche*, Brescia 1994, p. 27 sgg.

2 G. Garbini, *Le lingue semitiche. Studi di storia linguistica*, Napoli 1984².

3 G. Pettinato, "Testi cuneiformi del 3. millennio in paleo-cananeo rinvenuti nella campagna 1974 a Tell Mardikh-Ebla", *Or* 44 (1975), pp. 361 sgg.

un'unità di vedute tra gli studiosi (con l'eccezione di due soltanto) sul fatto che la lingua di Ebla non sia un dialetto dell'accadico. È stata confermata pure l'osservazione iniziale che l'eblaita non si può identificare con l'amorreo, donde la piena giustificazione dell'appellativo "nuova" riferito alla lingua di Ebla.[4]

a) La lingua di Ebla e la sua espansione

Come ho sottolineato a più riprese, il termine iniziale concordemente usato per designare la nuova lingua e cioè "paleo-cananeo" era da intendere piuttosto negativamente, in quanto sin da principio si voleva sottolineare che a Ebla non si parlava né accadico né amorreo, ma appunto una lingua propria dell'area geografica comunemente riconosciuta come ambiente cananeo, almeno nei periodi successivi al terzo millennio. Non si è voluto quindi mai mettere in evidenza, con il termine "paleo-cananeo", un rapporto generico con l'ebraico soltanto, come erroneamente è stato ritenuto da qualche autorevole collega, il quale ha scritto persino che il sogno nascosto coltivato dal sottoscritto fosse proprio quello di trovare nei nuovi testi la lingua della Bibbia, il libro sacro per eccellenza.

Anche se non sono d'accordo sull'uso riduttivo del termine "cananeo" per indicare l'ebraico, appunto perché esso abbraccia un ambito molto più vasto, comprendendo ad esempio sicuramente il fenicio, ho abbandonato il termine "paleo-cananeo", perché esso si rivelava restrittivo, per cui si è preferita la designazione "eblaita" o "lingua di Ebla" che, essendo generale, ci permette una certa flessibilità per quanto riguarda la classificazione ultima di questa nuova lingua. Volendo riferire la posizione aggiornata sul tema della classificazione dell'eblaita, possiamo affermare che gli studiosi sono divisi in due campi: quelli che preferiscono considerare la lingua di Ebla "semitico settentrionale" e gli altri che ritengono sia "semitico nord-occidentale", per non parlare della sparuta frangia che si ostina ancora a considerarla un semplice dialetto dell'accadico.

Nessuno nega le relazioni strettissime dell'eblaita con l'accadico parlato in Mesopotamia, soprattutto nel campo del sistema verbale, ma si è al contempo convinti che la lingua di Ebla per ragioni di natura fonologica, morfologica e lessicale è sicu-

4 Si vedano i contributi di vari studiosi in L. Cagni (Ed.), *La lingua di Ebla. Atti del Convegno internazionale [Napoli, 21-23 aprile 1980]*, Napoli 1981; *Idem*, *Il bilinguismo ad Ebla. Atti del Convegno internazionale [Napoli 19-22 aprile 1982]*, Napoli 1984; *Idem*, *Ebla: 1975-1985. Dieci anni di studi linguistici e filologici. Atti del Convegno internazionale [Napoli 9-11 ottobre 1985]*, Napoli 1986; P. Fronzaroli (ed.), *Studies on the Language of Ebla*, (*QdS*, 13), Firenze 1984. Si veda inoltre la nota 9.

ramente diversa dall'accadico; è appunto una nuova lingua semitica molto arcaica propria dell'area siriana. Qualche collega vede una relazione molto stretta con le lingue cananee del secondo e primo millennio, l'ugaritico, il fenicio e l'ebraico; altri, pur accettando connessioni con tali lingue, ne sottolineano la diversità, fermo restando il rifiuto a considerare l'eblaita un dialetto del semitico orientale.

È con profonda soddisfazione che ad appena venti anni dalla scoperta della nuova lingua di Ebla possiamo considerare chiuso il capitolo sull'appartenenza linguistica dell'eblaita, essendosi formata ormai una *communis opinio* sul carattere non orientale del semitico di Ebla. Lo studioso non al corrente delle gravi difficoltà rappresentate dalla classificazione di una lingua, non afferrerà appieno la portata straordinaria di un tale evento e non potrà apprezzare il significato ultimo della "profonda soddisfazione" che noi proviamo per tale fatto. Convinto infatti della centralità del tema "la lingua di Ebla", l'Istituto Universitario Orientale di Napoli si fece promotore, grazie all'impegno dell'infaticabile e lungimirante, compianto professor Luigi Cagni, ordinario di Assiriologia, non solo della pubblicazione della serie "*Materiali Epigrafici di Ebla*", ma anche di tre convegni internazionali dedicati allo studio del materiale epigrafico di Ebla ed in particolare della stessa lingua, a cui presero parte studiosi ed esperti d'Europa e d'America. I risultati di questi proficui incontri sono pubblicati e quindi a disposizione di tutti gli studiosi. Nonostante le naturali differenze di opinione su aspetti specifici, i partecipanti ai convegni sottolinearono tutti e il carattere "nuovo" della lingua di Ebla e la differenza sostanziale con l'accadico e l'amorreo, confermando in linea di massima la constatazione da noi fatta subito dopo la decifrazione. Parallelamente a Roma, a Firenze sono stati organizzati altri tre congressi, dove sono state affrontate le stesse tematiche, ed anche in tali occasioni i risultati sono stati simili, con l'eccezione di pochi studiosi cui si è fatto cenno più su.

A partire dal 1996, poi, l'Università di Heidelberg mi ha voluto come Professore Onorario, perché insegnassi regolarmente l'Eblaitologia, assurta così agli onori di disciplina insegnata ufficialmente al più alto livello. I temi che ho trattato sinora, seppur prevalentemente rivolti ai fenomeni puramente linguistici, non hanno trascurato l'aspetto comparativo che, soprattutto dopo la pubblicazione dei testi di Tell Beydar, è diventato un imperativo, e neppure l'altro della società e delle forme di governo in Siria alla metà del terzo millennio a.C.

Se sottolineo il comportamento esemplare di noi studiosi italiani non solo nell'aver messo a disposizione della comunità scientifica internazionale i documenti rinvenuti a Ebla, ma anche nell'aver promosso un dibattito serio e scientifico sulla lingua di Ebla, non lo faccio per ricevere il plauso generale, quanto piuttosto per evidenziare l'utilità e la proficuità di una discussione allargata nell'interesse esclusivo del progresso della scienza. Molte lingue restano da decifrare, molti documenti giacciono quasi dimenticati nei magazzini dei musei di tutto il mondo, mentre forse potrebbero venire studiati con successo, se si offrisse agli studiosi, così come abbiamo fatto noi Italiani, la possibilità di discuterli e di studiarli insieme.

Tornando ora al tema centrale di questo paragrafo, mi sembra opportuno non tanto entrare nei dettagli specialistici della nuova lingua semitica per la prima volta documentata a Ebla nel terzo millennio a.C., quanto piuttosto vedere la sua espansione al tempo degli archivi di Ebla e la sua eredità nel mondo semitico-occidentale dei millenni seguenti. Sono questi, infatti, i due aspetti rilevanti connessi con l'identificazione della lingua di Ebla.

Dalla semplice lettura dei testi economici di Ebla non è difficile trarre la conclusione che l'attività principale degli Eblaiti era il commercio internazionale, per cui la città siriana era in stretto rapporto con popoli e nazioni di diversa estrazione etnica e parlanti le lingue più svariate: sono ampiamente documentate negli Archivi amministrativi relazioni dirette di Ebla con Stati della Palestina, del Libano, della Siria stessa, dell'Anatolia, della Mesopotamia settentrionale e centrale, e persino dell'Iran e forse anche dell'Egitto faraonico.[5] La domanda che ora ci si pone è ovvia: in quale lingua comunicavano i mercanti siriani trattando dei loro importanti affari con gente che parlava idiomi diversi da quello parlato a Ebla e cioè l'eblaita?

Se è infatti indubbio che la scrittura adottata per redigere i rendiconti amministrativi ed in genere tutti i documenti era il cuneiforme di Sumer, cuneiforme che gli Eblaiti presero in prestito e studiarono intensamente nelle loro scuole, non altrettanto certi possiamo essere circa la lingua comunemente accettata come mezzo di espressione per le transazioni operate. E qui giunge puntuale la risposta che ricaviamo dagli stessi Archivi eblaiti: non andiamo infatti incontro ad errori di interpretazione e valutazione affermando che la lingua adottata nel terzo millennio come mezzo di comunicazione internazionale era proprio la lingua di Ebla. La portata eccezionale di tale constatazione non deve sfuggirci né va sottovalutata: Ebla con la sua biblioteca scritta in una nuova lingua semitica, non solo ci rivela di essere stata un centro politico molto rilevante che ha imposto la sua legge a innumerevoli Stati e che ha tenuto saldamente in mano il monopolio del commercio, ma anche ci fa capire in maniera

5 G. Pettinato, *Ebla. Nuovi orizzonti della storia*, Milano 1986, pp. 173 sgg.

estremamente chiara che la lingua franca del terzo millennio non era il sumerico, bensì l'eblaita. Come nel primo millennio la lingua internazionale è l'aramaico e nel secondo l'accadico o assiro-babilonese, nel terzo millennio è l'eblaita.

Scoprendo Ebla e decifrando la sua lingua noi abbiamo sì riportato alla luce una grande civiltà urbana, ma soprattutto abbiamo individuato il mezzo di comunicazione di cui ci si serviva nel terzo millennio in tutta la Fertile Mezzaluna. Ebla non finisce di sorprenderci: ultima ad essere stata scoperta nell'affollato panorama di civiltà del Vicino Oriente Antico, si rivela la prima e la più importante.

La prova che l'eblaita fosse la lingua franca del terzo millennio ce la forniscono documenti come il "trattato tra Ebla ed Assur",[6] la lettera diplomatica indirizzata a Ḫamazi, gli innumerevoli accordi stipulati con i più svariati Stati con cui gli Eblaiti erano in contatto politico-economico, tutti redatti in lingua eblaita. La notizia poi di frequenti e ripetuti viaggi di mercanti eblaiti in altri regni, come pure della presenza di mercanti stranieri e dignitari di altri Stati a Ebla, lascia supporre che la lingua con cui si comunicava fosse appunto l'eblaita.

Una conferma di quanto stiamo affermando la troviamo poi nel calendario dei mesi in uso nella Fertile Mezzaluna nella metà del terzo millennio. Come ho potuto dimostrare sulla base delle informazioni fornite dai testi amministrativi datati in base ai mesi in cui sono avvenute le transazioni o in cui esse sono state registrate, a Ebla furono in vigore in tempi diversi due calendari, completamente ricostruiti e studiati dal sottoscritto. In ambedue i calendari ogni mese ha un nome particolare, riferito a momenti produttivi, a fatti amministrativi o a feste religiose. Mentre il secondo calendario, in vigore nell'ultimo periodo del regno di Ebla, è costituito da nomi di mese prevalentemente sumerici, quello in vigore nel periodo precedente consta di nomi semitici, tanto che io nell'edizione lo chiamai "il calendario semitico del terzo millennio". Come ho scritto precedentemente, "tale denominazione non è certo dovuta a sensazionalismi tanto inutili quanto dannosi, ma trova il suo fondamento nel fatto che il vecchio calendario di Ebla si identifica con il calendario semitico o calendario accadico individuato da altri studiosi in documenti mesopotamici".[7]

Ormai siamo sicuri, dopo la ricostruzione integrale del "calendario vecchio" di Ebla, che esso fu in uso ad Abu Salabikh e a Mari nel periodo degli Archivi Reali,

---

6 Su questo pregevole documento si veda da ultimo G. Pettinato, *Fs. Kienast* 1999: "La formula ì-a(-)è nel trattato tra Ebla ed Assur", (in stampa).

7 G. Pettinato, "Il calendario semitico del 3.millennio ricostruito sulla base dei testi di Ebla", *OA* 16 (1977), p. 257.

ed in seguito a Gasur, Ešnunna, nella regione del Dijala e persino nelle città sumeriche di Adab, Kiš, Lagaš e Nippur. La fortuna di questo calendario, i cui nomi, tutti semitici, si riferiscono a momenti dell'agricoltura, dovette essere grande, se esso restò in vigore per circa 400 anni in aree geograficamente molto distanti tra loro.

Si comprende a questo punto perché io chiamo il "calendario vecchio" di Ebla "il calendario semitico del terzo millennio". Infatti l'uso del medesimo calendario non può non far pensare che ad una unità culturale di tutti i centri in questione; ora, ritrovando il medesimo calendario semitico nelle varie città della Siria e della Mesopotamia settentrionale e centrale, dobbiamo concludere che tutta quest'area geografica fosse culturalmente unitaria. Se poi si specifica che i nomi sono tutti prettamente semitico-occidentali, allora le conseguenze storico-culturali sono davvero sconvolgenti.

Non ci vuole molto, infatti, a trarre la conclusione che in tutta l'area di diffusione del calendario semitico si parlasse la stessa lingua, e che pertanto, essendo il calendario certamente non semico-orientale, si parlasse o almeno si comprendesse la lingua di Ebla. Ciò vale ovviamente per il terzo millennio, il periodo cioè in cui fiorì la civiltà di Ebla. Ma, come hanno rilevato diversi studiosi, tra cui M. Dahood e G. Garbini, il calendario semitico di Ebla assomiglia in maniera eclatante al famoso calendario di Gezer, tanto che sarebbe assurdo negarne un rapporto almeno indiretto.

b) Rapporto con le lingue semitiche di Mari e di Tell Beydar

Ancora recentemente lo studioso tedesco D. O. Edzard[8] ha confermato la sua convinzione che la lingua di Ebla sia identica a quella coeva di Mari, ed ambedue non siano altro che un dialetto dell'accadico.

Nel mio libro *Ebla. Nuovi orizzonti della storia*, Milano 1986, mi esprimevo, per quanto concerne la prima parte del suo discorso quasi alla stessa maniera; discutendo infatti della lingua franca nell'area siro-mesopotamica del terzo millennio, così scrivevo: "La prova indiretta della nostra asserzione ci viene dall'esame di documenti rinvenuti in centri diversi da Ebla, soprattutto a Mari e ad Abu Salabikh nel paese di Sumer; ebbene, a Mari si scriveva e parlava la stessa lingua di Ebla. Non diversa è la situazione proprio nel cuore di Sumer. Dobbiamo al grande studioso Gelb l'ipotesi di una *koiné* culturale di tutta l'area siro-mesopotamica avente come centro Kiš: ricordiamo che i professori ospiti presenti a Ebla provenivano quasi sicu-

8 "Ebla ou la grande surprise de l'histoire du Proche-Orient ancien", *Akkadica* 88 (1994), p. 19.

ramente da Kiš, come nel caso del professore di matematica. E la lingua di questa koinè culturale era appunto l'eblaita".[9]

Debbo riconoscere che oggi non sono più d'accordo su nessuno dei due punti or ora enunciati, in quanto la pubblicazione dei nuovi testi del terzo millennio rinvenuti a Tell Beydar evidenzia una realtà diversa da quella da noi finora ipotizzata, e si tratta di una realtà molto più complessa di quanto si potesse pensare. Io stesso, pur non avendo prove cogenti a mio favore, ero rimasto alquanto scettico, allorché Gelb formulò la sua ipotesi di dipendenza linguistica e culturale di Ebla e Mari dalla tradizione mesopotamica di Kiš, e ciò nonostante la presenza ad Ebla di "professori" o scribi provenienti dalla città sumerica. Nell'Introduzione a *MEE* 3, infatti, avevo avanzato dei dubbi sulla tesi avanzata da Gelb, appunto perché l'unico testo lessicale sumerico, la lista-Nagar, attestato sia ad Ebla sia a Kiš, presentava delle varianti non ortografiche tali che mi avevano convinto che la tradizione scribale di Ebla fosse differente da quella documentata a Kiš. Eppure tutti gli altri studiosi hanno accettato di buon grado la proposta di Gelb, anzi Steinkeller ha voluto estendere la dipendenza di Ebla da Kiš anche al campo istituzionale e politico, proponendo che il modello nordsiriano e centro-mesopotamico fosse diverso da quello in vigore nella Mesopotamia sumerica del Sud, cosa questa ampiamente criticata nelle pagine precedenti.

I testi semitici di Mari, d'altro canto, presentano varianti grafiche e peculiarità linguistiche che non permettono più di considerare la lingua di Mari identica a quella di Ebla, sicché non si possono più considerare le due lingue come identiche. Ma il colpo di grazia a quello che io chiamo ormai l'appiattimento linguistico delle parlate nordsiriane è venuto dalla pubblicazione dei testi di Tell Beydar: come hanno giustamente riconosciuto gli editori del volume *Subartu* II, la tradizione scribale di Mari e Beydar è differente da quella documentata dai testi di Ebla, sicché bisogna ipotizzare due vie di trasmissione del cuneiforme proveniente dalla Mesopotamia alla Siria, la prima che va verso Ebla e la seconda che va a Mari e Beydar. Non solo la grafia dei segni è diversa, ma anche le lingue semitiche attestate nelle città di Ebla da una parte e Mari+Beydar dall'altra sono chiaramente diverse.

Osservando poi l'uso dei grafemi notiamo che il sistema di scrittura di Ebla è più antico di quello in vigore a Mari e Beydar, come stanno a dimostrare il sillabario (per cui si confronti ad es. il valore del prefisso verbale /ba/, scritto ad Ebla coerentemente con ba_4 come a Fara e ad Abu Salabikh, mentre a Mari e Beydar è in vigore

---

9 G. Pettinato, *Ebla. Nuovi orizzonti*, *cit.*, p. 326.

ba), ed il sistema preposizionale - a Mari e a Tell Beydar è attestata la preposizione *iš* che manca sicuramente ad Ebla.

Se poi si allarga il discorso al mondo culturale, non possiamo non notare che il Calendario in vigore a Beydar corrisponde nella sua formulazione al Calendario Nuovo di Ebla, mentre Mari conserva il Calendario vecchio della città siriana. In base a questi e ad altri elementi non irrilevanti presentati dai documenti soprattutto di Ebla e Tell Beydar, sono pienamente convinto che i testi di Ebla sono certamente più antichi di quelli di Beydar, contrariamente a quanto ipotizzato dagli studiosi che si interessano all'elaborazione del materiale epigrafico di tale città.

Non vorrei anzi che la loro datazione sia viziata dagli errori fatti dagli archeologi ed epigrafisti di Ebla, che si ostinano a voler datare Ebla e la sua cultura al 2400-2350 a.C., mentre essa va innalzata di almeno cento anni.

c) Il Paleo-accadico e le lingue siriane

All'inizio di questo contributo abbiamo menzionato le varie posizioni degli studiosi circa l'appartenenza linguistica della lingua di Ebla. Esse si possono sinteticamente riportare a due concezioni, la prima che rivendica l'autonomia della lingua di Ebla rispetto al semitico orientale rappresentato dall'accadico, e l'altra che vuol vedere nella lingua di Ebla un dialetto dello stesso.

Già nel paragrafo precedente però sono state evidenziate alcune peculiarità non solo della lingua di Ebla, ma anche delle altre due lingue semitiche documentate a Mari e a Tell Beydar, che rendono sempre più difficile l'accettazione della tesi sostenuta dagli assertori del dominio del semitico orientale in tutta l'area siro-mesopotamica, sicché è opportuno elencare in questo terzo paragrafo gli elementi che vi si oppongono. Prima però di procedere, seppure schematicamente, alla menzione delle peculiarità distintive delle varie lingue, vorrei citare quanto scrive P. Fronzaroli a tal proposito:[10]

"Ma collocare la lingua di Ebla in rapporto alle altre lingue semitiche non dovrebbe essere considerato un semplice esercizio scientifico, rispondente agli intenti classificatori ereditati dalla linguistica del secolo scorso ed espressi nel modello dell'albero genealogico. Il problema dovrebbe invece essere posto nel quadro di una storia linguistica che appare non meno stimolante di altri aspetti della storia della cultura.

---

10 "La lingua di Ebla e le lingue semitiche", in P. Matthiae *et alii*, *Ebla. Alle origini della civiltà urbana*, Milano 1995, pp. 223 sgg.

Considerando tutti i dati linguistici disponibili da un punto di vista storico, possiamo supporre che nella seconda metà del III millennio a.C. l'area semitica fosse composta di un *continuum* di dialetti, che erano fissati in lingue letterarie (o lingue di cancelleria) soltanto nelle aree di più avanzata cultura urbana. In questo continuum dovevano esistere per lo meno due varianti principali, quella che è stato proposto di chiamare "semitico arcaico" e il cosiddetto "amorreo". Nella documentazione mesopotamica della fine del III millennio a.C. la variante amorrea appare propria dei seminomadi, in contrasto con l'akkadico parlato dagli abitanti delle città. Ciò nonostante sembra improbabile che popolazioni di cultura pastorale e organizzazione tribale, prive di istituzioni culturali e politiche unitarie capaci di imporre modelli linguistici, siano responsabili delle innovazioni che caratterizzano la variante amorrea. Il tipo amorreo potrebbe piuttosto avere avuto origine nelle città più meridionali dell'area siro-palestinese, città che esistevano anche se la loro lingua non è finora documentata.

Da un punto di vista diacronico la variante amorrea dovrebbe essere considerata innovativa rispetto al semitico arcaico, se non altro per la distribuzione periferica di quest'ultimo e per la sua scomparsa in quasi tutta l'area occidentale già nel II millennio a.C. Nell'ampio contesto afro-asiatico da cui si originano le lingue semitiche, innovativo significa anche più lontano dalle origini camito-semitiche, e quindi dai caratteri linguistici relativi.

Il tipo linguistico più antico (quello semitico arcaico) nella seconda metà del III millennio a.C. avrebbe occupato l'intera area settentrionale (lungo l'arco Ugarit-Ebla-Mari-Kiš) giungendo, attraverso la Mesopotamia meridionale, nell'area sudarabica dove certe caratteristiche arcaiche erano ancora presenti nel I millennio a.C. (la possibilità che una popolazione di lingua semitica fosse già arrivata nell'Arabia meridionale alla fine del IV o all'inizio del III millennio a.C. è stata suggerita di recente da più parti). Un secondo tipo linguistico (quello amorreo) potrebbe essere risalito dalle città meridionali lungo l'asse Hazor-Qatna e potrebbe essere stato condiviso dalle tribù seminomadi, o almeno da una parte di queste.

Se questa ipotesi è corretta, tutti i caratteri morfologici comuni all'akkadico e all'eblaita, e presenti anche in lingue di documentazione posteriore (come l'ugaritico o il sudarabico antico), dovrebbero appartenere al semitico arcaico. La documentazione di alcuni di questi caratteri anche in egiziano conferma la loro antichità, che può così risalire almeno in parte al camito-semitico. Caratteri morfologici appartenenti al semitico arcaico potrebbero essere la preferenza di *š*- nella formazione dei pronomi di terza persona e nel prefisso del tema causativo del verbo, l'esistenza di forme per il genitivo-accusativo e per il dativo nei pronomi personali indipendenti, così come i casi dativo e locativo.

I caratteri assenti in akkadico e in eblaita potrebbero essere considerati innovazioni meridionali (amorree). Tali potrebbero essere la preferenza per *h*- nella formazione dei pronomi di terza persona e del causativo, e la ristrutturazione del sistema degli aspetti verbali (*qatal(a), yaqtul* di contro a *yiqtul, yiqattal, qatil*). Altre innovazioni che potrebbero avere avuto origine nell'area urbana meridionale sono la perdita delle forme del dativo nei pronomi personali indipendenti e suffissi e la scomparsa delle forme di genitivo-accusativo nel pronome personale indipendente della seconda persona.

In ambedue le varianti saranno esistite naturalmente differenziazioni locali o tribali, e saranno sorte innovazioni rimaste limitate ad aree ristrette. Un esempio di ciò può aversi nel sistema pronominale del duale, dove le forme attestate in eblaita sembrano appartenere al patrimonio semitico più antico, e sono conservate in tutte le lingue che hanno mantenuto forme per il duale. Le forme attestate in akkadico, invece, sono il frutto di un'innovazione (per rimodellamento analogico sulle forme del plurale) e sono rimaste limitate all'area mesopotamica".

Se comprendiamo bene il pensiero di P. Fronzaroli, sia l'accadico sia l'eblaita sono da considerare espressioni del semitico arcaico; inoltre lo studioso, pur parlando di un *continuum* di dialetti, non prende posizione esplicita neanche su quest'ultimo aspetto e cioè se l'eblaita e l'accadico siano o no due dialetti differenti.

E veniamo a quelli che io chiamo elementi caratterizzanti dell'eblaita rispetto all'accadico, tanto che li considero due lingue diverse e non solo due dialetti della stessa lingua: e qui il discorso deve partire da una considerazione banale, quella cioè dell'esistenza nella lingua scritta di Ebla non solo di logogrammi sumerici, ma anche di accadogrammi, come ad esempio documenta l'attestazione del pronome suffisso di terza singolare *-sù*, da tutti riconosciuto e ritenuto appunto importazione dall'accadico.

Ora se ad Ebla sono attestati logogrammi accadici, ciò vuol dire che siamo chiaramente davanti a due lingue diverse. Se poi si passa all'esame del sillabario, alla morfologia e alla stessa sintassi, allora si comprende bene che l'eblaita e l'accadico non possono ricondursi alla stessa lingua, ma a due lingue ben diverse. Certo, quando il Fronzaroli scriveva il suo contributo, non erano stati pubblicati i testi di Tell Beydar: ora, come abbiamo riferito più su, i colleghi che hanno studiato tale materiale sono giunti correttamente alla conclusione che la tradizione scolastica e linguistica rappresentata da Ebla è diversa da quella documentata a Mari e Tell Beydar.

Io oserei andare ancora più avanti, affermando che tutte e tre le lingue siriane non solo sono differenti tra loro, ma lo sono ancor di più rispetto alla lingua accadica attestata cento anni più tardi nella Mesopotamia. Più sopra ho rifiutato la dipendenza linguistica di Ebla da Kiš, come pure l'affermata dipendenza culturale e istituzionale di Ebla e della Siria dalla Mesopotamia centrale. L'auspicio che esprimiamo è che nuovi ritrovamenti sia in Siria sia in Mesopotamia ci illuminino di più su questo interessante tema di carattere linguistico, che diventa ogni giorno più complesso e intricato.

Quanto finora è emerso è che la conclamata Kiš-tradition di I. J. Gelb[11] e P. Steinkeller[12] non trova riscontro alcuno nella documentazione siriana a nostra disposizione, come pure che conosciamo ben poco della o delle lingue semitiche attestate in Mesopotamia al tempo di Ebla.

---

11 *Thoughts about Ibla: A Preliminary Evaluation*, March 1977, *SMS* 1 (1977), pp. 1 sgg.; "Ebla and the Kish Civilization, in L. Cagni, *La lingua di Ebla* (cit.), pp. 83 sgg.

12 "Early Political Development in Mesopotamia and the Origins of the Sargonic Empire", in M. Liverani [Ed.], *Akkad. The First World Empire: Strukture, Ideology, Traditions,* Padova 1993, pp. 116 sgg.

HITTITE FRAGMENTS ON THE ATRAḪASĪS MYTH

ANNA MARIA POLVANI

University of Florence

The issue about the existence of a Hittite version of the Atraḫašīš poem (Atramḫašiš in Hittite), was put forward by J. Siegelová[1] who, on the basis of W. G. Lambert - A. R. Millard's work,[2] attributed the KUB XXXVI 74 fragment[3] to the epos of this hero wherein we read:

2' [ ] "we throw[4] (lit. saw) the weight!"
3' "Now however due to work the gods
4' opposed Enlil".
5' The god Nušku[5] lis[tened] to the words of the gods
6' and he then went back to his lord
7' and to his lord he [began] to say:
8' "My lord, after the assembly [of the gods] [you sent] me,
9' Well then I went, in front of the gods
10' and told them your words".
11' Not finished.

---

1 *ArOr* 38 (1970), p. 135 ss.

2 *Atra-ḫasīs. The Babylonian Story of Flood*, Oxford 1969.

3 The text was transliterated and translated by J. Siegelová, *op. cit.*, p. 136:
2' [ ]x a-im-p[a-a]n ar-du-me-ni

3' ki-nu-un-ma-wa KIN-ti ḫa-an-da-aš DINGIR^{meš}-i[š/-uš
4' ^{d}EN.LÍL-ya IGI-an-da ti-e-ir

5' ^{d}Nu-uš-qa-aš DINGIR^{meš}-aš ud-da-ar iš-t[a-ma-aš-ta
6' na-aš EGIR-pa EN-aš-ši kat-ta-an pa-it
7' nu EN-aš-ši EGIR-pa me-mi-iš-ki-u-wa-an [da-a-iš
8' EN-mi DINGIR^{meš}-aš-mu ku-it tu-li-ya[
9' nu-za pa-u-in DINGIR^{meš}-aš pí-ra-an du-[
10' nu-uš-ma-aš tu-e-el me-mi-an me-m[a-aḫ-ḫu-un
11' *U-UL QA-TI*

4 J. Siegelová, *op. cit.*, p. 136 translates: "... wir werfen die Last ab!".

5 J. Siegelová points out that in Hittite the god's name ends in *-a*.

The fragment was attributed to the Atra-ḫašīš myth by Siegelová for two reasons: the presence of the god Nuško, who has the duties of vizir to the god Enlil in the paleo-Babylonian version; and for its content, which can be compared to the third column in the first tablet of the version cited (rr. 146-157).[6]

It concerns the beginning of the myth when Enlil, surrounded by the Igigi, minor gods in revolt, worn out from the work assigned them by the major gods, decides to send his vizir, Nuško, to deal with them. Nuško, after learning the reasons for the rebellion against Enlil, returned to his lord to relate what he knew. The Hittite fragment seems to pick up the story again at the point when Nuško comes back from the god Enlil, having reported the results of his mission to him.

Even if the contents of r. 2' do not exactly correspond to the paleo-Babylonian version, the use of the first person plural (*ardumeni*) shows, according to the scholar, that it is the discourse directed to Nuško by the Igigi gods in which they tell of their revolt. It is worth noting that this passage contains the verb *ard-* "lit. to saw", the same verb used in the Ullikummi myth when the god Ea, while speaking to the "ancient gods", incites them to draw the ancient saw by which the sky and earth were separated and to cut under the monster's feet to remove him from Upelluri's shoulders.[7]

Even though the hero's name has not been preserved on the fragment, Siegelová's analysis clearly demonstrated that it is a Hittite version of the paleo-Babylonian epic poem. Since the scholar's analysis is focused only on this fragment, I think it opportune to take a look at the other Hittite fragment, KUB VIII 63, which at the time had already been transliterated and translated by Güterbock[8] entitled "Kumarbi und der Sintflutheld(?)". In this, unlike KUB XXXVI 74, appears the hero's name, both in the Hittite form ending in *-i* (Atramḫašiš IV 10') and in the pure form after the Accadian *A-NA* (Atramḫašiš I 5').[9]

6 For a new edition of tablet I, see W. von Soden, *ZA* 68 (1978), pp. 50-94.

7 KUB XXXIII 106 III 54: ᵈUl-lu-ku-um-mi-in ⁿᵃ⁴ŠU.U-zi-in GÌR^meš GAM-an ar-ḫa ar-du-[wa-an-du].

8 H. G. Güterbock, *Kumarbi. Mythen vom churritischen Kronos*, (*Istanbuler Schriften* 16) Zürich-New-York 1946, pp. 29-30; *29 -*30; 81, 93.

9 See H. G. Güterbock, *op. cit.*, p. 81.

The text is very fragmentary and difficult to interpret:[10]

I

1' [ ]. . . . .[
2' ". . . . [ ] I do, the friend to me/me[
3' sprin[g [11]] .[12] you'll die . ."

---

10 1' [ ]-pí ir-x-x-x-x[
2' x.x-x[ ]i-ya-mi a-ra-aš-wa-mu[
3' : wa-at-ta-[ru]-mi ak-ti-ma-wa [

4' [nu] GIM-an ᵐḪa-am-ša-aš *ŠA* ᵈKu-mar-pí INIMᵐᵉš iš-[ta-ma-aš-ta]
5' nu *A-NA* ᵐAt-ra-am-ḫa-ši DUMU-*ŠU* me-mi-iš-ki-u-wa-an [da-a-iš
6' ki-e *A-WA-TE*ᵐᵉš me-mi-iš-ta nu-wa-ra-at iš-ta-ma-a[š-tu
7' [x-x-pi-ru-x- x] *A-NA* EZEN-ma-wa-at-ta ku-e-da-ni ḫal-z[i (!)-iš-ša-i
8' [-u]n a-aš-ši-an-za(!) ku-it a-ra-aš e-eš-[ta/ zi
9' [ ]da-an-du-kiš-wa GIM an ak-kiš-kat-ta-[ri
10' [ ] ar-nu-ši ALAM *IZ-ZI* i-ya x-[
11' [ ]kiš-an me-mi ᵐḪa-am-ša-an-wa[
IV
1' [ ]x pi?-e-eš-ta(?)-[
2' [ᵐA]t-ra-am-ha-ši-iš ᵐḪa-am-š[a
3' [x a-]pi-el A.ŠAG₄ᵐᵉš da-me-ta-[ni?
4' [x x x] ḫi.a da-me-e-ta-[ni?
5' [x a- p]i-el A.ŠAG₄ᵇⁱ·ᵃ ku-e-[da-ni?
6' [ ]x-ma-za ku-i-e-eš da-[me-ta-ni?
7' [*I-NA*(?) M]U.3.KAM-ma-kàn ᵈKu-mar-[bi
8' [-r]i-e-ša-an ú-e-ri-i[r
9' [ḫ]a-ri-an-za nu hu-u-ma-an iš-ta-[ma-aš-ta(?)
10' ᵐḪa-am-ša-aš *A-NA* ᵐAt-ra-am-ḫa-ši x[
11' ᵈKu-mar-bi-iš ki-e-da-ni MU.KAM-ti at-[
12' la-la-ú-e-ša-aš ga-ra-pi nu ki-iš-š[a-an(?)
13': hu-ta-nu-en-zi da-a nu ma-a-an l[a-la-ú-e-ša-aš
14' :ḫa-ar-ša-an-ta-an-ma-kàn : ḫu-u-ta-nu-[en-zi
15' nu-wa ᵍⁱšMAR.GÍD.DAᵐᵉš pi-en-ni nu-wa[
16' pi-en-ni nu-wa-za ḫal-ki-in d[a]-[m]e-[ta-ni(?)
17' erasure
18' ᵐAt-ra-a[m-ḫa-ši]-iš ᵐḪa-am-ša-aš
19' [a]-ra-aḫ-z[a ᵏᵘš*A*(?)]-*RI-TUM*ᵇⁱ·ᵃ[
20' [ᵐ]At-r[a(?)-

11 The integration presupposes that the gloss sign precedes a Hittite word, a rare phenomenon but possible (see O. Carruba, Linguistic Contacts in Anatolia, on Languages and Culture in Contact with the Ancient and High Medieval World, Papers of the VIII International Congress on Linguistics, Milan 10-12 September 1992, Brescia 1993, p. 258. Different letters cannot be excluded: "10 *wa-at-ta-*[*ru*"

4’ When Ḫamša hea[rd] the words of Kumarbi
5’ then [he began] to speak to his son Atramḫaši:
6’ “These words (that)[13] (Kumarbi) said listen [to (them)!
7’ [“] . to which feast(?) he ca[lls] you[14]
8’ [ ] why is/wa[s] he a beloved friend[
9’ [ ] how a man dies[15][
10’ [ ] you will carry (away), make a wooden figure
11’ [ ]. . . speak (imp.) thus: “Ḫamša (acc.) .[

IV

1’ [ ] he gave (?)[
2’ [[At]ramḫaši Ḫamš[a[16]
3’ the fields of that [one] to anot[her](?)
4’ they [ ] to anot[her (?)
5’ [of th]at the fields to whom?[17]
6’ [ ] but which ones to an[other?[18]
7’ but [in the] third [ye]ar Kumar[bi
8’ [the an]t(?) he fe[ars?[19]
9’ [ ]](m/f)? buried(?)[20] and all lis[ten/ed

---

or “*u-wa-at-ta*-[. However the integration of the syllable *-ru* is still uncertain. H. G. Guterbock, *op. cit.*, p. *30 reads: *wa-at-ta*[(-).

12 Makes one think of the first person singular of a verb and therefore there is opposition between “I . .” and the following phrase “you’ll die”.

13 According to H. G. Güterbock, *op. cit.*, p. 81 “Ed. *ki-e,* man erwartet eher *ku-e*; dies nach Koll. möglich”, but to me the letter *ki-e* seems clear.

14 In reality the sign instead seems to be *-hu,* mistaken for *-zi.*

15 V. J. Puhvel, *HED*, p. 20 sub *ak(k)-,ek-*.

16 H. G. Güterbock, *op. cit.*, p. 30 : “zu (?oder :den?) Ḫamša”. In reality, the first hypothesis might be excluded, because the Accadian *A-NA* preposition is missing; it is more likely to be a nominative form.

17 Otherwise, H. G. Güterbock, *op. cit.*, p. *30, prefers not to integrate.

18 H. G. Güterbock, *op. cit.*, p. 30 translates “aber welche ne[hm-” and hence thinks of the verb form *dâ-*.

19 Thus B. J. Collins reads and translates, *The representation of wild animals in Hittite texts*, Ann Arbor 1989, p. 245. Otherwise H. G. Güterbock, *op. cit.*, p. 30 translates “riefen sie”.

20 The translation is based on the hypothesis of a]*ḫariyanza* and not a]-*ḫariyanza* reading as sustained by H. G. Güterebock, *op. cit.*, p. *30.

10' Ḫamša to Atramḫaši his son [speaks:
11' Kumarbi this year.[21][
12' an ant devours/will devour and s[o
13' *:ḫutanuenzi* you take and if the a[nt
14' *:ḫaršanta* and *:ḫutanu[enzi*
15' and guides /you push the carts and[
16' and guides/you push and the harvest.[
17' erasure [
18' Atra[mḫaši, Ḫamša[
19' [ar]ound [the shi]elds of hide(?)
20' [A]tr[amḫaši ??

The content of the fragment does not seem directly comparable to any passage in the Babylonian tale, however, some points may be considered: 1) the text shows a series of dialogues between Atramḫaši and his father Ḫamša, according to the literary model typical of these mythological texts; 2) the phrase "an ant devours/will devour" led both Collins[22] and Hoffner[23] to think of an allusion to a type of plague or famine. If this interpretation is correct, we understand from Ḫamša's words to his son that there would be a pestilence that year which would hit the harvest (lit. = wheat) and that Atramḫaši would have to prepare a cart and push it, and perhaps take it to safety. The episode may recall one of the three previous attempts by the god Enlil to destroy humanity through an epidemic, a famine and lastly a flood; 3) there is a phrase in r. 10 of column I that is difficult to interpret: "to make a wooden figure". At the point, in the paleo-Babylonian myth, when the hero asked the god Ea, who urged him to build a ship to rescue himself from the flood, to design one on earth as he did not know how to shape it, we wonder if this expression might not refer to a similar episode. Equally, the phrase (r. 16) "you take the harvest" recalls the episode in which Atramḫaši was requested to carry to safety not only his family and animals, but also the harvest. In this case the cart might be either a kind of poetic, literary definition to indicate the ship or to construct a real variant of the tale;

21 In the text we read *la*-[. Perhaps *lalauešaš* is to be integrated, as in line 12.

22 *Op. cit.*, p. 245.

23 *CHD* 3 (1980), p. 27.

4) the figure of the father, Ḫamša, unknown to the Babylon myth, seems here to play the role of the god Ea, protector of humanity.[24]

However, the text also shows phrases, albeit in a fragmentary and obscure context, that refer to different mythological contexts, such as the reference to a feast (?) (I 7'), a motif typical of the original Anatolian myths on the disappearing god, or the mention of a "dear/beloved friend" that recalls the theme of friendship between Gilgameš and Enkidu. One significant fact is that there are two Luwian glosses inserted in the text that seem to indicate specific parts of the cart; in particular, *ḫarsanta* is to be compared with the ^{giš}*ḫaršandanaḫit*[25] form shown in a text belonging to the Ullikummi[26] myth. It is an indication that gives strength to the hypothesis of the formation of, if not a real and proper poetic literary language, at least a lexical formulary peculiar to mythological texts.[27]

In addition to these two fragments, an Accadian version of the myth also existed in the Ḫattusa archives, as the fragment found in 1976 by H. Otten shows (819/z now published in KBo XXXVI 26): a text of 13 damaged lines in which it is not possible to deduce the exact point of the narration they refer to. Nevertheless, from a religious and historic point of view, the most interesting information is constituted by the figure of the god Kumarbi, who seems to have Enlil's role in this fragment, thereby confirming an identification between the two divinities, which can also be found in the fragment KUB VIII 62, a text belonging to the Hittite version of the Gilgameš myth.[28]

This assimilation process of the two divine figures also poses the problem about the role carried out by the Hurrian culture, not only in the transmission of the myth, but also in its reproduction in the Hittite language.

By entitling the fragment KUB VIII 63 "Kumarbi und der Sintfludheld?",[29] H.G. Güterbock thought, albeit dubitatively, that the episode was part of the original Hurrian mythological cycle centered on Kumarbi. At the present time, we do not know if a version of the Atramḫaši myth even existed in the Hurrian language, even

24 According to H. G. Güterbock, *op. cit.*, p. 81 the name can be linked to the Accadian *ḫamšu* "fünfter".

25 Cf. Starke, *StBoT* 21 (1990), p. 174; H. C. Melchert, *op. cit.*, p. 60.

26 Cf. H. G. Güterbock, *JCS* 6 (1952), p. 14.

27 See how it is observed with regard to the verb *ard-*.

28 See G. Del Monte in G. Pettinato, *La saga di Gilgamesh*, Milano 1992, p. 384.

29 *Op. cit.*, p. 29.

though it is very likely because versions of other famous myths, like those of Gilgameš and "Kešši the Hunter", exist in said language. However, from an overall evaluation of this text, it can seemingly be affirmed that it is a compilation that acknowledged and integrated themes and characters from different myths in a story that may be an episode from the Kumarbi cycle, as Güterbock thought, but that may also be, instead, a reproduction of the Atramḫaši myth written by the Hittite scribes.

The KUB XXXVI 74 fragment is particularly important because it preserves signs of the episode on the oppressed gods and their revolt over too much work, an episode in the paleo-Babylonian version already analysed by Burkert,[30] who prudently compared it with Book I of the Iliad.[31] If the scholar's statement were true, that this passage of the Atramḫaši poem had a possible influence on Homer's poem, the Hittite testimony would have particular value, as it would constitute a more direct connection between Homer and the Near Eastern culture, both in chronological and geographical terms.

The question of when the Hittites knew about the Atramḫaši myth remains. KUB VIII 63 is a later copy (13th century B.C.),[32] however, the analysis of the *ductus* in KUB XXXVI 74 clearly demonstrates that it is a copy of a more ancient text, probably of the Middle Hittite age,[33] a period to which the older version of the Accadian fragments on the Gilgameš myth found in Ḫattusa[34] also belongs.

We know that the principal, and the most complete, version of the Atramḫasi myth was copied by the Ku-Aya scribe during the reign of Ammisaduqua, the fourth successor of Hammurapi; and we also know that under Sansuditana, the last sovereign of the dynasty, the incursion of Babylon by Muršili I took place. Therefore, the myth might have been known and "imported" directly on this occasion, hence, in an age not so distant from the paleo-Babylonian version.

This thesis, which modifies the usual evaluation of the "go-between" role carried out by the Hurrians already put forward by both the writer and F. Pecchioli Daddi,[35]

---

30 W. Burkert, *The Orientalizin Revolution. Near Eastern Influence on Greek Culture in the Early Archaic Age*, Cambridge, Mass. 1992, pp. 104-106; *id.*, *Da Omero ai Magi*, Venezia, p. 31 ss.; M. L. West, *The East Face of Helicon. West Asiatic Elements in Greek Poetry and Myth*, Oxford 1997, p. 57.

31 Iliad I 396-406.

32 Cf. HW^2 p. 347 *sub* v. *ard(a)*-.

33 All the cuneiform signs with the exception of the sign for *e* seem to belong to the *ductus* OH/MS.

34 Cf. G. Wilhelm, *ZA* 78 (1988), pp. 99-121; G. Del Monte, *op. cit.*, p. 388, n. 6.

35 See. F. Pecchioli Daddi - A. M. Polvani, *La mitologia ittita*, Brescia 1990, p. 11.

finds, in my opinion, further confirmation in this case. Indeed, this does not mean to deny the undeniable cultural contribution of the Hurrian civilisation in its production of the mythological patrimony handed down by the Hittites, but to reconsider the history of contacts between these two cultures and their relationship with Mesopotamia in a different historical perspective. If a direct contact with the myths of the Mesopotamic tradition is hypothesised, it does not exclude either successive or coeval reproductions, but modifies the usual pattern that sees Hittite mythological literature of "foreign origin" exclusively as the fruit of Hurrian mediation.[36]

At the present time of documentation, we may therefore draw some significant conclusions:

1) The Hittites kept a written version of the Atramḫaši myth in Accadian, but we do not know how faithful it is to the paleo-Babylonian model.

2) KUB VIII 63 attests the existence of a version of the myth in the Hittite language that seems to be the closest to the paleo-Babylonian version, not only in content, but also for the likely dating of the tablets.

3) Instead, the KUB XXXVI 74 fragment shows elements of a later stage coming from myths of different traditions that were recreated in a tale which, we cannot presently say with any certainty, might not belong to the Kumarbi cycle, neither might it be a new version of the Atramḫaši myth.

No solution remains for the question posed by H. Otten,[37] who had observed the strange position of the colophon in KUB XXXVI 74 (displaced on the left side of the tablet), if in reality it might not be an Accadian-Hittite bilingual text.

---

36 Cf. G. Beckman, *JCS* 35 (1983), pp. 101-103.

37 Inahlt. KUB XXXVI, p. 3.

LA TERMINOLOGIA AMMINISTRATIVA DI EBLA: ŠU-DU$_8$ E TUŠ.LÚxTIL

FRANCESCO POMPONIO

Università di Messina

1. Il termine šu-du$_8$ dei testi eblaiti è stato di norma interpretato come definizione di un tipo di consegna: cf. da ultimo G. Pettinato, *MEE* 5, p. 20, § 25 r. IX 11: "consegna dovuta". Di contro, M. G. Biga e chi scrive, *MARI* 7, p. 115, n. 19 hanno proposto di considerarlo un nome di funzione, con il significato all'incirca di "collecteur". Da ultimo, F. D'Agostino, *MEE* 7, p. 100, r. III 3-8, ancorché non citi l'articolo di *MARI* 7, sembra accettare entrambe le ipotesi, e nota che il termine potrebbe riferirsi sia a una transazione, sia, se seguito da un toponimo, al nome di persona che lo precede: nel primo caso, egli accetta all'incirca l'interpretazione di G. Pettinato ("tassa dovuta"), nel secondo suggerisce la traduzione di "comandato, obbligato (a stare in ...)".

2. A parere di chi scrive, šu-du$_8$ ha un unico significato nella quasi totalità delle sue attestazioni eblaite,[1] da differenziare però in una forma verbale e in un nome di funzione. Il lessema dovrebbe assumere questi valori rispettivamente nei rendiconti di uscite di ovini e nei registri mensili di assegnazioni di tessili, le due categorie di testi in cui più spesso esso ricorre.

Nel primo tipo di documenti, in particolare nei grandi rendiconti mensili di ovini,[2] molte forniture di udu per offerte a divinità o per altri impieghi sono seguite dall'espressione NP šu-du$_8$, che l'Editore traduce "NP (ha) consegnato". In qualche passo questa formula è preceduta da quella NP nídba, che può essere resa solo come

1 Un significato diverso è da attribuire a šu-du$_8$ quando riferito a un pugnale: cf. 1 gír šu-du$_8$ kù-sig$_{17}$ 1 gír šu-du$_8$ zabar 1 gír šu-du$_8$ kù-bar$_6$ mu-DU *ar-ru$_{12}$-lum* (TM.75.G.1459 v. IV 1-5, citato da H. Waetzoldt, *OrAn* 29 [1990], p. 21): in questo caso il termine potrebbe designare o il manico o un particolare rivestimento del pugnale. Per il frequente impiego del verbo šu-du$_8$ nei testi letterari sumerici con il valore di "impugnare (un'arma, uno scettro)" cf. ad es. G. R. Castellino, *Two Šulgi Hymns (BC)*, Roma 1972, p. 248, 12; Å. Sjöberg, *Der Mondgott Nanna-Suen*, Stockholm1960, p. 51; W. H Ph. Römer, *SKIZ*, p. 23, 9.

2 Cf. i quattro testi editi da G. Pettinato, *OrAn* 18 (1979), pp. 85ss.

"NP ha offerto":[3] in tutti questi casi è probabile che la forma verbale šu-du$_8$ indichi la presa in consegna degli ovini.

A sostegno di questa resa si noti, in un rendiconto di uscite di beni vari, questa sequenza: 1 ma-na kù-bar$_6$ zi-du$_8$ *EN-mu*^{ki} *a-du-gu* šu-ba$_4$-ti 3 *mi-at* udu zi-du$_8$ *EN-mu*^{ki} *i-bí-iš-lu* šu-du$_8$ (1622 r. V 7-VI 8): ancorché sfugga a chi scrive il preciso significato del termine zi-du$_8$ che caratterizza i beni in oggetto, e che non ricorre in altri testi amministrativi di Ebla,[4] è pressoché certo che šu-ba$_4$-ti e šu-du$_8$ esprimano la stessa direzione dei beni:[5] quindi šu-du$_8$, alla pari di šu-ba$_4$-ti, deve essere una forma verbale che ha per soggetto il personaggio che prende in consegna i beni; l'uso differenziato dei due verbi potrebbe dipendere dal tipo di bene ricevuto.[6] Nei registri mensili di tessili, che esamineremo più sotto, i due termini possono essere menzionati a proposito della medesima assegnazione, poiché šu-du$_8$, come vedremo, si riferisce alla funzione dell'ufficiale e šu-ba$_4$-ti all'acquisizione dei tessili assegnatigli, che poteva avvenire anche in un luogo diverso da quello dove lo šu-du$_8$ svolgeva la sua specifica attività.[7] Si noti, ancora, che šu-du$_8$, avente per soggetto Iblul-Il e per oggetto il *qá-nu-um* (di Ebla) ricorre nella lettera di Enna-Dagan (G. Pettinato, *OrAn* 19 [1980], p. 240 r. VI 3-7), con il significato di "si impadronì"; nella parte finale dello stesso testo, parzialmente lacunosa, il medesimo verbo ha per oggetto gli scettri "unti" dei paesi, di cui avrebbe preso il possesso Enna-Dagan (*ma-ṭa-a in* ì-giš kalam-*tim* kalam-*tim* šu-du$_8$: v. IV 2-6).

---

3 Cf., ad es., 2 udu *a-ba-ti*^{ki} *ma-si-gi-ba-ad* nídba *i-da-ne* šu-du$_8$ (*ibid.*, p. 135 r. VIII 23-29).

4 Nel Vocabolario bilingue di Ebla zi-du$_8$ è tradotto *a/ʾà-ma-zu-um* (*MEE* 4, p. 314, 1048). Questo lessema potrebbe derivare dalla radice *ʿms*, attestata in ebriaco e ugaritico con il significato di "caricare", e indicare un tipo di tributo.

5 Nel Vocabolario bilingue di Ebla il lessema šu-du$_8$, non tradotto, segue immediatamente šu-ba$_4$-ti (*MEE* 4, p. 256, 504-505).

6 Il verbo šu-du$_8$ ricorre anche nei testi letterari di Ebla, con il medesimo significato di "prendere, reggere": cf. ki šu-du$_8$ *ba-ša-nu ba-ša-nu* "i serpenti hanno preso la terra" (*ARET* 5, 4 r. I 1-4); ^{d}utu šu-du$_8$ zi-kalam "Utu regge la la vita del paese" (versione di Abu Salabikh del passo parzialmente lacunoso di *ARET* 5, 6 r. I 1-3: cf. M. Krebernik, *QuSem* 18 [1992], p. 72). Per menzioni del medesimo verbo in tre passi di *ARET* 5, 7 di non facile comprensione, cf. *ibid.*, p. 140.

7 Cf., ad es., 3 mí-TÚG 3 íbx3-GÙN-TÚG *ti-ti-nu wa i-i-bù wa ar-si-a-ha* maškim *ḫa-ra-il* šu-du$_8$ *in ʾà-ra-bí-ig*^{ki} šu-ba$_4$-ti *in* u$_4$ *ib-rí-um* du-du *si-in ʾà-ra-bi-ig*^{ki} (*ARET* 4, 11 r. VII 18-VIII 16); 1 *ʾà-da-um*-TÚG-2 1 gu-dùl-TÚG 1 aktum-TÚG 1 sal-TÚG 1 íbx3-sa$_6$-GÙN-TÚG 1 íbx3-GÙN-TÚG maškim *ki-ti-ir wa* dumu-nita *ba-ti-lum* šu-du$_8$ *in za-bur-rúm*^{ki} *in du-u*$_9$^{ki} šu-ba$_4$-ti (*MEE* 7, 23 v. II 9-III 3); 4 *ʾà-da*-1 4 mí-TÚG 4 íbx3-GÙN-TÚG *a-bù-ru*$_{12}$ *ìr-ì-ba a-aḫ-du*^{ki} *du-bí NI.NE-du*^{ki} šu-du$_8$ *a-zu*^{ki} *ib-hur-lu ʾà-ša-rí-gú*^{ki} šu-du$_8$ *kab-lu*$_5$*-ul*^{ki} *in lu-ba-an*^{ki} šu-ba$_4$-ti (*ARET* 8, 542 v. IX 3-17).

Al di fuori della documentazione eblaita, alcune registrazioni aAcc. di bestiame grosso e minuto sono seguite dalla formula NP šu-du$_8$ (*MAD* 5, 25 r. II 2-4; F. Rasheed, *Himrin* 4, 8 v. 16-17; W. Sommerfeld, *Die Texte der Akkade-Zeit. 1. Das Dijala-Gebiet: Tutub*, Münster 1999, 28 v. 1'-2'; 34 r. 9; 54 r. 6-7), da rendere come "(il pastore) NP ha preso in consegna" (cf. anche P. Steinkeller, *TLAT*, p. 108).

3. La stragrande maggioranza delle citazioni di šu-du$_8$ nei testi di Ebla viene da registri di assegnazioni di tessili. In questa documentazione šu-du$_8$ ricorre insieme o in posizione analoga al termine TUŠ.LÚxTIL: l'un e l'altro caratterizzano il destinatario di un completo di tessili e in qualche caso di manufatti di metallo, ma non possono rappresentare propriamente un nome di professione, come dimostra la loro attribuzione a personaggi che di norma già risultano esercitare una precisa professione. I due termini devono, quindi, riferirsi a una funzione, svolta forse temporaneamente[8]. Sulla base del significato della forma verbale šu-du$_8$ nei testi esaminati nel paragrafo precedente, questo nome di funzione dovrebbe essere in rapporto con la presa in consegna di qualche bene o tributo. Sulla natura del primo e sulla motivazione del secondo non abbiamo elementi certi, anche se è verosimile che l'attività dello šu-du$_8$ riguardasse, anche, ovini.

Il nostro esame dei termini amministrativi šu-du$_8$ e TUŠ.LÚxTIL si inizia da quattro uscite in sequenza del testo *MEE* 2, 33, del periodo di Arrulum:

1 túg-NI.NI 1 íb-lá 1 *si-di-tum* 1 gír-kun kù-bar$_6$ 2 *gú-li-lum* kù-bar$_6$ kù-sig$_{17}$ *du-bí-zi-kir* maškim *en-bù-uš-li-im* TUŠ.LÚxTIL
1 túg-NI.NI 1 íb-lá 1 *si-di-tum* 1 gír-kun kù-bar$_6$ 2 *gú-li-lum* a-gar$_5$-a-gar$_5$ kù-sig$_{17}$ *i-bí-zú* maškim *ar-si-a-ha* TUŠ.LÚxTIL
1 mí-TÚG 1 *gú-li-lum* a-gar$_5$-a-gar$_5$ kù-sig$_{17}$ *a-ban-gú-nu* maškim *ar-si-a-ha* šu-du$_8$
1 mí-TÚG 1 gír-mar-tu 1 *gú-li-lum* a-gar$_5$-a<-gar$_5$> kù-bar$_6$ *i-ni-lum* maškim *en-bù-uš-li-im* šu-du$_8$ (r. VI 2-VII 9).

Il confronto tra di esse dimostra che a) TUŠ.LÚxTIL e šu-du$_8$ occupano la medesima posizione, e pertanto con ogni verosimiglianza devono essere assegnati alla medesima categoria di significato; b) che questi titoli non sono da riferire agli antroponimi che immediatamente li precedono, e che sono i nomi dei funzionari da cui dipendono i maškim, ma ai maškim stessi; c) che questi superiori dei maškim, nel

8 Nei testi giuridici aAcc. e di Ur III ricorre il termine šu-du$_8$(-a) con il valore di "garante, garanzia" (cf. *AAS*, p. 245, N.195, 5).

caso specifico Arsi-aha ed Enbuš-Lim, potevano avere sotto il loro controllo funzionari sia TUŠ.LÚxTIL, sia šu-du$_8$.

Sulla base del diverso valore dei beni assegnati si dovrebbe ricavare anche che il TUŠ.LÚxTIL era di livello leggermente superiore allo šu-du$_8$. Questa più o meno accentuata differenza si può notare anche da altri passi, dove TUŠ.LÚxTIL e šu-du$_8$, a differenza del testo precedente, precedono e non seguono il titolo di maškim NP:

1 mí-TÚG 1 *gú-li-lum* a-gar$_5$-gar$_5$ kù-sig$_{17}$ TUŠ.LÚxTIL 1 mí-TÚG 1 *gú-li-lum* a-gar$_5$-gar$_5$ kù-bar$_6$ šu-du$_8$ maškim *a-ʾà-lu* (*MEE* 2, 29 r. IV 1-6)
1 mí-TÚG 1 *gú-li-lum* a-gar$_5$-gar$_5$ kù-bar$_6$ *mi-ga-il* TUŠ.LÚxTIL 1 mí-TÚG šu-du$_8$ maškim *a-ʾà-lu* (*MEE* 2, 29 v. I 6-12)
2 *ʾà-da-um*-TÚG 2 aktum-ÚG 2 íbx3-sa$_6$-GÙN 1 *gú-li-lum* a-gar$_5$-gar$_5$ kù-bar$_6$ *NI-ba-ì* TUŠ.LÚxTIL *gi-UR*^{ki} *wa i-sar da-ʾà-zú*^{ki} šu-du$_8$ *ur-sá-um*^{ki} (*ARET* 4, 1v. III 22-IV 10).

Per l'ultimo passo sembra evidente che l'unico *gulilum* citato spetti al TUŠ. LÚxTIL. Si deve anche notare che nel primo dei passi succitati, non è precisato né il nome del TUŠ.LÚxTIL, né quello dello šu-du$_8$, nel secondo è indicato solo il nome del TUŠ.LÚxTIL, nel terzo quello di entrambi. I casi in cui il nome di persona dei funzionari TUŠ.LÚxTIL e šu-du$_8$ è indicato si alternano abbastanza regolarmente a quelli in cui tale nome manca; complessivamente, il nome degli šu-du$_8$ risulta omesso più frequentemente di quello dei TUŠ.LÚxTIL.

Inoltre, mentre nelle singole assegnazioni il TUŠ.LÚxTIL è di norma un solo personaggio, i funzionari che sono šu-du$_8$ possono ammontare ad alcune decine. Cf.:

1 túg-NI.NI 1 íb-III-GÙN-TÚG 1 *gú-li-lum* a-gar$_5$-gar$_5$ kù-gi TUŠ.LÚxTIL 35 mí-TÚG šu-du$_8$ maškim *ha-la* (1727 r. V 14-20).

Di contro, in altre uscite TUŠ.LÚxTIL e šu-du$_8$ ricevono i medesimi beni, anche se TUŠ.LÚxTIL è di regola citato al primo posto.[9] Così nel seguente passo dove il TUŠ.LÚxTIL Ibbišum e lo šu-du$_8$ Ibne, entrambi commissari di Dubi, ricevono lo stesso completo di tre tessili di medio valore:

2 *ʾà-da-um*-TÚG-1 2 mí-TÚG 2 íbx3-sa$_6$-GÙN-TÚG *i-bí-šum* TUŠ.LÚxTIL *ib-ne* šu-du$_8$ maškim *du-bí* (ARET 4, 11 r. XII 2-8),

9 In un solo caso l'assegnazione allo šu-du$_8$ precede quella al TUŠ.LÚxTIL, anche se la prima è meno ricca della seconda: 1 túg-NI.NI 1 mí-TÚG šu-du$_8$ 1 túg-NI.NI 1 *gú-li-lum* a-gar$_5$-gar$_5$ kù-bar$_6$ *ib-dur-i-šar* TUŠ.LÚxTIL maškim ⌜*iš*$_{11}$⌝*-a-il* (TM.75.G.1340 r. I 1-7).

e in un altro dove Išgi-Barzu, TUŠ.LÚxTIL in Ala, e Batilum di Batinu, commissario di Kitir e šu-du$_8$ in Niapinu, ricevono il medesimo completo di tre tessili di alta qualità e il medesimo *gulilum*:

2 *ʾà-da-um*-TÚG 2 aktum-TÚG 2 íbx3-GÙN-TÚG 2 *gú-li-lum* a-gar$_5$-gar$_5$ kù-sig$_{17}$ ab-si-2 *iš$_{11}$-gi-bar-zú* TUŠ.LÚxTIL *a-la*^{ki} *ba-ti-lum ba-ti-nu*^{ki} maškim *ki-ti-ir* šu-du$_8$ *NI-a-pi$_5$-nu*^{ki} (*ARET* 8, 523 r. VII 17-27).

Ancora, in un passo il TUŠ.LÚxTIL riceve un *gulilum* in più rispetto a uno dei due šu-du$_8$ con i quali è menzionato, ma questo manufatto risulta essere meno prezioso di quello ricevuto dal secondo šu-du$_8$:

1 mí-TÚG 1 *gú-li-lum* a-gar$_5$-gar$_5$ kù-bar$_6$ *i-da-am* TUŠ.LÚxTIL 1 mí-TÚG *NI-zi-ma-il* 1 mí-TÚG 1 *gú-li-lum* a-gar$_5$-gar$_5$ kù-sig$_{17}$ *Ib-ga-iš-ru$_{12}$* 3 maškim *ar-si-a-ha* šu-du$_8$ (*MEE* 2, 33 r. IX 5-12).

Si noti anche:

1 túg-NI.NI 1 íbx3-GÙN-TÚG *du-bí* maškim *du-bí* šu-du$_8$ 1 túg-NI.NI 1 íbx3-DAR-TÚG TUŠ.LÚxTIL 3 mí-TÚG 3 íbx3-GÙN-TÚG maškim-*sù* šu-du$_8$ *gàr-mu*^{ki} (*MEE* 10, 21 v. IX 5-15),

che deve essere interpretato nel senso che i 3 šu-du$_8$ in Garmu fungono da maškim del secondo Dubi della precedente assegnazione e non del TUŠ.LÚxTIL, menzionato immediatamente sopra e che riceve lo stesso completo di due tessili. Complessivamente nei due passi sono assegnati, quindi, 5 completi di 1 mí-TÚG e 1 íbx3-GÙN-TÚG, destinati a quattro šu-du$_8$, di uno dei quali è indicato il nome, Dubi, degli altri tre il centro, Garmu, dove svolgevano la loro specifica funzione, e a un TUŠ.LÚxTIL. Tutti questi funzionari erano maškim di un personaggio omonimo del primo šu-du$_8$.

4. Se di regola la funzione di TUŠ.LÚxTIL e di šu-du$_8$ era tenuta dai maškim, essa poteva essere attribuita anche a personaggi che svolgevano altre professioni: ad es. i lú-kar risultano agire sia da TUŠ.LÚxTIL, sia da šu-du$_8$. Cf.:

2 *ʾà-da-um*-TÚG-1 2 mí-TÚG 2 íbx3-GÙN-TÚG lú-kar *si-zú*^{ki} šu-du$_8$ in *u$_9$-ru$_{12}$*^{ki} (*ARET* 8, 533 v. I 6-11)

1 *ʾà-da-um*-TÚG-2 1 aktum-TÚG 1 íbx3-sa$_6$-GÙN-TÚG 1 *gú-li-lum* a-gar$_5$ kù-sig$_{17}$ *sa-ha-wa-*2 lú-kar *zi-mi-da-nu*^{ki} TUŠ.LÚxTIL *gàr-da-ne-du*^{ki} (*ARET* 8, 524 v. VII 17-21).

In altri esempi un *mazalum* e un lú-ká svolgevano la funzione di šu-du$_8$ e di TUŠ.LÚxTIL rispettivamente:

1 mí-TÚG 1 íbx3-GÙN-TÚG *en-na-ì ma-za-lum du-ub*^{ki} šu-du$_8$ *in* SAG^{ki} (*ARET* 8, 541 v. IV 1'-7')
1 íbx3-sa$_6$-GÙN-TÚG *i-ti-*^{d}*ga-mi-iš* lú-ká *bar-zi* 1 *'à-da-um-*TÚG 1 aktum-TÚG 1 íbx3-sa$_6$-GÙN-TÚG 1 dib-10 *ìr-ì-ba* lú-ká *en-zi-ma-lik* TUŠ.LÚxTIL (*ARET* 8, 524 v. VI 4-13).

In un caso la funzione šu-du$_8$ è tenuta da un dub-sar:

ku$_5$ kù-sig$_{17}$ 1 *gú-li-lum*-2 šušana 4 gín-dilmun šu-bala-aka 6 gín-dilmun kù-sig$_{17}$ šir-za-*sù en-zi-ì* dub-sar šu-du$_8$ *in HAR-ba-tum*^{ki} (2507 v. XX 9-19),

e da un artigiano:

[ ] *en-mar* nagar *lu-ba-an*^{ki} šu-du$_8$ *in 'à-la-ù*^{ki} (*ARET* 8, 532 v. III 1'-6').

La funzione di šu-du$_8$ era svolta anche da uno šu-i che era in relazione con l'en di Kakmium. L'eccezionalità del caso è sottilineata dalla particolare ricchezza della assegnazione:

1 *gu-zi-tum* 1 íbx3-sa$_6$-GÙN 1 íb-lá GÁxLÁ ša-pi kù-bar$_6$ maš-maš kù-sig$_{17}$ 1 dib GÁxLÁ šušana gín-dilmun kù-sig$_{17}$ šu-i šu-du$_8$ en *kak-mi-um*^{ki} (*MEE* 2, 37 r. I 14-II 6).

Il valore dell'assegnazione, che di norma è basso, può quindi elevarsi anche di molto secondo la professione svolta dal TUŠ.LÚxTIL o dallo šu-du$_8$.

Nei rendiconti mensili di tessili sono registrate di regola assegnazioni di tessili e manufatti di metallo a singoli funzionari, ma negli stessi testi possono anche essere citati in un'unica voce un centinaio di guruš con la funzione di šu-du$_8$ al servizio della "Tesoreria" SA+ZA$_x$^{ki}, come destinatari di misure di lana (*ARET* 3, 45 II; 92 I).[10]

5. Come su già accennato, le numerosissime menzioni della funzione di TUŠ.LÚxTIL e di šu-du$_8$ provengono quasi esclusivamente dai rendiconti mensili di tessili, e solo molto raramente, da alcuni rendiconti annuali di argento, i secondi limitatamente ai testi che sono da datare al periodo di Ibbi-zikir.

Una differenza è riscontrabile in questi documenti dei diversi periodi per quanto riguarda sia gli elementi che accompagnano šu-du$_8$ e TUŠ.LÚxTIL, sia la posizione

10 Allo šu-du$_8$ che qualifica 112 *na-si*$_{11}$, indicati come mah o come provenienti da tre diversi centri, al servizio del funzionario *ga-si-ru*$_{12}$ in TM.75.G.309 è dato il significato di "prigionieri" da G. Pettinato, in *Festschrift E. Lipinski*, Leuven 1995, pp. 236, 21 e 243. Sembra difficile attribuire a questa citazione un valore diverso da quello dei numerosissimi šu-du$_8$ che sono menzionati nei rendiconti mensili di tessili e, d'altro canto, è assolutamente da escludere che in questi ultimi testi siano registrate tante assegnazioni, anche di elevato valore, a prigionieri.

da essi tenuta.[11] Ripartendo la documentazione presa in esame nei tre periodi in cui operavano i successivi “viisr”, abbiamo i seguenti dati.

A. šu-du$_8$.

1) Periodo in cui Arrulum era “vizir”.

NP_1 šu-du$_8$ maškim NP_2 // NP_1 maškim NP_2 šu-du$_8$	63 menzioni
NP šu-du$_8$ NL[12] // NP NL šu-du$_8$	50 menzioni
NP_1 šu-du$_8$ (dumu-nita) NP_2 NL	3 menzioni
NP šu-du$_8$	2 menzioni
(NP_1) maškim NP_2 šu-du$_8$ gin NL	2 menzioni
(NP_1) šu-du$_8$ NL maškim NP_2	1 menzione
NL šu-du$_8$	1 menzione[13]

2) Periodo in cui Ibrium era “vizir”.

NP_1 šu-du$_8$ maškim NP_2 // NP_1 maškim NP_2 šu-du$_8$	59 menzioni
NP_1 maškim NP_2 šu-du$_8$ (in) NL // (NP_1) šu-du$_8$ NL maškim NP_2	20 menzioni
NP_1 NL šu-du$_8$ // NP šu-du$_8$ (in) NL	8 menzioni
NP NL_1 šu-du$_8$ (in) NL_2	7 menzioni
NP_1 lú/dumu-nita NP_2 šu-du$_8$ (in) NL	3 menzioni
NP NL šu-du$_8$	1 menzione
NP šu-du$_8$	1 menzione
NP_1 š NP_2	1 menzione

3) Periodo in cui Ibbi-zikir era “vizir”.

NP NL_1 šu-du$_8$ (in) NL_2	191 menzioni
NP_1 maškim NP_2 šu-du$_8$ (in) NL // NP_1 NL maškim NP_2 šu-du$_8$ // NP_1 NL šu-du$_8$ maškim NP_2	28 menzioni
NP_1 lú/dumu-nita NP_2 šu-du$_8$ (in) NL // NP_1 lú/dumu-nita NP_2 š (in) NL	17 menzioni
NP_1 NL_1 maškim NP_2 š NL_2 // (NP_1) maškim NP_2 šu-du$_8$ NL_1 in NL_2	17 menzioni
NP_1 lú/dumu-nita NP_2 NL_1 šu-du$_8$ (in) NL_2	9 menzioni
NP šu-du$_8$ NL	6 menzioni

11 I testi presi in considerazione nella lista che segue sono quelli editi in *ARET* 1. 2. 4. 7. 8; *MEE* 2. 7. 10. Per il periodo di Arrulum, per il quale i documenti editi sono pochi, sono stati utilizzati anche i rendiconti mensili di tessili dei quali chi scrive sta curando la pubblicazione per un volume di *ARET*. Ringraziamenti sono dovuti ad A. Archi e P. Matthiae per il generoso permesso di citare materiale inedito. I testi inediti sono citati con il solo numero di inventario senza l’aggiunta TM.75.G. Le numerose menzioni di šu-du$_8$ e TUŠ.LÚxTIL nei frammenti di *ARET* 3 non sono state inserite nella lista che segue, data la difficoltà di datare con precisione il materiale in questione, ma naturalmente i dati in essi contenuti sono stati utilizzati nella stesura dell’articolo.

12 L’abbreviazione NL si riferisce a un toponimo.

13 È questa l’unica menzione, a nostra conoscenza, della duplicazione di šu-du$_8$ in un testo amministrativo: 6 *ʾà-da-um*-TÚG-2 7 *ʾà-da-um*-TÚG-1 13 aktum-TÚG 6 íbx3-sa$_6$-GÙN-TÚG 10 gu-mug-TÚG 10 mí-TÚG 17 íbx3-GÙN-TÚG *ib-al$_6$*^{ki} šu-du$_8$ šu-du$_8$ (*ARET* 8, 533 r. IX 10-12).

NP$_1$ NL$_1$ maškim NP$_2$ šu-du$_8$ (in) NL$_2$	3 menzioni
NP$_1$ lú/dumu-nita NP$_2$ NL šu-du$_8$	1 menzione
NP$_1$ lú NP$_2$ šu-du$_8$	1 menzione
NP maškim NP$_2$ šu-du$_8$	1 menzione.

Nei due periodi più antichi il contesto più frequente nel quale è citato il funzionario che svolge l'attività di šu-du$_8$ menziona anche la sua carica di maškim di un altro funzionario; la differenza tra il periodo di Arrulum e quello di Ibrium riguarda quello che risulta essere il secondo contesto per numero di attestazioni: nei testi di Arrulum lo šu-du$_8$ è caratterizzato solo dal toponimo dove egli svolge la sua attività,[14] nei testi di Ibrium accanto a questa indicazione è conservata quella di maškim di un altro personaggio. In questi contesti, come in altri di diverso tipo, il toponimo può indifferentemente seguire o precedere šu-du$_8$ o TUŠ.LÚxTIL.

Per il periodo di Ibbi-zikir il contesto di gran lunga più frequente è quello in cui lo šu-du$_8$ è messo in relazione con due toponimi: il primo che segue direttamente il suo nome potrebbe indicare il luogo in cui egli in precedenza o regolarmente esercitava la sua attività, il secondo, che segue il termine šu-du$_8$, il centro in cui la funzione in oggetto era momentaneamente svolta. La menzione di due distinti toponimi in rapporto con lo šu-du$_8$ non ricorre mai nei testi di Arrulum e solo in sette casi in quelli di Ibrium. Nella documentazione di Ibbi-zikir seguono per ordine di frequenza i contesti in cui lo šu-du$_8$, oltre a esser messo in relazione con due toponimi, è definito maškim di un altro funzionario, e quelli in cui lo šu-du$_8$ è definito lú ovvero dumu-nita di un altro personaggio e menzionato insieme al toponimo in cui svolgeva la sua funzione. La caratterizzazione di uno šu-du$_8$ come lú/dumu-nita di un altro funzionario è rarissima nei documenti più antichi.

B. TUŠ.LÚxTIL

1) Periodo in cui Arrulum era "vizir".

(NP) TUŠ.LÚxTIL NL	14 menzioni
(NP) TUŠ.LÚxTIL	13 menzioni
NP TUŠ.LÚxTIL maškim NP$_2$ // NP$_1$ maškim NP$_2$ TUŠ.LÚxTIL	9 menzioni
NP$_1$ maškim NP$_2$ TUŠ.LÚxTIL NL	2 menzioni
NP$_1$ lú NP$_2$ TUŠ.LÚxTIL NL	1 menzione
NP$_1$ lú NP$_2$ TUŠ.LÚxTIL	1 menzione

---

14 Per quanto riguarda il significato del rapporto tra šu-du$_8$ e il toponimo che lo segue, in un passo tra i due termini è inserita la preposizione *mi-in* (*ARET* 3, 735 V), che almeno in questo caso suggerirebbe che sia indicata la provenienza del funzionario che svolge la funzione di šu-du$_8$. Cf. anche [ ] TUŠ.LÚxTIL *ma-ri*^{ki} *áš-ti du-du-lu*^{ki} (*MEE* 7, 47 r. VIIII 1-4).

2) Periodo in cui Ibrium era "vizir".

NP NL_1 TUŠ.LÚxTIL in NL_2	6 menzioni
NP_1 maškim NP_2 TUŠ.LÚxTIL NL	5 menzioni
NP_1 TUŠ.LÚxTIL maškim NP_2 // NP_1 maškim NP_2 TUŠ.LÚxTIL	5 menzioni
NP TUŠ.LÚxTIL NL	4 menzioni
NP_1 lú/dumu-nita NP_2 TUŠ.LÚxTIL NL	4 menzioni
NP_1 lú NP_2 TUŠ.LÚxTIL	2 menzioni
NP TUŠ.LÚxTIL	2 menzioni

3) Periodo in cui Ibbi-zikir era "vizir".

NP NL_1 TUŠ.LÚxTIL NL_2	41 menzioni
NP TUŠ.LÚxTIL (*in*) NL // NP NL TUŠ.LÚxTIL	17 menzioni
NP_1 lú NP_2 NL TUŠ.LÚxTIL // NP_1 lú NP_2 TUŠ.LÚxTIL NL	14 menzioni
NP_1 maškim NP_2/NProf NP_1 maškim NP_2/NProf T NL 11 NL	11 menzioni
NP_1 lú NP_2 TUŠ.LÚxTIL	3 menzioni
NP_1 NL_1 maškim NP_2 TUŠ.LÚxTIL NL_2	1 menzione
NP_1 maškim NP_2 T	1 menzione.

Complessivamente, per quanto riguarda i testi presi in considerazione, gli individui che svolgevano la funzione di TUŠ.LÚxTIL sono nettamente meno numerosi degli šu-du$_8$, dei quali rappresentano all'incirca un terzo per i periodi di Arrulum e di Ibrium e la metà per il periodo di Ibbi-zikir, per il quale la documentazione è molto più abbondante.

Per il periodo di Arrulum i passi più numerosi sono quelli in cui un funzionario è definito solo TUŠ.LÚxTIL ovvero TUŠ.LÚxTIL caratterizzato da un toponimo; seguono i passi in cui a questo titolo è affiancato quello di maškim di un altro funzionario. Per il periodo di Ibrium il tipo di contesto più frequente è quello in cui il nome di un funzionario è messo in relazione con due toponimi, uno dei quali precede, l'altro segue il titolo di TUŠ.LÚxTIL. Come per gli šu-du$_8$, questo contesto diviene di gran lunga il più frequente nella documentazione di Ibbi-zikir, nettamente superiore per numero di attestazioni a quelli in cui un personaggio è definito soltanto TUŠ.LÚxTIL in un centro oppure dipendente (lú) da un altro funzionario e TUŠ.LÚxTIL in un centro.

Per quanto riguarda il rapporto tra i due toponimi che nello stesso contesto rispettivamente precedono e seguono šu-du$_8$ o TUŠ.LÚxTIL, il primo (Adur, Abarsal, Burman, Dub, Dulu, Garmium, Hutimu, Ibubu, Imar, Kablul, Kiš, Mari, Muru, NIrar, Ra'ag, Ursaum) o il secondo (Adabig, Azu, Armium, Burman, Dub, Garmium, Harbatum, Hutimu, Ibal, Imar, Kablul, Kakmium, Manuwad, Mari, Martu, Mašadu, NIrar, Ursaum, Utigu, Zaburrum), o entrambi possono rappresentare uno stato indipendente da Ebla: in realtà tutti gli stati più importanti con i quali Ebla venne in contatto risultano, almeno in un passo, essere sede precedente o attuale di uno šu-du$_8$ o di un TUŠ.LÚxTIL. Nella maggioranza dei casi, tuttavia, i toponimi sono luoghi che dovrebbero far parte del territorio di Ebla o centri amministrativi di Ebla (soprattutto il SA+ZA$_x$^{ki} e poi il gigir^{ki}).

In alcuni esempi sono identici i due toponimi messi in rapporto con lo šu-du$_8$. Ciò non sembra avvenire con il TUŠ.LÚxTIL, forse perché le sue menzioni sono molto inferiori a quelle degli šu-du$_8$.

1 *ʾà-da-um*-TÚG 1 mí-TÚG 1 íbx3-GÙN-TÚG *du-bí gur-ad*^{ki} šu-du$_8$ *in gur-ad*^{ki} (*ARET* 4, 3 v. V 15-20)

2 *ʾà-da-um*-TÚG-1 2 mí-TÚG 2 íbx3-sa$_6$-GÙN-TÚG *a-lum ʾà-wa-ra ḫu-ti-mu*^{ki} šu-du$_8$ *in-ma ḫu-ti-mu*^{ki} (*ARET* 8, 523 r. IX 28-X 7)

2 aktum-TÚG 2 íbx3-sa$_6$-GÙN-TÚG 1 *gú-li-lum* a-gar$_5$-gar$_5$ kù-sig$_{17}$ *sa-ḫa-wa-2 i-ti-*^{d}*ʾà-da-bal ir-i-ne-du*^{ki} šu-du$_8$ *in-ma ir-i-ne-du*^{ki} *du-bí-šum gur-ad*^{ki} šu-du$_8$ *in-ma gur-ad*^{ki} (*ARET* 8, 526 r. VIII 8-18)

2 mí-TÚG 2 íbx3-GÙN-TÚG *mi-ga-ì i-šar a-ba-nu*^{ki} šu-du$_8$ *in-ma a-ba-nu*^{ki} (*ARET* 8, 526 r. VII 4-10)

3 aktum-TÚG 3 íbx3-sa$_6$-GÙN-TÚG 3 *gú-li-lum* a-gar$_5$-gar$_5$ kù-sig$_{17}$ ab-si-2 *iš*$_{11}$*-gi-bar-zú ù-nu-ub*^{ki} šu-du$_8$ *in-ma ù-nu-ub*^{ki} ... (*ARET* 8, 626 r. IX 12-17)

3 aktum-TÚG 3 íbx3-sa$_6$-GÙN-TÚG 2 *gú-li-lum sa-ḫa-wa-2* 1 *gú-li-lum* a-gar$_5$-gar$_5$ kù-sig$_{17}$ ab-si-2 *du-bí du-ub*^{ki} šu-du$_8$ *in du-ub*^{ki} ... (*ARET* 8, 526 v. V 13-18)

1 *ʾà-da-um*-TÚG-1 1 mí-TÚG 1 íbx3-GÙN-TÚG *ì-lum-bala gàr-ga-mi-iš*^{ki} šu-du$_8$ *in gàr-ga-mi-iš*^{ki} (*ARET* 8, 527 v. II 19-24)

3 gu-dùl-TÚG 3 mí-TÚG 3 íbx3-GÙN-TÚG ... *kum-a-ḫu a-na-bar-zu*^{ki} šu-du$_8$ *a-na-bar-zu*^{ki} (*ARET* 8, 532 r. VIII 19-IX 8)

4 mí-TÚG 4 íbx3-GÙN-TÚG *i-ti-*^{d}*ra-sa-ap du-bí maš-a*^{ki} šu-du$_8$ *in-ma maš-a*^{ki} ... (*ARET* 8, 538 v. II 1-7).

Questa ripetizione, sottolineata in qualche esempio dall'impiego della preposizione *in-ma* in luogo di *in*, dovrebbe precisare che l'ufficiale fungeva da šu-du$_8$ in quella che era la sua sede regolare di servizio. Awara del secondo passo ricorre in un altro testo con il medesimo toponimo di provenienza, ma con un differente toponimo come sede di svolgimento della sua funzione di šu-du$_8$ (*ARET* 8, 524 r. X 19-23): questo mutamento sembra aver comportato un'assegnazione migliore per l'aggiunta di un *gulilum*. Ilum-bala di Karchemiš e šu-du$_8$ in Karkemiš e Išgi-barzu di Unub e šu-du$_8$ in Unub ricorrono in altri testi caratterizzati dal medesimo toponimo, ma come TUŠ.LÚxTIL in un altro centro.[15] Nel primo caso questo passaggio di funzione e di sede comporta un'assegnazione di tessili di migliore qualità e in più l'aggiunta di 1 *gulilum*, nel secondo, invece, l'assegnazione già buona rimane del medesimo valore. La precisione di queste indicazioni,[16] che riguardano solo testi di Ibbi-zikir, suggerisce che almeno nel periodo più recente vi fosse un costante spostamento di personale da un centro all'altro con funzioni commerciali o di controllo amministrativo: non è possibile stabilire se la situazione fosse diversa nei periodi precedenti o se semplicemente gli scribi dei testi di Arrulum e di Ibrium non ritenessero necessaria una tale acribia.

6. Abbiamo visto che molto spesso chi svolgeva la funzione di šu-du_8 o di TUŠ. LÚxTIL è caratterizzato come maškim di un ufficiale, verosimilmente di rango medio-alto. A partire dai testi del periodo di Ibbi-zikir anche la formula lú NP_2 diviene relativamente frequente come elemento caratterizzante di uno šu-du_8 o di un TUŠ.LÚxTIL: non vi è di norma coincidenza tra il nome personale che ricorre nell'espressione lú NP_2 e in quella maškim NP_2. Fanno eccezione tre nomi che ricorrono come superiori di šu-du_8 o di TUŠ.LÚxTIL, Hara-Il (*ARET* 1, 10. 14. 17; 4, 10-13. 15; MEE 10, 29, quasi tutti del periodo di Ibrium), Ki-Tir (*ARET* 8, 523. 524. 531; *MEE* 7, 23. 35; 2429 v. II 13, del periodo di Ibrium e di Ibbi-zikir) e Ziti (*ARET* 4, 1, periodo di Ibbi-zikir) e che compaiono episodicamente nella formula lú NP riferita a uno šu-du_8 (rispettivamente *ARET* 8, 533 r. VIII 6; *ARET* 8, 542 v. VI 6; *ARET* 8, 542 r. X 12). È possibile che nei tre casi succitati, e anche in altri, lú sia una variante di maškim, ma vi sono passi in cui uno šu-du_8 è definito contemporaneamente lú di un funzionario e maškim di un altro (1414 r. III 4-10). Ne possiamo ricavare che, come uno šu-du_8, o un TUŠ.LÚxTIL, poteva essere messo in rapporto con un toponimo e temporaneamente agire in un altro, così poteva essere al servizio di un ufficiale e operare per un limitato periodo come maškim di un altro.

Tra i superiori diretti di un funzionario šu-du_8 poteva comparire eccezionalmente il re di Ebla:

1 *gu-zi*-TÚG 1 aktum-TÚG 1 íbx3-sa_6-GÙN-TÚG 3 aktum-TÚG ti-TÚG 1 gír-mar-tu kù-sig_{17} *a-da-um a*$^?$-[ ]^{ki} šu-du_8 en (*MEE* 10, 26 r. III 14-IV 3),

---

15 *i-lum-bala gar-ga-mi-iš*^{ki} TUŠ.LÚxTIL *ù-ti-gú*^{ki} (*ARET* 8, 533 v. V 5-9); *iš*$_{11}$*-gi-bar-zú ù-nu-ub*^{ki} TUŠ.LÚxTIL *a-la*^{ki} (*ARET* 8, 523 r. VII 18-21).

16 In un altro passo è precisato che un certo Awa-Išar era di Dub ed era šu-du_8 in Dub di Abatum (*ARET* 8, 526 r. XIV 23-28).

e nel testo *MEE* 2, 37, dove abbiamo visto menzionato uno šu-i che era šu-du$_8$ del re di Kakmium (*MEE* 2, 37 r. I 14-II 6), sono registrate assegnazioni di un completo di 1 *gu-zi-tum* e di 1 íbx3-GÙN-TÚG per tre šu-du$_8$ al servizio rispettivamente di due personaggi definiti di Kakmium (r. II 13-III 8) e di un dumu-nita del re della stessa città (r. IV 2-8). Lo stesso completo è fornito a un altro šu-du$_8$ del re di Kakmium in *ARET* 2, 14 v. VII 15-VIII 4.

Infine, in un testo già citato (TM.75.G.309) 112 *na-si*$_{11}$ sono definiti šu-du$_8$ al servizio del *ga-si-ru*$_{12}$, un alto funzionario, che riceve še-ba mensili di farina nel rendiconto settennale TM.75.G.427 (cf. G.Pettinato, *AfO* 25 [1974-1977], p. 4 r. II 18 *et passim*).

7. Il termine šu-du$_8$ in un buon numero di passi è seguito dall'elemento caratterizzante máš: šu-du$_8$-máš ricorre, alla pari di šu-du$_8$, nei testi mensili sia di uscite di ovini, sia di assegnazioni di tessili.

Nei registri di ovini (cf. G. Pettinato, *OrAn* 18 [1979], p. 124) šu-du$_8$-máš è sempre seguito dalla formula NP šu-du$_8$, in passi del tipo: 6 udu šu-du$_8$-máš *ìr-am*$_6$*-ma-lik* šu-du$_8$ (*ibid.*, p. 137 v. I 5-8). Il termine qualifica, quindi, l'assegnazione degli udu, che un funzionario prende in consegna. šu-du$_8$-máš, ridotto dopo la prima citazione al solo máš, ed evidentemente con lo stesso significato dei registri succitati, caratterizza anche l'uscita di molte centinaia di ovini nel testo TM.75.G.2096 (cf. G. Pettinato, *OrAn* 16 [1977], pp. 263ss.).

Le citazioni dello šu-du$_8$-máš sono relativamente frequenti nei rendiconti mensili di tessili di Arrulum:

1 gu-dùl-TÚG 1 íbx3-GÙN-TÚG dumu-nita *íl-gú-uš-da-mu* šu-du$_8$-máš-máš (1399 r. X 7-12)
1 mí-TÚG 1 íbx3-GÙN-TÚG šu-du$_8$-máš *bur-ma-an*^{ki} (1418 r. I 5-8)
1 gada-TÚG 1 íbx3-GÙN-TÚG *gú-nu-ga-aš-dar* šu-du$_8$-máš (1438 r. VII 6-9)
1 mí-TÚG 1 íbx3-GÙN-TÚG *kum-na-aš-dar* šu-du$_8$-máš (1438 r. XI 4-7)
1 gada-TÚG šu-du$_8$-máš (1441 r. IV 18-V 1)
1 íbx3-GÙN-TÚG *iš*$_{11}$*-a-da-mu* šu-du$_8$-máš *ib-al*$_6^{ki}$ (1590 r. VI 14-17)
1 mí-TÚG 1 gada-TÚG 1 íbx3-GÙN-TÚG *a-ti-aš-dar* šu-du$_8$-máš-máš (1590 v. I 3-6)
1 mí-TÚG 1 íbx3-GÙN-TÚG *a-ti-aš-dar* šu-du$_8$<<šu->>máš (1779 r. XII 23-XIII 4)
1 mí-TÚG *gàr-sa-ma-lik* šu-du$_8$-máš (1779 v. V 4'-5')
1 mí-TÚG *a-bí-ar* lú *i-ti-aš-dar* šu-du$_8$-máš (2629 r. VI 11-15),

sono del tutto assenti, a nostra conoscenza, in quelli di Ibrium e ricompaiono, ma con pochi esempi, in quelli di Ibbi-zikir:

8 íbx3-sa$_6$-GÙN-TÚG maškim *a-mur-da-mu* šu-du$_8$-máš (*ARET* 1, 4 v. VII 7-10)
2 gu-dùl-TÚG 2 aktum-TÚG 2 íbx3-sa$_6$-GÙN-TÚG 2 *ar-ḫa-du*ki šu-du$_8$-máš 1 aktum-TÚG 1 íbx3-GÙN-TÚG *ma-za-lum-sù* (*ARET* 4, 20 r. VII 9-14)
1 gu-dùl-TÚG 1 mí-TÚG 1 íbx3-GÙN-TÚG *a-bù-ma-lik du-lu*ki šu-du$_8$-máš 2 KIN$_x$ siki dam-*sù* (*ARET* 8, 521 r. VIII 19-IX 1)
2 *'à-da-um*-TÚG-2 2 aktum-TÚG 2 íbx3-sa$_6$-TÚG *ar-si-a-ḫu gar-ga-mi-iš*ki maškim *en-zi-ma-lik a-si-ma-lik du-lu*ki šu-du$_8$-máš (*ARET* 8, 523 r. VII 2-9)
2 gu-mug-TÚG 2 mí-TÚG 2 íbx3-GÙN-TÚG 2 dumu-nita *puzur$_4$-be* šu-du$_8$-máš (*ARET* 8, 523 r. IX 14-17).

Nel complesso, quindi, sembra che le menzioni di questo lessema vadano progressivamente diradandosi, anche considerando che la documentazione del periodo di Ibbi-zikir è naturalmente di gran lunga più abbondante di quella più antica. Per quanto riguarda il suo significato, i passi in cui è citato šu-du$_8$-máš sono del tutto simili a quelli in cui ricorre šu-du$_8$: è possibile, quindi, che šu-du$_8$-máš sia una semplice forma ampliata di šu-du$_8$, ma è più probabile che esso faccia riferimento a un particolare tipo di tributo preso in consegna. È degno di nota che in uno dei passi succitati un *mazalum* risulti al servizio di 2 funzionari šu-du$_8$-máš di Arhadu.

Lo stesso lessema, ma con l'ordine invertito dei due elementi che lo compongono, ricorre in alcuni articoli del Trattato di Ebla e Abarsal (cf. E. Sollberger, *SEb* 3 [1980], p. 152), dove in un caso la forma è duplicata: *al$_6$* ki-sur máš šu-du$_8$ máš šu-du$_8$ lú *we-dum* dar-dar. (*ibid.*, p. 141 299-307), e in una sezione del testo giuridico TM.75.G.2396, edito da P. Fronzaroli, *SEb* 7 (1984), p. 3 r. III 7-8. In questi passi šu-du$_8$ deve valere come verbo e máš come il suo oggetto anteposto.

Sebbene nel lessema su discusso máš debba avere il valore translato di "tributo", e non quello reale di "capretto", šu-du$_8$ è frequentemente seguito da altri nomi di animali. Il più ricorrente è il bovide ÉREN+x, che qualche volta risulta preceduto da un numerale (1 o 2) e unito al logogramma del femminile mí.

1) Periodo in cui Arrulum era "vizir".
1 mí-TÚG šu-du$_8$ ÉREN+x maškim *gú-gi-wa-an* (1340 r. VIII 8-11)
1 mí-TÚG *NE-ra-ad*ki šu-du$_8$ ÉREN+x (1364 r. IV 17-V 2)
1 mí-TÚG 1 íbx3-GÙN-TÚG šu-du$_8$ ÉREN+x (1537 v. I 1-3)
1 mí-TÚG 1 íbx3-GÙN-TÚG šu-du$_8$ ÉREN+x *a-la-ḫa-du*ki (1590 r. III 7-10)
1 mí-TÚG *en-na-il a-du-bù*ki šu-du$_8$ ÉREN+x (1727 r. V 1-6)
1 mí-TÚG 1 íbx3-GÙN-TÚG *ar-si-a-ḫa* šu-du$_8$ ÉREN+x *'à-mu-NI*ki (1779 r. XVI 21-XVII 4)
1 mí-TÚG 1 íbx3-GÙN šu-du$_8$ ÉREN+x (1779 v. VI 15-17)
1 mí-TÚG *GIBIL-za-ì du-hé-lu*ki šu-du$_8$ ÉREN+x (1862 r. V' 4-7)

2) Periodo in cui Ibrium era "vizir".
1 mí-TÚG ... šu-du$_8$ ÉREN+x *in* ... (*MEE* 10, 2 r. X 11-XI 7)

1 gu-dùl-TÚG 1 íbx3-GÙN-TÚG *ar-si-a-ḫa a-i-du*[ki] šu-du$_8$ ÉREN+x (*MEE* 2, 25 v. V 8-12)
1 gu-dùl-TÚG 1 íbx3-GÙN-TÚG *ar-si-aḫ a-i-ti-um*[ki] šu-du$_8$ ÉREN+x (*MEE* 2, 25 v. VIII 5-8)
1 mí-TÚG 1 íbx3-GÙN-TÚG *íl-ba-gú-nu* šu-du$_8$ ÉREN+x *in ne-er*[ki] lú *a-da-áš*[ki] (*MEE* 7, 50 v. I 7-13)
1 gu-dùl-TÚG 1 mí-TÚG 1 íbxIII-GÙN-TÚG *zi-kir-ra-ar* ( )*-du-bù*[ki] šu-du$_8$-ÉREN+x (*MEE* 10, 2 r. II 12-III 1)

3) Periodo in cui Ibbi-zikir era "vizir".
[ ] [ ]*-ar-⌜x⌝ šu-ti-gú*[ki] šu-du$_8$ 1 ÉREN+x-mí (*ARET* 3, 35 r. I)
1 mí-TÚG 1 íbx3-GÙN-TÚG šu-du$_8$ 1 ÉREN+x (*ARET* 3, 35 r. VI)
1 mí-TÚG 1 íbx3-GÙN-TÚG gigir[ki] šu-du$_8$-ÉREN+x (*ARET* 8, 542 r. X 1-4)
1 mí-TÚG 1 íbx3-GÙN-TÚG *na-zu-mu* šu-du$_8$-ÉREN+x *in aš-pú*[ki] (*ARET* 8, 532 v. II 3-8).

Anche per questo termine le menzioni più antiche sono proporzionalmente più numerose di quelle più recenti.

Più rare sono le citazioni di šu-du$_8$ con altri animali: la pecora (1 udu[17]), l'orso (2 az[18]), l'equide igi-nita,[19] la pantera nemur$_x$,[20] cui si deve aggiungere il mitico "dragone",[21] così come probabilmente mitico era il bovide ÉREN+x. Tutti questi passi appartengono alla documentazione più antica. Quale sia il significato preciso di questo collegamento della funzione šu-du$_8$ con vari animali ci sfugge. Per il resto, non sembrano esservi differenze tra queste specializzazioni di šu-du$_8$ e gli altri šu-du$_8$: i nomi dei personaggi in questione sono per lo più precisati, ma in qualche caso la citazione si limita al titolo di šu-du$_8$; con una certa frequenza la loro funzione è posta in relazione con un toponimo e, più raramente, sono definiti anche maškim di un altro personaggio. I beni ricevuti consistono di norma in tessili di qualità medio-bassa, ma il loro valore può mutare: così lo šu-du$_8$ messo in relazione con i due orsi nel passo succitato, e che era l'ugula di un centro, riceve un completo di tessili della migliore qualità.

Lo šu-du$_8$ sembra messo anche in rapporto con materiale umano:

1 nì-lá-sag *i-ba-zi-nu* šu-du$_8$ guruš *ḫa-zu-wa-an*[ki] *mug-rí-ni*[ki] (*ARET* 3, 506 III)
[ ] šu-du$_8$ 3 lú *in* ambar[ki] (*ARET* 3, 587 v. II)

---

17 [ ] ^{d}*be ga-na-núm NI-da-ba-du* šu-du$_8$ 1 udu šu-du$_8$-máš (*ARET* 3, 769 II).

18 1 *ʾà-da-um*-2-TÚG 1 aktum-TÚG 1 íbx3-sa$_6$-GÙN *rí-dam-ma-lik* ugula *šu-ti-gú*[ki] šu-du$_8$ 2 az (*ARET* 1, 11 r. VII 9-13).

19 *ARET* 2, 29 v. V 4-5: il testo, a differenza di tutti gli altri citati in questo paragrafo, non è un rendiconto mensile di tessili.

20 1 íb-3-GÙN-TÚG *la-ba-rí-ù* šu-du$_8$ nemur$_x$ *la-ra-ab*[ki] (2629 r. VI 1-5). Per la lettura /nemur/ di PIRIG.TUR cf. G. Marchesi, *SEL* 16, p. 6.

21 [ ] šu-du$_8$ gal:ušum (*ARET* 3, 822 II).

2 íbx3-sa_6-GÙN *in-gàr* lú *iš-má-da-mu wa i-rí-gu* lú *sá-gú-sum* šeš-2-eb kéš-da šu-du_8 dumu-nita $SA+ZA_x$[ki](*ARET* 4, 13 v. II 6-16).

In un passo del trattato di Ebla e Abarsal šu-du_8 sembra posto in relazione con categorie di lavoratori e anche qui, come nel caso di šu-du_8 e máš, l'ordine tra šu-du_8 e il suo elemento caratterizzante è invertito: [ ] *ib-la*[ki] géme ir_{11} šu-du_8 šub *du-tum* 50 udu-nita ḫe-na-sum (E. Sollberger, *SEb* 3, p. 144, 467-474).

8. Un altro elemento che accomuna šu-du_8 e TUŠ.LÚxTIL è la loro menzione nella formula di occasione di un'assegnazione. I passi in questione che riguardano lo šu-du_8 sono piuttosto rari: [ ] ne-di ne-di $SA+ZA_x$[ki] *in* u_4 šu-du_8 *mi-nu ḫal-sum*[ki] (*ARET* 3, 100 v. IV); 1 mí-TÚG 1 íbx3-GÙN-TÚG *a-BAN-rúm* maškim *ḫa-ra-il* šu-du_8 *in* u_4 *ḫa-lam*[ki] (*ARET* 3, 154 I); *i-bí-zi-kir* dumu-nita *ib-rí-um in* u_4 šu-du_8 *in ma-nu-wa-ad*[ki] (2359 r. XII, citato da A. Archi, *Amurru* 1, p. 82). Molto più frequenti sono le menzioni di TUŠ.LÚxTIL nel medesimo tipo di contesto; tutti i passi in questione provengono da testi del periodo di Arrulum, o, più raramente, della prima fase del periodo di Ibrium:

[ ] *i-bí-zi-kir* dumu-nita *ib-rí-um in* u_4 TUŠ.LÚxTIL *ḫal-sum*[ki] (*ARET* 3, 868 II)

1 *ʾà-da-um*-TÚG-2 1 aktum-TÚG 1 íbx3-sa_6-GÙN-TÚG 2 kù-sig_{17} 2 giš-PI-lá *ʾà-zi ma-lik-tum* ì-na-sum *in* u_4 nì-AN.AN.AN.AN *na-bù*[ki] šu-ba_4-ti *wa i-bí-zi-kir* TUŠ.LÚxTIL (*ARET* 4, 18 r. I 7-18)

1 *gu-zi-tum* 1 íbx3-sa_6-GÙN 1 íb-lá ku_5 kù-bar_6 2 *gú-li-lum* kù-bar_6 kù-sig_{17} *gi-ti-ir* lú *i-rí-gú-nu in* u_4 TUŠ.LÚxTIL *al_6-du-bù*[ki] (*MEE* 2, 32 v. II 3-10)

1 ⸢túg⸣-[ ] 1? [ ] 1 [ ] 1 [ ] kù-sig_{17} GÁxLÁ 1 ma-na kù-sig_{17} 4 kù-SAL 2 nì-anše-aka GÀxLÀ 1 ma-na kù-bar_6 *zé-ma-lik in* u_4 TUŠ.LÚxTIL *ḫa-zu-wa-an*[ki] (*MEE* 10, 26 r. I 9-15) ... 1 *gu-zi*-TÚG 1 íbx3-sa_6-GÙN 1 íb-lá kù-bar_6 2 *gú-li-lum* a-gar_6 kù-sig_{17} *i-bí-um* lú *i-bí-iš in* u_4 TUŠ.LÚxTIL *ḫa-zu-wa-an*[ki] (*ibid.*, r. II 12-III 4)

1 íb-lá GÁxLÁ 50 (gín) kù-bar_6 2 *gú-li-lum* a-gar_5-a-gar_5 kù-sig_{17} 1 gír-mar-tu MAŠ.MAŠ kù-gi *puzra*[ra]*-ḫa-al$_6$ in* u_4 TUŠ.LÚxTIL (1441 v. IV 11-16)

1 ma-na ša-pi kù-bar_6 šu-bala-aka šušana kù-sig_{17} 1 dib-10 *bar-za-ma-ù* ugula *ʾà-šu*[ki] *in* u_4 TUŠ.LÚxTIL *a-ʾà-lu*[ki] (1464 r. IV 3-10)

1 *gu-zi*-TÚG 1 íbx3-sa_6 1 íb-lá ša-pi kù-bar_6 1 dib TAR kù-gi *ib-da-am* TUŠ.LÚxTIL *ḫa-zu-wa-an*[ki] (1779 r. IX 7-12); [ ]-⸢x⸣-TÚG [ ]-TÚG 1 + [ ] íbx3-GÙN 1 íb-lá 1 ma-na kù-bar_6 2 *gú-li-lum* kù-bar_6 kù-gi 1 gír-mar-tu kù-sig_{17} níg-ba *dub-da-mu* lú *i-ti-ig in* u_4 TUŠ.LÚxTIL *ḫa-zu-wa-an*[ki] (*ibid.*, v. IV 7-15)

[ ]-⸢x⸣-TÚG [ ]-TÚG 1 + [ ] íbx3-GÙN 1 íb-lá 1 ma-na kù-bar_6 2 *gú-li-lum* kù-bar_6 kù-gi 1 gír-mar-tu kù-gi níg-ba *dub-da-mu* lú *i-ti-ig in* u_4 TUŠ.LÚxTIL *ḫa-zu-wa-an*[ki] (1861 v. IV 7-15)

1 *gu-zi*-TÚG 1 aktum-TÚG 1 íbx3-sa_6-GÙN-TÚG 1 íb-lá kù-bar_6 *za-bù-ru$_{12}$ kak-mi-um*[ki] *in* u_4 TUŠ.LÚxTIL *mi ma-rí*[ki] *áš-ti mu-ur*[ki] (1453 v. IV 19ss. [citato da A. Archi, *MARI* 4, p. 75, 34]; questo passo è da mettere in relazione con 2629 v. IV 12-21).

9. TUŠ.LÚxTIL è tradotto di regola "residente" sulla base della lettura del primo segno come tuš. Il secondo segno è considerato una variante di lú; anzi G.Pettinato adotta senz'altro questa lettura in *MEE* 2, seguito ad es. da F. D'Agostino, *Il sistema verbale sumerico nei testi lessicali di Ebla*, Roma 1990, p. 41. In realtà, il segno è LÚxTIL, come dimostra la sua grafia nei testi più antichi: solo in alcuni testi della seconda fase del regno di Iš'ar-Damu compare episodicamente la forma LÚ,[22] evidentemente un'abbreviazione grafica della prima, del tipo di quelle cui indulgono gli scribi eblaiti, ad es. KUL per BAL nel nome divino ^{d}*'à-da-bal* e nel toponimo *gú-ra-ra-bal*^{ki}.

Ora, gli stretti parallelismi sopra discussi di TUŠ.LÚxTIL e šu-du$_8$, che deve avere all'incirca il valore di "collettore (di tasse)", impongono un significato analogo per il primo termine. Ciò concorda straordinariamente bene, come già notato da P. Fronzaroli, *SEb* 1 (1979), pp. 79-80, con il valore semitico che il Vocabolario bilingue di Ebla assegna a TUŠ.LÚxTIL: *a-ḫa-sum* (*MEE* 4, p. 333, 1284'), da far derivare dalla radice semitica comune *'ḫḏ* con il significato di "ricevere, prendere possesso". Più precisamente questo *a-ḫa-sum* sarà da considerare una formazione nominale del tipo *parrās*, che soprattutto serve a designare nomi di professione.[23] Naturalmente questa ricostruzione richiede la lettura del primo segno come dab$_5$, che è il logogramma corrispondente al verbo accadico *aḫāzu*(*m*).

Resterebbe da spiegare il valore del logogramma seguente LÚxTIL. Chi scrive (*MARI* 7, p. 115, n. 19) aveva proposto dubitativamente di considerare il segno scritto all'interno di LÚ come la lettura dell'intero segno e questo un complemento fonetico (uš$_x$) per il logogramma TUŠ che precedeva. Questa ultima ipotesi è ora da abbandonare, ma vi è qualche elemento per sostenere che il segno LÚxTIL e il segno TIL, qualunque sia il valore loro da attribuire, abbiano la medesima lettura, cioè che TIL valga come un *Lautindikator* del segno nel quale è inserito.

Nei passi succitati, tutti ricavati da testi del periodo di Arrulum, in cui ricorre la formula *in* u$_4$ TUŠ.LÚxTIL, vi sono numerose assegnazioni caratterizzate da questa occasione di uscita, e più ricche della norma, che hanno in comune il toponimo

---

22 Ad es., nei testi editi da E. Sollberger, *ARET* 8, la grafia con il semplice LÚ ricorre in un decimo del numero di attestazioni di TUŠ.LÚxTIL.

23 F. D'Agostino, *Il sistema verbale sumerico nei testi lessicali di Ebla*, Roma 1990, p. 41 anche fa derivare il lessema del Vocabolario di Ebla *aḫd*(!), "prendere, possedere", ma, rispettando la lettura del lessema sumerico come tuš-lú, suggerisce il significato di "prendere possesso (di un luogo), abitare". Cf. anche M. G. Biga - F. Pomponio, *MARI* 7, p. 115, n. 19.

Hazuwan. Ora, in *MEE* 10, 26 sono registrate ben due di queste uscite seguite poco dopo da un'altra con la formula *in* u$_4$ kas$_4$-kas$_4$ *ḫa-zu-wa-an*^{ki} (*MEE* 10, 26 r. II 12x3 4).

Un'analoga relazione può essere stabilita tra due passi di un registro di uscite di oro, che menziona Iblul-Il e, verosimilmente, le esequie della sua regina Paba: la prima ricchissima assegnazione, collegata all' "unzione del capo del re (di Mari)", avviene *in* u$_4$ TIL.TIL *ga-sùr*^{ki} (*ARET* 2, 4 r. VI 6-8); la seconda che deve essere stata parimenti ricca, anche se la parte iniziale della sua elencazione è andata perduta in una lacuna del testo, avviene *in* u$_4$ kas$_4$-kas$_4$ *ga-sùr*^{ki} (v. III 4-6). Inoltre alcuni passi in cui TUŠ.LÚxTIL è citato insieme alla formula (*in* u$_4$) nì-AN.AN.AN(.AN)[24] potrebbero essere messi in rapporto con quelli molto numerosi che presentano la formula: *in* u$_4$ nì-AN.AN.AN(.AN) NL TIL.

Per stabilire approssimativamente il valore di TIL(.TIL)[25] in questi passi possiamo notare che in un paragrafo del "Trattato tra Ebla e Abarsal" (E. Sollberger, *SEb* 3, p. 140, 288-289) ricorrono in sequenza kas$_4$-kas$_4$ TIL.TIL preceduti da *a-sa-ma a-sa-ma*, che chi scrive (cf. *VO* 5 [1982], p. 200, n.13[26]) ha interpretato come derivante dalla radice *lsm*, "correre". In tutti questi passi TIL sembrerebbe indicare un particolare tipo di movimento di personale, differenziato da quello dei corrieri *a-sa-ma a-sa-ma* e dei viaggiatori kas$_4$-kas$_4$. Se questi accostamenti sono corretti, il nome di funzione TUŠ.LÚxTIL potrebbe essere formato da due distinti logogrammi: il primo è da leggere dab$_5$, con il significato all'incirca di "ricevitore",[27] mentre la lettura del secondo, ancora sconosciuta, deve essere quella del segno TIL, che in numerosi testi

---

24 1 mí-TÚG 1 íbx3-GÙN-TÚG 1 gír-mar-tu *ga-za-ab* kù-bar$_6$ *ù-du-ra-ù* giš-HÚB *in* u$_4$ nì-AN.AN.AN.AN *en-na-be* TUŠ.LÚxTIL (2629 r. IX 8-14); 1 *'à-da-um*-TÚG-2 1 aktum-TÚG 1 íbx3-sa$_6$-GÙN *lu-a-ì* maškim *du-bù-hu-*^{d}*'à-da* nì-AN.AN.AN.AN *du-bù-hu-*^{d}*'à-da* TUŠ.LÚxTIL *in* uru^{ki}-uru^{ki} *lu-a-tum*^{ki} (*ARET* 8, 521 r. IX 14-v. I 8). Anche in questa espressione šu-du$_8$ può ricorrere nella medesima posizione di TUŠ.LÚxTIL: nì-AN.AN.AN.AN šu-du$_8$ *en-zi-gú-núm* ugula-x-x *ib-rí-um* (*ARET* 3, 215 v. II).

25 Nelle formule di occasione di uscite TIL può anche apparire senza la duplicazione: *in* u$_4$ TIL *ḫu-sa-um*^{ki} (*ARET* 3, 459 r. VI; questa assegnazione è da mettere in relazione con quella di TM.75.G.2508 v. IX 14'-24').

26 La stessa ipotesi è presentata, dieci anni dopo, da D. O. Edzard, *QuSem* 18 (1992), p. 215.

27 In alcuni passi compare solo la forma TUŠ: 1 mí-TÚG maškim *ar-mi-um*^{ki} TUŠ *kak-mi-um*^{ki} (1347 r. II 10-11); 2 gu-dùl-TÚG 1 mí-TÚG 2 íbx3-GÙN-TÚG *NE-li íl-zi 'à-su*^{ki} TUŠ *ù-ra-ba-an*^{ki} (*ARET* 1, 12 v. I 2-7); 1 gu-dùl-TÚG 1 íbx3-GÙN-TÚG *'à-bí kak-mi-um*^{ki} TUŠ *ù-ra-kul*^{ki} (*ARET* 1, 12 v. I 8-II 1). Data la somiglianza con i contesti in cui ricorre TUŠ.LÚxTIL, qui TUŠ deve essere un'abbreviazione dell'altro termine. In altri casi invece TUŠ deve valere come forma abbreviata dell'al$_6$-TUŠ che discuteremo nel paragrafo seguente.

di Ebla dovrebbe indicare un particolare tipo di spostamento di personale o, se unito a nì-AN.AN.AN(.AN), di assegnazioni.

10. Vi è nei testi amministrativi di Ebla, in particolare nei rendiconti mensili di tessili, un altro termine cui è attribuito il valore di "residente": al$_6$-TUŠ. I passi in questione ricorrono per lo più nella documentazione di Ibbi-zikir e solo in due testi (*ARET* 4, 12; *MEE* 10, 3) del periodo di Ibrium.

Per lo più sono definiti al$_6$-TUŠ gruppi di lavoratori che arrivano ad alcune centinaia di componenti; in particolare, in più passi sono menzionati uomini di Mari, in qualche caso definiti lú-kar, che operano in Dunep o lavoratori, in un caso definiti "mietitori", di Armi che operano in Gizan o in Aalu:

1 *mi* 20 ha-zi urudu *ma-rí*^{ki} al$_6$-TUŠ *du-ne-éb*^{ki} (*ARET* 3, 118 v. III); 60 aktum-TÚG 80 *dam-ša-lu* 2 *mi-at* 47 mí-TÚG 1 *mi-at* íbx3-sa$_6$-TÚG 2 *mi-at* íbx3-GÙN-TÚG lú-kar *ma-rí*^{ki} al$_6$-TUŠ *du-ne-éb*^{ki} (*ARET* 4, 1 r. VII 9-17); 4 *mi-at* 70 KIN$_x$ siki tüg-MU 4 *mi-at* 70 *na-si*$_{11}$ lú-kar *ma-rí*^{ki} al$_6$-TUŠ *du-ne-éb*^{ki} (*ARET* 8, 522 v. VIII 21-IX 3); 30 gu-mug-TÚG 30 mí-TÚG 30 íbx3-GÙN-TÚG lú-kar *ma-rí*^{ki} al$_6$-TUŠ *du-ne-éb*^{ki} (*ARET* 8, 524 r. VI 13-17); [ ] + 20 KIN$_x$ siki túg-MU 3 *mi-at* 80 *na-si*$_{11}$ lú-kar *ma-rí*^{ki} al$_6$-TUŠ *du-ne-ep*^{ki} (*ARET* 8, 532 v. X 1-5); 20 íbx3-sa$_6$-GÙN-TÚG 2 *mi-at* 33 íbx3-GÙN-TÚG *ma-rí*^{ki} al$_6$-TUŠ *du-ne-éb*^{ki} (2330 r. VII 2-6, citato da A. Archi, *MARI* 4 [1985], p. 77, 92).

2 gu-dùl-TÚG 1 gu-mug-TÚG 2 aktum-TÚG 1 mí-TÚG 3 íbx3-GÙN-TÚG 3 *ar-mi*^{ki} al$_6$-TUŠ *gi-za-an*^{ki} kin$_x$-aka *ša-mu* (*ARET* 1, 13 r. V 7-13); 5 *mi-at* 50 KIN$_x$ siki *ar-mi*^{ki} al$_6$-TUŠ *gi-za-an*^{ki} DILMUN-ku$_5$ še-gur$_{10}$-*sù* (*ARET* 1, 15 v. VIII 20-IX 5); 2 *mi-at* gada-TÚG túg-MU *ar-mi*^{ki} al$_6$-TUŠ *gi-za-an*^{ki} (*ARET* 4, 5 r. IX 8-12); 1 *li-im* 1 *mi-at* 40 KIN$_x$ siti túg-túg *ar-mi*^{ki} al$_6$-TUŠ *gi-za-an*^{ki} (*ARET* 4, 25 v. III 1-5); 6 tùn-tur ku$_5$ 10 sum-12 al$_6$-TUŠ *gi-za-an*^{ki} (2428 v. VII 43-46); 33 šu-kešda al$_6$-TUŠ *gi-za-an*^{ki} (*ARET* 8, 529 v. IX 15-17); 1 *li-im* 34 KIN$_x$ siki *ar-mi*^{ki} al$_6$-TUŠ *a-a-lu*^{ki} (*ARET* 4, 8 v. III 8-12).

Meno frequentemente sono definiti al$_6$-TUŠ singoli individui, che alla pari dei funzionari šu-du$_8$ e LÚ.TUŠxTIL, sono caratterizzati da un sito e operano in un altro. Ma, a differenza di quel che avviene per šu-du$_8$ e LÚ.TUŠxTIL, i maškim non sono compresi tra gli al$_6$-TUŠ e possono essere definiti al$_6$-TUŠ, e ricevere quindi assegnazioni, anche le dam, oltre ai dumu-nita, di costoro:

1 mí-TÚG 1 íbx3-GÙN-TÚG *en-nu-lum* lú-kar *ma-nu-wa-ad*^{ki} al$_6$-TUŠ *šè-ra-du*^{ki} 1 íbx3-GÙN-TÚG 3 siki na$_4$ *i-ti-nu wa* 2 dumu-nita-*sù* lú-kar *ma-nu-wa-ad*^{ki} al$_6$-TUŠ *ib-su*^{ki} (*ARET* 4, 12 r. VIII 9-IX 4)

1 gu-dùl-TÚG 1 mí-TÚG 1 íbx3-GÙN-TÚG *a-ga-ma-al*$_6$ 1 gu-dùl-TÚG 3 na$_4$ siki dam-*sù* lú-kar *ma-nu-wa-ad*^{ki} al$_6$-TUŠ *'à-ma-ad*^{ki} (*ARET* 3, 470 r. I)

1 túg-NI.NI dam *i-ti-*^{d}*ga-mi-iš da-ra-um*^{ki} al$_6$-TUŠ *gar-ga-mi-su*^{ki} (*MEE* 10, 3 v. II 7-12)

Altrove un numero imprecisato di al_6-TUŠ, destinatari di lana, è messo in rapporto con la dea del sole (1442 v. IX 13-15) e altri con centri amministrativi di Ebla, il SA+ZA_x^{ki} (*ARET* 3, 904 I; 4, 12 r. IV 8-V 6) e l' é-ir_{11} (*ARET* 8, 527 r. X 13-16). E, per citare qualche altro esempio, in un registro mensile di tessili vi è l'assegnazione di uno $zara_6$-TÚG per un'addetta alla regina (di Ebla), che era al_6-TUŠ in Luban (*ARET* 4, 23 v. I 15-17) e 9 dumu-mí ne-di al_6-TUŠ *ì-ap*^{ki} sono citate in *ARET* 8, 521 v. II 19-21.

Per passare a testi di altre categorie, due passi dai rendiconti annuali di uscite di argento del periodo di Ibbi-zikir registrano 10 o 5 sicli di argento per alcuni guruš al_6-TUŠ giš-uštil, mentre nel frammento di un registro di personale sono citati 14 *na-si*$_{11}$ abba-abba al_6-TUŠ giš-uštil (*ARET* 3, 96 I). Questo manufatto, interpretato come "carro", "seggio, trono", "cippo, stendardo",[28] ricorre pure in rapporto con il termine al_6-TUŠ nel Rituale del matrimonio della coppia reale di Ebla: en *ù ma-lik-tum* è TUŠ *al*$_6$ 2 giš-uštil *a-bù-sù* (*ARET* 11, 1 v. IV 13-20); *mi-in* 5 u_4-gibil iti *ḫa-li-NI* al_6-TUŠ 2 giš-uštil a-ma-a-mu-*sù* (*ARET* 11, 2 r. VIII 12-21). Naturalmente in questi passi al_6-TUŠ non definisce una funzione amministrativa, ma un'azione o una situazione della coppia reale. Infine, in un testo di ovini alcune divinità sono definite al_6-TUŠ nel centro di Darib (*ARET* 7, 150 v. III 1-IV 2). Soprattutto questi ultimi passi stabiliscono per al_6-TUŠ una lettura al_6-tuš e il significato di "residente, che siede",[29] che conviene anche all'impiego del prefisso al_6, di norma utilizzato con verbi intransitivi.[30]

Infine, in due soli passi ricorre la formula TUŠ-ba//ba-TUŠ:

1 *ʾà-da-um*-TÚG-2 1 aktum-TÚG 1 íbx3-sa_6-GÙN-TÚG 1 *gú-li-lum* kù-bar_6-sig_{17} *nam-mi-su* TUŠ-ba *ag-ga* (*MEE* 2, 7 r. IX 10-14)

1 aktum-TÚG 1 *gú-li-lum* kù-bar_6-sig_{17} 10 (gín)-1 *wa-da-ʾà* ba-TUŠ *al*$_6$ giš (*ARET* 4, 6 v. VI 6-11).

La lettura ba-tuš sembra certa per il secondo passo, ma per il primo le si oppone l'eccezionale collocazione del prefisso di coniugazione dopo la radice verbale; così

---

28 Le citazioni bibliografiche di questi vari significati sono state raccolte da G. Pettinato, *Il rituale per la successione al trono ad Ebla*, Roma 1992, pp. 192-193.

29 Anche nell'inno al dio Sole proveniente da Ebla e Abu Ṣalabikh ricorre il termine al_6-tuš in parallelo con il verbo è: è *áš-mu* al_6-tuš *áš-mu* (cf. M. Krebernik, *QuSem* 18 [1992], p. 76, C7.5).

30 Come šu-du_8 e numerosi altri termini amministrativi, ad es. šu-mu-tag_x, al_6-TUŠ, oltre ad avere prevalentemente il su discusso valore di nome verbale, può assumere, in particolare in alcuni documenti giuridici, quello di forma verbale finita (cf. P. Fronzaroli, *SEb* 7 [1984], p. 12).

una lettura dab$_5$-ba con il secondo segno da interpretare come un complemento fonetico del logogramma che precede non è da escludere.

11. Dall'interpretazione di šu-du$_8$(-máš) e di dab$_5$-LÚxTIL come due nomi di funzioni si può ricavare che al servizio dell'amministrazione di Ebla operava un gran numero di ufficiali, dislocati in numerosi centri e con alto grado di mobilità, con due differenti incarichi di ricevute di beni, probabilmente sotto forma di tributi. Una delle due funzioni, quella resa dalla radice verbale šu-du$_8$, sembra operasse in particolare in relazione a bestiame. Queste funzioni erano assolte da personale che svolgeva diverse professioni, eccezionalmente anche di alto rango, pure se nella stragrande maggioranza dei casi esse erano affidate a maškim. Nei rendiconti mensili di tessili il pagamento relativo alle singole missioni comprendeva, di norma, l'assegnazione di un completo di due tessili di mediocre valore.

12. È consolidata norma che il primo paragrafo degli articoli scritti in onore di un collega sia impiegato a spiegare la scelta dell'argomento, per lo più basata su un comune interesse scientifico tra l'autore e lo studioso festeggiato.

Chi scrive ha preferito dedicare a questa gentile pratica l'ultimo paragrafo. Vent'anni fa, nei fascicoli di *Studi Eblaiti* 1 comparvero i primi lavori di Pelio Fronzaroli nel campo dell'Eblaitologia. Il valore del contributo dato alla nuova disciplina, per questo lungo periodo, sia dal prof. Fronzaroli, sia dai suoi allievi dell'Università di Firenze può difficilmente essere sopravvalutato. Ora, in uno di questi primi articoli, *Problemi di fonetica eblaita, I, SEb* 1 (1979), pp. 79-80 è stato esaminato uno dei due nomi di funzione che costituiscono l'argomento del presente studio. Dal 1979 sono state edite centinaia di citazioni di TUŠ.LÚxTIL, ma le conclusioni a cui era già arrivato il prof. Fronzaroli sia sull'etimologia del termine, sia sul suo significato sono state pressoché ignorate. Il presente articolo vuole ricordare queste conclusioni e fornire qualche altro elemento a loro sostegno, oltre, incidentalmente, a tentare di apportare nuovi dati alla conoscenza dell'amministrazione eblaita e allo studio della datazione interna dei suoi testi.

LA PARTE ALTA DEL CORPO NELLA PREISTORIA DELLE LINGUE

Umberto Rapallo

Università di Genova

1) Sul prolungamento della lessicografia comparativa semitica

Il contributo nasce da una riflessione sulla lessicografia comparativa delle lingue, a iniziare da quella delle lingue semitiche, per cui sembra di poter asserire che la tradizionale enfasi 'ideologica' sui requisiti più storico-culturali, assenti o quasi quelli più naturali, ha in molti casi comportato necessarie limitazioni sia areali sia anche temporali, che collocano le 'famiglie' linguistiche agli albori della storia, non oltre la protostoria. È un motivo che ha condizionato la ricerca etimologica, da sempre sbilanciata in eccessi non solo algebristici, ma anche storicistici. Una prospettiva più allargata, che includa con i requisiti più storico-culturali anche quelli più naturali, è implicita però già nel concomitante richiamo in atto a un lessico comune e a un lessico di base: il primo, non tutto storico-culturale, non esclude una conciliazione con il secondo, non tutto naturale, nel caso in cui parte del lessico di base sia comune a due o più lingue o gruppi linguistici. Si può credere che tale conciliazione possa rappresentare un utile correttivo nell'interesse, sempre più attuale, di una preistoria delle lingue, senza che la leibniziana tesi di una naturalità conduca a una stretta identificazione tra 'primitivo' e naturale e senza che ci sia tendenza a esagerare, esasperandolo, il dissidio tra natura e cultura. Nei limiti in cui la conciliazione si può dire praticabile e fruttuosa, può essere sostenuta per analogia dal fatto che una comparazione più storico-genealogica può non contrastare, ma piuttosto completarsi, con una più tipologica, garantendo anche, con una più estesa comparazione delle lingue (*total distribution*), una maggiore generalità.

Su questa via e nel superamento di sterili pregiudizi 'linguisticidi', si vogliono qui indicare come necessario prolungamento della tradizionale lessicografia comparativa e al di là dei lessici comuni, nella fattispecie di quello semitico (più un semitico comune che un protosemitico), convergenze lessicali più estese (macroareali) e più remote (preistoriche), sia che collimino con più specifiche e culturalmente più marcate convergenze tra lingue o gruppi linguistici, sia anche con più generiche e meno marcate convergenze, ipoteticamente anche della massima estensione. La validità-carisma di una protolingua 'nostratica', secondo una versione qual è quella di H. Pedersen, attualizzata a più o meno strette convergenze, per esempio a un camito-semitico-indeuropeo (CAM-SEM-IE), e non riconducibile perciò a un vuoto 'onni-comparatismo' pseudolinguistico, può non differire molto qualitativamente da quella di un SEM oppure IE.[1] La scelta poi di un CAM-SEM-IE, nell'àmbito di più estese convergenze linguistiche, può essere giustificata da una convergenza presumibilmente molto più antica rispetto ad altre 'nostratiche', più in particolare euroasiatiche.[2]

2) Il campo semantico del corpo (la parte alta)

In questa prospettiva, ci si è avvalsi di quella parte del lessico di base presente nel lessico comune delle lingue SEM che si riconosce più naturale e meno culturale per i suoi legami stretti con la vita, il movimento, le varie attività e la riproduzione, quella delle denominazioni del corpo (umano e/o animale). L'esemplificazione sulla parte alta del corpo, in particolare, ha imposto la considerazione di segni imitativi sì – caratterizzati in parte da associazioni tra i referenti e in contrasto con quel 'campo' semantico di J. Trier che definisce il significato in termini puramente relazionali di segni, e non di referenza alla realtà –, ma anche motivati culturalmente, tali cioè da indirizzare a una 'visione del mondo'. L'attenzione si è rivolta a undici 'metafore radicali' (M. Müller) CAM-SEM-IE.[3]

---

1 Varie considerazioni e testimonianze hanno finito per avvalorare una complementarità tra due ipotesi ricostruttive, una vicina (storica) e una lontana (algebrica), tra semantica ed etimologia, tra un'arcaicità filologicamente sostenuta dalla documentazione delle lingue e una più speculativa 'primitività'. Sui rapporti tra una ricostruzione 'lontana' e singole tradizioni linguistiche storiche, cfr. ora M. P. Bologna, "Realismo ricostruttivo e ricostruzione linguistica 'lontana': nota su alcuni aspetti della teoria laringalistica", in R. Ambrosini - M. P. Bologna - F. Motta - C. Orlandi (a cura di), *Scríbthair a ainm n-ogaim. Scritti in memoria di E. Campanile*, Pisa 1997, pp. 201-216; ma il problema è posto già da G. Devoto, *Origini indeuropee*, Firenze 1962, pp. 15-33. Inoltre sul rapporto stretto, anche se difficile, tra semantica ed etimologia, cfr. B. Nerlich, *Semantic Theories in Europe, 1830-1930*, Amsterdam - Philadelphia 1992, pp. 22 s. e 40 s.

2 Sulla marcata tardività di una branca euroasiatica rispetto a quella afroasiatica, cfr., nella loro critica ai nostraticisti moscoviti, A. R. Bomhard - J. C. Kerns, *The Nostratic Macrofamily. A Study in Distant Linguistic Relationship*, Berlin 1994, p. 18, anche pp. 34 s. (con bibl.).

3 Si è preferito mettere a confronto le radici dei varî sottogruppi linguistici (SEM, EG = egiziano, BERB = berbero, CUSC = cuscitico, comprensivo di omotico, CIAD = ciadico, IE), piuttosto che restituire una pre-proto-radice 'nostratica'; le radici sono indicate senza asterisco (*), separando le consonanti radicali con un trattino (-). Viceversa, sul piano del contenuto, si è cercato di rappresentare tra barre oblique verticali (/ /) un'area semantica di più significati (invarianti di contenuto o proto-proto-

[1] SEM *ʾ-n-š, n-š, ʾ-n* ; EG *n-š*; BERB *Ø-l-s* ; CUSC *n-s* ; IE *ə-n, n-s* /essere intimo, avere contatto fisico; respirare; **naso**; **bocca, labbro**; **gola volto**; uomo, donna, persona/

È un lemma del lessico di base difficile da etimologizzare per la sua antichità, il che vuol dire che può essere limitativo fermarsi a considerare la sua appartenenza al lessico comune SEM. Il campo lessicale è suscettibile di ampliamenti a etimologie 'seconde' per effetto di rideterminazioni morfologiche e reinterpretazioni semantiche. Sull'etimologia di *ʾ-n-š* può influire la paromonimia secondaria di *ʾ-n-ḥ* "respirare faticosamente" e di *n-p-š* "energia vitale". In altre parole, l''interpretante' (senso) del segno viene a coincidere con un rapporto paradigmatico, se pure sintagmatizzato, fra segni, secondo la definizione di Ch.S. Peirce (vd. §§ 6-7), in una loro tendenza ipodifferenziatrice (ipocodificazione) che li qualifica al tempo stesso come motivati (subicone e subindici) e immotivati (simboli), per una semiosi paradossalmente significativa e distintiva. Vi contribuiscono vischiosità foniche, contagi semantici, procedimenti metaforizzanti per doppia correlazione di suono e di senso. L'ampliarsi dell'etimologia va di pari passo con l'ampliarsi delle metafore radicali: di questo coerente allargamento possono dare conferma già anticamente gli usi dell'ebl. *ʾiškum* "testicolo", *nupuštum* "vita", *našū* "popolo", *napāḫum* "soffiare".[4] La motivazione del segno è direttamente proporzionale alla sua estensione, come indica già il concetto saussuriano di 'arbitrarietà relativa'. Gli usi testuali danno risalto a metafore radicali, avvalorandole, al tempo stesso che queste danno coerenza al

---

sememi) ricostruiti come 'nostratici'. I contenuti corrispondente alla parte alta del corpo sono indicati in grassetto. Per le radici IE ci si è avvalsi principalmente di Devoto, *Origini, cit.* (anche J. Pokorny, *Indogermanisches etymologisches Wörterbuch*, Bern 1949-1959), per quelle SEM specialmente di P. Fronzaroli, "Studi sul lessico comune semitico", *RANL* ser. VIII, 19 (1964) pp. 1-17; pp. 243-280; 20 (1965) pp. 135-150; pp. 246-269; 23 (1968) pp. 267-303; 24 (1969) pp. 1-36; 26 (1971) pp. 603-643 (anche D. Cohen, *Dictionnaire des racines sémitiques ou attestées dans les langues sémitiques*, Paris - La Haye 1970 ss. e *Id.*, *Études de linguistique sémitique et arabe*, The Hague 1970, pp. 7-30), integrato per il CAM-SEM – quando possibile – con M. Cohen, *Essai comparatif sur le vocabulaire et la phonétique du chamito-sémitique*, Paris 1947 e V. E. Orel - O.V. Stolbova, *Hamito-Semitic Etymological Dictionary. Materials for a Reconstruction*, Leiden - New York - Köln 1995. Fondamentali punti di riferimento per una comparazione più estesa CAM-SEM-IE, se pure da valutare con cautela e non sempre plausibili, sono stati soprattutto H. Möller, *Vergleichendes indogermanisch-semitisches Wörterbuch*, Göttingen 1911 (rist. 1970), A. R. Bomhard, *Toward Proto-Nostratic. A New Approach to the Comparison of Proto-Indo-European and Proto-Afroasiatic*, Amsterdam 1984 e Bomhard - Kerns, *Nostratic Macrofamily, cit.* Per cautela nei confronti di una diffusa tendenza a proiettare la comparazione molto al di fuori del tradizionale CAM-SEM, si è preferito per i varî sottogruppi, e spec. per il CIAD, registrare le corrispondenze più note e accreditate; sulle prospettive, tuttavia, di una comparazione 'afroasiatica', cfr. i contributi della recente miscellanea di A. Bausi - M. Tosco (a cura di), *Afroasiatica Neapolitana. Contributi presentati all'8° Incontro di Linguistica Afroasiatica (Camito-Semitica). Napoli, 25-26 genn. 1996*, Napoli 1997.

4 Su questi e altri casi in cui la metaforicità radicale di lemmi CAM-SEM-IE può essere sostenuta da attestazioni (parole ricostruite) dell'eblaita, rinvio al mio saggio "Il lessico ebraico di base: fra generalità e universalità", in S. Graziani *et al.* (a cura di), *Studi sul Vicino Oriente Antico, dedicati alla memoria di L. Cagni*, Napoli 2000, p. 2026 e nn. 18-21.

testo allargandone l'interpretazione. Al bivio tra una diacronia dinamica oppure storica, ogni metafora radicale dà luogo a considerare le transizioni di significato secondo una doppia concezione, logico-speculativa (dal proprio al figurato) oppure storico-cronologica (dal figurato al proprio: all'origine era la metafora!) Una comparazione multilaterale tra le lingue può evidenziare convergenze più o meno strette, difficile dire se primarie (antecedenti a uno stato di separazione) oppure secondarie (susseguenti a uno stato di separazione). Nel caso della radice [1], le convergenze di metafore radicali sono convergenze di lingue, più che di gruppi o sottogruppi linguistici. Particolarmente utili a stabilire delle convergenze primarie sembrerebbero le convergenze tra lingue molto lontane tra loro nel tempo (ant. indiano e BERB, accadico e gotico) e/o nello spazio (cimrico, ant. indiano, EG), ma anche in questo caso fluttuano i confini tra una temporalità interna (naturale, certo non 'fortuita'; vd. § 7) e una esterna (storico-culturale). Non sarà un caso che convergenze primarie, quali le tradizionali 'parentele' tra le lingue, sono qualificate indeterminatamente come 'storico-genealogiche'. Le metafore evidenziano differenze tra le lingue, che sono da ricondurre a diverse culture-ambienti e che complicano la ricostruzione di transizioni di significati: *ʾ-n-š* è "uomo-maschio-marito" in alcune lingue, "donna-sposa" in altre, mai "uomo-donna" nella medesima lingua. Rideterminazioni morfologiche e reinterpretazioni semantiche presiedono alle sovrapposizioni di denominazioni della parte alta del corpo, che si sviluppano da metafore radicali CAM-SEM-IE (vd. TABB. 1 e 2). Altre metafore radicali consentono di individuare indicatori semantici comuni ai varî organi: la /forza/ è comune a cranio [8] e testa [9], /signore, capo/ comune a capelli [4]. Meno sicura è la comunanza di /alto/ a capelli [4] e testa [9], di /barba/ a bocca, labbro [5], di /discendenza/ a capelli [4]. Con varie sfumature, /parola, voce/ è comune a bocca, labbro [2] e [5], gola [6] e [7] e forse occhio [11], /sapere, intelletto/ comune a bocca, labbro [2] e [5] e orecchio [10].

[2] SEM (*ʾ*) *p-* (*n*)*-w*, *ʾ-n-p*, EG. *w-p*, CUSC. (*ʾ/y*)*f/p/b-n/r*, BERB. *ʾ-m*, CIAD *p-n*, *ʾ-p* ; IE *ə-w-(s)* /**bocca**, **labbra**; **naso**; apertura, imboccatura, sbocco, foce; soffiare; aspetto, figura, **faccia**/ (vd. [1])

La consonante radicale *p* è prevalente nel CAM-SEM e attribuita a 'fonetica espressiva'. Rideterminazioni morfologiche e reinterpretazioni semantiche rendono difficoltosa la ricostruzione etimologica, anche se il monosillabismo della radice indizia di 'primitività'; il riferimento al campo semantico (lessico del corpo, parte alta) appare perciò prevalente. La sovrapposizione tra [1] e [2] si manifesta in SEM in una lunga serie di correlazioni di radici: con *p* "bocca", *ʾ-n-p* "naso", *p-n-w* "faccia", *n-p-š* "respirare", *p-w-ḥ* "soffiare, respirare, dire", anche *ʾ-n-š* "uomo; intimo", *ʾ-n-ḥ* "respirare faticosamente", *n-š-m* (anche *n-š-p/b*) "soffiare, respirare", *n-š-ḳ* "baciare". Da ultimo, nella sovrapposizione di [1]-[2] con orecchio [10] la convergenza coinvolge una correlazione di radici solo per l'IE, mentre per il [CAM-]SEM, per esempio per l'ebraico, è solo semantica. Möller (*Wörterbuch*, *cit.*, p. 176) accomuna *ʾ-n-p* "naso" e *n-p-š* "respirare". Una convergenza, chissà quanto secondaria, se già documentata dall'ebl. *ʾappu(m)*, acc. *appu* "naso", avvicina *ʾ-p* "naso" a *ʾ-p* "bocca", entrambi organi della parte anteriore del corpo e funzionalmente legati alla respirazione. Cohen (*Essai*, *cit.*, p. 171, NN. 380 e 380 *bis*) stabilisce anche una corradicalità tra parole ad alta frequenza, quali in ebraico *peh* "bocca" e **pāneh* "faccia, viso". C'è permutazione delle consonanti radicali in ebr. **pāneh* e **npš*. Di un'equivalenza contestuale tra ebr. *peh* "bocca", *pānîm* "faccia, viso" e

ʿayin "occhio" (anche se non è sempre chiaro quando *ʿayin* va tradotto "aspetto") è possibile il riscontro in IE (greco e ant. irlandese). Alcune particolari specificità semantiche impongono la necessità di considerare i legami stretti tra lingua e cultura-ambiente: vd. sir. *pantā* "dorso della mano", con ampliamento del campo semantico, mentre in CIAD la specificità del lessico religioso sviluppa un significato di "tempio". Difficile stabilire quale sia la radice e quali i determinativi-suffissi; per questi ultimi occorrerebbe anche valutare se siano presenti una forma e significato costanti. Il monoconsonantismo della radice e la sua natura espressiva fanno ipotizzare una etimologia quanto meno pre-SEM e pre-IE, com'è spesso quando il lessico comune delle lingue attinge al lessico di base. Una convergenza CAM-SEM-IE è ipotesi di lavoro utile a giustificare i parallelismi sui due piani delle lingue. Il CAM-SEM-IE è un utile complemento della comparazione CAM-SEM e di quella IE, specialmente (ma non solo) quando l'espressione o il contenuto delle radici sono incerti, da cui la necessità di tener conto di tutto il CAM-SEM-IE. Le transizioni dei significati sono chiarite da relazioni metaforiche (bocca-imboccatura/porta/foce) oppure metonimiche (bocca-soffiare/mangiare) all'interno del campo. Il lessico del corpo mostra frequenti connessioni non solo all'interno del CAM-SEM, ma anche del CAM-SEM-IE, e per quanto antico (preistorico) si mostra già subito culturalizzato (specialmente le metafore sono spia di una cultura), così da vanificare una rigida distinzione tra lessico di base e lessico culturale. Il CAM-SEM-IE attende di trasformarsi in una ipotesi storica, ma la comparazione preistorica consente forse già oggi una maggiore contestualizzazione (vd. §§ 5 e 7). Alcuni indicatori semantici sono comuni ad altri organi: /parola, voce/ è comune a gola, naso [1], bocca, labbro [5], gola [6] e [7] e forse occhio [11]. Con varie sfumature, /sapere, intelletto/ è comune a gola, naso [1], bocca, labbro [5] e orecchio [10], /mangiare/ a bocca, labbro [5] e gola, palato [7], /soffiare/ a naso, bocca e gola [1], /apertura/, /idronimia/, /luce/ a occhio [11], /orlo/ a testa [9].

[3] SEM *g-w-l, g-l-l, g-w* ; EG *ğ-ꜣ* ; BERB *k-l/r* ; IE k^w/g^w*-w* /circolarità, oggetto rotondo; ventre, intestino o altra parte del corpo; **testa**, **cranio**; **volto**/ (in IE anche /**bocca**, **labbra**; **capelli**; piede, gamba; natiche/)

L'espressività è indicata in CAM-SEM sia dalla reduplicazione, sia – non è una novità – dallo sviluppo metaforico, che è presente anche in IE, con caratteristiche di 'primitività' nel duplice riferimento alla cultura-ambiente (manufatti, paesaggio agreste, astronomia).[5] Caratteristiche analoghe mostra gola [7], per cui di nuovo la reduplicazione è prevalente in CAM-SEM, a sottolineare la compattezza del campo lessicale. L'illusorietà della distinzione tra un lessico di base, naturale, e uno culturale sarebbe confermata dalla ipotetica ricostruzione etimologica di una *Urbedeutung* più astratta (circolarità). Alla luce della comparazione, il significato "cranio" è proprio del CAM-SEM, nell'IE prevale quello di "intestino". È questione aperta quando nella diversità dei contenuti si sia autorizzati a parlare di un regolare sviluppo metaforico. Si avverte la necessità di princìpî semantici alla base delle transizioni da un significato

5 Per l'eblaita, F. Vattioni ("Osservazioni ai testi di Ebla", in L. Cagni (a cura di), *Ebla 1975-1985. Dieci anni di studi linguistici e filologici. Atti del Convegno Internazionale. Napoli, 9-11 ott. 1985*, Napoli 1987, pp. 199-219, spec. pp. 210 s.) individua uno sviluppo metaforico /rotolare → pietra, stele/.

all'altro, utili a costruire una 'scienza' dell'etimologia. Nell'ipotesi di una cronologia relativa delle lingue, difficilmente accertabile, la convergenza-divergenza può essere legata a sottogruppi (qui le due 'sottofamiglie' CAM-SEM e IE divergono, limitatamente al significato "testa", convergono nel significato "intestino"), più probabilmente a singole lingue: ciò vale sia per un generico significato di "circolarità, oggetto rotondo", sia anche per "intestino" e "gola; cesto, vaso; ruota", significati comunque ben differenziati. Alcuni indicatori semantici sono comuni ad altri organi: /rotondo/ a collo gola [6] e [7], /volta, cima/ a capelli [4] e testa [9], /organo sessuale/ (maschile oppure femminile) a bocca, labbro [5]. Con varie sfumature /paesaggio agreste/ è comune a collo, gola [6] e testa [9].

[4] SEM *p/b-r* ; EG *p-r* ; CUSC *f-r* ; IE *p-r* /crescere, scaturire; vegetazione; (**capigliatura**, **capelli** fluenti)/

È presente, come spesso, l'omologia tra parti del corpo e ambiente naturale, da indicare come caratteristica di 'primitività'. Di nuovo, come in [3], lo sviluppo metaforico di "capelli fluenti" è proprio del SEM (parzialmente), mentre i richiami alla "vegetazione" (vd. ebl. *paraytum* "frutteto") sono condivisi da tutto il CAM-SEM-IE, analogamente a quanto si è potuto rilevare per [3] relativamente a "intestino". Anche qui la comparazione oscilla tra sottogruppi e singole lingue, da indicare come convergenze primarie specialmente nei casi in cui le lingue sono lontane nel tempo (ant. indiano e CUSC, accadico e gotico) e/o nello spazio (irlandese, ant. indiano, EG), ma con fluttuazioni tra due diverse temporalità, interna ed esterna (vd. anche [1]). È un caso in cui il parallelismo tra [CAM-]SEM e IE è sostenuto dalle versioni bibliche.[6] Lo sviluppo metaforico si aggiunge ad altri del campo lessicale, di tipo 'proporzionale' (vd. anche [5], [6], [7], [8], [10] e [11]), per cui vale il ricorso a un indicatore fisiologico-funzionale o causa-effetto (vegetazione, capelli fluenti :: crescere).[7] Sulle oscillazioni fra naturalità e culturalità per il lessico di base, vale quanto già osservato a proposito di [3]: il significato più astratto di "crescere" può essere indicato come primario rispetto a quelli più concreti di "vegetazione" e "capelli fluenti", sempre che siano confermabili questa transizione semantica e questa ricostruzione etimologica. Per quanto riguarda indicatori semantici comuni ad altri organi, /alto/ è comune a testa [9] e forse naso, bocca [1]; anche /discendenza/ è forse comune a naso, bocca [1]. Con qualche sfumatura, /volta, cima/ è comune a testa, cranio [3] e [9], /signore, capo/ a naso, bocca [1], /vegetazione/ a gola, collo [6] (specialmente in aram. giud.) e orecchio [10].

6 Sulla possibilità che il letteralismo delle antiche versioni bibliche confermi e/o consolidi una convergenza macroareale CAM-SEM-IE, concretamente attualizzata in molteplici usi testuali, rinvio al mio saggio "Il sonno della morte: un problema interlinguistico", *AIΩN* 16 (1994) [1996] pp. 11-30, spec. p. 29.

7 Su varî parallelismi e simmetrie nell'organizzazione del lessico di base CAM-SEM-IE, in particolare su opposizioni privative oppure proporzionali, cfr. dello scrivente "I *nomina primitiva* nella costruzione delle pre-protolingue", in R. B. Finazzi - P. Tornaghi (a cura di), *Cinquant'anni di ricerche linguistiche: problemi, risultati e prospettive per il terzo millennio. Atti del IX Convegno Internazionale di Linguisti, Milano 8-10 ott. 1998*, Alessandria 2001, pp. 505-525.

[5] SEM *š-p* ; IE *s-p* /**labbro, bocca**; mangiare, gustare; percepire, sapere/ (in SEM anche /**barba**; vulva/)

È segnalata l'antichità del lemma, per l'origine biconsonantica della radice. Comparativamente, il parallelismo tra CAM-SEM e IE è affidato alla convergenza tra lingue lontane nel tempo e nello spazio, come accadico e russo (Möller, *Wörterbuch*, *cit.*, p. 106). Lo sviluppo metaforico /labbro → succhiare, mangiare/, proprio del SEM (ma presente anche in latino e armeno), più quello /labbro → percepire, sapere/, di tutto il CAM-SEM-IE, è di tipo proporzionale, affine ad altri del campo lessicale, con indicatore fisiologico-funzionale o causa-effetto. Vanno chiarite alcune variazioni morfonologiche, forse non dovute a convergenza primaria (la *s* dell'EG *sp.t*, quella dell'ar. *sabara*, semanticamente vicino al lat. *sapere*), ma a rideterminazione morfologica e reinterpretazione semantica. Lo sviluppo metaforico /labbro → percepire, sapere/ è largamente diffuso,[8] oscillante tra leggi storico-umane e organico-naturali. Di questa oscillazione occorrerebbe trovare conferma su entrambi i piani del segno; in questo caso, però, sul piano dell'espressione non c'è evidenza di espressività, cioè di motivazione iconica, ma solo di antichità. Indicatori semantici comuni ad altri organi sono: /mangiare/ comune a gola, palato [7] (però solo con varie sfumature in IE) e bocca, labbro [2]; /barba/ è forse comune a naso, bocca [1]. Con varie sfumature, /sapere, intelletto/ è comune a gola, naso [1], bocca, labbro [2] e orecchio [10], /organo sessuale/ (maschile oppure femminile) a testa, cranio [3], /parola, voce/ a gola, naso [1], bocca, labbro [2], gola [6] e [7] e forse occhio [11].

[6] SEM *ʿ-n-ḳ* ; EG *y-n-ḳ* ; CUSC *h-l-ḳ* ; IE *ə-n-k* /piegare, curvare; **collo, nuca**; **gola**; gomito/

Di nuovo, nel riferimento al campo lessicale, ritorna uno sviluppo metaforico di tipo proporzionale (indicatore fisiologico-funzionale) /collo → piegare/, che si ricostruisce come *Urbedeutung* in una comparazione formale astratta. La motivazione segnica associa collo-gola ad altre parti del corpo (il gomito non è parte alta) e soprattutto, in un'interessante omologia con cultura-ambiente, al paesaggio (idrico e agreste) e a varî manufatti, in un rapporto logico di somiglianza (iconicità). Una probabile conferma dell'uso già arcaico di questa metafora radicale viene dall'ebl. *ʿinḳu(m)*, *ʿenḳu(m)*, acc. *unḳu* "anello, sigillo". L'indeterminatezza /collo-piegare/ è CAM-SEM-IE, come altre, ma non tutte: /collana-anello/, /gancio-uncino/ e soprattutto /ramo/ sono forse specificazioni secondarie. Il significato di "gola" collide con [1] e [7], ma il valore dei lemmi nel campo non è pari a quello di tessere di mosaico, considerata la loro natura non interamente e non radicalmente arbitraria. Indicatori semantici comuni ad altri organi sono: /rotondo/ comune a testa, cranio [3] e gola, collo [7], /parola, voce/ a gola, naso [1], bocca, labbro [2] e [5], gola [7] e forse occhio [11]. Con varie sfumature, /paesaggio agreste/ è comune a testa, cranio [3] e [9], /vegetazione/ (specialmente in aram. giud.) a capelli [4] e orecchio [10].

---

8 Cfr. Fronzaroli, "Studi", *cit.* 26 (1971) pp. 607 e 630 (N. 7.11); G. Conti, "Arcaismi in eblaita", in P. Fronzaroli (a cura di), *Studies on the Language of Ebla*, Firenze 1984, pp. 159-172, spec. pp. 170 s.

[7] SEM *g-r* ; BERB. *g-r*, CUSC. *g-r*, IE *g^{w}-r/l* /rotondo, vortice; **gola**, **palato**; **nuca**, **collo**; rumore, suono, voce/ (in SEM anche /**criniera**/)

La reduplicazione è prevalente in CAM-SEM, presente tuttavia anche in ant. indiano, greco e latino; un'espressività legata al rumore del deglutire, in forma di *Schallwort*, è comune a tutto il CAM-SEM-IE. Anche il tipo proporzionale dello sviluppo metaforico è una caratteristica del campo lessicale comune al CAM-SEM-IE. Comparativamente, convergenze e divergenze riguardano specifiche lingue negli sviluppi metaforici, ma il significato di "gola", se non è esso stesso – come possibile – una metafora rispetto al più astratto "rotondo", è CAM-SEM-IE. Il lemma mostra un lessico di base oscillante fra natura e cultura, fra universalità e generalità. Una caratteristica di 'primitività' è legata, come spesso, al duplice riferimento a cultura-ambiente, con omologia tra parti del corpo e ambiente naturale, specialmente mondo animale, tale da riflettere una visione del mondo, in una contestualizzazione che – considerata l'antichità della radice, più 'primitiva' che arcaica – può qualificarsi come preistorica, ancor più tenuto conto che è preistorica, perché fuori della storia, già la ricostruzione di una protolingua. Indicatori semantici comuni ad altri organi sono: /rotondo/ comune a testa, cranio [3] e collo, gola [6], /parola, voce/ comune a gola, naso [1] e gola [6], bocca, labbro [2] e [5] e forse occhio [11], /mangiare/ comune a bocca, labbro [2] e [5], /desiderio, avidità/ comune a gola, naso [1].

[8] SEM *m-ḫ-ḫ* (*m-ḥ-ḥ*); EG. *m-ḥ*, CUSC. *m/b-ḥ/g* ; IE *m-s-g* /riempire, essere pieno; midollo; **cervello**, **cranio**/

Nell'ipotesi di uno sviluppo metaforico /midollo → riempire, essere pieno/, riaffiora il tipo proporzionale che è caratteristico del campo lessicale; ma la transizione di significati, che non è attestata dall'ebl. *muḫḫum* "la parte superiore (della testa)", è non si sa quanto logica (speculativa) oppure storica (temporale). In ogni caso il significato, più astratto come spesso nel lessico di base, di "riempire, essere pieno" è proprio del CAM-SEM, mentre quello di "midollo, cervello" è CAM-SEM-IE. Inoltre, in una comparazione formale astratta che mirasse alla ricostruzione etimologica di una *Urbedeutung*, il significato di "riempire, essere pieno" è l'unico in grado di giustificare un'ampia convergenza di significati diversi (midollo [anche di piante], cervello, tuorlo). Due divergenze, più di altre, sembrano variazioni da riferire a una cultura-ambiente: i significati in ebraico di "vigore, forza", in accadico di "cranio", forse una specializzazione secondaria. Un indicatore semantico comune ad altri organi è quello di /forza/, che è comune a naso, bocca [1] e testa, fronte [9].

[9] SEM *g-b-h*, CIAD. *g-b/p/w* ; IE *g^{h}-b^{h}* /alto; vetta; **testa**, **calvo**; **fronte**; cervello (?)/

Come per [8], e con maggiore evidenza, si può postulare una transizione di significati, da quello più astratto (come spesso nel lessico di base) di "essere alto" a "fronte, testa". "Fronte" è più CAM-SEM, "testa" più IE: una divergenza che riguarda in questo caso più i due sottogruppi linguistici, che non le specifiche lingue. Nell'appartenenza al campo lessicale, la metafora si costruisce su un indicatore topografico-anatomico, non fisiologico-funzionale. Un carattere di 'primitività' ha il riferimento alla cultura-ambiente: "vetta, monte" è CAM-SEM-IE.

Il significato dell'acc. *gabbu* (*gappu* ?) "cervello (di animale)", se confermato, sarebbe in collisione con [8]. Indicatori semantici comuni ad altri organi sono: /alto/ comune a capelli [4] e forse naso, bocca [1], /forza/ comune a gola, naso, bocca [1] e cranio, cervello [8], /volta, cima/ comune a testa, cranio [3] e capelli [4], /paesaggio agreste/ comune a testa, cranio [3] e collo [6], /orlo/ comune a bocca, labbro [2].

[10] SEM *ʾ -ḏ-n*, EG. *y-d-n*, CIAD. *ʾ-d-n* ; IE *ə-d* /acuto, appuntito; **orecchio**, attento; guglia; abete/

Fronzaroli ("Studi", *cit.* 19/1964, 255) ne rileva la 'primitività', al pari di *ʾ-n-p* "naso". In riferimento al campo lessico-semantico del corpo, un aspetto di motivazione segnica è evidenziato soprattutto dalla sovrapposizione di radici (omonimia) nell'àmbito dell'IE. Una reinterpretazione semantica può indicare il significato "vedere" dell'ittita, con estensione a un'altra parte vitale della testa. È una sovrapposizione non ben sostenuta da un CAM-SEM-IE, se pure la corradicalità 'nostratica' è più manifesta per [10] che non sia per [2], con interessanti sovrapposizioni semantiche anche per il [CAM-]SEM, come evidenzia in ebraico la sinonimia di *pānîm* (per Cohen, *Essai, cit.*, p. 171, NN. 380 e 380 *bis* corradicale di *peh* [2]) con *ʾōzen* [10] e con **ʿēnayim* ([11]). Le sovrapposizioni tra organi della parte alta del corpo sono frequenti, contravvenendo al ben noto *horror synonymorum*: l'ebr. *pānîm* può indicare lo sguardo degli occhi e diventare perciò quasi-sinonimo di **ʿēnayim* "occhi", analogamente *lipnê* rispetto a *leʿēnê*, il sintagma /*str*, hiph. + *pānîm*/ "nascondere lo sguardo" equivale a quello /*ʿlm*, hiph. + *ʾōzen*/ "nascondere l'orecchio", espressioni che richiamano la separazione totale di una persona da un evento. Parallelamente, in IE **ōus-* "bocca" e **ōus-* "orecchio" sono omonimi (Pok. pp. 784 e 785).[9] Alla radice [10] per orecchio può essere ricondotto forse l'itt. *auš-* "vedere". Che il rotacismo del lat. *auris* sia una rideterminazione morfologica è ipotesi gratuita, che servirebbe solo a far luce su una convergenza secondaria tra latino e accadico, che è però contraddetta dal carattere 'primitivo' dell'isoglossa. Un'altra variazione è quella *d-ǯ* che si manifesta nell'àmbito del CAM-SEM (EG *ỉdn* "orecchio") e che Orel-Stolbova, *Dictionary, cit.*, p. 126 valuta come inattesa; ma vd. anche in lat. *audio* e *oboedio* rispetto ad *auris* < **ausi-*. Il campo rende manifesti parallelismi e simmetrie, specialmente in quegli sviluppi metaforici-metonimici di tipo proporzionale, come bocca :: parlare, mangiare, baciare = orecchio :: fare attenzione, ascoltare (indicatori fisiologico-funzionali), oppure:

9 Sulle sovrapposizioni tra organi della parte alta del corpo in IE, specialmente testa, orecchio e occhio, cfr. anche C. A. Mastrelli, "Le denominazioni indeuropee della "testa"", in *Mille. I dibattiti del Circolo Linguistico Fiorentino. 1945-1970*, Firenze 1970, pp. 103-117, spec. pp. 110 s. Analoghe sovrapposizioni sul piano del contenuto trovano riscontro anche nelle lingue negro-africane, per esempio le denominazioni del naso, dell'orecchio e talvolta della testa (anche del dente) sono metafore riconducibili ai significati di "punta, vertice, estremità", quelle dell'occhio inoltre esprimono i significati sia di "faccia", sia anche di "vedere, intendere", quelle della bocca i significati di "orifizio, apertura"; cfr. L. Homburger, *Noms des parties du corps dans les langues négro-africaines*, Paris 1929, pp. 54-68, spec. p. 55 n. 1; pp. 59-66; pp. 69-80, spec. pp. 69 s. Su numerose concordanze e corrispondenze a varî livelli tra EG-copto e lingue negro-africane, nell'intendimento di dimostrare l'illusorietà delle tradizionali 'famiglie' linguistiche, cfr. anche Th. Obenga, "Égyptien ancien et négro-africain", *CFS* 27 (1970-1972) pp. 65-92.

bocca :: imboccatura, foce = orecchio :: guglia, abete = occhio :: acqua, fonte, pozzo. È un carattere anche questo di 'primitività', relativo a un'omologia tra parti del corpo e ambiente naturale, come evidenziano le estensioni di significato in varî àmbiti linguistici, negro-africano oppure austronesiano. Gli sviluppi metaforici sono particolarmente importanti, sia perché impongono la considerazione di uno stretto legame tra lingua e ambiente, sia perché danno forza a una convergenza CAM-SEM-IE: così /orecchio (spec. di animale) → guglia, abete/, come pure /bocca → imboccatura, foce/, anche /occhio → acqua, fonte, pozzo/, quest'ultimo uno sviluppo più marcatamente CAM-SEM (vd. però lat. *aestus*).Le convergenze CAM-SEM-IE, se non sono da valutare come del tutto 'elementari' (in certa misura sono sempre e anche elementari), hanno caratteristica di primarietà quando e quanto più le lingue sono lontane nel tempo e/o nello spazio. L'orecchio è sinonimo di /attenzione/ e di /ascolto/ in molte lingue lontane sia nel tempo che nello spazio, mentre per /guglia, abete/ la lontananza nello spazio è più marcata di quella nel tempo: in questo caso, però, la valutazione può essere anche molto diversa, in termini più speculativi di 'primitività' più che di arcaicità, investendo lingue (etiopico, ant. prussiano, ant. slavo eccl.) di grande spessore sul piano della comparazione-ricostruzione (spesso l'arealità supplisce alla documentazione cronologica tarda). Indicatori semantici comuni ad altri organi sono: /sapere, intelletto/ comune a gola, naso [1], bocca, labbro [2] e [5], /vegetazione/ comune a capelli [4] e collo [6], forse anche /vedere/ comune a occhio [11].

[11] SEM *ʿ-y-n*, EG. *ʿ-y-n/r/l*, *ʿ-n*, *ʾ/y-r*, CUSC. *ʿ-ğ-l/n*, *ʾ-n*, BERB. *ʿ-l/n*, CIAD. *ʿ-ğ-n*, *ʾ/y-n/r*, (*ʾ-d*); IE *ə-k*^{w} (*ə-y* ?) /**occhio**; vedere, guardare; faccia; acqua, fonte; finestra; ardere, splendere, giorno/

Il riferimento al campo semantico appare prevalente rispetto all'etimologia e i parallelismi tra le lingue – specialmente CAM-SEM-IE – appaiono come il risultato di rideterminazioni morfologiche e reinterpretazioni semantiche. Ciò dà forza alla motivazione (o relativa arbitrarietà) dei segni, motivazione implicita anche nel comune sviluppo metaforico, più marcatamente CAM-SEM (ma vd. lat. *aestus* : ebr. *ʿayām*), e – in una concezione storica – tale da accreditare una transizione di significati dal figurato al proprio, più che in senso contrario: ciò vale soprattutto per i significati di "fonte, sorgente" (per Cohen, *Essai*, *cit.*, p. 89, NN. 63-64 un'omonimia radicale). Specialmente in una prospettiva CAM-SEM-IE, la ricostruzione di una radice incontra difficoltà, ma anche all'interno del CAM-SEM sono manifeste variazioni legate a condizioni di subfonematicità (specialmente la seconda consonante radicale). Alla motivazione segnica, di cui non fornisce attestazione l'ebl. *ʿaynum* "occhio", danno sostegno le sovrapposizioni semantiche tra bocca, volto, orecchio, occhio, cui si aggiunge quella del gr. ὄψ "occhio" e "voce". Non c'è omonimia, invece, tra acc. *īnu*, *ēnu* e *wapū*, *apū*. Lo sviluppo metaforico /occhio → vedere, guardare/ è proporzionale ad altri (bocca :: parlare = orecchio :: ascoltare; oppure bocca :: apertura = occhio :: finestra). In questi casi, le metafore fanno luce sui 'primitivi' semantici, fissando i confini tra generalità e universalità. Indicatori semantici comuni ad altri organi sono: /apertura/ comune a bocca, labbro [2]; /parola, voce/ è forse comune a gola, naso [1], bocca, labbro [2] e [5], gola [6] e [7], /vedere/ è forse comune a orecchio [10], ma limitatamente all'ittita. Con varie sfumature /idronimia/ e /luce/ sono comuni a bocca, labbro [2].

Resta da accertare per questi lemmi in quale misura il loro carattere di 'monconi' lessicali,[10] che li proietta molto oltre la protostoria, nella preistoria delle lingue SEM, faccia riferimento a una più specifica e culturalmente più marcata convergenza di tipo CAM-SEM-IE oppure a una più generica e meno marcata convergenza da qualificare come massimale. Tra questi due orientamenti e ipotesi di lavoro oscilla da sempre la definizione di 'nostratico'.

3) La comparazione CAM-SEM-IE

È stata ribadita più volte la necessità di considerare tutti i dati comparativi utili. Metodologicamente, dunque, non ci sono limitazioni a convergenze anche arealmente molto estese, all'ampliarsi ('a ventaglio') dei confini da una convergenza all'altra, a partire dal SEM per giungere al CAM-SEM e al CAM-SEM-IE, da ultimo a un 'nostratico' che inglobi progressivamente altre relazioni 'intergenetiche' (o 'interphyletiche'), fino presumibilmente ad abbracciare tutti i gruppi linguistici del protomondo.[11] Le limitazioni sono semmai d'ordine pratico. Ma, a sottolineare la priorità del metodo rispetto alla verifica, va tenuto presente che le stesse tradizionali 'famiglie' linguistiche, se pure viziate da uno splendido isolamento, sono frutto di una generalizzazione e di uno schematismo logico, di una formalizzazione dei dati comparativi che si può ritenere così necessaria e così poco 'chimerica'[12] da porsi essa stessa come presupposto di una successiva e solo possibile storicizzazione. Una realtà storica non esclude una costruzione astratta, condizione anzi indispensabile per una comparazione più o meno estesa.[13]

---

10 Cfr. dello scrivente "Cimrico *eryr* "aquila" ($\mathit{\exists_\chi R}$-): problemi e prospettive della ricerca etimologica", *AIΩN* 13 (1991) pp. 129-170, spec. p. 134, con richiamo a G. van Langenhove ed E. Raucq.

11 Cfr. C. Montella, "La macro-famiglia linguistica nostratica", *AIΩN* 11 (1989) pp. 245-262, spec. p. 260. Alla base degli studi di V. M. Illič-Svityč, A.B. Dolgopol'skij e J. H. Greenberg c'è il tentativo di istituire una relazione genetica tra IE, cartvelico (caucasico meridionale), afro-asiatico (CAM-SEM), uralo-iucaghiro, elamo-dravidico, altaico, in parte anche sumero. È da tener presente anche che una convergenza più estesa, ad abbracciare con il 'nostratico' un proto-australiano, come nella proposta di M. Ruhlen, *On the Origin of Languages. Studies in Linguistic Taxonomy*, Stanford, Calif. 1994, pp. 261-276, innalzerebbe la cronologia a circa 40 mila anni fa.

12 Sulla chimericità già di un protoSEM, cfr. invece G. Garbini, "Convergenze indeuropeo-semitiche tra preistoria e protostoria", *AIΩN* 10 (1988) pp. 67-80, spec. p. 78.

13 Cfr. É. Benveniste, *Origines de la formation des noms en indo-européen*, Paris 1962 e A. Morpurgo Davies, "Il metodo comparativo, passato e presente", *AIΩN* 10 (1988) pp. 27-48, spec. p. 33, anche 43 e 45, a proposito dei coefficienti sonantici di Saussure e di un'opportuna distinzione tra formalizzazione e intuizione.

Della necessità che una comparazione – poco importa se più o meno estesa – approdi a un tentativo di ricostruzione danno evidenza i problemi stessi della lessicografia comparativa nei varî àmbiti, mettendo in risalto anche la tendenza ad abbracciare gruppi linguistici diversi. Quanto è già stato sottolineato per il SEM,[14] la difficoltà a distinguere tra isoglosse genealogiche (queste possono essere attestate da una sola oppure più lingue) e prestiti (questi, a loro volta, possono interessare il SEM comune oppure singole lingue storiche), trova riscontro anche fra gli stessi sostenitori moscoviti dell'ipotesi 'nostratica', sia pure con posizioni articolate e a volte contrastanti.[15] La comparazione 'nostratica' è da tempo e ancor oggi sempre più avviata al superamento del concetto di parentela pura, a favore di relazioni 'intergenetiche'. Che cosa rimane del lessico comune SEM tolti i lemmi di cui c'è attestazione fuori del SEM e quelli pre-SEM confluiti nelle lingue SEM? Il medesimo problema si può porre per altri gruppi linguistici. Lo sconfinamento nella preistoria è assicurato, tenuto conto che ogni convergenza, a partire dal SEM per giungere al CAM-SEM, anche senza procedere oltre, esige a livello ricostruttivo una cronologia notevolmente

14 Cfr. P. Fronzaroli, "Problemi della lessicografia comparativa semitica", *OA* 11 (1972) pp. 241-262, spec. p. 244, anche *Id.*, "On the Common Semitic Lexicon and Its Ecological and Cultural Background", in J. Bynon - Th. Bynon (a cura di), *Hamito-Semitica. Proceedings of a Colloquium held by the Historical Section of the Linguistic Association (Great Britain) at the School of Oriental and African Studies, University of London, on the 18th, 19th and 20th of March 1970*, The Hague 1975, pp. 43-53, spec. p. 43.

15 A margine e a conferma di questo diffuso orientamento, si può osservare che una comparazione 'di massa' (multilaterale) con riferimento al lessico di base dovrebbe essere garanzia di una comune origine delle lingue e non dovrebbe perciò essere messa in discussione da prestiti. È l'orientamento seguito, per esempio, da O. Rößler ("Berberisch-Tschadisches Kernvokabular", *Africana Marburgensia* 12/1979, pp. 20-32) e funzionale a un'estesa comparazione CAM-SEM. E tuttavia è facile rilevare come il lessico di base non sia esente da prestiti, così che la ricerca etimologica finisce per oscillare tra un approccio interno e uno esterno. Le convergenze potranno essere primarie (antecedenti a uno stato di separazione) oppure secondarie (susseguenti a uno stato di separazione), divise tra etimologie prime (isoglosse genealogiche) ed etimologie altre (seconde o terze, per conflitti omonimici e interferenze da contatto), tra monogenesi, allogenesi e/o poligenesi. Cfr. Y. Malkiel, "Between Monogenesis and Polygenesis", in J. P. Maher - A.R. Bomhard - E. F. K. Kœrner (a cura di), *Papers from the 3th International Conference on Historical Linguistics*, Amsterdam 1982, pp. 235-272; H. Wagner ("Indogermanisch-Vorderasiatisch-Mediterranes", *KZ* 75/1957, pp. 58-75, spec. pp. 66 s.), nell'escludere una *Urverwandtschaft*, proiettava già nel III millennio i più antichi contatti tra SEM (anche sumero) e IE. F. Ribezzo, nella 'Discussione' (p. 334) a H. Pedersen, "Il problema delle parentele tra i grandi gruppi linguistici", in B. Migliorini - V. Pisani (a cura di), *Atti del III Congresso Internazionale dei Linguisti, Roma 19-26 sett. 1933*, Firenze 1935, pp. 328-333, a sostegno di una diversità cronologica, parlava anche di una 'postaffinità', come affinità tra gruppi linguistici anche da 'sostrato'.

alta.[16] Il richiamo esclusivo alle specifiche protolingue è uno stadio fondamentale e obbligatorio, ma pur sempre uno stadio provvisorio nella formalizzazione dei dati comparativi, che non può essere troppo enfatizzato.

4) 'Primitivo' linguistico e migrazioni preistoriche

È in discussione il numero delle lingue da comparare: più si allarga il confronto e più appare vistoso lo sconfinamento nella preistoria, con valutazioni che sono il più delle volte negative, anche negli stessi nostraticisti. Ma nella convergenza tra CAM-SEM e IE può apparire pretestuosa, oltre che radicalizzata, la sottolineatura della debolezza dei confronti grammaticali.[17] Più correttamente, il CAM-SEM-IE può essere testimonianza di una neutralità grammaticale precedente una rigida dualità di fonologia e grammatica, uno stadio pre-grammaticale con sue specifiche modalità tipologiche, caratterizzato da istanze grammaticali 'naturali' di tipo analogico. Fermo restando l'interesse per l'individuazione di fasi più arcaiche, di cui per il SEM è preziosa testimonianza oggi l'eblaita malgrado un'ancora limitata conoscenza lessicale,[18] il 'terrore della preistoria'[19] e il sospetto 'pre-darwiniano' di speculazioni glottogoniche si pongono come pregiudiziali barriere a una ricerca sul 'primitivo' delle lingue, consigliando generalmente di bloccare la cronologia delle protolingue alla vigilia della storia. Eppure c'è la convinzione che la tradizionale grammatica stessa comparata non sia esente da speculazioni più glottogoniche e che le altrettanto tradizionali protolingue non differiscano molto da più ampie convergen-

16 Questa nella fattispecie può, secondo l'ipotesi formulata da I. M. Diakonoff ("An Evaluation of Eblaite", in Fronzaroli, *Language of Ebla*, *cit.*, pp. 1-10, spec. p. 2), oscillare tra 6/7 millenni fa per il SEM e 10/12 millenni fa per il CAM-SEM!

17 Cfr., per esempio, K. Petráček, *Altägyptisch, Hamitosemitisch und ihre Beziehungen zu einigen Sprachfamilien in Afrika und Asien*, Praha 1988, pp. 137-139.

18 Alla definizione da parte di P. Fronzaroli ("Lingua e testo negli Archivi di Ebla", *La parola del passato* 46/1991, pp. 220-236, spec. p. 223) dell'eblaita come tipo linguistico SEM arcaico che si è continuato nell'accadico, si aggiunge ancora recentemente la constatazione di una incompleta comprensione del lessico eblaita (*Id.*, "Fonti di lessico nei testi di Ebla, *SEL* 12/1995, pp. 51-64, spec. p. 57).

19 Come lo definisce Garbini, "Convergenze", *cit.*, p. 67; e, tuttavia, già P. Fronzaroli ("La semitistica", in *Gli studi sul Vicino Oriente in Italia dal 1921 al 1970*, I. *L'Oriente preislamico*, Roma 1971, pp. 11-31, spec. p. 18) qualificava come centrale alla definizione della semitistica il problema della preistoria dei popoli di lingua semitica e della formazione delle lingue storiche.

ze, incoraggiate dai medesimi schematismi,[20] comunque li si voglia valutare, spesso però non 'fortuiti'. Alla luce di queste considerazioni, è possibile forse cogliere una transizione tra arcaico e 'primitivo', ipotizzando alla lontana[21] e in parziale accordo con certo nostraticismo moscovita una forte rassomiglianza tra le protolingue e una loro convergenza attorno al paleolitico superiore, ventimila o più anni fa, prima del mesolitico e dopo il paleolitico superiore, in accordo con un orientamento ecologico e in una relazione stretta tra evoluzione genetica ed evoluzione linguistica, lasciando riaffiorare anche il fantasma di un 'caro estinto', la monogenesi del linguaggio.[22]

Le migrazioni preistoriche, argomento di cui si occupa la paleoantropologia, possono fare un po' di luce su convergenze e divergenze linguistiche, specialmente sugli antefatti di un CAM-SEM-IE.[23] Se pure a uno stadio di cronologia relativamente molto più bassa, una convergenza CAM-SEM-IE e, più sicuramente, una CAM-SEM si possono però ritenere analogiche di quell'origine africana dei moderni gruppi umani, giustificando l'ipotesi di una lingua ancestrale euro-afro-asiatica.[24] La

---

20 C. Vallini (*Speculazioni e modelli nell'etimologia della grammatica*, *AIΩN* 9/1987, pp. 15-81, spec. p. 74) valuta, perciò, che l'attuale grammatica comparata non debba più temere i rischi di una glottogonia a-scientifica, in quanto speculativa.

21 Cfr. R. W. Wescott, "Protolinguistics: The Study of Protolanguages as an Aid to Glossogonic Research", in S. R. Harnad - H. D. Steklis - J. Lancaster (a cura di), *Origins and Evolution of Language and Speech*, New York 1976, pp. 104 s.

22 Sull'analogia tra evoluzione biologica ed evoluzione linguistica, sul metodo linguistico-comparativo e sulle sue possibilità di cogliere interrelazioni tra le lingue già attorno a 15/20 mila anni fa, inoltre sulle incognite di una *Proto-Human hypothesis* proiettata molto tempo prima attorno a 100 mila anni fa, cfr. I. Dyen, "Genetic Classification in Linguistics and Biology", in G. Cardona - N. H. Zide (a cura di), *Festschrift for Henry Hoenigswald. On the Occasion of his Seventieth Birthday*, Tübingen 1987, pp. 101-108, spec. p. 101: "In fact there is now good reason to believe that all human (natural) languages have a common source".

23 I dati genetici basati sull'analisi del DNA mitocondriale del nucleo cellulare suggerirebbero un'origine africana recente per tutti i gruppi umani moderni, dando sostegno all'ipotesi *out of Africa* (o 'arca di Noè') e riformulando sotto forma di una teoria – detta della 'rapida sostituzione' – le vecchie teorie monogenetiche sull'origine dell'uomo, anche se si possono additare altre aree geografiche come ipotetiche culle dell'uomo moderno (dal medio-vicino oriente al sud della Cina e all'Australia). Ma una ricca collezione di fossili proviene dal Sudafrica, dalla Tanzania, dal Kenya, dall'Etiopia, dal Nordafrica ed è l'Africa l'unico continente a mostrare tutti i passi del genere umano, dai primi *Hominidae* all'*Homo erectus*, ai primi testimoni dell'*Homo sapiens sapiens*.

24 È da credere, infatti, che le caratteristiche del SEM discendano dall'Africa nord-occidentale del V millennio a.C. e che, in un processo ad andata e ritorno, le lingue berbere dell'Africa nord-occidentale possano costituire a loro volta – secondo l'ipotesi formulata da O. Rößler ("Der semitische Charakter der libyschen Sprache", *ZA* 50/1962, pp. 121-150) – un'emanazione-sopravvivenza di un antico idioma SEM. All'ipotesi ha dato sostegno W. von Soden, "Sprachfamilien und Einzelsprachen

possibilità, poi, di relazioni 'intergenetiche' molto più estese tra gruppi linguistici – al di là del CAM-SEM-IE un 'nostratico' massimale – è ancora al momento di difficile valutazione. Oltre a ciò, se le metafore 'nostratiche' del corpo siano garanzia di 'culturalità' oppure di 'naturalità' è prematuro dirlo: dipende dalla loro maggiore o minore diffusione areale, per cui resta enigmatico l'interrogativo dove finisca il 'nostratico': è una conferma che la distinzione tra un lessico di base e un lessico culturale è da ritenersi come largamente illusoria.[25]

5) Paleoecologia, lessico di base ed etimologie 'remote'

Il problema del rapporto tra cultura e ambiente investe più in particolare quello del rapporto tra lingue e dati extralinguistici attinenti in egual modo alla preistoria e alla storia. Nel richiamo all'ambiente tutto è ecologia, secondo un orientamento sempre più diffuso in tempi recenti, che fa appello a un'ecologia come termine di mediazione tra natura e cultura.[26] A sostegno di una ricostruzione non aridamente astratta,

---

im Altsemitischen: Akkadisch und Eblaitisch", in Fronzaroli, *Language of Ebla*, *cit.*, pp. 13 s. P. Zima ("Songhay, Hausa and Chadic. Preliminary Notes on Lexical Affinities", in S. Brauner - E. Wolff (a cura di), *Progressive Traditions in African and Oriental Studies*, Berlin 1988, pp. 185-192) parla di una 'creolizzazione' che investe per intero le lingue africane e chiama in causa per le lingue CIAD, in particolare, varie ipotesi ('nostratico', monogenesi, altre teorie e modelli di classificazione). All'ipotesi di un'emanazione del CAM-SEM dall'Africa dà sostegno K. Petráček, *Altägyptisch*, *cit.*, pp. 130 s. e p. 142 n. 25, sulla scia di un'antica tradizione di studi, coronata dal saggio di I. M. Diakonoff, *Semito-Hamitic Languages*, Moscow 1965, che ha portato anche ad avventurare un'antichissima origine africana dell'IE.

25 Occorre comunque ricordare come proprio i dati genetici mostrino l'esistenza di una certa affinità fra popolazioni geograficamente anche molto lontane, per esempio, tra asiatici e amerindi del sud, a riprova di una notevole facilità di 'meticciamento' tra i diversi gruppi umani. Al riguardo possono essere formulate varie ipotesi: con l'ipotesi di una monogenesi africana e quella di un'evoluzione multiregionale, una terza ipotesi postula un'ibridizzazione di popolazioni provenienti dall'Africa con popolazioni arcaiche di varie parti del mondo, in un incrocio fertile tra *Homo sapiens sapiens* e popolazioni pre-moderne. Sui varî apporti della paleoantropologia all'evoluzione umana e alle migrazioni preistoriche, cfr. spec. F. H. Smith - F. Spencer (a cura di), *The Origins of Modern Humans. A World Survey of the Fossil Evidence*, New York 1984 e P. Mellars - C. Stringer (a cura di), *The Human Revolution. Behavioural and Biological Perspective in the Origins of Modern Humans*, Princeton, N. J. 1989.

26 Cfr. W. Tyloch, "The Evidence of the Proto-Lexicon for the Cultural Background of the Semitic Peoples", in Bynon - Bynon, *Hamito-Semitica*, *cit.*, pp. 55-61, che attribuisce al *background* ecologico del SEM alcune radici relative all'allevamento e all'agricoltura. Anche per quanto riguarda Ebla, sono noti felici esempi di analisi dei testi amministrativi con ricorso alla paleoecologia, volti a dimostrare come Ebla sia stata una scoperta, oltre che archeologica, anche antropologica; cfr., per esempio, A. De Maigret, "La paleoecologia di Ebla alla luce dei testi amministrativi", in L. Cagni (a cura

proiettata in un passato più o meno definito, anche quando preistorico, il lessico di base – specialmente le denominazioni del corpo – manifesta un sapere non linguistico.[27] Il rilievo è importante per quanto riguarda le metafore CAM-SEM-IE del corpo, riunite ora da correlazioni di suono e di senso, ora da indicatori semantici comuni (vd. TABB. 1 e 2).[28]

Le denominazioni SEM del corpo verificano un'ampia convergenza CAM-SEM-IE, oltre che CAM-SEM, anche se la loro naturalità, più che culturalità – questa è minima rispetto ad altri 'campi', per eccellenza quello della religione[29]-, può essere di ostacolo a una visione etnobiologica del passato.[30] Il loro carattere elementare è insito in radici ora biconsonantiche, ora addirittura monoconsonantiche.[31] Per

---

di), *Il bilinguismo a Ebla. Atti del Convegno Internazionale. Napoli, 19-22 apr. 1982*, Napoli 1984, pp. 329-335 e K. Butz, "Ökologie: Ebla. Gegenstand und Wörter", in L. Cagni, *Ebla 1975-1985, cit.*, pp. 313-351.

27 È di rilevante interesse, a questo proposito, come P. Fronzaroli porti a sostegno di un metodo per 'campi associativi' esempi di associazioni lessicali che hanno origine dall'associazione stessa dei referenti, affiancando o anzi avvalorando i risultati della semantica strutturale. Non si tratta, come per altri 'campi', di una possibilità di contestualizzazione da mettere in relazione a circostanze ambientali e/o climatiche (cfr. P. Fronzaroli, "Réflexions sur la paléontologie linguistique", in A. Caquot - D. Cohen (a cura di), *Actes du premier congrès international de linguistique sémitique et chamito-sémitique, Paris 1969*, The Hague 1974, pp. 173-180, spec. p. 174; anche se Homburger, *Noms, cit.*, p. 66 ha avvertito la necessità di un esame etnografico e antropometrico relativamente a variazioni dialettali negro-africane sulle denominazioni del naso), ma piuttosto di una spia di 'primitività' insita in una concezione in qualche caso corporea del linguaggio, nel simbolismo fonetico di un esiguo numero di elementi significanti e submorfemici, in una nebulizzazione del significato in forma apparente di 'disordine' del linguaggio.

28 Vd. avanti, § 7; mancherebbe, infatti, secondo P. Fronzaroli ("Problems of a Semitic Etymological Dictionary", in *Id.* (a cura di), *Studies on Semitic Lexicography*, Firenze 1973, pp. 1-24, spec. p. 17), la possibilità di una contestualizzazione per una comparazione preistorica.

29 Come rileva P. Fronzaroli, "Antefatti semitico-comuni nella religione dei Patriarchi", *Bollettino dell'Amicizia Ebraico-Cristiana di Firenze*, N.S. 2 (1967) pp. 1-7, spec. p. 1.

30 Come evidenziava G. R. Cardona, "Dati linguistici e modelli antropologici", *AIΩN* 10 (1988) pp. 97-115, spec. pp. 104 ss.; vd. anche, più recentemente, l'importante e imponente miscellanea di H. Chappell - W. McGregor (a cura di), *The Grammar of Inalienability. A Typological Perspective on Body Part Terms and the Part-Whole Relation*, Berlin - New York 1996.

31 Per un confronto tra radici generalmente biconsonantiche EG e protoIE, mentre altre triconsonantiche sono riconoscibili come derivate da radici biconsonantiche, cfr. per es. P. Lavalade, "Correspondances entre l'égyptien et l'indo-européen", *BSLP* 80 (1985) pp. V-XII. Nella prospettiva di un'ampia convergenza linguistica, il richiamo esclusivo al consonantismo è d'obbligo in quanto solo le consonanti esprimono valori semantici in grado di assicurare alla comparazione un controllo parallelo sui due piani del segno, laddove il vocalismo assolve a varî livelli di analisi, per etimologie prime o altre, una funzione essenzialmente morfologica; cfr. A. Meillet, *Introduction à l'étude comparative des*

l'eblaita è un elemento arcaico importante la derivazione da una base biconsonantica, che è tangibilmente attestata in CAM-SEM a livello arcaico, anche nella fase preistorica dell'accadico, e che viene in soccorso di alcune etimologie.[32] Una convergenza CAM-SEM-IE può essere qualificata, poi, come storico-genealogica oppure anche tipologica, include inoltre – come ogni protolingua – tutto il lessico per intero, ivi compresi i prestiti, pur sviluppando di preferenza e per ipotesi di lavoro etimologie 'remote',[33] ma non solo queste. Soprattutto, essa non può essere relegata al modesto ruolo di *deus ex machina* – come tradizionalmente i 'sostrati' -, per la soluzione di problemi difficili o disperati, in ogni caso complementari: una 'nostraticità' solo di scarto è una formula un po' riduttiva. È possibile anzi che una convergenza CAM-SEM-IE dia nuova coerenza interpretativa ai testi delle lingue storiche, ampliando le nostre conoscenze lessicologiche.[34]

---

langues indo-européennes, Paris 1934[7], pp. 153 s. In accordo con questa prospettiva, è largamente accolta anche una larga supremazia del consonantismo sul vocalismo nella ricostruzione del CAM-SEM-IE.

32 Il determinativo non è spesso né identificabile con certezza, né forse necessario per una estesa comparazione CAM-SEM-IE; cfr. Conti, "Arcaismi", *cit.*, pp. 166 s. (sulle attestazioni eblaite della coniugazione bilittera) e Rapallo, "Cimrico *eryr*", *cit.*, p. 134 e n. 24 (sulla comparazione CAM-SEM-IE; con bibl.). La presenza in eblaita di tratti arcaici di eredità afroasiatica è sottolinata per esempio da Diakonoff, "An Evaluation of Eblaite", *cit.*, p. 7. Ma va fatta menzione anche, con K. Petráček ("Les catégories flexionnelles en eblaïte", in Fronzaroli, *Language of Ebla*, *cit.*, pp. 25-57, spec. pp. 25 s. e n. 2, con bibl.), di relazioni che l'eblaita intrattiene con lingue non SEM; con lui anche K. Butz ("Bilinguismus als Katalysator", in Cagni, *Il bilinguismo a Ebla*, *cit.*, pp. 99-138, spec. p. 111) parla di Ebla come punto d'incrocio di più influssi, fra Balcani, Anatolia e Mesopotamia e I. J. Gelb ("The Language of Ebla in the Light of the Sources from Ebla, Mari, and Babylonia", in L. Cagni, *Ebla 1975-1985*, *cit.*, p. 55) chiama in causa una più antica parentela 'nostratica' a spiegazione di alcuni teonimi che sfuggono a un'etimologia SEM.

33 Cfr., su entrambe le prospettive, P. Fronzaroli, "Problemi della lessicografia comparativa semitica", *OA* 11 (1972) pp. 241-262, spec. pp. 244 e 248 s. e *Id.*, "Common Semitic Lexicon", *cit.*, p. 45. Non vanno ignorati gli aspetti più tipologici della convergenza tra le lingue.

34 Per alcune verifiche dello scrivente, rinvio spec. a "Sangue camito-semitico e sangue indeuropeo: un'ipotesi 'nostratica'?", in F. Vattioni (a cura di), *Sangue e antropologia. Riti e culto*, Roma 1987, pp. 1765-1792 (= U. Rapallo, *La parola, il testo e la cultura. Linguistica e antropologia del "sangue"*, Roma 1985, pp. 57-84); "Cimrico *eryr*", *cit.*, pp. 129-170; "Linguistica e antropologia del sangue: convergenze macroareali", in F. Vattioni (a cura di), *Sangue e antropologia nel Medioevo*, Roma 1993, pp. 691-717; "Considerazioni sulle convergenze lessicali camito-semitico-indeuropee", in V. Brugnatelli (a cura di), *Sem Cam Iafet. Atti della 7ª Giornata di Studi Camito-Semitici e Indeuropei (Milano, 1° giugno 1993)*, Milano 1994, pp. 169-182; "Il sonno della morte", *cit.*, pp. 11-30. In una prospettiva indeuropeistica, non appare comunque metodologicamente corretta la pretesa di P. Meriggi ("Affinità strutturali fra indeuropeo e altre famiglie linguistiche", in *Indeuropeo e proto-*

È ipotizzabile inoltre un CAM-SEM-IE più o meno organico, anche se la ricostruzione include abitualmente rassomiglianze e differenze: ogni convergenza lessicale comporta, non l'eliminazione della diversità, ma un'omogeneizzazione e rimodellamento. Ma l'organicità delle lingue non può essere messa in discussione: per Humboldt tutte le lingue perché lingue, anche le più 'primitive', sono organiche e non è facile ipotizzare uno sviluppo graduale del linguaggio.[35] Ha interesse verificare che l'organicità sia risultato di dati al tempo stesso linguistici ed extralinguistici. Malgrado i tanti dubbi – etimologie fantasiose divise fra tradizionale e irrazionale, parziale utilizzazione delle lingue o loro documentazione lacunosa, arretratezza dell'indagine ricostruttiva e limiti individuali di conoscenza che renderebbero necessari gruppi di specialisti[36] -, la ricerca di grandi convergenze organiche trova sostegno, lontano nel tempo e in parallelo con i dati linguistici, in una grande omogeneità fra tutti i gruppi umani: non esistono infatti sottospecie in cui suddividere il moderno *Homo sapiens sapiens*.

6) Il campo lessicale del corpo: fra natura e cultura

La semantica del 'campo', di cui si conoscono precorrimenti nell'Ottocento, è utile a definire il significato in termini relazionali di parole, ma anche forse di referenza alla realtà.[37] Va sottolineata la compatibilità di una semantica strutturale con una ri-

---

storia. Atti del IV Convegno Internazionale di Linguisti. Milano, 6-10 sett. 1958, Milano 1961, pp. 31-38, spec. p. 33) che per una seria comparazione dell'IE occorra prima ricostruire il CAM-SEM.

35 Cfr., dopo L. Heilmann, "Strutturalismo e ricostruzione di protolingue. A proposito del nesso "ario-semitico"", in *Id.*, *Linguaggio, lingue, culture. Saggi linguistici e indologici*, Bologna 1983 [= in *Omagiu lui Alexandru Rosetti*, Bucureşti 1965, pp. 353-356], pp. 149-155, spec. p. 152, anche D. Di Cesare, "Origine del linguaggio e primitività delle lingue in Humboldt", *AIΩN* 12 (1990) pp. 115-140, spec. pp. 120 s. Ciò che vale per le lingue vale anche per i testi: questi, chissà quanto 'primitivi', per certo arcaici e conservativi, mostrano pur sempre una loro propria lingua funzionale; cfr., per l'eblaita, M. Bonechi, "Sulle attestazioni arcaiche del prefisso di coniugazione *ti*", in P. Fronzaroli (a cura di), *Miscellanea eblaitica*, 1, Firenze 1988, pp. 121-172, spec. p. 167.

36 Cfr. Fronzaroli, "Problemi della lessicografia", *cit.*, p. 241 e *Id.*, "Common Semitic Lexicon", *cit.*, p. 50; inoltre, W. G. Lambert, "The Language of ARET V 6 and 7", in P. Fronzaroli (a cura di), *Literature and Literary Language at Ebla*, Firenze 1992, pp. 41-62, spec. pp. 44 s., secondo il quale la lacunosità del materiale comparativo è di ostacolo alla collocazione del pur arcaico eblaita, tenuto conto che solo poche lingue SEM offrono una documentazione valida.

37 Affiora il ricordo dell''interpretante' di Peirce che, come rapporto paradigmatico tra segni, rende necessario il richiamo a una totalità-struttura. Cfr. Ch. S. Peirce, *Semiotica. I fondamenti della semiotica cognitiva*, Torino 1980 [trad. parziale da Cambridge, Mass. 1931-1935), spec. pp. 131-171 (con l''Introduzione' e la 'Presentazione' di M. A. Bonfantini, pp. XXI-LV e 119-130) e, su varî aspetti della semiosi peirciana, G. P. Caprettini, *Aspetti della semiotica. Principî e storia*, Torino 1980, pp.

cerca storico-culturale, ciò che equivale a dire che non esiste contraddizione tra un oggetto immediato, 'interno', in quanto conosciuto nel segno, un'idea o rappresentazione mentale secondo Ch. S. Peirce, e l'oggetto esterno, 'dinamico'. Lo studio della parte alta del corpo (ma non solo) conferma – come s'è detto – l'esistenza di associazioni lessicali che hanno origine dall'associazione stessa delle cose.[38] In questo senso, la scelta di un particolare 'campo', qual è quello del corpo, è stata mirata; i risultati dell'analisi variano, infatti, a seconda dei 'campi associativi'.[39] A un sommario controllo, il campo semantico – tra i cinque studiati da P. Fronzaroli – che registra il maggior numero di isoglosse CAM-SEM-IE è quello dell'anatomia e fisiologia, più del doppio della religione e dei fenomeni naturali, quasi il doppio rispetto alla natura domestica e all'alimentazione. È marcato anche il numero delle isoglosse nel campo della natura selvatica.

Ma una precisa quantificazione non è stata possibile per più motivi: 1) la disparità delle fonti bibliografiche: un massimo comun divisore, corrispondente al prodotto dei fattori comuni con l'esponente più basso, può venire dal confronto Fronzaroli-Devoto, suffragato da Möller e da Bomhard-Kerns, oltre che dall'*Essai* di M.

117-145 e V. M. Colapietro - Th. M. Olshewsky (a cura di), *Peirce Doctrine of Signs. Theory, Applications, and Connections*, Berlin 1995.

38 Vd. sopra, § 5. Secondo P. P. Friedrich ("Semantic Reconstruction", in W. Bright (a cura di), *International Encyclopedia of Linguistics*, Oxford 1992, III pp. 389-394, spec. p. 390), soprattutto il lessico del corpo, umano e animale, sarebbe determinato da fattori biologici di tipo universale, per quanto siano in gioco schemi logici probabili, mai necessari. Sulle strette corrispondenze tra 'tassie' linguistiche e 'tassie' biologiche in relazione all'origine del linguaggio, cfr. per es. Ruhlen, *Origin, cit.*, pp. 261 s. e p. 273. Al punto d'incontro ecologico fra natura e cultura, un campo semantico è basato su dati, oltre che linguistici, anche sempre biologici e storico-culturali, che la comparazione delle lingue mette in luce, con maggiore o minore evidenza in rapporto alla cronologia dei dati stessi. Ma, se l'astrattezza della ricostruzione non deve condurre fuori della storia, investendo per intero tutto il lessico, inclusi i prestiti, il lessico stesso oscilla tra natura e cultura, tra universalità e generalità, non escluse radici onomatopeiche, in àmbiti macroareali (più che 'macrofamiglie', in senso genealogico) anche molto estesi, molto al di là del CAM-SEM.

39 Ma è importante il riconoscimento che la distinzione tra un lessico di base, cui attingono molte denominazioni del corpo, e un lessico culturale è largamente illusoria; cfr. Fronzaroli, "Common Semitic Lexicon", *cit.*, pp. 44 s., che al proposito parla di 500 lessemi per cinque campi associativi: mancano purtroppo ancora sempre due campi, rispetto al piano annunciato, l'organizzazione sociale e le attività psichiche. Per questo la comparazione tra le lingue mette in evidenza convergenze e divergenze, in parallelo su entrambi i piani del segno. L'interrogativo che è emerso alla luce dei dati di cui sopra (§ 4) è se la paleoantropologia non offra oggi una maggiore contestualizzazione, tale da incoraggiare una comparazione preistorica. A questo proposito, occorre tener presente che le stesse protolingue tradizionali mettono in atto un compromesso tra 'primitivo' e arcaico.

Cohen, ma l'orientamento di Möller è marcatamente formalista, quello di Cohen sostanzialista; 2) l'appartenenza di alcune isoglosse a campi semantici diversi, per effetto della polisemia di quasi tutte le radici, con il rischio-necessità di computare la medesima isoglossa più volte; ci sono anche radici affini, come *ʾ-n-š*, *ʾ-n-ḥ*, *ʾ-n-p*, dove la radice può essere la stessa, cambiando solo il determinativo; 3) le isoglosse sono il risultato di parentele di diverso grado (primo, secondo o terzo), di più la stessa isoglossa può essere divisa tra parentele diverse: il maggior numero di isoglosse relative all'anatomia-fisiologia può essere interpretato come il risultato di una parentela di primo grado, ma, nei limiti in cui questa chiama in causa un lessico di base, da un lato porta tracce di una più remota antichità che va oltre la protostoria, dall'altro attinge a campi semantici diversi, ciò che vanifica una quantificazione per campi semantici (il lessico del corpo è una parte soltanto del lessico di base).

7) La motivazione del segno e il futuro della 'scienza' etimologica

Nel parallelismo dei due piani, ci si può attendere che la ricostruzione di un'invarianza radicale sul piano dell'espressione si accompagni a una *Urbedeutung* sul piano del contenuto, ovvero che le variazioni di significati emergenti dalla comparazione delle lingue – tanto maggiori quanto più estesa è la comparazione – siano sviluppi del medesimo significato 'originario'. Il ricorso a metafore nasce dal fatto che a corrispondenze fonologiche precise e regolari (*one-to-one*, oppure anche *one-to-many*!) non fanno riscontro uguali corrispondenze semantiche nelle lingue.[40] Nei limiti in cui si possono postulare etimologie a diversi livelli cronologici, dovrebbe essere possibile scaglionare le variazioni sui due piani, nel riconoscimento di etimologie diverse. Ma anche la distinzione fra etimologie prime (isoglosse genealogiche) ed etimologie 'altre' (seconde, terze...) è vanificata dallo spostamento progres-

40 A questo proposito, C. Watkins ("Culture History and Historical Linguistics", in W. Bright, *Encyclopedia, cit.*, I pp. 318-322, spec. p. 320) avanza la supposizione di un maggior numero di rassomiglianze nei testi di più antica documentazione. Su queste rassomiglianze si può ipotizzare, anche se difficilmente accertabile, una cronologia relativa (non assoluta) ovvero una stratificazione cronologica delle lingue. A riguardo del parallelismo dei due piani del segno, poi, si può ricordare con A. Meillet che una buona etimologia si basa su considerazioni sia morfonologiche (sul piano dell'espressione), sia semantiche. Per M. Bréal etimologizzare è ricercare i significati 'originari', secondo una concezione logica oppure storica. Ma non si può fare affidamento su singole lingue storiche, nessuna delle quali può essere investita da un'originaria primogenitura.

sivo (e indefinito) dei confini vicarianti di formalizzazione.[41] Ogni etimologia prima è suscettibile di divenire un'etimologia 'altra' per una successiva (ma non definitiva) etimologia prima. È una ricostruzione formale astratta che rischia di apparire acritica e puramente speculativa se non è calata nel 'tessuto' storico e filologico delle lingue, attraverso una contestualizzazione nei testi, a cominciare da quelli più arcaici, per esempio eblaiti. La verifica resta di importanza vitale, tenuto conto soprattutto che molte parole del lessico eblaita, grazie alla comparazione databili attorno alla prima metà del III millennio, appartengono al lessico di base, specialmente parti del corpo (umano e animale), attività fisiche e percettive collegabili a parti del corpo.[42]

Il futuro della 'scienza' etimologica risiede tutto in questo possibile compromesso ed equilibrio tra speculazione e arcaicità, alla ricerca non solo di principî diacronici evolutivi alla base delle transizioni da un significato all'altro (metafore-metasemie), ma anche di nuovi e coerenti allargamenti nella rilettura e nella critica dei testi, in grado di rinsaldare il rapporto stretto tra etimi e campi semantico-figurali. In questo senso ritorna di attualità quanto avvertito già da M. Bréal su una problematica oscillazione tra leggi organico-naturali e leggi storico-umane, alla base di un rigoroso statuto scientifico dei significati. Va rilevata la presenza nel lessico comune delle lingue, nella fattispecie in SEM, di radici onomatopeiche esposte a influenza di una 'fonetica espressiva',[43] a conferma di un nesso neuro-motorio tra suoni linguistici e processi motorio-visivi. Il carattere espressivo delle lingue non deve essere di ostacolo alla comparazione. Sono in gioco segni motivati e più o meno imitativi, in

41 Sull'esistenza di varî gradi di formalizzazione, con richiami alla teoria glossematica e alla logica di K. Gödel, cfr. dello scrivente *La ricerca in linguistica*, Roma 1994, p. 43 e n. 23. È un concetto metodologico interdisciplinare già da tempo in atto nella comparazione delle lingue, come attesta J. Ellis, "General Linguistics and Comparative Philology", *Lingua* 7 (1957-1958) pp. 134-174, spec. p. 155 n. 89 e p. 161.

42 Cfr. P. Fronzaroli, "The Eblaic Lexicon: Problems and Appraisal", in *Id.*, *Language of Ebla*, *cit.*, p. 127. Per H.-P. Müller ("Das Problem der Tierbezeichnungen in der althebräischen Lexikographie", in *The Lexicography of the Ancient Near Eastern Languages*, Verona 1995, pp. 135-147 [= *SEL* 12, 'Special Issue']) alcune convergenze tra eblaita ed ebraico (tre riguardano il corpo) sono riconducibili a una definizione 'nostratica'. L'arcaicità dell'eblaita è sostenuta anche dalla comparazione con CUSC, BERB, CIAD (Conti, "Arcaismi", *cit.*, p. 162).

43 Cfr. Fronzaroli, *Studi*, *cit.* 19 (1964) spec. pp. 10 s. 255; *Id.*, "Problems", *cit.*, spec. pp. 6-8; inoltre, A. Marra, "Modelli semiologici e semantici della protolingua originaria", *AIΩN* 15 (1993) pp. 193-224, spec. pp. 206 s. Più in generale, su simbolismo fonetico, onomatopea ed espressività, cfr. Y. Malkiel, "Etymology and General Linguistics", in R. Schmitt (a cura di), *Etymologie*, Darmstadt 1977, pp. 347-376, spec. pp. 374 s.; su semantica ed etimologia e sugli stretti rapporti tra etimologia e motivazione, S. Ullmann, "Semantik und Etymologie", *ib.*, pp. 421-450, spec. pp. 437 ss.

cui il parlante riconosce (o riconosceva) un rapporto naturale – o non del tutto arbitrario – tra immagine fonica e concetto. Sono comuni i tipi di onomatopea con raddoppiamento integrale oppure parziale (entrambi i tipi di raddoppiamento sono presenti per la rad. [7]).

Le denominazioni delle parti del corpo appaiono riccamente metaforiche (polifunzionali) e già per questo necessitano – come ogni metafora, per definizione – di una contestualizzazione: si tratta di sapere in che misura una loro contestualizzazione nei testi può far luce sulla preistoria delle lingue. La priorità di occorrenze contestuali rispetto a un'etimologizzazione solo ipoteticamente plausibile non può essere, però, disgiunta dal riconoscimento che un significato contestuale non è mai sufficiente a chiarire il significato totale di una denominazione.[44] Contestualizzazione ed etimologizzazione sono complementari l'una all'altra. La lessicografia comparativa giudaica, che sta alla base dell'esegesi talmudica, pur viziata talvolta da un *esprit de facilité*, è pur sempre un orientamento equilibratamente diviso fra comparatismo e analisi interna nella ricerca del corretto significato delle parole. Rideterminazioni morfologiche e reinterpretazioni semantiche sono frutto di contestualizzazioni, all'origine di parallelismi-convergenze tra le lingue. La tendenza allo sviluppo metaforico[45] è tendenza a trasformare il segno da segno-simbolo convenzionale (o arbitrario) in subicona e subindice, secondo la definizione di Ch. S. Peirce.[46] Si riscoprono i legami del lessico con una visione del mondo, si riconsiderano i rapporti stretti tra lingua e cultura, al tempo stesso con tutti i dati comparativi utili, oltre che CAM-SEM anche CAM-SEM-IE.[47] Gli 'interpretanti', nel sottolineare il primato dell'iconicità, in una ricerca sconfinata di correlazioni di suono e di senso, di-

---

44 Cfr. J. Bottéro, "La lexicographie accadienne", in Fronzaroli, *Studies on Semitic Lexicography*, *cit.*, pp. 25-60, spec. p. 48 e J. C. De Moor, "Ugaritic Lexicography", *ib.*, pp. 61-102, spec. p. 82.

45 Cfr. P. Dhorme, "L'emploi métaphorique des noms de parties du corps en hébreu et en akkadien", *RB* 29 (1920) pp. 465-506; 30 (1921) pp. 374-399 e pp. 517-540; 31 (1922) pp. 215-233 e pp. 489-517; 32 (1923) pp. 185-212.; anche P. Lacau, *Les noms des parties du corps en égyptien et en sémitique*, Paris 1970, spec. pp. 31-67, a proposito del quale, vd. G. Garbini, "Il corpo umano nella comparazione lessicale egitto-semitica", *RSO* 46 (1973) pp. 129-141; anche A. Boudot-Lamotte, "Notes sur des emplois métaphoriques des noms de quelques parties du corps humain", *Arabica* 18 (1971) pp. 152-160.

46 Cfr. Ch. S. Peirce, *Semiotica*, *cit.*, pp. 156-164.

47 Si può seguire l'etimologia delle parole anche prima del SEM comune, a condizione che si abbia in mente una precisa ipotesi di lavoro e ben definiti presupposti metodologici, non solo dichiarazioni di principî. Lo concede Fronzaroli, "Problems", *cit.*, p. 5; cfr. anche Ellis, "General Linguistics", *cit.*, p. 161.

ventano chiave di volta della convergenza linguistica. La motivazione (non-arbitrarietà) dei segni, superati i tradizionali pregiudizî sul rapporto fra etimologia ed espressività, per cui la ricerca tradizionale di convergenze storico-genealogiche tra le lingue relega abitualmente le convergenze elementari al ruolo (spesso non dimostrabile) di convergenze 'fortuite',[48] non vanifica, ma anzi valorizza, la comparazione tra le lingue e la ricerca etimologica.[49]

* * *

Lo studio di quel settore del lessico di base che si riferisce alla parte alta del corpo ha verificato la necessità di un coerente allargamento della lessicografia comparativa, in direzione di convergenze più estese (macroareali) e più remote (preistoriche). Le undici 'metafore radicali' CAM-SEM-IE prese in esame sono apparse da definire come segni imitativi e motivati, testimonianza di un 'primitivo' linguistico (concreto o astratto che sia) e di remote migrazioni preistoriche, in uno stretto rapporto tra natura e cultura. La semantica del 'campo' è valsa a definire i significati in termini relazionali di parole e – al tempo stesso – di referenza alla realtà, come hanno bene evidenziato le molte sovrapposizioni delle radici. Ne trarrà vantaggio forse la ricerca etimologica e la critica testuale, se rivitalizzate dalla considerazione di una formalizzazione mobile e dalla riscoperta complementarità tra etimologizzazione e contestualizzazione.

48 Cfr. A. Cuny, *Recherches sur le vocalisme, le consonantisme et la formation des racines en "nostratique", ancêtre de l'indo-européen et du chamito-sémitique*, Paris 1943, spec. p. V; anche Ruhlen, *Origin*, *cit.*, p. 274.

49 Come avverte già H. Wissemann, *Untersuchungen zur Onomatopoiie, I. Die sprachpsychologischen Versuche*, Heidelberg 1954, spec. pp. 7 s.

TAB. 1

sig.ti / radd.	[1]	[2]	[3]	[4]	[5]	[6]	[7]	[8]	[9]	[10]	[11]
naso	■										
faccia	■	■									■
bocca	■	■	■		■						
gola	■					■	■				
orecchio										■	
occhio											■
testa			■					■	■		
capelli			■	■							
collo			■			■	■				
alto	■			■					■		
barba	■				■						
discendenza	■			■							
forza	■							■	■		
parola, voce	■	■			■		■				■
rotondo			■			■	■				
volta, cima			■	■					■		
signore, capo	■			■							
intelletto	■	■			■					■	
mangiare		■			■		■				
org. sessuale			■		■						
paes. agreste			■			■			■		
vegetazione				■		■				■	
desiderio	■						■				
soffiare	■	■									
apertura		■									■
vedere										■	■
idronimia		■									■
luce		■									■
orlo		■							■		

La tabella evidenzia le principali sovrapposizioni di metafore radicali CAM-SEM-IE, relativamente a denominazioni della parte alta del corpo. Le sovrapposizioni sono espresse da celle ombreggiate e si riferiscono nella prima parte della tabella a significati strettamente attinenti al 'campo', nella seconda parte a significati secondari e/o a indicatori semantici).

TAB. 2

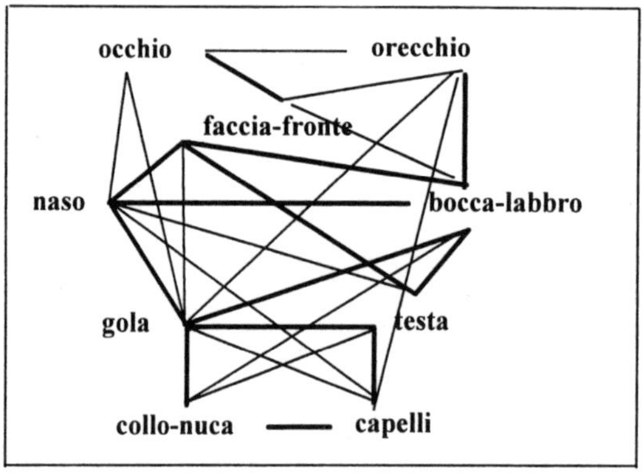

Il diagramma visualizza le principali sovrapposizioni di metafore radicali CAM-SEM-IE, di cui alla TAB. 1, non tenuto conto di ulteriori possibili sovrapposizioni risultanti da un'apertura del 'campo' verso altre denominazioni del corpo. Le sovrapposizioni che si riferiscono a significati strettamente attinenti al 'campo' sono notate con linee più marcate, quelle che si riferiscono a significati secondari e/o indicatori semantici con linee meno marcate.

SEMITIC AND INDOEUROPEAN. A LINGUISTIC STUDY IN COMPARATIVE ASPECTOLOGY

FRITHIOF RUNDGREN

University of Uppsala

Introduction

In our paper "On the Form of the Texteme in Tigriña" (*Festschrift Wolf Leslau*, II, p. 1363) we have called attention to Harald Weinrich's highly stimulating book *Tempus. Besprochene und erzählte Welt* (1964). In this text the author says: "Die literarischen Gattungen – geschrieben oder mündlich – sind prinzipiell als typisierte Sprechsituationen anzusehen und geben den ersten, sicheren Rahmen für eine grammatische Untersuchung. Die Literatur einer Sprache steht also nicht am Ende oder gar weit jenseits der Grammatik, sondern *an ihrem Anfang*. Es ist das grosse Verdienst der strukturalen Sprachwissenschaft, dass sie den Irrtum aufgedeckt hat, man könne eine Grammatik aus den kleinsten Elementen zu immer grösseren Einheiten aufsteigend aufbauen. Man hat mit den grössten Einheiten anzufangen und erkennt erst aus der Struktur der Ganzheit die kleineren Teile. Nun, die höchsten Einheiten sind nicht Sätze oder Perioden, sondern Sprechsituationen und Texte mit ihren literarischen Gattungsgesetzen. Mit ihnen fängt also die Grammatik an." (pp. 309-310). Now, after re-reading Weinrich's book many years later, we find the statement just quoted in principle correct. In *Festschrift Leslau*, II, p. 1363 we asked the question: "What is the macrostructure of language?", and we have later maintained the correctness of our postulate that the text is the first articulation of language (*WT*, p. 1). Moreover, the "text" in this sense might be said to constitute an entity that is its own reductionism and *vice versa*, and this maxim should guide our attempts to constructivism; cf. *Festschrift Wagner*, I, p. 134; *Aspectology*, pp. 57 ff.

"Semitic" is here represented throughout by *Arabic*. However, as we have already given a rather exhaustive textemic analysis of an old Arabic text in *Festschrift Knudsen*, pp. 283-295, we shall in Chapters I, II, and III give an account of the general linguistic results we have reached in our studies of the Semitic language type. Nowadays we consider this very old linguistic type to be of fundamental importance for the description of the Indoeuropean language type as this appears above all in Old Greek (Wackernagel, *Vorlesungen über Syntax*, I, p. 166; cf. below. p. 9). Antoine Meillet has said: "Il n'existe pas une grammaire comparée des langues sémitiques comparable à celle des langues indo-européennes". (*IA*, p. 16). This was once a well-grounded statement, but we cannot enter into his reasons for making it here; for the textemics of Accadian cf. *OS* 41-42, pp. 241-243.

The basis of our contributions to general linguistics is our prolonged study of the category of *aspect*, a category that happened to be the *Angelpunkt* from which we reached our results. However, the way to the concept of *textemics* turned out to be rather long. When we started our studies in this specific field its object was always formulated in terms of "the verbal system", "the verbal aspect" etc.[1] When necessary the undefined concept of "context" was introduced which only added to the linguistic confusion. Moreover, this *lexemic* point of departure for grammatic analysis led us astray for a long time until we fully realized that one had to *start* from *literature* as an overall linguistic notion. For as it appears already from the term *litteratura* itself (< τὰ γράμματα as a τέχνη) we are here confronted with an *ars litterarum sive phonematum*, with all that this implies for a description of the human language (*Eranos* 83, pp. 171-172; *CMS* 1, p. 42). "Art" should not be described in terms of the schoolmasters, that is, in terms like "noun", "verb", "Satz", "sentence" etc. (*CMS* 1, p. 45; *WT*, p. 8).

1. Language and Speech

Thus human language manifests itself first of all as literature, and then in its "letteral" sense so to speak, as "the art of letters", both in oral transmission and later in graphic tradition. Now what we can observe directly of the history of Man as a social being is very little. Under such circumstances the foremost source for his personal history will be on the one hand a deeper history of language, and on the other linguistic palaeontology (cf. *WT*, p. 7). However, by linguistic palaeontology we don't mean the "paléontologie linguistique" in the sense of Adolphe Pictet[2] but above all the exploitation of the early arising phenomenon which Jacques Monod calls "simulation personelle". Monod says: "Du jour, avons-nous dit, où l'Australan-

---

1 Cf. for instance David Cohen, *L'aspect verbal*, 1989 (an excellent work), and Stanley E. Porter, *Verbal Aspect in the Greek of the New Testament, with Reference to Tense and Mood*, 1989 (a learned work).

2 A. Pictet, *Les origines indo-européennes ou Les Aryas, primitifs. Essai de paléontologie linguistique*. I, 1859. II, 1863.

thrope ou quelqu'un de ses congénères parvint à communiquer, non plus seulement une expérience concrète et actuelle, mais le contenu d'une expérience subjective, d'une 'simulation' personelle, un nouveau règne était né: celui des idées. Une évolution nouvelle, celle de la culture, devenait possible. L'évolution physique de l'Homme devait se poursuivre longtemps encore, désormais étroitement associée à celle du langage, subissant profondément son influence qui bouleversait les conditions de la sélection." (*Le hasard et la nécessité*, p. 177).

Within the framework of a cosmic evolution which commenced milliards of years ago, Monod speaks here of a much later epoch of the history of the earth, namely the history of Man which is closely connected with the history of the earth, and whose earliest history for the time being extends from 200.000 to 40.000 years B.C. What we are interested in here in the first place is the genesis of the *articulated* language, and then more specifically not *when* it arose but *how* it might be imagined to have come into existence as the "institution sociale" that Meillet rightly considered it to be.

In Monod's statement the linguist can distinguish two stages of the human evolution, both of which correspond to stages in the development of the brain. Among the senses, *sight* and *hearing* play the largest part in establishing a social communication in a hereditary language. Suppose that an Arab catches sight of a "tomb" and then also through repeated perception of this object gets a memory-image of it, which as a conceptual image is incorporated with his consciousness. Here the phenomenon "consciousness" is of the greatest importance for the function we call "memory".

As regards the consciousness in the present case it is chiefly as "*conscientia* bei sich selbst, das Bewusstsein, die *volle Kenntniss* oder *Erinnerung*" that it is of interest to us (Georges, 514, II). As "tomb" in Arabic *speech* was and still is called *qabr*, this means that the conceptual image that the speaker (or, thinker) already has in his *mind* by him is pronounced *qabr*, a mainly cerebral event, the so-called "mentalism" being of primary importance in linguistics; cf. Benveniste, *Problèmes* 2, p. 19, and *WT*, p. 1 and p. 7. What we can observe in all the languages of the earth, happens through impulses from the brain. On the other hand, we can *infer* from the structure of these languages certain microbiological facts about the structure and function of the brain as a microbiological computer, so to speak.

Now we have said: "As is the case with many other important phenomena, the question of language is in the last resort a question of *chance* and *organization*."

(*Principia*, p. 36), and the title of Monod's book quoted above is "Le hasard et la nécessité" to which Gregory Chaitin's theory of chance should now also be added (Tor Nørretranders, *Världen växer*, pp. 9-20). As we have seen, Monod speaks of a new evolution within the framework of the general microbiologic evolution, an evolution implying *thought* and its *expression*, a phase between two biological states of aggregation, i.e. between microbiology and sociobiology. Thus, we can speak of a microbiological *heritage* common to the whole human race, and a sociolinguistic heritage distributed among the various languages of the earth, and constituting the various linguistic worlds (*WT*, pp. 7-8). This means that these languages in their *macrostructure*, in various ways, but all taken into account together might be said to *represent* the common microbiologic heritage, that is, the prerequisite of their existence.

Here it would not be out of place to quote a statement made by Monod's student and colleague, François Jacob. In a complicated microbiological connection Jacob says: "Mais on ne sait pas encore comment les circuits acquis se superposent au réseau de l'hérédité. On ignore comment s'articulent l'inné et l'appris. Car, aujourd'hui, ces derniers ne s'opposent plus: ils se complètent." (*La logique du vivant*, p. 337). This is an important remark. However, what is also important is the insight into the fact that the language acquisition of Man belongs above all else to l'appris. Thus we shall try to further elucidate the expression "ils se complètent", taking our bi-dimensional theory of language as the point of departure. In the light of this theory, *l'appris* will appear as the macro-structural *representation* of the corresponding micro-structural *l'inné*. Now, materially the above-mentioned *qabr* "tomb" is a linear *sound-image*, i.e. in reality an *ideomorpheme*, as the four elements *q-a-b-r* are materially image-sounds but in reality *ideomorphs*. Considered as a continuum, our *qabr* shows us an order of relation that is *iconically* pertinent, and thus we can easier understand the definition of the "word" as "an image that is its own pronunciation and *vice versa*" (*WT*, p. 1). Moreover, what has been established for Arabic has, of course, general validity.

In a speech-situation we can observe an interplay of two kinds of *complementarity*, on the one hand a *visual* image that is its own *acoustic* image, and *vice versa*, and on the other a *spatial* image that is its own *linear* image and *vice versa*. In *Festschrift Knudsen*, p. 289 and p. 294 we introduced the notion of "The recovering of the carrier", that is, in our case the *human being* as carrier of the microbiological as well as of the socio-phonemic behaviour we call "language". The mutual integration of these two kinds of behaviour, regulated in the brain, also appears, for the linguist, in the form of the two kinds of complementarity already mentioned. We consider these two complementarities to be macrostructural representations of the corresponding microbiological entities.

The sender (A) and the receiver (B) define each other in language as two persons, "I" and "You" (*WT*, p. 7) who communicate with each other *in* and *about* the "world" – in one of many possible worlds (*WT*, p. 7) – and between whom a mutual *consciousness* of the world in which they communicate exists. Thus we have for (A) and (B) not only with the "*conscientia* bei sich selbst" to do, but also with the "*conscientia* mit einem Andern" and "das Mitwissen mit einem Andern um etwas" (Georges, 514, I).

The genesis, and above all the mighty development of *this* consciousness through the genesis of the human completely articulated language has made the statement "la linguistique est la science pilote" appear well-founded. Moreover, we may well ask *how* the fact that the communication between (A) and (B) is based on a kind of "consciousness" existing between them, is to the halves of the brain; we know of differences in the flow of blood, when (A) speaks alone, and when (A) and (B) are communicating; cf. Nørretranders, *Märk världen*, pp. 159 ff.

In *Principia* (p. 36) we have said: "In virtue of its clear, transparent structure, which permits us sometimes to observe positively some of the main principles of language, the Semitic language type may be said to be to general linguistics what the fruitfly is or was to genetics or crystals to physics. For in Semitic the macrostructure of a phenomenon is sometimes quite directly a reflection of the underlying microstructure". To prove this rather profound statement, prolonged studies became necessary. In the first place we had to establish the true nature of the category of *aspect*. The studies in this difficult field led us to the discovery of the phenomenon of *apothematism* (*OS* 13, pp. 48-83), and the old doctrine of apophony (Ablaut) in Indoeuropean had to be given up (*Festschrift Johanson*, p. 197), as well as the *lexemic* orientation of aspectology. In *OS* 36-37, pp. 57-76 we introduced what we called *textemics* and the *linguistics* of the text; cf. *Festschrift Knudsen*, pp. 283-295.

We have spoken of two kinds of complementarity above. What in the first place is of interest to us here is the kind of complementarity that prevails between the linear image and the spatial image (*WT*, p. 4 and p. 16). This type of complementarity seems to have a parallel in the complementary structure of the crystals which shows us a remarkable relationship between macrostructure and microstructure. Here the complementarity is in principle absolute, so that a distance that in its macrostructure is measurable in centimeters is then in its microstructure measurable in corresponding Ångström (cf. Monod, *op. cit.*, p. 19).

Now in only orally transmitted and immediately vanishing speech its "script", so to speak, is invisible but audible and thus measurable in space-time (cf. *Cours*, p. 103), that is, in this connection in *phrasemes* (textemes), each of which in turn always is its own *text*, i.e. a conceptual image of the world. This kind of image might be considered to be a spatial continuum which is identical with the acoustic (linear) but invisible "script". Moreover, this conceptual image in the sense of a spatial continuum is, in exclusively orally transmitted speech, to be found in the brain of the speaker on a microbiological scale. This scenario implies that not only speech, audible in phrasemes, but also the speaker's own visual image – internal or external – are to be regarded as macrostructural representations of their microbiological equivalences in the brain.

Let us now visualize both possibilities: 1. Arabic قبر "It/is a tomb". The writing is visible but not its pronunciation nor its phrasemic function of a "pronouncement" = "statement". 2. The "script" is invisible but audible as *Qabrun* "It/is a tomb", i.e. audible in its phrasemic function as a statement about "It" = "the world" (*WT*, p. 17) being here a *qabrun* "tomb", an entity we call "word", that is, in actuality "a pronunciation that is its own conceptual image and *vice versa*".

This definition of the "word" is the definition of the *cognitio* that the human language has given to us, an epistemological term, cf. Georges, 440, I, A: "das Kennenlernen durch die Sinne", and I, B: "das geistige Kennenlernen = das Erkennen, die Erkenntnis". Given that a socio-biological heritage like *qabr* was, during the time of exclusively oral transmission, an invisible but audible "script" in an iconically pertinent order of relation, we are entitled to assume that the linguistic socio-biological heritage might generally be regarded as the macrostructural expression for its own microbiological, molecular heritage. This heritage is common to the human race and thus also constitutes the prerequisite for so many linguistic worlds on earth (*WT*, pp. 11-17), worlds macrostructurally representing, each in its own way, the common microbiological heritage.

2. The notion of the linguistic field

First of all we should learn to distinguish between two concepts, namely on the one hand *the field of the theory* (I), and on the other *the theory of the field* (II). Of these concepts (II) is, in some way, always to be regarded as a function of (I). For the text – the *web*[3] – as a linguistic category is the first articulation of language and thus an overall articulation, which already in its minimal entity, the *texteme* (phraseme) that is its own *text* (world), contains *in nuce* all theoretical and practical information necessary – *mutatis mutandis* – for the description of all languages known to us. This statement holds all the more true since we now have introduced the notion of "The recovering of the carrier" (*Festschrift Knudsen*, p. 289 and p. 294), that is, the human being; cf. *Aspectology*, p. 69.

Now the fact should be borne in mind that the texteme always *is* its own text and *vice versa*. From a structural point of view this state of things implies that the text as a continuum (process) consists of a *repetition* of its own unities, the textemes, that simultaneously are their own texts, i.e. various images of "the world". The functioning of this repetition we have described in *Festschrift Knudsen*, p. 291.

Within the framework of such a great number of linguistic worlds as we can observe on earth, where they constitute a linguistic *universe*, we may find the fact that they are translatable into each other in any case remarkable (cf. *Festschrift Johanson*, pp. 191 ff.). It is this translatability that connects all these languages with each other thus creating what we shall call the great field of communication, and hence an extension of our *theory of the field* (II). We can now communicate with other possible worlds through a renewed language acquisition or by the aid of translations. Unlike C. Hagège we are inclined to say: "*Il s'agira* de la définition même d'une langue, qui clôture le champ de l'enquête par le seul fait de s'énoncer, selon la conception minimaliste des structuralistes européens." (*La structure des langues*, p. 11).

3. The complexity of language and the cognitive phenomenon

The word "cognitive" is on the verge of being *à la mode*, much like the word "structure" that is nowadays used at all times. As the remark "La linguistique est la science pilote" first of all should be referenced to cognitive research, we have briefly

3 The term "text" in the sense of "web" is of capital importance to the linguistic theory; *WT*, p. 16, and *Festschrift Knudsen*, p. 288.

mentioned in *Festschrift Johanson*, p. 193 a linguistic starting-point for a theory of cognitive science; on *cognitio* and *conscientia* cf. above p. 590 and p. 587.

Nowadays a language is first of all described in a synchronic perspective. However such a description is, in a sense, also its own diachrony. Moreover, Man is a product of natural evolution and his language a phenomenon of great *depth*. A prehistorical epoch of great length precedes a short historical epoch. As far as Semitic is concerned we can from now follow this language type more than 5000 years, and we can hypothetically *infer* the structure of Semitic at least for the beginning of the prehistorical period but hardly more. However we can get some help from a study of the history of the script.

Old Egyptian shows us a pictorial script, in essence without pronunciation. Later on the pronunciation could summarily be indicated by alphabetic picture-signs, the sound-values of which were placed in an iconically pertinent order of relation. The cuneiform writing likewise goes back to a picture-writing. Moreover, since an exclusively *oral* transmission of speech and texts has preceded the tradition of writing we do not need much imagination to realize how great the intellectual difficulties must have been for generations of people struggling to transfer only spoken words to writing.

The Arabic word *faras* "horse" is, from an acoustic point of view, an alphabetical sound-image, composed of five image-sounds in the iconically pertinent order of relation *f-a-r-a-s*, a relation in which *-a-*^{1} and *-a-*^{2} are two different radicals but the same phoneme twice (*Festschrift Knudsen*, p.292); cf. *Farasun* "It/is a horse" with seven radicals but only six phonemes (thus to be read in *OS* 41-42, p. 224). Moreover, as the sound-image *faras* is iconically relevant we shall call its five radicals *positive* differences (cf. *Cours*, pp. 163 ff.); if our *faras* had *not* been iconically pertinent in Arabic we would have called the sequence in question *negative* differences or just a sequence of phonemes.

A serious question results from what has now been said. It seems in any case to us that the concepts "sound" and "image" do not belong together. How about "image" and "phoneme"? They do not belong together either as far as we can see. It hardly needs to be said that for certain purposes we not only can but must study phonetics as well as phonemics. However, as far as the *human* language is concerned it *can in the first place* only be a question of a study of the *Zeichenlehre* of language; cf. *Festschrift Knudsen*, p. 293.

In its conventional order, the 28 letters (*ḥurūf*) of the Arabic alphabet can be said to constitute a sequence of negative differences. From the point of view of what we would like to call the *semiotic energy* of language, the conventional order of this alphabet represents a maximum of semantic disorder (entropy), while an iconically pertinent order of relation like *frs* (radix) shows us an instance of order in the sense of communicative energy in terms of *understanding* (semantics). As regards *frs* "radix" it should not be understood as meaning "root", i.e. a metaphor taken from the vegetable kingdom, but as an "ideomorpheme", that is, an idea = conceptual image (*FRS*) that is its own morpheme, its own alphabetical form and *vice versa*; cf. *Festschrift Knudsen*, pp. 291-292. Thus, the monoliteral alphabet has *alone* been able to take over the double function of the linguistic sign, in virtue of the socio-biological heritage of Man, that is, the heritage, which enables him, with the help of the alphabet to create iconically pertinent orders of relation, for instance *F-a-r-a-s-u-n* "It/is a horse", a statement (*xabar*) about the world (*mawḍūᶜ*, subject matter); cf. *OS* 41-42, p. 225. In the phenomenon of the iconically alphabetical order of relation we also find the genesis of what is called "literarity", "literacy" and "literaturnost"; cf. *Festschrift Knudsen*, p. 284.

4. Greek. A textemic analysis. On the consecutio aspectuum

As far as the category of aspect in Indoeuropean is concerned, *Old Greek* comes first; cf. Wackernagel, *Vorlesungen*, I, p. 166. We have tried to elucidate the apothematic prerequisites of the aspectics of Greek in *OS* 41-42, pp. 221 ff., especially p. 237; cf. also *Festschrift Johanson*, pp. 196-197. The function of aspect in *Arabic* was definitively explained within the framework of the textemics introduced by us in the *Festschrift Knudsen*, pp. 263-295. As for Old Greek Bornemann-Risch very rightly points out: "Dazu kommt bei uns, dass besonders in der Syntax nicht alle Kategorien in gleicher Breite behandelt sind. Themen wie Verbalaspekt, Verbum infinitum und Konditionalsätze erforderten eine ausgedehntere Behandlung nicht nur wegen ihrer Wichtigkeit, sondern schon deshalb, weil sie teilweise auch in der Forschung noch umstritten sind." (*Griechische Grammatik*², Vorwort, p. VII). As regards the exposition in *Schwyzer-Debrunner*, *Griechische Grammatik*, II, pp. 246-301, full of details and to some extent out of date, we confine ourselves to a reference to *OS* 41-42, p. 238.

In Greek we have, in the first place, to deal with *consecutio aspectuum* to the structure of which the following textemic analysis will be a contribution.

For this purpose we have at random selected Thucydides, book III, 1 (Hude, p. 193-194). We want to also mention here what we said already in 1959: "Das Altsemitische kennt ferner grundsätzlich keine consecutio temporum, nur eine mehr oder weniger lokalisierte *consecutio aspectuum.*" (*IA*, p. 25). However, in Semitic this phenomenon could not appear in its full significance until we had introduced a textemic analysis and thereby also "literature" as also being a linguistic concept.

This, for Semitic, established "consecutio aspectuum" is also to a great extent to be found in Old Greek and this fact is of great importance to us when we try to reconstruct the category of aspect in Protoindoeuropean. It is appropriate to quote Harald Weinrich: "Besonders interessant wäre es, die Aspekte in den Sprachen zu untersuchen, an denen man sie zuerst abgelesen hat: den semitischen Sprachen. Oder an den Sprachen, in denen sie ihre sicherste Heimstatt zu haben scheinen: in den slavischen Sprachen." (*op. cit.*, p. 290).[4] However, it is in the nature of things that the category of aspect was the same in Protosemitic and in Protoindoeuropean, that is, a *textemic* opposition *Static/Non Static* = 1. *Fientic*. 2. *Neutral*. It is from this opposition that the *consecutio aspectuum* emanates, from which a later-arising tensification of the textemics has had to start. For the category of aspect in the Slavonic languages we refer to *IA*, p. 300 and *WT*, p. 24.[5] As Old Greek is fundamental to the discussion of the category of aspect in Indoeuropean in general, we shall now consider the category in question as it appears in Thucydides, III, 1 (Hude, p. 193).

Text (1). Τοῦ δ'ἐπιγιγνομένου θέρους Πελοποννήσιοι καὶ οἱ ξύμμαχοι ἅμα τῷ σίτῳ ἀκμάζοντι ἐστράτευσαν ἐς τὴν Ἀττικήν· ἡγεῖτο δὲ αὐτῶν Ἀρχίδαμος ὁ Ζευξιδάμου, Λακεδαιμονίων βασιλεύς "During the following summer the Pelo-

4 To this statement Weinrich has added the following reservation: "In beiden Bereichen fehlen mir alle Sprachkenntnisse, und ich würde meine Methode verleugnen, wollte ich nur aus Grammatiken und Monographien Auskunft schöpfen. Ich enthalte mich also gegenüber den semitischen und slavischen Aspekten des Urteils – nicht der Skepsis." (pp. 290-291).

5 As regards the terms "perfective", "imperfective", "accompli", "inaccompli" etc. they have nothing to do with the category of aspect as such (*WT*, p. 24). In this connection it is appropriate to quote A. Leskien: "Die *slavischen Sprachen* unterscheiden von jeher drei *Hauptaktionsarten,* die man als *perfektiv, imperfektiv, iterativ* bezeichnet. Perfektiv und Imperfektiv dürfen nicht, wie es oft geschieht, durch 'vollendet' (perfectus) und 'unvollendet' (imperfectus) übersetzt werden; das veranlasst eine falsche Auffassung, denn es handelt sich dabei gar nicht darum, ob eine Handlung abgeschlossen (vollendet) oder nicht abgeschlossen (unvollendet) ist, sondern, wie die Adjektivbildung durch -ivus auch andeuten soll, dass sie eine Beziehung zu den Begriffen der Vollendung oder Nichtvollendung hat." (*Grammatik der altbulgarischen Sprache*, 1909, pp. 215-216); cf. Roman Jacobson, "Zur Struktur des russischen Verbums" (*Charisteria*, pp. 74-84).

ponnesians and the allies, when the grain was ripening, made a campaign into Attica, Arkhidamos son of Zeuxidamos, king of the Lakedaimonians being their leader."

As far as the text (1) is concerned it is, for its author, a complex alphabetic *sign picture* that at the same time is its own alphabetic set of *picture signs* and *vice versa*, cf. *Festschrift Knudsen*, p. 293; *WT*, p. 16. This implies that the text (1) is a continuum of Greek *letters*, thus also a "letteral" continuum that is its own *literal* continuum. Moreover, we can also say that the text (1) is its own *literarity*, in a purely linguistic sense, this kind of literarity being immediately based on a "letterality", i.e. on an iconically pertinent "alphabeticallity", so to speak. For the alphabetical writing reproduced in text (1) represents here a maximal *order of relation* of the Greek phonemic inventory, i.e. its full communicative *energy* in terms of *understanding*, since the phonemes here function as positive, image-creating differences and thus not as phonemes but as *ideomorphs* (cf. above, p. 588). In the last resort this phenomenon is explained by the fact that the linguistic sign in its simplest form in living language, namely as the "word", always is a double entity, for instance θέρος "summer". In Greek this word constitutes an iconically pertinent order of relation, i. e. θ–έ–ρ–ο–ς, a pronunciation that is its own conceptual image, by the present writer symbolized with a cerebral ideogram: *THEROS*; cf. *Festschrift Knudsen*, p. 292. However such a "word-image" never occurs alone or as such in living language but only as its own "pronouncement", so to speak, i.e. as a phraseme: *Théros* "It/is summer". Here it is the predicate phrase of the phraseme.

We shall now consider the text (1) as a unity being composed of two textemes (phrasemes), namely … Πελοποννήσιοι καὶ οἱ ξύμμαχοι ... ἐστράτευσαν ἐς τὴν Ἀττικὴν (a), a fientic texteme in *casus rectus*, and ἡγεῖτο δὲ αὐτῶν Ἀρχίδαμος ... (b), another "imperfectic" texteme, so to speak, in the indicative but in our opinion in *casus obliquus*. Here, we are confronted with a problem. We must ask the following question: Is the texteme (b) fientic or is it neutral? For we have said that this texteme in any case is in the indicative. In the first place we can give the answer that an "imperfectic" predicate phrase in the indicative mood is in principle fientic, i.e. designates a cursive process, while an aoristic predicate phrase in the indicative only states an event. On the other hand, an event is also a process but in our case only the event as such.

Now in scientific Greek linguistics the term "syntax" means the relationship that exists *between* the textemes (phrasemes) in a textual continuum (*phrásis*); cf. *OS* 41-

42, p. 222. This relationship is of aspectual nature, aspect being the *inflection* of the text in its continuum. In our case we have to deal with the aspectual relationship obtained between texteme (a) and texteme (b) of the text (1), constituting what we shall call a "perspectivic scene". From the aspectual point of view we shall now, to begin with, say that the textemes, (a) and (b) taken together both have *Non-Static* aspect, that is, (a) has fientic aspect, and (b) neutral aspect, the latter within the framework of this kind of perspectivity which constitutes a for the literary style of Greek fundamental *consecutio aspectuum*. This "consecutio" is already superior to a *consecutio temporum* for the reason that aspect historically precedes tense (*WT*, p. 19). At this point of our exposition we must try to visualize this complicated state of things by introducing a theoretical distinction between an imperfectic predicate phrase as a purely *temporal* preterite, the imperfect – regarded now as a lexeme – considered here to be cursive in a temporal sense, and an imperfectic predicate phrase as a pure preterital *aspect*. In the last-mentioned case the text (1) should be analysed as follows.

Considering text (1) and comparing text (1a) = "foreground" with text (1b) "background" we can observe the following phenomenon. Within the framework of the linear simultaneity existing between (a) and (b) we obtain one single *spatial* image of the "world". In our text (1) we receive the impression of a dimension of *depth*, a feeling of a stereoscopic effect, so to speak. For a special reason we shall now give the following formulation of the state of the art. The texteme (b) turns out to be "en rupture perspectivique avec le textème (a)", and the special reason for this statement of ours is contained in the following words of Weinrich's: "Allerlei Erklärungen sind für dieses Imparfait de rupture vorgebracht worden, die allesamt nicht darüber hinwegtäuschen können, dass das Imparfait de rupture von einer wie immer aufgefassten Aspektlehre nicht erklärt werden kann." (*op. cit.*, p. 172), to our mind an unfounded statement. These are our arguments for the aspectual neutrality of the predicate phrase ἡγεῖτο δὲ αὐτῶν as well as for the positing of a *casus obliquus* for the texteme (1 b).

We shall now go on analyzing the text (1). In the first place we shall consider the construction Τοῦ δ'ἐπιγιγνομένου θέρους "During the following summer", a construction the "lexemic" schoolmasters call *genetivus absolutus*, a term which is only to a certain extent justified and for which we shall substitute the term "contracted texteme". Thereby we start from the old style (logographs), i.e. from the λέξις εἰρομένη, which in classic Greek was in the highest degree replaced by the λέξις κατεστραμμένη, the greatest rhetorical artifice of Greek, imitated in several languages both in the west (Latin) and in the East (Persian, Turkish). Thus "It was now the following summer. The Peloponnesians ... made a campaign into Attica.", that is, two textemes in *paratax*, the first one being later contracted, perhaps also in order to indicate a part of the space of time during which the campaign was made (cf. νυκτός), namely ἅμα τῷ σίτῳ ἀκμάζοντι, an expression which likewise can be regarded as a dative of a contracted texteme.

Now it is precisely this phenomenon of contraction that has made the rhetorically pertinent configuration that we have called the "frame-predicative" possible (*Festschrift Leslau*, II, p. 1365). We shall now sum up our analysis of the text (1) and now in terms of phrasemes, here in subject phrase and predicate phrase respectively.

Text (1a). Τοῦ δ'ἐπιγιγνομένου θέρους / = predicate phase / Πελοποννήσιοι καὶ οἱ ξύμμαχοι / = subject phrase / ἅμα τῷ σίτῳ ἀκμάζοντι ἐστράτευσαν ἐς τὴν 'Αττικήν / = predicate phrase. As we see, parts of a very long predicate phrase frame here the subject phrase. Text (1b) ἡγεῖτο δὲ αὐτῶν / = predicate phrase / 'Αρχίδαμος ὁ Ζευξιδάμου, Λακεδαιμονίων βασιλεύς / = subject phrase.

Text (2). καὶ ἐγκαθεζόμενοι ἐδῄουν τὴν γῆν "And settling down there they ravaged the land" < καὶ ἐγκαθέζοντο καὶ ἐδῄουν τὴν γῆν "And they were settling down there and (they) were ravaging the land", that is, a text composed of two textemes, while in text (2) the first texteme has been contracted, and its aspectual value is thus dependent on the aspectual value of the second texteme. In principle the "imperfectic" predicate phrase can in our opinion in Greek be fientic as well as neutral. In this connection it is appropriate to quote Wackernagel, who on the one hand says: "Aus allem dem geht die grundsätzliche Verschiedenheit zwischen *Aorist Ind.* und *Imperfekt* zur Genüge hervor." (Vorlesungen I, p. 182), and on the other: "Man kann höchstens, wenn man einen Unterschied machen will, gelegentlich feststellen, dass durch den Aorist mehr die Hauptmomente einer Reihe von Handlungen oder Vorgängen bezeichnet werden, während die Einzelausführung im Imperfekt gegeben wird." (p. 183); cf. Weinrich, *op. cit.*, p. 292. Now, since the text (2) is an immediate continuation of the text (1b), to which in the text (2) a further "Einzelausführung" in the sense of Wackernagel is added, we shall say that text (2) has neutral aspect in the *casus obliquus*.

Text (3). καὶ προσβολαί, ὥσπερ, εἰώθεσαν, ἐγίγνοντο τῶν Ἀθηναίων ἱππέων ὅπη παρείκοι (a), καὶ τὸν πλεῖστον ὅμιλον τῶν ψιλῶν εἶργον τὸ μὴ προεξιόντας τῶν ὅπλων τὰ ἐγγὺς τῆς πόλεως κακουργεῖν. (b) "And sallies, as they were usual, were made by the Athenian cavalry, wherever it was possible (a), and they prevented the greatest mass of the light-armed troops from moving forward, out from the watch-posts, laying waste the districts near the City."

This text is composed of two textemes, (a) and (b), which as being in the indicative, might *per se* be said to be aspectually fientic (*casus rectus*) as well as aspectually neutral, being a continuation to text (2), which in turn is a continuation of the text (1b), we shall for the text (3) prefer the second alternative, that is, "aspectually neutral" and "in the *casus obliquus*". Moreover, this case should here be regarded as aspectually superior to the first-mentioned alternative – in accordance with the linguistic phenomenon we have called *consecutio aspectuum*. Within the framework of the text (3a) we notice also two in (a) integrated neutral textemes in *casus obliquus*, namely ὥσπερ εἰώθεσαν and ὅπη παρείκοι.

Text (4). ἐμμείναντες δὲ χρόνον οὗ εἶχον τὰ σιτία ἀνεχώρησαν (a) καὶ διελύθησαν κατὰ πόλεις (b). "But remaining (there) the days for which they had provisions they returned (home), and they dispersed to the several cities." (b). Considering the text (4) as a unity, it consists *now* of two fientic textemes (phrasemes) in *casus rectus*, our ἐμμείναντες being contracted from a fientic < *ἔμμειναν to which the neutral texteme χρόνον οὗ εἶχον τὰ σιτία functioned as a "phrasème de rupture", in accordance with our doctrine of the *consecutio aspectuum*.

The specific doctrine of aspectology presented above is, in the last resort founded on the exposition in *OS* 41-42, pp. 236-237, more exactly on our reconstruction of the state of things in common Indoeuropean p. 237: **Bhor-ti* = Static / **Bher-ti*, **Bhir-ti* = Non-Static / = 1. Fientic. 2. Neutral (indifferent to fienticity as well as to stativity). These three forms are *textemes* (phrasemes) which are their own *texts* (images of the world). Why the terms of this system are indicated in forms that we generally call *praesentia*, this is a question upon which we cannot enter within the scope of this paper dedicated to my distinguished colleague Pelio Fronzaroli.

Bibliography

Aspectology = *Aspectology in the Light of Text Linguistics* (*OS* 36-37, 1989, pp. 57-76).
Benveniste, E., *Problèmes de linguistique générale*, 2, 1974.
Bornemann, E. – Risch, E., *Griechische Grammatik*[2],1978.
Charisteria = *Charisteria Guilelmo Mathesio quinquagenerio a disciplis et circuli linguistici Pragensis sodalibus oblata*, 1932.
CMS = *Centrum för Metriska Studier*, l, Göteborg, 1989.
Cours = F. de Saussure, *Cours de linguistique générale*[4], 1949.
Eranos. *Acta philologica Suecana*, 83, 1985, pp. 171-172.
Festschrift Lars Johanson, Swedish Research Institute of Istanbul. Transactions. Vol. 6, 1996.
Festschrift Ebbe Egede Knudsen, Ed. Elie Wardini, Oslo, 1997.
Festschrift Wolf Leslau. II. 1991. Ed. Alan S. Kaye.
Festschrift Ewald Wagner. I. 1994. Ed. W. Heinrichs.-G. Schoeler.
Georges, Dr., *Kleines lateinisch-deutsches Handwörterbuch*[2], 1869.
Hagège, C., *La structure des langues*[3], 1990.
Hude, C., *Thucydidis Historiae*. I. Libri I-IV, 1898.
IA = F. Rundgren, *Intensiv und Aspektkorrelation*, 1959.
Jacob, Fr., *La logique du vivant*, 1970.
Monod, J., *Le hasard et la nécessité*, 1970.
Nørretranders, T., *Märk världen*, Stockholm, 1993.
Nørretranders, T., *Världen växer*, Stockholm, 1997.
OS = *Orientalia Suecana*, Uppsala.
Principia = F. Rundgren, *Principia linguistica Semitica*, *OS* 29, 1981, pp. 32-102.
Wackernagel, J., *Vorlesungen über Syntax*[2], I. 1950.
WT = *The Word and the Text*, 1992.

NACHRICHTEN AN DEN PALAST VON EBLA. EINE DEUTUNG VON NÍĜ-MUL-(AN)

WALTHER SALLABERGER

Universität München

In so mancher Hinsicht bilden die Texte aus dem Palast von Ebla, dabei gerade auch die Verwaltungstexte, einen einzigartigen Befund im Bereich des Alten Orients. Doch der Auswertbarkeit der Urkunden stehen die nach wie vor bestehenden Schwierigkeiten entgegen, die Orthographie, Lexikon oder Terminologie bieten. Der Jubilar hat selbst viele Rätsel dieser Texte geklärt; ihm sei die folgende Studie zu dem nicht ganz seltenen, meist in besonders interessantem Kontext erscheinenden Begriff níĝ-AN.AN.AN.AN gewidmet.[1]

Einleitend will ich versuchen, auch die Methoden der Analyse zu thematisieren und ihre Berechtigung aus dem Charakter der Texte abzuleiten. Blickt man nämlich aus der Welt der mesopotamischen Verwaltungstexte nach Ebla, so erscheint einem vieles dort vertraut. Doch diese Vertrautheit beruht nicht nur auf dem gemeinsamen Hintergrund derselben Schrift, derselben Zahlen und teilweise Ideogramme sowie nahverwandter Sprachen/Dialekte, sondern auch auf vergleichbarem institutionellen Kontext.

1. Vorbemerkung zu den Textil- und Metall-Urkunden von Ebla

Metalle, insbesondere die Edelmetalle Gold und Silber, und Textilien aus Wolle und Leinen gehören im Alten Orient vorrangig zum Herrscherpalast: hier werden diese Güter eingeliefert oder produziert, verarbeitet, gehortet und von hier werden sie wieder verteilt. Dieses Bild bieten übereinstimmend die Archive des keilschriftlichen Bereiches, man denke zum Beispiel an das königliche Schatzarchiv von Puzriš-Dagān der Ur III-Zeit, die altbabylonischen Palastarchive von Mari, Šubat-Enlil oder Uruk, die Urkunden aus Nuzi oder Ugarit.

---

1 Bei den Abkürzungen orientiere ich mich an den in Arbeiten zu Ebla-Texten üblichen: MAT = "Monatliche Sammelurkunde der Ausgaben von Textilien" und JAM = "Jährliche Sammelurkunde der Ausgaben von Metallen"; Datierung mit Angabe der "Minister" Ar. = ArruLum, Ib. = Ibrium, IZ = Ibbi-zikir. n-AAAA = níĝ-AN.AN.AN.AN; Text-Nummern sind nur nach Jahr und *numerus currens* zitiert, also z. B. 75.1730 statt TM.75.G.1730. Deutungvorschläge von Wörtern werden aufgrund des raschen Fortschreitens der Forschung nicht ausführlich bibliographisch nachgewiesen. – Eine erste Fassung dieser Untersuchung stellte ich in einem Vortrag in Münster vor.

Der Befund von Ebla entspricht diesem Bild, denn gerade die Urkunden über Metalle und Textilien stellen den größten Anteil an den Texten, die im Hauptarchivraum L. 2769 am Eingangshof gefunden wurden (Archi 1986). Eine herausragende Bedeutung gewinnt diese Textgruppe in Ebla jedoch dadurch, daß die erhaltenen Urkunden weitgehend vollständig die Einnahmen und die Ausgaben dieser Materialien über mehr als dreißig Jahre dokumentieren (vgl. Archi 1996a. b).

1.1. Charakter und Gliederung der Sammelurkunden über Ausgaben

Vorliegender Aufsatz befaßt sich ausschließlich mit den Ausgabe-Urkunden über Metalle und Textilien. Dabei sind die wichtigsten erhaltenen Zeugnisse die Sammelurkunden der Ausgaben, die monatlich für Textilien, aber nur jährlich für die kostbareren und seltener vergebenen Metalle erstellt wurden. Entsprechend der italienischen Terminologie ("rendiconto mensile [di uscite] di tessuti", RMT, bzw. "rendiconto annuale [di uscite] di metalli", RAM) bezeichne ich diese beiden Gruppen als

MAT = "Monatliche Sammelurkunde der Ausgaben von Textilien" und
JAM = "Jährliche Sammelurkunde der Ausgaben von Metallen".

Die monatlichen Urkunden (MAT) führen auch Metalle an, wenn solche neben Textilien an einen Empfänger ausgegeben werden. Die Jahresurkunden (JAM) listen ausschließlich Metalle auf. Für diese etwa dreißig JAM legte Archi (1996b) eine chronologische Ordnung vor, die aufgrund innerer Kriterien erfolgte. Gemeinsame Ausgabevermerke zu Empfänger und Grund der Abbuchung erlauben es weiters, die monatlichen Texte (MAT) den jährlichen (JAM) zuordnen (Biga/Pomponio 1993, Biga 1996). Um einen Überblick zur Chronologie zu erleichtern, verweise ich bei den JAM und den jeweils zugeordneten MAT auf die chronologische Einordnung bei Archi (1996b, 81-92), z. B. JAM IZ 4 = 4. Jahresabrechnung über Metalle unter Ibbi-zikir; (MAT) // JAM IZ 4 = monatliche Urkunde über Textilien, die in das Abrechnungsjahr IZ 4 fällt.

Wesentlich ist bei beiden Typen, MAT und JAM, der Charakter als Sammelurkunden: die einzelnen verbuchten Ausgaben eines Textes verbindet das Material (Textilien bzw. Metall), die ausgebende Stelle, nämlich der Palast von Ebla, und der entsprechende Zeitraum (Monat bzw. Jahr). Das bedeutet insbesondere, daß verschiedene Ausgaben einer Urkunde aus demselben Anlaß erfolgen können, aber nicht müssen. Zudem sind die Einzelposten der Sammelurkunden nicht chronologisch gegliedert, wie die Gegenüberstellung von Jahres- und Monatsurkunden zeigt (vgl. Biga/Pomponio 1993). Die vorauszusetzenden Einzelurkunden sind nicht über den entsprechenden Zeitraum erhalten. Demgegenüber gibt es, gerade unter den älteren Texten (vgl. *ARET* 7), Zusammenstellungen von Ausgaben (und Einnahmen) nach inhaltlichen Kriterien.

Das zentrale Anliegen der Urkunden ist es, die Ausgaben mit allen relevanten Parametern zu verbuchen. Daraus ergibt sich folgender Aufbau der einzelnen Einträge (wobei nur 1. an erster Stelle steht, während die Reihenfolge von 2.-4. prinzipiell frei ist; vgl. 3.2.):

1. Objekt: Anzahl und Art der ausgegebenen Materie, insbesondere Qualität bei den Stoffen, Gewicht bei Metallen.
2. Der Empfänger, in der Regel eine Gottheit oder eine Person, wird meist mit Namen oder Funktion (z. B. "Herrscher von ON") bezeichnet, dazu kommen kennzeichnende Angaben wie Filiation oder Zugehörigkeit zu einem Patron, Herkunftsort, Funktion oder Beruf. Diese zusätzlichen Angaben begründen auch meist das verbuchte Geschenk.
3. Der Grund der Ausgabe (fakultativ), weshalb eben die genannte Person nun Textilien oder Metalle aus dem Palastschatz erhält, wird häufig als Temporalangabe formuliert (*in* u_4 ... "zur Zeit von, als", entsprechend Ur III u_4 ...-a oder altbabylonischem *inūma*) oder mit ŠÈ "wegen, weil" eingeleitet (entspricht Ur III mu ... (ak)-šè oder altbabylonischem *aššum*).[2] Häufig sind hier Angaben über Reisen, Aufenthalte an anderen Orten, Gaben für den Überbringer von Sendungen, besondere Anlässe wie Feste, ein Vertragsabschluß, Geburt, Hochzeit, Tod. In der Formulierung und inhaltlich läßt sich zwischen der näheren Bestimmung der Person, 2., und der Angabe des Grundes, 3., oft keine klare Grenze ziehen.
4. Administrative Angaben über Umstände bei der Ausgabe, etwa wer das Gut übergeben hat (i/ì-na-sum) oder es an einen anderen Ort gebracht hat (šu mu-$taka_4$), wenn der Ort der Geschenkübergabe nicht Ebla ist, oder wer die Materialien übernommen hat, wenn es nicht der intendierte endgültige Empfänger ist (šu ba_4-ti; z. B. Übernahme von Materialien, um bestimmte Endprodukte herzustellen).

2 Fronzaroli (1987, 268 f.), verweist auf die gängige Interpretation von ŠÈ als Präposition "für" und zeigt den Gebrauch von *šè* als Genitiv des Determinativ-Pronomens. Der Vergleich mit der Terminologie der Verwaltungstexte anderer Epochen legt demgegenüber - zumindest in vielen Fällen in den administrativen Texten - eine Deutung als kausales "wegen, weil" (wie babylon. *aššum*) nahe (aber nicht final, wie die bei Fronzaroli a. O. zitierten Autoren annehmen). Ein Beispiel unter vielen, *ARET* 1, 1 Rs. vii 3-7: (T.) ì-g̃iš sag̃ / *i-bí-zi-kir* / ŠÈ úš / *téš-má*-^{d}utu "(Textilien) (für) die Hauptölungs-Zeremonie des Ibbizikir, weil T. gestorben ist."

Die Interpretation wird bei den Sammelurkunden von Ebla wie andernorts dadurch erschwert, daß, wie gesagt, mehrere aufeinanderfolgende Einträge zusammengehören können, aber nicht müssen. Es ist oft erst durch das Zusammenstellen von Parallelen zu erkennen, wie weit etwa Personen- oder Ortsbezeichnungen, eine administrative Angabe oder der notierte Grund für vorangehende Ausgaben gelten, soweit diese nicht explizit (z. B. durch das Pronominalsuffix *-sù*) mit jenem Eintrag verbunden sind.

1.2. Methodische Ansätze zur Deutung der Verwaltungsterminologie

Im Palast von Ebla gebrauchte man wie in anderen Archiven eine begrenzte Anzahl von Termini zur Bezeichnung der üblichen Verwaltungsvorgänge, wobei den gewählten Ausdrücken innerhalb des Archives eine spezifische Funktion zukommt. Das Inventar an Begriffen, die den Grund einer Ausgabe angeben, ist dem Bedarf entsprechend größer, doch auch hier werden bestimmte Wendungen regelmäßig gebraucht.

Die Deutung der Verwaltungsterminologie muß daher grundsätzlich zwei Aspekte berücksichtigen:

1. Die wörtlich-lexikalische Bedeutung umfaßt in vielen Fällen zuerst eine Interpretation der sumerischen Ideogramme aufgrund deren ursprünglicher Bedeutung, wie sie in mesopotamischen Texten vorzufinden ist. Nicht jeder Begriff wird aber in etwa gleichzeitigen Texten Mesopotamiens belegt sein, nicht jeder ist sofort verständlich und zudem können sich Bedeutungen verschieben. Vergleichbar können Wörter des Ebla-Akkadischen etymologisch analysiert werden, und manchmal bieten die zweisprachigen Listen von Ebla (Pettinato 1982) eine Hilfe, Sumerogramm und eblaitisches Wort zu verbinden.

2. Die Gebrauchsbedeutung läßt sich demgegenüber durch das genaue Beobachten des Kontextes erreichen, in der ein Begriff gebraucht wird. Dieses Vorgehen bedeutet insbesondere die Analyse von Parallelen, das gemeinsame Vorkommen oder die Unvereinbarkeit mit anderen Begriffen oder auch eine komplementäre Verteilung. Besonders gute Beispiele für die Vertauschbarkeit von Begriffen bieten die Parallelen zwischen JAM und MAT. Neben der semantisch-pragmatischen ist auch die syntaktische Distribution zu berücksichtigen.

Es steht außer Frage, daß nur beide Wege der Interpretation gemeinsam zu einem überzeugenden Ergebnis führen können. Bisher wurde allerdings der folgende ergänzende Aspekt kaum gesehen:

3. Der Vergleich mit anderen Verwaltungsarchiven, insbesondere Palastarchiven, die dieselben Aufgabenbereiche abdecken, kann wichtige Hinweise zu Textaufbau und Terminologie im engeren Sinne ebenso wie zu grundlegenden inhaltlichen Gesichtspunkten bieten (z. B. welche Vermerke in solchen Urkunden überhaupt möglich und nötig sind, zu welchen Anlässen Geschenke gegeben werden, usw.).

Das Gesagte soll ein Vergleich administrativer Ausdrücke (vgl. oben 4. unter *1.1.*) von Ausgabeurkunden in Ebla und dem staatlichen Archiv von Puzriš-Dagān (nach Sallaberger 1999, 262 ff.) illustrieren; er wäre in ähnlicher Form durchaus mit anderen Archiven, etwa den altbabylonischen Texten aus Mari, durchführbar:

Ebla	Ur III (Puzriš-Dagān)	Erklärung
è	zi.g	Terminus für "ausgeben"
PN ì/in-na-sum	PN maškim; lugal ku$_{4}$-ra	Übergebender am Ort der Ausgabe
PN šu mu-taka$_{4}$	ĝìri PN (PN-e ...-de$_{6}$)	PN überbringt die Gabe vom Ausgabeort zum Empfänger an einen anderen Ort
in ON	šà ON	Ort der Übergabe (wenn nicht Ort der Ausgabe oder in nicht eindeutigen Fällen)

2. Der Terminus níĝ-AN.AN.AN.AN

2.1. Einige Beispiele für níĝ-AN.AN.AN.AN

Der hier zu behandelnde Terminus, níĝ-AN.AN.AN.AN, gehört sicher zu den Angaben, die eine Ausgabe von Metallen oder Textilien an eine Person begründen (Punkt 3. unter *1.1.*). Dieses níĝ-AN.AN.AN.AN ist nicht nur gut belegt, nämlich in veröffentlichten Texten oder Textzitaten [1999] etwa zweihundert mal,[3] sondern es ist auch recht oft mit zusätzlichen Angaben verbunden, die in den knapp

3 Ausgewertet sind *MEE* und *ARET*, für die Textzitate Baldacci (1992) = *PPET*, einzelne veröffentlichte Urkunden und insbesondere die zitierten Abschnitte der JAM bei Archi (1996b) und paralleler MAT bei Biga (1996).

formulierenden Urkunden eher etwas Seltenes und Besonderes darstellen. Einige charakteristische Beispiele sollen dies erläutern.

[1] *ARET* 1, 11 (MAT, // Ib. 1) Vs. xiii 6-12 = (35): 1 SAL-túg 1 íb+iii-gùn-túg / *mu-da-Lum* / níĝ-AN.AN.AN.AN / dam / *ig-rí-iš* / tu-da / dumu-nita
"(1+1 Textilien) (an) M. — (aufgrund von) n-AAAA: die Gemahlin des Igriš hat einen Sohn geboren."

[2] *MEE* 2, 37 (MAT, Ende Ar.) Rs. viii 3-9: 1 gu-dùl-túg 1 íb+iii-túg gùn / *in-ti* / ugula *ba-ti*-NE / níĝ-AN.AN.AN.AN / TIL / en / *kak-mi-um*^{ki}
"(1+1 Textilien) (an) I., 'Aufseher' von B. — (aufgrund von) n-AAAA: der Herrscher von Kakmi'um ist gestorben."

[3] *ARET* 8, 524 (MAT, um IZ 12) Vs. vi 4-12: 1 *'à-da-um*-túg-ii 1 aktum-túg 1 íb+iii-túg sa_6 gùn / *rí-ì-ma-lik* / *ì-mar*^{ki} / níĝ-AN.AN.AN.AN / en / *ì-mar*^{ki} / mar-tu^{ki} / TIL / *in* kur^{ki}
"(1+1+1 Textilien) (an) R. aus Emar — (aufgrund von) n-AAAA: der Herrscher von Emar hat die Amurriter im Bergland geschlagen."

[4] *MEE* 10, 29 (JAM IZ 4) Rs. iii 22-28: 1 ma-na babbar:kù / níĝ-ba / *šu-ga-du* / *ma-rí*^{ki} / níĝ-AN.AN.AN.AN / adab^{ki} / šu ba_4-ti
"1 Mine Silber (als) Geschenk (an) Š. von Mari — (aufgrund von) n-AAAA: Adab eingenommen."

2.2. Bisherige Deutungen und Schreibung

Der Begriff níĝ-AN.AN.AN.AN widersetzte sich bisher einer überzeugenden Deutung. Die meisten Vorschläge gehen von dem charakteristischen Zeichen AN aus, das meist vierfach, seltener auch dreifach gesetzt ist (vgl. Krecher 1987, 182), und das oft als Plural von diĝir "Gott" verstanden wird.

Der Befund ist nicht ganz einheitlich: vor allem ältere Texte schreiben unseren Begriff eher mit drei AN (níĝ-AN.AN.AN), jüngere dann níĝ-AN.AN.AN.AN, wobei die vier AN meist paarweise übereinander stehen, selten auch in einer Reihe nebeneinander (z. B. *ARET* 8, 525 x 7). Der Plural für "Götter" kann in Ebla mit dem erwarteten AN.AN (diĝir-diĝir), häufig auch AN.AN.AN (diĝir-diĝir-diĝir), selten sogar mit vier AN geschrieben werden (z. B. im Abarsal-Vertrag TM.75.G.2420 u. Rd. ii 6; s. Edzard 1992, 209; vgl. Krecher a. O.). Auf jeden Fall ist bei níĝ-AN.AN.AN.AN die Schreibung mit vier AN die übliche, beim Plural "Götter" dagegen die Ausnahme.

Weiters sind aber NAB, in Mesopotamien AN.AN, und MUL, in Mesopotamien AN.AN.AN, zu berücksichtigen. AN.AN.AN steht in Ebla für NAB oder MUL; MUL wird üblicherweise mit vier, selten mit drei AN geschrieben (Archi 1988b:1).

Ausgehend von der Schreibung versteht Pettinato (1980, 18) níĝ-AN.AN. AN.AN als "'appannaggio di divinità', nel senso forse di 'ex-voto', ed ha il valore di motivazione o giustificazione di spesa." Dieser Übersetzung folgen mehr oder weniger explizit viele (s. die Übersicht über bisherige Deutungen bei Baldacci 1991, 15). Die Lesung Pettinatos als níg-^{d}mul ist aufgrund der Unterschiede zur mesopotamischen Orthographie und der möglichen Varianten eine frühe Festlegung. Es bietet sich zwar aufgrund der knapp zitierten Ebla-Schreibungen eher níĝ-mul_x(AN.AN. AN.AN) an, doch gebietet der Befund von Fāra (*3.3.*) Vorsicht: níĝ-mul-an scheint ebenso möglich.

Eine Deutung als (wörtlich) "Sache der Götter" ist nicht nur wegen der Schreibung unwahrscheinlich, weil nämlich unser Terminus regelmäßig mit vier AN, "Götter" dagegen nur ausnahmsweise mit vier AN geschrieben wird. Das eigentliche Problem der Interpretation Pettinatos (und vergleichbarer) ist jedoch, daß sich hiermit keine überzeugende Beziehung zwischen dem Terminus "Gabe der Götter", dem Empfänger von Gewand oder Silber und dem nach n-AAAA genannten Sachverhalt erzielen läßt. Dieser Einwand wiegt umso schwerer, als gerade Ausgaben für den Kult recht gut bekannt sind und sich hier in den meisten Fällen keine Gemeinsamkeiten abzeichnen.

Aus demselben Grunde können daher vorsichtigere Umschreibungen des Terminus als "eine Zeremonie" nicht überzeugen (so etwa Bonechi 1990, 27 "un atto cultuale"; Urcioli 1995, 118 f. "ceremony n."). Das Wort blieb aufgrund solcher Schwierigkeiten oft ungedeutet oder wurde nur als "eine Zuweisung" umschrieben (z. B. Edzard 1981, 135; Sollberger 1986, 64; Krecher 1987, 182; Archi 1988a, 229); Baldacci (1991, 15) weist auf den nicht-kultischen Kontext hin. Auch die zweisprachigen lexikalischen Listen können nicht weiterhelfen, da sie den Begriff zwar aufführen (*MEE* 4: VE 48, EV 0264), aber nicht mit einer eblaitischen Glosse versehen.

Das immer bessere Verständnis der Ebla-Texte und die zahlreichen Vorkommen von n-AAAA fordern eine Deutung heraus, und so stammen aus neuerer Zeit zwei abweichende Vorschläge. Fronzaroli (1991, 1993) liest níg-mul und deutet dies ausgehend von mul = *nabāṭu* als "erstrahlen lassen" ("faire resplendir") usw., was jedoch den Vorkommen in administrativen Texten nicht gerecht werden kann.

Jüngst bot Archi (1997) eine völlig neue Wege weisende Übersetzung als "to assist, to take care of, to prepare; assistance", wobei er offensichtlich vom Kontext ausgeht und — zumindest vorerst — keine etymologische Stütze bietet. Die

Deutung Archis bereitet jedoch Schwierigkeiten bei nicht vorhersagbaren Ereignissen — und solche Gegenbeispiele sind in [1]-[4] auch aufgeführt — etwa der Geburt eines Sohnes, bei Tod, Sieg in der Schlacht und Zerstörung von Orten, insbesondere wenn z. B. explizit angegeben ist, daß "der Herrscher von Emar die Amurriter im Bergland besiegt" (wenn sich das "helfen" auf zukünftige Handlungen beziehen sollte). Auch daß etwa die Händler von Mari in Babylonien geholfen haben (oder helfen) sollen, die Städte Kiš oder Adab zu zerstören (s. unten *4.1.*), erscheint ebenso wie der Beistand eines Mannes bei einer Geburt, s. [1], nicht recht plausibel.

3. Deutung als "Nachricht"

Mein Vorschlag, den ich hier vorstellen und begründen möchte, geht in eine andere Richtung: meines Erachtens läßt sich níg-AN.AN.AN.(AN) als Ausdruck für "Nachricht, Botschaft, Kunde", bzw. verbal "Nachricht überbringen" oder als Personenbezeichnung (formal wohl ein Partizip) als "der die Nachricht überbringt" verstehen. Dieser Ansatz ergibt bei den oben gebotenen Beispielen [1]-[4] einen guten Sinn und läßt sich auch in allen mir bekannten Belegen anwenden (ohne daß damit freilich immer alle Probleme der jeweiligen Textstellen gelöst wären).

Der Vorschlag ist nun genauer zu prüfen, und zwar in Hinsicht auf

1. die Charakteristika von n-AAAA-Angaben im Vergleich mit anderen Einträgen der Ebla-Texte im Sinne der inhaltlich-terminologischen Deutung aufgrund des Kontexts,
2. die syntaktische Konstruktion innerhalb dieser Einträge,
3. die Herkunft des Sumerogramms n-AAAA und damit die Etymologie und ob sich auch von dieser Seite die Deutung stützen läßt. Hier wird sich eine Lesung als níĝ-mul-(an) anbieten.

3.1. Inhaltlich-terminologische Charakteristika von níĝ-AN.AN.AN.AN-Vermerken

Wodurch zeichnen sich in der administrativen Handhabung n-AAAA-Ausgaben gegenüber anderen aus? Stimmen diese Merkmale mit der angenommenen Interpretation "Nachricht" überein? Blicken wir dazu auf zwei wichtige Parameter von Urkundenvermerken, den Empfänger der Gabe und den Ort.

3.1.1. Zu den Personen

Im Inhalt der "Botschaft", nach dem "n-AAAA"-Vermerk, treten Mitglieder der königlichen Familie und die höchsten Beamten von Ebla oder die Herrscher (und ihre Familien) anderer Staaten auf (vgl. z. B. [2], [3]). Die Gaben-Empfänger dagegen gehören in der Regel diesem Personenkreis nicht an, obwohl sonst gerade dieser Personenkreis besonders häufig Geschenke erhält. Es läßt sich hingegen manchmal feststellen, daß der Empfänger der Gabe demjenigen unterstellt ist, von dem in der "Nachricht" die Rede ist; vgl. z. B.:

[5] *MEE* 2, 33 (MAT, etwa Ib.) Vs. x 2-5 (Umschrift nach Foto): 1 SAL-túg níĝ-AN.AN. AN.AN / maškim DUB-*da-ar* / DUB-*da-ar* / tuš:lú
"(1 Textilstück) (für) die Nachricht an den Beauftragen des D., daß D. *stationiert* ist."

In diesem Fall ist die Beziehung zwischen dem Empfänger der Gabe, also dem Überbringer der Nachricht, und seinem Patron, über den er berichtet, sogar im Text markiert (ähnlich maškim von PN als Empfänger, PN in der Nachricht: *ARET* 8, 521 ix 14-x 8; 529 v 9-vi 4). Prosopographie und/oder Beachten des Kontexts einer Urkunde zeigen in vielen weiteren Fällen eine solche Beziehung.

3.1.2. Zu den Ortsangaben

Ortsnamen begegnen ausgesprochen häufig in der Nachricht, dort auch weit von Ebla entfernte, sogar Kiš, Akšak und Adab in Babylonien (s. [4] und unten *4.1.*). Die Übergabe der Gabe dagegen findet fast ausschließlich im Palast von Ebla statt, denn nie erscheint der sonst so häufige Vermerk, die Gabe sei an einen anderen Ort zum Empfänger gesandt worden (šu mu-taka$_4$).[4]

Außerdem wird manchmal das Geschenk an den Boten persönlich von einem Mitglied der Herrscherfamilie übergeben (ì/in-na-sum; vgl. auch *3.2.*), selbst wenn von weit entfernten Orten die Rede ist; z. B.

[6] 75.2508 Vs. iv 37-46 (JAM IZ 7) // 75.1442 (MAT; Biga/Pomponio 1993, 124 f., PPET 2019): *ib-gi tíš-te-da-mu* in-na-sum níg-AN.AN.AN.AN *ib-al*$_6^{ki}$ šu ba$_4$-ti
(Satz von 3 Textilien und 2 Goldohrringe) "an Ibgi, Tište-Damu hat es übergeben, (für) die Nachricht, daß Ib'al eingenommen ist." (Tište-Damu ist Tochter König Iš'ar-Damus; s. Biga 1996, 69-71)

Es zeigt sich aber auch hier manchmal eine Beziehung des Beschenkten zum Ort, von dem die Rede ist: in [3] berichtet der Bote aus seinem Herkunftsort (vgl. ähnlich *ARET* 4, 8 [24]).

4 Die einzige deutliche "Ausnahme" ist nach meinem Kenntnisstand *MEE* 2, 1 Rs. vi 11-vii 5: (...) *bù-da-ma-lik* / *in* // *ša-ra-bi-ig*^{ki} / šu ba$_4$-ti / níg-AN.AN.AN.AN / *ma-ri*^{ki} / TIL "(Silberobjekte) hat B. in Š. empfangen (für) die Nachricht/(weil) er berichtet, daß Mari geschlagen wurde". - Der Betrag fehlt allerdings in der Metall-Summe, s. Pettinato (1980, 19), also bekommt der Bote wahrscheinlich seinen Lohn in Šarabig, muß ihn aber nicht abliefern.

Der Detailvergleich zum Textaufbau zeigt also wesentliche Merkmale, die sich bei der Bedeutung "Nachricht" leicht erklären lassen, damit diese Interpretation unterstützen und die anderen in *2.2.* angeführten Vorschläge meines Erachtens widerlegen.

3.2. Syntaktische Konstruktion von Vermerken mit níĝ-AN.AN.AN.AN

Im folgenden sind die möglichen Konstruktionen mit n-AAAA angeführt. Genannt sein müssen dabei die Materie, die ausgegeben, wird, der oder die Empfänger dieser Gabe, sowie nach dem Vermerk "n-AAAA" das Thema der Nachricht. Genannt sind manchmal auch der Empfänger der Nachricht, insbesondere der Herrscher oder seine Gemahlin, oder derjenige, der die Gabe im Palast übergibt.

In der folgenden Übersicht gelten zusätzlich folgende Abkürzungen (vgl. Anm. 1):

T/M = Textilien oder Metallgegenstände (z. B. Ohrringe) als Objekt der Gabe
E = Empfänger der Gabe, also der Überbringer der Nachricht
SV = Sachverhalt der Nachricht, ausgedrückt durch ein einziges Nomen ("Nachricht", n-AAAA, "(über) Wasser", "(über) Ort ON" usw.) oder einen Satz (vgl. [1]-[6])

1. Grundschema:
T/M — E — n-AAAA SV
"T/M (an) E für die Nachricht/der berichtet, daß SV/über SV"

1'. Varianten dazu:
T/M — níg-ba E — n-AAAA SV
"T/M als Geschenk (an) E für die Nachricht/der berichtet, daß SV/über SV"
T/M — n-AAAA SV — E
"T/M für die Nachricht, daß/über SV (an) E"
(75.10077 Rs. x = Archi 1996b, 81 [JAM Ib. 2a]; *ARET* 3, 465 Rs. i 5'-9')

2. Übergebender ist zusätzlich vermerkt:
T/M — E - | Tište-Damu/*ma-lik-tum* ì/in-na-sum | — n-AAAA SV
"T/M (an) E, — Tište-Damu/die Herrscherin hat es übergeben, — (für) die Nachricht, daß SV"
(75.2508 Vs. iv 36-46= [6]; *ARET* 8, 521 [30])

T/M — E - n-AAAA SV — | *ma-lik-tum* ì/in-na-sum
"T/M (an) E (für) die Nachricht, daß SV; die Herrscherin hat es übergeben"
(75.2428 Vs. vii 27-36 [JAM IZ 8], Biga/Pomponio 1993, 124 f.; 75.2429 Vs. xvi 22-xvii 8 [JAM IZ 9], Biga 1996, 70; *ARET* 3, 185 vi 1'-11' [JAM, Frgt.]; *ARET* 8, 527 [20])

M — E — | en/*ma-lik-tum* ì-na-sum | — ŠÈ n-AAAA SV

"M (an) E, — der Herrscher/die Herrscherin hat es übergeben wegen der Nachricht/weil er berichtet, daß SV"

(75.10074 Vs. xxx 20-26, Biga 1996, 53 [JAM IZ 6]; vgl. 75.10088+ Vs. xxii 1'-12', PPET 2309 [JAM IZ 3])

T — E — | *ma-lik-tum* ì-na-sum | — *in* u$_{4}$ n-AAAA SV

"T (an) E, — die Herrscherin hat es übergeben, als er berichtet, daß SV" (*ARET* 4, 18 [2], MAT // JAM IZ 6)

3. Empfänger der Nachricht ist vermerkt:

T — E — n-AAAA en/*ma-lik-tum*/ama-gal en SV

"T (an) E (für) die Nachricht (an) den Herrscher/die Herrscherin/die Königinmutter, daß SV"

(en: *ARET* 3, 801 ii; *ARET* 8, 522 (15); *MEE* 7, 48 Vs. iii. — *ma-lik-tum*: *ARET* 8, 525 x 5-13; 75.10013 Vs. ii', Archi 1997. — ama-gal en: *ARET* 3, 599 ii)

T — E — n-AAAA en *in* u$_{4}$ SV

"T (an) E (für) die Nachricht (an) den Herrscher, als SV"

(*ARET* 4, 1 [37]; Vermischung zweier Konstruktionen, der mit n-AAAA und der mit *in* u$_{4}$)

4. Einzelne, elliptische Konstruktionen:

T — E — *in* u$_{4}$ PN ur$_{4}$ n-AAAA [...

"T/M (an) E, als der ... PN berichtet, [..." (*ARET* 3, 176 ii)

M — n-AAA SV

"M für den, der SV berichtet" (75.2236 Rs. v, vi, Pettinato 1995, 105 f.; Ar.)

M — E — lugal al$_{6}^{?}$-DU n-AAAA

"M (an) E, der (dem/vom) König die Nachricht bringt/berichtet"(?) (*ibid.* Vs. iv 2-4)

Besonders deutlich sind die Möglichkeiten unterschiedlicher Realisierung des Ideogramms n-AAAA als Verb, Partizip oder Nomen actionis im Ritualtext zur Hochzeit der Königin (*ARET* 11; Partizip wohl auch dort 1 [33] = 2 [35]). Herrscher und Herrscherin haben sich am Hauptfesttag im Mausoleum der königlichen Familie niedergelassen und erwarten den Sonnenaufgang. Bei Sonnenaufgang beginnt die Musik, und vor Einsetzen der Hauptopfer und Feierlichkeiten heißt es nach der neuen Deutung:

[7] *ARET* 11, 1 (64)-(65) // 2 (67)-(68):

wa-(*a*) / du$_{11}$-(ga) / níĝ-AN.AN.AN.AN / ([níĝ]-⸢AN.AN.AN.AN⸣) / *wa-*(*a*) / níĝ-AN.AN.AN.AN / ^{d}TU / ^{d}*suḫ*$_{5}$*-ra* gibil / ^{d}*ba-ra-ma* gibil / en gibil / *ma-lik-tum* gibil

"und es spricht der, der Nachrichten bringt, (die Nachricht), und die Nachricht ist: (Nin)tu (die Geburtsgöttin) hat Šu'ra[5] erneuert, Barama erneuert, den Herrscher erneuert, die Herrscherin erneuert."

---

5 Lesung des bisher ^{d}KU-*ra* umschriebenen Gottesnamens als ^{d}*suḫ*$_{5}$*-ra* nach Bonechi 1997, 499-501. Die Form /suḫ/ statt eines für den GN zu erwartenden */šu(ḫ)/ (s. Bonechi a. O.) ergibt sich aus der Angabe zur Lesung in Proto-Ea 15 (MSL 14, 30).

Hier ist, darauf sei besonders hingewiesen, n-AAAA mit dem Verb "sagen, sprechen" (du_{11}-ga) verbunden.

3.3. Das Sumerogramm níĝ-mul-(an) und "Nachrichten" in Ur III-Urkunden

Bei der Interpretation des Sumerogramms níĝ-AN.AN.AN.AN ging ich vom Kontext der administrativen Texte aus, um die Gebrauchsbedeutung zu ermitteln. Der Ansatz ist auch beeinflußt von der Kenntnis vergleichbarer Terminologie in anderen Archiven, auf die ich sogleich zurückkommen werde.

Die Frage nach der Etymologie und damit Lesung von níĝ-AN.AN.AN.AN ist dagegen noch offen. Man wird annehmen wollen, daß dieses Sumerogramm aus der Verwaltungssprache Mesopotamiens nach Ebla übernommen wurde, wobei es durchaus zu Bedeutungsverschiebungen gekommen sein mag.[6]

3.3.1. "Botschaft" = á-áĝ-ĝá in Ur III-Urkunden

Das weitgehende Fehlen in mesopotamischen Texten deutet jedoch schon darauf hin, daß für "Nachricht, Botschaft" möglicherweise im späteren 3. Jt. ein anderer Begriff gebraucht wurde. Das ist in der Tat der Fall, wie einige Texte der Ur III-Zeit lehren, s. [8]: es handelt sich zweimal um Dankesopfer an die Götter, wenn die gute Nachricht vom erfolgreichen Feldzug gebracht wird. Der Terminus für eine solche "Nachricht" ist á-áĝ-ĝá, üblicherweise "Anweisung" (s. schon Sallaberger 1993.1, 208 Anm. 987, 278 mit Anm. 1288). Wichtig für den Vergleich mit Ebla sind die Belege aus Umma: jeweils werden Wolle, Gewänder bzw. 1 Silberring, also dieselben Materialien wie in Ebla, an einen Boten gegeben, der in die Provinz Umma die Nachricht vom siegreichen Feldzug bringt. Es handelt sich übrigens in diesen Fällen auch um den Feldzug, nach dem das jeweilige Jahr benannt ist.

[8] "Nachrichten" in Ur III-Urkunden:

a. MVN 13, 563:1-3; Puzriš-Dagan, [Datum nicht erhalten]:
1 gu_4 niga / ^{d}Nanna / u_4 á-ĝá sig_5 kaskal ì-im-de_6-a
"1 Mastrind (an) Nanna, als die gute Nachricht vom Feldzug gebracht wurde"

b. de Genouillac, ITT 3, 5271:14; Girsu, iv [ ]:
$sizkur_2$ á$^{!}$-áĝ-ĝá ugnim silim^{si-lim}-ma de_6-a

---

6 Ein deutliches Beispiel für Möglichkeiten der Bedeutungsverschiebung eines Sumerogramms ist gaba-ru "Empfang" (Lit. bei Milano 1990, 395: "ricevuta"). Hier liegt gaba ri/ru = *maḫārum* zugrunde, wobei allerdings das Akkadische zwei an sich verschiedene sumerische Begriffe mit demselben Wort wiedergibt (und in Ebla prompt das 'falsche' Sumerogramm gebraucht wird): *maḫārum* "jmdn. angehen" = sum. gaba ri/ru, dagegen *maḫārum* "empfangen" = sum. šu ti.

"(Mehlsorten für) Riten, als die Nachricht, daß die Truppen heil geblieben seien, gebracht wurde"

c. Yıldız/Gomi, UTI 4, 2315:1-5; Umma, i AS 6 (AS 6 = "Jahr, als Šašrum zerstört wurde"!)
1 ma-na ḫar kù-babb[ar$_2$] / níĝ-ba lugal-an-dùl / á-áĝ-ĝá sig$_5$ / *ša-aš-ru-um*[ki] / ḫul-a de$_6$-a
"1 Mine (schwerer) Silberring als Geschenk (an) L., der die gute Nachricht, daß Šašrum zerstört wurde, gebracht hat"

d. Schneider, AnOr. 1, 83:1-5; Umma, i AS 6 (den Hinweis auf diesen Text verdanke ich C. Wilcke)
2 gú siki gi / níĝ-ba lugal-an-dùl / á[!]-áĝ-ĝá sig$_5$ / *ša-aš-šú-ru*[ki] ḫul-a de$_6$-a
"2 Talente einheimische[?] Wolle als Geschenk (an) L., der die gute Nachricht, daß Šašrum zerstört wurde, gebracht hat"

e. Waetzoldt/Yıldız, MVN 16, 960:12-16, Umma, - ŠS 3 (ŠS 3 = "Jahr, als Simānum zerstört wurde"!):
(5 Gewänder) lugal-si-sá rá-gaba á-áĝ-ĝá sig$_5$ *si-ma-núm*[ki] ḫul-a de$_6$-a
"(5 Gewänder) für den 'Berittenen' L., der die gute Nachricht, daß Simānum zerstört wurde, gebracht hat"

3.3.2. Die altakkadische Belege für níĝ-mul-an-na "Nachricht"

Die Verbindung zwischen der Ur III- und der Ebla-Terminologie sowie die Lesung gelingt mit Hilfe zweier altakkadischer Texte:

[9] Grégoire, MVN 10, 124 (vgl. Krecher 1987, 182 Anm. 24), (spät)-sargon., Herkunft unbekannt:
(je ⅓, ½ oder ⅔ Sekel Silber, kù, an[?] 21 Personen:)
níĝ-mul(AN.AN.AN)-an-na / lagaš[ki] ḫul-a / tu-ru-UŠ sukkal[?]
"Nachricht, daß Lagaš zerstört wurde; T. Bote[?]." (Deutung der letzten Zeile unsicher)

[10] Pettinato 1997, Nr. 34; sargon., Umma:
0.1.0 šim *a-ga-dè*[ki] / 0.1.0 níĝ-àr-ra / 0.1.0 munu$_4$ / 0.1.0 dabin / é-zi aslag$_4$ / níĝ-mul(AN.AN.AN)-la-na / mu-de$_6$-a / 1 mu 5 iti
"(Lebensmittel) für den Wäscher E., der die Nachricht hergebracht hat. (Datum)."

MVN 10, 124 nennt wie die in [8] zitierten Ur III-Texte als Botschaft, daß ein Ort, nämlich Lagaš, zerstört (ḫul) sei; der Begriff für die "Nachricht", so müssen wir im Vergleich mit Ebla und Ur III annehmen, ist níĝ-mul an-na.

Die Lesung dieses seltenen Terminus erlaubt der jüngst von Pettinato (1997, Nr. 34) veröffentlichte Umma-Text [10] mit der Schreibung níĝ-mul-la-na, was wohl nur als gleichsam syllabische Schreibung von níĝ-mul an-na von MVN 10, 124 [9] aufgefaßt werden kann.

MVN 10, 124 bietet somit eine Brücke in der Terminologie zwischen Ur III und Ebla:

	"Nachricht"	"(Land, Ort) zerstört/besiegt"
Ebla	níĝ-mul-(an)(AN.AN.AN.AN)	TIL
MVN 10 124	níĝ-mul-an-na	ḫul
Ur III	á-áĝ-ĝá	ḫul

3.3.3. Zum Bedeutungsfeld von sumerisch mul (an-na)

Nun zur Semantik von níĝ-mul (an-na): die Gebrauchsbedeutung von níĝ-mul in Ebla ist wohl sicher "Nachricht", 'wörtlich' läßt sich níĝ mul an-na der altakkadischen Belege als "Sache der Himmelssterne" übersetzen. Lassen sich die beiden Bedeutungen verbinden? mul-an "Himmelsstern" oder nur mul "Stern" begegnet im Sumerischen vor allem in der literarischen Sprache Gudeas und Šulgis, [11], als Umschreibung für "Schrift", am besten zu verstehen über das Bild des Sternenhimmels als *šiṭirti šamê* "Schrift des Himmels"; die Keilschriftzeichen sind gleichsam die Sterne auf der Tontafel. Doch auch hier kann oft die (sekundäre?) Bedeutung "Botschaft, Nachricht" guten Sinn ergeben, insbesondere in Verbindung mit dem Verb gù dé "rufen, verkünden" in [11b-d].

[11] Einige Belege für mul-(an) "Himmelsstern" in der Bedeutung von "Schrift":[7]

a. Lexikalisch:
mul = *šiṭirtum* "Schrift" (MSL 14, 94, Proto-Aa 139:2), auch *šiṭrum* (s. *CAD* Š/3, 144 f. *s.vv.*)

b. Gudea, Zyl. A v 21-vi 2 (vgl. die Parallele iv 23-v 1):
ki-sikil ... / gi dub-ba kù-NE šu bí-du$_8$-a / dub mul-<an?> du$_{10}$-ga bí-ĝál-la-a / ad im-da-gi$_4$-a / nin$_9$-ĝu$_{10}$ ^{d}nisaba ga-nam-me-àm / é-a dù-ba mul kù-ba / gù ma-ra-a-dé
"Die junge Frau ..., die ein Schreibrohr aus *leuchtendem* Metall in Händen hält, die eine Tafel mit 'Sternen' auf den Knien hat, mit der sie sich berät, die ist in der Tat meine (= Nanšes) Schwester Nisaba. Des Hausbaus reinen 'Stern' hat sie dir verkündet." (vgl. Nisaba A 31 = Hallo 1970, 125; Lugale 715 f. und — gegen das Akkadische — 726; Nisabas Tempel é-mul-mul *v.s.*, TCS 3, 48:528; s. Alster 1976, 117-120)

c. Gudea, Zyl. A ix 10:
ĝarza-ĝá mul-an kù-ba gù ga-mu-ra-a-dé-e
"Den reinen 'Himmelsstern' meiner Riten will ich (= Ninĝirsu) dir (= Gudea) verkünden."

d. Šulgi B 307-310 (Ms. Geerd Haaijer, mit freundlicher Erlaubnis zitiert)

---

7 Mein herzlicher Dank gilt Pascal Attinger, Bern, für seine zahlreichen Belege zu mul-an, aus denen ich hier auswähle. mul-an mit gù dé erscheint außer bei Gudea auch in Šulgi B 364. Ähnlich wie der *sub* d. zitierte Abschnitt Šulgi B 307-310 lautet Šulgi E 246-248; vgl. die Übersetzung von Klein (1981, 19 f.). In anderen Belegen ist mul-an "Himmelsstern" in seiner primären Bedeutung anzusetzen, z. B. unter den Šulgihymnen Šulgi G 4, Šulgi C 19, oder Farmer's Instructions 38.

níĝ-DÉ-a èn-du-ĝu₁₀ ḫé-(en)-pà-dè mul-(an) ḫé-ù-tu / sig-šè uri₂ki-ma ki sikil-la bí-mú / É.ĜEŠTUG₂.(d).NISABA mul èn-du-ĝá-ka (//-ĝá-a-kam) / nim-šè nibruki-a ki gal-la bí-gub
"[Let him] choose my hymns for instruction; let him produce heavenly stars! / To that end I had built below, in Ur, on a pure place / a wisdom house of Nisaba for the writing of my hymns; / above, in Nippur, on a great place I had it founded!"

Um von 'wörtlichem' "Sache der Himmelssterne" und "Himmelsstern" zur übertragenen Bedeutung "Nachricht" bzw. "Schrift" zu gelangen, sind sicherlich beide Ebenen relevant: die Sterne des Himmels sind die 'Schrift' der Götter, die deren Botschaften zeigen; und die Keilschriftzeichen sind die 'Himmelssterne' auf der Tafel. Daß aber beide Ebenen zusammen gesehen werden müssen, und nicht nur eine allein (etwa allein das Astrale, wie dies Alster 1976, 117-120, annimmt), das zeigt meines Erachtens zweifelsfrei die enge Verbindung zwischen mul-(an) und der Göttin der Schreibkunst, Nisaba (s. besonders b. mit Anmerkungen, doch auch etwa d.).

Es sind auffälligerweise besonders relativ frühe sumerische literarische Texte, in denen mul-(an) in einer übertragenen Bedeutung "Schrift, Nachricht" erscheint, während es im umfangreichen sumerischen literarischen Corpus sonst seltener zu begegnen scheint.[8]

3.3.4. mul-an in frühdynastischen literarischen Texten

Die Göttin der Schreibkunst Nisaba und das Wort mul-an, das im späten 3. Jt. etwa als "Sternenschrift" wiedergegeben werden kann, sind ebenso eng verbunden in einer stereotypen Schlußwendung literarischer Texte aus Fāra und Abū Ṣalābīḫ.[9] Während Alster (1976, 117-120) daraufhin in den späten, oben [11b] angeführten Parallelen mul-an einzig als "Himmelssterne" deuten möchte, übersetzt Cohen (1976, 88 f.) ganz im Sinne dieser Ausführungen "shining/writing". Die Textabschnitte sind bis auf den Namen Nisaba, zà-me "Preis" und vielleicht ug₅ "erhaben" (so Cohen 1976) weitgehend unverständlich; dennoch erschiene eine Aussage, daß Nisaba den vorangehenden Text als mul-an = eine "Nachricht, Botschaft, Kunde" o.ä. verkündet, durchaus vorstellbar. In diese Richtung scheint mir besonders der Schlußabschnitt des ersten Textteiles von SF 18 zu weisen:

8 Pascal Attinger weist mich noch auf áĝ-mul-an-na (Emesal) in einer Bedeutung wie "Nachricht" im Eršemma CT 58, 5:15-17 hin (die Bearbeitung von S. N. Kramer, Eretz Israel 16*, 1982, 141-146, war mir nicht zugänglich).

9 Cohen (1976, 88 f.); Alster (1976, 116); s. Krebernik (1998, 323); die Abschnitte finden sich am Ende von SF 18 vii, SF 55, SF 56, NTSŠ 82, IAS 123; zu den Texten s. nun Krebernik (1998, 337 ff.). Vgl. Zu SF 18 (s. sogleich) den Beginn der Keš-Hymne, wonach Nisaba das Preislied Enlils niederschreibt (freundlicher Hinweis von A. Zgoll).

[12] SF 18 vii:
nisaba ug_5 / ... / ug_5 ug_5 / mul an [x?] / ^{d}inanna zà-me du_{11} / ^{d}inanna zà-me

Auf Nisaba mit den üblichen Epitheta(?) ug_5 ug_5 folgt wieder der uns interessierende Begriff mul-an, und die letzten Zeilen sind vielleicht ja zu verstehen als: "als Botschaft/Kunde spricht sie (= Nisaba) den Preis Inannas (= den vorangehenden Hymnus$^{?}$)"; es handelt sich laut Schlußdoxologie um ein "Preislied Inannas".

Diese literarischen Fāra-Belege sind insbesondere deshalb von Bedeutung, weil hier der Terminus mul-an in einer Bedeutung wie "Himmelsschrift", wie die späteren Parallelen zu Nisaba mit mul-an deutlich zeigen, in älteren Texten als Ebla belegt ist. Die Übernahme nach Ebla aus Mesopotamien - und damit vielleicht auch eine leichte Bedeutungsverschiebung - ist auf diese Weise plausibel. Aufgrund der Verbindung mit dem Verbum du_{11}-ga "sagen, sprechen" in [7] und aufgrund des Kontexts der administrativen Zeugnisse, etwa der hohen Anzahl von Boten oder der Tatsache, daß der Inhalt der Botschaft vermerkt wird, bedeutet níĝ-mul-(an) in Ebla nicht "Schrift, Text", sondern eben "(mündliche) Nachricht".

Unsere lexikographischen Schwierigkeiten mit dem Begriff mul-an ergeben sich deshalb, weil für "Nachricht" sich schon in Urkunden der Ur III-Zeit ein anderes Wort (á-áĝ-ĝá) eingebürgert hat, während mul-(an) in der literarischen Sprache noch weiterlebt.

Die Zeugnisse aus Fāra und Abū Ṣalābīḫ erlauben auch einen neuen Blick auf die Schreibung: die oben "mul-an" transkribierte Zeichengruppe wird wie folgt geschrieben: SF 18/1 (= [12]) und NTSŠ 82 zeigen deutlich MUL (Gruppe von drei kleineren AN) und daneben einzeln AN; IAS 123 schreibt zwei mal zwei AN paarweise übereinander; SF 55 und wahrscheinlich SF 56 schreiben vier AN in einer Reihe. Die beiden letzten Schreibweisen sind dieselben wie in Ebla (s. *2.2.*); SF 18/1 und NTSŠ 82 sprechen aber in Verein mit den altakkadischen Zeugnissen [9]-[10] und den Belegen aus der sumerischen Literatur [11] für eine Interpretation als mul-an, also eine Aufspaltung der so homogen erscheinenden Gruppe von vier AN.[10] Doch da auch "mul" neben "mul-an" in den literarischen Texten [11] begegnet, läßt es sich letztlich nicht endgültig entscheiden, ob níĝ-AN.AN.AN.AN in Ebla "níĝ-mul_x" oder "níĝ-mul-an" zu lesen ist.

10 Auch in MVN 10, 124, [9], stehen 4 AN nebeneinander, doch ist das letzte wegen des nachfolgenden -na sicher "an" zu lesen; eine solche Fortführung ist aber in der frühdynastischen Orthographie nicht zu erwarten.

Abschließend folgen kurz Bemerkungen zu möglichen ähnlichen Termini auf semantischer bzw. graphischer Ebene in Ebla-Texten. Eine "gute Nachricht" heißt in *MEE* 10, 3 Vs. v 12-20 du_{11}-ga sa_6, sie wird an den Herrscher "gesandt" (šu mu-$taka_4$), doch erhält hier der Absender eine Gabe. Recht unklar ist noch níĝ-áĝ in dem sehr frühen Text *MEE* 10, 27 (Vs. ix' 1-8, Rs. ii 7-iii 5), das ebenfalls "gesandt" (šu mu-$taka_4$) wird; es mag sich vielleicht weniger um eine "Nachricht, Information" als vielmehr um eine "Order" o. ä. handeln.

Nur auf den ersten Blick sieht unserem Begriff vielleicht níĝ-ba diĝir-diĝir-diĝir "Geschenk an die Götter" ähnlich. Dies hat aber mit n-AAAA nichts zu tun, wie schon die mögliche Schreibung über zwei Zeilenfächer (níĝ-ba / diĝir-diĝir-diĝir *MEE* 7, 29 Rs. x 17 f.) oder ein anderer administrativer Kontext zeigen (z. B. 75.10077, Archi 1996b, 81; mit šu mu-$taka_4$ wie nie bei n-AAAA, s. *3.1.*).

4. "Nachrichten" in den Urkunden von Ebla: Ein Überblick

Die Deutung von níĝ-AN.AN.AN.AN als níĝ-mul-(an) "Nachricht" erklärt nicht nur viele Textpassagen in den Verwaltungsurkunden, sondern nun tritt auch auf einmal das Nachrichtenwesen am Hofe von Ebla klar zu Tage, ohne daß entsprechende Briefe vorliegen würden. Denn die Urkunden von Ebla formulieren recht ausführlich, indem sie auch das Thema einer Nachricht angeben. Damit wird ein guter Überblick möglich, welche Nachrichten überhaupt als so wichtig erachtet wurden, daß der überbringende Bote entlohnt wurde. Somit läßt sich wenigstens ansatzweise im Spektrum der Themen der Informationsfluß an den Palast von Ebla erfassen, so wie er in späteren Zeiten in den umfangreichen Briefarchiven der Paläste, etwa derer von Mari oder Ninive, greifbar wird.

Der Palast entlohnt die Boten, die die Nachricht überbringen, mit einem Geschenk von Textilien, manchmal auch Ohrringen oder Silber. Die Informanten werden durch die kostbaren Gaben gereizt, ihr Wissen dem Herrscherhaus anzuvertrauen, womöglich dafür Mühseligkeiten auf sich zu nehmen. Der Palast kann sich so ein Informationsmonopol in seinem Lande sichern, denn für politische Entscheidungen ist die Kenntnis aktueller Entwicklungen unabdingbare Voraussetzung.

Es stellt sich weiterhin die Frage, ob die Nachrichten ungeprüft übernommen wurden. In der Tat gibt es einige wenige Fälle, in denen im selben Jahr oder Monat derselbe Tatbestand von zwei verschiedenen Personen überliefert wurde. Die deutlichsten Beispiele:

[13] 75.2359 (JAM Ib. 4; s. Archi 1996b, 82; PPET 1611. 1615; // *ARET* 3, 316 ii):
Drei verschiedene Personen ([x] aus Tuttul, AbNI und Warutum aus Mari) bringen während eines Jahres die "Nachricht über die Einnahme von Akšak" (*ag-sa-gú*^{ki} šu ba_4-ti; vgl. auch unten)

[14] 75.1464 (JAM Ib. 10; s. Archi 1996b, 84; PPET 0511, 0516, 0528):
Dreimal Nachricht über Niederlage/Zerstörung (TIL) von Kiš während eines Jahres.

[15] 75.10210 (JAM Ib. 15, s. Archi 1996b, 86):
Zweimal Botschaft über den Ort Duli während eines Jahres, das erste Mal "besiegt" (GÍN.ŠÈ), das zweite Mal "eingenommen" (šu ba_4-ti).

[16] *ARET* 4, 13 (MAT, Ib.) (6) und (25):
Zwei Beauftragte (maškim) von Ḫara'il berichten innerhalb eines Monats, daß "Arab hinausgeht" (*a-ra-ab*^{ki} è; unklar; ähnlich *MEE* 10, 2, ebenfalls mit doppelter Nachricht).

[17] *ARET* 8, 527 (MAT, IZ spät) xi 5-13 und xvi 3-8:
Zwei Personen berichten von der Zerstörung von Udig (*ù-ti-gú*^{ki} TIL).

Für Nachrichten aus dem Kult, von der Prozession des NIdabal von Luban (s. *4.4.*), begegnen ebenfalls manchmal mehrere Boten.

4.1. Politisch-militärische Ereignisse

Weitaus die meisten Ereignisse, die Boten berichten, betreffen militärisch-politische Ereignisse: Sieg und Eroberungen von Städten, der Ausgang von Schlachten, der Aufenthalt der eblaitischen Heerführer im Kriegsgebiet. Plastizität gewinnen solche Einträge, wenn sich mehrere Ausgaben derselben Urkunde einem Ereignis zuordnen lassen: etwa daß der ausziehende Feldherr, der Bote mit der Nachricht vom Sieg und dann der Feldherr selbst Geschenke erhalten. Im folgenden Beispiel [19] wird sogar noch vom anschließenden Friedensvertrag berichtet, der Zeremonie des "Öl opferns".

[18] 75.1419 (Biga 1996, 55 f.; MAT // IZ 8) Vs. iv 3-11:
(1+1+1 T.), 2 ^{giš}ĝeštu-lá *i-ti-*^{d}*ì*-LAM [níĝ]-AN.AN.[AN.AN] *ib-al*$_6^{ki}$ šu ba_4-ti *wa i-bí-zi-kir* tuš:LÚ×TIL
"1+1+1 Textilien, 2 Ohrringe (an) I. (für) die Nachricht, daß Ib'al eingenommen ist und Ibbi-zikir (dort) sich aufhält" (es folgen Geschenke an Personen, zuerst Ibbizikir, die sich in Ib'al aufhalten)

[19] 75.2508 (Biga/Pomponio 1993, 115; MAT // IZ 7) Rs. xvii 29-35:
(...) níĝ-AN.AN.AN.AN *du-bù-ḫu-*^{d}*'à-da* tuš:LÚ×TIL *wa* ì-ĝiš *ḫu-sa-um*^{ki} nídba
"(Objekte an PN) (für) die Nachricht, daß Dubbuḫ-Adda sich (dort) aufhält und einen Vertrag schließt mit Ḫuša'um" (vgl. dazu Rs. x 7'-12': *in* u_4 TIL *ḫu-sa-um*^{ki} "als Ḫuša'um geschlagen wurde ...")

Es entspricht durchaus dem aus anderen Palastarchiven gewonnenen Bild, wenn kriegerische Ereignisse, Feldzüge, an erster Stelle der Nachrichten stehen. Die Belege hierfür sind jedoch zu zahlreich und vielfältig, um an dieser Stelle im Detail behandelt zu werden.

Doch die Boten berichten nicht nur von den Taten Eblas. Wenn von Mari die Rede ist, kann es sich um Auseinandersetzungen mit Ebla handeln, doch ist auf jeden Fall das Interesse Eblas an der politischen Entwicklung dieses Staates verständlich, dem Ebla in der Frühzeit der Archive großen Tribut liefern mußte und der auch gegen Ende zu den mächtigsten Staaten Syriens zählte. Sogar Ereignisse von Nagar (Tell Brāk) im Ḫabūr-Gebiet werden überliefert:

[20] 75.2464 (Archi 1996b, 83; JAM Ib. 5) Rs. vi:
... *ba-du-lum ma-rí*ki níĝ-AN.AN.AN.AN *na-gàr*ki GÍN.ŠÈ
"(Objekte an PN), den 'Vizekönig' von Mari, (für) die Nachricht, daß Nagar besiegt (habe ?/sei ?)."

Daneben stehen noch Nachrichten über Ereignisse in Babylonien:

- Kiš "geschlagen/zerstört" (TIL): *MEE* 7, 47 (JAM Ib. 3) Rs. xii 21-xiii 6; 75.1464 (JAM Ib. 10 = [14]); unklar 75.2236 (Pettinato 1995, 105 f.) Rs. vii 8-13: "Söhne des Herrschers von Kiš *gefangen* (šu du_8)"; 75.1254 Vs. ix 25-x 9 (PPET 0204): PN *iš-du*-NI *Kiš*ki
- Adab "eingenommen" (šu ba_4-ti): *MEE* 10, 29 (JAM IZ 4) Rs. iii 22-28
- Akšak "eingenommen" (šu ba_4-ti): JAM Ib. 4 = [13] // *ARET* 3, 316 ii (... PN] / *du-du-lu*ki / níĝ-AN.AN.AN.AN / *ag*-[*sa-gú*ki] / š[u ba_4-ti])

Und interessanterweise sind die einzigen in Ebla belegten Orte Babyloniens außer Kiš, nämlich Akšak und Adab, im Kontext solcher Nachrichten belegt (vgl. *ARES* 2, *RGTC* 12/1).[11] Irgendein direkter Kontakt Eblas mit diesen Orten ist dabei nicht vonnöten. Es geht also nicht nur darum, daß "gute" Nachrichten an den Palast von Ebla geliefert werden, so wie dies bei den Ur III-Belegen [8] offenkundig ist, sondern daß der Palast über die politische Entwicklung informiert bleiben möchte.

Die Information über Babylonien wird fast vollkommen durch einige wenige Leute aus Mari gewährleistet, darunter URna und Warutum, die aufgrund ihres häufigen Auftretens in den Urkunden wohl regelmäßig die Strecke zwischen Ebla und

11 Zu den Orten Babyloniens in den Zeugnissen von Ebla vgl. Steinkeller (1993, besonders 244 mit Anm. 42 und 43 zu Adab und Akšak). Mit der Deutung von n-AAAA sind auch die Schlußfolgerungen Steinkellers zu modifizieren. Ich plane, an anderer Stelle auf die wichtigsten historischen Implikationen einzugehen.

Kiš auf sich nehmen.[12] Sie erhalten öfters Silberbeträge als "Geschenke" im Palast, meist ohne daß ein Grund dafür vermerkt sei. Offenkundig handelt es sich um Händler, die im Auftrag des Palastes Geschäfte mit Babylonien tätigen und dabei auch Informationen mitbringen — so wie wir das Jahrhunderte später etwa aus Mari kennen (vgl. Durand 1991, 49 f.).

4.2. Ereignisse im Leben der Herrscherhäuser

In den einleitend genannten Beispielen [1]-[2] sind es besondere Ereignisse in den benachbarten Herrscherhäusern oder in der Elite von Ebla, die eilends dem Hofe von Ebla gemeldet werden. Es sind Todesfälle oder vor allem die Geburt eines Sohnes,[13] die unter die wichtigsten Nachrichten gezählt werden, so daß der Bote die in den Urkunden genannten Geschenke, Stoffe oder Ohrringe, erhält. Es spricht übrigens auch für die vorgeschlagene Deutung, daß es gerade diese plötzlichen Ereignisse sind, die in Nachrichten (n-AAAA) erscheinen, nicht aber die lange vorbereiteten und durch den erforderlichen Geschenkaustausch gut dokumentierten Hochzeiten.

4.3. Verfügbarkeit von Delikatessen und Wasser

Ein anderes Thema der "Nachrichten" sind Informationen über die Verfügbarkeit von Delikatessen, die an den Palast geliefert werden sollen, Vögel,[14] Früchte,[15] Gemüse[16] und frisches Olivenöl,[17] sowie Trauben und der junge Wein.[18] Gut bezeugt

---

12 Vgl. zu ihnen die Belege in *ARES* 2, 363 f. *s.v. ma-rí*^{ki}, bei Archi (1985); (1996b).

13 Geburt eines Sohnes (dumu nita tu-da): 75.2429 Vs. xvi 22-xvii 8 (JAM IZ 9; s. Biga 1996, 7; vgl. *PPET* 1803), Tište-Damu; [1], Gemahlin des Igriš; *ARET* 3, 801, Gemahlin des Ibbi-zikir, Sohn Ibriums. Geburt (tu-da): *ARET* 1, 8 (65"), [Gemahlin] des Herrschers von Lub; *ARET* 4, 1 (37), "Schwiegertochter" (é-gi$_4$-a) des Herrschers; 75.1756 Rs. ii 11-15 (Biga 1996, 38 Anm. 18), Gemahlin des PN, "Aufseher" (ugula) von Ib'al. — Tod: [2], Herrscher von Kakmium; *MEE* 7, 48 Vs. iii 18 (MAT // IZ 9), PN, "Aufseher" (ugula) von Ib'al; 75.1559 Rs. i 5-10 (Archi, 1982, 155f. T 9): Sohn des *Za-ga*; *ARET* 4, 3 (31): MaNILum aus Armi (möglicherweise im Kampf gefallen?).

14 tu^{mušen} tur *ARET* 3, 465 Rs. i 5'-9'; NIN.UŠ^{mušen}-gi *ARET* 4, 4 (43); 15 (55); *MEE* 7, 14 Vs. v 1-5. tu^{mušen} tur werden an den Palast gesandt (wohl zum Verzehr) in ARET 3, 459 viii; MEE 2, 41 Vs. iv; NIN.UŠ^{mušen}-gi gesandt in *MEE* 7, 14 iv; *ARET* 4, 12 (24).

15 É.NE bzw. NE:É nach der Deutung von Krispijn (1991/92, 17 zu ZATU Nr. 251) als 'à-lém = ḫa-lu-úb = *ḫaluppu* (eine Baumfrucht): *ARET* 8, 532 (19a); *MEE* 7, 50 Vs. ii.

16 KASKAL^{sar} *ARET* 1,14 (31); x^{sar} *ARET* 3, 465 Vs. vii.

17 ì-ĝiš gibil *ARET* 4, 12 (49).

18 ^{giš}ĝeštin: *ARET* 4, 7 (54); *MEE* 2, 39 Vs. iv 19-22; ĝeštin gibil: *ARET* 2, 14 Vs. vii 9-12. Zum Wein in Ebla s. zum Inhaltlichen Milano (1994, 434 ff.), zusammenfassend Archi (1993, 28 ff.), dort auch S. 31 unter *Ma-na-na-du*^{ki}: "Nachricht", daß Weintrauben an den Wettergott von Aleppo gesandt wurden, also, daß der Kult ordnungsgemäß durchgeführt wurde.

sind übrigens die Sendungen (šu mu-taka$_4$) dieser Delikatessen an den Palast, für die der Überbringer mit Geschenken entlohnt wird (Pomponio 1986, 239 ff.).

Im Klima Syriens und der Abhängigkeit der Landwirtschaft vom Regen erhalten auch Nachrichten über "Wasser", das heißt wohl "Regen", ihren Sinn.[19]

4.4. Nachrichten von der Kultfahrt des NIdabal von Luban

Verwunderlich scheint auf den ersten Blick, daß eine ganze Reihe von Nachrichten in den Kult des Gottes NIdabal[20] von Luban gehören. Alle Texte sind in den xi. oder xii. Monat datiert, es handelt sich also um ein jährliches Fest dieses Gottes. Charakteristische Belege sind:[21]

[21] *ARET* 4, 23 (+ *ARET* 1, 2; Join Bonechi 1996; MAT // IZ 8):

(18) (1+1+1 T.) / *i-bí-šum* / níg̃-AN.AN.AN.AN // *ir-ti* / aga$_3$-ús / *in* / *ù-ra-mu*^{ki}
"(1+1+1 Textilien) an I. für die Nachricht, daß Irdi Bewacher$^?$ ist in Uram(u)"

(20) (1+1 T.) / ḪAR-*ra-ma-lik* / lú *ib-da-u*$_9$ / níg̃-AN.AN.AN.AN / *bù-ga-Lum* / aga$_3$-ús / *in* / *ar-u*$_9$*-gú*^{ki}
"(1+1 Textilien) an Ḫ., den des I., für die Nachricht, daß BugaLum Bewacher$^?$ ist in Arugu."

(21) (2+1+1+2 T.) / *šu-bí* // lú *i-ba-zi-mi-nu* / *ru*$_{12}$*-zi-da-ar* / lú *ib-dur-i-sar* / níg̃-AN.AN.AN.AN / *ir-ti* / šeš-ii-ib / *in ar-u*$_9$*-gú*^{ki}
"(2×(1+1+1) Textilien) an Š., den des I., und R., den des I., für die Nachricht, daß Irdi Begleiter ist in Arugu."

Im Kult wird also die Nachricht überbracht, wenn eine bestimmte Person den Gott NIdabal an einem Ort "bewacht" (aga$_3$-ús deutlich auch verbal) bzw. als "Begleiter" (šeš-ii-ib) an einem Ort übernimmt.[22]

Die Personen sind aus dem Text *ARET* 1, 2 + 4, 23 selbst bekannt: sie begegnen wieder unter den 12 Personen, die šeš-ii-ib-Funktion übernehmen, in *ARET* 1, 2 + 4, 23 v 3-vi 2: 12+12+12 Textilien an 12 PNN šeš-ii-ib / šu mu-nig̃in$_2$ // ^{d}NI-*da-bal* /

19 Meist formuliert als níg̃-AN.AN.AN.AN a (*in*) ORT "Nachricht über Wasser (in) ORT": *ARET* 3, 196 Vs. v und 322 Vs. iv im "Palast", sa-za$_x^{ki}$; *ARET* 3, 209 Vs. iii in Maʾbarra; 75.1399 Rs. (*PPET* 0359) in *i-da*-NE-NE^{ki}; *ARET* 4, 15 (46) "im Distrikt/am Tor", ká (unklar); *ARET* 3, 628 iv ohne Ortsangabe.

20 Zu einer Lesung *ʾa*$_5$*-da-bal* und möglichen Etymologien als einer Erscheinungsform des Wettergottes s. Fronzaroli (1997, 288 f.), Xella (1998).

21 Eine Liste von Belegen bietet Urcioli (1995).

22 Die Deutung von šeš-ii-ib als "Begleiter" oder ähnlich beruht auf der Annahme, daß šeš-"ii" = šeš-tab "Begleiter, Stellvertreter"; das auch als Personenbezeichnung (z. B. Milano 1990, 390 *s.v.*) bekannte Element IB bleibt unerklärt. šeš-ii-ib und aga$_3$-ús werden wie andere sumerographisch geschriebene Begriffe (z. B. níg̃-ba, nídba) wohl auch verbal gebraucht, etwa "begleiten$^?$, behüten$^?$".

*lu-ba-an*ki "die Begleiter? sind auf der Prozession[23] des NIdabal von Luban". In dieser Liste sind Irdi der zweite (*ARET* 1, 2 [11']) und BugaLum der letzte (*ARET* 4, 23 [8]) genannte Name.

Interessant sind auch die beiden Orte, bei denen der Gott von einer anderen Person betreut wird, *ù-ra-mu*ki und *ar-u₉-gú*ki, denn sie finden sich in der langen Liste der Ortschaften, die NIdabal auf seiner Rundreise (šu mu-niĝin₂) berührt.[24] Betrachtet man alle Belege für die Nachrichten über Begleiter des Gottes, so fällt auf, daß vor allem die Orte am Anfang und am Ende der Liste genannt sind, also die wichtigsten Punkte der Prozession.

Es ist hier sicher nicht der Ort, weiter auf dieses wichtige jährliche Fest einzugehen; die dauernden Berichte an den Palast über den Fortgang der Prozession zeigen aber einmal mehr die enge Verbindung des Gottes NIdabal und seines Hauptfestes mit dem Herrscherhaus.[25]

4.5. Einzelnes

Jeder weitere Themenkomplex der "Nachrichten" ist spannend und aussagekräftig, sind es doch immer besondere Ereignisse, die dem Palast gemeldet werden. Oft sind die "Nachrichten" noch kaum deutbar oder ihr Inhalt wird erst im weiteren Kontext der jeweiligen Urkunde interessant (vgl. etwa Archi 1997).

Als Ausklang seien aber noch zwei Belege zitiert, die ohne weitere Erläuterungen einen kleinen Einblick in die Aufrechterhaltung der inneren Ordnung erlauben:

[22] *ARET* 4, 13 (MAT, Ib.) (29):

(1 T.) / *iš₁₁-gi-li-im* / maškim / *zú-ba-lum* / níĝ-AN.AN.AN.AN / nu-zuḫ / é / *ib-rí-um* / šu-du₈

"(1 Stoff) an I., Beauftragten des Z., für die Nachricht, daß der Dieb des Hauses des ('Ministers') Ibrium gefaßt ist."

[23] 75.10079 Rs. ix 2-9 (PPET 2288):

(1 T.) *gur-da-Lum* maškim *a-mur-da-mu* níĝ-AN.AN.AN.AN nu-zuḫ udu-udu mar-tuki kar

---

23 šu mu-niĝin₂ wird in der Literatur nur selten mit einer Bedeutung wie "umkreisen", die dem Ideogramm adäquat ist, wiedergegeben; s. aber Krebernik (1983, 23 Anm. 78): "sich im Kreis bewegen" zu VE 629 á-niĝin₂ = *da-wa-lum, du-lum*, s. VE 509 šu mu-niĝin₂ = *da-lum*: vgl. akk. *dâlum*, **dūl*. Aufgrund des Sumerogramms weniger überzeugend erscheint mir die Interpretation von Conti (1990, 144. 173) und anderen, hier die zugrunde liegende Wurzel als **tūr* "zurückkehren" anzusetzen.

24 75.2377 v 6 *ù-ra-am₆*ki, Rs. i 1 *ar-u₉-gú*ki, // 75.2379; s. Archi 1979, 108 f.

25 Zu anderen "Nachrichten" im Zusammenhang mit dem Kult s. den Hinweis in Anm. 18.

"(1 Stoff) an G., Beauftragten des A., für die Nachricht, daß — Diebe — Schafe — Amurru/Amuriter — ..." (verschiedene Lösungen möglich).

5. Nachrichten an den Palast: Rückblick und Ausblick

Durch die Deutung des Begriffs níĝ-AN.AN.AN.AN = níĝ-mul-(an) als "Nachricht, Botschaft" bekommt man auf einmal einen sehr viel besseren Einblick in das Nachrichtenwesen am Hofe von Ebla. Zudem sind es nur die aus der Sicht des Hofes wichtigsten Nachrichten, die mit einer Gabe von Textilien oder Silber belohnt werden. Da für Ebla von einem weitgehend vollständigen Textcorpus der Metall- und Textiltexte auszugehen ist, lassen sich so die Nachrichten inhaltlich in verschiedener Hinsicht auch historisch auswerten, wenn die Texte einmal vollständig publiziert sein werden.

Am Beispiel der Nachrichten aus Babylonien (*4.1.*) wurde dargelegt, daß die Überbringer nicht nur für gute Botschaften belohnt werden, sondern daß der Herrscher der Informationen bedurfte. In diesen Kontext gehört, daß vom selben Ereignis auch mehrmals berichtet wurde.

Der Vergleich mit der Terminologie der Ur III-Urkunden (*3.2.*) hat gezeigt, daß Boten für Nachrichten auch andernorts mit Geschenken belohnt werden. Allerdings ist dies nicht so gut wie für Ebla zu belegen, da administrative Texte anderer, jüngerer Archive nicht so ausführlich die Ausgaben kommentieren. Eine knappe Angabe über den Grund des Geschenkes zählt dabei schon eher zu den Ausnahmen.

Eine rasche Durchsicht von einschlägigen Palastarchiven hat aber doch eine Handvoll Belege erbracht, in denen explizit das Übersenden von Botschaften genannt ist:

- Mari (Beispiele):

  ARM 18, 54 und 69: Je 1 Stoff an 2 Personen, "die beiden Ḫanäer, die einen Informanten herführten" (2 *ḫanû ša āhizam irdûnim*); ähnlich *ARM* 24, 184

  ARM 7, 75: Salböl "zum Salben von Nachrichten-Bringern, die von Išme-Dagān kamen" (*ana pašāš mubassirī ša ištu maḫar Išme-Dagān illikūnim*); vgl. *ARM* 7, 156:7: Sonnenscheibe und Waffe an 3 *mubassirū*

  ARM 25, 142: Silberringe an 2 Personen, "<als sie> eine Nachricht brachten" (<*inūma*> *bussurtam ubl*[*ūnim*])

- Uruk, Sîn-kāšid-Palast

Sanati-Müller (1993, 150 ff.) Nr. 202 Rs. vi 8'-13': ¼ bzw. $^{1}/_{6}$ Sekel Silber an 2 Personen, "die (Nachricht über) das Wohlergehen der Truppe von Dūrum herbrachten" (*ša šulum ṣābim ištu* BÀD^{ki} *ublūnim*)

ibid. 158 ff., Nr. 203 Rs. v' 22'-25'; vi' 17'-22', 32'-39'; vii' 2'-5', 6'-8' (Lesungen der Edition zu korrigieren): je $^{1}/_{6}$ Sekel Silber an Personen, "die einen Brief aus ORT herbrachten" (*ša unnedukkam*(ù-na-a-du$_{11}$) *ištu* ON *ublūnim*)

In Mari wird das Wort *bussurum* "eine Nachricht senden" gebraucht, die Boten erhalten Salböl, Silber oder Stoffe, die üblichen Arten von Geschenken in altorientalischen Palästen. Im altbabylonischen Uruk erhalten Boten Silber für das Übersenden von Briefen aus den Städten des eigenen Landes oder auch anderen Orten.

Boten, Gesandte, Läufer, Händler gehören jedoch im gesamten altorientalischen Bereich zu den am häufigsten genannten Empfängern von Gütern am Palast, ohne daß diese selbst zum üblichen Palastpersonal im engeren Sinne gehören.

Bibliographie

Alster, B. (1976): "On the earliest Sumerian literary tradition", *JCS* 28, 109-126.

Archi, A. (1979): "Diffusione del culto di ^{d}NI-da-kul", *SEb* I/7-8, 105-113.

Archi, A. (1985): "Les rapports politiques et économiques entre Ebla et Mari", *MARI* 4, 63-83.

Archi, A. (1986): "The archives of Ebla", in: K. R. Veenhof (Hrsg.), *Cuneiform Archives and Libraries*, Leiden, 72-86.

Archi, A. (1988a): *Testi amministrativi: Registrazioni di metalli e tessuti.* (*ARET* 7). Roma.

Archi, A. (1988b): "Minima eblaitica I", *NABU* 1988/44.

Archi, A. (1993): *Five Tablets from the Southern Wing of Palace G - Ebla.* (*Syro-Mesopotamian Studies* 5/2). Malibu.

Archi, A. (1996a): "Chronologie relative des archives d'Ébla", *Amurru* 1, 11-28.

Archi, A. (1996b): "Les comptes rendus annuels de métaux (CAM)", *Amurru* 1, 73-99.

Archi, A. (1997): "Minima eblaitica 10: /mapqad-um/ 'inspection, review'", *NABU* 1997/47.

Baldacci, M. (1991): "É×PAP and the Eblaite administrative terminology", *WO* 22, 10-20.

Baldacci, M. (1992): *Partially Published Eblaite Texts*, Napoli.

Biga, M. G. (1996): "Prosopographie et datation relative des textes d'Ébla", *Amurru* 1, 29-72.

Biga, M. G. - F. Pomponio (1993): "Critères de rédaction comptable et chronologie relative des textes d'Ébla", *MARI* 7, 107-128.

Bonechi, M. (1990): "Aleppo in età arcaica. A proposito di un'opera recente", *SEL* 7, 15-37.

Bonechi, M. (1996): "*ARET* I 2 + *ARET* IV 23", *VO* 10, 83 f., Tav. VI f.

Bonechi, M. (1997): "Lexique et idéologie royale à l'époque proto-syrienne", *MARI* 8, 477-535.

Cohen, M. E. (1976): "The name Nintinugga, with a note on the possible identification of Tell Abu Ṣalābīkh", *JCS* 28, 82-92.

Conti, G. (1990): *Il sillabario della quarta fonte della lista lessicale bilingue eblaita*, (*Miscellanea Eblaitica* 3). Firenze.

Durand, J.-M. (1981): "Espionnage et guerre froide: la fin de Mari", in: *id.* (Hrsg.), *Florilegium Marianum* [1], *Recueil d'études en l'honneur de Michel Fleury*, Paris, 39-52.

Edzard, D. O. (1981): *Verwaltungstexte verschiedenen Inhalts*, (*ARET* 2). Roma.

Edzard, D. O. (1992): "Der Vertrag von Ebla mit A-bar-QA", *QuSem* 18, 187-217.

Fronzaroli, P. (1987): "Le pronom déterminativ-relatif à Ebla", *MARI* 5, 267-274.

Fronzaroli, P. (1991): "Noms de fonction dans les textes rituels d'Ebla", *NABU* 1991/49.

Fronzaroli, P. (1993): *Testi rituali della regalità*, (*ARET* 11). Roma.

Fronzaroli, P. (1997): "Les combats de Hadda dans les textes d'Ébla", *MARI* 8, 283-290.

Hallo, W. W. (1970): "The cultic setting of Sumerian poetry", in: A. Finet (Hrsg.), *Actes de la XVIIe Rencontre Assyriologique Internationale* [...], Ham-Sur-Heure, 116-134.

Klein, J. (1981): *The Royal Hymns of Shulgi King of Ur: Man's Quest for Immortal Fame*, (*TAPS* 71/7), Philadelphia.

Krebernik, M. (1983): "Zu Syllabar und Orthographie der lexikalischen Texte aus Ebla. Teil 2 (Glossar)", *ZA* 73, 1-47.

Krebernik, M. (1998): "Die Texte aus Fāra und Tell Abū Ṣalābīḫ", in: P. Attinger - M. Wäfler (Hrsg.), Annäherungen 1. (*Orbis Biblicus et Orientalis* 160/1), Freiburg/Göttingen, 235-427.

Krecher, J. (1987): "Über Inkonsistenz in den Texten aus Ebla", in: L. Cagni (Hrsg.), *Ebla 1975-1985* [...], Napoli, 177-197.

Krispijn, Th. J. H. (1991/92): "The early Mesopotamian lexical lists and the dawn of linguistics", *JEOL* 32, 12-22.

Milano, L. (1990): *Testi amministrativi: assegnazioni di prodotti alimentari*, (*ARET* 9), Roma.

Milano, L. (1994): "Vino e birra in Oriente. Confini geografici e confini culturali", in: *id.* (Hrsg.), *Drinking in Ancient Societies* [...], (*History of the Ancient Near East, Studies* 6), Padova, 421-440.

Pettinato, G. (1980): *Testi amministrativi della biblioteca L. 2769*, (*MEE* 2), Napoli.

Pettinato, G. (1982): *Testi lessicali bilingui della biblioteca L. 2769*, (*MEE* 4), Napoli.

Pettinato, G. (1995): "'Napoleone' ad Ebla: un generale o un verbo?", *Aula Orientalis* 13, 75-106.

Pettinato, G. (1997): *L'uomo cominciò a scrivere. Iscrizioni cuneiformi della collezione Michail*, Milano.

Pomponio, F. (1986): "La terminologia amministrativa di Ebla. I: šu-mu-tag$_x$", *UF* 17, 237-252.

Sallaberger, W. (1993): *Der kultische Kalender der Ur III-Zeit*, (*Untersuchungen zur Assyriologie und Vorderasiatischen Archäologie* 7), Berlin/New York.

Sallaberger, W. (1999): "Ur III-Zeit", in: P. Attinger/M. Wäfler (Hrsg.), Annäherungen 3, (*Orbis Biblicus et Orientalis* 160/3), Freiburg/Göttingen, 121-390.

Sanati-Müller, Sh. (1993): "Texte aus dem Sînkāšid-Palast. Sechster Teil: Texte verschiedenen Inhalts III", *BaM* 24, 137-184.

Sollberger, E. (1986): *Administrative Texts Chiefly Concerning Textiles*, (*ARET* 8), Roma.

Steinkeller, P. (1993): "Observations on the Sumerian Personal Names in Ebla Sources and on the Onomasticon of Mari and Kish", in: M. E. Cohen [u. a.] (Hrsg.), *The tablet and the Scroll. Near Eastern Studies in Honor of William W. Hallo*, Bethesda Md., 236-45.

Urcioli, G.M. (1995): "Šeš-II-ib priests at Ebla", *Aula Orientalis* 13, 107-126.

Xella, P. (1988): "The Eblaite god NIdabal", in: M. Dietrich/I. Kottsieper (Hrsg.), "Und Mose schrieb dieses Lied auf", *Festschrift* [...] *für Oswald Loretz* [...], (*AOAT* 250), Münster, 883-895.

GIUSEPPE NELLA GENESI ED I FENOMENI ONIRICI

J. ALBERTO SOGGIN

Università di Roma "La Sapienza"
Facoltà valdese di Teologia, Roma

1. La figura di Giuseppe, il penultimo figlio di Giacobbe nella leggenda biblica, è passato alla storia tra l'altro per le sua qualità di sognatore e di interprete dei sogni altrui. Per molti esegeti le due attività vanno considerate intimamente connesse: perché sognatore egli stesso, Giuseppe sarebbe capace d'interpretare i sogni altrui.
1.1. Ho già segnalato nel mio commentario alla *Genesi* (Soggin 1997) ed in alcuni saggi precedenti (Soggin 1993 e 1996) l'insostenibilità di questa tesi e di questo vorrei occuparmi più dettagliatamente in questa sede, lieto di poter offrire un contributo all'omaggio al collega ed amico.
1.2. Ma sarà bene procedere per ordine. Giuseppe appare al lettore come sognatore in Gen 37,5-11, e si tratta di due sogni piuttosto caratteristici del personaggio. Non vorrei qui soffermarmi a descrivere il contenuto di questi sogni: ogni persona con una discreta cultura biblica sa di cosa si tratta. Non sono sogni che suscitano una grande attenzione nell'uomo moderno anche se modestamente versato in psicologia: essi testimoniano solo di un'ambizione sfrenata, tant'è che i fratelli nel primo sogno, i genitori ed i fratelli nel secondo vengono visti nell'atto di rendere omaggio, una specie di προσκύνησις, al giovinetto. Il fenomeno appare in un contesto psicologicamente normale, quello delle fantasie di un giovane alquanto esaltato, ambizioso e sognatore, e si tratta soltanto di quello che nel mondo anglosassone si chiamerebbe *wishful thinking*. La cosa non avrebbe quindi un particolare rilievo nell'economia della narrazione e non dovrebbe essere considerata importante, se non fosse per il fatto che i fratelli e una volta lo stesso padre, erano già adirati con lui per una serie di altre ragioni evidentemente ben motivate. Il fatto poi che questi sogni si avverano molti anni dopo, alla conclusione della narrazione, non è rilevante per una loro spiegazione, in sé ovvia.
1.3. E l'ira dei fratelli giunge, com'è noto, al punto da tentare prima il fratricidio, per poi contentarsi di vendere il fratello come schiavo ad una carovana di mercanti, 37,28 sgg., i quali lo trasportarono e lo vendettero in Egitto.

2. Sorvoliamo sulla varie avventure del nostro in quella terra lontana (nelle quali si distinse per onestà e pietà), avventure che lo conducono alcune volte alla miseria più profonda fino a farlo rinchiudere in prigione. E fu qui che Giuseppe manifestò le prime forme di capacità oniromantiche, per le quali passò alla leggenda popolare fino al giorno d'oggi.

2.1. Due alti funzionari egiziani, caduti in disgrazia presso il Faraone e associati alle carceri nelle quali Giuseppe era prigioniero, ma diventato frattanto per i meriti segnalati una specie di soprastante ai carcerati e uomo di fiducia del carceriere, ebbero ciascuno un sogno incomprensibile (dunque esattamente il contrario di quello che era capitato a Giuseppe ancora in patria), sogni che si rivelarono incapaci di comprendere. Secondo le credenze diffuse in tutto il Vicino Oriente antico, si trattava evidentemente di messaggi da parte della divinità, per cui era importante che fossero interpretati e, se necessario, decifrati.

2.2. Giuseppe procedette immediatamente alla spiegazione delle immagini che i funzionari avevano viste in sogno, immagini piuttosto generiche, che non hanno nulla di particolarmente egiziano, ed opera in due tappe successive. Giuseppe segnala anzitutto che l'interpretazione dei sogni è prerogativa divina ed è così ch'egli legittima una procedura in sé vietata in Israele: l'oniromanzia (Dtn c.13); più tardi, alla presenza del Faraone, egli ritornerà sull'argomento: con la dichiarazione che è stato Dio stesso ad ispirare questi sogni (41,16), per cui la loro interpretazione non è tanto il prodotto di tecniche apprese e generalmente diffuse nella regione, ma vietate in Israele, quanto di un caso d'ispirazione divina.

3. Il culmine della sua attività interpretativa dei sogni viene raggiunto da Giuseppe davanti al Faraone e alla sua corte. Il giovane insiste ch'è Dio ad ispirarlo e che non opera mediante una qualche tecnica o saggezza apprese con lo studio e la prassi. Tutto questo nel contesto della narrazione il cui scopo è appunto, come appare in molti passi, rendere testimonianza all'opera del Dio d'Israele.

3.1. Il primo sogno è quello delle vacche bene in carne e quello delle vacche magre, finché queste divorarono le prime, 41,1-4. Il motivo viene ripetuto nella narrazione che il Faraone fa a Giuseppe, 41,17-21.

3.2. Il secondo sogno è quello delle spighe rigogliose, divorate da spige malatticce, seccate dal vento d'oriente. Qui appare un elemento che non è certamente egiziano: il vento dell'est è infatti quello del deserto, *ḥamsīn* in arabo, *šārāb* in ebraico, che soffia appunto dall'est, dove si trova il deserto.

3.4. In seguito alla spiegazione dei due sogni, il Faraone riconosce in Giuseppe la persona più adatta per prendere i provvedimenti del caso, cosa non completamente logica, non essendo affatto certo che un interpretatore di sogni sia anche capace di gestire dal punto di vista economico una nazione con tutte le sue complessità. Ma Giuseppe assolve egregiamente il proprio compito, come del resto ci si aspetterebbe in una narrazione di questo tipo. Da allora sembra che Giuseppe non abbia più interpretato altri sogni.

3.5. L'episodio ha un interessante e tardivo parallelo: in Dan 2,1 sgg. e 4,1 sgg. l'eroe spiega i sogni di Nebucadnezzar, sogni che i saggi babilonesi non sono riusciti ad interpretare. Nei due casi abbiamo la figura di un ebreo che si trova contro la sua volontà nel paese del sovrano sognatore e che riesce a spiegarne i sogni per divina ispirazione.

4. Ho sostenuto in un passato recente che la narrazione di Giuseppe (come del resto quella dell'Esodo) va datata in un'epoca in cui in Canaan vi era una potenza ostile (dunque certamente non alla fine del II mill. o durante la prima metà del I mill. a.C.), che troppi sono gli elementi che rimandano ad una situazione palestinese (sull'Egitto abbiamo solo notizie generiche o addirittura insostenibili), che la topografia dell'Egitto è quella ellenistica (il paese di *gōšen*!), il parallelo col libro di *Daniele* e che tutto fa pensare all'epoca persiana o addirittura al II sec. a.C. (Soggin 1993 e 1997).

4.1. La cosa è stata contraddetta autorevolmente da P. Sacchi (1996).

In ogni caso la datazione che viene da lui proposta è posteriore al VI sec. a.C., quindi in epoca ben più recente da quella tradizionale.

4.2. Una cosa mi sembra però da mettere in dubbio: che la narrazione sia nata in Egitto: troppi elementi indicano un'origine palestinese, e questo spiega anche come mai il racconto non abbia che poche caratteristiche proprie della novella ellenistica.

Note bibliografiche

Per dettagli sono costretto a rinviare al mio *Das Buch Genesis*, Darmstadt, Wissenschaftliche Buchgesellschaft, 1997, 463-482.

Si vedano ancora:

Catastini, A. "Ancora sulla datazione della 'Storia di Giuseppe' (Genesi 37-50)", *Henoch* 20, 1998, pp. 208-224.

Sacchi, P. "Il problema della datazione della storia di Giuseppe (Genesi 37-50)", *Henoch* 18, 1996, pp. 359-366.

Soggin, J. A. "Notes on the Joseph Story", in *Understanding Poets and Prophets, Essays ... G. W. Anderson*, Sheffield 1993, pp. 336-349.

Soggin, J. A. "Uno sguardo alla narrazione di Giuseppe", in *Alle soglie della classicità. Studi... S. Moscati*, Roma, 1996, pp. 393-401.

AKKADISCHE LEXEME IM SUMERISCHEN*

GERD STEINER

Philipps-Universität Marburg

1. Umstände und Merkmale der Entlehnung

1.1. Im Verlauf der jahrhundertelangen Adstratsituation zwischen dem Sumerischen und dem Akkadischen sind nicht nur zahllose sumerische Lexeme in das Akkadische entlehnt – oder als technische bzw. "gelehrte" Fremdwörter übernommen – worden, sondern auch eine nicht unerhebliche Anzahl von akkadischen Lexemen in das Sumerische. Nicht immer ist dabei allerdings sicher zu erkennen, ob es sich um echte Entlehnung handelt oder um die Verwendung eines akkadischen Wortes in einem sumerischen Text, oder auch nur um eine akkadisierende Pseudolesung eines Logogramms, insbesondere in lexikalischen Texten. Auch ist nicht in allen Fällen, in denen ein Etymon im Sumerischen und im Akkadischen belegt ist, eindeutig zu entscheiden, in welcher Richtung die Entlehnung erfolgt ist, ganz abgesehen von Wörtern, die aus einer dritten Sprache in das Sumerische wie in das Akkadische übernommen wurden.[1]

1.2. Während aus dem Sumerischen in das Akkadische nahezu ausschließlich[2] nur Nomina oder nominale Syntagmen entlehnt wurden, finden sich im Sumerischen nicht nur Nomina, die allerdings auch hier bei weitem überwiegen, sondern auch einige Verben und sogar Morpheme aus dem Akkadischen. Wegen der strukturellen Unterschiede der beiden Sprachen und ihrer Wortstämme ist der morphologische Mechanismus der Entlehnung dabei jeweils verschieden.

(1) Nomina aus anderen Sprachen, speziell aus dem Sumerischen, werden in das morphologische System des Akkadischen dadurch integriert, daß ihnen ein Kasus-

---

* Für Abkürzungen und Zitate vgl. die Bibliographie sowie *PSD*, *CAD* und *AHw*.

1 Vgl. auch Lieberman (1977): 14-18 §§ 0.29-0.34, besonders 17 § 0.33.

2 Vgl. aber *unedukku* "Brief" < ù-na-dug$_4$ "wenn du (bitte) zu ihm sprichst" [vgl. Falkenstein (1960): 311]; sowie Lieberman (1977): 14f. § 0.30 mit Anm. 32 und 34. Für šu.bal = *šupêlu* "verändern" wird [gegen Falkenstein (1960): 310] Entlehnung aus dem Akkadischen in das Sumerische angenommen [vgl. § 2.1 Nr. 59].

morphem suffigiert wird, das bei vokalischem Stammauslaut mit diesem in der Regel Fusion eingeht. Dagegen verliert ein akkadisches Nomen im Sumerischen nicht generell das Kasusmorphem; vielmehr finden sich dabei drei Modelle:

(1a) Die reine Stammform,[3] die im Status constructus bzw. absolutus erscheint, dürfte die älteste Form von Lehnwörtern darstellen; sie entspricht einem sumerischen Nomen im Nominativ mit Kasusmorphem /= 0/, z. B. ḫa+zi(+in) "Axt".

(1b) Alt ist jedoch auch eine Form mit einem Morphem /=a/[3], z. B. dam+ḫa+ra "Kampf", das mit große Wahrscheinlichkeit das Morphem des akkadischen Akkusativs (Singularis) ist,[4] weil wegen der intransitiv-passivischen Verbalauffassung des Sumerischen ein akkadischer Akkusativ syntaktisch einem sumerischen Nominativ (Subjektskasus) entspricht.

(1c) Im Neusumerischen werden akkadische Nomina dann auch in der Form des Nominativs (Singularis) entlehnt, meistens verbunden mit der Mimation, /=u(m)/[5], z. B. pu+úḫ+ru+um "Versammlung".

(2) Akkadische Verben werden in einer Form entlehnt, die den Haupttypen der sumerischen Verbalstämme, /Konsonant – Vokal – Konsonant/ oder /Konsonant – Vokal – Konsonant – Vokal – Konsonant/, am ähnlichsten ist, nämlich der 3. Person Singularis masculini des Stativs des Grundstammes. Diese Form ergibt von Verben mediae infirmae einen sumerischen Verbalstamm des Typs /Konsonant – Vokal – Konsonant/, z. B. *kīn* > gin$_{6}$ "dauerhaft sein", von starken Verben aber einen Verbalstamm des Typs /Konsonant – Vokal – Konsonant – Vokal – Konsonant/, z. B. *labir* > libir "alt sein", oder auch einen Verbalausdruck des Typs šu.tag, wobei die erste Silbe als ein sumerisches Quasi-Nomen aufgefaßt wird, z. B. *šarik* > sa$_{12}$.rig$_{9}$ "schenken". Diese Verbalstämme können, wie ursprünglich auch generell der akkadische Stativ, sowohl intransitiv als auch transitiv konstruiert werden.

(3) Für die Entlehnung von Morphemen ist wegen der geringen Zahl von Beispielen keine Regel zu erkennen. Während etwa *ù* (*wa) "und, aber" in derselben Form ù und mit analoger Funktion entlehnt worden ist, wird *kīma* "wie" in der reduzierten Form -gim suffigiert als (Pseudo-)Kasusmorphem des Äquativs gebraucht.

---

3 Vgl. z. B. Falkenstein (1951): 13; Gelb (1961): 5, 141; Römer (1999): 54.

4 Vgl. auch Poebel (1923): 33 § 91; dagegen Falkenstein (1950): 69 Anm. 1 ("doch wohl ein sumerisches Bildungselement"); von Soden (1960): 170 ("diese könnte eine St. constr.-Endung sein"); Oberhuber (1981): 258 ("das sumerische Nominalisierungselement -a").

5 Vgl. Poebel (1923): 33 § 91; Falkenstein (1949): 47(f.) Anm. 5; ders., (1951): 13; Kraus (1969): 35-36 §§ 10-15; ders., (1970): 91f.; Römer (1999): 54.

1.3. Da das Sumerische genetisch isoliert ist, ein Vergleich mit verwandten Sprachen also nicht möglich ist, lassen sich Entlehnungen nicht immer ohne weiteres als solche bestimmen;[6] es gibt dafür jedoch gewisse Kriterien:

(1) Wesentlich ist auf jeden Fall Lautähnlichkeit wenigstens insoweit, daß die sich entsprechenden Konsonanten derselben Klasse angehören und daß die Bedeutung identisch oder doch sehr ähnlich ist.

(2) Ein graphisches Indiz für ein Lehnwort ist syllabische Schreibung, wobei nicht nur Morphogramme wie /a/, /ba/, /da/, usw. verwendet werden, sondern auch Zeichen, die sonst nur eingeschränkt, manchmal nur in einem einzigen Fall, auch "Silbenzeichen" sind.

(3) Formen des Nomens auf /=um/ sind in der Regel Entlehnungen aus dem Akkadischen oder aus einer dritten Sprache über das Akkadische [vgl. § 1.2 (1c)].

(4) Für eine Entlehnung aus dem Akkadischen spricht eine "semitische" Etymologie oder die Zugehörigkeit zu einer akkadischen "Wortfamilie".

(5) Ein semantisches Indiz für Entlehnung ist es auch, wenn das sumerische Lexem eine speziellere Bedeutung hat als das akkadische oder wenn ein sumerisches Wort mit synonymer Bedeutung bekannt ist.

2. *"Regelmäßige" Konsonantenentsprechungen*

2.1. Nach diesen Kriterien können – zum Teil nur mit Wahrscheinlichkeit und zum Teil mit modifizierter Bedeutung – folgende Entlehnungen von akkadischen Lexemen in das Sumerische angenommen werden:[7]

01	*abu*	Vater	> ab+ba	Ältester
02	*abullu*	Stadttor	> a+bul$_5$	*vgl.* ká
03	*akalu(m)*	Brot, Nahrung	> a+ka+la/lum	
04	*ālu*	Stadt	> a+la	Ansiedlung
05	*aplu*	Erbsohn	> ibila/ì+bí+la	
06	*arsānu*	Gerstengürtze	> ar+za+na	

6 Vgl. auch (*mutatis mutandis*) Lieberman (1977): 17 §§ 0.33.-0.35.

7 Vgl. Poebel (1923): 33f. § 91; Falkenstein (1950): 69 mit Anm. 1; ders., (1959): 15 § 2 b; ders., (1960); Gelb (1960): 266; Kraus (1969): 42f. § 13; ders., (1970): 91-93; sowie passim die Glossare in Bauer (1972): 577-668; Edzard (1968): 315-326; Falkenstein (1957): 89-175; Behrens - Steible (1983): 3-374.

07	*bēlūtu*	Besitzverhältnis	> pe+lu$_5$+da[8]	
08a	*dārī(tu)*	Dauer	> da+rí	
08b	*dūru*	Dauer	> du+rí	
09	*dulbum*	Orient-Platane	> tu+lu+bu+um	
10	*ebūru*	Ernte	> buru$_{14}$	
11	*emu rabû*	Schwiegervater	> murub$_5$	
12	*ḫarrānu*	Weg	> ḫa+ra+an	
13	*ḫaṣṣinnu*	Axt	> ḫa+zi(+in/na)	
14	*ḫazannum*	Bürgermeister	> ḫa+za+núm	
15	*ḫurrum*	Erdloch, Höhle	> ḫur+ru+um	
16	*illatu*	Gruppe, "Clan"	> ildú	
17	*k/gabābum*	Schleuder	> ka/ga+ba+bu+um	
18	*kam(m)ūnu*	Kümmel	> ga+mun	
19	*kaparru*	Hirtenjunge	> gáb+ra/ga+ba+ra	
20	*kar(a)šu*	Porree, Lauch	> ga+raš	
21	*karmu*	Weinstock	> ga+ra+an	
22	*kīma*	wie	> -gim	
23	(*kīn*)	dauerhaft sein	> gin$_6$	
24	*kīnātum*	Garantiebetrag	> gi+na+tum	
25	*kussiu*	Stuhl, Thron	> gu+za	
26	(*labir*)	alt sein	> libir	
27	*lē'um*	Tafel	> le+um	
28	*lulīmu*	Hirsch	> lu+lim	
29	*luppu*	Bohne(n)	> lu+úb	
30	*manā'u*	Mine	> ma+na	
31	*maškanu*	Ort	> maš+gan	Lagerplatz
32	*mātu*	Land	> ma+da	
33	*milku*	Rat	> ma+al+ga	[*vgl.* § 4.1 (1b)]

8 Im Hinblick auf sumerische Abstrakta wie nam.en "Herr(en)schaft", nam.lugal "Königsherrschaft" usw. ist das Abstraktum *bēlūtu* > pe+lu$_5$+da in der Bedeutung von *bēlu* "Herr = Besitzer, Eigentümer" aufzufassen; vgl. dagegen M. A. Powell, *ZA* 62 (1972) 210 Anm. 128 ("prevailing customs"); P. Steinkeller, *SEL* 1 (1984) 10 ("practices, (ritual) obligations"); ders., *JNES* 46 (1987) 58 ("power, rule, dominion, position of master"); G. Selz, in: dubsar anta-men (Fs W. Ph. H. Römer) = *AOAT* 253 (1998) 324 ("*Herrschaftsverhältnisse*"); H. Steible, l. c. 380 (Herrschaftsnormen); sowie *PSD* B 155f. s. v. biluda ("rituals, rites").

34	*miṭṭum*	eine Götterwaffe	> mi+tum	
35	*muška’’inu*	Palasthöriger	> maš+ka$_{15}$:en	
36	*nāgiru*	Ausrufer, Herold	> nimgir	
37	*nākidu*	Hirt	> na+gad	
38	*nisqu(m)*	Auslese	> ni+is+ku(+um)	edles Tier
39	*pašīšu*	p.-Priester	> pa$_4$+šeš	
40	*puḫrum*	Versammlung	> pu+úḫ+ru+um/rum	
41	*puršumu*	Greis	> bur+ša+ma	
42	*puzru*	Geheimnis	> buzur	
43	*rakbu*	Reiter	> ra/rá+gab	
44	*sabītum*	eine Leier	> za+bí+tum	
45	(*sām*)	rot(braun) sein	> sam$_x$ (SA$_5$)	
46	*ṣuḫāru*	junger Mann	> saḫar	Knappe
47	*šadû*	Berg	> sa+tu	
48	*šaggāšu*	Mörder	> sa+gaz	Räuber
49	*šāḫum*	(Wasch)Schale	> za+ḫum	
50	*šaknu*	Statthalter	> šagina	
51	(*šalim*)	unversehrt sein	> silim	
52	(*šām*)	kaufen	> šám/sám	
53	*šāpiru*	“Anweiser”	> šabra	Präfekt
54	(*šarik*)	schenken	> sa$_{12}$.rig$_9$	
55	*šāqiu*	Mundschenk	> sagi	
56	*šīmu*	Kaufpreis	> šám/šàm	
57	*šinipu/i*	zwei Drittel	> šanabi	
58	*šūmu*	Lauch, Zwiebel	> sum	
59	(*šupa’’il*)	vertauschen	> šu.bal	verändern
60	*tamḫāru*	Kampf	> dam+ḫa+ra	
61	*tamkāru*	Kaufmann	> dam+gàr	
62	*tīlu*	(Schutt)Hügel	> dul$_6$	
63	*ṭēmu*	Plan(ung)	> dím+ma	
64	*ummu*	Mutter	> um+ma	Alte, Klageweib
65	*ù* (**wa*)	und, aber	> ù	
66	*waklu*	Aufseher	> ugula	
67	*wardu*	Sklave, Diener	> warad/urda/*ird(?)	
68	(*w*)*āšipu*	Beschwörer	> išib	

69	(**wazz*)	Gans	> uz	Ente
70	(**wsm*)	Fest	> ezem/n	

2.2. Von den Konsonanten der entlehnten Lexeme bleiben im Sumerischen die Sonanten /l/ und /r/ sowie /ḫ/ in der Regel unverändert, die Nasale /m/ und /n/ weitgehend [vgl. aber unten 5c; § 4.1-2]. Bei den Labialen, den Dentalen, den Gutturalen und den Sibilanten zeigen sich nach den konventionellen Lesungen Veränderungen innerhalb derselben Konsonantenklasse; dabei ist jedoch zu berücksichtigen, daß die Art der Realisierung als Media, Tenuis oder Emphatica ohnehin nicht in allen Fällen bzw. Positionen graphisch eindeutig differenziert wird, im absoluten Auslaut sogar niemals.[9] Ferner ist für die Positionen der Konsonanten zu berücksichtigen, daß bei den Nomina ein Inlautkonsonant des akkadischen Lexems durch Abfall des Anlautvokals in den Anlaut gelangen kann, durch Abfall des Kasusmorphems aber in den Auslaut, wo er konventionell als Media wiedergegeben wird. Im einzelnen vgl.[10]

(1)	Labiale	(b, p)		
(la)	im Anlaut		b = b	10
			b > p	07
			p > b	41, 42
			p = p	39, 40
(lb)	im Inlaut		b = b	01, 02, 09, 17, 26, 44
			p > b	05, 19, 53, 57, 59
(lc)	im Auslaut		b = b	11, 43, 68
			p > b	29
(2)	Dentale	(d, t, ṭ)		
(2a)	im Anlaut		d = d	08
			d > t	09
			t > d	60-62
			ṭ > d	63

9 Vgl. von Soden (1952): 19f. § 19 a, 27f. § 27 b, 28 § 28 b, 29 § 29 b, 30 § 30 b.

10 Für die Nummern s. § 2.1.

(2b)	im Inlaut		d = d	67
			d > t	47
			t > d	07, 16, 32, 37
			t = t	24, 46
			ṭ > t	34
(2c)	im Auslaut		d = d	37, (67)
(3)	Gutturale	(g, k, q)		
(3a)	im Anlaut		g = g	(17)
			k = k	(17)
			k > g	18 – 25
(3b)	im Inlaut		g = (m) g	36
			(g) g = g	48
			k = k	35
			k > g	31, 33, 37, 43, 49, 61, 66
			q > g	55
			q > k	38
(3c)	im Auslaut		k > g	54
(4)	Sibilanten	(z, s, ṣ; š)		
(4a)	im Anlaut		s > z	44
			s = s	45
			ṣ > s	46
			š > z	49
			š > s	47, 48, 50, 51, 54, 55, 58
			š = š	50, 52, 53, 56, 57, 59
(4b)	im Inlaut		z = z	14, 42
			(s)s > z	06, 25, 70
			s = s	38
			ṣ > z	13
			š = š	31, 35, 39, 41, 68
(4c)	im Auslaut		z = z	69
			š > z	48
			š = š	20, 39

(5)	Nasale	(m, n)	
(5a)	im Anlaut	m = m	11, 30 – 35
		n = n	36 – 38
(5b)	im Inlaut	m = m	18, 41, 60, 61, 63, 64
		n = n	06, 14, 24, 50
(5c)	im Auslaut	m = m	03, 09, 14, 15, 24, 27, 34, 38, 40, 44, 49, 51, 52, 56, 58, (70)
		m > n	21, 70; [§ 4.2 (1) Nr. 86]
		n = n	12, 13, 18, 23, 31, 35

2.3. Diese Konsonantenentsprechungen sind – mit denselben Einschränkungen hinsichtlich der graphischen Differenzierung der Phoneme – nach den konventionellen Lesungen grundsätzlich reziprok denen bei der Entlehnung von sumerischen Lexemen in das Akkadische,[11] wobei ebenfalls die Sonanten /l/ und /r/ sowie /ḫ/ in der Regel, die Nasale /m/ und /n/ weitgehend unverändert bleiben; ein besonderer Fall ist das speziell sumerische Phonem /g̃/, der gutturale Nasal.[12] Für die Position der Konsonanten ist hierbei einerseits zu berücksichtigen, daß der Auslaut der ersten und der Anlaut der zweiten Komponente eines Kompositums grundsätzlich als Inlaute zu bewerten sind, andererseits aber, daß durch die Suffigierung eines akkadischen Morphems ein Auslautkonsonant ebenfalls zum Inlaut wird, so daß primäre (A) und sekundäre Inlautkonsonanten (B) zu unterscheiden sind. Im einzelnen vgl. z. B.

(1)	Labiale (b, p)				
(la)	im Anlaut	b = b	bappir	Malz	> *bappiru*
		b > p	baḫar	Töpfer	> *paḫāru*
			bala	Regierungszeit	> *palû*
(lb)	im Inlaut A	b = b	gab.raḫ	Brustschlagen	> *g/kabaraḫḫu*
		b > p	abgal	Weiser	> *apkallu*
		p = p	apin	Saatpflug	> *epinnu*

11 Vgl. Falkenstein (1960): 3l0f.; Krecher (1969): 161-164 §§ 11-16 (mit Literatur).

12 Zu dem Phonem /g̃/ vgl. Thomsen (1984): 44f. § 25 (mit Literatur); Römer (1999): 60 mit Anm. 131 (Literatur).

(lc)	im Inlaut B	b = b	lagab	Klumpen	> *lagabbu* (*lakappu*)
		b > p	ùb	Trommel	> *uppu*
			ab	Fenster	> *aptu*
(2)	Dentale (d, t)				
(2a)	im Anlaut	d > t	duraḫ	Steinbock	> *turāḫu*
		d > ṭ	dub	Tontafel	> *ṭuppu*
		t = t	tidap	Biermaische	> *titāpu*
(2b)	im Inlaut A	d = d	za.dím	Steinschneider	> *zadimmu*
		d > t	udul	Rinderhirt	> *utūlu*
		d > ṭ	gidim	Totengeist	> *eṭemmu*
		t = t	šitim	Baumeister	> *itinnu*
(2c)	im Inlaut B	d > t	askud	großer Riegel	> *aškuttu*
(3)	Gutturale (g, k)				
(3a)	im Anlaut	g = g	gú.gal	Kanalinspektor	> *gugallu*
		g > k	gala	Kultsänger	> *kalû*
		k = k	kiri$_6$	Obstgarten	> *kirû*
(3b)	im Inlaut A	g = g	tigi	(eine Trommel)	> *tigû*
		g > k	ašgab	Lederarbeiter	> *aškāpu*
			é.gal	Palast	> *ekallu*
		k = k	šukur	Lanze, Speer	> *šukurru*
(3c)	im Inlaut B	g > k	barag	Postament	> *parakku*
			ég	Graben	> *ēku*
		k = k	ensik	Regent	> *išši'akku*
			nu.èša(k)	(ein Priester)	> *nêšakku*
(4)	Sibilanten (z, s; š)				
(4a)	im Anlaut	z = z	zag̃.mu(k)	Neujahr(sfest)	> *zagmukku*
		z > s	zar	Kornstadel	> *sarru*
		s > š	sanga	Tempelverwalter	> *šangû*
		š = š	še	Gerste, Korn	> *še'u*
			šaḫ	Schwein	> *šaḫû*

(4b)	im Inlaut A	z > s	ezem/n	Fest	> *isinnu*
			a.zu	Arzt	> *asû*
		s = s	ensi	Traumdeuter	> *ensû*
			kissa	Grundmauer	> *ki(s)sû*
			absìn	Saatfurche	> *aps/šinnu*
		s > š	esi	Dunkelholz	> *ušû*
			gisal	Ruder	> *gišallu*
		š = š	ašlag	Wäscher	> *ašlāku*
		š > s	mušen.dù	Vogelfänger	> *usandû*
(4c)	im Inlaut B	z > s	sa+gaz	Räuber	> *sagassu*
		š = š	muš.ḫuš	Schlangendrache	> *mušḫuššu*
(5)	Nasale (m, n, g̃)				
(5a)	im Anlaut	m = m	mar	Schaufel	> *marru*
		n = n	nar	Musikant	> *nāru*
		g̃ > g	g̃iš.nimbar	Dattelpalme	> *gišimmaru*
(5b)	im Inlaut A	m = m	im.ḫul	böser Sturm	> *imḫullu*
		n = n	ensi	Traumdeuter	> *ensû*
		g̃ > g	zag̃.mu(k)	Neujahr(sfest)	> *zagmukku*
			si.g̃ar	Zwinge aus Holz	> *šigaru*
		g̃ > ng	ḫé.g̃ál	Überfluß	> *ḫe(n)gallu*
(5c)	im Inlaut B	m = m	me.lám	Schreckensglanz	> *melemmu*
		m > n	ezem/n	Fest	> *isinnu*
			šitim	Baumeister	> *itinnu*
		n = n	udun	Töpferofen	> *utūnu*
		g̃ > n	ur.sag̃	Krieger, Held	> *uršānu*

3. Vokalentsprechungen

3.1. Die Vokale der entlehnten Lexeme bleiben nach den konventionellen Lesungen der Zeichen weitgehend unverändert. Für Nomina sind es bei der reinen Stammform und der Form mit Morphem /=a/ [vgl. § 1.2 (la-b)] die Vokale des Status constructus bzw. absolutus, bei den Formen auf /=um/ [vgl. § 1.2 (1c)] die des Nominativs, für Verben die Vokale der 3. Person Singularis masculini des Stativs des Grundstammes [vgl. § 1.2 (2)]; vgl.[13]

13 Für die Nummern s. § 2.1; vgl. auch §§ 4.1-2.

(1)	bei einsilbigen Stämmen	
	a = a	01, 04, 32, 45, 52
	e/i = e/i	(16), (22), 23, 63
	u = u	(25), 29, 58, 64
(2)	bei zweisilbigen Stämmen	
(2a)	mit demselben Vokal in allen Silben	
	a + a = a + a	03, 06, 12, 19, 20, 21, 30, 31, 43, 48, 60, 61, (67)
	u + u = u + u	(10), 15, 40, 42
(2b)	mit verschiedenen Vokalen	
	a + e/i = a + e/i	08a, 13, 39, 44, 50, (54), 55
	a + u = a + u	02, 18, 47, 49
	e/i + u = e/i + u	07, 16, 27, 34, 38
	u + a = u + a	(59)
	u + e/i = u + e/i	08b, 28
(3)	bei dreisilbigen Stämmen	
(3a)	mit demselben Vokal in allen Silben	
	u + u + u = u + u + u	09
(3b)	mit verschiedenen Vokalen	
	a + a + u = a + a + u	(03), 14, 17
	e/i + a + u = e/i + a + u	24
	a + e/i + u = a + e/i + u	44

3.2. An Vokalveränderungen sind jedoch festzustellen

(1)	der Schwund eines Vokals	
(la)	im Anlaut[14]	10, 11
(lb)	im Inlaut	16, 53, 59
(lc)	im Auslaut	22, 25
(2)	Assimilation eines Vokals bei zweisilbigen Stämmen, und zwar	
(2a)	regressiv	
	a + i > a + a	37
	u + a > u + u	11

14 Vgl. Falkenstein (1949): 4lf. § 10/4 b; ders., (1959): 26 § 8 b 4 a; sowie von Soden (1952): 15f. § 14.

(2b)	progressiv	
	a + i > i + i	26, 36, 51, 68
	u + a > a + a	46
(3)	Lautwandel wa > u	65, 66, (67), 69
(4)	sonstige	
(4a)	bei einsilbigen Stämmen	
	a > e/i	(67)
	e/i > a	33, 56
	e/i > u	62
(4b)	bei zweisilbigen Stämmen	
	a + a > i + i	05
	u + u > u + a	41
(4c)	bei dreisilbigen Stämmen	
	u + a + e/i > a + a + e/i	35
	i + i + u/i > a + a + e/i	57

3.3. Wie bei den Konsonanten ist die Entsprechung der Vokale weitgehend gleich der bei Entlehnung von Nomina aus dem Sumerischen in das Akkadische. Meistens bleiben die Vokale unverändert [vgl. § 2.3], doch gibt es in einzelnen Fällen analoge Vokalveränderungen

(1) durch Schwund eines Anlautvokals [vgl. § 3.2 (1)], vgl.

/u/	ukúš	Gurke	> *qiššû*
	uzug	Heiligtum	> *sukku*

(2) durch Assimilation eines Vokals bei zweisilbigen Stämmen, und zwar

(2a) regressiv, vgl.

me.lám	Schreckensglanz	> *melemmu*

(2b) progressiv, vgl.

apin	Saatpflug	> *epinnu*
éš.dam	Wirtshaus	> *aštammu*

(3) sowie z. B.

mušen.dù	Vogelfänger	> *usandû* [vgl. § 4.3 (lb)]
esi	Dunkelholz	> *ušû*
ì.du$_8$	Pförtner	> *atû*
bur.gul	Steinschneider	> *parkullu*

4. Unregelmäßige Konsonantenentsprechungen

4.1. Eine Entlehnung kann – unter Berücksichtigung der übrigen Kriterien [vgl. § 1.3] – aber auch in einigen Fällen angenommen oder doch vermutet werden, in denen ein Konsonant nicht den "Regeln" [vgl. § 2.2] gemäß einem anderen entspricht, wenn die Bedeutung der beiden Lexeme identisch oder doch sehr ähnlich ist, insbesondere wenn sie in Texten oder lexikalischen Listen gleichgesetzt werden. Derartige unregelmäßige Konsonantenentsprechungen können auftreten

(1) im Anlaut

(la) durch Palatalisierung eines Gutturals, vgl.

71	g > z	*gurnu*	Durchschnitts-qualität	> za+rí+in	
72	k > z	**kinšu* (vgl. *kunāšu*)	Emmer	> zíz	[s. auch (2a)]
73		*kiššātu*	Schuld(sklaven)-dienst	> zíz+da[15]	
74	k > s	*kidītu*	Äußeres	> sa+ti	[vgl. § 3.2 (4a)]

(lb) in Einzelfällen, vgl.

75	p > g̃/m	*parṣu*	Kult(ordnung)	> g̃arza/ma+ar+za	
76		*parīsu*	Ruderstange	> má+rí+za[16]	
77	m > g̃	*milku*	Rat	> g̃alga	[vgl. § 2.1 Nr. 33]
78	m > d(?)	*mūru*	Eselfohlen	> dùr(?)	Eselhengst

(2) im Inlaut

(2a) durch Assimilation eines /n/, vgl.

79	nz > z	*enzu* > *ezzu*	Ziege	> ùz	[vgl. § 3.2 (4a)]
	nš > z	**kinšu* (vgl. *kiššatu*)	Emmer	> zíz	[s. auch (la)]

---

15 Vgl. H. Steible - H. Behrens, *ABW* 11 (1982) 161 Anm. 22, 164 Anm. 29 (mit Literatur).

16 Vgl. Kraus (1969): 38 mit Anm. 60.

(2b) in Einzelfällen, vgl.

80	n > r[17]	*tanattu*	Ruhm	> aratta	[vgl. § 4.2 (1)]
81	r > š	*sartu*	Falschheit	> za+áš+da	Verfehlung[18]
82	r > ḫ	*šuršu*	Wurzel	> suḫuš	Fundament

(3) im Auslaut, vgl.

83	q > m	(*ḫalaq*)	zugrunde gehen, D vernichten	> ḫa+lam	zugrunde gehen (lassen)[19]
84	r > š	*arratu*	Fluch	> áš	

4.2. Eine unregelmäßige Konsonantenentsprechung kann jedoch auch durch den Schwund eines Konsonanten bedingt sein, und zwar

(1) im Anlaut, vgl.

85	/b/	*bašmu*	Giftschlange	> usum	[vgl. § 3.2 (3)]
	/t/	*tanattu*	Ruhm	> aratta	[vgl. § 4.1 (2b)]
86	/ṣ/	*ṣalmu*	Bild, Statue	> alam/n	[vgl. § 2.2 (5c)]

(2) im (sekundären) Auslaut, vgl.

87	/n/	*dīnu*	Rechtsfall	> di	
88		*qanû*	Rohr	> gi	[vgl. § 3.2 (4a)]
89	/l/	*ašlu*	Meßleine	> éš	[vgl. § 3.2 (4a)]
90		*mišlu*	Hälfte	> maš	[vgl. § 3.2 (4a)]

4.3. Derartige Unregelmäßigkeiten der Konsonantenentsprechung finden sich ebenfalls bei der Entlehnung von Lexemen aus dem Sumerischen in das Akkadische

(1) im Anlaut durch

(la) Veränderung eines Konsonanten, vgl.

m > n	muḫaldim	Koch	> *nuḫatimmu*	[vgl. (2b)]
n > l	nu.bànda	Inspektor	> *laputtā'u*	"Leutnant"

17 Für den Lautwandel n > r (im Emesal) vgl. Falkenstein (1959): 28 § 9.1.

18 Vgl. Gelb (1961): 122 (III A l); P. Steinkeller, *RA* 74 (1980) 179.

19 Vgl. auch Poebel (1923): 33 § 91.

(1b) Schwund eines Konsonanten, vgl.

/g/	gidim	Totengeist	> *eṭimmu*
/m/	mušen.dù	Vogelfänger	> *usandû*
/š/	šitim	Baumeister	> *itinnu*

(2) im Inlaut durch

(2a) Assimilation eines Nasals, vgl.

mb > mm	g̃iš.nimbar	Dattelpalme	> *gišimmaru*	
mb > pp	ambar	Sumpf	> *appa(r)ru*	
ng > kk	engar	Pflüger	> *ikkaru*	
	kun.gal	"Großschwanz"	> *gukkallu*	(ein Schaf)
ns > šš	ensik	Regent	> *išši'akku*	
nš > šš	banšur	Tisch	> *paššūru*	

(2b) Veränderung eines Konsonanten, vgl.

d > p	ad.kid	Rohrmatten-flechter	> *atkuppu*	
g > b	agrig	Verwalter	> *abarakku*	
	gig	Weizen	> *kibtu*	
	níg̃.gig	Verbotenes	> *ikkibu*	
	šag$_4$.zu	Hebamme	> *šabsūtu*	
ld > t	muḫaldim	Koch	> *nuḫatimmu*	[vgl. (1a)]

5. Semantische Bereiche

5.1. Nach ihrem Bedeutungstyp sind die aus dem Akkadischen in das Sumerische entlehnten Verben[20]

(1) zur Hälfte qualitative Verben, nämlich gin$_6$ "dauerhaft sein" [23], libir "alt sein" [26], sam$_x$(SA$_5$) "rot(braun) sein" [45], silim "unversehrt sein" [51];

(2) fientische Verben

(2a) aus dem semantischen Bereich der Wirtschaft [vgl. § 5.2 (8)], nämlich šám "kaufen" [52], sa$_{12}$.rig$_7$ "schenken" [54],

(2b) zur Bezeichnung einer (negativen) Einwirkung, nämlich ḫa+lam "zugrunde gehen (lassen), vernichten" [84], šu.bal "verändern" [59].

---

20 Für die Nummern s. § 2.1 und §§ 4.1-2.

5.2 Die entlehnten Nomina sind Bezeichnungen für

(1) Berufe u. ä.: dam+gàr "Kaufmann" [61], gáb+ra/ga+ba+ra "Hirtenjunge" [19], ḫa+za+núm "Bürgermeister" [14], išib "Beschwörungspriester" [68], na+gad "Hirte" [37], nimgir "Ausrufer, Herold" [36], pa$_4$+šeš "*pašīšu*-Priester" [39], ra/rá+gab "Reiter" [43], sa+gaz "Räuber" [48], sagi "Mundschenk" [55], saḫar "Knappe", [46], šabra "Präfekt" [53], šagina "Statthalter" [50], ugula "Aufseher" [66];

(2) gesellschaftliche "Klassen" und Rollen: maš+ka$_{15}$:en "Palasthöriger" [35], warad/urda "Sklave; Diener" [67]; íldu "Gruppe, Clan" [16]; ibila/ì+bí+la "Erbsohn" [05], murub$_5$ "Schwiegervater" [11]; ab+ba "Alter, Ältester" [01], um+ma "Alte; Klageweib" [64], bur+ša+ma "Greis" [41];

(3) Tiere, insbesondere Nutztiere: dùr(?) "Eselhengst" [78], lu+lim "Hirsch" [28], ni+is+ku(+um) "edles Tier" [38], uz "Ente" [69], ùz "Ziege" [79], sowie ušum "(mythische) Giftschlange" [85];

(4) Pflanzen, insbesondere Nutzpflanzen, und deren Produkte: ar+za+na "Gerstengrütze" [06], ga+mun "Kümmel" [18], ga+ra+an "Weinstock" [21], ga+raš "Porree, Lauch" [20], gi "Rohr" [88], lu+úb "Bohne(n)" [29], sum "Lauch, Zwiebel" [58], tu+lu+bu+um "Platane" [09], zíz "Emmer" [72];

(5) Gegenstände: alam/n "Bild, Statue" [86], gu+za "Stuhl, Thron" [25], ḫa+zi(+in/na) "Axt" [13], k/ga+ba+bu+um "Schleuder" [17], le+um "Tafel" [27], má+rí+za "Ruderstange" [76], mi+tum "(Götterwaffe)" [34], za+bí+tum "(Leier)" [44], za+ḫum "(Wasch)Schale" [49];

(6) Messen und Maße: éš "Meßleine" [89], ma+na "Mine" [30], maš "Hälfte" [90], šanabi "zwei Drittel" [57], za+rí+in "Durchschnittsqualität" [71];

(7) Lokalia: a+bul$_5$ "Stadttor" [02], a+la "Ansiedlung" [04], dul$_6$ "(Schutt)Hügel" [62], ḫa+ra+an "Weg" [12], ḫur+ru+um "Erdloch, Höhle" [15], ma+da "Land" [32], maš+gan "Lagerplatz" [31], sa+ti "Äußeres" [74], sa+tu "Berg" [47], suḫuš "Fundament" [83];

(8) wirtschaftliche und politische Begriffe: a+ka+la/lum "Nahrung" [03], buru$_{14}$ "Ernte" [10], dam+ḫa+ra "Kampf" [60], di "Rechtsfall" [87], ezem/n "Fest" [70], gi+na+tum "Garantiebetrag" [24], g̃arza/ma+ar+za "Kult(ordnung)" [75], pe+lu$_5$+da "Besitzverhältnis" [07], pu+úḫ+ru+um "Versammlung" [40], šám/šàm "Kaufpreis" [56], zíz+da "Schuldsklaverei" [73];

(9) Abstrakta: aratta "Ruhm" [80], áš "Fluch" [82], buzur "Geheimnis" [42], da/du+rí "Dauer" [08], dím+ma "Plan(ung)" [63], g̃alga/ma+al+ga "Rat"

[77/33], za+áš+da "Verfehlung" [81]; sowie die Morpheme -gim "wie" [22], ù "und, aber" [65].

Einige dieser entlehnten Nomina sind – zum Teil mit modifizierter Bedeutung - sogar wieder in das Akkadische rückentlehnt worden, vgl.

[70	(**wsm*)]	> ezem/n	Fest	> *isinnu*	Fest
[68	(*w*)*āšipu*]	> išib	Beschwörungspriester	> *išippu*	Reinigungspriester
[07	*bēlūtu*]	> pe+lu$_5$+da	Besitzverhältnis	> *pelludû*	Kult
[04	*rakbu*]	> ra/rá+gab	Reiter	> *rakbû*	Gesandter
[48	*šaggāšu*]	> sa+gaz	Räuber	> *sagassu*	Räuber
[50	*šaknu*]	> šagina	Statthalter	> *šakkanakku*	Statthalter
[53	*šāpiru*]	> šabra	Präfekt	> *šabrû*	Tempelverwalter
[66	*waklu*]	> ugula	Aufseher	> *ukullû*	Aufseher
[69	(**wazz*)]	> uz	Ente	> *usu*	Ente, Hausgans
[71	**kinšu*]	> zíz	Emmer	> *zīzu*	Emmer

5.3. Zu berücksichtigen ist dabei aber auch, daß von einer erheblichen Anzahl von Nomina die primäre Sprachzugehörigkeit nicht eindeutig zu bestimmen ist. Das gilt nicht nur für z. B. Materialien, die aus dem "Fremdland" (kur) importiert wurden, wie eren = *erēnu* "Zeder; Konifere", zabar = *siparru* "Bronze", u. ä., sondern auch für Bezeichnungen von z. B.

(1) Berufen u. ä. wie uš+bar = *i/ušparu* "Weber", šà+tam = *ša(t)tammu* "Verwalter";
(2) Tieren wie az = *asu* "Bär", eštub = *arsuppu* "Karpfen";
(3) Pflanzen und deren Produkten wie ḫa+lu+úb = *ḫa/uluppu* "(ein Baum)", za+ḫi/aḫ+li(+a) = *saḫlû* "Kresse", zú+lum = *suluppu* "Dattel";
(4) Gegenständen wie gad = *kitû* "Leinen(kleid)", gu = *qû* "Faden", zà+mí(n) = *sammû* "Harfe;
(5) sowie Ortsnamen wie kiš^{ki}, nibru^{ki}.

Es wäre jedoch voreilig, diese Lexeme allein deshalb auf eine Substratsprache oder gar mehrere Substratsprachen zurückführen zu wollen.

Bibliographie

Generell ist zu verweisen auf

PSD *The Sumerian Dictionary of the University Museum of the University of Pennsylvania.*

CAD *The Chicago Assyrian Dictionary.*

AHw *W. von Soden, Akkadisches Handwörterbuch.*

Bauer, J. (1972) *Altsumerische Wirtschaftstexte aus Lagasch* = *Studia Pohl* 9.

Behrens H., Steible H. (1983) *Glossar zu den altsumerischen Bau- und Weihinschriften* = *FAOS* 6.

Edzard, D. O. (1960) "Sumerer und Semiten in der frühen Geschichte Mesopotamiens", in *CRRAI* IX = *Genava* n. s. 8: 241-258.

Edzard, D. O. (1968) *Sumerische Rechtsurkunden des III. Jahrtausends* = *ABAW* NF 72.

Falkenstein, A. (1949) *Grammatik der Sprache Gudeas von Lagaš* = *AnOr* 28.

Falkenstein, A. (1950) "Ibbīsîn – Išbi'erra", *ZA* 45 NF 15, 59-79.

Falkenstein, A. (1951) "Zur Chronologie der sumerischen Literatur", in *CRRAI* II: 12-30.

Falkenstein, A. (1957) *Die neusumerischen Gerichtsurkunden* III = *ABAW* 44.

Falkenstein, A. (1959) *Das Sumerische* = *Handbuch der Orientalistik*, l. Abt 2, 1-2, l.

Falkenstein, A. (1960) "Kontakte zwischen Sumerern und Akkadern auf sprachlichem Gebiet", in *CRRAI* IX = *Genava* n. s. 8: 310-314.

Gelb, I. J. (1960) "Sumerians and Akkadians in their Ethno-Linguistic Relationship", in *CRRAI* IX = *Genava* n. s. 8: 258-271.

Gelb, I. J. (1961) *Old Akkadian Writing and Grammar* = *MAD* II, 2nd edition.

Goetze, A. (1970) "Early Dynastic Dedication Inscriptions from Nippur", *JCS* 23: 39-56.

Kraus, F. R. (1969) "Altmesopotamisches Erbrecht", in *Essays on Oriental Laws of Succession* = *SD* IX: 1-58.

Kraus, F. R. (1970) *Sumerer und Akkader. Ein Problem der altmesopotamischen Geschichte.*

Krecher, J. (1969) "Verschlußlaute und Betonung im Sumerischen, in *lišān mitḫurti*" = *AOAT* 1 (Fs W. von Soden): 157-197.

Lieberman, St. (1977) *The Sumerian Loanwords in Old-Babylonian Akkadian* I.

Oberhuber, K. (1981) "Kontaktwirkungen der Symbiose Sumerisch – Akkadisch: Bemerkungen zum akkadischen Lehngut im Sumerischen", in *Al-Hudhud* (Fs M. Höfner): 257-261.

Poebel, A. (1923) *Grundriß der sumerischen Grammatik.*

Römer, W. Ph. H. (1999) *Die Sumerologie*, 2., erweiterte Aufl. = *AOAT* 262.

Thomsen, M.-L. (1984) *The Sumerian Language* = *Mesopotamia* 10.

von Soden, W. (1952) *Grundriß der akkadischen Grammatik* = *AnOr* 33.

von Soden, W. (1960) "Status rectus-Formen vor dem Genitiv im Akkadischen und die sogenannte uneigentliche Annexion im Arabischen", *JNES* 19: 163-171.

THE USE OF GLOSSES IN NEO-ASSYRIAN LETTERS AND ASTROLOGICAL REPORTS*

PHILIPPE TALON

Université Libre de Bruxelles

The question of literacy in the Ancient Near East has been a subject of a certain negligence among modern Assyriologists. Starting from the general idea that cuneiform writing was so difficult that it had to be restricted to a handful of specialized people, the common consensus has been, and still is, that most people did not master reading and writing and that literacy was limited to a a caste of scribes.[1] Nevertheless, some rather isolated examples seem to show that this was perhaps not the case, or at least, that the situation was perhaps a bit more complicated. One could start with the curious orthography, grammar and syntax of some of the Mari letters emanating from the city of Ilān-ṣurā.[2] Even if there is no definitive proof, it still remains possible that the peculiarities of these letters derive from the fact that their senders had been deprived of the use of their secretaries. An analogous example has recently been put forward by S. Parpola.[3]

Among the many letters and astrological reports written by Esarhaddon's and Assurbanipal's close advisors,[4] those emanating from Balasî and Nabû-aḫḫē-erība stand out in a fashion. These two scholars, respectively the crown prince's *ummānu*

---

* It is a pleasure to offer this small contribution to P. Fronzaroli as a humble token of my admiration.

1 See e.g. the humorous remark of J. Sasson about the mistakes in the Mari administrative accounts "Who's looking over their shoulders, "they would ask, "if not another scribe?", in "Accounting Discrepancies in the Mari NÌ.GUB [NÍG.DU] Texts", G. Van Driel *et al.* (eds.), *Zikir Šumim. Assyriological Studies Presented to F.R. Kraus*, Leiden 1982, pp. 326-341. The cited passage is on p. 341.

2 Cf D. Charpin, "L'akkadien des lettres d'Ilân-ṣurâ", in M. Lebeau and Ph. Talon (eds.), *Reflets des Deux Fleuves. Mélanges offerts à André Finet*, Akkadica Supplementum VI, Leuven 1989, pp. 31-40.

3 "The Man Without a Scribe and the Question of Literacy in the Assyrian Empire", in B. Pongratz-Leisten (ed.), *Ana šadî Labnāni lu allik. Festschrift für W. Röllig, AOAT* 247, 1997, pp. 315-324.

4 Published in S. Parpola, *Letters from Assyrian and Babylonian Scholars*, SAA 10, Helsinki 1993 (with earlier treatment in id., *Letters from Assyrian Scholars to the Kings Esarhaddon and Assurbanipal, AOAT* 5/1 and 5/2, Neukirchen-Vluyn, 1970 and 1983; H. Hunger, *Astrological Reports to Assyrian Kings*, SAA 8, Helsinki 1992.

(Balasî),[5] and the astrologer of both kings (Nabû-aḫḫē-erība), have the habit to include glosses in their messages. Apart from isolated examples of adding a simple sign to ensure the reading of a CVC-sign, such ^{I}*aš-šur-mu-kin*(*in*)-BALA-*u-a* (SAA 10, 298: rev. 3 and 300: rev. 5) or (*mu*)*muk* (SAA 10 34: 16 and 305:14),[6] all the glosses encountered in letters and reports can be attributed to these two scholars. It should be noted immediately that there is no common measure between both men as to the number of their glosses. Nabû-aḫḫē-erība is using them in almost every correspondence, whereas Balasî's explanatory glosses are only attested in three texts.[7]

I have been able to list a total of 155 cases, of which approximately half are written in dated documents. These dates show that the use of glosses by Balasî and his colleague do not represent a special moment in time. They span a period going from 675? to 666 BC, thus the last years of Esarhaddon and the first years of Assurbanipal.

The number of words glossed is also varying: from one single occurrence to a maximum of ten in some documents. Sometimes the same word is marked more than once in the same letter/report. The information is summarized in the following table (NAE = Nabû-aḫḫē-erība; texts are listed in chronological order, with undated texts first):

Reference	nb glosses	Author	day	month	year	glosses
SAA 10 79	3	NAE				MÚŠ.MEŠ-šu = zi-mu-šú qut-ri = qu-ut-ri MU = šá-at-ti
SAA 10 81	1	NAE				MUL.LI$_9$.SI$_4$ = li-si
SAA 8 44	3	NAE				TAR-[us] = ip-ru-[us] UD.NÁ.ÀM = UD bu-ub-bu-li AN-ú = šá-mu-u
SAA 8 57	6	NAE				AGA = a-gu-u SI = qar-nu ZAG-šú = i-mit-ti-šú AN-ú = šá-mu-u ḪI.GAR = bar-ti

5 See now K. Radner (ed.), *The Prosopography of the Neo-Assyrian Empire*, 1/II, Helsinki 1999, pp. 254-255; 2/II, Helsinki 2001, pp. 794-796.

6 All four letters emanate from the exorcist Nabû-naṣir.

7 SAA 10 44 (dated 670), written with his colleague Nabû-aḫḫē-erība, 51 (669) and the report SAA 8 82 (668).

						DIRI = di-ir
SAA 8 60	3	NAE				EME = [l]i-šá-a-nu BAR-tum = a-ḫi-tum i-be-e[l] = [i]-bi-il
SAA 8 62	1	NAE				KAB-šú = šu-me-li-šú
SAA 8 63	5	NAE				[GI]SKIM = [it]-tú me-ḫir = me-ḫi-ir GISKIM = it-ti PI.MEŠ = uz-ni GISKIM = it-tú
SAA 8 64	5	NAE				AN-ú = šá-mu-u AN-ú = šá-mu-u IM.[DIRI] = ur-[pa-ti] MUL.^{d}[IM.DUGUD] = mu-ul ^{d}[x x x x x] ba-ìl = ba-il
SAA 8 65	7	NAE				KA = pi-i UN.MEŠ = ni-ši IM.DIRI.MEŠ = ur-pa-a-ti IM.DIRI.MEŠ = ur-pa-a-ti DIRI-pu = i-qe-lip-pu AN-ú = šá-mu-u DUB-ik = šá-pi-ik
SAA 8 66	2	NAE				zi-qit = zi-qi-it NIGIN-šú = il-me-šú
SAA 8 68	1	NAE				MUL.a-nu-AGA = a-gu-u
SAA 8 70	8	NAE				[x ÚR] = [x x] ÚR IGI.BAR = tap-pal-la-as AN-ú = šá-mu-u KI = kaq-qa-ru kaš-du-ú = ka-áš-du-ú ZI = [ti]-ib TU$_{15}$ = šá-a-ri um-šum = um-šú
SAA 8 71	1	NAE				TÙR = tar-ba-ṣi
SAA 8 72	1	NAE				ZI = [ti]-ib
SAA 8 73	6	NAE				MUL.ŠUDUN = šu-du-un È-šú = a-ṣi-šú [MUL].KU$_{6}$ = [ku]-u MUL.UG[A] = mu-ul ú-ga KU$_{6}$.MEŠ = [x x] x MUŠEN.MEŠ = iṣ-ṣu-ri
SAA 8 74	3	NAE				MUL.ÙZ = mu-ul ú-za im-šu[ḫ] = im-šu-[uḫ]

						ARḪUŠ = re-e-mu
SAA 8 75	1	NAE				150 = šu-me-li
SAA 8 76	4	NAE				UD.DA = ṣi-is-su x [x x x x] = ú-[x x x] MUL = ka-ka-bu ša IGI = šá pa-ni
SAA 8 77	4	NAE				MUL.SIM.MAḪ = mu-ul ši-im-ma-a[ḫ] ZI-ut = ti-bu-ut ERIM-ni = um-ma-[ni] KASKAL-šú = ḫar-ra-ni-šú
SAA 8 78	3	NAE				SA$_5$ = sa-a-mu GAR.GAR-nu = it-ta-na-áš-kan TU$_{15}$ = šá-a-ru
SAA 8 39	3	NAE		2	-675 ?	K[I!.GUB-sà GI.NA] = m[a!-za-as-sa ke-e-né] KI.GUB.BA-sà I.NA = ma-za-as-sa ke-e-né ZI-ut = [t]e-bu-ut
SAA 8 40	9	NAE		4	-673	GI$_6$ = ṣa-al-mu a-dir = [a-di]-ir ḪUŠ-ma = e-zi-iz-ma IDIM.MEŠ-šú = kab!-tu-ti-šú GUR-ma = ú-tar-a-ma NU = la GAZ-ak = i-da-ak [x x] x-ú = [x x]-šu-u TUK-ši = i-ra-áš-ši
SAA 8 41	10	NAE	20	5	-672	GI! = ṣa-al-mu ITI = ar-ḫu A.AN = zu-un-nu ú-kal = ú-ka-la IM.DIRI.[MEŠ] = ur-pa-a-ti MÁŠ.ANŠE = bu-u-li KUR-MAR.TU.KI = ma-at a-mur-re-e MÍ.PEŠ$_4$.MEŠ = e-ra-a-ti NITA.M[EŠ] = zak-ka-⸢ri!⸣ [Ù].TU.MEŠ = [ul]-la-da
SAA 10 67	2	NAE	25	3	-671	GI$_6$-ma = ṣa-li-im-⸢ma⸣ Á.S[ÌG] = a-s[ak-ku]
SAA 10 68	1	NAE		6	-671	4 ITI = ra-ab-bi ur-ḫi
SAA 8 43	8	NAE		8	-671	IDIM = nag-bi UD = ú-me

						NU = la ŠÚ = er-pi MÍ.KÚR = nu-kur-te KIN-ka = iš-pur-u-ka SILIM-ma = sa-li-i-mu KIN-ka = i-šap-par-ka
SAA 8 69	2	NAE		3	-670	KUR-ma = ip-pu-ḫa-am-ma IGI-šú = pa-ni-šú
SAA 8 45	6	NAE	26	3	-670	MUL = ka-ak-ka-bu SUR-ma = iṣ-ru-ur-ma M[UL.x x x] = m[u-ul x x x] TU-ub = e-ru-ub ḪI.GAR = ba-ar-tú GÁ[L-ši] = ib-b[a-áš-ši]
SAA 10 44	1	Balasî + NAE		7	-670	ITI = ur-ḫu
SAA 10 70	3	NAE		10	-670	GARZA = pa-ar-ṣi DUMU-DUMU.MEŠ-šú = mar-mar-i-šú KASKAL = ḫu-u-li
SAA 10 71	2	NAE	16	12	-670	[par-s]u = [pa-a]r$^{!}$-su UD$^{!}$.DUG$_{4}$.GA.MEŠ = a-da-an-na-a-te
SAA 10 51	2	Balasî	26	3	-669	MUL = ka-ku-bu 1-en = is-si-i[n$^{!}$]
SAA 10 74	6	NAE	30	3	-669	ŠUG-su = ku-ru$^{!}$-ma-at-su KAŠ.SAG = ši-ka-ru ZAG = i-mit-tú GISKIM.BI = [it-ta-šú] GISKIM.BI = it-ta-šú KUR.SU.BIR$_{4}$.KI = šu-bar-ti
SAA 8 48	1	NAE	23	1	-668	KUR-ud = ik-šu-ud
SAA 8 49	10	NAE	15	3	-668	LÚ.SA.GAZ = ḫab-ba-a-tú$^{!}$ DIM$_{4}$ = is-niq ÁB.GUD.ḪI.A = ab$^{!}$-ba-gud-ḫa-a U$_{8}$.UDU. ḪI.A = uz-du-ḫa-a KASKAL = ḫar-ra-na 20 = ^{d}šá-maš KUR-ud = ik-šu-ud bu-lim = bu-u-li MUL.KA$_{5}$.A = mu-ul ka-a KUR-šú = ni-pi-iḫ-šú
SAA 8 82	1	Balasî	15	3	-668	GÁN.BA = ma-ḫi-ru
SAA 8 102	1	Akkulā	15	3	-668	ŠEŠ.UNUG.KI = [[ú$^{?}$]]-ri

		nu				
SAA 8 50	1	NAE	12	6	-668	TE-ma = iṭ-ḫu-ma
SAA 10 78	1	NAE	15	10	-667	EN.NUN-UD.ZA[L.LA] = e-nu-un ú-˹za-al˺-la
SAA 8 51	8	NAE	20	11	-667	MUL.˹ŠÁR.UR˺ = šá-ar-ur MUL.˹ŠÁR.GAZ˺ = ṣar-gaz AGA = a-gu-u MU = mu NÍG.SI.SÁ = ni-ig-si-sa AGA = a-gu-u GI$_6$ = ṣa-al-mu Ù.TU.M[EŠ] = ú-la-a-[da]
SAA 8 52	1	NAE	5	4	-666	MUL.ŠÁR.GAZ = ga-az
SAA 8 53	2	NAE	4	7	-666	15 = i-mit-ti 20 = ^{d}šá-maš
SAA 8 54	3	NAE	1	8	-666	A.ŠI.ŠI-ṣa = me-le-ṣa 3.20 = eš-šá-ba$^?$ MUL = ka-[ka-bu]
SAA 8 55	3	NAE		12	-666	TU$_{15}$.MEŠ = šá-ra-a-ni NU = la DÙG.GA.MEŠ = ṭa-bu-u-ti

It seems clear from this list that the dated tablets and reports cover the complete carreers of Balasî and Nabû-aḫḫē-erība.[8] Both were astrologers and they wrote letters together. It happens also that they separately write to the king about the same matter. It looks like they also shared this common writing practice, even if Nabû-aḫḫē-erība is much more prone to use it than his colleague.

What is more strange is the nature of the glosses themselves. The letters and reports are addressed to the king; since they span both the end of Esarhaddon's reign and the beginning of Assurbanipal's, one cannot use the argument of novelty or change to explain them. Was it really necessary for someone to remind the king that NU in omen texts had to be read *la*, or that KUR-*ud* stood for *ikšud*, or even that ITI is the logogram of *arḫu* 'month'? On the other hand, even if, as is often written today, the kings had only a very slight knowledge of writing, why is it then that the other correspondents of the monarchs did not feel necessary to clarify their letters or reports? It is known that Balasî was appointed *ummānu* to the crown prince. Since

8 Balasî is attested between 672 and 667, Nabû-aḫḫē-erība between 674 and 666 (two legal texts, dated 698 and 687, perhaps mention him, see SAA 6 100 and 157), cf S. Parpola, *LAS* I/2, pp. 468-469.

he was then probably involved in his education, it could be normal for him to use explanatory glosses in the letters sent to his pupil. But these letters are not sent (at least nominally) to the crown prince, but to the king himself. Everything thus points to a kind of idiosyncrasy or a particular habit of these two scholars.

Glossed words are given in the following table, in alphabetical order:

1-en	is-si-i[n$^{!}$]	SAA 10 51
15	i-mit-ti	SAA 8 53
150	šu-me-li	SAA 8 75
20	^{d}šá-maš	SAA 8 49
20	^{d}šá-maš	SAA 8 53
3.20	eš-šá-ba$^{?}$	SAA 8 54
4 ITI	ra-ab-bi ur-ḫi	SAA 10 68
A.AN	zu-un-nu	SAA 8 41
A.ŠI.ŠI-ṣa	me-le-ṣa	SAA 8 54
a-dir	[a-di]-ir	SAA 8 40
Á.S[ÌG]	a-s[ak-ku]	SAA 10 67
ÁB.GUD.ḪI.A	ab$^{!}$-ba-gud-ḫa-a	SAA 8 49
AGA	a-gu-u	SAA 8 57
AGA	a-gu-u	SAA 8 51
AGA	a-gu-u	SAA 8 51
AN-ú	šá-mu-u	SAA 8 44
AN-ú	šá-mu-u	SAA 8 57
AN-ú	šá-mu-u	SAA 8 64
AN-ú	šá-mu-u	SAA 8 64
AN-ú	šá-mu-u	SAA 8 65
AN-ú	šá-mu-u	SAA 8 70
ARḪUŠ	re-e-mu	SAA 8 74
ba-ìl	ba-il	SAA 8 64
BAR-tum	a-ḫi-tum	SAA 8 60
bu-lim	bu-u-li	SAA 8 49
DIM$_4$	is-niq	SAA 8 49
DIRI	di-ir	SAA 8 57
DIRI-pu	i-qe-lip-pu	SAA 8 65
DUB-ik	šá-pi-ik	SAA 8 65
DÙG.GA.MEŠ	ṭa-bu-u-ti	SAA 8 55
DUMU-DUMU.MEŠ-šú	mar-mar-i-šú	SAA 10 70
È-šú	a-ṣi-šú	SAA 8 73
EME	[l]i-šá-a-nu	SAA 8 60
EN.NUN-UD.ZA[L.LA]	e-nu-un ú-⸢za-al⸣-la	SAA 10 78
ERIM-ni	um-ma-[ni]	SAA 8 77
GÁ[L-ši]	ib-b[a-áš-ši]	SAA 8 45
GÁN.BA	ma-ḫi-ru	SAA 8 82

GAR.GAR-nu	it-ta-na-áš-kan	SAA 8 78
GARZA	pa-ar-ṣi	SAA 10 70
GAZ-ak	i-da-ak	SAA 8 40
GI$_6$	ṣa-al-mu	SAA 8 40
GI$_6$	ṣa-al-mu	SAA 8 41
GI$_6$	ṣa-al-mu	SAA 8 51
[GI]SKIM	[it]-tú	SAA 8 63
GISKIM	it-ti	SAA 8 63
GISKIM	it-tú	SAA 8 63
GISKIM.BI	[it-ta-šú]	SAA 10 74
GISKIM.BI	it-ta-šú	SAA 10 74
GUR-ma	ú-tar-a-ma	SAA 8 40
ḪI.GAR	bar-ti	SAA 8 57
ḪI.GAR	ba-ar-tú	SAA 8 45
ḪUŠ-ma	e-zi-iz-ma	SAA 8 40
i-be-e[l]	[i]-bi-il	SAA 8 60
IDIM	nag-bi	SAA 8 43
IDIM.MEŠ-šú	kab$^{!}$-tu-ti-šú	SAA 8 40
IGI.BAR	tap-pal-la-as	SAA 8 70
IGI-šú	pa-ni-šú	SAA 8 69
IM.[DIRI]	ur-[pa-ti]	SAA 8 64
IM.DIRI.MEŠ	ur-pa-a-ti	SAA 8 65
IM.DIRI.MEŠ	ur-pa-a-ti	SAA 8 65
IM.DIRI.[MEŠ]	ur-pa-a-ti	SAA 8 41
im-šu[ḫ]	im-šu-[uḫ]	SAA 8 74
ITI	ar-ḫu	SAA 8 41
ITI	ur-ḫu	SAA 10 44
KA	pi-i	SAA 8 65
KAB-šú	šu-me-li-šú	SAA 8 62
KASKAL	ḫu-u-li	SAA 10 70
KASKAL	ḫar-ra-na	SAA 8 49
KASKAL-šú	ḫar-ra-ni-šú	SAA 8 77
KAŠ.SAG	ši-ka-ru	SAA 10 74
kaš-du-ú	ka-áš-du-ú	SAA 8 70
KI	kaq-qa-ru	SAA 8 70
KI.GUB.BA-sà GI.NA	ma-za-as-sa ke-e-né	SAA 8 39
K[I$^{!}$.GUB-sà GI.NA]	m[a$^{!}$-za-as-sa ke-e-né]	SAA 8 39
KIN-ka	iš-pur-u-ka	SAA 8 43
KIN-ka	i-šap-par-ka	SAA 8 43
KU$_6$.MEŠ	[x x] x	SAA 8 73
KUR.SU.BIR$_4$.KI	šu-bar-ti	SAA 10 74
KUR-ma	ip-pu-ḫa-am-ma	SAA 8 69
KUR-MAR.TU.KI	ma-at a-mur-re-e	SAA 8 41
KUR-šú	ni-pi-iḫ-šú	SAA 8 49
KUR-ud	ik-šu-ud	SAA 8 48

KUR-ud	ik-šu-ud	SAA 8 49
LÚ.SA.GAZ	ḫab-ba-a-tú$^{!}$	SAA 8 49
MÁŠ.ANŠE	bu-u-li	SAA 8 41
me-ḫir	me-ḫi-ir	SAA 8 63
MI-ma	ṣa-li-im-⸢ma⸣	SAA 10 67
MÍ.KÚR	nu-kur-te	SAA 8 43
MÍ.PEŠ$_4$.MEŠ	e-ra-a-ti	SAA 8 41
MU	šá-at-ti	SAA 10 79
MU	mu	SAA 8 51
MUL	ka-ka-bu	SAA 8 76
MUL	ka-ak-ka-bu	SAA 8 45
MUL	ka-ku-bu	SAA 10 51
MUL	ka-[ka-bu]	SAA 8 54
MUL.a-nu-AGA	a-gu-u	SAA 8 68
MUL.^{d}[IM.DUGUD]	mu-ul ^{d}[x x x x x]	SAA 8 64
MUL.KA$_5$.A	mu-ul ka-a	SAA 8 49
[MUL].KU$_6$	[ku]-u	SAA 8 73
MUL.LI$_9$.SI$_4$	li-si	SAA 10 81
MUL.SIM.MAḪ	mu-ul ši-im-ma-a[ḫ]	SAA 8 77
MUL.⸢ŠÁR.GAZ⸣	ṣar-gaz	SAA 8 51
MUL.ŠÁR.GAZ	ga-az	SAA 8 52
MUL.⸢ŠÁR.UR⸣	šá-ar-ur	SAA 8 51
MUL.ŠUDUN	šu-du-un	SAA 8 73
MUL.UG[A]	mu-ul ú-ga	SAA 8 73
MUL.ÙZ	mu-ul ú-za	SAA 8 74
M[UL.x x x]	m[u-ul x x x]	SAA 8 45
MÚŠ.MEŠ-šu	zi-mu-šú	SAA 10 79
MUŠEN.MEŠ	iṣ-ṣu-ri	SAA 8 73
NÍG.SI.SÁ	ni-ig-si-sa	SAA 8 51
NIGIN-šú	il-me-šú	SAA 8 66
NITA.M[EŠ]	zak-ka-⸢ri$^{!}$⸣	SAA 8 41
NU	la	SAA 8 40
NU	la	SAA 8 43
NU	la	SAA 8 55
[par-s]u	[pa-a]r$^{!}$-su	SAA 10 71
PI.MEŠ	uz-ni	SAA 8 63
qut-ri	qu-ut-ri	SAA 10 79
SA$_5$	sa-a-mu	SAA 8 78
SI	qar-nu	SAA 8 57
SILIM-ma	sa-li-i-mu	SAA 8 43
SUR-ma	iṣ-ru-ur-ma	SAA 8 45
ša IGI	šá pa-ni	SAA 8 76
ŠEŠ.UNUG.KI	[[ú$^{?}$]]-ri	SAA 8 102
ŠÚ	er-pi	SAA 8 43
ŠUG-su	ku-ru$^{!}$-ma-at-su	SAA 10 74

TAR-[us]	ip-ru-[us]	SAA 8 44
TE-ma	iṭ-ḫu-ma	SAA 8 50
TU-ub	e-ru-ub	SAA 8 45
TU$_{15}$	šá-a-ri	SAA 8 70
TU$_{15}$	šá-a-ru	SAA 8 78
TU$_{15}$.MEŠ	šá-ra-a-ni	SAA 8 55
TUK-ši	i-ra-áš-ši	SAA 8 40
TÙR	tar-ba-ṣi	SAA 8 71
ú-kal	ú-ka-la	SAA 8 41
[Ù].TU.MEŠ	[ul]-la-da	SAA 8 41
Ù.TU.M[EŠ]	ú-la-a-[da]	SAA 8 51
U$_{8}$.UDU.ḪI.A	uz-du-ḫa-a	SAA 8 49
UD	ú-me	SAA 8 43
UD.DA	ṣi-is-su	SAA 8 76
UD$^{!}$.DUG$_{4}$.GA.MEŠ	a-da-an-na-a-te	SAA 10 71
UD.NÁ.ÀM	UD bu-ub-bu-li	SAA 8 44
um-šum	um-šú	SAA 8 70
UN.MEŠ	ni-ši	SAA 8 65
[x ÚR]	[x x] ÚR	SAA 8 70
x [x x x x]	ú-[x x x]	SAA 8 76
[x x] x-ú	[x x]-šu-u	SAA 8 40
ZAG	i-mit-tú	SAA 10 74
ZAG-šú	i-mit-ti-šú	SAA 8 57
ZI	[ti]-ib	SAA 8 70
ZI	[t]i-ib	SAA 8 72
zi-qit	zi-qi-it	SAA 8 66
ZI-ut	ti-bu-ut	SAA 8 77
ZI-ut	[t]e-bu-ut	SAA 8 39

The following table presents the glosses themselves, arranged alphabetically:

a-da-an-na-a-te	UD$^{!}$.DUG$_{4}$.GA.MEŠ	SAA 10 71
[a-di]-ir	a-dir	SAA 8 40
a-gu-u	AGA	SAA 8 57
a-gu-u	MUL.a-nu-AGA	SAA 8 68
a-gu-u	AGA	SAA 8 51
a-gu-u	AGA	SAA 8 51
a-ḫi-tum	BAR-tum	SAA 8 60
a-s[ak-ku]	Á.S[ÌG]	SAA 10 67
a-ṣi-šú	È-šú	SAA 8 73
ab$^{!}$-ba-gud-ḫa-a	ÁB.GUD.ḪI.A	SAA 8 49
ar-ḫu	ITI	SAA 8 41
ba-ar-tú	ḪI.GAR	SAA 8 45
ba-il	ba-ìl	SAA 8 64
bar-ti	ḪI.GAR	SAA 8 57

bu-u-li	MÁŠ.ANŠE	SAA 8 41
bu-u-li	bu-lim	SAA 8 49
^{d}šá-maš	20	SAA 8 49
^{d}šá-maš	20	SAA 8 53
di-ir	DIRI	SAA 8 57
e-nu-un ú-⸢za-al⸣-la	EN.NUN-UD.ZA[L.LA]	SAA 10 78
e-ra-a-ti	MÍ.PEŠ$_4$.MEŠ	SAA 8 41
e-ru-ub	TU-ub	SAA 8 45
e-zi-iz-ma	ḪUŠ-ma	SAA 8 40
er-pi	ŠÚ	SAA 8 43
eš-šá-ba$^{?}$	3.20	SAA 8 54
ga-az	MUL.ŠÁR.GAZ	SAA 8 52
ḫab-ba-a-tú$^{!}$	LÚ.SA.GAZ	SAA 8 49
ḫar-ra-na	KASKAL	SAA 8 49
ḫar-ra-ni-šú	KASKAL-šú	SAA 8 77
ḫu-u-li	KASKAL	SAA 10 70
[i]-bi-il	i-be-e[l]	SAA 8 60
i-da-ak	GAZ-ak	SAA 8 40
i-mit-ti	15	SAA 8 53
i-mit-ti-šú	ZAG-šú	SAA 8 57
i-mit-tú	ZAG	SAA 10 74
i-qe-lip-pu	DIRI-pu	SAA 8 65
i-ra-áš-ši	TUK-ši	SAA 8 40
i-šap-par-ka	KIN-ka	SAA 8 43
ib-b[a-áš-ši]	GÁ[L-ši]	SAA 8 45
ik-šu-ud	KUR-ud	SAA 8 48
ik-šu-ud	KUR-ud	SAA 8 49
il-me-šú	NIGIN-šú	SAA 8 66
im-šu-[uḫ]	im-šu[ḫ]	SAA 8 74
ip-pu-ḫa-am-ma	KUR-ma	SAA 8 69
ip-ru-[us]	TAR-[us]	SAA 8 44
is-niq	DIM$_4$	SAA 8 49
is-si-i[n$^{!}$]	1-en	SAA 10 51
iṣ-ru-ur-ma	SUR-ma	SAA 8 45
iṣ-ṣu-ri	MUŠEN.MEŠ	SAA 8 73
iš-pur-u-ka	KIN-ka	SAA 8 43
it-ta-na-áš-kan	GAR.GAR-nu	SAA 8 78
[it-ta-šú]	GISKIM.BI	SAA 10 74
it-ta-šú	GISKIM.BI	SAA 10 74
it-ti	GISKIM	SAA 8 63
[it]-tú	[GI]SKIM	SAA 8 63
it-tú	GISKIM	SAA 8 63
iṭ-ḫu-ma	TE-ma	SAA 8 50
ka-ak-ka-bu	MUL	SAA 8 45
ka-áš-du-ú	kaš-du-ú	SAA 8 70

ka-ka-bu	MUL	SAA 8 76
ka-[ka-bu]	MUL	SAA 8 54
ka-ku-bu	MUL	SAA 10 51
kab$^{!}$-tu-ti-šú	IDIM.MEŠ-šú	SAA 8 40
kaq-qa-ru	KI	SAA 8 70
ku-ru$^{!}$-ma-at-su	ŠUG-su	SAA 10 74
[ku]-u	[MUL].KU$_{6}$	SAA 8 73
la	NU	SAA 8 40
la	NU	SAA 8 43
la	NU	SAA 8 55
li-si	MUL.LI$_{9}$.SI$_{4}$	SAA 10 81
[l]i-šá-a-nu	EME	SAA 8 60
ma-at a-mur-re-e	KUR-MAR.TU.KI	SAA 8 41
ma-ḫi-ru	GÁN.BA	SAA 8 82
m[a$^{!}$-za-as-sa ke-e-né]	K[I$^{!}$.GUB-sà GI.NA]	SAA 8 39
ma-za-as-sa ke-e-né	KI.GUB.BA-sà GI.NA	SAA 8 39
mar-mar-i-šú	DUMU-DUMU.MEŠ-šú	SAA 10 70
me-ḫi-ir	me-ḫir	SAA 8 63
me-le-ṣa	A.ŠI.ŠI-ṣa	SAA 8 54
mu	MU	SAA 8 51
mu-ul ^{d}[x x x x x]	MUL.^{d}[IM.DUGUD]	SAA 8 64
mu-ul ka-a	MUL.KA$_{5}$.A	SAA 8 49
mu-ul ši-im-ma-a[ḫ]	MUL.SIM.MAḪ	SAA 8 77
mu-ul ú-ga	MUL.UG[A]	SAA 8 73
mu-ul ú-za	MUL.ÙZ	SAA 8 74
m[u-ul x x x]	M[UL.x x x]	SAA 8 45
nag-bi	IDIM	SAA 8 43
ni-ig-si-sa	NÍG.SI.SÁ	SAA 8 51
ni-pi-iḫ-šú	KUR-šú	SAA 8 49
ni-ši	UN.MEŠ	SAA 8 65
nu-kur-te	MÍ.KÚR	SAA 8 43
[pa-a]r$^{!}$-su	[par-s]u	SAA 10 71
pa-ar-ṣi	GARZA	SAA 10 70
pa-ni-šú	IGI-šú	SAA 8 69
pi-i	KA	SAA 8 65
qar-nu	SI	SAA 8 57
qu-ut-ri	qut-ri	SAA 10 79
ra-ab-bi ur-ḫi	4 ITI	SAA 10 68
re-e-mu	ARḪUŠ	SAA 8 74
sa-a-mu	SA$_{5}$	SAA 8 78
sa-li-i-mu	SILIM-ma	SAA 8 43
ṣa-al-mu	GI$_{6}$	SAA 8 40
ṣa-al-mu	GI$_{6}$	SAA 8 41
ṣa-al-mu	GI$_{6}$	SAA 8 51
ṣa-li-im-⸢ma⸣	MI-ma	SAA 10 67

ṣar-gaz	MUL.⌜ŠÁR.GAZ⌝	SAA 8 51
ṣi-is-su	UD.DA	SAA 8 76
šá pa-ni	ša IGI	SAA 8 76
šá-a-ri	TU$_{15}$	SAA 8 70
šá-a-ru	TU$_{15}$	SAA 8 78
šá-ar-ur	MUL.⌜ŠÁR.UR⌝	SAA 8 51
šá-at-ti	MU	SAA 10 79
šá-mu-u	AN-ú	SAA 8 44
šá-mu-u	AN-ú	SAA 8 57
šá-mu-u	AN-ú	SAA 8 64
šá-mu-u	AN-ú	SAA 8 64
šá-mu-u	AN-ú	SAA 8 65
šá-mu-u	AN-ú	SAA 8 70
šá-pi-ik	DUB-ik	SAA 8 65
šá-ra-a-ni	TU$_{15}$.MEŠ	SAA 8 55
ši-ka-ru	KAŠ.SAG	SAA 10 74
šu-bar-ti	KUR.SU.BIR'.KI	SAA 10 74
šu-du-un	MUL.ŠUDUN	SAA 8 73
šu-me-li	150	SAA 8 75
šu-me-li-šú	KAB-šú	SAA 8 62
tap-pal-la-as	IGI.BAR	SAA 8 70
tar-ba-ṣi	TÙR	SAA 8 71
[t]e-bu-ut	ZI-ut	SAA 8 39
ti-bu-ut	ZI-ut	SAA 8 77
[ti]-ib	ZI	SAA 8 70
[t]i-ib	ZI	SAA 8 72
ṭa-bu-u-ti	DÙG.GA.MEŠ	SAA 8 55
ú-ka-la	ú-kal	SAA 8 41
ú-la-a-[da]	Ù.TU.M[EŠ]	SAA 8 51
ú-me	UD	SAA 8 43
[[ú$^{?}$]]-ri	ŠEŠ.UNUG.KI	SAA 8 102
ú-tar-a-ma	GUR-ma	SAA 8 40
ú-[x x x]	x [x x x x]	SAA 8 76
UD bu-ub-bu-li	UD.NÁ.ÀM	SAA 8 44
[ul]-la-da	[Ù].TU.MEŠ	SAA 8 41
um-ma-[ni]	ERIM-ni	SAA 8 77
um-šú	um-šum	SAA 8 70
ur-ḫu	ITI	SAA 10 44
ur-pa-a-ti	IM.DIRI.MEŠ	SAA 8 65
ur-pa-a-ti	IM.DIRI.MEŠ	SAA 8 65
ur-pa-a-ti	IM.DIRI.[MEŠ]	SAA 8 41
ur-[pa-ti]	IM.[DIRI]	SAA 8 64
uz-du-ḫa-a	U$_{8}$.UDU.ḪI.A	SAA 8 49
uz-ni	PI.MEŠ	SAA 8 63
[x x] ÚR	[x ÚR]	SAA 8 70

[x x] x	KU$_{6}$.MEŠ	SAA 8 73
[x x]-šu-u	[x x] x-ú	SAA 8 40
zak-ka-⌜ri$^{!}$⌝	NITA.M[EŠ]	SAA 8 41
zi-mu-šú	MÚŠ.MEŠ-šu	SAA 10 79
zi-qi-it	zi-qit	SAA 8 66
zu-un-nu	A.AN	SAA 8 41

One could try to classify this material along some simple typology. A number of glosses fall in the category of sign-value explanation, what we could call 'phonetic complements', with the aim of clarifying the reading of a CVC-sign:

a-dir	[a-di]-ir	SAA 8 40
ba-il	ba-il	SAA 8 64
bu-lim	bu-u-li	SAA 8 49
i-be-e[l]	[i]-bi-il	SAA 8 60
im-šu[ḫ]	im-šu-[uḫ]	SAA 8 74
kaš-du-ú	ka-áš-du-ú	SAA 8 70
me-ḫir	me-ḫi-ir	SAA 8 63
[par-s]u	[pa-a]r$^{!}$-su	SAA 10 71
qut-ri	qu-ut-ri	SAA 10 79
ú-kal	ú-ka-la	SAA 8 41
um-šum	um-šú	SAA 8 70
zi-qit	zi-qi-it	SAA 8 66

Other types appear, which we could call 'exegesis' of signs:

15	i-mit-ti	SAA 8 53
150	šu-me-li	SAA 8 75
20	^{d}šá-maš	SAA 8 49
20	^{d}šá-maš	SAA 8 53
3.20	eš-šá-ba$^{?}$	SAA 8 54

If the first examples are relatively straightforward, the last one needs comment. The number 3.20 is used in SAA 8 54:7 as a logogram for *šarru* 'king': 3.20 *a-š[ar il-l]a-k[u li-is-su]* 'the king [will be victorious] wher[ever he] goes'. This expression is found in Group Voc. A (= CT 51 168 vii 1-27),[9] among learned and rare logograms for LUGAL, as 3 (*iš-še-bu*, var. *iš-eš-bu*) 30. The vocabulary may here be in error, with 3.30 instead of 3.20 of our text.

The main part of the glosses can be understood as relatively straightforward explanations of logograms:

---

9 *CAD* Š/2 77a; duplicates CT 18 29 i 1-31 and *RA* 16 166 i 1-31.

1-en	is-si-i[n!]	SAA 10 51
4 ITI	ra-ab-bi ur-ḫi	SAA 10 68
A.AN	zu-un-nu	SAA 8 41
A.ŠI.ŠI-ṣa	me-le-ṣa[10]	SAA 8 54
Á.S[!G]	a-s[ak-ku]	SAA 10 67
AGA	a-gu-u	SAA 8 57, 51 (twice)[11]
AN-ú	šá-mu-u	SAA 8 44, 57, 64 (twice), 65, 70
ARḪUŠ	re-e-mu	SAA 8 74
BAR-tum	a-ḫi-tum	SAA 8 60
DIM$_4$	is-niq	SAA 8 49
DIRI-pu	i-qe-lip-pu	SAA 8 65
DUB-ik	šá-pi-ik	SAA 8 65
DÙG.GA.MEŠ	ṭa-bu-u-ti	SAA 8 55
DUMU-DUMU.MEŠ-šú	mar-mar-i-šú	SAA 10 70
È-šú	a-ṣi-šú	SAA 8 73
EME	[l]i-šá-a-nu	SAA 8 60
ERIM-ni	um-ma-[ni]	SAA 8 77
GÁ[L-ši]	ib-b[a-áš-ši]	SAA 8 45
GÁN.BA	ma-ḫi-ru	SAA 8 82
GAR.GAR-nu	it-ta-na-áš-kan	SAA 8 78
GARZA	pa-ar-ṣi	SAA 10 70
GAZ-ak	i-da-ak	SAA 8 40
GI$_6$	ṣa-al-mu	SAA 8 40, 41, 51
GI$_6$-ma	ṣa-li-im-⌈ma⌉	SAA 10 67
GISKIM	it-ti	SAA 8 63
	it-tú	SAA 8 63 (twice)
GISKIM.BI	it-ta-šú	SAA 10 74 (twice)
GUR-ma	ú-tar-a-ma	SAA 8 40
ḪI.GAR	ba-ar-tú	SAA 8 45
	bar-ti	SAA 8 57
ḪUŠ-ma	e-zi-iz-ma	SAA 8 40
IDIM	nag-bi	SAA 8 43
IDIM.MEŠ-šú	kab!-tu-ti-šú	SAA 8 40
IGI.BAR	tap-pal-la-as	SAA 8 70
IGI-šú	pa-ni-šú	SAA 8 69
IM.[DIRI]	ur-[pa-ti]	SAA 8 64
IM.DIRI.MEŠ	ur-pa-a-ti	SAA 8 41, 65 (twice)
ITI	ar-ḫu	SAA 8 41
	ur-ḫu	SAA 10 44
KA	pi-i	SAA 8 65

10 This seems to be the only occurrence of this equation.

11 See also MUL.*a-nu*-AGA (a-*gu-u*) below.

KAB-šú	šu-me-li-šú	SAA 8 62
KASKAL	ḫar-ra-na	SAA 8 49
	ḫu-u-li	SAA 10 70
KASKAL-šú	ḫar-ra-ni-šú	SAA 8 77
KAŠ.SAG	ši-ka-ru	SAA 10 74
KI	kaq-qa-ru	SAA 8 70
KI.GUB.BA-sà GI.NA	ma-za-as-sa ke-e-né	SAA 8 39
K[I!.GUB-sà GI.NA]	m[a!-za-as-sa ke-e-né]	SAA 8 39
KIN-ka	i-šap-par-ka	SAA 8 43
KIN-ka	iš-pur-u-ka	SAA 8 43
KU$_6$.MEŠ	[x x] x	SAA 8 73
KUR.SU.BIR$_4$.KI	šu-bar-ti	SAA 10 74
KUR-ma	ip-pu-ḫa-am-ma	SAA 8 69
KUR-MAR.TU.KI	ma-at a-mur-re-e	SAA 8 41
KUR-šú	ni-pi-iḫ-šú	SAA 8 49
KUR-ud	ik-šu-ud	SAA 8 48, 49
LÚ.SA.GAZ	ḫab-ba-a-tú!	SAA 8 49
MÁŠ.ANŠE	bu-u-li	SAA 8 41
MÍ.KÚR	nu-kur-te	SAA 8 43
MÍ.PEŠ$_4$.MEŠ	e-ra-a-ti	SAA 8 41
MU	šá-at-ti	SAA 10 79
MUL	ka-ak-ka-bu	SAA 8 45
	ka-ka-bu	SAA 8 54, 76
	ka-ku-bu	SAA 10 51
MUL.a-nu-AGA	a-gu-u[12]	SAA 8 68
MÚŠ.MEŠ-šu	zi-mu-šú	SAA 10 79
MUŠEN.MEŠ	iṣ-ṣu-ri	SAA 8 73
NIGIN-šú	il-me-šú	SAA 8 66
NITA.M[EŠ]	zak-ka-⸢ri!⸣	SAA 8 41
NU	la	SAA 8 40, 43, 55
PI.MEŠ	uz-ni	SAA 8 63
SAÌ	sa-a-mu	SAA 8 78
SI	qar-nu	SAA 8 57
SILIM-ma	sa-li-i-mu	SAA 8 43
SUR-ma	iṣ-ru-ur-ma	SAA 8 45
ša IGI	šá pa-ni	SAA 8 76
ŠEŠ.UNUG.KI	[[ú?]]-ri	SAA 8 102
ŠÚ	er-pi	SAA 8 43
ŠUG-su	ku-ru!-ma-at-su	SAA 10 74
TAR-[us]	ip-ru-[us]	SAA 8 44
TE-ma	iṭ-ḫu-ma	SAA 8 50
TU-ub	e-ru-ub	SAA 8 45

12 The gloss clearly refers only to the last word, see above sub AGA.

TU_{15}	šá-a-ri	SAA 8 70
	šá-a-ru	SAA 8 78
TU_{15}.MEŠ	šá-ra-a-ni	SAA 8 55
TUK-ši	i-ra-áš-ši	SAA 8 40
TÙR	tar-ba-ṣi	SAA 8 71
Ù.TU.M[EŠ]	ú-la-a-[da]	SAA 8 51
	[ul]-la-da	SAA 8 41
UD	ú-me	SAA 8 43
UD.DA	ṣi-is-su	SAA 8 76
UD[!].DUG_4.GA.MEŠ	a-da-an-na-a-te	SAA 10 71
UD.NÁ.ÀM	UD bu-ub-bu-li	SAA 8 44
UN.MEŠ	ni-ši	SAA 8 65
ZAG	i-mit-tú	SAA 10 74
ZAG-šú	i-mit-ti-šú	SAA 8 57
ZI	[ti]-ib	SAA 8 70, 72
ZI-ut	[t]e-bu-ut	SAA 8 39
	ti-bu-ut	SAA 8 77

Most of these glosses are completely normal uses of simple and less simple logograms. Was it, for instance, really necessary to explain to the king that KUR-*ud* was to be read *ikšud*, when we find it in almost every line of the Assyrian annals? Of course, one could always argue here that it was glossed to avoid confusion with KUR = *napāḫu* or *nipḫu* 'to rise (for a star)', 'rising'. Other examples abound, such as MU = *šá-at-ti*, SI = *qar-nu*, AN = *šá-mu-u*, ITI = *ar-ḫu*, *ur-ḫu*, etc. and maybe above all NU = *la*. Once again, it could be said that AN, MU or NU all have other possible readings, but these are quite well attested and would not have posed a problem to anyone moderately acquainted with cuneiform writing.

The last category represents direct readings of logograms, where the sign is not translated into Akkadian, but simply phonetically explained:

ÁB.GUD.ḪI.A	ab[!]-ba-gud-ḫa-a	SAA 8 49
DIRI	di-ir	SAA 8 57
EN.NUN-UD.ZA[L.LA]	e-nu-un ú-⸢za-al⸣-la	SAA 10 78
MU	mu	SAA 8 51
MUL.^{d}[IM.DUGUD]	mu-ul ^{d}[x x x x x]	SAA 8 64
MUL.KA_5.A	mu-ul ka-a	SAA 8 49
[MUL].KU_6	[ku]-u	SAA 8 73
MUL.LI_9.SI_4	li-si	SAA 10 81
MUL.SIM.MAḪ	mu-ul ši-im-ma-a[ḫ]	SAA 8 77
MUL.ŠÁR.GAZ	ga-az	SAA 8 52
MUL.⸢ŠÁR.GAZ⸣	ṣar-gaz	SAA 8 51
MUL.⸢ŠÁR.UR⸣	šá-ar-ur	SAA 8 51

MUL.ŠUDUN	šu-du-un	SAA 8 73
MUL.UG[A]	mu-ul ú-ga	SAA 8 73
MUL.ÙZ	mu-ul ú-za	SAA 8 74
M[UL.x x x]	m[u-ul x x x]	SAA 8 45
NÍG.SI.SÁ	ni-ig-si-sa	SAA 8 51
U_8.UDU.ḪI.A	uz-du-ḫa-a	SAA 8 49

Most of them are star names and it seems quite understandable that in astrologer's parlance these would have been read and pronounced in Sumerian. It is to be noted that most of the time, MUL is included in the name, but some glosses omit this sign in their reading. The same cannot be said of ÁB.GUD.ḪI.A and U_8.UDU.ḪI.A (appearing together in the same text, SAA 8 49), or NÍG.SI.SÁ, which have 'normal' equivalents in Akkadian.

The use of writing in Ancient Mesopotamia is still in need of more study. The habit of 'glossing texts' that especially Nabû-aḫḫē-erība seems to exhibit may or may not be relevant. We could always explain it as an idiosyncracy or a particular turn of mind of this scholar. Concerning Balasî one could even say that it comes from the fact that he used to be the crown prince's mentor and that his pedagogic manners continue to show in his normal correspondence with the king. On the other hand, if letters were routinely read aloud to the monarch by secretaries, why include such information? The reports and letters which contain glosses do not seem to be special in any way, so there is no reason to believe that they were more 'private' than others, which could then explain that the king would have read them himself, without the help of his secretaries. This is sometimes the case, if we could judge by the fact that Issār-šumu-ēreš, chief scribe and king's scholar, could write: "Let them bring in that polyptych of *Enūma Anu Enlil* which we wrote, (and) let the king, my lord, have a look".[13] If we have to take this at face value, the king would have been able to read such difficult material as *Enūma Anu Enlil*. The same could again be said about the edition of the royal annals, which were, in my opinion, certainly written by members of the *inner circle*, but also approved by the king himself.[14]

---

13 SAA 8 19: rev. 1-3: GIŠ.LI.U_5.UM *am-mì-u*, *ša* UD-AN-[d]EN.LÍL *ša ni-iš-ṭur-u-ni*, *lu-še-ri-bu-u-ni* LUGAL *be-li le-mur*. In the same report, one could wonder what is meant by the "Akkadian tablet of the king" (rev. 4-5) GIŠ.*le-ʾu ak-ka-du-u*, *ša* LUGAL.

14 See Ph. Talon, "De mes frères aînés, j'étais le cadet... Une réinterprétation de l'apologie d'Assarhaddon", in *Cinquante-deux réflexions sur le Proche-Orient ancien*, Mél. De Meyer, Mesopotamian History and Environment, Occasional Publication, vol. II, Leuven 1995, pp. 339-353, esp. p. 340 and note 11; id. 'Neo-Assyrian Annals and Literacy' (forthcoming).

É = *BĪTUM* OR = *ʾÀ*? ABOUT EA IN EARLY DYNASTIC SOURCES

MARIA VITTORIA TONIETTI

University of Florence

According to onomastic documentation,[1] the Early Dynastic period seems marked by the presence of two main gods, Il(um) and Aštar; the other gods, which are well attested beginning with the onomastics of the Sargonic period, appear not to be documented at all or to be completely marginal.[2] In particular, the complete absence from Early Dynastic documentation has been remarked upon of two very important gods such as Ea e Adad.[3] The Sargonic period seems, therefore, to introduce a radical change with respect to the preceding one: from its very beginnings, in fact, the onomastics attest a massive presence of almost all the principle divinities which characterise the Mesopotamian Semitic pantheon of later Babylonian sources.[4] Turning our attention back to the absence of the two above-mentioned divinities, at least as far as Ea is concerned, the comparison with other contemporary sources suggests the possibility that such an absence may, in reality, be only apparent; due rather, that is, to the use of particular spellings.

---

1 By far the most important source for Pre-Sargonic Old Akkadian. See in particular the brilliant studies by A. Westenholz, "Personal Names in Ebla and in Pre-Sargonic Babylonia", in A. Archi (ed.), *Eblaite Personal Names and Semitic Name-Giving, ARES* 1, Roma 1988, pp. 99-117, partic. pp. 103-107; and *id.*, "The Old Akkadian Period: History and Culture" in Walther Sallaberger, Aage Westenholz, *Mesopotamien. Akkade-Zeit und Ur III-Zeit. Annäherung* 3, *OBO* 160/3, 1999, partic. pp.78 ff.

2 "We have plenty of Early Dynastic Akkadian theophoric personal names, and the religion they seem to reveal is basically ditheistic: there is one god and one goddess, named Il or Ilum, and Ashtar." Westenholz *OBO* 160/3, p. 78. For the interesting problem of the interpretation of *ʾil(um)* in Old Akkadian documentation - whether it is a divine name or a generic term for god, or even a personal god - see R. Di Vito, *Il in the Personal Names of the Third Millennium B.C. Studies in Third Millennium Sumerian and Akkadian Onomastics. The Designation and Conception of the Personal God,* Roma 1993; and A. Archi, "*Il* in the Personal Names", *OLZ* 91/2 (1996), pp. 134-151.

3 See Westenholz, *ARES* 1, p. 103; "Noteworthy is the complete absence of Adad and Ea, so popular from the time of Manishtusu onwards;" and *OBO* 160/3, p. 79, and n. 373.

4 Such as Sin, Šamaš, Ea, Adad, Dagan.

The mention of the god Adad/Hadda, to whom Pelio Fronzaroli devoted some important articles, provides me the opportunity to dedicate the present article to him, whose precious teaching and advice have been of enormous value to me in all these years.

As is known, in the texts of Abū Ṣalābīḫ there are some anthroponyms which as a second element present only the sign É.[5] Completely absent from the Names and Professions List these names appear in some colophons:

Im-lik-É	*IAS*[6] 126; and, fragmentary, 20 and 266;
I-ti-É	*IAS* 122;
PUZUR$_4$-É	*IAS* 487;

and, perhaps, in one case of difficult interpretation, in an administrative text:

Im-rí-iš-É *IAS* 494 II 8;[7]

The interpretation and even the reading of this latter name,[8] appear very problematic. The examination of photographic evidence seems to confirm the reading proposed by Krebernik.[9] Read in this way, however, the first part of the name does not seem to have a parallel in the onomastics of the III millennium, and remains of difficult interpretation. The following investigations will, then, concentrate on the three preceding names.

---

5 Names with É seem lacking in the remainder of Pre-Sargonic Babylonian documentation, with the sole possible exception of a PN from Fāra: *i*-[H]-I$^?$-É (*TSŠ* 453a II'3'), but its reading and interpretation are uncertain. See M. Krebernik, "Die Texte aus Fāra und Tell Abū Ṣalābīḫ", in J. Bauer, R. Englund, M. Krebernik, *Mesopotamien, Späturuk-Zeit und Frühdynastische Zeit, Annäherung 1, OBO* 160/1, Freiburg 1998, p. 262 and n. 230.

6 R. Biggs, *Inscriptions from Tell Abū Ṣalābīḫ, OIP* 99, Chicago 1974.

7 The text (with the field number AbS-T 14) is published by Biggs, "The Abū Ṣalābīḫ Tablets. A Preliminary Survey", *JCS* 20 (1966), pp. 73-88, partic. pp. 86-88. On p. 87 at l. 15 he reads: IM(!) SAḪAR É.DUB. For the reading given here see Krebernik, *OBO* 160/1, p. 267.

8 Absent in the onomastic lists compiled for the Early Dynastic period by Biggs (R.D. Biggs, "The Semitic Personal Names from Abu Salabikh and the Personal Names from Ebla", in *ARES* 1 pp. 89-98, partic. pp. 92-96) and Westenholz (*ARES* 1, pp. 110-117), and in Di Vito, cit.

9 Even if the sign *im* seems to have one vertical wedge too many, and in the right part of the case the superimposing of the two signs doesn't allow a clear reading: the lower sign is certainly É, the upper one seems to be URU, but note what Biggs, in *JCS* 20, p. 87, n. 107, writes: "É is written over the lower part of DUB and partially obliterates it". The text needs to be collated.

1. É= ʾÀ. *The evidence from Ebla.*

In *ARES* 1 both Westenholz and Biggs interpret the sign É in the cited names as a logogram for *bītum*.[10] A suggestion for a different interpretation comes from the Ebla texts. In these texts, in fact, some anthroponyms appear which have as a theophoric element the spelling ᵈEn-ki. The Semitic reading hidden by this Sumerian spelling clearly occurs in a variant of the name *I-ti-*ᵈEn-ki: *I-ti-*ᵈ*ʾÀ*(É),[11] which is a prosopographically certain variant, given that the two names appear in two parallel lists of nar musicians.[12] This reading is further supported by the Semitic rendering of the AN section of the bilingual word list, *VE* 803, source D: ᵈEn-ki = *ʾÀ-u*₉.[13] In accordance with the rules of Ebla syllabary,[14] *ʾÀ-u*₉ has been interpreted as /ḥayy-um/,[15] from West Semitic **ḥyy*; the spelling *ʾÀ* of the administrative text could be a

---

10 Westenholz, *ARES* 1, p. 111: *im-lik-*É = *yimlik-bītum, i-ti-*É = *yiddi(n)-bītum*, PU₃.ŠA-É = *puzra-bī tim* (?), and Biggs, *ibid.* p. 96: *I-ti-*É(*bītum*), "the temple has given"; *Puzur₄*-É(*bītum*) "the temple is protection".

11 Attested only once, in *ARET* III 498 rev. II 3. The writing *i-ti-*ᵈen-ki, instead, occurs more frequently: *ARET* I 6 rev. II 12; I 8 rev. VI 16; III 458 rev. V 9; III 468 obv. III 2; TM.75.G.1748 rev. VII 2 (my thanks to Vanna Biga for kindly letting me know of this unpublished attestation). ᵈen-ki is in fact the normal spelling for "Ea" in the Ebla texts (as in those from Early Dynastic Mari and Tell Beydar), even if this spelling does not refer exclusively to this god (see J. Pasquali, "Sul 'falco' [buru₄-mušen] di *Ra-sa-ab* ᵈenᵏⁱ a Ebla" *NABU* 2002/33).

12 In administrative texts. Cf. M.V. Tonietti, "La figura del nar nei testi di Ebla. Ipotesi per una cronologia delle liste di nomi presenti nei testi economici", in *MisEb* 1 (1988), pp. 93-94. This writing, then, is not to emend to *I-ti-*ᵈ*ʾÀ-da,* as proposed by Lambert, *BiOr* 56 3/4 (1999), p. 359. The interpretation of UR-É (*ARET* IV 10 obv. I 9; TM.75.G.1233 rev. IX 10), the other personal name containing as a second element the sign É attested at Ebla (but borne by a person from Mari), seems more doubtful. In this case it is difficult to exclude with certainty that it could be a Sumerian PN, especially because in the texts the PN UR-É-GAL (*ARET* VII 16 rev. IV 1; TM.75.G.1559 obv. III 9), equally borne by a person from Mari, also occurs. Cf. also Krebernik, *Die Personennamen der Ebla-Texte*, (=*PET*), Berlin 1988, p. 298. On PN UR-É see below, *2.2.*

13 See G. Conti, *Il sillabario della quarta fonte della lista lessicale bilingue eblaita, MisEb* 3, Firenze 1990, p. 193.

14 Where *ʾà* stands for /h/ and /ḥ/, excluding any possibility of first radical /ʾ/ or /ʿ/ etymologies (see for instance, Durand, in P. Mander, J.-M. Durand, *Mytología y religión del Oriente Antiguo II/1 Semitas Occidentales* [*Ebla, Mari*], Del Olmo Lete [ed.], Barcelona 1995, p. 190); *u*₉ stands for /h/, /ḥ/, /y/; and the diphthong /ay/ is normally expressed by a sign *(C)a*: *ba-du* /bayt-um/, *ma-sa-lu-um* /mayšar-um/, *mar-a-tum* /marʿayt-um/, *ba-la-um,* /barāy-um/, see P. Fronzaroli, "Materiali per il lessico eblaita, 1, *Seb* 7 (1984), p. 156; and G. Conti, *MisEb* 3, p. 35.

15 Cf. Krebernik, "Zu Syllabar und Orthographie der lexikalischen Texte aus Ebla. Teil 2 (Glossar)", *ZA* 73 (1983), p. 31; G. Conti, *MisEb* 3, p. 193; B. Kienast, "ᵈ*É-a* und der aramäische '*status emphaticus*'", *Ebla 1975-1985*, Napoli 1987, pp. 37-47. Cf. also I.J. Gelb, *Computer-Aided Analysis of Amorite*, Chicago 1980, p. 19; E. Arcari, *Or* 53 (1984), p. 443; Gordon, *Eblaitica* 1 (1987), p. 20.

defective spelling for /ḫayya/ or a spelling for the form /ḫay(y)/.[16] As other Semitic divine names present in the same section,[17] this theonym appears in a form with a nominative ending, and is not preceded by the divine determinative. The presence of the determinative in the spelling occurring in the administrative text, however, agrees perfectly with the normal praxis of Eblaitic administrative and chancery texts, where it is used systematically; very differently to what we find in Old Akkadian documentation, where, with some syllabically spelled divine names (as *É-a*, *Aš/Eš₄-dar*, *Ma-ma*) the determinative is normally omitted.[18] Nothing, therefore, from a formal point of view, seems to hinder a comparison between the names *I-ti*-É of Abū Ṣalābīḫ and *I-ti*-ᵈ*ʾÀ* of Ebla, the only difference between the two names being the presence or absence of the divine determinative, in accordance with the respective local practices. On the basis of this it is possible to hypothesise that as well as at Abū Ṣalābīḫ, as at Ebla, in *I-ti*-É and, by analogy, in *Im-lik*-É, PUZUR₄-É, and perhaps, *Im-rí-iš*-É, the sign É should be interpreted as the syllabogram *ʾà*, rather than as the logographic spelling of *bītum*, and that also in these cases it represents a

---

16 Absolute state forms are not rare in divine names, cf., *e.g.*, Adad and Šamaš.
Beside É, other particular spellings of Ea are attested in late III millennium Babylonia onomasticon, which have been considered as not supporting the above mentioned etymological interpretation (see Lambert, *BiOr* 56 3/4 [1999], p. 359, and *BaE* p. 399). These are syllabic spellings which employ the sign È rather than É: *Pù-zur₈-è-a, Šu-è-a, I-ti-è-a, Na-ra-am-è-a, È-a-ra-bi, È-a-sar*; or forms of *sandhi* writing, which seem to reflect the phonetic *continuum* of the spoken language: *I-ti-ne-a, Na-ra-me-a* (mostly from the late Sargonic or the beginning of Ur III, but some of them dating from the preceding period). To deal with this topic would go beyond the limits of this article, but see, by the present writer, the note on the name of Ea to be published in *NABU*. In her opinion, rather than hinder the aforementioned interpretation, these spellings simply testify to the process of weakening of laryngeals and fricative pharyngeals and (voiced) velar occurring toward the end of the III millennium in Babylonian Akkadian. Even if, as a rule, spelling conventions generally tend toward the conservation of etymological spellings, the distinct use of É or of È, strictly respected for as long as it actually corresponded to a contrast between different phonemes, may have ceased to be normative when and where (and not, it is, at the same time in all places) these phonemes coalesced into one (and caused in some cases the vowel change /a/ > /e/) (cf. *MAD* 2, p. 119). Compare the two Ur III spellings: *É-lu-núm* (*RA* 19, p. 192 N. 4: 8) and *È-lu-núm* (*YOS* 4 240).

17 See *VE* 799: ᵈEN.ZI / ᵈEN.ZU = *zu-i-nu*; *VE* 802: ᵈen-líl = *i-li-lu* (the latter spelling occurs also in Ebla literary texts: cf. D.O. Edzard, *ARET* V, p. 19, and A. Catagnoti, "Integrazione allo scongiuro *ARET* 5.2", *VO* 7 [1988], pp. 243-244). For the AN section of the bilingual word list, see W. Lambert, "The section AN", in L. Cagni (ed.), *Il Bilinguismo ad Ebla,* (=*BaE)*, Napoli 1984, pp. 393-401.

18 Cf. Gelb, *Old Akkadian Writing and Grammar, MAD* 2², Chicago 1961, p. 23.

spelling of the name of Ea: *I-ti-ʾÀ* /yiddin-ḫayy(a)/, *Im-lik-ʾÀ* /yimlik-ḫayy(a)/, PUZUR$_4$-*ʾÀ* /puzur-ḫayy(a)/, and *Im-rí-iš-ʾÀ* /yimriš-ḫayy(a)/.[19]

Given, however, the frequency of the onomastic type *i-ti*-DN, occurring in later periods with many different theophors,[20] even the perfect formal correspondence of the name of Abū Ṣalābīḫ with that of Ebla could be considered insufficient proof of an identical reading and interpretation. The fragmentary and rather casual nature of the documentation at our disposal does not allow categorical and definitive answers on this subject; but, in order to support this proposed hypothesis, other elements may be given, derived from a larger survey of the onomastic types occurring with É in Old Akkadian documentation, and, in particular, of the other theophors with which these types are attested. In fact, it is well known that, next to rather generic onomastic types, applicable more or less to any divinity, others exist which, because of the specificity of their semantic content, apply only to certain divinities and not to others, depending on their particular characteristics.[21]

2. É = bītum or = ʾÀ in Old Akkadian onomasticon.

2.1. Types /yiddin-DN/, /yimlik-DN/, /puzr(a)-DN/

Interesting data arises from examination of the theophors used in the III millennium with the same onomastic types as the three names mentioned above.

2.1.1. As far as the Abū Ṣalābīḫ documentation is concerned, /yimlik-DN/ and /puzr(a)-DN/ are uniquely attested with the theophors É and Il(um); only /yiddi(n)-DN/ is used with other divine names (^{d}ÍD, ^{d}*Ša-^{ga}gan*, UD.AN.GAM+GAM).[22] As we

---

19 It is worth stating the fact that in Ebla administrative texts a PN PUZUR$_4$-^{d}en-ki /puzur-ḫayy(a)/, borne by a Mari merchant, is also attested (TM.75.G.2372 III' [A. Archi, *MARI* 4, p. 77]). Cf. *PET* p. 275.

In *OBO* 160/1, p. 266 n. 324 (a footnote to PN *i-ti*-É, but referring to all names with É in Abū Ṣalābīḫ and Fāra texts), also Krebernik suggests: "Vielleicht liegt jedoch eine defektiv-syllabische Schreibung für /*ḫayy(a)*/ (Ea) vor". Similarly he proposes reading $^{d⌜}$*ʾÀ*$^{⌝}$, at l. 318 (line numbering by A. Alberti, "A Reconstruction of the Abū Ṣalābīḫ God-List", *SEL* 2 [1985], pp. 3-23) / l. 341 (line numbering by P. Mander (*Il Pantheon di Abū Ṣalābīḫ. Contributo allo studio del pantheon sumerico arcaico,* Napoli 1986, pp. 24-32) of the Abū Ṣalābīḫ God-List. Due to the context where this line is found, the aforementioned reading seems not easy to accept.

20 See, for instance, I.J. Gelb, *Glossary of Old Akkadian*, *MAD* 3, Chicago 1957, pp. 198-199.

21 A fact which can be clearly seen in the transition from Pre-Sargonic to Sargonic, when the various onomastic types, all more or less previously used almost solely with Il(um), are then distributed among the different divinities.

22 /yiddi(n)-nah(a)ru/, /yiddi(n)-Šakkan/, /yiddi(n)- .../; for an interpretation of this latter PN see Biggs, *ARES* 1, p. 94 n. 27. For ^{d}*Ša-^{ga}gan* being a spelling of Šakkan (and not Šamagan), see J.J. Roberts,

have seen, none of the names with É occur in the Names and Professions List: types /yiddi(n)-DN/ and /yimlik-DN/ appear in the list but with Il(um),[23] while type /puzr(a)-DN/ is completely missing.[24] This absence, however, is not limited to É, but also extends to the other, few, theophors occurring in the onomasticon of the colophons and of the administrative texts: Il(um) and, in only one name, Aštar are, in fact, the only certain Semitic theophoric elements attested in the NPL.[25] The absence from the NPL of other theophors could be due to a greater antiquity of the list compared to other texts.[26]

2.1.2. Particularly significant is the fact that all three onomastic types in question are usually employed with Ea in later Old Akkadian onomastics.[27] Furthermore, while /yiddi(n)-DN/ is attested with É also in this later phase,[28] the spellings *Im-lik*-É and PUZUR$_4$(-RA)-É never seem to occur outside of Abū Ṣalābīḫ.

Other significant data emerges from the examination of the occurrences of type /yimlik-DN/. In fact, if the types /puzr(a)-DN/ and /yiddi(n)-DN/ are widely used and they are found to be applied to a large number of theophors, the situation for

---

The Earliest Semitic Pantheon, (=*ESP*), Baltimore 1972, p. 50; Biggs, *ARES* 1, p. 97 n. 45; and recently Krebernik, *OBO* 160/1, p. 266 n. 326.

23 *I-t*[*i*]*-i-lum* (Ebla *I-ti-lum*) /yiddin-ʾilum/, NPL 118 (124); *Im-lik-il* (Ebla *Im$_4$-lik-il*) /yimlik-ʾil/, NPL 231 (244) (line numbering by Biggs, *OIP* 99, pp. 62-67, and, between brackets, by Archi, "La 'lista di nomi e professioni' ad Ebla", *SEb* 4 [1981], pp. 177-204). In Abū Ṣalābīḫ also the type /ND-mālik/ occurs, see Biggs, *Or* 36 (1967), p. 62.

24 Lacking in the NPL, the name PUZUR$_4$-*il* too occurs in the Abū Ṣalābīḫ texts: in the colophons (*IAS* 13; 142; 268), and in an administrative text (*IAS* 503 VII 6).

25 Besides, the element *me-ru* also occurs; for this, see recently M. Bonechi, "Lexique et idéologie royale à l'époque proto-syrienne", *MARI* 8 (1997), pp. 477-535, partic. pp. 494-496.

26 See below, *3*.

27 1- Sarg: *I-ti-É-a* (*MAD* 5 74: 8; *MDP* 14 50 obv. 5; *OIP* 104 40 C IV 7, IX 22, XI 9 [I.J. Gelb, P. Steinkeller, R.M. Whiting, *Earliest Land Tenure Systems in the Near East: Ancient Kudurrus, Chicago* 1991]); Ur III: *I-ti-É-a* (Ch. Jean, *RA* 19 p. 33, XVI rev. 11; *UET* 3 46: 13, 1581 r. II, 1681: 3; *UET* 9 140 obv. 17, 150 obv. 3, 1092 obv. II 9, 1094 obv. II 2; Owen *NATN* 918: seal); *I-din-É-a* (*RA* 19 p. 33, XVII obv. 7; *BIN* 3 624:6; Owen *NATN* 918 rev. 1); *I-ti-ne-a* (Oppenh. *CCTE* p.188).
2- Ur III: *Im-lik-É-a* (W. Hallo, *JCS* 14, p. 103 nr. 13 obv. 4; U 1736; *CT* 32 Pl. 12 IV 8, 103436).
3- Sarg: PUZUR$_4$-*É-a* (*MAD* 1 326 I 10; *OIP* 104 40 C V 8, XVI 11; *AIA* 14 obv. I 16 [Foster *ASJ* 4 10-13]; PUZUR$_4$-*È-a* (Nik II 21 [*USP* p.30]; Donbaz *STT* 123: 3; *TuM* 5 13: 5'); Ur III (*UET* 3 246: 5, 954: 7, 1521: 8; *UET* 9 452 left edge, 900 obv. 5).

28 *I-ti*-É, *CT* 1, 1a obv. 4, Sarg (according to Westenholz, *OBO* 160/3, p.79, this text, supposed to come from Kiš, is in fact from Sippar). Instead, in F. 1158 rev. I 2' (Loretz, *AOAT* 3/1 Pl. XXXVI) from Tell Brak (C.J. Gadd, *Iraq* 7 [1940], pp. 42-43, and I.L. Finkel, *Iraq* 47 [1985] p. 199, b2), according to the photograph, the restoration *I-ti-é-*[*a*$^?$] seems possible, even if not certain.

/yimlik-DN/ is completely different. This latter type, which is quite rare in the Old Akkadian onomastics,[29] appears exclusively with the theophors Il(um) and Ea; and, even more important, while it continues to be used with these DN even after the III millennium, it does not seem to be attested at all with *bītum*, even in later periods. The only theophors used with *Imlik-* seem to be: Il(um), Ea, É (uniquely at Abū Ṣalābīḫ), and Sin (only since the Old Babylonian period).[30] /yimlik-DN/ proves, then, to be an onomastic type strongly characterised and deliberately exclusive of very few divinities, probably because of its specific semantic content; on the basis of the examined documentation, it seems possible to note a particular specificity of this type with Ea, which covers the entire period during which it is attested. Its supposed use with *bītum* at Abū Ṣalābīḫ, therefore, appears completely isolated and in contrast to the remainder of the documentation.

All the three above examined onomastic types, then, show an evident continuity of use, in one case almost exclusive, with Ea, and a complete absence of post Old Akkadian usage either with É or with *bītum*. The other onomastic types in which É recurs shall now be examined, in order to verify if it is otherwise possible to assert with certainty a theophoric use of É=*bītum* in Pre-Sargonic and Sargonic onomastics.

2.2. Other onomastic types with É

In MAD 3,[31] Gelb writes: "apparently deified É in Sargonic and Ur III PN's" quoting, in support of this statement, some Old Babylonian anthroponyms.[32] The use

---

29 And, actually, in that of the following periods too.

30 This onomastic type is attested since the Fāra period: *Im-li[k?-X]* (*OIP* 104 16b B II 3', Kiš Stone); NPL 231 (244): *Im-lik-Il*; Abū Ṣalābīḫ: *Im-lik-*É; Sarg and Ur III see n. 27; OB: *Im-lik-É-a* (*CT* 8 Pl. 34b:23; *MDP* 28 508:2; *UET* 5 315:10; *VS* 7 154:14; *YOS* 5 127:17; *YOS* 14 156:22); *Im-lik-*^{d}*Sin* (*YOS* 14 93:9; *CT* 8 35 c:22, etc.); cf. *Im-ta-li-ik-*^{d}*Sin* (Figulla *CBT* 56:12865).
Cf. J.J. Stamm, *Die Akkadische Namengebung*, (=*ANG*), Leipzig 1939, p. 145 (only Imlik-Ea and Imlik-Sin); *MAD* 3 p. 176 (Ea is the only theophor cited here with verb *malākum*); Di Vito, cit. 17.8 (only Il in the Fāra Period and Ea in Ur III).
With the same root, the type ND-*malik*, occurs, as we have already seen in the Abū Ṣalābīḫ texts; with theophors other than Il(um) only since Ur III (cf. Di Vito, p. 394): *É-a-malik CT* 22 12 IV; *I-lí-ma-al-ki* Fish, *CST* p. 12; *É-a-ma-lik*, *ARM* XIX, 376 rev. 2; *Il-su-ma-lik UET* 2 Pl. XXXVI 308. Cf. *MAD* 3 p. 176 f. This type is much more common than the preceding one and since OB period occurs with many different DNs, cf. *CAD* M, p. 164, *s.v. māliku* d).

31 *MAD* 3, p. 93, *s.v. bītum*.

32 *Bi-tum-mu-ba-lí-iṭ*, É*-mu-ba-lí-iṭ*, É*-ga-mil*, É*-ra-bi*, É*-še-mi*.

of personal names with *bītum* is well attested in the Old Babylonian onomastics.[33] However, as Stamm points out, these names seem to belong only to the category of what he calls the "Attributnamen".[34] Moreover, the comparison with Old Babylonian syllabic and logographic variants does not seem binding as proof of a reading *bītum* for É in all of the Old Akkadian anthroponyms listed by Gelb: *Ba-luḫ*-É, DINGIR-É, ^{d}EN.ZU-É, *Eš*$_4$*-dar*-É, *I-ti*-É,[35] Ur-É, ^{d}UTU-É, LUGAL-É, *Ni-se*$_{11}$-^{d}É. In fact, the only anthroponym for which a diachronic continuity is documented, which could support such a reading, is *Ba-luḫ*-É (var. *Ba-lu-úḫ*-É), which Gelb compares with OB *Pa-luḫ-bi-tum*.[36] Examining the names belonging to this onomastic type occurring in Old Akkadian, however, we cannot help but notice that the only theophors attested besides É are Il(um)(DINGIR) and Ea;[37] and, moreover, that the occurrences have the following chronological distribution: Il(um) and É in Sargonic, and Il(um) and Ea in Ur III.

The name UR-É, widely attested in the Sumerian Early Dynastic documentation, also appears in Akkadian onomasticon, already in Pre-Sargonic and again in Sargonic period.[38] The type UR-DN already occurs in the Semitic onomastics from

Similarly, Roberts, *ESP*, p. 17 f., *s. v. bītum*: "The names (*Paluḫ-bītum*(É) *MDP* 14, 44, *Iddin-bītum*(É) *CT* 1,1a, *Ur-bītim*(É) *MAD* 3, p. 93) indicate that the temple was sometimes deified in the Old Akkadian period and thus could be used as a theophoric element just as in the later periods."

33 Cf. Stamm, *ANG* p. 91; *CAD* B, p. 287, *s.v. bītu* 1c) c'.

34 *Ibid.*: "Konnten wir also *ālu* als theophorisches Element nicht nachweisen, so finden wir dagegen *bītu* mehrfach in dieser Funktion, allerdings nicht in Dank- und Bittnamen, sondern nur in "Attributnamen", die mehr das Verhältnis zum Menschen als abstrakten Preis enthalten: *Bītum-še-mi, Bītum-rabi, Bītum-māgir, Bītum-muballiṭ, Ṣilli-bītum...Bītum-kīma-ilim-še-mi..*".

35 For this PN see above, *2.1*.

36 *PBS* VIII/1 101 II 5, 14.

37 Cf. *MAD* 3, p. 214 *s.v. palḫum*: *Ba-luḫ*-DINGIR (*MDP* XVIII 76), TE.NA-DINGIR (*MAD* 1, p. 222) (Gelb *OIAC* 18:17), *Ba-luḫ*-É (*MDP* 14 72 IV), *Ba-lu-úḫ*-É (*MDP* 14 44), *Ba-luḫ-É-a* (Yondorf a, Ur III).
Completely different theophors occur in another typology, using the same root: ND-*ba-luḫ* /ND-paluḫ/ (*ba-lìḫ* /paliḫ/ for Gelb *ibid.*): *Be-lí-ba-luḫ*, *Sar-ru-ba-luḫ*, LUGAL-*ba-luḫ* (see *MAD* 3 *ibid.* and Di Vito, p. 206), and *Aš-dar-ba-luḫ* (*FAOS* 19 Ki 2:2).

38 Cf. M.V. Tonietti, "The Mobility of the NAR and the Sumerian Personal Names in Pre-Sargonic Onomasticon", *Subartu* IV/2 (1998), pp. 83-101, partic. 93-95. For its presence in the Ebla texts, see above, at note 12.
Almost certainly to be interpreted as an Akkadian PN is UR-É in *OIP* 104 34 rev. I 4, a text from the Pre-Sargonic period, written in Akkadian, alleged to have been found in Uruk, but, according to the editors (p. 104), more likely from Northern Babylonia given the presence of Kish in ii 2 (from Matar possibly, if the PA.TE.SI *Il-su*-ERÍN+X at iv 10-11 is to be identified with the homonymous gover-

Fāra: UR-^{d}*aš-dar*,[39] UR-^{d}*e-lum*.[40] On the basis of the variant *gal-bù* in the NPL,[41] and the presence of parallel syllabic spellings already in Sargonic onomasticon,[42] it has been proposed that in Sargonic and even in Pre-Sargonic period the UR-DN personal names containing a Semitic theophoric element belong to the Semitic onomastic type *kalab*-DN.[43] As far as the theophoric element is concerned, besides É Sargonic names only attest Ea and Aštar.[44] Noteworthy is the absence, besides the aforementioned logographic and syllabic writings with *É-a* and *Aš-dar*, of spellings with *bí-tum*, or É^{ti}.[45] After the III millennium, this relatively rare onomastic type seems not to be attested until the Neo-Babylonian period.[46]

Several names follow in Gelb's list, all from the Diyala region, whose first member is a DN.[47] Here, the spelling É can clearly be interpreted as logographic for *bītum*. It is also clear, however, that in these names *bītum* does not act as theophor, but as a predicative element referring to the preceding theophor. In these cases,

---

nor of Matar). It can be noted that the sons of the figure in question as well as the PA.TE.SI mentioned here have Semitic names.

Also in *MM* 560 8 (M. Molina Martos, *AuOr* 9 [1991], p. 146), an Akkadian administrative text from Eshnunna (Naram Sin / Šarkališarri) where UR-É also occurs within a sequence of Semitic PNs: *Pù-su*-DÙG, *Im$_4$-da-lik, Da-ru-ru, Ik-ru-ub*-[DINGIR], it seems to be interpreted as Akkadian.

Instead, in P. Steinkeller, *Third Millennium Legal and Administrative Texts in Iraq Museum,* Winona Lake 1992, n. 35 l. 4, quoted by Gelb (as Iraq Museum 10630), *MAD* 3, p. 93 *s.v. bîtum*, UR-É occurs in a clear context of Sumerian PNs, and is likely to be considered as Sumerian.

39 *WF* 110 I.

40 *TMH* 5, 78, III 3, and *passim*. Cf. also *MAD* 3, p. 35. Absent in Di Vito.

41 NPL 45 (44) source F; other Abū Ṣalābīḫ sources and Ebla version: UR. See Tonietti, cit. p. 93 n. 124.

42 In such pairs as UR-*é-a* (*MAD* 1 255 III 1; Edzard 1968/69 [49]=Nr. 649) // *ga-la-ab-é-a* (*OIP* 104 40 B XI 4; *MAD* 5 19:4; Steinkeller, *Legal Administrative Texts in the Iraq Musem* 72 obv. 6); UR-*aš-dar* (*MAD* 1 186 [cf. p. 225], and Fāra, see n. 39) // *gal-pù-aš-dar* (*OSP* I 47), long before the OB evidence of spelling such as UR^{ab}-^{d}ba-ba$_6$ (*YOS* 14 127:8) // *ka-la-ab*-^{d}ba-ba$_6$ (*YOS* 14 228:9).

43 See Tonietti, cit. p. 93 f.

44 *Ibid.* p. 94-95. Cf. also *MAD* 3, p. 145 *s.v. kalbum*, and Di Vito, 37.2.

45 Attested outside of the onomastics, already since the end of the Sargonic period (*e.g.* [*in*] É-*ti* Gelb *OAIC* 36:10 ff., cf. ibid 29); and in onomastic since Ur III (for PN DÙG-*bí-ti-iš-zu* and *Na-si-bí-tum*, cf. below.

46 Cf. Stamm, *ANG*, p. 12 n. 2, and p. 261; NB *Kal-bi*-GN Nbn 95, 4.9; Camb 274, 12. Cf. *AHw* p. 424 *s.v. kalbu*, 5 b).

47 DINGIR-É (*MAD* 1 144 x+ i 5'; *CCTE* UU 16) cf. *ì-lí*-É (*PBS* 11/2 No. 59); ^{d}EN.ZU-É (*MAD* 1, p. 195); *Eš$_4$-dar*-É (*MAD* 1 A 7875 i; *MAD* 5 10:11); ^{d}UTU-É (*MAD*, 1 p. 226); ^{d}UTU-SA (*MAD* 1, p. 226). For SA = É see *MAD* 2, p. 62.

therefore, we are not dealing with a deified element. Also in the following name, LUGAL-É,[48] which perhaps belongs to the same typology as the preceding names, *bītum* has very probably a predicative function.

A different case is constituted by the last name reported by Gelb, *Ni-se*$_{11}$-^{d}É,[49] a late Ur III personal name where É is evidently a theophoric element. The interpretation of this name is problematic. Gelb's interpretation, seems not totally convincing.[50] It is, anyway, worth stating the fact that the sign É is preceded here by the divine determinative, a fact not otherwise attested in the Babylonian documentation we have considered here. May we interpret this as a scribal indication that a reading other than Ea is intended here?

3. Conclusion

As we have seen, the Ebla documentation suggests that the theophoric element É in the onomastics of Abū Ṣalābīḫ could be interpreted as a syllabic spelling of the name Ea, rather than as a logographic spelling of *bītum*. The synchronic and dia-

---

48 *MAD* 5 3 rev. 14.

49 *PBS* XI/3 No. 55, Ur III.

50 *MAD* 3, p. 208-209: "*nišî* (*enim*) 'favoured', Sarg and Ur III PNs: *Ni-se*$_{11}$-^{d}É, *Ni-se*$_{11}$*-e-ni-su*, *Ni-se*$_{11}$*-e-ni-sa* ". In fact, while the PN *Ni-se*$_{11}$*-e-ni-su*, and its feminine equivalent are well attested in Sargonic period, no uses of this word with theophoric elements seems to be attested. *Ni-se*$_{11}$*-e-ni-su*: *MAD* 1 79 rev. 6 (*Ni-se*$_{11}$*-e-n*[*i-su*]), 163 rev. X 8 (both from Tell Asmar), 267:2, 268:5 (both from Tell Agrab); Illingworth, *Iraq* 50 p. 92, r. 1 (⸢*Ni-se*$_{11}$⸣*-e-ni-s*[*u*]) (from Tell Brak); Edzard *AfO* 22 Abb. 157 (muḫaldim). *Ni-se*$_{11}$*-e-ni-sa*: *MAD* 1 163 v. VI $^{?}$ 13 (*Ni-se*$_{11}$*-e-ni-s*[*a*]) (from Tell Asmar); *MAD* 5 1:6 (=*RA* 24 96+) (from Kiš); (the same PN is attested in following periods too [*e. g.*, *Ni-ši-i-ni-šu* Bagh Mitt 2 pl 8a:7, OB, and see Ranke PN p. 192 s.; *Ni-iš-e-ni-šú KAJ* 45:20, and see Saporetti *RA* 68 p. 92]).
It would be very tempting to compare this PN with *Na-si-bi-tum* (Oppenheim *CCTE*, p. 197; see *MAD* 3, p. 93, *s.v. bītum*: "Meaning unknown") which, together with DÙG-*bí-ti-iš-zu* (*YOS* 4 284, Ur III, for which no logographic variants seem to be attested), constitutes the first example of a syllabic use of *bītum* in onomastics, in Ur III and previously unattested PNs. A possibility which, nevertheless, appears problematical. For the first element of the two PNs, in fact, one could think to *nišū* "people", a word for which many different spellings are employed in Old Akkadian. In Ebla, for instance, its normal spelling is *na-se*$_{11}$ (with *na-*), certainly not a local spelling, since *se*$_{11}$ is not employed in Ebla syllabary, and a very rare "Eblaite" spelling, *ne-sa*(*-a*), also occurs (see Fronzaroli, *Testi rituali della regalità*, *ARET* XI, Roma 1993, p. 45). Names with *nišū* "people" seem to be attested in Old Akkadian, from the Sargonic period (cf. *MAD* 3, p. 208, *s.v. nišū*) onwards; however, the word never appears as first element of the PN but always after a DN (Baba, Enlil, Ea, Eštar, Mama). Furthermore, the spelling *ni-se*$_{11}$, normally employed in Naram Sin period, does not seem otherwise attested in the onomastics, where instead one finds *ni-sa/ša/ša*$_{6}$. (In later Mari texts, the spelling *na-si* has been interpreted as a divine epithet or a DN, see H.B. Huffmon, *APNMT*, p. 240).

chronic analysis of the names in question, and of other onomastic types occurring with É in the third millennium has brought to light data that seems to confirm this hypothesis:

- all three of the names with É from Abū Ṣalābīḫ occur in Sargonic and/or Neo-Sumerian periods with Ea;

- none of the three types are later attested with *bītum*, while all three continue to appear with Ea, even after the III millennium;

- in particular the type /yimlik-DN/, occurs in the III millennium only with Il(um) and Ea: the occurrence with É from Abū Ṣalābīḫ being completely isolated.[51]

In the same way, all the other onomastic types in which É appears as a theophoric element occur with Ea in the third millennium. Moreover, in the majority of cases, the only theophors attested are Il(um), Ea and É.

It is worth noting that:

- none of these names occur in Old Akkadian with *bītum* either in syllabic or in logographic writing with phonetic complement, even if these spellings are normally widespread from at least Ur III onwards;

- none of them, with one sole exception,[52] belong to the onomastic typologies employed with *bītum* in Akkadian or Amorite onomastics of later periods.

All of this is in perfect agreement with what Stamm states regarding anthroponyms with *bītum*.[53]

The name of Ea, therefore, completely absent in the Names and Professions List, and probably in the texts of Fāra,[54] is thus attested for the first time with the spelling É=*ʾÀ*[55] at Ebla and, according to the hypothesis suggested here, at Abū Ṣalābīḫ. The same spelling continues to be used sporadically in personal names in the Sargonic and, even more rarely, in Ur III period. As we have seen, besides É other "non canonical" spellings are attested.[56] The sporadic use of É for Ea, still in the Sargonic

51 As we have seen above, this absence is in no way attributable to a clear religious caesura between Pre-Sargonic and Sargonic: also in this latter period, spellings with É are attested in other PNs.

52 *Ba-luḫ*-É. We have seen, however, that the onomastic type /paluḫ-ND/ in Sargonic and Ur III is only used with Il(um) and Ea.

53 See above, *2.2.* And seems to cancel Roberts objection, *ESP*, p. 73, n. 86: "If the interpretation of *Iddi(n)-Bītum* [from *nadānum*] is correct, Stamm's view that *bītum* does not occur in thanksgiving or entreaty names as a theophoric element (*ANG*, p. 91) will not hold for the Old Akkadian material."

54 See above, n. 5.

55 And *ʾÀ-u*$_9$.

56 See above n. 16.

period, could therefore be part of a phenomenon of particular spelling (which, in some cases, may, perhaps, reflect local pronunciation) used before the spelling É-a became definitively the norm;[57] or it could actually attest a different and probably less widespread form of the god name.[58]

Turning our attention back to Westenholz's observation,[59] the absence of Adad in Pre-Sargonic documentation is not particularly surprising: even in later phases his presence in the onomastics remains quite marginal in Babylonia, compared with his position of absolute importance in North-Western Mesopotamia and in the rest of Syria. Completely different is the case of Ea, who is always at the forefront in the onomastics already from the beginning of the Sargonic period, on the same level or, at times, above that of other important divine Mesopotamian figures. In the Old Akkadian period more than thirty different names with Ea can be listed.[60]

Considering, then, the huge presence of NPs with Ea during the Sargonic period, it seems very probable that their use[61] began already in the preceding period. At least in certain areas.[62] The texts of Abū Ṣalābīḫ bear witness to different onomastical levels (levels which may reflect either a local diachronic change or a more or less synchronic geographical heterogeneity). First of all, between the anthroponyms of the NPL, and those of the administrative texts and of the colophons: the absence from the NPL of theophors other than Il(um) and Aštar, as well as other features,[63] could be due to a greater antiquity of the list compared to the other texts, and could

57 Possibly accepted definitively also thanks to the false etymology 'house of the water'; an etymology probably modelled *a posteriori* on the syncretism Ea-Enki.

58 To compare, for instance with the name of Adad/Hadda/Addu, as an example of the coexistence of different forms of the same DN belonging to different cultural/linguistic traditions.

59 See above, p. 666 and n. 3.

60 Cf. Galter, *Der Gott Ea-Enki*, Graz 1983, pp. 217-269. Just on the obelisk of Maništušu there are 12 of them: *A-ar-É-a, A-ku-É-a,* BALA-*É-a, En-na-É-a, Ga-la-ab-É-a, I-ku-É-a, I-ti-É-a, Ik-ru-ub-É-a,* PUZUR$_4$-*É-a, Su-mu-É-a, É-a-ra-bí, É-a*-GÚ. The PNs *Su-mu-É-a, É-a-ra-bí* occur also in the Sippar Stone, *OIP* 104 41 (Sargonic). In the Old Akkadian *kudurru* inscriptions in comparison with 12 PNs with Ea, 9 with EN.ZU, 7 with Eštar, 6 with Malik (two of them without determinative), 3 with Dagan, 2 with Utu and 2 with Aba are attested (see *OIP* 104 pp. 163-182).

61 As that of other PNs with different Semitic divine names.

62 Which might not be documented on the basis of the sources currently available to us.

63 Such as the well attested presence of *me-ru*, completely lacking in the remainder of the Abū Ṣalābīḫ texts PNs.

therefore reflect a preceding onomastic (and, perhaps, religious) tradition.[64] But it cannot be excluded that even some of the names of the administrative texts and of the colophons, for instance the rare PNs with theophoric elements other than Il(um) and Aštar, may reflect onomastic realities different to local ones.[65] One of the most interesting data emerging from the Syrian Early Dynastic onomasticon[66] is the existence of several different Semitic onomastic traditions, related to the geographical distribution of the PNs.[67] It is well known that for this phase the documentation relating to Southern Mesopotamian centres with a dominantly Semitic culture is still meagre and partial. Furthermore, the absence even today of a consistent corpus of documents from Kish, which constitutes, if not the only, at least one of the principal cores of cultural diffusion in this area, makes it difficult to develop a satisfactory overall picture of the actual situation in this period. The available documentation, which is dispersed over a somewhat extensive area, seems to reveal a picture fairly fragmented into significant local peculiarities, rather than a really unified picture; local realities which, nevertheless, at a higher cultural level belong to a widespread *koinè* and are connected even at a distance by intensive cultural and commercial relations. Also on the onomastical level the scanty documentation in our possession seems to point to certain differences among the various centres. It is, for instance, a fact that PNs with É, attested at Abū Ṣalābīḫ in as many as three different onomastic types, are completely lacking in Early Dynastic documentation from other centres with the sole, isolated and dubious exception of the PN from Fāra,[68] It seems, there-

64 Not necessarily a local tradition: we do not know, actually, with certainty where the NPL was composed.

65 At Ebla, for example, the discrepancy between the onomasticon of the NPL and that of the administrative and chancery texts - where an extremely diffused use of theophors is attested - is self-evident, and not surprising seeing that both from a diachronic and geographic point of view the NPL belongs to a clearly different cultural-linguistic reality to the local one. But, more interesting is the fact that in the onomasticon of the administrative and chancery texts itself it is possible to detect different Semitic onomastic traditions according to the different areas of provenance of the persons named. On this basis, a map of onomastic regions of the Northern Syro-Mesopotamian area has also been proposed: see M. Bonechi, "Onomastica dei testi di Ebla: nomi propri come fossili guida", *SEL* 8 (1991), pp. 59-79.

66 Provided mainly by Ebla, Mari and Tell Beydar documentation.

67 Cf. Bonechi, cit.; P. Mangiarotti, "L'onomastica del palazzo a Ebla: confronti sincronici e diacronici" *MisEb* 4, (1997), pp. 153-216; Catagnoti, "The Third Millennium Personal Names from the Ḫabur Triangle in the Ebla, Brak and Mozan Texts", *Subartu* 4/2 (1998), p. 41-66, partic. pp. 61-62.

68 And even at Abū Ṣalābīḫ these PNs might not belong to the local onomastic tradition, or could be "professional names": it may be not purely by chance, in fact, that, with the single problematic

fore, possible to see in the unquestionable change occurring at the very beginning of the Sargonic period,[69] the establishment of a different predominant onomastic tradition which had remained until that moment marginal, and scarcely attested in the documentation available to us.

exception of *imriš*-É, these names are all borne by scribes. In Ebla, where 5 PNs with Enki/Ea are attested, these names hardly seem to belong to the Eblaite onomastic tradition.

69 As pointed out by Westenholz, *OBO* 160/3, p. 78, the PNs appearing in Maništušu Obelisk must have been given during Sargon's lifetime.

SULLA PIÙ ANTICA STORIA DEL DIO DEL VINO

PAOLO XELLA

CNR Roma - Universität Tübingen

In un recente studio sulle divinità documentate nei testi di Ebla ho proposto di riconoscere nel teonimo ᵈ*zi-la-šu* una figura legata etimologicamente e morfologicamente al vino, correlabile a Siraš in Mesopotamia, all'ugaritico *trṯ* e all'ebraico *tyrwš*, quest'ultimo riconosciuto ormai da molto tempo come uno dei vari teonimi "demitizzati" dal testo biblico.[1] In quella sede mi sono dovuto limitare ad affrontare per sommi capi il problema senza potere approfondire e discutere adeguatamente la documentazione relativa, che copre un arco cronologico e areale molto vasto, con implicazioni rilevanti anche per il mondo indoeuropeo e le sue credenze religiose. L'occasione attuale mi sembra particolarmente propizia per proporre alcune riflessioni più sistematiche su questa arcaica figura di dio delle bevande inebrianti, che fa risalire alla metà del III millennio la più antica attestazione di quello che W. F. Albright aveva definito anni or sono un "Bacco" cananeo.[2]

Lo spunto per il presente studio viene anche da una circostanza imprevista e assai opportuna, giacché legata all'attività dell'amico e insigne studioso al quale questo contributo è dedicato. Pelio Fronzaroli ha infatti di recente pubblicato un testo eblaita di estremo interesse che concerne l'uso farmaceutico di alcune erbe o sostanze di origine vegetale.[3] Tra gli ingredienti delle "pozioni" ivi menzionati figura il termine *ti-rí-šu*, che l'Autore ha giustamente riconosciuto come il corrispondente eblaita dell'ugaritico *trṯ* e dei termini semitico-occidentali apparentati, usualmente tradotti con "mosto" o "vino nuovo".[4] Egli inoltre non ha mancato di mettere in rilievo la connessione esistente tra il lemma eblaita e l'accadico *sirāš*- "birra", gene-

---

1 POMPONIO - XELLA 1997, pp. 346 ss. Su *tyrwš* cf. da ultimo HEALEY 1995.

2 ALBRIGHT 1955, p. 18, il quale notava (a proposito del teoforo amarniano su cui si veda *infra*, nota 15) che "this hitherto unknown divinity may perhaps have been a kind of Bacchus from whose name the Israelites got the poetic word *tîrōš* for wine".

3 FRONZAROLI 1999, in particolare p. 231, dove l'A. osserva che il "mosto", utilizzato in una pozione per curare una lacerazione cutanea, sembra avere qui la funzione usualmente attribuita alla birra nella farmacopea mesopotamica.

4 Sul problema specifico della resa del termine cf. *infra*.

ralmente (ma infondatamente) ritenuto imprestito sumerico,[5] a cui, come s'è detto, va riallacciato anche il teonimo eblaita ^{d}*zi-la-šu*.

*

* *

La documentazione di Ebla, intorno al 2350 a.C., ci fornisce pertanto la più antica attestazione di una divinità denominata in base (e quindi connessa) al vino. Il teonimo corrisponde al termine accadico per la (divinità della) birra, mentre nel testo farmaceutico eblaita sopra menzionato ricorre il corrispondente lemma in lingua locale, come nome comune e in una forma coerente con gli analoghi termini della documentazione semitica-occidentale posteriore. Questa circostanza obbliga tra l'altro a rivedere l'annoso problema dell'etimologia di *trṯ, un termine ritenuto da alcuni di origine indoeuropea, da altri semitica, da altri ancora un *Kulturwort* appartenente ad un più antico sostrato linguistico.[6]

Conviene dunque prendere le mosse dal dio eblaita Zilašu, un personaggio attestato a mia conoscenza finora soltanto due volte, in uno stesso testo di offerte, anzi nel medesimo passaggio. Si tratta di TM.75.G.2075 r. VI 5-11, pubblicato da G. Pettinato,[7] dove leggiamo:

1 udu ^{d}*zi-la-šu* lú-geštin 1 udu izi-gar ^{d}*zi-la-šu* lú-ŠÈ-làl
"1 ovino per Zilašu della vigna, 1 ovino (nel mese di) izi-gar per Zilašu del ... miele".

Da questo passo apprendiamo dunque che il dio in questione aveva almeno due manifestazioni diverse, una connessa con le vigne (e l'uva), l'altra con il miele.[8] Non abbiamo purtroppo elementi precisi onde poter stabilire se e quale relazione vi fosse eventualmente tra vino e miele per farne elementi riferibili alla stessa figura divina, se non che entrambi sono prodotti alimentari, di sapore dolce, utilizzati tra l'altro in

---

5 Opinione confluita nei lessici, cf. AHw, s.v. *si/erāšu*, p. 1050 ("Sum. Lw.", seguito però da un punto interrogativo); CAD S, s.v. *siraš*, p. 306. Si veda inoltre LIEBERMAN 1977, n. 728, p. 539. P. Fronzaroli puntualizza (*loc. cit.*) come la forma mesopotamica derivi probabilmente per dissimilazione dalla variante *ṯirāṯ.

6 Oltre ai correnti lessici, si vedano in particolare PAIRMAN-BROWN 1969; DELCOR 1974; NEUMANN 1977; DIETRICH - LORETZ 1978; GÖRG 1979.

7 PETTINATO 1979, p. 150.

8 Interpreto qui lú- come un nesso di relazione, giacché mi sembra meno probabile (per molteplici ragioni) che lú-geštin e lú-ŠÈ-làl (espressione, quest'ultima, non del tutto chiara) indichino dei mestieri e si riferiscano quindi a personaggi umani (cf. discussione in POMPONIO - XELLA 1997, pp. 346-347, con bibliografia).

libagioni, di risaputo impiego rituale (e medico) in tutta l'area siro-mesopotamica. Questi magri dati, insieme alle considerazioni etimologiche sul teonimo in questione, consentono comunque di ritenere che Zilašu fosse una figura probabilmente non (ancora) pienamente sviluppata in senso politeistico e correlata in generale alla sfera agricola, ma caratterizzata specificamente[9] dal legame con il vino. Le sue tracce (o quelle di un personaggio apparentemente analogo) possono essere ulteriormente seguite in epoche e documentazioni posteriori a Ebla, e anche al di fuori del mondo semitico.

In Mesopotamia, come accennato, è attestata una figura divina denominata Siraš,[10] della stirpe (uno degli otto figli) della dea sumerica Ninkasi, definita come "La signora che riempie la bocca", a sua volta figlia di Enki e antica "Schützerin der Braukunst".[11] Le fonti che la menzionano sottolineano particolarmente il suo ruolo nell'ambito magico-medico e rituale, certo spiegabile soprattutto con gli effetti prodotti dall'assunzione di bevande inebrianti nel mondo umano come in quello divino.[12]

Un confronto storico-morfologico tra l'eblaita Zilašu e Siraš (le cui prime attestazioni sono comunque posteriori a quelle eblaite e la cui comparsa/ascesa va probabilmente ascritta a speculazioni teologiche tarde) non può basarsi che su limitatissimi dati, ma sembra indubbio che si abbia a che fare con due figure analoghe, non solo per la loro etimologia. Non parla in senso contrario neppure la circostanza (del tutto prevedibile) che in Mesopotamia la bevanda di riferimento fosse la birra e non il vino,[13] giacché occorre soprattutto guardare al fatto che si tratta in entrambi i casi di un prodotto della fermentazione.

---

9 Non mi risultano infatti altri nessi di tale figura con il miele in altre documentazioni. Senza volere trarre alcuna conclusione da quella che può essere solo una coincidenza, colpisce la analogia con il caso miceneo della tavoletta di Khania (HALLAGER - VLASAKIS - HALLAGER 1992, p. 65 ss.: cf. *infra*, nota 28), in cui sono attestate offerte di miele a "Dioniso" (e a Zeus), nell'unica menzione diretta certa di questo dio in Lineare B.

10 Già inclusa in DEIMEL 1914, p. 239 (^{d}SIRIS, n. 2936); cf. HARTMAN - OPPENHEIM 1950, p. 10; RÖLLIG 1970, pp. 64 ss. Su ^{d}ŠIM cf. anche TALLQVIST 1974^{2}, pp. 448-449; CAD S, s.v. *siraš* b), p. 306.

11 Cf. WILCKE 1969, pp. 73-75; RÖLLIG 1970, p. 65.

12 Cf. ad es. in Šurpu V-VI 182 (Reiner), "la divina Birra che rilassa dio e uomo" (^{d}ŠIM *pāšir ili u amēli*).

13 Sulla regione siro-palestinese come area a cultura vinicola, di contro a quella mesopotamica caratterizzata da orzo e birra, cf. già FRONZAROLI 1972, pp. 613-614. Si veda in generale MILANO 1975; FINET 1977; RAMMANT-PEETERS 1991; MILANO (ed.) 1994; FRANKEL 1999.

Le tracce di questa divinità legata al vino e, in generale, alle bevande inebrianti, si colgono qua e là nelle culture del Vicino Oriente antico. Ma prima di passarle brevemente in rassegna, si noterà che i dati attualmente in nostro possesso dimostrano che il termine ittita (geroglifico) *tuwarsa* – sprovvisto di etimo convincente in ambito indoeuropeo[14] – così come gli apparentati greco θύρσος e latino *thyrsus* (denominazioni del celebre simbolo cultuale dionisiaco) – derivano certamente dall'Oriente semitico, con tutte le implicazioni di ordine linguistico, culturale e storico-religioso che tale circostanza comporta.

Per quanto riguarda la documentazione vicino-orientale risalente ad epoche successive, durante il Tardo Bronzo la suddetta divinità del vino compare come elemento teoforico nel nome del principe di Hazor, Abdi-tir-ši, menzionato dalle lettere di El-Amarna;[15] i testi di Ugarit, d'altra parte, documentano direttamente in cuneiforme alfabetico un termine *trṯ* usato sia come nome comune per designare il vino, sia come teonimo individuante una divinità evidentemente connessa a questa sfera e da ritenersi analoga allo Zilašu eblaita.

Per quanto riguarda l'ugaritico *trṯ* come nome comune, si tratta di un termine raro e d'uso poetico (è assente infatti dai testi economici ed epistolari) e viene impiegato anche in parallelo con *yn*.[16] Da riallacciare alla stessa radice (con m-) e di senso identico è *mrṯ*, anch'esso termine raramente usato ma documentato, oltre che nei miti, anche in prosa, in una lettera.[17]

Per quanto riguarda il teonimo, troviamo un dio *trṯ* in KTU^2 1.102:9, una lista divina la cui sequenza di nomi divini coincide con quella attestata in KTU^2 1.39, dove compare (linea 16) una forma *ṯrṯ* da ritenersi variante (meno plausibilmente

14 FRIEDRICH 1952, p. 336; MERIGGI 1976, pp. 116-119; cf. tra gli altri già ASTOUR 1965, pp. 187 ss.; PAIRMAN-BROWN 1969, pp. 168-169; NEUMANN 1977, p. 128; DIETRICH - LORETZ 1978. *Contra*, a torto, RABIN 1963, che pensava invece ad un imprestito dall'area asianica nelle lingue semitiche.

15 EA 228,3, cf. HESS 1993, p. 17 (Ì[R-]*tir-ši*). Il fatto che un personaggio di tale rango porti un nome simile suggerisce che il teonimo in questione godesse quanto meno di una certa popolarità nell'ambito delle tradizioni dinastiche di questo centro.

16 Cf. KTU^2 1.5 IV 20 (*tʿl trṯ* [*b bt bʿl*]); 1.17 VI 7; 1.114:4.16 (*//yn*). Altre indagini di tipo lessicografico (in parte discutibili): DAHOOD 1974, pp. 387 ss.; AARTUN 1984, pp. 35-36.

17 Cf. MILANO 1977; DIETRICH - LORETZ 1978. Testi: KTU^2 1.22 I 18-20; 2.34:32-33. Il termine si ritrova come imprestito in egiziano, cf. HOCH 1992, n. 183, pp. 140-141; si veda anche WARD 1961, p. 40. Si notino ancora aram. *myrtʾ* (DALMAN 1938, 235a) e sir. *m*(ʾ)*rytʾ* (BROCKELMANN 1966, p. 406a).

errore scribale) di *ṯrṯ*. In KTU^{2}1.148:28 abbiamo invece una sequenza di nomi divini del tutto diversa e troviamo attestato *ṯrṯy*, che potrebbe essere una forma/variante femminile di tale divinità, se non proprio un errore scribale.[18] Dai testi fin qui citati non emerge dunque alcun elemento che possa in qualche modo caratterizzare ulteriormente questo dio-vino, che appare comunque figura secondaria e alquanto sfumata in un pantheon peraltro ricco di divinità spesso ben personalizzate. Dal nostro punto di vista, va ricordato che il dio che mostra le maggiori connessioni con il vino e l'uva è addirittura Ilu,[19] suprema autorità e padre degli dèi, come dimostrano le celebrazioni in suo onore nel mese di *riš yn* e i dati espliciti di alcuni testi.[20] Ma non esistono indizi che mostrino la benché minima relazione tra il capo del pantheon ugaritico e la figura di *ṯrṯ* che si segnala quasi soltanto per il nome che la designa.

Come è noto, nelle altre documentazioni semitiche-occidentali il termine si ritrova in ebraico (*tyrwš*) e in fenicio (*trš*) e non è questione secondaria, nell'economia della presente disamina, la messa a punto del senso preciso di questo termine. È stato merito precipuo di L. Milano avere stabilito convincentemente che non esistono elementi per differenziare i significati di *ṯrṯ* / *tyrwš* e di (*y*)*yn*, come si fa abitualmente attribuendo ai primi il senso di "mosto" e ai secondi invece quello di "vino" vero e proprio. Le evidenze ugaritiche, come del resto quelle bibliche (anche qui *tyrwš* è d'uso letterario), indicano chiaramente che si tratta di due vocaboli entrambi molto antichi ma non differenziabili semanticamente; in altri termini, non vi sono prove per affermare che (*y*)*yn* fosse il prodotto fermentato, di contro a *ṯrṯ* / *tyrwš* che sarebbe il succo spremuto dell'uva. Entrambi appaiono infatti designare prodotti fermentati, dagli analoghi effetti su chi li assume (cf. ad es. Osea 4,11, etc.).

Uno sguardo alla documentazione fenicia conferma ulteriormente, se ve ne fosse bisogno, che *trš* indicava il vino *tout court* giacché, prescindendo dalle menzioni in ambito punico,[21] l'attestazione nell'iscrizione di Karatepe, come ha dimostrato A.

---

18 DIETRICH - LORETZ 1981, p. 76. Per la variante cf. quanto osservato da P. Fronzaroli, *supra*, nota 5. Problematico risulta il confronto con ^{d}x.tur in U 5 N 170:20 (che occupa il posto corrispondente a *ṯrṯy* in KTU^2 1.148), che non può facilmente essere integrato ^{d}[ni]n.tur per dedurne una natura femminile di questa divinità. L'oscillazione di sesso potrebbe comunque essere ammissibile richiamando il caso mesopotamico di Siraš, generalmente una dea ma talvolta ritenuta lo sposo di Ninkasi.

19 Cf. in particolare XELLA 1977.

20 KTU^2 1.41 // 1.87, il cui *incipit* è: *byrḫ riš yn . bym ḫdṯ / šmtr . uṯkl . lil . šlmm*; si veda ancora il ruolo che Ilu riveste in KTU^2 1.114. Cf. da ultimo DEL OLMO LETE 1999, pp. 106 ss.

21 Cf. BENZ 1972, s.v. (CIS I 2186:2; 3035:3; 3393:3; 4553:4; incerto il caso di 432).

Alt già 50 anni or sono,[22] indica chiaramente che si ha a che fare con il "vino" posto in parallelo con il "grano", quest'ultimo indicato metaforicamente da *šbʿ*,[23] nella frase che allude alla prosperità acquisita dai sudditi locali grazie alle "imprese" di chi si autocelebra nel testo.[24]

Per quanto riguarda il problema dell'etimologia di *trṯ, si propone usualmente all'origine una radice *yrṯ che significherebbe "premere", "pigiare", ma anche "espellere".[25] Questa ipotesi appare tuttora plausibile, ma non esime certo dalla ricerca di soluzioni diverse. La circostanza che in Mesopotamia Siraš fosse la (divinità della) birra, la cui produzione non prevede alcun procedimento di questo tipo, potrebbe suggerire – seguendo un'idea di M. Görg derivata dal Gesenius[26] – che il senso originario fosse piuttosto quello di "possedere", "occupare", "conquistare"[27] (la "mente" di chi beve?), con eventuale allusione agli effetti e non alle modalità di preparazione della bevanda. L'ipotesi – che di altro non si tratta – ha obiettivamente un fascino particolare, specie se ci si lascia suggestionare dal complesso miticorituale che culti dionisiaci e bacchici costelleranno in età posteriori. Non si può neppure escludere, infine, che la radice in questione si riferisse in qualche modo al processo di fermentazione, senza che ci sia più possibile coglierne il senso preciso.

Comunque stiano le cose, la scoperta che già a Ebla esisteva un dio del vino di nome Zilašu implica l'ammissione dell'origine semitica del teonimo e, di conseguenza, del personaggio, i cui contorni poco definiti non devono farci presumere che fosse una semplice "ipostasi" della bevanda dagli effetti così straordinari. Come si sia passati da Zilašu a *trṯ* / *tyrwš* e, attraverso l'ittita *tuwarsa*, al "tirso" con tutte le sue implicazioni resta ancora un processo in gran parte inafferrabile. È certo comun-

22 ALT 1949, p. 283.

23 In Prov. 3,10 si ritrovano in parallelo *šbʿ* // *tyrwš*.

24 Cf. KAI 26A iii 7,9; C iv 7,9: *bʿl šbʿ wtrš*. Vedasi BRON 1979, p. 108. Il termine è inteso ancora come "mosto/vino nuovo" in DNWSI II, p. 1234, s.v. $trš_1$.

25 Cf. in generale HAL, s.v. jrš II, p. 421. Si veda tra l'altro Michea 6,15. Cf. anche KAI 181:7, nell'iscrizione di Mesha.

26 GÖRG 1979, p. 9: "Warum die Annahme einer zweiten Basis, wenn die Konnotation von "in Besitz nehmen" von vorherein auch das "Vertreiben" implizierte, ein Vorgang, dessen bildliche Umsetzung keine Schwierigkeiten machen sollte". Egli ricorda le notazioni di G. Gesenius, *Thesaurus philologicus criticus linguae hebraeae et chaldaea veteris testamenti*, I, Leipzig 1829, 633b, a proposito di *tyrwš* ("*mustum, vinum novum*, ita dictum, quia inebriat, cerebrum occupat").

27 Cf. fen. *trš* "eredità" (?), DNWSI II, s.v. $trš_2$, p. 1234, che distingue dunque le due radici.

que che ogni approccio storico al culto di Dioniso non potrà non confrontarsi d'ora in poi con questa per certi versi imbarazzante eredità vicino-orientale, e più particolarmente semitica-occidentale, soprattutto da quando la documentazione micenea in Lineare B ha dimostrato non solo la presenza indiscutibile di Dioniso (di-wo-nu-so) in quel pantheon, ma anche la rilevante antichità del suo culto.[28*]

Bibliografia e abbreviazioni

AARTUN 1984 = K. Aartun, *Neue Beiträge zum ugaritischen Lexicon* I, *Ugarit-Forschungen* 16, 1984, pp. 1-52.

AHw = W. von Soden, *Akkadisches Handwörterbuch*, Wiesbaden 1959-81.

ALBRIGHT 1955 = W. F. Albright, *Recent Books on Archaeology and Ancient History*, *Bulletin of the American School of Oriental Research* 139, 1955, pp. 14-25.

ALT 1949 = A. Alt, *Die phönikischen Inschriften von Karatepe*, *Die Welt des Orients* 1, 1949, pp. 272-287.

ASTOUR 1965 = M. C. Astour, *Hellenosemitica*, Leiden 1965.

BENZ 1972 = F. L. Benz, *Personal Names in the Phoenician and Punic Inscriptions*, Roma 1972.

BROCKELMANN 1966 = C. Brockelmann, *Lexicon syriacum*, Hildesheim 1966 (ried. an.).

BRON 1979 = Fr. Bron, *Recherches sur les inscriptions phéniciennes de Karatepe*, Genève 1979.

CAD = *The Assyrian Dictionary of the University of Chicago*, Chicago-Glückstadt 1956--.

DAHOOD 1974 = M. Dahood, *Hebrew-Ugaritic Lexicography XII*, *Biblica* 55, 1974, pp. 381-393.

DALMAN 1938 = G. Dalman, *Aramäisch-Neuhebräisches Handwörterbuch zu Targum, Talmud und Midrasch*, Göttingen 1938.

---

28 Cf. PALAIMA 1998, in particolare sulla tavoletta di Khania (Creta occidentale) che attesta (cf. *supra*, nota 9) i nomi di Zeus e Dioniso, quest'ultimo associato al santuario del primo, entrambi destinatari di anfore di miele, rispettivamente 1 e 2. I nomi propri teofori con Dioniso risalgono a un'epoca compresa tra il 1200 a.C. e il 1325 a.C. circa ma, come osserva giustamente Palaima, l'uso del teonimo nell'antroponimia obbliga a risalire ancora più indietro nel tempo. Pur non essendo attualmente in grado di cogliere nessi diretti tra Dioniso e gli "dèi del vino" vicino-orientali, è indubbio che future ricerche dovranno essere indirizzate in tal senso, data la quantità e la qualità di indizi che spingono in questa direzione.

* Ringrazio cordialmente Oswald Loretz per aver voluto discutere con me vari aspetti di questo studio.

DDD = K. van der Toorn - B. Becking - P. W. van der Horst (edd.), *Dictionary of Deities and Demons in the Bible*, Leiden 1995.

DEIMEL 1914 = A. Deimel, *Pantheon Babylonicum*, Roma 1914.

DELCOR 1974 = M. Delcor, *De l'origine de quelques termes relatifs au vin en hébreu biblique et dans les langues voisines*, in A. Caquot - M. Cohen (edd.), *Actes du Ier Congrès International de linguistique sémitique et chamito-sémitique*, The Hague 1974, pp. 146-170.

DEL OLMO LETE 1999 = G. del Olmo Lete, *Canaanite Religion According to the Liturgical Texts of Ugarit*, Bethesda (Maryland) 1999.

DIETRICH-LORETZ 1978 = M. Dietrich-O. Loretz, *KTU 2.34:32 und die Herkunft von griech.* θύρσος, *Ugarit-Forschungen* 10, 1978, p. 426.

DIETRICH-LORETZ 1981 = M. Dietrich-O. Loretz, *Neue Studien zu den Ritualtexten aus Ugarit (I)*, *Ugarit-Forschungen* 13, 1981, pp. 63-100.

DNWSI = J. Hoftijzer - K. Jongeling, *Dictionary of the North-West Semitic Inscriptions*, I-II, Leiden 1955.

FINET 1974 = A. Finet, *Le vin à Mari*, *Archiv für Orientforschung* 25, 1974, pp. 122-131.

FRANKEL 1999 = R. Frankel, *Wine and Oil Production in Antiquity in Israel and Other Mediterranean Countries*, JSOT/ASOR Monograph Series 10, Sheffield 1999.

FRIEDRICH 1952 = J. Friedrich, *Hethitisches Wörterbuch*, Heidelberg 1952.

FRONZAROLI 1972 = P. Fronzaroli, *Studi sul lessico comune semitico VII. - L'alimentazione*, *Rendiconti dell'Accademia Nazionale dei Lincei*, ser. VIII, 26, 1971 (1972), pp. 603-643.

FRONZAROLI 1998 = P. Fronzaroli, *A Pharmaceutical Text at Ebla* (*TM.75.G. 1623*), *Zeitschrift für Assyriologie* 88, 1998, pp. 225-239.

GÖRG 1979 = M. Görg, *Ein semitisch-ostmediterranes Kultwort im Alten Testament*, *Biblische Notizen* 8, 1979, pp. 7-10.

HALLAGER - VLASAKIS - HALLAGER 1992 = E. Hallager - M. Vlasakis - B. P. Hallager, *New Linear B Tablets from Khania*, *Kadmos* 31, 1992, pp. 61-87.

HEALEY 1992 = J. F. Healey, *Tirash*, in DDD, 1642-45.

HELTZER 1990 = M. Heltzer, *Vineyards and Wine in Ugarit* (*Property and Distributon*), *Ugarit-Forschungen* 22, 1990, pp. 119-135.

HESS 1993 = R. Hess, *Amarna Personal Names*, Winona Lake 1993.

HOCH 1994 = J. E. Hoch, *Semitic Words in Egyptian Texts of the New Kingdom and Third Intermediate Period*, Princeton 1994.

KAI = H. Donner - W. Röllig, *Kanaanäischen und aramäischen Inschriften*, I-III, Wiesbaden 1962-1964.

KTU² = M. Dietrich - O. Loretz - J. Sanmartín, *The Cuneiform Alphabetic Texts from Ugarit, Ras Ibn Hani and Other Places*, Münster 1995.

LIEBERMAN 1977 = S. Lieberman, *The Sumerian Loanwords in Old-Babylonian Akkadian*, *Harvard Semitic Studies* 22, Missoula (Montana) 1977.

LORETZ 1977 = O. Loretz, *Hebräisch* tjrwš *und* jrš *in Mi 6,15 und Hi 20,15*, *Ugarit-Forschungen* 9, 1977, p. 354.

LORETZ 1993 = O. Loretz, *Ugaritisch-hebräisch* ḫmr/ḫmr *und* msk *(/mzg). Neu- und Mischwein in der Ägäis und in Syrien-Palästina, Ugarit-Forschungen* 25, 1993, pp. 247-258.

MERIGGI 1967 = P. Meriggi, *Manuale di eteo geroglifico*, II/1, Roma 1967.

MILANO 1975 = L. Milano, *Viticoltura ed enologia nell'Asia Anteriore antica dalle origini alla fine dell'Età del Bronzo*, Tesi inedita, Roma 1975.

MILANO 1977 = L. Milano, *Sul presunto giubileo a Ugarit (PRU V 9), Oriens Antiquus* 16, 1977, pp. 23-33.

MILANO (ed.) 1994 = L. Milano (ed.), *Drinking in Ancient Societies*, Padova 1994.

NEUMANN 1977 = G. Neumann, *Das Zeichen* vinum *in den ägäischen Schriften*, *Kadmos* 16, 1977, pp. 124-130.

PAIRMAN-BROWN 1969 = J. Pairman Brown, *The Mediterranean Vocabulary of the Wine*, *Vetus Testamentum* 19, 1969, pp. 146-170.

PALAIMA 1998 = Th. G. Palaima, *Die Linear-B Texte und der Ursprung der hellenischen Religion:* di-wo-nu-so, in AA.VV., *Die Geschichte der hellenischen Sprache und Schrift. Von 2. zum 1. Jahrtausend v. Chr.: Bruch oder Kontinuität?*, Altenburg 1998, pp. 205-222.

PETTINATO 1979 = G. Pettinato, *Culto ufficiale ad Ebla durante il regno di Ibbi-Sipiš*, *Oriens Antiquus* 18, 1979, pp. 85-215.

POMPONIO - XELLA 1997 = F. Pomponio - P. Xella, *Les dieux d'Ebla*, AOAT 245, Münster 1997.

RABIN 1963 = C. Rabin, *Hittite Words in Hebrew*, *Orientalia* 32, 1963, pp. 113-139.

RAMMANT-PEETERS 1991 = A. Rammant-Peeters, *De bereiding van bier en wijn bij de Oude Egyptenaren*, *Phoinix* 37, 1991, pp. 6-23.

RÖLLIG 1970 = W. Röllig, *Das Bier im Alten Mesopotamien*, Berlin 1970.

TALLQVIST 1974^2 = K. Tallqvist, *Akkadische Götterepitetha*, Hildesheim 1974^2.

WARD 1961 = W. A. Ward, *Egyptian and Ugaritic*, *Journal of Near Eastern Studies* 20, 1961, pp. 31-40.

WILCKE 1969 = Cl. Wilcke, *Das Lugalbandaepos*, Wiesbaden 1969.

XELLA 1977 = P. Xella, *Studi sulla religione della Siria antica-I. El e il vino, Studi storico-religiosi* 1, 1977, pp. 229-261.

I PRODROMI DELLA DEFINIZIONE DI VERBO PERFORMATIVO NELLE GRAMMATICHE TRADIZIONALI DELL'EBRAICO BIBLICO

IDA ZATELLI

Università di Firenze

Al Professor Pelio Fronzaroli
שפתי חכמים יזרו דעת
Prov. 15, 7

Della difficoltà di interpretare le diverse funzioni della forma *qaṭal* (perfetto, secondo il valore aspettuale, o passato in senso temporale) in ebraico antico offrono testimonianza già le grammatiche medievali.

wtdᶜ ky mnhg hᶜwbrym blšwn hqwdš lhštmš bw ᶜbr bmqwm ᶜtyd [...], wzh bnbwʾwt brwb, ky hdbr brwr kmw ʾm ᶜbr ky kbr ngzr.

"Sappi che nella lingua sacra si usa ricorrere a forme del passato invece del futuro, soprattutto nella profezia, dove l'evento è chiaro come se appartenesse al passato, poiché è già sancito".

Così scriveva probabilmente nella seconda metà del secolo XII Dawid Qimḥi nel suo *Miklol*,[1] cogliendo l'aporia tra piano presente / futuro del discorso e la compiutezza dell'evento espresso.

Il problema di interpretazione sorge nei grammatici medievali ebrei (ed arabi) per influsso degli studi grammaticali greci e per il confronto con le lingue romanze dotate di un sistema verbale a tre tempi, passato, presente e futuro, diverso dal sistema verbale semitico antico. ʾAbraham ʾIbn ᶜEzraʾ[2] sostiene che l'ebraico non ha il tempo presente, ma già *BTalmud Berakot* 52b riporta un'interessante discussione sulla forma participiale *boreʾ*, da alcuni intesa come passato, da altri come futuro, mentre sul perfetto *brʾ* considerato come passato, non ci sono dubbi, a dimostrazione

1 Dawid Qimḥi, *Miklol*, ed. Rittenberg, Lyck 1862, f. 37; vd. anche William Chomsky, *David Kimḥi's Hebrew Grammar (Mikhlol)*, New York 1952-5713, pp. 340-341.

2 ʾAbraham ʾIbn ʿEzraʾ, *Moznayim*, ed. W. Heidenheim, Offenbach 1791, 47 ab.

che il sistema verbale semitico si era trasformato nel suo interno rispetto ai tempi biblici.[3]

Le grammatiche di ebraico biblico di epoca moderna si soffermano quasi tutte[4] sulla questione delle funzioni del perfetto, fino ad arrivare in alcuni casi ad esprimere *in nuce* il concetto di performatività legato come è ben noto al verbo nel presente, che ricorre in una proposizione non negativa.

Wilhelm Gesenius nel suo *Lehrgebäude der hebräischen Sprache*[5] diceva che il *Praeteritum* ebraico può essere usato al posto del *Futurum* "wenn irgend eine andere *Bezeichnung der Zukunft* vorhergeht, und das *Praeteritum* durch *wᵉ* darangeknüpft wird". Cita, fra altri esempi che non rientrano nella nostra casistica, anche due passi in cui compaiono verbi con un chiaro valore performativo, da lui tradotti con dei futuri: Gen. 48, 4 *hnny mprk whrbytk wnttyk lqhl ʿmym (wntty ʾt-hʾrṣ hzʾt lzrʿk ʾḥryk ʾḥzt ʿwlm)*, "Con ciò ti rendo fecondo, ti accresco, ti faccio diventare un insieme di popoli (e do questo paese alla tua discendenza dopo di te in possesso perenne)" e Ez 30, 22 *hnny ʾl-prʿh mlk-mṣrym wšbrty ʾt-zrʿtyw ([...]whplty ʾt-hḥrb mydw)*, "Con ciò mi metto contro Faraone, re d'Egitto, gli spezzo il braccio ([...] e gli faccio cadere la spada di mano)". L'analisi delle funzioni del perfetto acquista un carattere molto più dettagliato nelle edizioni della *Hebräische Grammatik* di Gesenius rielaborate da Emil Kautzsch.[6] Risultano qui interessanti gli usi del perfetto così descritti:

"In direkter Rede zum Ausdruck von Handlungen, die, obschon äusserlich erst in Vollzug begriffen, doch als in der Vorstellung bereits vorliegende hingestellt werden sollen". Sono riportati alcuni esempi molto significativi in cui compaiono verbi con valore performativo come Gen. 14, 22 *hrmwty*, "alzo (si intende la mano per il giuramento)" o Deut. 8, 19 *hʿdty,* "attesto (oggi contro di voi che certo perirete)";

"Zum Ausdruck *zukünftiger* Handlungen, sofern solche durch eine ausdrückliche Versicherung des Redenden als abgemacht oder so gut wie vollzogen hingestellt werden sollen: a) bei vertragsmässigen oder sonstigen ausdrücklichen Zusicherungen (wiederum entsprechend dem deutschen Praesens)" - anche qui sono citati alcuni esempi molto interessanti, riconducibili alla casistica dei verbi performativi come Gen. 23, 11 "Ti do *(ntty)* il campo", cfr. Gen. 23, 13; 48, 22[...]; bei einer Drohung, es. 1 Sam 2, 16 [...] *wʾm-lʾ lqḥty*

---

3 Vd. Chomsky, *op. cit.*, pp. 361-362.

4 Sono esaminate qui le grammatiche di uso più comune.

5 Wilhelm Gesenius, *Ausführliches grammatisch-kritisches Lehrgebäude der hebräischen Sprache*, Leipzig 1817, in part. p. 765. I versetti biblici sono citati nel testo grammaticale solo parzialmente, ho aggiunto tra parentesi le parti mancanti che sono pertinenti alla nostra analisi; vd. anche *infra* le citazioni riportate in altri testi grammaticali esaminati.

6 *Wilhelm Gesenius' hebräische Grammatik* völlig umgearbeitet von Emil Kautzsch, Leipzig 1896, pp. 301-302. Compaiono pochissime varianti nell'edizione inglese curata da A. E. Cowley nel 1910.

bḥzqh, "[...] altrimenti (la) prendo con la forza". "So namentlich auch bei Zusicherungen von Seiten Gottes"; es. Gen. 1, 29; 15, 18 etc. "b) zum Ausdruck von zwifellos bevorstehenden, daher für das Bewusstsein des Redenden bereits vollzogenen Thatsachen (sog. *Perf. confidentiae*)", es. Num. 17, 27 *hn gwʿnw ʾbdnw klnw ʾbdnw*, "Ecco, moriamo, siamo perduti, siamo tutti perduti". Ricompare qui anche il cosiddetto *Perfectum propheticum*: "Am häufigsten findet sich dieser Gebrauch des Perfect in der profetischen Rede [...]; der Prophet versetzt sich so lebhaft in die Zukunft, das er das Zukünftige als ein bereits von ihm Geschautes oder Gehörtes beschreibt".

Un noto studioso italiano, Samuel David Luzzatto,[7] rileva in modo analitico, mantenendosi solo nell'ambito temporale, una serie di casi in cui il "passato" esprime il presente: accade quasi costantemente con il verbo *ydʿ*, "conoscere", "sapere" etc., e assai di frequente con i verbi indicanti "azioni dell'anima" come per es. *ʾhbty*, "amo" etc. (vd. Es. 21, 5) e talvolta con i verbi "qualitativi" come *mlʾ*, "essere pieno" etc. (vd. Is. 1, 15; Sal. 104, 24); infine l'autore si sofferma sul "passato" che esprime il "presente" nelle profezie dove si descrive "un avvenimento futuro quasi presente e già avvenuto" (vd. Is. 9, 1). Luzzatto quindi conclude: "Non è necessario, né ragionevole dire che il Passato faccia le veci del Futuro, ma sibbene che il Futuro venga poeticamente descritto siccome presente, e che il Passato faccia le veci del Presente". Egli conferisce al perfetto profetico un valore retorico, come è ormai consuetudine presso gli studiosi odierni, ma non affronta il problema dell'azione compiuta nel tempo presente propria di altre funzioni del perfetto ebraico.

Appare più aderente la definizione di Samuel Rolles Driver:[8] "The perfect is employed to indicate actions the accomplishment of which lies indeed in the future, but is regarded as dependent upon such unalterable determination of the will that it may be spoken of as having actually taken place: thus a resolution, promise, or decree, especially a Divine one, is frequently announced in the perfect tense". Gli esempi riportati sono tutti molto interessanti, con traduzioni pertinenti. Anche Driver pone particolare attenzione al *prophetic perfect* o *perfect of certitude*: "But the most special and remarkable use of the tense, though little more than an extension of the last idiom (vd. *supra*), is as the *prophetic perfect*: its abrupt appearance in this capacity imparts to descriptions of the future a forcible and expressive touch of reality, and reproduces vividly the certainty with which the occurrence of a yet

7 Samuel David Luzzatto, *Grammatica della lingua ebraica*, fascicolo VI, Padova 1869, p. 518.

8 Samuel Rolles Driver, *A Treatise on the Use of the Tenses in Hebrew*, Oxford 1892, pp. 17-19.

future event is contemplated by the speaker". Lo studioso sembrerebbe ammettere una qualche valenza performativa al perfetto profetico.

Risulta pertinente la definizione fornita da A. B. Davidson:[9] il perfetto è usato "in a class of actions which are completed just in the act of giving them expression. This usage appears chiefly with verbs denoting to speak, as verbs of swearing, declaring, advising, and the like, or their equivalent in gesture". Andrebbe aggiunto alla casistica dei verbi con cui Davidson illustra il suo assunto un esempio da lui classificato come *perfect of certainty*: Is. 42, 1 *hn ʿbdy ntty rwḥy ʿlyw*, tradotto con un futuro "*I will put* my spirit upon you" e che mi pare possa essere meglio inteso come verbo performativo.

È pregnante anche la formulazione di Eduard König,[10] che rileva come il significato di alcune forme del "*Qaṭal*" oltrepassi la sfera del passato e si inserisca in quella del presente e propone alcuni esempi classici come Gen. 30, 27 *nḥšty* o Gen. 14, 22 *hrmty* precisando: "Nicht einmal dies ist sicher, dass mit jener Form eine Handlung bezeichnet ist, die in ihrem Erfolge noch fortwirkte [...]; aber gewiss bezeichnete jene Form weder eine Act, der in Moment des Sprechens erst vollzogen wurde ("levo"; "ich erhebe" [...]), noch einen zukünftigen Act [...], denn was hinter dem Moment des Sprechens geschehen sollte".

È molto articolata la posizione di Gotthelf Bergsträsser:[11] "Präsentische Bedeutung gewinnt das konstatierende Perf. [...] in Fällen wie *brkty* "ich segne hiermit", wenn nämlich in der 1. Pers. von einer Handlung gesprochen wird, die entweder a) eben in dem Sprechen selbst besteht (wie in dem angeführten Beispiel), oder b) mit ihm zugleich ausgeführt wird; deutsch "hiermit". c) Eine Erweiterung dieser als ursprünglich anzusetzenden Gebrauchssphäre liegt vor, wenn eine Zeitbestimmung wie "heute" hinzutritt. d) Bisweilen werden solche Perf. durch Perf. cons. fortgesetzt". Vengono riportati molti esempi quali per a) e d) Gen. 17, 20 *wlyšmʿʾl šmʿtyk hnh brkty ʾtw whpryty ʾtw whrbyty ʾtw bmʾd mʾd,* "Anche riguardo a Ismaele ti ho esaudito: infatti lo benedico e lo rendo fecondo e molto, molto numeroso"; per b) Gen. 1, 29 *hnh ntty lkm ʾt-kl-ʿśb,* "Con ciò vi do ogni erba"; per c) Deut. 4, 26 *hʿydty bkm hywm*, "Chiamo oggi a testimonio contro di voi". Lo studioso riconduce essenzialmente il fenomeno della performatività al "perfetto constativo" e

---

9 A. B. Davidson, *Introductory Hebrew Grammar. Hebrew Syntax*, Edinburgh 1896, p. 60.

10 Eduard König, *Historisch-comparative Syntax der hebräischen Sprache*, Leipzig 1897, pp. 44-45.

11 Gotthelf Bergsträsser, *Hebräische Grammatik*, II. Teil: *Verbum*, Leipzig 1918[1], Hildesheim 1962, pp. 27-28.

nota molto opportunamente la presenza di deittici come "heute" che segnalano gli enunciati in cui compaiono i verbi performativi. Si sofferma inoltre[12] sul significato di futuro che può essere assunto talvolta dal perfetto nel discorso a forte connotazione emotiva. Fa riferimento anch'egli in particolare al "futuro profetico" sostenendo che l'uso del perfetto (o dell'imperfetto consecutivo) ha la funzione di rendere viva e attuale la rappresentazione di avvenimenti futuri e riporta come esempi, fra gli altri, Is. 9, 1-6 e Ger. 51, 29-32.

Driver, König e Bergsträsser hanno tracciato una linea che ormai tocca da vicino il concetto di performatività. Lungo di essa si pone anche Paul Joüon[13] con la sua definizione relativa al *qaṭal* dei verbi d'azione impiegato in casi particolari per il presente: "Le *qaṭal* s'emploie pour une action instantanée qui, s'accomplissant à l'instant même de la parole, est censée appartenir au passé". Quanto al perfetto profetico che tanto suscita l'attenzione dei grammatici osserva che nelle profezie un evento futuro è talora rappresentato come se si debba compiere immediatamente e puntualizza che non si tratta di un perfetto grammaticale speciale, ma di un espediente retorico. Takamitsu Muraoka nella sua revisione (1991)[14] della grammatica di Joüon perfeziona la definizione di *qaṭal* usato in funzione di presente per esprimere un'azione istantanea aggiungendo: "Hence this use of the perfect is sometimes called 'performative' [...]. It stands to reason that the performative perfect should not be used in negative clauses".

Carl Brockelmann, nella sua *Hebräische Syntax,*[15] introduce il concetto di *Koinzidenz* derivato dal linguista tedesco Erwin Koschmieder.[16] Tra le funzioni aspettuali del perfetto indica quella di "constatare" "den Zusammenfall (Koinzidenz) zwischen Aussage und Vollzug der Handlung" e riporta vari esempi classici come Gen. 15, 18 *ntty*, "io do" etc.

---

12 *Ibidem*, p. 29.

13 Paul Joüon, *Grammaire de l'hébreu biblique*, Roma 1923, p. 298.

14 Paul Joüon, Takamitsu Muraoka, *A Grammar of Biblical Hebrew*, Roma 1991, vol. II, p. 362.

15 Carl Brockelmann, *Hebräische Syntax,* Neukirchen 1956, p. 40.

16 Vd. Erwin Koschmieder, *Zeitbezug und Sprache. Eine Beitrag zur Aspekt-und Tempusfrage*, Leipzig, Berlin 1929, dove si affronta anche il problema dell'uso del perfetto in ebraico e inoltre, *id.*, *Durchkreuzungen von Aspekt - und Tempussystem im Präsens*, Zeirschrift für Slavische Philologie 7 (1930), pp. 341-358. Sulle tesi di Koschmieder si sono soffermati, fra gli altri, Andreas Wagner, *Sprechakte und Sprechaktanalyse im Alten Testament*, Berlin, New York 1997, in part. pp. 51-61 e Ida Zatelli, *Pragmalinguistics and Speech-Act Theory as Applied to Classical Hebrew*, Zeirschrift für Althebraistik 6 (1993), pp. 60-74, in part. pp. 63-64.

Osservazioni appropriate sulle funzioni del "passato" ebraico fornisce anche la grammatica di Mayer Lambert,[17] in particolare sul passato profetico o poetico inteso come procedimento retorico o quando afferma che "le passé peut exprimer des actions instantanées et coincidant avec l'énonciation même du fait". Riporta tre esempi validi tratti da Gen. 1, 29; 14, 22; 22, 16, mentre l'esempio di Es. 10, 3 non è assimilabile alla casistica addotta in proposito.

Il primo tuttavia a proporre considerazioni dettagliate ed esplicite sulla valenza performativa degli enunciati è Wolfgang Schneider nella riedizione della *Grammatik des biblischen Hebräisch*:[18]

> "Eine Sonderform besprechender Rede ist die performative Äusserung. 'Performativ' bedeutet, dass mit der sprachlichen Äusserung zugleich eine aussersprachliche Handlung vollzogen wird".

Usa sempre l'espressione "enunciato performativo" e non "verbo performativo" e inserisce le sue valutazioni relative alla performatività in una teoria temporale del verbo ebraico antico piuttosto che aspettuale. Schneider adotta i principi della linguistica testuale di Harald Weinrich.[19] Segnala giustamente la presenza di elementi deittici specifici di questi enunciati come *hnh*, *hywm* o *wʿth*.

Rileva infine come il cosiddetto "*perfectum propheticum*" non debba essere considerato un caso di espressione performativa e lo riconduce all'ambito letterario, retorico e teologico.

Bruce K. Waltke e Michael P. O'Connor introducono nel loro lavoro sulla sintassi ebraica[20] il concetto di "instantaneous perfective" che rappresenterebbe "a situation occurring at the very instant the expression is being uttered. This use appears chiefly with *verba dicendi* [...] or gestures associated with speaking". Gli esempi riportati possono entrare quasi tutti a buon diritto nella categoria dei performativi, come gli stessi Waltke e O'Connor riconoscono.

---

17 Mayer Lambert, *Traité de grammaire hébraïque*, Paris 1946[1], 1972, p. 241.

18 Wolfgang Schneider, *Grammatik des biblischen Hebräisch. Völlig neu Bearbeitung der "Hebräischen Grammatik für den akademischen Unterricht" von Oskar Grether*, München 1974[1], 1985, pp. 204-205.

19 Harald Weinrich, *Tempus. Besprochene und erzählte Welt*, Stuttgart, Berlin, Köln, Mainz 1964.

20 Bruce K. Waltke, Michael P. O'Connor, *An Introduction to Biblical Hebrew Syntax*, Winona Lake, Indiana 1990, pp. 488-489.

Recentemente il lavoro di Christo H. J. van der Merwe, Jackie A. Naudé e Jan H. Kroeze[21] riporta questa osservazione esplicita e sintetica: "The perfect form can indicate a performative action. A performative action is an action that occurs by means of speaking".

Negli ultimi anni sono usciti saggi dedicati alla performatività e alla teoria degli Speech - Acts in ebraico importanti e innovativi: si ricordano fra gli altri i contributi di Mats Eshkult,[22] Hubert Irsigler[23] e Delbert R. Hillers.[24] Un lavoro di grande rilievo è quello pubblicato da Andreas Wagner.[25]

Le funzioni del sistema verbale sembrano mutare in ebraico mishnaico, dove si riscontra un chiaro uso performativo del participio.[26]

L'indagine sulla performatività in ambito semitico non tocca ovviamente solo l'ebraico: da tempo sono state condotte ricerche sull'accadico da parte per esempio di Werner Mayer,[27] Dennis G. Pardee e Robert M. Whiting[28] e sull'ugaritico. La grammatica ugaritica di Stanislav Segert del 1984[29] riporta questa affermazione: "There is, in addition to the aspectual usage, a performative usage of the perfect, an

---

21 Christo H. J. van der Merwe, Jackie A. Naudé, Jan H. Kroeze, *A Biblical Hebrew Reference Grammar*, Sheffield 1999^1, 2000, p. 146.

22 Mats Eshkult, *Studies in Verbal Aspect and Narrative Technique in Biblical Hebrew Prose*, Stockholm 1990.

23 Hubert Irsigler, *Psalm-Rede als Handlungs-, Wirk - und Aussageprozess. Sprechaktanalyse und Psalmeninterpretation am Beispiel von Psalm 13*, in *Neue Wege der Psalmenforschung*, a cura di Klaus Seybold, Erich Zenger, Freiburg 1994, pp. 63-104.

24 Delbert R. Hillers, *Some Performative Utterances in the Bible*, in *Pomegranates and Golden Bells*, a cura di David P. Wright, David Noel Freedman, Avi Hurvitz, Winona Lake, Indiana 1995, pp. 757-766. Vd. anche Ida Zatelli, *La chiamata dell'uomo da parte di Dio nella Bibbia al vaglio della "discourse analysis"*, Rivista Biblica 38 (1990), pp. 13-26; *ead.*, *Pragmalinguistics and Speech-Act Theory*, *op. cit.*; *ead.*, *Analysis of Lexemes from a Conversational Prose-Text*: hnh *as signal of a performative utterance in 1 Sam. 25:41*, Zeitschrift für Althebraistik 7 (1994), pp. 5-11 e E. Talstra, *Text Grammar and Hebrew Bible. II. Syntax and Semantics*, Bibliotheca Orientalis 39 (1982), pp. 26-38.

25 Andreas Wagner, *Sprechakte und Sprechaktanalyse*, *op. cit.* Lo studioso propone distinzioni molto accentuate tra varie teorie e metodi di analisi come per esempio la distinzione tra Koinzidenzfall e teoria austiniana sui performativi/ constativi.

26 M. Azar, *tḥbyr lšwn hmšnh*, Yerušalayim 1995, p. 17.

27 Werner Mayer, *Untersuchungen zur Formensprache der babylonischen Gebetsbeschwörungen*, Roma 1976.

28 Dennis G. Pardee, Robert M. Whiting, *Aspects of Epistolary Verbal Usage in Ugaritic and Akkadian*, Bulletin of the School of Oriental and African Studies 50 (1987), pp. 1-31.

29 Stanislav Segert, *A Basic Grammar of the Ugaritic Language*, Berkeley, Los Angeles, London 1984, p. 89.

action is performed by saying the verb in the perfect". Buoni lavori sono comparsi di recente sull'aramaico e sul siriaco ad opera di Muraoka[30] e Max Rogland,[31] e sull'etiopico classico da parte di Stefan Weninger.[32]

I problemi affrontati riguardano soprattutto l'uso performativo della terza persona (in particolare quando è coinvolto un messaggero), la funzione performativa che dal perfetto passa in molti casi al participio e ad altre forme verbali e le molteplici difficoltà presentate dalle traduzioni di testi antichi in altre lingue o fasi diverse della stessa lingua (come spesso avviene con la Bibbia). Mi pare che il nodo più importante da chiarire sia il rapporto della performatività con i valori temporali e/o aspettuali del verbo. La forte incidenza di perfetti performativi in ebraico antico sembrerebbe un indizio del permanere di valori aspettuali accanto agli elementi temporali nel sistema verbale di tale lingua.

30 Takamitsu Muraoka, *Further Notes on the Aramaic of the Genesis Apocryphon*, Revue de Qumran 61 (1993), pp. 39-48; *id.*, *Classical Syriac*, Wiesbaden 1997, in part. p. 65; Takamitsu Muraoka, Bezalel Porten, *A Grammar of Egyptian Aramaic*, Leiden, New York, Köln 1998, in part. pp. 193-194 e 203.

31 Max Rogland, *A Note on Performative Utterances in Qumran Aramaic*, Revue de Qumran 74 (1999), pp. 277-280; *id.*, *Performative Utterances in Classical Syriac*, Journal of Semitic Studies 46 (2001), pp. 243-250.

32 Stefan Weninger, *On Performatives in Classical Ethiopic*, Journal of Semitic Studies 45 (2000), pp. 91-97.